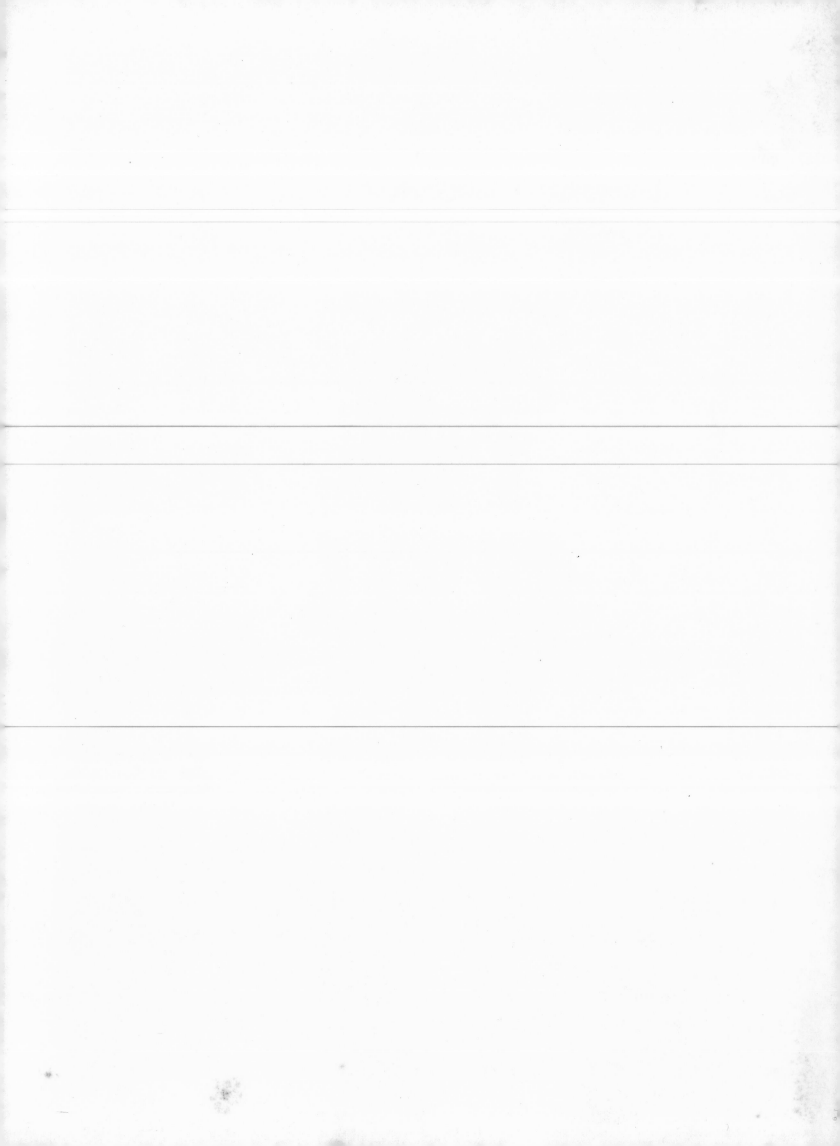

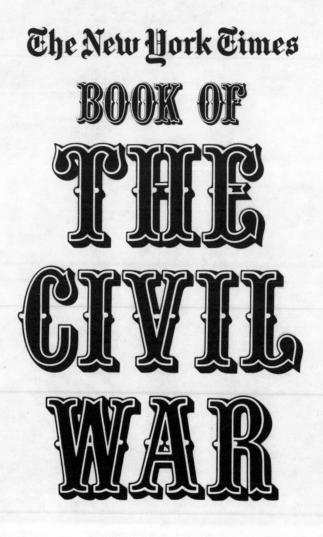

The New York Times
BOOK OF
THE
CIVIL
WAR

Rally round the Flag, boys!
  Rally once again;
There are traitors in the camp, boys,
  And pirates on the main;
There are rebels in the front, boys,
  And foes across the sea,
Who hate the proud republican
  And scoff at you and me.

Rally round the Flag, boys!
  Rally in your might;
Let the nations see how freemen
  Can battle for the right;
Make the throbbing mountains echo
  With the thunder of your tread;
With music sweet of martial feet
  Salute our gallant dead.

Rally round the Flag, boys!
  Rally with a cheer;
For all you love and cherish most,
  For all that hold you dear,
Defend the brave old banner,
  Unsullied from the earth —
Within its folds enshrined it holds
  All that this life is worth.

Then rally round the Flag, boys!
  Rally, rally still!
Rally from the valley,
  And rally from the hill;
Rally from the ship, boys,
  And rally from the plow;
Now or never is the word —
  Never! failing now.

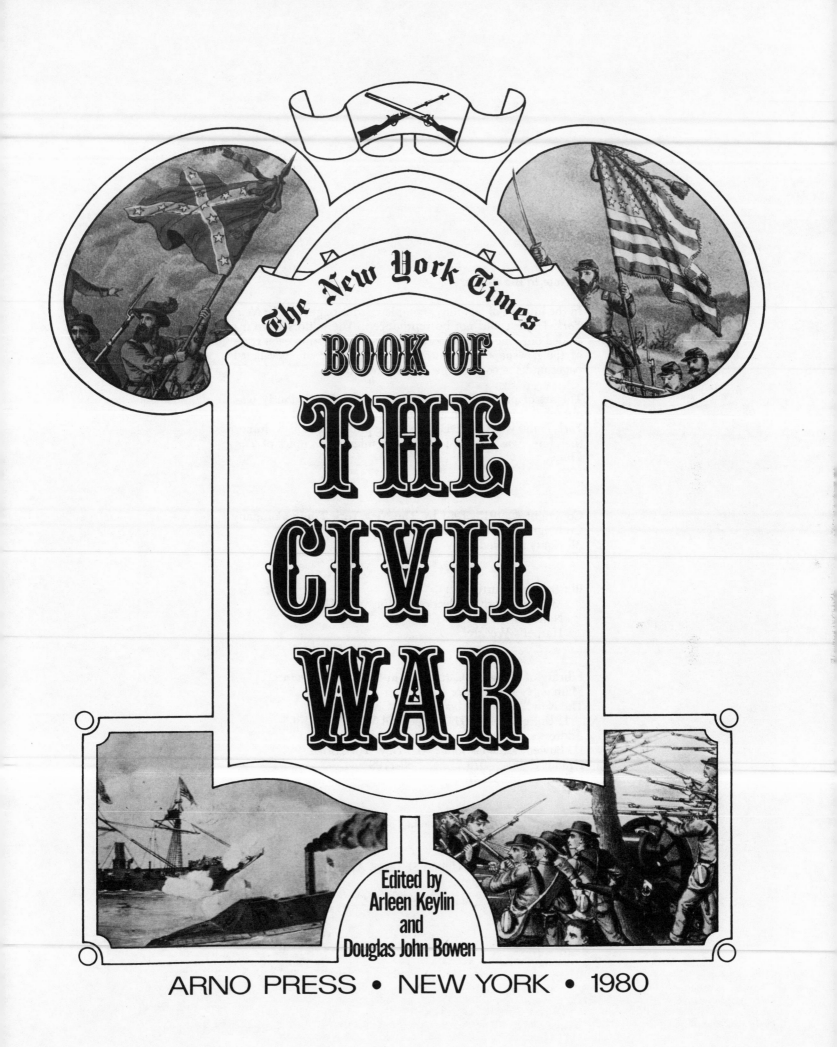

The New York Times
BOOK OF
THE CIVIL WAR

Edited by
Arleen Keylin
and
Douglas John Bowen

ARNO PRESS • NEW YORK • 1980

A Note to the Reader

In the interest of legibility, complete front pages of *The New York Times* could not be reproduced. The editors have included only the most important news articles from each issue of the newspaper. They appear in this book on redesigned pages under a copy of the original masthead.

The art of printing newspapers in the 1860's obviously was not what it is today. In addition, original copies of *The New York Times* were not available to the publisher. This volume, therefore, was created from 35mm microfilm copies of *The Times*.

Illustrations courtesy of:
    Mathew Brady Collection—Library of Congress
    National Archives
    Harper's Weekly

Library of Congress Cataloging in Publication Data
Main entry under title:
The New York times book of the Civil War.
    1. United States—History—Civil War, 1861-1865—
Addresses, essays, lectures. I. Keylin, Arleen.
II. Bowen, Douglas John. III. New York times.
E458.N48   973.7   80-7799
ISBN 0-405-13396-0

Book Design by Ernest Gusella

Manufactured in the United States of America

CONTENTS

Chronology of Events   vi

The Civil War:
A Centennial Perspective   vii

1861   1

1862   55

1863   151

1864   201

1865   255

The Golden Anniversary
of Peace Within the Union   283

Chronology of Events

1861

Mar. 5   Abraham Lincoln inaugurated as the 16th President of the U.S.

Apr. 12   Fort Sumter is fired upon by Confederate troops

Apr. 13   Fort Sumter falls

Apr. 15   Lincoln calls for 75,000 three-month volunteers

Apr. 17   Virginia secedes from the Union

Apr. 19   A Baltimore mob attacks the 6th Massachusetts Regiment, and is fired upon; Lincoln orders a Federal blockade of of all Southern ports

Jun. 3   Battle of Philippi, W. Va.

Jun. 21   First Battle of Bull Run (Manassas), Va.

Jun. 24   Gen. George McClellan assumes command of the Army of the Potomac

Nov. 7   Port Royal, S.C. bombarded by the U.S. Navy

Nov. 8   British steamer *Trent,* carrying two Confederate envoys, is detained by the U.S.S. *San Jacinto*

1862

Jan. 20   Battle of Mill Springs, Ky.

Feb. 6   Fort Henry captured by Northern troops under Gen. U.S. Grant

Feb. 16   Fort Donelson, Tenn. falls; first major U.S. victory

Mar. 7   Battle of Pea Ridge, Ark.

Mar. 9   The *Merrimac* and *Monitor* clash off Hampton Roads, Va.

Mar. 17   McClellan begins his Peninsular Campaign

Apr. 6-7   Battle of Shiloh, Tenn.

Apr. 7   Island No. 10, Tenn. surrenders to U.S. forces

Apr. 26   New Orleans falls to U.S. Navy under Commander Farragut

May 4   McClellan occupies Yorktown, Va.

May 31-Jun. 1   Battle of Fair Oaks, Va.; General Joseph Johnston wounded

Jun. 1   Gen. Robert E. Lee is assigned command of the Army of Northern Virginia

Jun. 26-Jul. 2   Seven Days' Battles (Mechanicsville, Gaines' Mill, Savage's Station, Frayser's Farm, Malvern Hill)

Aug. 29-30   Second Battle of Bull Run (Manassas), Va.

Sep. 17   Battle of Antietam (Sharpsburg, Md.); Lee's invasion of the North is checked

Sep. 22   Lincoln issues his Emancipation Proclamation

Oct. 8   Battle of Perryville, Ky.

Nov. 7   McClellan is relieved as head of the Army of the Potomac

Dec. 13   Battle of Fredericksburg, Va.

Dec. 31-Jan. 3, 1863   Battle of Murfreesboro, Tenn.

1863

Jan. 1   Emancipation Proclamation goes into effect

May 1   Grant begins his Vicksburg campaign by engaging Confederate troops at Port Gibson, Miss.

May 2-4   Battle of Chancellorsville, Va.; U.S. troops under Gen. Joseph Hooker defeated; Gen. Stonewall Jackson mortally wounded

May 22   U.S. troops under Grant begin siege of Vicksburg, Miss.

Jun. 7   Lee's troops cross the Potomac, beginning second Confederate invasion of the North

Jul. 1-3   Battle of Gettysburg, Pa.; U.S. Army, under Gen. George Meade, halts Lee's second invasion

Jul. 4   Vicksburg surrenders

Jul. 13-16   New York City draft riots

Sep. 19-20   Battle of Chickamauga, Ga., Confederate troops under Gen. Braxton Bragg besiege Chattanooga, Tenn.

Nov. 23-25   Battles of Chattanooga (Orchard Knob, Lookout Mountain, Missionary Ridge)

1864

Mar. 9   Grant appointed Lieutenant-General; assumes supreme command of all U.S. armies

May 5-6   Battle of the Wilderness, Va.

May 7   Gen. William T. Sherman invades Georgia

May 8-12   Battle of Spotsylvania, Va.

May 25-26   Battle of New Hope Church, Ga.

Jun. 1-3   Battle of Cold Harbor, Va.

Jun. 15-18   U.S. forces fail to take Petersburg, Va., but continue to besiege the city

Jun. 27   Battle of Kenesaw Mountain, Ga.

Jul. 2-13   Confederate forces under Gen. Jubal Early raid Pennsylvania and Maryland, threatening Washington, D.C.

Jul. 20   Battle of Peachtree Creek, Ga.

Jul. 22   Battle of Atlanta

Jul. 30   Battle of the Crater; Union frontal assault on Petersburg fails

Aug. 5   U.S. Navy under Farragut defeats Confederate forces in Mobile Harbor, Ala., blockading the port

Sep. 2   Atlanta falls; Sherman occupies the city

Sep. 19   Battle of Winchester, Va.

Oct. 19   Battle of Cedar Creek, Va., (Sheridan's Ride)

Nov. 8   Lincoln is elected to a second term

Nov. 14   Sherman begins his march to the sea

Nov. 30   Battle of Franklin, Tenn.

Dec. 10-21   Siege of Savannah, Ga.

Dec. 15-16   Battle of Nashville

Dec. 22   Savannah falls to Sherman

1865

Jan. 15   Fort Fisher, N.C., captured by U.S. Navy

Jan. 21   Sherman invades the Carolinas

Jan. 22   Port of Wilmington, N.C., falls to Union forces; the last major Confederate port is closed down

Feb. 3   Peace Parley at Hampton Roads, Va.

Feb. 17   Columbia, S.C., is captured and burned

Feb. 18   Charleston, S.C., falls

Mar. 4   Lincoln's second inaugural

Mar. 19-20   Battle of Bentonville, N.C.

Apr. 1   Battle of Five Forks, Va.; Lee's assault repulsed by Gen. Philip Sheridan

Apr. 2   Petersburg and Richmond are abandoned by the Confederate Army

Apr. 9   Lee surrenders to Grant at Appomattox Court House, Va.

Apr. 14   Lincoln assasinated at Ford's Theater, Washington, D.C.

Apr. 18   Confederate troops under Johnston surrender to Sherman under liberal terms later disavowed by U.S.; final surrender occurs April 26

THE CIVIL WAR
A Centennial Perspective

By
BRUCE CATTON

THE Çivil War was the continental divide of American history, the summit line beyond which everything was to be different. When we look back it is sometimes hard to tell just what we are seeing, because, although we know what happened, we still do not quite understand all of it. But if we want to measure modern America, the Civil War marks the spot where most of the tapes have to be anchored.

For the Civil War set this nation on the course it has followed ever since. The time before the war is part of the distant past; the time since it is, somehow, the beginning of the present. This was where the great change took place.

To begin with, in its own expensive and tragic way the war gave the country unity—an enforced unity, at first, but an enduring one. The chance that a new Europe, a tangle of separate, walled-off, competing small nations, might come into being on the vast continental expanse that runs from ocean to ocean was at last obliterated. This was going to be one country, able to use to the full its immense potential, fitted to take a great place on the world stage.

The political mechanism by which this nation would manage its own affairs passed its greatest test. As Lincoln remarked at Gettysburg, one of the fundamental questions which then came up for settlement was whether any nation conceived in liberty and dedicated to the proposition that all men are created equal could long endure. It could not endure if the political machinery were to collapse whenever unleashed emotions sub-jected it to great strain—if the appeal from ballots to bullets became an accepted procedure.

FURTHERMORE, the nation was obliged at some time to build on the broad base provided by its original assertion of independence: on the belief that a democratic society knows no grades or classes in its ranks, but makes freedom equal for everyone.

That the shining goal set forth in this way has not yet been reached makes no difference; the belief itself, as something which the nation must forever try to live up to, was riveted home in the Eighteen Sixties.

In addition, there was the world-changing industrial revolution, adjustment to which was imperative. No country on earth was as well fitted as the United States to develop the latent possibilities in this process with due regard for human values; in the century now closing, no country on earth has done so much with those possibilities as the United States. The Civil War not only removed the crippling anachronism of slavery, but immensely stimulated the nation's move toward full development of its industrial resources. The path the country has followed since then may indeed contain pitfalls or stumbling blocks, but for better or for worse the country got on that path through the Civil War.

One thing more. During the Civil War the United States flag became the living symbol of hope and freedom to a great many people who had never had any of either of those things; and a century afterward, the fact that these people were Negroes, recently transplanted (against their own will) from Africa, takes on profound meaning. Very few of our national assets today have a greater latent value than this one. We can still build something unshakable on it.

THESE are some of the significant dimensions of modern America, whose measurement has to begin in the Eighteen Sixties. They are among the principal things that define America's place in the world today. They help to lay out the American pattern. From them we can run our guide lines into the future with a measure of confidence.

It is odd that this should be so, because the Civil War began as an immense, uncalculated act of violence, born of misunderstanding and anger, doing much that nobody intended. It was something we blundered into; it came, really, because neither the North nor the South was quite ready to face up to the basic issue that was driving them into hostility.

That issue, of course, grew out of chattel slavery, yet this was not quite what men were arguing about. The argument before 1861 seemed to center around the question: Should slavery be continued or abolished? Actually, this was an empty question. The one certainty in an uncertain world was that human slavery in America could not possibly continue very much longer in the dynamic nineteenth century. It was a hopeless anachronism, and no matter what anyone did it was bound to become extinct sooner or later. The only real pertinent question had to do with the way in which its extinction was to come about.

THAT was going to make a great deal of difference to everybody, because slavery was deeply embedded in the nation's economic and social organization. It could not be suddenly uprooted without causing a revolutionary convulsion. To find some way by which the impending and wholly inevitable transition might be made with a minimum of shock and disturbance was the real imperative that faced America in 1860, and this imperative was the one thing hardly anybody was prepared to confront, because this problem that had to be solved seemed (when seen though a haze of anger, suspicion and hot impatience) to be utterly insoluble.

Instead of talking about what had to be done, people talked about what ought to be done. The chance to prepare for an orderly adjustment to slavery's disappearance was wholly missed. Consequently the disappearance was attended with an extremity of most expensive disorder.

Another oddity is that when the war began men were not fighting about slavery at all. They went to war over something very different—the right of one or more states to leave the Union and create a separate nation; or, to say the same thing in a different way, the right of the Union to enforce its own continental integrity. This issue would not have arisen if the slavery problem had not generated the pressure that forced it to the surface, but the fact does remain that it was the issue on which the war started.

THE South was fighting for independence, a great word in the American vocabulary, and the North was fighting for union, a word with equally powerful overtones. The fact that it was impossible for them to make this fight without, in the end, fighting also about slavery was something that became evident later.

The seven cotton states seceded because the result of the Presidential election of 1860 seemed to them to pose an intolerable threat to the Southern way of life. That Abraham Lincoln had no intention of interfering with slavery in the states where it existed made no difference; the Federal Government was apparently passing into the hands of people who disliked both the institution and the society which slavery supported, the inevitable and unwelcome change which was coming upon the Southland began to be too visible for comfort, and within six weeks of the election South Carolina left the Union.

It was followed in short order by Alabama, Florida, Georgia, Mississippi, Louisiana, and Texas. During February the Confederate States of America came into being, its capital at Montgomery, Ala. its President Jefferson Davis. By the time Lincoln took office in March he was faced with the fact of a broken Union, a fact that he steadfastly refused to recognize.

What had happened was that the issue between North and South had been changed

IN THE BLUE–The man with the haunted eyes and hard mouth: Grant in early 1864, after taking command of all Union armies.

from the question of slavery—about which hardly anyone was ready to fight—to the question of secession as opposed to union, about which a great many men were ready to fight very tenaciously. Unless one side or the other gave way there was bound to be a war, and on April 12 the war began when Confederate guns bombarded Fort Sumter, in Charleston harbor.

FORT SUMTER jarred things into focus. The slave states of Virginia, North Carolina, Tennessee and Arkansas promptly left the Union and entered the Confederacy. They had not seen in Lincoln's election adequate reason for secession, but they would have no part of armed action against the other Southern states; compelled to make a choice they made it with very little hesitation, and the Confederacy suddenly became a nation large enough to have a fair chance to win a fight for its independence.

Its chance was fair, that is, provided the war could be kept short. In a really long, all-consuming war the South's chance would come down to nothing better than the chance that the people of the North would

get tired and quit. Any realistic comparison of resources shows clearly that over the long pull the odds in favor of the North were all but overwhelming. In industrial capacity, manpower, money, transportation facilities, technical know-how, access to world raw materials, the North had all of the advantage. Drawing up a balance sheet, one is forced to wonder how the Southern leaders ever imagined that they could win.

CLEARLY enough, they had miscalculated. They believed so deeply in the legality and justice of secession that it was hard for them to believe that the rank and file in the North would actually fight to prevent it. To some extent they probably accepted at least part of the thesis that Yankees were a set of money-grubbers who really did not like to fight anyway. In addition, they overestimated the power of Southern cotton.

The great textile industries of England and France depended on that cotton; deprived of it, would not those countries be forced to intervene; guaranteeing Southern independence so that their mills could continue to operate? Thinking so, men would feel that the odds were a great deal better than they looked on the surface.

To this must be added that, if the North were to reestablish the Union, it would need every ounce of advantage it could get. It had to isolate and invade a very large area of land, occupied by pugnacious people who were deeply in earnest. The fight had to go to a finish; Lincoln's task was nothing less than to destroy the Confederate Government outright, which probably would mean destroying the armies which defended that Government and the economy which supported it. Only by harnessing all the resources the North possessed, and instilling into the Northern people a grim determination to keep on using those resources to the limit, could Lincoln hope to win.

It took him a little time to see this. At the start there seemed to be reason to hope that one quick blow would settle things. The blow was tried, at Bull Run, in mid-July of 1861, and it failed; and out of the ignominious defeat which that famous battle brought to the Northern cause came the realization that there would have to be an all-out effort. To such an effort Lincoln applied himself.

Basic strategy was simple enough. Begin with a blockade, using the Federal Navy (which was expanded with breakneck speed) to seal the Confederate coast line, shutting off essential supplies from the outside world, locking the new nation in with its inadequate resources. Extend the blockade by opening the Mississippi River all the way to the Gulf, cutting off Texas, Arkansas and most of Louisiana. Then send in armies to continue the fragmentation of the Confederacy, cutting it down piece by piece, reducing its area and its capacity to resist, weakening its armies and overwhelming them one after another. That was the plan adopted in the summer of 1861 and that was the plan on which the war at last was won.

It was not easy. Things went well at first,

and by the spring of 1862 it looked as if success might be near. Then the Confederacy produced its greatest single asset in the person of Robert E. Lee, who defeated Gen. George B. McClellan in front of Richmond, drove the invading army back to the Potomac, and launched his own invasion of Maryland.

By September the Confederacy's chance of winning looked very good—so much so that the British Cabinet prepared to consider outright recognition. Thrown abruptly on the defensive, the North began to see that a new and greater effort was needed. When Lee at last was checked, at the battle of Antietam, and compelled to return to Virginia, Lincoln made one of the decisive moves of the war, issuing the preliminary draft of the Emancipation Proclamation and thereby changing the whole character of the war.

Until then the Federal Government's war program was simply to restore the Union. Now the base was broadened; by Presidential edict, the war was also a war to destroy slavery. A powerful intangible was added. Lincoln not only won the support of the powerful but discontented anti-slavery minority in the North; in effect, he made European intervention impossible. The British Cabinet would discuss recognition no more. Cotton was not going to be the decisive factor.

The North resumed the offensive with renewed vigor, and its grip grew tighter. In the Virginia theatre, Lee continued to be unbeatable, but in the West things went according to plan. By the summer of 1863 the Mississippi was opened, the trans-Mississippi Confederacy was cut off and impotent, and the way was open for Union armies to invade the Deep South. Lee's counterstroke was repelled at Gettysburg, Chattanooga was taken, and in Ulysses S. Grant Lincoln at last found the general who would apply the North's superior resources remorselessly.

In the spring of 1864 the final campaigns of the war began, with Grant moving for Richmond and William T. Sherman leading an army into the heart of Georgia. A year of ruinously expensive fighting lay ahead, but the original plan was working. If the North retained its determination, victory lay ahead.

Meanwhile, the war was bringing immense changes. In the North it was a constant stimulus to business and industry. A boom was on; the productive mechanism that would display such explosive energy in the final decades of the nineteenth century was working up a full head of steam. Using its resources to the limit the North by that very act was immensely expanding them. By the end of the war it would be moving into the industrial revolution at incredible speed.

In the South, on the other hand, war was a constricting force. Progressive shortages in raw materials, in finished products, in factory capacity and in the ability to move goods to the places where they were vitally needed became more and more crippling. The blockade grew ever tighter, and the invaders' advance could be checked nowhere but in Virginia. As the South's ability to do so declined, month after month, its will to fight declined also.

And with all of this, slavery was being killed. This happened not so much because of the Emancipation Proclamation as because the invading armies simply dismantled the institution, chattel by chattel; the soldiers had nothing in particular against slavery, but they did see in it one of the chief sources of support for the Confederate war effort. Without realizing it, they were making war in the modern manner, breaking the South's economic potential, tearing up railroads, burning factories, seizing livestock and farm produce and, indeed, destroying all Southern property they could lay their hands on.

MEN IN BLUE–Officers of the 44th New York Infantry.

IN THE GRAY–Beaten, but still flashing fire, Robert E. Lee shows the face of a born soldier, a few days after Appomattox.

MEN IN GRAY–Southern volunteers after the firing on Sumter.

THE most obvious and most important property they encountered was the Negro slave, and they freed him in precisely the same spirit that they burned barns and shot cattle. Wherever they went, slavery died. It was the one institution on earth that could not be defended by force of arms; civil war was, beyond all other things, the one thing it could not survive.

So slavery died, and Southern ability to resist died, and at last the Confederacy itself died. Richmond was occupied. Lee surrendered finally, and by the middle of the spring of 1865 the last spark of resistance had been stamped out. The Civil War was over; and if the job of reconstructing the Union was so poorly handled that some of its subsidiary problems are still alive, at least the fighting had been ended. The greatest single chapter in American history had come to a close.

IT closed a century ago and we are still looking back at it. Why?

Partly, of course, because it tells us who we are, why we are whatever that is, and how we got that way—along with where we must be going. But there is also another matter. During this Civil War of ours, some 600,000 young Americans lost their lives. They did it, somehow, with valor and with confidence, believing in something they could not quite define, and although they were not trying to strike any attitudes they put a certain flavor on American life that will haunt us as long as we are a nation.

There are times, to be sure, when the whole Civil War looks like a strange, poorly directed pageant which got out of hand, erupting into violence just when it should have been most static and impressive.

A veil of sentiment lies over it, and the orchestration runs to haunting little tunes which turn the critical faculties rather numb; the business gets down under the mind and reaches the heart, with "Lorena" and "The Girl I Left Behind Me" all tangled up with Robert E. Lee, U.S. Grant, long files of Negro refugees running away from Old Massa toward the North Star and a chance to lead a new life without the irons on, and the marble statue of Abraham Lincoln brooding in the veiled twilight of the great memorial in Washington.

FOR the experts, of course, there is the technical business: Who marched where, and how did he get there, what did General So-and-So do at Wilson's Creek or Antietam, why was the Valley Campaign such an achievement, did Grant really know what he was doing when he crossed the Mississippi in 1863, and would Lee have won a stunning victory at Gettysburg if Stonewall Jackson had just been with him there?

These are the technicalities. They are of absorbing interest, if your mind runs that way, and it will be a long time before some of us get tired of examining these questions.

But there is more to it than that—more than sentiment, more than the question of strategy and its allied tactics, more than the matter of examining a weighty chapter in our history. Beyond all of this there is that haunting procession of 600,000 young Americans who gave up their lives in this war. They are the collective reason why our minds cannot leave this affair alone.

We are now at the centennial, and in observing its various ceremonies we are not celebrating anything at all. We are, however, commemorating something: the most significant and moving tragedy in American history. It is hard to add it all up. We can only say that the whole of it means more than the sum of its parts, that the innumerable heroic dead (no matter which uniform they wore) did not die in vain, and that here, coming down through one hundred years, is our Iliad and our Odyssey waiting for the proper poet.

Who, when he appears, will come straight out of the heart of America.

1861

President-elect Lincoln strikes a contemplative pose two weeks before his inauguration.

The New-York Times.

VOL. X–NO. 2925. NEW-YORK, TUESDAY, FEBRUARY 5, 1861. PRICE TWO CENTS.

THE NATIONAL TROUBLES.

Assembling of the Peace Congress at Washington.

THE SESSIONS TO BE SECRET.

Probable Ultimatum of the Border Slave States.

THE MONTGOMERY CONVENTION ORGANIZED.

Farewell Speeches of Messrs. Benjamin and Slidell in the Senate.

Statement of the Objects of a Southern Confederacy.

LATEST DISPATCHES FROM THE SOUTH.

Seizure of the Cutter Lewis Cass by the Alabamians.

ARRIVAL OF THE U. S. SHIP SUPPLY.

CONDITION OF AFFAIRS AT PENSACOLA.

Statement of Mrs. Lieutenant Slemmer and Mrs. Lieutenant Gilman.

OUR WASHINGTON DISPATCHES.

THE PEACE CONVENTION.

WASHINGTON, Monday, Feb. 4.

The Virginia delegation in the Peace Convention is determined to demand the equality of the South in all the territory hereafter to be acquired, as well as in that now held by the United States, in order, they say, that the present settlement may stand forever. Temporary expedients they ignore. In this they are supported by the entire Kentucky delegation, and a majority from Maryland. Missouri it is understood will take the same position.

The South will press for speedy action, as their Commissioners insist on a showing of hands immediately. The Northern delegations say they cannot see the policy of hurrying things, and will aim to take time for deliberation. The adjournment to-day, without permanent organization, looked at delay. Adjournments hereafter will be strenuously resisted by Virginia and Kentucky.

Mr. TYLER will be reported by the Committee for the Presidency of the Convention, but he does not desire it. He would much prefer being left free in the Convention, but will not decline.

The North Carolina men have indicated no policy as yet, but seem to be awaiting the developments from Virginia.

The Convention will hold its sessions secret, in order that Commissioners may confer more freely without public committal. Some of the Northern Commissioners were desirous to have open sessions, but the Southern men opposed it. They said they could hope for no good result with the conferences public.

The straightout Republican Congressmen, who are opposed to any and all compromises, about forty in number, are now in caucus at the Capitol, to canvass their future course, in view of the possible action of the Convention.

The Republicans in the Convention generally express themselves against any compromise, and have no expectation that anything will be agreed upon that will satisfy both sections. The chances are that the Convention will be utterly fruitless. The Vermont delegation did not act in the Convention, but are waiting for Massachusetts.

THE MONTGOMERY CONVENTION.

PERMANENT ORGANIZATION EFFECTED.
HOWELL COBB SELECTED TO PRESIDE—HIS ADDRESS, ETC.

MONTGOMERY, Ala., Monday, Feb. 4.

The Convention met at noon, R. W. BARNWELL, temporary Chairman.

An impressive prayer was offered by Rev. BASIL MANLEY.

On motion of R. B. RUITT, HOWELL COBB was selected for permanent President by acclamation, and JOHNSON F. HOOPER was selected as permanent Secretary.

All the Delegates were present except Mr. F. MORTON, of Florida.

In the course of Mr. COBB's address, after taking the Chair, he said, the occasion which assembled us together was one of no ordinary character. We meet as the representatives of sovereign and independent States, who by a solemn judgment have dissolved all the political association which connected them with the Government of the United States. It is now a fixed irrevocable fact. The separation is perfect, complete and perpetual. The great duty now imposed is to provide a Government for our future security and protection. We can and should extend to our sister States, and our late sister States, who are identified in interest and feeling and institutions, a cordial invitation to unite in a common destiny, and should be desirous at the same time of maintaining with our confederates friendly relations, political and commercial.

After the usual preliminary business was attended to, adjourned till to-morrow.

THE VIRGINIA ELECTION.

RICHMOND, Monday, Feb. 4.

This county elects one Secessionist and two Unionists. Henrico, Chesterfield, Dinwiddie, Prince George, Greenville, Surry, Alexandria, Petersburgh, Norfolk and Portsmouth elect Unionists.

WHEELING, Monday, Feb. 4.

The election, to-day, for delegates to the State Convention, resulted in the election of SHERRARD CLEMENS, and C. D. HUBBARD, Anti-Secessionists, by about 500 majority. The excitement was very great. Union candidates are elected in Marion, Taylor, Wood, Brooke and Hancock Counties. But very few votes were polled against referring the action of the Convention back to the people.

RICHMOND, Monday, Feb. 4.

Henrico elects three Unionists.

Augusta, three Unionists.

Campbell, two Unionists.

Charlotte County is for secession.

Amelia and Nottoway, probably so.

Pittsylvania and Halifax, Union.

Lynchburgh, Union.

The vote is generally in favor of a reference to the people.

HON. SHERRARD CLEMENS SUSTAINED.

WHEELING, Monday, Feb. 4.

Hon. SHERRARD CLEMENS and C. D. HUBBARD, anti-secession under any circumstances, were elected triumphantly to-day, to the State Convention, over their opponents, who refused to pledge themselves that they would not sign an ordinance of secession.

Reports from all the counties of the Pan Handle elect the anti-secession candidates by decided majorities.

A dead set was made at CLEMENS by the ultra-disunionists, reducing his majority somewhat, but he was triumphantly carried through. Thus was his position in Congress victoriously sustained.

THE NORTH CAROLINA LEGISLATURE.

RALEIGH, N. C., Monday, Feb. 4.

The House, to-day, passed, unanimously, a resolution declaring that in case reconciliation fails, North Carolina goes with the other Slave States.

The Legislature will adjourn, perhaps, and await results.

THE CUTTER LEWIS CASS SURRENDERED TO ALABAMA.

MOBILE, Saturday, Feb. 2.

The United States Revenue cutter *Lewis Cass* has been surrendered to the State of Alabama.

RUMORED ATTACK ON FORT PICKENS.

NEW-ORLEANS, Friday, Feb. 1.

There are flying reports that fighting has commenced at Pensacola, in consequence of the sloop-of-war *Brooklyn* trying to land troops at Fort Pickens, but no reliable authority can be found for them, though authoritatively stated by Alabamians.

[Dispatches of later date make no further mention of the matter, and the reports are doubtless unfounded.—EDS.]

A SOMEWHAT DIFFERENT REPORT.

BALTIMORE, Monday, Feb. 4.

The latest dates received here by mail from Pensacola, (27th ult.,) speak of the withdrawal of the troops. No mention is made of the *Brooklyn*.

The Montgomery and Milledgeville papers speak of the withdrawal of the troops from Pensacola as a thing fixed upon.

A Pensacola correspondent says it is deemed impossible to take Fort Pickens unsupported by a war vessel.

FROM LOUISIANA AND TEXAS.

NEW-ORLEANS, Saturday, Feb. 2.

The Convention has made the resolution to establish a standing army the special order for Tuesday.

The resolution conferring citizenship on persons residing in the State on the day of the passage of the ordinance of secession, was referred.

A resolution was referred to the Committee on Commerce that they report on the expediency of adopting an ordinance exempting from taxation for five years all property and capital employed in manufactures.

Adjourned till Monday.

Advices from Austin, Texas, state that the House has passed by a vote of 65 to 13, an act legalizing a Convention, under the bill of rights.

MASSACHUSETTS DELEGATES TO WASHINGTON.

BOSTON, Monday, Feb. 4.

The Senate this afternoon passed resolves for the appointment of seven Commissioners to confer with the General Government, with the separate States, or with any association of delegates from such States, and to report their doings to the Legislature at its present session. The House refused to suspend the rules to enable the resolves to go to the Governor to-night. The resolves will pass to-morrow and will receive the sanction of the Governor.

THE VIRGINIA LEGISLATURE.

RICHMOND, Monday, Feb. 4.

The Senate voted, to-day, to send back the Minnesota resolutions. A resolution was adopted that, in the opinion of the General Assembly, there is no just grounds for believing that the citizens of Virginia meditate an attack or seizure of the Federal property, or invasion of the District of Columbia, and all preparations are unnecessary, so far as this State is concerned.

THE RECENT SEIZURE OF ARMS.

ALBANY, Monday, Feb. 4.

The recent seizure of arms destined for Georgia, by Superintendent KENNEDY, is likely to create more trouble. It is said here to-night, that Governor MORGAN has received a communication from Governor BROWN, of Georgia, demanding the instant surrender of the muskets, and expressing a hope that a like outrage will not again be committed. A reply is desired. The Governor, it is understood, has not replied.

The New-York Times.

VOL. X–NO. 2949.　　　　NEW-YORK, TUESDAY, MARCH 5, 1861.　　　　PRICE TWO CENTS.

THE NEW ADMINISTRATION.

Abraham Lincoln President of the United States.

THE INAUGURATION CEREMONIES.

A Tremendous Crowd and No Accidents.

THE INAUGURAL ADDRESS.

How it was Delivered and How it was Received.

AN IMPRESSIVE SCENE AT THE CAPITOL.

Mr. Lincoln's First Audience at the White House.

Visit of the New-York Delegation to Senator Seward.

MR. SEWARD MAKES A SPEECH.

What was Done at the Grand Inauguration Ball.

MISCELLANEOUS INCIDENTS OF THE OCCASION.

OUR WASHINGTON DISPATCHES.

WASHINGTON, Monday, March 4.

THE DAWNING OF THE DAY.

The day to which all have looked with so much anxiety and interest has come and passed. ABRAHAM LINCOLN has been inaugurated, and "all's well."

At daylight the clouds were dark and heavy with rain, threatening to dampen the enthusiasm of the occasion with unwelcome showers. A few drops fell occasionally before 8 o'clock, but not enough to lay the dust, which, under the impulse of a strong northwest wind, swept down upon the avenue from the cross streets quite unpleasantly. The weather was cool and bracing, and, on the whole, favorable to the ceremonies of the day.

MR. LINCOLN.

Mr. LINCOLN rose at 5 o'clock. After an early breakfast, the Inaugural was read aloud to him by his son ROBERT, and the completing touches were added, including the beautiful and impassioned closing paragraph. Mr. LINCOLN then retired from his family circle to his closet, where he prepared himself for the solemn and weighty responsibilities which he was about to assume.

Here he remained until it was time for an audience to Mr. SEWARD. Together these statesmen conversed concerning that paragraph of the Inaugural relating to the policy of forcing obnoxious non-resident officers upon disaffected citizens.

When Mr. SEWARD departed, Mr. LINCOLN closed his door upon all visitors, until Mr. BUCHANAN called for him to escort him to the Capitol.

THE THRONG IN THE STREETS.

From early daylight the streets were thronged with people, some still carrying carpet-bags in hand, having found no quarters in which to stop.

THE NOTE OF PREPARATION.

The busy note of preparation for the parade was soon heard on every side. The New-York delegation, over two hundred strong, formed in procession on Pennsylvania-avenue at 9 o'clock, and proceeded in a body to Mr. SEWARD'S residence to pay their respects. J. H. HOBART WARD met them at the door, and JAMES KELLEY introduced the party to Mr. SEWARD in a pertinent speech.

Editorial

The Inaugural.

Mr. LINCOLN's Inaugural Address must command the cordial approval of the great body of the American people. The intellectual and moral vigor which pervades it will infuse new hope and loyalty into the American heart. The calm firmness with which it asserts the rightful authority of the Federal Government,—the declared purpose which it embodies to preserve, protect and defend the Union and the Constitution, the easy force with which it sweeps away all the cobwebs of secession logic, and vindicates the supreme duty of the Government to defend its own existence, cannot fail to impress even the most determined Secessionist with grave doubts as to the justice of his cause. The characteristic feature of the Address is its profound sincerity,—the earnest determination which it evinces to render equal and exact justice to every State, to every section, to every interest of the Republic,—and to administer the Government in a spirit of the most thorough and impartial equity. To this purpose every other consideration is made to bend. And no one who can understand and appreciate such a character as that of Mr. LINCOLN, will doubt that this spirit will mark every act of his Administration.

In our judgment the Inaugural cannot fail to exert a very happy influence upon public sentiment throughout the country. All men, of all parties, must feel that its sentiments are just and true,—that it sets forth the only basis on which the Government of this country can be maintained, while at the same time it breathes the very spirit of kindness and conciliation, and relies upon justice and reflection, rather than force, for the preservation of the Federal Union.

The President declares his purpose to "hold, occupy and possess the property and places belonging to the Government and to collect the duties and imposts." Anything less than this would be utterly and plainly incompatible with the existence of the Federal Government. The means by which these ends will be sought,—the kind and degree of force to which resort will be had, are open to the wise discretion of the Executive, and will undoubtedly depend, in a very large degree, upon the kind and character of the resistance that may be offered. We see nothing in this assurance to make war inevitable, or even probable, unless the seceded States are determined to precipitate an issue with the Government, as they have already precipitated their own people into revolution. The President's declaration that he will not send federal officers among them from other States,—that he will continue the postal service unless it be repelled, —that he relies on the returning good sense and loyalty of the South for the restoration of peace, and that he will do everything to inspire among the people "that sense of calm security which is most favorable to calm thought and reflection," must certainly dispel all fear of any unduly coercive policy or purpose on his part.

The Inaugural is equally explicit and emphatic in its proffer of concessions and guarantees to the alarmed interests of the Southern States. The President disavows in the most solemn manner,—and calls the record of his life to witness the justice of the disavowal,— all thought, purpose or inclination to interfere with Slavery in any State where it exists,—and declares his willingness to assent to an amendment of the Constitution which shall make such interference, on the part of Congress, irrevocably impossible. He declares that the obligation to return fugitive slaves is absolute and unquestionable, and calls for the enactment of laws which shall secure its fulfillment. In regard to differences of opinion as to the Territories, while he asserts the absolute necessity of yielding for the time, and while the decision stands unreversed, to the verdict of the majority and the decisions of the Supreme Court, he also declares his readiness to favor a Convention to amend the Constitution in these or any other particulars. It would scarcely be possible for him, in such an address, to go further towards the conciliation of all discontented interests of the Confederacy.

The Inaugural inspires the strongest and most confident hopes of the wisdom and success of the new Administration. It is marked throughout by consummate ability, a wise and prudent sagacity in the judgment of affairs, a profound appreciation of the difficulties and dangers of the crisis, a calm, self-possessed, unflinching courage adequate to any emergency, a kind and conciliatory temper, and the most earnest, sincere and unswerving devotion to the Union and the Constitution. If the dangers of the hour can be averted and the Union can be saved, this is the basis on which alone it can be accomplished. If the Union cannot be saved on this basis and consistently with these principles, then it is better that it should not be saved at all.

The New-York Times.

VOL. X—NO. 2983.　　　　NEW-YORK, SATURDAY, APRIL 13, 1861.　　　　PRICE TWO CENTS.

THE WAR COMMENCED.

The First Gun Fired by Fort Moultrie Against Fort Sumpter.

THE BOMBARDMENT CONTINUED ALL DAY.

Spirited Return from Major Anderson's Guns.

The Firing from Fort Sumpter Ceased for the Night.

Hostilities to Commence Again at Daylight.

The Correspondence which Preceded the Bombardment.

The Demand for a Surrender and Major Anderson's Refusal.

THE RELIEF FLEET OFF THE HARBOR.

How the News is Received in Washington.

Lieutenant-General P.G.T. Beauregard opened fire on Fort Sumter on April 12, 1861.

OUR CHARLESTON DISPATCHES.

CHARLESTON, Friday, April 12.

The ball has opened. War is inaugurated.

The batteries of Sullivan's Island, Morris Island, and other points, were opened on Fort Sumpter at 4 o'clock this morning.

Fort Sumpter has returned the fire, and a brisk cannonading has been kept up. No information has been received from the seaboard yet.

The military are under arms, and the whole of our population are on the streets. Every available space facing the harbor is filled with anxious spectators.

CHARLESTON, Friday, April 12.

The firing has continued all day without intermission.

Two of Fort Sumpter's guns have been silenced, and it is reported that a breach has been made in the southeast wall.

The answer to Gen. BEAUREGARD'S demand by Major ANDERSON was that he would surrender when his supplies were exhausted, that is, if he was not reinforced.

Not a casualty has yet happened to any of the forces.

Of the nineteen batteries in position only seven have opened fire on Fort Sumpter, the remainder are held in reserve for the expected fleet.

Two thousand men reached this city this morn-ing and embarked for Morris Island and the neighborhood.

CHARLESTON, Friday, April 12.

The bombardment of Fort Sumpter continues.

The Floating Battery and Stephens Battery are operating freely, and Fort Sumpter is returning the fire.

It is reported that three war vessels are outside the bar.

CHARLESTON, Friday, April 12.

The firing has ceased for the night, but will be renewed at daylight in the morning, unless an attempt is made to reinforce, which ample arrangements have been made to repel.

The Pawnee, Harriet Lane, and a third steamer are reported off the bar.

Troops are arriving by every train.

LATER DISPATCHES—HOSTILITIES STILL PROCEED-ING.

CHARLESTON, Friday, April 12.

The bombardment is still going on every twenty minutes from our morters. It is supposed that Major ANDERSON is resting his men for the night.

Three vessels-of-war are reported outside. They cannot get in. The sea is rough.

Nobody is hurt. The floating battery works well. Troops arrive hourly. Every inlet is guarded. There are lively times here.

CHARLESTON, Friday, April 12.

The firing on Fort Sumpter continues.

There are reviving times on the "Palmetto coast."

CHARLESTON, Friday, April 12—3 A. M.

It is utterly impossible to reinforce Fort Sumpter, to-night, as a storm is now raging.

The morter batteries will be playing on Fort Sumpter all night.

FROM ANOTHER CORRESPONDENT.

CHARLESTON, Friday, April 12.

Civil war has at last begun. A terrible fight is at this moment going on between Fort Sumpter and the fortifications by which it is surrounded.

The issue was submitted to Major ANDERSON of surrendering as soon as his supplies were exhausted, or of having a fire opened on him within a certain time.

This he refused to do, and accordingly, at twenty-seven minutes past four o'clock this morning Fort Moultrie began the bombardment by firing two guns. To these Major ANDERSON replied with three of his barbette guns, after which the batteries on Mount Pleasant, Cummings' Point, and the Floating Battery opened a brisk fire of shot and shell.

Major ANDERSON did not reply except at long intervals, until between 7 and 8 o'clock, when he brought into action the two tier of guns looking towards Fort Moultrie and Stevens iron battery.

Up to this hour—3 o'clock—they have failed to produce any serious effect.

Major Robert Anderson was in charge of the Sumter garrison.

Major ANDERSON has the greater part of the day been directing his fire principally against Fort Moultrie, the Stevens and Floating Battery, these and Fort Johnson being the only five operating against him. The remainder of the batteries are held in reserve.

Major ANDERSON is at present using his lower tier of casemate ordnance.

The fight is going on with intense earnestness, and will continue all night.

The excitement in the community is indescribable. With the very first boom of the guns thousands rushed from their beds to the harbor front, and all day every available place has been thronged by ladies and gentlemen, viewing the spectacle through their glasses.

The brilliant and patriotic conduct of Major ANDERSON speaks for itself.

Business is entirely suspended. Only those stores open necessary to supply articles required by the Army.

Gov. PICKENS has all day been in the residence of a gentleman which commands a view of the whole scene—a most interested observer. Gen. BEAUREGARD commands in person the entire operations.

It is reported that the Harriet Lane has received a shot through her wheelhouse. She is in the offing. No other Government ships in sight up to the present moment, but should they appear the entire range of batteries will open upon them.

Troops are pouring into the town by hundreds, but are held in reserve for the present, the force already on the island being ample. People are also arriving every moment on horseback, and by every other conveyance.

CHARLESTON, Friday, April 12—6 P. M.

Capt. R. S. PARKER brings dispatches from the floating battery, stating that up to this time only two have been wounded on Sullivan's Island. He

had to row through Major ANDERSON'S warmest fire in a small boat.

Senator WIGFALL in same manner bore dispatches to Morris Island, through the fire from Fort Sumter.

Senator CHESNUT, another member of the staff of Gen. BEAUREGARD, fired a gun, by way of amusement, from Mount Pleasant, which made a large hole in the parapet.

Quite a number have been struck by spent pieces of shell and knocked down, but none hurt seriously. Many fragments of these missiles are already circulating in the city.

The range is more perfect than in the morning and every shot from the land tells.

Three ships are visible in the offing, and it is believed an attempt will be made to-night, to throw reinforcements into Fort Sumpter in small boats.

It is also thought, from the regular and frequent firing of Major ANDERSON, that he has a much larger force of men than was supposed. At any rate, he is fighting bravely.

There have been two rain storms during the day, but without effect upon the battle.

Everybody is in a ferment. Some of those fighting are stripped to the waist.

IMPORTANT CORRESPONDENCE PRECEDING THE BOMBARDMENT.

CHARLESTON, Friday, April 12.

The following is the telegraphic correspondence between the War Department at Montgomery and Gen. BEAUREGARD immediately preceding the hostilities.

The correspondence grew out of the formal notification by the Washington Government, which is disclosed in Gen. BEAUREGARD'S first dispatches.

[No. 1.]

CHARLESTON, April 8.

L. P. WALKER, Secretary of War :

An authorized messenger from President LINCOLN, just informed Gov. PICKENS and myself that provisions will be sent to Fort Sumpter peaceably, or otherwise by force.

(Signed,) G. F. BEAUREGARD.

[No. 2.]

MONTGOMERY, 10th.

Gen. G. T. BEAUREGARD, Charleston :

If you have no doubt of the authorized character of the agent who communicated to you the intention of the Washington Government to supply Fort Sumpter by force, you will at once demand its evacuation, and if this is refused, proceed in such manner as you may determine, to reduce it.

Answer.

Signed. L. P. WALKER, Sec. of War.

[No. 3.]

CHARLESTON, April 10.

L. P. WALKER, Secretary of War :

The demand will be made to-morrow at 12 o'clock.

Signed, G. F. BEAUREGARD.

[No. 4.]

MONTGOMERY, April 10.

Gen. BEAUREGARD, Charleston :

Unless there are especial reasons connected with your own condition, it is considered proper that you should make the demand at an early hour.

(Signed) L. P. WALKER, Secretary of War.

[No. 5.]

CHARLESTON, April 10.

L. P. WALKER, Secretary of War, Montgomery :

The reasons are special for 12 o'clock.

(Signed) G. F. BEAUREGARD.

[No. 6.]

CHARLESTON, April 11.

L. P. WALKER, Secretary of War :

Demand sent at 12 o'clock. Allowed till 6 o'clock to answer.

(Signed) G. F. BEAUREGARD.

[No. 7.]

MONTGOMERY, April 11.

Gen. BEAUREGARD—Charleston:

Telegraph the reply of Maj. ANDERSON.

(Signed,) L. P. WALKER, Secretary of War.

[No. 8.]

CHARLESTON, April 11.

To L. P. WALKER, Secretary of War:

Maj. ANDERSON replies:

"I HAVE THE HONOR TO ACKNOWLEDGE THE RECEIPT OF YOUR COMMUNICATION DEMANDING THE EVACUATION OF THIS FORT, AND TO SAY IN REPLY THERETO, THAT IT IS A DEMAND WITH WHICH I REGRET THAT MY SENSE OF HONOR AND MY OBLIGATIONS TO MY GOVERNMENT WILL PREVENT MY COMPLIANCE." He adds: "Probably I will await the first shot, and if you do not batter us to pieces, we will be starved out in a few days."

Answer. G. F. BEAUREGARD.

[No. 9.]

MONTGOMERY, April 11.

Gen. BEAUREGARD—Charleston :

We do not desire needlessly to bombard Fort Sumpter, if Major ANDERSON will state the time at which, as indicated by him, he will evacuate, and agree that, in the meantime, he will not use his guns against us unless ours should be employed against Fort Sumpter. You are thus to avoid the effusion of blood. If this or its equivalent be refused, reduce the fort as your judgment decides to be the most practicable.

(Signed) L. P. WALKER, Secretary of War.

[No. 10.]

CHARLESTON, April 12.

L. P. WALKER, Secretary of War :

HE WOULD NOT CONSENT. I write to-day.

G. F. BEAUREGARD.

MR. FOX'S VISIT TO FORT SUMPTER.

CHARLESTON, Friday, April 11.

Intercepted dispatches disclose the fact that Mr. FOX, who had been allowed to visit Major ANDERSON on the pledge that his purpose was pacific, employed his opportunity to devise a plan for supplying the fort by force, and that this plan had been adopted by the Washington Government, and was in progress of execution.

THE KENTUCKY VOLUNTEER REGIMENT.

LOUISVILLE, Friday, Apr. 12.

Dispatches have come here to hold the Kentucky Volunteer Regiment in readiness to move at a moment's notice from the War Department at Montgomery.

EXCITEMENT IN MOBILE.

MOBILE, Friday, April 12.

There is intense excitement and rejoicing here. Fifteen guns have been fired in honor of the attack on Fort Sumpter

THE CONFEDERATE STATES CONGRESS.

MONTGOMERY, Friday, April 12.

An extra session of the Confederate States Congress has been called for April 29.

The New-York Times.

VOL. X....NO. 2984.   NEW-YORK, MONDAY, APRIL 15, 1861.   PRICE TWO CENTS.

FORT SUMPTER FALLEN.

PARTICULARS OF THE BOMBARDMENT.

The Fort on Fire and the Garrison Exhausted.

NO ATTEMPT AT REINFORCEMENT.

The Cessation of Firing and the Capitulation.

NO LIVES LOST ON EITHER SIDE.

Major Anderson and his Men Coming to New-York.

How the News was Received in Washington.

Call for Seventy-Five Thousand Militia.

AN EXTRA SESSION OF CONGRESS

War Feeling Throughout the Northern and Western States.

FORT PICKENS REINFORCED.

CHARLESTON, Saturday, April 13—Evening.

Major ANDERSON has surrendered, after hard fighting, commencing at 4½ o'clock yesterday morning, and continuing until five minutes to 1 to-day.

The American flag has given place to the Palmette of South Carolina.

You have received my previous dispatches concerning the fire and the shooting away of the flagstaff. The latter event is due to Fort Moultrie, as well as the burning of the fort, which resulted from one of the hot shots fired in the morning.

During the conflagration, Gen BEAUREGARD sent a boat to Major ANDERSON, with offers of assistance, the bearers being Colonels W. P. MILES, and ROGER PRYOR, of Virginia, and LEE. But before it reached him, a flag of truce had been raised. Another boat then put off, containing Ex-Gov. MANNING, Major D. R. JONES and Col. CHARLES ALLSTON, to arrange the terms of surrender, which were the same as those offered on the 11th inst. These were official. They stated that all proper facilities would be afforded for the removal of Major ANDERSON and his command, together with the company arms and property, and all private property, to any post in the United States he might elect. The terms were not, therefore, unconditional.

Major ANDERSON stated that he surrendered his sword to Gen. BEAUREGARD as the representative of the Confederate Government. Gen. BEAURE-

FORT PICKENS AND THE HARBOR OF PENSACOLA.

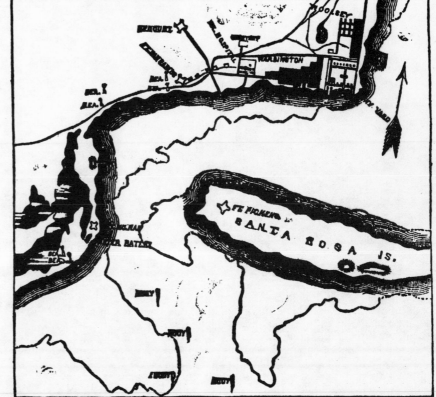

GARD said he would not receive it from so brave a man. He says Major ANDERSON made a staunch fight, and elevated himself in the estimation of every true Carolinian.

During the fire, when Major ANDERSON'S flagstaff was shot away, a boat put off from Morris Island, carrying another American flag for him to fight under—a noteworthy instance of the honor and chivalry of South Carolina Seceders, and their admiration for a brave man.

The scene in the city after the raising of the flag of truce and the surrender is indescribable; the people were perfectly wild. Men on horseback rode through the streets proclaiming the news, amid the greatest enthusiasm.

On the arrival of the officers from the fort they were marched through the streets, followed by an immense crowd, hurrahing, shouting, and yelling with excitement.

Several fire companies were immediately sent down to Fort Sumpter to put out the fire, and any amount of assistance was offered.

A regiment of eight hundred men has just arrived from the interior, and has been ordered to Morris Island, in view of an attack from the fleet which may be expected to-night.

Six vessels are reported off the bar, but the utmost indignation is expressed against them for not coming to the assistance of Major ANDERSON when he made signals of distress.

The soldiers on Morris Island jumped on the guns every shot they received from Fort Sumpter while thus disabled, and gave three cheers for Major ANDERSON and groans for the fleet.

Col. LUCAS, of the Governor's Staff, has just returned from Fort Sumpter, and says Major ANDERSON told him he had pleasanter recollections of Fort Moultrie than Fort Sumpter. Only five men were wounded, one seriously.

The flames have destroyed everything. Both officers and soldiers were obliged to lay on their faces in the casemates, to prevent suffocation.

The explosions heard in the city were from small piles of shell, which ignited from the heat.

The effect of the shot upon the fort was tremendous. The walls were battered in hundreds of places, but no breach was made.

Major ANDERSON expresses himself much pleased that no lives had been sacrificed, and says that to Providence alone is to be attributed the bloodless victory. He compliments the firing of the Carolinians, and the large number of exploded shells lying around attests their effectiveness.

The number of soldiers in the fort was about seventy, besides twenty-five workmen, who assisted at the guns. His stock of provisions was almost exhausted, however. He would have been starved out in two more days.

The entrance to the fort is mined, and the officers were told to be careful, even after the surrender, on account of the heat, lest it should explode.

A boat from the squadron, with a flag of truce, has arrived at Morris Island, bearing a request to be allowed to come and take Major Anderson and his forces. An answer will be given to-morrow at 9 o'clock.

The public feeling against the fleet is very strong, it being regarded as cowardly to make not even an attempt to aid a fellow officer.

Had the surrender not taken place Fort Sumpter would have been stormed to-night. The men are crazy for a fight.

The bells have been chiming all day, gun firing, ladies waving handkerchiefs, people cheering, and citizens making themselves generally demonstrative. It is regarded as the greatest day in the history of South Carolina.

Fort Sumter was recaptured by Federal forces in 1863, after another intense bombardment inflicted severe damage.

FORT SUMPTER EVACUATED.

CHARLESTON, via AUGUSTA, Saturday, April 13.

FORT SUMPTER HAS SURRENDERED.

The Confederate flag floats over its walls.

None of the garrison or Confederate troops are hurt.

Another correspondent says:

The bombarding has closed

Major Anderson has drawn down the stripes and stars, and displays a white flag, which has been answered from the city, and a boat is on the way to Sumpter.

CHARLESTON, Saturday, April 13—P. M.

The Federal flag was again hoisted over Fort Sumpter, when PORCHER MILES, with a flag of truce, went to the Fort.

In a few minutes the Federal flag was again hauled down by Major ANDERSON, and a white one unfurled.

CHARLESTON, Saturday, April 13.

Gen. BEAUREGARD, with two Aids, have left for Fort Sumpter.

Three fire companies from Charleston are now on their way to Sumpter to quell the fire before it reaches the magazine.

Fort Sumpter has unconditionally surrendered.

Ex-Senator CHESNUT, Ex-Governor MANNING and W. P. MILES have just landed and marched to Gov. PICKENS' residence, followed by a dense crowd wild with joy.

It is reported that the Federal flag was shot away by the Palmetto Guards at Morris Island.

In all two thousand shots have been fired. No Carolinians killed.

Major ANDERSON and his men, under guard, were conveyed to Morris Island.

The bells are ringing out a merry peal, and our people are engaged in every demonstration of joy.

It is estimated that there are nine thousand men under arms on the islands and in the neighborhood.

THE LATEST DISPATCHES.

CHARLESTON, Saturday, April 13.

I have seen W. PORCHER MILES, who has just returned from a visit to Fort Sumpter. He assured me that no one was killed at Fort Sumpter. This is reliable, and puts at rest all previous reports about Sumpter.

Maj. ANDERSON has reached the city, and is the guest of Gen. BEAUREGARD.

Our people sympathize with Maj. ANDERSON, but abhor those who were in the steamers off our bar and in sight of our people, and did not even attempt to reinforce him

The Fairfield regiment, one thousand strong, has just passed the *Courier* office, on their way to Morris Island.

There are now ten thousand men under arms in the harbor and on the coast.

Judge MAGRATH, who has just returned, reports that the wood-work and officers' quarters at Fort Sumpter are all burnt.

None of the officers were wounded.

The Fort will be taken possession of to-night by the Confederate troops.

A boat from one of the vessels outside the harbor communicated with Gen. SIMONS, in command of the forces on Morris Island, and made a request that one of the steamers be allowed to enter the port for the purpose of taking away Major ANDERSON and his command. An arrangement was agreed upon by the parties to stay all proceedings until 9 o'clock to-morrow.

CHARLESTON, Saturday, April 13.

Hostilities have for the present ceased, and the victory belongs to South Carolina With the display of the flag of truce on the ramparts of Sumpter at 1½ o'clock, the firing ceased, and an unconditional surrender was made.

The Carolinians had no idea that the fight was at an end so soon.

After the flag-staff of ANDERSON was shot away, Col. WIGFALL, Aid to Gen. BEAUREGARD, at his Commander's request, went to Sumpter with a white flag, to offer assistance in extinguishing the flames. He approached the burning fortress from Morris Island, and while the firing was raging on all sides, effected a landing at Sumpter. He approached a port-hole, and was met by Maj. ANDERSON. The Commandant of Fort Sumpter said he had just displayed a white flag, but the firing from the Carolina batteries was kept up nevertheless.

Col. WIGFALL replied that Major ANDERSON must haul down the American flag; that no parley would be granted; surrender or fight was the word. Major ANDERSON then hauled down his flag, and displayed only that of truce.

All firing instantly ceased, and two other of Gen. BEAUREGARD'S staff—Ex-Senator CHESTNUT and Ex-Governor MANNING—came over in a boat and stipulated with the Major that his surrender should be unconditional for the present, subject to the terms of Gen. BEAUREGARD.

Major ANDERSON was allowed to remain with his men in actual possession of the fort, while Messrs. CHESTNUT and MANNING came over to the city, accompanied with a member of the Palmetto Guards, bearing the colors of his Company. These were met at the pier by hundreds of citizens, and as they marched up the street to the General's quarters, the crowd was swelled to thousands. Shouts rent the air and the wildest joy was manifested on account of the welcome tidings.

After the surrender, a boat with an officer and ten men was sent from one of the four ships in the offing to Gen. SIMONS, commanding on Morris Island, with a request that a merchant ship or one of the vessels of the United States be allowed to enter and take off the commander and garrison of Fort Sumpter.

Gen. SIMONS replied that if no hostilities were attempted during the night, and no effort was made to reinforce or retake Fort Sumpter, he would give an answer at 9 o'clock on Sunday morning.

The officer signified that he was satisfied with this, and returned. This correspondent accompanied the officers of Gen. BEAUREGARD'S staff on a visit to Fort Sumpter. None but the officers were allowed to land, however. They went down in a steamer and carried three fire engines for the purpose of putting out the flames. The fire, however, had been previously extinguished by the exertions of Major ANDERSON and his men.

The visitors reported that Major ANDERSON surrendered because his quarters and barracks were destroyed and he had no hope of reinforcements. The fleet lay idly by during the thirty hours of the bombardment, and either could not or would not help him; besides, his men were prostrate from over-exertion.

There were but five of them hurt, four badly and one, it is thought, mortally, but the rest were worn out.

The explosions that were heard and seen from the city in the morning, were caused by the bursting of loaded shells. These were ignited by the fire, and could not be removed quick enough. The fire in the barracks was caused by the quantities of hot shot poured in from Fort Moultrie. Within Fort Sumpter everything but the casemates is in utter ruin. The whole thing looks like a blackened mass of ruins. Many of the guns are dismounted. The side opposite the iron battery of Cummings' Point is the hardest dealt with. The rifled cannon from this place made great havoc with Fort Sumpter. The wall looks like a honeycomb. Near the top is a breach as big as a cart. The side opposite Fort Moultrie is honey-combed extensively, as is that opposite the floating battery.

Fort Moultrie is badly damaged. The officers quarters and barracks are torn to pieces. The frame houses on the islands are riddled with shot in many instances, and whole sides of houses are torn out.

The fire in Fort Sumpter was put out, and recaught three times during the day.

Dr. CRAWFORD, Major ANDERSON'S surgeon, is slightly wounded in the face. None of the Carolinians are injured.

Major ANDERSON and all his officers and men are yet in Fort Sumpter. I approached near enough to the wall to see him bid adieu. In addition to this, conversations were had, which have been repeated to me.

A boat was sent from the Fort to-night to officially notify the fleet at the bar that Major ANDERSON had surrendered. It is not known when the

Virginia secessionist Edmund Ruffin fired the first shot at Fort Sumter, beginning the Civil War.

Carolinians will occupy Fort Sumpter, or what is to be done with the vanquished.

Everyone is satisfied with the victory, and happy that no blood was shed.

In the city, after the surrender, bells were rung and cannon fired.

CHARLESTON, Sunday, April 14.

Negotiations were completed last night. Major ANDERSON, with his command, will evacuate Fort Sumpter this morning, and will embark on board of the war vessels off our bar.

When Fort Sumpter was in flames, and ANDERSON could only fire his guns at long intervals, the men at our batteries cheered at every fire which the gallant Major made in his last struggles, but looked defiance at the vessels of war, whose men, like cowards, stood outside without firing a gun or attempting to divert the fire of a single battery from Sumpter.

Five of ANDERSON'S men are slightly wounded.

CHARLESTON, Sunday, April 14.

The steamer *Isabel* is now steaming up, and will take Gen. BEAUREGARD to Sumpter, which will be turned over by Major ANDERSON to the Confederate States. ANDERSON and his command, it is reported, will proceed to New-York in the *Isabel*.

CHARLESTON, Sunday, April 14.

Maj. ANDERSON and his men leave to-night in the steamer *Isabel* at 11 o'clock for New-York.

The fleet is still outside.

It was a thrilling scene when Maj. ANDERSON and his men took their formal leave of Fort Sumpter.

THE TIMES CORRESPONDENT IMPRISONED.

WILMINGTON, N. C., Sunday, April 14.

I saw the first gun fired at Fort Sumpter at 4 o'clock, A. M., April 12. I witnessed the battle for six hours. At noon I was arrested by order of Gen. BEAUREGARD as a Federal spy, and was imprisoned for twenty-four hours, and then sent out of the city by Gov. PICKENS, destitute of funds. In Wilmington I was aided by Mr. PRICE, of the *Daily Journal*, and will be with you in thirty-six hours.

There are conflicting reports as to the number killed. It is generally believed that nobody is hurt. JASPER.

THE NEWS IN WASHINGTON.

WASHINGTON, Sunday, April 14.
FORT PICKENS.

The Government has no advices from Fort Pickens, but you may rely upon it that relief has been sent to it. Dispatches hence to Pensacola have positively announced the fact to Gen BRAGG, and it is very probable that fighting has begun there also by this time. No apprehension is entertained on its behalf, as it has abundant men and supplies, and, if needed, additional forces can be sent it from Fort Taylor and Tortugas.

While the Executive does not indicate his purpose in that respect, it is generally understood tonight that the contest will be waged at Charleston vigorously for the vindication of the flag at that point and the recovery of the public property there.

FROM ANOTHER CORRESPONDENT.
WASHINGTON, Sunday, April 14.

THE RECEPTION OF THE NEWS.

The excitement consequent upon the news of the bombardment and surrender of Fort Sumpter is most intense. For a long time the accounts of the surrender were utterly discredited, even the Secessionists refusing to believe the statements transmitted by their friends. When, this morning, there was no room to doubt the story, the people warmly discussed the probable effects upon the country. The Avenue was crowded from the Treasury to the telegraph offices, and the one subject was the universal theme. It seemed difficult to comprehend the possibility that after twenty hours a fort pronounced impregnable had surrendered to its assailants without having inflicted the slightest injury upon the masses engaged in the assault.

Among the Northern men there was a general determination that Major ANDERSON had at last proved untrue to the trusts reposed in him by the Government, and unworthy of the praise bestowed upon him when he evacuated Fort Moultrie and retired to Fort Sumpter. Indeed, at this time, the first suspicion of his unfaithfulness has settled into a conviction so strong that nothing but an official report and justification to the Government will remove it.

I think the facts, when known, will, however, show that Major ANDERSON deserves the commendation of the country, for a most brave and vigorous defence of his command, and that he did not surrender until it became an inevitable necessity. He will probably show by his official communication to the Government, that his men had not tasted bread for the five hours previous to the surrender; that they were utterly exhausted with the labor of firing the heavy guns; that a shell from the Cummings Point Battery fell among the shells of the Fort, causing an explosion and setting fire to the wood-work of the Fort, and that the smoke of the burning structures was so dense as to render it impossible to continue the combat, and that his force was unable to put out the flames, or even to save their own private property.

It was under these circumstances that he was at last compelled to hoist a flag of truce, and eventually to stipulate for a surrender. He is now at sea with his command, and will probably soon be landed at New-York.

THE NEWS IN THE SOUTH.

HOW IT WAS RECEIVED IN MONTGOMERY.

MONTGOMERY, Saturday, April 13.
Gen. BEAUREGARD telegraphed to the Secretary of War, late last night, that there had been heavy firing all Friday; that four guns on Fort Sumpter had been dismounted; that the Confederate batteries were all safe; that nobody was hurt; that four steamers were off the Bar, and that the sea was quite rough.

Nothing of to-day's date has been received by the War Department from Charleston.

The President has appointed T. WARREN MORSE Judge for the District of Louisiana.

MONTGOMERY, Saturday, April 13—P. M.
Major CHAMBERS, of the Alabama army, has arrived here from Pensacola, bringing Lieut. REED WORDEN, of the Federal Navy, as prisoner of war. He was bearer of dispatches to Fort Pickens and the Federal Fleet off Pensacola bar. He is held by the Secretary of War, who sent a detachment to arrest him.

Lieut. WORDEN has been compelled to give up to the Secretary of War his dispatches from Lieut. SLEMMER to the Government at Washington. The Attorney-General's opinion is requested as to the law in his case. He violated his promise to report to Gen. BRAGG, and carried in secret dispatches to Fort Pickens, showing to Gen. BRAGG other dispatches, and failing to report himself on his return.

Dispatches from Gov. PICKENS to the Secretary of War here were read by the Clerk of the War Department from the Executive buildings, in presence of President DAVIS and his Cabinet.

Seven guns were fired in honor of the victory, and there is great rejoicing in all circles.

Fort Pickens was reinforced last night.

It is understood that Charleston harbor is blockaded.

The news of the surrender of Fort Sumpter was received with immense cheering by the people of this city.

Great crowds are gathered in the streets to-night, and the Confederate and Palmetto flags are flying everywhere. Cannon are firing, the bells ringing, and great rejoicing is manifested everywhere.

HOW RECEIVED IN BALTIMORE.

BALTIMORE, Sunday, April 14.
The Union feeling in this city has been unmistakably displayed since Friday. Men with cockades and secession emblems have been chased by crowds and protected by the police.

The bark *Fanny Fenshaw* hoisted the secession flag to-day, and a crowd compelled a boy on the vessel to take it down. The Captain afterwards rehoisted it and required a detachment of thirty police to protect it from the people. The indignation is intense. All the other vessels in port hoisted the American flag. The Captain is a Union man, but hoisted the flag under instructions from the owners of the vessel, the Messrs. CURRY, of Richmond. Va.

HOW RECEIVED IN ALEXANDRIA, VA.

ALEXANDRIA, Va., Sunday, April 14.
A meeting was held here last night to form a home guard. Resolutions to resist Northern aggression were adopted, while several speakers advocated secession. Others argue in favor of a Convention to unite the Border States.

to the Government at Washington. The Attorney-General's opinion is requested as to the law in his case. He violated his promise to report to Gen. Bragg, and carried in secret dispatches to Fort Pickens, showing to Gen. Bragg other dispatches, and failing to report himself on his return.

Dispatches from Gov. Pickens to the Secretary of War here were read by the Clerk of the War Department from the Executive buildings, in presence of President Davis and his Cabinet.

Seven guns were fired in honor of the victory, and there is great rejoicing in all circles.

Fort Pickens was reinforced last night.

It is understood that Charleston harbor is blockaded. The news of the surrender of Fort Sumpter was received with immense cheering by the people of this city.

Great crowds are gathered in the streets to-night, and the Confederate and Palmetto flags are flying everywhere. Cannon are firing, the bells ringing, and great rejoicing is manifested everywhere.

HOW RECEIVED IN BALTIMORE.

BALTIMORE, Sunday, April 14.

The Union feeling in this city has been unmistakably displayed since Friday. Men with cockades and secession emblems have been chased by crowds and protected by the police.

The bark *Funny Fenshaw* hoisted the secession flag to-day, and a crowd compelled a boy on the vessel to take it down. The Captain afterwards rehoisted it and required a detachment of thirty police to protect it from the people. The indignation is intense. All the other vessels in port hoisted the American flag. The Captain is a Union man, but hoisted the flag under instructions from the owners of the vessel, the Messrs. Curry, of Richmond, Va.

HOW RECEIVED IN ALEXANDRIA, VA.

ALEXANDRIA, Va., Sunday, April 14.

A meeting was held here last night to form a home guard. Resolutions to resist Northern aggression were adopted, while several speakers advocated secession. Others argue in favor of a Convention to unite the Border States.

IMPORTANT FROM VIRGINIA.

PROCEEDINGS OF THE STATE CONVENTION.

RICHMOND, Va., Saturday, April 13.

The Virginia State Convention reassembled to-day.

In Committee of the Whole the first three sections of the proposed amendments to the Constitution were adopted without material amendment.

A new section, offered by Mr. Wise, providing that compensation be made in all cases where property " in persons held to service or to labor" has been or may be taken for the public use, as in impressment, &c., was adopted.

The fourth section was then adopted.

The fifth section, prohibiting the importation of slaves, was taken up.

Numerous amendments to it were offered, and finally it was adopted, with an amendment providing that nothing herein contained shall apply to the Southern States which have or may declare their separation, in case their separation be acknowledged and continued.

The debate then turned exclusively upon the surrender of Fort Sumpter.

Messrs. Carlile and Early deprecated the action of South Carolina in firing, and expressed devotion to the Stars and Stripes.

Leading Secessionists replied, and applauded the gallantry of South Carolina, and maintained that, whatever the Convention might do, the people would now carry the State out of the Union.

The Committee here rose, when a communication was received from Gov. Letcher, inclosing a dispatch from Gov. Pickens, dated Charleston, to-day.

The dispatch gives an account of Friday's bombardment of Fort Sumpter, and says that not a man on our batteries is hurt. It adds:

" Fort Sumpter was furious in its fire on us. Our iron battery did great damage to the fort on its southern wall. Our shells fell freely into the fort, and the effect is supposed to be serious, as they are not firing from the fort this morning. Our battery dismounted three of the largest of the columbiads of the enemy. We will take the fort, and can sink the fleet, if they attempt to force their way up the channel. If they attempt to land elsewhere, we can whip them. We have now nearly seven thousand of the best troops in the world, and a reserve of ten thousand on the railroads. War is commenced, and we triumph or we perish. Please let me know what Virginia will do."

To this Gov. Letcher stated, that he replied that the Convention would determine.

Mr. Wise offered a resolution in view of the late information, recommending the people of Virginia at once to unite in defence of their institutions and make common cause with the Confederate States.

Without taking action on the resolution the Convention adjourned.

It was openly stated in debate that the Southern army would march through Virginia to the North, and that thousands would join them.

Mr. Early said this would be 'invasion and should be repelled.

Editorials

Major Anderson.

Our telegraphic advices from Charleston announce that Major Anderson and his fellow officers have left that port, in the steamer *Isabel*, for this City. Mrs. A. has been at the Brevoort House during the last few weeks.

Major Anderson will meet with a hearty welcome in this City, as, indeed, he would in any part of the country. It is very easy to say that he has done nothing more than his duty, and he would himself be the first to say it. But he has done it with a steady fidelity, and a degree of wisdom and discretion seldom surpassed in any service. He has been the first of our officers to bear the brunt of this great rebellion. It was a fearful and a trying emergency, but he has met it with the skill of a good officer, and the loyalty of a true American.

The Fall of Sumpter.

It is by no means impossible, after all, that what seemed at first to be a national calamity, and which rendered yesterday a memorably dark day in the experience of every patriot, was after all a substantial and crowning advantage, anticipated and provided for in the plans of the Administration. Its policy has been uniform and consistent—to protect the property of the Government, and enforce its laws. It will yield nothing belonging to it unless dispossessed by superior force, but it will not weaken the reputation of its military arm, by a reckless waste of men or means in the maintenance or attempted recapture of any comparatively valueless position. This arm is wielded by that illustrious Chief and Patriot, whose forty years of active service have never known dishonor or defeat, who, in the disappearance of our great leaders, is providentially left to us, and under whose guidance, though we may not for the time be advised of his plans, we are always sure of being led to substantial success.

I is altogether probable that Fort Sumpter could not, at any reasonable cost, have been relieved, after Mr. Lincoln assumed the reins of Government till he had collected the Army and Navy, dispersed by Mr. Floyd, in order to render Washington and the forts and magazines at the South an easy prey, and could assume something like vigorous offensive action. It was important that Fort Sumpter should be retained as a point upon which to concentrate the military strength of the rebels, securing to him precious hours in which to concentrate his forces upon more important and menaced points. To abandon it would instantly relieve a large force to operate against Washington and Fort Pickens. To hold this force inactive till they could be reinforced in a manner to defy attack, was a master-stroke of policy, and does credit even to Gen. Scott's military reputation.

This advantage being gained, the Administration was then prepared to test the question whether the Confederated States would allow the sending of supplies to a handful of famished soldiers, cooped up in Fort Sumpter. To relieve their wants was an act of mercy as well as peace. To prevent it, would be an act of war. This war the rebels have inaugurated. Major Anderson's orders were to act as he did at Fort Moultrie—to consult the emergency ; to yield, if necessary, to superior force. The fleet did not render assistance, as it could not without the risk of being disabled, and, perhaps, destroyed. Government was too weak in its naval arm to encounter any such risks. It would interfere with its proper command of the sea, and with its plans, to commence an immediate enforcement of the revenue laws at the ports of the rebel States. Fort Sumpter, as a strategetic point, is of no sort of consequence. It was constructed solely for defence against foreign invasion, which is not contemplated by the Government.

The port of Charleston, we learn by way of Montgomery, is *blockaded*. Every vessel entering or leaving it is to pass the *surveillance* of a ship-of-war. No wonder that "the Charlestonians regarded with execration the fleet that refused to come to the rescue of the gallant Anderson." It was not the plan of the Administration that they should go to his rescue at too great a peril. It was from the start destined to an entirely different field and mode of action. Neither the retention or surrender of Fort Sumpter could have any bearing on the policy the Government had marked out for itself. This was an isolated case, that stood solely on its own merits. Government could not allow its Flag to be disgraced by retreat. *It is strengthened in every part by the surrender of the Fort.* It may not attempt, at present, its recapture, but will notify the Confederated States that, till it is restored, *the commerce of Charleston must pass over the deck of a ship-of-war.*

The first act in the drama which has terminated in the surrender of Fort Sumpter, instead of being a defeat, is, when we come to look at its effects, a most brilliant success. It has thrown upon the Confederated States the entire responsibility of commencing the war. It has given us time to arm for offensive operations, and to *collect and to place before every Southern port a fleet sufficient to enforce the revenue laws, and to protect our commerce from Southern pirates.* We still hold every point of value in the Gulf—Fort Pickens, Key West and Tortugas. We turn the Confederated States upon themselves. We hold the command of the sea, upon which they cannot even float Alderman Boole's scows. Their armies, which they have collected and armed with such cost, they may turn against each other, to help to stifle the little freedom of thought or expression that may yet exist. They are harmless against us. The little commerce that may still seek their ports must submit to our revenue laws.

All this the Confederates at Montgomery may, in their impotent rage, contemplate with the same execration that the people of Charleston did the fleet that refused to expose itself to fire. Water is not their element. We command the avenue upon which their existence depends. They have commenced the war. We now propose to give them a taste of our power without exposing ourselves to their attacks. Mr. Jefferson Davis had good cause for being sick in bed at the reception of the news. The magnitude of the advantage gained at Washington, and the utter inability of the Confederate forces to cope with us in the arena we have chosen in which to carry on the contest, accounts for the lowered tone adopted at Montgomery and the feeble salvo of *seven* guns at their triumph. We are now prepared for a contest in a field in which we hold their lives in our hands, and on which they cannot harm us to the extent of a hair. We are prepared to follow up such a contest till they are entirely satisfied.

The New-York Times.

VOL. X....NO. 2986.   NEW-YORK, WEDNESDAY, APRIL 17, 1861.   PRICE TWO CENTS.

THE COMING STRUGGLE.

Patriotic Responses to the Government Appeal.

MEN AND MEANS IN ABUNDANCE.

How the Call for Volunteers is Received in the Border States.

THE EXPECTED ATTACK ON FORT PICKENS

Call on the Confederate States for 32,000 More Troops.

The Departure of Major Anderson and his Men from Charleston.

The Virginia Convention in Secret Session.

Volunteers swelled Union ranks in response to the President's requests for troops, but their fighting ability was doubted.

OUR WASHINGTON DISPATCHES.
WASHINGTON, Tuesday, April 16.

RUMORED BOMBARDMENT OF FORT PICKENS.

A rumor is circulating in town that the Government has received a dispatch from Pensacola announcing the commencement of the bombardment of Fort Pickens. This is erroneous, and if an attack has been made the Government has no advices of the fact.

MARYLAND RESPONDS LOYALLY.

Maryland has responded, through her constituted authorities, announcing that *she will promptly furnish her quota of men for the maintenance of the Government.*

Baltimore is reported as strong for the Union. There is to be a large meeting there of Minute Men to-night, and it is understood that two regiments will be raised on the spot to-night. The editor of the *Clipper* is among the leaders of the Union men. There are threats of destruction of the *Clipper* office, but it will not be permitted by the people, although some of the leading officials and military men in that City are rank Secessionists.

DELAWARE FOR THE UNION.

No official advices yet from Delaware. But there is good reason to believe that she will not fail in her duty in the present crisis.

KENTUCKY REFUSES HER QUOTA OF TROOPS.

The Secretary of War has received dispatches to-day from Gov. MAGOFFIN, of Kentucky, that he should not respond to the call for forces, and that no soldiers would, with his consent, leave the State to coerce any of the Southern sisters of Kentucky. A private dispatch is also received by a gentleman connected with a strong Union paper in Kentucky, stating that the State authorities would allow no troops to join the Federal forces, nor any Federal force to pass through the State. There was great excitement throughout the State upon the reception of the proclamation. A dispatch from Louisville says there is great danger of a mob attacking the *Journal* office, which, under the gallant PRENTICE, still stands out boldly for the Union.

GOVERNMENT RECRUITING IN KENTUCKY.

Major WOOD, of the Second Cavalry, has been ordered to Kentucky on recruiting duty.

NORTH CAROLINA, MISSOURI AND VIRGINIA TROOPS NOT FORTHCOMING.

Gov. ELLIS, of North Carolina, also telegraphed the President that he could not respond, as he had doubts of his authority and right to do so. His dispatch is regarded by the Administration as courteous and gentlemanly, which can hardly be said of Gov. MAGOFFIN's communication.

The Governor of Missouri also refuses to respond. Gov. LETCHER, of Virginia, also has unofficially refused.

INDEPENDENT CORPS COLLECTING.

The Secretary of War will accept an independent corps of Volunteers from any of the States where the Governors of such States refuse to call out the militia. Two regiments from Kentucky, two from Tennessee, and two from Missouri, "independent," it is expected will be tendered and accepted to-morrow. The War Department mustered in a large number of Volunteers to-day. The National Rifles of this city, of which so many members refused to take the oath, is now fully filled up by volunteers, all of whom took the oath and are each day performing guard duty. They were complimented by Adjt.-Gen. THOMAS, and cheered by the ladies from windows and the crowds in the streets as they passed.

KANSAS COMPLAINS OF NEGLECT.

The citizens of Kansas now here complain bitterly that their State was not called upon, and say they will tender a regiment anyhow.

THE MASSACHUSETTS QUOTA DOUBLED.

The quota of Massachusetts was doubled to-day, giving her one brigade of four thousand men. Gen. B. F. BUTLER, late the Democratic candidate for Governor of that State and member of the Charleston Breckinridge Democratic National Convention, will command the Brigade. Three companies will report at Washington and one at Fort Monroe.

GOV. SPRAGUE PROFFERS PERSONAL AID.

The voluntary offer of Gov. SPRAGUE of Rhode Island, to bring on his own forces and head them, has changed the mind of very many men, and excited a strong Union feeling in Maryland and elsewhere. The defection in the North was expected. This puts an end to it, and has an excellent moral effect.

THE SECESSIONISTS ENROLLING.

Dr. C. BOYLE, the Commander of the National Volunteers of this city, "secession corps," says that one hundred and twenty men joined the corps last evening. One advantage of martial law here would be that such men could be summarily disposed of at once.

CABINET COUNCILS.

The Cabinet has been engaged all day on military and naval affairs, and civil appointments have the go-by for the present. The sudden emergency which has arisen demanding instant preparation on a large scale for war, necessarily demands constant and severe labor on the part of the Executive Government, in considering and deciding upon the plans of operation presented by the military authorities.

The TIMES' articles of to-day upon the crisis have attracted marked attention here in official circles. I know at least one member of the Cabinet who expressed to-night decided admiration of their vigor and accurate measurement of the necessities of the hour.

WHAT WILL VIRGINIA DO?

Opinions here continue divided relative to the probable course of Virginia. Some of her citizens sojourning here are positive she cannot be dragged out of the Union, except by revolution, which would give her a civil war of her own. A greater number think her Convention will pass the Ordinance of Secession, but that her people will reject it. If Virginia secedes, it is a distinct declaration of war against the General Government, and the first thing she will have to do is to possess herself of Fortress Monroe, Harper's Ferry, and other public property, which will at once precipitate an hundred thousand men upon her in support of the Government, devastating her territory, and concentrating on her head all the plagues which the seven "Confederate States" have raised, and should share alone. Instead of preserving her domestic institutions by this, her own citizens are assuring her that war will make her a Free State within ninety days; while, if she continues to stand, she may yet stem the tide of disunion, and save blood and the dreadful arbitrament of the sword.

RUMORED IMMINENT ATTACK ON WASHINGTON.

There is a report here to-night that the Virginia Secessionists are approaching Washington. It created a sensation, but it is not true.

Capt. JUNIUS PALMER's company of Indiana cavalry, which arrived here only Saturday last, is already fully mounted and ready for efficient service.

THE VIRGINIA CONVENTION IN SECRET SESSION.
RICHMOND, Va., Tuesday, April 16.

The Virginia State Convention is in secret session this forenoon. Reporters are excluded, and consequently nothing is known of the proceedings.

A telegraph dispatch from Gov. PICKENS to Hon. HENRY A. WISE, says: "It is reported that eleven vessels are off the bar, and are stopping vessels engaged in regular trade."

The papers of this city express confidence that Gen. Scott will resign.

The Richmond *Whig* hauled down the Stars and Stripes this morning, and ran up the flag of Virginia.

LATEST DISPATCHES FROM MONTGOMERY

MONTGOMERY, Tuesday, April 16.

The Cabinet were in council this morning. Mr. LINCOLN's proclamation was read amid bursts of laughter.

The Secretary of War authorises the statement that 32,000 more troops were called out to-day to meet LINCOLN's men.

MONTGOMERY, Tuesday, April 16.

Gen. PILLOW guarantees to raise 10,000 men in Tennessee, in twenty days, if President DAVIS will accept of them, and there is no doubt expressed but what he will accept of the offer.

Hon. A. H STEVENS, in Atlanta, Ga., last night said that it would require seventy-five times seventy-five thousand men to intimidate the Confederate States and then it could not be done.

Of the 32,000 troops called out to-day, 5,000 are from each State except Florida, the number from that State being 2,000.

The Southern people say that they will suppress LINCOLN and SEWARD's combination, which is less of a Government than our's, and drive LINCOLN back to his abode in a quicker style than he came through Maryland.

There is perfect confidence expressed here that we can, with DAVIS, PILLOW, BRECKINRIDGE and BEAUREGARD, wipe out LINCOLN's 75,000 men. Our munitions of war will hold out longer than LINCOLN's money.

Gen. PILLOW's Division of Tennessee troops has been accepted by Mr. DAVIS. Gen. PILLOW returned to Tennessee immediately.

We have no controversy but with the Black Republicans.

Editorials

The Contest and the Relative Strength of Parties to It.

From the progress of the inventive arts, the chances of war among nations possessing an equal amount of courage and endurance are almost exactly measured by the amount of *money* a belligerent can command. Money is equivalent to numerical superiority in men, in ships, in means of locomotion and subsistence, and in the perfection and completeness of instruments of destruction. Success is no longer an attribute of a particular nationality, or the fortune of a particular General, or a matter of accident, but depends upon *mass*, and the skill with which this is wielded. The combatant excelling in these two conditions must in the end win, no matter what reverses it may at first suffer from want of preparation, or training, or habitude.

This premise, which is universally conceded, should relieve us of any concern as to the result of the contest in which we are now engaging, no matter how wide may be its range, or the extent to which it may be pushed. We may concede personal courage to our opponents, fully equal to our own, and still leave them in hopeless inferiority as to their ability to maintain anything like an equal fight. The Confederate States contain a white population of 2,560,000, or about one-eighth of the population of the Northern States. The latter can, if necessary, bring a force *eight times greater* into the field. All the Slave States together have a white population of only 8,000,000, against 19,000,000 in the North. Measured by numbers, the North is twice and a half as powerful, assuming all the Southern States to be a unit in sentiment and purpose. But this is impossible. Missouri in no contingency will join the Gulf Confederacy, neither will Delaware, nor Maryland, nor Western Virginia, nor Eastern Kentucky, nor Tennessee. In case of hostilities, the proper surveillance over the negro would compel at least one-half of the white males to remain at home as a local police, increasing the disparity to such a degree as to render it the

height of fool-hardiness for the South to venture upon the contest.

How is it with regard to munitions of war? In heavy ordnance and the like the South may be pretty well supplied, from the forts they have seized and plundered. But in the seceding States there is neither a powder-mill nor a foundry for the casting of cannon, nor an establishment for the manufacture of arms. Did any such establishment exist, they could never turn out material or arms that could match those manufactured at the North. The seceding States to day are being supplied from ourselves with everything they use. But for this source they could not put a regiment in the field. Disarm them, and they must remain so until they can again supply themselves by purchase. The Southern States are a people without artisans. Labor is held in disgrace. The greater portion of the white population are ignorant. To say that such a people can supply the very first conditions upon which success depends, a proper armament, and compete with the trained skill of the North, is an absurdity that carries its own refutation. Take away the arms the Federal Government have distributed through the South, or that have been stolen, and they would be impotent for any military exploit whatever.

They are equally weak in their commissariat. The seceding States cannot manufacture a yard of clothing fit for soldier's wear, nor raise the food for his rations. These must be supplied from the North, if at all. They are still weaker in the grand *sine qua non*—CASH. This the seceding States are literally without, and with the exception of one or two

points, never had any. It is the law there, that the crop is realized and spent long before it is gathered. Charleston was looked upon as the richest city South, in proportion to its population. Yet Charleston is almost completely exhausted. The State is so pressed that it cannot carry on the work necessary to complete its Capitol. All its banks are broken, with hardly a dollar of coin in their vaults. Its contributions to secession are forced loans. There is no other city South that had any money except New-Orleans, and this can be had only by forced loans from the banks. This resource will soon be exhausted, and then there must be an end both of borrowing and of forced loans. With all the bluster displayed, the $15,000,000 loan cannot be sold to voluntary purchasers. Nor can a second loan be put off, should this one be wrung from unwilling victims. The moment a State secedes its credit is ruined. The conviction is universal that secession will end in *repudiation*. A people that so readily trample under foot the most sacred obligations, will not be long in throwing off a debt the moment it is regarded as a burden. Nominally, Virginia is still a loyal State; but the fear that she will secede, has caused her bonds to fall to 57—the same bonds that a few years ago were sought after at 115, and but for secession would to-day be selling at a handsome premium!

Seceding States, individually, cannot borrow, because they deny all legal responsibilities. The Confederate States cannot, because they allow any one to secede from them at

Lieutenant General Winfield Scott, a hero of the Mexican War, was in command of Union forces at the outbreak of the war.

will, and because they embrace two *black sheep* among them, Mississippi and Florida. No one will trust a firm where these two are leading members, neither at home nor abroad, nor among themselves. In whatever direction the Confederate States may look, they can get no money, except by spoliation, which soon exhausts what it feeds on. Their people have none, and they can show their face in no foreign market.

The South lies entirely at the mercy of the North in their innumerable points vulnerable to attack. They want 200,000 men as a defence against 10,000 on board a well-appointed fleet. One day this force could threaten Norfolk; the next Wilmington; the next Charleston; the next Savannah; then Florida, Mobile, New-Orleans and Galveston. No one could tell where the blow was to be struck, and consequently every menaced point would have to be well guarded. Such a fleet and force could in six months put the whole South in a perfect frenzy, by constantly hovering upon their coast with hostile demonstrations. They could not touch it, and could only regard it from their shores with impotent rage.

What is the contrast the North presents to this picture? Vast wealth proffered to Government with a generous hand—hundreds of millions, if necessary, and with it a half a million of men, supplied by a homogeneous, united and enthusiastic people. Each State can place and maintain a respectable force in the field, and several of them, armies. Every one of them can raise any required amount of money at the legal, and many of them at much lower rates of interest. The credit of all is without stain. The value of their securities is unaffected by the civil war. Contrast the bonds of the State of New-York with those of Virginia, the former selling at *double* the price of the latter. The new war loan of New-York will be eagerly sought for; while, if Virginia secedes, she cannot borrow a dollar. Suppose these two States to be pitted against each other, does any one doubt the issue?

On the land, the Northern States alone constitute a first-class military power, in their wealth and the number of men they can arm and maintain in the field. The skill of their artisans is the admiration of the world. In food they can supply a continent. To say that such a people cannot overmatch one rude to the last degree in all its industries, capable of producing neither their food, nor clothing, nor arms, nor means of locomotion—a people, the greater portion of whom are unskillful and untrained, and impatient of all discipline or restraint—is to affirm that ignorance is stronger than intelligence, poverty than wealth, and wild insubordination than training and culture.

The North have an immeasurable advantage in its command of the sea. All the Southern produce must float upon it to market. We consequently hold in our hand the very elements of their existence. We could reduce them to beggary without moving or equipping a soldier. A few ships stationed off their forts would do all this. With the mercantile marine in our harbor, which could be got ready for sea at a week's notice, we could almost instantly throw 100,000 men upon any point to be attacked. We might threaten a dozen points at the same moment, and so divide and distract the enemy, that resistance at the point where the blow was to be struck would be impossible. With the command of the sea in our hands, the South, with ten times their present means, could not defend themselves. They have more than 5,000 miles of frontier

line to protect, requiring thrice the number of men they could bring into the field. With such a frontier to guard, how supremely silly are all threats of invading the *North*.

In this contest the Government has only steadily, but firmly, to pursue the course it has marked out, and ultimate success must follow with as much certainty as matter obeys its laws.

Sumter and the Administration.

The *Express* is doing its utmost to excite public distrust of the Administration. It publishes a letter from Washington, in which the writer says:

"*I am authorized to state that Gen. Scott, and Gen. Totten, the Chief of the Engineer Corps, wholly disapproved of the proposed reinforcement of Fort Sumter. Gen. Totten*, in particular, was decidedly opposed to it. Being a Connecticut man, and married to an Albany wife, Gen. Totten cannot be accused of complicity with Jefferson Davis. Nor will any Republican question Gen. Scott's loyalty. The attempt to reinforce the Southern forts, and to 'reoccupy' the Government property in the seceding States, was therefore made *without the sanction of the Lieutenant-General of the Army and the General of Engineers*—the two officers, whose counsels, above those of all other men, ought to have been eagerly followed. What is the consequence? So far as Sumter is concerned, failure—and the lowering of the American flag to the flag of the Southern Confederacy!"

By *whom* this writer is authorized to make so serious a statement, he does not say. It certainly will not command the belief of the people of the country, until it is sustained by evidence which will not admit of doubt.

President Lincoln knows no more of War than he does of Sanscrit,—nor has he a single military man in his Cabinet. But he has common sense, and is not at all likely to undertake the personal conduct of a military campaign, or to intrust it to anybody but the great Commander, who is the most skillful and scientific soldier living, and whose official position entitles him to take the lead in any military operations in which the country may be engaged. Gen. Scott is at Washington for the express purpose of giving his counsel in regard to the military operations which have been forced upon the Government. We shall not believe that the President would enter upon such an enterprise as the attempted reinforcement of Fort Sumter, without the support, and still less against the advice of Gen. Scott. Such an act would very seriously impair the confidence of the public in the wisdom of his Administration.

We adhere to the opinion we expressed on Monday—but which rests, we confess, on no positive information—namely, that it was never intended to provision or reinforce Fort Sumter, at the cost of an engagement between the fleet and the powerful batteries of the rebels. Such an engagement could have had but one result. The defeat of the attempt, with the destruction of the vessels and the ultimate reduction of the fort, was as certain as any future event could possibly be. War, especially a war of fortifications, has become purely and strictly a matter of science. Its result can be calculated with positive certainty. And we presume that no military man, whose judgment is of the slightest value, can be found at Washington or elsewhere, who would take the responsibility of attempting to reinforce and hold Fort Sumter with the forces available for that purpose.

If the President did really intend to do this—against the advice or without the sanction of General Scott, then his first step has been a gross and unpardonable blunder, one which, if the same policy were to be persisted in, would utterly destroy the public confidence in his ability to conduct a campaign. Our own belief is, that the attempt at reinforcement was a *front*— that its object was to put upon the rebels the

full and clear responsibility of commencing the war, and that no more obstinate defence was contemplated than would suffice to vindicate the honor of the Government. Upon this supposition, we are perfectly satisfied with the result. Upon any other, we should have very grave doubts of the wisdom and statesmanship that preside over our national councils.

Major Anderson.

The *Courier and Enquirer* makes a most disingenuous attempt to shuffle out of the responsibility of its gross attack upon the honor and loyalty of Major Anderson, for by quoting part of a paragraph from a telegraphic dispatch from Washington in the Times of Monday. Our correspondent stated that *suspicions* of Major Anderson's fidelity were excited in Washington by the news of his surrender; but he adds the following, which the *Courier and Enquirer* omits in its quotation:

"I think the facts, when known, will, however, show that Major Anderson *deserves the commendation of the country, for a most brave and vigorous defence of his command, and that he did not surrender until it became an inevitable necessity.* He will probably show, by his official communication to the Government, that his men had not tasted bread for the five hours previous to the surrender; that they were utterly exhausted with the labor of firing the heavy guns; that a shell from the Cummings Point Battery fell among the shells of the Fort, causing an explosion and setting fire to the wood-work of the Fort, and that the smoke of the burning structures was so dense as to render it impossible to continue the combat, and that his force was unable to put out the flames, or even to save their own private property. *It was under these circumstances that he was at last compelled to hoist a flag of truce, and eventually to stipulate for a surrender.*

The *Courier and Enquirer* has no right to quote the Times in support of its assault, and it certainly has no right to garble the paragraph by which it seeks to shield itself.

The *Courier and Enquirer* publishes the following extracts of letters written by Capt. Doubleday, from Fort Sumter:

Fort Sumter, Tuesday, Jan. 8, 1861.
I notice in the papers that the *Star of the West* has been sent here with 250 troops, but this is so improbable, we do not believe it. It requires a war-vessel to enter the harbor now. * * * So far they have staved off actual hostilities; but if *they fire upon any vessel which runs up the American flag, we will give them a taste of our columbiads.*

Jan. 9.—Early this morning I saw the *Star of the West*, with two American flags hoisted, approach the battery opposite to us on Morris Island. It was a beautiful sight, and my heart beat to see it. The battery is sheltered from our direct fire by some high sand hills. I saw a shot fired from it at the steamer, and immediately notified Major Anderson and caused the long roll to be beat. The men were rapidly formed at their guns. The enemy continued to fire upon the American flag; and as the steamer kept on her way, Fort Moultrie opened its fire in addition. I told the Major that guns were pointed and ready to fire. *but he would not permit us to do so. I felt deeply mortified to stand still and look on, without doing anything to assist the vessel. Though we did not see the steamer's name, yet we had no doubt it was the Star of the West, with troops on board.*

Jan. 14.—Major Anderson's orders from the Government, while in Fort Moultrie, were, to act strictly on the defensive.

Feb. 6—Major Anderson is a Southern man by birth and feeling, and sympathises with the South in its demands, but *considers secession as an unjustifiable means of securing them.* His situation here is a cruel one, and I feel deeply for him. He says if Kentucky secedes he will resign and go to Europe, for he will never fight against her nor the Stars and Stripes. I consider him as an honorable and brave man, placed in an exceedingly difficult situation. Much as we differ as to the propriety of some of his acts, and in political belief, I have a high respect for him as a man and an officer.

The *Courier and Enquirer* has quoted Capt. Doubleday as authority for its denunciations of Major Anderson. These extracts give an unqualified denial to the imputation. Instead of furnishing the slightest support for its censure, they afford the strongest possible evidence of its injustice.

The New-York Times.

VOL. X—NO. 2987.   NEW-YORK, THURSDAY, APRIL 18, 1861.   PRICE TWO CENTS.

Editorials

Prompt Action Demanded—Carry the War South!

It has been the misfortune of Government, throughout its contest with the seceding States, to have acted upon a policy purely *negative* in dealing with a party acting on a thoroughly *positive* one, and straining every nerve to accomplish its objects, before we could understand their full designs, or defeat them when discovered. Mr. BUCHANAN'S Cabinet was in league with the traitors, and purposely disarmed our forts, and scattered our army and fleet. Mr. LINCOLN was forced by his position to assume the parental attitude, and entreat the erring States to return.

Although these States were in open rebellion when he assumed the reins of government, public opinion would not at the outset have defended with sufficient unanimity the stand he has now taken. After his inauguration, the works were constructed that rendered Fort Sumter untenable. For months have the rebels, unmolested, been constructing works directly under the guns of Fort Pickens, for the purpose of reducing this fort as they did Fort Sumter. When the attack is made, an immense slaughter must follow whether the Fort is captured or not. A few shots at the right moment would have saved all this.

The preparations of the seceding States for war are now going on with unabated vigor in the loyal States. Immense shipments of arms are almost daily made through this City to the Confederate Government. All the mechanics of Richmond, Virginia, and the Tredegar works, an immense establishment in that city, have been for months turning off daily vast quantities of heavy artillery, shot and shell, for the seceding States. These can supply themselves with munitions of war from no other source but the North or Border States. They have been arming under our very noses, with as much impunity as they could in the interior of Alabama or Mississippi. It is certainly a singular spectacle to see an enemy, already in collision with us, quietly fabricating at our establishments the very weapons with which to deal us a mortal blow! Against such arming on our own soil, which is just as notorious to Government as the existence of the sun, not a step has been taken—not a protest uttered!

This is certainly discouraging, and shows how far our Government is still from realizing the real nature of the contest in which it is engaged. It is one of life and death; yet we are acting as if the seceding States were our own children, who would one day return in filial duty to their places in the domestic circle. An immense army has been called out, at the very moment it was entirely within our power, with the force on hand, to deal a heavier blow than 100,000 men could on land inflict. Why should the lives of 75,000 men be exposed, when the seceding States might be rendered utterly powerless and entirely at our mercy simply by closing their ports? From this instant, no ship should leave or enter those ports on any pretext. Every one should be sealed up. The idea that cotton should be allowed egress through them, is one of those weak fancies not yet worked out of the cranium of the Administration. Three-quarters of all the crop grown in the South can be delivered at the port of New-York at a cost not exceeding half a cent per pound that of sending it forward through their own ports. The closing of these would hardly exert an appreciable effect in reducing the exportation of cotton, as far as the matter of transportation is concerned. It would merely change its route, and send it to market over the public works leading to the Eastern cities, and compensate to a great degree the losses secession has occasioned.

We respect the humanity of the Administration, but humane wars are always the most cruel in the end, because they are interminable. The most humane act is a decided blow in the outset. A little resolution on the part of Mr. BUCHANAN would have averted secession altogether. The present Administration have, and are to a certain extent, copying his irresolution. It is still temporizing. Why can it not appreciate the crisis, and reflect the aroused sentiment of the country? In a few weeks we shall hear of the capture of our merchant ships by pirates and privateers fitted out at Southern ports. It will *then*, after the mischief is done, come into the head of the Administration that these ports should have been closed. Why not do this instantly, and avert a loss which otherwise must happen? Why not strike *the* decisive blow at the seceding States, one that will soonest bring them to terms? Why does the fleet sent to Charleston return from its bootless errand for instructions? Why did it not proceed at once to its more obvious duties?

Government should instantly wake up to a full consciousness of its position. Its destruction is the darling object of the conspirators. It is in a death struggle. A fleet of observation in the Gulf, carrying a land force of 10,000 men, and threatening every exposed point, would do more to keep JEFF. DAVIS from Washington than 50,000 troops concentrated in it. Let us at once carry the war into Africa, where we can deal a fatal blow, without exposing ourselves to the loss of a man.

Why Jeff. Davis Selects Virginia as the Seat of the War.

Mr. JEFFERSON DAVIS' bid to Virginia is a master-stroke of policy. He says to her, "Secede, make me Despot, and I will make your capital the seat of my Government." The State will very probably catch at the gilded bait. Mr. DAVIS well knows that he cannot carry on a campaign in the seceding States. His army, wherever placed, would soon starve, if collected in masses. All his dominions are barren of food. Great distress already prevails for the want of it among all classes. The only grain raised by them is corn. Some pork is grown, but no beef. The alternatives presented to him, consequently, are, to disband; to supply himself by purchase; or to move his forces to a theatre *where food can be seized*, so as to make war support war. Soldiers must live, and when hungry they are not very scrupulous as to the party who feeds them. The great crop of Virginia is wheat. The central and western counties raise a large amount of excellent *beef*. Towards this favored land, so well fitted for military operations, Mr. DAVIS, in the lack of cash, casts his longing eyes; and he tells its people if they will make him King he will transfer his army to their soil, and fight their battles!

Mr. DAVIS has another equally benevolent motive. The existence of a body of 75,000 men roaming over the seceding States would seriously affect the culture and production of Cotton. If these States are to be the theatre of hostilities, it may reduce the production one-half or two-thirds, or destroy it altogether. If he can transfer the war North, he thinks all will be peace and quietness in the Cotton States, while chivalrous Virginia may suffer the sack of her cities, the desolation of her fields, the liberation of her negroes, and see all her interests completely blasted. Of all the States that have seceded, or that threaten to secede, Virginia is the most vulnerable and exposed. The United States holding Fort Monroe, completely cut off her communication with the sea. From this fort expeditions may penetrate by water far into her interior. On the north, Washington will soon be a fortified camp of 25,000 men. On the west she will be threatened by her own free territory, and by Ohio and Pennsylvania. Between all these forces she will be ground to powder—eaten up by those who professed to come to her aid, and commanded at every turn by the overwhelming forces of the United States.

One would suppose that here was enough in prospect to make the State pause. To throw herself into the hands of the Secessionists is certain destruction. We are told that of her bonds issued, at least $10,000,000 are in the hands of her own people. Secession puts a wet sponge over these. She has 1,800 miles of railroad constructed, at a cost of $70,000,000, which must become almost entirely valueless. She has a *half a million* of slaves, that in good times would be worth $400,000,000. In case of hostility on her own soil, these would disappear, with very little return to their owners. The territory would become a prey to the contending forces, her property utterly destroyed, and her people subjected to the iron rule of a military despotism, which has *abolished the ballot-box*, and which pays no more regard to the popular will than the Emperor of Austria. And for what purpose are all these sacrifices to be made? To save the consistency of such fanatics as WISE and such knaves as FLOYD! Under the lead of these men she proposes to inaugurate her new career. What a contrast she presents to the days of the Revolution, when the types were WASHINGTON, JEFFERSON, MASON and HENRY! What blessings has she enjoyed under the Government they established, and which she has, to a great degree, controlled to the present time! If she goes, it will be another evidence of that unaccountable Pro-Slavery passion, which is sweeping like wildfire over the South, depriving men of all sense and reason, and impelling any one upon whom it seizes to certain destruction.

The New-York Times.

VOL. X—NO. 2989. NEW-YORK, SATURDAY, APRIL 20, 1861. PRICE TWO CENTS.

HIGHLY EXCITING NEWS:

SOUTHERN PORTS TO BE BLOCKADED.

A Day of Riot and Blood in Baltimore.

Pennsylvania and Massachusetts Volunteers Attacked.

Two Massachusetts Men Killed and Several Wounded.

They Return the Fire and Kill Seven of the Rioters.

The Secessionists Nonplussed at Harper's Ferry.

The Arms Destroyed and the Building Burnt.

Departure of the Seventh Regiment of New-York.

The Most Impressive Scene Ever Witnessed in Broadway.

THE WAR SPIRIT THROUGHOUT THE NORTH.

PROCLAMATION FROM PRESIDENT LINCOLN.

WASHINGTON, Friday, April 19.

The President has issued a proclamation, stating that an insurrection against the Government of the United States has broken out in the States of South Carolina, Georgia, Alabama, Florida, Mississippi, Louisiana and Texas, and the laws of the United States, for the collection of the revenue, cannot be effectually executed therein, conformably to that provision of the Constitution, which requires duties to be uniform throughout the United States, and further a combination of persons engaged in such insurrection have threatened to grant pretended letters-of-marque, to authorize the bearers thereof to commit assaults on the lives, vessels and property of good citizens of the country, carefully engaged in commerce on the high seas, and in the waters of the United States.

And whereas the President says an Executive proclamation has already been issued, requiring the persons engaged in these disorderly proceedings to desist, therefore calling out a militia force for the purpose of repressing the same, and convening Congress in extraordinary session, to deliberate and determine thereon. The President, with a view to the same purposes before mentioned, and to the protection of the public peace, and the lives and property of its orderly citizens, pursuing their lawful occupations, until Congress shall have assembled and deliberated on the said unlawful proceedings, or until the same shall have ceased, has further deemed it advisable to set on foot a BLOCKADE OF THE PORTS within the States aforesaid, in pursuance of the laws of the United States and the laws of nations, in such cases provided.

For this purpose a competent force will be posted so as to prevent the entrance and exit of vessels from the ports aforesaid.

If, therefore, with a view to violate such blockade, a vessel shall attempt to leave any of the said ports, she will be duly warned by the commander of one of the said blockading vessels, who will indorse on her register the fact and date of such warning; and if the same vessel shall again attempt to enter or leave the blockaded port, she will be captured, and sent to the nearest convenient port for such proceedings against her and her cargo as may be deemed advisable.

ABRAHAM LINCOLN,
President of the United States.

WM. H. SEWARD, Secretary of State.

OUR WASHINGTON DISPATCHES.

WASHINGTON, Friday, April 19.

The President's proclamation will be issued to-morrow, announcing the blockade of the Southern ports.

THE MASSACHUSETTS TROOPS ATTACKED.

The Massachusetts men were attacked on their passage to Baltimore. The Sixth Regiment turned and fired on the mob, killing several.

Our New York troops must be prepared to fight their way through.

THE SAFETY OF WASHINGTON.

Many people ask, "Will it be safe for women and children in Washington, in view of the threatened war?" and residents here are receiving numerous appeals from distant friends to leave the city for some more Northern refuge. All such indications of fear are idle. There has been danger of an outbreak here and in the neighborhood of the little squad of traitors who are scattered among the great mass of Unionists who comprise the population of the District; but there are not enough of them to get up a respectable riot, and they will not attempt it. As to the seizure of the Capital by a Southern army—that will never be effected if a million men can hold the Stars and Stripes over it,—for above all other points, this is the one which the Government will retain in its possession until it has been proven that the Secessionists can subjugate the rest of the American people,—and that time we apprehend here is not immediately at hand.

THE BENEFITS OF A FIGHT.

If there are still in the North any who hesitate about the propriety of effective measures to support the Government, and who fear and tremble lest a collision of arms is to render a perpetuation of the Union between the North and South impossible, it would do them good to hear the sentiments expressed by Southern gentlemen in this neighborhood—men who know the South, and who have independence enough to express their views freely and without stint. I remember that during the late session of Congress, an outspoken and honest Southern member, conversing with a member from New-England with respect to the disturbances between the sections, remarked, "We are going to have a fight with you, and somebody's going to get hurt; but after that we shall like each other better than we ever have since the foundation of the Government."

I confess that at the time it did seem as though the mode suggested was rather a rough sort of introduction to good fellowship; but in conversing to-day with another Southron, he expressed the same idea, in a form of argument which carried with it great force. "The masses of our people," he said, "don't understand the people of the North. You don't fight duels, nor do various other things which Southern education holds to be indispensable to a reputation for courage." They have consequently settled down into the conviction that 'Yankees' are 'cowards'—and while they despise them for that, they hate them also because they don't give them opportunity for more violent demonstrations upon their persons. They don't *respect* the people of the North—and so they don't believe Northern men when they disclaim any purpose of oppressing the South, and of interfering with Slavery in the States. Cowardice they look upon as the quintessence of meanness—and lying they consider its natural companion. Hence it is that they refuse to give the North credit for an honest motive in its Anti-Slavery sentiments, and hence they believe the demagogues, who profess to see nothing in your hostility to Slavery extension except an offensive purpose to humiliate the South, and force her to inequality in the Union. Now we are about to have a conflict; they will learn that Northern people are not cowards, but as brave and determined as themselves. The knowledge of that fact will inspire them with respect for you, give them confidence in your truth, and make us all better friends than the two sections ever can be until they have each learned, by a stern experience, that the other is worthy of respect and confidence."

There certainly is wisdom and sound logic in the argument,—and if the dread trial by the sword must come, there is some consolation in the anticipation that good will ultimately flow from the evil.

DISPATCH TO THE ASSOCIATED PRESS.

WASHINGTON, Friday, April 19.

It is reliably stated by parties direct from Richmond that the ordinance of secession was publicly proclaimed yesterday. The vote on its passage is kept secret.

On inquiry at the Post-office Department it is ascertained that no measures are in progress for discontinuing any of the Southern mails. On the contrary, the contractors from that section recently here have arranged for facilitating the transportation. The Postmaster-General has discretion to suspend them only in cases of obstruction.

Capt. PAULDING, Commander EMMONS, and Lieut. WOODHULL constitute the Board of Detail, through whom all the naval preparations are made.

The Chief Clerk's room is the only one in the Navy Department accessible at times to the public.

The city is comparatively quiet this morning.

Those who feared an attack on Washington during last night were not even alarmed by any extraordinary notes of warning or precaution.

Rumors have been circulating for a week that the Philadelphia appointments have been made. As soon as the President actually makes them they will be seen.

Major A. M. HANCOCK, of Kentucky, has been appointed Consul to Malaga.

HARPER'S FERRY BURNT.

The Post Deserted and Fifteen Thousand Stand of Arms Destroyed.

BALTIMORE, Friday, April 19—11 A. M.

Harper's Ferry was burnt last night, and abandoned by the United States troops.

CARLISLE, Penn., Friday, April 19.

Lieut. JONES, late in command at Harper's Ferry, arrived here with his command of 43 men at 3 P. M., to-day.

Lieut. JONES, having been advised that a force of 2,500 troops had been ordered by Gov. LETCHER to take possession of Harper's Ferry, and finding his position untenable, under directions of the War Department, destroyed all the munitions of war, Armory, Arsenal and all the buildings. He withdrew his command under the cover of night, and almost in the presence of 2,500 troops. He lost three men.

Fifteen thousand stand of arms were destroyed.

The command made a forced march of thirty miles,

Federal troops repulsed attacks by Baltimore mobs who tried to hinder their passage to Washington.

last night, from Harper's Ferry to Hagerstown, Md. Lieut. JONES and command look much worn and fatigued. They were most enthusiastically received by our entire population.

THE CUMBERLAND AT HAMPTON ROADS.
BALTIMORE, Friday, April 19.

The United States corvette *Cumberland* is at Hampton Roads, and not inside Norfolk harbor. She is caulked anew. It is said she got up anchor last night.

The *Illinois*, from Charleston, is due at Norfolk, with troops for Fort Monroe. Attempts may be made to prevent her from landing them, which the *Cumberland* can effectually oppose. Her presence is most opportune. Everything is quiet at Norfolk to-day.

STARTLING FROM BALTIMORE.

The Northern Troops Mobbed and Fired upon—
The Troops Return the Fire—Four Massachusetts Volunteers Killed and Several Wounded---Several of the Rioters Killed.

BALTIMORE, Friday, April 19.

There was a horrible scene on Pratt-street, to-day. The railroad track was taken up, and the troops attempted to march through. They were attacked by a mob with bricks and stones, and were fired upon. The fire was returned. Two of the Seventh Regiment of Pennsylvania were killed and several wounded.

It is impossible to say what portion of the troops have been attacked. They bore a white flag as they marched up Pratt-street and were greeted with showers of paving-stones. The Mayor of the city went ahead of them with the police. An immense crowd blocked up the streets. The soldiers finally turned and fired on the mob. Several of the wounded have just gone up the street in carts.

At the Washington depôt, an immense crowd assembled. The rioters attacked the soldiers, who fired into the mob. Several were wounded, and some fatally. It is said that four of the military and four rioters are killed. The city is in great excitement. Martial law has been proclaimed. The military are rushing to the armories.

Civil war has commenced. The railroad track is said to be torn up outside of the city. Parties threaten to destroy the Pratt-street bridge.

As the troops passed along Pratt-street a perfect shower of paving stones rained on their heads.

The cars have left for Washington, and were stoned as they left.

It was the Seventh Regiment of Massachusetts which broke through the mob. Three of the mob are known to be dead and three soldiers. Many were wounded. Stores are closing, and the military rapidly forming. The Minute Men are turning out.

BALTIMORE, Friday, April 19—2:30 P. M.

Affairs are getting serious. Before all the cars got through, great crowds assembled at various points and commenced obstructing the road.

Reports are now arriving that the mob are tearing up the track.

It is understood the principal portion of the troops have got through.

BALTIMORE, Friday, April 19—4 P. M.

A town meeting has been called for 4 o'clock.

It is said there have been 12 lives lost.

Several are mortally wounded.

Parties of men half frantic are roaming the streets armed with guns, pistols and muskets.

The stores are closed.

Business is suspended.

A general state of dread prevails.

Parties a short time ago rushed into the telegraph office, armed with hatchets, and cut the wires. Not much damage was done.

BALTIMORE, April 19—5 P.M.

R. W. DAVIS, of the firm of PEGRAM, PAYNTER & DAVIS, was shot dead during the riot, near Camden Station.

It is reported that the Philadelphians are now at the outer depot.

The President of the Road has ordered the train back, at the urgent request of the Mayor and Governor. They are already off.

The citizens who were mortally wounded are, JOHN McCAN, P. GRIFFIN and G. NEEDHAM.

Four of the Massachusetts troops were killed and several wounded, but it is impossible to learn their names.

As far as ascertained, only two of the Massachusetts soldiers were killed, belonging to Company C. Their bodies are now at the Police Station.

At the same Station are the following wounded:

Sergeant AMES, of the Lowell City Guard, wounded in the head, slightly.

Private COLUM, of the same place, shot in the head, not serious.

Private MICHAEL GREEN, of Lawrence, Mass., wounded in the head, by stones.

H. W. DANFORTH, Company C, Sixth Regiment, of Massachusetts, slightly wounded.

So far as known at present, seven citizens were killed, including Mr. DAVIS, before mentioned, and JAMES CLARK.

Half a dozen or so are seriously wounded, though it is believed not fatally.

Comparative quiet now prevails. The military are under arms, and the police are in full force.

There is a large mass meeting here tonight, addressed by the Mayor. The Governor was present.

PHILADELPHIA VOLUNTEERS SENT BACK.
PHILADELPHIA, Friday, April 19.

The Philadelphia Volunteers have been turned back, because without arms or equipments.

THE MASSACHUSETTS TROOPS IN WASHINGTON.
PHILADELPHIA, Friday, April 19.

A special dispatch from Washington says that the Massachusetts Regiment, except 120 men, arrived there at 5 o'clock. They report that three of their members were killed.

OUR BALTIMORE CORRESPONDENCE.

WARLIKE NEWS FROM THE SOUTH—VIRGINIA SECEDED—ATTACK ON HARPER'S FERRY—GOV. HICKS—EXCITEMENT IN BALTIMORE—RESIGNATION OF COL. HUGER, U. S. A., &C.

Correspondence of the New-York Times:

BALTIMORE, Thursday, April 18, 1861.

The news from the South is of the most warlike character. Every effort at preparation is being made for the anticipated conflict; and private dispatches, from unprejudiced sources, represent the feeling of resistance as unanimously extreme.

I have reason to believe, on reliable authority, that the Virginia Convention have, in secret session, by a large majority, repealed the ordinance by which she became a member of the Confederation; that it has not been made public, because of the desire first to mature some plan of prompt and general action; that some fifteen hundred or two thousand troops are now *en route* for Harper's Ferry, and that ere this reaches you that post will be in their possession.

Serious fears are entertained by the Baltimore and Ohio Railroad Company, in consequence of information imparted from different sources, that their bridge over the Potomac will be destroyed. The President, Mr. GARRETT, has this moment, by special engine, sent an influential agent there with a view to the protection of the Company's property.

The Norfolk boat of this morning also brings intelligence that the Navy-yard there had been seized, and that vessels had been sunk in the channel, to prevent the men-of-war, lying under the guns of Fortress Monroe, from leaving.

Gov. Hicks has not yet responded, either affirmatively or negatively, to the requirements of the Secretary of War, in regard to the quota of troops from Maryland. The statement in the papers of yesterday that he had done so, are not true.

There is great excitement in this city. A serious disposition is manifested in certain quarters to obstruct the passage of Northern troops through the State. Public opinion is, as yet, too equally divided to permit any open demonstration, and the Mayor and Board of Police are determined on preserving order. The Police force is a well disciplined and efficient one, but has no general authority beyond the Municipal limits.

Col. B. F. HUGER, commandant at the Pikesville Arsenal, near this City, on Monday resigned his commission in the United States service.

The clouds deepen, and all who seriously regard the political atmosphere, are trembling at the impending crash. CECIL.

The New-York Times.

VOL. X.—NO. 3009.   NEW-YORK, TUESDAY, MAY 14, 1861.   PRICE TWO CENTS.

THE SECESSION REBELLION.

Baltimore Occupied by Federal Troops.

MARTIAL LAW TO BE PROCLAIMED.

The Troops Encamped on Federal Hill.

The Direct Route Through Baltimore Open Again.

Outrageous Treatment of Northerners in Virginia.

One Hundred Maine Lumbermen in Prison.

The Anti-Secession Convention in Western Virginia.

The Collision Between the Federal Troops and the Mob at St. Louis.

WASHINGTON, Monday, March 13 Midnight.

At 7 o'clock this evening, Gen. BUTLER took possession of Baltimore, with 1,500 of the Massachusetts Sixth, 500 of the New-York Eighth, and one section of Cook's Battery. There was no resistance. Thousands welcomed them to the city. They camped on Federal Hill.

Gen. BUTLER sent out a car to Frederick with seventy-five Massachusetts troops, to take ROSS WINANS and bring him to Annapolis, on a charge of treason.

Martial law is proclaimed at Baltimore.

IMPORTANT FROM MARYLAND.

FOR WASHINGTON THROUGH BALTIMORE.
PHILADELPHIA, Monday, May 13.

It is understood that Col. LEWIS' Regiment (First Infantry) will receive marching orders to-morrow, through Baltimore, southward. They are fully equipped.

If Col. LYLE's Regiment can be got ready, it will also be sent off to-morrow, under command of Gen. CADWALLADER. They lack knapsacks and cartridge boxes.

A TRAIN THROUGH BALTIMORE.
BALTIMORE, Monday, May 13.

A train from Philadelphia came through this afternoon with mails and passengers. It was hailed with evident satisfaction by the people along the route, and as it passed through the city many expressions of welcome were given. The national flag was displayed at various parts of the city to-day, the prohibition having been removed. The citizens have been all day in expectation of the arrival of troops over the Northern Central road, but thus far none have arrived.

THE CONFEDERATE CONGRESS.
EIGHTH DAY.
MONTGOMERY, Ala., Monday, May 6.

Congress met to-day at noon, and was opened with prayer.

The journals of the preceding day were read and confirmed.

After the call of States,

Mr. BROOKE, of Mississippi, presented the ordinance passed by the Virginia State Convention, adopting the Provisional Constitution of the Confederate States of America, and also the resolution passed by the same Convention, authorizing the appointment or election of Commissioners to this Congress. Mr. BROOKE said that Messrs. HUNTER, RIVES, BURKENBROUGH, STAPLES and CAMERON had been selected as Commissioners, and that two of those gentlemen, Messrs. BURKENBROUGH and STAPLES, were now present, and he desired that they be invited to take seats in the Convention.

Mr. RHETT, of S. C., moved that Congress go into secret session, and that the Virginia Commissioners now present be invited to remain in the hall.

This motion prevailed, and Congress went into secret session.

VIRGINIA ADMITTED.

The only business transacted in secret session, and which have been made public, is the admission of Virginia into the Government of the Confederate States. Two of her members, Messrs. BARKENBROUGH and STAPLES, were sworn in and participated in the proceedings of Congress.

WESTERN VIRGINIA CONVENTION.

SPECIAL DISPATCH FROM WHEELING.
WHEELING, Monday, May 13.

The Convention met at 11 o'clock.

WM. B. SINN, of Preston Co., was appointed temporary Chairman.

A motion was made by Gen. JACKSON, of Wood County, to admit all gentlemen present from Northwestern Virginia to seats on the floor of the Convention.

The motion was opposed by Mr. CARLILE, on the ground that such a course would be inconsistent with their purposes as a deliberative body; that they were here to determine upon some action to insure the safety of Northwestern Virginia, where alone a Virginian could raise his voice in behalf of the Federal Union.

Mr. JACKSON, Jr. contended that they were not here assembled to take any definite action to establish a provisional Government, or to form a new State; that such a movement would be premature before the vote of the people on the question of ratifying the ordinance passed by the Richmond Convention.

After some discussion the motion of Gen. JACKSON was withdrawn, and the motion of Mr. HUBBARD, to appoint a committee of one from each county, to whom should be referred the subject of representation in the Convention, and also to report officers for the permanent organization of the Convention, was carried.

Subsequently it was moved and carried that the delegation from each county select its member of the committee.

The Convention then adjourned to 3 o'clock.

The Convention reassembled at 3 o'clock, and the Committee reported favorably to the admission of delegates from twenty-five Counties to seats. Permanent officers were appointed and resolutions adopted appointing a Committee on State and Federal Relations.

Before its adoption a discussion took place between Gen. J. J. JACKSON, of Wood County, who thought its division of the State premature, and JOHN S. CARLISLE, who said we must have immediate and prompt action. He wanted no paper resolves.

The Convention then adjourned until morning.

The ceremonies of hoisting a flag over the Customhouse this afternoon were very imposing. Thousands of people were on the ground; the national airs were sung and speeches were made by J. S. CARLISLE and others.

A large majority in the Convention are favorable to the separation from the State, or the establishment of a Provisional Government under the protection of the Federal Government.

The city is crowded. There is immense enthusiasm, and Union sentiment is increasing in Northwestern Virginia. There was speaking to-night from the balcony of the McLure House for three hours.

E. F. U.

Captain Nathaniel Lyon's volunteer troops clashed with a street mob in St. Louis, after parading captured state militiamen loyal to the Confederacy.

IMPORTANT FROM ST. LOUIS.

THE RECENT COLLISION BETWEEN THE MOB AND THE TROOPS.
ST. LOUIS, Monday, May 13.

An official statement, published this morning, says the first firing at Camp Jackson, on Friday evening, was some half-dozen shots near the head of the column of the First Regiment, headed by a volley of stones and a pistol shot from the crowd. No one was hurt at this point. The second firing occurred from the rear of the column guarding the prisoners. The crowd here was large and very abusive, and one man discharged three barrels of a revolver at Lieutenant FAXON, of the regular service, many of the mob cheering him and drawing revolvers and firing at the troops. The man who commenced the attack then laid his pistol across his arm and was taking deliberate aim at Lieut. FAXON, when he was thrust through with a bayonet and fired upon at the same time, and instantly killed. The column then moved on, having received orders to march, and the company, being assaulted by the crowd and several of them shot, halted and fired, causing the deaths already reported. The order was then given by Capt. LYONS to cease firing, which was promptly obeyed.

The principal arms taken from Camp Jackson were four large-size howitzers, two ten inch mortars, a large number of ten-inch shells ready charged, some 5,000 United States muskets, supposed to be a portion of those taken from the Baton Rouge Arsenal.

A thousand people left the city yesterday afternoon in consequence of the reports of insubordination among the German troops, and their threats to burn and sack the city, but the appearance of Gen. HARNEY's proclamation in a great measure restored confidence, and many of those who left will probably return to day.

The city is now quiet, and the highest hopes are entertained that no further disturbance will occur.

The New-York Times.

VOL. X—NO. 3028. NEW-YORK, WEDNESDAY, JUNE 5, 1861. PRICE TWO CENTS.

THE SECESSION REBELLION.

IMPORTANT FROM THE FEDERAL CAPITAL.

Official Account of the Battle at Philippi.

Complete Rout of Two Thousand Rebels.

COL. KELLY NOT KILLED.

An Advance of the Federal Troops To-day Towards Manassas Gap.

Night Alarms Along the Entrenchments.

IMPORTANT FROM FORTRESS MONROE.

The Yankee Gone to Norfolk with a Flag of Truce.

Gen. Butler Preparing for an Advance.

FATE OF THE NAVAL BRIGADE.

Rumored Withdrawal of the Insurgents from Harper's Ferry.

THE FIGHT AT PHILLIPPA.

A special Cabinet meeting was called to-day.

Important dispatches have just reached Gen. SCOTT, giving details of the fight at Phillippa, last night, twenty miles from Grafton. The enemy was some 2,000 strong, and was surprised in camp. Fifteen to twenty were killed in the conflict, several prisoners were taken, and a large quantity of arms and ammunition, tents, &c., fell into the hands of the Federal forces, commanded by Cols. KELLEY and CRITTENDEN. Col. KELLEY, of the First Virginia Union Volunteers, is reported killed The enemy was completely routed, and retreated into the interior of Virginia.

The Department Buildings are being draped in mourning to-day, on account of the death of Judge DOUGLAS, whose remains are expected here on Thursday or Friday for interment in the Congressional Burial Ground.

MOVEMENTS IN VIRGINIA.

Within the past twenty-four hours no movements have been made among the troops at Alexandria of material consequence. I passed a few hours in camp over the river to-day, and found about five or six hundred of the men busily engaged in squads at the trenches The weather continues intensely hot, but no serious illness prevails

The number of secession troops, in and around Fairfax, and between that point and Manassas Gap, is now set down at not exceeding four thousand six hundred in all.

A forward movement of a portion of our forces is ordered to-day, and an advance of some three or four miles will be made by the van in the next twelve hours.

General B.F. Kelley

AFFAIRS AT FORTRESS MONROE.

A messenger arrived from Fortress Monroe this morning. The troops there continue to enjoy good health. Some half-dozen members of the Troy (N. Y.) Regiment were on trial for the alleged robbery of a man and woman at Hampton. The Judge-Advocate on this occasion is N. ST. JOHN GREEN, a prominent Boston lawyer, and brother to DURELL GREEN, lately appointed Colonel in the United States Army. The citizens of Hampton and the residents in the immediate neighborhood of the Fortress, have conceived some alarm at the heavy augmentation of troops there, and appeared more especially concerned at the presence of Col. DURYEA'S Zouave Regiment, whom they stand in fear of. Most of the inhabitants are getting away from the vicinity and from Hampton as fast as it is practicable.

There are between eight and nine thousand troops now there, and accessions are constantly arriving. Gen BUTLER'S plans are not known, of course, but it is understood that he is preparing for a decisive and important movement.

The Massachusetts quota of the regular Army appointments was decided upon to-day. The old Bay State gets one Lieutenant Colonel. six Captains, twelve First Lieutenants, and six Second Lieutenants, as her portion of the officers in the new levy. The names of the fortunate appointees have not as yet been made public.

Sixty members of the Seventy-first Regiment came in this morning with the Scotch Regiment, and about thirty recruits for the Ninth New-York Regiment also accompanied them.

RUMORED EVACUATION OF HARPER'S FERRY.

CHAMBERSBURGH, Tuesday, June 4.

A person from Sharpsburgh, Md, states that the rebels have sent over five hundred sick back to Winchester. The prevailing diseases are small pox and diarrhœa

There are about 200 men at Sheppardstown on the Virginia side.

It is the general belief that Harper's Ferry has been evacuated by the secession troops, the evidence being the loading of cars.

COL KELLY NOT DEAD.
HOPES ENTERTAINED FOR HIS RECOVERY.

CINCINNATI, Tuesday, June 4.

Col. KELLY, wounded at the Philippi action, is not dead, as reported last night. He was seriously wounded in the breast. The ball has been extracted, and hopes are entertained for his recovery.

FROM FORTRESS MONROE.

FORTRESS MONROE, Monday, June 3, via BALTIMORE, Tuesday, June 4.

Only some fifty of the men belonging to the Naval Brigade will return to New-York in the steamer Coatzacoalcos to-day. The others will remain for one week, as citizens, laboring for their rations, and not as a military organization.

Col. BARTLETT is much better, and goes to Washington to-night with several of his officers. This is the best Gen. BUTLER can do for them.

It is believed that the Brigade was ordered back to New-York, partially on account of a misunderstanding between the President and Secretary of War, Mr. LINCOLN having accepted the Brigade without consulting Mr. CAMERON.

The steam tug Yankee left for Norfolk this morning with a flag of truce. Heavy firing from Sewall's Point was heard as she passed.

The Cambridge arrived this morning from Boston.

THE BORDER STATE CONVENTION.

FRANKFORT, Ky., Tuesday, June 4.

The Border State Convention adjourned yesterday sine die, after adopting the National and State address.

UNEMPLOYED NEGROES IN RICHMOND, VA.

LOUISVILLE, Ky., Tuesday, June 4.

The Richmond Whig says there are 5,000 unemployed negroes there. Manual labor is stagnant.

IMPORTANT FROM LOUISVILLE

LOUISVILLE, Ky., Tuesday, June 4.

Union flags are constantly raising amid great enthusiasm. They are flying at half mast to day, in consequence of the decease of Senator DOUGLAS.

Hon. JOHN J. CRITTENDEN consents to run for Congress in the Lexington District.

Mr. MALLORY was renominated for the Seventh District by acclamation, at Lagrange, yesterday.

Immense quantities of provisions day and night are going by way of Shepperdsville, 18 miles south of Louisville, on the Louisville and Nashville Railroad; thence to be sent by rail South, if the transmission thereto shall not be interdicted.

The Journal is informed that there are 2,000 soldiers at Camp Ironsdale, near Richmond, two miles from the Kentucky line; the same number at Camp Cheatham, near Springfield, Tenn.; that the measles was very prevalent among them; also, that well attended Union meetings had been held privately a Nashville Saturday, notwithstanding the suppression of the Union sentiment there by the Secessionists.

The Journal editorially says that Col. ANDERSON will take no military command here, but goes to the mountains of Pennsylvania on account of his failing health.

MORE SEIZURES IN ST. LOUIS.

The Missouri Democrat, of June 1, says:

"Having received information that a large quantity of munitions of war was expected to arrive by rail Thursday night or early Friday morning, Gen. LYON authorized Gen. SWEENEY, of the reserve corps brigade, to dispatch troops to each of the depôts in the city. Two companies attended the arrival of each of the trains, but nothing contraband was found. The troops were kept at the North Missouri depôt during most of the forenoon. An arrangement was at last made by which the Government is to select, and the Railroad Company to pay an Inspector, whose business shall be to see that no goods contraband of war pass over the lines without the approbation of the Government, and that such goods attempting to pass be seized. A similar arrangement will doubtless be made with each of the Railroad Companies.

From the above incident rumor projected the absurd story that the United States troops had taken possession of the various lines of railroad leading out of St. Louis.

On the previous day, seizure was made of five kegs of powder and a quantity of bar lead, shipped on the North Missouri Road, by order of Messrs. D. A. JANUARY, The S E TUTT & Co. and R. P. OBER & Co., to parties in the townships of Allen and Mexico. The shipper was Mr. LAFLIN, powder merchant, to whom Gen. LYON ordered the goods to be restored—this gentleman pledging himself to ship no more contraband articles without the consent of the United States military authority here, obtained in each instance.

THE BATTLE AT PHILIPPI.

WASHINGTON, Monday, June 3.

Lieut-Gen. SCOTT to-night received a dispatch from Gen. McCLELLAN, stating that the command under Gen. MORRIS, last night marched on Grafton.

It was raining at the time. They surprised a party of Secessionists, near Philippi, about 200 strong, and effectually put them to the route and killed some of them. A large quantity of arms, munitions, and a number of horses, which the Secessionists left in their alarm, fell into the hands of the Federals. The rebels retreated further into Virginia. Col. KELLY was mortally wounded.

The New-York Times.

VOL. X—NO. 3034.   NEW-YORK, WEDNESDAY, JUNE 12, 1861   PRICE TWO CENTS

THE GREAT INSURRECTION.

Startling Intelligence from Fort Monroe.

A Conflict with the Rebel Forces at Great Bethel.

The Rebels Intrenched in Force, with Batteries of Rifled Cannon.

Gallant Charge of the Federal Troops.

Their Ammunition Gives Out and They Retire with Loss.

INCAPACITY OF BRIGADIER-GEN. PIERCE.

The Loyal Forces Firing on One Another.

Thirty of the Federal Troops Killed and One Hundred Wounded.

The Batteries Reported to Have Been Subsequently Carried.

Rumored Evacuation of Harper's Ferry.

Withdrawal of the Rebels from Point of Rocks.

THE SKIRMISH AT WILLIAMSPORT.

FORTRESS MONROE, Va., Monday, June 10.

Last night about 2 o'clock quite a large force left camp, under command of Brig.-Gen. PIERCE, with the design of breaking up marauding expeditions on the part of the enemy, for the purpose of running off the negroes and white men to work on their batteries. The forces were transported safely over Hampton Creek in barges manned by the Naval Brigade, under supervision of Lieut. CROSBY, of the frigate *Cumberland*. The force had proceeded about three miles beyond the creek when they were fired upon by the New-York Seventh Regiment, who had marched down from Newport News, for the purpose of joining in the expedition.

The Seventh was established in a copse of wood at an angle of a road, and their fire was quite destructive. Sergeant CAREY, of Company A, Col. TOWNSEND'S Regiment, was killed. Lieut. STONE, of the same Regiment, a sergeant and nine privates, were wounded, some seriously. The fire was returned, and the Seventh fired one charge of grape from a howitzer, which passed over the heads of the troops of the Third, doing no harm.

The precise state of matters was then mutually ascertained, and the forces uniting proceeded towards Little Bethel church, five miles from Hampton. There they came upon the advanced guard of the enemy, defeated them and drove them back taking thirty prisoners, including one lieutenant.

Advancing towards Big Bethel, in York county, they came upon the enemy in force, and a sharp engagement ensued, in which the artillery played an important part on both sides.

No details have reached us of the action, and I must await them before I can give further accounts.

Gen. BUTLER was busy keeping open communication with the post.

The conduct of the men has been most admirable under the hottest fire. The Naval Brigade received the highest compliment for their efficient conduct. In working the boats they were of the greatest service throughout the night and day.

LATER.

The contest at Great Bethel was more severe than was at first apprehended. The enemy were so strongly intrenched in and protected by batteries, that after more than two hours and a half severe fighting, our ammunition giving out, we were obliged to fall back which we did in perfect order.

The details, as near as can be, in the confusion, ascertained, are as follows:

Brig.-Gen. PIERCE, with the First, Second and Third New-York, from this post, joined with detachments from Newport News from the Fourth Massachusetts, First Vermont, and Seventh and Ninth New-York, with two light field-pieces, under Lieut. GREBLE, and a squad of regulars, drove into the enemy, numbering four thousand men, and soon came upon their position, protected by the fire of six heavy batteries, mounted with six and twelve pound howitzers and heavy rifled cannon. The engagement immediately became warm, the guns under Lieut. GREBLE returning the intensely hot fire from the enemy's batteries.

After some time Gen. PIERCE gave the order to charge on the battery, and Col. DURYEE'S Zouaves gallantly marched in quick time under a scorching fire up to near the ramparts of the battery, where a broad ditch intervened, which could not be passed, when the gallant lads fell back.

Col. TOWNSEND'S Regiment also went near to the battery, but meeting the same obstruction were also compelled to retire.

After over two hours' hot contest the ammunition for the field pieces and the muskets gave out, and the order was given to retire, which was effected in perfect order.

Want of time prevents any details. We lament the loss of Lieut. GREBLE, of the United States artillery, one of the most brave, gallant and chivalrous officers in the service, who died bravely at his gun from a cannon shot, which struck him in the forehead, killing him instantly.

Our loss in killed and wounded is about seventy-five, among the latter I mention:

Capt. KILPATRICK, of the Zouaves, was shot in the leg.

Lieut. DUMONT, Company B, of the same regiment, had a bayonet wound in the leg, not serious, and others slightly wounded.

I shall forward a list at the earliest possible mo-ment. The enemy's loss was heavy. Every one on our side behaved most bravely and did their duty.

OTHER ACCOUNTS.

FORTRESS MONROE, Monday, June 10 *via* }
BALTIMORE, Tuesday, June 11. }

This has been an exciting and sorrowful day at Old Point Comfort. Gen. BUTLER having learned that the rebels were forming an intrenched camp with strong batteries at Great Bethel, nine miles from Hampton, on the Yorktown Road, he deemed it necessary to dislodge them; accordingly movements were made last night from Fortress Monroe and Newport News.

About midnight, Col. DURYEE'S Zouaves and Col. TOWNSEND'S Albany Regiment crossed the river at Hampton, by means of six large batteaux, manned by the Naval Brigade, and took up the line of march, the former some two miles in advance of the latter. At the same time, Col. BENDIX'S regiment, and detachments of the Vermont and Massachusetts regulars at Newport moved forward to form a junction with the regulars from Fortress Monroe, at Little Bethel, about half way between Hampton and Great Bethel. The Zouaves passed Little Bethel about 4 A.M. Col. BENDIX'S Regiment arrived next, and took a position at the intersection of the roads. Not understanding the signal, the German Regiment, in the darkness of the morning, fired upon Col. TOWNSEND'S column, marching in close order, and led by Lieut. BUTLER'S son, and aid of Gen. BUTLER, with two pieces of artillery. Other accounts say that Col. TOWNSEND'S regiment fired first. At all events, the fire of the Albany regiment was harmless, while that of the Germans was fatal, killing one man and seriously wounding two others, with several other slight casualties. The Albany regiment, being back of the Germans, discovered from the accoutrements left on the field, that the supposed enemy was a friend. They had in the meantime fired nine rounds with small arms and a field-piece. The Zouaves, hearing the firing, turned and also fired upon the Albany boys. At daybreak, Col. ALLEN'S and Col. CARR'S Regiments moved from the rear of the Fortress to support the main body; the mistake at Little Bethel having been ascertained, the buildings were burned and a Major with two prominent secessionists, named LIVERY and WHITING, made prisoners. The troops then advanced upon Great Bethel in the following order, namely: the Zouaves, Col. BENDIX, Lieut.-Col. WASHBURNE, Col. ALLEN, and Col. CARR. At that point our regiments formed and successively endeavored to take a masked secession battery. The effort was futile, our three small pieces of artillery not being able to cope with the heavy rifled cannon of the enemy, according to some accounts thirty in number. The rebel battery was completely masked, so that no men could be seen, but only the flashes of the guns. There were probably less than a thousand men behind the batteries of the rebels. A well-concerted movement might have secured the position, but Brig.-Gen. PIERCE, who commanded the expedition, appears to lost his presence of mind. The Troy Regiment stood for an hour exposed to a galling fire, when an order to retreat was at last given, but at that moment Lieut. GREBLE, of the United States Army, and in command of the artillery, was struck by a cannon ball and instantly killed. He had spiked his gun, and was gallantly endeavoring to withdraw his command.

Capt. GEO. W. WILSON, of the Troy Regiment, after the order to retreat was given, took possession of the gun, and with Quartermaster McARTHUR brought it off the field, with the corps of the beloved Lieutenant. Both were brought to Fortress Monroe this evening.

There are probably twenty-five killed, and one hundred of the Federal troops wounded.

Lieut. BUTLER deserves the greatest credit for bringing off the killed and wounded. Several of the latter are now in the Hospital here.

I should have stated that Col. McCHESNEY'S Regiment formed a reserve.

Col. HAWKINS' Regiment moved from Newport News during the day, and an armed vessel went up to Newport News, expecting the *Cumberland*.

All the regiments are now probably up at their former quarters.

Great indignation is manifested against Brig.-Gen. PIERCE.

Gen. BUTLER has been ubiquitous, doing all in his power to save our men and the honor of our cause.

SPECIAL DISPATCH FROM WASHINGTON.

WASHINGTON, Tuesday, June 11.

The unfortunate affair at Great Bethel, near Newport News, and its disastrous consequences, are the theme of conversation in every circle. The rashness of Gen. PIERCE is universally condemned, and his unfitness to command is as universally conceded. Such blunders as marching men into an enemy's country without food and without ammunition, are denounced as inexcusable crimes, and such as call for punishment.

Lieut GREBLE, among the killed, was one of our first officers,—probably one of the best artillerymen that we have. He leaves a young wife and two children, resident in Philadelphia. His father left Washington this morning, to visit his son, expecting to find him in command of the batteries at Newport News, and, of course, alive and well. It will be a terrible blow for him to find only the mangled corpse of his brave boy.

THE ENEMY'S WORKS CARRIED.

I am told that Postmaster-General BLAIR says that Gen. BUTLER last night assaulted the enemy's works at Bethel, where PIERCE was repulsed, and carried them by storm. I hope it is true.

GEN BUTLER'S CONTRABAND.

"Contrabands" are beginning to be plenty through all our camps over in Virginia. At a moderate estimate, there are five to ten chattels attached to each regiment, and "more a-coming." They are held subject to the claims of their owners, but not likely soon to be called for, as their owners just now appear to prefer straight necks to moveable goods.

MORE CONTRABAND.

Three slaves were taken into one of the camps yesterday. A Mr. WEBB, of Virginia, claimed to be their owner, and demanded them. The Colonel refused, deeming them contraband. They were sent over to Gen. SANDFORD's quarters, upon

BALLOON SERVICE.

Prof. LOWE, the balloon man, is in Washington, and has proposed to the Government a system of reconnoitering which promises to be effective. It will be tested to-morrow, if the necessary arrangements can be completed. The balloon will be sent up from the President's grounds, and will contain the Professor and an experienced telegraph operator. It will be held to the proper height by a cord. It will also be connected to the earth by insulated wires, which will be attached to the recording machine in the War Department. The operator in the balloon will thus communicate directly with the War Department. Of course, the same experiment would be practicable in the field, the operator in the balloon, above the smoke of the contest, giving information of all that was transpiring in the enemy's camp.

his order, where WEBB again presented himself, and Gen. SANDFORD sent for a wagon at his own expense, into which the three negroes were placed and sent back to Virginia, to the entire satisfaction of their secession master. This act on Gen. SANDFORD's part has given rise to much comment to-day, and he gets very little credit in any quarter save among the rebel slave owners over the river.

AFFAIRS AT HARPER'S FERRY.

TROOPS WITHDRAWN FROM POINT OF ROCKS.

FREDERICK, Tuesday, June 11.

From a gentleman well conversant with the localities in and around Harper's Ferry, who left Hagerstown early this morning, I learn that 10,000 United States troops are between the town of Greencastle, nine miles from the former place, and Chambersburgh, from whence they are marching.

Yesterday, the Virginians destroyed about twenty-five canal-boats in the vicinity of Harper's Ferry, with the intention, it is supposed, of preventing their being used to transport Federal troops across the Potomac.

The troops recently at Point of Rocks have certainly been withdrawn, and are now with the main body at Harper's Ferry.

Much disaffection is reported to exist among the Kentuckians on Maryland Hights, and a rumor is current here that in a few days they intend displaying the Stars and Stripes, and probably deserting in a body.

THE FIGHT AT WILLIAMSPORT.

BALTIMORE, Tuesday, June 11.

The Williamsport correspondent of the *American* says:

"The fight at Clear Spring continued all day yesterday between the Home Guard, of Clear Spring and Williamsport, and the Virginians, who were endeavoring to destroy Dam No. 5, on the Chesapeake and Ohio Canal.

No one on the Maryland side was hurt, but two horses and one man were killed on the Virginia side.

The Virginians had destroyed all the canal boats on the Maryland side, between Williamsport and the Ferry.

AFFAIRS IN WESTERN VIRGINIA.

RAPID MOVEMENTS OF FEDERAL TROOPS.

CINCINNATI, Tuesday, June 11.

A special dispatch to the *Gazette*, from Grafton, says that the Indiana Zouaves experienced no trouble in reaching Cumberland. No Secessionists were seen on the way. The people of Cumberland were friendly.

One hundred army wagons, with a full supply of horses, are at Parkersburgh, *en route* for Grafton.

Companies of Virginia Volunteers are rapidly organizing under Gen. MORRIS' proclamation.

Arms were issued to-day to two fully organized companies from Fairmount, and others are reporting themselves from the South and East.

The railroad is clear to Cumberland, and trains are running again. Travel is reviving.

Many delegates passed through Cumberland to-day, *en route* to the Wheeling Convention.

A special dispatch from Wheeling to the *Commercial* says that delegates to the Convention are fast arriving here. Over five counties east of the Alleghanies will be represented. The feeling predominant is for a Provisional Government.

A collision occurred at Glencoe, thirteen miles from Wheeling, on the Central Ohio Railroad to-day, killing four of the employes on the road, smashing an engine and shattering one or two cars.

Major-General Benjamin F. Butler and staff.

The New-York Times.

VOL. X–NO. 3037.   NEW-YORK, SATURDAY, JUNE 15, 1861.   PRICE TWO CENTS

HIGHLY IMPORTANT NEWS.

Harper's Ferry Evacuated by the Rebels.

The Bridge Blown Up and the Government Buildings Destroyed.

Retreat of the Rebels Towards Winchester.

THEIR DESTINATION MANASSAS JUNCTION.

Probable Retirement of the Combined Forces to Richmond.

IMPORTANT MOVEMENTS IN MISSOURI.

Open Treason of Gov. Jackson and the Other State Officers.

A Collision Expected Between the State and Federal Troops.

Latest Intelligence from Fortress Monroe.

A Flag of Truce Sent to Yorktown.

FORMIDABLE FORTIFICATIONS ALONG THE ROAD.

SPECIAL DISPATCH FROM WASHINGTON.

WASHINGTON, Friday, June 14.

The news of the evacuation of Harper's Ferry by the rebels was received at the War Department to-day about 12 o'clock. They went away with baggage down the road to Winchester, destroying all they could not carry, and, like a steam-plow, taking up the railroad track and burning the bridges as they run.

This result I telegraphed you three weeks ago must take place. They could not stay at the Ferry, and had to run. Where they have gone is the question now. Down to Winchester by rail, thence by a march of twelve miles to Strasburg or Front Royal, and then by railroad again to Manassas Junction; and doubtless to-night they are there or thereabouts, unless the Leesburgh column has taken the liberty of burning bridges and destroying a portion of the track from the Gap to the Junction.

How long will they stay at Manassas? There is a wide difference of opinion about this point. Some see in this evacuation of Harper's Ferry, and the retreat upon Manassas, an immediate attack upon Washington. Among some of the transient visitors and the oldest inhabitants, the danger of an attack on the city is very imminent—but, depend upon it, the rebels at Manassas will not move

towards Washington. Their next movement will be another retreat—a retreat in the direction of Richmond. They will stay at Manassas until, like locusts, they have eaten up the country, and then they will,

"Fold their tents, like the Arabs, and as quietly steal away."

There is no help for them. They must go. They have not provisions, nor transportation, nor field artillery in such quantity as will justify a forward movement, and least of all a movement that brings them face to face with the forty-five thousand men and two or three hundred field and siege guns. Depend upon it, the wind that next fills the sails of the rebel ship must blow from, not towards, the North.

A MOVEMENT OF THE SIXTY-NINTH.

At 1 A. M., this morning, two hundred and fifty of the Sixty-ninth, under Lieut. Col. NUGENT, accompanied by fifty of Company B, Second United States Cavalry, under Lieut. MASON, were hurriedly advanced to the two new bridges erected on the Loudon and Hampton Railroad, between BALL'S Cross Roads and Alexandria, Gen. McDOWELL having received positive information that an attempt in force to destroy the road would be made. The information was correct enough, but the strong force on the ground prevented any attack by the rebels, whose scouts were seen falling back as the cavalry advanced.

Two of the twenty-four-pounder columbiades were mounted yesterday on Fort Corcoran, the first being christened " Hunter," in honor of the officer commanding one brigade. The officiating Chaplain remarked that it was a promising and patriotic infant, being able to speak in thunder tones for the Union at the moment of its birth.

Great desire is felt by the men on Arlington Heights to have the Seventy-ninth sent over to join their brigade, the Highlanders now having no other employment than to kill the mosquitoes, which fasten on their bare legs just across the river, and within sight of the camp. The presence of the Seventy-ninth, abreast of the Sixty-ninth, would bring a generous emulation between Irishmen and Scotchmen, that could not fail to be of service. As Secretary CAMERON'S brother is Colonel of the Seventy-ninth, will the Secretary of War be pleased to make a not of this request?

SECRETARY SEWARD IN VIRGINIA.

Secretary SEWARD to-day visited Virginia, and the intrenched camp of the Sixty-ninth. He was honored with a hearty welcome and a *revielle*, which he repaid with a characteristic speech.

Col. MEIGS has entered upon his duties as Quartermaster-General. He retains Major SIBLEY in the Department, but the Major is promoted to be a Colonel.

UNIONISTS IN VIRGINIA.

A scouting party who visited Falls Church recently, nine miles from this city, were handsomely received by the residents there, who expressed the hope unreservedly that the Federal forces would shortly occupy that place.

At Fairfax Court-house about 700 Confederate troops are reported to be encamped at latest advices.

Several excellent field pieces have just been forwarded to Alexandria, for the use of the Zouaves there. They are to be mounted on the extensive entrenchments built by that regiment at Alexandria.

A BRUSH WITH THE REBELS.

At Annapolis, Major MORGAN, of the Thirteenth Brooklyn Regiment has just returned from Queenstown, where he had a brush with his forces with the enemy. He brought one prisoner and five hundred stand of arms. He was assaulted from the bushes, but drove the rebels out and secured their arms.

Several friends of the late Senator DOUGLAS met at the National, last evening, Hon. JOHN B. HASKINS in the chair. It was voted to procure a suitable monument in his honor, and arrangements

were discussed for pronouncing an eulogy upon Judge DOUGLAS' character on the 4th of July next. Another meeting will be held next week at the City Hall on this subject.

HARPER'S FERRY EVACUATED.

RETREAT OF THE REBELS AND DESTRUCTION OF THE BRIDGE.

FREDERICK, Md., Friday, June 14.

It is here reported, upon the authority of a messenger who arrived here this morning from within one mile of Harper's Ferry, that the bridge across the Potomac at that point was blown up and entirely destroyed, between 4 and 5 o'clock this morning. The explosion was distinctly heard, and the smoke of the burning structure seen by parties here.

The messenger further reports that all the troops have been withdrawn from the Maryland shore, and that the town of Harper's Ferry has been evacuated by the great body of the troops recently there. A small force is still there, probably the rear guard of the retreating army.

It is reported that eight car loads of provisions were destroyed to prevent them falling into the hands of the Federalists, who are supposed to be concentrating upon Harper's Ferry, from the directions of Greencastle and Cumberland.

The wife and family of Gen. HUGER were at the Ferry last night, and had engaged a private conveyance from the city to take them to a point further southward, but were compelled to accompany the column by its sudden flight.

The destruction of the bridge may be regarded as certain. Confirmatory intelligence of the fact has been received here within a few minutes. A gentleman of this city, who was at Harper's Ferry last night, saw the preparations being made for the blowing up of the structure.

The bridge at Shepardstown was also burnt last night.

IMPORTANT FROM MISSOURI.

OPEN TREASON OF THE STATE OFFICERS.

HERMANN, Mo., Friday, June 14.

A gentleman from Jefferson City, says the steamer *White Cloud* was loading at that place yesterday, with cannon and military stores. It was said that Gov. JACKSON and all the State Officers were to embark in her for Arrow Rock, a strong point about sixty miles above, on the Missouri River.

Capt. KELLY'S Guard, of one hundred men, were the only troops at the Osage Bridge, or Dodd's Island.

ST. AMHERST, (9 miles from Jefferson City,) FRIDAY, June 14—8. P. M.

A special agent, who was sent down from Jefferson City with the mail, has just returned here, having left here this P. M. He says the Governor and all the State Officers left there yesterday, and that the last of the soldiers left to-day at 2 P. M., taking with them all the locomotives (of which I understand there were five,) and cars, and burning the bridge at Grey's Creek, three miles west of Jefferson City, also one above there, after they had passed over them.

It is supposed the Governor has ordered his forces to concentrate either at Boonsville or Arrow Rock, probably the latter.

It is thought that Gen. LYON will push on after him, and should he meet with no detention, he will not be more than twenty-four hours behind him.

The Moreau bridge, forty-one miles this side of Jefferson City is unharmed, but the western span of the Osage bridge, nine miles this side, is burned.

The New-York Times.

VOL. X.....NO. 3041   NEW-YORK, THURSDAY, JUNE 20, 1861   PRICE TWO CENTS

HIGHLY IMPORTANT NEWS.

The Particulars of the Battle of Booneville, Mo.

Brilliant Ruse de Guerre of General Lyon.

UTTER ROUT OF THE REBEL FORCES

IGNOMINIOUS FLIGHT OF GOV. JACKSON.

IMPORTANT FROM WESTERN VIRGINIA.

Another Fight at Phillippa Expected.

Threatening Demonstrations on the Line of the Baltimore and Ohio Railroad.

A New Governor Nominated by the Wheeling Convention.

Position of the Federal Column Under Col. Stone

Unsuccessful Attempt of the Rebels to Cross the Potomac.

The Result of the Reconnoissance from Fortress Monroe,

IMPORTANT FROM MISSOURI.

THE SLAUGHTER OF REBELS AT BOONE-VILLE.

St. Louis, Tuesday, June 18.

The *Democrat* has just received the following dispatch from Jefferson City. Mr. Gordon, of St. Louis, and other gentlemen from above give the following account of the battle of Booneville:

Gen. Lyon landed four miles below Booneville, and opened a heavy cannonade against the rebels, who retreated and dispersed into the adjacent wood, whence, hidden by brushes and trees, they opened a brisk fire on our troops. Gen. Lyon then ordered a hasty retreat to the boats, and the rebels, encouraged by this movement, rallied and followed the troops into a wheat field. Gen. Lyon halted, faced his troops about, and bringing the whole force of his artillery to bear, opened a murderous fire on the rebels, *three hundred* of whom were killed, and the balance fled in all directions, leaving their arms on the field. Gen. Lyon then moved forward and took possession of Booneville.

Gen. Price was taken with violent diarrhœa at the beginning of the battle, and was taken on a steamer and carried to his home in Charaton.

Gov. Jackson viewed the battle from a distant hill,

and fled for parts unknown after the defeat of his forces.

There is great rejoicing among the Union men here, and the Stars and Stripes are hoisted on the Capitol, guns are fired and the Star-Spangled banner was played by regimental bands.

Scouting parties will be sent out in all directions to-morrow, to cut off the retreat of the rebels.

The steamer *J. C. Swan* has arrived with two cannon, ammunition and artillery men, which have been planted at Col. Boernstein's head-quarters.

John Fitzpatrick, one of the most violent Secessionists of the State, took the oath of allegiance to the United States Government in the presence of all the officers here to day.

REPORTS FROM JEFFERSON CITY.

Jefferson City, Wednesday, June 19.

People living near Syracuse have arrived to-day, saying that 600 State troops retreating from Booneville, with 6 cannon, reached Syracuse yesterday. They said they were going to draft men from the neighborhood and would take at least every one who could furnish a horse. Various reports as to the number of killed were in vogue. The probabilities are that about 150 were killed. There is no possible doubt that a battle was fought, and the State forces completely routed, but the telegraph being out of order between here and Booneville, we cannot get entirely authentic accounts of the affair.

BRIG.-GEN. LYON.

Brig. Gen. Nathaniel Lyon, whose brilliant exploit at Booneville is now the theme of every tongue, is a native of Connecticut, having been born near the birthplace of Hon. Gideon Welles, Secretary of the Navy. He graduated with honors at the West Point Academy, and entered the regular army as a Second-Lieutenant in the Second Infantry, his first commission bearing date on the 1st July, 1841. He was promoted to a Brevet First-Lieutenancy shortly afterward, subsequently to a Captaincy. He has occupied the latter rank practically since the 11th of June, 1851, and was booked for advancement to a higher position at the first opportunity, he being entitled to that title by brevet, before his recent appointments to a Lieutenant-Colonelcy and a Brigadier Generalship.

AFFAIRS IN WESTERN VIRGINIA.

OPERATIONS OF THE REBEL FORCES.

Grafton, Wednesday, June 19.

Information thought to be reliable says that 1,500 Confederate troops are in the neighborhood of Beverly and Phillippa, and that an attack will be made on the latter place; there is no doubt but the rebels in Western Virginia have been largely reinforced, and soon a grand movement is contemplated.

The Federal troops will be equal to the emergency. Large reinforcements will probably reach here in a few days.

A force sufficient to guard the Cheat River Bridge has been sent forward from here.

The rebel forces from Romney burned the railroad bridge over New-Creek, twenty miles west of Cumberland, early this morning, and marched on to Piedmont, which place they now hold.

The telegraph wires east of Piedmont were cut by them.

Their number is variously estimated at from 2,000 to 4,000.

Notice was given of their approach to the town, and the citizens were preparing to leave when our informant left.

All the engines belonging to the Baltimore and Ohio Railroad, were fired up and sent West, to Grafton, and the greatest excitement prevailed.

A company of citizen-soldiers, who were guarding the bridge, are reported to have retreated on the approach of the rebels.

The Piedmont telegraph operator closed the office and fled, and we have no means of ascertaining what damage is being done. Communication by railroad, between Cumberland and this place, is now cut off.

Francis P. Blair, Jr. brother of Lincoln's Postmaster General, was instrumental in aiding General Lynn and the Union cause in Missouri. Later a general, Blair became a competent politician-turned-soldier, a rare success amidst numerous failures.

PROCEEDINGS OF THE WHEELING CONVENTION.

Wheeling, Va., Wednesday, June 19.

The time of the Convention was occupied to-day with a debate on the ordinance for reorganizing the State Government.

Mr. West, of Wetzel, offered an amendment, that no one who voted for secession be allowed to hold office in the State during the war.

This was supported by Mr. West and his colleague, Mr. Martin, who, among other statements, said that the Secessionists in his County were in the habit of taking the oath of allegiance and afterwards repudiating it. There was no confidence in the oath of men, who had to learn to disregard an oath to be good Secessionists.

The amendment was lost—Ayes, 10; Nays, 66.

The ordinance was finally passed—73 to 3.

The ordinance provides for the entire reorganization of the State Government; every officer to be obliged to swear allegiance anew to the United States, and repudiate the Richmond Convention.

The Convention will now proceed to choose a Governor and Council. A new State seal and other emblems of authority had been ordered.

Wheeling, Va., Wednesday, June 19—P. M.

Frank Pierpont, of Marion County, was unanimously nominated for Governor by the Convention in caucus to day.

The New-York Times.

VOL. X....NO. 3061.   NEW-YORK, MONDAY, JULY 15, 1861.   PRICE TWO CENTS.

THE GREAT REBELLION.

Highly Important from Western Virginia.

Surrender of Col. Pegram and his Whole Force to Gen. McClellan.

ONE THOUSAND REBEL PRISONERS

Gen. McClellan in Full Pursuit of Garnett

IMPORTANT FROM MISSOURI.

Concentration of the National Forces at Springfield.

The Rebels Retreating Towards Arkansas.

Seven Hundred of them Killed in the Battle of Carthage.

Eight American Vessels Captured by the Rebel Steamer Sumter.

Latest Intelligence from Fortress Monroe.

Several of Col. Bendix's Men Taken Prisoners.

General George B. McClellan scored rapid victories in Western Virginia, encouraging those who looked for a quick end to the war.

REPORT OF GEN. McCLELLAN TO LIEUT.-GEN. SCOTT.

WASHINGTON, Sunday, July 14.

The following was received, July 13, from Beverly, Va.:

"I have received from Col. PEGRAM propositions for his surrender, with his officers and remnant of his command, say 600 men. They are said to be extremely penitent, and determined never again to take up arms against the General Government. I shall have near 900 or 1,000 prisoners to take care of when Col. PEGRAM comes in.

The latest accounts make the loss of the rebels in killed some 150."

Gen 'McCLELLAN's dispatches have diffused general joy here, and none share in it in a greater degree than Lieut.-Gen. SCOTT himself. The intelligence served to make the military hereabout impatient for an opportunity to achieve results simi- 'ar to those narrated.

LATEST FROM GEN. McCLELLAN.

CINCINNATI, Sunday, July 14.

A special dispatch to the *Commercial*, from Beverley, says that Gen. MCCLELLAN's advanced division is moving rapidly to Cheat Mountain Pass. The rebels burned the bridges at Huttonsville and will burn the Cheat Mountain Bridge, but it cannot delay us an hour.

At Rich Mountain, 131 dead rebels have been found. Our wounded are doing well. Ten commissioned rebel officers were killed and captured, including Capt. SKEPWITH, of Powhatan; Capt. D. E. LANGELL, late of the United States Army; and Capt. IRWIN, of Brunswick, are dangerously wounded. Dr. TYLER, late of the United States Army, and Dr. WALK, late of the United States Army, are prisoners.

Some Georgians and South Carolinians are among the dead, but the rebels dead are chiefly Eastern Virginians.

This morning Col. PEGRAM, commander at Rich Mountain, sent a letter to Gen. McCLELLAN, offering to surrender himself and command of 600 men. The surrender was accepted, and the prisoners will march in to-day. The prisoners are much reduced by hunger.

Franz Sigel enjoyed great popularity among German-Americans in Missouri who were Union loyalists.

IMPORTANT FROM MISSOURI.

CONCENTRATION OF NATIONAL FORCES.

St. Louis, Sunday, July 14.

Capt. SMITH, from Springfield, Thursday, reached here to-night, reports that a messenger arrived there that morning with intelligence that Gen. LYONS' command would reach there that day. The entire National force, comprising the commands under Gen. SWEENEY, Cols. SIEGEL, SOLOMON, BROWN, and four wounded Home Guards, under JOHN S. PHELPS, are concentrated at Springfield.

The last heard from the State forces they were in Neosho, going South, communication with Arkansas being open in consequence of Col. SIEGEL falling back on Mount Vernon.

A large number of Arkansas troops were engaged against Col. SIEGEL, in the battle near Carthage. The National loss in that battle was 10 killed, 43 wounded, and 4 missing. The rebels state their loss at 700 killed.

The guard of 120 men left at Neosho by Col. SIEGEL, previous to the battle, were taken prisoners by a large force of Arkansas troops, and a proposition was made to shoot them, but were finally released, on taking an oath not to bear arms against the Southern Confederacy.

OUR ST. LOUIS CORRESPONDENCE.

AUTHENTIC DESCRIPTION OF THE BATTLE OF CARTHAGE—RELATIVE STRENGTH OF THE FORCES ENGAGED—SUPERIORITY OF THE NATIONAL ARTILLERY—THE REBEL CAVALRY, ETC.

St. Louis, Wednesday, July 10, 1861.

Our city was thrown into a state of feverish excitement to-day, by the news of a great battle which was reported to have been fought in the vicinity of Carthage, between the United States forces, under Col. SIEGEL, and the rebel troops, under Gens. PRICE and RAINS. The most contradictory statements were afloat and published by the several newspapers, the *State Journal* affirming the total rout and destruction of Col. SIEGEL's corps d'armée, while, on the other side, it was maintained that our troops had achieved the most glorious victory which had yet shed lustre on the Star-Spangled Banner in the present campaign. The great numerical superiority of the enemy, whose forces were known to outnumber 7,000, while Col. SIEGEL's whole command did not reach 4,000, led us, at first, to doubt a real victory, and it was not until late in the evening that all doubts were dispelled, by the arrival of a messenger direct from Col. SIEGEL, with dispatches to the Commander of the Arsenal. This messenger, Lieut. M. TOSK, of the artillery attached to Col. SIEGEL's Regiment, came by the evening train of the Pacific Railroad, and brought a full account of the glorious victory.

After having made further endeavors to meet the enemy on the 4th, early on the morning of the 5th, Col. SIEGEL was advised that the enemy had been seen a few miles north of Carthage, Jasper County. Col. SIEGEL immediately ordered all troops under arms, and after a short march, had the good fortune to find the report confirmed, by meeting the enemy on an open prairie, about 10 miles noorth of Carthage. Col. SIEGEL's command consisted of eight companies of his own (Third) regiment, under Lieutenant-Colonel HASSENDEUBEL; seven companies of the Fifth Regiment, Col. SOLOMON, and two batteries of artillery, consisting of eight field-pieces, under Major BACKHOFF. The forces of the enemy numbered five thousand five hundred, at least three thousand of which were mounted, and a battery of artillery,—four six-pounders and one twelve-pounder. Generals PRICE and RAINS commanded the State troops in person.

The position of the State troops was well chosen and gave them a great advantage, which was more than balanced, however, by our superior artillery. Three flags floated over their ranks, two secession flags, which our splendid artillerists soon made to lick the dust, and in the centre the State flag of Missouri.

At half past ten o'clock the attack commenced by our artillery opening a strong fire against the centre of the enemy. The aim was so effective that in less than one hour the enemy's twelve-pounder was dismounted, and by noon the whole battery of the State troops was silenced. Repeatedly the columns of the enemy gave way under the heavy fire, but rallied again, until our infantry, which had heretofore remained in security behind the batteries, were ordered to advance, when the centre of the enemy at once was broken. To remedy this disaster, about seventeen hundred of the enemy's cavalry were ordered to fall back, and by a side movement try to get possession of Col. SIEGEL's baggage train, which had been left some three miles behind on the road, and thus encircle and cut him off from retreat. But this manœuvre did not succeed. The moment that Col. SIEGEL saw what was intended, he ordered his men to retreat, which was done in the greatest order, at the same time giving word to the baggage train to advance. Before the enemy's design could be carried out, Col. SIEGEL had his baggage train in safety. The wagons were placed in the centre of his column, protected in the front by Maj. BACKHOFF's artillery and Col. SOLOMON's battalion, and in the rear by Col. SIEGEL's eight companies.

By this time it was 4 o'clock P. M. Our troops had suffered a loss of only about twenty killed and forty wounded, while the enemy's loss was stated by some of their officers, who had been taken prisoners, to amount at least to two or three hundred. This difference in the list of killed is mainly due to the efficient use of our artillery, which mowed down the enemy, while our troops were scarcely hurt by the fire from the miserable battery on the other side.

Having thus placed his baggage train in a sure position, Col. SIEGEL followed the enemy, who had now taken position on the bluffs on the south side of a creek, cutting through the only road leading to Carthage. Here Gen. PRICE thought his State troops could cut off all further progress of SIEGEL's forces, and at the first show of a retreat fall in their rear with his cavalry and cut them to pieces. To Col. SIEGEL it was absolutely necessary to pass the creek and clear the road to Carthage, as he could not run the risk of being surrounded by an army of such a numerical superiority by remaining where he was, or of retreating. To dupe the enemy, he ordered his artillery to oblique, two pieces to the right and two to the left, following the movement with part of his force.

The enemy supposing it to be SIEGEL's intention to escape them by cutting a road at their extreme sides, immediately left the road leading over the bluffs, south of the creek, to Carthage, and advanced to the right and left, to prevent SIEGEL's forces from crossing their line. But scarcely had they advanced within four hundred yards of our troops, when our artillery suddenly wheeled around, and poured a most terrific volley of cannister on the rebel cavalry, from both sides. Simultaneously our infantry was ordered to advance at double quick step across the bridge, and in a few minutes the whole body of State troops was flying in all directions. Not a show of resistance was made. Eighty-one horses, sixty-five double shot-guns, and some revolvers fell into the hands of our troops. Some fifty prisoners were taken, and from them the number of killed was ascertained to amount to nearly three hundred. Very few on our side were lost.

After this splendid achievement, Col. SIEGEL proceeded to move toward Carthage, the road to which place was now open. But all along the road, squads of the State troops kept at the side of our forces, though not daring to attack, and occasionally saluted by a discharge from the rifles of our infantry. Arriving at Carthage, Col. SIEGEL found it in possession of the enemy; a secession flag, waving from the top of the court-house, was quickly shot down by our troops.

Col. SIEGEL now found it necessary to retire to Sarcoxie, eight miles southwest of Carthage, as his ammunition was beginning to give out, and it was necessary to connect again with the balance of our Southwestern Army, concentrated at Mount Vernon and Springfield. The road to Sarcoxie passes around Carthage, and is covered by heavy woods, which it was Col. SIEGEL's object to gain, since the State troops at Carthage, almost altogether cavalry, could not follow him there.

Fully aware of this, the enemy had taken his position on the road leading into the woods, prepared to dispute Col. SIEGEL's advance to the last. The most desperate conflict now commenced; the infantry on both sides engaging for the first time. Our troops fought splendidly, and for the first time the rebel troops screwed up some courage. But their arms were very inefficient, and their cavalry could be of little use. The battle raged for over two hours, from quarter-past six to half-past eight o'clock, and was altogether the most hotly contested encounter of the day. Over two hundred of the rebels bit the dust; our loss was eight killed, and some twenty wounded. One officer, Capt. STRODTMANN, was wounded. Our cannon fired 95 rounds. When the enemy retreated to Carthage, about a mile from the place of the engagement, Col. SIEGEL had got his troops into the wood, where they were secure from any further attack.

Although exhausted by ten hours' severe fighting in the heat, and suffering intensely from thirst, Col. SIEGEL ordered his forces to press on towards Sarcoxie, where they arrived on Saturday morning. On Sunday afternoon the retreat was continued to Mount Vernon, Lawrence County, where he has since been reinforced by Col. BROWN's Regiment of Home Guards, and Gen. SWEENEY with another detachment of Home Guards.

Thus the first serious conflict between the United States troops and the rebels has been fought in Missouri, by our brave German Missouri volunteers, resulted in a brilliant victory. Gen. LYON will perhaps now repent that he delayed so long at Booneville, and was thereby prevented from being present and sharing the honors of this glorious victory with Col. SIEGEL.

One battle more, and in all probability, secession will be crushed out in Missouri. A majority of the Committee, charged with the duty of convening the State Convention, have at last seen themselves forced to comply with the will of the people, and consequently issued a call for the meeting of that Convention at Jefferson City, on the 22d day of July. By that time, if Providence permits, Gov. JACKSON will be swinging at the gallows, and his followers adorning the battle-ground of Missouri, or the swamps of Arkansas.

The New-York Times.

VOL. X....NO. 3067.   NEW-YORK, MONDAY, JULY 22, 1861.   PRICE TWO CENTS.

CRUSHING REBELLION.

The Greatest Battle Ever Fought on this Continent.

The Whole Rebel Army of Manassas Engaged.

FEARFUL CARNAGE ON BOTH SIDES.

Advance of the National Army in Three Columns.

The Enemy's Position Attacked by Flank.

Incessant Roar of Artillery and Rattle of Small Arms.

The Rebels Routed and Driven Behind the Manassas Lines.

The Battle to be Renewed To-Day.

THE PRIVATEERS COMING TO GRIEF

Another Vessel Recaptured and Brought to This Port.

The Commander and His Mates Killed by the Colored Steward.

Meeting of the Rebel Congress at Richmond.

JEFF. DAVIS' MESSAGE.

TREMENDOUS BATTLE AT BULL'S RUN.

BULL'S RUN BRIDGE, Sunday, July 21—2 P. M.

The great battle occurred to-day, and the result is not certain at the moment I write. Both sides have fought with terrible tenacity. The battle has been hot and steady for three hours, and the loss must be very heavy—certainly not under one thousand on each side.

The Union Army advanced from Centreville in three columns at 3 o'clock this morning. Col. RICHARDSON commanded the column by the road to Bull's Run, where the action of Thursday took place, and Col. MILES lay on the

Prodded by an impatient Washington, Brigadier General Irwin McDowell marched ill-prepared Federal troops down the road to Richmond.

road and at Centreville to support him. Gen. TYLER commanded the centre division, which took the Warrenton Road—Gens. SCHENCK and Col. SHERMAN being in advance. He had the three Connecticut Regiments, two from Michigan, two from Wisconsin, and the Sixty-ninth and Seventy-ninth, from New-York. Gen. McDOWELL, with Col. HUNTER and a very powerful division, went out on this road, which leads directly forward to Manassas, crossing Bull's Run by a stone bridge, which had been mined.

The attack by these two points was intended mainly as a feint. The real attack was by HUNTER, who took a narrow road two miles out leading to the right, having HUNT'S and the Rhode Island batteries, and leaving Col. KEYES on the centre at the crossing of the roads as a reserve. His orders were to proceed high up the stream, cut himself a path through the woods, cross over, and turn the position of the rebels on the north.

I went out with the centre column. At ten minutes before six we halted about a mile this side of the position of the rebels. The Sixty-ninth and Seventy-ninth Regiments of New-York were thrown the to right, in the woods, and the First and Second Ohio and the Second New-York to the left in advance.

The thirty-pound Parrott gun was planted in the middle of the road, and at ten minutes past six it threw two shells into the battery of the enemy, but without eliciting any response. Ten minutes after, we heard firing on our left from RICHARDSON's column, which was continued at

intervals for two hours, but without eliciting any reply.

Our column remained silent, firing now and then a gun, and at twenty minutes to eight, AYRES' Battery, formerly SHERMAN'S, fired five or six rounds into the enemy, but without response. At a quarter before nine shots were rapidly exchanged between the opposing skirmishers, and GARDNER, of Lacrosse, belonging to the Rhode Island Regiment, was reported killed.

At about ten o'clock heavy clouds of dust showed that reinforcements were coming up to the rebels from Manassas, and was continued through the next three or four hours.

At 11 o'clock AYRES' Battery went to the front; the Sixty-ninth, New-York, was ordered to deploy into the field in front, and firing was heard from HUNTER's Division, on the extreme right, far in advance.

The Ohio regiments were pushed forward with the Second New-York, and ran upon a masked battery of four guns, which killed and wounded quite a number of both. Of the latter, MICHAEL McCARTY, Sergeant of Company H, was wounded, and afterwards was reported dead. Lieut. DEMSEY received a slight wound. Some twenty or thirty of the Ohio regiment broke and run, but the rest stood firm, as did the Second New-York.

CARLISLE's Battery was brought to the front on the right, and soon drove the rebels out of the masked battery.

It was now 11¼ o'clock, when HUNTER's column appeared across the Run, advancing on the flank of the rebels, and the engagement soon became very active in his position. He kept steadily advancing, pouring in a steady fire of artillery and musketry.

The whole Brigade under TYLER was ordered forward to his support. The Sixty-ninth and Seventy-ninth New-York, the First, Second, and Third Connecticut, and the Second Wisconsin were sent in. A constant roll of musketry marked HUNTER'S advance, and the artillery from our column played incessantly on the flank of the rebels. So far as I could see, the latter were pushed backward a considerable distance to the road directly in front of where I stood, across which they charged twice with the bayonet upon our troops, but were repulsed each time. Our men crossed the road and poured in upon them a terrible fire of artillery and musketry.

I write this at 2½ o'clock, and am compelled to close in order to avail myself of a special messenger to Washington. The fight is still going on with great energy. The rebel batteries have again commenced firing upon us, and their balls and shells fall thick upon the road and in the field which I had selected as my observatory.

Gen. SCHENCK and two batteries are ordered up to repulse an attempt of cavalry to outflank us. I shall try to send the result in a later dispatch.

H. J. R.

SPECIAL DISPATCHES FROM WASHINGTON.

WASHINGTON, Sunday, July 21—2 P. M.

Fronting Bull's Run is the main battery of the rebels, flanked on each side by slanting batteries, which protect the entire crossing of the creek. The right battery can be flanked, but the left cannot.

Our troops moved onward last night at 6 o'clock, numbering about forty-five thousand. Gen. PATTERSON'S column is reported moving down the Winchester Road with about fifteen thousand men, and is expected to join to-day. Eleven thousand troops left Alexandria this morning, so that by night we shall have a superior force there, although this morning we stood forty-five thousand against sixty thousand rebels.

What was done last night we do not know positively, but I am just in receipt of a report that a battle was commenced last night, and has continued all day.

The frequent discharge of heavy guns can be heard distinctly at Long Bridge, and this has continued since 6 this morning.

WASHINGTON, Sunday, July 21—5½ P. M.

This morning a general engagement took place along the entire line. After a terrific fight, with great slaughter on both sides, each and every battery was taken.

The fight progressed most fiercely, and the firing only ceased when the rebels were forced within their Manassas lines.

The principal fight took place three and a half miles this side of Manassas. Couriers have been dispatched for further intelligence, and may be expected in very soon.

This news is corroborated by dispatches now before President LINCOLN, Gen. SCOTT and Gen. MANSFIELD. Gen. MANSFIELD says the enemy's guns and equipments are in the hands of our forces.

Now, on to Richmond!

WASHINGTON, Sunday, July 21—8 P. M.

That this city has been in the greatest possible excitement you can well imagine. Bulletins have been received hourly by the President, and at the War Department. Several of them have been made public, being read at the corner of Willard's Hotel to vast crowds, who cheered vehemently, and seemed fairly intoxicated with joy.

Dr. PULLISTON, who has just returned, says that our artillery was played beautifully, and with terrific effect. Very many prominent men were on the field, and others were stationed at a distance of three-quarters of a mile. Senator BIGLER was one of the former.

It seems idle to add anything to the detailed account of Mr. RAYMOND, with the exception of what I learn from official sources. Gen. SCOTT received the following from an official courier.

FAIRFAX C. H., 5½ P. M.

The enemy accepted battle in full force. A great battle was fought and a victory won. The rout of the enemy was complete.

The Fourth Regiment, Pennsylvanians, are on their way from Centreville, their time being up. They had legal a right to leave, but there can be but one opinion as to their courage. Dr. PULLISTON met them on their way hither, and accosting the Major of the Regiment, said. "where are you going?" "Home," replied he—"our time is up." "But didn't they want you to stay?" "Oh, yes, they would have been glad of us, but we have done much hard work, and didn't care to stay." Whereupon the Doctor gave him a good blowing up, and went on.

An eye-witness informs me that members of a regiment on the right made a stampede, but were brought up by Col. BLENKER'S regiment, which supported them, and brought them again to order.

The Zouaves. of New-York, were very badly cut up, but behaved with great gallantry, and are spoken of by all as being worthy of the highest praise.

I hope to send later confirmatory news.

WASHINGTON, Sunday, July 21—11½ P. M.

Quartermaster SAMPSON, of the New-York Thirty-first, has just come in. He left Mr. RAYMOND at Fairfax Court-house. Mr. SAMPSON agrees with Dr. RAY, of the Chicago Tribune, in the belief that the battle will be renewed to-morrow. Col. HUNTER, who was shot through his cheek, has arrived, and though seriously, is not mortally wounded.

From all accounts it is evident that this has been the greatest battle ever fought on this continent. It has resulted in serious mortality on both sides.

Col. HUNTER'S column did most of the fighting, and suffered very severely. Col. SLOCUM, of the Second Rhode Island, is reported dead.

It would be gratifying to know of the safety of several Senators and hosts of Representatives who were spectators, and who have not been heard from. HOWARD.

FROM ANOTHER CORRESPONDENT.

WASHINGTON, Sunday, July 21.

An arrival from the battle-field, as late as 5½ o'clock, says that the conflict was being carried on with vigor and success beyond Bull's Run, and three miles in advance of the battle-field of last Thursday. Reports of cannonding were heard here so late as 10 o'clock this evening, and it is supposed that our troops were still engaging the enemy at or near Manassas Junction.

From the thousand and one rumors around the city, it is impossible to send anything reliable.

Each man tells a different story, and all profess to have been eye-witnesses to the events they narrate. It is certain, however, that there has been a desperate and destructive fight, and that the contest has been equally stubborn on both sides. The supremacy of the cavalry of the rebels gave them great advantage. They charged repeatedly upon our infantry, and caused great harm. The Fire Zouaves sustained several of these charges, and were finally broken.

It is now 12 o'clock. Mr. RAYMOND has not yet reached Washington. LEO.

PREPARATIONS FOR THE BATTLE.

CENTREVILLE, Sunday, July 21,
via Fairfax Court House, Sunday, July 21.

We have successfully outflanked the enemy. At 2½ o'clock this morning the various regiments about Centreville were formed for march, and at 3 o'clock they were in motion in the direction of Perryville, leaving Bull's Run to the left. At 6 o'clock the first gun was fired by a thirty-pound rifled cannon, sent ahead to batter the masked batteries that might be encountered on the road. There was no reply from the enemy, and the advance moved on.

At Gen. McDOWELL'S head-quarters, three miles beyond Centreville, the greater part of the army moved to the right, to avoid a bridge some distance beyond, said to have been undermined. They will pass over upon pontoons prepared by Capt. ALEXANDER, of the Engineer Corps, and who has inspected the country minutely in a previous reconnoisance, and to whom, in a great measure, the plan of the campaign is due.

A general battle is expected to-day or to-morrow, and which will probably decide the fate of the whole campaign.

If Gen. JOHNSON has not yet formed a junction with Gen. BEAUREGARD, he will be entirely cut off by this manoeuvre. Thrown back upon the mountains, his army will become utterly demoralized, and probably fall into the hands of Gen. McCLELLAN, who is advancing beyond the Blue Ridge. And if he has formed a junction with Gen. BEAUREGARD, it opens our communication with Gen. PATTERSON'S column; and thus reinforced, the National army can crush out opposition.

If we are driven back the army can retreat upon Centreville, and keep open the communication with Washington. If Gen. BEAUREGARD remains where he is, his communications in the rear are endangered, and Manassas Junction being situated in the apex of a triangle formed by railroads, a movement in his rear would destroy his communications with Richmond.

The only danger the National troops run by this flank march would be by a sudden advance of Gen. BEAUREGARD upon Centreville, interrupting communications and cutting off our supplies. But this manoeuvre would be desperate, as cutting himself off from supplies, and placing himself in an exhausted country, and between the National troops and the Potomac.

The Sixty-ninth New-York Regiment was assigned the post of honor in advance. The members of this regiment have agreed unanimously to serve, although their time is now out.

All the New-York regiments will follow this example.

The New-York Times.

VOL. X....NO. 3068. NEW-YORK, TUESDAY, JULY 23, 1861. PRICE TWO CENTS.

DISASTER TO THE NATIONAL ARMY

Retreat of Gen. McDowell's Command from Manassas.

Full Details of the Engagement.

But 20,000 of the National Forces in Action.

90,000 REBELS IN THE FIELD.

The Retreat of Our Forces on the Eve of Victory.

A Panic Among the Teamsters and Civilians.

Exaggerated Statements of Our Losses.

Measures of the Government to Retrieve the Disaster.

GENERAL M'CLELLAN IN COMMAND.

Offensive Operations to be Resumed Immediately.

GEN. PATTERSON AT HARPER'S FERRY.

Latest Intelligence from Western Virginia and Missouri.

These Confederate defenders were among the first to fall at the Battle of Manassas.

Editorial Correspondence of the N. Y. Times.

WASHINGTON, Monday Morning, July 22, 1861.

I came in from Centreville last evening for the express purpose of sending you the latest intelligence of the great battle of yesterday. I left Centreville at half-past 5 and reached here at midnight. I sent a dispatch to the office, but, as it is to be subjected to the censorship of the Government, which gives no hint of what it refuses permission to pass, I have no means of knowing whether its contents reached you or not. I must therefore repeat its contents.

The battle yesterday was one of the most severe and sanguinary ever fought on this Continent, and it ended in the failure of the Union troops to hold all the positions which they sought to carry, and which they actually did carry, and in their retreat to Centreville, where they have made a stand and where Gen. McDowell believes that they are able to maintain themselves.

As I telegraphed you yesterday, the attack was made in three columns, two of which, however, were mainly feints, intended to amuse and occupy the enemy, while the substantial work was done by the third. It has been known for a long time that the range of hills which border the small, swampy stream known as Bull's Run, had been very thoroughly and extensively fortified by the rebels,—that batteries had been planted at every available point, usually concealed in the woods and bushes which abound in that vicinity, and covering every way of approach to the region beyond. These are the advanced defences of Manassas Junction, which is some three miles further off. Until these were carried, no approach could be made to that place; and after they should be carried others of a similar character would have to be overcome at every point where they could be erected. The utmost that military skill and ingenuity could accomplish for the defence of this point was done. Gen. McDowell was unwilling to make an attack directly in face of these batteries, as they would be of doubtful issue, and must inevitably result in a very serious loss of life. After an attack had been resolved upon, therefore, he endeavored to find some way of *turning* the position. His first intention was to do this on the Southern side,—to throw a strong column into the place from that direction, while a feigned attack should be made in front. On Thursday, when the troops were advanced to Centreville, it was found that the roads on the south side of these positions were almost impracticable,—that they were narrow, crooked and stony, and that it would be almost impossible to bring up enough artillery to be effective in the time required.

This original plan was, therefore, abandoned; and Friday was devoted to an examination by the topographical engineers of the Northern side of the position. Maj. BARNARD and Capt. WHIPPLE reconnoitred the place for miles around, and reported that the position could be entered by a path coming from the north,—though it was somewhat long and circuitous. This was selected, therefore, as the mode and point of attack.

On Saturday the troops were all brought closely up to Centreville,—and all needful preparations were made for the attack which was intended for the next day. Yesterday morning, therefore, the Army marched—by two roads—Col. RICHARDSON with his command taking the Southern, which leads to Bull's Run, and Gen. TYLER the Northern—running parallel to it at a distance of about a mile and a half. The movement commenced at about 3 o'clock. I got up at a little before 4, and found the long line of troops extended far out on either road. I took the road by which Colonel HUNTER with his command, and Gen. McDowell and staff, had gone, and pushed on directly for the front. After going out about two miles Colonel HUNTER turned to the right—marching obliquely towards the Run, which he was to cross some four miles higher up and then come down upon the intrenched positions of the enemy on the other side. Col. MILES was left at Centerville and on the road, with reserves which he was to bring up whenever they might be needed. Gen. TYLER went directly forward, to engage the enemy in front, and send reinforcements to Col. HUNTER whenever it should be seen that he was engaged.

I went out, as I have already stated, upon what is marked as the northern road. It is hilly, like all the surface of this section. After going out about three miles, you come to a point down which the road, leading through a forest, descends;—then it proceeds by a succession of rising and falling knolls for a quarter of a mile,—when it crosses a stone bridge and then ascends by

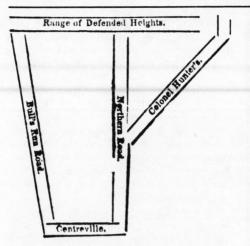

a steady slope to the heights beyond. At the top of that slope, the rebels had planted heavy batteries, and the woods below were filled with their troops and with concealed cannon. We proceeded down the road to the first of the small knolls mentioned, when the whole column halted. The 30-pounder Parrott gun, which has a longer range than any other in the army, was planted directly in the road. Capt. AYRES' battery was stationed in the woods a little to the right. The First Ohio and Second New-York Regiments were thrown into the woods in advance on the left. The Sixty-ninth, New-York, the First, Second and Third Connecticut regiments, were ranged behind them, and the Second Wisconsin was thrown into the woods on the right. At about half past six o'clock the 30-pounder threw two shells directly into the battery at the summit of the slope, on the opposite height, one of which, as I learned afterwards, struck and exploded directly in the midst of the battery, and occasioned the utmost havoc and confusion. After about half an hour Capt. AYRES threw ten or fifteen shot and shell from his battery into the same place. But both failed to elicit any reply. Men could be seen moving about the opposite slope, but the batteries were silent. An hour or so afterwards we heard three or four heavy guns from Col. RICHARDSON'S column at Bull's Run, and these were continued at intervals for two or three hours, but they were not answered, even by a single gun. It was very clear that the enemy intended to take his own time for paying his respects to us, and that he meant, moreover, to do it in his own way. Meantime we could hear in the distance the sound of Col. HUNTER'S axemen, clearing his way, and awaited with some impatience the sound of his cannon on the opposite heights. Time wore along with occasional shots from our guns, as well as those of Col. RICHARDSON'S column, but without, in a single instance, receiving any reply.

At a little before 11 o'clock, the First Ohio and Second New-York, which were lying in the wood on the left, were ordered to advance. They did so,—passing out of the road and climbing a fence into a wood opposite, which they had barely approached, however, when they were met by a tremendous discharge of a four-gun battery, planted at the left in the woods, mainly for the purpose of sweeping the road perpendicularly and the open field on its right by which alone troops could pass forward to the opposite bank. They were staggered for a moment, and received orders to retire. Capt. AYRES' Battery (formerly SHERMAN'S) was advanced a little, so as to command this Battery, and by twenty minutes of vigorous play upon it, silenced it completely.

At half-past 11 we heard HUNTER'S guns on the opposite height, over a mile to the right. He was answered by batteries there, and then followed the sharp, rattling volleys of musketry, as their infantry became engaged. The firing was now incessant. HUNTER had come upon them suddenly, and formed his line of battle in an open field, at the right of the road. The enemy drew up to oppose him, but he speedily drove them to retreat and followed them up with the greatest vigor and rapidity. Meantime, for some three hours previous, we had seen long lines of dense dust rising from the roads leading from Manassas, and, with the glass, we could very clearly perceive that they were raised by the constant and steady stream of reinforcements, which continued to pour in nearly the whole day. The Sixty-Ninth, Seventy-ninth, Second and Eighth, New-York—the First, Second and Third Connecticut, and the Second Wisconsin, were brought forward in advance of the wood and marched across the field to the right, to go to Col. HUNTER's support. They crossed the intervening stream and drew up in a small open field, separated from Col. HUNTER's column by a dense wood, which was filled with batteries and infantry. Our guns continued to play upon the woods which thus concealed the enemy, and aided materially in clearing them for the advance. Going down to the extreme front of the column, I could watch the progress of Col. HUNTER, marked by the constant roar of artillery and the roll of musketry, as he pushed the rebels back from point to point. At 1 o'clock he had driven them out of the woods and across the road which was the prolongation of that on which we stood. Here, by the side of their batteries, the rebels made a stand. They planted their flag directly in the road, and twice charged across it upon our men, but without moving them an inch. They were met by a destructive fire, and were compelled to fall still further back. Gradually the point of fire passed further away, until the dense clouds of smoke which marked the progress of the combat were at least half a mile to the left of what had been the central position of the rebels.

It was now 2½ o'clock. I was at the advanced point of the front of our column, some hundred rods beyond the woods, in which the few troops then there were drawn up, when I decided to drive back to the town, for the purpose of sending you my dispatch. As I passed up the road the balls and shell from the enemy began to fall with more than usual rapidity. I did not see the point from which they came; but meeting Capt. AYRES, he said he was about to bring up his battery, supported by the Ohio Brigade, under Gen. SCHENCK, to repel a rumored attempt of cavalry to outflank this column. As I went forward he passed down. Gen. SCHENCK's Brigade was at once drawn up across the road, and Capt. AYRES' guns were planted in a knoll at the left, when a powerful body of rebels, with a heavy battery, came down from the direction of Bull's Run, and engaged this force with tremendous effect. I went to Centreville, sent off my dispatch, and started with all speed to return,—intending to go with our troops upon what had been the hotly contested field, never doubting for a moment that it would remain in their hands. I had gone but a quarter of a mile when we met a great number of fugitives, and our carriage soon became entangled in a mass of baggage-wagons, the officer in charge of which told me it was useless to go in that direction, as our troops were retreating. Not crediting the story, which was utterly inconsistent with what I had seen but a little while before, I continued to push on. I soon met Quartermaster STETSON, of the Fire Zouaves, who told me, bursting into tears, that his Regiment had been utterly cut to pieces, that the Colonel and Lieutenant-Colonel were both killed, and that our troops had actually been repulsed. I still tried to proceed, but the advancing columns rendered it impossible, and I turned about. Leaving my carriage, I went to a high point of ground and saw, by the dense cloud of dust which rose over each of the three roads by which the three columns of the Army had advanced, that they were all on the retreat. Sharp discharges of cannon in their rear indicated that they were being pursued. I waited half an hour or so, to observe the troops and batteries as they arrived, and then started for Washington, to send my dispatch and write this letter. As I came past the hill on which the Secessionists had their intrenchments less than a week ago, I saw our forces taking up positions for a defence if they should be assailed.

Such is a very rapid and general history of yesterday's engagement. I am unable to be precise or profuse in matters of detail, and must leave these to a future letter.

I hear nothing, on every side, but the warmest and heartiest commendation of our troops. They fought like veterans. The rebels did not, in a single instance, stand before them in a charge, and were shaken by every volley of their musketry. I do not mean to praise any one at the expense of another. The Sixty-ninth fought with splendid and tenacious courage. They charged batteries two or three times, and would have taken and held them but for the reinforcements which were constantly and steadily poured in. *Indeed it was to this fact alone* that the comparative success of the rebels is due. We had not over 26,000 men in action, the rest being held behind as reserves at Centreville; while the enemy must have numbered at least 60,000.

The Fire Zouaves before they had fairly got into action, were terribly cut up by a battery and by musketry, which opened on their flank. They lost a great many of their officers and men.

Col. HUNTER, who led the main column of attack, received a severe wound in his throat; he was brought to this city, but I understand that he cannot recover, if indeed he is not already dead. I have heard the names of many others reported killed or wounded, but deem it best not to mention them now, as the rumors may prove to be unfounded.

About a mile this side of Centreville a stampede took place among the teamsters and others, which threw everything into the utmost confusion, and inflicted some very serious injuries. Mr. EATON, of Michigan, in trying to arrest the flight of some of these men, was shot by one of them,—the ball taking effect in his hand. Quite a number of Senators and members of the House were present at the battle.

I shall be able to ascertain to-morrow the cause of the retreat of Col. HUNTER's column after the splendid success it achieved. I would gladly, though in the face of evidence unable, believe what is rumored here, that this column did indeed hold its ground, and that the retreat was confined to the other columns. I fear this will not prove to be the fact.

H. J. R.

SPECIAL DISPATCHES TO THE N. Y. TIMES.

WASHINGTON, Monday, July 22.

Stragglers from the Army create great but needless excitement, by stories that the rebels are coming to Washington. There is not the slightest cause for any such apprehension. The Army is falling back upon Arlington, and new regiments are constantly arriving from the North.

It is not easy to account for the panic which occasioned the first movement of retreat, but the most probable account is, that it was caused by a charge of cavalry. which was repulsed by the regiment upon which it was made, but which threw another, upon which in turn, it fell into confusion.

The Army, in its retreat from Centreville, was protected in rear by Col. MILES' Reserve.

Some fifty or one hundred of the Fire Zouaves have just arrived here. The rumor is circulated that this is all that is left of the regiment, but this is not so. These are only those who have come on singly in advance.

Exaggerated statements about the losses of individual regiments increase the excitement and cause heedless grief. The official list will be published as speedily as possible. All access to the Army across the Potomac is impossible.

DISPATCH TO THE ASSOCIATED PRESS.

WASHINGTON, Monday, July 22.

After the latest information was received from Centreville at 7½ o'clock last night, a series of events took place in the intensest degree disastrous.

Many confused statements are prevalent, but enough is known to warrant the statement that we have suffered in a degree which has cast a gloom over the remnants of the Army, and excited the deepest melancholy throughout Washington.

The carnage is tremendously heavy on both side, and on ours it is represented as frightful. We were advancing and taking the masked batteries gradually but surely, and driving the enemy towards Manassas Junction, when the enemy seemed to have been reinforced by Gen. JOHNSTON, who, it is understood, took command, and immediately commenced driving us back, when a panic among our troops suddenly occurred, and a regular stampede took place.

It is thought that Gen. McDOWELL undertook to make a stand at or about Centreville, but the panic was so fearful that the whole Army became demoralized, and it was impossible to check them either at Centreville or Fairfax Court-house.

Gen. McDOWELL intended to make another stand at Fairfax Court-house, but, our forces being in full retreat, he could not accomplish the object.

Beyond Fairfax Court-house the retreat was kept up until the men reached their regular encampments, a portion of whom returned to them, but a still larger portion coming inside the intrenchments.

A large number of troops fell on the wayside from exhaustion, and scattered along the route all the way from Fairfax Court house.

The road from Bull's Run was strewed with knapsacks, arms, &c. Some of our troops deliberately threw away their guns and appurtenances, the better to facilitate their travel.

Gen. McDOWELL was in the rear of the retreat, exerting himself to rally his men, but only with partial effect.

The latter part of the Army, it is said, made their retreat in order. He was completely exhausted, having slept but little for three nights. His orders on the field did not at all times reach those for whom they were intended.

It is supposed that the force sent out against our troops consisted, according to a prisoner's statement, of about 30,000 men, including a large number of cavalry. He further says, that owing to reinforcements from Richmond, Strausburgh, and other points, the enemy's effective force was 90,000 men.

According to the statement of two Fire Zouaves, they only have about 200 left from the slaughter, while the Sixty-ninth and Seventy-ninth Regiments frightfully suffered in killed and wounded. The number cannot now be known.

SHERMAN'S, CARLISLE'S, GRIFFIN'S, and the West Point Batteries, were taken by the enemy, and the eight siege and 32 rifle cannon, the latter being too cumbrous to remove. They were two miles the other side of Centreville. Such of the wounded as were brought to the Centreville Hospital were left there, after having their wounds

properly dressed by Surgeon FRANK H. HAMILTON.

The panic was so great that the attempt to rally them to a stand at Centreville was entirely in vain. If a firm stand had been made there our troops could have been reinforced and much disaster prevented. Gen. McDOWELL was thus foiled in his well-arranged plans.

It is supposed all the provision trains belonging to the United States Government were saved. Some regimental wagons were overturned by accident, or the wheels came off, and had, therefore, to be abandoned. Large droves of cattle were saved by being driven back in advance of the retreat.

It is supposed here, to-day, that Gen. MANSFIELD will take command of the fortifications on the other side of the river, which are able, it is said, by military engineers, to hold out against any force the enemy may bring against them. Large rifled cannon and mortars are being rapidly sent over and mounted.

An officer just from Virginia, (10:30,) reports that the road from Centreville to the Potomac is strewed with stragglers. The troops are resuming the occupations of the fortifications and intrenchments on the line of the Potomac.

Col. MARSTON'S New-Hampshire Regiment reached here this morning. He was wounded. Col. HEINTZELMAN was also wounded in the wrist. In addition to those reported yesterday, it is said that Col. WILCOX, the gallant commander of a brigade, was killed. Also Capt. McCOOK, a brother of Col. COOK, of Ohio.

The city this morning is in the most intense ex-

Fairfax Court House

citement. Groups are everywhere gathered inquiring the latest news.

Wagons are continually arriving, bringing in the dead and wounded. Soldiers are relating to greedy listeners the deplorable events of last night and early this morning. The feeling is awfully distressing. Both telegraph communication and steamboat communication with Alexandria is suspended to-day to the public. The greatest alarm exists throughout the city, especially among the female portion of the population.

GEN. McCLELLAN ASSIGNED TO THE COMMAND OF THE POTOMAC.

WASHINGTON, Monday, July 22.

Gen. McCLELLAN has been summoned by the Government from Western Virginia to repair to Washington to take command of the Army of the Potomac.

Gen. ROSENCRANZ takes his place in command of the Army of Western Virginia.

The *Corps d'Armée* at Washington is to be instantly reorganized and increased. The orders have already been given. Offers of regiments already raised and being made, will be accepted with such rapidity as to insure that this will be accomplished in a few days. Large reinforcements from various districts are already on the way hither, orders having been telegraphed for them yesterday, while the battle was in progress.

REBEL ACCOUNT OF THE FIRST FIGHT.

LOUISVILLE, Monday, July 22.

A special dispatch to the Nashville *Union* from Manassas, 18th, says that at the fight at Bull's Run Gen. BEAUREGARD commanded in person. The enemy was repulsed three times in great confusion and loss. The Washington Artillery of New-Orleans, with seven guns, engaged SHERMAN'S fifteen guns, and, after making the latter change position fifteen times, silenced and forced them to retire. Large quantities of arms were taken. Our loss was trifling. Maj. HARRISON and two privates were killed. Capts. DULANY, CHITTMAN and three privates were wounded. A National officer of high rank was killed, and $700 in gold taken from his body.

POSTSCRIPT

TUESDAY, FOUR O'CLOCK, A. M.

THE BATTLE OF SUNDAY.

Latest Reports from Our Special Correspondents.

Exaggerated Character of the First Reports.

List of Casualties so Far as Known.

SPECIAL DISPATCHES FROM WASHINGTON

WASHINGTON, Monday, July 22.

The disaster of Sunday is less overwhelming than was at first reported. The army was not routed, nor cut to pieces; nor were our losses, although heavy, such as cannot be repaired by a few weeks of vigorous preparation. The Government will give its exclusive attention to this matter, and will profit in many respects from the experience acquired.

Only a small portion of the camp equipage was captured. Our heaviest loss, aside from men, is that of artillery. No time must be lost in repairing it.

Brigadier General P.G.T. Beauregard positioned Southern troops to meet McDowell's advance.

It is universally agreed that up to 2 o'clock our troops were steadily gaining upon the rebels. They had beaten them in every open encounter, had resisted every attempt to charge by cavalry, had silenced three of their batteries, and had pressed them back a mile from their advanced position; but they had been marching and fighting twelve hours, and were physically exhausted, so that, when they saw new batteries opening upon them and fresh reinforcements marching against them, it was impossible to continue the fight; but they proved their superiority in the open field beyond all question. In no instance did the rebels stand their ground against a charge or in the open field with musketry. They had a prodigious advantage in number, and a still greater in their intrenchments.

The censure of the public will fall upon the authority which decided on a battle against such fearful odds. Whether that was Gen. McDowell, Gen. SCOTT, or the Cabinet, we shall probably know ere long. The *Evening Star* announces that Gen. McDowell has been superseded by McCLELLAN. It is not at all likely that any such precipitant judgment and execution will be passed upon him.

FROM ANOTHER CORRESPONDENT.

WASHINGTON, Monday, July 22.

The disaster of yesterday is not so great as was at first supposed. Our troops retired in order from Centreville last night, falling back to the intrenchments opposite this city—the brigade under Gen. BLENKER covering them, and bringing down the stragglers and destroying the bridges in the rear.

We shall not lose, in killed, wounded and missing, to exceed one thousand men. We have lost from eighteen to twenty-three pieces of artillery, including five of the Rhode Island Battery, and some of the Sherman, Carlisle and Griggin Batteries. About sixty to seventy baggage wagons will be lost. As near as can be ascertained the number of muskets thrown away on the retreat and lost on the field will reach four thousand. At least one-half of the blankets and haversacks were thrown away previous to the battle, and on the retreat. We have lost but little provisions, and no ammunition.

The rebels continued in pursuit of our retreating columns, pushing their cavalry as far as Cen-

treville, at which place they were checked for a time, but of which they took possession when our troops retired.

Our men fought with determined vigor, and accomplished results worthy of veterans. The Seventy-first, the Zouaves, the Sixty-ninth, and the Fourteenth Militia, are most frequently mentioned as among the New-York regiments that most resolutely contested the field.

The city is full of stragglers from the different regiments. They are mostly those men who first left the field. They give the most exaggerated accounts of disasters to our regiment. One says his regiment is entirely decimated; another that his regiment is cut to pieces, and another that his regiment is totally lost. Of course out of all these rumors it is impossible to gather anything reliable.

A number of the ladies of Washington promptly provided succor for the hungry and tired troops. Though it was raining hard, many went into the streets with baskets of provisions and wine, and distributed them among the soldiers.

The causes of our defeat are yet unexplained, at least officially, but that it was due to a stampede among our troops is generally admitted. The cause of that stampede will, I think, be traced to the failure of the supply of ammunition of one of the batteries engaged. When more ammunition was wanted, an order was given to the commandant of a caisson to go for ammunition to the wagon, about a half mile distant. The drivers at once started their horses on a full run, and then arose the cry that the column was being attacked by a mass of cavalry; that it had wavered, and that the artillery was already in retreat. This panic spread rapidly, and in a short time the entire army was *en route* for Centreville.

Gen. McDOWELL was so overcome by fatigue, that while writing a short dispatch in the telegraph office, at Fairfax, he fell asleep three times. He had been busy all the night preceding in making preliminary arrangements, and had been in the saddle from 2 o'clock in the morning until 10 at night. A 9½ his dispatch was received here, announcing his retreat and his purpose to make a stand at Centreville. At 1½ it was announced that he would fall back to Fairfax. It was left to his own judgment whether to retire to the Potomac line or not.

The New-York Times.

VOL. X....NO. 3069.   NEW-YORK, WEDNESDAY, JULY 24, 1861.   PRICE TWO CENTS.

THE GREAT REBELLION.

The Victory of Sunday, and How it was Lost.

Exaggerations of the First Reports Corrected.

THE NATIONAL ARMY NOT ROUTED.

A Body of Troops Still at Centreville.

Our Loss in Killed and Wounded not Over Six Hundred.

The Rebel Loss Estimated at Three Thousand.

THEIR TROOPS IN NO CONDITION TO PURSUE.

Shocking Barbarities Perpetrated by the Rebels.

They Make Targets of the Wounded Soldiers, Mutilate them with Knives, and Fire at the Hospital.

Brilliant and Dashing Bravery of the Fire Zouaves.

They Annihilate the Black Horse Cavalry.

Lists of Our Killed and Wounded.

SPECIAL DISPATCHES FROM WASHINGTON.
WASHINGTON, Tuesday, July 23.

The feeling is much better here to-day. The enormous exaggerations of the runaway soldiers have ceased to have the effect which attended them yesterday. Our loss in killed and wounded will not much exceed six hundred, though the missing may be three times that number.

It is understood that the Government has already taken the necessary steps to bring one hundred thousand men into the field here, and this renews the confidence and determination of the people.

Col. RAMSAY's regiment has been accepted, and ordered to report at Washington within twenty days, and muster in by hundreds.

The losses of the New-York and other regiments have been greatly overstated. The Sev-

A soldier pauses among soldiers' graves at Bull Run.

enty-first has not lost over thirty in killed and wounded. The Fire Zouaves suffered more severely, as did also the Sixty-ninth. Capt. T. F. MEAGHER had a horse shot under him, but is untouched. All our losses were in advancing—none in falling back. There was no panic in front. This was confined mainly to the wagon drivers, straggling soldiers and fugitive officers, at the rear of the columns.

Our greatest deficiency was in cool and competent officers. The men fought nobly, and were ready for anything which experienced commanders would order them to do.

Gen. McDOWELL behaved admirably. He was active, cool, and attended to everything in person, so far as possible; but he had not a sufficient staff, and was not properly supported by his subordinates. Major WADSWORTH, of New-York, one of his aids, showed the utmost gallantry and devotion. He exerted himself to rally the forces when they first fell back, and towards the close, after having his horse shot under him, seized the colors of the wavering New-York Fourteenth, and called on the boys to rally once more to the glorious old flag. Private TYLER took hold of the colors with him, and the regiment rallied to another charge, but without success. Major WADSWORTH, as the Army retreated, remained at Fairfax Court-house, and devoted himself to purchasing everything needful for the wounded, of whom about a hundred and fifty were at that place.

Gov. SPRAGUE behaved with conspicuous gallantry, and insisted on making a stand for another fight at Centreville, but the men were too much demoralized by the panic which sprung up in the rear.

Col. BURNSIDE displayed great activity and courage at every stage of the fight, and is eager to renew it. Cols. HUNTER and HEINTZELMAN have sent word that, in spite of their wounds, they will take the field again in two days, if desired. When the Fourteenth New-York entered the field, they passed a wounded major of the rebel army, who begged for water. A private gave it to him, and he offered his gold watch in return. The private declined to take it, but the Major insisted, as he said some one else would get it if he

The ruins of Henry House testify to the ferocity of the Battle at Manassas.

did not. The testimony is universal to the barbarity and ferocity with which our wounded were treated by the rebels. Gen. SCOTT is in good spirits, and hard at work. RUSSELL got a report of the fight off in time for the Boston steamer.

WASHINGTON, Tuesday, July 23—2 P. M.

Capt. TODD, of Brattleboro, Vt., and the Major of the Second Vermont, are among the wounded.

The stragglers are gradually gathering together, but very slowly. Most of them are ambitious of telling their own stories, and as they have crowds of listeners, they do not like to go again into camp.

The Government has taken possession of the rolling stock and tracks between this city and Baltimore, and will hold all for the use of Government.

Two hundred volunteer surgeons came from Philadelphia this morning.

The body of Col. KENNEDY, of the Tammany Regiment, will be sent to New-York by the train this afternoon.

The first installment of Col. VAN ALLEN's regiment of cavalry, from New-York, reached Washington last night. It consisted of Capt. FITZSIMMONS' company from Rochester, eighty-five men and horses.

The remnants of the regiments composing Gen. McDOWELL's Army occupy the lines they left before their advance upon Manassas.

Many of the citizens of Washington are again leaving the city, fearful of an attack from the rebels under BEAUREGARD. The Secessionists of Washington make no concealment of their exultation. The prisoners taken from the rebels and in confinement in Washington are liberally supplied with cakes, pies, wines and clothing by women who commend them as the greatest patriots in the country.

Among the dispatches received at the Washington office to-day, was the following, addressed to a member of one of the regiments quartered at Arlington Heights, of course of the Sixty-ninth:

NEW-YORK, July 23, 1861.

Your wife wishes to know if you are dead, alive or wounded. If dead, please send the body on.

A spectator of the scene tells me that the Zouaves literally decimated the Black Horse

Cavalry, the celebrated rebel troop. About the middle of the battle the Zouaves fired by platoons upon the rebel infantry stationed in the woods. After they had fired they discovered a troop of horse coming down on their rear. They carried the American flag, which deceived Col. HEINTZELMAN, and made him believe they were United States Cavalry, and he so told the Zouaves. As they came nearer, their true character was discovered, but too late for all the Zouaves to reload. The regiment faced and received the cavalry as they came down, with leveled bayonets, which threw them into confusion. Then away went muskets, and the Zouaves went in with their knives and pistols. They siezed horses and stabbed their riders. In this hand-to-hand conflict the Black Horse Troop were handled in their own professed way of fighting. The sequel showed the Zouaves to be the most expert handlers of the knife.

When the fight was over, there were not twenty of the four hundred cavalry left alive. Men and horses had been cut to pieces by the infuriated red-shirts. This troop of cavalry had boasted they would picket their horses in the grounds of the White House.

The telegraph office here is besieged by a crowd sending messages to friends. The capacity of the office is not equal to the extraordinary demand upon it, which will account for any delay in the receipt of answers to inquiries.   LEO.

INCIDENTS OF THE BATTLE.

Correction of Exaggerations—The Enemy in No Condition for Pursuit—Another Solferino Stampede—Straggling Soldiers— Treatment of the Wounded by the Rebels.

Editorial Correspondence of the New-York Times.
WASHINGTON, Monday Evening.

Public feeling grows somewhat more settled and resolute in regard to the defeat of Sunday. The first reports brought by the stragglers and fugitives from the Army, and marked by all the exaggerations of men in a panic, created a feeling of consternation and intense alarm. Men were looking for the instant appearance of the rebel army against Washington,—for an immediate uprising of the Secessionists of Baltimore, and for the immediate overthrow of the Government. Reflection and more accurate intelligence has

Stone Church, Centreville.

modified this feeling very essentially;—and the Washington public begin to realize that the American Government is not so near its end as they were inclined at first to suppose, and perhaps to hope. The earliest reports represented the defeat as an entire and disgraceful rout, which had completely broken up the Union Army.

It was asserted that the entire baggage train of the force, with all their horses, wagons and equipage of every kind collected at such an enormous cost, had fallen into the hands of the enemy, and that the rear of the Army was left without protection of any kind. It now appears that our Army retreated in very good order as far as Centreville, where it was protected from pursuit by the reserves, under Col. MILES; that no attempt was made to capture the baggage wagons which had nearly all been left between Centreville and Fairfax, and went back with the Army to the latter place, and that the only material which fell into the hands of the rebels was such as had been hastily, and not very creditably, abandoned on the road between Bull's Run and Centreville.

It is pretty evident that the enemy was in no condition for pursuit. A powerful force of cavalry might have done great execution upon the rear of our retreating columns; and they did make an attempt of this sort upon the Warrenton Road, but a volley from Col. BLENKER's regiment, which was sent out from Centreville to cover the retreat, soon put them to flight. The pursuit extended but a short distance, and was attended by no important results.

It will delight the heart of my excellent old friend of the *Herald*, to learn that I became involved in another stampede, not quite so extensive or disastrous as that of Solferino, but one sufficiently disgraceful to answer his purpose. As soon as it was understood in the crowd of teamsters, fugitive soldiers and miscellaneous hangers-on of the army at Centreville, that our columns were retreating, they became very considerably excited,—and this feeling rose to panic when they heard the sound of cannon in the rear, as they supposed it to indicate that the enemy was pursuing in force. After I had driven something over a mile from the village on my way to Washington, the crowd in the rear became absolutely frenzied with fear, and an immense mass of wagons, horses, men on foot, and flying soldiers, came dashing down the hill at a rate which threatened destruction, instant and complete, to everything in their way. The panic spread as they proceeded, and gathering strength by its progress, the movement became absolutely terrific. The horses caught the frenzy of the moment, and became as wild as their masters. My driver attempting to check the speed of our carriage, found it suddenly crushed under the weight of an enormous Pennsylvania Army wagon which crushed it like an egg-shell. The opportune arrival of another carriage containing a couple of Congressmen, relieved me from the dilemma, and took me to Washington. Previous to my mishap I was overtaken and passed by a solitary horseman, who proved to be Mr. RUSSELL, of the London *Times*, who was profoundly disgusted with this movement, and was making all possible haste to get out of it.

THE SIXTY-NINTH.

The following private dispatch has been placed at our disposal:

WASHINGTON, Tuesday, July 23—12 M.

Col. CORCORAN is still missing up to this hour (12 M.,) and Lieut. BAGLEY, Col. SHERMAN's Aid-de-Camp is also missing. Col. CORCORAN was wounded and is probably taken prisoner.

Lieut.-Col. NUGENT is not killed as reported. A great many of the Sixty-ninth are still missing.

Sudley's Springs, Bull Run.

IMPORTANT REPORTS FROM BALTIMORE.

BALTIMORE, Tuesday, July 23.

A gentleman from the Valley of Virginia says that Gen. JOHNSON left Winchester on Thursday noon. He reached Manassas during the battle, 20,000 strong. He left behind only his sick to the number of 1,800.

It was confidently asserted at Winchester that Gen. JOHNSON and Col. HUNTER were both killed at Manassas. It was also rumored, but not certain, that Gen. JACKSON was also killed.

There had been great sickness and numerous deaths at Winchester. The slaughter of the Confederates at Manassas is represented as very great.

Messengers sent here from Manassas, represent the Army as in a starving condition, and all the produce in the neighborhood was being seized and sent down.

The suffering at Winchester was very great. Provisions and groceries were very scarce. Sugar was $1 a pound.

FROM THE SEAT OF WAR IN THE WEST

CAIRO, Ill., Tuesday, July 23.

The rebels are rapidly organizing opposite here, in Kentucky.

It is currently reported that WATKINS, with 2,000 men, is encamped within seven miles of Bloomfield, Mo. He has no field pieces, and his men are poorly armed.

CLAIB JACKSON and staff were at Memphis on Saturday last.

An attack on Bird's Point is threatened.

At Memphis the loss of the rebels at the fight at Manassas is estimated at 3,000.

FROM FORTRESS MONROE.

FORTRESS MONROE, Monday, July 22, }
via BALTIMORE, Tuesday, July 23. }

Mr. WHITNEY, Quartermaster's Sergeant, of the Vermont Regiment, was shot this morning by some rebels at Newport's News. With two others, he was in search of a strayed bullock not far from the camp. His body was pierced with half a dozen bullets.

An infernal machine, intended by the Confederates to blow up some of the ships of war in the Roads, washed ashore this morning. It is of ingenious construction. This is the second attempt of the kind, and one of the atrocious methods of warfare employed by the high-minded chivalry. It landed within a few rods of Floyd's House.

The *Roanoke* steamed up the Roads this morning. She has been as far South as St. Augustine, Florida. During her cruise she burned a Confederate vessel, supposed to be a privateer, the name of which we have not been able to learn. The crew escaped to shore in small boats.

The *Quaker City* is up from the Capes.

A heavy gale from the southeast is prevailing.

The railroad at Old Point is in rapid progress of construction. By means of it FLOYD's gun will be moved to a position where it can be brought to bear upon Sewall's Point. The Union gun will also soon be mounted.

Important news may be expected from Old Point in the course of a few days.

The New-York Times.

VOL. X....NO. 3072. NEW-YORK, SATURDAY, JULY 27, 1861. PRICE TWO CENTS.

THE GREAT REBELLION.

Highly Important News from Washington.

ANOTHER CRY OF DANGER TO THE CAPITAL

Plans and Intentions of the Rebel Leaders.

A Corps d'Armee to Cross the Potomac and Make an Attack in the Rear.

Simultaneous Movements to be Made Against McClellan, Butler, Banks and Rosencranz.

Troops Still Pouring into Washington.

An Important Expedition from Fortress Monroe.

Capture of Ten Rebel Schooners and Sloops.

RETURN OF WAR-WORN HEROES.

Enthusiastic Reception of the Eighth and Seventy-first.

THE CAPITAL IN DANGER.

Project of the Rebels for Capturing Washington—Lee to Arouse Baltimore—Beauregard to Engage McClellan and Henningsen to Dislodge Rosencranz.

From Our Own Correspondent.
WASHINGTON, Thursday, July 25, 1861.

In these exciting times, when so many rumors, having only an imaginary foundation, are gaining currency, it is bad policy to add to their number, but I will be pardoned for communicating a project which a military officer of high rank has just assured me is now entertained by the rebels for gaining possession of the Capital. The recent success of the Confederate forces at Manassas has determined their leaders to adopt another plan of campaign,—to give up the offensive and take up the defensive. They think it is useless now to defend Richmond, but they deem it necessary to occupy this city and Baltimore,

and to accomplish that end they have not only agreed upon the following plan of operations, but they have begun to put it into practice.

According to my authority, Gen. LEE, who has now, as you know, set his *corps d'armée* in motion, under the pretext of attacking our army in Western Virginia, really intends to direct his force upon the upper Potomac, which he will cross at a distance of about forty miles from Washington. Once there, he will be joined by the Secessionists, who are secretly organizing all over Maryland, and will then attack Washington on its unfortified and defenceless side. At the same time, BEAUREGARD will make a movement against McCLELLAN, whom he will keep busy within his own lines, thus preventing his taking part in the defence of the city. JOHNSTON will be left to watch and counteract PATTERSON's movements; a strong column will be sent against BUTLER from Richmond, and PRYOR, the chevalier of the bowie-knife, and HENNINGSEN, the companion of WALKER, the fillibuster, will dislodge ROSENCRANZ from the position he occupies in Western Virginia. Such, according to the information I have received, is the plan the rebels have adopted.

I know the Administration expressed the opinion, the other day, that Washington cannot be taken. I know such is not their opinion to-day; and that they are expecting momentarily to hear of the approach of Gen. LEE. I know also that a great many persons, mainly the politicians, will lull the people into mistaken confidence. What will be the consequence? The nation suddenly aroused by the catastrophe at Bull's Run, will, under these soothing assertions, go to sleep again, until awakened by a new disaster. Shall we suffer this to take place, or shall we prepare ourselves against all contingencies of the kind? Shall be maintain our Army on the same footing, allowing lack of discipline to rule supreme, soldiers to leave their camps for the indulgences of cities, regiments to remain disorganized, the city unfortified, soldiers commanded by lawyers and merchants, officers in peace, civilians in war? Shall we continue to have no camps in which our soldiers may be in-

ured to the fatigue of a long march, no schools to instruct them in the tactics of war, and in the evolutions indispensable to the success of a campaign? to evolutions by battalions, regiments and divisions?

NOTES OF THE REBELLION.

THE REVERSE.

Red Tape and the Wounded Soldiers—Gen. Scott Unmanned—Incidents of the Fight—Instances of Incompetency among the Officers.

Correspondence of the New-York Times.
WASHINGTON, Wednesday, July 24, 1861.

A monstrous instance of red-tapeism occurred in connection with the ambulance train which reached Jackson City at 8 o'clock on Monday morning. I would not have believed it if I had not been on one of the wagons and heard the order given by an officer on horseback. We had over one hundred poor sufferers on these wagons. We had made them as comfortable as circumstances would permit, and were cheering them with the prospect of a speedy admission to the hospital here. As we approached the city of three houses, the official rode up and ordered the train to stop, telling the drivers that "the horses were probably hungry, and there was some good grass for them." I told him that we were hastening to relieve our wounded, that many of them were suffering intensely, etc., but his only reply was a brutal oath, and the remark that "Gen. SCOTT himself could not pass the Long Bridge at present." I hastened to the gate, showed my special pass from Gen. SCOTT, and came over without difficulty. The order applied to all the routed soldiers, but the stupid and brutal officer could not make any discrimination, and probably hastened the death of several who had poured out their blood so freely on that fatal Sunday.

Gen. SCOTT is almost unmanned by this defeat, and told the President Monday that this fatal and only military error of his long and well-spent life, was brought about by rabid civilians, who goaded on the Cabinet and the Cabinet him before his plans were fully matured. It seems hardly credible, but it is a fact, that the old hero wished to send over to Gen. McDOWELL nine additional regiments on Sunday morning, but the Commander of Arlington telegraphed "that he did not want them, they were equal to any emergency," &c.

In walking the streets one finds soldiers sleep-

Federal encampments such as this were set up in numerous locations ringing Washington.

The Long Bridge, which spanned the Potomac River, had its planks removed each night by Federal troops, to prevent access to Washington by Confederate troops.

ing still on the sidewalks, in alleys and on stoops. Their varied stories of the fight would fill a volume. All of the Twenty-seventh of New-York agree in saying that in their first charge an American flag was waved by some troops whom they mistook for some Massachusetts men, and thus lured on to join their friends, as they supposed, a masked battery opened on them with terrific effect. This regiment is badly cut up. The Fire Zouaves tell me the same story. Their exploits with the "Black Horse" remind Washingtonians of their gymnastic performances at WILLARD'S, during the fire there in April. Charged by a battery in front, and by this cavalry troop in the rear, they turned on the Virginia horse, mounted the horses by the tails, pitched the riders out of the saddle, and knifed the men with a fearful *nonchalance*. These fire boys swore so strongly about the cruelties practiced on their wounded by the Confederates, that I fear in the next battle they will bring in no prisoners alive. The death of ELLSWORTH, and the cowardly waving of the American flag by the enemy, have so exasperated them that when next they meet "no quarters" will be the word. Although Col. CAMERON was killed, and his body still remains on the field, his sword was recovered by a wounded Captain of the same regiment, who although horribly shot in the neck, managed to escape, and is now at the infirmary near my hotel. I met a New-York lieutenant at Willard's yesterday, who had a truly miraculous escape. He was advised to take off his showy kepi and put on a plain felt. At that moment a Minié flew by and tore through the visor just as he was lifting it. An instant after a Black Horse trooper came thundering up, and presented his heavy horse pistol at his head. It snapped, and before the Virginian could recover his aim the trusty "Colt" of my friend had sent the enemy to his last long account. A corporal of the Twelfth New-York State (the Salt Boilers Regiment,) told me, during the retreat from Fairfax that the reflections cast on their regiment by a large proportion of the Press were unjust in the extreme. At that unauthorized reconnoissance at Bull's Run, the terrible responsibility of which rests upon Gen. TYLER, the Twelfth were thrown into a masked battery not more than ten yards in front. The fatal mistake was made, too, of mistaking a large force of the enemy for Michigan troops, they being costumed alike. They cheered them, too, as they advanced, and then opened fire, supported by these batteries. The Twelfth were not supported, as he assured me, on either flank; they retired under a horrid fire, after having fired nine rounds. In justice to the regiment, it seems proper that these facts should be known. It was very remarkable to see how the colors were riddled by bullets, shot and shell. One flag that I bore on the retreat from Bull's Run had over fifty holes in it. The superb collar of the California flag, presented to the Maine Second, had every silver star covered with blood, while the delicate embroidery on the leather, done by fair hands in El Dorado, was covered with deep blood stains. While the men were worthy of their flag, the officers were in many cases fearfully incompetent.

REPORTS FROM ALEXANDRIA.

ALEXANDRIA, Friday, July 26.

The conduct of the soldiers in Alexandria, to-day, has been very excessive, drunkenness being predominant, and the guard-houses, slave-pens and jail are nearly all full.

The Provost Marshal's Guard visited three drinking-houses, to-day, which had been selling liquor after having been notified, and destroyed all remaining on hand.

Gen. RUNYON has issued an order to arrest, after to-day, all soldiers found in the streets after 5 o'clock, excepting those having passes.

JOHN HUGHES, of Company A of Mozart Regiment of New-York, broke and ran from the guards about dusk this evening, while they were endeavoring to handcuff him, and being called on to halt he refused, when he was shot down dead by a member of his own company.

—— CHAMBERLAIN, of Company A Second Maine Regiment, died at the hospital to-day.

It is stated on military authority that the secession pickets extend to within three miles of Fort Corcoran, in the vicinity of the former Camp Upton.

Union men were seized early this morning near the Chain Bridge, two miles above Georgetown, by secession scouts.

It is ascertained as a fact that the rebels were kept well informed of all our movements. Their gradual withdrawal from Fairfax Court-house and advanced posts, was a portion of their plan in drawing our troops into the ambuscades which led to ruin and death. Hence the imperfect condition of their earthworks at Fairfax and other points, which excited ridicule among military men.

ANOTHER REBEL REVERSE IN WESTERN VIRGINIA.

CINCINNATI, Friday, July 26.

Gen. COX occupied Charleston on the Kanawha yesterday, the rebels retreating and burning the bridges. A rebel steamer was abandoned and burnt. It is supposed the rebels will be met by Col. ROSENCRANS's column, sent out some days ago to intercept their retreat.

The New-York Times.

VOL. X....NO. 3072   NEW-YORK, SUNDAY, JULY 28, 1861   PRICE THREE CENTS.

Editorials

Our Defeat to Inaugurate a Plan for the War.

The reverse at Bull's Run is undoubtedly the first step of our Government toward the adoption of a competent plan of military operations, if not of a well defined policy as to the war; the absence of such policy is the only explanation for our defeat. Unless a person has some definite object, he wastes his strength in extravagant, futile, and often contradictory efforts, in precisely the same manner that our own has been wasted in the campaign in the Eastern States. In Missouri, Gen. LYON was instructed to clear the State of rebels, which he did in a most summary manner. There were really no difficulties in the way of a skillful commander, because he had a definite object and abundant means for its execution. Common sense was the only other element wanting to insure success; and this Gen. LYON appears to possess in an eminent degree. There was no sufficient motive to thwart him while he was too far from Washington to have his plan of operations interfered with. To Gen. MCCLELLAN was confided the task of driving the enemy out of Northwestern Virginia—a duty which he promptly accomplished, because a straightforward one, to which he could direct his undivided energies and skill. In a short month his campaign was brought to a glorious termination, allowing him to be called to duty elsewhere.

The campaigns in Missouri and Western Virginia have shed lustre upon our arms; but when we come to the Eastern States, this agreeable picture is wholly reversed. We call out vast bodies of troops, keep them in positions and cantonments where they are almost entirely unemployed till the period of the enlistment expires; the monotony of their camp life being broken only by a few ill-considered and ineffectual attacks upon the positions of the enemy, in which our soldiers make a prodigal display of personal daring to be stung to the quick by defeats. Our movements seem to be the result of a momentary impulse, not of any definite or great plan. Why was the enemy allowed to collect 90,000 men at Manassas Junction, to receive the attack of some 20,000 of our own troops, while nearly twice that number, charged with the duty of preventing a junction of the forces under JOHNSTON with those under BEAUREGARD, were idling their time away in camp at Harper's Ferry? It does not help the matter to say that the period of enlistment of one-half of PATTERSON's command had nearly expired, paralyzing his movements to such a degree that he could not act offensively. If PATTERSON could not move safely against JOHNSTON, then the attack on Manassas Junction was sheer madness. But the force directed against this position was in the same condition that PATTERSON alleges his to have been. The time of a number of regiments in MCDOWELL's command was to expire within four days from the first real battle of the campaign. Suppose we had held the advance gained only by the united exertions of the whole Army, what was to become of those left behind, when deserted by one-half of their comrades? Who ever heard of a campaign being inaugurated with an Army so composed? A regiment has no sufficient motive to fight to-day whose time is

Major-General Robert Patterson

out to-morrow. It encounters all the dangers without reaping any advantage of the contest; the day after the battle the men composing it go into private life. Nothing can be more demoralizing to those left behind than to see, perhaps in the midst of battle, regiment after regiment leaving for home to be disbanded. It is no wonder that our men were repulsed, but that they fought as well as they did.

We know that Gen. SCOTT is not responsible for such follies. But who is? The President does not claim to be a military man, or to direct the movements of our forces. Where does this power, so potent for mischief, and never for good, reside? Is it not the same influence to which are to be referred the blunders and mismanagement in the organization of the Army, and the entire indifference and neglect shown to meritorious officers seeking to have accepted their services and those of their men, and dancing attendance in Washington week after week, often with the strongest recommendations from the President and Gen. SCOTT, to come home at last utterly wearied and disgusted with the treatment received? To get anything like satisfactory answers to proffers of service has frequently been impossible, unless made through particular channels through which alone the official ear could only be reached and influenced.

Upon this power, busied with its own schemes, the disaster at Bull's Run has fallen like a clap of thunder. Since the battle sixty thousand men have, without shuffling or equivocation, been accepted for the war. Henceforward the necessities of the crisis, not schemes of petty personal ambition, are to guide and direct affairs. A definite plan of the campaign must now be entered upon. The real magnitude of the contest has just burst upon us. We shall be compensated for our defeat by the lesson it has taught. Its causes will be so thoroughly sifted, that their recurrence will be effectually guarded against. The machinery of the War Department will be thoroughly overhauled and ventilated. Hereafter troops will be collected in large bodies with some definite object; and more than all, capable officers will take the place of those incapable. The reverse, for the first time, will set us in the Eastern States, methodically at work. The instant a right beginning is made a successful issue of the contest is not far distant.

The Hard-hearted Confederates.

Some months ago the plan of the Confederates for quieting the revolution they were about inaugurating in this country was, to frame a new Constitution for the seceding States, and then let into their league such of the Middle and Western States as, on due contrition for past hostility to Pro-Slavery rule, and good promise of dutiful behavior in the future, should be found worthy of Southern association. But New-England it was thought best to exclude entirely, as sinners too hardened for salvation in the Black Republic.

Mr. JEFFERSON DAVIS modified the plan slightly in his message to the Montgomery Congress, wherein he prayed to be "let alone," and expressed the extreme pleasure with which he would drop the sword, and make friendly and favorable treaties with the free-soil, semi-barbarians of the United States. But the hardness of the Union heart to these tenders of the rebel olive-branch, has quite disgusted the organs of Mr. DAVIS, and they now are taking new and higher ground. Whenever the United States are fairly whipped, ruined and starved (as they unquestionably will be, by rebel accounts, in a few weeks,) and shall ask Mr. DAVIS to call off his war-dogs, and grant them a peace, the Richmond (Va.) *Examiner* suggests a clause to be put into the treaty, the nature of which will be gathered from the following extract from its columns:

"There is a greater danger to be apprehended from a hasty and incautious peace than any we have as yet suggested, and which we have, therefore, reserved for separate consideration. It is bad enough to deal with Northerners—to have them visit us, and to be forced to visit them—but it would be ruinous to have them come down upon us in shoals as numerous as the mackerel and cod about their coasts, to seize the ballot-box and control the helm of State. Unless the terms of peace exclude them this they will certainly do. The Yankees are not farmers, and few will remove to the Northwest. We have been their customers—have bought most of their manufactures—and, if we refuse to go to them, they will certainly (unless prevented) come to us. Lowell and Salem, Boston and Hartford, and every other town and village in New-England, will empty their scoundrel bosses, their filthy factory hands and starving laborers upon us. They will change the whole tone and character of our society, and soon, uniting with the Submissionists, abolitionize one-half of the South.

No treaty of peace will be worth a fig that does not effectually exclude Yankee notions and Yankee people. Our tariff should discriminate against their goods, and our naturalization laws against themselves."

That is, indeed, the unkindest cut of all. Dixie's land has proved to be so good a place for "permanent investments" of Northern capital; so delightful a place for Northern born bem to sojourn in; so difficult a country for them to "tear themselves away from," when the heat of war made migration to the northward politic, that it will be a heart-breaking matter to find that not only are they expelled from the comforts of Southern hospitality, but that the door is to be irrevocably closed, bolted and barred against them. How will they survive it?

The New-York Times.

VOL. X....NO. 3087.　　　NEW-YORK, WEDNESDAY, AUGUST 14, 1861.　　　PRICE TWO CENTS.

IMPORTANT NEWS.

Great National Victory in Missouri.

Defeat of 23,000 Rebels by 8,000 National Troops.

Tremendous Slaughter of the Rebels.

Our Loss About Eight Hundred Killed and Wounded.

The Rebel Generals McCulloch and Price Killed.

Death of Gen. Lyon at the Head of his Troops.

Destruction of all the Rebel Tents and Camp Equipage.

Subsequent Retirement of the National Forces to Rolla.

Important from Fortress Monroe.

Prisoners Captured at Bull Run Released on Parole.

THEIR ARRIVAL IN WASHINGTON.

Highly Interesting Statements Made by Them.

SPECIAL DISPATCH FROM WASHINGTON.

WASHINGTON, Tuesday, Aug. 13.

The following persons were to-day appointed:

Brig.-Gen. DAVID HUNTER to be a Major-General of Volunteers.

Lieut.-Col. H. STONEMAN, United States Cavalry, to be Brigadier-General of Volunteers.

Major W. T. SMITH, Topographical Engineers, United States Army, to be a Brigadier-General of Volunteers.

Capt. HENRY W. BENHAM, Engineers, United States Army, to be Brigadier-General of Volunteers.

OPERATIONS DOWN THE POTOMAC.

The river steamer *Resolute* to-day brought up ten contrabands, the property of a Secessionist named BROWN, living near Machaedge. The steamer was fired on from the house, when the crew went ashore, burned the buildings, and brought off the contrabands.

NO NEGROES TO BE TAKEN HOME.

Gen. PORTER, the Provost-Marshal, has issued an order forbidding the troops from taking negroes home with them. The Zouaves were taking quite a number in the direction of the North Star.

CONSULS COMMISSIONED.

The following Consuls were commissioned to-day:

Leeds—JAMES W. MARSHALL, of Pennsylvania.
Shanghai—JAS. H. PARTRIDGE, of Maryland.
Batavia—ISAAC S. DIEHL, of California.
Leghorn—ANDREW J. STEVENS, of Iowa.
Geneva—To. CROSBY, of Kentucky.
Commercial Agent at Amoor River—ISAAC PLATT, of New-York, and editor of the Poughkeepsie *Eagle*.

Mr. PARTRIDGE, who is appointed to Shanghai, was Secretary of State of Maryland, and warmly sustained the Union cause. When Gov. HICKS caved in, on the 20th of April, he resigned.

CHASSEURS D'AFRIQUE.

The Secretary of War has accepted a company from Philadelphia of one hundred men, to be commanded by Capt. COLLIS. They are to be equipped as *Chasseurs D'Afrique*, and every man of this company served in the Crimean War.

GEN. ANDERSON IN THE FIELD.

Gen. ANDERSON, though advised by his physicians to refrain from active duty, has nevertheless determined at once to take the field. When warned that he might break down, he answered that the Union men of Kentucky were calling him to lead them, and that he must and would make the attempt, and if he failed he would fail in a most glorious cause.

THE REBELS AT MANASSAS.

From a source upon which I place implicit reliance, I learn that the rebel forces at Manassas, Fairfax Court-house, Centreville and Vienna are within a fraction of sixty thousand men, and that all the forces engaged in the battle of Bull Run yet remained in that vicinity. The same authority assures me that the supplies of this force are exceedingly short. A lady who reached Washington *viâ* Tennessee and Kentucky, tells me that large numbers of water tanks are being constructed in Richmond and sent to Manassas These are used to bring supplies of water by rail to the troops at the Junction.

MINISTER TO VIENNA.

J. LETHROP MOTLEY, Minister to Vienna, arrived in Washington this evening. He comes for instructions, and will leave for Vienna at once.

THE BLOCKADE.

At the Cabinet meeting to-day it was formally resolved to make the blockade of the rebel States effectual, providing for closing every inlet, and that vessels enough should be procured to make it certain that the work is thoroughly done.

ANOTHER BATTLE IN MISSOURI.

DEFEAT OF THE REBEL TROOPS.

ST. LOUIS, MO., Tuesday, Aug. 13—P.M.

Rumors are current on the street, in which reliance is placed, that Gen. LYON's command in the Southwest has been defeated by the rebels.

Gen. LYON himself was killed, and Gen. SIEGEL was in full retreat with the remnant of the National forces.

This information is said to have been received by Secessionists last evening.

The messenger who brought the news killed four horses between Springfield and Rolla, in his haste to outstrip the Government messenger.

It is also reported that Gen. FREMONT received dispatches about midnight, corroborating the above, but that their contents have not yet been divulged.

Great anxiety is felt by the Union men here, and most serious apprehensions are indulged for the safety of our Army.

We shall probably get something reliable on the arrival of the train to-night.

OFFICIAL ANNOUNCEMENT OF THE BATTLE.

WASHINGTON, Tuesday, Aug. 13.

The War Department to-day received a dispatch from Major-Gen. FREMONT, saying, among other things, that Gen. LYON's Aid reports an engagement, with a severe loss on both sides, and that Gen. LYON was killed.

Gen. SIEGEL was in command, and retiring in good order from Springfield toward Rolla.

The following is the official report received to-night by Gen. SCOTT:

HEAD-QUARTERS WESTERN DEPARTMENT,
ST. LOUIS, Aug. 13, 1961.

Col. E. D. Townsend:

General LYON, in three columns under himself, Gens. SIEGEL and STURGES, attacked the enemy at half-past six o'clock on the morning of the 10th, nine miles southeast of Springfield. The engagement was severe. Our loss was about eight hundred killed and wounded. Gen. LYON was killed in a charge at the head of his column. Our force was eight thousand, including two thousand Home Guards. The muster-roll reported taken from the enemy gives their forces at twenty-three thousand, including regiments from Louisiana, Tennessee and Mississippi, with the Texan Rangers and Cherokee half-breeds. This statement is corroborated by prisoners. Their loss is reported as heavy, including Gens. McCULLOCH and PRICE. Their tents and wagons were destroyed in the action. Gen. SIEGEL left one gun on the field, and retreated to Springfield, whence, at 3 o'clock on the morning of the 11th, he continued his retreat on Rolla, bringing off his baggage trains and $250,000 in specie from the Springfield Bank.

J. C. FREMONT,
Major-General Commanding.

FULL DETAILS OF THE BATTLE.

ST. LOUIS, Tuesday, Aug. 13.

The following is the official report of the fight near Springfield on Saturday last, forwarded by one of Gen. LYON's aids:

To Major-Gen. Fremont:

Gen. LYON, in three columns under himself and Gen. SIEGEL, and Major STURGES, of the cavalry, attacked the enemy at 6½ o'clock on the morning of the 10th, nine miles southeast of Springfield. The engagement was severe. Our loss is about 800 killed and wounded. Gen. LYON was killed in a charge at the head of his column. Our force was 8,000, including 2,000 Home Guards. The muster rolls taken from the enemy give his strength at 23,000, including regiments from Louisiana, Mississippi and Tennessee, with Texan Rangers and Cherokee half-breeds.

Their loss is reported heavy, including Gens. McCulloch and Price. This statement is corroborated by prisoners. Their tents and wagons were destroyed in the action.

Gen. Siegel left only one gun on the field, and retreated to Springfield with a large number of prisoners at 3 o'clock in the morning of the 11th. He continued his retreat upon Rolla, bringing off all his baggage trains and $250,000 in specie from the Springfield Bank.

The following is a verbal report, taken from a special messenger, who brought dispatches for Gen. Fremont:

Early on Saturday morning Gen. Lyon marched out of Springfield to give battle to the enemy. He came up to him on Davis Creek, on Green's Prairie, a few miles southwest of Springfield, where he had taken a strong position, on rolling ground, at 20 minutes past 6 o'clock in the morning.

Gen. Lyon fired the first gun, when the battle immediately begun. Severe cannonading was kept up for two or three hours, when the fire of Capt. Totten's artillery proving too severe for the enemy, they gradually fell back towards their encampment on Wilson's Creek. Gen. Lyon's cavalry posted on the enemy's left flank, and Gen. Siegel's artillery on the right, there began a terrific attack, and spread slaughter and dismay in the ranks of the enemy, pursuing them to their camp, shells from Totten's artillery setting fire to their tents and baggage-wagons, which were all destroyed.

A Louisiana regiment and a Mississippi regiment seemed to have suffered most in the fight and were almost annihilated.

Some time in the afternoon, as Gen. Lyon was leading on his column his horse was shot from under him. He immediately mounted another, and as he turned around to this men, waving his hat in his hand and cheering them on to victory, he was struck in the small of the back by a ball and fell dead to the ground.

The command then devolved on Gen. Siegel. Pursuit continued till night fall, when our little Army rested for the night in the encampment of the enemy.

Sunday morning Gen. Siegel, fearing the enemy might recover and attempt to cut his command off from Springfield, fell back upon that city, where the Home Guards were stationed. On reaching Springfield, fearing the great numbers of the enemy might induce them to get between him and Rolla, Gen. Siegel concluded to fall back upon Rolla with his provision trains and meet the reinforcements which were on the way to him. At the latest moment of the departure of the messenger, the enemy had not been seen, and it is probable Gen. Siegel has not been disturbed in his march.

Ninety of the rebels were captured, among whom a Colonel of distinction, the messenger not remembering his name.

The sword and horse of Gen. McCulloch were the trophies taken.

Reinforcements are on the way to Rolla, and Gen. Siegel and his Army may be considered safe.

NEWS OF THE DAY.

A dispatch from St. Louis, published in the evening papers yesterday, announced the defeat of the National Army at Springfield, Missouri, and the death of Gen. Lyon. The information was first received in St. Louis by the Secessionists, on Monday evening, through a special courier from the vicinity of the battle, who rode several horses to death in his haste to be before the Government courier with the news. Gen. Fremont, however, is stated to have received his dispatches about midnight. The rebel reports announced the total rout of the National Army; but the dispatches of Gen. Fremont

simply announced an engagement, with severe loss on both sides, the death of Gen. Lyon, and the retirement of the National forces towards Rolla in good order, under the command of Gen. Siegel. Still later dispatches, however, turn the National defeat into a most glorious victory, although the report of the death of Gen. Lyon is confirmed. The engagement took place on the 10th inst. The National forces, in three columns, under the command respectively of Generals Lyon, Siegel and Sturges, made the attack at 6 o'clock in the morning, at a place nine miles southeast of Springfield. The enemy, according to the muster rolls captured on the field, numbered *twenty-three thousand*, including regiments from Louisiana and Tennessee, with Texas Rangers and Cherokee half-breeds, while our forces were but *eight thousand* strong, including some two thousand Home Guards. Gen Lyon fired the first gun, when the engagement immediately became general. After two or three hours' severe cannonading, the execution done by Capt. Totten's Artillery proved too much for the enemy, and they commenced to fall back, when the National cavalry, posted on the enemy's left, and Gen. Siegel's artillery on the right, commenced a terrific onslaught, which spread slaughter and dismay in the rebel ranks. They were pursued to their camps, and shells from Totten's artillery set fire to their tents and baggage, and completely destroyed them. The rebel Gens. McCulloch and Price were both killed. Gen. Lyon was killed while leading a charge at the head of his column, after having one horse shot under him. The command then devolved upon Gen. Siegel, who deemed it prudent to retire to Springfield, and subsequently to Rolla, as before stated, carrying with him a large amount of specie taken from the Springfield Bank, to prevent its falling into the hands of the enemy.

Editorial

Spies in Washington.

It is now well ascertained that the whole plan of the advance of our forces upon Manassas Junction, the deviations of the different columns, the movements designed as feints as well as for attack, were as thoroughly known to the rebel Generals as to our own. Hence they were fully prepared to receive it with an overwhelming force, and defeat was almost inevitable, as it is in nine times out of ten, in such cases. It is the object of strategy to mislead the enemy, and to assail him in his weakest point. But up to this time, we have had no strategy in the campaign in the East, because the rebels, through spies, with which Washington is swarming, are kept constantly informed of all our plans and the condition and strength of our forces, and can always adapt the strength and mode of their resistance to our plan of attack. Hence the disasters, or perhaps we should say, the uniform want of success in Eastern Virginia, the campaign in which is directed from Washington, while in other parts of the country our arms have made steady progress.

Such a condition of things is very mortifying. But we must not forget that if one-third of the people of Washington are now rebels and spies, nearly the whole were, only a few months ago, including the President and nearly every member of his Cabinet. The master spirits both of Mr. Pierce's and Mr. Buchanan's Administrations have been plotting, for eight long years, the overthrow of the Government, and have been earnestly occupied in fomenting the rebellion that is now seeking its destruction. With both of these Administrations secession was at a premium. The greater part of all the offices of Government were filled by persons who openly and heartily advocated the destruction of the Confederacy, in the event of the election of a person to office not acceptable to their tastes or ideas. Such an event being foreseen under Mr. Buchanan's Administration, his confidential advisers immediately began to prepare for the outbreak by disarming the North, by corrupting the Army, and by putting the South in position for the stupendous resistance it is now making.

Many of these efforts were as open as the day, yet a large portion of the North denounced all measures calculated to thwart or check them. There was to be no coercion; no forts were to be held against the wishes of those designing to seize them. Mr. Floyd, with impunity, stole our arms; Mr. Toucey scattered and dismantled our fleet, and Mr. Cobb visited New-York with the express purpose of putting an end to the operations of Government, by destroying its credit. Mr. Yancey was received with open arms by a great political party in this State, and *feted* all the way on his political tour from New-York City to Niagara Falls. For a time the moral sense of a large portion of the community seemed completely debauched. Washington, made up of office-holders appointed by such Administrations, could not be otherwise than the very focus of the disunion schemes and sentiment. Dissolution had been plotted there for years. The *haut ton* there was as intensely Pro-Slavery and hostile to Northern institutions as Charleston itself. It was not to be expected that such a sink could be purged in a day, or in a month, or in a year. A whole community had to be newly made. Till this work is completed, the place will swarm with traitors. It is their life and habit. Instead of wondering that there are so many, we really ought to congratulate ourselves that there are so few; that we have a loyal Administration there—a loyal Congress; a lever with which to work, to ferret out the rascals. The Administration is gradually waking up to the crisis. It is always unpleasant to proceed against one's neighbors; but the arrest of Mr. Faulkner shows that this false delicacy is no longer to be respected. Only let this be followed up by a little more such decided action, and we can move our forces without the conviction that every step they take and every plan we lay out is instantly communicated to the enemy. We shall then begin to achieve successes in the East, that have so signalized our arms elsewhere.

The New-York Times.

VOL. X....NO. 3103.   NEW-YORK, MONDAY, SEPTEMBER 2, 1861.   PRICE TWO CENTS.

THE GREAT REBELLION.

HIGHLY IMPORTANT NEWS

A Great National Success at Hatteras Inlet.

Capture of Forts Hatteras and Clark.

Upwards of Seven Hundred Rebels Taken Prisoners.

Twenty-five Cannon, a Thousand Stand of Arms, and a Quantity of Munitions and Stores.

Three Vessels, One Loaded with Cotton, Made Prizes.

A Number of Rebels Killed and Wounded.

"NOBODY HURT" ON OUR SIDE.

A SERIOUS CHECK TO PRIVATEERS.

The Minnesota Coming to New-York with the Prisoners.

THE HARRIET LANE AGROUND.

SPECIAL DISPATCH FROM WASHINGTON.

WASHINGTON, Sunday, Sept. 1.

The news of the brilliant success of the Naval Expedition has been received here with that intense satisfaction which can hardly be described. It has aroused the feelings of the troops, and inspired them to rival the gallantry of their associates at Cape Hatteras.

SERENADE TO GEN. BUTLER.

This evening Gen. BUTLER was serenaded at the National Hotel, in honor of his success. In response to the compliment of his friends, the General made a characteristic speech. Gen. BUTLER goes to Massachusetts in the morning, to recruit his health.

GEN. FREMONT'S PROCLAMATION.

If anything could be received here with greater satisfaction than the success at Hatteras, it was

General Benjamin F. Butler

the proclamation issued by Gen. FREMONT. I have not seen or heard of one man who does not warmly approve the declaration that the rebels must lose their property, and that the Government will hold its existence as paramount above all consideration for the individual rights of the rebels. Declaring negroes free whose masters are in arms against the Government, strikes at the root ; and while the leading rebels of the South cannot be incensed to greater efforts for the overthrow of the Government than they have already made, the heavy owners of negroes will hesitate

to risk their all by encouraging and aiding the chief traitors.

GEN. BUTLER IN WASHINGTON.

WASHINGTON, Sunday, Sept. 1.

Gen. BUTLER, accompanied by Commander STEELWAGEN, and others connected with the military and naval forces, arrived here early this morning, in special train from Annapolis. The brilliant exploit on the North Carolina coast soon spread throughout the city, and occasioned unbounded joy among all loyal people. The Government, of course, was promptly informed of the gladsome news. The returned party, with several members of the Cabinet, visited the President, between 10 and 11 o'clock. The result of the expedition is claimed to be the possession of the entire North Carolina coast.

A BRILLIANT VICTORY.

CAPTURE OF THE FORTS AT HATTERAS INLET.

UNITED STATES CHARTERED STEAMER ADELAIDE,
OFF CAPE HATTERAS, Thursday, Aug. 29.

I am now on my way from Hatteras Inlet, N. C., having left Fort Monroe on Monday P. M., the 26th inst. The Expedition had been in contemplation for some days. The materials were being carefully gathered and all the details arranged, but the precise nature, extent and destination of the fleet and troops were kept profoundly secret.

On Monday A. M. the signs of the departure of ships with regulars and volunteers on board began to be evident. Detachments of the Virginia Coast Guard under Capt. NIXON and JOHNSON, and Lieut. C. A. WEILY; of MAX WEBER'S Regiment, under WEBER'S command, and that of Lieut.-Col. WESS, of the New-York Ninth, Col. HAWKINS, and of the United States Marines, under Maj. SHUTTLE, appeared in the streets of Old Point Comfort, and on board the transport vessels at the wharves. They bore several standards of colors, and were accompanied by one band of music.

As soon as the troops were on board the signal for starting was given. The fleet consisted of the following vessels:

Minnesota, Flag Ship, Commodore STRINGHAM.
Wabash, Capt. MERCER.
Harriet Lane, Capt. FAUNCE.
Pawnee, Capt. THOMPSON.
Monticello, Capt. GRILLIS.
Adelaide, Capt. STEELWAGEN.
Peabody, Capt. LOWREY.
Fanny, Capt. CROSBY.

The *Adelaide*, *Peabody* and *Monticello* had vessels without masts, and boats and batteaux in tow. Most of the troops were on board the *Adelaide* and *Peabody*. The steam tug *Tempest* soon after followed, making a fleet of nine vessels in all, with a body of about a thousand fighting men.

We steamed out of Hampton Roads in fine style. The weather was beautiful, and the sea smooth. It was about the hour of two in the afternoon, and the sun shone forth in all the splendor of the tropics. The evening drew on, with a steady breeze from the southeast. The *Monticello* took the lead, while the *Adelaide*, not being armed with large guns, immediately followed. No one but those specially authorized knew of our destination and object. It was understood that we went out under sealed orders, which would be opened at the proper time.

We soon passed Cape Henry, although the speed of the leading steamer was limited to a certain point. As the night advanced, a mild August moon rose to light our passage, while the winds continued to blow gently and the waves were smooth. The troops on board the *Adelaide* suffered but little from sea-sickness, and the night passed pleasantly away.

As the morning broke, we were opposite Cape Hatteras, and the *Adelaide*, *Pawnee*, *Lane* and *Peabody* were in sight of each other. No lights greeted us along the whole coast from Cape Henry to Hatteras — a proof of the dangerous condition in which secession has left the coast.

On Tuesday morning, the 27th, as the morning advanced, and the part of the fleet already off Hatteras gathered together, following the *Monticello* in toward shore, the *Minnesota* and *Wabash* hove in sight, and afterwards the frigate *Cumberland*, Capt. MARTIN, was signaled [coming up. The *Wabash* bore down to her and took her in tow towards a point for which the *Minnesota* was steering.

It was now announced that our destination was Hatteras Inlet, and that our purpose in coming on the coast of Secessia, with such a force, was to destroy certain rebel fortifications erected there, and perform certain other duties for the welfare of the Union

but the day had now so far advanced, and the ships *Fanny* and *Tempest* not having arrived, it was decided to lie by for the night and carefully complete all our preparations for an attack in the morning. All night the sea remained as smooth as a Summer lake; the swell was regular and slow; the moon came out again with unwonted beauty, lighting up the sky with splendor. The squadron lay silent at its post through all the watches of the night.

On Wednesday morning, the 28th, the day broke upon us beautifully, indeed, and the glassy calmness of the sea still continued. The *Fanny* and *Tempest* having arrived the previous evening, the squadron was now all mustered, with the exception of the *Susquehannah*, soon to arrive. Orders were issued for the disembarkation of troops on the beach to the east of Hatteras Inlet.

It was now discovered that there were two forts and one camp at the inlet and vicinity. The first is called Fort Hatteras, the second Fort Clark, after the Governor of North Carolina, while Camp Gwinn is at the end of a clump of trees near by.

The landing was effected in the following order: HAWKINS on the right; the Regulars, Union Coast Guard and Marines in the centre; MAX WEBER on the left. The advance of the ships to effect and protect the landing was a splendid sight — such a one as it was worth going to see. It was now a little after 8 o'clock. We steadily and firmly advanced towards the two forts, which were in plain sight on the point of Hatteras Inlet, with the disunion flag flying on a small staff.

Fort Hatteras, the principal fort, was erected in June last; Fort Clark within a few weeks past. They are composed of rude materials. The number of guns is as follows: Fort Hatteras, twelve mounted guns, 32-pounders; some eight-inch shells. Fort Clark, five mounted guns, 32-pounders; some eight-inch shells. The number of troops in the forts and camp was nearly seven hundred.

GEN. WOOL'S ANNOUNCEMENT OF THE VICTORY.

BALTIMORE, Sunday, Sept. 1.

The following is General Order No. 8, issued by Gen. WOOL:

HEAD-QUARTERS, DEPARTMENT OF VIRGINIA,
FORTRESS MONROE, Aug. 31, 1861.

[GENERAL ORDER NO. 8.]

The Commanding General has great satisfaction in announcing a glorious victory achieved by the combined operations of the Army and Navy at Hatteras Inlet, North Carolina, under the command of Commodore STRINGHAM and Major-Gen. BUTLER. The result of this gallant enterprise is the capture of 715 men, including the Commander, BARRON, and one of the North Carolina Cabinet, 1,000 stand of arms, and 75 kegs of powder, 5 stand of colors and 31 pieces of cannon, including a 10-inch Columbiad, a tug loaded with cotton, a sloop loaded with provisions and stores, two light boats, 150 bags of coffee, &c.—all of which was achieved by the Army and Navy, and 800 volunteers and 60 regular artillery of the Army. This gallant affair will not fail to stimulate the regulars and volunteers to greater achievements. Obedience, order, discipline and instruction are indispensible to maintain the interest, honor and humane institutions of the Union.

By command of

(Signed)   Major-Gen. WOOL,
CHAS. CHURCHILL,
Captain Third Artillery, A. A. G.

IMPORTANT RESULTS OF THE EXPEDITION

WASHINGTON, Sunday, Sept. 1.

The Navy Department, by able and experienced officers, has carfully studied the whole line of the coast, with a view to making the best use of such forces as it could secure. The expedition was planned before the meeting of Congress, and when that body placed the necessary funds at the disposal of the Department, active preparations were made. As the coöperation of the War Department was necessary, other preliminaries, requiring time, were indispensable, so that it was not till Monday, the 26th ultimo, that the expedition sailed. The success is

perfect, and every anticipation of the Departments realized.

Among the papers captured was a press copy from the late American Consul at Rio Janeiro, ROBERT G. SCOTT, giving a list of all the vessels leaving, or to leave that port during a month, with a full description of their cargoes and destination. By the information the rebel privateers knew just when and where to look for the vessels, and six, named in the list, were captured.

The report of their Engineer-in-Chief was also among the papers. It states that all the good guns at Norfolk are expended. Also the whole amount of fuses.

Some hand-made percussion caps were found, and it was ascertained that the copper had been stripped from one of their prizes—the bark *Linwood*—to furnish material for caps, the manufacture of which is of tolerable good quality. Among the guns captured was one large 16-inch columbiad from the Tredegar Works, Richmond, which had not been mounted.

Our vessels took three prizes; one brig, the *Henry C. Rogers*, of New-York, and two light boats belonging to the United States, but in the employment of the Confederates, with miscellaneous cargoes.

A gentleman connected with the expedition, reports the forces were landed and drawn up in line on the beach, when it was found that there were three hundred and nineteen men under Col. WEBER, of the Twentieth New-York Regiment. At this time, the wind raised a little, and it was found impossible to land more troops. Pickets were immediately posted under command of Lieut. LEDER, of the Regulars. A scouting party, under Lieut.-Col. WEISS and Lieut. WPEGEL, proceeded up the beach, capturing one brass field-piece and a horse. The force then advanced to Fort Clark, which had been evacuated, but were compelled to retire again, owing to the shells of the fleet falling therein, and marched back to the place of landing, and there bivouacked for the night. Early next morning they again returned and the fleet commenced bombarding the second fort, called Fort Hatteras, which soon after displayed the white flag, when the fort was entered by Capt. NIXON, of the Union Coast Guard, Lieut. WEIGEL, of Gen. BUTLER's Staff, and Sergeant DUBIVAGE. They were conducted to the tent of Commodore BARRON, who was in command of the forces. After some preparatory and common-place remarks, the Commodore placed in the hands of Lieut. WIEGEL the following proposition, which was immediately carried to Gen. BUTLER:

MEMORANDUM.

Fort Hatteras, Aug. 29, 1861.

Flag-officer SAMUEL BARRON, C. S. N., offers to surrender Fort Hatteras, with all the arms and munitions of war—the officers to be allowed to go out with side arms, and the men without arms to retire.

S. BARRON, Commanding
Naval Defences of Virginia and North Carolina.

The following reply was dispatched by Capt. CROSBY, U. S. N., and Lieut. WIEGEL:

MEMORANDUM.

BENJAMIN F. BUTLER, Major-General Commanding, U. S. A., in reply to the communication of SAMUEL BARRON, commanding the forces at Fort Hatteras, cannot admit the terms proposed. The terms offered are these: Full capitulation, the officers and men to be treated as prisoners of war. No other terms admissible. Commanding officers to meet on board the flag-ship *Minnesota*, to arrange details.

On the reception of this, the Commodore called a council of war of his field-officers, and accepted the terms offered, and proceeded to the flag-ship to arrange the details, after which the prisoners were put on board the flag-ship, and the Stars and Stripes hoisted by Capt. CROSBY, U. S. N., and Lieut. WIEGEL, amid cheers and the booming of the cannon lately in possession of the enemy.

BALTIMORE, Sunday, Sept. 1.

The Major ANDREWS captured at Hatteras Inlet, is R. SNOWDEN ANDREWS, architect, of this city. Many of the prisoners are Baltimoreans.

Among the prizes is a ship-load of cotton, which was all ready to run the blockade. It is rumored that a member of the Southern Cabinet was taken prisoner.

The gun-boat *Harriet Lane* is ashore, but will soon be relieved.

The footing thus obtained in North Carolina will be permanently held, and Wilmington ultimately taken, thus giving fire in the rebels rear.

The New-York Times.

VOL. XI....NO. 3132.   NEW-YORK, SATURDAY, OCTOBER 5, 1861.   PRICE TWO CENTS.

THE GREAT REBELLION.

FIGHTNG IN WESTERN VIRGINIA.

Everything Quiet Around Washington.

Arrival of Gen. Wool on his Way to the West.

Gen. Fremont Not Superseded nor Ordered to Washington, nor to be Court-martialed.

IMPORTANT NEWS FROM MISSOURI.

The Reported Evacuation of Lexington.

Price Said to be Moving Towards Independence.

The Strength and Position of the National Forces.

Interesting Facts and Rumors From the South.

Gustavus W. Smith a Major-General in the Rebel Army.

SPECIAL DISPATCH FROM WASHINGTON
Washington, Friday, Oct. 4.

GEN. WOOL AND GEN. FREMONT.

Gen. Wool arrived in this city to-day, and I am now entirely satisfied that my statement in this morning's TIMES was correct. Gen. Fremont has neither been superseded nor ordered to this city under arrest.

THE CHARGES AGAINST GEN. FREMONT.

The following is the result of inquiries to-day, in official quarters : The charges preferred by Col. Frank P. Blair against Major-Gen. Fremont, on the 26th of September, have not yet reached Washington. According to the revised Army Regulations, charges are required to be transmitted through the superior officer, which in this case is Gen. Fremont himself. A copy of the charges, however, has been received to be filed, in the event that Gen. Fremont himself shall neglect or decline to transmit the original document to the War Department.

Gen. Wool, it is thought by those well-informed in military circles, will proceed to the West under specific instructions.

John C. Fremont, a skilled explorer, was nonetheless unable to command effectively as a Union general.

THE SITUATION IN MISSOURI.

Gen. Fremont's Position---His Action Contrasted with that of Gen. Lyon---Number of the National Forces---Movements of the Rebels, etc.

From Our Own Corrrespondent.
Jefferson City, Tuesday, Oct. 1, 1861.

Notwithstanding the very small attention with which Western operations are regarded, (unless a defeat occur,) this place is just now one possessing military elements of the greatest interest. Not only is it a point at which Gen. Fremont is to demonstrate to an anxious public his fitness or unfitness for the tremendous responsibilities he has assumed, but it is also one at which are being created events and circumstances which ere long will decide the long-disputed question as to the fate of Missouri. Here are concentrating all the talent, the material, the energies, of the Department of the West—here are the actors rehearsing their parts preparatory to another drama, such as was shown at Springfield, Carthage, Booneville, Lexington.

One Thursday of some months ago, Jackson issued his treasonable proclamation from this very place. Friday Gen. Lyon drove him a fugitive from his Capital, and the next Monday dislodged him from Booneville and hunted him from the State. People who remember this are disposed to grumble as they reflect that two weeks have elapsed since the fall of Lexington—for two weeks has secession held high carnival over the spot rendered sacred by the gallant defence of Mulligan—for two weeks has it been permitted to rejoice, to fortify, to recover its breath—and as yet nothing more has been done than to transport an army to this point, which, in point of time and difficulty of travel, is not half way to Lexington.

If two weeks are required to get a sufficient force to this point, how long will it take to get that same force over the balance of the route?

I believe that Gen. Fremont is a hard worker; he labors incessantly to promote the cause in which he is engaged; he leaves nothing undone that can be done by personal effort, or advanced by personal sacrifice; yet, in spite of all this, things seem to advance with supernatural slowness. Never seemed there motions before, which looked so exactly like rest; but possibly, in view of the gigantic task before the National troops, it is well that nothing should be done hastily—that nothing should be adventured prematurely.

When one reviews the course of Gen. Lyon—sees him routing secession from two distant and important points in less than a week—the rapidity of his march in the hottest months of Summer from Booneville to Springfield—the wind-like velocity with which he swooped upon Forsyth, Dug Springs and Curran—his omnipresence, his untiring vigilance, the facility with which he clapped an extinguisher upon every blaze of treason that broke out in or near the scene of his operations; when one remembers all this, he cannot but at least contrast the light, effectual movements of then, with the ponderous slowness of those of to-day. May it not be that Gen. Fremont is too much embarrassed with the etiquette of war—with a cumbrous, unwieldy staff—with the panoply and externals of conflict? There may be use of private secretaries of private secretaries of private secretaries—of certain ceremonies, head-quarters approachable through a pathway lined by glittering swords, bands making the air sick in languishing with the stirring music of silver instruments, red tape formalities, and a thousand other similar things and operations; but yet their effect, although brilliant to friend and observer, is of doubtful utility upon the ragged Secessionists who hide themselves and their shot guns behind every bush in Northern Missouri.

If our foe was a polite one, his appreciation might be moved, his loyalty excited, by witnessing the gallant efforts made on his account, were he to see the magnificent trappings and caparisons, hear the beautiful music, watch the admirable evolutions. But, unfortunately, our Secession friend is an unkempt blackguard—wrapped in the contemplation of "treasons, stratagems and spoils." His soul has no appreciation for the beautiful music of Hungarian airs, poured upon the resonant and delighted air from costly silver instruments. Clad in a shirt innocent of soap and water, he appreciates not at all the gilded trappings of our gallant array; sneaking in the recesses of the dim woods, and coolly priming his old flint-lock rifle, he cares absolutely nothing for the gleam of beautiful muskets, the clank of heavy sabres, or the intricate deadliness of improved revolvers.

To him, Lyon, with his old white hat, his stern countenance, his common every-day soldiers, was a dreaded reality—they feared him in life and respected him in death. One long roll from his battered old drums carried a more wholesome terror into the hearts of secession than will a thousand airs from Norma, born under the breath and manipulations of skillful Teutonic artistes. They knew he was never fettered by formalities, and only found courage to attack him when confident in the strength of an overwhelming force.

But it is to be hoped that ere long Gen. Fremont will demonstrate that, in spite of all these apparent drawbacks, he is competent to the position he has undertaken to fill—and thus at once satisfy the earnest hopes of the country, and make good his own assertion to that effect.

THE SEAT OF WAR IN MISSOURI.

The above map of Missouri will be found full of interest at the present moment, when all eyes are turned toward that State, in view of the extraordinary events occurring there. If a line be drawn from a point just back of Bird's Point, bearing northward and verging towards Cape Girardeau, then deflecting westward, passing a little south of Ironton, and continuing on in the same general direction between Rolla and Waynesville to Versailles; thence, circling around to the west of Sedalia and Georgetown, and turning sharply eastward to Arrow Rock; and thence taking both banks of the Missouri, westward to Kansas City, the northern limit of insurrectionary domination in Missouri will be very accurately described. All south and west of the line thus drawn is under subjection to the rebels, and it is nearly one-half of the territory of the State.

The head-quarters of Major-Gen. FREMONT are now removed to Jefferson City. He has concentrated nearly his whole force there, and is pushing his columns freely up the railroad to Syracuse, to the Lamine Bridge, to Otterville, a few miles beyond the Lamine, and to Sedalia, the terminus of the railroad, which is four miles south of Georgetown. He is supposed to have 15,000 men at these points. Gens. SIEGEL and DAVIS are in command at Sedalia of these advancing forces. There were a few Union troops stationed at Booneville, and at a point some distance above on the opposite side of the river, but we believe they have been withdrawn to join the columns advancing from Jefferson City towards Georgetown. There were about 5,000 troops at Rolla, where there is an immense amount of valuable stores. Three regiments of these men have been ordered to march overland towards Georgetown, a distance of full sixty miles, leaving Rolla quite weak—two regiments being a very small force to defend so much property.

Certain steamboats have gone up the Missouri River from Jefferson City with troops, destination not known. In addition to this, it should be known that the new gun-boat *New Era*, just completed at St. Louis, has gone up the Missouri, to aid the Army in its present advance. This vessel is shot and shell-proof. The engines, boilers and wheels are all protected beyond any peradventure by heavy iron, and the sharp-shooters (300 in number) and gunners aboard are in no danger from bullets from shore. She has several Dahlgren guns—84-pounders—in place, under bomb-proof decks, directed by experienced gunners, and it is expected that they will destroy with the greatest ease any obstacle within a distance of three miles. It is added that she can't be sunk, perforated, burned, nor blown up. If this boat shall reach Lexington, and break up PRICE's control of the river, his situation will be much worse than it now seems. Gen. STURGIS was last reported on his return from Kansas City toward Jefferson. His whereabouts and Gen. LANE's, we are not certain of.

Our Missouri letter, to-day, says that the troops now in the field, under FREMONT, are splendidly equipped, accompanied by unsurpassed artillery, and at least 2,500 cavalry.

Of Gen. PRICE's position and purposes, we can know but little. He is believed to command fully 40,000 men—all at Lexington recently, and all his best generals around him. What will be his policy now, we can only conjecture. If he has evacuated Lexington and gone West, then he is safe again, and will elude capture.

The New-York Times.

VOL. XI....NO. 3149. NEW-YORK, FRIDAY, OCTOBER 25, 1861. PRICE TWO CENTS.

THE GREAT REBELLION.

Highly Important News from Various Points.

Quiet Along the National Lines Across the Potomac.

Full Particulars of the Battle of Monday.

Approximate Estimate of the National Loss.

THE OBSEQUIES OF COL. BAKER.

The Rebel Steamer George Page Cruising on the Lower Potomac.

From the Mouth of the Mississippi and Fort Pickens.

EXPOSURE OF REBEL MENDACITY.

Hollins' Story of the Defeat of the National Fleet a Humbug.

The Rebels Terribly Whipped at Santa Rosa.

SPECIAL DISPATCH FROM WASHINGTON.

WASHINGTON, Thursday, Oct. 24.

THE NATIONAL LOSS ON MONDAY.

The official number of the killed, wounded and missing at the Leesburgh fight have been received. We had 79 killed and drowned, 141 wounded, and there are 193 missing. The missing may be prisoners or straggling.

THE RECENT REBEL MOVEMENT.

An evidence that the falling back of the Confederates at Fairfax Court-house, three weeks ago, was a sudden and unexpected movement, is furnished in the fact that they set up telegraph poles, and stretched the wires upon them, from Fairfax to Falls Church, and had only completed the work on the Thursday previous to the Sunday when our troops advanced. They removed the wire as they fell back, but had not time to remove the poles, which are still standing, ready for

Colonel E. D. Baker

Government wires, when our troops shall make an advance.

THE BATTLE AT EDWARDS' FERRY.

FULL DESCRIPTION OF THE ENGAGEMENT.

Repulse of the Union Forces—Heavy Loss—Gallant Conduct of the Men.

LIST OF THE KILLED AND WOUNDED.

From Our Special Correspondent.

EDWARDS' FERRY, UPPER POTOMAC, Sunday—6 P. M.

The Union troops have commenced shelling the rebels on the Virginia shore across the river, whether merely to drive them out or as preliminary to an advance, we shall probably know in the morning. As I intend to make my letter, as far as possible, a journal from hour to hour of what actually takes place under my own observation, I shall not attempt to anticipate movements, but only record what I see and hear. The firing commenced at 4:35 this afternoon, from VAN ALLEN's Battery of two Parrott guns,—12-pounders,—the shells going well over to the Virginia side, to the north of Goose Creek. Their explosion is very distinctly heard. Seven shells have been thrown within ten minutes, without eliciting any response from our friends across the water. Gen. STONE is directing the movement. The tenth and eleventh shells fired were long range, the explosion not being heard for ten seconds. The next two exploded in five. The direction given to the shells is varied so as if possible to find out the location of the rebels, who are supposed to be concealed in a thick wood to the southwest, on the hill, and apparently a mile from the mouth of Goose Creek. The fourteenth sounded like a solid shot, and the three following shells, which made a loud explosion, brought no answering shot from the rebels.

MONDAY MORNING.

The engagement has been renewed this morning. At daylight, portions of the Massachusetts Twentieth, Col. LEE, and the Massachusetts Fif-

teenth, Col. DEVENS, not over 300 in all, crossed over three-quarters of a mile below Conrad's Ferry. They crossed the island, which at this point is about 150 yards wide, and three miles in its extreme length. These two companies—viz., I and D, commanded respectively by Captains BARTLETT and CROWINGSHIELD—met with no opposition on landing, and pushed on until they had reached the open space. This company (II, of the Fifteenth Regiment) went ahead as skirmishers, and were met in an open field by a company of 70 rebels, who fired the first volley, wounding ten and taking two prisoners. The company charged on them, and drove them back, but were in return driven back by a large cavalry force, besides a Mississippi rifle company.

This ended the contest for the morning; but a straggling fire was kept up on both sides until 1:30 P.M., when the rebels renewed the engagement with great fury. They attacked in front and on the right flank. At this time Gen. BAKER's Brigade was arriving. They consisted chiefly of the Philadelphia Zouaves, under command of Col. BAXTER.

Col. VAUGHAN, of the Rhode Island, had also arrived, and, with the greatest difficulty, succeeded in getting one of his six-pounder guns up the ascent, being obliged first to dismount the gun. This piece, with the two mountain howitzers belonging to the Twentieth Massachusetts, were all the heavy guns on the field. The fire was kept up from the right flank and front with great activity, the rebels raining a perfect storm of balls upon the Union forces. The Twentieth, although mostly raw recruits, stood the enemy's fire like veterans. They ran up to the brow of the hill, delivered their fire, and only fell back to reload and repeat. This continued until 5½ P.M., the Union forces maintaining their position steadily against the deadly, raking cross-fire from the front and left of the woods.

At this juncture Gen. BAKER, who had dismounted from his horse, and was advancing at the head of his command, coolly, but resolutely encouraging his men, received a ball through his head, killing him instantly. The General's blood bespattered Cap. CROWNINGSHIELD, who stood beside him at the moment. He never spoke. His body was immediately taken to the rear by his men, who freely wept at their loss. He was placed in a scow, and transported to the island, and thence to the Maryland shore. His remains were sent to Edwards' Ferry, and thence to Poolsville. His horse, which had been left standing, was afterwards shot. A small canvas satchell, containing his papers, I saw in the hands of a young man to whom they were delivered shortly before he fell.

This was the turning point of the battle. The rebels were five to one of the Union force, and the latter were finally ordered to leave the field. The retreat was made after the Bull Run pattern, with slight improvements, the men rolling, sliding, and almost turning summersaults down hill, to escape the galling fire which now assailed them from all points. The rebels were constantly reinforced, screaming like furies at each onset. Before retreating they threw the six-pounder down the hill into the river. The howitzers were left on the field, and fell into the enemy's hands.

The Fifteenth and Twentieth Massachusetts Regiments suffered very severely, losing a large part of their numbers in killed and wounded.

The Tammany Regiment covered itself with glory, Capt. O'MEARA often rallied his command, throwing defiance into the very teeth of the enemy, and showing the rebels that he could scream equal to the worst of them. Capt. O'MEARA took charge of the landing, and refused to let any but wounded men enter the boat, ordering the sound troops to go back and pepper the rebels. His conduct was very gallant throughout, evincing a true and lofty courage. Lieut. MESSRS took command of the scow, and continued to ferry over the wounded, who poured down the hill. Several times the rebels fired upon him as he was crossing with the wounded men. The fourth boat-load was capsized, by the men rushing into it in too great numbers, and the whole party, about fifty in number, well and wounded, were precipitated into the stream. Ten of the party, at least, were drowned. A great many tried to swim the river, and sank from exhaustion. One half of those who are missing were drowned in this manner. It is not yet known how many of our men have fallen into their hands. The destruction of life has been far greater, in proportion to the numbers engaged, than at Bull Run.

The New-York Times.

VOL. XI....NO. 3166.   NEW YORK, THURSDAY, NOVEMBER 14, 1861.   PRICE TWO CENTS.

THE GREAT EXPEDITION.

Arrival of the Bienville with Official Dispatches and Correspondence.

The Accounts of Capt. Dupont and Gen. Sherman.

A Full Narrative of Events by Our Own Correspondent.

COMPLETE SUCCESS OF THE EXPEDITION.

How Forts Beauregard and Walker were Taken.

Terrific Bombardment of Between Four and Five Hours.

Gallant Conduct of the National Vessels.

The Defeat and Utter Rout of the Enemy.

Forty-three Pieces of Cannon Captured.

Beaufort Abandoned by All but the Negroes and One Drunken White Man.

Fifteen Thousand National Troops Landed.

Proclamation of Gen. Sherman to the South Carolinians.

The U. S. gunboat *Bienville*, Commander CHAS. STEEDMAN, and A. E. R. BENHAM, Executive Officer, arrived at this port at 6½ o'clock last evening, from the Great Naval Expedition, *viâ* Fortress Monroe, where she left dispatches for Commodore GOLDSBOROUGH, and whence Capt. STEEDMAN proceeded to Washington with dispatches for the Army and Navy Departments. These dispatches, from Capt. DUPONT, who commanded the naval portion of the Expedition, and from Gen. SHERMAN, who commanded the military branch, will be found below, together with a detailed narrative of the operations of the Expedition since it left Hampton Roads.

The fleet arrived at Port Royal on Monday, the 4th inst.

S. F. Dupont commanded the South Atlantic Blockading Squadron.

Tuesday the smaller gunboats rounded into the channel under a fire from the forts, which did no damage.

On Wednesday the weather prevented active operations, but on Thursday morning, 7th inst., the men-of-war and the gunboats advanced to the attack.

The action commenced at 10 A. M., and was hotly carried on on both sides, and lasted about four hours, at the end of which time the rebels were compelled by the shower of shells to abandon their works and beat a hasty retreat.

The day after the fight the *Seneca*, and two other gunboats, under the command of Lieut. AMMEN, proceeded up to Beaufort, and found but one white man in the town, and he was drunk.

After the capture of the forts the whole army, about 15,000 men, were safely landed and established on shore.

THE GOVERNMENT ACCOUNTS.

WASHINGTON, Wednesday, Nov. 13.

Capt. STEEDMAN arrived here at noon to-day bringing official dispatches from the great naval expedition. He is also the bearer of two rebel, Confederate flags, one Palmetto flag, and the American flag first hoisted in South Carolina over Fort Walker. Capt. STEEDMAN reports that the captured forts are magnificent, with covered ways, and bomb-proof. All that our troops had to do was to occupy them. They can be held against any opposing force.

Among the most efficient vessels were found to be the new gunboats, and of which the Navy Department had twenty-three constructed expressly for such purposes, and their success both in the gale and under fire was perfect.

Commander DRAYTON, who commanded the *Pocahontas*, is the brother of Gen. DRAYTON, who commanded the rebel forts.

Capt. STEEDMAN, who brings the dispatches, is the son of a former Mayor of Charleston.

On the reception of the official dispatches, the following order was issued:

GENERAL ORDER.—The Department announces to the navy and to the country its high gratification at the brilliant success of the combined navy and army

Brigadier-General T. W. Sherman

forces, respectively commanded by Flag-Officer S. F. DUPONT and Brig.-Gen. J. W. SHERMAN, in the capture of Forts Walker and Beauregard, commanding the entrance to Port Royal harbor, South Carolina. To commemorate this signal victory, it is ordered that a national salute be fired from each Navy-yard at meridian on the day after the reception of this order.

(Signed) _____ GIDEON WELLES.

PRIVATE LETTER FROM CAPT. DUPONT.

The following is a portion of a private letter from Flag-Officer DUPONT, to the Assistant Secretary of the Navy:

WABASH, PORT ROYAL, Nov. 9, 1861.

MY DEAR MR. FOX: During the disheartening events of our passage my faith never gave way, but at some moments it seemed appalling. On the other hand, I permit no elation at our success, yet I cannot refrain from telling you that it has been more complete and brilliant than I ever could have believed. I have been too fatigued to send a detailed official account of the battle. My report is full up to the eve of it, and I think will interest you; but I had to content myself with a succinct account, which I think will be liked as well as a more detailed narrative. This I will however, forward in time for the Secretary's report. I kept under way and made three turns, though I passed five times between the forts. I had a flanking division of five ships to watch, and old TATNALL, too, who had eight small and swift steamers ready to pounce upon any of ours, should they be disabled. I could get none of my big frigates up. I thought the *Sabine* would have gotten clear up to the *St. Lawrence*, I sent no word, however, and the *Savannah* was blown off. I do not regret it now, except on their account. I believe my plan was clever. I stood against the tide, and had the management the better in consequence. Their confidence was extreme that they could drive us away. They fought bravely, and their rifle guns never missed. An 80-pounder rifle ball went through our mainmast in the very centre, making an awful hole. They aimed at our bridge where they knew they could make a hole if they were lucky. A shot in the centre let water into the after-magazine, but I saved a hundred lives by keeping under way and bearing in close. We found their sights graduated at six hundred yards. When they once broke the stampede was intense, and not a gun was spiked. In truth I never conceived of such a fire as that of this ship on her second turn, and I am told that its effect upon the spectators outside of her was intense. I learn that when they saw our flag flying on shore the troops were powerless to cheer but wept. Gen. SHERMAN was deeply affected, and the soldiers are loud and unstinting in their expressions of admiration and gratitude. The works are most

PORT ROYAL HARBOR AND BEAUFORT.

The Scene of the Engagement.

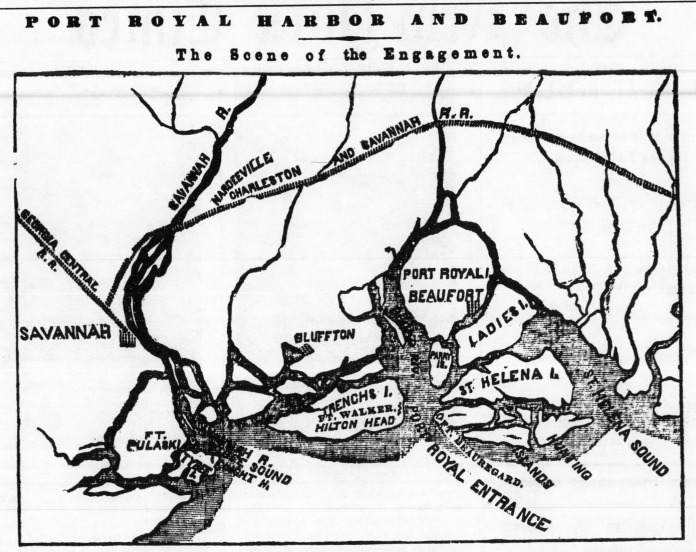

scientifically constructed, and there is nothing like Fort Walker on the Potomac. I did not allow the victory to check our ardor, but dispatched some vessels, under Capt. GILLIS, over the other side. To-day I have sent an expedition to Beaufort to save the light vessels, but they were fired instantly after the surrender.

Beaufort is deserted. The negroes are wild with joy and revenge. They have been shot down, they say, like dogs, because they would not go off with their masters. I have already a boat at Skull Creek, and the communication between Savannah and Charleston is cut off."

PRIVATE LETTER FROM ANOTHER OFFICER.

The following is an extract from a private letter from one of the officers engaged in the bombardment:

"I am sure our success will rejoice your hearts; it has been complete, and terror runs over the whole country. The negroes are wild, and plundering their masters' houses. The whites have been driving the negroes away by force, and shooting them down, but they still come to the gunboats. The moment Gen. DRAYTON took to his horse in the panic of the 7th, his two hundred servants went directly to the Wabash. This is worthy of notice, as putting down the nonsense that the slaves were ready to fight for their masters. They surrounded Capt. AMMEN in crowds at Beaufort, one of them, calling out, in the joy of his heart, 'I didn't think you could do it, massa.'"

CAPT. DUPONT'S OFFICIAL REPORTS.

The following are the official dispatches to the Navy Department:

SECOND DISPATCH.

FLAG-SHIP WABASH, OFF HILTON HEAD,
PORT ROYAL HARBOR, Nov. 8, 1861.

Hon. Gideon Welles, Secretary of the Navy, Washington:

SIR: I have the honor to inform you that yesterday I attacked the batteries of the enemy on Bay Point and Hilton Head, and Forts Walker and Beau-

regard, and succeeded in silencing them after an engagement of four hours' duration, and driving away the squadron of rebel steamers under Commander TATNALL.

The reconnoissance of yesterday made us satisfied with the superiority of Fort Walker, and to that I directed my especial efforts, engaging it at a distance of eight hundred, and afterwards at six hundred yards. But the plan of attack brought the squadron sufficiently near Fort Beauregard to receive its fire, and the ships were frequently fighting the batteries on both sides at the same time. The action was begun on my part at 26 minutes after 9, and at half-past 2 the American ensign was hoisted on the flag-staff of Fort Walker, and this morning at sunrise on that of Fort Beauregard. The defeat of the enemy terminated in utter rout and confusion. Their quarters and encampments were abandoned without an attempt to carry away either public or private property. The ground over which they fled was strewn with the arms of private soldiers, and the officers retired in too much haste to submit to the incumbrance of their swords. Landing my marines and a company of seamen, I took possession of the deserted ground, and held the forts on Hilton Head till the arrival of Gen. SHERMAN, to whom I had the honor to transfer their command.

We have captured forty-three pieces of cannon, most of them of the heaviest calibre, and of the most improved design. The bearer of these dispatches will have the honor to carry with him the captured flags, and two small brass field-pieces, lately belonging to the State of South Carolina, which are sent home as suitable trophies of the success of the day.

I inclose herewith a copy of the general order which is to be read in the fleet to-morrow morning at muster.

A detailed account of this battle will be submitted hereafter. I have the honor to be, very respectfully, your obedient servant, S. F. DUPONT,

Flag-Officer, Commanding South Atlantic Blockading Squadron.

P. S.—The bearer of dispatches will also carry

Fort Beauregard was among the installations recaptured by Federal naval bombardment and assault.

with him the first American ensign raised upon the soil of South Carolina since the rebellion broke out.
S. F. D.

GENERAL ORDER TO THE FLEET.

FLAG-SHIP WABASH, HILTON HEAD,
PORT ROYAL BAY, Nov. 8, 1861.

GENERAL ORDER No. 2.—It is the grateful duty of the Commander-in-Chief to make a public acknowledgment of his entire commendation of the coolness, discipline, skill and gallantry displayed by the officers and men under his command, in the capture of the batteries at Hilton Head and Bay Point, after an action of four hours' duration.

The New-York Times.

VOL. XI....NO. 3168. NEW-YORK, SUNDAY, NOVEMBER 17, 1861. PRICE THREE CENTS.

THE GREAT REBELLION.

Highly Important and Gratifying Intelligence.

Capture of the Rebel Commissioners, Slidell and Mason.

The Frigate San Jacinto Takes Them from the English Mail Steamship Trent.

Particulars of the Capture—Protest of the Rebels.

Sketch of the Commissioners, and of Capt. Wilkes, Commanding the San Jacinto.

HOW THE NEWS WAS RECEIVED IN WASHINGTON

Highly Important News from Kentucky.

A Rebel Army of Forty Thousand Threatening Cincinnati, Louisville and Lexington.

Floyd's Forces Driven Back in Western Virginia.

The Armies of McCulloch and Price Gone to Arkansas.

The Late Movement of National Troops into Eastern Virginia.

Terrible Panic in the South Following the Battle of Port Royal.

THE CAPTURE OF MASON AND SLIDELL.

DISPATCHES FROM FORTRESS MONROE.
FORTRESS MONROE, Friday, Nov. 15.
The United States steam-frigate *San Jacinto.* Capt. WILKES, arrived in the Roadstead at 12½ P. M., having on board the rebel Commissioners, SLIDELL and MASON.

James M. Mason represented the Confederate effort for recognition in visiting England.

They were taken from the English mail steamer on the 8th instant off Bermuda.

Lieut. FAIRFAX and thirty-five armed men went from the *San Jacinto* with five officers, who boarded the steamer and picked out the Commissioners.

Messrs. SLIDELL and MASON made feeble resistance, but were induced to leave with Lieut. FAIRFAX.

The captain of the steamer raved and swore, called the United States officers " piratical Yankees, " and other abusive names.

One of the secretaries of the rebel Commissioners, named EUSTACE or HURSTACE, also showed resistance; but himself and colleague accompanied their employers to confinement.

Mr. SLIDELL had his wife and four children on board, who were allowed to proceed to Europe.

Commodore WILKES came ashore and had a lengthy conversation with Gen. WOOL.

He expressed his opinion that he had done right, and said that, right or wrong, these men had to be secured, and if he had done wrong, he could do no more than be cashiered for it.

When it became known that these two worthies were in Hampton Roads, the excitement was immense.

Some reported that quarters would be provided them on the Rip Raps, but either the frigate will proceed to New-York, or some other vessel will be sent there with the prisoners on board, and deliver them at Fort Lafayette.

FROM ANOTHER CORRESPONDENT.
FORTRESS MONROE, Friday, Nov. 15,
The U. S. steamer *San Jacinto* has just arrived from the Coast of Africa, *viâ* the West Indies, where she has been cruising for some six weeks.

Old Point was electrified by the tidings that the *San Jacinto* had on board Messrs. SLIDELL and MASON, who were going abroad as Ministers of

John Slidell represented the Confederacy in France.

the Southern Confederacy to France and England.

Capt. WILKES reported the news at headquarters in person, and will forward his dispatches to Washington to-night.

They had embarked on board an English mail steamer. Hearing of the fact, Capt. WILKES determined to take them, and coming up with the steamer in the Bermuda Channel, he sent aboard and demanded the surrender of the arch rebels. The reply was, that there was not force enough to take them.

Capt. WILKES thereupon sent an additional force and at the same time put the *San Jacinto* into a convenient position.

Messrs. SLIDELL and MASON were then surrendered.

The English steamer took them on board, knowing who they were, their destination and business.

Capt. WILKES is understood to have acted on his own responsibility.

Messrs. SLIDELL and MASON asked permission of Gen. WOOL to send letters to their friends, which was granted. The letters were open, of course.

The *San Jacinto* will leave for New-York direct this evening.

FURTHER PARTICULARS FROM BALTIMORE.
BALTIMORE, Saturday, Nov. 16.
An officer of the *San Jacinto* has arrived here on the steamer from Old Point, with dispatches for the Government. He hurried off to the railroad depôt immediately upon his arrival and took a special train to Washington. We shall, doubtless, soon hear something official in regard to the arrest of Messrs. SLIDELL and MASON.

The name of the British vessel from which Messrs. MASON and SLIDELL were taken has not as yet been ascertained.

All the documents and papers of Messrs. SLIDELL and MASON were seized. Their families were allowed to proceed.

The captain of the British vessel delivered up Messrs. SLIDELL and MASON under a protest.

This is the substance of the reports by the passengers by the Old Point boat.

FROM ANOTHER CORRESPONDENT.

BALTIMORE, Saturday, Nov. 16.

I have been enabled to gather a few facts concerning the arrest of MASON, SLIDELL, McFARLAND and EUSTIS. After Capt. WILKES had brought the English steamer to, he sent his First Lieutenant and other officers to board her. The Lieutenant informed the Captain that his object was to arrest the four gentlemen, who, with the other passengers, had gathered on deck to see what was going on. MASON asked if he would take them by force, to which he replied, he was ordered to bring them along with him, and he always obeyed orders. The families of the traitors felt terribly aggrieved, and after consultation it was decided to offer them free passage to New-York with their husbands. This they declined, and continued their journey to St. Thomas.

Capt. WILKES stood at the side of his vessel when the prisoners came up. MASON and SLIDELL, both of whom knew him perfectly well, passed over the side quietly, but without recognition. EUSTIS followed, and was swaggering offensively by, when Capt. WILKES said, "I am Captain of this ship, Sir;" whereupon EUSTIS, touching his hat, said, "I beg your pardon, Sir," and passed on.

Capt. TAYLOR, a passenger home from the Coast of Afcica, and who was bearer of dispatches to the Government, gave up his room to MASON. They did not leave the vessel at Fort Monroe, but coals having been obtained, they were put at once *en route* for fort Lafayette.

SEMI-OFFICIAL ACCOUNT OF THE ARREST.

WASHINGTON, Saturday, Nov. 16.

Capt. TAYLOR, who has arrived here with dispatches, reports that when the *San Jacinto* stopped at Cienfuegos, the escape of SLIDELL and MASON was ascertained. Proceeding thence to Havana, it was understood they had taken passage on the 7th inst. on the British mail steamship *Trent*, plying between Vera Cruz, by way of Havana, and St. Thomas and Southampton.

While the *San Jacinto* was in the narrowest part of the Bahama Channel, about twenty-four miles to the westward, she met the packet, and, as usual in such cases, fired a shot across her bows and brought her to. Two boats were sent to her, under the command of Lieut. FAIRFAX, who, boarding the packet, arrested MASON and SLIDELL, who were personally known to him.

They at first objected to being removed without the employment of force for that purpose. However, they were soon after removed without further trouble, and conveyed to the *San Jacinto.* Their respective Secretaries, EUSTIS and McFARLAND, were also brought on board, and are now on their way to New-York.

The packet had no other save her own flag.

The remainder of the passengers, including the ladies connected with the Slidell and Mason party, were not molested, and were therefore left free to pursue their journey.

The official dispatches are voluminous, and include several accounts of the capture, together with the protest of MASON and SLIDELL against being taken from a British ship.

SKETCH OF THE REBEL COMMISSIONERS.

JAMES M. MASON.

JAMES MURRAY MASON is a native of Virginia, and springs from one of the very first of its families. He was born in 1797, in what was at that time a part of Fairfax County, on Anadostan Island, which is encircled by the Potomac River, just above the present metropolis of the Union. His first ancestor in Virginia was GEORGE MASON, who was a member of the English Parliament in the reign of CHARLES I. He was a strong upholder of the King, and resisted the measures adopted against him by the Parliament. Subsequently he became an officer in the army of CHARLES II., and commanded a regiment of cavalry in the campaign against the "Roundhead" troops of OLIVER CROMWELL. After the defeat of the royal forces at Worcester, in 1651, he made his escape disguised as a peasant, and, embarking for America, landed at Norfolk. Soon afterward he established a plantation in Westmoreland County, on the Potomac, on which river he and his lineal descendants have lived for more than two hundred years.

Our present subject began his education at the primary schools in Virginia and in Georgetown, D. C.; and graduated in 1818, at the University of Pennsylvania, in Philadelphia. He commenced the study of law at the College of William and Mary, Williamsburgh, Va., afterward entered as a student the office of the late BENJAMIN WATKINS LEIGH, at Richmond, and obtained a license to practice in 1820. In the same year he removed to Winchester, where he entered upon the practice of his profession. In 1826 he was elected to the Virginia House of Delegates, and was twice reelected. He also served as a member of the Convention called in 1829 to revise the Constitution of that State.

In 1837 he was elected to Congress, where he served but one term. In 1847, he was elected to the Senate, to fill the seat of JOEL PENNYBACKER who died during the session. He was reelected in 1849, for the term commencing on tne 4th of March, 1851, (the session of the Legislature being biennial,) and he was again elected to the Senate in December, 1855, for the term commencing on the 4th of March, 1857, and to expire on the 4th of March, 1863. He was thus a member of the Senate for fourteen years. His position as Chairman of the Senate Committee on Foreign Relations, which he held for several sessions, may be said to have given him a *quasi* superintendence of the proceedings of the State Department, and brought him into intimate contact with BUCHANAN and other dignitaries and conspirators at home and abroad. During his long Congressional career, he has never distinguished himself by bringing forward or carrying out any of those great and beneficent acts of legislation which alone can make a prominent position illustrious. He was, violently, pro-Slavery, and took a memorable part in the debates on the Fugitive Slave law, on the Kansas-Nebraska bill, and on all questions which involved in any way the everlasting negro. He will be remembered as the principal concocter of the Fugitive Slave bill.

MASON is a man of narrow and feeble intellect, of virulent temper and of insolent manners; and why JEFF. DAVIS ever sent him as a plenipotentiary to England, is one of those Confederate mysteries which it is not given to ordinary mortals to comprehend. His position in the Senate made him somewhat acquainted with foreign affairs, and it is most likely on this plea that he has got himself appointed. The probability, however, is that, morally and intellectually blind though he be, he had eyesight enough to foresee the disaster that was about to fall upon the cause on which he had staked his neck, and, being an arrant coward, obtained the appointment as a means of escape from the ruin which he saw would soon overtake him. Even this miserable subterfuge, however, has failed him, and he is now in the iron clutch of the Government over whose utter destruction he has lately been reveling.

MASON is not only a knave, but a hypocrite. He found it convenient through life to class himself as a Democrat, though a man with less democracy in his composition or manners never existed. He wrote disunion letters to South Carolina, and Union letters to Massachusetts, and in the debatable ground of Washington, when it suited his schemes, or his plans of personal advancement, he was everything to all men—except being honest and truthful. As far back as September, 1855, he wrote to a public affair in South Carolina: "But one course remains for the South—*immediate, absolute and eternal separation.* Better, far better, to stand toward the Northern States as we stand to the rest of the world—enemies in war, in peace friends—than to remain halting under a common Government, enemies in the guise of peace, or friends at war." And yet, only two years later, he said, in a speech delivered to an audience assembled on Bunker Hill: " I shall tell it in old Virginia, when I return to her hallowed land, that I found the spirit of Massachusetts as buoyant, as patriotic, as completely filled with the emotions that should govern patriotism, when I visited Bunker Hill, as it was when that battle was fought."

During the secession excitement in the last regular session of Congress, when one State after another was rushing out of the Union, MASON was equally double-faced. As long ago as March last, he said in the Senate that "he recognized no allegiance to this Government; he recognized and acknowledged no allegiance to this government; none whatever." And yet, for a considerable time after this, he retained his seat in the United States Senate. He will now, it is to be hoped, have an opportunity to straighten up and rectify his mischievous political career.

JOHN SLIDELL.

This arch-conspirator is a native of the State of New-York, to which he now returns loaded with eternal infamy. He was born in the year 1793, and as soon as he reached manhood, he went to New-Orleans, to seek his fortune. He arrived there " poor, friendless and alone ;" but, as he had received a good education in his native State, he shortly undertook the practice of law in that city. His skill and adroitness soon won for him a high place at the New-Orleans bar. His success as a lawyer was unparalleled even in that city of sudden successes ; and he was retained on one side or the other, in almost every important lawsuit which arose. After fifteen or twenty years' toil at the bar of New-Orleans, he accumulated a princely fortune and a wide reputation. His first public service appears to have been as United States District Attorney at New-Orleans, to which office he was appointed by Gen. JACKSON. He was frequently sent to the State Legislature of Louisiana, and was afterwards chosen one of the Louisiana delegation to Congress. In the House he was remarked for his tact and skill as a manager, and his shrewdness and coolness in debate. At times, under provocation, he would become excited, and the words would flow from his lips in a torrent ; but this rarely happened. His temper was generally thoroughly under command.

While a member of Congress, SLIDELL was selected by the President to act as Minister-Plenipotentiary and Envoy-Extraordinary to Mexico. The circumstances imparted unusual importance to the mission. War was actually on the point of breaking out. TAYLOR was on the Rio Grande, and the American squadron lay off Vera Cruz. Previous to firing the first gun, however, President POLK, professing still to be anxious to preserve peace, and Mexico having intimated that a new Envoy from the United States would be received, SLIDELL was accredited. The mission did not achieve any useful purpose. After many and futile discussions, the Mexican Government refused to receive SLIDELL, and he finally demanded his passports and returned home.

After his return, he began to develop his ideas of the necessity of conquering Mexico, and subjugating the Spanish, Indian, and other races, not excepting the negroes, which added greatly to his popularity in the South.

When Mr. SOULE vacated his seat in the Senate to fill the post of Minister to Madrid, SLIDELL was appointed to succeed him for the unexpired term ; and, at the close of this term, he was reëlected for six years. In the caucuses of the extreme Southern Party with which he acted, no member's advice carried more weight than SLIDELL's. He spoke little, but kept a close eye on affairs and on the wires.

During BUCHANAN's reign, he was the controlling spirit of that miserable old man ; and all the atrocious acts of the late Administration, particularly for the last year of its existence, are traceable to him. He taught COBB how to swindle, and FLOYD how to steal, and twisted old BUCK's nose and conscience as if they were wax He has been mentioned for many important diplomatic missions, but, excepting the unsuccessful one to Mexico, obtained none. He was, when caught, on his way as JEFF. DAVIS' Plenipotentiary to France ; but in this, too, he has wretchedly failed. In person, SLIDELL is striking ; of middle height, stout figure and with a bold mein. He is utterly unprincipled, and his political career in Louisiana a record of villainies that it would be heard to parallel. In 1844, by the celebrated Plaquemine frauds, he defrauded the Whigs of the vote of Louisiana, and thereby defeated HENRY CLAY and made POLK President. For his infamous work at this time he acquired the soubriquet of Baron Plaquemine. Again, at a later day, in the matter of the Houmas Land Grants, in Louisiana, he was guilty of frauds so palpable and outrageous that even New-Orleans, with its easy virtue, almost spewed him out. By this he acquired the nom de plume of Old Houmas. But his crowning fraud on the people of Louisiana and on his country was when he swindled his adopted State out of the Union.

In catching him we have undoubtedly caught the most accomplished scoundrel, and the ablest engineer of conspiracy in all the South—JEFF DAVIS himself not excepted.

CAPTAIN CHARLES WILKES.

The name of Capt. CHARLES WILKES, who so neatly nabbed SLIDELL and MASON, is a name known both in navigation and in science. He was born in this State in 1805, and originally entered the naval service of his country in 1818, at the early age of 13 years. In 1838, having previously distinguished himself by his scientific ability, he received from the American Government the command of a naval expedition intended to explore the countries bordering on the Pacific and Southern Oceans. His command consisted of two sloops-of-war, a brig and two tenders, and he himself had the grade of Captain. Leaving here shortly after his appointment, he doubled Cape Horn, crossed over to Polynesia, Van Dieman's Land and Australia, advancing as high as the 61st degree of south latitude ; he then visited the Feejee Islands and Borneo, and returned to New-York in 1842, after having visited Singapore and the Cape of Good Hope. This memorable expedition of four years was fertile in useful observations, which Capt. WILKES recounted in a very able work in five octavo volumes, entitled *A Narrative of the United States Exploring Expedition.* In 1848 the Geographical Society of London presented him with a gold medal, as a token of their appreciation of his labors. He has also, since then, published a work entitled *Western America,* which contains valuable statistical details and geographical facts and maps relating to California and Oregon. Commodore WILKES received his present commission in 1855. He has been in the service altogether forty-three years. Ten of these years he has been on sea service ; twenty-six engaged on shore or other duty, and seven years unemployed. For some years, latterly, he has been assigned to special duty near Washington. He is now returning from the Coast of Africa with the United States steamer *San Jacinto.* On his way home he found orders to cruise around the coast of the West Indies to look out

Captain Charles Wilkes removed the Confederate delegates from the English steamship *Trent.*

for privateers or vessels attempting to run the blockade, which duty he has been performing for the past six weeks. While engaged in this business he fell in with the vessel containing the two rebel Plenipos. The whole country now rings with applause of his bold action.

THE NEWS OF THE CAPTURE IN WASHINGTON.

WASHINGTON, Saturday, Nov. 16.

The city was made joyful to-day by a rumor which gained currency about noon, to the effect that ex-Senators MASON and SLIDELL, the Envoys of JEFF. DAVIS to England and France, respectively, had been taken at sea, and were now prisoners on board a United States vessel of war. An hour later, Capt. ALFRED TAYLOR, of the navy, arrived by a special train from Baltimore, bearing dispatches to the Government, from Commodore WILKES. These official documents, numbering near a dozen, give full particulars of the capture, and are at present in the hands of the Government, to be fully examined before publication. The general facts connected with the arrest are as follows :

Commodore WILKES, while returning from the Coast of Africa, in the *San Jacinto,* stopped at Havana to take in coal, and while *there,* learned that Messrs. MASON and SLIDELL were to leave on the 7th, on the British Mail steamer *Trent,* for England. Capt. WILKES heard, about the same time, that the *Sumter* was off Laguayra, and he determined to capture her if possible.

While steaming through the Bahama Channel he encountered the *Trent,* and brought her to by firing two shots across her bow. Lieut. FAIRFAX, of the *San Jacinto,* was immediately sent on board with a boat's crew and marines, and asked of the master of the *Trent* to see his passenger list. This was denied, and Lieut. FAIRFAX then stated that his purpose was to take into custody Messrs. SLIDELL and MASON, whom he knew to be on board, and those who accompanied them·

The rebel envoys were soon recognized, and they refused Lieut. FAIRFAX's demand that they should proceed aboard the *San Jacinto,* and immediately went below to their state-rooms. They were followed, and Lieut. FAIRFAX told them that if they refused to go peaceably, he should be compelled to use force. They still refused, when the marines, stepping forward and taking them by the shoulder, they made no further opposition.

Messrs. EUSTIS and McFARLAND, the Secretaries of the rebel Envoys, were also arrested. SLIDELL and EUSTIS had their families on board the *Trent,* and the prospect of a separation occasioned an affecting scene. Commodore WILKES subsequently offered to allow their families to accompany them, but the ladies refused, preferring the voyage to England and a protracted separation from their husbands, rather than the risk of an imprisonment in the North. SLIDELL's family consisted of his wife, four children and two servants ; EUSTIS' of his wife, two children and a servant. The baggage of the prisoners was transferred to the *San Jacinto,* and it is said that i contains important documents, and among them their instructions from JEFF. DAVIS' Government. Any mail matter which had been intrusted to them had probably been transferred to the English mail.

No opposition was offered by the officers of the *Trent* to the arrest, other than a verbal protest though one man who has charge of the mails on board indulged in some gasconade about the outrage committed, and was loud in his assertions that the blockade would be raised within a month after the news reached England.

Of course everybody is rejoiced that the arch rebels are in custody, but the circumstances connected with their arrest have created some apprehensions of consequences. The right of search has always been asserted by Great Britain, and has been denied by the United States. England and France have not recognized the rebel States as a nation, but have recognized them as belligerents, and the point is now presented of an insurgent claiming to be a diplomatic envoy from a State not yet recognized, arrested while traveling, on a vessel of the nation to whom he is accredited, and taken from it by a vessel of the nation against which he is in rebellion, and which still claims him as its subject. It seems to be conceded that Commodore WILKES acted in the matter without instructions, and whatever instructions may have been given to the Atlantic fleet to effect their capture in the *Theodora,* it was hardly contemplated that they should be taken in a British vessel. In view of the intricate question of international law likely to be raised, there is a casting about for precedents, and in the streets even GROTIUS, PUFFENDORF, VATTEL and WHEATON are learnedly appealed to for justification. I am informed that the Secessionists of Baltimore called upon the British Consul to-day and asked what Great Britain would do in the matter, and that he expressed the opinion that the act did not interfere with any law of nations ; and that, in view of all the facts, probably no notice would be taken of it. Members of the Cabinet think that the case presents an opportunity to test the point whether the British Government will accept its own doctrines when the American Bull goads the British Ox and the general feeling seems to be that the most that will be required will be, that the United States Government apologize for the act, which it will do and hold on to the prisoners.

The New-York Times.

VOL. XI....NO. 3170.   NEW-YORK, TUESDAY, NOVEMBER 19, 1861.   PRICE TWO CENTS.

THE GREAT REBELLION.

IMPORTANT NEWS FROM WASHINGTON.

Attempt of the Rebels to Capture the Brooklyn Fourteenth.

They are Repulsed, with Considerable Loss.

The Expedition to the Eastern Shore of Virginia.

Landing of the Troops in Accomac.

Favorable Reception of General Dix's Proclamation.

IMPORTANT FROM SANTA ROSA ISLAND.

Preparations for the Rebels at Newport's News.

SPECIAL DISPATCH FROM WASHINGTON.

WASHINGTON, Monday, Nov. 18.

CAPT. WILKES AND THE REBEL COMMISSIONERS.

Capt. WILKES was sent to the coast of Africa' especially to bring home the *San Jacinto*, and it was only when he arrived in the West Indies that he heard of the escape of Messrs. MASON and SLIDELL. Therefore, his arrest of them could not have been pursuant to orders. Capt. WILKES acted in accordance with the principle of international law. He tendered to the ladies accompanying the Mason and Slidell party a passage on his ship, and the use of the cabin, with all the delicacies and attentions they might require, but they declined his gallant and considerate invitation.

THE ARREST NO VIOLATION OF LAW.

The *Intelligencer* of this morning has an able article, reviewing the act of Capt. WILKES in the light of international law. Its purpose is to show the entire justification of the arrest, and I learn upon good authority, that in the estimation of diplomats the positions therein assumed are well founded, and are sustained both by precedent and the teachings of standard writers.

THE EXPEDITION TO ACCOMAC.

Four Thousand Troops Preparing to Land—Favorable Reception of Gen. Dix's Proclamation, &c.

BALTIMORE, MONDAY, NOV. 18.

The steamers *Georgia* and *Georgiana* arrived this morning from Newtown, Worcester County, Maryland. Four thousand Federal troops were preparing to go into Virginia. On the way up the Potomac River a boat was sent ashore with Gen. DIX's proclamation, which was read to a large number of Virginians in a farm house, who declared it entirely satisfactory, and claimed the protection of the Government against the Secessionists; who were forcing them into the rebel ranks against their will. The gunboat *Resolute* had been giving them protection through the day, but at night they would have to seek shelter in the woods.

AFFAIRS AT FORTRESS MONROE.

A Spanish Bark Captured off Charleston—Preparations for a Fight at Newport's News, &c.

FORTRESS MONROE, Sunday, Nov. 17,
via BALTIMORE, Monday, Nov. 18.

There has been no flag of truce, to-day, and there is no intelligence whatever from the South.

A Spanish bark, taken off Charleston by the *Alabama*, has arrived, in charge of a prize crew, and will sail to-night for New-York. She has no cargo on board, and will probably be released.

Our naval force at Newport's News has been increased in order to check the rebel expedition fitting out in James River, of which three formidable fireboats are said to form a part.

Gen. PHELPS' command are building comfortable huts for Winter quarters, and Newport's News, will, in a few days, present the appearance of a large frontier village.

IMPORTANT FROM MISSOURI.

Gen. Halleck in St. Louis—Positions of the Different Divisions of the National Army.

ST. LOUIS, Monday, Nov. 18.

Gens. HALLECK and HAMILTON arrived here this morning.

Gens. STURGIS and WYMAN arrived here last night.

The Divisions of Gens. HUNTER, STURGIS and POPE have reached different points on the Pacific Railroad, where they will await orders from Gen. HALLECK.

Gen. WYMAN's Brigade reached Rolla on Saturday, and the Divisions of Gens. SIEGEL and ASBOTH will arrive here to-day or to-morrow.

Gen. WYMAN brought a number of rebel prisoners, among them Col. PRICE and several other officers.

NEWS FROM THE SOUTH.

The Retribution Threatened by the Rebels.

What the Confederates Think of the War and Northern Financial Movements.

Miscellaneous Facts and Rumors.

THE NATIONAL OFFICERS SENTENCED TO BE HUNG.

The Richmond *Examiner*, of Nov. 13, publishes the following correspondence:

C. S. A. WAR DEPARTMENT,
RICHMOND, Nov. 9, 1861.

SIR: You are hereby instructed to choose by lot from among the prisoners of war of highest rank, one who is to be confined in a cell appropriated to convicted felons, and who is to be treated in all respects as if such convict, and to be held for execution in the same manner as may be adopted by the enemy for the execution of the prisoner of war SMITH, recently condemned to death in Philadelphia. You will also select thirteen other prisoners of war, the highest in rank of those captured by our forces, to be confined in the cells reserved for prisoners accused of infamous crimes, and will treat them as such so long as the enemy shall continue so to treat the like number of prisoners of war captured by them at sea, and now held for trial in New-York as pirates. As these measures are intended to repress the infamous attempt now made by the enemy to commit judicial murder on prisoners of war, you will execute them strictly, as the mode best calculated to prevent the commission of so heinous a crime. Your obedient servant,

J. P. BENJAMIN, Acting Secretary of War.

To Brig.-Gen. JOHN WINDER, Richmond, Va.

HEADQUARTERS DEPARTMENT OF HENRICO,
RICHMOND, Va., Nov. 11, 1861.

Hon. J. P. Benjamin, Secretary of War:

SIR: In obedience to instructions contained in your letter of the 9th inst., one prisoner of war of the highest rank in our possession was chosen by lot, to be held for execution in the same manner as may be adopted by the enemy for the execution of SMITH, recently condemned to death in Philadelphia. The names of six colonels were placed in a can. The first name drawn was that of Col. CORCORAN, Sixty-ninth Regiment N. Y. S. M., who is the hostage chosen to answer for SMITH. In choosing the thirteen from the highest rank to be held to answer for a like number of prisoners of war captured by the enemy at sea, there being only ten field officers, it was necessary to draw by lot three captains. The first names drawn were Capts. J. B. Ricketts, H. McQuade and J. W. Rockwood. The list of thirteen will therefore stand: Cols. Lee, Cogswell, Wilcox, Woodruff and Wood; Lieut.-Cols. Bowman and Neff; Majors Potter, Revere and Vogdes; Capts. Ricketts, McQuade and Rockwood. Respectfully, your obedient servant,

JOHN H. WINDER, Brigadier General.

HEADQUARTERS DEPARTMENT OF HENRICO,
RICHMOND, Va., Nov. 12, 1861.

Hon. J. P. Benjamin, Secretary of War, Richmond, Va.

SIR: In obedience to your instructions, all the wounded officers have been exempted as hostages to await the result of the trial of prisoners captured by the enemy at sea. I have, therefore, made selections by lot of Capts. BOWMAN and T. KEFFER to replace Capts. RICKETTS and McQUADE, wounded.

The list of thirteen will now stand: Cols. Lee, Cogswell, Wilcox, Woodruff and Wood; Lieut.-Cols. Bowman and Neff: Majors Potter, Revere and Vogdes: Capts. Rockwood, Bowman and Keffer. Respectfully, your obedient servant,

JOHN H. WINDER, Brigadier-General.

SUNBEAMS FROM CUCUMBERS.

The Richmond *Examiner* of Nov. 14, has a very cheerful review of the aspect of the war. It claims that the blockade in reality benefits them, by arousing the resentment of France and England against the North, and preparing the way for breaking the blockade. There is good reason to believe that St. Louis will yet fall into the hands of the Confederates, and in Kentucky everything is encouraging; for Gen. Johnston is pushing on to Louisville, and the dispatch thinks that he will get there—of course. It proceeds:

Upon the Virginia campaign it is hardly necessary to dwell in detail. In the West, the latest phase of the campaign is favorable to our arms. Gen. FLOYD has followed up the enemy, assaults him in his position, and threatens his communications. Gauley is more than an equivalent to Rich Mountain. In the Valley, PATTERSON was not only completely foiled by Gen. JOHNSTON's superior strategy, but has retired in disgrace to private life. Instead of conquering and holding, the enemy limits himself to marauding. In the Peninsula, MAGRUDER holds the enemy securely in check. In the single battle there fought the enemy was ignominiously routed. At Manassas our army has held its ground firmly, proudly and defiantly. It awaited with confidence the onset of the finest army that had hitherto been organized on this Continent, and drove it back with a loss, not so much of numbers as of honor, that will never be forgotten. In its old stand-point it defies the advance of the enemy. It is a standing menace and insult to the enemy. It is within twenty miles of his capital, and it means to stay there or to advance—not to fall back. Meantime, McCLELLAN has let the best period for an attack go by. We still believe he will assail Gen. JOHNSTON in this position, but we have no apprehension about the result.

Next to the army of SCOTT, which was defeated, and of McCLELLAN, which devotes itself to ditchwork and drill, the greatest efforts of the Yankees have been bestowed upon their late naval expedition. And what have they effected by it? With thirteen powerful ships-of-war and upwards of two hundred heavy guns they have silenced some twenty badly served pieces of artillery. They have captured no important city. They will not even get the town of Beaufort, for, like Hampton, it will be burned by its inhabitants ere they shall have it. We imagine they will get but little cotton—not half enough to freight a ship. If they dare to advance into the interior, they will be crushed, and none will go back to tell the story. Our people are tired of having their homes burned, their women ravished, and their property devastated without adequate retaliation. They have captured no important city. It will not even humbug Europe, as is confidently expected by its projectors. The people of England will liken it to the Welcheren expedition of a former day. In fact, the attempt of PACKENHAM on New-Orleans in 1814 promised much greater results. The reason why the Crimean expedition succeeded was that Russia was, from a want of military roads, further off from the scene of hostilities than her powerful antagonists. So we see no cause to be troubled about Port Royal if but ordinary energy is used by our Commander, and the people of Carolina show, as we believe they will, the same spirit that was exhibited in the first struggle for liberty.

Upon a full and calm survey of the whole ground, we see no cause for gloom or despondency, but every reason for gratulation and triumph. We have, in truth, done wonders. We have maintained our position, and the universal opinion of disinterested Europe is that we will be able to achieve our liberties.

FAMINE PRICES IN NEW-ORLEANS.

From the New-Orleans Crescent, Nov. 9.

Passing by the talk on battles and disruptions in the army, we come to the steadily-increasing scarcity of breadstuffs and other necessaries of life. Even the article of rice, which is selling in Charleston and Savannah at 2½ to 3 cents per pound, is now retailing here at 7½ cents per pound. It has been the current opinion that this nourishing article would at least have been restrained from advancing to famine prices. It would be supposed that an interchange of commodities would follow the political changes; that is, the sugar of Louisiana would be exchanged for the rice of Carolina. Possibly such may attend the course of trade. The system of credit which has been in vogue for years, appears to have been struck down, wholly repudiated. Therefore, unless rice is forwarded hither on Carolina account, we may not have a tierce this season.

According to returns before us, the crop of rice of Louisiana for 1860 was 29,502 barrels. The Charleston table of exports says there were shipped from that port for New-Orleans, between the 1st of September, 1861, and the 31st of October, 1861, (two months,) 1,020 tierces of rice. Has this quantity been received here? *Quien sabe?* We have merely to say that 7½ cents for rice for family use, and at the corner groceries say about 15 cents, which the public pay, are rather high prices. Irish potatoes, (excuse the bull,) which might be raised in almost any quantity on our prolific soil, are selling at one cent. each, or about $2 50 per bushel. Corn has now advanced to $1 25 to $1 35 per bushel, and we have for months past been reading of the greatest crop of corn and wheat ever known. We judge the country is abundantly supplied, and that farmers and raisers intend to hold on and starve us out here in the Crescent City. If planters have these heavy yields secured, we urge them to send a share to market. Flour is advancing to famine figures. Each succeeding day is attended with an advance of 25 cents or more per barrel.

Other articles—such as soap, candles, starch—are advancing from day to day. Soap, candle and starch factories could be made profitable. Soap, which can be made for 6 to 8 cents per pound, is held at 30 to 35 cents. Starch, another necessary article, commands 40 cents per pound; in fact, the supply of this article is running so short that shirt collars will have to follow a wilted cabbage leaf. For candles the poor folks have to pay 15 to 20 cents each at the corner grocery. Is it not time that some of our leading citizens should take action, and move in the establishment of manufactories for these and other articles? It requires but very little capital. If dealers in scrip, stocks and paper ever expect to confer any good on the country now is the accepted time. But we fancy, if the war should be brought to a close, many of our moneyed citizens would leave us and go Northward, or to Europe, and our good city would be a secondary thought with them.

It is asked what has forced up the price of cottonseed oil. Six or seven months ago it was selling at from 50 to 75 cents per gallon—now it is held at from $1 50 to $2 and $2 50. There is no scarcity of cotton seed in the country—in fact it is a drug where planters have ginned their cotton. Are there any solid reasons for an advance of 200 per cent., simply for the cost of transmuting the seed into oil?

We present above a minute and faithful map of the eastern shore of Virginia, the destination of an expedition which Major-Gen. DIX has dispatched from his command at Baltimore. The counties of Accomac and Northampton occupy the lower extremity of the peninsula, of which Delaware is the base, the Atlantic and Chesapeake Bay washing the two sides. The seaboard exhibits the common characteristics of the Atlantic coast, in its numerous islands of sand, with inlets and interior sounds; the principal of these being Chincoteague Island, inlet, and sound, famous for oysters, the favorites of epicures. It is from the Atlantic side of Accomac and Northampton that the Northern supplies of the bivalves are chiefly drawn. The Chesapeake shore is closely indented with bays and inlets, often the estuaries of small inland streams. From Cape Charles, the Southern extremity, to Cape Henry, the opposite gate-post of the Chesapeake waters, the distance is about fifteen miles. To Old Point Comfort it is nearly thirty.

Accomac County is only known to fame as long

THE EASTERN SHORE OF VIRGINIA.

Our Map of Accomac and Northampton Counties, the Destination of Gen. Lockwood's Expedition.

time the home of Ex-Gov. WISE, whose seat "Only, near Onancook," was the place at which his not infrequent letters, public and private, were for many years dated. The county covers some 480 square miles, principally of a sandy alluvium, naturally fertile, but sadly abused by slave cultivation. The population, which is represented to be mainly loyal to the Union, numbered in the census of last year 10,687 whites, and 4,507 slaves. Northampton County, at the southward of Accomac, with one-fourth less area than the latter county, has less than one-half the population. It numbers 2,994 whites, 3,872 slaves; the preponderance being dangerously in favor of the latter; and we discover, what is always noted where such disproportion exists, a community almost unanimously given over to treason. It is not the

practice of the insurgent Government to leave such dispositions without encouragement. Troops have therefore been sent across the bay; the inhabitants have joined them in large numbers; and, pushing into Accomac, they have found sympathy at a village, euphoniously named Pungoteague, which they have intrenched and surrounded with batteries more or less formidable.

It is to repress this this demonstration, and to afford support to the alarmed Unionists, that Gen. DIX has sent a force of about 4,000 men to occupy the peninsula. These entering the Pocomoke Sound and River, had, at the latest advices, landed at Newtown, a point just above the Maryland line, whence they will be able to advance without difficulty in pursuit of the rebels. From this point also the judicious proclamation of Gen. DIX has been promulgated, and, as we learn, with satisfactory effect.

The New-York Times.

VOL. XI....NO. 3180.   NEW-YORK, SATURDAY, NOVEMBER 30, 1861.   PRICE TWO CENTS.

THE GREAT REBELLION.

Further Reports About the Engagement at Fort Pickens.

The Navy-Yard Destroyed, and Bragg Calling for Reinforcements.

Official Announcement of the Capture of Tybee.

The Island Within Easy Mortar Distance of Fort Pulaski.

The National Flag now Flying in all the Rebel States but Two.

Important Results Accomplished by the Eastern Virginia Expedition.

CONDITION OF AFFAIRS AT WASHINGTON.

Another Reconnoissance to Fairfax Court-house.

SKIRMISHING ON THE UPPER POTOMAC.

SPECIAL DISPATCH FROM WASHINGTON.
WASHINGTON, Friday, Nov. 29.
OFFICIAL ANNOUNCEMENT OF THE CAPTURE OF PORT ROYAL.

Dispatches have been received at the Navy Department from Flag-officer DUPONT, dated Port Royal, 25th Inst., giving the gratifying intelligence that the flag of the United States is flying over the territory of the State of Georgia. Tybee Island, which he says is within easy mortar distance of Fort Pulaski, has been taken possession of, and the approaches to Savannah completely cut off. On the Island is a strong martello tower, with a battery at its base.

ONLY TWO STATES LEFT.

The National flag now floats over the soil of every seceded State except Alabama and Arkansas. In Virginia it floats over one-third of the State; in North Carolina, at Hatteras Inlet; in South Carolina, at Port Royal and a half-dozen neighboring Islands; in Georgia, on Tybee Island; in Florida, at Key West, Santa Rosa Island and other points; in Mississippi, at Ship Island; in Louisiana, at Chandeleur Island; in Texas, at El Paso; and in Tennessee, at Bristol Elizabethtown, and other points in the eastern part of the State.

RUMORS FROM FORT PICKENS.

Further Rebel Accounts of the Engagement.

No Breach Made in the Walls of the Fort.

The Navy-Yard and a Considerable Quantity of Army and Ordnance Stores Destroyed.

Pensacola Evacuated by Order of Gen. Bragg.

A LOUD CALL FOR REBEL REINFORCEMENTS

The Reported Damage to the National Vessels.

REBEL ACCOUNTS VIA NORFOLK.
Correspondence of the Philadelphia Inquirer:
FORTRESS MONROE, Wednesday, Nov. 27, P. M.

Passengers by a flag of truce from Norfolk, this morning, furnish some further particulars in regard to the fight at Fort Pickens. These particulars, it must be remembered, come through rebel sources. Gen. BRAGG had not made a breach in the fort, as was before reported.

Great excitement was prevalent throughout the South respecting the battle, but it was thought that BRAGG would be able to force Col. BROWN to surrender.

A messenger arrived from Pensacola on Sunday last, with a peremptory order for reinforcements.

Gen. BRAGG was at that time hopeful of early success, and was replying at intervals upon the fortress with great effect. His regular salvos are described as being really terrible.

The General was perfectly cool and confident. No breach had yet been made, but on Monday one would be manifest, when BRAGG expected reinforcements, and would storm with fresh troops and ordnance.

Col. BROWN had concentrated a perfect storm of hot shot and shell upon the Navy-yard, and it had been burned down, together with all of the out-buildings, and a considerable quantity of army and ordnance stores.

Pensacola had been evacuated by order of Gen. BRAGG.

Col. BROWN had called to his assistance five vessels of war, all of which had been driven off by the batteries. The steam-frigate *Niagara* was almost riddled with bullets, and the *Colorado* was thoroughly disabled.

Gen. BRAGG had declared to his troops that he would never surrender, and the greatest enthusiasm prevailed among the men.

On Tuesday, Gen. BRAGG would engage Col. BROWN in front, and land a large force on the island so as to take him in the rear.

The United States steam gunboat *Cœur de Lion*, Capt. ALEX. HAMILTON, arrived at Fortress Monroe on Wednesday, from Washington, which place she left on Sunday last, having successfully run the Potomac blockade. She had forty-two shots aimed at her, of which she received but one, doing very little harm. The *Cœur de Lion* had on board Prof. LOWE, the Government aerial navigator, and Prof. STARKWEATHER, of Boston, his assistant. Prof. STARKWEATHER goes to Port Royal, with apparatus complete, to aid Gen. SHERMAN in making reconnoissances.

On Tuesday evening a rebel flag of truce was brought to by a blank shot from the gun-boat *Gen. J. E. Wool*, and upon boarding her she was found to have on board a few letters from our poor fellows who are prisoners of war, and one gentleman with a foreign air, a consumptive cough, and a trunk full of generalities.

This gentleman said he had very urgent business in Baltimore, and would like to go up on the *Louisiana*; but Capt. DAVIS, the Provost Marshal, detained him, and then started for the headquarters of Major-General WOOL for instructions.

After Captain DAVIS had explained matters, Gen. WOOL determined to detain the man and await orders from Washington.

The "poor refugee" entered his name on the register of the hotel as "BRIAN O'HARRA, Puerto Rico, W. I."

He says the new iron British steamer *Fingal* arrived off Tybee about two weeks since from Southampton, *via* Puerto Cabello, where she had seen the rebel steamer *Sumter* often.

The *Fingal* was loaded with arms and munitions of war of the most approved pattern, some of which were being used against Fort Pickens. She ran into Beaufort in a storm, and is now at Charleston, about to be fitted for a man-of-war, and will carry a powerful battery of Whitworth rifled cannon.

The gentleman spoke in a manner to lead us to believe that he must have been either an officer or a special agent on board of the *Fingal*.

He says the Southerners have raised a great deal more grain than usual this season, and that they are not suffering for the want of anything but luxuries, which they are willing to forego for the sake of their so-called independence.

When we asked this man how he got South, he said he left New-York and went through Kentucky and when we asked how he got to Puerto Cabello he seemed confused and refused to explain.

Upon examining his trunk some valuable papers were found, the contents of which it would not be proper to publish. Some were sealed and stamped by "ROBERT BUNCH, Her Majesty's Consul at Charleston, S. C." These were directed to "His Excellency, Lord LYONS, H. B. M. Minister Plenipotentiary at Washington," &c., &c., and were carefully consigned to the care of a special agent, who will take them to Mr. SEWARD for inspection.

A LATER DISPATCH—NO NEWS.

BALTIMORE, Friday, Nov. 29.

The boat from Old Point has arrived. A flag of truce had brought down two or three ladies from Norfolk, but no news. The rebels are evidently endeavoring to keep back Southern news.

THE FORT PICKENS AFFAIR.

The news from Western Florida is still very meagre, and, being from rebel sources, is still very dubious. The rebels, however, talk a good deal less loudly of their own doings, while they are singularly reticent about ours. They had not breached the walls of Fort Pickens nor captured the Fort, but they *were* greatly excited, were calling for reinforcements, and swearing they would never *surrender* alive, while Col. BROWN had burned down the Navy-yard and the town of Warrington, and the rebels had evacuated Pensacola. This is certainly a considerable "come down" from the news of two days ago. But still it is so unsatisfactory that the public will not be contented till reliable advices arrive, and these must now be very close at hand.

We give to-day a map, more concise and definite than any that has yet been published, of the immediate scene of the action, and of the different forts, batteries and camps, both of the National forces and the rebels. The entrance of the bay, between Santa Rosa Island on the east, and the mainland on the west, is about a mile wide, but within it expands into a capacious harbor, from 4 to 10 miles in width, and entirely landlocked. Fort Pickens is on the extreme point of the long, narrow Santa Rosa, and various batteries and other works, described by us three days ago, have been erected here.

On the mainland to the west are the rebel works and rebel encampments, which have been so often described. Opposite the lower part of the island is Fort McRae, and about a half a mile to the north, and immediately in front of the entrance, (the west shore making an abrupt turn to the east,) stands Fort San Carlos de Barrancas. In rear of this fort is situated Gen. BRAXTON BRAGG's main camp. Near the fort are the lighthouse, extensive barracks and the naval hospital. About a mile above the hospital is the navy-yard, situated on Tartar Point, where the shore bends again to the north. The village of Warrenton lies immediately adjacent to the wall of the Navy-yard.

THE SCENE OF OPERATIONS IN WESTERN FLORIDA.

Map Showing Santa Rosa Island, Forts Pickens, Barrancas and McRae; Warrington, the Navy-Yard, and the Positions of the Rebel Batteries.

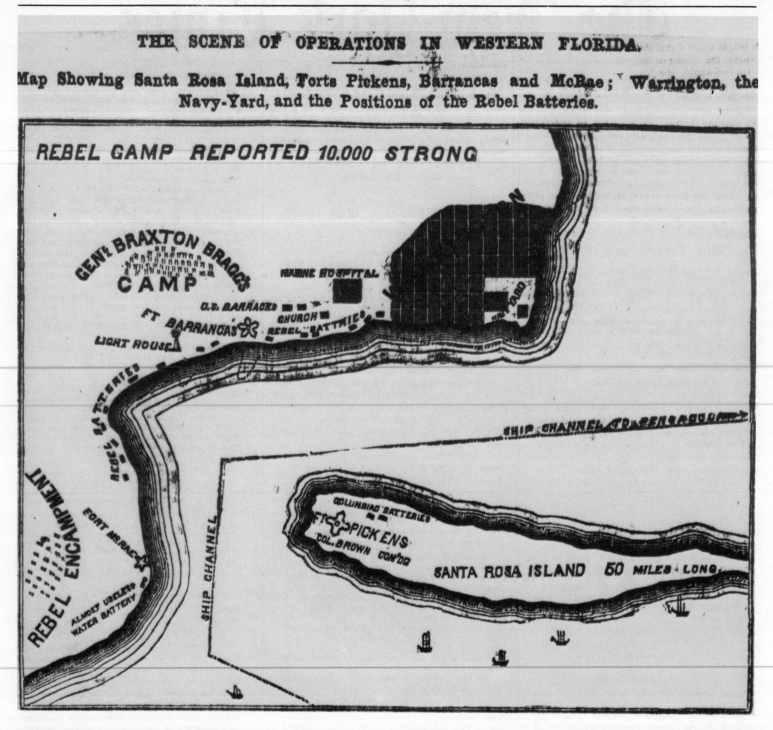

The town of Pensacola, reported as evacuated, is eight miles in a northeasterly direction from the Navy-yard, and why Gen. BRAXTON BRAGG should have ordered its evacuation, if he had positively determined to breach Fort Pickens "on Monday," it is hard to see. It appears much more likely that BRAGG anticipated the destruction of his forts and batteries by the very troops he was on the point of "forcing to surrender," and an immediate assault on Pensacola by the vessels of war which he had just "riddled with bullets." It will be seen, by the line of the ship channel to Pensacola, in our map, how close to rebel forts, and their line of shore batteries, our vessels had to run when playing on the enemy, or when making their way to the city. (The ship-channel line running westward in the map, does not of course indicate the direction in which lies Pensacola; just about the point at the tip of the arrow, the channel turns sharply up the bay to the city.)

It is hardly likely that Col. BROWN could have seized and held Pensacola or Warrington, or either of the rebel forts. His force is too small to permit him to spare a detachment for any such work as that. If he shelled out the rebels in front, kept them at bay in the rear, (from which they had been for some time preparing to attack him,) burned their army and ordnance stores, their barracks and towns, and maintained his own position, it will be a triumph sufficient-

ly great, and will, moreover, have prepared the way for the occupation of the mainland at our convenience. The whole number of National troops at Pickens, as we stated the other day, was but eleven hundred regulars and Wilson's Zouaves, while the rebels claimed to have something like ten thousand men. As to the "five vessels" which Col. BROWN called to his assistance, it is impossible to conjecture what ships they were; but it is quite likely that the frigate *Colorado*, which had just returned from a run down to the vicinity of the Balize about the time the bale opened, brought along with her some of the blockading vessels, which had been released from duty by the completion of the fortifications on Ship Island.

The whole account we take to be eminently favorable to the National arms; and if BRAGG had not bragged that he would never surrender alive, we should soon expect to see him and his men along here, to keep company with his fellow-North Carolinian and fellow-traitor, Commodore BARRON.

PENSACOLA BAY AND CITY.

Pensacola harbor is the best harbor on the Gulf of Mexico. It is completely landlocked, and has twenty-two feet of water on the bar at low tide. East Bay admits frigates of the largest class, and is entirely sheltered from all winds. The town of Pensacola, which is the principal seaport of West Flori-

da, had, a year ago, a population of about 4,000; but a great part of these fled from the ruin and terror that had overtaken the city. The houses are generally old-fashioned Spanish structures. The Alabama and Florida Railroad, which connects the town with Montgomery (Ala.,) was completed shortly after secession. That part of the road then unbuilt was finished with great haste by DAVIS' orders, so that troops and munitions might be hurried forward for the capture of Fort Pickens. Although that is nine months ago, however, Pickens is as yet uncaptured—nor, we judge by the latest news, is it likely soon to be captured. The climate is exceedingly healthful, except for occasional and rare visitations of yellow fever. The creole element predominates in the resident population. In 1814, Gen. JACKSON drove out the British, who had established themselves there by permission of the Spaniards, and assaulted and took the city and adjacent forts. Again in 1818, Gen. JACKSON, in consequence of Indian incursions on United States territory, took possession of Pensacola, and obliged Fort Barrancas, to which the Spanish Governor had retired, to capitulate. In 1821, the whole territory was ceded to the United States. We hope it will turn out that Col. BROWN is no unworthy successor of Gen. JACKSON.

The New-York Times.

VOL. XI....NO. 3192.   NEW-YORK, SATURDAY, DECEMBER 14, 1861.   PRICE TWO CENTS.

IMPORTANT FROM THE WEST.

Preparations for a Great Battle in Kentucky.

Expected Collision Between Schoepf and Zollicoffer.

Gen. Buell's Army Moving Forward to Green River.

Sixty Thousand National Troops on the Line between Louisville and Nashville.

TROOPS STILL POURING INTO KENTUCKY

A Simultaneous Movement at all Important Points Expected.

POSITION OF THE OPPOSING FORCES.

REPORTS FROM CINCINNATI.

CINCINNATI, Friday, Dec. 13.

The Frankfort (Ky.) *Gazette* has a dispatch, which says that when the stage left Somerset, at 11 o'clock, on Wednesday, there had been no fighting.

The Postmaster wrote as follows:

"We are expecting to fight hourly. The enemy are close upon us, with a force estimated at from 8,000 to 15,000 men. Our force is about 5,000 effective men. Both citizens and soldiers complain of Gen. THOMAS for not having sent reinforcements to Gen. SCHOEPF."

As it cannot interfere with the plans laid down, it is not improper to state that the plans of Gen. BUELL was that Gen. THOMAS should get in the rear of Gen. ZOLLICOFFER.

Letters to-night express apprehensions about the result, should Gen. ZOLLICOFFER force Gen. SCHOEPF to an engagement before Gen. THOMAS arrives.

An officer arrived from London this evening says that the rumor there was that after some picket fighting Gen. ZOLLICOFFER began to retreat again. If this should prove true Gen. THOMAS will not be in time to intercept him.

Troops continue pouring into Louisville. Four regiments passed through yesterday.

The *Commercial* of this city has a dispatch which says: "The Paymaster from London reports that Gen. CRITTENDEN is at Cumberland Gap with fifteen hundred men and a large force in the vicinity."

A letter to the Representative from Wayne County says that Major HALVETI, and three others captured with him by the rebels, were killed after their capture.

All the leading men have been driven from Owensville, Bath County, and the town is in possession of 400 rebels, who are committing the greatest excesses.

The Louisville *Journal* of yesterday, says that all Indiana regiments which have a minimum number of men, have been ordered into Kentucky. This order will throw from nine to ten thousand troops into Kentucky during this and the coming week.

Gen. ROSECRANS arrived at Cincinnati the day before yesterday. A public reception was given him at the hall of the Catholic Institute last night.

FORWARD MOVEMENT OF THE NATIONAL FORCES.

From the Cincinnati Commercial, Dec. 11.

A dispatch from Louisville last night informs us that Gen. BUELL's army (which, on the direct Louisville and Nashville line, is not less than sixty thousand strong) is moving forward to Green River.

IMPORTANT FROM REBELDOM.

A Renewal of the Fight at Fort Pickens Anticipated.

AN EXPECTED ATTACK ON NORFOLK.

Arrest of Slaves on their Way North.

The Late Destruction of Property Near Port Royal.

Excitement Relative to Drafting in Tennessee.

Gov. Harris Driven from Nashville to Memphis.

THE CONDITION OF LOUISIANA

COMMERCIAL AND FINANCIAL INDICATIONS.

NEWS BY WAY OF FORTRESS MONROE

FORTRESS MONROE, Thursday, Dec. 12, *via* BALTIMORE, Friday, Dec. 13.

A flag of truce left here this morning for Norfolk, in charge of Capt. MILWARD, with a large quantity of letters and express matter for the South. The boat returned with passengers from Richmond, who are British subjects, and two from Norfolk.

The Norfolk *Day Book* has dates from Pensacola to Dec. 2. There had been no further fighting, but Gen. BRAGG hourly anticipated a renewal of the attack from Fort Pickens. The National vessels were flitting in and out of the harbor in the most bewildering manner to the rebels. Sometimes there would be a dozen in the evening, and all but two disappear before morning.

The Montgomery *Mail*, of the old inst., congratulates its readers on the report that old HARVEY BROWN has died of a wound received in the late fight at Fort Pickens. Passengers up from that city this morning, say that the report is firmly believed, but not positively known to be true.

The *Day Book* of Thursday was considerably excited in relation to a rumor that Norfolk is to be attacked. It suggests that additional obstructions, be placed at the entrance of the harbor, and if not done by the military authorities, urges that the City Councils take it in hand.

The Norfolk *Day Book* speaks of an important arrest there of a number of slaves in the act of making their escape to the North. They had with them fifteen hundred dollars in stolen money. An examination of their case was had before the Mayor, but for prudential reasons the report of it is withheld.

The Richmond *Dispatch*, of Wednesday, contains the following mail items:

The Charleston *Courier*, of the 9th, says that on Wednesday a detachment of the Beaufort Artillery, 22 men, passed over to the island and visited Beaufort, where the utter desolation and abandonment were relieved only by the presence of one light and a barking dog.

There were no signs of the enemy, either on land or water. Our men then proceeded to the work of destruction. The chief object was to destroy the crops of cotton and provisions on Paris Island, which being near the enemy, was crowded with negroes, who had flocked there to escape from the control of their owners. Owing to the want of boats, this object was but partially effected. Seven hundred bales of cotton, and seven hundred bushels of corn, were burnt on Dr. THOMAS FULLER's plantation. Returning to Battery Plantation, the work of destruction was resumed. The torch was successively applied to the cotton of twelve other plantations, and the contents of five barns were emptied and consumed. Seventeen crops, amounting to nearly four thousand bales, were thus effectively removed from the fangs of the destroyer.

The *Courier* says that the English steam ship-of-war *Racer* arrived off Charleston harbor on Friday, and brought dispatches to the British Consul. The *Racer* left next day for Port Royal.

The *Courier*, of the 9th, says: "On Friday last, there were in sight near this harbor the steamship *Susquehanna*, two side-wheel gunboats, a store ship, a large schooner, supposed to be laden with coal, and the Swedish bark *Winona*. We hear that this last vessel was bound to this port, supposing there was no blockade, which want of information will be unfortunate for her owners, as she will no doubt be seized."

THE ESCAPE OF THE SUMTER.

Serious Charge Against the Commander of the Gunboat Iroquois.

The brig *Thomas W. Rowland*, Capt. ROWLAND, from Rio Janeiro *via* St. Thomas, Nov. 27, arrived at this port on Thursday night.

Capt. ROWLAND states that the Captain of the United States gunboat *Iroquois* is entirely and alone to blame for the escape of the *Sumter* from Port Royal, Martinique. The captain of the gunboat sent a man on shore at Port Royal with signal lights, and gave him instructions to signalise to him the movements of the *Sumter*, and on the night of the 23d of November, signals were made by the man on shore that she was leaving the harbor, but no notice was taken of it by the Captain of the *Iroquois*. His first Lieutenant tried to persuade him to give chase, which they could easily have done, as the *Sumter* drew one foot more water than the *Iroquois* did, but he would not comply, saying it would be very unpleasant for him to capture her, as he and Capt. SEMMES had been schoolmates, and had sailed together, and Capt. SEMMES had been his superior officer; and another reason was that he did not want to break the neutrality laws. The movements of the *Sumter* were seen from the deck of the *Iroquois*, she (the *Sumter*) taking a southerly course, when the captain of the *Iroquois* gave orders to proceed to St. Thomas, not making the least effort to capture the privateer, although he had been lying off the port several days for that purpose. On these facts becoming known at St. Thomas, the greatest indignation prevailed among the Americans in port, and all others friendly to the United States.

RUMORS ABOUT THE REBEL COMMISSIONERS.

HALIFAX, Friday, Dec. 13.

It has been strongly reported here to-day that Messrs. BRECKINRIDGE and HUNTER applied for passage by the *Canada*, but were refused, in consequence of a telegram from Secretary CAMERON, warning the agents of the Cunard line against conveying rebels. Mr. CUNARD emphatically contradicts the report.

DOWN THE MISSISSIPPI.

FROM CAIRO TO MEMPHIS.

One of the boats of the great naval river expedition, now nearly ready at Cairo, has a flag-staff erected on its upper deck, from the top of which floats the American flag, while on the bottom is nailed a sign, "For Memphis and New-Orleans." The impression generally prevails in our Western Army, as well as among the river rebels, that the grand flotilla will shortly cut its moorings at Cairo, and start on this perilous voyage down the Mississippi among the innumerable river batteries and river rebels—flanked on the land sides by fifty or a hundred thousand Union soldiers. Whether the belief is correct that it will certainly go down the Mississippi, in preference to any of the other streams in the vicinity, a short time now will tell. But the fact that we have a choice of navigable rivers near by, which penetrate into the very heart of the South, may well keep the rebels in a terrible state of perturbation as to where the blow *will* be struck. For fear it *should* start down the Mississippi one of these fine Winter mornings, however, we give a map of the course and windings of that river, from Cairo to Memphis, indicating also the towns, forts, and other natural and artificial points of defence between these two places.

THE NAVAL FORCE.

Cairo at present presents as much the appearance of a marine town as it does of a military post. Naval uniforms, jolly jack tars, jaunty young officers, naval supplies, iron-clad gunboats, and all the paraphernalia of "life on the river wave," now give a novel appearance and furnish a new phase of life to that marshy, muddy and unhealthy, but all-important military and naval strategical point. At the latest advices, the last gunboat for the fleet, building at St. Louis, had left for Cairo, and the mortar-floats, &c., building at other points, were leaving for the point of rendezvous daily. The dispatch with which these boats have been built and equipped exceeds anything in our naval history. Some of them are already in fighting condition—the guns lashed, ammunition taken aboard, machinery adjusted, and men and officers all aboard; and it looks as if it could not be long before the whole thing was under way—for somewhere.

The expedition will consist of a fleet of eleven gunboats, 38 floating batteries, and 28 river steamers. There are now over two hundred pieces of cannon of the heaviest calibre, at Cairo, ready to be mounted on them.

Rear Admiral Andrew H. Foote was the flag officer of the Union naval campaign advancing down Mississippi River.

THE MISSISSIPPI, FROM CAIRO TO MEMPHIS.

1862

The New-York Times.

VOL. XI....NO. 3223.   NEW-YORK, TUESDAY, JANUARY 21, 1862.   PRICE TWO CENTS.

GLORIOUS NEWS.

A Great National Victory in Kentucky.

Zollicoffer's Army Twice Defeated and Routed.

DEATH OF ZOLLICOFFER.

Attack on Gen. Schoepf at Somerset.

A Battle Lasting from Daylight until 3 o'clock P. M.

The Rebels Utterly Routed and Driven Back to Their Intrenchments.

Combined Attack upon Them by Generals Schoepf and Thomas.

THE ROUT RENDERED COMPLETE.

Capture of All the Rebel Cannon. Quartermaster's Stores, Tents, &c.

The National Flag Flying Over "Zollicoffer's Den."

HEAVY LOSS OF LIFE ON BOTH SIDES.

THE BATTLE AT SOMERSET.

CINCINNATI, Monday, Jan. 20.

A battle took place at Somerset, Ky., on Saturday, between Gen. SCHOEPF's and Gen. ZOLLICOFFER's forces.

The battle lasted from early in the morning till dark.

Gen. ZOLLICOFFER was killed and his army entirely defeated.

The loss is very heavy on both sides.

A CONFIRMATION FROM LOUISVILLE.

LOUISVILLE, Ky., Monday, Jan. 20.

Gen. THOMAS telegraphs to headquarters that on Friday night, Gen. ZOLLICOFFER came up to his encampment, and attacked him at 6 o'clock on Saturday morning, near Webb's Roads, in the vicinity of Somerset.

At 3 o'clock on Saturday afternoon Gen. ZOLLICOFFER and BAILIE PEYTON had been killed, and the rebels were in full retreat to their intrenchments at Mill Springs, with the National troops in hot pursuit.

No further particulars have been received in regard to the losses on either side.

Confederate Brigadier-General Felix K. Zollicoffer was killed as Federal forces solidified their hold on Kentucky.

THE SECOND BATTLE, ON SUNDAY.

LOUISVILLE, Monday, Jan. 20.

Gen. THOMAS, on Sunday afternoon, followed up the rebels to their intrenchments, 16 miles from his own camp, and when about to attack them, this morning, he found their intrenchments deserted, the rebels having left all their cannon, quartermaster's stores, tents, horses and wagons, which fell into our hands. The rebels, dispersing, had crossed the Cumberland in a steamboat and nine barges at White Oak Creek, opposite their encampment at Mill Springs. Two hundred and seventy-five rebels were killed and wounded, including Gen. ZOLLICOFFER and BAILIE PEYTON dead, who were found on the field. The Tenth Indiana lost seventy-five killed and wounded. Nothing further of the National loss has yet reached here.

THE STARS AND STRIPES FLOATING OVER THE REBEL FORTIFICATIONS.
THE DEATH OF GEN. ZOLLICOFFER CONFIRMED.

CINCINNATI, Monday, Jan. 20.

A combined attack was made, to-day, (Sunday,) on Gen. ZOLLICOFFER's intrenchments at Mill Springs, Wayne County, Ky., resulting in a complete victory. The Stars and Stripes now float over the fortifications. We captured all their camp property and a large number of prisoners. Our loss is heavy. Gen. ZOLLICOFFER's dead body is in the hands of the Nationals.

DETAILS OF RESULTS ACHIEVED.

CINCINNATI, Monday, Jan. 20.

A Lexington correspondent of the *Commerical* gives the following account of Saturday's battle:

Gen. ZOLLICOFFER, learning that the National force had appeared in his rear, marched out of his intrenchments at 3 o'clock Saturday morning, and attacked Gen. SCHOEPF in camp. The pickets were driven in at an early hour, and the attack was made before daylight. The battle is reported to have raged with great fury until 3 in the afternoon, when Gen. ZOLLICOFFER, having been killed, the whole force of rebels fled in confusion to their camp. The loss is not stated, but is thought to be heavy. The BAILIE PEYTON killed is a son of the ex-member of Congress from Tennessee of that name. Our victory has been very decisive, and will result in a rout of the whole force defending the right flank of Bowling Green.

THE NEWS IN WASHINGTON.

WASHINGTON, Monday, Jan. 20.

The news from Kentucky causes intense delight. It is everywhere credited. No official confirmation, however, has been received up to 9 o'clock to-night.

One o'clock, A. M., 21st.—The Government, this morning, received official intelligence of the victory in Kentucky similar to that previously received by the Press.

THE LOCATION OF THE BATTLE.

We have more good news this morning from Eastern Kentucky. Our last advices from that quarter, a week ago, announced the rout of HUMPHREY MARSHALL; to-day we chronicle an action and a victory of far greater importance.

The column of Gen. THOMAS, when he left Columbia to move forward, consisted of 15,000 well-appointed men. They were nearly all Western troops—mostly from Ohio, Indiana and Kentucky. In Gen. SCHOEPF's Brigade were the two famous regiments of East Tennessee, who have been burning for a fight with their enemies and persecutors for nearly half a year.

This victory opens the way for our gallant army of the West to penetrate into East Tennessee, through Cumberland Gap; [See map;] and if promptly followed up to the capture of the Virginia and East Tennessee Railroad, will *compel the rebels to evacuate Bowling Green, and will compel Beauregard to retire from Manassas.* The position of the different points mentioned, and their relation to Cumberland Gap and the Tennessee and Virginia Railroad, to Knoxville, Nashville, Bowling Green and Columbus, and to our main body at Munfordsville, will all be found on our map. The rebels propose to make the Ohio River the boundary line of their bloody despotism, but they are rapidly retreating from that line.

IMPORTANT FROM CAIRO.

The Late Movement Down the River Explained—A Reconnoissance in Force—Evacuation of Camp Beauregard by the Rebels, &c.

CHICAGO, Monday, Jan. 20.

A special from Cairo to the *Journal* says that Gen. GRANT and Staff arrived in town yesterday morning. Gen. PAINE's Brigade reached Fort Jefferson on Saturday night. Gen. McCLERNAND's Brigade will arrive to-morrow. The object of the expedition was a reconnoissance in force of all that part of Kentucky upon which portion operations against Columbus will necessarily be performed, and a demonstration to aid Gen. BUELL's right wing, our forces have been eminently successful—the Engineer Corps, under Gen. WEBSTER, having a full and accurate knowledge of the country.

It is understood that Gen. SMITH has taken the camp equipage and whatever was left in Camp Beauregard, and the rebels fled to Columbus. Gen McCLERNAND's Brigade went to within seven miles of Columbus, and encamped Thursday night in sight of the rebel watch-fires. They afterwards visited the towns of Milburne, Lovelaceville, Blandville, surveying all the roads as they went. Part of Gen. SMITH's command will return to Paducah to-day.

The New-York Times.

VOL. XI—NO. 3228. NEW-YORK, MONDAY, JANUARY 27, 1862. PRICE TWO CENTS.

THREE DAYS LATER FROM EUROPE.

ARRIVAL OF THE EUROPA AT HALIFAX.

How the Rendition of Mason and Slidell was Received.

Mr. Seward's Dispatch Perfectly Satisfactory.

Insulting Tone of the British Press Toward the Rebel Commissioners.

The British Government would Have Done as Much for Two Negroes.

Further Denunciation of the Stone Blockade.

The Nashville Still Watched by the Tuscarora.

THE SUMTER EXPECTED AT SOUTHAMPTON

Commercial and Money Affairs.

HALIFAX, Sunday, Jan. 26.

The R. M. steamship *Europa*, Capt. ANDERSON, from Liverpool at 3 P. M. of the 11th, and Queenstown on the 12th, arrived here at 10½ o'clock last night. The wind was then and is still blowing a hurricane, with a heavy sea.

The *Europa* has neither troops nor stores, the Government having discontinued shipments by the Cunarders.

The *Europa* has 18 passengers for Boston, £6,500 for Boston and £64,000 for Halifax.

THE TRENT AFFAIR.

It was said that notwithstanding the pacific solution of the American question, warlike preparations at Woolwich have not been relaxed. The steamers *Spartan* and *Ajax* continued to take in heavy stores for Halifax and Jamaica.

No official notice had yet been given at Portsmouth respecting any discharge of hired mechanics or laborers, but it was understood that the reduction takes place in April.

A Cabinet council, summoned for the 14th, had been countermanced, Mr. SEWARD's dispatch having been considered in a council held on the 9th.

The *Times* understands that an answer will be returned, expressing gratification at the disavowal of Commodore WILKES' act, accepting the satisfaction rendered, and assuming that the precedent in the *Trent* case will rule the case of the schooner *Eugenia Smith*. As to the general discussion of the law of neutrals, the Government will decline any answer until they have had an opportunity of submitting the whole note to their law officers. There are propositions in this note which are not at all admissible, and after the de-

Lord Palmerston, the British Prime Minister, was incensed over the American seizure of Confederate envoys off the English Steamer Trent.

livery of the prisoners these points may be properly raised and discussed.

The *Morning Post* announces that a thorough understanding had been arrived at with the American Government. Not only had they given the required reparation, but in doing so Mr. SEWARD will have succeeded in impressing on the English Government the notion that they have not only present indemnity, but also no small pledge of future security.

The *Times* says rumor fixes England's expenses, owing to the late difficulty, at £2,000,000 ; but the *Times* expects that when all the bills are in, it will be double that sum, and that the money has not been thrown away.

The *Daily News* is eulogistic of the course pursued by the Washington Government, and bitterly denounces the policy of the *Times* and *Post*.

The *Times* has a strong editorial on the reception due to MASON and SLIDELL; says they are *about the most worthless booty it would be possible to extract from the jaws of the American lion*—having long been known as blind and habitual haters and revilers of England.

The *Times* sincerely hopes that Englishmen will not give these fellows anything in the shape of an ovation. The civility due to a foe in distress is all they can claim. England has returned them good for evil; and even now, if they can, they will only entangle her in a war with the North. *England would have done just as much to rescue two negroes.* Let MASON and SLIDELL, therefore, pass quietly on their way, and have their say with anybody who may have to listen to them.

The other journals advise a similar course, and allude to MASON's strong advocacy of the Fugitive Slave law, to prejudice the public against him.

THE STONE BLOCKADE.

The *Times* reiterates its denunciation of the stone blockade of Charleston harbor, and says among the crimes which have disgraced the history of mankind it is difficult to find one more atrocious than this. Even the fierce tribes of the desert will not destroy the well which gives life to the enemy.

The *Times* protests in the strongest terms against

such proceedings, and asserts that no belligerent has the right to resort to such a warfare.

THE TUSCARORA AND NASHVILLE.

Great interest had been excited relative to the movements of the *Tuscarora* and *Nashville*. At the latest dates they continued at Southampton, watching each other. The *Tuscarora* remained at her anchorage, about a mile from the dock mouth, with her fires banked up and ready to slip her anchor and start at a moment's notice. She only required coals, water and provisions, which were being supplied her. On her arrival Capt. CRAVEN communicated with the captain of the frigate *Dauntless*, expressing regret at Prince ALBERT's death, and asking if he might fire, as a tribute of respect, twenty-one minute guns. He was notified that the Queen had requested that no guns be fired in the vicinity of Osborne. The compliment, therefore, although fully appreciated, could not be accepted.

The *Nashville* continued in dock. The Government had observed the strictest neutrality towards her, and nothing whatever had been permitted to be done to her but what was absolutely necessary to make her seaworthy. Neither powder, guns, nor munitions of war had been put on board. During the night of the 9th, three armed men from the *Tuscarora* were discovered reconnoitering the *Nashville*, and were ordered off by the dock superintendent. Fires were lighted on the *Nashville* on the 10th, and there was an impression she was about to sail, but she made no movements. The *Tuscarora* was on the alert with steam up.

The *Sumter* was reported to have left Cadiz for Southampton.

It was also reported that another National vessel was cruising in the channel, and might be expected at Southampton.

The *Morning Herald* is surprised that the Government has not given orders to the authorities at Southampton to warn the *Tuscarora* that she must either quit port at once, or wait until twenty-four hours have elapsed after the departure of the *Nashville*. We should not, says the *Herald*, have allowed the *Nashville* to lie in wait within the mouth of the Mersey for American packets and merchantmen. Therefore, we cannot, without a gross violation of our duty as neutrals, allow the *Tuscarora* a license we should have refused her enemy. The *Herald* holds out the course

British Foreign Secretary Earl Russell protested strongly to the American government, demanding an apology from Secretary of State Seward.

of the French authorities at Martinique between the *Iroquois* and *Sumter* as an example to follow.

GENERAL ENGLISH NEWS.

Dr. RUSSELL, in his correspondence to the *Times*, predicts the fate of the American Government will be sealed if January passes without some great victory.

McLARIN, mate of the American ship *Ganges*, had been committed for trial in London, for murdering one of the crew at sea.

The London Money market on the 10th opened firm, but toward the close showed some slight reaction, Consols closing at ½ decline, attributed solely to realizations after the advance.

The market on the 11th was dull but steady.

Since the reduction of the Bank *minimum* of Thursday, to 2½ per cent., money has been pretty plentiful in the open market, at 2½ per cent, for the best bills and was offered on the Stock Exchange at 1 per cent'

There had been a considerable advance in Salt, petre, under the idea that the export prohibition would soon be removed.

WAS IT THE SUMTER?

The Montreal *Advertiser*, which is in the interest of the rebels, and has manifested an accurate knowledge of their affairs, makes the following statement concerning the rebel privateer at Cadiz:

" The Confederate privateer, or rather public armed ship, which has been playing the mischief with American ships off Cadiz, is not the *Sumter*, which is yet on her old beat ; but one of the new vessels for which the *Nashville* took officers to Europe. Her name and that of her consorts will be known soon enough ; in the meantime there will be weeping and wailing among the underwriters of Federal war risks."

Editorial

The End of the Trent Affair— England Satisfied.

The news received this morning from Europe sets all doubt at rest as to the reception encountered by the surrender of MASON and SLIDELL. The London Journals—the extracts furnished by the telegraph are unfortunately drawn exclusively from those of the most belligerent antecedents—accept the dispatch of Mr. SEWARD and the rendition of the two rebels, as a full satisfaction of the British demand, and as a restoration of the tarnished lustre of the British crown. It is conceded that the act of the American Government was at once graceful and consistent. Of that spirit of bravado, and disposition to represent

cowardice as the motive at the back of our conciliatory temper, which there was too much reason to apprehend from journals so malignant as the London *Post* and *Herald*, we have no evidences whatever. The absence of these offensive traits may be merely due to the meagreness of the telegraphic summary. But we are disposed to think otherwise, and to believe that the *amende* of America has been as frankly received as it was frankly offered. It is, indeed, significant of the real direction of public opinion that the Press bespeaks anything but a welcome for the restored Commissioners. They are stigmatized as a brace of conspirators who have been balked in an attempt to embroil England in war; and who are entitled to no more respectful consideration than a pair of negroes fortuitously extricated by diplomacy from the clutches of a slave-catcher. In this curt dismissal of the candidates for a British ovation, the South will find little prospect of instant recognition and alliance.

And thus the accident of the *Trent* loses its character of a *casus belli*. There will be a further discussion of the questions of international law it has raised. The points presented in the dispatch of Mr. SEWARD have already been submitted to the law officers of the Crown. They will be the topic of interesting negotiations, to which, not only England and the United States, but all the maritime States of Euope will be parties, and all pledged to the support of the doctrines so long sustained singly by this Government; and there is little doubt that England will have to yield much that she declined to concede in 1856. A semi-official organ of the Russian Government announces the intention of the Emperor to lend the weight of Russian diplomacy to the advocacy of the American positions. But these discussions have no practical bearing on the contest which is our immediate occupation as a people. It must take its place in that long category of deferred business to be adjusted at the end of the war.

But while a threatening issue has been laid to rest, there is an ominous readiness on the part of the London *Times* and the *Moniteur* to raise other questions, which, without being strictly international, may lead to complications, involving results only less hazardous than the one just settled. The blockade is the most important weapon we possess in the task of subduing this rebellion. By energy almost superhuman we have made it little less than perfect; and have studiously avoided in the effort to this end, the employment of any means not fully authorized by historical precedent. The single port of Charleston has been made an exception to this punctiliousness. Its various and difficult channels defied the vigilance of our cruisers. Vessels, large and small, were constantly passing between Charleston and Nassau or Havana; and a squadron of coast-guarding steamers was insufficient to stop this traffic. The Government thought proper to solve the difficulty by closing the larger channels leading to Charleston, with a stone blockade; taking the step in that particular case the more readily because Charleston had no claim to exemption from the weightiest punishment an outraged nation could inflict; and because it had preceded the measure by opening to the commerce of mankind the harbor of Beaufort, a port superior in convenience, accessibility and health, to the one to be closed. These reasons may be insuf-

ficient to justify such extreme rigor; they certainly palliate it; and when we remember how noisily the rebel agents in Europe proclaimed the folly and impotence of the attempt thus to close a harbor, when the obstructions would only lead to the formation of other and equally commodious passages through the shifting sands of the bar, we can well understand that the criticisms of the French and English semi-official journals are not prompted by any amicable temper. They indicate, in fact, a shrewish disposition to find a flaw in the blockade, which may justify them in disregarding it altogether.

The premonition of such a tendency points us our duty. We are warned that the two leading Powers of Europe only suspend their design to intervene in our quarrel until they find occasion for intervention. Our inability to end the war within a year from its commencement, will be the occasion; anything, even the hypocritical lamentation over the stone blockade, will serve as a pretext. The civil war must be ended, or enlarge into a foreign war of unmanageable proportions. If the plans by which Gen. MCCLELLAN proposes to subdue the rebellion can be realized at once, this added danger will be averted. The matter is entirely in our own hands. The same blow that strikes the insurrection to the earth, will rivet our pacific relations with every Power in Christendom. The true peacemaker is a victory.

THE BATTLE AT MILL CREEK.—The earliest detailed accounts of the engagement at Mill Creek, in Kentucky, are laid before our readers in other columns. The *Herald*, with characteristic enterprise, anticipated the arrival of mail and express by publishing in its Saturday issue, a letter from Kentucky, curiously uniform in tone and matter and volume with the scattered telegraphic reports previously received. We have only to say, no genuine descriptive report of the battle could have reached this City before yesterday; a fact that sufficiently demonstrates the character of the *Herald's* enterprize.

Lord Lyons delayed giving Seward the ultimatum, giving the U.S. time to save face.

The New-York Times.

VOL. XI....NO. 3239.　　　NEW-YORK, SATURDAY, FEBRUARY 8, 1862.　　　PRICE TWO CENTS.

ANOTHER GREAT VICTORY.

The Capture of Fort Henry on the Tennessee River.

THE WAR CARRIED INTO TENNESSEE.

Official Dispatches from Gen. Halleck and Commodore Foote.

The Battle Fought Entirely by the Gunboats.

Desperate Resistance of the Rebels under Command of Gen. Tilghman.

The Rebel Commander and a Large Number of Officers and Men Captured.

Panic and Flight of Four Thousand Rebel Infantry.

EVERYTHING LEFT BEHIND THEM.

The Gunboat Essex Disabled by a Shot Through Her Boiler.

Immense Strategic Importance of the Victory.

DISPATCH FROM MAJ.-GEN. HALLECK.

ST. LOUIS, Friday, Feb. 7.

The following is announced from Headquarters

Fort Henry is ours! The flag of the Union is re-established on the soil of Tennessee. It will never be removed.

By command of Maj.-Gen. HALLECK.

W. W. SMITH,

Captain and Ai...le-Camp.

DISPATCH FROM FLAG OFFICER FOOTE.

WASHINGTON, Friday, Feb. 7.

Secretary WELLES has received the following dispatch:

U. S. FLAG SHIP CINCINNATI, off FORT HENRY, TENNESSEE RIVER, Feb. 6, 1862.

The gunboats under my command, the *Essex*, commander PORTER; the *Carondelet*, Commander WALKER; the *Cincinnati*, Commander STEMDEL; the *St. Louis*, Lieut.-Commanding PAULDING; the *Conestoga*, Lieut.-Commanding PHELPS; the *Taylor*, Lieut.-Commanding GWINN, and the *Lexington*, Lieut.-Commanding SHIRK, after a severe and rapid fire of one hour and a quarter, have captured Fort Henry, and have taken Gen. LLOYD TILGHMAN and his Staff, with sixty men, as prisoners.

THE SCENE OF OUR NAVAL VICTORY IN NORTHERN TENNESSEE.

Diagram Showing the Location of Fort Henry and its Guns, together with its Relations to Fort Donelson, the Nashville and Memphis Railroad, and Other Important Points.

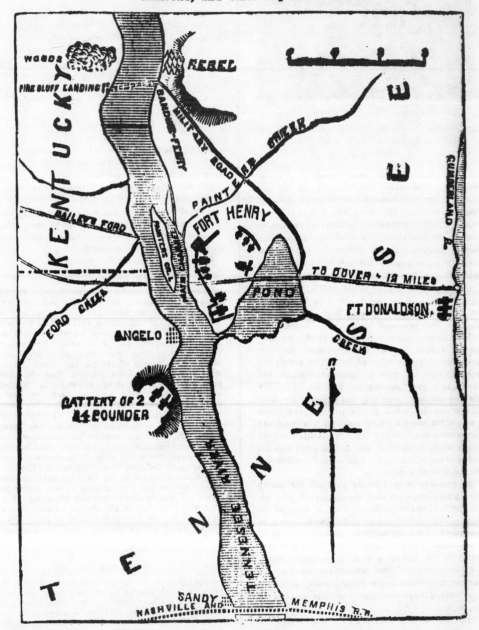

The surrender to the gunboats was unconditional, as we kept an open fire upon the enemy until their flag was struck.

In half an hour after the surrender, I handed the fort and prisoners over to Gen. GRANT, commanding the army, on his arrival at the fort in force.

The *Essex* had a shot in her boilers, after fighting most effectually for two-thirds of the action, and was obliged to drop down the river. I hear that several of her men were scalded to death, including the two pilots.

She, with the other gunboats, officers and men fought with the greatest gallantry.

The *Cincinnati* received thirty-one shots, and had one killed and eight wounded, two seriously.

The fort, with twenty guns and seventeen mortars,

was defended by Gen. TILGHMAN with the most determined gallantry.

I will write as soon as possible.

I have sent Lieut.-Commanding PHILLIPS and three gunboats after the rebel gunboats.

(Signed,)　　　A. H. FOOTE, Flag-Officer.

DETAILS FROM CINCINNATI.

CINCINNATI, Friday, Feb. 7.

The *Gazette* and *Commercial's* Cairo correspondence give the following account of the bombardment and capture of Fort Henry:

Yesterday at 12½ P. M., the gunboats *Cincinnati*, *St. Louis*, *Caroudelet*, and *Essex*, the *Tyler*, *Conestoga*, and *Lexington*, bringing up the rear, advanced boldly against the rebel works, going

59

Commodore W. D. Porter was scalded by an exploding boiler caused by a bullet. Others were scalded to death.

to the right of Painter Creek Island, [see TIMES' diagram,] immediately above where, on the east shore of the river stands the fortifications, and keeping out of range till at the head of the island, and within a mile of the enemy, passing the island in full view of the rebel guns. We steadily advanced, every man at quarters, every ear strained to catch the Flag-Officer's signal-gun for the commencement of the action. Our line of battle was on the left, the *St. Louis* next, the *Carondelet* next, the *Cincinnati* (for the time being the Flag-ship, having on board Flag-Officer FOOTE,) and the next the *Essex*. We advanced in line, (the *Cincinnati* a boat's length ahead, when at 11:30, the *Cincinnati* opened the ball, and immediately the three accompanying boats followed suit. The enemy was not backward, and gave an admirable response, and the fight raged furiously for half an hour. We steadily advanced, receiving and returning the storm of shot and shell, when getting within three hundred yards of the enemy's works we came to a stand, and poured into him right and left. In the meantime the *Essex* had been disabled, and drifted away from the scene of action, leaving the *Cincinnati, Carondelet* and *St. Louis* alone engaged.

At precisely forty minutes past one, the enemy struck his colors—and such cheering, such wild excitement, as seized the throats, arms, or caps, of the four or five hundred sailors of the gunboats can be imagined. After the surrender, which was made to Flag-officer FOOTE by Gen. LLOYD TILGHMAN, who defended the fort in a most determined manner, we found that the rebel infantry encamped outside the fort, numbering four or five thousand, had cut and run, leaving the rebel artillery company in command of the fort.

The fort mounted seventeen guns, most of them 32-pounders, one being a magnificent 10-inch columbiad. Our shots dismounted two of their guns, driving the enemy into the embrasures. One of their rifled 32-pounders burst during the engagement, wounding some of their gunners. The rebels claimed to have but eleven effective guns worked by fifty-four men—the number all told of our prisoners. They lost five killed and ten badly wounded. The infantry left everything in their flight. A vast deal of plunder has fallen into our hands, including a large and valuable quantity of ordnance stores.

Gen. TILGHMAN is disheartened. He thinks it one of the most damaging blows of the war. In surrendering to Flag-Officer FOOTE the rebel General remarked, "I am glad to surrender to so gallant an officer." Flag-Officer FOOTE replied, "You do perfectly right, Sir, in surrendering, but you should have

blown my boat out of the water before I would have surrendered to you."

In the engagement the *Cincinnati* was in the lead, and flying the Flag-officer's pennant, was the chief mark-Flag-Officer FOOTE and Capt. STEMBEL crowded her defiantly into the teeth of the enemy's guns. She got thirty-one shots, some of them going completely through her.

The *Essex* was badly crippled when about half through the fight and crowding steadily against the enemy. A ball went into her side-forward port through the heavy bulkhead and squarely through one of her boilers, the escaping steam scalding and killing several of the crew.

Capt. PORTER, his Aid, L. P. BRITTON, Jr., and Paymaster LEWIS, were standing in a direct line of the balls passing, Mr. BRITTON being in the centre of the group. A shot struck Mr. BRITTON in the top of his head, scattering his brains in every direction. The escaping steam went into the pilot-house, instantly killing Messrs. FORD and BRIDE, pilots. Many of the soldiers, at the rush of steam, jumped overboard and were drowned.

REPORTS FROM LOUISVILLE.

LOUISVILLE, Friday, Feb. 7.

Three large steamers—*Benjamin J. Adams, E. H. Fairchild* and *Baltic*—left here for the Cumberland and Tennessee Rivers this evening.

All quiet along the line of the Louisville and Nashville Railroad.

A dispatch from Gen. HALLECK to Gen. BUELL, this evening, says: "We have taken Fort Henry. The enemy has retreated on Paris, leaving part of his guns. Our cavalry are in pursuit.

Gen. GRANT will attack Fort Donelson to-morrow.

COMMODORE FOOTE.

Commodore ANDREW H. FOOTE, who so gallantly led the gunboats in the action at Fort Henry, is a native of Connecticut, and entered the service from that State in 1822. Since that time he has been continually in service, making the whole time of his naval career extend over forty years. He is still, however, full of the fire and vim of youth, and is one of the best specimens of the old sea dogs in America. Over twenty years of his time he has been on ocean service, cruising in almost every sea; ten years he has been on shore duty, and twenty years of his time has been what is designated as unemployed. He received his commission as commander in 1852, and was last at sea in 1858. Since that time he has been on service in the Brooklyn Navy-yard; but about eight months ago was assigned to the duty of superintending the putting up of the great Mississippi flotilla. Commodore FOOTE is known in the navy as one of its most efficient officers, and distinguished himself greatly in China by the bombardment and breaching of a Chinese fort, the fort, in all respect, a superior work of masonry. The feat called forth the praise of all foreign naval officers on that coast. Commodore FOOTE is an affable gentleman, and, as will be seen by his reply to the rebel TILGHMAN, *never surrenders.*

CAPT. PORTER.

Capt. PORTER, of the gunboat *Essex*, who is reported as badly scalded by the bursting of his boat's boiler, is a native of Louisiana, but entered the navy from Massachusetts in 1823. He is a son of the renowned Commodore PORTER, who figured so prominently in the war of 1812. He has been thirty-eight years in the service, and has seen twelve years sea duty, five years shore duty, and the rest of the time unemployed. He was last at sea in 1850, and was then and has been since until recently in command of the sloop *St. Marys*. His commission as naval commander dates only since 1855. When the Mississippi flotilla was projected, he was detailed to the command of a gunboat. The Captain christened his boat the *Essex*, after his father's renowned vessel, and judging from precedent, Capt. PORTER is the "bull-dog," or fighting man of this expedition. He has Dahlgren guns for his armament, and delights in "shelling." He worked prodigiously getting his boat ready, and since then he has been cruising round, stirring up the rebels wherever he could find them.

It was the boast of Commodore PERRY that he built some of his vessels on Lake Erie in twenty-six days. Capt. PORTER took the ferry-boat *New Era*, completely stripped her of everything but the framework of her

The Confederate force in Fort Henry was commanded by Brigadier-General Lloyd Tilghman.

hull, and entirely remodeled, rebuilt, and planked her, strengthened her with additional timbers and knees, caulked her, put in bulkheads, built strong and ample gun-decks, cased her hull with iron plates, in fact, constructed a new vessel, carrying nine heavy guns, and floated her out of her dock in *fourteen days*. The mechanics tell with considerable zest how, on the fourteenth day, Capt. PORTER, who had been crowding the work night and day, without giving notice, opened the gates of the floating dock, let on the water, and, to the astonishment of the industrious artisans aboard, the craft was in her element.

It is earnestly to be hoped that the gallant Captain will speedily recover, and be ready once more for active duty on his loved element.

GEN. TILGHMAN.

The rebel commander of Fort Henry, who was so gallantly captured by our navy boys, is a native of Maryland; entered West Point as a cadet in 1831; was made brevet Second Lieutenant in the First Dragoons in 1836, but shortly after resigned, and became division engineer on the Baltimore and Susquehanna Railroad, and afterward on the Baltimore and Ohio Railroad. In the Mexican war he reëntered the service as volunteer Aid-de-Camp to Col. TWIGGS, and was present at the battles of Palo Alto and Risaca de la Palma. He commanded a Volunteer till October, 1846, and in January, 1847, was made Superintendent of the defences of Matamoras; finally he acted as Captain of Volunteer Artillery in HUGHES' regiment from August, 1847, till July, 1848. At the close of the war he again entered civil life, and was chosen principal Assistant Engineer in the Panama Isthmus Railroad. On the breaking out of the war he was acting as railroad engineer, but joined the rebels, and was appointed to command at Fort Henry, where he has been ingloriously captured.

THE NEWS IN WASHINGTON.

WASHINGTON, Friday, Feb. 7.

The news from Fort Henry has diffused general joy, and stimulated the openly expressed desire for additional victories.

Mr. SEDGWICK caused the dispatch from Flag-Officer FOOTE to Secretary WELLES, to be read to the House, and it was received with great demonstrations of applause.

CONFIDENCE OF THE REBELS.

The following dispatch, received by way of Fortress Monroe, shows that the rebels were confident of being able to repulse an attack upon the fort:

MEMPHIS, Thursday, Feb. 5.

Three Federal gunboats appeared on the Tennessee River yesterday, and opened fire on Fort Henry. The latter responded. There was no damage done to the Fort. The Federals are landing troops two miles from the fort. An attack is expected. The Confederates are in full force on the Tennessee River. No damage from the Federals is apprehended.

The New-York Times.

VOL. XI....NO. 3247.　　　NEW-YORK, TUESDAY, FEBRUARY 18, 1862.　　　PRICE TWO CENTS

GLORIOUS VICTORY.

THE FALL OF FORT DONELSON.

Johnston and Buckner, the Rebel Generals, Captured,

FIFTEEN THOUSAND OTHER PRISONERS.

Escape of Floyd and Pillow with Five Thousand Men.

Floyd Denounced by the Rebels as a Black Hearted Traitor and Coward.

Heavy Losses in Killed and Wounded on Both Sides.

Immense Amount of War Material Captured.

THE OFFICIAL DISPATCUES.

Flag-officer Foote Gone to Attack Clarksville.

AUTHENTIC PLAN OF FORT DONELSON.

The following brief telegrams announcing the surrender of Fort Donelson to the land forces under Gen. GRANT, were received in this City, yesterday, and appeared in "Extras" and in the afternoon papers.

CHICAGO, Monday, Feb. 17.

Fort Donelson surrendered yesterday forenoon.

Gen. BUCKNER and JOHNSTON, with 15,000 rebels, are prisoners.

Gen. FLOYD, by his great experience in the business, stole away with 5,000 men on Saturday night.

CINCINNATI, Monday, Feb. 17.

Fort Donelson surrendered yesterday forenoon. Fifteen thousand prisoners were taken, including Gens. BUCKNER and JOHNSTON.

ST. LOUIS, Monday, Feb. 17.

Dispatches from Gen. GRANT to Gen. HALLECK announce the surrender of Fort Donelson, with 15,000 prisoners, including Gens. JOHNSTON, BUCKNER and PILLOW.

Further official advices from Fort Donelson say that Gen. FLOYD escaped during the night, and the rebels in the fort denounced him as a black-hearted traitor and coward.

The enemy is known to have had thirty thousand troops, fifteen thousand of whom are our prisoners.

Given no choice but "unconditional surrender", General Simon Buckner turned over Fort Donelson and 15,000 Confederate troops to U. S. Grant.

Five thousand escaped, and the rest reported killed and wounded, or otherwise disabled. Our loss is not stated, but the slaughter in our ranks is mentioned as terribly severe.

The casualties on the gunboats at Fort Donelson were as follows: On the *St. Louis* there were three killed, including P. R. RILEY, of Cincinnati, two wounded, among them Lieut. KENDALL.

On the *Louisville*, five sailors were killed, four were slightly wounded, and two severely, each having both arms shot away.

On the *Carondelet* four were killed, six badly wounded, including WILLIAM HINTON, the pilot, and two severely wounded.

On the *Pittsburgh* two were wounded.

The force *en route* for Fort Donelson had mostly come up, and were located on the left.

Gen. LEW WALLACE, with the steamer *Missouri* and the Eleventh Indiana Regiment, arrived on Friday.

NEWS RECEIVED IN WASHINGTON.

WASHINGTON, Monday, Feb. 17.

Gen. MCCLELLAN has received a dispatch fully confirming the capture of Fort Donelson.

NEWS RECEIVED FROM RICHMOND.

FORTRESS MONROE, Sunday, Feb. 16.}
VIA BALTIMORE, Monday, Feb. 17.}

By a flag of truce to-day, we learn that Fort Donelson surrendered to Gen. GRANT yesterday.

Gens. PILLOW, FLOYD, JOHNSTON and BUCKNER were taken, together with 15,000 other prisoners.

DETAILS RECEIVED LAST NIGHT.

The following more detailed dispatches reached the City, last night, from the points indicated in the dates:　　　ST. LOUIS, Monday, Feb. 17.

Fort Donelson surrendered at 9 o'clock yesterday morning to the land forces. The gunboats were present at the time. *An immense amount of war material are among the trophies of the victory.*

Gen. FLOYD skulked away the night before the surrender.

The gunboat *Carondelet* has arrived at Cairo with a large number of our wounded. Many have also been taken to the Paducah hospital.

This city is wild with excitement and joy. The news was read at the Union Merchants' Exchange,

creating the most intense enthusiasm. "The Star Spangled Banner" and the "Red, White and Blue" were sung by all present, after which they adjourned and marched to headquarters, twelve or fifteen hundred strong, where three rousing cheers were given for HALLECK and FOOTE. Gen. HALLECK appeared at the window, thanked the people for the hearty demonstration, and said:

"I promised when I came here, with your aid, to drive the enemies of the flag from your State. This has been done, and they are now virtually out of Kentucky, and soon will be out of Tennessee."

The "Star Spangled Banner" was repeated, and with louder cheers for the Union the crowd dispersed.

Judge HOLT wept for joy when he heard the news. Many of the stores were closed, the city decorated with flags, and evidence of the greatest joy everywhere manifest.

GOV. YATES, Secretary HATCH and Auditor DUBOIS of Illinois, left for Fort Donelson this morning to look after the wounded Illinois troops.

A requisition has been made for all the steamboats in this vicinity to be held in readiness for transportation of troops or Government stores.

CHICAGO, Monday, Feb. 17.

A special to the *Times*, dated Fort Donelson, 16th, says:

"Fort Donelson surrendered at daylight this morning unconditionally. We have Gens. BUCKNER, JOHNSTON, BUSHROD and 15,000 prisoners, and 3,000 horses. Gens. PILLOW and FLOYD, with their brigade run away on steamers without letting BUCKNER know their intentions.

Gen. SMITH led the charge on the lower end of the works, and was the first inside the fortifications. The Fort Henry runaways were bagged here.

The prisoners are loading on the steamers for Cairo.

Our loss is heavy—probably 400 *killed and* 800 *wounded.* We lose a large per centage of officers: Among them are Lieutenant-Colonels IRWIN of the Illinois Twentieth, WHITE of the Thirty-first, and SMITH of the Forty-eighth; Colonels JOHN A. LOGAN, SAWYER and RANSOM are wounded. Maj. POST, of the Eighth Illinois, with 200 privates, are prisoners, and have gone to Nashville, having been taken the night before the surrender. The enemy's loss is heavy, but not so large as ours, as they fought behind entrenchments.

We should have taken them by storming Saturday, if our ammunition had not given out in the night.

Gen. MCCLERNAND's Division, composed of Gens. OGLEBIE's, WALLACE's and MCARTHUR's Brigades, suffered terribly. They were composed of the Eighth, Ninth, Eleventh, Eighteenth, Twentieth, Twenty-ninth, Thirtieth, Thirty-first, Forty-fifth, Forty-eighth and Forty-ninth Illinois Regiments.

Gen. LEWIS WALLACE, with the Eleventh Indiana, Eighth Missouri, and some Ohio regiments, participated.

TAYLOR's, WILLIARD's, MCALILTER's, SCHWART's and DECESSES' Batteries were in the fight, from the commencement.

The enemy turned our right for half an hour, but our lost ground was more than regained.

Gen. LANMAN's Brigade of Gen. SMITH's Division was the first in the lower end of the enemy's works, which was done by a charge of bayonets.

As nine-tenths of the rebels were pitted against our right, our forces on the right were ready all night to recommence the attack.

On Sunday morning they were met on their approach by a white flag, Gen. BUCKNER having sent early in the morning a dispatch to Gen. GRANT surrendering.

The works of the fort extend some five miles on the outside.

The rebels lost forty-eight field-pieces, seventeen heavy

guns, twenty thousand stand of arms, beside a large quantity of commissary stores.

The rebel troops are completely demoralized, and have no confidence in their leaders, as they charge PILLOW and FLOYD with deserting them.

Our troops from the moment of the investment of the fort, on Wednesday, lay on their arms night and day, half the time without provisions, all the time without tents, and a portion in a heavy storm of rain and snow.

PLAN OF FORT DONELSON.

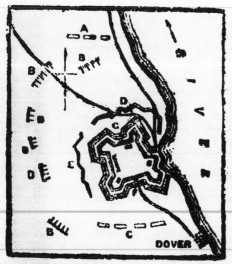

REFERENCES TO THE PLAN.

A.—Gen. SMITH.
B.—Union Field Batteries.
C.—Gen. McCLERNAND.
D.—Rebel Redoubts.
E.—Rebel Rifle Pits.
F.—Draw Bridge.
G.—Ditch around the Fort.

OFFICIAL BULLETINS OF THE VICTORY.

REPORT OF FLAG-OFFICER FOOTE.
CAIRO, Monday, Feb. 17, 1862.
Hon. Gideon Weltes, Secretary of the Navy:

The *Carondelet* has just arrived from Fort Donelson, and brings information of the capture of that Fort by the land forces, yesterday morning, with fifteen thousand prisoners.

JOHNSTON and BUCKNER were taken prisoners.

The loss is heavy on both sides.

FLOYD escaped with 5,000 men during the night.

I go up with the gunboats, and as soon as possible will proceed up to Clarksville.

Eight mortar boats are on their way, *with which I hope to attack Clarksville.*

My foot is painful, but the wound is not dangerous.

The army has behaved gloriously.

I shall be able to take but two iron-clad gunboats with me, as the others are disabled.

The trophies are immense.

The particulars will soon be given.
A. H. FOOTE, Flag-Officer.

REPORT OF BRIG.-GEN. CULLUM.
CAIRO, Feb. 17, 1862.
To Major-Gen. McClellan:

The Union flag floats over Fort Donelson. The *Carondelet*, Capt. WALKER, brings the glorious intelligence.

The fort surrendered at 9 o'clock yesterday (Sunday) morning. Gens. JOHNSTON (A. SYDNEY) and BUCKNER, and fifteen thousand prisoners, and a large amount of material of war are the trophies of the victory. Loss heavy on both sides.

FLOYD, the thief, stole away during the night previous, with five thousand men, and is denounced by the rebels as a traitor. I am happy to inform you that Flag-Officer FOOTE, though suffering with his foot, with the noble characteristic of our navy, notwithstanding his disability, will take up immediately two gunboats, and with the eight mortar boats which he

will overtake, will make an immediate attack on Clarksville, if the state of the weather will permit. We are now firing a National salute from Fort Cairo, Gen. GRANT's late post, in honor of the glorious achievement.

(Signed,) GEO. W. CULLUM,
Brig.-Gen. Vols. and U. S. A., and
Chief of Staff and Engineers.

SIMON BOLIVAR BUCKNER.

Gen. BUCKNER, the second prisoner in rank captured at Fort Donelson, is a Brigadier-General in the rebel army, and for some months was in chief command in the rebel Western Department. He is a native of Kentucky, a graduate of West Point, and is now 38 years of age. In 1841, he was appointed, by brevet, Second Lieutenant in the Second Infantry, and next year he was Acting Assistant-Professor of Ethics at West Point. In 1846, he was transferred to the Sixth Infantry, in which he went to Mexico, and was breveted First Lieutenant for gallant conduct at Contreras and Cherubusco, at which latter battle he was wounded. He was subsequently breveted Captain for gallant conduct at Motino del Rey. In 1847 he was Regimental Quartermaster, subsequently Assistant Instructor in Infantry Tactics, and in 1852, Commissary of Subsistence, with the rank of captain. When the secession movement began, he took an active but secret part with them, and as commander of the Kentucky State Guard, he exercised a powerful influence on the fighting element of his native State. Last Summer he visited Washington, represented himself there as loyal, ingratiated himself into Gen. SCOTT's confidence, obtained permission to inspect all the fortifications in that vicinity, made Hon. ROBERT MALLORY and others believe that he wished to take active service in the army of the United States, returned to Louisville, and remained for a brief period, without giving public indication that he contemplated any disloyal movement, but all this time was holding conference with JEFF. DAVIS and the conspirators. Subsequently he managed to seduce a large part of the State Guard into the rebel service, and for this was appointed to command at Bowling Green. He is an adroit, skillful, bad man. The days of his active treason, however, are now ended.

GEN. BUSHROD.

Gen. BUSHROD, we believe, is a Kentucky Militia General. He is not a graduate of West Point, and is unknown to fame either in military or civil life.

IMPORTANT FROM KENTUCKY.

The Evacuation of Bowling Green.

PART OF THE TOWN BURNED.

Movements of the National Forces.

Eighty Thousand Men Concentrating on the Cumberland.

CINCINNATI, Monday, Feb. 17.

This morning's *Commercial* has the following special dispatch:

"On learning that the rebels were evacuating Bowling Green, Gen. BUELL ordered a forced march by Gen. MITCHELL to save if possible the railroad and turnpike bridges on Big Barron River. They, however, had all been destroyed when Gen. MITCHELL reached the banks of the river.

The brigades of Gen. BRECKINRIDGE and Gen. HINDMAN were, until Thursday evening, at Woodland Station.

The rebels left nothing at Bowling Green except a few old wagons.

A part of the town, it is reported, is being burnt.

It is believed now that no rebel forces exist in Ken-

Union forces led by General C. F. Smith stemmed a desperate Confederate escape attempt from Fort Donelson.

tucky east of the direct road from Bowling Green *viâ* Franklin to Nashville.

Gen. CRITTENDEN is trying to organize another army at Carthage, on the south bank of the Cumberland. This is the only rebel force on the line from Bowling Green to Nashville.

Gens. BRECKINRIDGE and HINDMAN's Brigades have fallen back on Russellville, where Gens. BUCKNER's and FLOYD's Brigades have been stationed for some time. Gens. JOHNSTON and HARDEE were also believed to be at that point on Friday.

It is believed that, with the exception of the above brigades, the whole rebel army has been moved to Fort Donelson and Clarksville.

What movements may have been made by the rebel forces can only be conjectured, but the probabilities are that they have concentrated their whole force on the Cumberland.

If, however, they have not done so, the divisions of Generals NELSON and MITCHELL will be ample to cope with all they may have between Bowling Green and Nashville.

It is believed that the divisions of Gens. McCOOK and THOMAS embarked at the mouth of Salt River, on steamers for Cumberland, on Saturday night, and that the troops who have been in camps of instruction at Bardstown, were at Louisville yesterday embarking for the Cumberland.

Three Indiana regiments, and a battery of artillery, leave New Albany to-day.

The aggregate of these reinforcements is perhaps 40,000.

Gen. BUELL, we understand, goes with Gen. McCook's Division, to take command in person on the Cumberland, where our forces will be, by to-morrow night, 80,000. While he presses the enemy on the Cumberland with his tremendous force, their flank and rear are pressed by the heavy divisions under Gens. NELSON and MITCHELL.

Since writing the above we learn, that ten regiments now in Ohio camps are ordered at once to the Cumberland.

The New-York Times.

VOL. XI.—NO. 3248. NEW-YORK, WEDNESDAY, FEBRUARY 19, 1862. PRICE TWO CENTS.

THE GREAT VICTORY.

Further Particulars of the Capture of Fort Donelson.

Desperate Nature of the Fighting on Saturday.

Attempt of the Rebels to Cut Their Way Through Our Lines.

HOW THE SURRENDER WAS MADE.

Correspondence Between Gen. Buckner and Gen. Grant.

Some of the Names of the Killed and Wounded.

THE NATIONAL FORCES ENGAGED.

The End of the Rebellion in Tennessee at Hand.

The following dispatch, giving a somewhat detailed account of occurrences at Fort Donelson, on Saturday and Sunday, with the correspondence between the commanding officers of the opposing forces preceding the surrender, and the names of some of the National killed and wounded, appeared in but a portion of our morning edition yesterday, owing to the late hour at which it was received:

CHICAGO, Monday, Feb. 17.

A special from Fort Donelson says: The forces were about equal in numbers, but the rebels had all the advantage of position, being well fortified on two immense hills, with their fort near the river, on a lower piece of ground. From the foot of their intrenchments, rifle-pits and abattis extended up the river, behind the town of Dover. Their fortifications on the land side, back from the river, were at least four miles in length. Their water battery, in the centre of the fortifications, where it came down to the river, mounted nine heavy guns.

The rebels were sure of success. In any other cause and against less brave troops, they could easily have held the position against a hundred thousand men.

The business of getting the different brigades in position for attaching the new arrivals to the different divisions, took up the greater portion of Friday night.

At daylight Saturday, the enemy opened on the Eighteenth Illinois, when Col. OGLESBY's Brigade was soon engaged, and was soon followed by WALLACE's and McARTHUR's Brigades, the latter acting under Gen. McCLERNAND, as the position of the troops had been changed during the night, and Gen. GRANT had been called away during the night to the gunboats.

The movements of all the troops, except those attached to McCLERNAND's Division, were made without anything except general orders.

At a suggestion from Gen. McCLERNAND, Gen. WAL-

LACE sent up four regiments to support his division, who were nearly out of ammunition.

From the commencement till near 10 o'clock the fighting was terrific. The troops on the right were disposed as follows: McARTHUR's Brigade, composed of the Ninth, Twelfth, Forty-first, Seventeenth, and Nineteenth Illinois Regiments; next Gen. OGLESBY's Brigade, consisting of the Eighth, Thirteenth, Twenty-ninth, Thirtieth, and Thirty-first Illinois Regiments, SCHWARTZ's and DRESSER's batteries; next was Gen. WALLACE's Brigade, of the Eleventh, Twentieth, Forty-fifth, and Forty-eighth Illinois Regiments. These three brigades composed Gen. McCLERNAND's Division, and bore the brunt of the battle.

It was found that the enemy was concentrating his main force to turn our right, which was done by our men getting out of ammunition, and in the confusion of getting up reinforcements, retreating about half a mile. As soon as the division, which had stood its ground manfully for three hours, retired, the enemy occupied the field, when Gen. GRANT ordered Gen. SMITH to move forward his division and storm the enemy's works on our left. This order was obeyed with great alacrity, and soon the cheers of our daring soldiery were heard, and the old flag displayed from within the enemy's intrenchments.

Gen. GRANT then sent word to Gen. McCLERNAND that Gen. SMITH was within the enemy's intrenchments and ordering their forces to move forward and renew the attack on the right. One of Gen. WALLACE's Brigades—the Eleventh Indiana, Eighth Missouri and some Ohio Regiments—was rapidly thrown into position and Company A, of the Chicago Light Artillery, was planted in the road, and as the rebels, supposing we were in retreat, came, yelling, out of their works into the road, the Chicago boys poured a hailstorm of grape and canister into their ranks, slaughtering dozens of them.

Simultaneously with this the infantry commenced firing at will, and the rebels went pell-mell back into their works, our men advancing and taking possession of the ground lost, and a hill besides. Fresh troops who had not been in the action were then thrown forward, and as the shades of night drew on were in a strong position to participate in a simultaneous attack to be made on Sunday morning.

Gens. OGLESBY, WALLACE and McARTHUR's brigades did the hardest fighting, and have suffered terribly. They would undoubtedly have held their first position but for the failure of their ammunition. The ammunition wagons were some distance off the hills preventing their being moved.

Some of our best officers and men have gone to their long homes.

Hardly a man that went over the field after the battle, but discovered some comrade who had fallen.

We lost three Lieutenant-Colonels, and at least one-quarter of all the other officers were wounded or killed.

During Saturday night a contraction of all our

Confederate General J.B. Floyd escaped from Fort Donelson and avoided capture.

Major-General Lew Wallace led the Federal troops that saw the brunt of the battle.

The North discovered that they had not captured General Albert S. Johnson at all, but "only" General Bushrod R. Johnson.

lines was made for a simultaneous assault from every point, and orders were given by Gen. GRANT to take the enemy at the point of the bayonet. Every man was at his post. The Fifty-seventh Illinois was on the extreme right.

HOW THE SURRENDER WAS MADE.

At daylight the advance was made, and when the full light of day broke forth, white flags were hung in many places on the enemy's works.

An officer at a convenient point was informed that they had stacked their arms and surrendered early in the morning, the following correspondence having passed between the commanders:

GEN. BUCKNER TO GEN. GRANT.

HEAD-QUARTERS, FORT DONELSON, Feb. 16.

SIR: In consideration of all the circumstances governing the present situation of affairs at this station, I propose to the commanding officer of the Federal forces the appointment of Commissioners to agree upon terms of capitulation of the forces at this post under my command. In that view I suggest an armistice until 12 o'clock to-day.

I am, very respectfully, your obedient servant,
L. B. BUCKNER, Brig.-Gen., C. S. A.
To Brig.-Gen. U. S. GRANT, commanding United States forces near Fort Donelson.

GEN. GRANT TO GEN. BUCKNER.

HEADQUARTERS ON THE FIELD, FORT DONELSON, Feb. 16.

To GEN. S. B. BUCKNER—Sir: Yours, of this date, proposing an armistice and the appointment of Commissioners to settle the terms of capitulation is just received. *No terms except unconditional and immediate surrender can be accepted.*

I propose to move immediately on your works.

I am, very respectfully, your obedient servant,
U. S. GRANT, Brig.-Gen., Com'd'g.

GEN. BUCKNER TO GEN. GRANT.

HEADQUARTERS, DOVER, Tenn., Sunday, Feb. 19.
Brig.-Gen. U. S. Grant, U. S. A.:

SIR—The distribution of the forces under my command incident to an *unexpected change of commanders,* and the overwhelming force under your command compels me, *notwithstanding the brilliant success of the Confederate arms,* to accept the ungenerous and unchivalrous terms which you propose.

I am, Sir, your servant,

S. B. BUCKNER, *Brig.-Gen., C. S. A.*

Our force was soon in the enemy's works, when the rebel officers gave up their swords.

The bulk of the rebels are chagrined, as they knew of the surrender long before our men were apprised of it. PILLOW and FLOYD had planned and executed their escape during the night, taking with them FLOYD'S Brigade and a few favorites, occupying what few small steamers they had. The prisoners are loud in their denunciations of the runaways.

Many of them acknowledged the hopelessness of their cause, and intimated a willingness to take an oath of allegiance, and return to their homes. To the question put to an officer, as to how many prisoners we had, he replied, *"You have all out of twenty-five thousand who were not killed, or did not escape."*

DISPATCHES RECEIVED LAST NIGHT.
REPORTS FROM CHICAGO.

CHICAGO, Tuesday, Feb. 18.

The Chicago *Tribune's* special dispatch from Fort Donelson, says that the position of the ground occupied by our troops in the attack on Fort Donelson, was such that not more than one regiment could operate at the same time, while the rebels could bring nearly their whole force to bear against us.

The first regiment to receive the rebels was the Eighteenth Illinois, which fought with desperate courage until their ammunition was exhausted, when they were forced to retire.

They were replaced by the Eighth Illinois, who were also driven back, after firing their last round.

Meanwhile the other regiments were lending such feeble assistance as their positions would admit.

Gen. LEW. WALLACE was then ordered to reinforce Gen. McCLERNAND, and he sent two brigades from the centre.

The Thirty-first Illinois Regiment, Col. LOGAN, fought like veterans, defending SCHWARTZ'S Battery under the most galling fire until every horse at the battery was killed, together with all the officers who had charge of the guns, as well as the Lieutenant-Colonel, the Acting-Major, seven Captains, and a number of Lieutenants of the Thirty-first Illinois Regiment had been killed, and the Colonel wounded.

Being nearly surrounded, Capt. COOK, who was left in command, drew off what there was left of the regiment, not, however, until their last round was expended, and they had commenced driving the rebels before them.

The Second Brigade then came up and took the place of the retired one, and fought desperately, losing a great number of killed, but with the assistance of a portion of WALLACE'S Division, the Forty-ninth and Fifty-ninth Ohio Regiments, drove the rebels back to their intrenchments, gaining a portion of the ground lost.

The object of the rebels was, evidently, to cut their way through our troops.

The Gen. JOHNSON taken prisoner is BUSHROD JOHNSON, a Brigadier-General from Tennessee.

REPORTS FROM ST. LOUIS.

ST. LOUIS, Tuesday, Feb. 18.

The *Republican's* Fort Donelson correspondent gives the following account of the fighting on Saturday:

"Yesterday morning, just at daylight, a heavy sortie was made by the garrison from the left portion of their works. This attack was made upon the extreme right wing of the Union army, where it was the weakest. Part of Gen. McCLERNAND'S Division, under Col. OGLESBY, consisting of his brigade, which was stationed there; also, SCHWARTZ'S and McALLISTER'S batteries. The point was upon a ridge leading into the right redoubt, and was situated just above the main fort.

During the night the enemy could be heard busily at work, but what at it is impossible to tell, as a thicket and woods encompassed the Union troops on every side, rendering the view in almost any direction almost impossible. At daylight, a large body of the enemy suddenly appeared on the extreme right wing of Col. OGLESBY'S command, and opened a terrible fire from cannon from their redoubts, playing at the same time on our forces from guns placed in position on the night previous.

BUSHROD R. JOHNSON.

It seems, after all that it was not Gen. SIDNEY JOHNSTON who was captured at Fort Donelson, but quite a different personage and one of small enough consequence. BUSHROD R. JOHNSON is a graduate of West Point, in the class of 1836, and a native we believe, of Kentucky. He was Second-Lieutenant, and afterward First-Lieutenant in the Third Infantry; resigned from the army in 1847, and next year became Professor of Mathematics at the Western Military Institute, Georgetown, Ky., which post he filled until last year. When the rebellion broke out in Kentucky, he raised and commanded an artillery company, known as Company A., of the First Tennessee Artillery, and has been in command of it quite recently. Whether the rebels have of late elevated him to the rank of "General," or whether the telegraph has given him the title, or console us for the disappointment at not having caught SIDNEY JOHNSTON is, like the fellow himself, a thing of no consequence.

J.A. McClernand was promoted to Major-General after the battle of Fort Donelson.

REJOICING OVER THE VICTORY.

IN THE EAST.

CAPE RACE, Tuesday, Feb. 18.

Fifty flags, being all we have got, are floating to the breeze here, in honor of the glorious victory at Fort Donelson. The news gives great satisfation at St. Johns, N. F., and here.

BOSTON, Tuesday, Feb. 18.

Gov. ANDREW has ordered national salutes to be fired to-morrow, at noon, in Boston, on Bunker Hill and at Lexington and Concord, in honor of the recent victories.

CANANDAIGUA, N. Y., Tuesday, Feb. 18.

Guns are booming, bells are ringing, and flags are flying at the glad news from Tennessee.

There is universal regret that the thief FLOYD escaped.

AUBURN, Tuesday, Feb. 18.

Guns are firing, bells ringing, flags flying, and general rejoicing is being had over the capture of Fort Donelson.

TRENTON, (N. J.,) Tuesday, Feb. 18.

A national salute was fired to-day, and the bells of the city rung in honor of the victories of our arms in the recent attack on Fort Donelson and Savannah.

Resolutions of thanks to our brave officers and men, and of sympathy with the wounded and friends of the dead engaged in the recent battles in Tennessee and Georgia, passed both houses this morning.

PHILADELPHIA, Tuesday, Feb. 18—Noon.

The city is decorated with flags, our people believing that Savannah has surrendered, though no confirmation has been received.

BALTIMORE, Tuesday, Feb. 18.

Demonstrations of joy are visible all over the city. Flags are flying from all public and private buildings, and from all the newspaper offices except the *Republican* and *News* sheet. A salute of 34 guns was fired at noon by Capt. NIMS' Boston Battery. A salute was also fired yesterday from Fort Marshall.

WASHINGTON, Tuesday, Feb. 18.

A national salute was fired at the Navy-yard to-day in honor of the recent victories.

IN THE WEST.

CINCINNATI, Monday, Feb. 17.

News of the capture of Fort Donelson was received here at 11 o'clock this morning, and caused intense excitement and joy. The enthusiasm on 'Change was unbounded.

To-night a general illumination with bonfires and fireworks will take place. A salute will be fired from the heavy guns on the fortifications around the city, at noon to-morrow. Troops have been passing through the city all day, *en route* for the Cumberland River.

CLEVELAND, Tuesday, Feb. 18.

There was firing of cannon all day yesterday, and bonfires, and very general rejoicing all last night in honor of the taking of Fort Donelson.

LOUISVILLE, Monday, Feb. 17.

There is great excitement and rejoicing here at the Fort Donelson capture, in honor of which a supper is given at the Galt House this evening, to Gen. BUELL and Staff, and other officers in the city.

National salutes were fired from the Benton Barracks, the Arsenal, Jefferson Barracks, and all the forts surrounding the city to-day in honor of the victory.

The New-York Times.

VOL. XI—NO. 3253.   NEW-YORK, TUESDAY, FEBRUARY 25, 1862.   PRICE TWO CENTS.

THE CAMPAIGN IN TENNESSEE.

MORE GOOD NEWS.

Nashville Occupied by General Buell's Forces.

The Tennessee Troops Called in by Gov. Harris.

A Strong Reaction in Favor of the Union.

Flag-Officer Foote's Proclamation to the People of Clarksville.

IMPORTANT ORDER FROM GEN. HALLECK.

St. Louis, Monday, Feb. 24.

A special dispatch from Cairo to the *Democrat* says the latest intelligence from the Cumberland is that Gen. Buell's forces occupy Nashville; that Gov. Harris has called in all the Tennessee troops, and that a strong reaction has occurred among the people.

THE SURRENDER CONFIRMED.

Louisville, Monday, Feb. 24.

Reliable private information received to-night assures us that Nashville is virtually in possession of the National forces.

THE CITY OF NASHVILLE.

By the capture of Nashville, we obtain possession of the largest city in the rebel States which has yet been occupied by our troops. Nashville, the capital of the State of Tennessee, is a city of 30,000 inhabitants. It is situated on the Cumberland River, 200 miles (following the windings of the stream) above its junction with the Ohio. The city is built chiefly on the south side of the river, on the slopes, and at the foot of a hill rising from it. It stands upon a solid rock, elevated to the height of from 50 to 175 feet above the level of the stream. It is a place of great trade, and is an important railroad centre. There are five railroads radiating from the city, namely: the Tennessee and Alabama, the Louisville and Nashville, the Edgefield and Kentucky, the Nashville and Chattanooga, and the Nashville and Northwestern. Steamboats and *gunboats* ascend from the mouth of the Cumberland to Nashville, and the river is navigable by boats of 1,500 tons for 50 miles above the city, and by smaller boats to the Falls, 500 miles.

Nashville is generally well built, and there are numerous imposing public edifices. One of the finest of the former is the new capitol, situated on an eminence 175 feet above the river, and constructed of a beautiful variety of fossiliferous limestone. It is built in the Grecian style of architecture, cost over a million of dollars, and is considered the handsomest State Capitol in the Union. There are many other fine public buildings. There were at secession time, five daily newspapers, eight weeklies, and eight monthlies.

The commerce of Nashville was very large, and was carried on by river, rail and turnpike. The average annual shipments are 30,000 bales of cotton, beside tobacco, wheat, corn, bacon and hogs. The neighborhood is a famous stock-raising country, and has a high reputation for blood-horses and other stock. The value of taxable property is about $15,000,000.

Twelve miles east from the city is the Hermitage, the famous residence of ANDREW JACKSON, over which will once again be raised the glorious flag which the stern old hero loved. Among the residents of the city is the late JOHN BELL; and there are known, also, to be a strong and more enduring Union element than he was made of.

By the possession of Nashville, taken in connection with our late occupation of Cumberland Gap, and Forts Henry and Donelson, we gain military possession of nearly the entire State of Tennessee. The rebels of the Southwest are now all crowded into Columbus and Memphis. These strongholds, too, must now soon fall.

FROM FORT DONELSON.

COMMODORE FOOTE'S PROCLAMATION TO THE CITIZENS OF CLARKSVILLE, ETC.

Cairo, Saturday, Feb. 22.

Everything is quiet at Fort Donelson.

The rebels, before evacuating Clarksville, fired a railroad bridge crossing the Cumberland at that point.

Commodore Foote issued the following proclamation:

Inhabitants of Clarksville at the suggestion of Hon. CAVE JOHNSON, Judge WISDOM and the Mayor of the city, who called upon me yesterday after our hoisting the Union flag on the forts, to ascertain my views and intentions towards the citizens and private property. I hereby announce to all peaceably disposed persons that neither in their persons nor property shall they suffer molestation by me or by the naval forces under my command, and they may safely resume their business avocations with assurances of my protection. At the same time I require all military stores and army equipment shall be surrendered, no part of them being withheld or destroyed; and further, that no secession flag or manifestation of secession feeling shall be exhibited. And for the faithful observance of these conditions I shall hold the authorities of the city responsible.

(Signed,)   ANDREW H. FOOTE.

The Nashville papers advise the undermining of some of the bluffs on the Cumberland River, on the approach of our gunboats, either to destroy them or obstruct the channel.

IMPORTANT FROM THE SOUTH.

How the Fall of Fort Donelson is Received.

Shrieks of Wrath from the Rebel Press.

Lessons to be Learned from Northern Perseverance.

The Rebels Whistling to Keep their Courage Up.

A Warning Against the Foreign Residents of Richmond.

THE FALL OF FORT DONELSON.

AN OUTBURST FROM THE REBEL PRESS—"THE BLOODY BARBARIANS."

From the Richmond Dispatch, Feb. 19.

After three days of the most desperate fighting ever witnessed on this continent, (so declares a veteran regular officer,) the most desperate fighting against the most tremendous odds, in which day after day the multitudinous host of invaders were driven back past their own camps, our glorious Spartan band, from sheer exhaustion, has been borne down by a new avalanche of reinforcements piled upon the already enormous weight against which they have hitherto struggled with complete success, and has suffered one of those misfortunes which are common to war, but which entail no dishonor on our cause, and which will only animate to the most stern and undying resistance every true Southern heart.

If these bloody barbarians, whose hands are now soaked to the elbows in the life-blood of men defending their own homes and firesides, dream that they are now one inch nearer the subjugation of the South than when they started on their infernal mission, they prove themselves to be fools and madmen, as well as savages and murderers. They have taught us a lesson, we admit; they have admonished us to be more wary and circumspect, to husband with greater care our limited resources, and not to underrate our enemy.

But they have also placed between them and us a gulf that can never be crossed by their arts or arms, and a universal determination to die, if die we must, for our country, but never permit her to be subjugated by the most malignant, the most murderous, the meanest of mankind, whose name is at this very moment such a by-word of scorn and reproach throughout Europe, for their combined cruelty and cowardice, that their own ambassadors cannot stand the scorn of the world's contempt, and are all anxious to fly back to the United States.

Their success at Fort Donelson, gained only by vast superiority of numbers, will only have the effect of converting the whole population of the South—men, women and children—into an immense army, who will resist them at every step, and everywhere "welcome them with bloody hands to hospitable graves." The glorious valor of our troops at Fort Donelson is not dimmed in the slightest degree by their inability to hold their ground against overwhelming odds; but, on the contrary, shines through the black clouds of disaster with a radiance that will kindle the whole South into a blaze, and surround their own names with a halo of imperishable venom.

THE CRISIS.

From the Richmond Dispatch.

The crisis of the war is upon us, and reverse upon reverse comes in quick succession. We have scarcely recovered from the depression consequent upon our defeat at Fort Henry and Roanoke, ere we are called upon to meet a still heavier calamity in the fall of Fort Donelson, and the surrender of our brave troops holding that important post. It is true the facts concerning this last disaster have not yet reached us from sources entitled to belief; but enough is known to convince us that we have sustained another staggering blow.

We have not been of those who entertained the belief that our arms would always be successful, or that it was within the bounds of possibility our small army could meet and drive back the overwhelming hordes of the enemy at every point at which they could penetrate, and are not, therefore, taken by surprise, nor greatly discouraged, by the untoward events which have taken place in the West and on the Atlantic coast. We have not known our own strength, although we have been greatly too confident of the weakness and cowardice of our foe. If these disasters shall turn our thoughts in upon ourselves, and shall arouse us to the full comprehension of our perilous situation, and to the energy and activity requisite for the occasion, they will not have overtaken us in vain.

We do not believe the defeat at Fort Donelson is of the proportion our telegraphic colums would give us to understand. It must be remembered, the intelligence they furnish comes from the enemy, who are not apt to depreciate the victories they gain. And we see much to encourage us even in this dark hour. Our permanent Government is launched upon the stormy sea, it is true, but we think her timbers are stout enough to bear the strain, and that the noble structure will be none the worse for the rough usage to which it has thus early been subjected.

The War Department received, on Monday evening, from Gen. A. JOHNSTON, a telegram, announcing the fall of Fort Donelson, but couched in so ambiguous a style that it becomes necessary to request more intelligible information. No answer has as yet been received from that officer, probably on account of the interruption of telegraphic communication, occasioned by the severity of the weather.

The New-York Times.

VOL. XI—NO. 3264.　　　NEW-YORK, MONDAY, MARCH 10, 1862.　　　PRICE TWO CENTS.

HIGHLY IMPORTANT NEWS.

Desperate Naval Engagements in Hampton Roads.

Attack Upon our Blockading Vessels by the Rebel Steamers Merrimac, Jamestown and Yorktown.

The Frigate Cumberland Run Into by the Merrimac and Sunk.

Part of Her Crew Reported to be Drowned.

SURRENDER OF THE FRIGATE CONGRESS.

Engagement of the Rebel Steamers with the Newport's News Batteries.

The Minnesota and Other Vessels Aground.

CESSATION OF FIRING AT NIGHT.

Opportune Arrival of the Iron-Clad Ericsson Battery Monitor.

A Five Hours' Engagement Between Her and the Merrimac.

The Rebel Vessel Forced to Haul Off.

THE MONITOR UNINJURED

FORTRESS MONROE, Saturday, March 8.

The dullness of Old Point was startled to-day by the announcement that a suspicious looking vessel; supposed to be the *Merrimac*, looking like a submerged house, with the roof only above water, was moving down from Norfolk by the channel in front of the Sewell's Point batteries. Signal guns were also fired by the *Cumberland* and *Congress*, to notify the *Minnesota*, *St. Lawrence* and *Roanoke* of the approaching danger, and all was excitement in and about Fortress Monroe.

There was nothing protruding above the water but a flagstaff flying the rebel flag, and a short smokestack. She moved along slowly, and turned into the channel leading to Newport's News, and steamed direct for the frigates *Cumberland* and *Congress*, which were lying at the mouth of James River.

Lt. John L. Worden commanded the *Monitor* at the Hampton Roads battle.

As soon as she came within range of the *Cumberland*, the latter opened on her with her heavy guns, but the balls struck and glanced off, having no more effect than peas from a pop-gun. Her ports were all closed, and she moved on in silence, but with a full head of steam.

In the meantime, as the *Merrimac* was approaching the two frigates on one side, the rebel iron-clad steamers *Yorktown* and *Jamestown* came down James River, and engaged our frigates on the other side. The batteries at Newport's News also opened on the *Yorktown* and *Jamestown*, and did all in their power to assist the *Cumberland* and *Congress*, which, being sailing vessels, were at the mercy of the approaching steamers.

The *Merrimac*, in the meantime, kept steadily on her course, and slowly approached the *Cumberland*, when she and the *Congress*, at a distance of one hundred yards, rained full broadsides on the iron-clad monster, that took no effect, the balls glancing upwards, and flying off, having only the effect of checking her progress for a moment.

After receiving the first broadside of the two frigates, she ran on to the *Cumberland*, striking her about midships, and literally laying open her sides. She then drew off, and fired a broadside into the disabled ship, and again dashed against her with her iron-clad prow, and, knocking in her side, left her to sink, while she engaged the *Congress*, which laid about a quarter of a mile distant.

The *Congress* had, in the meantime, kept up a short engagement with the *Yorktown* and *Jamestown*, and having no regular crew on board of her, and seeing the hopelessness of resisting the iron-clad steamer, at once struck her colors. Her crew had been discharged several days since, and three companies of the Naval Brigade had been put on board temporarily, until she could be relieved by the *St. Lawrence*, which was to have gone up on Monday to take her position as one of the blockading vessels of the James River.

On the *Congress* striking her colors, the *Jamestown* approached and took from on board of her, all her officers as prisoners, but allowed the crew to escape in boats. The vessel being thus cleared, was fired by the rebels, when the *Merrimac* and her two iron-clad companions opened with shell and shot on the Newport's News batteries. The firing was briskly returned. Various reports have been received, principally from frightened sutler's clerks. Some of them represent

Confederate Commander Franklin Buchanan led the *Merrimack* in successful battle against Union vessels *Cumberland* and *Minnesota*.

that the garrison had been compelled to retreat from the batteries to the woods. Another was that the two smaller rebel steamers had been compelled to retreat from their guns.

In the meantime the steam-frigate *Minnesota*, having partly got up steam, was being towed up to the relief of the two frigates, but did not get up until it was too late to assist them. She was also followed up by the frigate *St. Lawrence*, which was taken in tow by several of the small harbor steamers. It is rumored, however, that neither of these vessels had pilots on board them, and after a short engagement, both of them seemed to be, in the opinion of the pilots on the Point, aground. The *Minnesota* either intentionally or from necessity, engaged the three steamers at about a mile distance, with only her two bow guns. The *St. Lawrence* also poured in shot from all the guns she could bring to bear, and it was the impression of the most experienced naval officers on the point that both had been considerably damaged. These statements, it must be borne in mind, are all based on what could be seen by a glass at a distance of nearly eight miles, and from a few panic-stricken non-combatants, who fled at almost the first gun from Newport's News.

In the meantime darkness approached, though the moon shone out brightly, and nothing but the occasional flashing of guns could be seen. The *Merrimac* was also believed to be aground, as she remained stationary, at a distance of a mile from the *Minnesota*, making no attempt to attack or molest her.

Previous to the departure of the steamer for Baltimore, no guns had been fired for half an hour, the last one being fired from the *Minnesota*. Some persons declared that immediately after this last gun was fired, a dense volume of vapor was seen to rise from the *Merrimac*, indicating the explosion of her boiler. Whether this is so or not, cannot be known, but it was the universal opinion that the rebel monster was hard aground.

Fears were of course entertained for the safety of the *Minnesota* and *St. Lawrence* in such an unequal contest; but if the *Merrimac* was really ashore, she could do no more damage. It was the intention of the *Minnesota*, with her picked and gallant crew, to run into close quarters with the *Merrimac*, avoid her iron prow, and board her. This the *Merrimac* seemed not inclined to give her an opportunity to do.

At 8 o'clock, when the Baltimore boat left, a fleet of

steam-tugs were being sent up to the relief of the *Minnesota* and the *St. Lawrence*, and an endeavor was to be made to draw them off the bar on which they had grounded. In the meantime the firing had suspended, whether from mutual consent or necessity, could not be ascertained.

The rebel battery at Pig Point was also enabled to join in the combined attack on the *Minnesota*, and several guns were fired at her from Sewall's Point as she went up. None of them struck her, but one or two of them passed over her.

The Baltimore boat left Old Point at 8 o'clock last night. In about half-an-hour after she left the wharf, the iron-clad Ericsson steamer *Monitor* passed her, going in, towed by a large steamer. The *Monitor* undoubtedly reached Fortress Monroe by 9 o'clock, and may have immediately gone into service; if not, she would be ready to take a hand early on Sunday morning.

The foregoing are all the facts as far as can be at present ascertained, and are, probably, the worst possible version of the affair.

LATER AND BETTER NEWS.

A Five Hours' Engagement Between the Ericsson Battery and the three Rebel Steamers.

The Rebel Vessels Driven Off---The Merrimac in a Sinking Condition.

WASHINGTON, Sunday, March 9—6:45 P. M.

The telegraph line to Fortress Monroe is just completed, and a message from there states that after the arrival of the *Monitor*, last night, she was attacked by the *Merrimac*, *Jamestown*, and *Yorktown*. After a five hours' fight they were driven off, and the *Merrimac* put back to Norfolk in a sinking condition.

OFFICIAL.

[BY TELEGRAPH FROM FORTRESS MONROE.]
WASHINGTON, Sunday, March 9—7 P. M.

The *Monitor* arrived at Fortress Monroe last night.

Early this morning she was attacked by the three vessels—the *Merrimac*, the *Jamestown* and the *Yorktown*.

After five hours' contest they were driven off—the *Merrimac* in a sinking condition.

The above is official.

John Ericsson was commissioned by the U.S. to build a successful ironclad vessel.

DISPATCH AUTHORIZED BY GEN. WOOL
FORTRESS MONROE, Sunday, March 9.

The *Monitor* arrived at 10 P. M., last night, and went immediately to the protection of the *Minnesota*, lying aground just below Newport's News. At 7 A. M. to-day the *Merrimac*, accompanied by two wooden steamers, the *Yorktown* and *Jamestown*, and several tugs, stood out toward the *Minnesota*, and opened fire. The *Monitor* met them at once, and opened fire, when the enemy's vessels retired, excepting the *Merrimac*. *The two iron-clad vessels fought, part of the time touching each other, from 8 A. M. till noon, when the Merrimac retreated.* Whether she is injured, or not, it is impossible to say.

Lieut. J. L. WORDEN, who commanded the *Monitor*, handled her with great skill, assisted by Chief-Engineer STIMERS.

The *Minnesota* kept up a continuous fire, and is herself somewhat injured. She was moved considerably to-day, and will probably be off to-night.

The *Monitor* is uninjured, and ready at any moment to repel another attack.

[Sent by order of Gen. WOOL.]

WASHINGTON, Sunday, March 9.

The following was received to-night by Major-Gen. McCLELLAN from Gen. WOOL, dated Fortress Monroe, at 6 o'clock this evening:

"Two hours after my telegraphic dispatch to the Secretary of War last evening, the *Monitor* arrived. She immediately went to the assistance of the *Minnesota*, which was aground, and continued so until a few moments since. Early this morning she was attacked by the *Merrimac*, *Jamestown* and *Yorktown*. After a five hours' contest they were driven off, the *Merrimac* in a sinking condition. She was towed by the *Jamestown*, *Yorktown* and several smaller boats toward Norfolk, no doubt, if possible, to get her in the dry-dock for repairs. The *Minnesota* is afloat and being towed toward Fortress Monroe."

THE VESSELS ENGAGED.

THE ERICSSON BATTERY MONITOR.

The new Ericsson battery, or, as she is now called, the *Monitor*, which left this port for Southern waters last Wednesday, has already had her first engagement with the enemy, and has come out victor. It appears that she arrived in Hampton Roads last Saturday night, just after the rebel battery *Merrimac*

The *Merrimack*.

had been playing havoc with our blockaders. She came to the rescue precisely at the right moment. Yesterday morning she was set upon by the *Merrimac*, the *Jamestown* and the *Yorktown*. After a five hours' fight she drove them all off, the *Merrimac* putting back to Norfolk in a sinking condition. As the public will now be anxious to know something of the style and power of this iron-clad vessel, which has thus routed the famous rebel iron-clad floating battery, we append a full account of her, furnished by our correspondent, who accompanied her on a recent trial trip from this harbor.

DESCRIPTION OF THE VESSEL.

The designer and builder of the *Monitor* was Capt. ERICSSON, famous in connection with the invention of a mode of propelling vessels and working engines by the motor-power of caloric, or heated air. Capt. ERICSSON is a Swede by birth, but his remarkable and persevering scientific efforts have been carried on principally in this City for the last ten years.

By an act of Congress passed last Summer, the Secretary of the Navy was authorized to advertise for proposals to build one or more iron-clad vessels, all proposers to furnish their own plans. An appropriation of $1,500,000 was made to build such vessels, providing that the plans met with the approval of three commanding officers of the navy. The Board appointed consisted of Commodores JOSEPH SMITH, HIRAM PAUL-

DING, and Capt. CHAS. H. DAVIS. Capt. ERICSSON sent in a plan which was accepted, with the understanding that the vessel was to be finished in one hundred days. The contract bears date the 4th of October, 1861.

The keel of this vessel was laid on the 25th of October, and so rapidly was the work performed, that the engines were put into the vessel and operated on the 31st of December last. The construction of the vessel was under the superintendence of Engineer ALBAN C. STEINERS, and Assistant Engineer ISAAC NEWTON, who were detailed from the frigate *Roanoke*, by Government, for that purpose.

THE ARMAMENT.

The armament consists of two 11-inch Dahlgren guns, which are the heaviest now used by the navy. The lower part of the gun-carriages upon which the upper part slides when the gun is run in or out, consists of solid, wrought iron beams, extending the whole diameter of the turret, with their ends, secured to it in such a manner that they essentially form a part of it. These beams are planned perfectly true, are seven inches deep by four inches wide, and are placed perfectly parallel in the turret, both guns pointing in the same direction. This permits the officer working the guns to take his aim by sights fixed with the turret instead of with the guns, in the usual way, which requires personal exposure when taking the aim. The ports through the side of the turret are only sufficiently wide to permit of the passage through them of the muzzle of the guns, and with just enough addition, vertically, for the elevation required. Inside of these

swing iron pendulums, which close them against the enemy as soon as the gun recoils. The whole is made to revolve by a pair of steam engines placed beneath the deck, the handle which governs them passing up into the turret convenient to the hand of the officer who aims the gun.

HER AMMUNITION.

At the Novelty Iron Works a quantity of solid wrought iron shot was forged for the *Monitor*; each one weighing 187 pounds. These were intended for perforating and sinking iron clad vessels of the enemy whose sides are the ordinary height above the water line. Besides these she carries a quantity of cast iron shots, weighing 175 pounds each, and one hundred round of shells, in weight 155 pounds each.

THE MACHINERY.

Mr. C. H. DELAMATER fitted this vessel with machinery. It consists of two horizontal tubular boilers containing 3,000 square feet of fire surface, and two horizontal condensing engines, of forty inches diameter of cylinders, by twenty-two inches stroke of pistons. The propeller is nine feet diameter, sixteen feet pitch, and has four blades. Her speed is about six and a half knots an hour. All her machinery is below water-line.

FOR WHAT THE MONITOR WAS INTENDED.

The Ericsson Battery was not intended for an ordinary cruiser, but for the defence of our harbors and coast, and for operations such as those in which she has just achieved such a signal success. She is enabled to carry eight days' fuel, and thus can proceed easily from port to port along our seaboard. Provisions for three months can be stowed away in her, and a condensing apparatus for supplying fresh water to the officers and crew is fitted up on board.

THE LAST TRIAL TRIP OF THE MONITOR
AND ITS RESULTS.

Last Monday the *Monitor* went on a trial trip down the Bay, about five miles beyond Fort Lafayette. Her steering qualities were found to be all that could be desired.

The guns were fired to test the question which had been mooted, of whether the concussion within the turret would not be so great as to injure seriously the ears of the men. First, a blank cartridge was fired, with the hatches in the roof open. Then a charge of canister, weighing 135 pounds, with 15 pounds of powder, with the hatches still open, and finally the same charge with the hatches closed, as they will be under the fire of the enemy. It was found that in every case the concussion in every part of the Interior of the turret was considerably less than when standing near such a gun fired in the open air. The sailors stationed at the guns, and who expected to handle them shortly against the enemy, all expressed themselves delighted at the success of the trial. The speed of the vessel by the ship log was 6¼ knots, the engines making 65 revolutions.

The last heard of the *Monitor* previous to this news of her success, was by a bark which arrived here yesterday morning. The bark reported that, on the 7th inst., at 10 P. M., off Barnegat, she passed the *Monitor* in tow, bound for Fortress Monroe.

This magnificent success in her first trial, will settle all questions as to her efficiency.

LIEUT. WERDEN.

Lieut. J. R. WERDEN, it will be recollected, at the commencement of the rebellion was captured by the rebels, after having conveyed dispatches from the Government to the National fleet off Pensacola, and imprisoned several months at Montgomery. He was exchanged a short time ago, and was immediately assigned to the *Monitor*, in which, as will be seen from the dispatches, he has done most efficient service.

NORFOLK AND ITS NEIGHBORHOOD

A Map Showing the Locality of the Great Maritime Action in Hampton Roads, and the Railroad Connections of Norfolk with Richmond and Petersburgh. Reproduced from Our Sunday Edition.

THE MERRIMAC.

The *Merrimac*, the iron-plated rebel steamer which attacked the Ericsson Battery, was formerly the United States screw-frigate of the same name. She was built at the Navy-Yard at Charlestown, Mass., in 1855; and her last active service was in the Pacific Squadron. At the time of the rebel attack on the Norfolk Navy-Yard, she was lying there in ordinary, as a store and receiving ship. She was a ship of 3,200 tons burden, and was pierced for forty guns. When the Navy-yard was assailed, she was set fire to, scuttled and sunk, by the National officers, in preference to letting her fall into the hands of the rebels. A recent official report on the subject, made to the rebel authorities, stated that she was sunk and burned to her copper line and down through to her berth-deck, which, with her spacious gun-decks were also burned. After the rebels had got possession of the Yard, they proceeded to raise the hull of the *Merrimac*, and to convert her into a vessel of war for their own purpose. Her hull was cut down to within three feet of her water-work, and a bomb-proof house built on her gun-deck. She was then iron-pleated, and her bow and stern steel clad, with a projecting angle of iron for the purpose of piercing a vessel. She had no marts, and there was nothing to be seen over her gun-deck, with the exception of the pilot-house and smokestack. The bomb-proof was three inches thick, and made of wrought iron. Altogether she looked like a most formidable war-ship. But when her iron sheathing was half on, it was tested by columbiads and found inefficient. She was then additionally strengthened, until she was so heavy that she bade fair to become unmanageable, and even to sink by her own weight. In a description published some two or three months ago, her armament was stated as consisting of four 11-inch navy guns on each side, and two 100-pounder Armstrong guns at the bow and stern. But no doubt great changes have been made in her armament before this time. The Norfolk *Day Book* of the 6th ult. had an article describing the attempt to convert the *Merrimac* into an impregnable iron plated man-of-war as a failure. It began thus:

"We have scarcely patience enough left to condemn in temperate language the reckless impropriety of two of our cotemporaries, who have seen fit, in their thirst for notoriety, to thrust before the public the fact that the *Merrimac* has proved an abortion."

It was further said, that

"The calculation in displacement was erroneous. An error amounting to more than two hundred tons was discovered when the ship was floated off. The chief subject of regret is, that when she was shored up again the ship caught upon the blocks and received a considerable strain; consequently, some parts of the machinery have been taken up, and a quantity of dead-wood will have to be introduced to correct the tendency to log. Her great draught of water will prevent her taking part in active operations. This draught originally was about twenty-four feet, but it has been considerably increased."

The editor, however, comforted himself that at all events she could be used as a floating battery.

Her bow is armed with a steel plough, projecting six feet under water, to strike and sink the vessels of the blockading fleet. Her decks are protected by a covering of railroad iron, in the form of an arch, which it was hoped would be proof against shot and shell.

Perhaps this story of its failure was intended as a rebel ruse, to throw our naval force on the Potomac off its guard. The rebels have previously boasted of the immense power and strength of the *Merrimac* in the most extravagant manner. They had frequently averred that she was about to run out, sink the blockading vessels, and run along the Atlantic coast, and by destroying our men-of-war effectually raise the blockade. And indeed the first reports yesterday seemed as if the threat was actually about to be carried out. It was flashed over the wires that she had sunk the *Cumberland*, captured the *Congress*, and run the *Minnesota* ashore. The prospect seemed to be that she would rush along the Atlantic and Gulf coasts to the Rio Grande, sweeping the seas as she went. But she was no match for the *Monitor*, who has now effectually admonished her to keep out of the Road hereafter.

THE YORKTOWN (REBEL.)

The rebel steamer *Yorktown*, which took part in the fight, was formerly used on the New-York and Virginia line of steamers, running from here to Norfolk, Petersburgh and Richmond. She is a side-wheel steamer of 1,400 tons burthen, was built in this City in 1859, and her size is as follows: Length, 251 feet; breadth, 34 feet; depth, 18 feet. She was seized by the rebels last Summer while in Virginia waters, and was taken to Norfolk and fitted out as a man-of-war. Her sides were plated with iron, and other means were taken to render her strong. Our correspondent at Fortress Monroe, writing on the 6th inst., says he saw her a day or two before when up the James River with a flag of truce, and describes her as quite a formidable looking and formidably armed vessel. She carried six broadside guns rifled, one of which was an Armstrong, and two pivot guns. We believe she was commanded by Capt. PARRISH, late of the United States Navy.

JAMESTOWN, (REBEL,)

The *Jamestown* was another vessel of the same kind, running in the same line, and was almost a twin

to the *Yorktown*. The flag-of-truce correspondent, already mentioned, described her thus in yesterday's issue:

"As she approached us we perceived she was the *Jamestown*—one of the Confederate crack vessels. Yet, in comparison with our own boat, it must be confessed that she was not particularly formidable. She was worked with double engines, had a sharp iron prow at her bow, which will probably never come near enough any craft to do it much harm. She carried two 32-pound rifled cannon, Parrott style, fore and aft, and both guns were furnished with telescopic sights. The vessel looked trim; the officers wore a profusion of gold lace, while the marines and sailors were smart and active in appearance."

MINNESOTA—(NATIONAL.)

The *Minnesota*, which was run ashore after doing good duty against the rebel steamers, is a screw-frigate of 3,200 tons' burthen, pierced for 40 guns, built at Washington Navy-yard in 1855, and was manned by 400 officers and men. She is one of our largest screw steam-frigates, and is what is termed an auxiliary propeller. Her engines are 450 horse-power. Two of her guns are of 11-inch calibre, capable of throwing balls of 160 pounds weight. She has made but one regular cruise since she was built, and that was in the East India waters, from which she returned in 1858. On her return, she went to the Charlestown (Mass.) Navy-yard, where she was overhauled and repaired throughout. In May she sailed from Boston, and did various coast duty, under Capt. SILAS D. STRINGHAM, who was flag-officer of the Atlantic blockading squadron. In August she was the flag-ship of the expedition at the capture of the Hatteras forts by Commodore STRINGHAM, and did effective and brilliant duty in that affair. In September she arrived in this port, with the captured Hatteras prisoners. Shortly after she again went South, but under another commander, and has been doing duty of late at or near Hampton Roads. It is not known whether much damage has been done to her in the engagement.

THE CUMBERLAND (NATIONAL.)

The *Cumberland*, which was attacked and sunk by the rebel iron-clad steamer *Merrimac*, is a sailing sloop-of war, which has been engaged in the blockade of James River. She was a vessel of 1,726 tons burthen, was pierced for 24 guns, and carried 300 officers and men. She was built at Charlestown, Massachusetts, twenty years ago. Previous to the war she was in commission as one of the vessels of the Home Squadron. She was a leaky old affair, and her loss is by no means serious.

THE CONGRESS (NATIONAL.)

The *Congress*, which was captured on Saturday by the rebels was an old sailing frigate, employed also in blockading the Virginia waters. She was built at Kittery in 1841, was a vessel of 1,867 tons burthen, and was pierced for 50 guns. She was manned only by a few men of the Naval Coast Squadron, and was just about to be put out of commission, on account of unworthiness, when she was attacked by the rebels. In April last she returned from Montevideo, on the coast of Brazil, where she had been cruising; when she arrived here a large number of her officers, being big rebels, resigned. She was retained at Boston, and in September last sailed for duty on the Southern coast.

THE NEWS IN WASHINGTON.

WASHINGTON, Sunday, March 9.

The most intense excitement was created in Washington, to-day, by the news from Fortress Monroe, which came by the Baltimore boat. Visions were freely indulged in, of the *Merrimac* running the blockade of the fort, getting to sea, entering New-York harbor, and burning all the shipping at your docks, and holding your city itself at its mercy. The completion of the telegraph line to Fortress Monroe seems providential, in lifting these gloomy fears from the public mind. We only hope that the *Monitor* has done all that is claimed for her; but it is undeniable that yesterday's event in Hampton Roads is of the most exciting character, and should make New-York merchants and shipowners look instantly to their harbor defences. The Stevens battery, that the TIMES has in vain vindicated and urged to completion, might have been finished months ago, and could have sunk the *Merrimac* in twenty minutes; but she has been virtually abandoned by the Government, after the expenditure of half a million dollars on her. It is to be hoped that immediate action will be taken by Congress to-morrow to finish this iron velocipede and put her in commission.

Secretary STANTON gave orders this morning that the fullest reports of the Hampton Roads affair should be allowed to pass over the lines, so as to save the people of Northern cities from any vague fears.

The *Merrimac* is understood to have been under the command of Commandant BUCHANAN, late of the Navy-yard.

The Telegraph Line to Fortress Monroe.

WASHINGTON, Sunday, March 9.

The telegraph line to Fortress Monroe was built by order of the Secretary of War, under the direction of the General Manager of Military Telegraph Lines. The extension of the Government line from Harrington, Del., to Cape Charles, was constructed in twenty-three days. Thirty miles of the submarine cable was manufactured for the channel crossing in twenty days from the date of the order, by S. C. BISHOP, of New-York City.

The sixteen miles that was laid before the recent gale was recovered in good condition. The cable to replace the portion lost off Cape Henry was furnished by Mr. BISHOP in five days.

The shore end was landed at Cape Charles, at 4 o'clock this Sunday afternoon, by Mr. W. H. HEISS, Assistant-Manager of the Government Telegraphs, who has had the immediate charge of the work. Its completion at this opportune moment, bringing the news of the splendid victory of the *Monitor*, and the disabling of the *Merrimac*, has saved the country from great anxiety and expense.

The delay in completing the cable connection has been owing entirely to the continued boisterous weather.

The crew of the *Monitor* examine dents in the ship's armor from shellfire by the *Merrimack*.

The Officers of the *Monitor*.

The New-York Times.

VOL. XI—NO. 3265.　　　　　NEW-YORK, TUESDAY, MARCH 11, 1862.　　　　　PRICE TWO CENTS.

ANOTHER GREAT BATTLE.

A Most Glorious Victory in Arkansas.

The Combined Rebel Army Under Price, McCulloch, Van Dorn, and Mc-Intosh, Defeated.

A Desperate Battle, Lasting Three Days.

FINAL ROUT OF THE ENEMY.

OUR CAVALRY IN FULL PURSUIT.

Capture of Guns, Flags, Provisions, &c., in Large Quantities.

Our Loss in Killed and Wounded One Thosand.

THAT OF THE ENEMY STILL LARGER.

St. Louis, Monday, March 10.

The following is an official dispatch to Maj.-Gen. McClellan:

The army of the Southwest, under Gen. Curtis, after three days' hard fighting, has gained a most glorious victory over the combined forces of Van Dorn, McCulloch, Price and McIntosh. Our loss in killed and wounded is estimated at *one thousand!* That of the enemy was still larger. Guns, flags, provisions, &c., were captured in large quantities. Our cavalry are in pursuit of the flying enemy.　　(Signed)

H. W. Halleck, Major-General.

THE SOUTHWESTERN ARMY AND ITS MOVEMENTS.

St. Louis, Monday, March 10.
Correspondence of the Missouri Democrat.
Cross Hollows, Ark., Saturday, March 1.

Vigorous reconnoissances are kept up to watch the enemy's movements, and foraging parties are active in obtaining supplies. Pork and beef are purchased in the vicinity in abundance, and about half the quantity of flour required is obtained in the same manner and all our forage.

Price, whose retreat is acknowledged on all hands to have been ably conducted, has found refuge in Boston Mountains. From two deserters who came into camp yesterday, it is ascertained that he is encamped on Cove Creek road, while McCulloch is posted one and a half miles distant. The latter had burnt the village near the Indian frontier, known as Caul Hill. The supplies of the rebel army are obtained from Van Buren.

Brigadier-General Samuel R. Curtis defeated Confederate troops in the Battle of Pea Ridge.

It is stated on good authority that Price and McCulloch had a violent quarrel before leaving Cross Hollows.

At Fayetteville we found all the telegraphic dispatches up to the time of the evacuation by the rebels. A dispatch from McIntosh to Herbert, in command at Cross Hollows, urges him to press forward and reinforce Price at Springfield at all hazards, as that point is important to be held by the Confederates.

Ex-Senator Johnson, of Missouri, who opened a recruiting office at Springfield for the rebels previous to Price's departure, was the first to reach Fayetteville, where he stopped several days.

The clemency of Gen. Curtis, and judicious policy inaugurated in relation to the treatment of the citizens of Benton County, is bringing its reward in the general confidence already showing indications of being restored among fugitives who fled at our approach. Confederate bills, which were 25 cents discount on our arrival in Benton County, have suddenly become valueless, and the inhabitants refuse to take them.

Maj. Wright learns that the citizens of Keetsville knew of the intended attack on that place, and communicated the intelligence to the rebels, but kept all intimation of it from Capt. Montgomery. On the afternoon before the fight, the ladies of the village left, one by one, and during the attack all were out. Maj. WRIGHT learns that there are 5,500 rebels in Cedar County and in Dade County, Mo. These parties are committing depredations, and swearing vengeance against Union men.

The health of the troops has been good, particularly on the march.

THE REBELS FALLING BACK

Their Lines Along the Potomac Being Withdrawn.

Evacuation of Centreville, Winchester, and Other Important Points.

Their Batteries on the Lower Potomac Deserted.

EVIDENCES OF A GREAT PANIC

Splendid Pieces of Artillery Left in Position.

SPECIAL DISPATCH FROM WASHINGTON.
WASHINGTON, Monday, March 10.

My dispatch last night stated that the appearance of rebel scouts near Vienna was a feint, to cover their retreat. The latter part of the message failed to reach you—why, I know not, as it would have informed you of the great event that to-day convulses Washington—the general abandonment by the rebels of their Potomac line of defences.

From Winchester on the west, to the Cockpit batteries on the east, covering a front of one hundred miles, the rebels have precipitately withdrawn. Their retreat bears many evidences of a panic. Splendid guns were left in position in the Potomac batteries—some of them spiked, some not harmed. Valuable ammunition and stores were left at some places, that came into quiet possession of our troops. It can hardly be doubted that their wary leaders, as usual, obtained full information from traitors among us of the impending advance of our great army, and that they fled to get out of danger.

There seems to be uncertainty to-night whether the rebels have evacuated Manassas, but they are certainly gone from Centreville—at all events, after a diligent search in the extensive trenches there, late this afternoon, none were found.

OPERATIONS ON THE COAST

Brilliant Successes of the Fleet Under Commodore Dupont.

Capture of Brunswick, Ga., and Fernandina, Fla.

Inglorious Flight of the Rebels from Both Places.

Cannon and Munitions of War Captured.

Confederate General Sterling Price failed to regain a Rebel foothold in Missouri.

Old Fort Clinch "Retaken, Held and Possessed."

An Exciting Race Between a Gunboat and a Railroad Train.

BALTIMORE, Monday, March 10.

The United States steam gunboat *Alabama*, Capt. LANIER, arrived here this morning, direct from Fernandina, Fla., bringing Capt. DAVIS, late Flag-Officer of the South Atlantic Squadron, as bearer of dispatches from Commodore DUPONT to the Navy Department, announcing the capture of Fernandina and Brunswick by the fleet under his command.

We are indebted to Capt. DAVIS for an outline of the operations of the fleet since it left Port Royal about the 1st of March, on what was announced as an important expedition, the place of destination having been held back at the request of the Government.

The first point of the coast approached by the fleet was the town of Brunswick, Ga., the enemy abandoning their works and precipitately flying at the approach of the gunboats. It was taken possession of, and gunboats left in charge. This gives the Government the control of the whole coast of Georgia from South Carolina to Florida.

Brunswick being disposed of, the fleet moved twenty miles further to Cumberland Sound, the entrance to the harbor of Fernandina, Fla.

THE BATTLES IN HAMPTON ROADS.

Interesting Details of the Two Days' Fighting.

How the Cumberland was Sunk by the Merrimac.

The Congress Set on Fire and Blown Up.

Probably About a Hundred Lives Lost on the Cumberland.

The Terrific Engagement Between the Merrimac and the Monitor.

"THE BATTLE OF THE GIANTS."

A Large Hole Stove in the Side of the Merrimac.

LIEUT. WORDEN WOUNDED.

SPECIAL DISPATCH FROM WASHINGTON.
WASHINGTON, Monday, March 10.

A gentleman who witnessed the naval engagement in Hampton Roads, on Saturday and Sunday, says that only one man was killed by the shelling of Newport's News. The fire of our ships had no effect on the *Merrimac* until the arrival of the *Monitor*. The *Merrimac* can do no damage to a vessel or fort, unless within a half mile, on account of the lowness of her guns, which are barely above the level of the water In a gale she would be powerless.

The report of the *Monitor's* guns was much heavier than those of the *Merrimac's*. Not a man was to be seen on either ship—all being housed.

Our informant says the *Merrimac* is a "devil," but the *Monitor* a little more so : and that unless a gun explodes on the *Monitor*, she would have the advantage over her adversary.

The *Monitor* has the advantage of being all the time broadside on, and able to deliver her fire from any position. Her guns being so arranged that she can rake her own decks, if necessary.

The *Merrimac* was struck seventy-five times, but no perceptible effect was produced, though she hauled off and returned to Norfolk. The *Monitor* was wholly uninjured.

WASHINGTON, Monday, March 10—P. M.

The Government has no uneasiness about the *Merrimac*. The *Monitor* is considered, by naval men to have clearly established her superiority in the conflict of Sunday. The *Merrimac* cannot escape.

Lieut. WORDEN, who handled the *Monitor* so splendidly, and who was the only man wounded in the engagement, arrived in Washington to-day, and reported to the Navy Department in person. WORDEN is injured about the eyes, which are closely bandaged, and he has to be led from place to place. He gives many interesting incidents of the fight, and is quite sure that three of his heavy shot penetrated the *Merrimac*.

When the news was received in Washington of the *Merrimac's* advance, and the havoc she was committing among our war-vessels, there was a burst of indignation against the Navy Department for not having been prepared to meet her. It was for the moment forgotten that Congress had made no appropriation to enable Secretary WELLES to build iron-plated ships, although he had urged it three months ago, and, if Congress had acted, the iron-plated ships might now be in service.

Editorials

A PANIC ON A SMALL SCALE.—We hope the recent news from Hampton Roads has somewhat reassured the timid souls who were certain, on Sunday night, that the *Merrimac* would speedily visit this harbor and lay New-York in ashes. Their magnificent project of sinking stone-boats in the channel, for the purpose of keeping her out, may safely be postponed for a few weeks. Naturally enough the exploits of the *Merrimac* excited some consternation. Her movements were bold and brilliant, and if she had met nothing more formidable than the ordinary wooden frigates of our navy, it is not easy to limit the amount of mischief she might have done. But it was absurd to suppose that, under any circumstances, she could have been tempted to visit New-York. In the first place, it is very doubtful whether she could possibly stand the sea voyage. In the next, there is scarcely one chance in three that she could pass the forts that guard the entrance to the harbor. And in the third place, even if she could get in, it is not easy to see how she could possibly get out. In any event, she is not likely to enter upon such an adventure as a hostile visit to this port; and it is not worth while to destroy the harbor by way of protecting the City just yet.

Iron-clad Vessels.

The affair of the *Merrimac* has proved incontestibly the absolute necessity of iron-clad vessels in naval warfare. All the experiments and speculations in the world become of little importance in presence of the decisive test which she encountered. All our best and most formidable wooden vessels proved to be utterly ineffective against her mail-clad sides; and nothing but the most fortunate circumstance that we had just completed *one* war vessel of the same sort, enabled us to resist her raid upon our naval defences. But for the opportune presence of the *Monitor,* we do not see what could have prevented the *Merrimac* from destroying every one of our vessels in Hampton Roads, and then proceeding by a similar process to clear the Southern coast of our blockading squadron.

We trust this incident, disastrous as it has been to us, will convince Congress of the absolute necessity of at once ordering the construction of enough iron-clad gunboats to meet every probable emergency. Not long since, they rejected a proposition to appropriate $15,000,000 to this purpose. Recent events have shown that there is no possible way in which that sum of money can be put to better uses. We shall always need vessels of precisely this class. Even if the rebellion should end at once, and all danger of foreign war should for the time pass away, we need them as part of the permanent defences of the country; and there is no better time than this for entering upon the work of their construction.

There is another point, in this connection, which needs explanation. During the last eight or ten years, the Government has invested over half a million of dollars in STEVENS' Battery—an iron-clad vessel, resting upon substantially the same principles as those just tested, and certain to be, if successful, the most formidable engine of the kind ever constructed. The inventor has invested a very large private fortune in the work, and a few hundred thousand dollars more would insure its completion. Every dictate of interest and of honour—every motive of economy and of public safety—requires that this tremendous weapon should be made effective at the earliest possible moment.

Just at this point a Congressional Committee steps in, and, without assigning a single valid reason, arrests its progress and forbids its completion. They admit that, upon the testimony of professional men in every department, it promises to fulfil all the conditions

A complex military maneuver by Major-General Earl Van Dorn backfired when his Confederate troops were cut off from their supply depots.

that can be required of it. They acknowledge its power, its speed, its invulnerability, its easy management, and everything essential to its success. But—as will be seen by reference to an article in another column—without witnessing a single experiment, although the inventor had prepared them at his own cost,—without assigning a single valid objection, or alleging anything beyond a vague conjecture in disparagement of its claims, the Committee has pronounced judgment against it, and Congress refuses to authorize its completion.

Why is this? Why, at such a moment, when the country needs everything it can secure in the way of effective preparation for defence, does the Committee refuse to sanction the completion of such a work? Is it because the contract is already made—because there is no room for further speculation, no chance to make money out of it as a Government job? We trust Congress will give renewed attention to this subject, and take pains to procure such information as will enable it either to satisfy the country that the Battery is a failure, or else take early steps for its completion. Those who are best acquainted with its capabilities assert that it could sink the *Merrimac* in half an hour. If this is so, the country cannot afford to dispense with its services.

Coast and Harbor Defence.

We give in another column an abstract of an elaborate memorial to Congress, recapitulating the great features of the Stevens Battery, as approved by the whole Board of Government Examiners, completely refuting the objections of the majority, and setting forth, in detail, the fighting qualities and the results of experiments relative to that vessel.

Nothing could be more erroneous than the impression which generally obtains, that the report of this Board, taken as a whole, and with reference to the several professions of its distinguished members, is unfavorable to the completion of this great work. On the contrary, the Board *unanimously approved* all its great

features. They admit that all the parts of the vessel above water, and intended to be shot-proof, are "efficiently protected against the heaviest ordnance now afloat in any part of the world;" that the speed, even at one-half the boiler pressure proposed, will be seventeen knots, or nearly twenty statute miles an hour; that the vessel's facilities of manœuvring are remarkable and unprecedented; and that the weight and efficiency of broadside are 50 per cent. greater than those of our heaviest steam frigates.

The majority of the Board then make certain objections, which, according to the standard authorities in such matters, are wholly of an engineering character. Now, the only engineering experts on the Board—Prof. HENRY (who made an entirely favorable minority report) and Mr. STIMERS—were equally divided in opinion on these objections; therefore, there is *no majority report of experts against any feature of this vessel.*

Hence it was eminently proper for Mr. STEVENS to put to the highest possible test those points which were left in dispute by the experts of the Board. As the only material objection of the majority, according to Prof. HENRY, was that the Battery was not strong enough to go to sea, Mr. STEVENS therefore invited the very men who *have built* above two-thirds of the iron ships that the country has produced—and they will be admitted by Congress to be the highest possible authority—to decide the matter finally; and their unanimous report was that the Battery would be strong enough to stand any weather at sea.

The following objections of the majority—the demolition of the decks by firing over them; the inability of the sides to support their load; and the choking of the pumps by coal and the *débris* of the bilge, are refuted by the results of *actual trial,* as witnessed and verified by experts. The objection that the boilers can safely carry but twenty-five pounds of steam, is answered by the certificate of the United States Supervising Inspector of boilers, who, having tested them, states that they can carry fifty pounds according to law. The other objections are just as fully and satisfactorily answered, in the memorial referred to.

If it is possible to make a clearer case than this, we cannot divine the process by which it would be done. In fact, the costly and elaborate experiments made by Mr. STEVENS, and these certificates of the highest professional authorities, not only relieve Congress of the responsibility it must ordinarily feel in acting upon such novel questions, but they convert the report of this Board into an indorsement of his plans, by settling in his favor the points left unsettled by them.

In addition to all this, the facts that the Government already has an interest of half a million dollars in the vessel; that its total cost will be about half that of the European iron-clad vessels of the same size, but of inferior speed, protection and broadside, as admitted by the Board; and that the smaller iron-clad vessels now ordered, cannot possibly cope with such fast and heavy vessels as the *Warrior,* for instance—these facts must, and will, we think, speedily settle the question of completing this great work. We cannot see any pretext, much less a reason, why Congress should longer refuse to grant the necessary appropriation.

The New-York Times.

VOL. XI–NO. 3266.　　　　NEW-YORK, WEDNESDAY, MARCH 12, 1862.　　　　PRICE TWO CENTS.

MANASSAS EVACUATED.

The Rebel Stronghold Occupied by the Union Forces.

Evidences of the Precipitate Flight of the Rebels.

Jackson's Force Deserted at Winchester.

Hospital and Commissary Stores and War Materiel Left Behind.

The Works and Quarters Left Uninjured.

Accommodations for One Hundred and Fifty Thousand Men.

Supposed Stand of the Rebels at Gordonsville.

SPECIAL DISPATCH FROM WASHINGTON.

WASHINGTON, Tuesday, March 11.

The rebels have evacuated Manassas. We occupied it this morning.

Dispatches received at headquarters this forenoon stated positively that the rebels had not evacuated Winchester. If this is so,—and those best authorized to know report it,—Gen. JACKSON's rebel army is assuredly cut off and will be captured.

This abandonment of a splendid army corps at Winchester could not have been designed, and is further proof of the haste and confusion of the fight from Centreville and Manassas.

The officer commanding the Union forces at Manassas sent in a messenger to-night. I had the fortune to meet him, and get many particulars concerning the condition of things at Manassas. That famed rebel post was occupied this morning about 10 o'clock, and the Union flag was unfurled over the works.

Everything at Manassas was found in great confusion, the flight of the rebels having been precipitate in the extreme. Persons in the vicinity allege that the abandonment of the place was quite recently resolved on, and the guns were begun to be removed about a week ago. Intense alarm seized the rebel forces, and thenceforward a wild haste characterized all their movements.

The last rebel troops left the place last Friday. Their works were left entire and unharmed, and finer, it is said, are not to be found in the country. The log-huts are remarkably comfortable, and the accommodations ample for one hundred and fifty thousand men. Our army have come into possession of commissary and hospital stores in large quantities, besides wagons, tents, caissons and hundreds of other valuables. It is proper to add, however, that statements quite contradictory of these are received,

and it is hard to decide which are true.

The statements of all persons in the vicinity concur that the rebel forces have retired to Gordonsville. This would place them behind the Rappahannock River, the crossing of which by the Union army could be strongly resisted, as the bridge is 1,200 feet long, and that the rebels will doubtless destroy. The country about Gordonsville is rolling, and susceptible of good defences, though the Rappahannock bottom is wide, and only about two feet higher than the water in its usual Winter Stage. But though the rebel officers may have designed to stop at Gordonsville, it is by no means certain they have done so, as they retreated in a most excited and disorderly manner.

At Gordonsville the rebels would have the advantage of a narrower front than at Manassas, and less easily flanked. The reason of their sudden retreat from Manassas was the belief they had of an intention on the part of Gen. McCLELLAN to turn their right flank by a march through Fredericksburgh.

If the rebels are pursued from Manassas to Gordonsville ever so vigorously, it is not likely they could be caught up with under a week, if they destroy the railroad as they go. Those persons who are so exasperated because the rebels were not advanced upon two months ago, forget that they could have run away as easily then as now, and the pursuit of them been far more difficult and dangerous.

Dispatches from Gen. HEINTZELMAN, to-day, confirm in every particular the report of the panic retreat of the rebels from the Potomac batteries. Confusion reigned everywhere. For miles in the interior, men were burning their houses, their fodder, and other farm wealth, and fleeing in dismay to the South.

The *Stepping Stones*, late yesterday evening, towed from Quantico to Budd's Ferry a barge containing the picket guards of 500, and, returning, towed to the Maryland shore the barge containing the stores mentioned.

The rebel steamer *Page* is lying in Quantico Creek, burned to the water's edge.

A reconnoissance was made this forenoon across the Occoquan, scouring the country for five miles west of that stream. All the late rebel camps in that vicinity were found deserted and destroyed.

The Lincoln Cavalry, while scouting in the vicinity of Burke's Station, on the Orange and Alexandria Railroad, fourteen miles out, yesterday captured thirteen secession prisoners. Eleven of these prisoners passed through Pennsylvania-avenue this morning, in charge of a guard.

BATTLE OF PEA RIDGE.

Official Report of Gen. Curtis to Gen. Halleck.

BEN McCULLOCH KILLED.

Brilliant Manœuvres by the Union Army.

DESPERATE FIGHTING ON BOTH SIDES.

FINAL ROUT OF THE REBELS.

ST. LOUIS, Tuesday, March 11.

The following is the official report of Gen. CURTIS to Gen. HALLECK:

HEADQUARTERS ARMY OF THE SOUTHWEST. }
PEA RIDGE, Ark., March 9. }

GENERAL: On Thursday, the 6th inst., the enemy commenced an attack on my right wing, assailing and following the rear guard of a detachment under Gen. SIEGEL to my main lines on Sugar Creek Hollow, but ceased firing when he met my reinforcements, about 4 P. M.

During the night I became convinced that he had moved on so as to attack my right or rear. Therefore, early on the 7th I ordered a change of front to the right—my right, which then became my left, still resting on Sugar Creek Hollow.

General Ben McCulloch was another Rebel commander lost in battle against the North.

General James McIntosh, one of three Confederate field commanders at Pea Ridge, Arkansas, was mortally wounded.

This brought my line across Pea Ridge, with my new right resting on Head Cross Timber Hollow which is the head of Big Sugar Creek. I also ordered an immediate advance of the cavalry and light artillery, under Col. Osterhaus, with orders to attack and break what I supposed would be the reinforced line of the enemy. This movement was in progress, when the enemy, at 11 A. M., commenced an attack on my right. The fight continued mainly at these points during the day, the enemy having gained the point held by the command of Col. Carr, at Cross Timber Hollow, but was entirely repulsed with the fall of the Commander, McCulloch, in the centre, by the forces under Col. Davis. The plan of attack on the centre was gallantly carried forward by Col. Osterhaus who was immediately sustained and supported by Col. Davis' entire division, supported also by Gen. Sigel's command, which had remained till near the close of the day on the left. Col. Carr's division held the right, under a galling, continuous fire, all day. In the evening, firing having entirely ceased in the centre, and the right being now on the left, I reinforced the right by a portion of the Second Division, under Gen. Asboth. Before the day closed I was convinced that the enemy had concentrated his main force on the right. I commenced another change of front, forward, so as to face the enemy where he had deployed on my right flank in a strong position. The change had only been partially effected, but was in full progress, when, at sunrise on the 8th, my right and centre renewed the firing, which was immediately answered by the enemy with renewed energy along the whole extent of his line. My left, under Gen. Sigel moved close to the hills occupied by the enemy, driving him from the heights, and advancing steadily toward the head of the Hollows. I immediately ordered the centre and right wing forward, the right turning the left of the enemy, and cross-firing on his centre. This final position of the enemy was in the are of a circle. A charge of infantry, extending throughout the whole line, completely routed the whole rebel force, which retired in great confusion, but rather safely, through the deep, impassable defiles of Cross Timber. Our loss is heavy. The enemy's can never be ascertained, for their dead are scattered over a large field. Their wounded, too, may many of them be lost and perish. The force is scattered in all directions, but I think his main force has returned to Boston Mountains.

Gen. Sigel follows him toward Keitsville, while my cavalry is pursuing him toward the mountains, scouring the country, bringing in prisoners and trying to find the rebel Major-Gen. Van Dorn, who had command of the entire force at this, the battle of Pea Ridge.

I have not as yet statements of the dead and wounded, so as to justify a report, but I will refer you to a dispatch which I will forward very soon.

Officers and soldiers have displayed such unusual gallantry that I hardly dare to make distinction. I must, however, name the Commanders of Divisions: Gen. Sigel gallantly commanded the right, and drove back the left wing of the enemy; Gen. Asboth, who s wounded in the arm, in his gallant effort to reinforce the right; Col. and Acting-Brig.-Gen. Davis who commanded the centre, where McCulloch fell on the 7th, and pressed forward the centre on the 8th; Col and Acting-Brig.-Gen. Carr is also wounded in the arm, and was under the continuous fire of the enemy during the two hardest days of the struggle.

Illinois, Indiana, Iowa, Ohio and Missouri may proudly share the honor of victory, which their gallant heroes won over the combined forces of Van Dorn, Price and McCulloch at Pea Ridge, in the mountains of Arkansas.

I have the honor to be, General,

Your obedient servant,

SAMUEL R. CURTIS, Brigadier-General.

LATEST REPORTS FROM SPRINGFIELD.

Special to the Missouri Republican.

SPRINGFIELD, Mo., Monday, March 10.

A messenger who arrived this morning at 3 o'clock reports that the battle lasted from Thursday morning till Saturday evening, and that our loss was about 450 killed and wounded. The rebel loss was about 1,000 killed and wounded, and 1,000 taken prisoners, among them Col. McRea, of an Arkansas Regiment.

The attack was made from the North and West our army being completely surrounded. Gens. Van Dorn, Price, McCulloch and McIntosh were present with about 25,060 men. Gens. McCulloch and McIntosh are reported mortally wounded.

The attack from the rear was made by Gen. McCulloch, and was met by Gen. Sigel, who routed him completely. His corps scattered in wild confusion. We have also captured a large amount of stores, cannon, teams and ammunition.

THE LOCATION OF THE BATTLE.

The location of the battle can be seen from any ordinary map of Arkansas, or of the United States. It was in the extreme northwestern part of the State, and in the northwesternmost county (Benton.) A range of hills (of the Ozark range) will be seen sweeping from Missouri through this corner of the State, and from thence branching into the Indian Territory, where that section known as the Boston Mountain is known. Big Sugar Creek, near which the fight began, is a short distance north of Bentonville, the capital of Benton County, and Pea Ridge, which is a part of the mountain range, is but a short distance from the same town. Cross Timber Hollows, to and from which the rebels were chased, is four miles from the head-waters of the Osage Creek. The enemy retreated in two directions, part of them through one of the mountain defiles toward the Indian Territory, and part in a southeasterly direction. At the time when Gen. Curtis' report ends they were being pursued in both directions by our cavalry and infantry. The section of country where the battle took place is a wild, hilly region, where, in case of a rout, it would be extremely difficult to pursue the routed enemy.

GEN. CURTIS.

Maj.-Gen. Samuel R. Curtis, who comes so prominently before the public in connection with the battle and victory of Pea Ridge, is a native of Ohio, and a man of 54 years of age. He was a resident of New-York when, as a Cadet, he, in 1827, entered West Point; he was breveted Second Lieutenant Seventh Infantry, 1831, and next year resigned from the army. He devoted himself to the law and to civil engineering, and in 1837-9 was Chief Engineer of the Muskingum River Improvement. He was for years an Engineer of the Ohio Board of Public Works, and in 1846 he was appointed Adjutant-General of that State. In June of that year, having prepared the military outfit of the Ohio volunteers for the Mexican war, he took the field himself as Colonel of the Third Ohio. At the close of his year's service he acted as Assistant Adjutant-General to Gen. Wool; he was subsequently Civil and Military Governor of Saltillo; also, in 1847, of Matamoras, Camargo and Monterey. When he returned to the United States, he practiced law for a time, but when the State of Iowa entered on the project of removing the obstructions at the Des Moines Rapids of the Mississippi River, he was chosen Chief Engineer, and took up his residence at Keokuk. He was elected to Congress from Iowa, as a Republican member of the Thirty-fifth Congress, and reëlected to the Thirty-sixth. On the breaking out of the war he resigned his seat to accept a commission as Brigadier-General, and in May last entered on his duties. He was assigned to duty in Missouri, which was then in the throes of revolution. He did much active service under Fremont, and shortly after Gen. Halleck took command of the Department, he was appointed to command the expedition intended to clear the rebels out of Southwestern Missouri. He left Rolla, in January, with a force twenty thousand strong, drove Price from Springfield, routed him at Cross Hollows, and now has defeated the combined commands of all the rebel Generals in Arkansas. Congress, a few days ago, signified their approval of his merits by appointing him a Major-General of Volunteers.

BEN. McCULLOCH.

The career of Gen. Ben. McCulloch, who is reported by Gen. Curtis as having been killed at the battle of Pea Ridge, is so well known that it is hardly necessary to recapitulate now. But, if he be killed, this will be the last of him. As, however, since the war began, he has not only been ubiquitous in his presence, but has been slain several times, he may, perhaps, turn up again. He is a Tennesseean by birth, and 48 years of age. He first became famous in his native State, as a bear-killer. In 1835 he went to Texas with Davy Crockett to take part in the Texan revolution, and Sam Houston assigned him to the artillery and made him captain of a gun. He afterwards settled in Texas and became celebrated in Indian fights. When the Mexican war broke out he raised a band of Texans on the Guadaloupe, whose services were accepted by Taylor. He was employed in scouting expeditions and took a hand in various battles of the war; for which services President Pierce afterward appointed him United States Marshal for Texas. When the Mormon rebellion broke out, he was appointed one of the Peace Commissioners to Utah, though a more unfit person could not have been discovered in the country. When the present rebellion broke out, he was sought for by Jeff. Davis, and has been engaged everywhere, and in all sorts of rebel service. He took a body of Texans to Missouri and assisted Gen. Price in various engagements, and particularly in the battle of Springfield. After that he quarreled with Price, and retired with his army to Arkansas, and stationed himself at Fort Smith. When Gen. Curtis gave the present chase to the rebels, he again came north to the Arkansas northern line, with all the other rebel commanders in that section; and has now fallen, a traitor to his country. In person he was remarkable—six feet high, slender but athletic, and with the appearance and air of a frontier fighter. He was undoubtedly a partisan leader of capacity, but was utterly unfit to command a large body of men.

WINCHESTER NOT EVACUATED.

JACKSON'S FORCES STILL THERE.

An Armed Reconnoissance to Within Five Miles of the Place.

BUNKER HILL, Tuesday, March 11.

The intelligence of the evacuation of Winchester, yesterday, was premature. It was Berryville that the reconnoissance reported evacuated. The latest intelligence from Winchester is to the effect that the town is occupied by at least one brigade of infantry. Other troops are also there. There is a strong suspicion that a portion of the forces which evacuated Centreville have been ordered to reinforce Winchester.

The pickets were undisturbed last night. An active scouting was continually kept up.

The New-York Times.

VOL. XI–NO. 3267.　　　　NEW-YORK, THURSDAY, MARCH 13, 1862.　　　　PRICE TWO CENTS.

NEWS FROM MANASSAS

Reports of Our Correspondent with the Advance of the Army.

The Rebel Evacuation Commenced on Friday Last.

THE PANIC AMONG THE REAR GUARD.

The Rebels at Winchester Now Said to Have Escaped.

Great Strength of the Rebel Fortifications.

Concentration of the Rebel Army at Gordonsville.

SPECIAL DISPATCHES FROM WASHINGTON.

WASHINGTON, Wednesday, March 12.

A courier from the Union troops in the direction of Brentsville, Va., brings reports to 5 P. M. yesterday. Up to that time they had sustained their difficult march with much fortitude, and but few lagged behind. All are much disappointed at the flight of the rebels. The smoke of burning property near Manassas can be plainly seen from camp.

The roads in many places are very bad.

Contrabands coming into our lines report that officers commanding the twelve months "Confederate" troops advised their men to disband and repair to their homes.

Great columns of smoke seen in the direction of Brentsville, indicated the abandonment and destruction of the enemy's works.

A correspondent of the TIMES, who accompanied the advance upon Centreville and Manassas has just come in. He was in every fort at Centreville, and went with the first column that crossed the Bull Run battle-field and entered the famous stronghold, Manassas. He corrects many previous statements we have had of the evacuation of those places by the enemy.

It was only last Friday that the retreat of the rebels from Centreville commenced. Gen. JOHNSTON left on Friday morning; Gen. SMITH left on Saturday afternoon, and Col. STUART last Monday, the day our army left camp on the Potomac.

The retreat was conducted very orderly at first. Everything was carefully cleaned up at Centreville —nothing left that could be useful to us. The forts were well planned and very formidable. They command the roads, and the fire of not less than a hundred guns could be converged upon any approach to the defences; but the guns were never brought from Manassas to mount the Centreville forts. A railroad track extended from Manassas to Centreville, and a telegraph line. The rebel Generals had their headquarters at Centreville all together, and a more convenient and complete military establishment could not be found in Washington than they had.

Through Manassas the enemy continued their re-

THE GREAT PLAN OF THE CAMPAIGN.

Diagram Exhibiting the Grand Lines of Military Movement of the Union Armies, as Planned by Lieut. Gen. Scott, and now being Carried Out.

1. STARTING POINT OF THE PIVOT.
2. DIAGONAL TERMINUS OF THE PIVOT.

treat as quietly as it began. They carried off all their heavy guns from Manassas—forty to sixty in number —part of their army marching by turnpike to Warrenton, and part to Gordonsville, where it was said they would make a stand.

It was on Monday evening that the first sign of panic was noticed at Manassas. A part of STUART's rear column was preparing a train to move Southward by railroad, when they learned some excited rebels had set fire to the bridges ahead of them. They immediately began to burn, destroy, and run away in general confusion. Five hundred barrels of flour, piled up in ranks, had their heads stove in. Barrels of molasses suffered the same way, with more loss to the commodity; and a hundred and sixty barrels or kegs of powder were left which they did not well know how to destroy in safety to themselves.

It seems to be confirmed that the enemy had, two weeks since, between fifty and sixty thousand troops

at Centreville and Manassas, and that they only began their retreat last Friday. Why they went is a mystery, as that number of men, in the fortifications they had prepared, would have been equal to three times their force assailing them from without. They must have feared to trust their men whose enlistments were expiring, or their powder, which many accounts agree is of very inferior quality.

But the strangest news brought by the TIMES correspondent is that Gen. JACKSON and one-half his army, whom Gen. BANKS yesterday supposed he was closely watching in Winchester, went down the railroad to Manassas one week ago, and quietly marched off southward. The other half are said to be moving southward in the valley of the Shenandoah.

Reconnoissances beyond Manassas show that all the damage possible to be done in a brief time has been done to the railroad that took the rebels off. The last of the rebels left Manassas on Monday evening. On Monday night our scouts approached the place. On Tuesday, about 1 o'clock, P. M., the correspondent of the TIMES, attended by a detachment of Union troops, entered the works.

FROM ANOTHER CORRESPONDENT.

WASHINGTON, Wednesday, March 12.

Information received from a gentleman direct from Manassas, who left there at 10 o'clock this morning, represents the condition of the army as about the same as it was yesterday afternoon. The report prevalent that the rebels were again concentrating in that vicinity is without foundation; on the contrary, there is little if any doubt that the rebels have retired toward Gordonsville, and that they rest, with their advance at the Rapidan River, their camps extending back to Gordonsville, twelve miles.

WASHINGTON, Wednesday, March 12—P. M.

Accounts received from Manassas to-night state that nothing of much value to our army was found at that place. The wagons, about thirty in number, were old and worn out, and had evidently been impressed into the service. The "contrabands" from the surrounding country came in and helped themselves to whatever clothing they could find, and also to the commissary stores, such as flour, bread, meat and cooking utensils, which the enemy had left behind them.

It was ascertained from the prisoners captured yesterday, namely, Capt. WOODS and four privates of the Louisiana Tigers, at the first station on the Orange and Alexandria Railroad, beyond Manassas, that a company of that corps had just retired as our forces advanced into Manassas.

The works deserted by the enemy are not occupied by our troops.

A large number of rebels in leaving Bull Run took the Warrenton Turnpike leading towards Richmond.

The rebel rear guard, on passing through Gainesville, six miles from Bull Run, fired and destroyed the village.

MOORE's extensive flouring mills, at the foot of Bull Run Mountain, and six miles from the Stone Bridge, were also burned.

The railway stations and bridges, for the distance of about fifteen miles, were also destroyed yesterday morning.

It is supposed from what could be gathered, making a fair average for the number the huts could contain, that the rebel troops at Manassas did not at any time exceed 60,000 men, and not more than 30,000 have occupied that section within the last two months.

Information to-night, received from Winchester, is that our forces to-day took possession of that town.

Major-General McDowell.

Logs shaped and painted like cannons — "Quaker guns" — were found throughout the abandoned Confederate defensive works around Manassas.

IMPORTANT FROM WASHINGTON.

War Bulletins Issued by the President.

THE ORDER FOR A FORWARD MOVEMENT

Gen. McClellan Relieved of the Command-in-Chief.

He Takes the Field at the Head of the Army of the Potomac.

A NEW DIVISION OF DEPARTMENTS.

Gen. Fremont Assigned to a Command in Western Virginia and Eastern Tennessee.

Gen. Halleck in Command of the Department of the Mississippi.

Enthusiastic Reception of Gen. McClellan by the Army.

IMPORTANT PROCEEDINGS OF CONGRESS.

[OFFICIAL.]

WAR BULLETINS.

EXECUTIVE MANSION,
WASHINGTON, Jan. 27, 1862.

THE PRESIDENT'S GENERAL WAR ORDER, NO. 1.

Ordered, That the 22d day of February, 1862, be the day for a general movement of the land and naval forces of the United States against the insurgent forces.

That especially,

The army at and about Fortress Monroe,

The army of the Potomac,

The army of Western Virginia,

The army near Munfordsville, Ky.,

The army and flotilla at Cairo,

And a naval force in the Gulf of Mexico,

be ready for a movement on that day.

That all other forces, both land and naval, with their respective commanders, obey existing orders for the time, and be ready to obey additional orders when duly given.

That the Heads of Departments, and especially the Secretaries of War and of the Navy, with all their subordinates, and the General-in-Chief, with all other commanders and subordinates of the land and naval forces, will severally be held to their strict and full responsibilities for the prompt execution of this order.

ABRAHAM LINCOLN.
EXECUTIVE MANSION,
WASHINGTON, March 8, 1862.

THE PRESIDENT'S GENERAL WAR ORDER, NO. 2.

Ordered, First, that the Major-General commanding the army of the Potomac proceed forthwith to organize that part of said army destined to enter upon active operations, including the reserve, but excluding the troops to be left in the fortifications about Washington, into four army corps, to be commanded according to seniority of rank, as follows:

First corps to consist of four divisions, and to be commanded by Maj.-Gen. I. McDOWELL.

Second corps to consist of three divisions, and to be commanded by Brig.-Gen. E. V. SUMNER.

Third corps to consist of three divisions, and to be commanded by Brig.-Gen. S. P. HEINTZELMAN.

Fourth corps to consist of three divisions, and to be commanded by Brig.-Gen. E. L. KEYES.

2. That the divisions now commanded by the officers above assigned to the commands of corps shall be embraced in, and form part of their respective corps.

3. The forces left for the defence of Washington will be placed in command of Brig.-Gen. JAMES WADSWORTH, who shall also be military Governor of the District of Columbia.

4. That this order be executed with such promptness and dispatch as not to delay the commencement of the operations, already directed to be undertaken by the army of the Potomac.

5. A fifth army corps to be commanded by Maj.-Gen. N. P. BANKS, will be formed from his own and Gen. SHIELDS' (late Gen. LANDER's) Division.

ABRAHAM LINCOLN.
EXECUTIVE MANSION,
WASHINGTON, March 11, 1862.

Confederate fortifications are surveyed by Federal troops.

THE PRESIDENT'S GENERAL WAR ORDER, NO. 3.

Major-Gen. McCLELLAN having personally taken the field at the head of the army of the Potomac, until otherwise ordered, he is relieved from the command of the other Military Departments, he retaining command of the Department of the Potomac.

Ordered, further, That the two Departments now under the respective commands of Generals HALLECK and HUNTER, together with so much of that under Gen. BUELL as lies west of a north and south line, indefinitely drawn through Knoxville, Tenn., be consolidated and designated the Department of the Mississippi, and that until otherwise ordered Maj.-Gen. HALLECK have command of said Department.

Ordered, also, That the country west of the Department of the Potomac and east of the Department of the Mississippi be a Military Department, to be called the Mountain Department, and that the same be commanded by Major-General FREMONT; that all the Commanders of Departments, after the receipt of this order by them respectively, report severally and directly to the Secretary of War, and that prompt, full and frequent reports will be expected of all and each of them.   ABRAHAM LINCOLN.

THE NEW MILITARY DEPARTMENTS.

GEN. McCLELLAN'S DEPARTMENT.

The Department of the Potomac, to which Gen. McCLELLAN is now confined by the President's War Order, No. 3, has the following geographical boundaries:

The States of Delaware and Maryland, the District of Columbia, and that portion of Virginia east of the Alleghany Mountains and North of James River, excepting Fortress Monroe and sixty miles around the same.

GEN. HALLECK'S DEPARTMENT.

The Department of the Mississippi, as newly constructed, embraces the late Departments of HALLECK and HUNTER, and the greater part of that under BUELL. It will extend over the following region:

Dacotah, Nebraska, Colorado, the Indian Territory west of Arkansas, and Kansas—being HUNTER's late Department; Missouri, Arkansas, Iowa, Minnesota, Wisconsin, Illinois, Indiana, and the States of Kentucky and Tennessee as far west as the town of Knoxville, and to a line from thence run north and south indefinitely—being all of HALLECK's and nearly all of BUELL's late Departments. This Department is by far the largest, geographically, of the three newly-constructed Departments, and comprises more than one-half of the entire territory of the United States.

GEN. FREMONT'S DEPARTMENT.

The new Mountain Department will include the following sections:

That part of Virginia west of the Alleghany Mountains, lately commanded by Gen. ROSECRANS; that part of Tennessee west of Knoxville, that part of Kentucky west of a line drawn north from the same town, and the States of Ohio and Michigan.

OUR SPECIAL WASHINGTON DISPATCHES.

WASHINGTON, Wednesday, March 12.
GEN. M'CLELLAN AND THE ARMY OF THE POTOMAC.

The department having formally announced that Gen. McCLELLAN has taken the field in person, it is not improper to say that he left Washington last Monday, and is leading his great Potomac army upon the flying rebels of Virginia. His reception among the troops, as he passed to their head, was one of the grandest ever witnessed in the country. The largest body of men ever put in motion at once since the battle of Solferino moved from the banks of the Potomac on that day. For many miles, on divers roads, the embattled ranks pressed forward, and the cheers that hailed the General at one point of the lines was taken up by regiment after regiment, and division after division, until the whole vast army rent the heavens with shouts of welcome.

Gen. McCLELLAN rode through the ranks in motion his cap ever in his hand, returning the salutes of the enthusiastic soldiers. It is only hoped by his friends that the country will patiently give him half the time

that was accorded to the Western General who pursued his foe from Lexington, Missouri, to Arkansas.

GEN. M'CLELLAN'S POSITION.

The relief of Gen. McCLELLAN from the command of the Western Department, is only just to him. It would be wrong to keep him responsible for campaigns which, while he is in the field, he cannot personally supervise. While his enemies see in this change his humiliation, his friends see his justification and safety.

GEN. FREMONT'S RESTORATION TO COMMAND.

The restoration of Maj.-Gen. FREMONT to a command, was, under the circumstances, a proper deference to the opinions of a very large, intelligent and respectable body of men in Congress, whose good will it is desirable for the President to retain. The President's action would have been more gratifying if FREMONT's new command had been more important. It includes only ROSECRANS' and GARFIELD's troops, and there are no rebels in arms in the Department for even this small force to operate against.

NO COUNCIL OF WAR HELD.

The statement published that last week a council of war in Washington decided, eight to four, that the army of the Potomac could not be moved against the enemy at present, is entirely untrue. The Generals were unanimous that an advance was possible and proper. The only difference was as to the plan of the proposed attack.

NO TAX ON FLOUR.

Hon. ALFRED ELY having received about fifty letters from millers residing in New-York, appeared before the Committee on Ways and Means, recently, in opposition to the proposed tax of ten cents on every barrel of flour. The result was this tax was stricken from the bill.

THE CLAIMS COMMISSION AT ST. LOUIS.

JOSEPH HOLT arrived here to-day from St. Louis. The Commission for the settlement of the claims in the Department of Missouri, under FREMONT's administration, have completed their labors. They will make their report in a few days. The aggregate amount of claims presented amounted to $10,000,000. The sum awarded is considerably below that figure.

THE SECRETARY OF WAR AND HARBOR DEFENCES.

The Secretary of War was before the Military Committee of the Senate to-day for two hours. The Secretary has under consideration the important subject of harbor defences in the Northern cities.

VOTES OF THANKS.

The speedy action taken by Congress, in passing resolutions of thanks to our gallant Naval Commanders, will have a good effect in the service. The Naval Committee of the Senate have reported two to-day—one to Commander FOOTE and Capt. WORDEN.

COST OF THE MONITOR.

The *Monitor* cost less than $250,000, and was contracted to be finished in ninety days.

THE STEVENS BATTERY.

Mr. STEVENS is here with a model of his battery. It has been visited and examined with deep interest to-day, by Naval Committees of Congress, and receives universal applause. Can New-York do nothing to promote its completion? By working day and night it could be finished in sixty days.

THE AQUIA CREEK BATTERIES.

By an arrival at the Navy-yard to-day it was ascertained that the rebel batteries were evacuated at Aquia Creek yesterday morning. Whether permanently or not, there are no means of ascertaining.

GEN. FREMONT.

Gen. FREMONT will return to Washington either this evening or to-morrow morning.

THE RAILROAD TO MANASSAS.

Repairs have already been commenced on the bridges injured by the rebels at Bull Run, and the probability is the railroad to Manassas will be in running order this week.

The New-York Times.

VOL. XI–NO. 3290.　　　　　NEW-YORK, WEDNESDAY, APRIL 9, 1862　　　　　PRICE TWO CENTS.

GLORIOUS NEWS.

"ISLAND NO. TEN IS OURS."

Surrender of the Rebel Stronghold to Com. Foote.

Evacuation of the Shore Batteries in the Night.

The Whole Rebel Force Captured by Gen. Pope.

Three Generals, 6,000 other Prisoners, 100 Siege Pieces, Several Field Batteries, Immense Quantities of Small Arms, &c.

The Great Rebel Floating Battery and the Whole Rebel Fleet.

NOT A UNION SOLDIER LOST.

CHICAGO, Tuesday, April 8.

The steamer *Alp* arrived at Cairo at 8 o'clock this morning, bringing Second Master LORD, of the Flagship *Benton*, with dispatches from Commodore FOOTE, announcing the surrender to him, at midnight, of the entire position of the rebels, including men, guns and transports. The number of prisoners is not yet known, nor the amount of ordnance-stores.

DISPATCH FROM GEN. HALLECK.

ST. LOUIS, Tuesday, April 8.

Gen. HALLECK has just telegraphed the War Department that Island No. 10 was abandoned by the enemy last night, leaving all their artillery, baggage, supplies and sick.

FIRST REPORT OF COMMODORE FOOTE.

STRAMER BENTON, OFF ISLAND No. 10,
April 8, 1862—3:25 A. M.

To Hon. Gideon Welles, Secretary of the Navy:

Two officers of the rebel navy have this instant boarded us from Island No. 10, by order of their commanding officer; they were ordered to surrender Island No. 10 to the commander of the naval forces. As these officers knew nothing of the batteries on the Tennessee shore, I have sent Capt. PHELPS to ascertain something definite on the subject. Gen. POPE is now advancing in strong force to attack the rear. I am ready with the gunboats and mortars to attack in front. BUFORD is ready to cooperate; but it seems as if the place is to be surrendered without further defence.

(Signed,)　　　A. H. FOOTE,
　　　　　　　Flag-Officer.

THE SIEGE OF YORKTOWN.

RECONNOITERING THE ENEMY'S POSITION

A Line of Defence from Yorktown to the James River.

The Batteries on Each Flank Attacked by Our Artillery.

Berdan's Sharpshooters Picking off the Rebel Gunners.

EVERYTHING PROGRESSING FAVORABLY.

NEWS BY WAY OF BALTIMORE.

FORTRESS MONROE, Monday, April 7,
via Baltimore, Tuesday, April 8.

Nothing has been done to-day in front of Yorktown, with the exception of a reconnoissance in that direction and some cannonading.

A telegraph line is built to our headquarters near Yorktown.

The *Spaulding* came in this morning from Ship Point. The rebel works abandoned there are quite formidable. The rebels took off their guns, but left their barracks complete. Ship Point is about eight miles from Yorktown, affording a fine base of operations.

A great crowd of Norfolk people assembled on the shore near Sewall's Point on Sunday, including men, women and children, all eagerly engaged in watching the Yankees.

DISPATCH FROM GEN. WOOL.

WAR DEPARTMENT,
WASHINGTON, Tuesday, April 8.

The Secretary of War received a letter this afternoon from Gen. WOOL, stating that at 2 o'clock yesterday afternoon, nothing was doing at Yorktown except preparations for attacking the fortifications; that the enemy's force was reported to be from 25,000 to 30,000, and at 2 o'clock P. M., the *Merrimac, Yorktown, Jamestown*, and four tugs were lying at Craney Island.

THE ENEMY'S LINE OF DEFENCE.

From the National Intelligencer of Yesterday.

From the seat of war in Lower Virginia private information up to Sunday noon has been received. Gen. McCLELLAN's army then confronted the enemy's line of defence, which extended across the peninsula, from Yorktown to James River, embracing three batteries and several mill-dams.

An artillery engagement had occurred with MAGRUDER's Battery at Winn's Mill, near James River, and another with the battery at Lee's Mill, two miles from Yorktown. The battery in the centre had not been attacked. The peninsula at this point is six miles wide.

The first shell from MAGRUDER's battery killed three men in the Seventh Maine Regiment, but 200 shells afterwards thrown did no injury whatever.

Yorktown was seen to be in flames, and it was conjectured that the rebels had fired the town, perhaps with an intention of evacuating their position. The place, it was supposed, would be taken and occupied by Gen. McCLELLAN on Sunday night. So far there had been no infantry engagement.

MORE GLORIOUS NEWS.

A Great Battle Fought at Pittsburgh Landing, Tenn.

VICTORY OF THE UNION FORCES.

"The Hardest Battle Ever Fought on this Continent."

Beauregard and Johnston in Command of the Rebel Army.

Gen. Grant in Pursuit of the Flying Rebels.

HEAVY LOSSES ON BOTH SIDES.

CHICAGO, Tuesday, April 8.

A PRIVATE DISPATCH RECEIVED IN THIS CITY, TO-NIGHT, FROM ONE OF GENERAL GRANT'S STAFF, SAYS THAT "WE HAVE FOUGHT AND WON THE HARDEST BATTLE EVER FOUGHT ON THIS CONTINENT." THE DISPATCH IS DATED PITTSBURGH LANDING, 6TH.

ST. LOUIS, Tuesday, April 8.

In response to a serenade to-night, Gen. HALLECK said that *Gen. Beauregard with an immense army advanced from Corinth and attacked the combined forces of Gens. Grant and Buell. The battle began at daybreak yesterday, and continued till late in the afternoon with terrible loss on both sides. We have gained a complete victory, and driven the enemy back within his fortifications.*

He also announced his departure for the field to-morrow morning.

DISPATCH FROM GEN. HALLECK.

To Hon. E. M. Stanton, Secretary of War:

The enemy attacked our works at Pittsburgh, Tenn., yesterday, but were repulsed with heavy loss. No details are given.　　(Signed,)

H. W. HALLECK, Major-General.
WASHINGTON, Tuesday, April 8.

The following message was received by the Secretary of War this evening:

"On the 6th Inst. the rebels, in overwhelming numbers, attacked our forces at Pittsburgh Landing. The battle lasted from morning till late in the afternoon, and resulted in the complete defeat of the rebels with heavy loss on both sides. Gen. GRANT is following up the enemy."

Gen. BUELL has arrived in Tennessee. Two divisions of his army were in the battle.

Gen. POPE is scouring the country round Island No. 10, and so far has captured Gen. MAKALL and Staff, and 2,000 men.

The above is not from an official source, but is deemed authentic, and corresponds with the expectations formed upon previous official information.

Lieutenant-General Leonidas Polk led the Confederate left-flank attack against Union troops at Shiloh.

NEWS OF THE DAY.

THE REBELLION.

"Island No. 10 is ours!" This time the announcement is founded, not on conjecture or belief, but on positive knowledge. The imminence of the danger threatening them after the crossing of Gen. POPE to the Tennessee shore, and the running of two of our gunboats by their batteries, proved too much for the rebels, and on Monday night, at midnight, they hastily evacuated their shore batteries, leaving everything behind them, and surrendered the island into the hands of Commodore FOOTE. The gallant Commodore, in a dispatch dated at 3:25 A. M. yesterday, announced to the Navy Department that he had just been boarded by two officers of the rebel navy, by order of their commanding officer, with instructions to surrender to the Commander of the Union naval forces. The Commodore, of course, made no delay in availing himself of the rebel offer. By this surrender, a large number of heavy cannon, quantities of munitions of war, the famous floating battery, and a number of gunboats and steamtransports come into our possession. The number of prisoners is not stated in our dispatches.

Later dispatches make it certain that our triumph at Island No. 10 has been most complete. Gen. POPE, we are informed, succeeded in cutting off the retreat of the flying rebels, and captured three Generals, with 6,000 other prisoners of war, 100 siege pieces, several field batteries, immense quantities of small arms, tents, wagons, horses, and provisions,—without the loss of a single man in the Union army. As we write this, we are still without the particulars.

Still more glorious news! Brief dispatches announce that a great battle was fought at Pittsburgh Landing, Tenn., on Sunday last, which resulted in a complete National victory. It appears that the rebels made the attack upon our position there, intending, probably, to strike an effective blow before we could fully concentrate our forces, but were signally repulsed. A private dispatch received in Chicago, from a member of Gen. GRANT'S Staff, calls the battle the hardest one ever fought on this Continent. At last accounts, Gen. GRANT was in full pursuit of the flying rebels

We have, this morning, quite full particulars of the advance from Fortress Monroe to Yorktown, and of the preliminary skirmishing, which finally settled down into regular siege operations before the city. Gen. MCCLELLAN and Staff arrived at Fortress Monroe on Wednesday last; and Friday, the 4th inst., having been fixed upon for the advance, about daylight on that day the army struck tents and commenced the march. The advance on the first day reached Cockeysville without encountering the enemy in any force. On Saturday, the 5th, a rain-storm commenced, which put the roads in a horrible condition, but our troops pushed on with enthusiasm, anxious to reach the scene of operations. About 10 o'clock on the 5th the first gun was fired from the rebel works, and it was soon answered by our batteries, which lost no time in getting into position, and our line of battle was immediately formed. The fight was carried on entirely by the artillery, assisted by DERDAN'S Sharpshooters, which did excellent service in picking off the rebel artillerists at long ranges, with their telescopic rifles. Several of the rebel guns were silenced during the day, and on the morning of the 6th (Sunday) the enemy commenced evacuating some of their works on the right, our artillery and rifle practice proving too much for them. In the meantime, Ship Point, about eight miles from Yorktown on the river, had been abandoned by the rebels, under the pressing influence of our gunboats and land forces, and all the fortifications there fell into our hands, though the rebels succeeded in saving their artillery. This point afforded a fine place at which to land siege supplies for operations against Yorktown, and the advantage was at once seized. On Monday, very little was done except to reconnoitre the enemy's position, which, as before stated, was found to be a very strong one.

From the *National Intelligencer* of yesterday morning, we obtain a definite statement relative to the position of the rebel fortifications on the peninsula. The enemy's line of defence extends across from Yorktown to the James River, and embraces three batteries and several milldams in addition to the main fortifications at Yorktown. The *Intelligencer's* information extends to Sunday noon, at which time an artillery engagement had occurred with MAGRUDER'S battery at Winn's Mill, near the James River, and another with the battery at Lee's Point, two miles from Yorktown, while the centre battery had not been attacked. The peninsula at this line of defence is six miles wide.

The officers who were recently released from Richmond, and who arrived at Baltimore on Sunday last, report that the Confederate Congress recently appropriated $20,000 for the repair of the *Merrimac.* One of the officers was the room-mate of Col. CORCORAN, who is confined in a warehouse in Richmond. He reports him well.

A correspondent of the Philadelphia *Inquirer,* who returned to Washington from the Rappahannock on Saturday, states that our troops have advanced to the north side of that stream. No rebels are in sight on the opposite side. They may, however, be concealed behind the hills in that direction. The magnificent railroad bridge over that stream was entirely destroyed by fire, as were also all the bridges over the smaller streams on the whole railroad route. For the space of four miles, near Warrenton, the track was torn up and the bars placed in piles, and a fire kindled beneath them, warping them so as to render them unfit for use. Our troops are all in good health, though fatigued with rapid marching. It is currently reported through the entire neighborhood, that WHITE'S and STEWART'S cavalry are prowling about the country, plundering property and capturing stray Union troops. There is some mystery about these rebel troopers, who disappear suddenly when they are pursued. Knowing ones say that the residents of that section will be found to be those who pursue this villainous system of ruffianism.

Gen. SICKLES received, on Sunday morning last, an order from Gen. HOOKER, depriving him of his command of the Excelsior Brigade, the reason assigned being the failure of the Senate to confirm his nomination as Brigadier. Gen SICKLES has protested against this action, and has gone to Washington to consult the President in the matter. Before leaving his command he issued an address to the men composing it, regretting the necessity which caused the separation.

Gen. BUTLER was at Port Royal on the 2d inst., on his way from Ship Island to Boston.

Editorials

The Great Victory in the West.

The great victory achieved by the combined military and naval forces of Gen. POPE and Commodore FOOTE at Island No. Ten, on the Mississippi River, and the capture of six thousand rebels, and their arms and a hundred siege guns, without the loss of a single man on our side, crowns in a worthy manner the long siege of the famous river stronghold. In its importance, it is second only to the capture of Fort Donelson—if, indeed, it be second to that achievement. The fall of Fort Donelson opened our way into the States of Alabama and Mississippi, and gave us virtual possession of all of Tennessee, excepting its southwestern corner. The fall of Island No. Ten must soon give us possession of that rebel corner, and will thus open our way through the entire rebel territory to New-Orleans and the Gulf of Mexico. Fort Donelson was won by terrific fighting, and after the loss of between one and two thousand brave men; Island No. Ten is gained by pure strategy, and without the loss of a single National soldier. At Fort Donelson, we took twice the number of rebels prisoners; but we did not get half the number of siege and other heavy guns that now fall into our hands, which latter are a far greater loss to the rebels than men would be. The artillery and warlike munitions the rebels cannot supplement; and they will soon have to stop the war, if but from the lack of

Troops under Major-General Don Carlos Buell began to reinforce Grant's beleaguered forces at Shiloh as the first day of battle drew to a close.

the death-dealing implements. At Forts Henry and Donelson, at New-Madrid, and now at Island No. Ten, we have captured nearly three hundred pieces of ordnance, besides immense quantities of small arms and miscellaneous material. Gen. POPE and Commodore FOOTE have raised themselves even higher than the position they have heretofore achieved ; and their persistence and spirit have won for them unmingled admiration. With such heroes and such strategists on the side of the nation, there is not a shadow of danger of the success of this atrocious rebel war.

The operations at Island Ten, which have culminated in its evacuation by the rebels, have been conducted with a skill, gallantry and patience beyond praise. It was twenty-three days from the time that Commodore FOOTE opened fire upon it until the date of its fall ; and during all that time, acting in conjunction with Gen. POPE, he has persistently and by every means possible, labored for its reduction. The position was really a formidable one. There were not merely the works and batteries upon the Island itself, but there was a powerful line of supporting batteries upon the eastern land shore ; there were also a number of coöperating rebel gunboats and an iron-clad floating battery. The force of rebel troops was sufficiently strong.

On Sunday morning, the 20th of March, Commodore FOOTE anchored his gun and mortarboats in safe position and saluted the rebels with a monstrous shell. After a time they responded ; but so briskly did he keep up the action, and so successfully did it seem to proceed, that on the next day Gen. HALLECK announced publicly in St. Louis that the island stronghold was ours. It was soon discovered, however, that the works were more extensive than had been thought, and that their reduction would not be such an easy, off-hand matter. FOOTE and POPE then went to work systematically to reduce the position—in the meantime keeping up, night and day, a lively bombardment from the boats, for the purpose, as the gallant

Commodore said, of keeping the rebels awake. Gen. POPE, who had previously taken the rebel fortifications at New-Madrid, below Island No. Ten, planted his batteries on the river at Point Pleasant, a little further down stream, to prevent the escape of the rebels or their gunboats in that direction. He then began the herculean work of cutting a water-passage for FOOTE's gunboats through a swamp or bayou on the mainland west from the island. FOOTE now sent Col. BUFORD, with three thousand men, to disperse the rebel force at Union City, on the mainland east from the island ; and the work of dispersion was gallantly accomplished. He then dispatched that famous midnight expedition (so well described by our correspondent " Galway " in another column) to destroy the main rebel battery on the island ; and the battery was destroyed. He then directed his mortar-fire to the rebel iron-clad floating battery ; and that was discomfited and floated down stream. Then, on the dark and stormy nights which closed last week, he ordered one, two, three of his gunboats to run the gauntlet of the rebel batteries, and take position below the island ; and that was successfully accomplished. The water-passage on the Western mainland was by this time cut, and boats and transports were thus enabled to outflank the island by that line. And now everything having been made ready for the grand assault, on Monday of this week, Gen. POPE's troops, infantry, artillery and cavalry, were conveyed across from the Missouri bank of the river to the Tennessee shore. Things began to look bad for the rebels. They were virtually surrounded ; and there was known to be only a narrow road along the river bank, which was nearly always submerged, by which they could possibly retreat. They prudently resolved not to die in the last ditch, but to surrender the island, ditches and all ; and on Monday midnight they sent word to Commodore FOOTE to that effect. The rebel force on the mainland was at the same time intercepted by the troops under Gen. POPE, and surren-

der being thought by them preferable to death, they too, to the number of six thousand, have laid down their arms. And so the long agony of Number Ten has at last come to an end. This terrible blow must utterly discourage the rebels, and show the futility of further resistance to the Government. Before the close of this week, the Corinthian rebels will probably follow suit of those at Number Ten.

AT THE END OF THEIR TETHER.—We are enabled to say that, even before the surrender of Island No. 10, Gen. SCOTT expressed the opinion that the rebels were so disorganized and demoralized that they would offer little further armed resistance to the authority of the Government, and only make such stands and take to such shifts as their desperate leaders could intimidate or cajole them into. This opinion from one who has judged and dealt so wisely upon all public affairs, in peace or war, heretofore, and who appreciated in the very beginning the magnitude of the task of the Government in putting down the rebellion, and saw that it was not to be accomplished by a direct march into the hostile country, is, we need hardly say, of great importance, and will add much to the feeling of confidence which is now universal.

THE SIEGE OF YORKTOWN.—The most exciting and important action of the war, thus far, the siege of Yorktown, is veiled in great part from the people's eyes by the mandates of the military authorities, and we only get the dryest and most meagre outline of what is going on. This is all unlike the glowing pictures we have heretofore had of battles, sieges and bombardments, even while they were in progress; and it is to be feared that posterity will lose as much as we do from the lack of special telegrams and special correspondence. But the work is, nevertheless, going on. The progress of the siege daily shows favorable signs; and, added to the glorious news from the West, we shall probably soon have news of the fall of Yorktown.

Union forces in Virginia hoped to rely on superior artillery support, such as this battery in front of Yorktown.

The New-York Times.

VOL. XI—NO. 3291. NEW-YORK, THURSDAY, APRIL 10, 1862. PRICE TWO CENTS

THE BATTLE OF PITTSBURGH.

Important Particulars of the Terrible Struggle.

The Fight Continued Through Two Days.

Partial Success of the Enemy on Sunday.

Opportune Arrival of Gen. Buell's Forces.

Final Defeat and Flight of the Rebels.

Gen. Albert Sidney Johnston's Body Left on the Field.

Other Prominent Rebel Officers Killed.

Our Probable Loss in Killed, Wounded and Missing Five Thousand.

Gen. Wallace Killed and Gen. Prentiss taken Prisoner.

Occupation of Corinth by Our Forces.

Confederate General Albert Sidney Johnston, a West Pointer, lost his life at Pittsburg Landing.

Northern casualties included Brigadier-General W.H.L. Wallace, who had been promoted after Fort Donelson.

CAIRO, Wednesday, April 9.

Further advices from Pittsburgh Landing give the following about the battle:

The enemy attacked at 4 o'clock Sunday morning, the brigades of Gens. SHERMAN and PRENTISS being first engaged. The attack was successful, and our entire force was driven back to the river, where the advance of the enemy was checked by the fire of the gunboats.

Our force was then increased by the arrival of Gen. GRANT, with the troops from Savanna, and inspirited by reports of the arrival of two divisions of Gen. BUELL's army.

Our loss this day was heavy, and, besides the killed and wounded, embraced our camp equipage and 36 field guns.

The next morning our forces, now amounting to 80,000, assumed the offensive, and by 2 o'clock P. M. had retaken our camp and batteries, together with some 40 of the enemy's guns and a number of prison-

ers, and the enemy were in full retreat, pursued by our victorious forces.

Our casualties were numerous, and include:

Gen. GRANT, wounded in the ankle, slightly.

Gen. W. H. WALLACE, killed.

Gen. SMITH, severely wounded.

Col. HALL, Sixteenth Illinois, killed.

Col. LOGAN, Thirty-second Illinois, wounded severely.

Col. DAVIS, Forty-sixth Illinois, wounded, severely.

Major HUNTER, Thirty-second Illinois, killed.

Col. PEABODY, Twenty-fifth Illinois, severely wounded.

Our killed, wounded and missing are not less than 5,000.

CHICAGO, Wednesday, April 9.

The *Times'* account of the battle at Pittsburgh Landing on Sunday and Monday, says that the enemy surprised Gen. PRENTISS' Brigade, which was in the advance, five miles beyond Pittsburgh, at 5 o'clock on Sunday morning, taking two regiments prisoners and capturing the General. The fight continued during the entire day, the enemy driving our forces back to Pittsburgh with fearful loss.

Gen. BUELL, with Gen. NELSON's Division, arrived at 4 o'clock, and turned the tide of battle.

The enemy was commanded by Gens. POLK and BEAUREGARD, who suspended the attack about 6 o'clock.

On the morning of Monday, the troops having rested on the field, and being reinforced by Gen. NELSON's Division, supported by the gunboats, drove the enemy back and occupied their former position, completely routing the rebels, who were immediately followed by several thousand cavalry, who at last accounts were some miles beyond Corinth.

The *Tribune* places our loss at from 500 to 1,000 killed and 3,000 to 4,000 wounded. The rebel loss is twice that number. *Six of our batteries were taken and retaken six times.*

The *Times* says that Gen. BEAUREGARD had given orders not to destroy any of the camp equipage taken

on Sunday, as he *expected a complete victory the next day.*

CHICAGO, Wednesday, April 9.

The *Tribune's* special from Cairo, 9th, gives the following summary of reports gathered from persons who witnessed the battle at Pittsburgh Landing:

The National army was posted between two streams, about four miles apart, that run into the Tennessee nearly at right angles, within about two miles from Pittsburgh. The left front was commanded by Gen. PRENTISS, who had several raw regimens. In his rear was Gen. SHERMAN, with his division, completely cutting it off from the main army.

Gen. MCCLERNAND put himself at the head of his troops and cut his way through the rebels, and rejoined the army.

The fight had now become desperate, and on Gen. GRANT's assuming command, the enemy were driven back, and the National forces occupied at night nearly the same position they did in the morning. The fight lasted 15 hours.

During the night, Maj.-Gen. LEW. WALLACE came up from Crump's Landing, with 19,000 troops, and in the morning the battle was renewed with great fury, neither party seeming disposed to yield. Between 11 and 12 o'clock the fight was terrific.

Soon after noon, Gen. BUELL had crossed the Tennessee, and attacked the enemy in flank with 40,000 men. The rebels were soon routed, Gen. BUELL pursuing them with 12,000 men, mostly cavalry, and *the latest rumors were that he had taken Corinth.*

Eight hundred wounded are reported to be on one steamer, on the way down. Gen. HALLECK is expected here in the morning *en route* for Tennessee. Several barges of ice are ordered to go up the Tennessee to-night for the use of the wounded.

THE FIRST DETAILED REPORTS.

The following dispatch reached us yesterday

morning too late to be inserted in our regular morning edition, but was issued at an early hour in an "Extra:"

PITTSBURGH, via FORT HENRY,
Wednesday, April 9—3:20 A. M.

The greatest battle of the war has just closed, resulting in the complete rout of the enemy, who attacked us at daybreak Sunday morning. The battle lasted without intermission during the entire day, and was again renewed on Monday morning, and continued undecided until 4 o'clock in the afternoon, when the enemy commenced their retreat, and are still flying toward Corinth, pursued by a large force of our cavalry. The slaughter on both sides is immense.

The fight was brought on by a body of three hundred of the Twenty-fifth Missouri Regiment, of Gen. PRENTISS' Division, attacking the advance guard of the rebels, which were supposed to be the pickets of the enemy in front of our camps. The rebels immediately advanced on Gen. PRENTISS' division on the left wing, pouring volley after volley of musketry, and riddling our camps with grape, cannister and shell. Our forces soon formed into line and returned their fire vigorously, and by the time we were prepared to receive them, had turned their heaviest fire on the left centre of SHERMAN's Division and drove our men back from their camps, and bringing up a fresh force, opened fire on our left wing, under Gen. McCLERNARD. This fire was returned with terrible effect and determined spirit by both infantry and ar-

tillery, along the whole line for a distance of over four miles.

Gen. HURLBURT's Division was thrown forward to support the centre, when a desperate conflict ensued. The rebels were driven back with terrible slaughter, but soon rallied and drove back our men in turn. From about 9 o'clock, until night closed on the bloody scene, there was no determination of the result of the struggle. The enemy exhibited remarkably good generalship. At times engaging the left with apparently their whole strength, they would suddenly open a terrible and destructive fire on the right or centre. Even our heaviest and most destructive fire upon the enemy did not appear to discourage their solid columns. The fire of Maj. TAYLOR's Chicago Artillery raked them down in scores, but the smoke would no sooner be dispersed than the breach would again be filled.

The most desperate fighting took place late in the afternoon. The rebels knew that if they did not succeed in whipping us then, that their chances for success would be extremely doubtful, as a portion of Gen. BUELL's forces had by this time arrived on the opposite side of the river, and another portion was coming up the river from Savannah. They became aware that we were being reinforced, as they could see Gen. BUELL's troops from the river bank, a short distance above us on the left, to which point they had forced their way.

At five o'clock the rebels had forced our left wing back so as to occupy fully two-thirds of our camp, and were fighting their way forward with a desperate de-

gree of confidence in their efforts to drive us into the river, and at the same time heavily engaged our right.

Up to this time we had received no reinforcements, Gen. LEW. WALLACE failing to come to our support until the day was over, having taken the wrong road from Crump's Landing, and being without other transports than those used for Quartermaster's and Commissary stores, which were too heavily laden to ferry any considerable number of Gen. BUELL's forces across the river, those that were here having been sent to bring up the troops from Savanna. We were, therefore, contesting against fearful odds, our force not exceeding thirty-eight thousand men, while that of the enemy was upwards of sixty thousand.

Our condition at this moment was extremely critical. Large numbers of men, had straggled toward the river, and could not be rallied. Gen. GRANT and staff, who had been recklessly riding along the lines during the entire day, amid the unceasing storm of bullets, grape and shell, now rode from right to left, inciting the men to stand firm until our reinforcements could cross the river.

Col. WEBSTER, Chief of Staff, immediately got into position the heaviest pieces of artillery, pointing on the enemy's right, while a large number of the batteries were planted along the entire line, from the river bank northwest to our extreme right, some two and a half miles distant. About an hour before dusk a general cannonading was opened upon the enemy, from along our whole line, with a perpetual crack of musketry. For a short time the rebels replied

THE FIELD OF CONFLICT IN THE SOUTHWEST.

Showing Number Ten, and the Rebel Defences on the River to Memphis; also, Pittsburg Landing, Corinth and the Line of the Tennessee River.

with vigor and effect, but their return shots grew less frequent and destructive, while ours grew more rapid.

The gunboats *Lexington* and *Tyler*, which lay a short distance off, kept raining shell on the rebel hordes. This last effort was too much for the enemy, and ere dusk had set in the firing had nearly ceased, when, night coming on, all the combatants rested from their awful work of blood.

Our men rested on their arms in the position they had at the close of the night, until the forces under Major-General WALLACE arrived and took position on the right, and General BUELL'S forces from the opposite side and Savanna were now being conveyed to the battle-ground. The entire right of Gen. NELSON'S Division was ordered to form on the right, and the forces under Gen. CRITTENDEN were ordered to his support early in the morning.

THE SECOND DAY'S BATTLE.

Gen. BUELL having arrived on Sunday evening, in the morning the ball was opened at daylight, simultaneously by Gen. NELSON'S Division on the left, and Major-Gen. WALLACE'S Division on the right. Gen. NELSON'S force opened up a most galling fire on the rebels, and advanced rapidly as they fell back. The fire soon became general along the whole line, and began to tell with terrible effect on the enemy. Generals MCCLEENAND, SHERMAN and HUELBURT'S men, though terribly jaded from the previous day's fighting still maintained their honors won at Donelson; but the resistance of the rebels at all points of the attack was worthy a better cause.

But they were not enough for our undaunted bravery, and the dreadful desolation produced by our artillery, which was sweeping them away like chaff before the wind. But knowing that a defeat here would be the death blow to their hopes, and that their all depended upon this great struggle, their Generals still urged them on in the face of destruction, hoping by flanking us on the right to turn the tide of battle. Their success was again for a time cheering, as they began to gain ground on us, appearing to have been reinforced; but our left, under Gen. NELSON, was driving them, and with wonderful rapidity, and by eleven o'clock Gen. BUELL'S forces had succeeded in flanking them, and capturing their batteries of artillery.

They however again rallied on the left, and recrossed, and the right forced themselves forward in another desperate effort. But reinforcements from General WOOD and Gen. THOMAS were coming in, regiment after regiment, which were sent to Gen. BUELL, who had again commenced to drive the enemy.

About three o'clock in the afternoon Gen. GRANT rode to the left, where the fresh regiments had been ordered, and finding the rebels wavering, sent a portion of his body-guard to the head of each of five regiments, and then ordered a charge across the field, himself leading, as he brandished his sword and waved them on to the crowning victory, while cannon balls were falling like hail around him.

The men followed with a shout that sounded above the roar and din of the artillery, and the rebels fled in dismay, as from a destroying avalanche, and never made another stand.

Gen. BUELL followed the retreating rebels, driving them in splendid style, and by 5½ o'clock the whole rebel army was in full retreat to Corinth, with our cavalry in hot pursuit, with what further result is not known, they not having returned up to this hour.

We have taken a large amount of their artillery and also a number of prisoners. We lost a number of our forces prisoners yesterday, among whom is Gen. PRENTISS The number of our force taken has not been ascertained yet. It is reported at several hundred. Gen. PRENTISS was also reported as being wounded. Among the killed on the rebel side was their General-in-Chief, A. Sydney JOHNSTON, who was struck by a cannon ball on the afternoon of Sunday. It is further reported that Gen. BEAUREGARD had his arm shot off.

This afternoon Gens. BRAGG, BRECKINRIDGE and JACKSON were commanding the rebel forces.

THE HEROES OF THE BATTLE.

Sketches of Some of the Commanders at the Battle at Pittsburgh Landing, and of Some of the Killed and Wounded Officers.

The hasty dispatches that were received yesterday of killed and wounded officers are probably both incomplete and incorrect in many particulars. Indeed, some of those reported dead have already turned up, and others will doubtless do so: Under these circumstances it might be both injudicious and painful to give sketches of the officers reported fallen until

Ulysses S. Grant began to emerge as a major military figure after repulsing the Confederate thrust at Shiloh.

the facts are definitely ascertained. We will briefly notice some of those honorably engaged in the battle, and some of the fallen, regarding whom the statements seem to be authentic. The officers in chief command were Major-Gen. GRANT, who acted so gallantly on Sunday, and Major-Gen. BUELL, who was in joint command on Monday.

MAJ.-GEN. ULYSSES S. GRANT.

Gen. GRANT is just forty years of age, is a native of Ohio, a graduate of West Point, and served honorably in the Mexican War, having been attached eleven years to the Fourth Regiment United States Infantry, serving as Second and First Lieutenant, as Quartermaster and as Captain. After his resignation he settled in Missouri, and moved from there to Illinois, in 1850. Upon the breaking out of the present war, he offered his services to Gov. YATES, and was appointed Colonel of the Twenty-first Illinois Volunteers, and served until promoted as a Brigadier-General, with commission and rank from the 17th of May, 1861. He was engaged as Colonel and Acting-Brigadier-General in several of the contests in Southeastern Missouri; and his course as Commander of the Southern District of Missouri has been thoroughly scrutinized, and among his most praiseworthy acts was the occupation of Paducah and stoppage of communication and supplies to the rebels *via* the Tennessee and Cumberland Rivers. He was the planner of the battle of Belmont, and had chief command of the troops at the capture of Fort Donelson. After the latter event, a new district was created, under the denomination of the District of West Tennessee, and he was created a Major-General, and assigned to the command of it. But it was reported that he was under a cloud with the superior military authorities, and the most absurd stories were circulated as to the cause thereof. The simple fact was that there was some dissatisfaction with his "strategy" at Fort Donelson. When the expedition went up the Tennessee, he was not at first put on duty; but was very soon after assigned to the command of that heavy column. His personal bravery and dash is undoubted. He is a man of plain exterior, light hair, blue eyes, five feet nine in height, plain and retiring in his manners, firm and decisive in character, esteemed by his soldiers, never wastes a word with any one, but pays strict attention to his military duties. He is one of the hard-fighting school of Generals.

GEN. BUELL.

Gen. DON CARLOS BUELL is 42 years old, was born in Ohio, reared in Indiana, graudated at West Point, has been twenty years in the army, and his service has been almost continuous. He served with great distinction in the Mexican war, as Lieutenant, Captain and Adjutant, until at Churubusco he received a severe wound from a bullet, which passed through the upper part of his chest. At the time the present war broke out, he was a Lieutenant-Colonel in the Regular army, in California, but he was appointed a Brigadier-General by Congress, and was ordered to take command of a division of the army of the Potomac. On the resignation by Gen. ROBERT ANDERSON of the command of the Department of the Ohio, he was assigned to that important position, and it was under his eye that the magnificent army which lately marched from Bowling Green to Nashville, was raised and drilled. The various battles of Gen. GARFIELD against HUMPHREY MARSHALL, the battle of Mill Springs, where ZOLLICOFFER was killed, and various other important actions in Kentucky, were the emanations of his skill, and his military management in Kentucky was of the highest order. On the recent reconstruction of Departments in the Southwest, he was subordinated to Gen. HALLECK, but was at the same time created a Major-General. He left Nashville with his fine army a fortnight ago, and arrived at Pittsburgh Landing, at a most opportune moment to achieve a triumph for the previously wavering National arms. Gen. BUELL is remarkable for industry and energy; his coolness and self-possession are such that it is believed he could think as calmly, and form his plans as deliberately in a tempest of grape as in the quiet of his tent; and in the regular army he is esteemed as emphatically a fighting man. He is of compact frame, very deep chest, indicating great vital power, possesses almost herculean strength in his arms, and can lift prodigious weights at arm's length; has light hair and full beard; blue eyes, which are steady and unmoved in danger; carriage erect, step measured; and, in short, is such a type of man as is produced by long service in the American army.

GEN. W. H. WALLACE.

Brig.-Gen. W. H. WALLACE, who was the only General officer killed at Pittsburgh Landing, was a native of Illinois, a graduate of West Point, and, previous to the present war, had seen service on the Pacific frontier, as a Captain of the Washington Territory Mounted Volunteers, in which position he took part in the Indian War of 1855. At the opening of this war, he raised and obtained the Colonelcy of the Eleventh Illinois Regiment of Volunteers. With his regiment he was at Fort Henry, and from there went to Fort Donelson, at which battle he was Acting Brigadier-General, and immediately afterward was confirmed as Brigadier-General by Congress. He was a very skillful and gallant officer, and his loss will be deeply mourned by the brave soldiers of the West.

GEN. C. F. SMITH.

Major-Gen. SMITH, who was severely wounded at the battle, is already well known to the country for his immense personal bravery at Fort Donelson. He is a Pennsylvanian, graduated at West Point in 1825, and held successively several responsible positions in the Academy until 1843. He went to Mexico as Captain, but, for various gallant acts, was soon breveted Colonel. In 1854 he received regular promotion as Major of the First Artillery, and in 1055 was made Lieutenant-Colonel of the Tenth Infantry, which rank he held up to the opening of the war. He then received a commission as Brigadier-General, and was appointed to the command of the forces at Paducah, Kentucky. Various preposterous charges of disloyalty were here brought against him by personal enemies, but all these he has since disproved in a most splendid manner.

THE REBEL GENERAL KILLED.

GEN: ALBERT SIDNEY JOHNSTON.

Gen. JOHNSTON, the bogus report of whose capture at Fort Donelson gave him a biographical fame two months ago, is now certainly disposed of at last, as his dead body is in our hands. He was one of the five rebel "Generals," the other four being BEAUREGARD, LEE, COOPER and JOE JOHNSTON. He was for half a year commander of the rebel Department of Kentucky, with his headquarters at Bowling Green, which famous stronghold he evacuated six weeks ago. He is 60 years of age, a native of Kentucky, and graduated at West Point in 1826. He was engaged in the Black Hawk war, in the Texan war of independence, in the Mexican war, and in the war against the Mormons. He was Brigade-General in command of the Military District of Utah, and at the opening of this rebellion, was in command of the Department of the Pacific. Shortly after the rebellion got under way, his loyalty was suspected, and Gen. SUMNER was sent out to supersede him. Before Gen. SUMNER reached California, JOHNSTON had left to join the rebels For fear of being caught, he took the overland route, with three or four companions, on mules, and passed through Arizona and Texas, and thence to Richmond. At first he was appointed to a rebel command on the Potomac; but upon the great importance of the Western Department being seen by JEFF. DAVIS, he was appointed to take chief command at Bowling Green. He did everything to strengthen that position, and bring as large a force as could be got for its defence. But, on being outflanked by our advance up the Cumberland, he incontinently deserted his stronghold, fled to Nashville, from thence to Decatur, and from thence to Corinth, and now has fallen—a traitor to his native State and to his country. JOHNSTON was a little over six feet high, of a large, bony, sinewy frame, with a grave, gaunt and thoughtful face; of quiet, unassuming manners—forming, in all, a soldier of very imposing appearance. He was considered by military men the ablest General, for command, in the rebel service, and his loss will be a severe blow to the tottering rebellion.

The New-York Times.

VOL. XI—NO. 3292. NEW-YORK, FRIDAY, APRIL 11, 1862. PRICE TWO CENTS.

THE BATTLE OF PITTSBURGH.

A Clear and Graphic Account of the Two Days Action.

Splendid Generalship Displayed on Both Sides.

Indomitable Bravery of Our Troops Against Great Odds.

Opportune Service of the Gunboats Tyler and Lexington.

The Movement of the Union Army which Caused the Rebel Retreat.

Seventy Thousand Men Engaged on Each Side.

The Rebels Reinforced by Price and Van Dorn.

Reported Capture of John C. Breckinridge.

CINCINNATI, Thursday, April 10.

A correspondent of the *Times* writes the following account of the Pittsburgh battle:

Our forces were stationed in the form of a semi-circle, the right resting on a point north of Crump's Landing, our centre being in front of the main road to Corinth, and our left extending to the river in the direction of Hamburgh, four miles north of Pittsburgh Landing.

At 2 o'clock, on the morning of the 6th, 400 men of Gen. PRENTISS' Division were attacked by the enemy, half a mile in advance of our lines. Our men fell back on the Twenty-fifth Missouri, swiftly pursued by the enemy. The advance of the rebels reached Col. PEABODY's Brigade just as the long roll was sounded, and the men were falling into line. Resistance was but short, and they retreated under a galling fire, until they reached the lines of the Second Division.

At 6 o'clock the attack had become general along our whole front. The enemy, in large numbers, drove in the pickets of Gen. SHERMAN's Division, and fell on the Forty-eighth, Fiftieth and Seventy-second Ohio Regiments. Those troops were never before in action, and, being so unexpectedly attacked, made as able a resistance as possible, but were, in common with the forces of Gen. PRENTISS, forced to seek the support of the troops immediately in their rear.

At 10 o'clock the entire line on both sides was fully engaged—the roar of cannon and musketry was without intermission from the main centre to a point extending half way down the left wing. The rebels made a desperate charge on the Fourteenth Ohio battery, which, not being sufficiently supported by infantry, fell into their hands. Another severe fight occurred for possession of the Fifth Ohio battery, and three of its guns were taken by the enemy.

By 11 o'clock, a number of commanders of regiments had fallen, and in some cases not a single field officer remained ; yet the fighting continued with an earnestness which showed that the contest on both sides was for death or victory. Foot by foot the ground was contested, and finding it impossible to drive back our centre, the enemy slackened their fire, and made vigorous efforts on our left wing, endeavoring to outflank and driving it to the river bank. This wing was under Gen. HURLBURT, and was composed of the Fourteenth, Thirty-second, Forty-fourth and Fifty-seventh Indiana ; Eighth, Eighteenth and Twenty-first Illinois. Fronting its line, however, was the Fourteenth, Fifty-seventh and Seventy-seventh Ohio, and Fifth Ohio Cavalry of Gen. SHERMAN's Division. For nearly two hours a sheet of fire blazed from both columns, the rebels fighting with a vigor that was only equaled by those contending with them.

While the contest raged the hottest, the gunboat *Tyler* passed up the river to a point opposite the enemy, and poured in broadsides from her immense guns, greatly aiding in forcing the enemy back.

Up to 3 o'clock the battle raged with a fury that defies description. The rebels had found every attempt to break our lines unavailing. They had striven to drive in our main column, and finding that impossible, had turned all their strength upon our left. Foiled in that quarter, they now made another attempt at our centre, and made every effort to rout our forces before the reinforcements which had been sent for should come up.

At 5 o'clock there was a short cessation in the fire of the enemy, their lines falling back for nearly half a mile, when they suddenly wheeled, and again threw their entire forces upon our left wing, determined to make a final struggle in that quarter, but the gunboats *Tyler* and *Lexington* poured in their shot thick and fast, with terrible effect.

Meanwhile Gen. WALLACE, who had taken a circuitous route from Crump's Landing, appeared suddenly on the enemy's right wing. In the face of this combination of circumstances, the rebels felt that their enterprise for the day was a failure, and as night was approaching, fell back until they reached an advantageous position somewhat in the rear, yet occupying the main road to Corinth. The gunboats continued to throw shells at them until out of range.

After a wearied watching of several hours of intense anxiety, the advance regiments of Gen. BUELL appeared on the opposite bank of the river. The work of passing the river began, the Thirty-sixth Indiana and Sixty-eighth Ohio being the first to cross, followed by the main portions of Gens. NELSON and BRUCE's Divisions. Cheer after cheer greeted their arrival, and they were immediately sent to the advance, where they rested on their arms for the night. All night long steamers were engaged ferrying Gen. BUELL's force across, and *when daylight broke, it was evident the rebels, too, had been strongly reinforced.*

The battle was opened by the rebels at 7 o'clock, from the Corinth road, and in half an hour extended along the whole line. At 9 o'clock the sound of artillery and musketry fully equalled that of the previous day. The enemy was met by our reinforcements and the still unwearied soldiers of yesterday, with an energy they certainly could not have expected.

It became evident they were avoiding the extreme of our left wing, and endeavoring, with perseverance and determination, to find some weak point by which to turn our force. *They left one point but to return to it immediately, and then as suddenly would, by some masterly stroke of Generalship, direct a most vigorous attack upon some division where they fancied they would not be expected; but the fire of our lines was as steady as clock-work, and it soon became evident that the enemy considered the task they had undertaken a hopeless one.*

Further reinforcements now began to arrive, and took position on the right of the main centre, under Gen. WALLACE. Gens. GRANT, BUELL, NELSON, SHERMAN and CRITTENDEN were everywhere present, directing movements for a new stroke on the enemy. *Suddenly both wings of our army were turned upon the enemy, with the intention of driving them into an extensive ravine. At the same time a powerful battery, stationed in the open field, poured volley after volley of canister into the rebel ranks.*

At 11½ o'clock the rear of the battle shook the earth. The Union guns were fired with all the energy that the prospect of the enemy's defeat inspired, while the rebels' fire was not so vigorous, and *they evinced a desire to withdraw.* They finally fell slowly back, keeping up a fire from their artillery and musketry along their whole column as they retreated. They went in excellent order, battling at every advantageous point, and delivering their fire with considerable effect ; but from all the divisions of our lines they were closely pursued, a galling fire being kept upon their rear.

The enemy had now been driven beyond our former lines, and were in full retreat for Corinth, pursued by our cavalry.

The forces engaged on both sides in this day's battle are estimated at about 70,000 each.

OPERATIONS ON THE MISSISSIPPI.

The Prisoners and Spoils Captured at Number Ten.

Nearly the Entire Rebel Force Prisoners.

One Major-General and Three Brigadiers

Seventy Rebels Killed and Wounded on the Island

ST. LOUIS, Thursday, April 10.

A special to the *Republican*, from Island No. 10, says that two hundred hogsheads of sugar, and several hundred barrels molasses, eighty cannon, four hundred wagons, one hundred and twenty-six horses, sixty mules, five thousand stand of arms, thirty pieces of light artillery, and great quantities of blankets, clothing, &c., have fallen into our hands.

The total number of prisoners captured is five thousand. One Major-General, (MAKALL,) and three Brigadier-Generals, (GAULT, WALKER and SCHAUM,) The prisoners are being embarked as rapidly as possible for Illinois.

We also took about 10,000 solid shot, and immense quantities of ammunition.

The New-York Times.

VOL. XI.—NO. 3306.   NEW-YORK, MONDAY, APRIL 28, 1862.   PRICE TWO CENTS.

NEW-ORLEANS OURS !

Acknowledgment of its Capture by the Rebels.

Dispatches from Gen. Wool and Gen. McDowell.

Fort Jackson Passed by Our Forces on Thursday Morning.

GREAT EXCITEMENT IN THE CITY.

Strict Martial Law at once Proclaimed.

Cotton and Steamboats Reported to be Burnt.

The National Forces Before the City on Friday at Noon.

Last Gasp of the Rebel Telegraph Operator.

DISPATCH FROM GEN. WOOL.

FORTRESS MONROE, Sunday, April 27.

Hon. E. M. Stanton, Secretary of War :

A fugitive black, just arrived from Portsmouth, brings the Petersburgh *Express* of yesterday, which contains the following dispatch :

NORFOLK, Friday, April 25.

The enemy passed Fort Jackson at 4 o'clock yesterday morning.

When the news reached New-Orleans, the excitement was boundless.

Martial law was put in full force, and business was completely suspended.

All the cotton and steamboats, excepting such as were necessary to transport coin, ammunition, &c., were destroyed.

At 1 o'clock to-day the operator bade us good by, saying that *the enemy had appeared before the city.*

This is the last we know regarding the fall. Will send particulars as soon as they can be had.

The negro bringing the above, reports that the rebels have two iron-clad steamers nearly completed, and that it is believed that the *Merrimac* will be out to-morrow.   JOHN E. WOOL.

DISPATCH FROM GEN. McDOWELL.

HEADQUARTERS OF THE DEPARTMENT OF THE RAPPAHANNOCK, April 27, 1862.

Hon. E. M. Stanton, Secretary of War :

I have just returned from the camp opposite Fredericksburgh. I was told the Richmond *Examiner* of the 26th had been received in town, announcing as follows:

"New-Orleans taken." "Great destruction of property, cotton and steamboats." "Steamboats enough saved to take away the ammunition." "Great consternation of the inhabitants."

IRWIN McDOWELL, Major-General.

THE CITY OF NEW-ORLEANS.

The population of New-Orleans, by the last census, was 168,472. This has, undoubtedly, been largely decreased since the rebellion. The commerce of the city, which was its main support, has been totally ruined, and thousands of the people have fled to the country, or anywhere that they could find a scanty subsistence, while other thousands have been drafted into the rebel army. The city is the emporium of the Mississippi Valley, and is situated on the left bank of the river, about a hundred miles from its mouth. The older portion of the city is built on the convex side of a bend of the river, which here sweeps around in a northeast, east, and southeast course. From this location it derives its familiar soubriquet of the "Crescent City." In the progress of its growth up stream, the city has now so extended itself as to fill the hollow of a curve in the opposite direction, so that the river front presents an outline somewhat resembling the letter S. It stretches or straggles along the bank of the river some six or seven miles, with an average depth of one mile, it only being possible to build on the narrow strip of land lying immediately on the edge of the river, the highest point being in front, and then rapidly *sinking in the rear until lost in interminable swamps.* In the rear of New-Orleans, a half a mile, perhaps, beyond the suburbs, is the Metarie ridge, a narrow strip of high land two or three feet above high water mark, of an average of a half mile in width ; then you come again to the swamp, which continues to the shores of the lake beyond, almost as dense as any in the surrounding valley, gloomy and peculiar and uninhabited, except by alligators and bitterns. The front of New-Orleans is of course on the river, and from the peculiarity of the country, and the levée which serves to protect the city from being overflowed by the Spring rise, our fleet, when it reached the city, *must have been above the ground on which the city is built, and commanded it as from an eminence.* This circumstance, with the fact that the breaking of the levée by a cannon-shot, or a few minutes' work with the spade, *would submerge the whole place,* makes New-Orleans, with its defenceless rear, the weakest and least protected place of any commercial importance in the world. The defences of the city were so fully and, as the event has proved, accurately described in the TIMES of Monday last, that it is not necessary now to rehearse the facts. What has become of the rebel gunboats and rams, of which we have heard so much, it is hard to conjecture.

The most important railroads terminating at New-Orleans, are the New-Orleans, Jackson and Great Northern, which, until lately, united it with the great railroad systems of the Eastern and Northern States, and the New-Orleans, Opelousas and Great Western, extending westwardly a short distance into Texas. The great avenue, however, of the trade and commerce of the city, is the Mississippi River. Along the river front of the city the levée, or artificial embankment to keep the city from inundation, is extended by a continuous series of wooden wharfs. A sort of esplanade is thus formed, several miles in extent, which, during the busy season, presents a scene of wonderful variety and animation. Cotton bales, sugar hogsheads, negroes and mule-drays are in great abundance. Among the notable buildings are the branch mint of the United States—which the rebels seized a year ago and stole a part of the coin—the Custom-house, one of the most massive structures in America, but not yet completed, the cathedral of St. Louis, and sixty other churches, the St. Charles Hotel, which cost $590,000 ; the hospital, banks and benevolent institutions. On Jackson-square is a bronze equestrian statue of Gen. JACKSON, by CLARK MILLS. The New-Orleanians will now remember Gen. JACKSON as the man who said, "The Union must and shall be preserved."

The population of New-Orleans has long been remarkable for the diversity of its elements. About one-half of the whites are of foreign birth, and among these the French and Spanish are predominant. There is also a large number of Northerners. Those who know the city best believed that it would surrender when the forts defending it should fall. The mass of the permanent population is composed of intelligent men, and the commercial interests have always had a more clear idea of the folly of this rebellion than the people in the interior. At all events, after the forts alluded to fall, and the gunboats, which are not really formidable, are taken, New-Orleans is helpless—more helpless indeed than any other city can be.

THE NEWS IN WASHINGTON.

WASHINGTON, Sunday, April 27.

The city is wild with rejoicing to-night over the news of the advance of our gunboats upon New-Orleans, in spite of the resistance of Forts Jackson and Philip, and the probable surrender of that city from the vile clutches of rebeldom, and its return to loyalty and trade with all the world. New-Orleans is probably in possession of Gen. BUTLER at present writing. The President is in high glee over the news.

A large naval squadron led by Captain David G. Farragut (later an Admiral) assaulted and captured New Orleans.

The New-York Times.

VOL. XI — NO. 3309   NEW-YORK, THURSDAY, MAY 1, 1862   PRICE TWO CENTS

Editorials

THE PRESIDENT AND THE ARREST OF GEN. STONE.—The President declares himself solely responsible for the arrest of Gen. STONE. It was only the other day he assumed the responsibility of the arrest of Mr. PIERCE BUTLER and others, effected by the direction of the Secretary of War. This is not only just and characteristic, but it is satisfying. We have heard much of intrigues about the State and War Departments, to procure the imprisonment of suspected men, solely to indulge private malice or to serve a personal end. We have been told that Gen. McCLELLAN sacrificed Gen. STONE, to avoid the odium of his own bad Generalship. All this we now know to be the coinage of fancy. Whatever has been done of this kind has been done by President LINCOLN himself, whose character is fortunately beyond all suspicion of partiality, injustice or oppression. When the time comes, we shall no doubt find that, whoever has been wrong, the President has been right.

The News from New-Orleans.

The news we receive from the rebels concerning New-Orleans is a remarkable medley, and the only fact that appears in it clear and certain is that the city is really in our possession. The fleet passed Fort Jackson just a week ago this morning, and by noon of next day it appeared before the Crescent City. A demand for the surrender of the city was immediately made by the commander of the naval squadron, which the rebel General refused to comply with; but immediately after his refusal, he and his forces evacuated the city, and fled northward by railroad, nearly a hundred miles. Commodore FARRAGUT, instead of opening fire upon the rebellious city, then entered into a correspondence with the civil authorities, the result of which is not told; but the terms of the dispatch we give this morning, dated Mobile, Sunday, indicate that the city functionaries were trying to induce our naval commander to ask *them* to surrender the city; and the only thing they seemed to fear was that he would not renew his demand. It is said that "*he promised* the Mayor's Secretary, who visited the fleet by flag of truce, *that he would make a renewed demand* for the surrender of the city; but," alas! "he has not done so up to this hour, 5 o'clock" (Sunday.) That certainly looks exceedingly like a parallel to the authentic tale of Capt. SCOTT's coon, whose anxiety to avoid the bullets of the huntsman led him to invite himself down from the tree—a historical narrative, well known and much admired by all Orleanians. But if Commodore FARRAGUT had not repeated his demand for a capitulation by 5 o'clock, it is probable he did so by 5½ o'clock; or, more likely still, the Mayor, waiving all needless ceremony in the matter, chivalrously took the initiative, and offered to give up what he knew he could not keep. For the Richmond papers, of Monday morning, definitely proclaimed to the startled rebels of the capital, and in the ears of JEFF. DAVIS himself, that

"New-Orleans was in the possession of the enemy." The latest of our dispatches concerning the city is from Mobile, Monday, and that announces the evacuation of all the fortifications erected for the defence of New-Orleans on the lake in its rear—so that, from the battered forts, sixty miles below the city, to the point to which LOVELL retreated, eighty miles above it, there was nowhere an enemy who offered any resistance. No mention is made in any of the dispatches of Gen. BEN. BUTLER, who was in chief command of the whole expedition, military and naval; and it is evident that he was not with the fleet when it appeared before the city, as, if he had been, the negotiations for capitulation would have been carried on by and with him, instead of Commodore FARRAGUT. It is very likely that FARRAGUT was waiting for his appearance from Friday, when the first demand for surrender was made, until Sunday night at five o'clock, when the second demand had not yet been sent to the anxious Mayor. It was understood, however, that Gen. BUTLER was to approach New-Orleans, with the Army of Occupation, by way of the Lakes, reduce the fortifications on their shores, and march to the possession of the City *via* the famous Shell Road; and this view is confirmed by our special dispatch from Washington this morning. If he reached his point of debarkation by Sunday or Monday of this week, however, as he must have done, he would find no hostile batteries or forts lining the shore, as the rebels themselves had destroyed them all; and the way would be clear for a triumphal march into the greatest city of rebeldom. By this route (*i. e.* by Lakes Borgne and Pontchartrain) our vessels could keep up free communication with the city; and if the forts on the Lower Mississippi were not reduced, they will now be cut off from supplies, and a speedy surrender is inevitable. They were only of value as defences to the city; and that being in our hands, it is better not to waste powder on their destruction, but to preserve as much of them as possible for our own uses. But we shall have authentic details concerning the whole affair before many days, as a steamer was doubtless dispatched North as soon as the work was completed. In the meantime, the rebel dispatches we already have, leave no doubt of the fact that our forces are in actual possession of the city.

The rebels, it would seem, propose making another stand—probably a "desperate stand"—for the defence of the capital of the State. Baton Rouge is 120 miles above New-Orleans, on the eastern bank of the river; and the rebel steamboats, at the lastest advices, were running with the rebel troops, stores and ordnance to Manchac, fifteen miles below that place, while the forces of Gen. LOVELL were said to have fled to Tangapaho, which is within supporting distance of the capital, to its northeast. The rebel papers mentioned last Summer that Baton Rouge and Manchac had been strongly fortified, as an extra safeguard in case the fall of New-Orleans, that impossible event, should possibly happen. They hope here not only to defend the State Capital, but also to prevent the advance of

our steamers into the rich cotton valley of the Red River. But, if all their gunboats that were not captured by us were burned by themselves, they must have a poor hope now of preserving the capital, or any part of the State, or of the Mississippi Valley. Gov. MOORE, of Louisiana, will doubtless soon be added to the list of fugitive rebel Governors.

MILITARY POLICE FOR SOUTHERN CITIES.—The rebel leaders count largely upon the aid they are presently to receive from the climate in repelling the Union armies. The occupation of New-Orleans cannot, they believe, continue longer than June, because of the Summer heat, malaria, and fevers, to which Northern troops will be exposed; and as last Fall they argued that if they could only hold out until Winter, Europe would come to their assistance, so they now persuade themselves that Summer will bring to their redemption that tremendous destroyer, the yellow fever.

It is not to be doubted that with the coming Summer sickness will very seriously affect the usefulness of our unacclimated soldiery in the South. On the Atlantic, as on the Gulf shores, bilious diseases will make sad havoc among rank and file; and if the yellow fever appear, as it is likely to, such places as New-Orleans and Mobile will be wholly untenable. It will be for the Secretary of War to meet this difficulty. The only means seems at this moment to be the enrollment and arming of the negroes in the various cities we may hold on the coast, furnishing them with white officers of skill and accustomed to the climate, who shall drill and discipline them, and exert over them a proper military control. We know no reason why the preservation of order may not be safely intrusted to this class of persons. They have been employed in the ranks by the rebels themselves; they make good and tractable soldiers; the English have no better troops in the West Indies; and we can safely reckon not only on their fidelity, but on their immunity from climatic diseases.

The subject, we are happy to see, is engaging the attention of the Government. A communication, in another column, from our Port Royal correspondent, shows that the temper of the blacks has been tested, by the direction of the War Department, and they have shown an unexpected alacrity in volunteering to bear arms, and do their devoir in field or garrison.

THE COMMANDERS OF THE NEW-ORLEANS EXPEDITION.—The merit of capturing New-Orleans will only be apportioned when we receive the official accounts. It is so common, however, to hear the achievement ascribed wholly to "PORTER's Mortar Flotilla," that it is well worth while to recall that the expedition was composed only partially of mortar-boats; a very powerful squadron of men-of-war, under command of Capt. THEODORUS BAILEY, constituting a very material portion. Of the entire naval expedition, composed of these two divisions, the command was in the hands of Capt. FARRAGUT. The details will probably show that the credit is to be divided equitably between FARRAGUT, BAILEY and PORTER

The New-York Times.

VOL. XI—NO. 3317.　　　　NEW-YORK, SUNDAY, MAY 11, 1862.　　　　PRICE THREE CENTS.

OPERATIONS IN VIRGINIA.

Another Cannonade of Sewall's Point.

The Object of the Demonstration on Thursday.

Official Report of Commodore Goldsborough.

The Measures Taken to Dispose of the Merrimac.

The Work of Gen. McClellan's Army.

Detailed Reports of the Battle of Williamsburgh.

OFFICIAL LISTS OF KILLED AND WOUNDED.

FORTRESS MONROE, Friday May 9. }
via BALTIMORE, Saturday, May 10. }

The *Merrimac* remained off the point all night. The *Monitor* went up this forenoon and fired a few shots into Sewall's Point.

The Rip Raps battery also opened briskly, a large number of the shots striking in the wood.

Many comparisons are drawn between the enterprise of the naval fleets here and at New-Orleans.

REPORT OF COMMODORE GOLDSBOROUGH.

U. S. FLAGSHIP MINNESOTA, }
HAMPTON ROADS, Va., May 9, 1862. }

His Excellency the President of the United States:

SIR: Agreeably to a communication just received from Hon. EDWIN M. STANTON, I have the honor to report that the instructions I gave yesterday to the officers commanding the several vessels detailed to open fire on Sewall's Point, were—that the object of the move was to ascertain the practicability of landing a body of troops thereabouts, and to reduce the works if it could be done; that the wooden vessels should attack the principal works in enfilade, and that the *Monitor*, to be accompanied by the *Stevens*, should go up as far as the works, and there operate in front. On the *Merrimac's* appearance outside of the works, the *Monitor* had orders to fall back into fair channel-way, and only to engage her seriously in such a position that this ship, together with the merchant vessels intended for the purpose, could run her down. If an opportunity presented itself, the other vessels were not to hesitate to run her down, and the *Baltimore*, an unarmed steamer of light draught, light speed, and with a curved bow, was kept in the direction of the *Monitor*, expressly to throw herself across the *Merrimac*, either forward or aft of her plated house, but the *Merrimac* did not engage the *Monitor*, nor did she place herself where she could have been assailed by our ram-vessels to any advantage, or where there was any prospect whatever of getting at her. My instructions were necessarily verbal, and, in giving them, I supposed that I was carrying out your wishes in substance, if not

to the letter. The demonstration resulted in establishing the fact that the number of guns at the principal works on Sewall's Point has been essentially reduced, and is not greater than about seventeen, and that the number of men now stationed there is comparatively quite limited. The quarters connected with this work were set on fire by our shells, and no doubt are ously injured.

I am, very respectfully, your obedient servant,
(Signed,)　　　L. M. GOLDSBOROUGH,
Commanding Naval Blockading Squadron.

THE BATTLE OF WILLIAMSBURGH.

Connected Account of the Engagement—Strength of the Rebel Position—Fort Magruder—The Forces Engaged on Each Side—Seventeen Pieces of Artillery Captured from the Rebels.

[From Our Own Correspondent.

WILLIAMSBURGH, Va., Wednesday, May 7, 1862.

Now that the smoke of the battle has somewhat cleared away, I am able to give you a more connected account of the engagement, on Monday, between our advance guard and a large force of rebels who opposed our entrance into this town. The position from which the rebels assailed our forces was an exceedingly strong one, being along the line of defences established by them just below Williamsburgh, last Spring, previous to their fortification of Yorktown and Warwick Creek. Near the centre of a broad plain, at the upper side of which stands Williamsburgh, and right across the turnpike road leading to the city, they erected a substantial bastion, large enough to accommodate six or seven thousand men, and commanding the place in every direction, so that a force approaching it from any point must be exposed to a raking fire for three-quarters of a mile or more. Well supplied with artillery, and defended with determination by a force of 5,000 men, this bastion would give a world of trouble to an army of five times that number. It was supported by five smaller flanking works of the same pattern, on the right, and

two on the left, each of them having platforms for two guns, the large work being fitted for five guns.

The approach to the plain thus defended from the direction of Yorktown was by two roads; the one on the left, taken by Hooker's Division and its supports, being a straight path through the woods. That on the right, along which Hancock advanced, led over a brook or creek, which had been dammed at this point, where the road crossed it through a defile in such a way as to convert the defile into a deep pond, passed at the lower side by a narrow causeway, commanded by an earthwork looking down upon it at a height of fifty feet, and from a bold bluff on the further side. Over this causeway troops would be compelled to march four abreast for a distance of more than one-eighth of a mile, exposed to the fire of a fort above the reach of their artillery. For some reason, however, this position has never been occupied. Probably it was intended to mount artillery there, as the occasion demanded. The fact that this work, and the flanking works about Fort Magruder, were none of them occupied on Monday, shows plainly that the rebels had not proposed to make any decided stand against us here. Indeed, the command of the York River, secured to us by the evacuation of Yorktown, made their position at this point of the Peninsula untenable, as we could easily throw a force above them to take them in the rear.

The rebels had, in fact, pushed on several miles beyond Williamsburgh with their main body, before our advance approached on Sunday night, retaining a small force only at the forts in their rear. But, leaving everything behind them, our troops pushed on so rapidly after the rebels, struggling through the mud with their heavy wagons, that they found it absolutely necessary to hold us in check long enough to secure their retreat. Accordingly, on Monday morning, troops were hurried back to the support of their rear guard, occupying Fort Magruder. They continued to come in all through the day, supplying fresh troops to oppose our men. Commencing with a small force, each party continued to swell its numbers with reinforcements, until the rebels had finally fifteen or twenty thousand men on the ground, and we about the same number. The rebels had the advantage of hurrying their troops along more rapidly, so that some of our men were compelled to stand their ground for hours against a much superior force opposing them.

Confederate troops withdrew towards Richmond before these Union mortar batteries could be used.

The New-York Times.

VOL. XI–NO. 3318.   NEW-YORK, MONDAY, MAY 12, 1862.   PRICE THREE CENTS.

GLORIOUS NEWS

Norfolk and Portsmouth Captured Without a Battle.

The Gosport Navy-yard Repossessed.

THE MERRIMAC BLOWN UP.

Five Thousand National Troops Landed at Willoughby Point.

THE ADVANCE ON NORFOLK.

Our Forces Met by a Delegation of Citizens.

THE CITY FORMALLY SURRENDERED.

No Property Destroyed by the Retreating Rebel Troops.

The Monitor and the Naugatuck Gone Up to the City.

DISPATCH FROM SECRETARY STANTON.
WASHINGTON, Sunday, May 11.

The following was received at the War Department this morning :

FORT MONROE, Saturday May 10—Midnight.

Norfolk is ours, and also Portsmouth and the Navy-yard.

Gen. WOOL, having completed the landing of his forces at Willoughby Point, about 9 o'clock, this morning, commenced his march on Norfolk, with 5,000 men.

Secretary CHASE accompanied the General.

About five miles from the landing-place a rebel battery was found on the opposite side of the bridge over Tanner's Creek, and after a few discharges upon two companies of infantry that were in the advance, the rebels burned the bridge.

This compelled our forces to march around five miles further.

At 5 o'clock in the afternoon our forces were within a short distance of Norfolk, and were met by a delegation of citizens.

The city was formally surrendered.

Our troops were marched in, and now have possession.

Major-General John E. Wool considered Federal possession of Norfolk essential.

Gen. VIELE is in command, as Military Governor.

The city and Navy-yard were not burned. The fires which have been seen for some hours proved woods on fire.

Gen. WOOL, with Secretary CHASE, returned about 11 o'clock to-night.

Gen. HUGER withdrew his force without a battle.

The *Merrimac* is still off Sewall's Point.

Commander ROGERS' expedition was heard from this afternoon ascending the James River.

Reports from Gen. McCLELLAN are favorable.   EDWIN M. STANTON.

DESTRUCTION OF THE MERRIMAC.

DISPATCH TO THE NAVY DEPARTMENT.
FORTRESS MONROE, Sunday, May 11.

To Hon. J. H. Watson, Assistant Secretary of War :

The *Merrimac* was blown up by the rebels at two minutes before 5 o'clock this morning. She was set fire to about 3 o'clock. The explosion took place at the time stated. It is stated to have been a grand sight by those who saw it. The *Monitor*, *E. A. Stevens* (*Naugatuck*) and the gunboats have gone up toward Norfolk.

THE PREPARATORY MOVEMENTS.

SPECIAL DISPATCH FROM FORTRESS MONROE.

MOORE'S RANCHE, PLEASURE POINT, }
Saturday, 3 P. M., via WASHINGTON, May 11. }

I have just arrived here, and meet intelligence from the army in advance. It seems that five regiments of infantry were sent forward this morning, and pushed forward as far as the bridge across Tanner's Creek, about seven miles from this place, on the road to Norfolk. They arrived just in time to see the secession troops *burn the bridge* in their faces, and plant four pieces of rifled cannon on the opposite bank to protect them in doing it. It was then discovered that our artillery, which had been ordered over, was still on board the transport, not a single piece having been landed. The result was, that we were absolutely helpless.

It was decided to take a roundabout road, which leads around the head of Tanner's Creek. Gen. MANSFIED, who had been requested by Gen. WOOL to leave his command at Newport's News, overtook the advancing troops, MAX WEBER's Regiment taking the lead, just after the bridge had been fired, and was at once placed in command. He attended to everything in person, and has now gone back to attend to the landing and forwarding of the artillery, and to bringing up reinforcements. Five regiments are already in advance.

By the road which the destruction of the bridge has compelled them to take, our troops will be obliged to march some eight miles further—not far from twenty in all—to Norfolk, which they will scarcely be able to reach before morning.   H. J. R.

DISPATCHES TO THE ASSOCIATED PRESS.

FORTRESS MONROE, Friday, April 9—Evening.

Old Point this evening presents a most stirring spectacle. About a dozen steam transports are loading troops. They will land on the shore opposite the Rip Raps and march direct on Norfolk. At the time I commence writing, (9 P. M.,) the moon shines so brightly that I am sitting in the open air, in an elevated position, writing by moonlight. The transports are gathering in the stream—they have on board artillery, cavalry and infantry, and will soon be prepared to start. The Rip Raps are pouring in shot and shell into Sewall's Point, and a bright light in the direction of Norfolk leads to the supposition that the work of destruction has commenced.

President LINCOLN, as Commander-in-Chief of the Army and Navy, is superintending the expedition himself. About 6 o'clock he went across to the place selected for the landing, which is about a mile below the Rip Raps. It is said he was the first to step on shore, and, after examining for himself the facilities for landing, returned to the Point, where he was received with enthusiastic cheering by the troops who were embarking.

The *Merrimac* still lies off Craney Island, and the *Monitor* has assumed her usual position. The fleet are floating quietly at their anchorage, ready at any moment for action.

It is evident that the *finale* of the rebellion, as far as Norfolk is concerned, is rapidly approaching. The general expectation is, that the troops now embarking will have possession of the city before to-morrow night.

10 P. M.—The expedition has not yet started, the delay being caused by the time required for stowing the horses and cannon on the *Adelaide*. The batteries at the Rip Raps have stopped throwing shells, and all is quiet. The scene in the Roads, of the

transports steaming about, is most beautiful, presenting a panoramic view seldom witnessed.

11 P. M.—The vessels have not yet sailed.

The *Merrimac* exhibits a bright light.

It is said the *Seminole* will go up the James River in the course of the night.

BALTIMORE, Sunday, May 11.

The Old Point boat has arrived.

Our troops crossed to the Virginia shore during Friday night, whilst the Rip Raps shelled the rebel works at Sewall's Point.

A landing was effected at Willoughby's Point, at a spot selected the previous day by President LINCOLN, who was among the first who stepped ashore.

The rebels fled as our troops advanced.

At last advices Gen. MAX WEBER was within three miles of Norfolk.

The *Merrimac* remained stationary all day off Craney Island.

LATER.

WILLOUGHBY'S POINT, Saturday Morning, May 10.

The troops left during the night, and at daylight could be seen from the wharf landing at Willoughby's Point, a short distance from the Rip Raps. Through the influence of Secretary STANTON, I obtained this morning a permit to accompany Gen. WOOL and Gen. MANSFIELD and Staffs to Willoughby's Point, on the steamer *Kansas*, and here I am, on "sacred soil," within eight miles of Norfolk. The Point at which we have landed is known as Point Pleasant, one of the favorite drives from Norfolk.

The first regiment landed was the Twentieth New-York, known as MAX WEBER's regiment, which pushed on immediately, under command of Gen. WEBER, and were at 8 A. M. picketed within five miles of Norfolk. The First Delaware, Col. ANDREWS, was pushed forward at 9 o'clock, accompanied by Gens. MANSFIELD and VIELE and Staff. They were soon followed by the Sixteenth Massachusetts, Col. WYMAN. The balance of the expedition consists of the Tenth New-York, Col. BENDIX, the Forty-eighth Pennsylvania, Col. BAILEY, the Ninety-ninth New-York, (Coast Guards,) Major DODGES' Battalion of Mounted Rifles, and Capt. FOLLETT's Co. D of Fourth (regular) Artillery. Gen. WOOL and staff remained to superintend the landing of the balance of the force, all of whom were landed and off before noon.

The President, accompanied by Secretary STANTON, accompanied Gen. WOOL and Staff to the wharf, and then took a tug and proceeded to the *Minnesota*, where he was received with a National salute. It is generally admitted that the President and Secretary STANTON have infused new vigor into both the naval and military operations here, and that the country will have no cause for further complaint. As to the insulting course of the rebels in this quarter, the

President has declared that *Norfolk must fall, that the Merrimac must succumb to the naval power of the Union*, and that the Government property at Norfolk must be repossessed at whatever cost it may require. What is more, he has determined to remain until it is accomplished.

The iron-clad gunboat *Galena*, accompanied by the *Port Royal* and *Aroostook*, went up the James River on Wednesday night, and although I have been unable to obtain any positive information from them since they silenced the forts on the lower part of the river, it is understood that the President has received dispatches from Gen. McCLELLAN to the effect that they have given him most valuable aid in driving the enemy to the wall. It is even stated to-day that the *Galena* not only captured the *Yorktown* and *Jamestown*, but has put crews on board and ran them up within shelling distance of the river defences of Richmond. Of the truth of this, however, I cannot vouch, as Old Point is becoming famous for fabulous rumors.

THE CITY OF NORFOLK

Norfolk, by last census, had a population of 14,609, about 3,300 of whom were slaves. But on account of the fearful state of perturbation in which the city has been kept for the last year, and also on account of the rebel conscription, it is now probably reduced to a half of that number. It is situated on the right bank of the Elizabeth River, just below the confluence of the two branches, 8 miles from Hampton Roads, 32 miles from the Ocean, and 106 by land and 160 by water southeast from Richmond. The situation is low; the streets are irregular and mostly wide, with good brick and stone buildings.

The harbor is safe and spacious, admitting the largest vessels. The entrance to it is over a mile in width, and Fortress Monroe and Fort Calhoun, on the Rip Raps, were built for its defence.

Among the principal buildings, are the City Hall, having a granite front, and a cupola 110 feet high; the Norfolk Military Academy, Mechanics' Hall, and Ashland Hall. The city contains a court-house, jail, custom-house, three banks, and fourteen churches. There is a beautiful cemetery, handsomely laid out, and adorned with cypress trees. In the vicinity, at Gosport, is the celebrated United States Navy-yard, which was seized by the rebels last year, and at which they clad in iron the *Merrimac* and other vessels. The yard contains a dry dock, constructed of granite, at a cost of a million of dollars.

The foreign commerce of Norfolk exceeds that of any other place in Virginia; and there are only two towns in the State of greater population, Petersburgh and Richmond.

The Dismal Swamp Canal connects Chesapeake Bay and Albemarle Sound, and opens an extensive water communication from Norfolk to the South.

The locks of this canal were recently partially destroyed by Gen. RENO, when the battle of Camden insued; and the canal was subsequently obstructed by a detachment of Commodore ROWAN's naval force. There is a line of railroads running from Norfolk to Suffolk, in the adjoining county of Nansemond, which connects it with the whole Southern system of railroads.

Norfolk was the scene of important military events in the war of the Revolution. The British fleet, to which Lord DUNMORE, the Governor of Virginia, fled at the outbreak of hostilities, made Norfolk harbor its principal rendezvous. On the 1st of January, 1776, the town was bombarded by the British at the order of DUNMORE, and a party of troops were landed, who set fire to the houses. The fire raged three days, and the horrors of conflagration were heightened by the thunder of cannon from the ships; and many women and children lost their lives. The remaining edifices were afterward destroyed, and the mournful silence of gloomy depopulation reigned where once was the principal town of Virginia. But it rose again from its ashes, and has now, for the second time been taken, but by a more humane and civilized Government than the British.

THE TOWN OF PORTSMOUTH.

Portsmouth, directly opposite Norfolk, is a place of 9,500 inhabitants. It is built on level ground, has various institutions of learning, a military academy, five newspapers, and six churches. By the seaboard and Roanoke Railroad, and James River, it has extensive communications North and South. It, of course, falls with the fall of Norfolk. The Navy-yard is more properly said to be here than at Norfolk. It is half a mile from the central part of the town, or that part of it called Gosport.

THE NEWS IN WASHINGTON.

WASHINGTON, Sunday, May 11.

Washington has been in a state of tumult all day, growing out of the extraordinary war bulletins that have been posted at the hotels. People are bewildered, and their joy made grave and inexpressible by the unexpected immensity of the Union triumphs. Willard's Hotel has been crowded, the War Office besieged, and every place of public resort thronged by eager crowds pressing and breathless for news. Extra editions of the Sunday papers were issued, and sold at fabulous prices, until every man, woman and child of Washington knew the wonderful tidings. Shall I add it—need I add it—that the chorus of every congratulation between the people was the same—a pean of enthusiastic praise of the noble General of the Union, who, in the unanimous declaration of Congress, has accomplished such great results with such small sacrifice of human life.

Contrary to first reports, retreating Confederates destroyed what they could of the Norfolk Navy Yard.

The New-York Times.

VOL. XI–NO. 3319. NEW-YORK, TUESDAY, MAY 13, 1862. PRICE TWO CENTS.

THE CAPTURE OF NORFOLK.

Editorial Correspondence of the New-York Times.

Interesting Particulars of the Advance Upon and Occupation of the City.

The Destruction of the Navy-Yard by the Rebels.

Proclamations Issued by Gens. Wool and Viele.

THE LAST OF THE MERRIMAC.

Character of the Rebel Fortifications on Craney Island.

Gen. Wool's Report to the War Department.

About Two Hundred Cannon Captured.

OCEAN VIEW, OPPOSITE FORTRESS MONROE, }
Saturday evening, 8 o'clock. }

NORFOLK and Gosport Navy-yard again belong to the United States! Our troops under Gen. WOOL entered and took possession of the town at 5 o'clock this afternoon, receiving its surrender at the hands of the Mayor and Common Council. All the troops who had been holding it under Gen. HUGER were withdrawn yesterday,—the public buildings and public property in the Navy-yard were all destroyed,—the people remained in the city, and our forces entered into peaceable possession, being encamped two miles out of the town, in what is called the intrenched camp, which was very strongly fortified, and in which 30 pieces of cannon fell into our possession. Brig.-Gen. EGBERT L. VIELE has been appointed Military Governor of the place, and the strongest assurances were given by Gen. WOOL and by Secretary CHASE, who accompanied him throughout the march, that the persons and property of all the inhabitants should be treated with the utmost respect.

VISIT OF PRESIDENT LINCOLN AND SECRETARIES STANTON AND CHASE TO NORFOLK.

President LINCOLN, who has been staying here, as have also the Secretaries of War and the Treasury, for several days, and whose presence and personal participation in the movements of the last week, have been of the utmost importance to the country, decided to start for Washington this morning in the steamer Baltimore. On hearing the reported destruction of the Merrimac confirmed he concluded first to take a look at this latest of the cities which had been recovered for the Union. Taking Gen. WOOL on board the steamer accordingly,

under charge of Commodore GOLDSBOROUGH, they went down to Norfolk, where the Commodore left for his flagship, and Gen. WOOL remained to transact business connected with the affairs of this new Department. The President did not go ashore, but after taking a look at the city started immediately for Washington. His visit here has been of the most unostentatious, but certainly of the most useful sort. He has given his personal attention and care to every department of operations here, and has brought a very excellent and safe judgment to bear upon matters which required something more than mere professional knowledge and skill for their solution. And I do no injustice to others in saying that much of the vigor and success of the recent operations here is due to the stimulus of his presence.

Latest from Norfolk.

NORFOLK, Sunday, May 11—2 P. M.

I seized the first opportunity, to-day, to take a look at the fortifications by which Norfolk has been so long defended against our fleet. It is easy to see that their strength has not been exaggerated. The works on Sewall's Point are quite extensive, intended for forty guns, only twenty-three of which, however, have ever been mounted, and of these only seven now remain. Craney Island—long, low and level—stands just at the entrance of the channel, and has upon it a very formidable series of skilfully constructed earthworks, intended for fifty guns, of which thirty-nine had been mounted,—mostly nine and ten inch Dahlgrens, though there were also rifled and Parrot guns among them. There were also nine finished casemates on the north bastion, and five unfinished. The works are all admirably constructed. Next beyond Craney Island, on the right, is a most beautiful semi-circular water battery, with eleven casemates, and finished in as fine style as any works of a similar kind I have ever seen. Still further on, upon the same side, is still another battery, while on the opposite shore stands Fort Norfolk. All these works together constitute a gauntlet which it certainly would not be prudent in any but the most powerful vessel of war to attempt to run. Then, too, just below these batteries, directly across the channel, has been driven a line of piles, an opening being left in the middle for the passage of vessels, intended, however, to be closed in an emergency by sinking the immense hulk of the old United States, which lies close by for preparation. Upon these piles, the San Jacinto, as she was going in to-day, stuck fast for a couple of hours, but finally extricated herself without injury.

The rebels succeeded in almost completely destroying the Navy-yard last night. Hundreds of them were busy in setting fire to all the buildings and all the vessels, and this morning little remained but smoking ruins and a dismal desolation. The great Eastern and Western ship-houses, the marine barracks, officers' quarters, smiths' shops, engine houses, &c., were all consumed. The rebels had built and launched two iron vessels, mounting four guns each and built in water-tight compartments, so as to be raised or sunk at pleasure. These were not intended to be propelled, but to be used as stationary batteries for harbor defence, or else to be towed out to operate against our wooden vessels. They were burned, but not so seriously injured as to be entirely useless. A number of small vessels and schooners were also burned. Great efforts were made to destroy the dry dock, but they were unsuccessful.

The magnificent Naval Hospital remains untouched. Even the vandalism which has marked so many of the acts of the rebels during this war, shrank from the sacrilege of firing this splendid structure.

Brigadier-General Egbert L. Viele was appointed Military Governor of Norfolk.

GEN. McCLELLAN'S ADVANCE

News from the Army up to Sunday Evening.

Our Cavalry in Possession of White House.

Large Quantities of Wheat and Corn Captured.

The Enemy's Rear Guard Five Miles Distant.

TWO AND A HALF MILES FROM KENT COURT-HOUSE, }
CUMBERLAND, Va., Sunday morning, May 11. }

A company of the Sixth Cavalry passed on last night to White House, five miles from here, on the Pamunkey River, better known as the Curtis estate, owned by a son of Gen. ROBERT E. LEE. The company secured 7,000 bushels of Wheat and 4,000 bushels of Corn. The rebels had burnt the railroad bridge and town, and torn up the road for some distance toward Richmond. The distance from White House to Richmond is 23 miles.

The gunboats arrived here this morning and are now on their way to White House. The rebels had blockaded the river two miles below here by sinking vessels, but they were blown up without much trouble.

The rear guard of the enemy is at Tunnel's Depot, five miles from White House.

A contraband who left Richmond on Friday reports the city full of sick soldiers, and that the citizens are flocking in from the surrounding country.

The New-York Times.

VOL. XI.—NO. 3337.　　　　　NEW-YORK, TUESDAY, JUNE 3, 1862.　　　　　PRICE TWO CENTS.

THE GREAT BATTLE.

Full Particulars from Our Special Correspondent.

The Attack on Gen. Casey's Position.

The Temporary Disaster There, with Loss of Artillery and Camp Equipage

The Divisions of Gens. Kearney and Hooker Brought up.

GALLANT BAYONET CHARGE

The Rebels Driven Back Like Sheep.

The Crossing of the Chickahominy by Our Reinforcements.

DESPERATE NATURE OF THE FIGHTING.

The Great Victory of Our Forces On Sunday.

Our Advance Now Some Distance Beyond the Battle Ground.

FIELD OF BATTLE BEFORE RICHMOND, }
Sunday A. M., June 1, 1862. }

A battle before Richmond has at last put to the test the rebel boast as to what they would do with Gen. McClellan's army when they should get it beyond the protection of the gunboats. Though the advantage of a sudden movement, against the weakest point in our lines, gave the enemy a temporary success, the final result has not been such as to afford encouragement to their disheartened and demoralized troops, or occasion any fears as to our ultimate possession of the rebel capital.

The attack commenced shortly before 1 o'clock on Saturday, on the left wing of the army, on the further or south side of the Chickahominy, where the advance position was held by the division of Gen. Casey, much the weakest in the army, composed almost entirely of raw regiments, and reduced by disease to an effective force of some 6,000 men.

THE POSITION HELD BY GEN. CASEY

Was on the Williamsburgh Stage Road, within six

Major-General Silas Casey.

or seven miles of Richmond, and on a line so extended at the front that the troops required to maintain picket guards of sufficient strength, made no slight draft on his weakened forces. The right of the line was held by his First Brigade, under Gen. H. M. Naglee, as brave and vigilant an officer as is to be found in the army of the Potomac. Gen. Naglee's pickets extended across the railroad (running parallel with the Williamsburgh road, about a mile to the right) to near the sixth mile-post from Richmond, and so on further to the right and a little to the rear until within a short distance of a point on the Chickahominy, where Gen. Sumner had thrown a bridge across the stream, and was hourly expected to cross to complete the line of pickets to the river.

The centre of Gen. Casey position, held by the Second Brigade, Gen. Wassell's, (formerly Gen. Keims',) extended from Gen. Naglee's lines to the left a short distance across the Williamsburgh Road, where it joined the Third Brigade, Gen. Palmer's, stretching some distance further to the left, and joining the lines of Gen. Couch, who guarded the left flank, the main portion of his force being a short distance to the rear of Casey, on the Williamsburgh Road.

THE NATURE OF THE GROUND.

The position occupied by the main body of these two divisions was a clearing of about one mile square, surrounded on the left and the front by a belt of forest, in which Gen. Casey's pickets were stationed. On the right, a wooded swamp divided the clearing from a similar opening in the forest, along the railroad, which was occupied by Gen. Naglee with his brigade. Just beyond the woods to the front were similar clearings with woods on their further side, where the rebels lay concealed, their pickets occupying the edge of the forest, and separated from our pickets by the width of the fields, forming a sort of neutral ground between the two armies, over which

each kept close watch lest his neighbor should take possession. The position of Gen. Casey and other Generals, the nature of the ground, etc., will be made clear by reference to the map accompanying this account.

Step by step Gen. Casey had pressed on to this point, overcoming such opposition as met him, until it became evident that the rebels had reached the limit of their retreat, and further advance could not be ventured without the risk of a general engagement, for which the plans were not yet ripe. Our proximity to the rebels was evidently annoying to them, and on Thursday, and again on Friday, they made an unsuccessful attempt, with a force of a few hundred, to drive in the pickets and discover what mischief was plotting behind the belt of woods sheltering Gen. Casey from their view. Their attack was resolutely met by the pickets, who fell back on the reserves and held their ground, defeating the purpose of the enemy.

Meanwhile Gen. Casey was actively at work securing his position, a large force of men being placed under the skillful direction of Lieut. E. W. West, of his Staff, digging rifle pits and felling trees for abattis. A similar line of defensive works had been commenced and partially completed at Gen. Casey's former position, at the Seven Pines, three miles further to the rear, and just back of these was a line of earthworks, constructed by Gen. Couch, and more carefully finished.

Failing in the two attempts to gather information by forcing back Gen. Casey's pickets, the rebels apparently resolved upon an *advance in force against the left wing of the army*, doubtless determined to drive it beyond the Chickahominy, should the opportunity offer, and put themselves in a position to turn Gen. McClellan's left flank.

THE ATTACK ON SATURDAY.

Shortly after noon the grand attack commenced, Gen. Casey's pickets being driven in all along the front, after a spirited resistance, the rebels advancing in force along three roads—the Williamsburgh road, to our left, the railroad, in the centre, and the "Nine-mile Road," as it is called, on the right. With his feeble division greatly weakened by extension, Gen. Casey had no backbone to oppose to this sudden attack. But no thought of yielding his ground entered the mind of the old soldier, scarred with the wounds of Mexico and disciplined to danger by a hundred fights. His troops were immediately formed into position, the three brigades maintaining their relative positions on the right, left and centre, and as thorough preparations were made for resisting the attack as its suddenness would admit of. Regan's New-York Battery was stationed just to the right of the Williamsburgh road, Bates' Battery of Napoleon guns further to the left across the road, and Fitch's Battery three or four hundred yards to the rear, the last sending its shell over the heads of our troops at the enemy beyond. The fourth battery was near the railroad, further to the right.

The vigor with which the enemy pressed forward to the attack indicated the confidence of superior strength. A battalion of two regiments pressed against Gen. Naglee on the right, another fell on Gen. Wassell at the centre, and a third on Gen. Palmer to the left, pouring in at once a fire hot and heavy, and advancing with great resolution in face of the steady fire of canister and grape from the guns in front, and shell from those further to the rear, moving down their ranks in all directions. The rebels had but little artillery, and were evidently disposed to make good the deficiency by pressing to

SCENE OF THE GREAT BATTLE BEFORE RICHMOND.

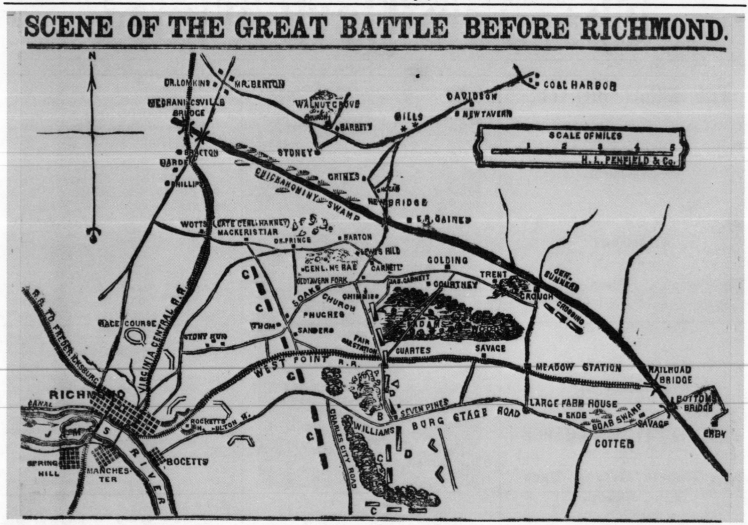

close quarters with their superior force, to bear down at once by weight of numbers the feeble skeleton regiments of three and four hundred men who composed the advanced division.

Most of Gen. CASEY's troops were thrown forward to the edge of the woods in front of his position to meet the advance of the rebels, a few regiments being left behind the partially completed rifle-pits, a short distance to the rear. Thus a division, nearly new to warfare, was suddenly exposed, in an open field, to the heaviest of fire from an enemy covered to a considerable extent by the woods through which they were advancing. Terribly the tempest raged, the air almost growing thick with musket balls; officer after officer fell, or was borne from the field a wounded man; the men drooped by scores, and the usual number of weak-jointed ones were falling to the rear. But in spite of the rapid thinning of their ranks, the regiments generally held their ground until the enemy succeeded in rushing around on the left flank, and poured in an enfilading fire from that direction, against which the rifle-pits were no protection. The sixty rounds of ammunition with which they entered the fight were nearly exhausted, and no more was at hand.

ARRIVAL OF REINFORCEMENTS.

Meantime one of Gen. COUCH's brigades, commanded by Gen. ABERCROMBIE, was ordered up to the support of Gen. NAGLEE on the right, Gen. DEVENS, of the same division, sustaining Gen. WASSELL on the center, and Gen. PECK, with the remaining brigade, supporting Gen. PALMER on the left. When Gen. CASEY's troops were forced to give way, the rebels fell on these brigades of COUCH's Division, who disputed every inch of ground, until sustained by Gen. KEARNEY, pressing up the Williamsburgh road with reinforcements to meet them, supported by the Division of Gen. HOOKER in his rear. Pressing rapidly forward

Gen. KEARNEY advanced along the Williamsburgh road to within a short distance of our original position, where he bivouacked for the night in front of the enemy.

It was along this Williamsburgh road that the main attack was made, and here our troops were forced back for half a mile or more, before the arrival of Gen. HEINTZELMAN's corps, the feeble brigades of CASEY's Division, averaging less than 2,000 men, being completely broken up, many, if not most of the officers killed, wounded or missing, and the privates scattered through the woods and along the road. Bravely and well did Gen. CASEY do his duty, pressing on to the extreme front and cheering on his men, regardless of the storm of fire and hail that raged about him, cutting down his officers on all sides, but strangely escaping his own person. Bravely and well did most of his officers stand by him, until, one after another, they were borne from the field dead or wounded.

THE LOSS OF ARTILLERY.

Col. BAILEY, Chief of Artillery, was shot early in the afternoon, the ball striking him in the head and causing his death after a short period of insensibility. Maj. VAN VAULTENBERG, the second in command of the First New-York Artillery, was killed, Adj't WM. RAMSAY wounded, while every battery but one lost its quota of men, and some of them lost nearly all their horses. BATES' Battery of Napoleon guns—12-pound brass pieces—which was to the front, thus deprived of locomotion and stuck fast in the mud, was left behind in the retirement of our troops, but not until Gen. NAGLEE had taken it upon himself to see that several of the pieces were spiked. In addition to this, one 3-inch Parrot gun of Battery H was disabled by a shot, and fell into the hands of the enemy. The Pennsylvania Reserve Battery, of COUCH's Division, also lost one of their guns—these eight pieces of ordnance constituting our entire loss, so far as I could learn. We can bet-

ter afford to spare the pieces than we can afford to have the rebels profit by their gain. They show every indication of being much in want of artillery, and the need is evidently stimulating their efforts to profit by the chances of war to possess themselves of our guns.

GEN. SUMNER'S ADVANCE.

Meantime Gen. SUMNER had succeeded in bringing his troops across the Chickahominy, and was advancing on the right there, where less ground had been lost. After several days of labor, Gen. SUMNER had thrown two bridges across the creek between Bottom's Bridge and New Bridge, where local reports held it to be impossible to find any foundation for piles to support the superstructures. One of these bridges was some two miles above Bottom's Bridge, the other a mile further up the stream. The lower of these was carried away during the heavy storm of Friday night, and Gen. SUMNER was obliged to depend upon a single shaky structure for the passage of his troops, who nearly all, however, succeeded in crossing that night, the head of the column reaching the Nine-mile Road, along which the rebels were pressing our troops, at about 7 o'clock, holding the enemy in check for the night, preventing them from following up in that direction the advantage they had gained during the day.

THE FIGHT ON SUNDAY.

Flushed with their seeming victory of Saturday the rebels awoke with confidence on Sunday to follow up their movements, sure of driving us this time to the Chickahominy and beyond. But they had made the unfortunate mistake of estimating the strength of our reserves by the weakness of our advance. *Most bitterly did they pay for their mistake.* Pressing eagerly forward with confidence of victory, they were met by the trained troops of HEINTZELMAN and SUMNER, whose unyielding columns

The Peninsula Campaign saw the use of observation balloons by Federal troops; here the balloon *Intrepid* is inflated.

checked their fierce assault, turning the tide of battle everywhere against them, *and forcing them at the point of the bayonet on toward Richmond.* It was their turn now to break and run, and their losses of the Sabbath left them little cause for rejoicing over the trifling gain of Saturday. Terribly did the rebels suffer on this, as well as the previous day, from the well-directed fire of our artillery, *piling the ground with the slain.* Terrible also to them were the frequent charges of our solid columns, pressing them back, step by step, to the last point of endurance, *when they broke and ran,* ingloriously leaving behind them many of their men and officers, as well as privates, prisoners in our hands. The number of these it is not yet possible to ascertain, several days necessarily elapsing after every engagement before a full inventory can be taken.

OUR LOSS IN KILLED AND WOUNDED.

Even of our loss it was impossible to form any correct idea at the time I left the field of battle. The only source of information was the wounded, who gave such particulars, in regard to their respective regiments as they could, as they were borne by from all parts of the field. To the oft-repeated question :

Well, how did your regiment stand it ?" I got uniform answers.

" O, Sir, our regiment was all cut to pieces—cut to pieces, Sir ; nothing left of it."

I, of course, was able to rely little on such stories from my disabled informants, knowing the tendency, not only among soldiers, but equally among people in civilized life, to magnify their own misfortune into a measure of the public calamity. They took no account of their nimble-footed comrades, who had disappeared without damage to life or limb. It is impossible, so soon after the affair, to give even a rough estimate of the loss in an engagement spread over so great a space of country, and in the confusion which always ensues after a battle. That the loss is very severe, and particularly so in the matter of officers, there is no matter of doubt. The difficulty of rightly estimating our loss is also enhanced by the fact that many

of those falling were unavoidably left upon the ground subsequently occupied by the enemy in his first successful attack. The number of these we cannot learn until regimental rolls are compared. It is sincerely to be regretted, in view of the tales we have of the barbarous treatment of our wounded by the rebels, when once they fall into their hands, that necessity should have compelled any to be left upon the field, to receive "the tender mercies of the wicked." That the rebel loss was greater by far than our own I do not doubt. Besides our superiority in artillery, our small arms were much more effective, having all the superiority in fatal power, which the Minié ball has over the round rifle ball. The wounds inflicted by the enemy were mainly by the latter. Had the leaden hail in which our men were obliged to stand so long, been composed of conical instead of round shot, many more Rachels would be mourning over the lost, and many more homes draped in funeral weeds. Your correspondent feels particularly grateful to the blockade, being morally certain that had the ball which lodged so harmlessly in his legging been a Minié, he would have been obliged always hereafter to write standing on one foot—a good figure of speech for JUVENAL, but one which he would rather be excused from practically embodying. As it is, the slight abrasion left upon his leg by the ball, after forcing two thicknesses of leather and one of cloth, is sufficiently suggestive of a reward to satisfy his moderate ambition for military adventure.

THE CASUALTIES OF SATURDAY.

Of those who entered into close range of the enemy's guns, scarcely one of the officers that I saw escaped without some mark of the enemy's bullets on clothes or person, when no positive wound was inflicted. Gen. NAGLEE was struck four times by balls that pierced his clothes, inflicting slight bruises on his person. Lieut. WEST, Aid-de-Camp to Gen. CASEY, who continued constantly under fire while actively discharging his duties, had his clothes badly torn by a piece of shell. Lieut. FOSTER, who was equally cool and energetic, I heard reported as wounded, but discredit the statement, which I should be sorry to believe true of so efficient an officer. Capt. SMITH, Gen. CASEY's Assistant Adjutant-General, and Lieut. HARRINGTON RAYMOND, Aid-de-Camp, were disabled, by sickness—Lieut. RAYMOND fretting upon his sick bed at the thought that he should be compelled to inaction at a time when his services were so much needed by his General.

Of the line officers not positively wounded, Col. C H. VAN WYCK, of the Fifty-sixth New-York Regiment, seems to have met with the most narrow escape, being struck by a spent shell which doubled up his sword-sheath, and severely bruised his left knee. Had the shell been nearer its initial velocity, the Colonel would have lost a pair of limbs, of essential service to a man of his active habits ; and had it exploded, Congress would have been minus one of its working members.

All sorts of reports were afloat immediately after the engagement in regard to accidents to prominent officers, in Gen. CASEY's Division more particularly. The General himself was reported to me first as wounded, and then as killed, but I was happy to be able to congratulate the brave old soldier on his entire safety before leaving the field with my dispatches

Gen. CASEY's son-in-law, Col. HUNT, received a ball through the fleshy part of his thigh, inflicting a wound more painful than dangerous. Col. HUNT, who is a Captain in the Twelfth United States Infantry, had taken command, only the week previous, of the Ninety-second New-York Regiment, to which he had been appointed. He has seen fifteen years of service in the regular army, and is an officer whose services we can ill afford to spare at this juncture.

REPORT FROM THE PRESS CORESPONDENT

McCLELLAN'S HEADQUARTERS, }
Monday, June 2—P. M. }

A Union soldier in the gondola of the *Intrepid* prepares to survey Confederate movements.

Two days of the battle of Richmond have been fought, on both of which our troops have been victorious. The loss on both sides is heavy. The battle was opened by the enemy's making an attack on Gen. CASEY's Division encamped near the Seven Pines, on the turnpike leading over Bottom's Bridge and within seven miles of Richmond. The attack was made about one o'clock on Saturday, by Gen. HILL's Division, composed of five rebel brigades, the rebel troops being for the most part from South Carolina, Virginia and Georgia. The fight there was disastrous.

Gen. CASEY's troops were forced to retire before superior numbers, leaving all their camp equipage and twelve batteries. Col. BAILEY, in endeavoring to save his batteries, was killed. Some of the troops in this division from New-York and Pennsylvania behaved very badly. Many of the officers were killed and wounded in endeavoring to rally their men.

Gen. HEINTZELMAN, on ascertaining the result, ordered forward a portion of the divisions of Gen. KEARNEY and HOOKER, to regain the day. Gen. KEARNEY's men, on being brought into action, charged with the bayonet, driving the rebels before them like sheep, regaining all the lost ground but about half a mile. Night coming on operations were brought to a close.

Gen. SUMNER's two Divisions, Gens. SEDGWICK and RICHARDSON's, crossed the Chickahominy about 3 o'clock on Saturday afternoon, taking a position on Gen. HEINTZELMAN's right. Here they encountered Gens. LONGSTREET, RAINS and HUGER's Divisions, the flower of the rebel army. The fighting was desperate, every foot of ground being hotly contested, but our soldiers were too much for them.

The enemy would stand manfully at a distance of sixty yards and be fired at, but they were afraid of the bayonet ; and in every instance that our men charged they were victorious. These two divisions did nobly, driving the rebels at every point until dark.

The enemy's loss was very heavy, many of them being killed by the bayonet. Gen. PETTIGREW, of South Carolina, was taken prisoner. We have about 300 prisoners, among whom—

[NOTE.—At this point of the message the line ceased to work between Wilmington and Cherrystone, probably on account of a storm.—REPORTER.]

GREAT IMPORTANCE OF THE VICTORY.

WASHINGTON, Monday, June 2.

Dispatches of an unofficial character, received from the headquarters of the army of the Potomac, say that the importance and dimensions of our victory increase as they are hourly developed.

A LATER DISPATCH.

I have information that I deem reliable, that dispatches are in hand here *giving far more conclusive evidences of our great victory before Richmond than the Government has published.*

LATEST FROM THE ARMY.

No More Fighting Yesterday—Our Advance Considerably Beyond its Former Position.

WASHINGTON, Monday, June 2.

Advices from the army of the Potomac, dated this afternoon, show that there has been no fighting to-day. Our advance is considerably in front of the position it occupied previous to the battle of Saturday.

OUR CORRESPONDENCE FROM THE ADVANCE.

INDICATIONS OF THE GREAT BATTLE.

The Rebels Appearing in Force—They Attack Our Pickets and are Driven Back in Confusion—Major Kelley of the Ninety-sixth New-York Killed—Illness of Col. Van Wyck.

WILLIAMSBURGH STAGEROAD, NEAR RICHMOND, Thursday, May 29, 1862.

Five and six miles from Richmond seems to be the limit of our present advance in this direction, without a decisive action; for the enemy, who have thus far yielded so readily to our movements, now exhibit great irritability at the slightest symptom of further progression. They have been showing themselves in considerable force for the past two days, just in front of our lines, between the railroad and the Chickahominy, where they have a portion of a regiment in line of battle on the edge of wood bounding the further edge of a plain intervening between us and them. Cavalry and artillery are also to be seen there, and a large force is apparently in reserve under cover of the woods. One of their guns at this point is a smooth-bore 12-pounder, which they fire on the slightest provocation, the adventurous disposition of Gen. NAGLEE, who occupies this position, making him the especial subject of their attentions. It is to the well-considered enterprise of Gen. NAGLEE that we are chiefly indebted for our rapid progress from beyond Bottom's Bridge to this point, he having led the way with ——s of reconnoissances in which enterprise and boldness have shown themselves, united to the rarer quality of quick and correct military judgment.

The rebels made an attempt to inform themselves as to the exact position of Gen. KEYES' outposts this morning, taking advantage of a thick fog which obscured the air just at sunrise, to advance on our pickets with a force of 300 men, from EARLEY'S Brigade of North Carolinians. The men on duty, though from some of Gen. CASEY'S "raw regiments," showed the discipline of veterans, rallying without confusion on the reserves, and, thus reinforced, driving the enemy promptly back—a force of 90 men on our side sending 300 rebels flying in confusion, each man for himself. The excellent conduct of the pickets was due in no slight measure to the presence of Maj. JNO. E. KELSEY, of the Ninety-sixth New-York Volunteers, who, while encouraging them with his commands and his example, fell mortally wounded, and died in a few moments, after being assisted to a house near the scene of action. A private of the One Hundred and Third Pennsylvania Regiment, NEWTON JOSEPH, of Company B, was also killed—shot through the heart. Two others were wounded—First Sergt. DAVID LANCASTER, Company C, Eighty-fifth Pennsylvania, losing an arm, and private WM. LEEP, of Company C, Eighty-fifth Pennsylvania, receiving a slight wound in the hand.

Confederate thrusts by Stonewall Jackson in the Shenandoah Valley kept troops under Major-General John C. Fremont (above) preoccupied.

The rebels must have suffered some loss, one of their wounded men being left behind in their hasty flight, and he reporting another, whom he knew of, as wounded. The name of this man is SIGEL, a private in the Twenty-third North Carolina Regiment, and kin, as he says, to our Gen. FRANZ SIGEL. Though every attention has been paid to him, there is little prospect of his recovery, the upper third of the thigh being badly shattered. His case excites more than usual commisseration, as he is an intelligent fellow, who, it is evident, has entered into the rebel service with no very good heart. He confirms previous reports of dissatisfaction in the rebel ranks, especially apparent of late among the North Carolinians, owing to the position of that State toward the Confederate Government. Like all of the privates we have taken, he is ignorant of the number and position of the rebel troops. Gen. EARLEY, he says, is again on duty, having nearly recovered from the wound received at Williamsburgh in the left arm.

Major KELLEY, of the Ninety-sixth New-York, (Col. FAIRMAN,) whose death is here recorded, is an officer deserving of more than a passing notice. For fifteen years he has seen service in the regular army, last holding the position of Orderly-Sergeant under Gen. (Col.) CASEY. He was one of the few in the volunteer service who have a military ambition, pure and simple. Having made arms his profession, he was earnest to excel and prompt in every duty; energetic, and yet quiet, he had made for himself a place which it will not be easy to fill. I hear on all sides expressions of more than ordinary regret at his loss.

We are still in doubt as to what is before us in this direction. The rebels, after submitting so quietly to the crossing of Bottom's Bridge, are threatening opposition to the passage of New-Bridge, holding tenaciously to their positions in that vicinity. It would seem that having been driven from their extended lines of defence, they are seeking a position where they will have a narrower field of action, though they can have halted at Richmond only under the pressure of political necessity. Why they should have suffered our occupation of so many excellent positions, to fall back so hastily on Richmond, does not appear evident, except as the lack of confidence in their troops may derange the plans of the Confederate leaders. They clearly feel themselves out-generaled by MCCLELLAN, and this would be provocative of uncertainty and indecision in their movements.

I can hear of no very elaborate defences about Richmond, though having access to information which seems complete and reliable.

Another smart shower visited us yesterday. The days are warm, but the nights quite cool.

The friends of Col. VAN WYCK (M. C.) will regret to learn that he has been so unwell for a week past as to be unfit for duty, though now convalescent.

PIERREPONT.

FROM THE MOUNTAIN DEPARTMENT

Extraordinary March of Gen. Fremont Across the Shenandoah Mountains.

Jackson Encountered Near Strasburgh in Full Retreat.

He Declines an Engagement After a Brief Skirmish.

Occupation of Strasburg by Gen. Fremont.

FREMONT'S HEADQUARTERS, NEAR STRASBURGH, Sunday, June 1.

Gen. FREMONT, with a strong column, left Franklin last Sunday, and, by rapid forced marches, has *crossed the Shenandoah Mountain ranges, marching nearly 150 miles over difficult roads, with little means of transportation, and no supplies in the country.*

This morning, five miles from Strasburgh, he overtook Gen. JACKSON in full retreat with his whole force, on the road from Winchester to Strasburgh. Col. CLUSERET, commanding the advance brigade, came upon the enemy strongly posted with artillery, which opened as soon as the head of his column approached.

Gen. FREMONT rapidly brought his main column up, and formed in line of battle. *Gen. Jackson declined to fight,* and while holding CLUSERET in check with a portion of his troops, withdrew his main force and continued his retreat.

In the skirmish, five of the Eighth Virginia, and two of the Sixtieth Ohio were wounded.

The enemy's loss is unknown. Twenty-five prisoners were taken by our cavalry.

Lieut.-Col. DOWNEY, of the Third Regiment, Potomac Home Brigade, in a skirmish Thursday morning, drove a large party of ASHBY's Cavalry through Wardensville, killing two and wounding three.

GEN. FREMONT'S HEADQUARTERS, STRASBURGH, Monday, June 2.

Gen. FREMONT's advance brigade, under Col. CLUSERET, *occupied Strasburgh last night without opposition. Jackson is rapidly retreating before our forces.*

A midnight reconnoissance, three miles beyond Strasburgh, came upon a rope barricade and ambush of JACKSON's rear guard and retired successfully with the loss of only three wounded. Col. FIGGELMENCIL, of Gen. FREMONT's staff, with only fifteen men, brilliantly charged and put to flight a body of cavalry commanded by ASHBY in person.

The New-York Times.

VOL. XI—NO. 3338.   NEW-YORK, WEDNESDAY, JUNE 4, 1862.   PRICE TWO CENTS.

THE GREAT VICTORY.

Full Details of the Second Day's Fight.

Interesting Letter from one of Our Special Correspondents.

How the Battle was Fought and How the Battle was Won.

The Rebels Driven Back at Every Point with Great Slaughter.

Twelve Hundred of Their Dead Left on the Field.

Distinguished Gallantry of Gen. Sickles.

The Bayonet Charge of the Second Excelsior.

INCIDENTS OF THE BATTLE-FIELD.

BATTLE-FIELD, Monday, June 2, 1862.

The rebel army still occupied the camps of CASEY's and COUCH's Divisions on Sunday morning, with a strong picket force guarding the road facing SNEAD's house and the wheat field where our earthworks were thrown up, extending from our extreme left to the railroad, near Fair Oak Station. The distance from the point where our earthworks were located to the edge of the wood could not have been more than four hundred yards. This position the rebels held until day dawned on Sunday morning.

To our right, on the other side of the railroad, the divisions of Gens. RICHARDSON and SEDGWICK were found, in a semi-circle, with their left resting on Gen. HOOKER's right, at the railroad, and their left flanking the enemy. These divisions were composed of parts of the brigades of Gen. BURNS, Gen. FRENCH, Gen. T. F. MEAGHER, with four batteries of artillery.

Gen. HOOKER's Division were camped in the wood fronting SNEAD's house, on the Williamsburgh road, occupying the centre, and a little in advance of our right and left wings. On our left the remaining portions of COUCH's and CASEY's Divisions rested, with reserves of fresh troops extending to our extreme left, near the middle road, under Gen. KEYES.

Gen. HEINTZELMAN was on the ground at the front as soon as day dawned, accompanied by two Aids. Gen. HOOKER met him, and the two Generals sat down at the foot of a tree behind our breastworks, arranging a plan for the day's proceedings.

Gens. JAMESON, KEYES and SICKLES arrived at the front soon after, and the fight of Saturday was talked over as one of no particular advantage to the enemy, as they had concentrated their main force upon this portion of our front lines, and the effect was more

The Comte de Paris and the Duc de Chartres were two of the distinguished foreign guests that accompanied General McClellan on his campaign.

disastrous to them. *Their loss in killed in Saturday's fight exceeded ours two to one*, and of their number wounded it is impossible to form an estimate. Several of their men brought in as prisoners gave their loss in killed and wounded upward of three thousand. They made a desperate attack, it is true, and gained considerable ground, besides a large number of guns, camps, equipage, &c., as trophies, *which they immediately sent to Richmond* to dazzle the eyes of its pent-up inhabitants, who doubtless secretly wish to see the City fall into the hands of McCLELLAN.

PREPARATIONS FOR THE BATTLE ON SUNDAY.

Gen. HEINTZELMAN, at 6 A. M., ordered a reconnoissance to be made by a small force on the left of the wood and to the right, toward the railroad. A Lieutenant with two cavalrymen crossed over the wheatfield behind SNEAD's house, and was about to penetrate the wood near the Williamsburgh road, when the enemy's pickets appeared at his front. He immediately turned back and reported to Gen. HEINTZELMAN the close proximity of the enemy.

In the meantime, the other parties sent out came in, and reported the enemy in great force in front of our right and left flanks.

Gen. HEINTZELMAN then ordered out Gen. HOOKER's Division,—part of which had been left to guard the camp, and a certain position on our extreme left. The regiments Gen. HOOKER brought on the field were the five regiments comprising the Excelsior Brigade, under command of Gen. D. E. SICKLES, and the Fifth and Sixth New-Jersey regiments; Gen. HEINTZELMAN having resolved to attack the enemy, and drive them from the wood.

THE BATTLE.

It was about a quarter of seven when Gen. HEINTZELMAN ordered Gen. HOOKER to attack the rebels in his front, and drive them from the woods. The Excelsior Brigade marched out from their camp in the woods to the Williamsburgh road, the New-Jersey Fifth and Sixth following. The Excelsior Brigade filed in the wheat-field in front of our earthworks, to the right of the road, while the two regiments of New-Jersey troops took a position to the left. As the Second Regiment, Excelsior Brigade, was forming in position to the front of the wood, the rebels opened a rapid and heavy fire upon it,

killing two or three privates, and wounding about six. Among those wounded at the first fire of the rebels was Lieut. LAWRIA (formerly an aid to Gen. SICKLES) and Capt. NOLAN.

The fire of the enemy immediately became simultaneous along their entire line.

The New-Jersey troops fought splendidly, loading and firing without flinching from their position. Gen. SICKLES' regiments did great execution, advancing at every fire upon the rebels masked by the wood. However, it was plainly to be seen the enemy had every advantage, and *it was resolved to clear the woods at the point of the bayonet.*

Gen. SICKLES rode along the front of his men, in the midst of an iron hail which the rebels poured in, and gave orders for the Second Regiment, Col. G. B. HALL, to charge bayonets. No sooner was the order given than the men fixed bayonets. Col. HALL gallantly led the charge—*one of the most brilliant ever made in any battle. Not a man shirked or straggled from the ranks.*

The rebels presented a strong front to the gleaming bayonets of our men, not a hundred yards distant.

As the Second advanced on the double quick, cheering and shouting, the rebels held back their fire until our men were hardly one hundred feet from their line, when they fired a murderous volley into the ranks of the Second. It proved too low, and few were killed or wounded.

Immediately after the rebels fired this volley, they broke ranks and fled through the wood. A few of their bravest remained to resist our passage, but they were soon mowed down by the steel front of the gallant Second Excelsior.

Major HERBERT, of the Eighth Alabama Regiment, was taken prisoner at this time. His horse had been shot under him, and as he fell he received a shot in his side. He sprang to his feet, however, almost instantly, and seeing several of our men in front of him, mistook them for some of his own regiment. "Rally once more, boys!" he cried, but they corrected his mistake by presenting their bayonets and demanding him to surrender, which he did with all the grace and finish that an original Secessionist, as he afterwards informed me he was, could do under the circumstances. The rebels made two or three attempts to flank us on the left, after retreating from their centre, but they were beat back with great loss, our troops pursuing them for nearly two miles.

RICHARDSON's Brigade, before the enemy's centre gave way, had a hard fight ; the ground was hotly contested by the rebels. The Fourth and Fifth Excelsior Regiments were sent to support one of RICHARDSON's Batteries, but before the battery got in fair working order, the enemy began to show signs of a retreat. The rebel officers could be heard distinctly, urging the men to fight, but they would run away. The Irish Brigade fought splendidly, and routed the rebels at the point of the bayonet.

None of our forces on the left flank participated in the fight. The rebels were defeated and driven back by HOOKER's and RICHARDSON's Divisions.

Advance parties scoured the woods on both sides of the Richmond road, and succeeded in capturing nearly two hundred of the rebels, among them three Lieutenants.

At 11 o'clock the firing on both sides ceased. The rebels had fallen back to beyond our original lines, leaving guards stationed to watch our advance and also to bring their wounded off the field.

The enemy were driven from every position they occupied by our troops. The main column rested a mile in advance of their position, at the commencement of the fight.

At about 12 o'clock Gen. McCLELLAN rode up to the front, accompanied by his Staff and body guard, and met Gen. HEINTZELMAN seated at the foot of a tree. Little MAC democratically seated himself at side of HEINTZELMAN, on the ground, when his Staff grouped themselves, resting on stumps of trees and logs. There was the Prince de Joinville, Count de Paris, and the Duc de Chartres, forming a select group of three, conversing quite animatedly in French, and the other members of McCLELLAN's Staff joining in with a little English.

" They fight on Sunday always," said the Duc de Chartres, alluding to the rebels.

Gen. McCLELLAN had been seated probably a half an hour, conversing with Gen. HEINTZELMAN, when Gen. HOOKER rode up from the extreme advanced line gained that morning, and as he was dismounting from his horse Gen. McCLELLAN rose from his seat, and, advancing, shook him warmly by the hand, and congratulated him and his noble division in terms of the highest praise. A long conversation took place between them. It was plainly seen no further advance was to be made that day, as no troops were ordered up to the front.

At a little after one o'clock Gen. McCLELLAN mounted his horse and rode along the lines of his troops, back and forth, until all the soldiers had a good opportunity of seeing him. NAPOLEON never was received by his enthusiastic troops with greater manifestation of delight than was McCLELLAN by his army, showing that he possessed the confidence as well as the hearts of his men. They feel that they must ever be victorious under his guidance.

Prisoners continued to be brought in very fast; we had captured nearly five hundred. They were immediately handed over to Provost-Marshal YOUNG, of Gen. HOOKER's Division, who sent them properly guarded to HEINTZELMAN's headquarters, at Savage's Station. Many of them were dressed in new clothes, captured in CASEY's camp,—a large supply having been sent up to CASEY's Division a few days before the battle, but had not been distributed to the men. The result was that the enemy, who had been wearing faded, worn-out home-spun, doffed their forms in our genteel uniforms. This was the cause of many serious mistakes, our men unfortunately mistaking them for our own.

INCIDENTS OF THE FIELD.

Gen. SICKLES had several narrow escapes; he was always to be found in the thickest of the fight. Had those gifted Senators who refused to confirm his nomination, but witnessed the enthusiasm of his troops when serving under him, and his military qualification for the office, they would do penance until re-elected.

The rebels during the fight had their sharpshooters posted in trees to pick off our officers—a fact discovered in the early part of the action. One of these sharpshooters had been wounded, and lay down at the foot of a tree; as Gen. SICKLES was riding in the wood, he took deliberate aim and fired, but fortunately missed his mark. Some of our men rushed at the wounded rebel, and were about dispatching him with their bayonets, when Gen. SICKLES ordered them not to harm him, but take him prisoner.

As I stood watching the regiments of HOOKER's Division march in the battle-field, I recognized, marching at the head of his company, Capt. JOHNSON, belonging to the Third Regiment Excelsior. Capt. JOHNSON was in the battle of Williamsburgh, where he acted with the most heroic courage, and was wounded badly in the left arm by a minié ball; so dangerously was he wounded, that the surgeons at one time, thought an amputation of his arm would become necessary to save his life. The wound, however took a favorable turn, and he is now in a fair way of recovering. At the head of his company marched this gallant officer, his bandaged arm resting in a sling. As he passed by me smiling, an Aid from Gen. KEYES, who, with his Staff, was on the opposite side of the road, rode up to me and inquired the name of the wounded officer. I gave it to him; he exclaimed, " He is a brave man." If his country rewards her heroes, Capt. JOHNSON's name will stand among the foremost.

There were many incidents illustrating fully the mettle of our men engaged in this struggle. Many a private displayed deeds of bravery worthy of record. The officers bore themselves well, and shared the dangers in advance of their men.

THE REBEL COMMANDERS.

The rebel Generals, commanding in this engagement, were Gens. LONGSTREET, ROGER A. PRYOR, HILL, BRONK, HOWELL COBB, RAINS, HUGER and five others whose names I could not learn.

A STAGE AND FOUR HORSES CAPTURED.

A small party of our men reconnoitering, met an omnibus drawn by four fine bay horses, on the New Bridge road, going at a speedy gait toward Richmond, and containing two officers. Driving the horses were two contrabands. Lieut. LEE cried out for them to stop, but no attention was paid to the summons, and he ordered the men to fire. One of the officers jumped out and made good his escape in the woods. The other was shot as he had his head out of the window urging the contrabands

Professor T.S.C. Lowe was employed by the North as a balloonist.

to go faster. The driver now held up, and Lieut. LEE mounted the box, first placing the negroes inside, in charge of private BOYD, One Hundredth New-York. The Lieutenant brought the stage safely within our lines. As it made its appearance, emerging from the wood on the Williamsburgh road, where but a few hours ago the enemy were disputing our advance, it created the most intense excitement and curiosity among our men. Many supposed it was sent down by Gen. McCLELLAN, from Richmond, with the news of his occupation of the city. The stage is comparatively new. In size and shape it is about the same as our Broadway stages, perhaps a trifle lighter. From the fact of its being built by " JOHN STEPHENSON. New-York," (painted on a panel on the inside,) I seriously doubt if JOHN S. has received payment for it. Over the windows, on the outside, " Columbia Hotel" is painted.

THE BATTLE-FIELD.

In company with Gen. SICKLES, Col. GRAHAM, Col. HALL and Lieut. GRAHAM, I rode out upon the battle-field on Sunday afternoon at 4 o'clock. The scene witnessed here baffles all description. Caissons, with horses shot dead in their traces, ambulances, wagons, &c., &c., filled the road in front of CASEY's camp. There were about two hundred of our wounded still lying where they fell on Saturday. Some of them spoke kindly of the rebels, saying they treated them very well. Dead rebels, as well as our own men, were lying in every part of the field and wood. I counted fifty-seven dead rebels in front of a small piece of woods not forty feet square. One wounded rebel was lying on the ground, unable to move; he was shot in both legs. On each side of him lay some dead rebels. As we passed by, he begged us for God sake to take the dead men away from him. The stench was intolerable.

NUMBER OF GUNS LOST.

We lost 19 guns in the fight of Saturday. Not one of them has been recovered. The rebels ran a train down near Fair Oak Station, and carried away our commissary stores, guns, etc., etc., to Richmond.

The rebels destroyed what they could not conveniently carry away, including the new tents of CASEY and COUCH's Division.

The two contrabands captured with the stage had left Richmond on Sunday morning, with a party of gentlemen who had chartered the stage to take them out to see the fight. They have furnished the authorities with much information relative to the number and movements of the rebel force, which is highly important. It is not improbable that Gen. McCLELLAN, with his Generals, will dine at Richmond on Sunday next.

I inclose you a list of the casualties, but some days will elapse before a full and perfectly correct list can be obtained.

ACCOUNTS FROM THE PRESS REPORTER.

[The following is the conclusion of the dispatch from Gen. McCLELLAN's headquarters, part of which was published in our morning edition of yesterday. —ED.]

McCLELLAN'S HEADQUARTERS, Monday, June 2—P. M.

We have taken some 500 prisoners, among whom are several prominent officers.

On Sunday, as soon as it was light, the fight was renewed by Gen. SUMNER with marked success, the fight lasting nearly the whole day. The rebels were driven at every point with heavy loss. The ground gained by Gen. SUMNER was about two and a half miles ; Gen. HEINTZELMAN on Sunday morning retaking the ground lost the day before by Gen. CASEY, after a severe struggle.

Our loss in the two days' engagement, in killed and wounded, will amount to about three thousand. A great number are missing who will probably return, having strayed away.

All of the enemy's killed, and most of their wounded, fell into our hands.

The country in which the battle was fought is swampy, with thick underbrush, and most of the fighting was in the woods. Owing to the nature of the ground very little artillery was used.

Both balloons were up nearly all day yesterday.

All the troops left Richmond, and marched out in the direction of the battle-field.

The railroad has been of inestimable service, the cars running within a mile and a half of the battle-field, bringing forward ammunition and supplies. The wounded were immediately put aboard the cars and sent to the White House.

Gen. McCLELLAN arrived on the battle-field on Saturday evening, where he has remained ever since, directing all the movements in person. His presence among the troops had a most inspiriting effect.

Four separate charges with the bayonet were made yesterday. In one instance, *the enemy were driven a mile, during which one hundred and seventy-three rebels were killed by the bayonet alone !*

Lieut. WASHINGTON, Aid to Gen. JOE JOHNSTON, was taken prisoner.

The enemy's dead left on the field, amounted to over twelve hundred.

Gen. HOWARD was wounded twice in the arm.

Col. MILLER, of Eighty-first Pennsylvania, and Col. RIPLEY, of Pittsburgh, were killed.

Col. CAMPBELL, of Pennsylvania, was wounded in the thigh.

HEADQUARTERS, Monday, June 2.

The rebel officers were unable to rally their troops this morning, and have retreated back toward Richmond. Our men have moved forward to Fair Oak, five miles from the city.

JEFF. DAVIS and LETCHER were both at the fight yesterday.

The dead are now being gathered and buried.

HEADQUARTERS, Monday, June 2—9 P. M.

Gen. HOOKER made a reconnoissance to-day on the Williamsburgh Turnpike to within four miles of Richmond, without meeting the enemy in force. Their pickets kept in sight, but retreated on his approach.

Every one feels sanguine of the fall of the rebel capital when our troops advance for an engagement.

The fight of Saturday and Sunday seals the fate of that city. They threw the main body of the army, composed of the best troops, on our left wing, with a view of crushing it. They were defeated after two days hard fighting, and forced to retreat.

Among the wounded were Col. HUNT, Ninety-second New-York, in the leg ; Lieut.-Col. PERRY, of the Eighty-fifth Pennsylvania, in the leg, Lieut.-Col. MORRIS, of the One Hundred and First Pennsylvania, in the leg, and Col. VAN WYCK, Tenth Legion, slightly in the leg.

THE KILLED AND WOUNDED.

HEADQUARTERS, Tuesday, June 3.

As all the wounded and many of the dead have been sent to Whitehouse by railroad, it is impossible to obtain any correct list of the casualties of the past three days.

The New-York Times.

VOL. XI—NO. 3340. NEW-YORK, FRIDAY, JUNE 6, 1862. PRICE TWO CENTS.

FROM THE POTOMAC ARMY.

Stirring Address of Gen. McClellan to his Soldiers.

A Dispatch from Gen. McClellan to the War Department.

A Correction of his Dispatch Regarding the Battle of Fair Oaks.

The Services of Gen. Sumner Acknowledged.

Effects of the Severe Storm of Wednesday.

Great Rebel Losses in the Late Battle.

WASHINGTON, Thursday, June 5.

The following dispatch was received to-day at the War Department:

NEW-BRIDGE, June 5—10:30 A. M.

To Hon. E. M. Stanton, Secretary of War:

My telegraphic dispatch of June 1, in regard to the battle of Fair Oaks, was incorrectly published in the newspapers. I send with this a correct copy, which I request may be published at once. I am the more anxious about this, since my dispatch, as published, would seem to ignore the services of Gen. SUMNER, which were too valuable and brilliant to be over-looked, both in the difficult passage of the stream and the subsequent combat. The mistake seems to have occurred in the transmittal of the dispatch by the telegraph.

(Signed) G. B. McCLELLAN,
Major-General Commanding.

THE CORRECTED DISPATCH.

FIELD OF BATTLE, 12 o'clock, June 1.

Hon. E. M. Stanton, Secretary of War:

We have had a desperate battle, in which the Corps of SUMNER, HEINTZELMAN and KEYES have been engaged against greatly superior numbers. Yesterday, at 1 o'clock, the enemy taking advantage of a terrible storm, which had flooded the valley of the Chickahominy, attacked our troops on the right bank of the river. CASEY's Division, which was the first line, gave way unaccountably and discreditably. This caused a temporary confusion, during which some guns and baggage were lost, but HEINTZELMAN and KEARNEY most gallantly brought up their troops, which checked the enemy. At the same time, however, Gen. SUMNER succeeded, by great exertions, in bringing across SEDGWICK's and RICHARDSON's Divisions, who drove back the enemy at the point of the bayonet, covering the ground with his dead. This morning the enemy attempted to renew the conflict, but was everywhere repulsed.

We have taken many prisoners, among whom are Gen. PETTIGREW and Col. LORING. Our loss is heavy; but that of the enemy must be enormous. With the exception of CASEY's Division, our men behaved splendidly. Several fine bayonet charges have been made. The Second Excelsior made two to-day.

Headquarters of the Army of the Potomac, at Savage Station, June 1862.

(Signed) G. B. McCLELLAN,
General Commanding.

THE LATEST NEWS FROM HEADQUARTERS.

McCLELLAN'S HEADQUARTERS,
Thursday Evening, June 5.

The severe storm which set in Tuesday afternoon lasted during the whole of yesterday. The water in the Chickahominy rose to an unprecedented height. The railroad trains from White House to the late battle-field were detained several hours, and the telegraph line was down in many places.

A contraband, who left Richmond Monday night, states that all the carts, furniture cars, omnibuses and carriages to be found were impressed into the service for the carrying of the dead and wounded from the battle-field; and that the Spottswood and Exchange Hotels, together with a number of public and private buildings, were turned into hospitals. All the information shows that the enemy suffered terribly.

The rebels opened with artillery this morning from five different points opposite New-Bridge, with a view of preventing its reconstruction. Three of our batteries opened on them, causing them to retreat after a hot fire of two hours. Our loss was one killed and two wounded. No further interference took place during the day.

GEN. McCLELLAN TO HIS SOLDIERS.

McCLELLAN'S HEADQUARTERS,
Tuesday evening, June 3.

The following address was read to the army this evening at dress parade, and was received with an outburst of vociferous cheering from every regiment:

HEADQUARTERS ARMY OF THE POTOMAC,
CAMP NEAR NEW-BRIDGE, Va., June 2, 1862.

SOLDIERS OF THE ARMY OF THE POTOMAC: I have fulfilled at least a part of my promise to you. You are now face to face with the rebels, who are held at bay in front of the Capital. The final and decisive battle is at hand. Unless you belie your past history, the result cannot be for a moment doubtful. If the troops who labored so faithfully, and fought so gallantly, at Yorktown, and who so bravely won the hard fights at Williamsburgh, West Point, Hanover Court-house and Fair Oaks, now prove worthy of their antecedents, the victory is surely ours.

The events of every day prove your superiority. Wherever you have met the enemy you have beaten him. Wherever you have used the bayonet, he has given way in panic and disorder.

I ask of you now one last crowning effort. The enemy has staked his all on the issue of the coming battle. Let us meet him and crush him here, in the very centre of the rebellion.

Soldiers, I will be with you in this battle, and share its dangers with you. Our confidence in each other is now founded upon the past. Let us strike the blow which is to restore peace and union to this distracted land. Upon your valor, discipline and mutual confidence the result depends.

(Signed,) GEO. B. McCLELLAN,
Major-General Commanding.

A heavy shower that set in about dark had the effect of again raising the water in the Chickahominy.

Gen. BIRNEY, of Philadelphia, was relieved of his command on the battle-field by Gen. HEINTZELMAN, he having failed to bring his brigade into action when ordered on Saturday.

Reconnoissances made to-day show no material change in the enemy's position.

Further information shows that our troops on Saturday and Sunday engaged six divisions instead of four, making a force of 75,000 rebels.

FROM FORTRESS MONROE.

The Wounded in the Great Battle.

An Unsuccessful Attempt to Exchange the Rebel Privateers.

COL. CORCORAN NOT YET SURRENDERED.

BALTIMORE, Thursday, June 5.

The Old Point boat arrived here about 7 o'clock this morning. Passengers state that three steamers, full of wounded, had arrived at the fort.

FORTRESS MONROE, Wednesday, June 4.

The steamer *C. Vanderbilt* arrived this morning from White House, with 560 wounded soldiers in the recent engagements.

The steamer *Metamora*, which took to City Point Mrs. GREENHOW and party, returned last night. The steamer *Massachusetts*, with the privateers on board, was lying alongside the wharf at City Point. In answer to the notice given of her arrival, a train of three baggage-cars came to City Point from Petersburgh, yesterday forenoon, with two rebel officers on board. They came after the privateers, but not having brought down Col. CORCORAN's party, the privateers were not given up. Nothing later in relation to the subject had transpired up to yesterday afternoon, when the *Massachusetts* was still awaiting some further communications from Petersburgh.

The New-York Times.

VOL. XI.—NO. 3363. NEW-YORK, THURSDAY, JULY 3, 1862. PRICE TWO CENTS.

HIGHLY IMPORTANT.

A Reliable History of Events Before Richmond from Our Special Correspondents.

FULL DETAILS TO MONDAY NIGHT.

Five Days of Almost Continuous Fighting.

Repulse of the Enemy Near Mechanicsville on Thursday.

Desperate Battle at Gaines' Hill on Friday.

Retreat of Our Forces Across the Chickahominy.

Repulse of the Enemy in Front on Saturday.

Continuous Skirmishing Along the Rear on Sunday.

Another Desperate Battle in Our New Position on Monday.

OUR GUNBOATS ON JAMES RIVER IN ACTION

The Position of Affairs on Monday Night.

From the Special Correspondents of the New-York Times.

ARMY OF THE POTOMAC, ON THE JAMES RIVER, }
Monday Evening, June 30, 1862. }

Events of the gravest character have transpired within the last five days, touching the condition and prospects of the army on the Peninsula. Acting under the necessity which the Commanding General has long foreseen, the widely-extended lines of the army, with its miles of well-constructed defences, stretching almost from the James River on the left, to, and beyond the Chickahominy on the right, have been abandoned, and the army before Richmond has fallen back to a more practicable line of defence and attack, upon the James River. Hither the grand army, with its immense artillery and wagon train; its Commissary and Quartermaster's stores; its ammunition; its cattle-drove, of 2,540 head; in fact, its entire *materiel*, horse, foot and dragoons, bag and baggage, have been transferred. This manœuvre, however—one of the most difficult and dangerous for a commander to execute in the face of the enemy—has been accomplished safely, though under circumstances of difficulty and trial which would have taxed the genius of a Napoleon. *The army has been engaged in constant conflict with the enemy for six days*, during which their highest energies have been taxed to the uttermost. We have had no moment of repose—no opportunity scarcely to properly care for the wounded and to bury the dead. The enemy have closely watched every movement, and, with an army more than double that of our own, have had the ability to constantly launch fresh troops upon our rear, an advantage which they have been quick to discover, and remorseless in improving. Their perfect knowledge of the roads, paths and bridges, and the topography of the country, which has taken us *time* to learn, has placed an immense advantage in their hands. Heaven grant that here, under the shadow of these hills, and with the co-operation of the gunboats, our overtaxed soldiers and officers may have that brief repose which is so essential to them, and to the existence of the army itself.

The interruption of all communication with the Government has, no doubt, convulsed the country with anxiety and alarm. A knowledge of the facts, however, will relieve this feeling, while any effort to conceal the truth will not only be fruitless, but will leave the public to imagine a thousand evils which do not exist.

Beginning with the fight at Mechanicsville on Thursday, our advance forces, while steadily falling back, have had a continuous running fight.

On Friday one of the severest battles which was ever fought on this continent occurred on the right of the Chickahominy, near Gaines' Hill. On Saturday, after our forces had retired in good order across the creek and destroyed the bridges, we were attacked in front of our encampment, but Gen. SMITH repulsed the enemy, leaving the ground strewn with his dead.

On Saturday morning, the arrangements having been completed, the wagon train was started on its way to James River, and was followed on Sunday morning by the artillery and Commissarys train.

Meantime the enemy, getting scent of our movement, strongly reconnoitered our front, and finding that several of our positions had been abandoned, pushed in and attacked us vigorously. Gens. HOOKER and RICHARDSON drove them back, and Gen. MEAGHER's Brigade, always on hand at the right time, charged, and captured two of their guns. The rebels paid a dear price for the information which they obtained. The chief struggle was near Savage's Station.

Anticipating a movement on our right flank, the railroad bridge over the Chickahominy was destroyed on Saturday morning. The rebels, supposing we had fallen back on the White House, sent a large force of infantry, cavalry and artillery in that direction, but after a long, rapid and weary march, discovered they had gone on a wild goose chase in the wrong direction. They only found a small force of our infantry and cavalry scattered down to guard the rear, who fell back and escaped from White House Landing. The rest was one of those "howling wildernesses" which the rebels intend to leave for us. All the quartermaster and commissary stores had been removed two days before, and the rubbish burned.

Gen. McCLELLAN and Staff left the headquarters at Savage's Station at daylight on Sunday morning, with a body guard of the Fourth United States Cavalry, and halted some five miles out, after crossing the White Oak Creek.

There were, on Saturday, about one thousand of the wounded and sick, chiefly accumulated from the battle of Friday, many of whom it was found impossible to remove, owing to the nature and severity of their wounds, and as a matter of humanity, as well as of necessity, they were left behind. A great many, however, who could walk slowly followed the track of the army, and the ambulances brought away a great many others.

WITHDRAWING FROM THE FRONT.

Gen. HOOKER's Division broke camp in the intrenchments at 3 o'clock Sunday morning, and Gen. SICKLES' and GROVER's Brigades proceeded to the outposts to relieve Gen. PATTERSON's New-Jersey Brigade. At 5 o'clock A. M. the three brigades fell back to the second line of redouts, where they formed a line of battle with RICHARDSON's and KEARNEY'D Divisions, and remained until 8 o'clock P. M. On discovering that Gen. HOOKER had fallen back, the enemy advanced his scouts with two field-pieces, and opened a brisk fire upon his rear, along the line of the railroad. Gen. MEAGHER's Brigade made a movement on both the enemy's flanks, while the Eighty-eighth New-York charged in front, and captured two of their guns. The enemy then fell back under cover of the wood. None were killed in HOOKER's Division. In the Twenty-sixth Pennsylvania three were wounded; the First Massachusetts lost two prisoners. One man lost both legs by a shell. KEARNEY's and RICHARDSON's Divisions were the last off the field.

On the approach of the rebel force to the Savage's Station, where the hospital was established, a white flag was sent out, and it was met by a Lieutenant-Colonel of the Confederates, who gave assurance that the hospital should be respected. There was no firing, purposely, in that direction, and, if an occasional shell exploded near the house, it is believed to have been accidental.

About 120 rebel prisoners, who were captured on Friday, accompanied us under guard. On Sunday forenoon an advance body of our cavalry, who were reconnoitering in front, discovered a body of rebel cavalry near a small church, and, after a sharp engagement, put them to flight, killing a considerable number of horses, and capturing some twenty-five prisoners, who were added to the group already in hand.

SEDGWICK's Division left the front at daylight, and were engaged by the enemy half way to Savage's Station, which they reached at 5 P. M. Here the enemy's infantry, with a battery, came out of the woods on the right, and attacked them.

The First Maine were advanced on the left, with a line of skirmishers in front. They had twelve wounded, three mortally, viz: SMITH, WREN and TAYLOR. C. W. HASKELL, Company C, was slightly wounded in the hand by a shell.

SEDGWICK's Division crossed the creek at White Oak Swamp about 4 o'clock A. M., Monday. His rear was not annoyed during the night.

KEYES' and PORTER's Divisions had already preceeded us on the march, and had reached a position on the James River, near Turkey Island, which is about ten or twelve miles above City Point.

The Engineer Brigade of Gen. WOODBURY preceded the army, and constructed corduroy roads where they were necessary. At the Four-mile Creek, a bridge was built across the run. At the White Oak Swamp Creek two bridges were also constructed by the same valuable corps. One for the passage of the main army train, and the other to accommodate Gen. HEINTZELMAN's Division, who, with HOOKER and RICHARDSON, covered the retreat.

DESTRUCTION OF THE BRIDGES.

As the army resumed its march on Monday morning, information was received, through Gen. RICHARDSON, that the enemy were pursuing, and orders were given to destroy the bridges.

The Engineer Corps was detailed for this duty, and also to defend the approach to the place. A wide space of trees had been felled across the creek, and the brigade was deployed as skirmishers at the right and left of the passage. AYRES' battery of six guns was also left to hold the position, and was stationed on the hill overlooking the swamp.

HOW THE RETREAT WAS CONDUCTED.

The retreat was conducted in the most perfect order. There was no trepidation or haste; no smashing up of wagons by careless or fast driving, and not a single accident of any consequence is believed to have occurred. A drove of 2,500 fat cattle, under the charge of Col. CLARK, Chief Commissary, and Capt. E. M. BUCHANAN, Commissary of Subsistence on Gen. MCCLELLAN's Staff, were successfully driven along.

They had been brought up from the White House, and narrowly escaped stamping by the rebels.

The country through which we passed contained some of the finest farming lands I had seen in Virginia. Broad farms, with well-grown crops of oats and wheat, were passed along the roads, in which the horses and cattle found abundant forage. The forage of the army had all been consumed the day before, thus relieving the train of an immense burden. Instead of the expected swamps and impassable roads, we found well-traveled country roads in excellent condition, along which the immense artillery and wagon train passed with the greatest ease. After approaching within about five miles of the river, the train was divided, part being sent by each of three roads which converged near the landing. An occasional halt was ordered, to enable the advance to examine the roads and woods in front for a concealed force or masked batteries, but nothing of the kind interrupted our progress. A teamster or some mischievous person would occasionally report that we were attacked in front, which would produce a temporary scare, but beyond this, nothing delayed the movement. The soldiers regarded it as the carrying out of part of a necessary plan—the only dissatisfaction expressed being at the leaving behind of so many of the sick and wounded.

Plenty of provisions and medicines were left for them, however, and if they are permitted to use them, their situation for some time to come will be much better there than with the army in the midst of conflict and alarm.

At Savage's Station the Government had made arrangements for the sick and wounded as they were brought from the field. It was under the care of Dr. JOHN SWINBURNE. Dr. BAUNOT, of Pittsburgh, Penn., arrived on Monday with a corps of surgeons and nurses. How many of these remained with the patients I am not able to state. There is a report that a large part of them ran away when the army left. It was certainly a severe test of their philanthropy to be left in rebel hands. The demand for nursing and surgical attendance was so great that large numbers were obliged to wait for long hours before their cases could be reached. The worst cases were attended to first, but there was and have been a great many who never received attentions at all. The entire area in the back and on both sides of the house was covered with the wounded, and there were also some twenty large tents pitched in the garden at the east of the house, filled with sick and wounded. The stores for Mrs. HARRIS, the benevolent lady, who, assisted by Mrs. SAMPSON, are devoting themselves to the sick, were delayed at White House, and if they reached Savage's at all, it is doubtful whether the good things

This Union field hospital at Savage Station was abandoned to the Confederates.

99

were not appropriated by the rebels as soon as they got possession of the place.

Many poor fellows who were scarcely able to drag themselves along, clung to the skirts of their comrades, or hobbled on crutches, apparently dreading more than death itself, falling into the hands of the rebels. Many became so exhausted that they fell by the wayside, and could only be roused and helped forward by the greatest exertion.

THE APPROACH TO JAMES RIVER.

When an aid of Gen. McCLELLAN rode back and reported that *the way was all open to James River*, a thrill of relief ran through the whole line, and the sight of the green fields skirting its banks was indeed an oasis in the terrible desert of suspense and apprehension through which they had passed. The teams were now put upon a lively trot in order to relieve the pressure upon that portion still in the rear.

Gen. McCLELLAN and Staff rode ahead and took possession of the old estate known as Malvern Hills, owned by B. F. DEW, one mile back from "Turkey Island Bend." It is a large, old-fashioned estate, originally built by the French, and has near it, in front, an old earthwork constructed by Gen. WASHINGTON during the Revolutionary war. It has a spacious yard shaded by venerable elms and other trees. A fine view of the river can be had from this elevated position. Gen. McCLELLAN expressed the opinion that *with a brief time to prepare, the position could be held against any force the enemy can bring against us.*

Exhausted by long watching and fatigue, and covered thickly with the dust of the road over which we had passed, many of the officers threw themselves upon the shady and grassy lawn to rest. The soldiers also attracted by the shady trees, surrounded the house, or bivouacked in the fields near by.

Gen. McCLELLAN immediately addressed himself to the task of preparing dispatches for the Government.

THE FIRE IN OUR REAR.

At 2 o'clock P. M. firing was heard in the direction of White Oak Swamp, where it was supposed AYRES was holding in check the rebel force who were attempting to cross. This continued for nearly two hours, when sudden and heavy firing began further to the left, in the direction of Charles City Cross Roads. At this point an immense body of fresh troops, with artillery and cavalry, had made their appearance direct from Richmond, and were engaging our batteries still left to guard the road.

Orders were sent immediately to put the troops in line of battle ; and Gens. PORTER's and KEYES' commands were soon on the way up the hill, returning from their comfortable encampment beyond Malvern Hills. By 4½ o'clock P. M. the road was thronged with these troops, with artillery and cavalry, hastening to resist the advance of the enemy.

The firing now became more and more rapid, and was evidently approaching our line. The roar of cannon was incessant, and the dust of the contest swept upward and whirled in eddying clouds above the forest trees, which concealed friend and foe from view.

Members of the Staff and messengers hurriedly mounted and rode to and fro with important orders to the commanding officers. The wagons were drawn up on the right of the field as a kind of temporary breastwork, and the troops were disposed in line of battle at the westward, from which direction the enemy were advancing.

THE GUNBOATS BROUGHT INTO ACTION.

The firing now became incessant, the explosion of shells constant and most terrific from both lines, and the roar of musketry, mingled with the shouts and cheers of the contending forces. If we could have seen them, and estimated their strength or number, it would have been some relief, but they were advancing, apparently, to within less than a mile of our

Robert E. Lee assumed command of the Army of Northern Virginia, replacing the wounded Joseph E. Johnston. Lee's decisive victories over McClellan proved that Jefferson Davis' choice for a replacement was a timely one.

The Grapevine Bridge, destroyed by retreating Federal forces, was restored by pursuing Confederates.

position, under cover of woods. It was very evident that *our men were being driven in, and that, too, by an overwhelming force.* At this juncture two of our gunboats, the *Galena* and *Aroostook* moved forward some half a mile and opened fire upon the left with their 54-pounders, the shells exploding in the edge of the woods along the line of hills where it was supposed the enemy would attempt to turn our left. No doubt these terrific missiles had an excellent effect in deterring them from this enterprise, and in retarding their advance. In so long a range there was danger that some of our own men might be hit, and a signal station was established on the top of an old house overlooking the field, and also commanding a view of the river. The firing from the *Galena* was directed in front by these signals. The *Jacob Bell* and also the *Aroostook* fired several shells during the last part of the battle.

During the evening, and while the fight was going on, crowds of dusty men rushed down to the river, and plunged in to bathe. Considering the circumstances of the army, this was hardly the time to adjust one's toilet.

Meantime the contest raged with terrible fury along our whole front and right. Exploding shells filled the air, and rifled shot screamed overhead. So thick was the cloud of dust enveloping the field, it was impossible, except from the sound, to determine which way the tide of battle ebbed or flowed. The gunboats kept up a discharge of their heavy shells upon the enemy's position. Provost-Marshal PORTER meantime took charge of the disabled and sick soldiers, and conducted them to the rear. A large number of stragglers filled the road, who seemed to have

business in an opposite direction from that in which the enemy was coming.

The *Prince DE JOINVILLE*, with the Duke DE CHARTRES and the Count DE PARIS, took charge of dispatches for the Government, and Gen. McCLELLAN accompanied them as far as the gunboat *Jacob Bell*, on board of which he bade them a final adieu toward evening. The crew manned the rigging, and cheered as the General returned to headquarters.

The day's contest wound up by a diminuendo of musketry, and by dark all firing, except an occasional shot, had ceased. It was too late to obtain any list of killed and wounded, or in fact to learn definitely the result of the fight. The *Jacob Bell* went down to City Point ordering up the *Southfield*, and all the other vessels lying below.

It should be borne in mind that the wide bottoms along the river separate the gunboats in many places, some two miles from the forces operating on the hills. The gunboats *Galena, Maratanza, Aroostook, Maraska* and *Port Royal*, are near by, and ought to be able to render valuable assistance to the army until it can be placed in position to operate. The indications are that the *enemy will continue to harass our position* *and give the troops no rest, day or night, until they have* *been dislodged or compelled to embark.* Should affairs reach the latter crisis, where are the transports to receive such an army on board, with its immense *materiel* of war? There are scarcely vessels enough now in the James River to take on board the wounded and sick, to say nothing of the army.

The *Jacob Bell* having returned from City Point, was dispatched, about 10 o'clock P. M., to Fortress Monroe, with the Prince DE JOINVILLE and companions

who, it was understood, carried dispatches to the War Department.

When the steamer left, all was quiet along the river, and was supposed that our forces were holding their position at Malvern Hills.

The results of this contest are not known. The fight was a most determined one on both sides.

Transports and steamers were proceeding up the river; among them the *Wilson Small*, of the Sanitary Commission. All their vessels will be needed to remove the sick and wounded. Early arrangements will no doubt be made by the Government for the recovery of the wounded from Savage's Station and from the battle-field of Gaines' Hill.

THE BATTLE OF GAINES' HILL.

Full Details of the Desperate Battle of Friday

Had the enemy possessed full information of the purposes of our Commanding General they could not have taken better advantage of our position than they did. The fact that our front gave way at Mechanicsville on Thursday, after making a successful stand, and fell back toward Gaines' Hill, seems to have suggested to them that a general retrograde movement was contemplated; and it became their policy to follow and fight us on the retreat. With the Chickahominy in our rear, it was, of course, impossible for our army to cross, successfully, under the enemy's fire; and there is no doubt but that they expected to overtake and compel us to fight or be cut to pieces at the bridges.

On Thursday nearly all the wagons were sent across, to have them out of the way. This movement was going on all day and night, and, if known to the enemy, must have revealed the fact that our army was either about to retreat or to change its position. This was too valuable an opportunity to be lost, and was improved to the best advantage. Our troops had been engaged in an exhausting contest at Mechanicsville the day before. They had plenty of fresh soldiers, and were near their base of operations, from which whole masses could be drawn at an hour's notice. We were separated from our centre by the bridges of the Chickahominy, from which we could obtain reinforcements only by a comparatively tardy and uncertain process. That they brought nearly their whole force against us on that side of the river shows that a determined effort was to be made to compel us to cross the river, and then to pass to the rear and turn our right.

Foreseeing this plan, and without the necessary force to guard against the movement, *the only expedient left was adopted by the Commander of the Union forces. The enemy were to be held in check as long as possible, to enable him to safely withdraw his whole force to the James River, and take up a new position.* Another day and night would, no doubt, have found our entire right abandoned, and the commands of PORTER, McCALL and STONEMAN withdrawn safely to the left of the Chickahominy, and the bridges destroyed, without a battle. That this was not permitted was owing to the watchfulness of the enemy, or to the treason of some one within our lines who possessed a knowledge of our plans.

A precipitate retreat was out of the question. It would have resulted in the sacrifice of the entire right wing. With our retreating forces massed in front of the Woodbury and Grapevine Bridges, along the river bottoms, a pursuing force commanding the eminence at Dr. WILLIAMS' house, would be able to cut them to pieces, or compel a surrender. From the attacking party we here, for the first time, took a position of defence, and accepted the battle which was offered.

THE ATTACK IN THE MORNING.

The enemy's skirmishers made their appearance beyond Gen. MORELL's encampment at an early hour in the morning, and were met by the advance pickets of the Ninth Massachusetts, who engaged them sharply, steadily retiring toward Gaines' Hill. During this hour's contest, the Ninth Massachusetts lost a considerable number of their men. They fell back slowly and in good order on the road toward Coal Harbor.

Meantime, McCALL's Brigade of Pennsylvania reserves, and SYKES' Brigade of regulars took up a position upon the high land overlooking the valley of the Chickahominy, eastward of and near the roads leading from Gaines' Hill to Coal Harbor. Your correspondent arriving at this place just as the troops were coming up, watched with much care the forming of the line of battle, and the disposition of the troops. SYKES' Brigade, consisting of the Third, Fourth, Twelfth and Thirteenth United States Infantry, DURYEA's Zouaves and WEED's Battery, commanded by Lieut.-Col. R. C. BUCHANAN, were disposed on both sides of the road leading north from Gaines' Hill, and parallel to the road to Coal Harbor. The Zouaves were drawn up in the open field, facing the line of the enemy's approach, while the regulars were placed to the right, left and rear, in the same field and along the road. Capt. WEED, in anticipation of the attempt of the enemy to push their lines up the Coal Harbor road to our right, found an admirable position for his battery of 3-inch Parrots, in a wheat-field about forty rods to the right of his original position, on a slight eminence which commanded a cross-road intersecting that to Coal Harbor. Here he could sweep a mile of the cross-road, and effectually prevent the passage of any considerable body

of the rebels to the right. Experience soon showed that this position was well chosen, for it proved, during the day, one of the hottest in the fight. Capt. DE HART's Battery was posted further to the left, and directly confronted the rebel line, whose position, though not as yet precisely known, was partially revealed by the sound of his artillery and musketry beyond a belt of woods toward Gaines' Hill Capt. DE HART's Battery consisted of six 12-pounder Napoleon guns, besides which there was a battery of 3-inch rifled guns, of wrought iron, belonging to the reserves. Capt. EATON's Battery was on his left, and Capt. KERN's further to his left.

This Capt. EATON, of Drainsville memory, was killed ; Capt. KERNS was wounded ; Capts. WHITING' CHAMBLISS, Lieut. SWEET killed, and Lieuts. ARNOLD, WATKINS and one other officer were all wounded during the day. Lieut. HAYDEN, of EDWARDS' Battery, and Lieut. PIPER were also wounded.

McCALL's troops came rather wearily into line They had been fighting nearly all the previous day and night, and did not relish being called so soon to a repetition of the entertainment.

MORELL's Division were disposed in the centre and to the left of the hospital, nearly abreast of Gen. PORTER's headquarters.

There was now an intermission of the fire beyond the woods lasting for half an hour—an ominous silence,—and all eyes were directed toward the enemy's position to detect, if possible, any movement right or left. The field of conflict about to take place was bounded by the road leading to Coal Harbor, on the west ; the meadow or bottom of the Chickahominy on the south and east, and a belt of woods stretching northward nearly parallel with the river. The land is elevated, somewhat undulating, and near the centre contains a thinned growth of pine. Near the north line of this space, and along the road leading to the military bridges are three houses, the first SALLY McGEE's ; the second, JOSEPH McGEE's, at first taken for a hospital, and the third, Dr. WILLIAMS' house on the hill, to which all the wounded who were brought off the field were conveyed. Gen. PORTER's headquarters was at ADAMS' house, about a third of a mile distant.

About 10 o'clock the pickets at our right were driven back from the woods skirting the field, and shortly afterward those stationed on the Cross Roads toward the Coal Harbor road, were also driven in The enemy were silently creeping up to the right. Simultaneously he made his appearance in a green field, directly in front, drawn up in line of battle, and in five minutes their batteries opened on our lines with shell. Following this the enemy had also placed a battery in position, fronting that of Capt. WEED's, and commenced fire—the fire of the two rebel batteries being at an angle of 45 degrees to our position, enfilading the troops. There was a temporary panic among horses, men and servants, who plunged, dodged, scampered and skedaddled to get out of range. Your reporter, perfectly cool himself—of course—was twice tossed nearly out of his saddle or thrown over the horse's head, as he raced uncontrolled about the field. A small party of cavalry disgracefully started down the road to get under cover of the woods, but your reporter hailed and brought them to by a word of gentle admonition. They turned and took a short path out to McGEE's. Here we found the rifled shot of the rebels flying overhead, and going nearly a mile beyond, close up to WILLIAMS' house. Capt. WEED opened his battery, as did those of TIDBALL's, which was stationed near the same position. The battery of Capt. DE HART also replied vigorously. The Zouaves, who were drawn up in line nearest to the enemy, stood motionless and stern awaiting the onset, while the regulars occupied the field and road, ready to receive and return the rebel fire as soon as they should get within range. The whiz-z-z of Minié bullets, and scream

of shell and shot from a dozen different directions now showed that the work had begun in earnest. The people, old, young, white and black, male and female, occupying the houses near the field, now ran across the field to get under cover of the woods.

The force of the enemy could not be ascertained, as they kept concealed to a great extent, and fired across a small ravine at our line. As they advanced, the Zouaves and regulars also met them, and sturdily maintained their ground.

The position of these batteries and of SYKES' command was not essentially changed during the day. They held their own under a most terrific fire, and to WEED's and TIDBALL's Batteries is unquestionably due the credit of preventing the flanking of our right.

As the contest thickened, the enemy showed themselves in constantly augmenting numbers. The tide of battle swayed to the left, and finally covered the entire rolling land overlooking the river valley. Details from the Zouaves and other ambulance corps began to bring in the wounded from the field, and soon the hospital was full of the badly wounded. One man whose arm had been torn from his shoulder by a shell, cried with vexation because he could not have time to discharge his musket.

By 2 o'clock, the woods covering the hill were thronged by the two contending armies. The enemy generally advanced in three lines, the first firing and falling down while that behind repeated the same movement. By the time the third line had discharged their pieces, the first had loaded and were ready to rise and fire again.

Thus the battle raged, the enemy at times giving way before the impetuous charges of our men, and again recovering and advancing. The fiercest portion of the fight was near the brow of the hill. Batteries thundered, musketry roared, and the din and noise of the contending forces were terrific.

It was apparent that the rebels were constantly bringing fresh troops upon the field, and there was literally no end to their number.

As soon as it could be done, orders were sent back for reinforcements, and SLOCUM's Division came over the bridge and marched to the support of our hard-pressed forces. About 5 o'clock the Irish Brigade of Gen. MEAGHER came upon the field, and with a shout of defiance went in and for a few moments staggered the rebel lines by their persistent and courageous conduct. A few thousand more of such desperate heroes would have turned the tide of battle. The rebels who fell into our hands were furiously drunk, having got a supply of whisky from one of our encampments, where it had been carelessly left by a Commissary.

At this point I find myself obliged to stop writing in order to send forward my copy by my brother reporter I will finish the account by the next conveyance.   E. S.

ADDITIONAL DETAILS.

Graphic Particulars of the Events of Thursday, Friday, Saturday, Sunday and Monday.

ON BOARD THE GUNBOAT STEPPING STONES, JAMES RIVER, Monday, June 30, 1862.

The right wing of our army has at length been attacked by the enemy—an event which was not wholly unanticipated by us. For several days previous to the attack, preparations were being made by the right wing to resist, if possible, to some extent, any advance movement of the rebels from the direction of Hanover or Mechanicsville, but the extent of the preparations were not sufficient to justify the belief that a vigorous stand was to be made on the west side of the Chickahominy.

At the time the enemy first made their appearance to our pickets on the right, which was on the 26th, our force at Mechanicsville consisted of the Eighth

Lieutenants Jones, Bowen and Custer.

Illinois Cavalry, Col. FARNSWORTH; six companies of the Bucktail regiment, under command of Maj. STONE, and five companies of Pennsylvania Reserves. This force was distributed about the town, also on the road leading to Richmond, the road leading to Ashland, and the road leading to Hanover. The videttes were keeping special watch on the Hanover road.

The Pennsylvania Reserves were guarding the Richmond road, and having received timely information of the near approach of the enemy, returned to camp before the rebels could get between them and it. It was fortunate for Gen. McCALL that he had the assistance of the five companies later in the day. They performed their part gallantly, and defended the rifle-pits to the last moment.

At 10 A. M. on Thursday, the 26th, videttes on the Hanover road came into Mechanicsville with the intelligence that the enemy was approaching the town from the direction of Hanover. Three companies of the Bucktail Regiment immediately moved out to a distance of 1½ miles on the road indicated, in order to support the pickets already there. The strength of the enemy was not then known, neither could it be

ascertained that he intended anything beyond a reconnoissance.

THE ENEMY'S ADVANCE.

No sooner had the reinforcements reached their destination than it was discovered that the rebels were advancing in considerable force from the direction of Hanover, they evidently having crossed the railroad at Meadow Bridge. The design of the rebels to turn our right could not now be doubted, and as it was clear that our small force would be insufficient to meet the attack, Gen. REYNOLDS sent back to Gen. McCALL for reinforcements.

Meantime, and before the reinforcements could arrive, the enemy had pushed steadily onward and was fast closing in upon Maj. STONE's force. The small command, however, was drawn up in line, ready to receive the rebels, and was determined to do its utmost, even if it lost the life of every man. The cavalry took their position in the rear of the infantry, and remained at their posts until it was evident that the superior number of the rebels would ultimately drive us, when they retired further to the rear, but still within supporting distance of the infantry. On-

ward came the rebel columns, and firmly stood our small force to combat them. When the rebels had approached within rifle distance, Maj. STONE gave the command to fire, and a volley was poured into the enemy's ranks which told with terrible effect. At this fire a rebel Major was seen to fall.

The enemy returned the fire, and pushed his cavalry to our right, in order to surround our men. They at last succeeded in getting round to the rear, which circumstance placed our men in an exceedingly critical position. Major STONE, observing the importance of immediate action, rode up to his men, and shouted, "Shall we fight or surrender?" "*Fight!*" was the hearty response of the Bucktails; and, after giving one more volley to the rebels in front, wheeled, charged through the cavalry in the rear, and gained a piece of woods, where they took temporary refuge. Here they were again surrounded, and again they cut their way through the rebel cavalry, and proceeded in a direction toward Gen. McCALL's camp.

Company K, and a portion of Company B, who were on picket duty on the Ashland road, were too far distant too join their comrades in season to make a retreat with them. It is feared that this portion of the Bucktails were captured by the rebels, as nothing has been heard from them since the commencement of the fight.

THE WESTERLY APPROACHES TO MECHANICSVILLE.

There are two roads leading into Mechanicsville from the west side. The one nearest Hanover we will designate as the upper road, and the other as the lower road. The object of our men was to fall back on the upper road, but the rebels having got possession of the road on the right, our men were compelled to take to the fields and woods.

Gen. McCALL's Division was upon the ground, and drew up in line of battle on the west side of a small stream, over which the lower road crosses. A part of the force was placed on the right and a part on the left of the road. The stream referred to is about one mile from Mechanicsville. The First and Second Brigades of Gen. MORELL's Division, the former under command of Gen. MARTINDALE, and the latter under command of Gen. GRIFFIN, also arrived upon the ground and took positions at the right and left of the main road leading to the White House, near the junction of the upper Mechanicsville road. Gen. MARTINDALE advanced to the right of the main road, in a direction toward a place called Old Church. Gen. GRIFFIN occupied the woods at the left, and supported the right of McCALL's Division.

THE LINE OF DEFENCE.

The space between the Chickahominy and the lower road, the small stream and the upper road, and open field for some distance on the right of the upper road, formed our line of defence. The left was held by McCALL's Division, including the Bucktails that fell back from Mechanicsville; the centre by Gen. GRIFFIN's Brigade, and the right by Gen. MARTINDALE's Brigade. We had a rifle-pit on each side of the lines, and a short distance from the stream.

THE POSITION OF THE BATTERIES.

EASTON's Pennsylvania Battery occupied positions at the rear of the rifle-pits, so as to command the lower road. The other batteries of McCALL's Division were placed at different points along the left of the line. We also had two batteries, of six pieces each, to protect the right and centre.

THE REBEL POSITION.

We did not have the advantage of the rebels in position. Their right rested in a piece of woods, and upon an eminence which was admirably adapted for artillery practice, knowing which they brought to bear a large number of guns from that point. The remainder of the line extended for the most part along the edge of the woods. The enemy had batteries stationed at different points of the line, the number of their guns equaling if not exceeding that of our own.

ADVANCE OF THE FIRST BRIGADE.

The First Brigade (Gen. MARTINDALE) proceeded through a field at the extreme right of the line, in order to repel any demonstration of the rebels that might be made in that quarter. They had not advanced far before the rebel skirmishers were discovered prowling in the woods directly in front, and soon after the enemy began to appear in considerable force all along the right of the line. Gen. MARTINDALE quickly disposed his force, and prepared to give the rebels a most severe drubbing should they attempt to turn the right. The artillery was then brought into action, and did good service in shelling the woods. No attempt was made by the enemy at the time to push forward, and Gen. MARTINDALE having become convinced of the much superior force of the enemy, did not consider it prudent to do anything more than hold his position.

It was nearly dark before our line was formed and the battle had commenced in earnest. The battle was principally between the artillerists, although late in the evening the rebels attempted to turn our right, and were repulsed with a severe loss. The pieces used on both sides were of 10 and 12-pound caliber, the range being too short for guns carrying heavier metal. When the engagement had really commenced, and all the guns were in practice, it seemed as though both armies were destined to immediate annihilation, so terrific and deafening was the sound. The very earth seemed to quiver, and at times the whole heavens would be lighted up with a red glare.

This was the first night engagement of any consequence that had taken place since the army arrived on the Peninsula. The firing continued rapidly and earnestly until about 8 o'clock, without any apparent advantage being gained by either side. The rebels, for the most part, fired over, consequently our men suffered but little from their shells. The shells fired from our guns appeared to explode directly over the heads of the rebels, and we have reason to believe that they did not escape without a heavy loss from that cause alone.

At about 7 o'clock the enemy attempted to break our centre. To accomplish this he made most vigorous efforts, but was boldly and successfully met by Gen. GRIFFIN, who arranged his men in excellent order and encouraged them by his presence and daring. The Fourth Michigan, Col. WOODBURY, and the Fourteenth New-York, Col. McQUADE, especially distinguished themselves for the many brilliant and prompt movements they made. The Ninth Massachusetts and Sixty-second Pennsylvania are also deserving of much credit for the successful manner in which they repelled the enemy's charge.

While the rebels were endeavoring to force back our centre, the left of the column was also busily engaged in keeping the enemy from crossing the bridge over the stream on the lower road. The Pennsylvania Reserves fought bravely, and their unflinching perseverance was the only thing that prevented the rebels from gaining ground in that quarter. The enemy seemed to concentrate his whole strength first at the centre, and then at the left of our line, but in each attempt he failed to cross the stream. Our batteries did not spare the canister and grape, and whenever an opportunity offered a most terrible fire was poured into the rebel ranks. The Pennsylvania Reserves, who were in the rifle-pits, kept up an unceasing fire upon the rebels on the other side of the stream and finally compelled them to abandon their original front position at that end of the line.

At 9:30 P. M. the firing had entirely ceased, the rebels had been repulsed, and we held our ground Our loss was comparatively small, not exceeding 250 killed and wounded.

AFTER THE BATTLE.

The shrieks and groans of the rebels when the battle was ended indicated that their loss was heavy. The air was filled with the wails of the wounded and dying, and all night long the rumbling of ambulance trains and the suppressed voices of those engaged in burying the dead and caring for the wounded could be distinctly heard.

By order of Gen. PORTER a strong picket force was stationed along the lines, and every precaution taken to resist any renewed attack that the rebels might make.

Gen. McCALL and Staff bivouacked in the open air upon a field situated near the battle-field, and necessarily passed a sleepless night.

The silence of the night was frequently broken by the discharge of a picket-gun, and every one was on the alert for the enemy save the wearied soldier, who had become exhausted from the night's effort, and was indulging in a short but sweet repose.

THE MORNING.

At 3 o'clock the next day the sleepers were aroused, and a whisper passed from ear to ear that the enemy were on the move. The picket firing became more frequent, and it was evident that the rebels were preparing to renew the attack. Our men were again formed in battle array upon nearly the same ground occupied by them the preceding night, and everything was ready on our part to again flay the rebels.

That the rebels received strong reinforcements during the night was a fact not to be disputed, and the event was certainly not unexpected by us. Intimations that the rebels intended to attack our right had been in circulation for a week, at least, and we had no reason to suppose that so important a movement would be attempted by a light force. The enemy came prepared not only to force us from the stream and the Mechanicsville road, but also to *drive us across the Chickahominy.* Later in the day the rebel force was estimated *to be not less than seventy-five thousand men.* The force we brought to bear numbered about 20,000. Of course, to hold our position against such fearful odds was an impossibility, and the next best thing had to be done.

At daybreak, finding the enemy was rapidly closing on our right flank, Gen. PORTER *issued orders for the whole force to slowly fall back toward Gaines' Hill.*

This movement was conducted in the most orderly and satisfactory manner, and had I not known the nature of the movement, it would have been impossible for me to decide whether the army was advancing toward or retiring from the enemy. No hasty demonstrations were made, and every gun-carriage and every wagon held its place in the column. One accident only came under my notice, which was the breaking of the trail of one of the ammunition-wagons. Extra horses were subsequently sent back, and the disabled wagon taken to the rear.

The rear of our column, as it marched toward GAINES' Hill, was admirably protected by ROBERTSON's United States Battery, EASTON's Pennsylvania Battery and the Ninth Pennsylvania Reserve Regiment. The enemy followed slowly and cautiously, as if he feared being decoyed into some trap. The firing was not rapid, and we lost but few men. Good order prevailed.

As the column moved forward toward the Chickahominy, the regiments in the advance wheeled into position, forming the left of the line, and the regiments following took positions at the centre and right. The ground selected was well adapted to the purpose, it being a range of hills extending from a point near the Chickahominy to Coal Harbor. On the extreme left was the Chickahominy, then came a meadow, adjoining which was a succession of hills reaching to Coal Harbor. The front was lined most of the distance by woods. A ditch, in some places difficult to cross, extended through the woods and formed the infantry line of defence.

THE ENEMY'S POSITION.

On the enemy's right was the Chickahominy and a meadow, the same as on our left. Then came Gaines' Hill, which had been our camping ground, at the left of which was another hill, the road to Coal Harbor separating the two. An elevated plain formed the extreme left.

If the rebels were in hopes of securing a vast amount of plunder, they were sadly disappointed. On the night of the 26th, orders were given to remove all the Commissary stores, forage, tents, camp equipage, and everything that transportation could be provided for, to the east side of the Chickahominy. That which could not be removed was to be burnt and destroyed. All the wagons were brought into requisition, and the larger portion of the supplies were safely removed. A considerable amount of Commissary stores belonging to MARTINDALE's Brigade was destroyed, also the tents and camp equipage belonging to GRIFFIN's Brigade. The property destroyed belonging to McCALL's Division was valued at several thousand dollars.

OUR FORCE.

As has been previously stated the rebel force was estimated to be 75,000 men.

Our force consisted of MORELL's, McCALL's and SYKES' Divisions, and COOK's Cavalry Brigade, numbering altogether about 20,000 men.

Our force was distributed as follows :

Gen. MEAD's Brigade of the Pennsylvania Reserve troops on the extreme left, and near the Chickahominy.

Gen. BUTTERFIELD's Brigade, the left at the right of Gen. MEAD's Brigade.

Gen. MARTINDALE's Brigade, the left, joining Gen. BUTTERFIELD's right.

Gen. GRIFFIN's Brigade on the right of Gen. MARTINDALE's.

The Division under command of Gen. SYKES at the right of Gen. GRIFFIN's Brigade.

Gen. REYNOLDS' Brigade of Pennsylvania Reserve troops at the extreme right of the line, reaching to Coal Harbor.

Gen. SEYMOUR's Brigade of Pennsylvania Reserve troops held a position in about the centre of the column, within supporting distance of the force in front.

Gen. COOK's Cavalry Brigade took a position in the rear of the extreme right.

ROBERTSON's United States Battery, of six pieces. HART's United States Battery, of six pieces, EASTON's Pennsylvania Battery, of four pieces, and KERN's Pennsylvania Battery, of six pieces, took positions on eminences at the left ; ALLEN's Massachusetts Battery, of six pieces, MARTIN's Massachusetts Battery, of six pieces, WEEDEN's Rhode Island Battery, of six pieces, and GRIFFIN's United States Battery, of six pieces, held positions in about the centre. At the right were TIDBALL's, WEED's and CARLISLE's United States Batteries, a German battery of four 20-pounders, and a battery attached to the Pennsylvania Reserve Corps.

At 12 o'clock M., the rebels fired the first shot, from a battery stationed on the hill in front of GAINES' house. It was a solid shot, and struck in the woods at the rear of Gen. MARTINDALE's Brigade, and between his advance and reserve columns. This shot was followed by several others before any of our batteries responded.

At 1 o'clock, sharp skirmishing was heard in front of the centre. By this we knew the rebels to be steadily advancing, and expected every moment to see them make their appearance on the brow of the hill before our line of defence. The firing became more rapid, but up to this time we had not heard any volleys.

The Fifth New-York were in advance of the column acting as skirmishers, consequently they were the first to receive the enemy's fire.

MOVEMENTS OF TROOPS.

Before the battle actually commenced, Gen. NEWTON's Brigade crossed the bridge from the other side of the Chickahominy and drew up in battle line on the left, and in advance of McCALL's troops. After remaining here for about one hour they recrossed the bridge. I did not understand the object of the last movement, unless it was to assist the other brigades in case the rebels attacked them on that side of the river. In fact, the rebels had already commenced shelling SMITH's force from their pieces on Gaines, Hill, and we thought that within an hour's time a general battle would be raging.

COMMENCEMENT OF THE BATTLE.

At about 1 o'clock our guns began to respond to those of the enemy. The skirmishers were already engaged in front of the centre, and soon after they got to work along the whole extent of the lines. The firing became more frequent as the enemy's pickets advanced. The skirmishers were at length called in and took their position in the line.

By far the heaviest battle in which the army of the Potomac had yet been engaged was now progressing. Little did we think as we stood two days previous in the midst of the army that it was so soon to meet with a reverse. The rebels came down from Richmond in tremendous force, and they fought with the desperation of madmen.

We had taken the precaution the preceding night to remove all the siege guns on the right to the other side of the river, and then destroyed all the bridges above the one which crossed just at the rear of SMITH's Division.

I have no idea that it was originally designed by Gen. McCLELLAN to make a stand on the right side of the Chickahominy, but to quietly withdraw the force on that to the other side. We had thrown up but few earthworks, only two of which were mounted. Five 30-pound Parrots were mounted on an earthwork near GAINES' house, and five more 32-pound Rhodmans were placed in position behind an earthwork near HOGAN's house.

On Wednesday he opened these guns on the enemy, keeping up the fire from 10 A. M. till late in the afternoon. The fire was directed to the rebel batteries on the bluff across the river opposite GAINES' house. This bluff was lined with open and masked batteries, and I believe that to have taken possession of the bluffs would have required the united force of the whole army. This was the strong point of the enemy, and he could have held it against terrible odds. During the fire of Wednesday we succeeded in dismounting one of the enemy's guns.

At 2 o'clock P. M., on Thursday, the artillery on both sides were hotly engaged. The infantry in force had not yet got into the fight, but not many minutes elapsed before they were also engaged.

At one time we could not have had less than sixty guns in practice, and the enemy had as many, if not more. The roar of cannon was truly awful. Shells were bursting in every direction, and a dense cloud of smoke covered the entire field.

The enemy now advanced in columns toward our centre. MARTINDALE's Brigade stood firmly to receive the charge, as also did the Fifth New-York Zouaves, who were on the right of MARTINDALE. The rebels were repulsed, but at the loss of numbers of our brave men. Hundreds of the rebels were seen to fall, but their places were quickly filled by others.

Failing to break our line at the first attempt, the rebels sent over a large force to the right, for the purpose of turning our flank. We immediately strengthened that end of the column by a change of position.

When the enemy had advanced to within about three hundred yards of our batteries, our guns opened with canister and grape. The slaughter was terrible, and the rebels were compelled to withdraw. Not only did the artillery do good execution on this occasion, but also the infantry, who kept up a constant fire.

It was near three o'clock, and during the hour following there seemed to be a lull in the terrible conflict. The enemy was apparently bringing down reinforcements from Richmond, notwithstanding their force already exceeded ours by over 50,000.

We also found it indispensable to have a larger force. Accordingly, Gen. SLOCUM's Division crossed the river at Grapevine Bridge, and proceeded to the right of the line. FRENCH's and MEAGHER's Brigades subsequently crossed over the same bridge and took positions further to the left.

The enemy had made two charges and been repulsed in both.

It was now approaching 5 o'clock, and the enemy was preparing to make a charge on the left wing of this portion of our force. With this view he seemed to have concentrated the larger portion of his force on the hill directly opposite GAINES' house. He had been largely reinforced by fresh troops, and seemed determined to make one more vigorous effort to break our line. The rebels descended Gaines' Hill six columns deep, and in compact order. This mass of men gave our artillerists on the left a splendid opportunity for practice, and when the proper time arrived, a deadly fire was opened upon the advancing columns. An immense weight of canister and grape was thrown among them, and hundreds of their number were seen to bite the dust. The rebels, however, were not checked by our artillery, and onward they come toward our left. Gen. BUTTERFIELD, with up lifted hat, passed from one to the other end of his Brigade, cheering and encouraging his men, calling upon them to fight like soldiers, and, if need be, die like soldiers. The conduct of Gen. BUTTERFIELD during the whole engagement elicited the admiration of every one who saw him. The presence of Gen. MARTINDALE among his men seemed to inspire them with double zeal, and they fought like men who were fighting for the noble cause of country.

Every man stood at his post resolved to do his utmost to repel the enemy. Volley after volley was exchanged, but neither side wavered. At last the rebels poured a tremendous volley into our ranks, which thinned them out to an alarming extent. After a while, the superior numbers of the rebels also began to tell, and it became evident that our troops would soon be obliged to give way. The troops under command of Gen. McCALL were nearly exhausted, having been in the battle of the preceding day, and having passed the night without sleep. Our men fought well, but they could not do impossibilities. One man could not contend against three, and come out the winner. The left wing began to fall back. The centre and right of the column were necessarily forced to do the same, and *our entire line commenced retreating toward the river.* The enemy seized upon the auspicious moment, and, with furious yells, rushed forward upon our broken ranks. The horses attached to the batteries on the left were nearly all shot, consequently many of the pieces had to be abandoned. Teamsters and ambulance drivers began to whip up their horses, and try to get up another Bull Run. Some portions of cavalry were galloping helter-skelter, and confusion among the infantry would have taken place, had not the officers leveled their pistols, and threatened to shoot the first man that ran.

But to contend longer was useless. We had lost our position, and all attempts to rally the men for the time were vain. *The command for the troops to retire in order across the Chickahominy was given, and the regiments commenced moving in that direction.* It was nearly dark. The fight had been desperate, and the enemy did not seem inclined to press hard.

With the assistance of the reinforcements previously mentioned, another line of battle was formed, about half a mile in the rear of the first position. The object, however, was more for the purpose of covering the retreat than for renewing the contest. The battle was ended.

Throughout the day Gen. PORTER was upon the field, and gave his commands in a manner as cool and definite as if the spectacle before him was nothing but a game at football. The disaster cannot be attributed to inefficient officers or cowardly men, but simply to the fact of our being overpowered in numbers.

THE HOSPITALS.

Three buildings, the only ones on the field, were used as hospitals. Late in the afternoon the wounded commenced to be brought in by the dozens. All the skill that surgeons possessed was employed in treating their wounds. The accommodations were not ample, and, in fact, they scarcely ever are on the field of battle. All that could be done was done.

OUR LOSSES.

No tidings had been heard from Gen. REYNOLDS up to Saturday night. It was supposed he had been captured by the enemy.

Lieut. WELD, Aid to Gen. PORTER, went out with a detachment of cavalry early in the morning, for the purpose of reconnoitering the position of the enemy. When near Gaines' Hill he left the cavalry and went to water his horse at a stream running through a piece of woods. In about twenty minutes the Lieutenant having failed to return, the cavalry followed the road in the direction taken by him, and when within a few yards of the stream were fired upon from an ambuscade. It is inferred from this that the Lieutenant was captured by the parties concealed by the brush.

Lieut. EDWARD M. FISHER, Aid to Gen. BUTTERFIELD, was killed while conveying an order to some portion of the command. His loss is greatly lamented, not only for his military merits, but also for his social qualities.

Col. BLACK, of the Sixty-second Pennsylvania; Col. GORE, of the Twenty-second Massachusetts, and Col. MCLANE, of the Eighty-third Pennsylvania, were killed while leading their men forward in the battle.

Capt. KINSTRY, Assistant Adjutant-General to Gen. REYNOLDS; Lieut.-Col. SKILLON, Fourteenth New-York; Capt. EASTON, of EASTON'S Pennsylvania Battery, and Lieut. MORTIMER, of MARTIN'S Massachusetts Battery, are also among the killed.

Maj. S. TILTON, Twenty-second Massachusetts, was wounded and taken prisoner.

Col. MCQUADE, of the Fourteenth New York, is wounded, but not seriously.

Col. STOCKTON, of the Sixteenth Michigan is missing. When last seen he was walking up the hill in front of his men, for the purpose of getting a view of the enemy. He was probably surrounded and taken prisoner.

The Fifth New-York Zouaves went into the battle with over 700 men. They returned with less than 300.

The Forty-fourth New-York went in with about 400, and returned with 250.

The Sixteenth Michigan lost about 300 men.

The Pennsylvania Reserves suffered terribly, as did nearly all the regiments stationed on the left of the line.

Gen. BUTTERFIELD'S Brigade was cut up fearfully.

EASTON'S Pennsylvania battery of four pieces, was lost; ALLEN'S Massachusetts battery lost four; WEEDEN'S Rhode Island battery, three; EDWARDS' Pennsylvania battery, two; WEED'S United States battery, two, and KERN'S Pennsylvania battery, three pieces of artillery.

Several other pieces were lost, but I am not yet informed to what batteries they were attached.

A SEPARATE MOVEMENT.

The Seventeenth New-York and Eighteenth Massachusetts Regiments, under command of Col. LANSING, were ordered Thursday morning to proceed to Old Church and intercept the movements of Stonewall JACKSON, who, it was reported, was on his way to cut off our communication in the rear. Arriving upon the ground, pickets were posted and scouts sent out to ascertain the location of JACKSON, should he be in the vicinity. Scouts soon fell in with the rebel pickets and discovered that the enemy was coming down on the Hanover road with a large force of infantry, cavalry and artillery. This is the same force that engaged Gen. MARTINDALE on the main road leading to the White House.

Col. LANSING immediately withdrew his force, keeping a good guard on the rear, and proceeded to Tunstall' Station, on the railroad.

The next day, (Friday,) learning that the rebels were still pursuing, he destroyed everything of value at the station, and then went to the White House, where he remained until Sunday morning. The rebels were close on his heels, and it was only by masterly manœuvring that he managed to keep them at bay.

Before leaving the White House, Col. LANSING ordered his men to burn a large quantity of sutler's stores, some Commissary stores, and a large lot of damaged forage. This the men did under the protection of the gunboats which lay opposite the White House. Most of the Government supplies that were of any value, had been placed on board transports and were on their way to Fortress Monroe.

The next thing in order was to burn the White House and all the out-buildings. This having been accomplished, Col. LANSING placed his command on four different gunboats, and protected the rear of the retiring vessels. Arrived at Cumberland the force landing and destroyed a small amount of property, and then proceeded to West Point, where another lot of property of little value was also destroyed. The whole force then moved down to Fort Monroe, where they arrived Tuesday morning.

MOVEMENTS OF OUR LEFT WING.

THE RETREAT TO JAMES RIVER—EVENTS OF SATURDAY—CHANGE OF POSITION BY OUR ENTIRE FORCE.

Early in the morning of Saturday our entire force which had been engaged the day before, left the east side of the Chickahominy and crossed over to the opposite side. The bridges, four in number, were then blown up, and batteries were planted on Trent Hill, to command the river below.

At 10 o'clock A. M., it was discovered that the rebels were crossing the river at New Bridge, from the west side, and were ascending Gaine's Hill in large numbers. From this it was inferred that they intended to move round towards Bottom,s Bridge and cut off our railroad and telegraphic communication. That they had not done this before was surprising, for they certainly had free access to that portion of the Peninsuta.

Confederate General Huger

No attack was made during the day. The enemy was probably busily engaged in burying the dead and attending to the wounded. They had not only their own but ours to attend to. We were obliged to leave our killed on the field of battle, also those of our wounded who were not able to walk away.

Gen. MCCLELLAN had removed his headquarters from Trent Hill on Friday morning, and has located in a field near Savage Station.

On Friday afternoon at 5 o'clock a train of cars left Savage Station for the White House. The cars, nine or ten in number, were filled with wounded soldiers, and got safely through, although much apprehension was felt for them. The train returned during the night and early in the morning proceeded again to the White House with another lot of wounded. It then came back to Savage's, and was preparing to make one more trip down when the telegraph wire was found to be cut and Dispatch Station to be in possession of the rebels.

We immediately sent down a force *to destroy the railroad bridge* which was done by pouring turpentine on the timbers and then igniting it.

In the afternoon MORELL'S Division left Trent Hill, where they had been since Friday night, and marched to Savage Station, around the railroad and the Williamsburgh road, and proceeded over a road running between White Oak Swamp and Bottom's Bridge. They halted at a point near Charles City until the next day, when they were joined by other portions of the army.

On Saturday night orders were given Gens. FRANKLIN, SUMMER and KEYES, whose forces held the centre and right of our line on the west side of the Chickahominy, to destroy everything in the way of camps, commissary stores, ammunition and hospital supplies that transportation could not be furnished for, and to *gradually withdraw their forces toward Savages.* Word was also sent to the wounded at Savages, for those who were able to walk, *to move immediately toward Carter's Station on James River.* All the ambulances belonging to the army were brought down to the station and filled with the severely wounded. But transportation could not be provided for all, and about three hundred were left to fall into the hands of the enemy.

Four carloads of ammunition sent up from the White House on Thursday, for the use of the siege train, was replaced in the cars, and *the entire train, including the locomotive, was let loose, to run down the railroad, and so off the burnt railroad bridge into the Chickahominy.* The whole train moved down the track, increasing in speed at every yard, and when it reached the bridge went tumbling into the river with a terrible crash.

A small amount of Commissary stores and camp equipage was destroyed at Savage's. The larger portion of the army supplies were at Fair Oaks. Here we were obliged to burn vast quantities, for the lack of transportation.

At 12 o'clock, midnight, the transportation train—the head of which was across the railroad, on the road crossing the railroad at Savage's Station—began to move toward Charles City, following the direction taken by MORELL'S Division in the afternoon. The transportation train was preceded by a long line of artillery.

At 3 o'clock Sunday morning Gen. McClellan ordered his tents to be struck, which, having been done he, with his staff and body-guard, proceeded to Charles City.

The train was several hours in passing, and did not reach Charles City till late the next morning.

Gen. SMITH was ordered to hold his position on the Chickahominy till the train was at a safe distance, and then to follow, acting as a guard to the rear.

At about daylight on Sunday morning, Gen. SMITH began to retire over the same road that the transportation train had taken. Gens. SUMMER, KEYS and HEINTZLEMEN, also began to bring their forces round so as to make their front extend at right angles with the rear of the wagon train.

As soon as the enemy diszerned the movement, he began to close in but did not press hart until later in the day.

By noon, all our artillery, except that which was required to protect the rear of the retiring column, also all our wagons, had arrived at Charles City. Gen. MCCALL'S Division came next. Then followed other divisions in regular order, Gens. HOOKER and KEARNEY bringing up the rear and covering the retreat.

On two or three occasions the rebels made attempts to flank HOOKER and KEARNEY, but they were unsuccessful each time. The retreat was conducted in perfect order.

The main body of the army was now at Charles City, distant from James River, by one road six miles, and by another fifteen miles.

McClellan's object was to reach James River at a point opposite Turkey Bend.

During the day the Eighth Illinois Cavalry had been sent over the road, fifteen miles in length and which ran through dense woods in a circuitous manner, to ascertain if it was clear.

They reported favorably, and at about dark a train of transportation wagons, preceded by the Eighth Illinois cavalry, commenced moving toward James River. KEYES' corps brought up the rear of this column. The column reached a point two miles west of Carter's Landing at an early hour Monday morning, without accident and without meeting the enemy.

The other road, which was nearer Richmond, was not so free from the rebels. In the morning a squad of cavalry was sent out to reconnoitre, and found the enemy in possession of the road at a point five miles from James River. He did not know their strength, but concluded it was not great.

At 7 o'clock in the morning, the pickets brought word that a squadron of rebel cavalry was coming down this road toward the Charles City Road. We sent up two pieces of artillery and planted them in a concealed position, so as to command the range of the road upon which the cavalry was approaching. When they had come sufficiently near a volley of canister was poured into their column, which caused them to retreat in a most precipitate manner. A number were killed and several wounded.

Gen. MARTINDALE'S Brigade then marched up and occupied the ground at the point where the two roads meet.

At about the time the column moved on the fifteen mile road toward James River, MORELL'S Division, MCCALL'S Division and a large amount of artillery were sent forward to open the way on the upper road. This they succeeded in doing after having several slight skirmishes with the rebels. They were obliged to move cautiously, however, and did not reach Turkey Bend till after the column that took the long route had reached the point near Carter's Landing.

A train of wagons was then sent forward on the six-mile route, and was followed by infantry.

Gen. MCCLELLAN arrived at Turkey Bend on Monday morning.

When I left the ground the new position to be occupied by our forces was not made known, but I presume the right of the line will rest on the Charles City road.

Several gunboats, including the *Monitor* and *Galena*, were lying in James River, off Turkey Bend, prepared to shell the rebels should they attack MCCLELLAN'S force.

At Carter's Landing the gunboat *Stepping Stones* was lying at the wharf, receiving on board the wounded who had walked from Savage's Station. The ground in the vicinity of the landing was covered with sick and wounded soldiers.

Carter's Landing is three miles above City Point and about twenty-two miles from Richmond. Turkey Bend is eight miles above Carter's Landing.

The gunboat *Stepping Stones* was the first vessel to leave the landing after the army had arrived at James River. Your correspondent secured a passage, and on the way to Fortress Monroe collected a list of wounded and sick soldiers on board.

On the way down we met the gunboat *Southfield*, protected on each side by a barge loaded with hay.

I understand that Carter's Landing is to be the main dépôt for supplies and storage.

On Tuesday several transparts left Fort Monroe with provisions and forage, which they probably landed at Carter's.

WHIT.

The New-York Times.

VOL. XI–NO. 3364. NEW-YORK, FRIDAY, JULY 4, 1862. PRICE TWO CENTS.

FROM GEN. MCLELLAN.

The Great Battle Continued Through Seven Days.

IMMENSE LOSSES ON BOTH SIDES.

Terrific Onslaught of the Rebels on Our New Position.

Final and Overwhelming Defeat of the Enemy.

Death of Stonewall Jackson and Gen. Barnwell Rhett.

Gen. Magruder Reported to be a Prisoner.

Gen. McClellan Safe and Confident in His New Position.

Arrival of Considerable Reinforcements.

OFFICIAL ADVICES FROM GEN. McCLELLAN.
WASHINGTON, Thursday, July 3—3:12 P. M.

A dispatch from Gen. McCLELLAN, just received at the War Department, dated "From Berkley, Harrison's Bar, July 2, 5:30 P. M," states that he has succeeded in getting his army to that place, on the banks of the James River, and *had lost but one gun*, which had to be abandoned last night, (Tuesday,) because it broke down ; that an hour and half ago *the rear of the wagon train was within a mile of the camp, and only one wagon abandoned* ; that we had a severe battle yesterday (Tuesday ;) *that we beat the enemy to-day*, the men fighting even better than before ; that all the men are in good spirits, and that the *reinforcements from Washington have arrived.*

ADVICES FROM FORTRESS MONROE.
FORTRESS MONROE, Tuesday, July 1.

A gunboat has just arrived here from the scene of action yesterday, ten miles above City Point.

That division of our army has been fighting four days, and has retreated about 17 miles.

The fight of yesterday was most terrific, the enemy having three to our one.

The battle commenced with our land forces, and after about four hours' fighting, our gunboats got in range, and poured into the rebels a heavy and incessant fire.

This fire the rebels stood about two hours and then retreated.

Our troops have captured, notwithstanding their disadvantages, a large number of artillery pieces and 2,000 prisoners.

Among the prisoners captured is the Rebel General MAGRUDER.

The place where this last action took place is near Turkey Creek.

The retreat of the rebels last evening was with great disorder, and their loss has been very heavy, much greater it is thought than ours.

There is nothing definite, however, in regard to losses.

In the retreat forced upon Gen. McCLELLAN by the superior numbers of the enemy, I learn that he had to spike his siege guns and leave them on the field, after burning the carriages. The nature of the ground rendered it impossible to move them.

[This, it will be seen, is denied by Gen. McCLELLAN himself.]

In the retreat many of our sick and wounded were necessarily left behind. There are, of course, innumerable reports and rumors here, but I send only what appears to be authentic.

FORTRESS MONROE, Tuesday, July 1.

The loss of the enemy in killed and wounded alone yesterday (Monday) is said not to have been less than four thousand, but we hear nothing definite of the loss on either side.

Gen. Shields' army arrived here this morning, and have proceeded up the James River. They came in vessels viâ Annapolis.

FORTRESS MONROE, Wednesday, July 2,—9 P. M.

The steamer *Daniel Webster* has just arrived here from City Point with upwards of 300 wounded on board.

A gentleman who came down in charge of them informs me that *yesterday was the sixth day that the battle has been going on, with the most terrific fighting the sun ever shone upon.* It has extended the whole length of our line.

After deceiving McClellan and skillfully defending Richmond, Confederate General J.B. Magruder harassed retreating Federal troops in constant rearguard clashes.

Brigadier-General James Shields commanded relief forces that aided McClellan's withdrawal.

We have lost a great many men in killed, wounded and missing, *probably fifteen to twenty thousand.*

He informs me that Gen. McCLELLAN's headquarters are at Hardy's Landing to-day, and his lines extend five miles above toward Richmond. This move of the right wing of the army was predetermined upon and planned ten days ago, and would have been carried out sooner, but for certain reasons well known in the army, but which it would not be proper to state. The enemy's forces have greatly outnumbered ours in almost every action, *but notwithstanding this they have been repulsed oftener than we have and their loss far exceeds ours.*

Yesterday Gen. McCLELLAN is said to have *captured a whole rebel brigade, and took from them several rifle cannon, and other pieces.*

It is now said that we have lost very few of our siege guns, most of them having been recovered in safety.

There have been a great many wounded prisoners taken on both sides.

Our informant says that Gen. McCLELLAN and his Staff all agree that the present position of our army is *far more advantageous as a base of operations against Richmond than that hitherto occupied.*

The gunboats can now be brought to bear, and materially aid in carrying on the work.

Some of our regiments have suffered terribly, while others have but little. The New-York Fifth suffered terribly. They made a most heroic struggle, and made great havoc among the enemy. About one-half their number are killed, wounded, and taken prisoners. They were in the fight at Cold Harbor, and fought against desperate odds.

Our left wing was engaged yesterday, July 1, up to 2 o'clock, with the enemy, mostly with artillery.

The enemy's force, gathered from prisoners, who were members of Beauregard's Western

The legendary Confederate cavalry commander, General James E.B. ("Jeb") Stuart.

army, was 185,000 men, whilst our effective force did not exceed 95,000.

The Richmond *Dispatch*, of Monday, announced the death of Gen. "Stonewall" JACKSON, and of Gen. BARNWELL RHETT, of South Carolina.

ADVICES RECEIVED IN THIS CITY.

A person arrived in this City last evening from the field of battle before Richmond, having left there on Tuesday evening, July 1, at 9 P. M.

At that time Gen. McCLELLAN'S advance was three miles northwest of Hardin's Landing, and within fifteen miles of Richmond.

The enemy was terribly repulsed in the battle of Monday, which was sanguinary in the extreme. We were attacked at four different points, and summarily repulsed the enemy three, when they pressed HEINTZEMAN'S left very hard, but SUMNER went to his relief, and they were finally repulsed with great slaughter. HEINTZLEMAN captured eight guns and a whole brigade of rebels, 1,600, including their Colonels—PENDLETON, of Louisirna, ex-Congressman LAMAR, of Georgia, and McGOWAN, of South Carolina.

Our transportation was all safely removed but seventy-five wagons, which were burned in camp.

The enemy's attack, on Monday, was fierce in the extreme. Kearney, Hooker, Richardson, Sedgwick, Smith and McCall participated.

The reserve under McCall suffered severely, and Gens. McCall and REYNOLDS were probably taken prisoners, as they were missing Tuesday night. Gen MEADE is severely wounded, and Gens. BURNS and BROOKS slightly.

Stonewall JACKSON is undoubtedly killed. Gen Mc-CLELLAN, after the fullest investigation, credits the report; all the prisoners corroborating it.

The rebel General J. R. ANDERSON was mortally wounded in the action at Savage's Station on Sunday.

On Monday night intrenchments were begun and prosecuted as rapidly as possible. The first boat of reinforcements arrived just as our correspondent left. Supplies were also coming in in abundance.

Our total loss in the whole six days' terrific fighting, from Wednesday up to Monday night, is about twelve thousand, seven thousand five hundred of which were lost in the battle of Friday on the right.

Col. McQUADE of New-York; Col. CASS, of Massachusetts; Maj. PATTERSON, of Pennsylvania, and all the field officers of the Duryea Zouaves heretofore reported killed or wounded, and many others, are alive and well.

OUR FORTRESS MONROE CORRESPONDENCE.

OLD POINT, Wednesday, July 2, 1862.

I did not write you yesterday, because the reports were coming in so thick and contradictory, that, without having time to thoroughly sift, them, you would be just as likely to receive wrong as right information. What little I am now permitted to tell you is, therefore, reliable; for I have taken pains to obtain it from trustworthy eye-witnesses, or from parties who ought to be thoroughly well posted.

Whatever may be the impression in New-York, there is but one conclusion arrived at here by all intelligent people, in spite of all that the army pedlers and other skedaddling croakers have to say, and that is that the terrific battle which has been raging for the last four or five days has exhibited the most masterly strategy on the part of McCLELLAN, and bravery in himself, his officers and his men. So far from there being anything like defeat in his position, it is eminent success, and the enemy, without intending it, could not have better contrived to play into his hands.

I have just been on board the *George Washington*, which arrived this morning with 821 sick and wounded; among others, Gen. MEADE, and Brig.-Gen. W.

A. GORMAN, of SEDGWICK'S Division—the former wounded very severely by the fragment of a shell passing through his body, and the latter prostrate by sickness. I have had a long and interesting conversation with one of the patients—a Captain of the Twenty-third Pennsylvania, and a man of great intelligence—and I was glad to find, not only in the facts he advanced, but in the cheerful and confident view he took of the dreadful struggle now going on, a full corroboration of the opinion so earnestly sustained by the TIMES and its correspondents.

The whole affair is simply this: As soon as Mc-CLELLAN discovered—by the bold raid of STUART near the White House, and other indications—that the enemy had an intent upon that point, he at once came to the conclusion to turn that to account; and, by luring them on to a spot that could be of no ultimate use to them, and too far removed from his own base of operations, concentrated his forces on the James River, where he could have the aid of our gunboats—the terror of the rebels. For this reason —and long before any descent was made upon POR-TER'S right wing—Gen. McCLELLAN had caused to be removed to his centre all the army stores, provisions, &c., from the White House, and all the rest by transports down the York River, leaving but a small portion there (variously estimated at from $5,000 to $50,000, though probably nearer the first sum) to be destroyed, in the event of the enemy approaching sooner than they could remove it.

So certain is this, that many days elapsed before there was any demonstration at the White House, loaded vessels were seen coming down the York River and up the James, with what intent people did not *then* know, though they do *now*. All this being arranged, orders were given for PORTER'S wing to fall back, add *he was doing so when attacked by the rebels*. The result was that, after great slaughter on both sides, McCLELLAN has reached the very spot he intended on the James River, with all his equipments, and allowed the rebels to go into the very trap he had prepared for them. Does this look like defeat?

Much excitement prevailed here yesterday (Monday) when news came of the bloody work of the last two days, and the information that our army was on rations which must soon be exhausted. This fear is now, however, entirely removed. Boats, loaded with provisions, are rapidly going up the James River in abundance, and twelve vessels had already unloaded when my informant left, which was at 6 o'clock last evening. I was also informed that Gen. McCLELLAN is in a strong position, under cover from gunboats, and able to hold his own until reinforcements come. The latter we know are rapidly on the way to him— though whence and in what number I am not at liberty to say. Well sustained in the position he now holds, there can be no doubting his success.

Some people here are contemplating not only the possibility but the probability of the rebels venturing down the peninsula as far as Yorktown, and even further. It is almost to be hoped they will have the foolhardiness to do so. They might thereby gain the glory of shedding more human blood, but they will only be rushing on their own destruction. Shut up between the York and James rivers, without a plank afloat to confront our gunboats on them, it is difficult to see how they could either hold anything or sustain themselves there, while every man taken from their forces to go there is only increasing McCLELLAN'S chances of entering Richmond.

It is the province of those of your correspondents who were on the battle-field to give the details of what passed under their own eyes. I am merely giving you impressions derived from those who actually took a part in the fights, and who betray not the remotest symptoms of despondence. They all assured me that never did a General live who commanded more thoroughly the love of his men, and one of them said, with deep emotion, that there was not a man in his army who would not die for him. Should calamity befall our noble young chieftain before Richmond, through lack of strength before overwhelming numbers—and under no other circum-

Major-General J.F. Reynolds was captured by Rebel troops during a Confederate breakthrough at Frayser's Farm.

stances could he fail—God help the trucking politicians, who will have brought him and his country to such extremity! He has done all that man can do. He has the indorsement of men, both at home and from abroad, who stand high in the ranks of war; and if disaster attends him, the responsibility not only should, but *will* be placed upon other shoulders than his. To know how deeply the army feel upon this subject, one should mix with them, as we correspondents are compelled to do; and you may depend upon it, a long account is being scored up against some political marplots of the Press and Congress.

Among the reports here which I have heard, but know not whether to credit or not, is that Gen. Mc-CALL was wounded in the neck on Sunday, and is now a prisoner in Richmond; also that "Stonewall JACKSON" is killed. Dr. STRONG, Chaplain of the Fourth Michigan, who is unceasing in his attentions to his men, begged me to correct the following mistakes in one of your contemporaries:

Col. McQUADE, of the Fourteenth New-York, reported as killed on Friday last, was seen yesterday at the head of his regiment in good health.

Col. ROBERTS, First Michigan, also reported killed, is not dead, but only slightly wounded.

Capt. SPALDING, Fourth Michigan, also reported killed, was seen in perfect health yesterday.

Capt. R. G. DEPUY, Company K, Fourth Michigan, was instantly killed on Friday last; also Lieut. T. B. JONES, Company B, Fourth Michigan, in the same engagement.

We are awaiting, with intense excitement, the result of the next two or three days; but unless something worse arrives than we have yet heard, Richmond must and will be ours in a few days.

NEMO.

NATIONAL LOSSES BEFORE RICHMOND.

BOSTON, Thursday, July 3.

A special dispatch to the *Journal*, states that Col. POWELL T. WYMAN, of the Massachusetts Sixteenth, was killed in the Richmond battle. Col. EDWARD W. HINKS, of the Nineteenth Massachusetts, was wounded. The reported loss of the Twenty-second Massachusetts is 350 in killed, wounded and missing; that of the Massachusetts Ninth, 311. The Eleventh also suffered severely, having only four line officers left.

The National loss is stated at 15,000. The loss of officers in the Massachusetts regiments engaged is very great.

WOUNDED SOLDIERS AT BALTIMORE.

BALTIMORE, Thursday, July 3.

The steamer *Daniel Webster* has arrived here, with a large number of soldiers wounded in the recent great battle before Richmond.

REBEL ACCOUNTS OF THE PRELIMINARY FIGHTING.

From the Richmond *Whig*, of Friday last, (27th inst.,) we obtain the following interesting items:

THE BATTLE OF THURSDAY.

"Yesterday afternoon an engagement opened a few miles northeast of the city, which we have no reason to doubt is the beginning of the great conflict that is to decide the fate of this capital, and, perhaps, of the Confederacy itself. The cannonading, till an hour or more after dark, was quick and heavy, exceeding in rapidity and volume that at Seven Pines. Not a word from the field has reached the city. The reason probably is, that the attack was made and the fight waged on the enemy's rear. The city is confident and calm.

LATER.

Information came to hand last night that the attack was made by Gen. A. P. HILL'S Division on the enemy's position near the Meadow Bridge, about 3 o'clock. The enemy recoiled, leaving a battery, as is reported, in the hands of our troops.

Retreating about two miles, the enemy made a stand in their intrenchments at Mechanicsville, and offered vigorous resistance for two or three hours. But they could not stand the impetuous onset of our victorious troops, and again broke and made for the main body of McCLELLAN'S army, leaving three batteries to their pursuers. Darkness put an end to the chase. We have no reports of casualties. The battle opens gloriously. May this morning's sun be our sun of Austerlitz.

THE FIGHT ON WEDNESDAY.

We are permitted to take the following extract from a letter from a member of a company of the Forty-eighth North Carolina Regiment, dated yesterday:

"We have had nothing to eat since yesterday morning, and then only a slice of bread and a cup of coffee to each of us. We had to lie all day in the sun. The Yankees were shelling us most of the time, but did not hurt us. About 6 o'clock P. M., we were ordered to fix bayonets and charge the Yankees—that is, four companies of our regiment (the Twelfth Virginia)—the other position being held as a reserve and support for our artillery. We had to charge across a wheat field about three-quarters of a mile. The Yankees were under cover, in a dense wood, and at least eight to our one.

We crossed the field with a yell, and so quick and unexpected was the movement that the Yankees broke and fled, but not until many of them had been made to bite the dust. I don't mean that our battalion did all this. We were nobly aided by the Forty-eighth North Carolina and Fourth Georgia. The woods were filled with the dead and wounded Yankees. None of our company were killed, but seven were wounded: Sergeant Wm. Woodson, in the knee; R. Edyson, through the lungs, mortally; J. B. Old, in calf of leg; A. Gathwright, in small of back, seriously; John Leatmont, in arm; Sergeant John E. Laughton, slightly, in leg; David Wilson, in foot, slightly. We took some twenty or thirty prisoners.

We have been unable to obtain any further particulars of the fighting in the early part of the day, and until the Generals in command concede some facilities to reporters and correspondents of the Press, will have to trust to chance for whatever news we may obtain from the lines.

The Forty-eighth North Carolina, alluded to in the above extract, is a new regiment, commanded by Col. HILL. The regiment marched from the Capitol-square, Wednesday morning, about 8 o'clock, and went into action soon after reaching the lines. About twenty of the regiment were killed, and a considerable number wounded, including Major HOLPE, who was struck in the right foot by a ball.

Early Wednesday morning 'Long Tom' again operated on the Yankee breastworks, north of the Williamsburgh road, and demolished a considerable portion of the intrenchments. The Yankees fled in dismay from the shells of this powerful engine. The gun was manned, we learn, by Capt. SNOWDEN ANDREWS' Artillerists, the infantry support being a portion of Gen. PENDER'S Brigade."

THE NEWS FROM RICHMOND.

Effect of the Times Account of the Battle.

The first and only thorough and reliable account of the fearful struggle through which the Army of the Potomac has just passed, was published in the TIMES of yesterday.

The details fell upon the community with the most disheartening effect, and produced a shock which has never before been felt.

Probably the first thing done on Thursday morning by nine-tenths of the citizens of New-York was to open and glance through the paper that they might learn of the state of affairs with the army. Those who had the TIMES were informed ; others were not.

All over the City, in Brooklyn, and Williamsburgh, and Jersey City, the greatest excitement prevailed. Hope, that the account was exaggerated, struggled with the fear that all was not yet told, and the most gloomy forebodings were uppermost in the minds of the majority.

The TIMES office was thronged by those who had heard of, but had not seen the account, and thousands of extras were sold in addition to the vast regular edition of the morning.

One of the correspondents of the paper was known to be in the City, and the editorial rooms were beseiged by anxious parents, brothers and wives, who sought confirmation of the reports concerning the fate of their relatives, who desired to know the worst, and to be kept from further suspense about their friends.

Secretary of War Edwin M. Stanton insisted upon maintaining a large body of troops to defend Washington, refusing to send reinforcements to aid McClellan in the Peninsula Campaign.

Some of these went away rejoicing, for of the safety of their friends they were assured ; while the sad countenances of others were made sadder yet by the narration of details which placed the death or wounding of their loved ones facts beyond further question.

At a public resort in Brooklyn there was gathered quite a little crowd of gentlemen to whom one of the group was reading the graphic account given in the TIMES by "E. S." Until the description was ended all kept quiet, and then one person said, "Well, that may be so, but these first accounts are always greatly exaggerated, you know, and I think we'll find matters better than this correspondent says." To this a well-known clergyman of the City, who formed one of the listeners said, "Gentlemen, that letter is signed 'E. S.,' and is from a man whose probity and veracity are unquestioned, who writes the truth and nothing else. Whenever I see a statement signed by him, I know what to believe, and there is no use in blinking these facts. We are badly whipped, and all we have to do is to rise up en masse, make another effort, let the Government see that we are in earnest, that we mean war, and I think we will have no cause to regret it."

On the ferryboat Union, the passengers were gathered about three gentlemen, who were excitedly discussing the effect which the disastrous news will have upon recruiting. Said one: "If the account in the TIMES of to-day is correct—and I see no reason to doubt it, for it is full of details—I'll bet my head that LINCOLN not only won't get 300,000 men, but he won't get 30,000 men." "Nonsense," said his friend ; "the news of the defeat of the army of the Potomac will sting our people like the bite of a serpent. It was so after the Bull Run defeat; and I am of the opinion that men will crowd the recruiting stations, anxious and eager to show to the world generally, and the South particularly, that this rebellion must be stopped."

At this one of the outside listeners said, interrupting: "For one, I believe in Mayor WOOD'S words, though not with the meaning he desired to convey. I believe we must have a change of measures or a change of men. Either the President must announce that he is determined to go to work in earnest, or else that he is disappointed in the way this campaign is managed, and will put some one else at the head of the army. Otherwise, I believe he will get no recruits." This was received with signs of satisfaction, and seemed to be the prevalent feeling of that particular crowd.

In Wall-street excited groups met everywhere and at every corner ; in each the one topic was the "great battle," the "great battle." Speculations as to the course of France and England, as to the dread possibility of further disaster, as to McCLELLAN's next movement, and so on, ad infinitum, were current and indulged in by all.

They would have been glad to disbelieve the story; but it was told too well, entered too minutely into details and facts, to be set aside, and, as a consequence, was credited universally.

In the Park a company of youthful cadets attracted a large and admiring crowd—a crowd of the floating population from whose lips fell many curious remarks about the battle and its results. Many were talking of going into the army at once, others were fighting (verbally) about the "strategic movement," others blamed the President for not giving the young Napoleon more troops, others hurrahed yet for the old flag, and predicted its eventual success, and others yet did not hesitate to avow themselves believers in the Star of the South to this extent—that having won so great a victory they were deserving of recognition at once.

At CROOK & DUFF's the usual 12 o'clock gathering convened at about 10 A. M. Blood ran high—McClellan and Anti-McClellan, confidence and suspicion, sorrow and slimly-disguised joy, had their consultations and their squabbles, as together they took the mutual "smash."

In many places we heard the question of possible and probable recognition discussed. Those who two weeks since would not dare to say a word about the impolicy of the peninsular movements, whose mouths were closed concerning the rights of the South, did not hesitate in a certain half-and-half way to express the opinion that so soon as the news could be gotten across the ocean the Confederacy will be recognized. Saying, too, that they really could not see upon what ground it could be denied them.

Bull Run they say was a Union rout, Corinth a mismanaged occupation, Ball's Bluff a slaughter-house, Williamsburgh a victory on paper, and the last movement a terrible disturbance of the confidence of the people. Upon whom to lay the responsibility no set of men agreed. The plans of McCLELLAN, the inaction of STANTON, the non-reinforcement by the President, the possible weakness of the troops. Who ? What ? Where ? No one knew, no one could decide, though every one had his opinion and his say.

The New-York Times.

VOL. XI–NO. 3366.　　　　　NEW-YORK, TUESDAY, JULY 8, 1862.　　　　　PRICE TWO CENTS.

GEN. M'CLELLAN'S ARMY.

Details of Events to the Afternoon of the Fourth.

The Battles which Followed the One at Gaines' Hill.

Allen's Farm, Savage's Station, Nelson's Farm and Malvern Hills.

Vain Attempts of the Rebels to Force Our Lines.

A SKIRMISH ON THE FOURTH.

Reported Capture of a Thousand Rebel Prisoners and Three Batteries.

LIST OF CASUALTIES.

From the Special Correspondent of the New-York Times.

HARRISON'S BAR LANDING, JAMES RIVER,
Friday, July 4, 1862.

The Army of the Potomac rests to-day, after six consecutive and connecting battles, after toils which few armies have ever endured, after a week of continual fighting and marching, leaving behind it thousands of brave men on hard-fought and well-contested battle-fields—after all this, it rests this Independence Day by the side of the beautiful James, to recover strength and proudly tell and retell the story of the memorable movement so happily and yet so sadly accomplished. As I write, my ears catch the unwonted strains of the regimental bands, discoursing patriotic and martial music. Massed around are the solid columns of the great army, forgetful of the toils of the past in the memory of its glory, and the hope of future success. For the first time since last week Thursday, more than a week ago, there is opportunity to pause and collect the events of the week in a continuous story. You have already had full and careful accounts of the great battle of Friday, which strewed the north bank of the insignificant, swampy, pestilential Chickahominy Creek with thousands of the slain and the disabled. I shall, therefore, confine myself to a statement of the events connected with the great military movement, whereby a vast army, in the face of an enemy of superior numbers and intense activity, has *changed its front and defeated every attempt at interference with the plan.*

PREPARATIONS TO FALL BACK.

The great mass of the army, occupying the intrenchments extending for miles from the Chickahominy to the left, were not apprised until midnight of Friday last, after PORTER's hard-pressed corps had

Major-General Fitz-John Porter used Federal artillery to great advantage in savaging the Confederate drive up Malvern Hill.

partially yielded to the overwhelming force of the enemy, of the intention of Gen. McCLELLAN to change his base from the York to the James River. At that hour orders were received to put everything in readiness for a movement at daylight. Accordingly tents were quickly struck, baggage packed, wagons loaded, and everything prepared for a march, the men meantime getting with alacrity under arms. At 4 o'clock Saturday afternoon the long line of wagons moved down the Williamsburgh and other roads toward the rear—an immense train. The army remained in the intrenchments during the night standing to arms. It commenced moving at 4 o'clock in the morning, just before the appearance of the sun above the tops of the trees to the east, and amid a considerable fog, which threw its kindly obscuring veil over the movement, and blinded the sharp eyes of the enemy. During the evening of Saturday, in various places in the rear of our lines, bonfires had been made of Commissary and Quartermaster's stores, that nothing might fall into the eager hands of the hungry enemy. TURNER's, HEINTZELMAN's and FRANKLIN's corps fell back, nearly simultaneously, at 4 o'clock Sunday morning, a distance of one mile, one hour after drawing in their pickets and taking up their position in line of battle at Orchard Station.

Gen. KEYES' corps had, at about noon of Saturday moved from their line, as the advance toward White Oak Swamp and the Chickahominy, the Engineer corps, the Fiftieth and Fifteenth New-York, the latter under the efficient command of Col. McLEOD MURPHY, whose services in this movement the whole army appreciate, going before to prepare the way and build bridges. The first duty of our troops, after reaching Orchard Station, was to destroy the large quantity of stores which had been gathered there, and which our rebel friends, still ignorant of our movement, had long laid covetous eyes upon. Some ten thousand boxes of crackers, a large number of packages of coffee, barrels of sugar, molasses, beef and other stores, a great quantity of intrenching tools, ammunition and Quartermaster's stores, a rocket battery, powder and shell for siege guns, &c., were burned or otherwise so destroyed as to be of no use to the enemy soon to occupy this ground. This important work done, the smoke and noise it occasioned giving the alarm to the enemy, our brave soldiers

stood to arms, awaiting the advance of the rebels, who soon were reported to be rushing in great numbers, with cheers and yells, into our abandoned and beautifully constructed intrenchments, and exploring in vain the deserted camps for booty. There was no chance for loot. Everything was gone.

At nine o'clock the enemy, who had formed into line and commenced the pursuit, made their appearance, to the left of SEDGWICK's Division, driving in the Fifth New-Hampshire, one of Gen. CALDWELL's admirable regiments, and of the brigade which was acting as the advance guard. Our forces were ready for the attack. SEDGWICK's Division held the left, resting on the railroad, joining HEINTZELMAN's right held by HOOKER's Division, RICHARDSON's Division occupying the right of SEDGWICK, these two latter divisions being of Gen. SUMNER's corps. Gen. FRANKLIN's corps occupied the extreme right, thus putting Gen. SUMNER's force in the centre. The firing soon extended along the line, until it reached the left of RICHARDSON's Division. Gen. SEDGWICK soon repulsed the enemy, who had been pouring upon his firm columns a steady galling fire of artillery and musketry. The enemy, then, next appeared opposite Gen. RICHARDSON's centre, opening fiercely with artillery. Capt. HAZZARD's Fourth Regular Battery responded handsomely, assisted by one of Gen. SMITH's batteries, while the Fifty-third Pennsylvania, of Gen. FRENCH's Brigade, opened a heavy fire of musketry upon the rebels, advancing in solid and numerous columns upon us. The firing soon extended through RICHARDSON's Division, continuing with almost unexampled intensity for something like fifteen minutes, when the rebels were driven back. Three times they repeated the attack, and three times were driven back as at first. The ammunition of Capt. HAZZARD's Battery, which had been most beautifully served and doing terrible execution among the enemy, now giving out, Capt. PETTIT's Battery—Battery B, of the First New-York Artillery—came up, got immediately into position, and opened its eight 10-pounder Parrots upon the enemy. Capt. PETTIT almost immediately got the range of the rebels' cannon and soon silenced them. This engagement was fought on ALLEN's farm, and derives its name from that place.

The enemy now discovered the weak place in our lines, endeavoring to get into the gap necessarily left between SUMNER and FRANKLIN. We accordingly fell back in admirable order to Savage's Station, about two miles to the rear, with a view of destroying the material which had been there concentrated, and to make a further stand at that place. The work of destruction was forthwith commenced. A long line of cars loaded with ammunition and stores was blown up, the sound of the grand explosion reaching for miles, the smoke of the burning mass arising in a vast and beautiful column, which soon touched the sky and mingled with the clouds. Along the sides of the railroad, piles of stores were then given to the flames and the work of demolition was completed. Several engines which had been collected were fastened together, steam was gotten up, and they were sent at full speed to plunge into the mud and water of the Chickahominy, whose bridge a few miles below had been previously destroyed.

BATTLE AT SAVAGE'S STATION.

Our forces now took position in the large open field to the left of the railroad, opposite SAVAGE's house, the left occupying the edge of the woods, and the right extending down by the side of the railroad. It was now late in the afternoon; the men had already fought one battle, and been under arms two nights, yet they were ready for battle, and had no thought of yielding to the enemy—troops who never yet had been beaten, nor would be. At about 6 o'clock in the evening, the enemy, who had come down the Williamsburgh Road in pursuit, deployed in the woods to the left, and, in great numbers, opened the attack with artillery and musketry. The columns of Gen.

SEDGWICK, posted in the plain to the right of the Williamsburgh Road, were first attacked. A fierce fire soon extended along the whole line of SEDGWICK, working destruction among his men. It was promptly and efficiently responded to by our troops, the rebels suffering terribly. The Eighty-eighth and Sixty-ninth New-York Regiments, of Gen. MEAGHER'S Brigade, were now sent to SEDGWICK'S support. Meantime. Gen. HEINTZELMAN'S Corps had fallen back, taking the road towards White Oak Swamp, and leaving Gens. SUMNER'S and FRANKLIN'S Corps to carry on the fight. The contest continued until dark—8½ or 9 o'clock—when the enemy were again driven back, having suffered severe loss. We had also lost heavily in the two battles. In this affair, also, PETTIT'S and HAZZARD'S batteries did splendid service. Our troops during the morning, commenced to retire towards the James River, FRANKLIN'S Corps leaving first, SUMNER'S following, RICHARDSON'S Division acting as rear guard; Gen. FRENCH, of this division, handsomely executing the difficult task of protecting the extreme rear, and bringing all of his men off. At 12 o'clock, midnight of Sunday, all our forces were moving down the road to White Oak Swamp in good order, the enemy having suffered so severely as to be unable to continue the pursuit that night. The most painful thing connected with this falling back was the imperative necessity which compelled us to leave many of our sick and wounded in the battles upon the field and in SAVAGE'S house, in the hands of the enemy. Several physicians and nurses, with hospital stores, were, however, left with them, and they doubtless will be and have been well cared for. Including the wounded of the battles of Mechanicsville and Gaines' Hill, with those of Allen's Farm and Savage's Station, *at least from three to five thousand wounded must have been left in the hands of the rebels.* I hazard much in making this estimate, but think I must fall below rather than exceed the actual number; but I would avoid any exaggeration in this painful matter.

BATTLE OF NELSON'S FARM.

The last of our forces falling back, reached the White Oak Swamp, and crossed the bridge at daylight—5 o'clock—Monday morning. Gen. RICHARDSON bringing up and protecting the rear, succeeded in getting over the bridge a long transportation train, which was in imminent danger of falling into the hands of the enemy, and in collecting and driving forward a large number of stragglers, who had got separated from their regiments during the night. Everything over, he destroyed the bridge, and formed line of battle adjacent to the Swamp, placing his batteries on some commanding hills, his Division taking the centre, SMITH on his right, KEARNEY, HOOKER and McCALL on the left. PORTER and KEYES, who had advanced beyond, moved back and connected to the left of HOOKER. At about 10 o'clock in the morning, the rebels, who had got twelve rifled guns, most of them three-inch bore, opened a terrific fire on Gen. RICHARDSON'S Division, who, though sheltered as much as possible by the hills, lost heavily under it—some 200 men—the shell pouring in with terrible intensity for two hours. Capt. HAZZARD'S Battery, of RICHARDSON'S Division, MOTT'S and AYRE'S Batteries, of Gen. SMITH'S Division, responded shot for shot. MOTT, however, lost one gun, which was spiked, after having been dismounted, and several caissons. Capt. HAZZARD'S Battery, after fighting splendidly for three hours, had so suffered in the loss of cannoneers, and its gallant commander himself having been wounded in the leg, that it was obliged to retire. He was relieved by Capt. PETTIT'S Battery, which came trotting upon the field, and speedily opened a well-directed fire upon the rebels. This skilful artillerist succeeded in silencing the enemy's guns after some three hours' fire. At Nelson's Farm, our infantry soon became engaged in a fight with the forces of the enemy pressing on in great force.

The rebels opening on HEINTZELMAN at about 3 o'clock, McCALL'S, HOOKER'S and KEARNEY'S Divisions now became actively engaged. The fight continued during the afternoon, with great intensity, the loss on both sides being heavy. Toward evening, the overpowered reserves of Gen. McCALL'S Division were evidently wavering, and it looked to an observer as if the battle was going against us. Gen. HEINTZELMAN now sent to Gen. RICHARDSON for help, whereupon Lieut. CHARLES DRAPER, his Aid, brought up to the field of battle, through a most murderous fire, Gen. CALDWELL'S already well-tested brigade, and they forthwith plunged into the engagement. At this hour—6½ o'clock in the evening—the roads were lined with exhausted soldiers, and batteries broken and empty of ammunition were hurrying from the field. Gen. CALDWELL did not arrive a moment too soon. Riding rapidly through the clouds of dust and smoke, so

A transport and monitor on the James River.

thick and heavy that all view of the operations was obstructed, the gallant General led his hardy men on into the fight, every man in order, a column not large, but powerful in courage and will. The tide of battle was soon turned, Gen. MEAGHER bringing his fiery brigade up a little later, and assisting in holding the ground. Night closed in, the enemy again driven back, leaving the field strewn with his wounded and slain, but not yet beaten sufficiently to prevent continued pursuit in the morning.

During the night our forces continued the line of march toward the James River, Gen. FRENCH again covering the retreat. At six o'clock on Tuesday morning they arrived at Haxall's Landing, weary with the exhaustion of five battles and continuous night marches, with little food and scarcely any sleep, unable to understand, and therefore bewildered and partially discouraged by the constant falling back, but not prepared to be beaten, nor exhausted of courage. A portion of the army were already concentrated on Malvern Hills, two miles back of the landing, near the residence and on the place of Mr. DEW, a wealthy Virginia planter, whose sharp-gabled, old-fashioned and eminently comfortable mansion had, during the Revolutionary war, been occupied for a short time by Gen. WASHINGTON as his headquarters, and near by which that General had built a redoubt, commanding with its guns the James River, whose clear waters could easily be seen from the grounds. Here was subsequently fought

THE BATTLE OF MALVERN HILLS.

At eight o'clock Tuesday morning, our forces having been concentrated at this point, the line of battle was formed, Gen. FRANKLIN holding the right, resting on the James River, and Gen. PORTER the extreme left, Gens. KEYES and HEINTZELMAN occupying the centre. Gen. SUMNER'S corps was held in reserve. At nine o'clock the rebels opened the battle with a heavy fire of artillery, to which we responded from numerous batteries which had been placed along the hill-sides in commanding positions. The day was a beautiful one, clear and cloudless, unless from the smoke of the incessant artillery fire; the position a fine one; an open country, with rolling ground fringed by thick woods; the James River in sight, and on its waters, cleared for action, two gunboats, the *Jacob Bell* and *Galena*, kindly auxiliaries, whose 100-pounders poured awful missiles of death into the woods above the river, by whose sides rebel reinforcements were coming, in heavy numbers. The fire of the artillery on the hills was kept up during the day, the rebels getting decidedly the worst of it. They, beyond disparagement, fought nobly. We could see several of their batteries pushed out beyond the woods, and almost hear the commands of their officers. Their infantry marched up in solid columns by brigades of ten to the support of the batteries, and would press forward in the face of galling fires toward our artillery, determined to make trophies of our guns. Maintaining their close columns, they pushed forward to receive first our shot and shell, and then drawing nearer, to be mowed down by grape and canister. Facing this as long as they could, they would at

length wheel around and march back again in good order, leaving the ground covered with their fallen. *Again and again, with new regiments, this was repeated, and again and again shot and shell, grape and canister gave them awful punishment.* It was too much to be borne, and at last they no longer marched back in columns, but ran hurrying for life from the terrible ministers of death.

At three o'clock in the afternoon the enemy opened a fierce musketry fire upon COUCH, which quickly extended along the line, including KEARNEY and PORTER in its fire. For three hours the battle raged fiercely, the sound of musketry and artillery deafening the ear. Up to six o'clock it was an equal game—if anything, we were getting the worst of it. At 6 o'clock in the evening Gen. PORTER sent word by an aid, who drove hastily up, dust-covered and well-nigh exhausted, to Gen. SUMNER, who, as Senior General, was in command, saying that he must have reinforcements or lose the day. Gen. SUMNER immediately directed that two of RICHARDSON'S Brigades—Gen. CALDWELL'S and Gen. MEAGHER'S—be sent to his assistance. Gen. HEINTZELMAN at the same time sent two of HOOKER'S—Gen. SICKLES' Excelsior Brigade and Gen. PATTERSON'S New-Jersey Brigade. These new men, fighting with a courage and determination of which the annals of war cannot furnish a superior, drove the enemy until dark, and decided the fate of the Battle of Malvern Hills and the Army of the Potomac. Night coming on, we held the hard-fought and thickly strewn field, having in every engagement during the progress of the movement toward James River beaten and held in check a powerful and superior enemy, at Allen's Farm, Savage's Station, Nelson's Farm and Malvern Hills—a series of battles scarcely paralleled in history. The rebels were so thoroughly beaten that they could no longer pursue with the rapidity or vigor which had characterized their movements, since our movement for a change of position was inaugurated.

TO CAMP ON JAMES RIVER.

The firing of artillery continued until near midnight, at which hour we commenced to fall back on this position. Gen. McCLELLAN having meantime gone forward and selected it, Gen. HEINTZELMAN covered the movement, and at an early hour on Tuesday morning the army was collected here, transportation trains, artillery and troops, welcomed by a beating rain-storm, for which the incessant smoke of the artillery fire was largely responsible. The men were, many of them, exposed for hours, unsheltered, to the beating rain, after they arrived, as they had been during the march; but it was impossible to prevent it. Toward night, however, they had camps arranged, and to-day, after a good night's rest, they marched out to a Fourth-of-July review, as if they had gone through nothing more than a series of sham fights in Washington or on Boston Common.

WE TAKE A BATTERY.

In the afternoon of yesterday, the rebels got a couple of rifled field pieces in position on a hill commanding our camps, and commenced a shelling which did some damage among our crowded wagon camps.

The gunboats responded with a few shot, but did not get the range. The little pests must be stopped, and the Fifth Maine undertook the work. Advancing stealthily through the woods they came suddenly upon the battery, flanking it and taking both the guns, and all the cannoneers and their officers. It was a handsomely executed manœuvre, and the Maine men deserve great credit for it. At the battle of Nelson's Farm the Sixty-first New-York captured a splendid stand of colors from the enemy, on which was inscribed "Williamsburgh and Seven Pines." At the battle of Malvern Hills Couch's Division also captured a rebel flag.

OUR LOSS IN KILLED, WOUNDED AND PRISONERS in all the engagements, Mechanicsville and Gaines' Mill included, can hardly fall far short, or much exceed *twenty-five thousand men*. Our loss in prisoners is heavy, the enemy's cavalry making easy captives of thousands of stragglers who lined the roads in our rear, and besides these we have left thousands of wounded in their hands. Their loss must be at least as heavy, and probably heavier in killed and wounded than our own, but in prisoners it fell far short, though we have taken about two thousand from them. Included in our loss were many of our finest officers, the number of line, company and staff officers killed and disabled, being unusually large. I inclose a list as complete as it is possible to get together, and shall see that the TIMES is soon provided with the whole of the official reports of casualties. Our loss of guns is stated at forty, and we have taken from the enemy perhaps two-thirds that number. To compute the value of the property—stores, cars, ammunition, &c.—destroyed by us in our change of position is impossible, with the scanty data I have at hand, but it must amount to two or three millions of dollars.

THE CHANGE OF BASE

was necessitated by the impossibility of holding our extended lines with the army which Mr. STANTON would grant to Gen. McCLELLAN. Our front extended from Mechanicsville on the right to White Oak Swamp on the left, a distance of fifteen miles. Besides defending this against a greatly superior force of the rebels, to say nothing of satisfying the ambition of the Secretary of War and Congress for an immediate advance, we were obliged to guard some twenty miles of railway from White House to Fair Oaks. *Gen. McClellan had not enough men to hold this position* after the reinforcement of the rebels by Stonewall JACKSON and others, and he became convinced of this after the dash of Gen. STUART's Cavalry. Our right was constantly subject to the danger of being turned, and our army being surrounded. The rebels knew that this was our weak position, and when they could bring an overwhelming force to bear against it and were sure of success, they made the attempt. Our right wing, held by Gen. PORTER, was turned last Friday, and *the army has only escaped a terrible fate by the masterly accomplishment of one of the most difficult and delicate movements which an army can undertake, the change of its base in face of the enemy by a flank movement.* The glorious success of the movement is the defeat of the rebels, and the order with which our soldiers have gone through it, proves them to be of the very best kind, reliable and worthy of the world's applause. Gen. McCLELLAN owes everything to his soldiers and to some of his leading Generals, for the success which has attended a movement upon which he hazarded the safety of his whole army.

The position which we now occupy is one which our engineers say we can defend against anything JEFF. DAVIS or any other monarch can bring to bear upon us. Our line, instead of being fifteen miles front, with twenty miles of railway to defend, is scarcely five miles long. One of our flanks is the James River, not a railroad to be torn up, nor a highway that may be obstructed, but a sure means of conveying supplies, and easily defended by gunboats. Our other line is readily held by the force we can bring. We occupy the centre of a circle, which greatly facilitates celerity of movement, and are so positioned that no artillery can be brought to bear upon us by the enemy within effective range. If we could only have occupied this same position six weeks ago, instead of the difficult one we took, your correspondent would now be dating his letters at Richmond, instead of twenty odd miles below there. Though further from Richmond than we were last Thursday, in miles and furlongs, in effect we are nearer that stubborn capital, and surer of its capture. I will not venture to name the exact date when we shall exchange the hardships of the camp for such luxuries as Richmond will afford, but the day cannot be far distant, if other coöperative movements are properly conducted. The army is in excellent spirits to-day, and disposed to let off a deal of

Fourth of July patriotism and powder. The *Galena*, the *Jacob Bell*, the *Aroostook*, the *Monitor* and other gunboats are with us, and they are welcome visitors. The river is already full of craft, and is rapidly getting to look the same great mart of commerce which distinguished the Pamunkey at White House.

MERITORIOUS OFFICERS.

The number of these is so great that it is impossible to mention any without leaving out many more equally meritorious. Of the Generals great and just praise is accorded to Gens. SUMNER and HEINTZELMAN, Corps Commanders; Gens. Richardson, Kearney, Hooker, Couch, Smith and Sedgwick, to whom, as Division Commanders, the historian of this war and this movement will give such meed of praise as to satisfy the ambition of the most ambitious. Gen. CALDWELL, who, since the battle of Fair Oaks, and the wounding of Gen. HOWARD, has commanded that gentlemanly and Christian officer's Brigade, has demonstrated rare soldierly ability, and won the enthusiastic confidence of his men. His Brigade was in every fight but those of Mechanicsville and Gaines' Hill, and lost perhaps more severely than any other in proportion to the number of men he brought into action. I was personally a witness of the gallantry of Lieuts. DRAPER, MILLER and HURLBURT, of Gen. RICHARDSON's Staff, and Capt. MILES, of Gen. CALDWELL's, and hear a like good tale of the other Staff Officers of the different Generals. Gen. FRENCH receives great and deserved praise for the masterly manner in which he covered the rear of our retreating columns, during the whole of the movement. To Gen. Meagher, Gen. Brooks, Gen. Burns, Gen. Dana, and Gen. Gorman, the country cannot accord too much credit.

F. P. C.

CAMP AT HARRISON'S BAR, }
JAMES RIVER, July 4. 1862. }

Worn as the soldiers are after their long continuous marches and severe fighting, they responded heartily to the following order, issued from headquarters early in the morning :

HEADQUARTERS ARMY OF THE POTOMAC, }
CAMP NEAR HARRISON'S LANDING, July 3, 1862. }

CIRCULAR.—I. A National salute will be fired at noon to-morrow, at the headquarters of each Army Corps. Immediately thereafter, the bands will play appropriate National airs.

The General Commanding will visit all the troops during the afternoon, when the troops will be paraded and a Major-General's salute fired in each corps. The troops will be notified of the hour of the visit.

II. Regimental commanders must now see that the sick are taken care of, within the limits of their respective regiments, and not permitted to be sent away, except by orders from these headquarters.

III. The camp of General Headquarters has been removed into the woods, a short distance further up the river, than this morning's camp.

By command of Maj.-Gen. McCLELLAN.
(Signed)   S. WILLIAMS, Asst. Adjt.-Gen.

The storm which yesterday drenched many a poor fellow's dusty uniform and chilled his tired frame, and which reduced the clayey soil to that pasty adhesive condition which offends the patience of the pedestrian and tries the nerves of horse and rider alike,

passed over during the night, and Independence Day came in with a gladdening sun to cheer the hearts of the army. During yesterday, in spite of mud and rain, the mass of troops which had been poured in here so hastily was reduced to order, and corps and divisions had their definite positions assigned to them, prepared camp grounds, and the men spread couches to enjoy the first real rest which had been permitted them for a week. The long pull of sleep they got last night told on the troops. It was a far happier, brighter, stronger set of men who stood about the camp-fires this morning than that which the day before shivered in the rain. At about noon the bands, such of them as still have musicians and instruments wholly or partially complete, played National airs, which unusual sounds did much to enliven the camps, for months debarred the luxury of music by an imperative order, necessitated by the near proximity of the rebels, who could, from our music, discover our position. A little after noon Gen. McCLELLAN, with his staff, in costumes cleaned of the mud and rust of the long journey, commenced the round of visits to the different corps. The Commanding General looked in excellent spirits, not discovering in the least any appearance of fatigue. He took the different corps in order, reviewing the men, his arrival welcomed in every division by the firing of a Major-General's salute, and he himself received by the troops with hearty cheers, which kept mingling along the whole line, as he passed from brigade to brigade. It was a touching sight to view the thinned ranks drawn up before their General, the warn-worn veterans, no longer the scholar-soldiers whom he reviewed in Washington last November, but heroes of six, eight and ten battles, who had attested their courage and devotion, and had won the right to the name of soldiers. Gen. McCLELLAN looked with particular interest on brigades which had suffered very severely in the late battles, and expressed his sorrow at the gaps in their lines, but as Gen. CALDWELL told in answer to such an expression of regret in regard to his Brigade, they died in doing their duty, and the rest were ready to do the same thing. The visit and review of the General occupied nearly the whole of the afternoon, during all which time, the hills resounded with the salutes. The whole ceremony was one of the most impressive and touching that could possibly be witnessed, and cannot be without its good effects upon commander and men. The soldiers on their own part celebrated the Fourth with the popping of guns—forbidden sport—and best of all, by quietly resting and going over the story of the last week's fights.

In the afternoon the enemy had a sharp skirmish with our pickets on the edge of James River, in which we gave them a few artillery reminders, which stopped their demonstrations, but not until they had killed and wounded some twenty of our men. Otherwise, everything is quiet along the lines.

F. P. C.

Lieutenant George A. Custer poses with a former classmate of his, James Washington, taken prisoner during the Seven Days Battles.

The New-York Times.

VOL. XI—NO. 3397.   NEW-YORK, WEDNESDAY, AUGUST 13, 1862.   PRICE TWO CENTS.

FROM GEN. POPE'S ARMY.

Retreat of Jackson's Army Across the Rapidan.

Our Cavalry and Artillery in Pursuit.

Gen. Pope Reinforced by Gen. King's Division.

Further Particulars of the Battle of Cedar Mountain.

Terrible Nature of the Fire on Both Sides.

The Rebels Believed to be Badly Crippled.

Safe Return of the Madison Court-House Expedition.

WASHINGTON, Tuesday, Aug. 12.

The War Department has information from the Army of Virginia in front of Slaughter's Mountain up to yesterday evening. Gen. KING, with his whole division, was then within a few miles of the battle-field of Saturday, and has doubtless joined Gen. POPE ere this. No fighting has occurred in that quarter since Saturday night last.

RETREAT OF THE REBELS ACROSS THE RAPIDAN.

HEADQUARTERS, ARMY OF VIRGINIA,
CEDAR MOUNTAIN, VA.—7:30 A. M., Aug 12.

To Maj.-Gen. Halleck :

The enemy has retreated under cover of the night. His rear guard is now crossing the Rapidan towards Orange Court House. Our cavalry and artillery are in pursuit.

(Signed,)   JOHN POPE, Major-General.

FURTHER PARTICULARS OF THE BATTLE.

WASHINGTON, Tuesday, Aug. 12.

Accounts from Culpepper, dated yesterday, speaking of Saturday's fight, say that so heavy was the fire to which our comparatively small number of men was exposed, the only wonder is that the entire command was not completely annihilated at the end of half an hour, instead of our bringing off so large a proportion of our force at the expiration of an hour and a half.

The prisoners report that their own troops were mowed down by our fire like grass. Three times were they reinforced by fresh regiments and brigades, and when our troops retired they were too crippled to pursue in the open ground.

The prisoners also report that the heavy guns used by the enemy were of recent English manufacture, with English fixed ammunition.

Major-General John Pope was in charge of the Army of Virginia, but was to be continuously beguiled by the Confederate army throughout August, 1862.

We lost but one gun, which was left behind in a ditch, spiked, several of the horses having been killed.

The gun was not lost while changing our position for the night, but under the fire of the enemy's sharp-shooters.

Col. CHAPMAN, of the Fifth Massachusetts, was shot in the breast, and is probably dead.

Lieut.-Col. STONE fell, with many wounds.

Major BLAKE also fell, and, if alive, is a prisoner.

Adjt. SMITH is wounded or dead.

Major SAVAGE, of the Second Massachusetts, is believed to be killed, as well as many of the Captains and Lieutenants belonging to the regiment.

Dr. LELAND was shot in the eye.

Capt. GEORGE JANNETT, of Gen. PRINCE'S Staff, was shot in the breast, and mortally wounded.

The casualties in other regiments have not yet been heard from definitely.

Stragglers from the battle-field to town have been arrested by the orders of Major-Gen. POPE, and by to-morrow a list of the missing will be obtained.

The Twenty-eighth Pennsylvania Regiment escaped without loss, having been detached to guard a signal station eight or ten miles southwest of the battle-field, early in the day. They returned yesterday, escorting safely the signal officers without being compelled to pass near the enemy's pickets.

On Sunday night, about 11 o'clock, while Gen. POPE and Gen. BANKS were in conference in the rear of our advanced batteries, a body of rebel cavalry charged in the most daring manner through the woods on our front upon the group. The discharge of muskets and the whizzing of balls near gave them timely notice of the approach of the rebels. They speedily mounted their horses, and a regiment of infantry fired a volley at the approaching rebels, thus checking their charge, and probably saving both commanders.

Gen. BUFORD with his cavalry command arrived at Culpepper yesterday from Madison.

Previous to Gen. BUFORD'S departure, he made a reconnoissance to the Rapidan, where he found a force of the enemy on the south side, but none north of the river.

A telegraph dispatch dated to-day, states that all was quiet last night and this morning.

Col. DONNELLY is still alive but is in a sinking condition.

Other wounded officers are generally doing well.

THE PLANS OF JACKSON FOILED.

CULPEPPER COURT-HOUSE, VA.,
Tuesday, Aug. 12—7 P. M.

The battle of Saturday, the 9th, is one of the most important of the war, not merely on account of the desperate valor and unfaltering discipline displayed by

Major-General Nathaniel P. Banks

our troops, the obstinacy of the contest, and the heavy loss on both sides, but because of its important effect on the campaign of which it makes a part. The campaign on the part of JACKSON is an attempt to penetrate and recover the Valley of the Shenandoah, whence the richest supplies of the enemy are drawn, and the possession of which was of a practical importance in the endeavor to hold Virginia as a part of the attempted Confederacy hardly to be estimated. At the same time the rebel leaders hoped by this movement to so threaten Washington and Maryland as to relieve Richmond, and withdraw again our armies to the line of the Potomac. To secure such objects as these, and knowing that the Government was now relatively weaker, and the rebellion stronger than could again occur in the war, the Richmond leaders sent the flower of the Southern infantry, under their most popular and enterprising generals, a large body of cavalry, under their most distinguished cavalry officer, Maj.-Gen. STUART, and an abundance of artillery. When JACKSON had arrived with his forces as far as Louisa Court-house and Gordonsville, and found the disposition of Gen. POPE'S troops such that not only his purpose to enter the valley was foiled, but his own direct communications with Richmond were interrupted, he called for further reinforcements, and with those, which were freely furnished, attempted to stem POPE'S further advance upon that railroad, the destruction or even the permanently threatening of which must bar from Richmond all hope of the material or political control of Central Virginia.

JACKSON attempted, by a feint upon Madison Court-house and Sperryville, to detain our force at the latter point, while at the same time he threw the mass of his forces, numbering 35,000 men, by way of Orange Court-house, upon us at Culpepper, expecting to find only a portion of our forces there, which he could overwhelm, and then march on Sperryville from Culpepper, and crush the army corps of SIGEL.

His plans were completely foiled by the rapid concentration of our forces at Culpepper, and their advance to meet him at Cedar Run. The cool and determined temper of BANKS accepted the proffered battle as soon as offered, and the battle of Saturday afternoon was fought between the advance under Gen. BANKS and the advance of JACKSON, under himself and EWELL.

After endeavoring in vain to rout and drive BANKS' corps, JACKSON found himself compelled at night, by the rapid movements in front of him, to fall back to a strong defensive position in Cedar Mountain, and finding his line of retreat growing insecure, in the succeeding night he retreated altogether, retiring beyond Robertson's River and again beyond the Rapidan. The result is JACKSON is again foiled, and forced to abandon his operations, and his prestige seriously impaired. He will be rapidly followed.

The New-York Times.

VOL. XI—NO. 3399.　　　　NEW-YORK, FRIDAY, AUGUST 15, 1862.　　　　PRICE TWO CENTS.

FROM THE ARMY OF VIRGINIA.

Gen. Pope's Report of the Battle of Cedar Mountain.

A Clear and Comprehensive Document.

DESPERATE CHARACTER OF THE BATTLE.

The Conspicuous Gallantry of General Banks.

Retreat of the Rebel Forces to Gordonsville.

Jackson's Army Swelled to Seventy Thousand Men.

GEN. POPE'S OFFICIAL REPORT.

HEADQUARTERS OF VIRGINIA, CEDAR MOUNTAIN,
Aug. 13, 1862—5 P. M.

To Major-Gen. Halleck, General-in-Chief:

On Thursday morning the enemy crossed the Rapidan at Barnett's Ford, in heavy force, and advanced strong on the road to Culpepper and Madison Court-house. I had established my whole force on the turnpike between Culpepper and Sperryville, ready to concentrate at either place, as soon as the enemy's plans were developed.

Early on Friday it became apparent that the move on Madison Court-house was merely a feint to detain the army corps of Gen. SIGEL at Sperryville, and that the main attack of the enemy would be at Culpepper, to which place I had thrown forward part of BANKS' and McDOWELL's corps. Brig.-Gen. BAYARD, with part of the rear of McDOWELL's corps, who was in the advance, near the Rapidan, fell slowly back, delaying and embarrassing the enemy's advance as far as possible, and capturing some of his men.

The forces of BANKS and SIGEL and one of the Divisions of McDOWELL's Corps were rapidly concentrated at Culpepper during Friday and Friday night, BANKS' Corps being pushed forward five miles south of Culpepper, with RICKETT's Division of McDOWELL's Corps, three miles in his rear.

The Corps of Gen. SIGEL, which had marched all night, was halted in Culpepper to rest for a few hours.

On Saturday the enemy advanced rapidly to Cedar Mountain, the sides of which they occupied in heavy force.

Gen. BANKS was instructed to take up his position on the ground occupied by CRAWFORD's Brigade, of his command, which had been thrown out the day previous to watch the enemy's movements. He was directed not to advance beyond that point, and, if attacked by the enemy, to defend his position, and send back timely notice.

It was my desire to have time to give the corps of Gen. SIGEL all the rest possible after their forced march, and to bring forward all the forces at my disposal.

The artillery of the enemy was opened early in the afternoon, but he made no advance until nearly 5 o'clock, at which time a few skirmishers were thrown forward on each side, under cover of the heavy wood in which his force was concealed.

The enemy pushed forward a strong force in the rear of his skirmishers, and Gen. BANKS advanced to the attack.

The engagement did not fairly open until after 6 o'clock, but for an hour and a half was furious and unceasing.

Throughout the cannonading, which at first was desultory and directed mainly against the cavalry, I had continued to receive reports from Gen. BANKS that no attack was apprehended, and that no considerable infantry force of the enemy had come forward.

Yet towards evening the increase in the artillery firing having satisfied me an engagement might be at hand, though the lateness of the hour rendered it unlikely, I ordered Gen. McDOWELL to advance RICKETT's Division to support Gen. BANKS, and directed Gen. SIGEL to bring his men upon the ground as soon as possible.

I arrived personally on the field at 7 P. M., and found the action raging furiously. The infantry fire was incessant and severe.

I found Gen. BANKS holding the position he took up early in the morning. His losses were heavy.

RICKETT's Division was immediately pushed forward, and occupied the right of Gen. BANKS, the brigades of CRAWFORD and GORDON being directed to change their position from the right and mass themselves in the centre.

Before this change could be effected it was quite dark, though the artillery fire continued at short range without intermission.

The artillery fire at night by the Second and Fifth Maine Batteries, in RICKETT's Division, of Gen. McDOWELL's corps, was most destructive, as was readily observable the next morning in the dead men and horses, and broken gun-carriages of the enemy's batteries which had been advanced against it.

Our troops rested on their arms during the night in line of battle, the heavy shelling being kept up on both sides until midnight.

At daylight the next morning, the enemy fell back two miles from our front, and still higher up the mountain.

Our pickets at once advanced and occupied the ground.

The fatigue of the troops from long marches and excessive heat, made it impossible for either side to resume the action on Sunday. The men were, therefore, allowed to rest and recruit the whole day, our only active operation being of cavalry on the enemy's flank and rear.

Monday was spent in burying the dead and in getting off the wounded.

The slaughter was severe on both sides, most of the fighting being hand to hand.

The dead bodies of both armies were found mingled together in masses over the whole ground of the conflict.

The burying of the dead was not completed until dark on Monday, the heat being so terrible that severe work was not possible.

On Monday night the enemy fled from the field, leaving many of his dead unburied and his wounded on the ground and along the road to Orange Court-House, as will be seen from Gen. BUFORD's dispatch.

A cavalry and artillery force under Gen. BUFORD, was immediately thrown forward in pursuit, and followed the enemy to the Rapidan, over which he passed with his rear guard by 10 o'clock in the morning.

The behavior of Gen. BANKS' corps during the action was very fine. No greater gallantry and daring could be exhibited by any troops.

I cannot speak too highly of the coolness and intrepidity of Gen. BANKS himself during the whole of the engagement. He was in the front and exposed as much as any man in his command. His example was of the greatest benefit to his troops, and he merits and should receive the commendation of his Government.

Brigadier-General G.D. Bayard

Gens. Williams, Augur, Gordon, Crawford, Prince, Green and Geary behaved with conspicuous gallantry.

AUGUR and GEARY were severely wounded, and PRINCE, by losing his way in the dark, while passing from one flank to another, fell into the hands of the enemy.

I desire publicly to express my appreciation of the prompt and skillful manner in which Gens. McDOWELL and SIGEL brought forward their respective commands and established them on the field, and of their cheerful and hearty coöperation with me, from beginning to end.

Brig.-Gen. ROBERTS, Chief of Cavalry of this army, was with the advance of our forces on Friday and Saturday, and was conspicuous for his gallantry, and for the valuable aid he rendered to Gens. BANKS and CRAWFORD.

Our loss was about 1,500 killed, wounded and missing, of whom 290 were taken prisoners. As might be expected, from the character of the engagement, a very large proportion of these were killed.

The enemy's loss in killed, wounded and prisoners, we are now satisfied is much in excess of our own.

A full list of casualties will be transmitted as soon as possible, together with a detailed report, in which I shall endeavor to do justice to all.

JOHN POPE, Major-General Commanding.

REPORTS FROM CULPEPPER COURT-HOUSE.

Special Dispatch to the New-York Times.

WASHINGTON, Thursday, Aug. 14:

The following dispatches have just been received from Culpepper Court-house, dated Aug. 13:

The rebels have fallen back to Gordonsville, where it is supposed they will make a stand. Our cavalry to-day entered Orange Court-house. A number of rebel prisoners, stragglers, were captured by them.

A man named MATHEW PEASE, who was identified by some of our men as a bushwhacker, was arrested as a spy while prowling about our camps. He was sent to Gen. SIGEL's headquarters, in company with other prisoners. The prisoners captured state that JACKSON's force is 70,000 men. He was heavily reinforced from Richmond the day following the battle. They represent great dissatisfaction as existing among JACKSON's army, owing to the scarcity of food and raiment. Eleven dead rebels were found in the woods. They were buried by our troops.

Gen. PRINCE, though a prisoner, was not wounded in the late battle. He was taken prisoner while leading a charge with his brigade. The rebel Gen. WINDER was killed by a shell fired from Capt. McGILVERY's Sixth Maine Battery. He was partaking of lunch at the time, in a house occupied by the enemy as a signaling post. The shell killed several other officers who were sitting near him. The rebels were commanded by Gens. Jackson, Hill, Stuart and Ewell.

I have sent a list of 300 killed and wounded by mail.

Gen. POPE threatens to make quick work with correspondents, if they do not stop scribbling nonsense. He told me to warn them of that fact.

The rebels are to concentrate at Gordonsville.

WASHINGTON, Thursday, Aug. 14.

Letters from Culpepper contain no news of interest. On Saturday night, after the action, Dr. STEELE, of the Twenty-sixth New-York, while endeavoring to find his way to his regiment, encountered two rebel soldiers, fully armed. He sternly demanded a surrender, and they were so alarmed, apprehensive of their proximity to our forces, that they surrendered, and the doctor marched them into camp as prisoners.

ADDITIONAL ACCOUNTS OF THE BATTLE.

WAR DEPARTMENT, WASHINGTON, D. C., Thursday, Aug. 14, 1862.

The following has been received here from Cedar Mountain, 6 P. M., 13th:

Gen. MILROY and Gen. BUFORD, with their brigades of infantry and cavalry, followed the enemy beyond the Rapidan. Gen. JACKSON's baggage trains are seen in the distance, and it is said JACKSON will not make a stand this side of Orange Court-house.

Thirty deserters came within our lines this morning. Nearly all of them are from Louisiana and South Carolina regiments. They tell a very pitiful tale of cruelty, starvation, and distress, and say it will be impossible to hold the Southern army together three months longer. They confirm the reports of the prisoners taken in the late battle about the number of the killed and wounded, and say our artillery fire at night was terribly destructive.

Rev. K. P. SLAUGHTER, of Cedar Mountain, on the side at the foot of which the battle was fought, is a strong Union man, and an ardent advocate of the cause of colonization, His library was destroyed by the Rebel soldiers upon discovering among his papers letters favoring the abolition of Slavery.

Scouting parties from Gen. MILROY's Brigade passed the Rapidan yesterday, and nearly reached Orange Court-house, where a large body of rebels remained. The bodies of rebels are constantly found in the woods and corn-fields around the battle-ground. Some of our shells nearly reached the summit of Cedar Mountain, near which the battle was fought, and from which it takes its name.

FROM THE PRESS CORRESPONDENT.

CULPEPPER COURT-HOUSE, Va., Monday, Aug. 11—Midnight.

In an interview with some of our prisoners today they stated that the enemy had treated them with kindness; but one instance of gross outrage came under your correspondent's notice. It was that of Capt. O'BRIEN, of the Third Wisconsin Regiment, who was mortally wounded. The rebel Surgeon told him that he had no chance of living, gave him some water to drink, and left him on the field. Some rebel soldiers subsequently came up, took his watch, and cut his pocket out, containing $260, leaving him to die there. He was brought off the field under the flag of truce, but cannot survive the night. I had the statement from the dying man's lips.

The view of the battle-field was a sight never to be forgotten. It was full of horror. For nearly a mile the dead lay scattered or in heaps, many disemboweled, decapitated and mangled by shells. At the point where CRAWFORD's Brigade twice dashed on the enemy the sight was fearful.

The rebel General, CHARLES WINDER, was killed and Major SNOWDEN ANDREWS, of Baltimore, of Gen. EWELL's Staff, mortally wounded.

The advance lines of the enemy extended nearly up to the line of our batteries on the day of the battle.

A reporter of the Press, by missing his way, got further to the rear than laid down by the flag of truce, and was thus enabled to view the location of the enemy's forces. Their batteries, seven in number, occupy nearly the same positions as when they opened on us on Saturday. He learned that the rebel infantry were to the right of their batteries, and that a large rebel reserve was behind the mountain.

One of the rebel Generals told a Union officer he would be in Culpepper to-night, but up to the small hours of the morning he has not attempted to perform his promise.

It is now estimated that our wounded will reach twelve hundred men. Many amputations have been performed, and many have died from their wounds.

The atmosphere in the town is fetid with fever and perspiration.

Most of the wounded are comfortable. Every Surgeon with his assistants, are at their posts, and admirably have they performed their arduous duties. The Division of Medical Directors have managed the whole arrangements in such a manner that it is believed not a single wounded soldier has been unattended to, or left to suffer a moment longer than absolute necessity required.

The following statistics of Gen. WILLIAMS' command on the day of the battle are the only returns obtainable to-day:

GEN. CRAWFORD'S BRIGADE.

Tenth Maine Regiment—Went into the action with two field, twenty-one line officers and two acting Lieutenants. Present to-day: Two field and twelve line officers and 254 men. Capt. Cloudman and Lieut. Folsom are known to be killed. Capt. Adams, Capt. Nye, Lieut. Rankin and Lieut. Freman are wounded. Fifteen men are known to be killed and 140 wounded.

Forty-sixth Pennsylvania Regiment—Col. Knipe, Maj. Mathews, Capts. Eusebius, Luckenback and Brooks, Lieuts. Selheimer, Craig and Scott, wounded; Capts. Foulke and Griffiths, Lieuts. Greatrake, Wilson, Gorman, Selfridge and A. Caldwell, missing. The total in killed, wounded and missing reaches 246. Every company in this regiment suffered in nearly equal proportion.

Fifth Connecticut Regiment—Wounded and probably prisoners: Col. Chapman, Lieut.-Col. Stone and Major Blake. Missing: Capt. Corliss, Lieut. Chaney and Lieut. Doyle. Wounded: Capt. Packer, Capt. Lane, Lieut. Daniels, Lieut. Dutton, Lieut. Whitney, and Adjutant Smith.

Twenty-eighth New-York Regiment—There is no report of this regiment. It is completely broken up and has been removed from the field. The brave and noble Col. DONNELLY is now breathing his last. Lieut.-Col. BROWN suffered the amputation of his arm to-day.

GEN. GORDON'S BRIGADE.

Second Massachusetts Regiment—Went into action with 22 officers and 474 men. Capt. Abbot, Capt. Cary, Capt. Williams, Capt, Goodwin and Lieut. Perkins are known to be dead. One hundred and ten men are known to have been killed and wounded. Eighty are missing. Among the wounded are Lieut. Robertson, Lieut. Grafton, Lieut. Brownin and Lieut. Okey—all of whom are doing well.

Twenty-seventh Indiana Regiment—Went into action with 511 men and 15 officers. One officer was killed, 2 wounded and 1 is missing. Eleven men were killed, 29 were wounded and 32 are missing.

Third Wisconsin Regiment—Lieut.-Col. CRANE and Capt. O'BRIEN are killed; Maj. SCOTT is seriously wounded. Two officers are missing. This regiment went into action with 11 o[illegible] and 426 men. It was in the hottest of the battle. Lieut.-Col. CRANE was shot three times. Either of the wounds would probably have been fatal.

COTHRAN's Battery, attached to this brigade, lost three men.

On Saturday night, when the enemy shelled our camp, this battery fired four shots, which silenced the enemy. A Lieutenant, two men and eight horses belonging to the latter were found dead next morning.

REBEL ACCOUNTS.

The Battle Called by Them the Battle of Southwest Mountain—A Great Victory Claimed, of Course.

From the Richmond Dispatch, Aug. 12.

The prelude to the battle of Saturday evening occurred on Friday, in Culpepper County, beyond the Rapidan River, in a skirmish between the advance of our army and a large force of the enemy. The latter retreated with some loss in killed and wounded, and twenty-one prisoners fell into our hands, including three commissioned officers, who arrived here by way of Lynchburgh, on Sunday night. The pursuit was continued for some distance, and

Major-General John Buford

the Yankee forces made a stand at Southwest Mountain, near Mitchell's Station, about six miles beyond the Rapidan. Slight skirmishing was kept up on Saturday morning, and in the afternoon of that day, about 4 o'clock, an attack was made upon the enemy by a portion of the division of Gen. EWELL, and a brigade under Gen. C. S. WINDER. Over 300 prisoners were captured in this engagement, including thirty commissioned officers.

One of the latter admits that a Federal division was cut to pieces while endeavoring to surround the Stonewall Brigade, and the general belief is that the enemy's loss in killed and wounded is at least four times greater than ours. It was while bravely leading on the men under his command that Gen. WINDER was shot through the breast and almost instantly killed. At one moment the fate of his brigade seemed in doubt, when his supports came up, and the enemy was driven back under an impetuous onset. On Saturday night the division of Gen. A. P. HILL was engaged, and the whole Federal force retreated, the pursuit being kept up for a distance of some five miles. Heavy and rapid firing was heard after midnight, and the supposition is that a battle took place immediately on the Rappahannock River, near the line of Fauquier County.

The prisoners were sent back to Gordonsville, whence they were transferred by railroad to Richmond, guarded by a detachment of the First Maryland Regiment, under Capt. WM. GOLDSBOROUGH.

According to the statements of the prisoners, the force under POPE amounts to 40,000 men.

From the Richmond Enquirer, Aug. 12.

The news from JACKSON's army, which appeared in yesterday's issue, diffused a lively pleasure throughout our city; and well it might, for it told of a very handsome and most cheering victory, and in the right quarter! All honor to the laurel-crowned hero, and his glorious army!

Although "Stonewall" JACKSON was in the front of our new lines, and notwithstanding he was never known to lose time, or to idle away a single hour, yet the amateur Generals had already begun to indulge in heavy censures at the delay. Folly, stupidity, weakness, criminal trifling, &c., were the terms that were coming freely into use, although they fell on JACKSON and his foot-cavalry, whose fame fills the whole Confederacy! The result shows that JACKSON has not been idle. Those preparations and plans, which are as necessary to victory as are skill and courage in the battle itself, had to be completed. To the impatient, the time seemed to be lost; but as the plowman reaps the recompense of his toil in the harvest which follows, so JACKSON is now rewarded by success.

At the time of writing this, we have not received any additional particulars of the battle of Saturday. Such as may reach us before our paper goes to press, will appear in our news column. The battle must have been a hot one, as the heavy roar of artillery was heard in this vicinity for three hours commencing at 3 o'clock Saturday afternoon.

The capture of Gen. PRINCE and the other commissioned officers, will tend to bring the two warring powers to a speedy understanding as to the future policy of the war. LINCOLN will either relieve the hostages we now hold, by revoking his new war policy as set forth in his own General Orders and in those of POPE, or he will respond by counter-retaliation. This will require further action on our part, and the speedy result must be the discarding of all restraints on both sides, and a war of extermination. We hope, however, that our enemies are not so demented and demoniac as to have seriously resolved to force this upon us and upon themselves.

The New-York Times.

VOL. XI—NO. 3412.   NEW-YORK, SUNDAY, AUGUST 31, 1862.   PRICE THREE CENTS.

HIGHLY IMPORTANT.

Defeat of the Rebels on the Old Bull Run Battle-Ground.

DISPATCH FROM GEN. POPE.

A Terrific Battle on Friday, Lasting All Day.

The Combined Forces of the Enemy Engaged.

The Rebels Driven from the Field.

Our Losses Not Less than Eight Thousand Killed and Wounded.

The Rebel Losses Probably Double.

Important Captures Made by our Forces.

Retreat of the Rebels toward the Mountains on Friday Morning.

PROMPT PURSUIT BY GEN. POPE.

ANOTHER GREAT BATTLE YESTERDAY.

OFFICIAL DISPATCH FROM GEN. POPE.

HEADQUARTERS FIELD OF BATTLE,
GROVETON NEAR GAINESVILLE, Aug. 30, 1862.

To Major-Gen. Halleck, General-in-Chief, Washington, D. C.:

We fought a terrific battle here yesterday, *with the combined forces of the enemy,* which lasted with continuous fury from daylight until after dark, by which time *the enemy was driven from the field,* which we now occupy.

Our troops are too much exhausted to push matters, but I shall do so in the course of the morning, as soon as FITZ-JOHN PORTER'S corps come up from Manassas.

The enemy is still in our front, but badly used up.

We have lost not less than *eight thousand men killed and wounded,* and from the appearance of the field, *the enemy have lost at least two to our one.* He stood strictly on the defensive, and *every assault was made by ourselves.*

Our troops have behaved splendidly.

The battle was fought on the identical battle-field of Bull Run, which greatly increased the enthusiasm of our men.

The news just reaches me from the front that *the enemy is retreating toward the mountains.* I go forward at at once to see.

We have made great captures, but I am not able yet to form an idea of their extent.

JOHN POPE, Major-General Commanding.

DISPATCH FROM GEN. McDOWELL.

WASHINGTON, Friday, August 30.

Secretary CHASE received this afternoon, through Gen. POPE's messenger, the following note from Gen. McDOWELL, dated on battle field at 6:15, morning:

"DEAR GOVERNOR—Please telegraph Mrs. McDowELL that I have gone through a second battle of Bull Run, on the identical field of last year, and unhurt. The victory is decidedly ours.

Very sincerely,   IRVIN McDOWELL."

ANOTHER BATTLE YESTERDAY.

WASHINGTON, Aug. 30.

Information has reached Washington from private sources that Gen. POPE came up with and attacked the enemy again shortly after nine o'clock this morning.

Gen. FITZ-JOHN PORTER had probably arrived on the field by that time from Manassas, only seven miles distant.

The cannonading was distinctly heard in Washington.

The railroad was regularly run this forenoon from the town of Warrenton to Bristoe, so it is already clear that the only damage remaining to be repaired to the railroad is to build the Bull Run and Rappahannock bridges. The former should be completed to-night, and the latter may be in four or five days.

The news received from the army has occasioned the greatest excitement throughout this city.

Orders were issued by the Heads of the different Bureaus, calling upon the employes to repair to the battle-field, for the purpose of attending to the condition of our wounded.

The order required each man to provide himself with two days' rations.

A prompt response was made to the call, and not only the persons employed by the Government, but many others, left the city for the purpose stated.

Although the engagement with the enemy is of a most appallingly sanguinary character, yet such is the confidence of Union men in the skill and strength of our army, that an abiding faith in our ultimate success is everywhere discernible.

THE SECOND BULL RUN BATTLE.

WASHINGTON, Saturday, Aug. 30.

To-day's *Evening Star,* speaking of the battle of yesterday, says:

"The battle was continued by the army corps of Generals HEINTZELMAN, McDOWELL and SIGEL, on our side, against a rebel force believed to number from fifty to sixty thousand strong—that is, against the army corps of JACKSON, and, we presume, a portion of the rest of LEE's army that had succeeded in making its way down from White Plains through Thoroughfare Gap.

The location of the battle of the day was in the vicinity of Haymarket, and from Haymarket off in the direction of Sudley Church, or, in other words but a few miles northwest of the scene of the never to-be-forgotten battle of Bull Run.

HEINTZELMAN's Corps, if we are correctly informed, came up with the enemy's rear about 10 A. M., seven

Confederate Major-General James Longstreet set up 30,000 troops against the Union left flank. Reports of his presence were dismissed by General Pope.

miles from Centreville, which point he left at daybreak.

He found Stonewall JACKSON fighting with McDOWELL or SIGEL, or both, on the right, in the direction of Haymarket, the position they took by going north from Gainesville, to command the entrance to and exit from Thoroughfare Gap.

Our own informant, who left Centreville at 4 o'clock in the afternoon, a cool and clear-headed man, says that, up to that hour, the impression prevailed there that nothing had definitely resulted from the day's fighting, which, though continuous, had not been a very bloody battle.

Persons subsequently arriving, who were on the field of action themselves until 4 P. M., however, represent that the tide of success was decidedly with the Union army, which pushed the rebels successfully on both sides.

An impression prevails that the reserve of LEE's army, supposed to be from twenty to forty thousand strong, might suddenly appear near the field, and we know that the heavy corps under FITZ-JOHN PORTER was so posted that it could instantly move upon LEE with equal ease, whether attacking McDOWELL, SIGEL or HEINTZELMAN.

The railroad, we are happy to say, has already been repaired quite up to Bull Run, and supplies, etc., are now being transported over it to that point.

By midnight we have every reason to believe that the Bull Run bridge will again be passable, when the trains can again run to Manassas.

Ere evacuating Manassas, the rebels paroled the 700 Union prisoners they had taken since the commencement of the movement for which they are paying so dearly.

The rebels realized that prisoners in their present strait were an elephant in their hands, and wisely thus got rid of them.

These 700 prisoners covered all the stragglers they had taken, as well as the 500 of TAYLOR's Brigade."

WASHINGTON, Saturday, Aug. 30.

The following is gathered from private sources:

On Wednesday morning, or rather Tuesday night, a report reached Warrenton Junction that JACKSON was again in our rear, and that, instead of making an

Stonewall Jackson's raid on General Pope's base at Manassas gained valuable knowledge of Union troops for the Confederacy, and left the North with destruction.

attack and retiring, as his cavalry did on Friday night last, at Catlett's Station, he had taken up a position on the railroad near Bristor, four miles south of Manassas; had burned two railroad trains, torn up the railroad track, cut the telegraph, and took prisoners all the guards along the road.

These reports prove to have been true, and the events of Wednesday showed his determination not to be easily driven from the neighborhood.

It seems from what can be learned from the rebel wounded in our hands, that JACKSON and EWELL started from the vicinity of Warrenton Springs on Sunday, with three divisions, crossed the Rappahannock some six miles south of the Blue Ridge, and proceeded by way of Orleans and Salem to Bristor, making the distance in about two and a half days.

On reaching this point their first object of attack was the house of Mr. Lipscomb, where ten officers were stopping, and who were on the back porch at the time, smoking.

The house was attacked both front and rear, and the bullet-holes in the wood and plaster, with the fact that none of the party were wounded, showed what poor marksmen these rebel cavalry were. The entire party, however, with the exception of Capt. O. A. Tildenmonn, were taken prisoners.

The names of the officers taken prisoners are as follows:

Lieut.-Col. Pinxson, First New-York Volunteers.

Lieut. Allen, and two other Lieutenants of the same regiment.

A Lieutenant of the Fifty-Seventh Pennsylvania Regiment.

First Lieutenant of Company B, One Hundred and Fifth Pennsylvania Volunteers.

A Captain of the Fourth Maine Regiment.

Lieuts. Prendergast and Johnson of the Thirty-Eighth New-York Volunteers.

The next attack of the rebels was upon a company of the One Hundred and Fifth Pennsylvania Infantry and some dozen of Pennsylvania Cavalry, left to

guard the road, two or three of whom were killed, and the remainder are supposed to be captured.

A train of empty cars then came along from Warrenton, and was fired into by a regiment of infantry and one of cavalry, but escaped without serious injury.

Orders were then issued by JACKSON to tear up the railroad track, which was done, and a second train coming along, ran off the track, and was fired into.

A third train following ran into the second and was also fired into, and some persons on board were taken prisoners.

A fourth train made its appearance, but the Engineer suspected something wrong, stopped at a distance and blew a whistle, and being answered by one of the others, backed and returned toward Warrenton.

The two trains were then fired, under the direction of JACKSON, and entirely consumed, excepting the iron-work.

The rebels then proceeded a mile down the track, burned the bridge at Cattle Run, tore up some thirty feet of the track, and cut the telegraph.

They also burned the bridge across Broad Run, at Bristor.

On Wednesday morning, EWELL's Rebel Division was placed in position on each side of the railroad, having three batteries, one on the right, one on the left, and the other near the railroad, with infantry and cavalry between, the entire force being concealed behind brush-woods and the rail car track, with an open field in front.

Our troops sent down from Warrenton Junction to attack them consisted of HOOKER's Division, with a portion of KEARNEY's, but the latter, it is said, did not get a chance to enter into the contest.

Gen. HOOKER was in command, and not expecting the enemy to be in any large force, ordered a change through a piece of woods and into the cleared space, when a most murderous fire was opened upon him from the entire line of the rebels, their batteries throwing grape and canister, the most of

which, however, went over the heads of our troops; but the fire from the rebel line of infantry was very destructive, and some of HOOKER's regiments were compelled to fall back to the woods, but on being supported by others rallied, and, after firing several volleys, repeated the charge, when the rebels broke and retreated, our boys pursuing them, shouting and yelling.

The Third New-Jersey Brigade was commanded by Col. Carr, who had his horse shot under him while urging his men on to an attack. This is the Brigade, though somewhat changed, which so nobly held the extreme left at the battle of Williamsburgh for four hours, sustaining a loss there of over six hundred killed and wounded.

Adjutant BENEDICT's horse was also shot during the action.

Lieut.-Col. Potter, of the Second Regiment, Excelsior Brigade, was shot in the hand while leading his men.

The pursuit continued till dark, the enemy retreating towards Manassas.

The result of this action was that the enemy was beaten and driven from the field, sustaining a loss about equal to our own.

Our loss was about fifty killed and over two hundred wounded, a complete list of which was collected, but stolen.

The Second New-York regiment lost about ten officers and some ninety or one hundred killed and wounded.

The Excelsior Brigade suffered severely.

The physicians on the ground (Dr. Morrow of the Second New-Hampshire being the only name I can now recollect) exerted themselves to relieve the wounded; and although the accommodations to operate were very poor, they succeeded during the afternoon and night in attending to all.

Gen. Pope arrived on the ground late in the evening and proceeded towards the scene of action, but the fighting was then over and the enemy in full retreat.

Jackson had left for Manassas during the day with his division, where he pillaged the place, capturing a large number of prisoners, and burning every building, except the telegraph building and a few shanties, after taking off their own old rags, and putting on our good clothing, and helping themselves to food of all kinds, arms, equipments, and whatever else they could carry away out of the cars, about a hundred of which were at that place, for the greater part loaded with supplies for our army.

The rebels then set fire to all the cars, and they now present a mass of bleached ruins.

On their arrival, they found a portion of two New-Jersey Regiments of Infantry, which had arrived there during the forenoon. They immediately attacked them, our troops defending themselves for some time, but finding the number of the enemy so great, and that they were being flanked, they retreated towards Centreville, and got away with the loss of some forty wounded and about twelve killed. The rebels captured six hundred and twenty-five of them, but they were paroled yesterday morning just before the battle commenced.

The pursuit was continued towards Centreville on Thursday afternoon, and a squadron of the Second Pennsylvania Cavalry, with Gen. BIRNEY, was in the advance, and stopped at Centreville to inquire the route taken by the enemy. While there a woman waved a flag from the back window, at which signal a force of rebel cavalry, about 2,000 strong, under Gen. LEE, emerged from the woods. Our men had scarcely time to mount their horses and escape, coming down the road at full speed, the enemy in swift pursuit. They were followed until they came to where our infantry were drawn in line of battle on each side of the road, at which point the rebels received a volley which caused them to retreat at more than a double-quick.

Our troops took up the line of march, and followed the rebels during the night on the Gainesville or Warrenton road, and soon came in sight of the old Bull Run battle-ground in strong position, and under cover of the woods.

The action commenced about 9 o'clock, our batteries having been placed in position, and MILROY's Brigade having the advance, was ordered to charge the rebels through the woods, and to cross toward the railroad switch, when the enemy poured into our troops a perfect storm of grape and canister.

This caused them to fall back, but they soon rallied, and paid the enemy with interest.

The rebels here rose en masse behind the railroad track, and again caused our men to fall back, which they did behind HAMPTON's Pittsburgh Battery, which opened upon the rebels terrifically. The enemy were at the time only about thirty yards distant, and

the effect of the fire destroyed at least 600 of them. In this action, however, HAMPTON lost one of his guns. He had to change his position to the left, as he was unable to maintain himself under the fire which the rebels poured into him.

The battle in other quarters raged furiously; the general result of which has already been stated from other sources.

The position of the forces on Thursday night remained about the same as it was at the commencement of the action.

The loss on both sides is heavy.

Gen. DURYEA, while engaged in making a reconnoissance to-day, was wounded in the hand.

The fighting up to 12 o'clock to-day was of a desultory character.

We occupy the ground where the rebels had buried their dead.

PREVIOUS NEWS IN WASHINGTON.

From the Washington Star of Friday Evening.

PHILADELPHIA, Saturday, Aug. 30.

We have information that satisfies us that the rebel force that suddenly appeared between the position of the army of Gen. POPE, and at Bristoe and Manassas, on Tuesday night last, was the army corps of JACKSON, and STUART's independent cavalry corps. They consisted of infantry and artillery, and marched about thirty thousand strong from near Waterloo, on the head waters of the Rappahannock, around by White Plains to Manassas, about forty miles in two days, without wagons, tents, blankets, or even knapsacks, thus leaving their baggage of every description to be transported by wagons, with the other army corps of LEE's following on behind them.

Instead of fighting merely a portion of STUART's Cavalry at Manassas, on the day before yesterday, TAYLOR's Brigade were actually confronted by a greater portion of JACKSON's corps d'armée, Maj.-Gens. Jackson, Ewell, Talliaferro, A. P. Hill, and Stuart, and the General-in-Chief, Robert Lee, or his son, Brig.-Gen. FITZHUGH LEE, being present at Manassas during the engagement.

Yesterday, at 1 o'clock P.M., JACKSON's advance occupied Fairfax Court House in force of cavalry, and had collected their own wounded of the action of the day before with TAYLOR, if not their wounded of the engagement on the same day with HOOKER, and also the prisoners they took from TAYLOR.

In the afternoon, about 800 of this cavalry force under STUART in person, moved down from Fairfax Court-house to Vienna.

HOOKER's battle, of the day before yesterday, was with EWELL's division, and was a gratifying success.

Maj.-Gen. POPE, by 9½ o'clock yesterday morning, had concentrated his very large army, so as to sadly interfere with the calculations upon which the rebel Generals must have ventured their bold and extraordinary movement.

At 4 P. M. yesterday an engagement commenced between POPE and JACKSON's rear or LONGSTREET's advance, somewhere about Manassas. If with the former, then HEINTZELMAN's Corps d'Armée, or a portion of it, were engaged on our side. If with the latter, then McDOWELL or SIGEL, or both, commenced it. It continued through the balance of the afternoon.

We had gotten McDOWELL's force, including SIGEL's probably, between JACKSON's and LONGSTREET's front, and had also all the rest of his army well up within supporting distance. Thus it continued through the balance of the afternoon.

Facts within our knowledge lead to the impression that in twenty-four hours direct communication will have been established between Washington and Maj.-Gen. POPE's army; more especially as there are signs that JACKSON's army corps is endeavoring to proceed northwardly, as though making for the experiment of opposing the reëstablishment of such communication with his immediate front, with POPE's army practically between him and the other rebel corps d'armée.

We may add that Gen. McCLELLAN is disposing of his heavy Union force around Washington and Alexandria, and the fortifications, so as to make it play an important part in the eventful drama of the hour.

Railroad destruction at Manassas.

In the battle of yesterday, the attack certainly came from our side.

CARE FOR THE WOUNDED.

WASHINGTON, Saturday Aug. 30.

Hundreds of the convalescents of the various hospitals reached their quarters to-day, and will be sent out of Washington to make room for patients from the recent battle-fields, who are already arriving.

The conduct of Maj.-Gen. POPE is highly commended in Government as well as in other quarters.

Between five hundred and a thousand Governmen Clerks repaired to the battle-field, in compliance with a request from the War Department, not in pursuance of an order, as erroneously stated in a previous dispatch, this afternoon, the report having reached here that the dead and wounded on both sides needed attention.

Col. PULESTON, the military agent of Pennsylvania, accompanied by Majors GILLILAND and PINKERTON, and a number of other Pennsylvanians, left immediately on the receipt of the news for Manassas, with large supplies of stimulants and hospital stores for the wounded.

The Pennsylvania Relief Association also sent off with alacrity quantities of stores in the charge o agents.

Dr. PAGE, of the Columbus Hospital, left this evening for Centreville, in charge of two hundred ambulances and the citizen nurses from the different Government departments.

Dr. WEBSTER, of the Douglas Hospital, also left for the battle-field in charge of a large train of medical supplies and the Citizen Volunteer Surgeons of this District.

Gen. WADSWORTH has taken possession of all the hacks in this city and sent them forward as a train to transport the sick and wounded to this city.

OUR CORRESPONDENCE FROM THE FIELD.

THE GUERRILLA RAID UPON THE ORANGE AND ALEXANDRIA RAILROAD—THE ATTACK NEAR WHITE PLAINS—CAPTURE OF A NEW-YORK BATTERY AT MANASSAS—THE FIGHT AT BULL RUN, &c.

HEADQUARTERS IN THE FIELD, BETWEEN ALEXANDRIA AND BRISTOE STATION, Thursday, P. M., Aug. 28, 1862.

I have fortunately been able to obtain some reliable and interesting details of the transactions during Tuesday night and a portion of yesterday, (Wednesday,) on the line of the Orange and Alexandria Railroad and vicinity. Tuesday evening, between 5 and 8 o'clock, five trains of empty cars were captured and mostly destroyed by a rebel cavalry force on the road between Bristoe Station and Manassas Junction, and on the same evening the enemy destroyed the bridge across Broad River, and subsequently the bridges across other small creeks on the railroad. There were stationed at Manassas Junction, Tuesday, the Twelfth Pennsylvania Cavalry, numbering between 500 and 600 men, Col. WHITE, and the First New-York Battery—10 pieces—with about 590 men to serve them. At 5 o'clock, a dispatch was received by telegraph from Warrenton Junction, directing the cavalry to proceed immediately to White Plains, (15 miles,) on the Manassas road, and keep a sharp look out for the enemy, who, it was understood, had crossed the Rappahannock in force on Sunday, and by the way of Jeffersonton and Little Washington, was making his way for some point on the line of the Orange and Alexandria Railroad, with a view, no doubt, to divide our forces and isolate the command of Gen. POPE—a position which the commander of the Union forces desired him to take, and a fatal one to the enemy it is certainly believed to be. The Pennsylvania cavalry left for the point directed, but finding none of the enemy at White Plains, at a late hour the corps started to return to the Junction. When within eight or nine miles of the latter place, they found a corps of about 1,000 cavalry, supposed to be commanded by FITZHUGH LEE, drawn up to dispute their further progress. A brisk skirmish took place, when our cavalry cut their way through the rebel ranks, losing a number in killed, wounded and prisoners. There was a kind of running fight kept up until the Junction was reached, at about 1 o'clock A. M. of Wednesday, when the rebels apparently retired satisfied. The cavalry fell back to a position one mile north of the Junction, known as BEAUREGARD'S Headquarters, and were under arms all night, without knowing what had transpired at the Junction during their absence at White Plains. In this interval the rebels had fallen upon the First New-York Artillery by surprise—the officer in command supposing the approaching force to be our own cavalry until too late—and captured eight of their ten guns. This was not done, however, until after a most sanguinary resistance, resulting in the killing and wounding of quite a number on both sides. A member of the Pennsylvania cavalry, not knowing that the Junction was in possession of the rebels, walked very deliberately to the plane at sunrise, and finding himself in **a trap, coolly asked the first rebel he met "how things were going," and in reply the rebel soldier said, "All right—we have had lots of fun and plunder." Our soldier then attempted to set loose a number of Government horses tied in a stable, when an officer said, "That is not one of our men—shoot him." At about this time the two guns saved from the New-York Battery commenced throwing shell, and this soldier escaped and reached his own command. It was now 7 o'clock Wednesday morning. The rebels occupied the earthworks near the Junction, but after a time advanced from their position and made an unsuccessful attempt to take the remaining guns of the New-York Battery. A running fight was kept up along the line of the railroad, our troops gradually falling back until near mid-day, when at a point one mile south of Fairfax Station, they were met by a force of infantry and artillery under the command of Brig. Gen. TAYLOR, of New-Jersey, and the rebels were driven back to Manassas Junction forthwith. A fact especially worthy of notice in this connection is, that upon the person of a prisoner captured was found a copy of the identical dispatch sent by telegraph from Warrenton Junction, between 4 and 5 o'clock P. M. of Tuesday, directing the cavalry at Manassas Junction to leave for White Plains, so that they were enabled to attack the place when the least resistance could be offered. It is believed by many that this dispatch could not have been obtained in any other way than through the agency of some employe of the Government.**

Of the fight that took place Wednesday afternoon, with Gen. TAYLOR'S force, on the road between Manassas Junction and Bull Run, and at the latter place, but little reliable information can be obtained at this time. The engagement was a sharp and deadly one —the rebels holding their position at night; but those who ought to know what occurred this morning look very good-natured, and hence we, who are in the dark, draw the inference that the rebels got their dessert this morning. The rebel force in action at Bull Run, Wednesday evening, is believed to have been about 5,000 men, principally cavalry and artillery. Our force consisted of ten regiments of infantry, and ten guns. Gen. TAYLOR was so badly wounded in one of his legs, by the explosion of a shell, that the leg was amputated to-day. The Eleventh and Twelfth Ohio Regiments, it is said, suffered the most the latter having, according to a statement of a member, eighty wounded and twelve killed. The wildest rumors were circulated in Alexandria to-day about the result of the fight yesterday and this morning, but there is no occasion for any alarm. A force of —— men left the vicinity of Alexandria early this morning for the scene of action—a force which, with that under Gen. POPE'S immediate command, is sufficient to crush a very respectable force of the enemy. I shall send forward additional details as soon as anything reliable can be obtained. The excitement was somewhat intensified in Alexandria last night, by the 12th Virginia Cavalry rushing into the city in a panic; and the excitement was again renewed this morning by the return of a train of cars that started for Manassas Junction. The train was fired upon when fifteen miles out, and returned.

I escaped from the Rappahannock just at the right moment. Had I been 20 minutes later on Tuesday night, I should have been captured by the rebels. The train that kept us company all the way up was nabbed. It is supposed that JACKSON had nearly his whole force near White Plains. If so there is no escape for them, so far as I can see. POPE must have 200,000 well-disciplined troops south of JACKSON. There are 75,000 fresh troops encamped about Washington, and then there is an immense force of tried men—say 50,000 men—between this point and JACKSON'S position. Gen. McCLELLAN reached Alexandria Wednesday morning, and was at the telegraph office writing dispatches—orders—nearly all night. He can write with facility with either hand. To-day he is confined to his room by reason of slight indisposition. The rebels captured a saddle of mine at Manassas Junction, and a small bundle of papers and clothing. They were placed on the train just behind the one in which I took passage, by mistake. I hope that HALLECK'S infamous order about correspondents will be modified soon. It is very unsatisfactory to be compelled to obtain information as we do now. The Tenth New-York Cavalry, 750 men (new corps), is now passing to the front. They are the finest set of men, and best mounted, in the service. They elicit the admiration of every one.

New regiments are rolling in upon us here almost every hour in the day—quite as fast as they can be accommodated. Three hundred paroled prisoners, I suppose, left Washington yesterday for Dixie, *via* Fortress Monroe. But these matters you get by telegraph.

The reports in the *Tribune* of the fighting on the Rappahannock are, for the most part, grossly erroneous.

THE OPERATIONS OF GEN. TAYLOR'S BRIGADE AT BULL RUN AND VICINITY, WEDNESDAY, AUG. 27 —JACKSON COMPLETELY CUT OFF ON THURSDAY, BY GENERALS HOOKER AND KEARNEY.

FAIRFAX COURT-HOUSE, Friday, Aug. 29, 1862.

In my last I gave you a correct and somewhat detailed account of the operations of the Twelfth Pennsylvania Cavalry, and First New-York Battery, at Manassas Junction and vicinity, on Wednesday, the 27th inst., down to the time when they were relieved by the arrival of reinforcements. To continue in order as the events occurred, Brig.-Gen. TAYLOR, in command of the New-Jersey Brigade, 1,600 strong —*all infantry*—left Alexandria early on Wednesday morning, to reinforce the command at Manassas Junction. When one mile north of Bull Run Bridge, they found the track obstructed by the *débris* of a destroyed train of cars, and, disembarking, proceeded on foot toward Manassas Junction. Upon arriving in sight of the latter place, they saw the Stars and Stripes flying, and heard the roar of cannon; as the flag was there, and no shots were directed toward Gen. TAYLOR'S column, that officer concluded that our forces were firing upon a force of the enemy beyond, and consequently pressed forward at a double-quick. Too late the discovery was made that the troops at the Junction were rebels, and that the raising of the "Stars and Stripes," and the aiming of their guns in an opposite direction was a ruse of the enemy. When within half gunshot distance, the rebels opened upon Gen. TAYLOR'S command, right, left and front, with the eight 32-pound cannon which they had captured a few hours before from the New-York battery. Their cavalry immediately fired a volley and charged at the same time, which for a moment created a panic in our ranks. Gen. TAYLOR speedily obtained order, and gradually fell back to Bull Run Bridge, he having no artillery or cavalry to use against the rebels. At the latter place Gen. TAYLOR was reinforced by the arrival of the Eleventh and Twelfth Ohio Volunteers— the latter a cavalry corps—and quite a brisk fight took place, when the rebels were finally repulsed. Gen. TAYLOR was wounded in the leg while gallantly rallying his men against a superior force of the enemy, composed of cavalry and artillery. Late at night the commander of our forces, learning that the rebels had received large reinforcements, fell back to Fairfax Station, and at 11 o'clock at night moved on to this place, as the advance of a large force which left Alexandria on Thursday morning. The rebels had disappeared.

It is alleged that the Twelfth Pennsylvania Cavalry acted in the most scandalous manner at Bull Run, and the bulk of the regiment made a rapid retreat toward Alexandria. Of the truth of this, however, I cannot vouch.

JACKSON CUT OFF.

The movements on Thursday, the 28th, were more important than any that have taken place on this line during the present campaign. POPE'S strategy is being developed. Gens. HOOKER and KEARNEY, with their thoroughly disciplined commands, advanced upon the rear of JACKSON and have forced him toward Leesburgh, where he is completely cut off, and must, with his whole force, be captured or destroyed, unless some stupendous error is made on our side. JACKSON will **probably get into Washington somewhat sooner than he expected, and in a manner less agreeable than he anticipated.**

There is heavy firing northwest of this place this morning, and it is supposed that our forces have compelled JACKSON to face about and fight.

The New-York Times.

VOL. XI—NO. 3413.   NEW-YORK, MONDAY, SEPTEMBER 1, 1862.   PRICE TWO CENTS.

ANOTHER BATTLE WEEK.

Desperate Battles on Thursday, Friday and Saturday.

Defeat of the Rebels on the Bull Run Battle-Ground.

Our Losses Not Less than Eight Thousand.

Important Captures Made by our Forces.

The Enemy Heavily Reinforced on Friday Night.

Renewal of the Fighting on Saturday.

Gen. Pope Forced to Fall Back to Centreville.

ARRIVAL OF REINFORCEMENTS.

No Fighting of Consequence Yesterday.

PARTIAL LISTS OF KILLED AND WOUNDED.

HEAVY LOSSES AMONG OUR OFFICERS.

Arrival of a Thousand Prisoners in Washington.

THE GREAT BATTLE OF FRIDAY.

OFFICIAL DISPATCH FROM GEN. POPE.

HEADQUARTERS FIELD OF BATTLE, GROVETON NEAR GAINESVILLE, Aug. 30, 1862.

Major-Gen. Halleck, *General-in-Chief, Washington, D. C.:*

We fought a terrific battle here yesterday, *with the combined forces of the enemy,* which lasted with continuous fury from daylight until after dark, by which time *the enemy was driven from the field,* which we now occupy.

Our troops are too much exhausted to push matters, but I shall do so in the course of the morning, as soon as FITZ-JOHN PORTER'S corps come up from Manassas.

The enemy is still in our front, but badly used up.

We have lost not less than *eight thousand men killed and wounded,* and from the appearance of the field, *the enemy have lost at least two to our one.* He stood strictly on the defensive, and *every assault was made by ourselves.*

Our troops have behaved splendidly.

The battle was fought on the identical battlefield of Bull Run, which greatly increased the enthusiasm of our men.

The news just reaches me from the front that *the enemy is retreating toward the mountains.* I go forward at once to see.

We have made great captures, but I am not able yet to form an idea of their extent.

JOHN POPE, Major-General Commanding.

DISPATCH FROM GEN. M'DOWELL.

WASHINGTON, Friday, August 30.

Secretary CHASE received this afternoon, through Gen. POPE'S messenger, the following note from Gen. MCDOWELL, dated on battle field at 6:15, morning:

DEAR GOVERNOR—Please telegraph Mrs. MCDOWELL that I have gone through a second battle of Bull Run, on the identical field of last year, and unhurt. The victory is decidedly ours.

Very sincerely,   IRVIN McDOWELL.

THE SECOND BATTLE OF BULL RUN

The Washington *Star,* of Saturday evening, in speaking of the engagement of Friday, says:

"The battle was continued by the army corps of Generals HEINTZELMAN, McDOWELL and SIGEL, on our side, against a rebel force believed to number from fifty to sixty thousand strong—that is, against the army corps of JACKSON, and, we presume, a portion of the rest of LEE'S army that had succeeded in making its way down from White Plains through Thoroughfare Gap.

The location of the battle of the day was in the vicinity of Haymarket, and from Haymarket off in the direction of Sudley Church, or, in other words, but a few miles northwest of the scene of the never-to-be-forgotten battle of Bull Run.

HEINTZELMAN'S Corps, if we are correctly informed, came up with the enemy's rear about 10 A. M., seven miles from Centreville, which point he left at daybreak.

He found Stonewall JACKSON fighting with McDOWELL or SIGEL, or both, on the right, in the direction of Haymarket, the position they took by going north from Gainesville, to command the entrance to and exit from Thoroughfare Gap.

Our own informant, who left Centreville at 4 o'clock in the afternoon, a cool and clear-headed man, says that, up to that hour, the impression prevailed there that nothing had definitely resulted from the day's fighting, which, though continuous, had not been a very bloody battle.

Persons subsequently arriving, who were on the field of action themselves until 4 P. M., however, represent that the tide of success was decidedly with the Union army, which pushed the rebels successfully on both sides.

An impression prevails that the reserve of LEE'S army, supposed to be from twenty to forty thousand strong, might suddenly appear near the field, and we know that the heavy corps under FITZ-JOHN PORTER was so posted that it could instantly move upon LEE with equal ease, whether attacking McDOWELL, SIGEL or HEINTZELMAN.

The railroad, we are happy to say, has already been repaired quite up to Bull Run, and supplies, etc., are now being transported over it to that point.

By midnight we have every reason to believe that

Troops commanded by Major-General John Gibbon put up a stout defense on Henry House Hill, allowing Federal troops to escape the advancing Confederate sweep.

the Bull Run bridge will again be passable, when the trains can again run to Manassas.

Ere evacuating Manassas, the rebels paroled the 700 Union prisoners they had taken since the commencement of the movement for which they are paying so dearly. The rebels realized that prisoners in their present strait were an elephant in their hands, and wisely thus got rid of them.

These 700 prisoners covered all the stragglers they had taken, as well as the 500 of TAYLOR'S Brigade."

THE GREAT BATTLE OF SATURDAY.

WASHINGTON, Friday, Aug. 30.

Information has reached Washington from private sources that Gen. POPE came up with and attacked the enemy again shortly after nine o'clock this morning.

Gen. FITZ-JOHN PORTER had probably arrived on the field by that time from Manassas, only seven miles distant.

The cannonading was distinctly heard in Washington.

The railroad was regularly run this forenoon from the town of Warrenton to Bristow, so it is already clear that the only damage remaining to be repaired to the railroad is to build the Bull Run and Rappahannock bridges. The former should be completed to-night, and the latter may be in four or five days.

The news received from the army has occasioned the greatest excitement throughout this city.

Although the engagement with the enemy is of a most appallingly sanguinary character, yet such is the confidence of Union men in the skill and strength of our army, that an abiding faith in our ultimate success is everywhere discernible.

WASHINGTON, Sunday, Aug. 31—10:55 A. M.

The enemy was heavily reinforced yesterday, and attacked Gen. POPE'S army before the arrival of Gens. FRANKLIN and SUMNER.

The attack was boldly met, and a severe battle followed. The advantage, on the whole, was with the enemy, [and Gen.] POPE fell back to Centreville with his whole army in good order.

He has been joined at Centreville by FRANKLIN, and SUMNER was on the march to him last night. He occupies the strongest position in the vicinity of Washington, and is expected promptly to renew the contest and repeat the successes of Friday.

Every effort should be used to hasten the forwarding of the new troops.

THE OPERATIONS OF SUNDAY.

WASHINGTON, Sunday, Aug. 31.

Gen. POPE'S statement that HEINTZELMAN'S Corps would move on the enemy at daylight to-day, is confirmed by the heavy firing heard from that vicinity. Rumors of various successes have reached here, but need confirmation.

Yesterday rebel scouts were seen at Langley's, in the vicinity of Chain Bridge!

Every precaution has been taken to prevent a surprise in that direction.

The impression prevails that the rebels have been entrapped, and the result of the recent manœuvring is looked for with intense eagerness.

WASHINGTON, Sunday, Aug. 31—Evening.

Information received here indicates that there has been but little, if any, fighting to-day.

Our army is well concentrated and the men in good condition and spirits.

REPORTS FROM ALEXANDRIA.

ALEXANDRIA, Saturday, Aug. 30.

There has been heavy firing heard to-day in the direction of Centreville, and the contest of yesterday was undoubtedly renewed this morning.

Telegraphic communication has been reëstablished to Mannssas, and the cars are running as far as Bull Run. The bridge and railroad are being repaired with the greatest dispatch, and trains will probably extend their trips to-morrow.

There are still a large number of troops in Alexandria awaiting transportation to the field of battle. A Pennsylvania Brigade, comprising the One Hundred and Twenty-third, One Hundred and Thirty-third, One Hundred and Thirty-fourth and One Hundred and Thirty-sixth Regiments, under Gen. COOK, were to march to-day.

Those who were able to be moved from the Alexandria hospitals have been taken to Washington, to make room for the wounded who are to arrive to-day.

REBEL PRISONERS IN WASHINGTON.

WASHINGTON, Sunday, Aug. 31.

About a thousand rebel prisoners have just arrived in the city, representing nearly all the seceded States.

OUR CORRESPONDENCE FROM THE FIELD.

THE MOVEMENT ON FAIRFAX COURT-HOUSE—A LETTER FROM THE REBEL COL. LEE—CAPTURE OF MASSACHUSETTS SOLDIERS—REBEL SPIES CAPTURED—NO STORES LOST AT RAPPAHANNOCK STATION, ETC.

FAIRFAX COURT-HOUSE, Friday, Aug. 29, 1862.

The troops which had been concentrated at Fairfax Station, yesterday morning commenced a movement upon this place—to find the enemy. In the woods, just above the village, a large force of rebel cavalry was discovered, and skirmishing was at once commenced. The Second New-York Artillery delivered one fire and skedaddled; the Twelfth Pennsylvania Cavalry discharged their duty but little better. The Fourteenth Massachusetts, Col. GREENE, of Essex County, seized two guns of the Eleventh New-York Battery, and soon compelled the rebels to retire to cover. The Fourteenth then passed into the woods, occasionally exchanging shots with the enemy, and remained until late at night, when the rebels retired, and our forces were ordered upon another expedition. But few of our men were killed at this point, and only some thirty wounded, so far as known. A rebel corps, un-

Major-Geneal Phil Kearney was killed at the Second Battle of Bull Run.

der Col. LEE, during the day, captured from the Fourteenth Massachusetts a one-horse hospital wagon, a four-horse ambulance, and the following-named persons, all of whom were at a house used as a temporary hospital.

Surgeon DANA and Assistant-Surgeon MASON, and

JUDSON RILEY, hospital steward.

JOHN B. WORTHING of Lawrence, driver of ambulance.

HENRY FOLSOM, of Lawrence, driver of hospital wagon, and JONATHAN FORCE, of Ipswich.

The surgeons and assistant-surgeons were at once sent back, by Col. LEE, who sent a note to Col. GREENE, with his compliments, saying that he (LEE) would have bagged the whole command had not Col. GREENE been so sharp. LEE and GREENE were together at West Point.

During Thursday evening the Fourteenth Massachusetts captured half a dozen spies within their lines, two of whom were in the tops of trees, observing the movement of our troops. They have been sent forward to Washington. The Fourteenth has been stationed for a long time in the fortifications near Harper's Ferry, and although only a few days in the field, it has rendered efficient service, especially in saving Gen. BANKS' baggage train on Tuesday night last. But for the prompt advance of this corps, the whole train, numbering several hundred wagons, would undoubtedly have been lost.

All the bridges on the railroad between Fairfax Station and Warrenton Junction have been destroyed by the rebels within the last two days. At Manassas Junction on Tuesday night they succeeded in destroying a considerable quantity of commissary stores, but elsewhere their raids upon the railroad has not amounted to much. I see that the correspondent of a cotemporary states that a large amount of commissary stores were destroyed by our troops at Rappahannock Station and Bealeton Station, to prevent the rebels from having the benefit of them. This is a mistake. Nearly every article of value was safely removed to the rear from both of the stations named.

As I write there is heavy firing off to the northwest of us, and I must close. *Don't be surprised, however if in my next is recorded the capture of the arch-rebel Jackson.*

Our pickets were attacked last night and driven in at Burke's Station, between Fairfax and Alexandria. There was tall running on both sides and nobody hurt. A man who walked from Warrenton Junction to Fairfax Station to-day, says that he did not catch a glimpse of a rebel.

A DISASTER IN KENTUCKY.

Defeat of Our Forces Under General Manson.

Six Regiments Engaged Against a Rebel Force of 15,000 or 20,000.

RETREAT OF OUR FORCES TO LEXINGTON.

CINCINNATI, Sunday, Aug. 31.

Friday afternoon, the rebels, beyond Richmond, Ky., drove in our cavalry. Gen. MANSON, with the Sixty-ninth and Seventy-first Indiana, moved up, and after throwing a few shells, the enemy retreated rapidly beyond Rogersville, leaving one gun behind. MANSON bivouacked for the night, and, on Saturday morning, advanced with two regiments and four guns, and coming up with the enemy, an artillery fight began, with heavy loss on both sides. The enemy attempted to turn our left flank, when sharp fighting occurred between tee skirmishers.

The Sixty-ninth Indiana advanced through a dense fire of shot and shell, to the relief of our skirmishers, and behaved like old soldiers; but the rebels finally turned our left flank and advanced in full force on our column. Gen. MANSON ordered a retreat; fell back three miles and re-formed in line of battle on high hills, with artillery in position on the right and left flanks.

The firing by artillery was recommenced and kept up by both sides very briskly. After fighting about two hours, the enemy advanced on our right flank, under cover of the woods, and after severe fighting succeeded in turning it. Retreat immediately took place to the original camping ground. Here Gen. NELSON came up, and after great efforts succeeded in rallying the men, and formed another line of battle. Our artillery ammunition was nearly exhausted, and some of the guns were kept without a man to work them—all having been killed or wounded.

Gen. MANSON was wounded at about 3 P. M., when the men again fell back, retreating to Lexington. The enemy's force numbered 15,000 to 20,000. The Federal forces engaged were the Ninety-fifth Ohio, Twelfth, Sixteenth, Sixty-sixth, Sixty-ninth and Seventy-first Indiana, and MUNDY'S and METCALF'S Cavalry. The loss in killed and wounded is heavy on both sides. The number is not yet known.

Lieut.-Col. TOPPING, Maj. KEMBLE, of the Seventy-first Indiana, were killed.

Gen. WRIGHT left this morning to take the field. Gen. WALLACE leaves to-night to join him. A large number of regiments are on route to Lexington.

MEDICAL SUPPLIES FOR THE FIELD.

WASHINGTON, Sunday, Aug. 31.

Forty-three wagon-loads of hospital supplies left here Saturday evening for the battle-field. Medical Inspector COOLIDGE, Surgeon PAGE, Assistant-Surgeon WEBSTER and other medical officers of the army and private physicians, have proceeded to the same locality.

CARE OF THE CONVALESCENTS.

WASHINGTON, Sunday, Aug. 31.

The following was issued this evening from the Medical Director's office:

MEDICAL DIRECTOR'S OFFICE, MILITARY DISTRICT OF }
WASHINGTON, Aug. 31, 1862. }

All persons who are willing to receive into their houses convalescent soldiers whom it may be necessary to remove from the hospitals in order to make room for the wounded from the recent battles near the city, will please inform this office of their names, residence, and the number of such convalescents they can receive and provide for.

JOHN CAMPBELL, Surgeon U. S A.,
Medical Director.

The New-York Times.

VOL. XI.–NO. 3414.   NEW-YORK, TUESDAY, SEPTEMBER 2, 1862.   PRICE TWO CENTS.

THE WAR NEWS.

NO FIGHTING YESTERDAY.

OUR ARMY HEAVILY REINFORCED.

The Union Forces Concentrated at Centreville.

GENERAL BANKS SAFE

Details of the Recent Engagements.

LISTS OF THE KILLED AND WOUNDED.

Commodore Wilkes Demolishes City Point.

Movements of the Western Guerrillas Checked.

THE STATE OF AFFAIRS AT ALEXANDRIA.

CARE FOR THE WOUNDED.

NEWS VIA ALEXANDRIA.

ALEXANDRIA, Sunday, Aug. 31.

According to all accounts Stonewall JACKSON, yesterday, succeeded in forcing his way through the National troops surrounding him, and effected a junction with the remainder of the Confederate forces. This result was not attained without fearful loss on both sides, as the most desperate fighting took place.

From all that can be learned, in the absence of any regular report, the corps of Gens. McDOWELL, HEINTZELMAN, PORTER and SIGEL were engaged, the former having the left, the latter the right, and the others operating about the centre.

The principal part of the fighting seems to have been on the left and centre.

The left was thrown up from Manasses Junction toward Thoroughfare Gap, the right at about Centreville, and the centre on the old Bull Run battle-field out from Manassas.

The action was commenced by the enemy opening his batteries upon our left, between 1 and 2 o'clock in the afternoon.

Their guns were strongly and advantageously posted upon a ridge, while our batteries had to fire from the open plain. Gen. MORELL's Division supported our batteries at this point.

After some severe cannonading, Gen. BUFORD's Brigade of Cavalry, comprising the First Michigan, the First Virginia, and the First Vermont Cavalry were ordered to our extreme left to reconnoitre, and guard against any attempt to turn our left flank, which movement was threatened by the enemy.

Riding beyond our left, where our infantry were formed close behind our batteries—which were playing with great precision upon the enemy, while our troops were cheering vociferously—our cavalry reached a slight eminence, and were about to send out a detachment to explore, when the enemy were seen coming up in force along the line of the adjacent woods.

A rebel battery was seen to whirl into position, and then came shell thrown into the midst of our cavalry, followed by canister and grape.

Thus was discovered the intention of the enemy to attempt a flank movement.

Long lines of rebel infantry could plainly be seen hurrying up to take position, and soon other rebel batteries were brought up, and opened upon our left.

Our cavalry, forced to retire, retreated behind a low ridge, but the clouds of dust revealing their place of retreat, the rebels continued shelling them, and another change of position was made.

Here a body of cavalry were observed riding toward the spot, and the sabres of our cavalry were drawn to meet the coming foe. The squadron proved to be friends—the Fourth New-York Cavalry. Where they had come from, as Gen. SIGEL was on the right, was and is a mystery. They reported the rebel cavalry under Gen. STUART as about making a charge.

The New-York Cavalry fell in behind Gen. BUFORD's Brigade, the bugles sounded, and over the hill galloped our men to meet the advancing rebels. As our men approached them, the rebel cavalry discharged double-barrelled shot guns and then met us in full charge. Our men broke the enemy's line and pursued them. The rebels rallied in splendid style and dashed forward again to meet the charge. Again their line was broken, and as our cavalry was preparing to charge again the rebels opened fire upon them from their batteries and with musketry, compelling them to retire.

Meanwhile, our left had given way, and was on the retreat, passing the cavalry.

A battery, which had run short of ammunition, was on the point of being captured, but under the determined resistance of our cavalry it was safely brought off.

The troops fell back upon Gen. FRANKLIN's Division, which had just come up, and were formed in line to prevent straggling and anything like a panic.

Had Gen. FRANKLIN's corps arrived two hours ear-

lier upon the field, the result of the day's fighting would have been different.

The fact of Gen. STUART's Cavalry being armed with double-barreled shot-guns is proved by a number of the guns being captured and several of our cavalry having buckshot wounds.

Col. BROADHEAD, commanding the First Michigan Cavalry, was captured.

Lieut. MERRIAM was wounded and taken prisoner.

Lieut. MORSE was killed.

Gen. FRANKLIN's Division retired to Centreville after preventing confusion and giving our retreating troops time to rally.

During the fight a body of the enemy concealed in the woods annoyed our forces much by their rifle practice. Gen. MARTINDALE's Brigade charged them and drove them from the woods amidst the cheers of our men.

Gen. HARTSUFF's Brigade made a similar charge but with a different result. They penetrated into the woods, when a deadly fire of grape and canister was opened upon them from a masked battery. At the same time a murderous volley of rifle balls came from one side and a desperate charge of the enemy from the other. Our men fought bravely, but were forced to retire.

The enemy remained upon the battle-field over night.

To-day there has been some skirmishing.

Reinforcements are going up to-day, and a battle is anticipated to-morrow.

The road from Alexandria, extending to Centreville, was densely crowded all this day with wagon trains, ambulances, hacks and private conveyances, on their way to and from the latter place.

The number of wounded sent to Washington was comparatively small.

Not a few persons who had reached Centreville and intermediate points, intending to aid the sick and wounded, were turned back for the reason that the battle-field of Manassas was in the possession of the rebels, and that their services were not needed. Many who had ridden to Centreville have returned to Alexandria on foot.

Pickets had been thrown out all along the road to prevent stragglers from deserting the front.

Four Government employees, who had started from Gen. McCLELLAN's headquarters last night, in company with a mail carrier, (intending to act as nurses,) were arrested at Ball's Cross Roads, on suspicion of being spies, but on being returned to Gen. McCLELLAN's headquarters were discharged.

OUR CORRESPONDENCE FROM THE FIELD.

A DETAILED ACCOUNT OF THE RECENT MOVEMENTS—JACKSON'S TACTICS AND HOW THEY WERE MET—DESPERATION OF THE REBELS.

General Sykes and staff.

CENTREVILLE, Va., Sunday, Aug. 31, 1862.

The commencement of the conflict now pending between the National and rebel forces may be said to date from Tuesday, the 26th inst., upon the night of which day Stonewall JACKSON appeared with a large force at Bristor, where he destroyed about fifty cars and two locomotives. He also tore up the railroad track for some distance and burnt two bridges. The cars were on the way to Alexandria, having conveyed a portion of Gen. HOOKER's Division to Warrenton Junction a few hours previous. One of the locomotives was thrown down an embankment and, upon examination, was found to have been pierced with sixty-three rifle shots. The other locomotive, which was remaining on the track, showed marks of having been shot at twenty-five times. One of the engineers jumped from his locomotive and surrendered himself as prisoner, but the rebels did not heed the usage of civilized warfare and shot him upon the spot. At the time of the raid but few persons were aboard the trains, and those were parties employed by the Government to superintend and assist in their running. The cars were empty. The telegraph wire was cut in several places and one of the poles severed.

From Bristor Station JACKSON proceeded to Manasses Junction, two miles below, where he burned about one hundred other cars which were standing upon a side track in readiness to be drawn to Warrenton Junction. The cars destroyed here were heavily laden with subsistence stores, ammunition and saddlers and blacksmiths materials. All, or nearly all the ammunition, consisting of three car loads was secured, and carried away. A few shells had been left in the cars as the fragments of ragged iron found upon the ground testified. All the subsistence stores that he could conveniently dispose of were taken by JACKSON. A half-dozen barrels of hard bread were discovered near the track, also a quantity of hams. At the Junction the rebels burned another bridge, tore up more railroad track and also burned a large bakery and several small buildings in the immediate vicinity of the same. Half an hour before the rebels appeared Gen. STURGIS, who, with his brigade, had been guarding the Junction, was ordered to report with his force to Warrenton. When Gen. STURGIS had left the Junction, six pieces of artillery, belonging to a New-Jersey battery, was left almost entirely unsupported, consequently the rebels found it an easy matter to overcome the artillerists and capture the guns. At about the time the rebels arrived at the Junction, Gen. DANA's New-Jersey Brigade, which was stationed at the railroad bridge over Bull Run, acting upon orders previously received, were advancing to Manassas. The bridge is situated about five miles from the Junction, and, of course, as the Brigade approached that place, they were surrounded by the rebels, and a great many taken prisoners. All the prisoners, however, taken at the Junction by JACKSON were paroled on the following day, he doubtless considering that they might occasion him much trouble before he could get them safely into Richmond

From the Junction JACKSON proceeded to the railroad bridge over Bull Run and destroyed it. The reflection of the burning cars, bridge and building, could be seen distinctly at Warrenton Junction. The mass continued to burn throughout the night.

Until Thursday morning JACKSON remained in the vicinity of Bristor and Manassas Junction, and dined on Wednesday with a family living near the dépôt, at the former place. When preparing to leave, he ordered his temporary landlord to pack up his wordly goods and make ready to depart with his family into the land of Secessia. The host, however, was too keen to observe the import of the command, and began at once to conjecture how he should escape being forced into the rebel service. He gained permission of JACKSON to go a short distance from his home for the ostensible purpose of procuring a wagon, in which he might convey his family and goods from the Union line ; but instead of returning immediately, he remained concealed in the woods until our forces appeared and drove the rebels from the line of the railroad, on the following day.

Although the rebels commenced their depredations early on Tuesday evening, it appears that no effort was made to repel them until the next morning, when HOOKER's Division and one brigade of KEARNEY's, (ROBINSON's,) the whole under command of Gen. HOOKER, were sent from Warrenton Junction down the railroad, to meet and drive away the enemy. The ground in the vicinity of Bristor is undulating, thereby affording good points upon which to plant batteries, and also a fine protection for the men against the enemy's fire. Before reaching Bristor from the Warrenton side, the railroad is lined on each side by dense woods which fringe an open field of many hundred acres in extent. Along the skirt of these woods. JACKSON had posted a portion of his force, while he held the remainder in reserve, and out of sight, behind the hills in the rear. He had two batteries of six pieces each, planted one on either side of the railroad, which the rebels commenced using with destructive effect at the opportune moment. HOOKER ordered his men to advance cautiously and deployed skirmishers through the woods who reported the presence of the rebel pickets at the further end. Soon after, several shots were exchanged by the advance guard on both sides. But instead of moving his troops down the railroad, HOOKER took a sweep round the woods at his left and entered the open field upon the right wing of the enemy's advance. This movement caused the rebels to fall back, and not without confusion, and it being a propitious moment for the Union force to deal a good blow, Gen. HOOKER gave the command to fire, which was followed by a tremendous volley of musketry. More of the enemy fell at this fire than by any succeeding one. Our force suffered mostly from the effect of the batteries stationed on the hills in front of them. The projectile used by the enemy was grape and canister shot. The fight lasted from 3 to 5 o'clock. HOOKER succeeded in forcing the rebels from their position and bivouacked at night on the battle-ground. Our casualties amounted to fifty killed and about one hundred and fifty wounded. The rebels left their dead and over one hundred of their wounded on the field. On Thursday morning the bodies were buried by order of the Commanding-General.

Prisoners captured on this occasion agree in the statement that JACKSON had a force of 30,000 men. They also state that he came to Bristor on the road leading from Centreville to Manassas Gap, and followed the same road on his retreat. He commenced retiring from Manassas Junction Thursday morning, burning all the bridges that he crossed, including the one over Bull Run. KEARNEY and HOOKER closely pursued, and did not stop until the rebels had been driven to Haymarket, and night overshadowed the chase.

It was expected that the rebels would receive reinforcements from Richmond ; but, in order to detain the reinforcements as long as possible, KING's Division was sent round to Thoroughfare Gap to oppose the entrance of the rebels. KING's Division took the road leading from Catlett's Station to Manassas. They arrived upon the ground early Thursday evening, and in the course of a couple of hours were engaged with the rebel LONGSTREET, who was endeavoring to force his division through the Gap. The rebels were held in check for some hours, which was a great advantage to POPE, as he had an opportunity to march his troops and properly dispose them.

The attempt of JACKSON to come in upon our rear has evidently been anticipated by POPE for some days before the event actually happened. On Tuesday, the 26th, orders were issued for the troops to proceed to Manassas Junction, and on that same day the line of the Rappahannock was abandoned, with the exception of that portion near Fredericksburgh. During Tuesday night and all day Wednesday the supply and baggage trains were moving towards Manassas Junction, from which place they were sent to Centreville and subsequently to Fairfax Court-house. They were at length concentrated in a valley just outside the limits of Centreville. Three locomotives and about one hundred and fifty cars loaded with the sick and wounded and medical supplies at Warrenton Junction, were waiting at that place for the burnt bridge to be reconstructed and the track relaid, so that they might pass on to Alexandria. On Thursday, however, it was deemed advisable to tranfer the sick and wounded who could not walk to ambulances, by which means they were conveyed to Alexandria. The medical supplies were placed in wagons. It will be inferred from that movement that the event of the rebels occupying Warrenton Junction was not wholly unanticipated by POPE.

The battles of Friday and Saturday took place upon the old Bull Run battle-ground. On Friday the fight was on our right, which was held by SIGEL in the morning, and in the afternoon and evening by HEINTZELMAN. KING's Division had suffered considerably in the engagement the night previous, and was held in reserve, with the remainder of McDOWELL's Corps.

PORTER's Corps arrived at Warrenton Junction from the Rappahannock on Thursday, and were ordered to proceed to the battle-ground. They took a position on the road leading to Centreville. At the left of the road were stationed McDOWELL's and BANKS' Corps.

At daylight on Friday morning the fight was commenced by the rebels endeavoring to turn our right, or the troops under command of SIGEL. They brought to bear a heavy artillery fire, and received in return one equally as energetic from us. Three times during the morning they advanced in mass upon SIGEL, but were successfully resisted each time. The rebels had the choice of position, and had the advantage of us in that respect. They had woods for cover, and from the rising and falling of the ground, could keep up a rapid and decimating fire, without exposing any large bodies of their troops. SIGEL and his men fought nobly till about 2 o'clock in the afternoon, when they were relieved by KEARNEY and HOOKER of HEINTZELMAN's Corps. The rebels, as is their usual practice, frequently relieved their troops, and had fresh men to meet those of HEINTZELMAN. In the afternoon the fight became desperate, the enemy seeming determined to force back our right. After his usual custom, KEARNEY was at the head of his column, cheering on his men, and throwing defiance at the rebels. HOOKER was equally conspicuous, and fought—as he always fights—with the coolness, judgment and daring of a brave man. The contest lasted till dark, the enemy having been driven a mile from his original position. The loss on both sides was heavy, but it is impossible to make an approximate estimate. SIGEL took 800 prisoners, and captured seven pieces of artillery.

The battle was renewed by us at 7 o'clock on Saturday morning. The disposition of our forces was about the same as on the previous day ; HEINTZELMAN held the extreme right ; PORTER and McDOWELL the centre, and BANKS the extreme left. SIGEL was held in reserve in the rear of PORTER's corps. The fight was sustained on our part by PORTER's force until afternoon when the enemy concentrated his entire force upon McDOWELL. The engagement was almost entirely with the artillery until 1 o'clock in the afternoon. Up to this time little damage had been sustained on either side. The rebels at length became desperate and charged with solid columns upon PORTER's men. They did not succeed in breaking the line, however, and were compelled to fall back to their original position. The result was in our favor, inasmuch as we drove the enemy, although we suffered severely in so doing. The rebel loss must have been frightful, as our artillerists fired at excellent range.

At 3 P. M. the enemy changed tactics, and moved the major part of his force toward McDOWELL, who was on the left of the centre. At this point we had stationed three batteries—LAPINE's Fifth Maine, of four pieces ; THOMPSON's New-York, of six pieces, and HOWELL's Battery, of four pieces. For some reason, LAPINE's battery, which was in the extreme front, was unsupported by infantry. This was certainly a great oversight on the part of McDOWELL. Then again, the troops under McDOWELL were too much scattered to effectually resist an enemy's advance. It was particularly observed that an immense number of stragglers were loafing about the field. Stragglers are a nuisance to an army, and the discipline of troops can be ascertained by observing if many of them leave the ranks during a march.

The enemy charged at first upon LAPINE's Battery and succeeded in capturing it. They then advanced eight columns deep toward McDOWELL's force ; but, strange to say, instead of offering any opposition, McDOWELL ordered his men to fall back, which they immediately commenced doing. All three of the batteries were then left unsupported, and, of course, to fall into the hands of the enemy. It is reported, however, that three pieces out of the sixteen were drawn from the field by the artillerists. Soon as McDOWELL's troops commenced retiring, the cowardly stragglers set up a shout and ran pell-mell to the rear. Teamsters and ambulance drivers were the next to follow, and it was feared that another Bull Run fight was about to be inaugurated. The breaking of the line in the centre of course compelled the right and left to fall back. If the movement had been conducted systematically all might have been well, but the fear of being the last man seemed to seize the troops, and they made a rush for Centreville. Before reaching Bull Run

The Confederate victory at Manassas hastened the withdrawal of all Union troops in Virginia by General Halleck, to be consolidated for an expected attack on Washington. Here, a gunwork at Fort Totten is shown.

Ex-slaves, known as "Contraband," were employed as servants in the Army of the Potomac.

they were partially rallied, which had the effect to hold in check the advance of the enemy. Several attempts were made to arrest the flight of the men between Bull Run and Centreville, but they all failed. Men with loaded rifles and fixed bayonets behind a breastwork at Centreville were the only barrier sufficiently strong to keep back the troops.

Darkness soon come on, and it being ascertained that the enemy was not rushing upon them with the celerity of lightning, the men became calm and set about preparing something to eat.

FRANKLIN's entire corps had arrived two miles beyond Centreville when the stampede commenced. They drew up in line of battle at that point and remained there during the night.

The battle of Saturday was a loss to us on account of mismanagement somewhere. McDOWELL is blamed by both officers and men for not standing firm upon the approach of the enemy. His men assert that they will not fight under him again.

Our forces have now fallen back to Centreville. SUMNER's corps passed up from Alexandria to-day. The road from Alexandria is lined with reinforcements. It is doubtless the intention of the rebels to make the next a decisive battle. All their available force is at Manassas. Prisoners state that JACKSON in an address to his men, told them that he would take Washington within eight days or sacrifice his whole army.

The Union and the rebel armies are now face to face with each other. It remains to be seen which side shall conquer. Our casualties in the two days' fight will probably amount to about 5,000 killed and wounded. **WHIT.**

THE RECENT BATTLES AS VIEWED FROM WASHINGTON—POSITION OF THE CONTENDING ARMIES, AND THEIR RELATIVE FORCE—WHAT WE MAY EXPECT.

WASHINGTON, Sunday Evening, Aug. 31, 1862.

That the greatest battle of the war has been raging for several days past in the vicinity of Manassas, is now known in Washington, although the information is not allowed to go over the wires. That this fight, up to the present time, has *not* resulted in a success to the National arms, is also now known. The same mail that carries this will convey to you an account of this fearful contest, by one of your special correspondents on the field, and hence I shall not attempt any account in detail; but I will give a few observations from this point of view, and the conclusions to which the intelligent public here has arrived in regard to the present " situation."

When JACKSON threw himself with a comparatively small force, in the rear of POPE, he executed one of those bold inspirations of genius whose very audacity almost insures success. POPE's retreat had been a feat of such astonishing rapidity that he may almost be excused for not conceiving it to be possible for JACKSON to thus overtake and flank him. At the same time, JACKSON's daring subjected him to a terrible risk, but promised brilliant rewards. The risk, thanks to his prompt reinforcement by LEE and LONGSTREET, he has survived, and the rewards he has realized in the capture of immense stores, giving the rebels a welcome supply of ordnance stores and ammunition, as well as of provisions, of which, in consequence of their rapid march, they were destitute.

Had our military leaders, however, possessed the boldness and promptitude of JACKSON, he would inevitably have fallen a sacrifice to his enterprise and courage. Probably he estimated all the chances, as in his raid in the Shenandoah Valley, and the fact shows that his estimate was correct.

Both armies have now been reinforced; JACKSON by a force estimated at from 40,000 to 60,000; POPE by divisions from the corps of McCLELLAN and BURNSIDE. The enemy made an overpowering attack on McDOWELL's corps, when LONGSTREET came up and drove it back with great loss of men and ordnance. The fighting of our men was superb. Since that reinforcement we have been on the defensive, and are now back as far, at least, as Centreville—*perhaps further* The retreat has been made with entire steadiness' and the men exhibit the utmost coolness and courage' But little fighting has been done to-day; the enemy, who occupy the old battle ground of Bull Run, apparently seeking some means of turning our flank. Our Generals are, of course, ignorant of what the morning will bring forth.

In case our troops prove too weak to hold the present line of defence, they will still be able to fall back in good order to the fortifications in front of Washington,

unless the enemy, by some daring flank movement, succeed in occupying them first. In the former case, Washington is entirely safe till the new levies arrive—in the latter contingency, its fate would seem to be sealed.

I think confidence is lost in Gen. POPE. To-night an officer of some prominence, who was in the fight, announces, after visiting the War Office, that to-morrow morning will see a new Commander in the field. Whom it can be, I can only guess. McCLELLAN has not been in the field at all, nor has BURNSIDE; but there is confidence in the latter, who is now said to be at Centreville, and *must* be the man, if a change is made.

Yesterday afternoon, the War Department invited everybody to go out to the battle-field and assist in tending and nursing the wounded. Washington responded almost *en masse*. From 3 to 7 o'clock the streets swarmed with people and conveyances, armed with blankets and baskets and rolls of lint. A thousand, I should say, went out, and this morning, notwithstanding the rain, a large number more. But at 10 o'clock this morning the order was countermanded and passes were refused, and it turns out that the whole affair was ill-advised, and that very few of those who went were allowed to go far enough to find the wounded they sought. Scarce a hack or omnibus was left in the city; this evening sees them returning. But the affair was not altogether bootless, and the result is very creditable to the loyalty and charity of the citizens of Washington.

The wounded are now arriving in, and are well cared for. Our loss is heavy—probably 15,000 to 20,000 already. We have also some prisoners—1,000 are already in.

On the whole, if our Generals show average *brains*, and the loyal citizens of the country *at once fill up the new regiments*, the war was never in better shape; for though this last kick of the enemy is severe, it is final, and a dying spasm. His present army, all of which is at Manassas, is the *last* he can raise. **J. M. W.**

SECURE POSITION OF THE UNION ARMY

Judge WHITE, of the New-York Supreme Court, telegraphed the *Tribune* from Washington at 3 o'clock yesterday afternoon as follows:

" I have just returned from our army close to the battle-field. Our men are in good spirits and as firm as veterans. They hold Centreville and its vicinity, with part of the old battle-field of Bull Run."

GEN. BANKS SAFE.

WASHINGTON, Monday, Sept. 1.

Dispatches received from Fairfax Court-house, seven miles from Centreville, state that no firing has been heard up to 12 o'clock to-day.

Gen. BANKS' forces were heard from last night, and were in a favorable position for joining Gen. POPE's army.

THE PLANS OF THE REBEL GENERALS.
Correspondence of the Philadelphia Inquirer.

WASHINGTON, Sunday, Aug. 31, 1862.

The audacity of the rebel troops in approaching so near to Washinton as they have, has led me to speculate as to their probable object in doing so, their purposes, and the means at their command for accomplishing the same. As I am the fortunate possessor of some " facts not generally known," bearing directly upon the subject, these speculations may not be incorrect. First, as a basis, let me premise a few facts which *may* be generally known. These facts are not pleasant ones, and they are as well known in the rebel capital as in ours.

1. The masterly retrograde movement of Gen. POPE from Culpepper to the Rappahannock, and from the Rappahannock towards Manassas, although a brilliant and successful exploit in itself, has been attended with the loss, and capture by the enemy, of the whole of Gen. POPE's official papers. Gen. LEE, therefore, and the Rebel War Department, are fully and accurately informed as to every minute particular respecting the forces composing Gen. POPE's army, and his own and Gen. HALLECK's plans for conducting the campaign.

2. The rebel army now holds both sides of the Rappahannock, in strong force. On the Southern side, they have some forty-three thousand troops, and about as many negroes, all of whom, whites and blacks, are busily engaged, working night and day, in building new fortifications, and in enlarging and making stronger those works which already exist. When these works are completed, it is not too much to say that the rebels will then have a chain of forts along the entire south bank of the Rappahannock, from the Rattlesnake Mountain (southwest of Warrenton) to Fredericksburgh, a distance of thirty-five miles. The object of these fortifications cannot be misunderstood. It is to make the future passage of the Rappahannock by the Union forces almost an impossibility. The forts will command every ford and crossing-place on the river.

3. The capture of POPE's official papers and his entire baggage train, at Catlett's, on Friday last, and the attack of the rebel cavalry at Manassas, on Tuesday, the 26th, and the terrible battles near Bull Run, on Wednesday, the 27th, show that the rebel troops not only hold both sides of the Rappahannock, but also that they dispute with the Union troops the occupancy of the line of Bull Run. According to the best estimates they have at least 100,000 troops so engaged, of whom 12,000 are cavalry, with a large train of field artillery.

4. And most serious of all—in spite of all POPE's efforts to prevent them—the rebel troops have succeeded not only in crossing the Rappahannock, but also in getting a strong position between Gen. POPE's army and Washington. The details of the battles of Wednesday are still confused, and I will not attempt to repeat them. The result of the affair is, however, that the main body of Gen. LEE's army is within striking distance of Centreville.

Here then my speculations begin. It is evident that ever since this movement of Gen. LEE against Gen. POPE began, it has been Gen. LEE's object to turn POPE's flank, or else to get in his rear, in order that he might annihilate his army, and then march on to Washington. It would seem that the first part of his design has been accomplished. What amount of loss Gen. POPE's army has sustained up to this time, it is impossible to ascertain. How can the truth be learned, when all newspaper correspondents are excluded from the army.

But whether POPE has been defeated or not, Gen. LEE will learn from POPE's official papers that Gen. McCLELLAN and the Army of the Potomac have arrived from the Peninsula. He will understand, therefore, that this city is safe; that it is beyond his reach. It is probable that Gen. LEE will now endeavor to take possession of Centreville, so that the rebel army may occupy, during the coming Fall and Winter, the same positions near Washington which they held last Winter. If Gen. LEE succeeds in taking Centreville, it will release two-thirds of the rebel army now in Virginia. The remaining third will be sufficient to hold Centreville and the line of the Rappahannock, and to defend Richmond, while the two-thirds will be sent to the West.

THE WAR IN THE WEST.

UNION VICTORY AT BOLIVAR, TENN.

The Rebels About to Attack Fort Donelson.

GUERRILLAS IN MISSOURI.

WASHINGTON, Monday, Sept. 1.
GRANT's HEADQUARTERS, Aug. 31, 1862.
Maj.-Gen. Halleck, General-in-Chief, Washington:

GENERAL: The following dispatch is received from Bolivar, Tenn.:

Col. HOGG, in command of the Twentieth and Twenty-ninth Ohio Infantry and some cavalry, was attacked by about 4,000 rebels yesterday.

Our troops behaved well, driving the enemy, whose loss was over one hundred.

Our loss is twenty-five men killed and wounded, Col. HOGG being one of the number.
(Signed,) U. S. GRANT,
Major-General Commanding.

THE REBELS MARCHING ON FORT DONELSON.

CAIRO, Ill., Sunday, Aug. 31.

Dispatches are received at headquarters here that the rebels are marching on Fort Donelson, with the purpose of attacking it.

The number of the rebels is not known.

THE CAPTURED REBEL STEAMER " FAIR PLAY"—GEN. CURTIS.

CAIRO, Ill., Sunday, Aug. 31.

The rebel steamer *Fair Play* captured up the Yazoo River a few days since, has arrived here.

Gen. CURTIS and his Staff have also arrived here.

The General has leave of absence to attend the Pacific Railroad meeting at Chicago.

GUERRILLAS IN MISSOURI.

ST. LOUIS, Mo., Sunday, Aug. 31..

Advices from Greenville state that guerrillas 1,500 strong, under McBRIDE, threaten that place. 1,400 Union troops, under Col. SIMPSON, are there to meet them. The rebels for some days have been congregating all available forces at that point. They hourly make offensive demonstrations. An attack was soon expected. No fears are entertained for the result. There is no further news of raids throughout the State.

The steamer *Adriatic* arrived to-day with 00 negroes, freed by Gen. CURTIS, on board. ne 500 more are expected to-night.

The Twentieth Wisconsin regiment arrived this evening.

The New-York Times.

VOL. XI—NO. 3429.   NEW-YORK, FRIDAY, SEPTEMBER 19, 1862.   PRICE TWO CENTS.

THE GREAT BATTLES.

The Fighting Continued Through Wednesday.

The Advantages on the Side of the National Army.

THE BATTLE NOT RENEWED YESTERDAY.

Great Extent and Magnitude of the Struggle.

The Entire Rebel Army in Maryland.

A Dispatch from the Gallant General Hooker.

He Claims a Great Victory on Wednesday.

DREADFUL CARNAGE ON BOTH SIDES

Our Losses Estimated at Ten Thousand Killed and Wounded.

DISPATCH FROM GEN. HOOKER.

CENTREVILLE, Md., Wednesday, Sept. 17.

A great battle has been fought, and we are victorious. I had the honor to open it yesterday afternoon, and it continued until 10 o'clock this morning, when I was wounded, and compelled to quit the field.

The battle was fought with great violence on both sides.

The carnage has been awful.

I only regret that I was not permitted to take part in the operations until they were concluded, for I had counted on either capturing their army or driving them into the Potomac.

My wound has been painful, but it is not one that will be likely to lay me up. I was shot through the foot.

J. HOOKER, Brig.-Gen.

NEWS BY WAY OF HARRISBURGH.

HARRISBURGH, Penn., Thursday, Sept. 18.

The news received during last night indicates that the result of yesterday's fight was decidedly in our favor ; but still another battle is necessary to determine who shall finally be the victor.

It was expected that the battle would be again renewed this morning, but no firing has been

Major-General George B. McClellan with his wife. McClellan was reinstated as head of the Army of the Potomac.

heard, and it is supposed that burying of the dead is the order of the day.

Gen McCLELLAN's headquarters are at Sharpsburgh.

Surgeon-Gen. SMITH dispatched a special train to Hagerstown yesterday to attend our wounded.

The number of wounded in Gen. McCLELLAN's army is very large ; most of them will probably be brought into Pennsylvania.

The rebel prisoners taken have been sent to Fort Delaware.

HARRISBURGH, Thursday, Sept. 18—P. M.

Information received here this morning direct from the battlefield, represented that the battle would undoubtedly be resumed to-day, but up to this hour no firing had been heard at Hagerstown. The forces remain about in the same position as in yesterday's fight.

Preparations are now being made here for receiving the sick and wounded from the late battle. Citizens are anxious to do all in their power for the comfort of those who are fighting for the support of the National Government.

Troops are still coming in by thousands and are immediately forwarded.

The Government having complete control of the road to Chambersburgh and Hagerstown. The regular trains to these points were suspended to-day, but will be resumedd in a few days.

NEWS BY WAY OF PHILADELPHIA.

PHILADELPHIA, Thursday, Sept. 18.

A special dispatch, dated Hagerstown, yesterday, to the *Press*, says of the fight on Tuesday:

"The battle raged with great spirit. The firing on either side was very heavy, until toward sundown, when the rebels were flanked by HOOKER and PORTER, and severely punished. Their fire became desultory, and it was evident that their ammunition was giving out.

This morning the battle was renewed by the rebels with renewed vigor. They acted as if they had been reinforced and furnished with fresh ammunition. The battle lasted until 4 o'clock this afternoon, when the rebels retreated, leaving Gen. LONGSTREET and the remnant of his division in our hands as prisoners.

The entire rebel army will be captured or killed. There is no chance left for them to cross the Potomac, as the river is rising and our troops are pushing them continually and sending prisoners to the rear.

Six batteries of artillery belonging to Gen. LONGSTREET's Division were captured yesterday and to-day, and it is said that we have taken nearly 15,000 prisoners since Sunday.

Stonewall JACKSON's army is with Gen. LEE and other distinguished officers will be forced to surrender within a day or two at furthest.

Our immense army is in motion, and our Generals are certain of ultimate and decisive success.

Stores for our army are coming by way of Harrisburgh and Baltimore.

Gen. BURNSIDE has retaken the position of Harper's Ferry, and is advancing on a special mission with his troops.

NEWS BY WAY OF BALTIMORE.

BALTIMORE, Thursday, Sept. 18.

I was on the battle-field up to 10 o'clock yesterday morning, and left with confidence that all was going on right. It was a grand battle—the most severe of the war—every division of the rebel army being on the field.

From Harrisburgh dispatches and other movements, I think there has been some change in the position of the armies at the close of the day, but have no doubt all is well. Army trains were moving forward from Frederick this morning.

OUR DISPATCHES FROM WASHINGTON.

WASHINGTON, Thursday, Sept. 18.

A special dispatch from Fredericksburgh states that fighting has been desperate at Sharpsburgh, and that among the wounded are Gen. HOOKER. Gen. MEAGHER, and Col. HINKS of the Nineteenth Massachusetts, and the Surgeon of the Twelfth Massachusets ta reported killed.

The churches in Frederick are all taken for hospital uses. A great many rebel prisoners have been captured.

WASHINGTON, Thurday, Sept. 18—10 P. M.

The rebel prisoners captured by our scouts

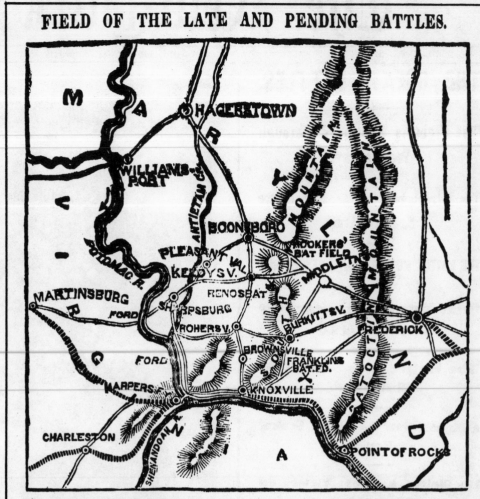

FIELD OF THE LATE AND PENDING BATTLES.

THE GREAT BATTLES IN MARYLAND.

The accompanying map will give a succinct view of the scene and localities of the great battles of the present week, and of the course of the rebel movements from the time they crossed the Potomac until Wednesday night. On Friday evening last, one week ago to-day, our army entered Frederick, having driven the rebel forces up to and beyond that place, from the point at which they crossed the Potomac, above and below the Point of Rocks. Our forces followed the retreating rebels from Frederick across the Catoctin Mountains, and on Sunday HOOKER and RENO came up with their rear guard at the gap in South Mountain, indicated in our map, (incorrectly called "Hagerstown Heights,") while Gen. FRANKLIN engaged another body of them on the same day, at a point to the southeast. Of these battles, the TIMES on Wednesday and Thursday gave by far the fullest and best accounts that have been published. The different bodies of the rebels seem to have then swept around southwesterly on Monday from these localities and from Hagerstown—skirmishing briskly as they retired—until on Tuesday all their forces were concentrated in the neighborhood of Sharpsburgh, at a point east of Antietam Creek, and probably at the intersection of the roads leading from Middletown to Sharpsburgh, and Rohersville and Williamsport. Here was fought the great but indecisive battle of Tuesday; and during the day's fighting, we drove the rebels south and west for some distance—our army at night occupying the ground where the battle closed. The tremendous engagement of Wednesday was fought closer to Sharpsburgh, or between Sharpsburgh and Rohrersville; and though we do not definitely know the course and result of the battle, we know that at night we occupied Rohrersville, and that Gen. Mc-CLELLAN had destroyed the aqueduct at the mouth of the Antietam Creek, and the bridge across that creek upon the road leading to Sharpsburgh. So that from all we can gather, it would appear that the rebel army is now collected in the great bend of the river, (see map,) which will be observed as running some ten miles north from the junction of Antietam Creek with the Potomac. There are mountain ridges on both sides of the creek, and the whole country in this vicinity is thickly covered with hills, so that it is necessarily slow work pursuing the rebels, and they are able to contest many points. One dispatch asserts that the greater part of the rebel army, instead of being west of Antietam, has retreated southward in the direction of Harper's Ferry. When it is considered, however, that Gen. BURNSIDE, with a large force, holds Harper's Ferry, and that other troops, under Gen. SIGEL, are moving in this direction from Washington, it would seem that wherever the rebel army may be placed, or in whatever direction it may be retreating, it will find escape a difficult matter if our troops are thrown upon it with skill and vigor. There will likely be another, and a decisive, battle fought speedily on this part of the line off the Upper Potomac; and on the space covered by our little map is, very probably, located the ground which will see the death, as it is now seeing the dying, struggles of this great rebellion.

near Leesburgh, were brought into the city last evening. They say that the rebel force under Gen. HOOD, lately stationed at Leesburgh, left that place on Monday morning for Williamsport, for the purpose of reinforcing LONGSTREET. The prisoners were unable to accompany their regiments on the march to Williamsport, on account of exhaustion. HOOD's force was about 5,000 men.

A great many straggling and wounded soldiers from the battle-fields in Maryland had arrived at Leesburgh. The prisoners say they all concurred in the fact that the hardest fighting of the war is now going on in Maryland; that LEE was getting badly whipped, and that he would be annihilated unless reinforcements speedily came to his assistance.

A division lately encamped at Waterford had also left to reinforce LEE. It numbered about 6,000 men.

Stonewall Jackson's forces completed a raid of Federal supplies at Harper's Ferry, before rejoining Lee at Antietam.

The prisoners state that the whole of the rebel army is in Maryland.

WASHINGTON, Thursday, Sept. 18th—Midnight.

We have no reliable news from Gen. Mc-CLELLAN to-day, though the city is full of rumors. The general belief is that our army has not gained any decisive advantage, though still acting on the offensive. Apprehensions are felt that JACKSON may succeed in executing some dangerous flank movement with fresh troops, which will imperil our forces, but with Pennsylvania in their rear, constantly sending on reinforcements, he will scarcely venture to place himself between them and McCLELLAN.

The continued silence of the Government adds greatly to the disposition of the public to apprehend disaster to our arms.

FROM ANOTHER CORRESPONDENT.

WASHINGTON, Thursday, Sept. 18.

The latest information received here up to 11 o'clock to-day, was dated from the seat of war at 11 o'clock last night, when it was telegraphed that Gen. McCLELLAN had a severe engagement throughout the day, *resulting in gaining the position for which our army fought.*

Information from a point within four miles of the battle-ground, up to 9 o'clock this morning, says nothing of the engagement having been renewed previous to that hour. It merely states that a thousand rebel prisoners were taken yesterday, and that they were being marched to the rear past that point under a guard.

A reconnoissance in force, made yesterday, has demonstrated that *there are no rebel troops between Washington and Bull Run,* while our scouts yesterday reported that they were in full force at Drainesville on Tuesday evening.

NO BATTLE FOUGHT YESTERDAY.

HARRISBURGH, Thursday, Sept. 18—Evening.

Advices just received at headquarters, from Hagerstown, confirm the report that no fight had taken place to-day; that the rebels are supposed to be short of ammunition, and that the fight would probably commence at daybreak tomorrow.

Our troops are said to have behaved nobly, and talk confidently of gaining a great victory tomorrow.

Gov. CURTIN had arrived safely at Hagerstown, together with Col. J. A. WRIGHT, Surgeon-General SMITH, and his corps of Surgeons. Gov. CURTIN and staff are using every exertion in preparing for the comfort of the wounded brought into that place.

A telegraph line is being extended to Boonsboro, thus bringing us much nearer to Gen. Mc-CLELLAN's Headquarters. It will be completed to-morrow.

DETAILS OF THE BATTLE OF WEDNESDAY

HEADQUARTERS ARMY OF THE POTOMAC, }
Sept. 17, *via* Frederick, Sept. 18. }

This has been an eventful day in the history of the rebellion. A battle has taken place, in which the army of the Potomac has again been victorious, and which exceeded in extent any battle heretofore fought on this continent.

At the dawn of day the battle was resumed on the centre and right, by HOOKER and SUMNER, who, after a sharp contest of two hours, drove the enemy about one mile. The rebels rallied shortly afterward, and, with terrible loss, regained much of the ground. At this time the fearless and indomitable HOOKER received a shot in the ankle, and was carried from the field. The command of his troops now devolved upon SUMNER.

Gen. RICHARDSON, commanding a division, was severely wounded at the same time. Gen. SUMNER, determined to take the lost ground, ordered the troops to advance, which they did with a will, driving the rebels before them with great slaughter. They not only retook the ground, but drove drove them a quarter of a mile beyond.

In this action Gen. MANSFIELD was shot through the lungs, and died soon after.

During this time the troops under BURNSIDE and PORTER had not been idle. They drove the rebels from the line of Antietam Creek, on the main road to Sharpsburgh, built a bridge, (the old one having been destroyed, and occupied the opposite bank. The loss here was considerable. The troops now held both banks of the creek. To get possession of the ridge of hills on the right and left hand sides of the road, from which the rebels were thundering away with artillery, was a task not easily accomplished. SYKES' Brigade, with the assistance of SUMNER, carried the ridge on the right hand side after considerable trouble and loss, the rebels running in all directions.

It is now 4 o'clock, and all the enemy's positions have been carried except the one on the left hand side of the road. To do this duty BURNSIDE was assigned. The arttllery opened and the infantry advanced. The point was carried, but we were forced to retire before a superior force. Knowing that if they lost this ridge, a complete rout of their army would be the result, they fought with great desperation.

Darkness now overlooked the two armies, and hostilities ceased as though by mutual consent.

The battle lasted from 5 o'clock in the morning till 7 at night witnout a moment's cessation.

The conduct of all the troops, without exception, was all that any General could wish. Several regiments of new troops, who wsre in action for the first time, behaved admirably.

Hundreds of Marylanders were present to witness the battle, which could be seen from many of the surrounding hills. The sharp rattle of fifty thousand muskets, and the thunders of a hundred pieces of artillery is not often heard, nor the consequent excited movements of such armies witnessed.

It is impossible at this writing to form any correct idea of our loss, or that of the enemy. It is heavy on both sides; ours will probabaly reach in killed and wounded ten thousand. That of the enemy will not exceed it.

The enemy's dead, which nearly all fell into our hands, were thickly strewn over the fields, in many places lying in heaps.

Our wounded were immediately carried from the field, and the best possible attention given them.

When Gen. HOOKER fell, Gen. MCCLELLAN immediately proceeded to the right, where he was, enthusiastically received, and by his presence added much to our success in recovering the ground lost. He was in the centre and on the left as well, anxiously watching the progress of the battle, and giving directions as to the manner of attack. He is in his tent to-night for the first time since he left Frederick City.

We took some 1,500 prisoners during the day, while the enemy obtained but few.

The following officers were among the killed and wounded :

Gen. Hartsaff, wounded.

Gen. Duryea, wounded.

Gen. Sedgwick, wounded in the shoulder.

Col. Childs, Eleventh Connecticut, seriously wounded.

Lieut.-Col. Parisen, Fifty-seventh New-York, killed.

Capt. Andenreid, Aid to Gen. Sumner, wounded.
Maj. Sedgwick, killed.

Col. McNiel, of the Bucktails, and Lieut. Allen were killed.

Col. Polk, Second United States Sharpshooters, wounded.

Maj. Burbank, Twelfth Massachusetts, wounded. Several other prominent officers were reported killed and wounded, but nothing positive is known concerning then.

A FIGHT AT LEESBURGH.

A Reconnoisance from Gen. Sigel's Force.

Rebel Force Driven Back at Leesburgh at the Point of the Bayonet.

WASHINGTON, Thursday. Sept. 18th—9 P. M.

A force, consisting of artillery, infantry and cavalry, under command of Lieut.-Col. KILPATRICK, left Gen. SIGEL'S headquarters, yesterday morning, on a reconnoisance toward Leesburgh.

On arriving at Goose Creek, the passage of that stream was disputed by a squadron of rebel cavalry, who, however, were soon put to flight by our artillery.

Our force then proceeded to Leesburgh, which place they found occupied by one regiment of rebel infantry and a battalion of cavalry. After a short engagement the enemy were driven out of town with considerable loss. Our loss was slight.

We captured the regimental flag of the enemy, a number of guns and a number of prisoners.

The Tenth New-York Regiment behaved with great gallantry, driving the enemy through the town at the point of the bayonet.

SECESH REPORTS IN BALTIMORE.
WASHINGTON, Thursday, Sept. 18—10:20 P. M.

By a special dispatch from the TIMES correspondent in Baltimore we learn that orders have

Confederate dead lie along the fence of the Cornfield, scene of heavy fighting at Antietam.

An artillery spotter surveys Confederate positions at a signal tower on Elk Mountain. Once again, Union artillery accuracy was a Federal strength.

been received there to prepare for the arrival of a number of wounded to-morrow.

The Secessionists in Baltimore claim to be in receipt of private intelligence from the seat of war favorable to the rebel cause, and are in excellent spirits.

THE TWELFTH NEW YORK MILITIA,

BALTIMORE, Thursday, Sept. 18.

The Twelfth New-York Militia, paroled at Harper's Ferry, leave for New-York to-night. None of the regiment were injured. The officers retain the side arms and personal effects.

Col. MILES' body arrives here this afternoon.

LIEUT.-COL. DWIGHT WOUNDED.

BOSTON, Thursday, Sept. 18.

A private dispatch states that Lieut.-Col. DWIGHT, of the Second Massachusetts Regiment, was badly wounded in the late battle.

OUR SPECIAL CORRESPONDENCE.

LETTER FROM BOONSBORO.

The Rear-Guard of the Rebels Overtaken on Monday—An Artillery Duel—Commencement of the Great Battle of Sharpsburgh on Tuesday—The Rebels Driven Back at all Points, &c.

BOONSBORO, Md., Tuesday, Sept. 16, 1862.

The pursuing Union army came up with the rear guard of the rebel forces in Pleasant Valley yesterday. The enemy made a stand, for the evident purpose of gaining time for their advance to cross the river, and erected batteries upon the heights two miles beyond Boonsboro. Gen. SUMNER's corps, with BANKS' command, occupied the advance, and shelled the rebels steadily during the afternoon. There was no infantry engagement, and but slight loss on our side. Our guns, however, seemed to tell with good effect, and soon silenced the rebel batteries, and they pushed on toward the river, whither our forces pursued them to within five miles of the Potomac, skirmishing all along the way.

The rebel troops took advantage of the confusion existing in their ranks, and concealed themselves by hundreds in the woods, awaiting the approach of our troops, when they would come out and give themselves up. They seem thoroughly disgusted and tired of fighting. They do not manifest any leaning toward the Union cause, but simply wish to get out of a bad scrape. A squad of seven hundred of them will be sent to the rear, under a strong guard, to-night. I incline to the belief that the well-known character of Gen. BURNSIDE for clemency in the treatment of his prisoners has had a powerful effect upon the rebel army, and is fast depleting their ranks. They seem to regard him with a feeling almost akin to veneration.

RENEWAL OF THE CONFLICT TO-DAY

About 8½ A. M., our batteries, supported by Gen. BANKS' column in the centre, began to shell the enemy, who had crossed Antietam Creek, a stream about as large as the Monocacy, and at a point about five miles from the Potomac. The cannonading was continued up to 2½ o'clock P. M. without bringing on any general engagement. The enemy appears to have expended his stock of shells, and uses principally round shot. One of their missiles struck near the root of a tree where a group of our men were sitting, and killed and wounded three or four. There had been no great loss, apparently, on either side, up to the time above-named. *The enemy, however, were steadily dislodged and driven back from every place where he made a stand,* and it was reported at the front, at 2½ o'clock, that the rebels were skedaddling in disorder. "*Sauve qui peut*" had become the cry in the rebel ranks, and each man, on his own hook, was making for the river. I cannot vouch for the correctness of the report. A heavy firing wound up the day.

Gen. McCLELLAN's headquarters are now at the extreme front. His presence inspires the troops with emulation and enthusiasm.

The reports from Harper's Ferry have been conflicting. I have seen some soldiers belonging to the Maryland Brigade, who assert that Col. MILES surrendered Maryland Heights to the rebel forces yesterday morning. That he held out in expectation of reinforcements, but failing to receive them, gave up the position, after spiking the guns and throwing some of the heavier cannon down the precipice. It is also reported that the whole force, some 8,000 strong, were paroled and dismissed, Gen. LONGSTREET taking possession of the Heights.

On the contrary, the report to-day at headquarters is that Col. MILES had three times repulsed the rebel troops, and still held out. In the midst of so many conflicting rumors, it is difficult to decide what is true and what false. I shall press forward in that direction in the morning.

PHELPS' Georgia Legion and COBB's Legion have suffered heavily by desertions since they came into Maryland. They do not seem to relish a return to Virginia, with the prospect of another long Winter campaign before them, and the State wasted by the ravages of war, and destitute of crops and subsistence for the troops.

There are now strong indications of an easterly storm—perhaps we are about to have the usual equinoxial storms, in which case the chances of the rebels escaping across the Potomac, swollen by heavy rains, will be very poor indeed.   E. S.

P. S.—Our loss at the battle of Crampton's Gap was not heavy. I have not yet heard the report of the numbers killed and wounded, but judge it does not exceed 75 or 100. Some dozen of the wounded were last evening sent to Middletown, where they ought not to have been sent, considering the already crowded condition of the town.

The New-York Times.

VOL. XI—NO. 3430   NEW-YORK, SATURDAY, SEPTEMBER 20, 1862.   PRICE TWO CENTS.

GREAT VICTORY.

The Rebel Army in Full Flight Out of Maryland.

The Dead and Wounded Left Behind.

Our Cavalry Pushing Them Across the Potomac.

The Whole National Army in Good Condition.

Further Details of the Great Battle of Wednesday.

No Fighting of Consequence on Thursday.

Official Dispatches from Gen. McClellan.

HE ANNOUNCES A COMPLETE VICTORY.

DISPATCHES FROM GEN. McCLELLAN.

FIRST DISPATCH.
HEADQUARTERS ARMY OF POTOMAC.}
Sept. 19—8:30 A. M. }

Maj.-Gen. H. W. Halleck, General-in-Chief:

But little occurred yesterday, except skirmishing.

Last night the enemy abandoned his position, leaving his dead and wounded on the field.

We are again in pursuit.

I do not yet know whether he is falling back on an interior position, or crossing the river.

We may safely claim a victory.

GEORGE B. McCLELLAN,
MAJOR-GENERAL.

SECOND DISPATCH.
HEADQUARTERS ARMY OF POTOMAC.}
Friday, Sept. 19—10½ A. M. }

Maj.-Gen. H. W. Halleck, General-in-Chief:

PLEASANTON is driving the enemy across the river.

Our victory was complete.

The enemy is driven back into Virginia. Maryland and Pennsylvania are now safe.

GEO. B. McCLELLAN, Major-General.

Major-General Joseph K.F. Mansfield, killed at Antietam.

OUR LATEST WASHINGTON DISPATCHES.

WASHINGTON, Friday, Sept. 19—11½ P. M.

A special dispatch from the TIMES' Baltimore correspondent says that Gen. McCLELLAN's bulletins have greatly discouraged the rebels there. They are inclined to believe that the Confederate combinations have failed, and that their cause is ruined.

WASHINGTON, Friday, Sept. 19—12 Midnight.

It is now clearly apparent that the rebel army is repelled from Maryland. Probably nearly or quite the whole has succeeded in crossing the Potomac, with slight additional loss of men, wagons and artillery. It is believed that the rebels can sufficiently defend the most important crossings to enable the bulk of their forces successfully to retreat to Winchester, which is probably their base, or to any other point they choose.

LATEST REPORTS FROM HEADQUARTERS.

HEADQUARTERS OF THE ARMY OF THE POTOMAC.}
Friday Morning, Sept. 19, 1862. }

Yesterday was occupied in burying the dead and caring for the wounded.

The rebels sent in a flag of truce in the morning, asking permission to bury their own dead, which was granted.

At first the orders were very stringent against holding intercourse with the rebels, but during the afternoon they were relaxed, and the troops of both sides freely intermingled.

The following is a list of some of the killed and wounded:

Brig.-Gen. Rodman, commanding a brigade in Major-Gen. Burnside's Division, was wounded.

Col. Stear, of the Fourth Rhode Island Regiment, was wounded in the hip.

Lieut.-Col. Appleman, of the Eighth Connecticut Regiment, was wounded.

Capt. Griswold, of the Eleventh Connecticut Regiment.

Lieut. Arenberg, of SEAMAN's Ohio Battery, lost a leg.

Major Giles, of the Eighty-eighth Pennsylvania Regiment, was severely wounded.

Col. Barlow, of the Sixty-first New-York Regiment, was wounded.

Col. Goodrich, of the Sixty-first New-York Regiment, was killed.

Col. Reall, of the Tenth Pennsylvania Regiment, was wounded.

Col. Crossdale, of the One Hundred and

Twenty-eighth Pennsylvania Regiment, was killed.

Maj. Dwight, of the Second Massachusetts Regiment, was wounded.

At daylight, this morning, it was discovered that the enemy had changed their position. Whether their whole force has crossed the river, or taken a new position nearer the river, is not at present known.

Had the rebels remained, a general engagement between both armies would have taken place this morning.

OUR DISPATCHES FROM HARRISBURGH.

HARRISBURGH, Friday, Sept. 9—1 P. M.

A dispatch just in from Gov. CURTIN, on the battle-field, says that the battle is raging fearfully, and progressing favorably for our side.

McCLELLAN has been largely reinforced. The Pennsylvania militia were also advancing to the field, under Gen. REYNOLDS.

Surgeon-Gen. SMITH has telegraphed to prepare for the wounded to be brought here, and all the churches and other buildings are being got ready.

There is intense excitement, but every one is full of hope.

HARRISBURGH, Friday, Sept. 19—3 P. M.

By an official telegram just received, we learn that our victory is complete. The enemy is in full retreat, and our forces are driving them to the river.

No details at present.

FROM THE ASSOCIATED PRESS CORRESPONDENT
HARRISBURGH, Friday, Sept. 19.

Information just received from the battle-field says our victory is complete, and that Gen. PLEASANTON is in hot pursuit of the enemy, and driving them across the Potomac. The whole Federal army is in good condition, and the enemy has been badly punished.

THE GREAT BATTLE OF WEDNESDAY.

BALTIMORE, Friday, Sept. 19.

A gentleman who left the battle-field at 9 o'clock on Wednesday night, confirms the statement of the reporter of the Associated Press at headquarters, in every particular.

He says that our forces occupied the position chosen by the enemy at the commencement of the battle, and that the rebels were driven back a mile and a half at all points, except upon our extreme right, which they still held at the close of the day.

Our informant was all day within a hundred yards of Gen. McCLELLAN, and says that the results of the day were regarded by him and his Staff as a glorious victory, though not a final one.

There was no faltering at any point of the line of our whole army.

Our soldiers were exultant at the results of the day's fight, and Gen. McCLELLAN was in the highest spirits.

The opinion of Gen. McCLELLAN and those around him was that the final result would depend on who got reinforcements first.

Our informant says that nothing had been heard on the field of the capture of Gen. LONGSTREET or

Confederate Major-General D.H. Hill's center lines held against a Federal onslaught at Bloody Lane.

the killing of Gen. HILL, and that there is no truth in either report.

Twenty thousand more reinforcements were expected to reach the field yesterday from Harrisburgh.

Our informant thinks the loss of the rebels fully equal to ours.

The gentleman who furnished us with the foregoing intelligence is one of our most respectable and intelligent citizens, and says that the battle of Wednesday was not a decisive one. It was a contest in which all the advantages were with Gen. McCLELLAN, who occupied the field of battle at the close of the day.

GEN. MANSFIELD.

Brig. Gen. J. K. F. MANSFIELD, killed at the battle of Sharpsburgh on Wednesday, was a native of Connecticut, from which State he was appointed a cadet to the West Point Military Academy in Oct., 1817. He was at the time of his death about sixty years of age. He graduated on the 30th of June, 1822, standing No. 2 in a class of forty members, among whom are the names of Gens. HUNTER, McCALL, and others noted during the present war. On the 1st of July, 1822, he was brevetted a Second Lieutenant of a corps of Engineers, and received his full rank the same day. On the 5th of March, 1832, he was promoted to a First Lieutenancy, and on the 7th of July, 1838, became Captain. He served in the Texan and Mexican wars, and on the 9th of May, 1846, was brevetted Major for gallant and distinguished services in the defence of Fort Browne, in Texas. On the 23d of the following September, he was brevetted Lieutenant-Colonel for gallant and meritorious conduct in the several battles of Monterey, in Mexico, on the 21st, 22d and 23d of September, 1846.

On the first of those days he was severely wounded. He was breveted Colonel on the 23d of February, 1847, for gallant and meritorious conduct at Buena Vista. During the campaigns of 1846 and 1847 of the war with Mexico he held the position of Chief Engineer of the army under Gen. TAYLOR. Previous to the war he had been appointed as member of the Board of Engineers, viz.: From Dec. 8, 1842, to Sept. 8, 1845, and after the war he resumed this same position, which he kept for some time. On the 28th of May, 1853, he was appointed an Inspector-General of the United States Army, with the rank of Colonel. This position he held at the breaking out of the rebellion. On the 6th of May, 1861, he was brevetted a Brigadier-General of the Regular United States Army, and on the 14th of May, 1861, was commissioned a full Brigadier-General. He was placed in command of the position at Newport's News, which he held until the advance upon Norfolk transferred his services to the other shore of the James River.

He was next placed in command at Suffolk, Va. When Gen. Pore met with his reverses in Virginia, and demanded a Court of Inquiry to examine into the conduct of certain of his officers, Gen. MANSFIELD was ordered to proceed to Washington to sit as one of the Court. The inquiry having been postponed, by order of the President, at the request of Gen. McCLELLAN, Gen. MANSFIELD was assigned a post of duty in the field. In the discharge of that duty he fell, at the post of honor.

COL. McNEIL.

Among the killed in this week's terrible battles in Maryland, is COL. McNEIL, the commander of the justly celebrated "Bucktail" Regiment, while leading a charge at the head of his men, near Antietam Creek. HUGH WATSON McNIEL was a son of Rev. A. McNIEL, a Cameronian clergyman, and was born in Seneca County, New York, in 1830. He was educated at Yale College, and entered upon the study of the law in the office of CLARENCE W. SEWARD, at Auburn. In 1857 he commenced practice in this City, but was obliged to abandon his profession two years afterward, by reason of ill health. He removed to Pennsylvania, and engaged in banking. Upon the breaking out of the rebellion he enlisted as a private in a company known as "Wild Cats," commanded by Capt. STONE, which was afterwards incorporated with the famous Bucktail Regiment. In a short time he was chosen First Lieutenant and then Captain. In this capacity he led the regiment in a magnificent bayonet charge at Drainesville. The exploits of the regiment are familiar to all. While with McDOWELL on the Rappahannock; while in pursuit of Stonewall JACKSON up the Shenandoah Valley, under FREMONT, and particularly at the spirited battle of Cross Keys, the Bucktails gained the foremost name for valor and vigor. And since then they have not ceased for a day to harrass the enemy. They accompanied Gen. HOOKER in the recent expedition up the Potomac in quest of Stonewall JACKSON. On Tuesday they came up with the enemy under LEE, near Sharpsburgh. The National troops were disposed in order of battle. The Bucktails were at the front. The action commenced at dark and lasted two hours. Col. McNEIL had just charged upon the rebel forces, driving them back half a mile, when he received his death wound.

He was a daring and intrepid officer, a generous friend and kinsman, the idol of his family and regiment, and his loss cannot be replaced.

BATTLE OF ANTIETAM CREEK.

Full Particulars from Our Special Correspondent.

The Most Stupendous Struggle of Modern Times.

The Battle Won by Consummate Generalship.

The Rebel Losses Estimated as High as Thirty Thousand.

A GREAT NUMBER OF PRISONERS CAPTURED.

BATTLE-FIELD OF ANTIETAM CREEK, }
Thursday, Sept. 18, 1862. }

Another great battle has been fought, and the cause of the Union has once more been vindicated upon one of the most bloody and well-contested fields known to ancient or modern times. Wednesday, Sept. 17, 1862, will, we predict, hereafter be looked upon as an epoch in the history of the rebellion, from which will date the inauguration of its downfall. On that day about one hundred and sixty thousand men met in deadly strife upon the field of Antietam—a name which will occupy a leading position in the history of the war—and there, marshaled by brave and able men, fought with a desperation and courage never before excelled, and rarely, if ever equaled, for twelve hours, leaving the Union army in possession of the contested ground. This victory was not gained, however, without the sacrifice of many valuable lives, and the maiming of thousands of individuals.

PRECEDING EVENTS.

Before attempting to present even a glance at this battle, let us first prepare the reader for a correct understanding of it by relating—in continuation of my last letter—the events immediately preceding the great contest. My last brought Gen. McCLELLAN's

Major-General Israel Richardson was another Union casualty, killed while assaulting D.H. Hill's troops.

advance into Maryland up to midday on Tuesday, Sept. 16, at which time the army occupied a position in close proximity to the road leading from Boonesville to Sharpsburgh, and upon and near the left bank of the little creek known by the name of Antietam, which rises in Central Pennsylvania, and, after running in a southerly direction, its waters are mingled with the turgid waters of the Potomac, about five miles above Harper's Ferry.

The enemy occupied a position on the right bank of the Antietam, favorably located for both offensive and defensive operations, and in this respect had the advantage. To circumvent the enemy, and secure an equally favorable position, was the first object to be obtained. That this required the genius of a great leader, needed no military man to elucidate, for the whole position of affairs could be taken in at a glance. How well and successfully this object was accomplished, the success of our arms is abundant evidence. Of some of the details of the movement to this end we shall give in the proper place. Just across the creek, in plain view from the eastern bank, the enemy's skirmishers could be distinctly seen, and from elevated positions massed forces of infantry and cavalry could be discovered in every little valley and ravine for miles on either hand. Two hundred thousand men was what the enemy pretended to have within the scope of the eye, and from repeated personal inspection, aided by an excellent glass, while standing in a favorable position, I should judge the figure named not an exaggerated one.

PREPARATIONS FOR A MOVEMENT.

Between 12 and 2 o'clock P. M. all was silent along the lines. The German Battery of sixteen 20-pound Parrott guns, upon the eminence overlooking the river's bank were silent. Major ARNDT had fallen, and the infantry battalions were quietly resting upon the ground under the hill, upon the tops of which were planted our artillery. This quietness was like the quietness that precedes the storm. The Commanding General had arrived upon the ground at an early hour the day before, and had made himself familiar with the position, and [at the time of which we write was busily engaged in giving the necessary instructions to the Commanders of Corps, so as to render our success in the impending conflict as much a matter of certainty as possible.

THE MOVEMENT.

Soon after 2 o'clock P. M. the Parrott guns, to which allusion has been made before, were opened upon the enemy and worked with great rapidity, and nearly every shell thrown, as I afterward ascertained, did fearful execution in the massed columns of the enemy. In a brief space after this terrible fire had been opened, there was a movement of the troops inexplicable to the uninitiated at the moment, but the object of which was soon revealed to the careful observer. The Antietam was to be crossed! Gen. HOOKER's Corps, by a flank movement, gained a point to the north of between two and three miles, and changing direction to the left reached the river at Kelly's Ford. A portion of the Pennsylvania Reserve, under command of Brig.-Gen. MEADE, were thrown across the river and were deployed as skirmishers, and under their cover and the support of the German New-York Battery, Gen. HOOKER's column very speedily gained a foothold upon the opposite bank. Our skirmishers were met with a galling fire, poured in by the skirmishers of the enemy and the fire from a battery of four or six pieces, so located as to give a raking fire to the advancing column. Fortunately this battery was not well managed and most of the missiles were thrown too high, hence our loss at this point was comparatively trifling. This battery was speedily silenced, and the rapid movements of Gen. HOOKER's column soon placed it in jeopardy; but the enemy, always on the alert, managed to get their pieces out of the way before a battery could be thrown across to sustain the infantry column in its local movements. The enemy's skirmishers were forced back step by step by the Reserves to their main body, by which time the whole of the advancing column was in position, and ready for more decisive offensive operations. The enemy rushed forward seemingly bent upon annihilating the comparatively small force sent against them, and several times there was some wavering under the terrible and impetuous resistance —but the troops quickly rallied, and, under the lead of their able commander, secured the much coveted and a necessary position to secure success. This movement across the river was one for which Gen HOOKER was peculiarly qualified, and he executed it in a manner highly creditable to his skill as a General. Here the battle of Antietam commenced in earnest. Until nightfall set in Gen. HOOKER pressed the enemy back, and every step was gained by hard fighting.

THE BATTLE OF ANTIETAM.

On Wednesday morning, Sept. 17, the sun rose in a cloudless sky, and all nature seemed to smile as if the world were filled with the elect of God. But its splendors were soon dimmed with the smoke rising from the battle-field.

To enable the reader to understand the events of this day, he should look at a map which has laid out the principal roads throughout the State of Maryland. With a pencil follow the road or "pike" from Boonsboro' direct to Sharpsburgh—which is nearly three miles west of the river, at the point where the road crosses it; the battle-field is on both sides of that road—between the river and Sharpsburgh—the bulk of it being north of the Boonsboro' road, and in the triangle formed by the roads connecting Bakersville and Middletown and Bakersville and Sharpsburgh. The surface is interspersed with hill and vale, and covered with cornfields and grass land, and skirting and stretching toward the centre from different points are thin belts of forest trees—all of which gives advantage to the enemy acting on the defensive, he having an opportunity to select his position for defensive operations, and when forced from one position he has only to fall back a short distance to find a position naturally as strong as the first. The engagement was opened early Wednesday morning by the advance of a strong line of our skirmishers. They were met by a similar movement on the part of the enemy. The latter were forced back until the right of our line (Gen. HOOKER's,) came into action with the enemy's left, commanded by Gen. HILL, who commands a portion of LONGSTREET's corps. BANKS' corps was, within a half an hour, at work, and was followed soon after by Gen. PATTERSON's command. The first fire was at about 5 o'clock, and at 6 o'clock the infantry arm entered upon its work. The line thus formed.

THE ENEMY'S LEFT WAS FORCED BACK

for nearly three miles from the ford, where the bulk of

our troops crossed the creek before 9 o'clock, when they were relieved by Gen. SEDGWICK's coming to the front. Just previous to this, MORRIS' Brigade, of HOOKER's command, had advanced from a belt of timber across a plowed field into a piece of woods, where the enemy, massed in great force, were repulsed, and the troops fell back to the belt of timber in some disorder, but soon rallied again, and regained the field in front. It was at this time that Gen. MANSFIELD, in command of Gen. BANKS' corps, was mortally wounded, carried from the field and died soon afterward. Gen. WILLIAMS succeeded to the command of the corps, and Gen. CRAWFORD took command of WILLIAMS' Division until he was wounded and taken from the field. The repulse of MORRIS' Brigade was accomplished by an old and contemptible trick of the enemy. As the corps advanced to the woods across the plowed field, the rebels unfurled the Stars and Stripes, and waving them, cried out, "What the h—l are you doing? Don't fire upon your friends!" Our troops, deceived by this ruse, ceased firing, when the rebels opened upon them a murderous volley of musketry and cross fire, and creating a temporary panic. They rallied and drove the rebels back, but it was done at a great sacrifice of life.

These troops were relieved by

GEN. SEDGWICK'S COMMAND

coming up on their left. The enemy who had gained a point of timber extending some distance in front of our line, at the left of Gen. BANKS' corps, were driven out, and across a plowed field in front, to the timber beyond, with great slaughter—AYER's battery opening upon them with great effect, strewing the ground with the dead. At one point, just on the brow of a little roll of the ground that the infantry, emerging suddenly upon the open field, supposed that it was a rebel force in waiting for them and the dead rebels got an extra volley. This corps came into action by brigades, between 9 and 9 o'clock—GORMAN's, DANA's and HOWARD's. While preparing for action, the enemy appeared from an unexpected quarter, and opened a terrific fire with a view of breaking the line by a sudden attack with musketry and artillery, he believing that it was composed of raw troops. But they soon discovered their mistake; these veterans, notwithstanding the sudden attack, though their lines were broken for a moment, were not disconcerted, but received it with cheers. While under this galling fire the Fifteenth Regiment Massachusetts Volunteers made a dash forward and seized the battle-flag of one of Gen. HILL's regiments, and now have it to show to their friends as a trophy of the day. In this connection it should be mentioned that Capt. HOWE and Lieut. WHITTIER, of Gen. Sedgwick's Staff, distinguished themselves in the action by rallying the left of Gen. Sedgwick's division, and on several occasions, by their example, they encouraged the men in discharging their duties faithfully. Gen. Sedgwick's horse was killed, and he was wounded twice, but remained on the field until he was ordered to the rear with his command.

FRENCH'S DIVISION.

The division under Gen. FRENCH occupied a position to the left of Sedgwick's, and was fairly engaged by 10½ o'clock. The fighting on the extreme right at this time was confined mostly to artillery, while the tide of infantry fighting swept along toward the left of our line. The left of this division gave way and fell back from the superior force they had to contend against—the rebel hordes making pell mell after them. The left fell back in pretty good order, and upon a walk, under as galling a fire of musketry as is often experienced. This movement was evidently no fault of the men. The rebels advanced, and as they ventured a little to the rear of our line at that point, Col. BURKE (acting Brigadier-General in Gen. RICHARDSON's Di-

vision,) changed his front, and poured in several volleys upon their flank, strewing the ground with dead. The balance, hastened somewhat by a cross fire from AYER's battery, fled in utter dismay. The left of FRENCH's Division advanced again, and fought like heroes until ordered to the rear.

RICHARDSON'S DIVISION.

Three Brigades of this Division, commanded by Gen. MEAGHER, Gen. CALDWELL and Col. BURKE' Tenth Pennsylvania, did not cross the creek until Wednesday morning, when Gen. RICHARDSON was ordered to form on the left of FRENCH's Division The Division crossed the river and moved up with alacrity near the line of battle, ready for action. Having filed about through the valleys to avoid letting the enemy know of the movement, the Division laid down under the brow of a hill, just in rear of the line of battle, until wanted. It was now about 9 o'clock.

THE IRISH BRIGADE.

In less than half an hour after taking this position Gen. MEAGHER was ordered to enter the line with the Irish Brigade. They marched up to the brow of the hill, cheering as they went, led by Gen. MEAGHER in person, and were welcomed with cheers by FRENCH's Brigade. The musketry fighting at this point was the severest and most deadly ever witnessed before—so acknowledged by veterans in the service. Men on both sides fell in large numbers every moment, and those who were eye-witnesses of the struggle did not suppose it possible for a single man to escape. The enemy here, at first, were concealed behind a knoll, so that only their heads were exposed. The brigade advanced up the slope with a cheer, when a most deadly fire was poured in by a second line of the enemy concealed in the Sharpsburgh road, which at this place is several feet lower than the surrounding surface, forming a complete rifle-pit, and also from a force partially concealed still further to the rear.

At this time the color-bearer in the right wing advanced several paces to the front, and defiantly waved his flag in the faces of the enemy; as if by a miracle, he escaped without serious injury.

The line of the brigade, in its advance up the hill was broken in the centre temporarily by an obstruction, the right wing having advanced to keep up with the colors, and fell back a short distance, when Gen. MEAGHER directed that a rail fence which the enemy a few minutes before had been fighting behind should be torn down. His men, in face of a galling fire, obeyed the order when the whole brigade advanced to the brow the hill, cheering as they went and causing the enemy to fall back to their second line—the Strasburgh road, which is some three feet lower than the surrounding surface. In this road were massed a large force of infantry, and here was the most hotly contested point of the day. Each brigade of this Division was in turn brought into action at this point and the struggle was truly terrific for more than four hours—the enemy finally, however, were forced from their position. In this work the New-York German Battery, stationed on the hill across the Creek, rendered efficient service by pouring in upon their massed forces a constant stream of 20-pound shells.

Gen. CALDWELL's Brigade was next ordered into action by Gen. RICHARDSON in person. They two advanced in good order, cheering, and were received with cheers by the Irish Brigade. It was at about this time that the left of FRENCH's Division, commanded by Col. BROOKS, of the Tenth Pennsylvania, was directed by Gen. RICHARDSON to wheel to the right, and a murderous flanking fire was poured into the flank of an advancing division of the enemy, causing him to recoil, and fall back in disorder.

This division was actively engaged for nearly five hours, and lost nearly half of the men taken into action.

A Confederate battery and the fallen who manned it testify to the ferocity of fighting at Dunker Church, a scene of heavy fighting at Antietam.

The New-York Times.

VOL. XI–NO. 3432.   NEW-YORK, TUESDAY, SEPTEMBER 23, 1862.   PRICE TWO CENTS.

HIGHLY IMPORTANT.

A Proclamation by the President of the United States.

The War Still to be Prosecuted for the Restoration of the Union.

A DECREE OF EMANCIPATION.

All Slaves in States in Rebellion on the First of January Next to be Free.

The Gradual Abolition and Colonization Schemes Adhered to.

Loyal Citizens to be Remunerated for Losses' Including Slaves.

WASHINGTON, Monday, Sept. 22.

By the President of the United States of America:

A PROCLAMATION.

I, ABRAHAM LINCOLN, President of the United States of America, and Commander-in-Chief of the Army and Navy thereof, do hereby proclaim and declare, that hereafter, as heretofore, the war will be prosecuted for the object of practically restoring the constitutional relation between the United States and the people thereof in which States that relation is, or may be suspended or disturbed; that it is my purpose, upon the next meeting of Congress, to again recommend the adoption of a practical measure tendering pecuniary aid to the free acceptance or rejection of all the Slave States so called, the people whereof may not then be in rebellion against the United States, and which States may then have voluntarily adopted, or thereafter may voluntarily adopt, the immediate or gradual abolishment of Slavery within their respective limits; and that the efforts to colonize persons of African descent with their consent, upon the Continent or elsewhere, with the previously obtained consent of the governments existing there, will be continued.

That on the first day of January, in the year of our Lord one thousand eight hundred and sixty-three, all persons held as slaves within any State, or any designated part of a State, the people whereof shall then be in rebellion against the Unit- ed States shall be then, thenceforward, and forever, free; and the Executive Government of the United States, including the military and naval authority thereof, will recognize and maintain the freedom of such persons, and will do no act or acts to repress such persons, or any of them, in any efforts they may make for their actual freedom.

That the Executive will, on the first day of January aforesaid, by proclamation, designate the States and parts of States, if any, in which the people thereof, respectively, shall then be in rebellion against the United States; and the fact that any State, or the people thereof, shall on that day be in good faith represented in the Congress of the United States by members chosen thereto at elections wherein a majority of the qualified voters of such State shall have participated, shall, in the absence of strong countervailing testimony, be deemed conclusive evidence that such State and the people thereof have not been in rebellion against the United States.

That attention is hereby called to an act of Congress entitled "An act to make an additional article of war," approved March 13, 1862, and which act is in the words and figure following:

"Be it enacted by the Senate and House of Representatives of the United States of America in Congress assembled, That hereafter the following shall be promulgated as an additional article of war for the government of the army of the United States, and shall be obeyed and observed as such.

ARTICLE—All officers or persons in the military or naval service of the United States are prohibited from employing any of the forces under their respective commands for the purpose of returning fugitives from service or labor who may have escaped from any person to whom such service or labor is claimed to be due, and any officer who shall be found guilty by a Court-martial of violating this article shall be dismissed from the service.

SECTION 2. And be it further enacted, that this act shall take effect from and after its passage."

Also to the ninth and tenth sections of an act entitled "An act to suppress insurrection, to punish treason and rebellion, to seize and confiscate property of rebels, and for other purposes," approved July 17, 1862, and which sections are in the words and figures following:

SEC. 9. And be it further enacted, that all slaves of persons who shall hereafter be engaged in rebellion against the Government of the United States, or who shall, in any way, give aid or comfort thereto, escaping from such persons and taking refuge within the lines of the army; and all slaves captured from such persons or deserted by them and coming under the control of the Government of the United States, and all slaves of such persons found on (or being within) any place occupied by rebel forces and afterward occupied by the forces of the United States, shall be deemed captures of war and shall be forever free of their servitude and not again held as slaves.

SEC. 10. And be it further enacted, That no slave escaping into any State, Territory or the District of Columbia, from any of the States, shall be delivered up, or in any way impeded or hindered of his liberty, except for crime or some offence against the laws, unless the person claiming said fugitive shall first make oath that the person to whom the labor or service of such fugitive is alleged to be due, is his lawful owner, and has not been in arms against the United States in the present rebellion, nor in any way given aid and comfort thereto, and no person engaged in the military or naval service of the United States shall, under any pretence whatever, assume to decide on the validity of the claim of any person to the service or labor of any other person, or surrender up any such person to the claimant, on pain of being dismissed from the service.

And I do hereby enjoin upon and order all persons engaged in the military and naval service of the United States, to observe, obey and enforce, within their respective spheres of service, the act and sections above recited.

And the Executive will in due time recommend that all citizens of the United States who shall have remained loyal thereto throughout the rebellion, shall (upon the restoration of the constitutional relation between the United States and their respective States and people, if the relation shall have been suspended or disturbed,) be compensaed for all losses by acts of the United States, *including the loss of slaves.*

In witness whereof, I have hereunto set my hand, and caused the seal of the United States to be affixed.

Done at the City of Washington, this Twenty-second day of September, in the year of our Lord one thousand eight hundred and sixty-two, and of the Independence of the United States the eighty-seventh.

ABRAHAM LINCOLN.

By the President.

WILLIAM H. SEWARD, Secretary of State.

GENERAL NEWS FROM WASHINGTON.

OUR SPECIAL WASHINGTON DISPATCHES.

WASHINGTON, Monday, Sept. 22.

THE PRESIDENT'S PROCLAMATION.

The great event of the day here is the proclamation of the President ordering the execution of the war measures of the last Congress, and promising freedom to the slaves in all States that persist in the rebellion against the Government. This act, so long expected, so long delayed, bids fair to simplify at once the issues of the war, and immediately to array against each other the unconditionally loyal and the rebellious of all shades and grades. If the cause of the Union and free institutions is strongest, this test will show it, and the only question of its triumph will then be the power in the Government to execute its policy with courage and vigor.

THE NEWS FROM KENTUCKY.

A special private dispatch, just received from Cincinnati, announces that BRAGG is marching on Louisville, Ky., and that Gen. NELSON has ordered the women and children to leave the city. BUELL is believed to have been outgeneraled, and to be several hours behind. The dispatch closes—"A General wanted for the West."

THE LATEST WAR NEWS.

A Raid of Stuart's Cavalry Across the Potomac at Williamsport.

NO DAMAGE DONE.

The Reoccupation of Maryland Heights by Our Forces.

THE REBELS CONTINUING THEIR RETREAT

No Further Collisions at Last Accounts.

LATEST REPORTS FROM HEADQUARTERS.

HEADQUARTERS OF THE ARMY OF THE POTOMAC,
Saturday Evening, Sept. 20, 1862.

The firing heard last evening in the direction of Williamsport, turns out to have been a raid of STUART'S rebel cavalry. He crossed the Potomac on Friday night into Maryland, at that point, with his cavalry, one regiment of infantry, and seventeen pieces of artillery. The force sent up to drive him back, arrived near the town late in the afternoon. The firing heard was principally from the rebel guns. During the night they recrossed into Virginia and this morning they had disappeared from the opposite shore. No one was hurt.

The work of burying the dead is still continuing. They average about one thousand per day. To-morrow will probably finish it.

The Maryland Heights were yesterday occupied by a National force.

The indications are that the rebels are continuing their retreat into Virginia, leaving the line of the Potomac.

Divine worship was held at headquarters this evening, Bishop WHIPPLE, of Minnesota, officiating.

HEADQUARTERS, ARMY OF THE POTOMAC,
Monday Evening, Sept. 22.

The following is the official report of loss in SUMNER'S corps at the battle of the Antietam:

GEN. RICHARDSON'S DIVISION.

Killed	212
Wounded	800
Missing	24

GEN. SEDGWICK'S DIVISION.

Killed	335
Wounded	1,577
Missing	321

GEN. FRENCH'S DIVISION.

Killed	293
Wounded	1,321
Missing	203
Total loss in Gen. SUMNER'S Corps	5,208

The loss in missing may be somewhat reduced by stragglers returning.

A train of cars crossed the Monocacy this morning. The road is now open to Harper's Ferry, where there is a sufficient Federal force for all purposes.

The rebels, in their hasty retreat from Maryland, left between 1,100 and 1,200 wounded between Sharpsburgh and the river. They are being paroled.

Twenty-six stands of colors were taken during the battle of the Antietam, and have been received at headquarters. Seven more are known to have been captured, and are in the hands of the different regiments which captured them.

OUR LATEST WASHINGTON DISPATCHES.

WASHINGTON, Monday, Sept. 22.

A special dispatch from Frederick states that some surgeons, just arrived from the army, report rebels still falling back from the Potomac. Not even their pickets are now to be seen.

Another dispatch states that our losses in the last fight are not nearly as great as at first reported, especially in SUMNER'S Corps. In the California Regiment only one commissioned officer was killed (Lieut. WILSE) and one hundred and fifty privates killed and wounded.

The last reports from headquarters represented "All quiet along the lines."

REVIEW OF THE WEEK'S BATTLES

Is McClellan a Great General?

NEW-YORK, Monday, Sept. 22, 1862.
To the Editor of the New-York Times:

The force of circumstances, seconded by the reckless valor of our troops, have crowned the arms of the Republic with a sound success; and from this moment we may reassure ourselves that the rebellion must go down.

The Confederates, intoxicated by the strange sacrifice of POPE into their hands at Centreville, and being withal driven to take desperate risks by the poverty of their resources, decided to press too much upon their luck, and consequently made a fatal error. They had hurried toward Washington in the hope of seizing it while comparatively undefended, and being impressed, afterward, with a deep disdain for our generalship, adopted the hair-brained scheme of putting to sea in Maryland, in expectation that the seditious gales and risings of that State, would enable them to sail on, and winter in Philadelphia and New-York. The alternatives of this programme were extreme, for unseconded by Mary-

President Lincoln and his Cabinet consider the Emancipation Proclamation.

land, they must perforce retire, and if intercepted while thus hastening back, might suffer the loss of their entire army. But the demands of hunger, the temptations of success, and the established slowness of our anaconda, decided them to make the throw This last reliance was probably their leading calculation, and they believed they could at least get a full belly by the raid, and gather from the unravaged fields a week's rations before they were disturbed.

They entered Maryland on the 2d of September, JACKSON going first and LEE following with the main army. They ate the country out like locusts, but the expected rising was a failure; so LEE, feeling that he had sustained a virtual defeat, without any intervention by our forces, had no course left but to withdraw and bear back with him as much provender and spoil as possible.

To provide for his retreat, he sent JACKSON and HILL to Harper's Ferry, and then lingered about Frederick in the hope that the latent influence of his proclamation might still fructify in treason and in troops. Though McCLELLAN had set out in pursuit of him as early as the 7th, LEE remained at Frederick till the 11th, and then his rear guard yielded to the advance of HOOKER, who entered on the morning of the 12th.

On this very morning Harper's Ferry was attacked by HILL. That place was of the last importance to both armies. Without its protection the rebels would hardly be able to escape, while with it, the Union troops might make the destruction of their army sure. The force we had in that strong position numbered some 13,500 men, 2,000 of whom were cavalry. Col. MILES, who was the officer in command, finding himself attacked in unexpected force, sent couriers to McCLELLAN, urging him for aid. McCLELLAN was at Frederick on Saturday the 13th, and it would seem he got the news for we learn, through your paper that on the same date the Government sent him an urgent inquiry as to the strait of MILES, and that, "in reply to distinct orders from Washington, he at once telegraphed that reinforcements would reach Harper's Ferry *that* night." Now, it happened to be the case that his only two advanced columns, which had been pushed ahead of him from Frederick, were the corps under HOOKER, which was to attack Hagerstown heights away to the north on the next morning, and the divisions of FRANKLIN, which were en route for Crampton's Gap, where they also were to fight the next day. Both of these points were two days' march from Harper's Ferry—indeed, four good days' tramp, at the rate the main army had hunted after LEE. You may, therefore, be in error as to this answer of McCLELLAN's, but whether you are or not, we are quite sure McCLELLAN did not truly appreciate the value of Harper's Ferry. To our mind it was worth his earliest march and the protection of his consolidated army, for with it we could have made a better base of operations than the Confederates did on the following Wednesday, because, in our possession it would have been attended with the advantage of the Pennsylvania troops advancing on the rebel rear, while the forces at Washington would be menacing their left.

LEE, on his part, however, seems to have fully appreciated the importance of Harper's Ferry, for while MILES was sending couriers for reinforcements, he orders JACKSON to unite with HILL and overwhelm MILES, while he stayed the columns of HOOKER and of FRANKLIN with his best divisions. It turned out that this strategy was successful. He obliged HOOKER and FRANKLIN both to fight on Sunday, the 14th, while poor MILES, who was miles and miles away, and pressed by the swarming divisions of JACKSON and HILL together, capitulated on the following morning. This was, by long odds, the heaviest disaster of the war, for it gave the rebels one hundred guns, vast military stores, a pontoon bridge, a safe road home, and virtually struck dead 11,538 of the flower of our troops for the remainder of the war. Compared with the disasters of an ordinary battle the mortal summing up is equal to the loss in killed and wounded inflicted by the conflict of a hundred thousand men, and will probably exceed the number of all our slain in the terrific battles that ensued on the three following days. Those of our citizens well know how to appreciate the blistering shame of that surrender who saw our brave fellows of the Twelfth march up Broadway on Friday last, without a gun among them, and nothing but a naked flag-staff in their hands.

LEE having accomplished this fine achievement, and probably being encouraged by it, to have a trial of strength with the Union army before retiring, now that his power to retreat was sure, ordered JACKSON and all the disposable forces of HILL to come to him and thus having got the whole of the rebel forces of

Virginia together, stretched them along the line of Antietam creek on Tuesday afternoon, in a formidable line of battle. The subsequent day's fight showed that his ground was well chosen. The creek was deep, ran in a crescent toward our forces, almost parallel with the Potomac, and was fordable only at one place to the north, and by a stone bridge, at some three miles distance to the south. McCLELLAN came up on Tuesday, and formed his plan of battle on the only fashion left him. The simple choice he had, was the wing on which to make his main attack, and he chose the right, for his chief demonstration, as LEE knew he must, in order to gain possession of a projecting piece of wood, which would constantly threaten our right wing. FRANKLIN and SUMNER were to be more toward the center, and were to support and feed the exigencies of our right. FITZ JOHN PORTER was to act as a reserve, while BURNSIDE was to go to the left, force his way over the stone bridge, occupy the attention of the enemy's right, and when HOOKER succeeded in fascinating the main power of the enemy to his position, BURNSIDE was to make a vigorous flank movement, in order to throw the enemy into confusion. In pursuance of this plan, which, though blindly lauded as a flash of genius, was, from the very nature of the ground and position of the enemy, in accordance with the simplest military "A, B, C," Gen. HOOKER was intrusted with the main portion of the action. He forced his way across the upper ford on Tuesday afternoon, steadily obliging the rebels to give ground, and fighting every footstep till darkness settled on the scene.

The hostile soldiers slept so near, that at the first peep of dawn they could actually look into each other's eyes, and, by spontaneous action, each side, on that morning, seized its arms and vehemently recommenced the battle.

It is not our purpose to describe the details of the day; suffice it, that the contest raged fiercely on all sides from morn till night, and only ceased through mutual exhaustion when darkness had set in. On our side, HOOKER had been wounded early in the action, and MANSFIELD had been slain; but we had gained upon the enemy's position, and the advantage of the day remained unmistakably with us. BURNSIDE, it is true, had by the tameness and tardiness of his assault upon the bridge, placed us at one time in exceeding peril; but he worked out of it himself, and the division of FITZ JOHN PORTER was never once required in the action. The plan of the morning had been steadily followed out during the day. There was no strategy, no flashes of genius, no special manœuvering from headquarters.

It was a simple, downright, equal, forward pressure of resistless valor on our part, in which officers and men deserved alike, and which, in its limited display of generalship, is creditable to McCLELLAN. It must be obvious, however, to every intelligent mind, that he could have followed no other method than he did, and if he be reasonably modest, he must secretly have smiled at the hosannas of those besotted flatterers who, in the servile European style of journalism, have eagerly proclaimed that he deserves the undying gratitude of the country! As if it were not a sufficiently good thing, for a man of his moderate capacity, to have the station and income of a prince, without being thanked on bended knees by the entire people, for the gracious boon of his accepting them!

These are the movements of the first five days. Now, let us examine the result. On Thursday, the 18th, the rebels sent a flag of truce to ask the privilege of burying their dead, but making a mere show of this religious service, they used the opportunity to suddenly abandon their position, and, during the night, retreated in mass across the river. The dispatch of Gen. McCLELLAN, which announces this result, closes with the sentence: "The enemy is driven back into Virginia. Maryland and Pennsylvania are now safe." He might have added, without any violation of the truth, "and the rebel army is safe also."

The next day's telegram to the Associated Press chronicles the same facts in the following paragraph:

HEADQUARTERS ARMY OF THE POTOMAC,
Saturday Morning, Aug. 20.
The rebel army has succeeded in making its escape from Maryland. They commenced to leave about dusk on Thursday evening, and by daylight yesterday morning were all over, except a small rear guard. They saved all their transportation, and carried off all their wounded but 500.

We have nothing beyond this, at the present time of writing, than the fact that the reserve of PORTER reached the Potomac on Saturday; but, after crossing, and capturing a few prisoners from the enemy's rear guard, he was repulsed in force, and necessitated to come back.

And here the performance of the week concludes; and the summing up is, that the rebels have suffered but little at our hands that would not have resulted to them, had they retreated of their own accord. Their losses proceeded mainly from the failure of their own exaggerated expectations, while the battle portion of the drama, counting in the moral annihilation of twelve thousand of our own troops at Harper's Ferry, can scarcely entitle us to claim a victory. Our soldiers and division leaders gained superb triumphs on Sunday, Tuesday and Wednesday, but our leading General has lost the grand opportunity, and LEE may now freely challenge the admiration of the South, by telegraphing exultingly to DAVIS that "*the Army of Richmond is safe.*" In fact, his retreat over the Potomac was a masterpiece, and the manner in which he combined HILL and JACKSON for the envelopment of Harper's Ferry, while he checked our columns at Hagerstown Heights and Crampton Gap, is probably the best achievement of the war. The rapidity of his movements, as well as the perfection of his combinations, contrasts strangely with the marches of McCLELLAN; and when we behold JACKSON crossing and recrossing the Potomac, at long distances, in four days, we look with surprise at the tardiness of our early movement toward the enemy by a series of marches that barely averaged four or five miles a day. Does any one suppose, for an instant, that POPE, who found sixteen days of fighting out of thirty-five, between Centreville and the Rapidan, would not have found LEE at the end of fifty miles of well-known road in less than ten days? Or can any one believe that NAPOLEON, who is so honored in the adoption of his name by Little MAC, would not have first flung himself upon the base of Harper's Ferry, and selecting the ground which the enemy defended so effectively, have placed his presumptuous foe between two fires, and effectually prevented his retreat?

But the mistakes in the matter are not entirely those of McCLELLAN. HALLECK could have ordered him what main course to pursue (if McCLELLAN be not already superior even to his control,) and HALLECK should have made provision for attacking the retreating enemy on the right bank of the Potomac, in case he eluded the forces of McCLELLAN. His neglect to do so, while he had ample forces for that purpose, (if he supposed it possible for LEE to escape,) is just as gross an error as that of McCLELLAN, in making a ten-day march to get in front of LEE at Frederick, instead of getting behind him at Harper's Ferry, and obliging him to defend both front and rear.

We thus freely analyze the conduct and capacity of our military leaders, because they obviously challenge it, and because there is a servile disposition being hatched to render them imperial. Moreover, we perceive that the generous and unsuspicious public, inflamed by loyal happiness at results which have fallen to us merely through rebel exhaustion of resources, may heedlessly contribute to the scheme. Thousands cannot even yet bring themselves to comprehend the danger of dictatorship. They say, that in a country so irreverent as this, a military despotism is impossible. It strikes them, that such a mental revolution, with a people free and intelligent as we, would be a miracle not to be accomplished; but do they not see that treason against such a Government as this, is a greater mental marvel than admiration for a conqueror? Everything is possible to a debauched and corrupted public mind, and while any spark of constitutional liberty is still alive, it is worth the watching. Above all things, we wish the Government to remain in the hands of its constituted leaders, and the general management and policy of the campaign to be with the President and his civil counselors. After the scene at Centreville, where the legions of the Republic were betrayed to the enemy by Major-Generals who refused to fight, we are justly jealous of West Point, and we do not want its hand in the policy or settlement of the campaign. It is too largely represented on the rebel side to be safely trusted in that way, and the amenities and courtesies between its representatives in either army has already sufficiently amazed and perturbed the people. What we *do* want, is a full understanding with it, through a keen investigation of the late treason at Bull Run; and in the meantime, we want a leader from the President, who is equal to the spirit of our troops. We want no more caution, no more solemn, snail-like strategy. Our army has recently proved itself the finest ever seen on earth. It requires a leader who knows how to march, who has a stomach for fighting, and fast following up, and its motto should be that of the first NAPOLEON—"*Audace, toujours audace.*"

GEO. WILKES.

The New-York Times.

VOL. XI—NO. 3134.　　　　　NEW-YORK, THURSDAY, SEPTEMBER 25, 1862.　　　　　PRICE TWO CENTS.

IMPORTANT FROM WASHINGTON.

Another Proclamation by the President.

The Punishment of Rebels and Their Aiders and Abettors.

Suspension of the Writ of Habeas Corpus.

The Rebel Army Said to be Concentrating at Winchester.

THE REBELS FORTIFYING THE PLACE.

BY THE PRESIDENT OF THE UNITED STATES OF AMERICA:

A PROCLAMATION.

Whereas, It has become necessary to call into service, not only volunteers, but also portions of the militia of the States by draft, in order to suppress the insurrection existing in the United States, and disloyal persons are not adequately restrained by the ordinary processes of law from hindering this measure, and from giving aid and comfort in various ways to the insurrection;

Now, therefore, be it ordered:

First—That during the existing insurrection, and as a necessary measure for suppressing the same, all rebels and insurgents, their aiders and abettors, within the United States, and all persons discouraging volunteer enlistments, resisting militia drafts, or guilty of any disloyal practice affording aid and comfort to the rebels against the authority of the United States, shall be subject to martial law, and liable to trial and punishment by courts-martial or military commissions.

Third—That the writ of *habeas corpus* is suspended in respect to all persons arrested, or who are now, or hereafter during the rebellion shall be, imprisoned in any fort, camp, arsenal, military prison or other place of confinement, by any military authority, or by the sentence of any Court-Martial or military commission.

In witness whereof I have hereunto set my hand, and caused the seal of the United States to be affixed.

Done at the City of Washington this twenty-fourth day of September, in the year of our Lord one thousand eight hundred and sixty-two, and of the Independence of the United States the eighty-seventh.

Signed,　　ABRAHAM LINCOLN.

By the President.

WILLIAM H. SEWARD, Secretary of State.

OUR SPECIAL WASHINGTON DISPATCHES.

WASHINGTON, Wednesday, Sept. 24.

SERENADE TO THE PRESIDENT.

The city was enlivened last evening by a serenade to the President, in token of satisfaction with his proclamation. The crowd formed with a band of music at the National Hotel, and marched with continually increasing numbers to the White House, and arriving at which place it had swelled to a small army. After the preliminary music, calls were made for the President, who obediently appeared at a window over the front entrance, and addressed them very briefly.

Similar compliments were paid to Secretaries CHASE and BATES. The crowd was large, and very enthusiastic, vociferously cheering all loyal and Anti-Slavery sentiments.

REBEL PRISONERS.

Several rebel prisoners, captured by Gen. SIGEL's scouts near Centreville, were brought here to-day. They gave the loss of the rebels in the late battle in Maryland at about twenty thousand. The rebels have concentrated their forces at Winchester, which place they are fortifying. They regard the capture of Harper's Ferry as an offset to the loss of the battle on the Antietam, and say their retreat from Maryland was affected in the best order. These prisoners report the loss of rebel officers in the late engagements as very great.

REBEL CAVALRY NEAR LEESBURGH.

A dispatch from a TIMES special, just received, says that Lieut. KARNAY has just returned from a scouting expedition to Leesburgh and vicinity. The rebels have cavalry in all directions in that neighborhood. There are no rebel soldiers between Washington and Centreville.

ALL QUIET IN THE ARMY.

A private dispatch from the vicinity of the headquarters of the army of the Potomac, represents matters there as very dull.

FROM THE ARMY OF THE POTOMAC.

No Troops Yet Crossed Into Virginia.

The Rebels Expected to Dispute the Crossing at Williamsport.

A BATTLE PROBABLE IN THAT VICINITY.

HARRISBURGH, Wednesday, Sept. 24.

A gentleman from Williamsport this morning, says no troops had passed into Virginia up to Tuesday afternoon at 3 o'clock. Neither had any of the different divisions received any orders for a forward movement. The impression seemed to prevail among the soldiers that when they did move, they would proceed into Western Virginia, crossing at Williamsport. The enemy, he says, will undoubtedly dispute the crossing here, and when Gen. McCLELLAN orders a forward movement, a battle will, no doubt, take place at that point.

This gentleman dined at a house in Hagerstown where Gen. LEE and Staff had made their headquarters. The lady of the house says she heard LEE instruct his officers to see that no depredations were

Governor Andrew G. Curtin of Pennsylvania.

committed by the soldiers while in Maryland, but when they entered Pennsylvania, they might pillage and destroy everything on their route.

Quartermaster-General HALE visited the different hospitals at Hagerstown to-day, and reports the sick and wounded properly cared for. They have bandages and all necessary appendages for their comfort, but jellies and other delicacies are much needed.

LATEST REPORTS FROM HARRISBURGH.

HARRISBURGH, Wednesday, Sept. 24.

Gov. CURTIN has ordered the restriction on travel removed. All persons, therefore, will be permitted to leave the city without passes from the Mayor.

Information from Hagerstown reports our army along the Potomac in good condition, notwithstanding the terrible crosses it has sustained during the late battles in Maryland.

Regiments are returning from Hagerstown by every train.

THE PENNSYLVANIA MILITIA.

PROCLAMATION OF GOV. CURTIN DISCHARGING THE VOLUNTEERS.

HARRISBURGH, Wednesday, Sept. 24.

The Governor issued a proclamation discharging the volunteers under his call from the service of the State. He says:

A threatened invasion of Pennsylvania by a rebel army has been arrested by the prompt and patriotic response of the loyal men of the State, and a signal victory has been achieved by Gen. McCLELLAN's army on Antietam. The alacrity with which the people in every section of the Commonwealth rushed to the rescue of their brethren on the Cumberland Valley border is worthy of the highest measure of praise. Although not required by the terms of the call to pass the border of the State, our brave men, unused to the rigors of war and untrained in military movements, not only entered Maryland, but held Hagerstown against an advancing foe, pressed forward to the Potomac, and resisted the threatened movement upon Williamsport until troops in the United States service arrived and relieved them.

Their timely and heroic action has saved the State from the tread of an invading enemy, whose necessities made even military strategy subordinate to plunder.

In the name of our mighty State, and in behalf of our threatened people on the border, I tender them the grateful acknowledgments of the rescued Commonwealth, and recommend that the companies hereby discharged from active service should take prompt measures to preserve and perfect their organizations, and that new ones should be formed in every county, so that they may at all times be ready to answer the call of the State, should their services again be required.

139

The New-York Times.

VOL. XII–NO. 3445.   NEW-YORK, WEDNESDAY, OCTOBER 8, 1862.   PRICE TWO CENTS.

THE VICTORY AT CORINTH.

The Enemy Intercepted in their Flight by Gens. Hurlbert and Ord.

Another Battle of Seven Hours' Duration.

The Rebels Driven Back Again Toward Corinth.

They Are Again Attacked by Rosecrans and Completely Routed.

Everything Thrown Away in Their Flight.

HEADQUARTERS OF GENERAL GRANT, JACKSON, Tenn.,} October 6, 1862—12:20 o'clock, }

To Major-General Halleck, General-in-Chief:

Generals ORD and HURLBERT came upon the enemy yesterday, and General HURLBERT having driven in small bodies of the rebels the day before, after seven hours' hard fighting, drove the enemy five miles back across the Hatchie towards Corinth, capturing two batteries, about three hundred prisoners, and many small arms.

I immediately apprised Gen. ROSECRANS of these facts, and directed him to urge on the good work. The following dispatch has just been received from him:

CHEVALLA, Oct. 6, 1862.

To Major-Gen. Grant:

The enemy are totally routed, throwing everything away. We are following sharply.

W. S. ROSECRANS, Major-General.

Under previous instructions, Gen. HURLBERT is also following, Gen. McPHERSON is in the lead of Gen. ROSECRANS' column. The rebel Gen. MARTIN is said to be killed. U. S. GRANT,

Major-General Commanding.

[The rebel General MARTIN, who is reported in the above dispatch as killed, is probably Brig.-Gen. JAS. G. MARTIN, a North Carolinian, who was a Captain and Brevet-Major in the Quartermaster's Department of the United States Army when the war broke out. He lost an arm in Mexico. Some years ago he was stationed at the United States Arsenal in Philadelphia.]

SOME DETAILS OF THE FIGHTING.

CAIRO, Tuesday, Oct. 7.

As yet we can only state the general results of the fighting at Corinth. Skirmishing commenced Tuesday last, and there has been more or less fighting every day since. The rebel loss is about 800 killed and from 1,500 to 1,800 wounded. We have 2,500 prisoners at Corinth and 300 on the Hatchie River and more constantly coming in.

We have taken several thousand stand of arms thrown away by the rebels in their fight. They are mostly new and of English make.

Our loss, it is believed, will be 300 killed and 1,000 wounded.

Many houses in the town were badly shattered by shot and shell.

On Sunday Gen. ORD drove the enemy five miles, over hills, and through woods and valleys, the rebels taking advantage of every wood for their infantry and every hill for their artillery. The fight lasted seven hours.

The rebel Gen. ROGERS was killed. Gen. OGLESBY has died of his wounds. Gen. ORD is slightly wounded.

Prisoners taken say their effective force in the vicinity is 65,000 men. This is probably an over-estimate, but it is certain that they have outnumbered us two to one.

IMPORTANT FROM KENTUCKY.

The Rebels Believed to be Retreating to Hall's Gap—A Stand to be Made There.

LOUISVILLE, Tuesday, Oct. 7.

Gen. GILBERT with his corps is at Lebanon. It is supposed here by military men that the whole rebel force is retreating to Hall's Gap, a few miles south of Crab Orchard, where they intend to make a stand.

The bridges at Shepherdsville will be completed by Sunday. Nearly all the bridges between us and the rebels have been burned by them, and some three weeks will elapse before they can be reconstructed.

The story of the capture by the rebels, near Elizabethtown, of three companies of Ohio cavalry last week, is untrue.

LEXINGTON BEING EVACUATED.

LOUISVILLE—Midnight.

Lexington is mostly evacuated by the rebels, there being only 100 remaining. They took and sent to Camp Dick Robinson 7,000 barrels pork from CHENAULT & Co., packed on their own account and for other parties, mostly Secessionists.

They also took $9,000 worth of jeans and linseys from OLDHAM, SCOTT & Co., which they have manufactured into clothing. The rebels paid for these goods in Confederate scrip, unless owners refused to receive it, in which event no consideration was given.

Reliable individuals from Lexington, who have conversed with rebel soldiers, are confident that a battle must ensure before the rebels leave Kentucky. Rebel soldiers tell them they prefer being killed, or captured and paroled, rather than march over the mountains again. This seems to be the conclusion of the whole rebel crew.

THE SITUATION IN KENTUCKY.

From the Indianapolis Journal, Oct. 4.

Dr. CHITTENDEN, Surgeon of the Sixteenth Regiment, returned from Kentucky yesterday, leaving Richmond on Monday and Lexington on Tuesday. He has been attending on our wounded, and in constant contact with the rebels, and is therefore able to speak intelligently of their strength, and the events of the past few weeks. He says that about three weeks ago our Gen. MORGAN, on his way from the Gap to the Ohio, near Manchester, captured KIRBY SMITH's ammunition train, and all the supplies he had there. He also seized all the salt and flour which had been stored there by the rebels. This news, which we have not heard before, was learned by Dr. C. from the rebels themselves, and is doubtless correct.

About two weeks ago the guerrilla MORGAN started out with 800 cavalry to disperse a band of Home Guards near Irvine, but was completely defeated, and his men came back terribly demoralized and disordered. A number of wounded were brought in, and several young men belonging to Richmond, who had joined the rebel force, were killed. The Doctor saw this himself, and heard the rebels talk of their discomfiture repeatedly.

tor saw a large number of the rebel wounded brought to Richmond. They filled the African church with them. On last Monday evening, while at Lexington, to which place our wounded were taken, he saw a number of rebel stragglers coming in, and heard from the citizens that they admitted they had been badly whipped by MORGAN, and had lost all their artillery, but one gun. This news comes directly, and we have no doubt is true. Nothing has been said of it because nothing definite has been learned of it either at Cincinnati or Louisville. The Doctor says that Gen. WRIGHT had some intimations of such news, but it was so uncertain that he would allow no publication of it made.

Of the Union feeling in Kentucky, and the conduct of the loyal citizens, the Doctor speaks in enthusiastic terms. He says that as our ambulance train entered Lexington, the citizens cheered the soldiers openly and heartily. Both BUCKNER's and KIRBY SMITH's staffs were on the corner of the street, by the Phœnix Hotel, and the windows above, and on all sides of them, were crowded with ladies, displaying Union flags. Over three hundred ladies met the train at the hospital, to take care of the wounded, and supply them with everything they needed. Every delicacy that money could get was furnished in profusion. No men were ever more nobly cared for. The Doctor says our soldiers express the deepest gratitude for the generous treatment they received from the Lexington people and especially the ladies. At Paris, the Union feeling was exhibited with great enthusiasm. At Richmond, the citizens came for miles in carriages to take our wounded from the hospitals to their homes, and 300 of them were kept by the people for four weeks without a cent of compensation. The wealthiest and most refined ladies of the neighborhood almost made their homes in the hospitals, working at whatever was found necessary for the comfort of the men, no matter how hard or unpleasant.

An amusing incident is related by the Doctor of a Union lady near Paris. As the train of wounded came up, she came out to the gate with a Union flag and waved it and cheered with all her might. While she was in the midst of her enthusiastic welcome one of our guards who happened to have on a rusty grey suit, very like the rebel uniform, rode up, and asked the lady to give him that flag as he wanted to keep it. She took him to be rebel, and said, "Sir, I thought you were a Union soldier. I see you are a rebel. You shan't have this flag." And she tore it all to rags before his face. The Union feeling in Kentucky, the Doctor says, is in no way affected by the President's proclamation. The people say they want the Government and they will preserve it, let what will perish in doing so. The Doctor speaks with special gratitude of the kindness of Mrs. Judge GOODLOE, Mrs. Col. HOLLOWAY, Mrs. Judge EMBRY, Mrs. GREEN CLAY, Mrs. CASSIUS M. CLAY, Mrs. Dr. SMITH, and Mrs. Dr. LYMAN.

A VICTORY IN MISSOURI.

Gen. Schofield Whips 15,000 Rebels at Newtonia.

The Advantage Followed Up.

ST. LOUIS, Tuesday, Oct. 7.

Dispatches received at headquarters bring intelligence to the effect that on Saturday morning Gen. SCHOFIELD advanced upon the rebels at Newtonia, a small town about fifty-four miles south of Springfield, and after a two hours' engagement the rebels broke and fled in all directions. The force of the enemy is estimated at 15,000 men. Our loss is trifling.

Dispatches intercepted after the fight acquainted Gen. SCHOFIELD of the intention of the enemy to concentrate their whole force at a point twelve miles distant from Newtonia, to which point he was pushing rapidly with the expectation of renewing the battle on Sunday.

No further particulars have been received.

Missouri Politics.

ST. LOUIS, Tuesday, Oct. 7.

FRANK P. BLAIR was unanimously nominated for Congress in the First District, by the Union Emancipation Convention yesterday.

The New-York Times.

VOL. XII–NO. 3446.   NEW-YORK, THURSDAY, OCTOBER 9, 1862.   PRICE TWO CENTS.

THE VICTORY AT CORINTH.

Desperate Assault Upon the Place by Fifty Thousand Rebels.

The Battle Continued Through Two Days.

The Final Repulse of the Enemy with Terrible Slaughter.

The Rebel Losses Much Heavier Than Ours.

PROMINENT OFFICERS KILLED.

CORINTH, Miss., Sunday, Oct. 5.

The correspondent of the St. Louis *Democrat* has the following details of the battle at Corinth:

"On the morning of the 3d, our outposts were attacked by the enemy in force, about six miles northeast of Corinth, and before 9 o'clock the engagement became general and fierce, and a sanguinary battle was fought.

Our men under ROSECRANS stood up manfully, and fought with great coolness and bravery; but regiment after regiment, and brigade after brigade poured in upon us, and we were forced slowly backward, fighting desperately. The rebels pushed forward with determined obstinacy, and held every foot of their advantage ground.

They outflanked our inferior force and were forming in the rear, and we were obliged to fall back still further to prevent this movement from being accomplished. The enemy were now inside our breastworks pushing us backward toward the town when darkness put an end to fighting that day.

During the day's fight our loss was heavy, but that of the enemy must have largely exceeded ours.

Three pieces of the First Missouri Battery were captured after having stood for hours before the enemy's fire. Brig.-Gen. HACKLEMAN fell mortally wounded at the head of his men, and died the same evening. Gen. OGLESBY was shot in the breast.

About 4 o'clock A. M. of the 4th, the enemy opened on the town with shot and shell. Our batteries replied, and for an hour or more a heavy cannonading was kept up. At the expiration of that time, two rebel guns had been disabled, and, shortly after daylight, their battery of seven guns was captured.

A portentous quiet soon occurred, and it was evident that some movement was being made by the enemy. The Western Sharpshooters, under Col. BURKE, were ordered forward as skirmishers, to feel the enemy. At 9½ they met him three-quarters of a mile in advance of our line of battle, advancing rapidly in heavy columns upon the town. Immediately a murderous fire was opened on this heavy line by our skirmishers, who slowly began to retire, returning the fire of the enemy with effect.

The woods seemed alive with rebels, and it appeared impossible for this gallant regiment to escape destruction in their retreat over the three-quarters of a mile of open ground which intervened between them and our temporary works of defence.

In a few moments the engagement became general; our batteries opened a destructive fire on the exposed ranks of the rebels, mowing them down like grass. Their slaughter was frightful, but with unparalleled daring and recklessness they pushed impetuously forward.

They charged our works desperately, broke our lines of infantry, and captured a small fortification, in which a battery of the First Missouri was planted. All seemed lost, and a temporary panic seized our men, and the rebels once more marched into the streets of Corinth; but new batteries opened on them, and our men, under the direction of a few courageous officers, and stimulated by their example, fought desperately, and the advance of the enemy was checked.

They wavered, and then fell back. Our lost battery was regained, and once more it hurled destruction into their ranks. The day was saved, and the enemy was in full retreat.

Our loss was comparatively small during this charge. That of the enemy *was fully twenty to our one killed.*

Among the rebels killed and left on the field were Brig.-Gen. RODGERS, of New-Orleans; Col. and Acting Brig.-Gen. JOHNSON, of Mississippi, and another Colonel commanding a brigade, whose name was not learned.

The enemy was commanded by VAN DORN, PRICE and VILLIPIGUE, with their respective army corps, which swelled their forces to 50,000 men.

It is impossible now to give a list of the casualties. Our proportion of officers is thought to be large. We lost but four taken prisoners.

Heavy Losses Among the Rebel Officers.
CHICAGO, Wednesday, Oct. 8.

The Chicago *Tribune's* Cairo special says that the rebel Cols. JOHNSON, ROGERS, ROSS, MORTON, McLAIN and Major JONES were killed, and Cols. DALY and PRETCH were severely wounded in the late battle at Corinth.

THE WAR IN KENTUCKY.

Gen. Morgan's Forces Occupying Frankfort.

LOUISVILLE, Wednesday, Oct. 8.

A reliable report, just received, says that Gen MORGAN's advance reached Frankfort at 1 o'clock this afternoon, and that 3,000 more of his men are rapidly approaching that place. Our troops had left Frankfort for Lawrenceburgh, Ky.

On Saturday, near Hardensville, SCOTT's rebel Cavalry cut off and dispersed Co. A Ninth Kentucky Cavalry, under Lieut. MORRIS. The Company has not since been heard from. It is reported that Lieut. MORRIS and two privates were shot after capture by the rebels.

Gen. DUMONT's Division is still at Shelbyville.

An Exciting March from Louisville to Mount Washington—Skirmishing with the Flying Enemy, &c.

From Our Own Correspondent.

MOUNT WASHINGTON, }
SEVENTEEN MILES EAST OF LOUISVILLE, }
Thursday, Oct. 2, 4 o'clock P. M., 1862. }

This has been rather a stirring day with our men. We left camp, twelve miles this side of Louisville, at 8 o'clock this morning, the Brigade, commanded by Col. BEATTY, leading the advance. The First Ohio Cavalry and the Fourth Indiana Cavalry went in front. We knew that the rebels, in scouting and skirmishing parties, were all along the route, and that their guerrilla bands infested every hill and hollow. Capt. DRURY's Third Wisconsin Battery of Parrot guns, preceded us, feeling the way with an occasional shot that made it unpleasant for the rebels.

Major-General Edward O.C. Ord and staff.

The two regiments—the Ninth Kentucky and Nineteenth Ohio—which had been on picket all night, fell into line one mile from camp, and our whole corps, led by Gen. CRITTENDEN in person, moved forward in splendid order, and with buoyant feelings, anticipating an engagement with the rebels before night.

We had proceeded but about two miles when brisk musketry was heard between our advance cavalry and the enemy's pickets. We were now near Floyd's Fork, at which place the rebels were reported in considerable force. Gen. CRITTENDEN rode along the lines of the entire corps, and showed by his looks the highest confidence in his gallant men.

Shortly came the order to keep the ranks closed and to "fire low," in case we met the enemy. The breeze of battle began to snuff quite strongly. A little on ahead we reached a beech grove ; a very brief halt was ordered, the canteens were filled with fresh water, and every gun loaded. Here we left the turnpike, turning to the left and ascending an elevated hill that overlooked the valley of Floyd's Fork.

Again the rattle of musketry was heard in front. Then followed the reports of cannon in rapid succession. We galloped to the front, where we found Capt. DAVAY, of the Third Wisconsin Battery, with his guns planted upon an eminence that projected into a curve of Floyd's Fork, and commanded the turnpike to our left, and quite an area of country around. Two hundred rebel cavalry, just this side the creek, were making their way in hot haste for the ford, to avoid our advance. Capt. DRURY was pouring his Parrot pills at them in fine style. These rebels were all in their shirt sleeves, but were apparently well mounted. They succeeded in effecting their escape across the river, pursued and harassed by our cavalry. Two of their men were killed by our firing.

Our advance now drew up in line of battle upon the eminence referred to, while the cavalry were sent across the creek to ascertain the position of the flying enemy. Very soon Gen. VAN CLEVE came riding up, and ordered us forward. Col. BEATTY, the acting Brigadier of the Eleventh Brigade, which had the advance, had in the meantime inspected our position with a lorgnette, and, with the quick eye of a regular veteran officer, pronounced it admirable. The cavalry on the opposite bank of the creek had sent back for infantry and artillery, and when the order was given it was obeyed with alacrity. We proceeded cautiously, but steadily, down the steep declivity into the bottoms of Floyd's Fork, preceded by DRURY's Battery, with our cavalry, the First Ohio and Fourth Indiana in advance of it. The turnpike bridge across the creek had been burned by the rebels. It was a two-span wooden structure. The creek, being not much over our shoe-tops, the burning of this bridge was a piece of wantonness and foolery. Our men and artillery turned a little to the right and crossed the creek, making their way through a field of heavy corn without obstruction.

It was reported that the rebels, after leaving the creek in such haste, would make a stand at Mount Washington, and that they would be reinforced at that point. Immediately after crossing the creek, as we ascended the hill, two rebel horses were found lying in the road. One of them was in a dying condition, his nostrils distended, and blood flowing from them copiously. The prints of the rowels of the spur were visible in his sides. The other was quite dead, quantities of blood having come from his nose. They were both evidently run to death.

Just as we had reached the top of the hill, boom came the sound of the rebel cannon in our front. The firing became more rapid, and our men were, in a double-quick, ordered into line of battle. These cannon were fired from Mount Washington, two miles ahead. DRURY's Battery hurried up the road, unlimbered, and took a position to our right. The guns then let loose upon Mount Washington and High Grove, where the rebels had just been encamped. Hoarsely and loudly they thundered, as the balls and shells went screaming through the air, cutting limbs and tops from the trees. All now was eagerness, and every round we expected a reply from the enemy. They did not reply, however.

Presently we saw a man coming toward us from Mount Washington with a white flag. With Maj. MANDISON we galloped forward to meet him. The bearer proved to be Capt. CHURCH, of Col. BAYLES' Kentucky Cavalry, who being at home at Mount Washington when the rebels came there, had been forced to conceal himself till the sound of our cannon proclaimed his deliverance. We now learned that the rebels had left Mount Washington, as they had done Floyd's Creek, and fallen back toward Salt River. The rebels which have been here and along the road are

FORREST's Cavalry. They number near twelve hundred. The rebels expected to make a stand at this point. All the fences have been torn away to assist in cavalry movements. They had two brass six-pounders, which they withdrew on our approach. So rapid was their flight from this place, that slice bacon was found on their camping ground, and wood gathered for fires which had not been kindled. The rebels are reported as being extremely destitute of clothing and food. The hotels and the citizens here have been entirely stripped of all they had.

The rebels are represented as being in strong force and with a large amount of artillery at Salt River. We are four miles from Salt River, and about eighteen from Bardstown. We push forward in the morning.

P. S.—As I close this, heavy cannonading is going on in the direction of Salt River. We may have hot work in a short time. Two rebel prisoners have just been brought in, captured at Mount Washington.

THE ARMY OF THE POTOMAC

FROM ANTIETAM.

Rebel Demonstrations—Winter Quarters in Prospect—Sentiment of the Army—Impatience of Delay—Visitors at Headquarters—The Order of Gen. Burnside on the Death of Gen. Rodman, &c.

From Our Own Correspondent.
ANTIETAM IRON WORKS, Md., Monday, Oct. 6, 1862.

The rebels made their appearance yesterday, in small force opposite this place, for the evident purpose of—showing themselves. They were mounted, and numbered two hundred or less. As they seemed anxious to attract attention, a section of a Parrot battery was brought up, and a few shells were sent after them across the river. Of course, they made tracks.

The best information that can be derived from Virginia confirms the theory I have already put forth, that the body of the rebel army, which lingered for a time on the south bank of the Potomac, retired up the Valley from the direction of Martinsburgh *over a week ago.* They succeed, however, in keeping up the semblance of a force along the Potomac, for their own purposes. Thus this splendid Fall weather, with its invigorating air and excellent roads inviting to activity, will soon give place to storms and muddy thoroughfares, which will forbid us to move. By the time the Potomac has been swollen by rains, which will secure "My Maryland" against another rebel raid, the roads, by the same natural agencies, will have been rendered impassable. We shall then be ready, I suppose, to go into Winter quarters, where the army will waste away by sickness and inaction, and be ready (?) for active operations *in the Spring.*

There is nothing the soldiers desire so much as to have the war brought to a close. With them *time* is everything. They are tired of the business and want to go home. This is as true of the rebel soldiers as of our own ; and with a certain class—not, I hope, by any means the best or largest—every hour's delay makes them more and more indifferent as to *how* the fighting ends, so that it *ends.* Remove the *legal* restraint which holds the army together, and half of them would go home to "see their parents" to-morrow—the other half would vote to send Commissioners to Richmond, or to welcome propositions from the rebels for winding up the struggle—rather than drag through another Winter campaign in the swamps of the Chickahominy, or in any other part of Virginia. But give them the word "Forward," and with the needful leaders and reinforcements, they will not stop until they have chased the rebels into the Gulf.

There is nothing the soldiers so much dread as this eternal delay, and the prospect of an indefinite prolongation of the war. "Let us whip or get whipped, and have an end of it," is the language of every man I meet and talk with on the subject. The officers (who are worth a copper) would say the same thing if they possessed the independence of those in the ranks, and would speak their minds. I mention these things, not willingly, but for the purpose of showing the *temper of the army,* and the absolute necessity of *keeping their energies employed* and *their minds easy.*

Confederate dead at the battle of Corinth.

The New-York Times.

VOL. XII—NO. 3473.   NEW-YORK, MONDAY, NOVEMBER 10, 1862.   PRICE TWO CENTS.

IMPORTANT NEWS.

Gen. McClellan Relieved of the Command of the Army of the Potomac.

Gen. Burnside Appointed in his Place.

The Order of Displacement Delivered on Friday Night.

A FAREWELL ADDRESS TO THE SOLDIERS

General McClellan on his way to Trenton, N. J.

How the News was Received in Washington.

HEADQUARTERS OF THE ARMY OF THE POTOMAC, SALEM, Va., Saturday, Nov. 8—12 o'clock, noon.

The order relieving Major-Gen. McCLELLAN from the command of the army of the Potomac was received at headquarters at 11 o'clock last night. It was entirely unexpected to all, and therefore every one was taken by surprise.

On its receipt, the command was immediately turned over to Gen. BURNSIDE.

Gen. McCLELLAN and his Staff will leave to-morrow for Trenton, where he is ordered to report.

The order was delivered to him by Gen. BUCK-INGHAM, in person.

His last official act was the issuing of an address to his soldiers, informing them in a few words that the command had devolved on Gen. BURNSIDE, and taking an affectionate leave of them.

THE NEWS IN WASHINGTON.

Special Dispatch to the New-York Times.

WASHINGTON, Sunday, Nov. 9.

The removal of Gen. McCLELLAN, and the significant fact of his being ordered to report to his family at Trenton, have produced some excitement here to-day. At the hotels, crowds have been discussing the subject, and occasionally the feelings of some have found expression in language disrespectful to the President and disloyal the Government. The truly loyal and more sensible of Gen. McCLELLAN's friends, however, whilst they regret his removal, acquiesce ie the action of the President, as the friends and admirers of other Generals have done on like occasions. It is certain that Mr. LINCOLN never performed a duty which gave him so much pain as did the removal of McCLELLAN just at this time; but facts recently presented in an official shape by the General-in-Chief made it clear to the President that he had but one course to pursue, and when these facts are given to the public, as they will be soon, all true supporters of the Government will not hesitate to concede the wisdom of the act, whilst those who are blinded by prejudice, and those animated by a spirit of disloyalty, will, of course, seize this occasion as an opportunity for renewing their expressions of hostility to the Administration.

A few gentlemen, wearing shoulder straps, have been rendering themselves. to-day, fit subjects for the Old Capitol Prison, by talking loudly against the act of relieving McCLELLAN of his command. A Lieutenant-Colonel said publicly, to-night, that if by fighting another hour he could put down the rebellion, he would not do so.

It is understood that Judge HOLT has written a long letter to a gentleman of your City, strongly condemnatory of Gen. McCLELLAN's course, which it is said will be made public.

Dispatch to the Associated Press.

WASHINGTON, Sunday, Nov. 9.

The first information the public received of the relief of Gen. McCLELLAN from the command of the Army of the Potomac, was through the telegram published this morning. It affords a general theme of conversation and comment, and excites surprise, the event occurring unexpectedly. The cause of the Executive action in the premises does not appear to be known outside of official circles, and hence the absence of facts gives rise to conflicting speculations.

Gen. McCLELLAN, it is said, passed through Washington to-day, on his way to Trenton.

THE ELEVATION OF BURNSIDE.

REJOICING IN PROVIDENCE.

PROVIDENCE, Sunday, Nov. 9.

By order of Gov. SPRAGUE, a salute of 100 guns is to be fired here to-morrow noon, in honor of the appointment of the Rhode Island-General, BURNSIDE, to the command of the Army of the Potomac.

THE NEWS IN PHILADEELPHIA.

PHILADELPHIA, Sunday, Nov. 9.

The removal of Gen. McCLELLAN has caused much excitement throughout the city, and is the universal topic of conversation. Among the rumors as to the cause, it is said that some instructions from the General-in-Chief were not followed, and that the escape of LEE followed as a consequence.

FORNEY'S *Press* of to-morrow, in speaking of the removal, says:

It was purely a military act, and was the result of a military consultation and decision, although recommended to the President and approved by him some time ago. It was only finally resolved upon after the change became inevitable. No act of the present Administration, we might say no Executive act since the beginning of the Government, has been the subject of more careful deliberation.

GENERAL McCLELLAN.

Letter from Gen. Halleck to the Secretary of War Concerning Gen. McClellan's Complaints of Lack of Supplies.

HEADQUARTERS OF THE ARMY, WASHINGTON, Oct. 28, 1862.

HON. E. M. STANTON, Secretary of War—*Sir*: In reply to the general interrogatories contained in your letter of yesterday, I have to report:

First—That requisitions for supplies to the army under Gen. McCLELLAN are made by his Staff officers on the Chiefs of Bureaus here; that is, for Quartermaster's supplies by his Chief Quartermaster on the Quartermaster-General; for commissary supplies by his Chief Commissary on the Commissary-General, &c. No such requisitions have been to my knowledge made upon the Secretary of War, and none upon the General-in-Chief.

Second—On several occasions Gen. McCLELLAN has telegraphed to me that his army was deficient in certain supplies. All these telegrams were immediately referred to the heads of Bureaus with orders to report.

It was ascertained that in every instance the requisitions had been immediately filled, except one, where the Quartermaster-General had been obliged to send from Philadelphia certain articles of clothing, tents, &c., not having a full supply here. There has not been, so far as I could ascertain, any neglect or delay in any Department or Bureau, in issuing all supplies asked for by Gen. McCLELLAN or by the officers of his Staff. Delays have occasionally occurred in forwarding supplies by rail, on account of the crowded condition of the dépôts or of a want of cars; but, whenever notified of this, agents have been sent out to remove the difficulty. Under the excellent superintendence of Gen. HAUPT, I think these delays have been less frequent and of shorter duration than is usual with freight trains. An army of the size of that under Gen. McCLELLAN will frequently be for some days without the supplies asked for, on account of neglect in making timely requisitions, and unavoidable delays in forwarding them, and in distributing them to the different brigades and regiments. From all the information I can obtain, I am of opinion that the requisitions from that army have been filled more promptly, and that the men, as a general rule, have been better supplied than our armies operating in the West. The latter have operated at much greater distances from the sources of supply, and have had far less facilities of transportation. In fine, I believe that no armies in the world, while in campaign, have been more promptly or better supplied than ours.

Third—Soon after the battle of Antietam, Gen. McCLELLAN was urged to give me information of his intended movements, in order that, if he moved between the enemy and Washington, reinforcements could be sent from this place. On the 1st of October, finding that he purposed to operate from Harper's Ferry, I urged him to cross the river at once and give battle to the enemy, pointing out to him the disadvantages of delaying till the Autumn rains had swollen the Potomac and impaired the roads. On the 6th of October he was peremptorily ordered to "cross the Potomac and give battle to the enemy, or drive him south. Your army *must* move now while the roads are good." It will be observed that three weeks have elapsed since this order was given.

Fourth—In my opinion, there has been no such want of supplies in the army under Gen. McCLELLAN as to prevent his compliance with the orders to advance against the enemy. Had he moved to the south side of the Potomac, he could have received his supplies almost as readily as by remaining inactive on the north.

Fifth—On the 7th of October, in a telegram in regard to his intended movements, Gen. McCLELLAN stated that it would require at least three days to supply the First, Fifth and Sixth Corps; that they needed shoes and other indispensable articles of clothing, as well as shelter tents. No complaint was made that any requisitions had not been filled, and it was inferred from his language that he was only waiting for the distribution of his supplies. On the 11th, he telegraphed that a portion of his supplies, sent by rail, had been delayed. As already stated, agents were immediately sent from here to investigate this complaint, and they reported that everything had gone forward. On the same date (the 11th) he spoke of many of his horses being broken down by fatigue. On the 12th he complained that the rate of supply was only "150 horses per week for the entire army there and in front of Washington." I immediately directed the Quartermaster-General to inquire into this matter and report why a larger supply was not furnished. Gen. MEIGS reported on the 14th, that the average issue of horses to Gen. McCLELLAN's army in the field and in front of Washington, for the previous six weeks, had been 1,459, per week, or 8,754 in all. In addition, that large numbers of mules had been supplied, and that the number of animals with Gen. McCLELLAN's army on the Upper Potomac was over thirty-one thousand. He also reported that he was then sending to that army all the horses he could procure.

On the 18th, Gen. McCLELLAN stated in regard to Gen. MEIGS' report that he had filled every requisition for shoes and clothing: "Gen. MEIGS may have ordered these articles to be forwarded, but they have not reached our dépôts; and unless greater effort to insure prompt transmission is made by the Department of which Gen. MEIGS is the head, they might as well remain in New-York or Philadelphia, so far as this army is concerned." I immediately called Gen. MEIGS' attention to this apparent neglect of his Department. On the 25th he reported as the result of his investigation, that 48,000 pairs of boots and shoes had been received by the Quartermaster of Gen. McCLELLAN's army at Harper's Ferry, Frederick and Hagerstown; that 20,000 pairs were at Harper's Ferry dépôt on the 21st; that 10,000 more were on their way, and 15,000 more ordered. Col. INGALS, Aid-de-Camp and Chief Quartermaster to Gen. McCLELLAN, telegraphed on the 25th: "The suffering for want of clothing is exaggerated, I think, and certainly might have been avoided by timely requisitions of regimental and brigade commanders." On the 24th he telegraphed to the Quartermaster-General that the clothing was not detained in cars at the dépôts. "Such

complaints are groundless. The fact is, the clothing arrives and is issued, but more is still wanted. I have ordered more than would seem necessary from any data furnished me, and I beg to remind you that you have always very promptly met all my requisitions so far as clothing is concerned. Our depôt is not at fault. It provides as soon as due notice is given. I foresee no time when an army of over one hundred thousand men will not call for clothing and other articles."

In regard to Gen. McCLELLAN's means of promptly communicating the wants of his army to me or to the proper Bureaus of the War Department, I report that in addition to the ordinary mails, he has been in hourly communication with Washington by telegraph.

It is due to Gen. MEIGS that I should submit herewith a copy of a telegram received by him from Gen. McCLELLAN. Very respectfully, your obedient servant, H. W. HALLECK, General-in-Chief.

UNITED STATES MILITARY TELEGRAPH.
(Received Oct. 22, 1862—9:40 P.M.)
FROM McCLELLAN'S HEADQUARTERS.
To Brig.-Gen. Meigs:
Your dispatch of this date is received. I have never intended in any letter or dispatch to make any accusation against yourself, or your department, for not furnishing or forwarding clothing as rapidly as it was possible for you to do. I believe that everything has been done that could be done in this respect. The idea that I have tried to convey was, that certain portions of the command were without clothing, and the army could not move until it was supplied.
(Signed.)   G. B. M'CLELLAN, M. G.

ARMY OPERATIONS IN VIRGINIA.

Stuart Again Defeated by Gen. Pleasanton.

Three Pieces of Artillery and Several Officers Captured.

The Bridge Across the Rappahannock Held by Gen. Bayard.

THE STRUCTURE UNINJURED.

Details of Recent Skirmishes During the Advance.

HEADQUARTERS, WARRENTON, Sunday, Nov. 9.
Gen. PLEASANTON yesterday, in a skirmish with STUART, near Little Washington, captured three pieces of artillery, also a Captain, Lieutenant and five privates. No loss has been reported.

Gen. Bayard yesterday occupied and now holds the railroad bridge across the Rappahannock. The bridge is not injured.

The bridge across Broad River has been destroyed.

There is nothing new up to this writing from the front at the Rappahannock.

The weather is clear and cold.

THE GUERRILLAS IN KENTUCKY.

A Fight with a Rebel Force Under Fowler—Fowler Killed and his Gang Routed.

CINCINNATI, Sunday, Nov. 9.
A special to the *Commercial* from Indianapolis says: Wednesday night a battalion of Col. SHACKLEFORD's Eighth Kentucky Cavalry was attacked by a large force of guerrillas under Col. FOWLER, on Pond River, eleven miles from Madisonville, Ky.

The attack was gallantly met, and the rebels compelled to retire. Their loss was eight killed, including Col. FOWLER, and a large number of wounded and prisoners.

President Lincoln reviewed General McClellan's troops in October, 1862. One month later, Lincoln dismissed McClellan, frustrated by the latter's reluctance to actively engage the Confederate army.

The New-York Times.

VOL. XII—NO. 3492.　　　　　NEW-YORK, MONDAY, DECEMBER 1, 1862.　　　　　PRICE TWO CENTS.

FROM THE ARMY OF THE POTOMAC.

New Earthworks Thrown up by the Rebels Near Fredericksburgh.

Some of Our Batteries Similarly Protected.

Five of Our Gunboats Advanced up the Rappahannock.

A Position Taken Opposite the Rebel Right Wing.

A Few Shots Thrown Across the River by One of Our Batteries.

The Significance of the Recent Visit of the President.

HEADQUARTERS ARMY OF THE POTOMAC, }
Sunday, Nov. 30—7½ P. M. }

Some camps of the enemy, visible yesterday, disappeared last night. They probably have retired to the valley behind the range of hills in the rear of Fredericksburgh.

New rebel earthworks almost daily make their appearance, and the range in the rear of the town is crowned almost continuously with redoubts and rifle pits.

Some of our batteries, whose guns bear directly upon the town, have recently been protected by earthworks.

Five gunboats are reported to have advanced up the Rappahannock opposite King George Court House. The right wing of the enemy extends nearly to that point, but at some distance from the river.

A few shots were thrown over the river, yesterday, by one of our left wing batteries, probably to try the range of the guns.

Gen. BURNSIDE has returned to camp from his temporary visit to Washington.

All is quiet, to-night, along our lines.

LATEST REPORTS FROM FALMOUTH.

WASHINGTON, Sunday, Nov. 30.

We learn, by a special dispatch from the TIMES' correspondent at Falmouth, that three hundred infantry, belonging to the Twelfth and Seventeenth New-York Regiments, were reported surprised and captured, last evening, a few miles above that point on the Rappahannock.

About dusk, last evening, the enemy commenced throwing up a new line of earthworks below Fredericksburgh, from five to eight hundred workmen being visible from our signal station.

It is considered certain that Gen. LEE is in command.

THE OPPOSING ARMIES ON THE RAPPAHANNOCK.

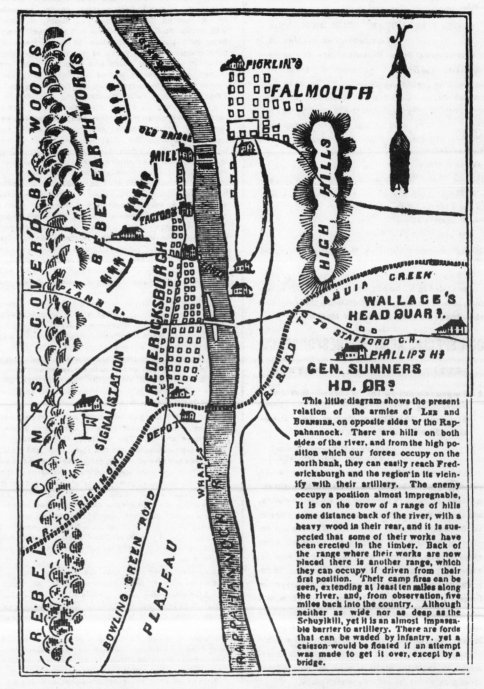

This little diagram shows the present relation of the armies of LEE and BURNSIDE, on opposite sides of the Rappahannock. There are hills on both sides of the river, and from the high position which our forces occupy on the north bank, they can easily reach Fredericksburgh and the region in its vicinity with their artillery. The enemy occupy a position almost impregnable, It is on the brow of a range of hills some distance back of the river, with a heavy wood in their rear, and it is suspected that some of their works have been erected in the timber. Back of the range where their works are now placed there is another range, which they can occupy if driven from their first position. Their camp fires can be seen, extending at least ten miles along the river, and, from observation, five miles back into the country. Although neither as wide nor as deep as the Schuylkill, yet it is an almost impassable barrier to artillery. There are fords that can be waded by infantry, yet a caisson would be floated if an attempt was made to get it over, except by a bridge.

THE PRESIDENT'S VISIT TO GEN. BURNSIDE.

WASHINGTON, Saturday, Nov. 29.

The object of the President's visit to Gen. BURNSIDE continues to be the theme of speculation. I think that, without departing from the line of strict propriety, I can say that it had reference to the delay which has attended the advance across the Rappahannock. When Gen. BURNSIDE assumed command of the Army of the Potomac, he at once wrote to the Government proposing a change of base, and a rapid advance, and specifying certain supplies which would be *indispensable* to the movement. He based his movement on the assurance of receiving them. His plan was approved, and the supplies promised. He executed his part of the programme with a rapid-ity and vigor of which the country has already been informed. But when he reached the designated point, *he found none of the promised supplies*—neither pontoons, forage nor provisions. The Government had failed, and his movements were of necessity arrested.

I surmise that the President went down to see about it—to ascertain precisely where the responsibility for this failure rested,—to assure Gen. BURNSIDE of his steady and hearty support—to renew promises of all the supplies and reinforcements he might need, and to tell him that, whatever might be the pressure upon him, he wished him to fight no *indecisive* battle there. The visit was intended and calculated to aid Gen. BURNSIDE'S advance.

We learn here that the rebels continue to strengthen their position in the outskirts of Fredericksburgh,—

that they are throwing up earthworks nearer the town, and that *four or five* separate forts have already been completed and made ready for their guns, which had not, however, been mounted on Friday morning. The rebels are evidently preparing for an obstinate resistance. We shall see whether a combination of pluck and strategy cannot circumvent and overcome them.

HIGHLY IMPORTANT FROM RICHMOND.

WASHINGTON, Sunday, Nov. 30.

Our advices from Richmond are of the most important character. The removal of Gen. McCLELLAN, and the rapid movements of Gen. BURNSIDE, have caused the greatest consternation, and an entire change in the programme for the Winter. The expectation of Winter quarters was suddenly exchanged for the certainty of active operations, and Gen. LONGSTREET was recalled to Richmond, while on his way to North Carolina, and ordered at once to hold the line of the Rappahannock, while JEFF. DAVIS has instructed Gen. LEE at all ways to retard the advance of the Federal forces, supposed to be half a million, on the rebel Capital.

The rebel army on the Rappahannock consists of about 60,000 men, besides about 25,000 in the works about Richmond.

Immense stores of beef, pork and flour have been accumulated in Richmond, but the army still suffers from lack of clothing, notwithstanding the continual violation of the coast and interior blockade.

OUR SPECIAL ARMY CORRESPONDENCE.

LETTERS FROM HEADQUARTERS.

An Improvement in the Weather—Reviews—Perfecting Arrangements for the Great Struggle—The Work Before Gen. Burnside—The Rebel Forces, &c.

CAMP NEAR FREDERICKSBURGH, Thursday, Nov. 27, 1862.

Contrary to general expectation, the weather, yesterday, proved better than the signs of the night and morning indicated. There was no rain after 9 o'clock, and though the sky remained overcast, nothing checked the usual routine of the camp. There was a review of artillery and infantry of the Ninth Army corps by Gen. SUMNER; and Gen. HOOKER also reviewed a portion of his troops, including Gen. WHIPPLE's Division. There were several other reviews by Brigade Commanders, and the day, on the whole, was one of the most stirring the army has experienced since its arrival in this region. The troops appeared to very great advantage, considering the bad weather of the previous night, and went through their movements in excellent style in view of the softened ground on which the evolutions took place.

Artillery drills have been very frequent of late, in all the batteries, and when called upon, they will, no doubt, give a good account of themselves.

Thus every hour is being improved in perfecting the troops preparatory to the coming struggle. Col. J. H. H. WARD returned after a brief leave of absence, yesterday, and it is expected that he will be assigned to the command of his old brigade, Gen. BIRNEY being now in command of the division. He is strongly recommended for the position, and he is deservedly popular with the soldiers.

Yesterday morning revealed a large camp of the enemy, which had located during the previous night, northwest of the town, in plain view of the signal station. Their tents, wagons and camp fires, with thick clusters of troops moving about, could be distinguished almost by the naked eye. This is, no doubt, what gave rise to the rumor that Gen. JACKSON had arrived with his army of 50,000 strong.

Deserters from that side of the river state—as is customary with them—that the enemy are in strong force, and that they have many and heavy guns in position. These deserters have come to be regarded with suspicion, and one was put under arrest. Even some more distinguished personages who have lately arrived here, are not wholly above suspicion, though they profess to be subjects of a foreign Government. I doubt if they will obtain Staff appointments. The rebel army have paid particular attention to the defence of the Gordonsville road, which is the chief one leading out of the city to the north and west. A long line of earthworks, freshly thrown up during the night, rose to view in the morning on the line of this road. To say nothing of these accumulating works of defence, the formation of the hills back of the town renders the position one of the strongest that can be imagined. The first line of hills, which rise like an amphitheatre from the river plain occupied by the town, is traversed by indentations or ravines running at various angles, the sides of which are covered by preparations for batteries, and several of them have guns in position, capable of pouring a raking cross-fire upon any advancing column. Behind the first range, with an intervening valley of irregular width, known as the Mattoponix Valley, is a still more formidable range of hills, which in turn will no doubt be strongly fortified. There are also their favorite woods for shelter. To cross this river, and carry the positions I have described, with a large army to oppose us, *is the most stupendous undertaking which has been presented to any military commander during the war !*

Nothing has passed between the town and our own lines for several days. The *status quo*, at least on our part, being observed. The enemy have no large military force in the town, but do not hesitate to come and go at will, in small squads of cavalry. The pickets, near the place, of course, have quarters in the houses of the town, and at our distance it is difficult to decide as to how much good faith the authorities observe in keeping their own promises not to allow stores or supplies to pass out of the town.

The rest of the pontoon train was expected last evening, and horses and mules, in considerable numbers, have arrived. The weather, this morning, is cool, clear and bracing, the sun rises rosy and clear, and gives promise of a fine, crisp day—just such as gives elasticity to the step, and life to the spirit of the soldier. The frosty temperature of the night must have stiffened and dried the roads, so that the wagon trains can move with greater ease. A wagon-master, yesterday, told me that one of the teams became "stalled" on the way hither from Bellplain, and that after the load of hard bread had been all taken out, eight horses and mules could not haul the wagon out of the mud.

Last evening we could hear the welcome sound of the steam-whistle, near Potomac River, to which point the locomotive now travels with materials for completing repairs of the bridge. Gen. HOOKER, yesterday, stated that it would take two days more to finish the work. We shall then be ready to receive the locomotive and cars which are already on the way from Alexandria. The former were safely conveyed away when the troops evacuated this position last August. The freight cars were destroyed.

No one who has not given his attention to the subject is aware of the enormous amount of stores which is required for the simple subsistence of a large army. Allowing four pounds per day per man, it will require 2,850 net tons for one week's subsistence for 200,000 men. To supply the *current demand* of an army of 150,000 men at five pounds each, and *accumulate* a ten day's supply, will necessitate the transportation of 7,500 tons. This estimate does not include the most bulky portion of supplies—forage for the animals. A large part of this, in the present bare condition of the country, must also be hauled in wagons over the same roads by which the food is transported. This would furnish a full cargo for four first-class Liverpool ships each ten days. The forage will keep in constant employment a fleet of 200 schooners of 150 tons each. To all this let it be remembered there should be added the cumbrous pontoon trains, and transportation for thousands of horses and mules required for keeping up the working force of the army. No estimate is here made for ammunition and miscellaneous supplies.

General Ambrose Burnside commanded the Army of the Potomac as it neared Fredericksburg.

How Thanksgiving Day was Observed—Depredations on the Inhabitants—Movements of the Enemy—New Earthworks, &c.

CAMP OPPOSITE FREDERICKSBURGH, Friday, Nov. 28, 1862.

Yesterday was a comparatively a quiet day in the army, and one also of comparative rest and festivity to the troops. Upon the slender materials afforded by army rations, pieced out by an occasional fowl—the weather has been that way of late—many a mess was rendered savory and thanksgiving-like. The absence of the warm mince and pumpkin pies, and mugs of good cider out of the cellar, was lamented in some localities, but as a general thing these luxuries were voted unhealthy, and there was no disposition to overload the stomach. In the presence of so much desolation and distress, it is difficult to be thankful, except upon the principle practiced by the old lady, when her son had both legs and arms blown off by the premature discharge of a canon, and his eyes put out by the powder—she was thankful it was not worse.

ACTIVITY OF THE REBELS.

The arrival of Gen. LEE on the opposite side is said to be definitely ascertained. There was great cheering there some two days ago, upon the occasion of his coming. So it is said. Yesterday morning a fresh line of breastworks, thrown up during the night, appeared in view from the Signal Station. I counted four different sections, at short distances apart, on which working parties of forty to fifty men were busily engaged. One new intrenchment was observed in rear of the town. They are also building magazines near the centre of the main sections. No guns are yet in position on these works—only those mounted a week ago are visible.

On our side the note of preparation is heard, and as soon as all things are ready, the forward movement will begin. Any plans of attack it would be improper to hint at even if they were known to me.

E. S.

The New-York Times.

VOL. XII—NO. 3503.　　　　　NEW-YORK, MONDAY, DECEMBER 15, 1862.　　　　　PRICE THREE CENTS.

IMPORTANT FROM VIRGINIA.

The Great Battle Fought on Saturday at Fredericksburgh.

Storming of the First Line of the Enemy's Works.

FAILURE TO CARRY THE POSITION.

TERRIFIC FIGHTING UNTIL DARK.

Splendid Success of Gen. Franklin on the Left.

Stonewall Jackson Driven Back About a Mile.

Several Hundred Prisoners Captured.

A Number of Our General Officers Killed and Wounded.

NO GENERAL ENGAGEMENT YESTERDAY.

THE OPERATIONS OF SATURDAY.

HEADQUARTERS OF THE ARMY OF THE POTOMAC,
Saturday, Dec. 13, 1862.
IN THE FIELD—11 o'clock, A. M.

The great battle, so long anticipated between the two contending armies, is now progressing.

The morning opened with a dense fog, which has not entirely disappeared.

Gen. REYNOLDS' Corps, on the left, advanced at an early hour, and at 9:15 A. M., engaged the enemy's infantry. Seven minutes afterward the rebels opened a heavy fire of artillery, which has continued so far without intermission.

Their artillery fire must be at random, as the fog obstructs all view of almost everything.

Our heavy guns are answering them rapidly.

At this writing, no results are known.

HEADQUARTERS OF THE ARMY OF THE POTOMAC,
Saturday Dec. 13—11 P. M.

The fog began to disappear early in the forenoon, affording an unobstructed view of our own and the rebel positions.

It being evident that the first ridge of hills, in the rear of the city, on which the enemy had their guns posted behind works, could not be carried, except by a charge of infantry, Gen. SUMNER assigned that duty to Gen. FRENCH'S Division, which was supported by Gen. HOWARD'S.

The troops advanced to their work at ten minutes before 12 o'clock at a brisk run, the enemy's guns opening upon them a very rapid fire. When within musket range, at the base of the ridge, our troops were met by a terrible fire from the rebel infantry, who were posted behind a stone wall and some houses on the right of the line. This checked the advance of our men, and they fell back to a small ravine, but not out of musket range.

At this time another body of troops moved to their assistance in splendid style, notwithstanding large gaps were made in their ranks by the rebel artillery. When our troops arrived at the first line of the rebel defences, they "double quicked," and with "fixed bayonets" endeavored to dislodge the rebels from their hiding places. The concentrated fire of the rebel artillery and infantry, which our men were forced to face, was too much for them, and the centre gave way in disorder, but afterwards they were rallied and brought back.

From that time the fire was spiritedly carried on, and never ceased until after dark.

Gen. FRANKLIN, who commanded the attack on the left, met with better success. He succeeded, after a hard day's fight, in driving the rebels about one mile. At one time the rebels advanced to attack him, but were handsomely repulsed, with terrible slaughter and loss of between four and five hundred prisoners belonging to Gen. A. P. HILL's command. Gen. FRANKLIN's movement was directed down the river, and his troops are encamped to-night not far from the Massaponox Creek.

Our troops sleep to-night where they fought to-day. The dead and wounded are being carried from the field.

The following is a list of officers killed and wounded as far as yet known:

Gen. JACKSON, of the Pennsylvania Reserves, killed.

Gen. BAYARD struck in the thigh by a shell, and afterward died.

Gen. VINTON wounded in the side, but not seriously.

Gen. GIBSON wounded in the hand.

Gen. KIMBALL wounded in the thigh.

Gen. CALDWELL wounded in two places, but not seriously.

Col. SINCLAIR, of the Pennsylvania Reserves, wounded seriously.

Capt. HENDERSON, commanding the Ninth New-York State Militia, wounded seriously.

The following is the loss of officers in the Fifth New-Hampshire Regiment:

Col. CROSS, wounded in the abdomen.

Major STURTEVANT, killed.

Adjutant DODD, killed.

Capt. MURRAY, killed.

Capt. PERRY, killed.

The firing of musketry ceased about 6 o'clock

Rifle pits lace the lawn of Marye's House, situated on Marye's Heights, overlooking Fredericksburg.

this evening, but the Rebels continued throwing shell into the city until 8 o'clock.

The position of the rebels was as follows:

Gen. LONGSTREET on the left, and holding the main works.

Gen. A. P. HILL and "Stonewall" JACKSON were in front of Gen. FRANKLIN, with JACKSON's right resting on the Rappahannock, and HILL's forces acting as a reserve.

The troops are in good spirits and not the least disheartened.

FROM ANOTHER CORRESPONDENT.

HEADQUARTERS ARMY OF THE POTOMAC,
Saturday, Dec. 13—10 P. M.

Last night our troops were rapidly pushed across the river, and every preparation made for a battle. Gen. FRANKLIN's Division crossed two miles below the city, while Gen. SUMNER's troops occupied a portion of the town. Gen. FRANKLIN's line was moved forward at sunrise, with his right resting on Fredericksburgh, his centre advanced a mile from the river, and his left resting on the river three miles below.

Skirmishing commenced on the left about daylight. Soon after a rebel battery opened on our lines, and the Ninth New-York Militia was ordered to charge, but after a fierce struggle was compelled to retire. The remainder of the Brigade, under Gen. TYLER, then charged the enemy's guns, when the fight became general on the extreme left.

Gen. MEAD's and Gen. GIBBON's Divisions encountered the right of Gen. A. P. HILL's command.

The cannonading was terrific, though our troops suffered but little from the enemy's artillery. Gradually the fight extended around to the right. Gen. HOWE's division went in, and then Gen. BROOKS' division. About 10 o'clock A. M. Gen. SUMNER's troops engaged the enemy back of the city, since which time the battle has raged furiously along the whole line. The enemy, occupying the woods and hills, had a much more advantageous position, but were driven back on their right a mile and a half early in the day.

About noon Gen. GIBBON was relieved by Gen. DOUBLEDAY, and Gen. MEAD by Gen. STONEMAN Afterward Gen. NEWTON's Division moved round to the support of the left, when the firing ceased in that portion of the field for a short time, and broke out with greater fierceness in the centre, where our troops were exposed to a plunging fire from the enemy's guns and earthworks from the hills.

Along the whole line the battle has been fierce all day, with great loss to both sides. To-night each army holds its first position, with the exception of a slight advance of our left. Cannonading is still going on, and the musketry breaks out at intervals quite fiercely.

Gens. GIBBON, VINTON, BAYARD and CAMPBELL are wounded. Gen. BAYARD was struck in the hip by a solid shot, while conversing with Gen. FRANKLIN and his Staff, and cannot survive. His right leg has been amputated, but the operation will only serve to prolong his life a short time.

Several hundred prisoners have been taken, who report that Gen. LEE's entire army is in the immediate vicinity. Gen. HILL's troops were withdrawn this morning and started down the river, but afterwards returned. Gen. FRANKLIN is to-night opposed to Stonewall JACKSON.

It is impossible to form an accurate idea of the loss on either side, as the firing is still going on, rendering it extremely difficult to remove the killed and wounded.

The city suffered terribly from the enemy's artillery, and is crowded with our troops, the front extending but a short distance beyond.

The balloon has been up all day. During the morning but little could be seen, owing to the dense fog; but the afternoon was remarkably clear.

This evening the rebels have been shelling Fredericksburgh, endeavoring to drive our troops out of the place, but without success.

THE OPERATIONS OF SUNDAY.

HEADQUARTERS ARMY OF POTOMAC, }
Dec. 14—11:30 A. M. }

There is no fog to-day, the sun shining brightly, with a strong breeze. At daylight this morning there was a heavy fire of artillery and infantry in front of the first line of works, where Gens. SUMNER and HOOKER were engaged yesterday. The fire slacked about an hour afterward, and was heard only at intervals until now. The same occurred in front of Gen. FRANKLIN's Division down the river. The object of both parties was evidently to feel the other.

During last night and this forenoon the rebels have considerably extended their works and strengthened their position. Large bodies of troops are now to be seen where but few were to be seen yesterday.

Our dead which were killed yesterday, while charging in front of the enemy's works, still remain where they fell. When attempting their removal last night, the rebels would open fire with infantry, but the wounded have all been removed

Major-General Burnside and his staff, prior to the Fredericksburg campaign.

from the field, and all the dead obtained are now being buried.

The indications are that no decisive battle will be fought to-day, unless the rebels should bring on the engagement, which they will not probably do.

REPORTS BY WAY OF WASHINGTON.

WASHINGTON, Sunday, Dec. 14.

It is thought here that about 40,000 of our troops were engaged in yesterday's battle.

From information received early this morning, preparations were making all night for a conflict to-day, Gen. BURNSIDE remaining on the field, giving orders, looking to the position and condition of his forces.

Additional surgeons, and everything which the necessities of the wounded require, have been dispatched from Washington to the battle-ground.

It is proper to caution the public against hastily crediting the many unsupported rumors concerning yesterday's battle. Some of them here prevalent have no other basis than surmise, and are mere inventions in the absence of facts. Rebel sympathizers are responsible for not a few of these fictions.

Gentlemen in high public positions repeat the assertion, as coming from Gen. BURNSIDE, that *he has men enough, and, therefore, desires no further reinforcements.*

OUR SPECIAL ARMY CORRESPONDENCE.

Details of Operations to Saturday Morning.

The Crossing of the Rappahannock--The Movement Splendidly Performed--Preponderance of the Union Forces--Condition of Fredericksburgh, &c., &c.

CAMP OPPOSITE FREDERICKSBURGH, }
Saturday, Dec. 13, 1862. }

Affairs are rapidly culminating here, and the crisis of battle, the grandest—probably the most decisive—of the war, approaches apace.

The nation may well pause and hold its breath, in the terrible suspense now impending. The prelude of the conflict has passed. The taking of the town by assault, and after a determined fight with the enemy's sharpshooters and skirmishers, and the crossing of the river by a considerable portion of the Union force, are fast bringing the two great armies face to face. To-day—to-morrow at furthest—must witness events which will long live in history. May we hope that the battle will be as decisive as it now promises to be bloody and terrible.

The events of yesterday may be briefly summed up as follows:

Gen. SUMNER's Corps, the Right Grand Division, were across and occupied the town; one Division took possession the first night, and the remainder of the column passed across the upper bridges in the morning. They filled the whole length of Caroline or Main-street to the lines of the railroad, and by degrees extended their front to Commerce-street, and the streets running up from the river, until the body of the town was filled up. They remained under cover of the houses, the streets running nearly North and South being parallel to the line of the enemies' batteries behind the town. The completion of a second pontoon bridge during the first night greatly facilitated the passage of the troops. The first artillery thrown across were the Napoleon batteries attached to Gen. SUMNER's Division.

The enemy's pickets stubbornly occupied the outskirts of the town, and a fusilade between them and our own advance pickets was kept up during the day. The remainder of FRANKLIN's column crossed their two pontoon bridges during the forenoon, two miles below the centre of the town. Their passage, as well as that of Gen. SUMNER's Corps, was disputed by occasional but not very persistent firing from the rebel batteries, which are chiefly to the South and rear of the town, so as to command the line of the railroad, and also the Bowling Green.

Gen. REYNOLDS' First Corps brought up the rear of FRANKLIN's column, and occupied the broad plateau South of the town, extending for miles down the river.

Gen. HOOKER's Grand Division, which had been on foot since Thursday, when they broke camp, remained with the head of its column pointed toward the upper bridges, but up to 3 o'clock awaited Gen. BURNSIDE's orders to advance.

Three times during the day the enemy's battery commanding this crossing opened fire upon the troops which came down, their shells exploding with uncomfortable accuracy just at the hither end of the bridge, on the slope of the hill, and even beyond on the level plain by which they approached.

Shortly after 3 P. M. HOOKER's column began to move down the river, as if with the design of crossing on the bridges below, where FRANKLIN crossed. Up to a late hour, however, they had not gone over. It is believed they passed the river during the night.

This change in the line was no doubt occasioned by the extraordinary activity displayed by the rebel batteries southeast of the town.

At 2½ P. M. the whole semi-circle of batteries in that direction opened fire upon the pontoon bridges, and upon the lower part of the town, where our troops were quartered. Their other batteries, north of the plank-road, and toward Falmouth, simultaneously poured in their contribution upon the upper crossing, and that part of the town lying in front of it.

Five separate batteries below, working ten or twelve guns, and four above, with eight or ten, kept up a fire of shot and shell until near sundown. Many of their shells fell short, but some took effect in the town, and near the river. What damage they did to the troops I could not learn at that late hour.

Several shells burst near the Lacey House, and one close by the north end of the building while I was getting the names of the wounded lying in that place. One man, a few minutes afterward, was brought in with his arm terribly shattered by a piece of shell. A considerable body of cavalry and infantry were partially sheltered behind these buildings, which are of brick. It being used as a hospital, and occupied by the rebels in common with the Union, wounded soldiers is a guarantee (?) that it will be respected. Its position being only a little to the left of the crossing, and nearly in line of one of the main rebel batteries, probably accounts for these shells bursting so near it.

We must presume that they were accidental shots, as I believe there is no well authenticated instance of their intentionally firing upon a hospital. It is situated only two hundred yards north of Lieut. MILLER's battery, which is protected by earthworks, and very prominent on the high land below the house. These circumstances render the place unsafe, and it will only be used as a temporary hospital. The wounded will, for the present, be carried to the rear, where tents have been established for their accommodation.

The main body of the rebel army is believed to be in position some five or six, perhaps ten miles west, with a strong rear guard for cooperating with and supporting their batteries.

If estimates which I have heard be correct, we have an aggregate of over sixty thousand men more than the estimated strength of the rebel army. Our artillery figures up over five hundred guns. Considering the difficulties of the situation, the completion of six pontoon bridges, and the crossing of such an army in twenty-four hours, is worthy of all military achievement. The events of the last two days have increased the enthusiasm of the whole army toward its Commander, and strengthened confidence in the Generals leading the Grand Divisions. With town and river behind we must fight—there is no backing out.

THE TOWN—ITS CONDITION.

Our shot and shell have riddled a great many of the houses in town; and most of the churches, from foundation to steeple, have been *accidentally* perforated by the storm of missiles which were sent into the town. As the monuments and representatives of a priesthood and people thoroughly baptized in treason, they deserved no exemption from the common doom, but being larger than any other buildings, and very prominently in the range of our fire, they naturally received their full share of the iron storm. The clock in the steeple of the Episcopal church was untouched, and continues to toll off the eventful hours, for the benefit of the Union forces in the town.

In spite of prompt and general efforts to guard the houses from intrusion and pillage, by the establishment of guards, a good many residences have suffered more or less spoliation. Household articles, such as cooking utensils and crockery, pickles, sweetmeats and flitches of bacon, were observed among the troops, as I passed through the different streets. The latter, taken from the meat houses of the first families, no doubt, were generally transfixed on the end of bayonets, and carried in triumph on their shoulders.

There has been, as yet, no general pillaging of the town, and it will not be permitted. The principal stores have each a strong guard to protect the small stock of goods left behind in the flight of their proprietors.

Not over twenty houses all told, have been burned and the total damage to the place, by the bombardment and flames, I estimate at not over two hundred thousand dollars.

The few dead who were shot in the streets, have been buried, necessarily in the town, near where they fell. Considering all the terrible circumstances of provocation, the preservation of the town from total destruction, and its wholesale pillage by the army, are in the highest degree creditable to the Union troops, and to their discipline. Inclosed is a list of the killed and wounded as far as ascertained.

In haste to send the mail.   E. S.

Fredericksburg in March 1863. Scattered fighting would occur here again in May, as part of the Battle of Chancellorsville.

The New-York Times.

VOL. XII—NO. 3504.　　　NEW-YORK, TUESDAY, DECEMBER 16, 1862.　　　PRICE THREE CENTS.

FROM THE ARMY OF THE POTOMAC.

No General Engagement on Sunday or Yesterday.

Desultory Skirmishing Along the Advanced Positions.

The Position of the Two Armies Unchanged.

Continued Preparations for the Second Great Conflict.

Removal of the Wounded to the Washington Hospitals.

Over Seven Hundred Prisoners Captured by Us.

Engagement Between the Gunboats and a Rebel Battery.

HEADQUARTERS OF THE ARMY OF THE POTOMAC, MONDAY MORNING, Dec. 15, 1862—11 o'clock.

There was considerable firing yesterday, between the advanced troops of the two armies.

At one time the rebels showed a disposition to move upon Gen. FRANKLIN's forces.

Occasionally the rebels would throw a few shells among our troops, just to remind us that they were still there.

With these exceptions, everything was quiet.

There is some skirmishing this morning, with considerable artillery firing.

The body of Gen. BAYARD left for Washington to-day. He was to have been married next Wednesday.

HEADQUARTERS, Monday, Dec. 15—P. M.

The weather to-day has been clear and warm, with a strong southerly wind. The roads are in very good condition.

The position of the two armies remain nearly the same. There was not much artillery firing this afternoon by either party. Those shots the rebels did fire were thrown into the city.

The enemy, who are in plain view, are not idle, but busily employed in strengthening their position.

Most of the wounded, to-day, were removed from the city to this side of the river, as on the renewal of the battle the rebel guns would likely cause its destruction.

Over seven hundred prisoners have been taken since our army crossed the river.

REPORTS FROM WASHINGTON.

WASHINGTON, Monday, Dec. 15.

A large number of the wounded from Fredericksburgh are expected here to-night or early to-morrow. A number of steamers have been dispatched to Aquia Creek for that purpose. The hospitals here are being rapidly depleted of such as are able to bear removal, to make room for the fresh comers.

Gen. VINTON, who is severely, but not dangerously, wounded in the side, is here under the care of his father, Rev. Dr. VINTON, who came on this morning.

GUNBOAT FIGHT ON THE RAPPAHANNOCK.

WASHINGTON, Monday, Dec. 15.

On Wednesday evening, our gunboats at Port Royal, about twenty-seven miles from Fredericksburgh, were fired into by a rebel battery from the shore supposed to number twenty heavy guns.

One of the rebel shots struck a coal schooner, wounding Capt. SIMMONS, who has since died.

Another shot struck the *Currituck* on the larboard side, pushing into the engine-room and wounding H. F. SMITH, of Rhode Island, who has since died; also, wounding JEREMIAH DAILY dangerously, and two others slightly.

The firing was very rapid and continued, until sun-down, when the rebel batteries were silenced.

Two schooners, at the commencement of the fight were lying directly in range of the rebel guns, near the shore, but were brought off safely by the *Teaser*.

Our gunboats laid off the shore until morning, when they again opened upon the rebel battery, but met with no response.

THE OPERATIONS OF FRIDAY.

Continual Skirmishing Throughout the Day—About Two Hundred of our Men Killed and Wounded, &c.

From Our Special Correspondent.

FREDERICKSBURGH, Va., Friday, Dec. 12, 1862.

As I stated in my last letter, the National troops occupy the town of Fredericksburgh. During the preceding night FRANKLIN's and a portion of SUMNER's Grand Divisions passed over the river and bivouacked on the opposite bank. Skirmishers were sent to reconnoitre the several streets, and met with much opposition from the rebel sharpshooters, who were posted behind buildings, chimnies and fences. The night was quite dark, and it was with considerable difficulty that the rebels could be discovered in their hiding-places. The skirmishers, however, understood their duty, and displayed much courage in ferreting out the foe. They finally gained their point, and drove the rebels out of the town. As may be naturally supposed, our loss in casualties was not light. Numbers of our men were shot dead, and a great number, considering the nature of the fight, wounded. During the day and evening our casualties were about 200 killed and wounded. The rebel loss cannot be estimated, as they removed their killed and wounded before we got possession of the place.

This morning our troops were massed on the two principal streets of the town running parallel with the river. The upper portion of the town was occupied by the skirmishers, while just at the outside the pickets were stationed. Our force has not made any material change in position to-day. FRANKLIN's troops are bivouacked at the lower end of the place. The troops have not as yet ventured far to the upper end of Fredericksburgh, in consequence of the rebel sharpshooters being in position some five hundred yards distant.

This morning, while the rear of SUMNER's column was passing over the upper pontoon, the rebels opened fire from guns in their second tier of earthworks. The shots were well directed, but fortunately our men escaped injury. After firing a few rounds, the rebels ceased. Our batteries near Falmouth replied, and possibly had much to do in silencing the enemy's guns. Nearly all of our batteries, which were planted along the river bank yesterday, were taken across the bridges to-day. They were not, however, excepting those which accompanied FRANKLIN's troops, placed in position, but remained upon the streets, their commander awaiting orders.

This afternoon HOOKER's troops appeared at the upper bridge for the purpose of crossing. The rebels immediately opened a heavy fire upon them. The order was at length countermanded and the troops were marched down to the vicinity of the lower bridge upon which FRANKLIN crossed, and upon which they will cross early to-morrow morning.

To-day, Gen. FRANKLIN sent out artillery and skirmishers to the left of the rebel fortifications. They were met with a vigorous fire from the rebel guns, and made but little progress toward an advance.

Four companies of the Eighth Illinois Cavalry, under Major BEVERIDGE, made a reconnoissance toward the rebel earthworks. They went sufficiently near to count the guns—eight in number—in one battery. The rebels did not offer to fire upon them, probably from the fact of their being unable to depress their guns to the proper degree.

Lieut KERNES, of the Sixth United States Cavalry, with four men, forded the river just above Fredericksburgh. The water was ascertained to be four feet deep, which rendered the crossing of artillery and supply wagons by the same means impracticable. It is decided that the entire army must cross the river over bridges. There are now four bridges constructing, two at the upper and two at the lower end of the town.

The appearance of Fredericksburgh after the severe cannonading it received yesterday can be readily imagined. Hardly a house stands that has not been penetrated by more or less shots. In the midst of all the shelling, however, some of the citizens remained in their houses, taking refuge in the cellars. Among the citizens I notice a few women. No reliable information could be obtained from the inhabitants in regard to the position and strength of the rebels. As near as I could learn the town was defended yesterday by two Mississippi Regiments, one of which was the Seventeenth.

The number of prisoners taken yesterday and to-day amount to over two hundred. A deserter came in this morning. He reports that the rebels have their lines of earthworks extending a distance of two miles. They are so built as to command every street leading from the river.

Our next movement will be to flank the rebels on their right. Gen. BUTTERFIELD has issued orders to his Staff, to-night, to prepare themselves with five days' rations, it being the intention to pursue the enemy until he is forced to fight or surrender. This order would imply that it is not impossible that the enemy may evacuate his position before morning. It is considered a singular circumstance that he has not opened upon us with more continuous and vigorous fire. It is the intention to cross Gen. HOOKER's Grand Division in the morning. The three Grand Divisions will then be across the river. To-morrow a strenuous effort will be made to take the rebel earthworks. If the rebels stand we shall certainly have a terrible conflict.

WHIT.

The New-York Times.

VOL. XII—NO. 3518. NEW-YORK, THURSDAY, JANUARY 1, 1863. PRICE THREE CENTS.

A BATTLE AT MURFREESBORO.

A General Advance of Rosecrans' Army on Monday.

The Enemy Pushed Back Seven or Eight Miles.

A Sharp Brush on the Nolinsville Road.

A Rebel Gun and Caisson Captured.

Our Army Sweeping Down all the Roads on Tuesday.

A GENERAL ENGAGEMENT IMMINENT.

CINCINNATI, Wednesday, Dec. 31.

The *Enquirer* has advices from Nashville, stating that ROSECRANS' army had moved on the enemy, driving them before him with considerable heavy skirmishing. The Federals are in high spirits and anxious for a fight. On Monday ROSECRANS' advance was in sight of Murfreesboro, with the enemy in full view, drawn up in line of battle. A battle was expected on Tuesday.

A DISPATCH FROM THE ARMY.
CINCINNATI, Wednesday, Dec. 31.

The following is a special dispatch to the *Commercial:*

NEAR MURFREESBORO, Tenn., Tuesday, Dec. 30.

The Fourteenth Army Corps made a general advance yesterday, and pushed the rebels back seven or eight miles. COLLINS' Brigade, of Gen. McCOOK's Corps, had a sharp brush with the enemy just beyond Nolinsville. Cannonading took place for an hour, the enemy wasting considerable ammunition. Our troops reserved their fire, until advancing briskly, by a dexterous flank movement, the One Hundred and First Ohio captured one gun and a caisson. We lost one killed, and three wounded.

A general engagement is imminent. Our army is sweeping down all the roads to Murfreesboro. Heavy artillery firing is now heard on the Nolinsville Road, where Gen. McCOOK is engaging the rebel HARDEE. The weather is damp and the ground very heavy.

A LATER DISPATCH.
CAMP, TEN MILES FROM MURFREESBORO,
Wednesday, Dec. 31.

Gen. CRITTENDEN reports the enemy drawn up in line of battle on the east side of Stone River, menacing Gen. ROSECRANS. He is ordered to form in line of battle, two divisions in front, one in reserve and covering his flanks, and Gens. NEGLEY and ROSSEAU to close up.

Gen. McCOOK also reports his command on Wilkinson's Creek, seven miles from Murfreesboro. The enemy is in line of battle on Stone's River, from Murfreesboro to Franklin Pike. A similar disposition of McCOOK's forces is ordered as on Gen. CRITTENDEN's line.

It now appears that a great battle will be fought on Stone's River to-morrow, in front of Murfreesboro.

LATEST REPORTS FROM LOUISVILLE.
LOUISVILLE, Wednesday, Dec. 31.

All is quiet south of here, as far as headquarters are advised.

FROM CORINTH AND OTHER POINTS.
CAIRO, Wednesday, Dec. 31.

Information from Corinth to Saturday night states that the garrison at that place were on half-rations. Foraging parties, however, were able to supply the deficiency.

Col. LEE, with a large cavalry force, is still in pursuit of VAN DORN.

Trains are running from Corinth to Jackson, and from Jackson to Holly Springs. The road is also repaired from Jackson to a point nine miles north of Trenton. Every station-house and all the bridges between Trenton and Moscow, within twelve miles of Columbus, are burned. All the bridge-timber along the route is also destroyed, and much of the tracks torn up.

A National force, to the number of 3,000, which had left Trenton in the direction of the Tennessee River, on a reconnoissance, had not returned when the information left.

A construction train left Columbus yesterday. It went as far as Union City without meeting any obstacle. Two regiments and a battery left to-day to assist in putting the road in order. The rebels have evidently left the road. It will be repaired in a week.

FROM ALBANY.

Arrival of Gov. Seymour—Preparations for the Inauguration, &c.
ALBANY, Wednesday, Dec. 31.

Gov. SEYMOUR and Lieut.-Gov. JONES arrived to-day. A large number of prominent citizens of the State are in the City, to witness the ceremonies of the inauguration, to take place in the Assembly chamber at 11 o'clock to-morrow. New-York is liberally represented. The Court of Appeals adjourned to-day. In the Forest divorce case, judgment was affirmed.

The Missouri Legislature.
JEFFERSON CITY, Tuesday, Dec. 30.

Both Houses of the Legislature completed their organization to-day by the election of all the Emancipation candidates.

There seems to be a general desire that Congress should lead off in the Emancipation movement, and there is no doubt that a prompt, liberal tender of compensation would greatly facilitate the Emancipation measure in the Legislature.

There is a strong prospect that the Senatorial question will be disposed of this week. Under the Constitution of this State a simple majority only is required to pass any bill over the Governor's veto.

FROM THE ARMY OF THE POTOMAC.

An Important Reconnoissance in Force.

A Portion of the Rebel Army Supposed to Have Moved up the Rappahannock.

HEADQUARTERS ARMY OF THE POTOMAC,
Wednesday, Dec. 31.

A reconnoissance in force went out yesterday morning, which will probably be heard from in a few days.

It is believed here that a considerable portion of Gen. LEE's army has moved from its late position in our front, and gone up the Rappahannock. Its destination, however, is not known.

It has been ascertained by flag of truce that Capt. SWEARENGEN, of the late Brig.-Gen. JACKSON's Staff, who was reported killed in the battle of the 19th, was only wounded and captured. He is now doing well at a farm-house about four miles in the rear of the enemy's front.

Lieut. EDDY, ordnance officer of Gen. WHIPPLE's Staff, is a prisoner in Richmond. He was unhurt on the battle-field.

Major-General William S. Rosencrans replaced General Buell as commander of the Union Army of the Cumberland.

The New-York Times.

VOL. XII—NO. 3519.   NEW-YORK, SATURDAY, JANUARY 3, 1863.   PRICE THREE CENTS.

A TERRIBLE BATTLE.

Attack Upon the Rebels at Murfreesboro by Gen. Rosecrans.

Severe Fighting All Day Wednesday.

The Rebel Centre Broken by Gen. Thomas.

Their Intrenchments at Murfreesboro Captured.

Gens. Rousseau, Palmer and Stanley Wounded.

The Rebel Gens. Cheatham and Rains Killed.

NEAR MURFREESBORO, Wednesday, Dec. 31.

Our whole line suffered terribly this morning. Four regiments of regulars lost half their men and all their commanding officers.

Gen. ANDERSON's troops suffered severely.

Majors ROSENGARTEN and WARD are killed.

Generals STANLEY, ROUSSEAU and PALMER are wounded.

Two o'clock P. M.

Gen. THOMAS has just broken the rebel centre, and driven the enemy a mile.

We are advancing our whole line.

Gen. ROSECRANS is personally superintending the movements. One shot killed two of his Staff officers.

The Fifteenth Wisconsin Regiment has lost seven Captains.

Gen. NEGLEY's artillery is still mowing the rebels in the centre.

Gen. CRITTENDEN's left wing has taken the intrenchments at Murfreesboro.

The rebel Generals CHEATHAM and RAINS are killed.

REPORTS RECEIVED IN WASHINGTON.

WASHINGTON, Friday, Jan. 2.

The Secretary of War to-day received the following advices:

CLEOELAND, Friday, Jan. 2.

The following has just been received by telegraph from Cincinnati, dated Murfreesboro, Jan. 1, 1863:

A terrible battle was fought yesterday. The latest from the field is up to noon. The rebel centre had been broken, and things looked favorable. The losses are reported to be enormous. STANLY, ROUSSEAU and PALMER are wounded, and the rebels CHEATHAM and RAINS are killed.

Gen. ROSECRANS occupies Murfreesboro.

(Signed.)   J. T. BOYLE, Brigadier-General.

LATER PARTICULARS.

The Rebels Driven Out of Murfreesboro—The Losses Very Severe.

NASHVILLE, Friday, Jan. 2.

The Federals encountered the rebels on the 30th ult., near Stewart's Creek. After heavy skirmishing, the rebels were driven back. We captured one hundred prisoners, and killed and wounded a large number of rebels. Our loss was seventy killed and wounded.

At daybreak, on the 31st, the fight was resumed with great fury. McCOOK's corps was opposed to HARDEE. After desperate fighting, with heavy loss on both sides, McCOOK retreated two miles. He soon rallied, and was driven back. At night he was four miles this side of the ground occupied in the morning. The fight continued until 10 o'clock P. M., at which time we had maintained our position.

The Federal Loss is very heavy.

The Twenty-first, Twenty-fifth and Thirty-fifth Illinois, lost two-thirds, and the Fifteenth and Thirty-eighth Ohio, one half their number. The One hundred and first Ohio lost 125 men, the Thirty-eighth Indiana about the same number.

The total killed and wounded is estimated at 2,500. The rebel loss exceeds ours.

Gen. J. E. RAINES was killed. Gen. CHEATHAM was wounded and taken prisoner.

We have captured 500 prisoners.

RENEWAL OF THE BATTLE ON THE 1ST.

The fight was renewed at 3 A. M., on Jan. 1. The cannonading was heard at Nashville. At 10 A. M. WOOD's and VAN CLEVE's Divisions were in Murfreesboro driving the enemy, who were in full retreat.

Three hundred prisoners reached Nashville at 6 P. M., on Jan. 1, including the following commissioned officers:

Maj. J. J. FRANKLIN, Thirtieth Arkansas.
Capt. W. E. JOHNSON, Second Arkansas.
Capt. J. P. EAGLES, Second Arkansas.
Capt. S. C. STONE, First Tennessee Cavalry.

Many buildings have been taken for hospital purposes. Great numbers of wounded are being brought in now.

The river has fallen 18 inches on the shoals.

Soldiers from General Sheridan's division holding the Union right were forced to retire due to lack of ammunition.

The New-York Times.

VOL. XII—NO. 3597.   NEW-YORK, SATURDAY, APRIL 4, 1863.   PRICE THREE CENTS.

THREE DAYS LATER FROM EUROPE.

Arrival of the Canada at Halifax.

Still Further Depredations by the Alabama.

The Washington, Golden Eagle, Olive Jane and Palmetto Captured by Her.

The Washington Released on Bond---The Others Burnt.

The Rebel Cotton Loan all Taken.

PROGRESS OF THE POLISH REVOLUTION.

Close of the Debate in the French Senate.

Loud Calls for More French Troops in Mexico and Cochin China.

HALIFAX, Friday, April 3.

The Royal Mail steamship *Canada*, Capt. GRACE, from Liverpool on Saturday, the 21st of March, at 10 A. M., *via* Queenstown 22d, arrived here at 3½ P. M. to-day. She had been detained off the harbor since this morning by fog.

The *Canada* sailed from Halifax at 7 P. M. Weather clear.

The *Canada* has $10,000 in specie and 43 passengers for Halifax, and 30 for Boston.

She passed on the 21st, ships *Elvira*, *Ben. Nevis*, and bark *Solo*, going into Liverpool.

22d, at 6 A. M., off Saltas, Royal Mail steamship *Africa*, for Liverpool.

23d, lat. 51°, long. 13°, steamship *City of New-York*, for Liverpool.

26th, lat. 46°, long. 30°, steamship *Kangaroo*, for Liverpool.

The ship *Benj. Bangs* arrived at Queenstown 22d, and the *Dashaway* at Gravesend 22d.

The *Canada* also passed at 6 A. M., April 2, lat. 43°, long. 59°, the steamship *Nova Scotian*, from Liverpool March 19, for Portland.

The steamers *City of Cork*, of the Inman line, and the *Louisiana* would leave Liverpool, shortly after the *Canada*, for New-York. The former would call at Queenstown, sailing thence on the 23d.

The steamship *Jura*, from Portland, reached Liverpool on the evening of the 19th.

The steamship *Glasgow*, from New-York, arrived at Queenstown, and the *Borussia*, from New-York, at Southampton, early on the morning of the 20th. The *Glasgow* reached Liverpool on the 21st.

The steamship *Damascus*, from New-York, arrived at Liverpool 21st.

The departure of the *Great Eastern* is postponed till the 18th of April.

AMERICAN AFFAIRS ABROAD.

FURTHER DEPREDATIONS BY THE ALABAMA.

The ship *Washington*, from Callao for Antwerp, arrived at Southampton on the 20th, having been captured by the pirate *Alabama* Feb. 20, but released on a bond for $50,000. She brought the crews of the ships *Golden Eagle*, *Olive Jane* and *Palmetto*, burnt by the *Alabama*.

THE REBEL COTTON LOAN.

The Confederate Loan would close on the afternoon of the 21st, the bids having greatly exceeded the amount needed, particularly in London. Report says the applications in Liverpool were not very heavy, and there was considerable diversity of opinion there as to the merits of the scheme.

Paris telegrams say the loan was quite the rage there.

The *Times* City Article says:

"Very little political feeling is manifested in the business, and it seems evident, so far as London is concerned, that it is in viewing it as a cotton speculation, that any attractions it possesses are to be found. In other respects there can be no doubt the majority of merchants and capitalists would have wished it had not been introduced. As the affair will not be officially recognized on 'Change, the dealers agreed among themselves to fix the 24th of April as the settling day."

The London *Star* cannot believe *bona fide* investors will be found to take the loan even at par, without better security than that offered by the hypothecation of cotton, which it may never be in the power of JEFF. DAVIS & Co. to deliver.

The *Daily News* editorially denounces the loan. It says:

"Its flagrant indecency and immorality will strike and scandalize most Englishmen who care for the reputation of their country. Those who subscribe to the loan are *aiding and abetting the Slave Power in a most direct and emphatic manner*, and all who have an enlightened regard for the true reputation of England, will regard this open assistance to traffickers in human flesh as a desecration and pollution to English exchange.

There was rather less excitement in regard to the loan on Friday, the 20th, and after touching 5½, it closed that day at 4½@4¾ premium. The bids reached £10,000,000 sterling, and were expected to be £15,000,000 to £18,000,000 at the close.

The *Times* again asserts that it is regarded as a cotton transaction, and not a political loan, and there is nothing in it to prevent any one from subscribing.

THE REBEL STATES.

The Connecticut Copperheads as Seen in Richmond.

The Hopes for Peace More Remote

THE DEFENCES OF CHARLESTON HARBOR

State of the Markets in Richmond

We have received our usual files of late Richmond and Charleston papers. They contain no news in addition to that which has already been transmitted by telegraph, but the following extracts will be found of interest:

"TWO NATIONS."

Under this caption the Richmond *Enquirer* has a long article, which has for its text the Connecticut election. It says:

"Democratic men in Connecticut, then, finding that fire and sword are unlikely to bring in the money invested in them, with cent. per cent. interest, bethink themselves, it seems, of resorting to 'reason'—to see if *that* will pay. We know exactly what they mean by *reason*. We shall even put the proposition they would make us thus: 'Come now, ye wayward sisters!' Has not enough been done for honor, as you call it? After all, what do you make by this war and carnage? We 'Democrats' have tried it, and behold! it did not pay. On the contrary, all the pay and all the profits go to those wretches, the 'Black Republicans,' whom you and we together so long abused and kept out in the cold. You know we abhor them as bitterly as yourselves can do. It is true we joined with them in the employment of a gentle coercion to retain you in our glorious and lucrative old Union; but we are reasonable; when a speculation is found not to pay, we drop it; shall we throw good money after bad? God forbid! We think it is *time*—we are now ready—to make common cause with you against the common enemy—namely, the party that is *in*. Suffer the Democratic party to lead you over once more into the green pastures of Federal office, and by the still waters of Federal patronage, and we shall make fair division of the spoil on the word of patriots and gentlemen. What shall stand in the way of such a blessed reunion? Shall the blood of sons and brothers slain, the shrieks of violated women, and smoking homesteads and desolated fields, and all the price and passion and agony of the mortal strife, be suffered to rise up between us on the sacramental day when we meet 'in that august and immortal Convention to distribute the patronage of a hemisphere, and feel that the wide, unbounded Continent is ours! Perish the thought! Let us drop from our hands these bayonets and bullets, and make a peaceful Presidential kind of campaign, as to the golden days of 'TYLER, too;' let us marshal the gallant old legions of the Unterrified, and *charge* at the rate of two hundred millions per annum, to the war-cry of *Pluribus Unum*!"

This is the sort of "reason" which those Connecticut Democrats propose to try. *To them it seems reason; to us the very extremity of hopeless delirium. We shall watch those "Confederates" (so called) who may show any inclination to hearken unto those eloquent Democrats; who may praise their lofty patriotism, or sympathize in their noble struggle for their Constitution. Such Confederates will be fit subjects—to say the least—of medical treatment as lunatics.* To shave their heads and half-drown them with shower-baths might do them good; but to answer them according to their folly would only exasperate their paroxysm. If there be few such Confederates, or none, so much the better."

THE PEACE PROBLEM.

From the Charleston Mercury, March 14.

The march of events during the last thirty days has done much to dispel the hopes of early peace, so generally entertained at the opening of the year. Since the bloody affair at Murfreesboro, the hostile forces in Tennessee, as well as those upon the Rappahannock and the Mississippi, appear to have been at a dead lock. But though the military *status* is in the main, unchanged, our enemies have not been idle. *Never have their preparations to crush us been so active and energetic as during the present lull in the tempest of the war.* In the desperate resolve to rob us of our rights, they have madly thrown away their own. With a bankrupt Treasury, with a Constitution trampled in the dust, with an army which has invariably been beaten in every pitched battle, by troops inferior in number and equipments, and with a Government derided abroad and despised at home, the Yankees have deemed all that was left to them—the shadow of a free and constitutional Government—not worth preserving, and *they have deliberately cast the lives and the liberties of their whole people in the scale against the hitherto invincible sword of the South.* The Northern States have welded together all that remains to them of strength and wealth, to form an *efficient weapon, in the hands of the vulgar despot at Washington, for our destruction.* They have learned already to applaud the tyrannies of their master, and they salute him Dictator. There are some among us who hope that the spirit of republican government will yet assert itself at the North and that the people of the Northwest, at least, will ere long rise up to wrest their independence from the grasp of the new Autocrat. But in vain do we look for any material indication of this counter revolution. The whole Yankee nation, from Cape Cod to the prairies of the far West, is this day substantially a unit in the determination to subjugate these Confederate States, if their subjugation be possible. *Meantime, the dreams of foreign intervention that have so long deluded our people are passing away.* England was never so resolute in her policy of non-interference as now; France stirs not in our behalf without the coöperation of her jealous rival. Thus, to our cost, we have learned the wholesome lesson that upon the blows yet to be struck by our own right arms rests the only hope of peace and independence. Henceforth let our Government bend all its energies to strengthen our armies in the field; and let our planters everywhere, as they desire the salvation of our cause, as they prize the success of our living defenders and the cherished memory of our glorious dead, see to it that the soil is tilled with the single view of feeding the armies, whose breasts are the barriers that protect that soil from the tide of desolation.

AFFAIRS AT CHARLESTON.

A letter to the Mobile *News* gives the following regarding affairs at Charleston, and the measures taken to repel our forces:

The orders just issued by Gen. RIPLEY, who is the Brigadier commanding this district of Gen. BEAUREGARD'S Department, are significant. *No more blockade running steamers to pass Forts Sumter or Moultrie by night;* if they succeed in running the gauntlet of the Federal squadron, they must anchor until daylight outside and under the guns of the forts, and report by a small boat at Fort Sumter. Every channel in the harbor bristles with torpedoes, and woe to the hostile vessel that tries to pass in, without a pilot familiar with the position of the submerged and slumbering thunderbolts. By another general order all furloughs are revoked and absentees recalled to their commands. The hospitals are to be immediately cleared, and all the preparations which denote the expectations of an action at any moment are going on with great energy.

The struggle, when it comes, will certainly be of a fearful character. It will be the shock of tremendous forces, the relative powers of which are yet untried. The long-mooted question of the fighting value of ships against batteries will be brought to a test more conclusive than any to which human warfare has yet subjected it. In other words, the Monitor iron-clads, which the Federals claim to be the most impenetrable vessels ever constructed, will necessarily come within point-blank range of the most numerous and powerful batteries that ever yet have been used in a single engagement. We have good reason, too, to believe that our guns will be managed with admirable tact and precision. The more important batteries are manned by the South Carolina regulars, for whom the credit is claimed, and I think justly, of being the most expert and practical heavy artillerists in the Confederate army. The forts are well officered, and Gen. RIPLEY, who has made the study of heavy ordnance a specialty for years, and whose excellence in that particular branch of military knowledge is an admitted fact, will himself take command of Fort Sumter as soon as the enemy makes his appearance.

It is scarcely possible that any floating thing can breast unharmed the concentrated storm of heavy metal from the guns of Sumter, Moultrie, and Battery Bee, the three principal works commanding the throat of the harbor. Nor can the peril of running the gauntlet be diminished by any attempt to pass under the cover of darkness, as has been the case at Vicksburgh and New-Orleans. So tortuous and intricate is the channel leading to the forts that the most experienced pilots of the harbor would not venture to bring in a vessel by night, under the conditions which the enemy cannot escape, namely, without a light or a landmark to guide the way. Even when the blockade-running vessels leave the harbor, it is always necessary to aid their exit by previously arranged lights (shaded) and signals; so that it is reasonably certain that the attacking iron-clads must either enter in open day, or incur the immense hazard of getting aground upon one of the most treacherous bars on the Southern coast, which seldom yields a vessel once it has grasped the keel. But if, perchance, despite of mazy channel, multiplied torpedoes, and the combined batteries of the forts, some of the nine Monitors should chance to get into port, they would still have to encounter a concentrated fire from other batteries, which, as the Northern papers have learned from contrabands, "line the shores of the interior of the harbor." And then will come the "tug of war" which will determine the possession of the honored old city.

The captured gunboat *Isaac P. Smith*, now called the *Stono*, has been repaired, and is now in good fighting trim. She will be the flag ship of Commodore INGRAHAM.
W.

THE WAR IN TENNESSEE.

JOHNSTON AND BRAGG.

Correspondence of the Richmond Enquirer.

TULLAHOMA, Tenn., Sunday, March 22, 1863.

Gen. JOHNSTON reviewed the troops on yesterday. The spectacle was by no means brilliant in point of pageantry, but as an exhibition of swarthy strength was imposing in the extreme. Gen. BRAGG

was not on the field; he is with Mrs. BRAGG, who is lying dangerously ill at Winchester.

There are lively hopes expressed on all hands that the army will pass under the immediate command of Gen. JOHNSTON; and in any event, that the next engagement may be directed by him. Let me, in this connection, sketch briefly the main features of objection to Gen. BRAGG, rumors of which have reached Richmond. In the first place, Gen. BRAGG does not understand the *personnel* of our army. He is what may be called a "fidgety" person, full of whim and, occasionally, of caprice; often unreasonable, and sometimes not altogether dignified. I do not regard him as a cruel man, although the prejudices of the soldier so estimate his dealing in cases of life and death. The chief objection to him proceeds out of a general disbelief in his capacity to *achieve*. No one doubts his industry, his energy, his perfect knowledge of the minutiæ of his office. Nor does any one of an unbiased disposition question his loyalty and courage. But, as some one said after the battle of Murfreesboro, there "is a superstition against him." *He is invested with the idea of "failure."* Hence the army, officers and privates, lose no opportunity of speaking ill of his "luck," as they descant freely of his unreliability.

On the other hand, Gen. JOHNSTON is invested with just so much *eclat*, beyond his own fame, as is taken from Gen. BRAGG. Gen. JOHNSTON is a full man; he has a large, manly, round-hearted soul of his own, and the men love him. They believe him to be a man of genius. They respect him, and are perfectly confident of success if led by him. They look upon his presence as a good omen, and are impatient for a battle before he gets away.

He should not be absent on the expected day!

When will that be? I cannot say. Perhaps not in a month: perhaps in a fortnight. I do not believe ROSECRANS will attack us here—it is so far from his base; such a wild, rugged country, and steep retreat so impossible, if necessary. And yet, how can he dodge us, either with honor or without risk? He has a dissatisfied army to keep in temper—a discontented "constituency" to appease. Nothing short of a meeting with the "rebels" will do, and then a meeting when he shall come off victor. No one conceives this possible in two events: 1. His advance here; 2. The personal presence of Gen. JOHNSTON.

There is a rumor of the resignation of Gen. Breckinridge. This surely cannot be so. A fact of the kind would be extremely unfortunate. I do not credit it.

OUR FLAG.

From the Richmond Enquirer.

There is a general prejudice against the stars and bars; though in itself a handsome banner, it is said to be too like the old Yankee concern, which has become so hateful. Fortunately, it is not the flag under which our armies have won their most signal successes; and many believe that it will be hard now to supersede the crimson battle flag with its starred St. Andrew's Cross of Blue. It has claims upon us now; for was not this the banner that waved along the lines of the Confederates when they pressed fiercely upon McCLELLAN's hosts through the woods and marshes of the Peninsula, until its crimson flutter was a vision of terror, and vengeance to the flying foe? Was not this the glorious flag that struck panic into the legions of POPE when they saw it flash upon their rear like a crimson star? It has waved defiance from the heights of Fredericksburgh, and Potomac, from the mountain to the sea, has fondly reflected its blood-red gleam. Under its shadow great soldiers have died with one last look upon its

dear cross, and in the hour of victory it has seemed transfigured into something godlike when the rapturous shout of our Southern soldiery shook its fold like a storm. It will be hard to supersede this battle-flag.

RICHMOND MARKETS.

From the Dispatch.

SATURDAY, March 28, 1863.

SPECIE AND BANK-NOTES—Gold has declined to $4 premium—selling rate. The brokers are paying from $3 50@$3 75. according to amount. Silver is quotable at about 25 ℔ cent. below these rates. Bank-notes are heavy at 75 ℔ cent. premium, some asking 70. The buying rate is 60 ℔ cent.

PRODUCE—We notice a general upward tendency in all articles of indispensable necessity, caused partly by a lack of transportation facilities, and partly by the hesitation of producers to send supplies to market, through fear of impressment. The bill which lately passed Congress, insuring just compensation for all articles impressed, has been signed by the President, and is now a law—in addition to which the Adjutant-General has issued an order forbidding the impressment of supplies on their way to market, for sale on arrival. Surely the people of the interior need have no further hesitation in performing their real duty of relieving the distress occasioned in the cities by a scarcity of provisions. We quote Apples at $30@$60 ℔ bbl., according to quality. Bacon, hog-round, $1 50@$1 75 ℔ ℔. White Beans, $11@$12 ℔ bushel.

GROCERIES—Coffee, $4 37½ ℔ ℔. Brown Sugar, $1 25, with an upward tendency. Molasses, $10 50 ℔ gallon. Salt, 40c. ℔ ℔. Rice, 30c. ℔ ℔.

LIQUORS—Common Whisky, $25 ℔ gallon, good do., $30. Apple Brandy, $24 ℔ gallon.

THE PRICES IN TEXAS.

In Wharton County, Texas, a few days since, the sale of a wealthy bachelor's estate came off, the owner having died. The Galveston *News* gives the following account of the prices realized:

"Common field hands (negro men) brought from $3,000 to $3,500; negro girls, from $2,000 to $3,000; negro boys, (from 12 to 16 years old,) from $2,500 to $3,000, &c., prices somewhat raising according to age and condition. One family of negroes—a woman 45 years of age, with seven children, the oldest a boy of 22 years, the youngest a child of 3 years old—brought the handsome sum of $18,000. The whole lot, consisting of 138 negroes, of all ages, sex, size and condition, ran up to the round sum of $280,000 and upward. Mules and oxen also seemed to be in great demand; mules sold at from $400 to $800 per pair; oxen at from $200 to $280 per yoke. Eight pair of hames and traces brought $146, and everything else went in proportion. The two plantations known as Clark's upper and lower plantations, and comprising the best quality of old Caney soil, were certainly among the best bargains of the sale. The upper place brought $35 per acre; the lower place brought $34 per acre."

REBEL GENERALS QUARRELING.

The Jackson *Mississippian*, of the 12th inst., says:

"It is said that, in retaliation for the order of Gen. PEMBERTON stopping supplies from being sent to Mobile by railroad from this State, Gen. BUCKNER has issued a similar order in regard to supplies from his department coming in this direction. Hence we learn that flour advanced in this city yesterday to $110 ℔ barrel."

Many Confederate ships were built or refitted in British ports, despite Britain's tenacious claim to neutrality. This photo shows the *Old Dominion* docked at Bristol.

The New-York Times.

VOL. XII–NO. 3624.　　　　　NEW-YORK, WEDNESDAY, MAY 6, 1863.　　　　　PRICE THREE CENTS.

FROM HOOKER'S ARMY.

Letters From Our Special Correspondents to Monday Morning.

Further Details of the Great Battles of Saturday and Sunday.

The Storming of the Heights at Fredericksburgh.

Prodigies of Valor Performed by Our Troops.

THE PRISONERS AND GUNS CAPTURED.

Unsuccessful Attempt of the Rebels to Recapture the Heights.

Gen. Lee Said to be Calling for Reinforcements.

Fitzhugh Lee Reported a Prisoner in Washington.

RUMORS ABOUT STONEMAN

A Partial List of Casualties on the Left.

HEADQUARTERS IN THE FIELD, NEAR CHANCEL-
LORSVILLE, Sunday Evening, May 6, 1863.

At this hour of writing, it is impossible to estimate the loss in to-day's battle on either side. We know that ours is heavy—heavier than ever before in a battle of so short duration. We further know that the loss of the enemy is admitted by themselves to be perfectly frightful. We had the advantage in artillery, and our shells and canister tore and mangled their ranks fearfully. The prisoners are silent as to the loss of prominent officers, but some of the Alabamians in A. P. HILL's division say that he was killed early in the day, and that Gen. RAYNOR is now in command of the division.

THE BATTLE-GROUND.

Probably no battle was ever fought upon ground more unfavorable for the manœuvring and deploying of troops. Nearly the whole country in this vicinity is covered with dense forest, much of it being of the same character as "The Wilderness," lying only a short distance west of this point. The timber is mostly dead, and still very dense; then, to make the forest still more impenetrable, there is a denser growth of dead underbrush, so that it is hardly passable for man—certainly not for beast—and the worst place conceivable for handling troops. Yet a very great part of to-day's terrible battle was fought in this almost impenetrable jungle, and many dead and wounded on both sides still lie there, concealed in the gloomy depths of "The Wilderness." The only open ground upon which the battle was fought, was the plain on the south side of the plank-road, near Chancellorsville, half a mile long, and perhaps three hundred yards wide. The only open ground in

our present position is a semi-circular crest, extending from the left of Gen. SYKES' position to the right of Gen. HOWARD's. Immediately in front of this are dense woods, concealing our skirmishers and those of the enemy. This crest is our artillery position, and here guns enough are massed to blow to atoms the armies of a dozen Southern Confederacies. The enemy seem to have a proper appreciation of the courtesies in waiting for them from this position. Twice to-day they have essayed out of the woods toward our guns, and twice have those guns sent to their earthly doom untold numbers of desperate wretches. The artillery at this point is in charge of Capt. WEED, Chief of Artillery of the Fifth Army Corps.

PRISONERS.

The exact count of prisoners thus far taken, during the battle of Sunday, is not yet known, but it must be, all told, *nearly, if not quite, two thousand*. They were brought in singly, in squads, in companies and by regiments; and our men say that they could have taken many more, "but for the trouble of bothering with them on the field of battle." They would rather shoot than capture. Two regiments were taken entire—the Twenty-third Georgia and the Fourth Alabama—the former yesterday and the latter to-day. Then there are detachments from fifty or sixty other regiments, including many North and South Carolina, Virginia, Mississippi and Louisiana regiments. The enemy has undoubtedly taken several hundred of our men, mostly wounded, with some from the Eleventh Corps, who couldn't run fast enough to get away.

THE ELEVENTH CORPS.

The unaccountable and inexcusable conduct of a large portion of this corps, was the means of turning to ashes a grand victory almost within our grasp, while the position was only retrieved by the superb generalship of the Commanding General. A portion of the troops, the brigades of Cols. BUSHBECK and McLEAN, stood their ground manfully until overpowered by vastly superior numbers. Gen. BARLOW's brigade was absent with Gen. SICKLES.

The manner in which Gen. HOOKER proposed to checkmate the rear attack of JACKSON strikingly illustrates the bold and daring character of our commander. Finding that JACKSON was marching by the old Catharpin road past our right front, Gen. HOOKER promptly ordered Gen. SICKLES to attack that impudent column on the flank. This was not more quickly conceived than vigorously executed. In one hour and a half from the time the movement began the head of Gen. BIRNEY's division was engaging the enemy, and our force and vigorous attack were so great that the enemy's left flank was speedily turned, his columns doubled back one upon the other, and his men seized with demoralization and panic. WILLIAMS' division ably assisted this dashing movement,

while Gen. GEARY attacked sharply on our centre front, and the prospects were cheering indeed. The Eleventh Corps was strongly intrenched. Its position ought to have been held, and *somebody* is to blame for this disgraceful affair which smote us so sorely, just as we were about to reap rich fruits from the boldest move yet projected since we crossed the river. And to remedy the effect of this disaster, we have spent this day in fighting which only puts us in our former condition, and the enemy once more in our front. Albeit we have inflicted on LEE a murderous loss, and so shattered his columns that he must have time and reinforcements to enable him to fight again as savagely as he fought to-day. Beside, his position is now such that he must inevitably attack our strong position, or retreat. Retreat in his case, with our swift-marching army after him, is most surely disastrous. He may precipitate his whole force upon SEDGWICK, who can retire to the Heights of Fredericksburgh, and wait for HOOKER to follow up in his rear. Two or three times Gen. HOOKER has said that he would compel the rebels to come out of their fortications and attack him on his own ground. It is brilliant generalship, indeed, that has so faithfully fulfilled this promise. To-day the enemy literally leaves his fortifications, and stands before our intrenched camp, essaying its capture.

The question of supplies must now be of great moment to the enemy. His communication by rail, if not totally severed by our cavalry, must be seriously interrupted by the presence of our forces in the vicinity of Hamilton's Crossing, five miles below Fredericksburgh, which has been the rebel supply depot during the Winter. The prisoners taken to-day had nothing to eat, and some of them say no rations had been issued to them for three days.

SPIRIT OF OUR TROOPS.

Our men never behaved more magnificently. Cool, confident and brave, they fought with splendid valor, and were even complimented by the prisoners who fell into our hands. The demoralization of the Eleventh Corps did not affect the rest of the army in the least. Some how or other they looked upon it as a matter of course. Gen. HOOKER's appearance on the field, under severe fire, created tumultuous enthusiasm among the men, and he was cheered to the echo time and again. When it became known that he had been struck by a piece of spent shell, (although uninjured,) the cheers grew louder still.

To the indefatigable efforts of Major-Gen. HOWARD, commanding the Eleventh Corps, is due the fact that before daylight this morning this corps was so far reorganized as to be placed on duty again in an important position. Gen. HOWARD is one of our bravest and best officers. His emotions at the conduct of some of the brigades cannot be described. Had he been longer in command of these men, undoubtedly this stampede would not have occurred.

Union artillery under Major-General John Sedgwick are seen here, photographed during the actual assault on Marye's Heights.

OUR OWN SUPPLIES.

When the army started on its present movement, the troops took eight days' rations in their haversacks and knapsacks. The prospect of having to carry this amount of food on a long march was not very palatable to the troops, and mutterings were loud and frequent. But the eight days' rations are just what has enabled the army to do so much and march so far in so short a time. The rations will be used up tomorrow, and large amounts are already coming forward in supply trains to United States Ford, and on the backs of pack mules from that point hither. The mules carry the boxes of hard bread on their packsaddles, while the meat ration is fresh beef, driven on foot.

RETURN OF GEN. AVERELL.

Gen. AVERELL, with his cavalry command, returned to United States Ford to-day, and reported in person to Gen. HOOKER this afternoon. Gen. A. has been out 23 days, and been as far south as Rapidan Station, on the Orange and Alexandria Railroad, where he destroyed the bridge and track of the road. During his trip, he drove LEE and STUART out of Culpepper, and captured there about five thousand dollars' worth of salt and bacon belonging to the rebel Government, which he did not destroy, but distributed among the poor and suffering people of that vicinity. This made Gen. A. very popular, and hereafter the people there will prefer his visits to those of LEE and STUART.

Gen. AVERELL has received instructions for more important work, and our communications may be considered entirely safe so long as his force is in reach.

HEADQUARTERS.

The headquarters of the Army of the Potomac in the field are to-night under a large tree, just in the rear of the front line of rifle-pits and abattis. Gen. HOOKER has just dined on hard tack and cold ham. The gentlemen of the Staff are looking for their "pack mule."   L. L. CROUNSE.

THE FIGHTING AT FREDERICKSBURGH.

HEIGHTS ABOVE FREDERICKSBURGH, }
Monday Morning, May 4, 1 o'clock. }

The Stone Wall under Marye's Heights in Fredericksburg, scene of a futile Union charge in December, 1862, was wrested from the Confederates in the Battle of Chancellorsville, but only briefly.

Yesterday was a proud day for the Union arms. The boasted heights of Fredericksburgh were stormed by our brave boys, and the Stars and Stripes now wave triumphantly over this Gibraltar of America. Whatever may have been the result of the fighting on the right, that on the left has crowned our arms with imperishable renown. This crest of hills, wrote the London *Times'* correspondent, after the battle in December, constitute one of the strongest positions in the world—impregnable to any attack from the front. Yesterday's achievements have again demonstrated, for the twentieth time, that what is impossible with John Bull becomes possible with Jonathan.

The going down of the sun on Saturday found our troops of the left scattering out on both sides of the river, some two miles below the city. The Flying division had advanced to the old Richmond road. Gen. BURK's command lay back, nearer to the river. Gen. HOWE's and Gen. NEWTON's forces were on the plain opposite. To mention where the other troops were would not be prudent.

Under cover of night Gens. HOWE and NEWTON crossed over the river. (Gen. NEWTON's division is now temporarily commanded (by Gen. WHEATON, he having assumed command of Gen. SEDGWICK's corps.) About 2 o'clock in the morning orders came to move at once on the enemy. The greater portion of the forces moved quietly up the Richmond road 'and winding down through the gully just below the city reached the outskirts of Fredericksburgh, between 4 and 5 o'clock. Gens. HOWE and NEWTON's divisions were in the advance, then followed the "flying division," or "light brigade," and Gen. BROOKS' forces were extended on the extreme left. Meantime companies of the Fiftieth New-York engineers had constructed pontoon bridges directly across to the city, both above and below the Lacey House, and the Forty-second New-York, Nineteenth and Twentieth Massachusetts, Fifty-ninth New-York and the One Hundred and Twenty-seventh Pennsylvania, constituting HALL's—DANA's old brigade. Second corps—together with three other regiments, including the Second New-York and Fifteenth Massachusetts, crossed on the upper bridge and deployed out along the bank above the city. Batteries were also brought up and planted close to the city; among them HARNE's, MARTIN's, Battery B, Second Rhode Island. Lieut. BROWN; Battery G, Eighth Rhode Island, Capt. ADAMS; and Battery D, Second artillery The First Maryland and "HEXAMER's" Pennsylvania Battery were posted on the plain further below, where they could deliver a fire either up or down the range of hills. The object of this movement to the city was to storm the first line of rebel earthworks above, which Gen. SUMNER attempted in vain to take, last December, losing 7,000 men in the effort. Nor did the idea of again charging against those formidable intrenchments appear so insane to the troops as one might think, So buoyant and hopeful were the boys that they felt as if they could go anywhere and surmount any and every obstacle. The reader will remember that this line of earthworks is about one-third of a mile from the city, extending close along the monument erected to MARY, the mother of WASHINGTON, which' is erected on a sort of natural bluff. Beneath runs the famous stone wall and a road leading off in the direction of Richmond. Between this road and the city is an open plain commanded by the rebel works. Across this plain and over the stone wall the charging column had to advance before reaching the fortified bluff. About 5½ o'clock in the morning COCHRANE's old brigade, (NEWTON's division,) now commanded by Col. SHALER, and led by him in person, charged over the plain, and succeeded in nearly reaching the stone wall, but were obliged to fall back. The Sixty-second New-York, it is said, endeavored to storm the works before this hour of the morning. The rebels kept up a constant fire of musketry from behind earthworks, buildings and rifle pits, while the guns from above rained down a perfect storm of grape and canister on the troops. Gen. BROOKS' division, which was on the extreme left, suffered least, though fired at the most, owing to the fact of most of the enemy's missiles passing over the heads of the troops. It was now 11 o'clock, continuous fighting had been going on for full six hours, and the rebels still held their works. Gen. SEDGWICK now determined on having the "light brigade" charge the heights. Col. BURNHAM commanding moved his forces along under the protection of abandoned earthworks, and the hill-side formed by the sloping down of the plain near the city, until he had arrived directly in front of the most formidable position, known as the "Slaughter pen." Knapsacks and any article of clothing which might impede their rapid movement were cast aside by the men, and they were deployed out in the following order: one half of the Fifth Wisconsin, Col. ALLEN, as skirmish line; Thirty-first New-York, Col. JONES, on the left; Sixth Maine, Lieut.-Col. HARRIS commanding, and the remaining portion of the Fifth in the rear of, and supporting the Thirty-first at the same time. At the same time a force consisting of the Forty-third New-York, and Sixty-first Pennsylvania, and one or two other regiments were sent up the road at the right of the stone wall. Going on to the regiments of the Light Brigade, prepared for a charge were the Thirty-sixth New-York, and Seventh Massachusetts, and still further on other regiments. At twenty minutes past eleven the lion-hearted men rose from their feet. Every one of the thousand spectators on the hills in the rear held their breath in terrible suspense, expecting to see them all the next moment prostrate in the dust. "Forward!" cried the General, and they dashed forward on the open plain when instantly there was poured upon them a most terrific discharge of grape and cannister. Many lay dead, but not one faltered. Full 400 yards must be passed over before gaining the stone wall. As they press forward, delivering the battle-cheer, which is heard above the roar of artillery. The rebel guns further to the left are turned upon them. But they falter not. A moment more they have reached the stone wall, scaled its sides, are clambering the green bank of the bluff, and precisely as the City clock struck, they rush over the embrasure of the rebel guns and the Heights are ours. The enemy, with the exception of the cannoniers, fled in wild confusion, secreting themselves in the houses, woods and wherever a place of concealment was afforded. The guns captured proved to be the Washington Artillery, the battery so highly complimented by Gen. LEE in his report of the last battle of Fredericksburgh, and which has figured more or less since the outbreak of the rebellion. "What men are these," was the interrogatory of one of the astonished and terrified members, as our brave boys appeared over the ramparts. "We are Yankees, —— —— you; do you think we will fight now," was the response from one of our men. "Boys," remarked the Commander of the Battery, "You have captured the best battery in the Confederate service." The Sixth Maine were the first regiment to reach the scene. Lieut.-Col. HARRIS, with unparalleled bravery, rushed right up to the mouth of one as it was belching away, and through the mist and smoke his form could just be discerned as he cheered his men forward. He, together with Capt. FURLONG, were the first to lay hold of the rebel pieces.'

The rebels succeeded in getting one gun away to some distance, when the force which had gone round to flank the battery perceived it, and immediately starting in hot pursuit, captured it with seventy-five prisoners. A wagon train was ahead which they might have secured, had they not received orders to proceed no further. On the Washington Artillery being surrendered the other batteries to the right did not make much resistance, but fled hastily before our charging forces. Gen. MILLS' Brigade consisting of the Seventy-seventh New-York, Twenty-first New-Jersey, Forty-ninth New-York, Thirty-third New-York, and Second New-York, made a very gallant charge.

The Rhode Island batteries at the right of the road kept up an animated fire during the storming of the works. The rebels on the extreme left, in front of the Barnard House, retreated up the hills when we obtained possession of the city.

THE CAPTURES AT FREDERICKSBURGH.

One of our correspondents, writing from headquarters, near Falmouth, gives the following facts concerning Gen. SEDGWICK's captures at Fredericksburgh:

"Among the prisoners taken are the Sixteenth and Eighteenth Mississippi, of BARKSDALE's brigade, who have usually defended the river passages during the past Winter.

There is also a whole company of the famous Washington Artillery, of New-Orleans, and a more aristocratic and intelligent lot of Southern chivalry I have never seen. The officers are Capt. SQUIRES, Lieut. GALBRAITH, and Lieut. EDWARD OWEN, formerly of Cincinnati. A fine-looking young man introduced himself to me as Private MORGAN E. HARRIS, formerly of Cincinnati, and desired that his friends should know where he was. Most of them appeared much chagrined at their capture, and said it was the first misfortune of the kind. Four of their guns were taken; also two of ALEXANDER's battery. These were all the guns captured, I believe."

IMPORTANT FROM MISSISSIPPI.

Some of the Results of the Great Cavalry Raid.

Destruction of the Jackson and Meridian Railroad.

The Communications with Vicksburgh Severed

Failure of the Attempt to Occupy Grand Gulf.

Preparations to Attack Vicksburgh Above and Below.

LANDING OF GEN. SHERMAN ABOVE THE CITY

Gen. Grant on the Eastern Side of the Mississippi

CHICAGO, Tuesday, May 5.

The Jackson *Appeal* of the 28th of April, says of Col. GRIERSON's Federal raid, that besides tearing up the railroad, he has destroyed two bridges, each 150 feet long, seven culverts, burned twenty-eight freight cars, blown up two locomotives, and burned the railroad depot and two commissary buildings at Newton. He also destroyed the telegraph line by destroying five miles of wire, and captured two trains.

Special dispatches from Cairo say that the report that the Federal troops have occupied Grand Gulf is premature, the rebels having planted batteries on the hill, and repulsed our troops.

IMPORTANT FROM VICKSBURGH.

Preparations for an Attack on the Rebel Stronghold.

CHICAGO, Tuesday, May 5.

A special dispatch from Cairo says the steamer *Lady Franklin* has arrived from Vicksburgh on Thursday night last. She reports that on that morning Gen. SHERMAN, with a fleet of transports, accompanied by gunboats, passed up the Yazoo and made an attack on the rebel batteries. In the afternoon several more transports followed with troops aboard.

It was reported that Gen. SHERMAN landed precisely in the same place he landed when he made the former attack.

Cannonading and musketry were distinctly heard at Young's Point, on Thursday, till long after nightfall.

A gentleman who left New Carthage on Wednesday last, states that a very heavy force of Gen. GRANT's army has been landed on the eastern side of the river, eight miles above Grand Gulf, and that our gunboats had been shelling the latter place for several days.

The New-York Times.

VOL. XII—NO. 3626.　　　　　NEW-YORK, FRIDAY, MAY 8, 1863.　　　　　PRICE THREE CENTS.

FROM HOOKER'S ARMY.

Abandonment of the South Side of the Rappahannock.

NO BATTLE ON TUESDAY.

The Withdrawal Commenced on Tuesday Night.

Our Losses in the Great Battles Estimated at Ten Thousand.

GEN. STONEMAN HEARD FROM.

All the Railroads and Telegraphs Communicating with Lee's Army Cut.

Our Cavalry Within Five Miles of Richmond.

Important Movements in Other Directions.

Interesting Reports from the Richmond Papers.

Our intelligence this morning puts beyond doubt the fact that Gen. HOOKER's army has again retired to the north side of the Rappahannock. From various sources we collect the following facts in regard to the movement.

There was no fighting on Tuesday of any consequence, and the rumors to that effect were founded on a misapprehension.

The sharpshooters were quite active, and the artillery opened occasionally, but results were unimportant. The enemy had evidently massed his army on our right.

About 5 o'clock in the morning it commenced raining. The water fell in torrents over an hour, deluging the roads, tearing up the corduroys, sweeping away bridges, and threatening the destruction of the pontoons. The river rose with great rapidity, and soon overflowed the ends of the pontoons, rendering crossing impracticable. The upper pontoon was taken up, and used in lengthening out the others, and after several hours of very hard labor the bridges were once more ready. It was soon evident that Gen. HOOKER, seeing his position was rendered temporarily untenable by the storm, had determined to cross over again to this of the Rappahannock. On Tuesday the order was given to retreat. New roads were cut. The trains and reserve artillery were sent back, and the evacuation was commenced.

Pine boughs were spread upon the pontoons to prevent the noise of crossing, and at 10 o'clock Tuesday night the troops commenced falling back. The First Corps (COUCH's) was the first to cross. The Fifth (MEADE's) Corps remained in the intrenchments to cover the retreat. The Sixth Corps also recrossed

the United States Ford, and are marching back to Falmouth. At 3 o'clock on Wednesday morning wagon and mule trains and the artillery had all passed, and the infantry was crossing on two bridges at United States Ford. COUCH's corps was in the advance. The retreat was covered by the Fifth, MEADE's corps. By dark, the wagons, extra caissons, pack mules, &c., were at Falmouth. The wounded were hastily removed from the hospitals, and sent to Washington, leaving nothing on the other side except our infantry and artillery.

After fighting the severe battle of Sunday morning, Gen. HOOKER continued to strengthen his lines, throwing up double lines of rifle pits, and constructing abattis along the entire line of his camp. The enemy continued to make demonstrations along the works, driving in the pickets, and delivering volleys of musketry at men most exposed.

SEDGWICK, at Fredericksburgh, was overwhelmed by numbers, and pressed hard on both front and rear, and was hardly able to make good his escape near Banks' Ford. Fredericksburgh and the heights beyond have been reoccupied by the enemy.

SEDGWICK has lost in killed and wounded about 5,000 men. His artillery and trains were safely brought over on Monday night.

Richmond papers of the 5th, state that STONEMAN's cavalry had completely severed all LEE's communications with Richmond, and that the only reports of the fighting were received there from mounted messengers. These journals also state that Gen. PECK's forces were pressing on after the rebel forces, which had abandoned the siege of Suffolk ; and that KEYES' corps at Yorktown was also moving.

Reports are said to have been received in Washington that, after cutting the railroad lines leading into Richmond, STONEMAN deployed his forces along the road leading from LEE's army to Gordons-

ville. It was also said that troops were arriving at the latter point, en route to LEE's army, but that they came from Lynchburgh, and not from Richmond.

The most intelligent estimates place our losses during this brief campaign at not more than 15,000. The rebel army is thought to have lost at least one-third more, as they charged upon our batteries in masses, and were fearfully slaughtered by our artillery.

Our correspondent with the left wing alludes to a rumor that Gen. SICKLES had fallen in the fight on the right. The report lacks confirmation, however.

We subjoin the letters of our correspondents detailing the important movements which transpired previous to Gen. HOOKER's withdrawl from the south bank of the Rappahannock. The lists of casualties, so far as they have been received, are also given.

A SEMI-OFFICIAL STATEMENT.

From the National Intelligencer of Yesterday.

Official nformation received ast evening at the War Department authorizes us to state that Gen. HOOKER, after waiting in vain near Chancellorsville, on Tuesday last, for a renewal of the battle by the enemy, recrossed the Rappahannock on the evening of that day, influenced by prudential motives, springing, doubtless, in part, from the great and sudden rise of the Virginia rivers, in consequence of the recent heavy rains.

We do not learn that Gen. HOOKER was apprized, before making this retrograde movement, of the success which is alleged to have attended the operations of Gen. STONEMAN in breaking the enemy's communications with Richmond. If this fact had been known to him, (assuming it to be a fact,) it may be doubted whether Gen. HOOKER would have deemed it necessary to take a step which must

Major-General O.O. Howard's XI Corps, holding the Union right, was smashed by Stonewall Jackson's troops when Howard became isolated.

159

to deprive him of some, at least, of the advantages resulting from Gen. STONEMAN's coöperative expedition.

Among events which have not transpired officially, but of which there are rumors having the appearance of truth, it may be stated that Gen. SEDGWICK, in endeavoring, on Monday last, with the greater part of his command, to effect a junction with Gen. HOOKER's army near Chancellorsville, encountered the enemy in force and met with a serious reverse, the particulars of which are not yet known.

LATEST NEWS FROM THE ARMY.

WASHINGTON, Thursday, May 7.

It is ascertained from the front that the Army of the Potomac has arrived, with all its material, at their old camps at Falmouth.

The demonstration of Gen. HOOKER has proved no disaster, but simply a failure, owing to the impracticability of the position which the army had gained with so much skill and energy. Less than three-eighths of the whole force was engaged as could be engaged, the ground being covered with forest, and being without any practicable roads.

Our entire loss in killed, wounded and missing does not exceed 10,000. The enemy's loss must have been double of this—honorably to the army, but lamentably for the country, the greatest proportion of them in killed and wounded.

Our loss of prisoners does not exceed 1,700. We have received 2,450 prisoners of the enemy.

We lost eight guns, and took the same number of pieces from the enemy.

The relinquishment of the position was made simply because it afforded no field for the manœuvreing of the army, and not from any reverse or injury sustained by it. The General and the entire army are in excellent heart and ready for a new movement. We will probably not know where this is to be made after it has been commenced.

Richmond papers show that STONEMAN's corps went within two miles of Richmond and effected many captures and a great destruction of property. At least a part of all this gallant force has reached Gloucester, in KEYES' command, opposite to Yorktown, on the York River.

There can now be no impropriety in saying that the President and Major-Gen. HALLECK visited Gen. HOOKER and the army yesterday, and returned to the city to-night.

At nearly 1 this morning information was received that Gen. STONEMAN has safely arrived at Rappahannock Station, with the remainder of his force. He has cut the railroad connections of the enemy in all directions, and thus won a noble distinction.

THE NEWS IN WASHINGTON.

WASHINGTON, Wednesday, May 6.

The news that HOOKER and his army had recrossed the Rappahannock, flashed through Washington about 5 o'clock this afternoon. The impression produced by it was profound. Men's minds were cast down from the congratulatory cheerfulness with which all had for three days discussed the events which succeeded the brilliant passages of the Rappahannock and the Rapidan. The fact that our army had recrossed was all-sufficient. Scarcely any interest was excited by the details attempted here and there of the restoration of headquarters at Falmouth—of intrenchments thrown up in the rain—of this measure for security or that measure.

It made men silent and thoughtful beyond anything I have ever seen in Washington.

And yet what is the fact ? The immense downfall of rain had swollen the Rappahannock so deep and so rapid as to endanger the existence of HOOKER's bridges. One statement is, that the water rose seven feet in 24 hours.

A Council of War is said to have unanimously agreed that the army should be transferred to the other bank of the river in anticipation of the loss of the bridges, and it was accordingly transferred. The artillery crossed at 3 o'clock this morning. The infantry followed.

All who have come from Fredericksburgh, and from the upper fords to-day, unite in unstinted praise of the heroic fighting done by SICKLES' and SEDGWICK's corps. BIRNEY's, BERRY's and WHIPPLE's divisions—particularly BIRNEY's—covering themselves with glory. The sad losses we have sustained fell principally on these brave organizations. The large captures made were mostly made by SICKLES' regiments. Experienced witnesses of the panoramic contest at Fredericksburgh agree in their estimate that SEDGWICK's fifteen thousand fought at least twice the number of the rebels.

The losses at Chancellorsville and Fredericksburgh are about even on each side. The numbers of killed and wounded are about even, and of prisoners captured, and of guns lost and taken; and justice requires me to say that the fighting of the two armies was equal. Each walked right up to the muzzles of the other's guns.

WASHINGTON, Thursday, May 7—11:15 P. M.

Brig.-Gen. STOUGHTON arrived to-day from Richmond, exchanged. He says that on Monday morning the neighboring farmers rushed into Richmond, bringing the startling news that STONEMAN, with his cavalry and artillery, was at the suburbs of the city ; that they had destroyed all the railroads and public property, and were gobbling up everybody as prisoners.

The alarm spread like wildfire. The bells were rung, and the news carried from street to street. A fearful consternation ensued. All business was immediately suspended, and families who could do so packed up their property to leave. The military guard at Libby Prison were ordered off to the fortifications, and the clerks in the departments were put in their places.

The panic continued throughout the day and night, and not until it was known that STONEMAN was on his way down the peninsula was quiet restored.

Gen. S. thinks that a detachment of STONEMAN's force struck the Richmond and Fredericksburgh Railroad, above Chesterfield, north of the junction of the Gordonsville road going South ; destroyed the bridges over the North and South Anna, Chickahominy, and other streams, and tore up the road at frequent points to within two miles of Richmond. Second detachment destroyed portions of the Gordonsville Railroad, and crossed it, striking the James River at Columbia, breaking the canal banks, and passing down the river, burned considerable property at Goochland, within twenty miles of Richmond, and joined the first detachment near Richmond.

The whole force threw aside worn out horses and took fresh ones wherever they could find them, and appropriated property available for the expedition. They captured two rebel trains, and paroled many

Stonewall Jackson, photographed in 1863, two weeks before his fatal wounding at Chancellorsville.

prisoners. They got within sight of the Richmond churches, and citizens riding out in barouches encountered our cavalry with Union flags, and went marching back, shouting that the Yankees were upon them, that LEE's army was defeated, and Richmond summoned to surrender.

The intrenchments surrounding the city were very weakly garrisoned, if at all. Gen. STOUGHTON thinks there were no troops in Richmond except a battalion of 400 men. One of our officers and two men were taken within a mile and a quarter of the town.

Gen. S. heard it reported that "Stonewal" JACKSON was wounded, and had his left arm amputated.

ESTIMATES OF LOSSES.

WASHINGTON, Thursday, May 7.

The *Evening Star* says:

"Gen. HOOKER, it is understood, estimates his losses in the late battles at about ten thousand, all told, killed, wounded and missing; also, that he brought all his material away safely from his late position; and that while we were so unfortunate as to lose some artillery, we have taken at least as many pieces as we have lost."

ACCOUNTS FROM WASHINGTON PAPERS
From the Washington Star, April 6.

STONEMAN's force was divided into three columns, one of which, that moving in the direction of the Richmond and Fredericksburgh railroad, he commanded in person, though the havoc worked from Hanover Junction down to within five miles of Richmond, was made by a subdivision under the command of Col. DAVIS.

One of the three columns, commanded by Brig.-Gen. AVERILL, after crossing the Rappahannock at Kelly's Ford, pushed on to Brandy Station, where it met the enemy's pickets and drove them back in a short skirmish. It then pushed on direct to Culpepper Court-house, where Gens. FITZHUGH and WILLIAM HENRY LEE were found with a rebel force of perhaps 500 cavalry, which fled precipitately back across Cedar Mountain.

At Culpepper Court-house Gen. AVERILL captured a lot of rebel Government flour, and then pushed on after the retreating LEES, following them to Rapidan Station, where they burned the railroad bridge, over which they retreated, after a smart fight, in which they lost Col. ROSSER, (late of the United States Army,) who commanded one of their brigades. Our loss there was inconsiderable, and they lost several killed besides Col. ROSSER, and also thirty-one prisoners, whom Gen. AVERILL brought back with him. The object of AVERILL's expedition seems to have been to destroy this (Rapidan) bridge, which the enemy in their panic did for him. After proceeding as far as Orange Court-house, he returned with his force to the main army, joining it at Chancellorsville on Sunday last.

Another column of STONEMAN's force, under command of Gen. BUFORD, which left the Rappahannock at the same time, pushed on directly toward Gordonsville, and positive information has just been received announcing its success in cutting the Central Railroad between Gordonsville and Richmond, and also between Gordonsville and Charlottesville, thus (with the achievements of the column in destroying the railroad between Fredericksburgh and Richmond) completely stopping rail communication in any direction out from LEE's main army, and breaking up for the time being the enemy's facilities for forwarding supplies or reinforcements to it from any direction.

According to the Richmond papers of yesterday, LONGSTREET, in person, joined LEE some days ago, but was accompanied by none of the troops with which he had been operating before Suffolk.

We regret to have to say that Brig.-Gen. A. W. WHIPPLE, who was wounded in the recent engagement in which Gen. BERRY was killed, died yesterday at 2 P.M.

The latest information from the field states that the aggregate rebel loss in the four days' fighting has been far larger than ours—which is natural enough, as they were necessarily in every case the attacking party, and followed their old practice of massing their troops very heavily against the points they selected to assail, thus presenting numerous opportunities for our artillery to mow them down in great numbers.

The Richmond papers of yesterday claim that LEE took in the engagement of Saturday 5,000 of the Eleventh Army Corps as prisoners. This is the corps that behaved so badly on Saturday, but the number of prisoners taken from it is nothing like this number.

It is but fair to the Eleventh corps to say that they retrieved their reputation measurably by good conduct on Monday and yesterday, showing that their bad behavior previously was from one of those panics that will sometimes overtake the best troops.

OUR SPECIAL ARMY CORRESPONDENCE.

MOVEMENTS ON THE LEFT.

FALMOUTH, Va., Tuesday, May 5, 1863.

Major-General Alfred Pleasonton.

Yesterday two terrible battles were fought by the Sixth corps, Gen. SEDGWICK, resulting in fearful carnage on both sides. Owing to the sudden appearance of the enemy in rear, I was unable yesterday to complete my account of Sunday's operations, and will now go back and refer briefly to them. After the charge of the flying division on the Washington Artillery, portions of HOWE's charged up the hill further to the right, under a most galling fire, capturing four guns. They were taken by MILLS' brigade and the Vermont ——, which suffered the most. One brass twelve-pounder was charged and taken by the Thirty-third New-York, Col. TAYLOR—which afterward, together with the Seventy-seventh New-York, pushed on after the fleeing rebels, who, getting under the protection of woods, returned a hot fire. They stood, however, but a short time and then fled. The earthworks were stormed, twelve guns captured, and the stars and stripes planted.

The various divisions of the corps (Sixth, Gen. SEDGWICK's) moved rapidly forward up the Gordonsville turnpike, to the distance of four miles, skirmishing all the way, where they found the enemy in force, when another battle ensued, in which BROOKS', NEWTON'S, and the Flying division, were engaged—the

IMPORTANT REBEL ACCOUNTS.

Extracts from the Richmond Papers to the 5th.

Official Dispatches from Gen. Lee Announcing the Battle of Saturday.

The Great Raid of Stoneman on the Rebel Communications.

FRIGHT IN RICHMOND

GEN. LEE'S OFFICIAL DISPATCH.

MILFORD, May 3, 1863.

TO PRESIDENT DAVIS: Yesterday, Gen. JACKSON penetrated to the rear of the enemy, and drove him from all his positions from the Wilderness to within one mile of Chancellorsville.

He was engaged at the same time in front by two of LONGSTREET's divisions.

Many prisoners were taken, and the enemy's loss in killed and wounded is large.

This morning the battle was renewed.

He was dislodged from all his positions around Chancellorsville, and driven back toward the Rappahannock, over which he is now retreating.

We have again to thank Almighty God for a great victory.

I regret to state that Gen. PAXTON was killed, Gen. JACKSON severely, and Gens. HETH and A. P. HILL slightly wounded.　　　　R. E. LEE,
(Signed)　　　　General Commanding.

UNOFFICIAL DISPATCHES.

MILFORD, Va., Sunday, May 3.

Yesterday Gen. JACKSON penetrated to the rear of the enemy, and drove him from his positions in the Wilderness to within one mile of Chancellorsville. He was engaged at the same time, in front, by two of LONGSTREET's divisions.

The losses on both sides are heavy. Gen. PAXTON was killed, Gen. JACKSON severely wounded, and Gens. HETH and A. P. HILL slightly wounded.

FROM GORDONSVILLE.

GORDONSVILLE, Monday, May 4.

Dr. W. S. WOOLFOLK left Chancellorsville at 3 o'clock P. M., yesterday. He reports that the fight was still going on at Fredericksburgh. Gen. JACKSON occupies all the fords except Ely's, and had taken five thousand prisoners, and prisoners were still coming in. Our men are in good condition. Our loss is heavy. All seems quiet in front. No enemy in Culpepper.

GORDONSVILLE, Monday, May 4.

The fight is still going on. JACKSON occupies all the fords except Ely's. Our loss is heavy. No enemy in Culpepper.

WHAT THE RICHMOND PAPERS SAY.
From the Enquirer, 5th.

Acting like a charm upon the public mind, amidst the *furore* of patriotic excitement which pervaded the community on yesterday, came the following dispatch from Gen. LEE. It tells the tale of the enemy's second charge upon our gallant army on the Rappahannock, in language as simple as it is cheering, and eclipses forever the futile raid which was, no doubt, intended by the enemy to be one of their fancy embellishments to what is now (alas for them!) a spoiled picture. It will be seen, by a dispatch in another column, that the number of our prisoners is estimated at 5,000.

This battle was, from all we can hear, one of the most hotly contested of the war. The gallant men on our side who fell numbered among them some of our ablest heroes, whose virtues on this occasion shone out with ten-fold lustre, as they dashed amidst the storm of shot and shell and cheered their followers to victory.

From the Whig, 5th.

We bring our readers good tidings of great joy this morning. In the language of the noble and invincible LEE, "we have again to thank Almighty God for a great victory." We cannot furnish particulars, but the public know the moderation with which that great leader expresses himself, and will understand how much is meant by the language he employs. The intelligence that JACKSON is severely wounded will bring the prayer to millions of lips, that his injury may not be mortal, and that it may not keep him long from the field.

THE WOUNDED.

None of the wounded have arrived in Richmond, owing to the destruction of the railroads between Richmond and Fredericksburgh. Many of the business houses in Richmond were closed yesterday, in consequence of the exciting news from the Rappahannock.

The New-York Times.

VOL. XII—NO. 3640.   NEW-YORK, MONDAY, MAY 25, 1863.   PRICE THREE CENTS.

VICKSBURG.

An Official Announcement to the President that Vicksburgh has Fallen.

The Stars and Stripes Floating Over the Rebel Stronghold.

THE VICTORY COMPLETE.

Probable Capture of the Entire Rebel Army Under Pemberton.

Official Details of Gen. Grant's Progress After Leaving Jackson.

Two Great Battles Fought on Saturday and Sunday, 16th and 17th.

Fifty-Seven Pieces of Artillery Captured.

Heavy Losses of the Enemy in Killed, Wounded and Prisoners.

THE CROSSING OF THE BIG BLACK.

Capture of Haines' Bluff and Investment of the City.

Co-operation by Admiral Porter's Gunboats.

THE REBELS KEPT BUSY, DAY AND NIGHT.

The following dispatch was received in Washington on Saturday, and appeared in our Sunday edition:

MEMPHIS, Tenn., Saturday, May 23.

Col. Anson Stager, Washington, D. C.:

Official information from below, to Wednesday, states that Gen. Grant has captured Haines' Bluff and the outer works of Vicksburgh, a large number of prisoners, and fifty-seven pieces of artillery.

The battle is still raging, *with every prospect of capturing the entire force in Vicksburgh.*

We hold Jackson, Black River Bridge and Haines' Bluff.

A report is making up for Washington.

(Signed,)   W. G. FULLER,

Ass't Manager of Telegraph.

HIGHLY IMPORTANT OFFICIAL DETAILS.

WASHINGTON, Saturday, May 23.

The following dispatch has just been received at the War Department:

MEMPHIS, Tenn., Saturday, May 23.

I forward the following, just received from Col. JOHN A. RAWLINS, Assistant Adjutant-General:

REAR OF VICKSBURGH, Wednesday, May 20, 1863.

The Army of the Tennessee landed at Bruinsburgh on the 30th of April.

On the 1st of May we fought the battle of Port Gibson, and defeated the rebels under Gen. BOWEN, whose loss in killed, wounded and prisoners, was at least 1,500, and loss in artillery five pieces.

On the 12th of May, at the battle of Raymond the rebels were defeated with a loss of 800.

On the 14th of May we defeated Gen. JOSEPH E. JOHNSTON, and captured Jackson with a loss to the enemy of 400, besides *immense stores and manufactures, and seventeen pieces of artillery.*

On the 16th of May we fought the bloody and decisive battle of Baker's Creek, in which *the entire force of Vicksburgh, under Gen. Pemberton, was defeated with the loss of 29 pieces of artillery and 4,000 men.*

On the 17th of May we defeated the same force at the Big Black River Bridge, *with the loss of 2,600 men and seventeen pieces of artillery.*

On the 18th of May we invested Vicksburgh closely.

To-day Gen. STEELE carried the rifle-pits on the north of the city.

The right of the army rests on the Mississippi above Vicksburgh.   JOHN A. RAWLINS,

Assistant Adjutant-General.

POSTSCRIPT.—I learn further that there are from fifteen to twenty thousand men in Vicksburg, and that *Pemberton has lost nearly all his field artillery, and that the cannonading at Vicksburgh closed at about 3 P. M. on the 20th of May.*

Gen. Grant has probably captured nearly all.'

The Great Battles at Baker's Creek and Black River Bridge.

The following dispatch was received by the War Department yesterday:

MEMPHIS, Tenn., May 23—11½ A. M.

Hon. Edwin M. Stanton, Secretary of War:

The following dispatch has been received at these headquarters, and is forwarded as requested.   S. A. HURLBUT, Major-General.

REAR OF VICKSBURGH, May 20, 1863—6 A. M.

Hon. E. M. Stanton, Secretary of War:

Gen. GRANT won a great and momentous victory over the rebels under PEMBERTON, on the Jackson and Vicksburgh road at Baker's Creek, on the 16th inst.

PEMBERTON had a most formidable position on the crest of a wooded hill, over which the road passes longitudinally. He had about 25,000 men. The battle begun at 11 A. M., and was gained at 4 P. M. Its brunt was borne by HOVEY's division of McCLERNAND's corps, and by LOGAN's and CROCKER's divisions of McPHERSON's corps.

HOVEY attacked the hill, and held the greater part of it till 2 o'clock P. M., when, having lost 1,600 men, he was succeeded by BOOMER's and HOLMES' brigades of CROCKER's division, by which the conflict was ended in that part of the field. BOOMER lost 500 men.

LOGAN operated on the right, and cut off the enemy's direct retreat, so that he was compelled to escape by his right flank through the woods. LOGAN lost 400 killed and wounded. We took about 2,000 prisoners.

On the 17th, advancing to the Big Black, we fought PEMBERTON again at the bridge there, and captured 3,000 more prisoners. He fought in rifle-pits, protected by a difficult bayou full of abattis. LAWLE's brigade of McCLERNAND's corps charged the rifle-pits magnificently, and took more prisoners than their own numbers. PEMBERTON burned his bridge, and returned to Vicksburgh with only three cannon out of sixty that he had taken out.

Building four bridges over the Big Black, Gen. GRANT arrived before the town on the evening of the 18th, and now holds it closely invested. He had opened a line of supplies *via* Chickasaw Bayou, having cut the town off from Haines' Bluff, which is abandoned by the enemy, and which Gen. GRANT will occupy.

There was sharp fighting through the day yesterday.

STEELE won and holds the upper bluffs, and the enemy's upper water batteries, and gets water from the Mississippi.

SHERMAN's corps lost yesterday 500 killed and wounded.

McPHERSON, who holds the centre, lost little, as did McCLERNAND, who holds the left.

The gunboats kept the enemy alert during the night, and probably the town will be carried to-day. There are from 15,000 to 20,000 men in it.

PREVIOUS DISPATCH FROM GEN. HURLBUT.

Union cavalry under Colonel Benjamin H. Grierson disrupted railroads and depots throughout Mississippi, confusing Confederate strategists and providing a cover for Grant's plans for assault on Vicksburg.

MEMPHIS, TENN., Thursday, May 21, 1863—11 A.M.
Maj.-Gen. H. W. Halleck, General-in-Chief, Washington:

A citizen has arrived at Lagrange who left Canton on Saturday morning. He reports that Gen. JOE JOHNSTON was at Calhoun, seventeen miles north of Jackson, with 6,000 men, endeavoring to effect a junction with Gen. PEMBERTON, at Edwards' Station. At Holly Springs he saw a dispatch from Canton, dated the 19th, as follows:

"General GRANT was reinforced and drove the enemy into his intrenchments on the Big Black. General JOHNSTON ordered all his provisions from Canton. The Pearl River Bridge at Jackson and the trestle work at Brandon were burned."

S. A. HURLBUT, Major-General.

REPORTS RECEIVED FROM CAIRO.

CAIRO, Sunday, May 24.

It is reported that Gen. SHERMAN has taken Haines' and Chickasaw Bluffs, with 8,000 prisoners, 100 guns, and ammunition and commissary stores. The prisoners were paroled and sent across the Yazoo.

Another report says these points were evacuated, and SHERMAN took quiet possession.

Gen. GRANT attacked the upper batteries of Vicksburgh Sunday, while the gunboats attacked the water batteries.

Tuesday the upper batteries were captured and turned on the water batteries.

The paroled prisoners who were brought across from Vicksburgh say our forces have possession of the entire line of outer fortifications, and rebel officers told these men since the capture of Haine's Bluff that there was no chance of escape.

The rebel force is estimated from 20,000 to 30,000. *The wildest confusion existed among them.* Officers were unable to keep the line of battle.

The *Empress*—the last boat up—says when she left Wednesday evening the firing had ceased. There is no doubt but that the rebels surrendered.

Gen. BLAIR reached Chickasaw Bluffs on Tuesday, and was sent down for rations. The Federal loss is reported heavy.

Operations of the Fleets under Porter and Farragut.

WASHINGTON, Sunday, May 24.

The Navy Department has received information that Admiral PORTER has been cooperating with Gen. GRANT in the siege of Vicksburg. His fleet was cannonading the city and its works (still in the hands of the rebels) by night, while GRANT's army assailed it by day, thus giving the rebels within the town and intrenchments not a moment's relaxation from the perils of their situation.

The same department has also received official information that Admiral FARRAGUT's fleet is actively engaged in bombarding Port Hudson.

REBEL ACKNOWLEDGMENT OF DEFEAT.

FORTRESS MONROE, Sunday, May 24.

The Richmond *Dispatch* of May 23 contains the following;

"MOBILE, Thursday, May 21.
In Saturday's fight we lost thirty pieces of artillery, which were spiked and abandoned.

On Saturday the Federals advanced to take the Big Black bridge, but were repulsed. They crossed higher up, and took us in the rear where the bridge was burned and the works abandoned. Our loss is heavy.

Vicksburgh is closely besieged. The enemy is closing in on every side."

The Richmond *Enquirer*, in addition to the Mobile telegram of May 21, says:

"Gen. LORING has assumed command of Jackson. No official confirmation has been received here of the crossing of the Big Black by the Federals, or of the destruction of the bridge and abandonment of the works. Private dispatches from Jackson up to the 22d say nothing of these events."

HEADQUARTERS ARMY OF THE POTOMAC, }
SUNDAY, May 24. }

The latest published rebel intelligence from Vicksburgh is in effect that Gen. GRANT had crossed the Big Black above the burnt bridge, and had circumvented Vicksburgh, taking thirty rebel guns. The papers speak mournfully of their prospects in the Southwest, and hope that affairs there may prove less disastrous than reported.

———

ADDITIONAL REBEL ACCOUNTS.

From the Montgomery (Ala.) Advertiser, May 18.
The rumors as to the fall of Jackson, Miss, in circulation yesterday, were so vague and uncertain, that we had well nigh despaired of hearing anything intelligible from that quarter.

It appears that the fight began at an early hour Thursday morning, some eight miles southwest of Jackson, and continued nearly all day, *our troops commanded by Johnston and the enemy's by Grant.* We were finally driven back to Jackson, and fought them through the streets until overpowered by greatly superior numbers, and were compelled to evacuate the city, the enemy's forces amounting to about 20,000 or 30,000. and our own only to about 9,000. Gen. JOHNSTON then retreated on Canton, twenty-four miles due north of Jackson, situated on the wagon road connecting thence by Vaiden to the road running due east to the Yazoo River, and leading directly to Vicksburgh, some seventy miles from Jackson by this route.

When heard from yesterday morning, the enemy's cavalry were at Brandon, on the Southern Road, twenty odd miles this side of Jackson, near which point we had a force to protect the road. This fact is official, and may be relied on.

Gen. JOHNSTON had arrived at Jackson 11 A.M. Wednesday, and the fight commencing so early the next morning, left him no time to reorganize and concentrate the forces, and he no doubt made a desperate resistance under great disadvantages. *It is stated that some days before leaving Tennessee Gen. Johnston sent Gen. Pemberton an order to somewhat change his plans which was forthwith set aside by the latter as very improper directions to so consequential a commander, whereupon Gen. Johnston received an order at the last moment on Saturday to go to Mississippi and take command of the army. He left the same day, and arrived in unprecedented time, as before stated*—Wednesday morning. We are glad to learn that his complacent predecessor had so far anticipated the evacuation as to have the most important supplies and the archives and other articles of value removed. *Our army has four months provisions at Vicksburgh.* We have ample forces in communication in Mississippi, under the masterly lead of JOHNSTON, to meet and repel the invaders; but it may require some little time to put our forces in the proper position.

GEN. JOE JOHNSTON IN FULL COMMAND OF THE REBEL FORCES AROUND VICKSBURGH.

From the Richmond Enquirer, May 20.

The "retreat towards Vicksburgh" of Gen. GRANT's army, mentioned in a late dispatch, proves to have been *an advance of the Federals upon Vicksburgh.* They have been met by Gen. PEMBERTON, near the eastern bank of the Big Black River.

Vicksburgh, therefore, may now be said to be besieged both by land and water; *and if some happy combination be not made between the forces under PEMBERTON and JOHNSTON the heroic city may possibly fall.* Gen. JOHNSTON *is in the supreme command in that department.*

Grant had not captured Vicksburg by May 25, but his siege of the city was secure and became airtight.

The New-York Times.

VOL. XII — NO. 3641   NEW-YORK, TUESDAY, MAY 26, 1863   PRICE THREE CENTS

Editorial

Gen. Grant and His Splendid Success at Vicksburgh.

The track of this war is strewed with faded and with ruined military reputations. As we look back to the first year of the war, we are absolutely amazed to find how few who then stood out as Generals of mark have retained their place in the public regard. Of course we leave those who have lost their lives—such as LYON, SMITH, KEARNEY, MITCHEL, RENO, STEVENS and SUMNER—out of the question. They died illustrious, but whether they would have kept that lustre, had they lived, no one can say. Aside from these, we think it would be rather difficult to name more than five or six of all the early Major-Generals whose military career has justified the expectations of the people. Their names have all suffered more or less, some from one cause, some from another; McDOWELL's from a humiliating defeat, for which he was not at all responsible, STONE's for a 'disastrous miscalculation, PHELPS' for a foolish proclamation, BENHAM's for a proneness to strong drink, McCLELLAN's for "pedantic slowness," FITZ-JOHN PORTER's for jealousy and treachery, FREMONT's for deserting his post because of personal feeling, MILKS' for drunkenness and suspected treason, BUELL's for lack of earnestness and energy, POPE's for falsehood and bombastic vaporing, SIGEL's for unjust treatment of a fellow-General, BURNSIDE's for self-distrust, HOOKER's for unfulfilled promises, CURTIS' for mercenary dealing in cotton, &c., &c. This loss of former prestige probably has not been in all cases fully deserved, but it is none the less an undeniable fact. Of the very few who have escaped it, BANKS, ROSECRANS and GRANT are the chief, and of these, the last named is the one most notable instance.

Gen. GRANT's fame has been steadily gaining from the outset. Though but a man of forty, at the commencement of the war he had seen more hard fighting than any other officer, having been in every battle of Mexico except that of Buena Vista. Yet, when he took command at Cairo, he was not much known, and attracted little attention. The public had set its heart upon other favorites. If he obtained some little praise for crossing the Ohio so promptly and seizing Paducah in anticipation of the rebels, it was lost the same season, by his battle of Belmont, which the public in its inexperienced judgment of that time, insisted upon styling a defeat because an advance was followed by a retreat. It was, in fact, simply an expedition with a definite purpose—namely to break up the enemy's camp, and to prevent reinforcements from being sent from Columbus to PRICE's army in Missouri. This was effectually accomplished, and therefore the movement, though it cost blood, was a complete success. At Fort Donelson, where Gen. GRANT next appeared on the stage, he won a

Lt. General John C. Pemberton commanded the Confederate forces besieged within Vicksburg by Grant.

victory unexampled in its results; but the public still were inclined to attribute it to good fortune rather than to any special military capacity, and were even disposed to find fault that a quarter of the rebel army had been allowed to escape in the night before the surrender. At Pittsburgh Landing, his next scene of action, it was conceded that he fought splendidly; but he was reproached for having been on the enemy's side of the river at all, without intrenchments and without open communications in the rear. The ultimate victory was again ascribed to nothing but good fortune. At Vicksburgh, his next theatre of operations, he has labored, everybody admitted, with great energy, yet the impression has generally prevailed that it would be to no purpose. The manifold expedients that he adopted, in order to get a chance at the rebel stronghold, were regarded with a good deal of curiosity, but with very little confidence. The expedient, which at last succeeded, struck the public with not a little surprise. He got his chance at last. The style in which he followed it up—his extraordinary celerity of movement, his striking at unexpected points, his success in thwarting the attempts of the enemy to concentrate, his whipping them in detail every time in six distinct battles, and the magnitude and completeness of his final conquest, which casts into the shade all of the other achievements of the war—all this is now a marvel, and the public is quite ready to accept the conclusion, which the Army of the Tennessee long since formed—that, take him all in all, Gen. GRANT is the most *serviceable*, and, therefore, the most valuable, officer in the national army.

Why has Gen. GRANT thus at last distanced every other commander? In natural brilliancy he is probably surpassed by many of them; in science he certainly is. It all lies simply in the fact that he is a *man of success*. Unfavorable as have been the constructions that have been put, by very many, upon his past successes, yet the fact stood that *some*how they were achieved; and that was enough of itself, constantly, to brighten his fame, for success is precisely the thing which the people want. But we believe that there are solid reasons for this remarkable success. Gen. GRANT, though perhaps possessed of no great military genius, yet combines qualities which, in such a war as this, are even better calculated to insure success, and which scarcely any of his brother Generals have exhibited in similar complete combination.

First, he has absolute singleness of purpose. From the beginning he has addressed himself strictly to the *military* work he had in hand, without a thought about cotton speculations or about political advantage; without a look either toward Washington for favor, or toward home for popularity.

Second, his Spartan simplicity of character, his abstemiousness, his readiness to share any privation with his soldiers, his impartial justice, his strict discipline, and his absolute personal fearlessness, have given him an unsurpassed moral command over his soldiers, and there is nothing which they are not ready to do and to suffer with him.

Third, his modesty, his straightforwardness, his entire freedom from jealousy, and his manly bearing every way challenge the admiration and whole-souled support of every officer in his army, and in like manner secure the most cordial and effective coöperation of every navy officer who has been associated with him, from Admiral FOOTE to Admiral PORTER.

Fourth, whether he has genius or not, he has sound judgment and sterling sense, which, after all, are the prime intellectual qualifications for success in any sphere of action.

And, *Fifth*, he has, what tells more than all else, a most extraordinary combination of energy and persistence. In these two moral elements, he probably has not his equal. Nothing daunts him, nothing discourages him. There is nothing he does not dare to undertake, there is nothing he can bear to give up. In that one great point at least, he is a perfect counterpart of the NAPOLEON who said that the word "impossible" was not in his vocabulary. Thus, indomitable resolution and perseverance is that element which, of all others, contributes most to make up the master-spirit in war. It is only GRANT's preëminence in this that has done most to give him preëminence in everything. It is the motive power that brings into the intensest play every other faculty and quality. Without it the most splendidly endowed mind would be as worthless in military life, as would the most superbly constructed engine without the propelling force of steam.

U. S. GRANT—or, as his soldiers style him, Unconditional Surrender GRANT—has given the Confederacy blows such as no other arm has dealt; and, if he is let alone, as we trust he will be, he will in due time bring the whole concern to the dust.

The New-York Times.

VOL. XII—NO. 3655.   NEW-YORK, THURSDAY, JUNE 11, 1863.   PRICE THREE CENTS.

GREAT CAVALRY FIGHT.

The Engagement at Beverley's Ford and Brandy Station.

Full Details from Our Special Correspondents.

Desperate and Gallant Fighting by Our Forces.

THE REBELS DRIVEN BACK THREE MILES.

THEIR CAMPS CAPTURED AND OCCUPIED

Two Hundred Prisoners and One Stand of Colors Taken.

Highly Important Information Gained.

Stuart Proposing to Start on his Great Raid Yesterday Morning.

His Force 12,000 Cavalry and 16 Pieces of Artillery.

Our Losses About 400 Killed, Wounded and Missing.

THE REBEL LOSS MUCH HEAVIER.

IN BIVOUAC AT BEALETON, VA., }
ORANGE AND ALEXANDRIA RAILROAD, }
Tuesday Evening, June 9, 1863. }

This has truly been an exciting day. An hour since I sent you the mere skeleton of the day's operations, which scarcely affords any idea of the extent or character of our achievements. I informed you by letter on Monday what might be expected to-day, and I have now the result to record.

About the middle of last week, information of a pretty positive character was received at headquarters, concerning the massing and drilling of a large force of the enemy's cavalry in the vicinity of Culpepper. Numerous reports had been received before, but they were more or less conflicting, especially that portion of them which concerned the movement of the rebel infantry forces in a westerly direction. In my letter of Monday I gave in substance such information as I had concerning the strength and character of the enemy's augmented cavalry force. It was in the main correct; but, in the light of to-day's operations, I can give you the details as specifically as you can desire, for, beside defeating the enemy in a severe battle, we have ravaged his camp, ascertained his strength to a figure, and frustrated a bold plan, the execution of which was to have begun to-morrow morning at daylight.

The bold reconnoissance across the Rappahannock on Friday last, below Fredericksburgh, which we rightly thought would startle the indifferent public, had more than one object. Its first object was to discover the exact whereabouts of the rebel army, which was accomplished Saturday morning. Its second object was to remain where it was as a diversion, while we hastily gathered together a force to feel of, and if prudent, to attack this threatening mass of cavalry opposite our extreme right flank.

Gen. HOOKER conceived the whole plan very quickly, and caused its execution to be begun with that rapidity and secrecy for which he is noted.

Saturday evening the composition of the force was determined upon, and all the cavalry that could be made immediately available was detailed for the work under command of Gen. PLEASANTON, (Gen. STONEMAN having been relieved,) assisted by Gens. BUFORD and GREGG, and Col. DUFIE, as subordinate commanders. In addition, two small brigades of picked infantry, under Gen. AMES, of the Eleventh corps, and Gen. RUSSELL, of the Sixth corps, were detailed to accompany the expedition. A detail of artillery was made in the proportion of one battery to each brigade, the horse-batteries, with the cavalry, being in charge of Capt. ROBERTSON, chief of artillery on Gen. PLEASANTON's Staff.

The infantry force selected challenged particular admiration. The regiments were small, but they were reliable—such for instance as the Second, Third and Seventh Wisconsin, Second and Thirty-third Massachusetts, Sixth Maine, Eighty-sixth and One Hundred and Twenty-fourth New-York, and one or two others of like character.

The force, when completed, did not, by several thousand, reach the reported number of the enemy, from twelve to fifteen thousand, but then as far as cavalry was concerned we sent all that could be spared, and as far as infantry was concerned the sequel proved that fully as much was sent as could be used to advantage. And then there was a strong supposition that the force of the enemy had been exaggerated.

General PLEASANTON's cavalry rendezvoused during Saturday and Sunday at Catlett's Station and Warrenton Junction, getting supplies of forage and food from both places, by the Orange and Alexandria Railroad. Gen. AMES' infantry moved Saturday evening to the Spotted Tavern, and on Sunday to near Bealeton Station. Gen. RUSSELL's brigade moved on Sunday to Hartwood Church, and on Monday to Kelly's Ford. The plan was to rendezvous the command at the two points on the Rappahannock, Beverly's Ford on the right, and Kelly's Ford on the left, the two being six miles apart, and then move the column forward toward Culpepper, on roads converging at Brandy Station, where a junction of the forces was to be formed, or sooner, if necessary.

On Monday evening, therefore, Gen. BUFORD's column left Warrenton Junction, and followed by Gen. AMES from Bealeton, bivouacked for the night near the Bowen Mansion, about one mile from Beverly's Ford. Gen. GREGG, taking his own and Col. DUFIE's command, moved to the left from the Junction, and encamped for the night in close proximity to Kelly's Ford, where Gen. RUSSELL had already arrived. No fires were allowed, and a vigilant watch was kept to prevent disturbances or anything which might give any indication of our presence.

The orders were to arouse the command at 3 A. M., and to make the passage of the river as soon as it was daylight.

At dawn Gen. BUFORD's command was in motion. Col. DAVIS' brigade, led by two squadrons of the Eighth New-York, and supported by the Eighth Illinois and Third Indiana, had the advance. The morning was cool and pleasant, a thick mist hung over the river, and objects on the other side were rather indistinct. Our cavalry soon reached the river, dashed in, dashed up the bank, and were well on the opposite side before the rebels in their fortifications were aware of their presence. The suddenness of the movement completely surprised them, and they at once broke for the first friendly timber, which was about one-fourth of a mile in their rear. Our cavalry followed rapidly, and in these woods the first severe skirmish occurred, in which we speedily lost one of the most valued officers of the command, Col. B. F. DAVIS, of the Eighth New-York cavalry, and captain in the First Regular cavalry, and the same gallant officer who led the gallant charge out of Harper's Ferry last Fall, and captured LONGSTREET's ammunition train. When the rebels, who were dismounted reached the woods, they began to skirmish, and detained our force there long enough to give the alarm to JONES' brigade, they being encamped just beyond in the outer edge of the woods. Though their horses were grazing in the fields, yet they speedily fell in, and in a very short time two or three squadrons came charging down the road and through the timber. Hurling their force upon the Eighth New-York, they broke it and forced it back, and killed and wounded quite a number. Col. DAVIS, who was gallantly leading the advance, turned to rally them, and waiving his sword to the Eighth Illinois, shouted, " Come on boys," when a rebel rode out in front of him, and fired three shots from his pistol at him, the last one taking effect in his forehead, and inflicting a mortal wound. Quick as thought, Lieut. PARSONS, acting A. A. General to Col. DAVIS, was at the side of the rebel, and raising, in his stirrups, with one well directed blow of his sabre, he laid his head open midway between eyes and chin, and the wretch fell dead in the dust at his horse's feet. PARSONS is but a youth ; his adversary was a strong, athletic man, yet the former, though young in years and slight stature, nobly avenged his Commander's fall.

By this time the gallant Eighth Illinois, though meeting with a hot reception, in which Capt. CLARK and Capt. FORSYTH were both wounded, had charged upon the rebels, and driven them back upon the main body of the enemy, who were now engaged in deploying and forming in the rear of the woods, and just beyond their camp, nearly two miles from the river.

Maj. WHITING's command now came up to the support of the Illinois and Indiana troops. Gen. AMES also brought his infantry over, and deployed them on the left of the road as skirmishers, and then pushed them out in line of battle to the edge of the woods, in front of which the enemy was drawn up by squadrons, with artillery at the intervals, which omitted no opportunity to shell everything in sight that had motion to it. Thus far the enemy evidently had but one brigade at hand, and a few prisoners taken said they belonged to the Sixth, Seventh and Twelfth Virginia cavalry, of General JONES' brigade. When asked if he was " JONES, the guerrilla," they indignantly denied the imputation. Nevertheless he was. Gen. PLEASANTON now directed Gen. BUFORD to make preparations to charge this force in the flank, while the infantry and artillery engaged it in front. It was desirable to do this as soon as possible, as the enemy might be getting reinforcements at any moment. Gen. BUFORD having driven the enemy's pickets and skirmishers in the open fields on the right of the road, sent in the Sixth Pennsylvania, supported by the Fixth and Sixth regulars, to charge this line on the flank. The Pennsylvanians came up to their work in splendid style. This is the regiment formerly known as the " Lancers," and they had a matter of pride to settle in this charge. Steadily and gallantly, they advanced out of the woods, in excellent order, and then dashed across the open field in an oblique direction toward the enemy's guns. They went up almost to their very muzzles, through a storm of canister and shell, and would have taken them, when suddenly there dashed out of the woods on their right flank, in almost the very spot from which they themselves had issued, two whole regiments of the enemy, on the full charge. Retreat was almost cut off, but the regiments, now subjected to a fire in front, and on both flanks, charged back, cutting their way out with considerable loss. The Sixth regulars came to the rescue, but the fire was so severe that even these veterans could not stand it, and they fell back with some loss. In this charge we lost about the only prisoners captured by the enemy during the day. Maj. MORRIS, of the Sixth Pennsylvania, was seen to fall from his horse, and is probably wounded and a prisoner. Capt. DAVIS, of the same regiment, was killed. Capt. LIKER was wounded, and Maj. HAZELTINE had his horse shot under him. Capt. DAHLGREN, of Gen. HOOKER'S Staff, a model of cool and dauntless bravery, charged with the regiments, and his horse was shot in two places. He describes the charge as one of the finest of the war.

The enemy was now being reinforced very rapidly, and in a short time Gen. PLEASANTON found that BUFORD'S small division was opposed by three strong brigades of rebels, with artillery to match.

After the repulse of the Sixth Pennsylvania, the rebels made two rapid attempts to gain our rear and the approaches to the ford, both on our right and on our left, but particularly on the right. But they were handsomely foiled by BUFORD, and for two hours there was very sharp skirmishing, rapid shelling and admirable manœuvering by both sides, in the open and undulating fields on our extreme right. A brigade of the enemy's cavalry came down the road which branches off to the right from Beverley's, and made a dash for the ford. But they were too late. A couple of squadrons and a section of artillery interposed. They never got nearer than a mile to the point, and during the two hours that they remained in position they suffered severely from our shells and skirmishers.

At this stage of the engagement, Gen. PLEASANTON plainly saw that the division under Gen. BUFORD was far outnumbered, and much anxiety was expressed to hear from Gen. GREGG, whose column was considerably stronger than BUFORD'S. Word had been received from him at 8 o'clock, saying that he had crossed with scarce any opposition, and that he was driving the enemy before him, but his guns had not yet been heard. Matters thus remained in *statu quo* until twelve o'clock, nothing being done save some artillery pratice, which was pretty accurate on both sides. We dismounted one gun of a section that the enemy had on the extreme right, and compelled the enemy to move the other. During this interem the skirmishers of each party would frequently become very annoying. Gen. AMES formed his skirmish line, and they picked off the rebel officers without mercy. Although our infantry were masked by the timber, yet the enemy seemed to know what we had, and always refused to meet them, save by dismounted cavalry as skirmishers against skirmishers. They were very profuse of their shells and canister, however, and opened whenever any of our cavalry approached near enough. Many of our men were wounded by canister shot, a thing almost heretofore unknown in cavalry fighting.

At one time, on the left of Gen. AMES' brigade, the rebel cavalry skirmishers had advanced and concealed themselves in some bushes, where they were annoying a body of the Ninth New-York. Major MARTIN, of that regiment, was finally ordered to take a squadron and drive them out. This he most gallantly did, though it was right in the teeth of the enemy's artillery, and he was met by a perfect storm of canister. He captured fifty prisoners, but owing to the severity of the enemy's fire, could bring but a portion of them away. The gallant Major was himself wounded in the shoulder.

About 1 o'clock BUFORD again began to press the enemy, and this time he showed evident signs of uneasiness, and soon withdrew his force from our right flank as though he had a fire in the rear. About the same time we heard GREGG'S guns, and some prisoners taken from ROBINSON'S North Carolina brigade just then reported Gen. RUSSEL'S infantry advancing through the woods on their right flank and rear. Gen. GREGG, from the sound of the firing, was evidently in the vicinity of Brandy Station. PLEASANTON now pushed forward, but the rebels soon gave way, and fell back rapidly. They were in a bad predicament—for GREGG was almost directly in their rear, RUSSELL was on their right flank, and BUFORD on their front. They therefore made a hasty retreat, abandoning their old camp entirely, part of which we had already occupied, and two regiments were very near being cut off, as KILPATRICK moved off toward the right, to make connection with BUFORD. They had but a narrow strip of land, not covered by our force, through which to escape.

Gen. PLEASANTON'S headquarters were moved forward to where the rebel Commander's had been, and the lines of the two columns were soon connected.

Gen. GREGG reported that his two brigades, under KILPATRICK and WYNDHAM, had been hotly engaged all the morning, but had driven the enemy uniformly from the river back to Brandy Station. Our troops, especially the First New-Jersey, First Maine and Tenth New-York, fought most gallantly, and repulsed the enemy in repeated charges, though losing heavily themselves. The artillery with Gen. GREGG also suffered considerably, and the Sixth New-York battery was almost totally disabled. It did excellent service, however. In the charges by Gen. GREGG'S column, a stand of colors and over one hundred and fifty prisoners were taken. Col. WYNDHAM'S brigade captured the heights commanding Brandy Station, and there discovered rebel infantry being brought up by the cars. A portion of it drew up and fired a volley at our cavalry. Another correspondent will give you further particulars about the gallant fighting of this column. Col. WYNDHAM was shut through the calf of the leg by a bushwhacker, but his wound is not serious, and he still keeps the saddle.

While a junction was being effected with GREGG'S column on the left, BUFORD and AMES were pushing out on the right, and, with VINCENT'S battery, BUFORD had by 2 o'clock carried all the crests occupied by the enemy during the forenoon, and had forced him back over three miles from the river. In these exploits the regulars, especially the Second and Fifth regiments, distinguished themselves by their intrepidity. The Third Wisconsin skirmishers also won praise by the accuracy of their fire, which was fatal to many a rebel.

The fact that the enemy were now falling back upon strong infantry supports, and we being already numerically inferior to them, induced Gen. PLEASANTON to consult with his subordinates, and it having been left discretionary with the former to advance or return, it was finally deemed prudent to return, and at 4 o'clock our forces began falling back. The enemy was not inclined to "pick a fight" on the return, and, save some slight skirmishing, we were not molested. BUFORD'S division fell back to Beverley Ford, and GREGG'S division to Rappahannock Ford, a mile and a half below. We brought off all our dead and wounded, and also some of the enemy's, while many of the latter were still remaining on the field when we retired. By dark our forces were all over the river, and the wounded of BUFORD'S division all loaded in the cars and on the way to Washington. The loss in his division is about one hundred and eighty, and in GREGG'S about the same. The rebel prisoners report their loss as heavier than ever before, and express admiration of the gallantry of our cavalry. The total number of prisoners taken is about two hundred and twenty-five, and we lost about fifty.

Though our force was not large enough to thoroughly defeat the rebels, yet they received a sound thrashing, and it will result in postponing their "grand raids" into the North for some time, if not indefinitely; for, beside chastising them, we have gained full information of their strength, character and designs. Witness the following letter captured on the battle-field, which I have copied from the original *verbatim*:

CAMP NEAR BRANDETH STATION, CULPEPPER COURT-HOUSE, June 8, 1863.

DEAR BROTHER: We have made another change of base. We left Dayton one week ago to-day, and after five days of marching, we encamped at this place. We have had two grand reviews of *five brigades of cavalry, about 12,000 in number,* under Gen. STUART. The first took place on Saturday, when we were inspected by STUART; and I have just now returned from the second, when we were inspected by Lieut.-Gen. ROBERT E. LEE, in person. He was a fine looking man, but very gray haired. We are now in a battery *numbering about sixteen pieces,* under the command of Major BECKHAM. *Longstreet's division passed us on Saturday.* The Wise artillery was along. You can look out for some *small fighting before a week.* We are now about two miles from the Rappahannock, at Beverley's Ford. I expect, from the preparations that is being made, that *we are going to make a grand raid toward the Potomac, as soon as the valley is cleared.*

You must excuse the shortness of this letter, as I have just returned from the review, and I feel tired from riding so much. Direct your letter to CHERO'S battery, JONES' cavalry brigade.

Please write immediately, *as we may leave in a couple of days.*

Your affectionate brother,   J. M. D.

I leave the name blank for the sake of the writer. This confirms all the information we previously had. FITZHUGH LEE, W. F. LEE, G. W. JONES, ROBINSON, of North Carolina, and FIELD, of Virginia, commanded the brigades. In the latter's brigade is all the mounted infantry they had—reported at 800 men.

An order was found from Gen. STUART, dated June 6, ordering the commands to be held in readiness to move at fifteen minutes' notice.

A Captain, who was taken prisoner, said *they were under orders to move on Wednesday morning at daylight.* They moved a day sooner, and backward at that.

The prompt manner in which these plans of the enemy have been baffled will elicit the admiration of every one. *A day longer, and it would have been too late.* Their plans are now known, and we can prepare accordingly. Pennsylvania and Maryland will awake to the importance of the occasion, and make all needful preparations to receive this horde of raiders. They will probably only defer, not abandon, their designs; and such a body of cavalry once loose in a defenceless State they can take the whole of it. But Gen. HOOKER has unmasked them, and given time for preparation. Shortly he will be fully ready himself to take them thoroughly in hand.

L. L. CROUNSE.

THE SIEGE OF VICKSBURG.

AFFAIRS PROGRESSING FAVORABLY.

Our Total Loss thus Far Not Over Seven Thousand.

Arrival of Admiral Farragut with Additional Gunboats.

AN ALMOST CONSTANT BOMBARDMENT.

CINCINNATI, Wednesday, June 10.

The *Commercial* has advices from Vicksburgh through an officer of the Forty-eighth Ohio Volunteers.

The condition of affairs there was favorable.

The troops were impressed with the idea that Vicksburgh must fall, and have no idea of failure.

Our losses are greatly exaggerated.

The total loss since the crossing of the Mississippi will not exceed 7,000.

FROM GEN. HOOKER'S HEADQUARTERS.

Our Force Still Across the River Below Fredericksburgh.

A Brief Cannonade, but No Damage Done

WASHINGTON, Wednesday, June 10.

The latest news from the Rappahannock is as follows:

Yesterday afternoon the enemy opened several of their crest batteries upon our ranks and the forces on the plain west of the river and south of Fredericksburgh. They also threw several shells on this side of the river. Our batteries replied to them. There was no loss on our side. The cannonading lasted only a few minutes. This was the first time the enemy have opened their guns on our new position.

The respective lines remain the same as yesterday morning. It is said the enemy has but one corps opposed to our front below the town.

The New-York Times.

VOL. XII—NO. 3659.   NEW-YORK, TUESDAY, JUNE 16, 1863.   PRICE THREE CENTS

INVASION!

Rebel Forces in Maryland and Pennsylvania.

Their Advance to Hagerstown, Md., and Greencastle and Chambersburg, Penn.

HARRISBURG IN IMMINENT DANGER

A PROCLAMATION BY THE PRESIDENT.

One Hundred Thousand Militia Called Out.

Pennsylvania to Furnish 50,000, Ohio 30,000, and Maryland and West Virginia 10,000 Each.

A Subsequent Call for Twenty Thousand from New-York.

NEW-YORK TROOPS HURRYING TO ARMS.

The Advance of the Rebels Up the Shenandoah Valley.

A Desperate Battle at Winchester on Saturday and Sunday.

Gen. Milroy Surrounded by Jackson's Old Corps.

He Cuts His Way Out, and Falls Back to Harper's Ferry.

TWO OTHER BATTLES IN THE VALLEY.

WASHINGTON, Monday, June 15.

By the President of the United States of America:

A PROCLAMATION.

Whereas, the armed insurrectionary combinations now existing in several of the States are threatening to make inroads into the States of Maryland, Western Virginia, Pennsylvania and Ohio, requiring immediately an additional military force for the service of the United States,

Now, therefore, I, ABRAHAM LINCOLN, President of

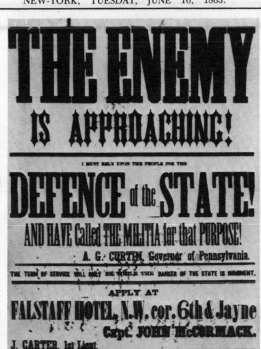

the United States and Commander-in-Chief of the Army and Navy thereof, and of the militia of the several States when called into actual service, do hereby call into the service of the United States one hundred thousand militia from the States following namely :

From the State of Maryland 10,000.

From the State of Pennsylvania 50,000.

From the State of Ohio 30,000.

From the State of West Virginia 10,000.

To be mustered into the service of the United States forthwith, and to serve for the period of six months, from the date of such muster into said service, unless sooner discharged, to be mustered in as infantry, artillery and cavalry, in proportions which will be made known through the War Department, which Department will also designate the several places of rendezvous.

These militia are to be organized according to the rules and regulations of the volunteer service, and such orders as may hereafter be issued.

The States aforesaid will be respectively credited under the Enrollment act for the militia service rendered under this Proclamation.

In testimony whereof, I have hereunto set my hand and caused the seal of the United States to be affixed. Done at the City of Washington, this 15th day of June, in the year of our Lord 1863, and of the independence of the United States the 87th.

(Signed,)   ABRAHAM LINCOLN.

By the President,

WM. H. SEWARD, Secretary of State.

A CALL UPON NEW-YORK.

ALBANY, Monday, June 15.

The Governor received, to-day, a telegram from Washington calling for 20,000 militia men immediately.

He has summoned the several Major-Generals of the State Militia to Albany for consultation, and taken steps for the rapid organization of the militia.

Gen. SANFORD telegraphs that he can bring out 5,000 men without delay, and the General commanding the Eighth division promises 2,000 more.

A draft will be made under the State law to fill up to their maximum number all the militia regiments in the State, and from these the 20,000 will be supplied.

They are called upon to serve six months, and will be credited to the State as three years' men under the impending National draft. They are to serve without State or National bounties.

CALL FOR THE FIRST BRIGADE.

HEADQUARTERS FIRST BRIGADE, N. Y. S. N. G., NEW-YORK, June 15, 1863.

SPECIAL ORDERS.—By order of the Commander-in-Chief of the State of New-York, the several regiments of this brigade will hold themselves in readiness to depart for Philadelphia at once—short service.   By order of

Brig.-Gen. C. B. SPICER.

R. H. HOADLEY, Brigade Major and Inspector.

WM. D. DIMOCK, A. D. C.

CALL FOR THE THIRD BRIGADE.

HEADQUARTERS THIRD BRIGADE, No. 543 BROADWAY, NEW-YORK, June 15, 1863.

ORDER: Commandants of regiments are hereby directed to report to Gen. WM. HALL, at his quarters, at 11 o'clock A. M. Tuesday morning. By order of the Commander-in-Chief, HORATIO SEYMOUR. The brigade drill for the 17th inst., is hereby countermanded.   By order of   Gen. WM. HALL.

J. R. SMITH, Quartermaster.

THE BROOKLYN THIRTEENTH.

HEADQUARTERS, THIRTEENTH REGIMENT, N. G. S. N. Y., ARMORY, CORNER HENRY AND CRANBERRY STS., BROOKLYN, June 16, 1863.

GENERAL ORDERS : This regiment will assemble at the City Armory, corner of Henry and Cranberry streets, this Tuesday morning, at 9 o'clock, in full fatigue, knapsack, overcoat and canteen ; having received orders from the Commander-in-Chief " to proceed to Philadelphia for short service."

By order,   Col. JNO. B. WOODWARD.

WM. AUGUSTUS McKEE, Adjutant.

THE NEW-YORK SEVENTH.

PHILADELPHIA, Monday, June 15.

The New-York Seventh have offered their services to aid in resisting the invasion of Pennsylvania, and are expected to leave for Harrisburgh tomorrow.

PROCLAMATION OF GOV. CURTIN.

HARRISBURGH, Monday, June 15.

The following Proclamation has just been issued by the Governor of Pennsylvania :

In the name and by the authority of the Commonwealth of Pennsylvania and ANDREW G. CURTIN, Governor of the said Commonwealth :

A PROCLAMATION.

The State of Pennsylvania is again threatened with invasion, and an army of rebels is approaching our borders. The President of the United States has issued his Proclamation calling upon the State for fifty thousand men. I now appeal to all the citizens of Pennsylvania who love Liberty and are mindful of the history and traditions of their Revolutionary fathers, and who feel that it is a sacred duty to guard and maintain the free institutions of our country, who hate treason and its abettors, and who are willing to defend their homes and firesides, and do invoke them to rise in their might and rush to the rescue in this hour of imminent peril. The issue is one of preservation or destruction. It involves considerations paramount to all matters of mere expediency and all questions of local interest. All ties, social and political, all ties of a personal and partizan character, sink by comparison into insignificance. It is now to be determined by deeds, and not by words alone, who are for us and who are against us. That it is the purpose of the enemy to invade our borders with all the strength he can command is now apparent. Our only defence rests upon the determined action of the citizens of our free Commonwealth.

I therefore call upon the people of Pennsylvania, capable of bearing arms, to enroll themselves in military organizations and to encourage all other to give aid and assistance to the efforts which will be put forth for the protection of the State and the salvation of our common country.

The New-York Times.

VOL. XII—NO. 3672.　　　　NEW-YORK, WEDNESDAY, JULY 1, 1863.　　　　PRICE THREE CENTS.

THE REBEL INVASION.

Important Intelligence Regarding the Movements of Lee.

Sudden Withdrawal of His Forces from Before Harrisburgh.

Hurried Evacuation of York and Other Places.

Probable Concentration of the Rebel Army at Shippensburgh.

The Army of the Potomac Pressing it Closely.

A Great Battle Expected in the Cumberland Valley.

Pleasanton's Outer Pickets Reported Near York.

A Cavalry Fight and Defeat of the Rebels at McConnellsburgh.

MARTIAL LAW IN BALTIMORE.

SPECIAL DISPATCHES FROM WASHINGTON.

WASHINGTON, Tuesday, June 30.

Advices received here this evening indicate that Lee is at last thoroughly aroused to the peril of the position in which he has entangled his army. He is drawing in his forces to the neighborhood of Shippensburgh, *where a great battle will probably be fought.*

The position of our army cannot be stated, but the public may rest assured that it is rapidly forcing conclusions with the enemy. Its present numbers, and moral and physical condition are such as to give informed parties here to-night the most sanguine expectations. The tide has turned to-day, and will hardly flow again in the enemy's favor.

TELEGRAMS FROM HARRISBURGH.

HARRISBURGH, Tuesday, June 30—1 o'clock P. M.

The city is now as quiet as though it was Sunday.

There is no excitement in the city.

The soldiers are all at their posts.

Yesterday 400 cavalry, belonging to Col. PIERCE's command, late MILROY's, had a fight with IMBODEN's cavalry at McConnellsburgh, defeating them and driving them through the town.

The rebels had three killed. On our side two men were wounded. We took thirty-three prisoners.

The rebel division of Gen. EARLY left for York this morning, taking the road to Carlisle.

Gen. LEE is now concentrating his army in the valley between Shippensburgh and Chambersburgh,

Major-General George B. Meade became the fifth man to command the Army of the Potomac within a year. Surprised by the designation, Meade in turn surprised others by proving to be a competent leader.

evidently anticipating an attack from the Army of the Potomac.

Gen. EWELL's rebel corps is still in front of Harrisburgh, and may commence the attack at any time.

THE REBELS RETIRING.

HARRISBURGH, Tuesday, June 30.

All is quiet. The rebels have retreated beyond Carlisle.

TELEGRAMS FROM COLUMBIA, PENN.

COLUMBIA, PENN., Tuesday, June 30.

S. S. BLAIR, Train-master on the Northern Central Railroad, left York at 8 o'clock this morning, when the rebels had all left, except their rear-guard, which was beginning to move off when he left.

The rebels are supposed to be moving toward Harrisburgh. They left unexpectedly, and in a hurry.

It was reported that Gen. PLEASANTON's outer pickets had been seen within four miles of York.

The total demand on York by the rebels, amounted to three hundred thousand dollars.

The citizens raised $30,000 in cash and subsistence, and the rebels allowed them twenty days to raise the balance.

No private families were molested. The citizens were all treated with respect.

The railroad property was not disturbed, with the exception of about thirty old cars that were at the shops awaiting repairs.

The railroad south of Glen Rock was not injured in any way.

The rebel force at York was not over 8,000, with eighteen pieces of artillery.

The rebel force at Wrightsville was 3,000, with five pieces of artillery.

TELEGRAMS FROM PHILADELPHIA.

PHILADELPHIA, Tuesday, June 30—2 P. M.

Intelligence has been received here to-day that Gen. LEE and his Staff were at Carlisle last night.

A rebel infantry force was seen this morning, about fourteen miles from Harrisburgh, marching toward that city. They may come up to our forces some time this afternoon. An engagement is then expected to take place, although it may be postponed until the morning.

The telegraph wires are uninterrupted along the whole line of the Pennsylvania Railroad. The trains are running also, but slowly and cautiously, so as to avoid surprise.

The Reading *Adler*, the organ of the Democrats, and generally known as the Berks-County "Bible," has come out with a stirring appeal to the farmers to quit their fields and rally for the defence of the State.

A camp has been formed, and it is expected that there will be 20,000 men assembled there immediately.

PHILADELPHIA, Tuesday, June 30—3:15 P. M.

A dispatch from Harrisburgh, received this morning, states that the authorities at Harrisburgh have information, apparently reliable, that EWELL's corps, with portions of HILL's and LONGSTREET's, will move this day toward Harrisburgh.

They number about forty thousand men.

The report that several companies of Col. THOMAS' regiment had been captured is incorrect. They have arrived safe, with but small losses.

PHILADELPHIA, Tuesday, June 30.

Fifty rebel prisoners from Harrisburgh arrived here to-day.

TELEGRAMS FROM BALTIMORE.

PHILADELPHIA, Tuesday, June 30—8½ A. M.

A special dispatch to the *Inquirer*, from Baltimore, says:

" A train came in this morning from Union Bridge, the western terminus of the Western Maryland Railroad, having passed through Westminster. No rebels had appeared anywhere along the route.

It is ascertained that a large body of National cavalry reached Gettysburg, took possession of the town, and captured quite a number of rebels. Our army is gradually moving in that direction.

The trains on the Northern Central Railroad run this morning to Parkton, twenty-six miles from Baltimore.

Several bridges have been destroyed north of Parkton.

No apprehensions are felt for the Baltimore and Washington Railroad, as it is strongly protected. The same may be said of the Philadelphia, Wilmington and Baltimore Railroad.

The gunboats are in each of the gunpowder rivers, and at Havre de Grace and at Bush River.

The defences of Baltimore are now very strong.

All the negroes that can be found, without distinction, are impressed into the service and made to work in building fortifications.

The cars from Baltimore to Frederick, this morning, were obliged to return after reaching Sykesville, where a large force of rebel cavalry were seen tearing up the track and burning bridges.

The train narrowly escaped being captured.

BALTIMORE, Tuesday, June 30.

The *American*, this morning, publishes the following paragraphs:

A portion of the First Delaware cavalry regiment, which were stationed at Westminster, twenty-eight miles from the city, were attacked, yesterday, by rebel cavalry, and a running fight ensued, in which our cavalry were chased to within seven miles of the city, but few of the detachment reporting at headquarters.

Later in the evening it was reported that a considerable force of rebel cavalry were advancing toward the city on Keister's town road. The preconcerted signal was immediately given, and the members of the Union Leagues promptly assembled at their different headquarters, received their arms and marched to the barricades. The promptness with which the call was answered was highly creditable to their patriotism and courage.

The *American* also says:

We are gratified to be able to announce that the Army of the Potomac is in rapid and successful motion under its new commander, Maj.-Gen. MEADE. The character of this movement is such as will satisfy the country of the vigor, skill and good judgment of the new commander. We feel that we ought not to explain this grand movement in its present stage, but we assure our readers that it will give great satisfaction.

BALTIMORE, Tuesday, June 30.

The following definite information relative to the rebel cavalry force which crossed the Potomac River at the Point of Rocks on Saturday night, has been received by the *American*, in a letter from a Methodist clergyman residing at Brookville, Md. :

Very much to the astonishment of the citizens the rebels came in there on Sunday evening about 6 o'clock.

Gen. STUART was with the rebel force, and took possession of the Reverend gentleman's house.

The rebels had with them captured wagons, prisoners, contrabands and mules, besides other plunder. On Monday morning the rebels left, going northward, as is learned from another source.

The Reverend gentleman says he entertained five of the National prisoners (officers,) at breakfast, among them Major DOANE and Capt. MECKLING, of the United States Engineers.

This was doubtless the same rebel force which struck the Baltimore and Ohio Railroad yesterday morning.

It is equally certain that it is the same rebel force which passed northwest of this city last evening, in the direction of Westminster, doubtless aiming to reach their forces at York or Gettysburgh, which gave rise to the alarm here last night.

BALTIMORE, Tuesday, June 30.

The *American* says:

"The response of the Union Leagues of this city last night to the call of Gen. SCHENCK for the public defence, was most prompt and enthusiastic. Old and young flocked to the armories to obtain arms, and the supply was not sufficient for one-half of those who presented themselves. By previous concert each company marched to its post at the barricades, and stood guard during the night.

We learn from a citizen of Westminster, who arrived here this morning, that the First Delaware cavalry made a most excellent fight, and fought with sabres and revolvers when first attacked, and until the enemy appeared in overwhelming numbers. The enemy came on by the Washington road, and at the time our cavalry were getting their horses shod and preparing for a scout beyond. They captured two or three horses and men at a blacksmith's shop at the end of the town, when the balance charged on them in an effort to recover the prisoners. A fierce fight ensued, in which a number were wounded on both sides.

While the fight was going on about 300 more rebel cavalry came in sight, when a retreat was ordered, and they passed through the length of the town, skirmishing and fighting the whole distance, in which one of the rebels was shot by a civilian who joined the Union troops. There were not more than sixty of the Delaware cavalry in the engagement, and it is feared that the greater portion of them were killed, wounded or captured. Not more than fifteen out of 110 in the command have reached this city."

Commodore DORUIN has, at the request of Gen. SCHENCK, placed two gunboats near the end of Broadway, and one at the bridge on the western side of the city, in an admirable position to bear upon the city and its approaches.

One o'clock P. M.—The mail train that left Baltimore at 8½ has just arrived at Monocacy. The timber for the burnt bridges, sent out on that train, was unloaded, and the bridge rebuilt in twent-five minutes, and the train crossed safely with its passengers."

MARTIAL LAW PROCLAIMED IN BALTIMORE.

BALTIMORE, Tuesday, June 30.

The *American* contains the following:

HEADQUARTERS MIDDLE DEPARTMENT,
EIGHT ARMY CORPS, BALTIMORE, June 30, 1863.

The immediate presence of a rebel army within this Department and in the State of Maryland requires, as a military necessity, a resort to all the proper and usual means of defence and security. This security is to be provided against known hostilities, and opposition to the lawful and National Government, from every quarter and in every form. Traitors and disaffected persons within must be restrained, and made to contribute to the common safety; while the enemy in front is to be met and punished for this bold invasion.

Martial law is therefore declared and hereby established in the City and County of Baltimore, and in all the counties of the western shore of Maryland.

The Commanding General gives assurances that this suspension of the civil Government within the limits defined shall not extend beyond the necessities of the occasion. All the civil courts, tribunals, and political functionaries of State, county or city authority, are to continue in the discharge of their duties, as in time of peace, only in no way interfering with the exercise of the predominant power assumed and asserted by the military authority.

All peaceful citizens are requested to remain quietly at their homes and in the pursuit of their ordinary avocations, except as they may be possibly subject to calls for personal services, or other necessary requisitions for military purposes or uses hereafter.

All seditious language or mischievous practices tending to the encouragement of rebellion are especially prohibited, and promptly be made the subject of observation and treatment. Traitorous and dangerous persons must expect to be dealt with as the public safety may seem to require.

To save the country is paramount to all other considerations. When the occasion for this proclamation passes by, no one will be more rejoiced than the Commanding General that he can revoke his order and return to the normal condition of a country at peace and a Government sustained by a united and loyal people.

(Signed) ROBERT C. SCHENCK,
Major-Gen. Commanding.

EXCITEMENT AT OXFORD, PENN.

OXFORD, Chester County, Penn.,
Tuesday, June 30.

The excitement at this point is increasing.

The merchants are moving away their goods.

Rebel scouts have been seen passing down the banks of the Susquehanna River, on the Harford side, and they have been reported as far down as Peach Bottom.

OUR HARRISBURG CORRESPONDENCE.

The Report of a Spy — His Adventures in Carlisle and Vicinity — Ewell's Corps There, Numbering 20,000 Men — Lee's Movements — The Work of the Copperheads — Information to the Enemy — The Rebel Intentions, &c.

HARRISBURGH, Monday, June 29, 1863.

I have just had an extremely interesting conversation with a young man whose name I dare not mention, because if the rebels should ever catch him they would surely shoot or hang him as a spy—for such he was. He voluntarily went within their lines, and traversed all their camps in the vicinity of Carlisle, with which country he is entirely familiar. While in Carlisle he met an old friend now in the

Union cavalry headed by John Buford (seated) stymied Confederates descending upon Gettysburg the first day. Eventually the Rebel advance proved irresistible.

rebel army, and through him was introduced to several of the rebel Generals, who talked with him very freely. They said he could not get out of town, and they did not care how much they told him. He is brave, adventurous, and as cool as a man can be, though he is but a mere boy. He made his escape over the South Mountain, though the rebel soldiers were in pursuit of him, and he arrived in Duncannon at 2½ o'clock this morning. He walked twenty miles in three hours and a half, having left Carlisle at 11½. He arrived here in the 12 o'clock train.

Nearly the whole of EWELL's corps is at and about Carlisle, and it numbers about 20,000 men. Gen. EARLY left yesterday, with a considerable body of troops, for Gettysburgh. All the expeditions hereabouts have been made from this corps. Gen. ANDERSON's corps is close behind at Chambersburgh, and advancing. Gen. LEE passed through Chambersburgh yesterday, on his way to Gettysburgh. He holds the centre, which is composed, in part at least, of LONGSTREET's corps. EWELL is on the left, and A. P. HILL, who is now at Hagerstown, on the right. The whole rebel army is on this side of the Potomac, and most of it in Pennsylvania. It consists, probably, of not far from one hundred thousand men.

The information of the rebels is very full and accurate. They showed my informant a complete map of the fortifications here, and told him of fords on the river. They know as well as we do the number of men that we have, and their character. They say that our militia won't be able to stand two volleys of musketry, and that they are not afraid of as many as we can bring against them. There are plenty of Copperheads, who furnish them all the information they want, and point out to them the places where goods are hidden. While they use these men, they despise them. "There," said a rebel officer to my informant, "do you see that man?" (pointing to one of these sympathizers.) "Well he is a —— rebel; and if I were in the place of you people that are loyal, I would hang him as soon as we get away from here." The individual alluded to felt the force of the remark, and left. The rebels concurred in saying they honored an open enemy, but despised a snake. The more I think of it, the more I wonder that a Northern man can be found who will aid the rebels while invading the Free States. That some Southern people retain their loyalty to the Union, and their affection for the old flag, is not surprising, but a traitor to the Union in the Free States is an anomaly.

Gen. EWELL said he should encamp in front of Harrisburgh to-night, and would have done so last night but that he preferred not to travel on Sunday, where it could be avoided. Several of the other Generals said the intention of the rebel army was to capture Harrisburgh at all events, and then march on Philadelphia. They all appear to be in the greatest spirits, particularly the officers, who have of late had very superior quarters to those they are accustomed to. The privates are many of them better clad than the wretched tatterdemalions who are brought in as prisoners; but they seem to feel very well, and marched through the streets of Carlisle singing "Dixie" at a great rate. They are very rude and unfeeling in their conduct toward our prisoners, tantalizing and abusing them when they are taken through the camps. They told my informant that HOOKER had retreated to Washington and that GRANT had been repulsed at Vicksburgh, both of which statements they profess to believe.

A great many desert from the rebel army. The mountains are full of deserters, and they come into Harrisburgh every day. The picket guard has been doubled in order to prevent this. I apprehend Gen. LEE will find a good deal of trouble on this score. Thousands of the privates are tired of fighting and have no heart in the cause. Now that they have got into a Free State and having a good chance, if they once get beyond the pickets, of escaping North, many will leave and regain their freedom. After the first great fight, when the usual precautions to catch deserters are necessarily somewhat intermitted, the rebel army will unquestionably lose heavily in deserters and stragglers. Heretofore, if they escaped, they could only go south. Now the case is quite different. The most of them, however, are very plucky. They say they are fighting for their rights, and that if they can only succeed in staying North during the Summer they are sure to be recognized.

They make requisitions on the inhabitants for all they want. They made one requisition on Carlisle yesterday morning for 1,500 rations, and later in the forenoon another for 500 barrels of flour. They strip the stores, but touch nothing in private dwellings, and they are courteous and polite to citizens, particularly ladies. I am happy to be able to say, also, that our ladies do *not* follow the example of Southern ladies in their treatment of the rebel soldiers.

Thus, while we of the North have been quibbling, grumbling and criticising, instead of aiding the Government—manœuvring for the next President instead of fighting for our country, and quarreling about our Generals instead of following them cheerfully, a powerful, desperate and determined foe has invaded our soil and driven our citizens from their homes. While our peace Democracy have been advocating an armistice, and resisting all our preparations for men, the character of the issue has changed, and now we are obliged to fight or be conquered. Why don't FERNANDO WOOD go down to Gettysburgh and ask LEE if he won't consent to an armistice? I think Mr. LEE would say, if he deigned to answer him at all, that he would talk about that when he should get to Philadelphia. Even now, appalling as the danger is, I hear from all quarters, both high and low, scarcely less vindictive denunciations of the War Department and the Abolitionists than of the rebels. "Why don't the President send up 10,000 men from HOOKER's army," they whine, "and defend Harrisburgh." As though any one would think of such a thing as dividing the army, which is our only hope, to save such a contemptible little village as this. People have got so into the habit of blaming and finding fault that it seems as though they could do nothing else. They are doing better now, however, than they yet have. The whole population is ready to take up arms; very many are formed into companies. The veterans of 1812 have taken their muskets and cartridge boxes. Two companies of negroes were armed yesterday and marched through the streets, strange to say, without being insulted. The thought seemed to impress itself on every mind that there was bone and muscle even if the skin was black. The darkies themselves are highly delighted. They polish up their muskets and stuff their cartridge boxes full, laughing and chatting all the time as merrily as possible—tickled as a child with a new toy. These men have never been drilled much, and are officered by colored men, but I am inclined to think they will fight as well as the militia. When we consider the fearful risk they run we must acknowledge that it requires a high order of courage for a negro to enlist.

The fortifications are finished, and there are now a great many troops to defend them. They are impregnable, if well defended, and I hope the rebels will find cause to change the contempt they feel for our militia into admiration, when once they test their mettle. I do not suppose the great battle will be fought here; but I have very little doubt of their intention to take Harrisburgh if they can do it. Though they made no use of the capture, it would be a great thing to say that they had taken the capital of Pennsylvania. It would be worth five thousand men to them. If, however, they mean to stay in the North the whole Summer, they could not do better than to occupy Harrisburgh permanently. In the meantime, a few days longer will explain the whole plan up to the first battle.

The Philadelphia *Age* published on its bulletin-board to-day that there were no rebels near Harrisburgh. A message was sent to Gen. COUCH that the statement was believed in many quarters, and that it had the effect which was undoubtedly intended—to stop enlistments—and asking for the facts. He answered that the rebels were within four miles of Harrisburgh and advancing, and that an attack was hourly expected.

Col. COPPIE is relieved of his onerous duties, and his place is filled by WAYNE MCVEIGH, Esq., who is an old newspaper man, and will, I hope, be able to give us more news than we obtained from Col. COPPIE.

There was a slight skirmish over the river to-day. Nobody hurt, but some a good deal frightened. The Seventy-first New-York was engaged; also, SPENCER MILLER's battery. The rebels were about one hundred and fifty cavalry. They have made no advance this afternoon, so far as heard from. A detachment was seen at a point about thirty miles north of Harrisburgh, on the river, but no report has yet come of their operations.

The bridge company at this place keep an account of all the soldiers and teams that cross the river, and

Casualties of the first day's fighting at Gettysburg.

intend to present their bill to the State or the National Government, whichever they think will be fool enough to pay it. Patriotic!

THE SITUATION

just at present, seems to be this: LEE's whole army is in Pennsylvania and the borders of Maryland. LEE himself is at the centre, at or near Gettysburgh, with LONGSTREET's corps. A. P. HILL is on the right, and EWELL on the left. The latter corps is much the strongest, and numbers, according to information received by Gov. CURTIN, *thirty-seven thousand men.* Other accounts place it at thirty-four thousand. LONGSTREET's corps is said to be only ten thousand, but this, it seems to me, must be a mistake. ANDERSON's corps is in reserve, and is now at Chambersburgh. The whole rebel army must number at least one hundred thousand men.

EWELL's corps, which consists largely of cavalry and mounted infantry, and were the first to advance into the Cumberland Valley, is charged with the double duty of watching our movements and making excursions to various points for the purpose of plunder, and also to break our railroad connections. IMBODEN is advancing on Bloody Run, probably to capture MILROY's remnant, at the same time a force is at Perryville, thirty miles north of Harrisburgh, and will probably cut the Pennsylvania Railroad at some important point. A force is also at York, and has laid that unfortunate city under contribution to the amount of $150,000 in money and a large amount of flour and other edibles. These points are at least one hundred miles apart. A large force is threatening Harrisburgh, and all these detachments are parts of EWELL's corps. I think the other corps, LONGSTREET's, A. P. HILL's and ANDERSON's, are to be held in hand, while EWELL's does the work of burning bridges and cutting off our communications with the North, East and West, and at the same time collects together horses and supplies for the main army. I can no longer doubt that the rebels intend to carry on the Summer campaign in the North. It is a desperate movement, but it is their only hope. They must neutralize our victories in the West if they can. If we can beat them the rebellion is crushed, for whether we capture and destroy their army, or whether we only drive them back to Richmond, they cannot live through another Winter. The "black cloud" is gathering in the Southwest. A counter fire is gathering in the Northeast. When the fire and the cloud meet, the bolt that falls will destroy the last vestige of the rebellion. The people of the North must realize the fact that the rebels have actually attempted their conquest, for such is the fact. They trust to the machinations and schemes of their friends here to succeed. May this be discouraged and foiled now and forever.

Gen. COUCH has issued an order forbidding all newspaper correspondents to cross the river.

The New-York Times.

VOL. XII.—NO. 3673.   NEW-YORK, THURSDAY, JULY 2, 1863.   PRICE THREE CENTS.

THE REBEL INVASION.

Highly Important from the Army of the Potomac.

Defeat of Stuart's Cavalry in Three Fights.

The Rebels Driven from Westminster to Hanover by Gen. Gregg.

Their Defeat at Hanover by Gen. Kilpatrick.

Another Defeat of the Rebels at Hanover Junction.

Their Loss Four Hundred Men and Six Pieces of Artillery.

A Supposed Heavy Battle Between Gens. Meade and Lee.

Rapid Cannonading Heard at Harrisburgh Last Evening.

Probable Position of the Main Rebel Army.

Special Dispatch to the New-York Times.
HEADQUARTERS ARMY OF THE POTOMAC,
Tuesday Evening—8 P. M.

I am just in from the front, and send by a messenger to Frederick a brief dispatch of the occurrences of yesterday and to-day. The rebel force which made the raid on the Baltimore and Ohio Railroad consisted of STUART'S whole force, with eight pieces of artillery. On Monday night they arrived at Westminster and interrupted the Western Maryland Railroad. They threw out strong pickets, and shot two citizens who attempted to escape and give us information. Early this morning, Gen. GREGG attacked STUART and drove him all the way from Westminster to Hanover, Pennsylvania—a distance of eighteen miles. During the forenoon Gens. KILPATRICK and CASTAR drove STUART out of Hanover after a splendid fight, and they are still pursuing him; part of his force going toward Gettysburgh and part toward York.

During the day Gen. BUFORD drove a regiment of rebel infantry out of Gettysburgh, who also retired in a northeasterly direction.

You may expect to hear of brilliant news.

The whole army is in splendid spirits.

The rebels are reported to have burned Cashtown, Penn., yesterday. It is between Gettysburgh and Chambersburgh.

Confederate Lieutenant-General R.S. Ewell succeeded Stonewall Jackson as corps commander.

HEADQUARTERS ARMY POTOMAC,
Wednesday, July 1, 1863—8 A. M.

Gen. KILPATRICK captured fifty prisoners, including a Lieutenant-Colonel and a Lieutenant yesterday afternoon. They belonged to FITZHUGH LEE's cavalry brigade. The rebels retreated by way of the road to York, which is the nearest route to Harrisburgh. The column of infantry which was driven out of Gettysburgh, also fell back east toward York by way of Berlin and Abbottsville. This looks like a concentration of their forces near Harrisburgh.

LATER.
WEDNESDAY, 12 M.

From the best information we can obtain the rebels appear to be concentrating their forces on a line running from Cashtown to Berlin. LONGSTREET and A. P. HILL were near Cashtown yesterday. They are ripping, stripping and stealing everything. Citizens report that they burned twenty-five houses in Shippensburgh a couple days ago. In Gettysburgh they took everything that was left—most of the goods having been sent away in advance.

Our cavalry received a glorious welcome in Gettysburgh.

It looks at this hour as though the rebels were preparing to clear from the State with their plunder, or else to concentrate and give us battle.

York, Penn., was evacuated by the enemy last evening.   L. L. CROUNSE.

DISPATCHES FROM WASHINGTON.

WASHINGTON, Wednesday, July 1.

Letters of to-day's date have been received from the Army of the Potomac, in which the following facts are stated:

Our last movements have been characterized by a marked willingness on the part of the soldiers to undergo any fatigue within the bounds of human endurance.

The rebels recently sent only a small scouting or reconnoitering party to the vicinity of Frederick. Sharing in the general belief that there is no force of the enemy between that city and Hagerstown, the stage proprietor this morning sent out his team from the former for the latter place. This fact is stated to show that the intervening distance is now believed to be safe to travelers.

A portion of our forces surrounded Emmettsburg on Monday, and captured without conflict a battery—the only reble force there.

Notwithstanding various reports to the contrary, our pontoon bridges at Edwards' Ferry have been taken up and safely secured by the Engineer brigade.

Gen. STAHL was relieved from his cavalry command by Gen. HOOKER on Sunday, and Gen. KILPATRICK appointed in his place.

Brigadier-Gen. COPELAND has been assigned to other duty, and his late command has been reorganized.

The very best spirit pervades the army, and the hope of an early and decisive battle is the prevailing sentiment of the troops.

The portion of Maryland occupied by our army is teeming with rich agricultural products, affording large supplies. The most friendly disposition is evinced toward us by the inhabitants generally, and every precaution is taken to prevent the wanton destruction of property.

The following circular has been issued:

HEADQUARTERS ARMY OF THE POTOMAC,
June 30, 1863.

The Commanding General requests that previous to the engagement soon to be expected with the enemy, corps and all other commanding officers address their troops, explaining to them the immense issues involved in the struggle. The enemy is now on our soil. The whole country looks anxiously to this army to deliver it from the presence of the foe. Our failure to do so will leave us no such welcome as the swelling of millions of hearts with pride and joy at our success would give to every soldier of the army. Homes, firesides and domestic altars are involved. The army has fought well heretofore. It is believed that it will fight more desperately and bravely than ever if it is addressed in fitting terms. Corps and other commanders are authorized to order the instant death of any soldier who fails to do his duty at this hour.

By command of   Major-Gen. MEADE.
S. WILLIAMS, Assistant Adj.-Gen.

Our cavalry is actively scouting in every direc-

Brigadier-General Francis T. Nicholls of the Confederate Army.

tion, and no fears of surprise are for an instant entertained by any one.

WASHINGTON, Wednesday, July 1.

Official advices from the Army of the Potomac state that a portion of our cavalry under Gen. KILPATRICK had a handsome fight yesterday with the enemy's cavalry at Hanover. We captured a battle-flag, Lieutenant-Colonel, a Captain, and 45 privates. Fifteen or twenty of the enemy were killed.

MOVEMENTS OF THE ENEMY.

Special Dispatch to the New-York Times.

WASHINGTON, Wednesday July 1.

Parties arriving to-night assert that LEE is nearer Frederick than we supposed this morning, and that the relative positions of the two armies is more complicated than indicated in yesterday's dispatches.

LEE is believed to be striving to make headway in a south-east direction.

An extended reconnoissance made beyond the fortifications of Washington develops no signs of the enemy. All have left for more northern regions.

TELEGRAMS FROM HARRISBURGH.

HARRISBURGH, Penn., Wednesday, July 1.

Everything is quiet.

There is no news from any quarter this morning.

Gov. CURTIN leaves at 1 o'clock for Philadelphia. He will stop at the Continental Hotel, and return here at 10 o'clock.

Gov. CURTIN desires to see the citizens, that they may know and appreciate the danger which they have been so loth to believe, that they may not relax their efforts until the danger is over.

HARRISBURGH, Wednesday, July 1—9:30 P. M.

A battle took place yesterday afternoon at Hanover Junction, between PLEASANTON and the rebel cavalry. It lasted nearly the whole afternoon. The result was that the enemy lost 400 killed, wounded and prisoners, besides six pieces of artillery. Our loss is reported at 200.

It is believed that the main body of LEE's army is between Gettysburgh and Chambersburgh.

The indications are, that a battle has been fought to-day between LEE and MEADE, but to what extent and with what result is unknown; nor is it likely to be known to-night.

Heavy firing has been heard here the whole evening in the direction of Carlisle. It is a long way off and at times very rapid. The river banks are lined with persons listening and discussing the probable results.

OUR FORCES AT HANOVER JUNCTION.

The Lancaster *Express*, of Tuesday evening, publishes the following important intelligence :

"We have just learned from a reliable source that Gen. MEADE has taken Hanover Junction, thus cutting into the rebel lines, and turning their right. Gen. EARLY has retreated from York, and EWELL from in front of Harrisburgh.

The position of our army is such now that LEE must either beat a hasty retreat at great disadvantage, or give battle to Gen. MEADE on his chosen ground. In either event it is of the utmost importance that the new levies be pushed on as rapidly as possible. Now is the hour in which to strike the decisive blow."

TELEGRAMS FROM WASHINGTON.

NO REBELS WITHIN TEN MILES.

WASHINGTON, Wednesday, July 1.

It was ascertained by our scouts yesterday, who completed a circuit extending ten miles from the city, that there was not a single rebel soldier to be seen.

Our scouts are confident that there are no rebel soldiers anywhere between Frederick and the Potomac.

Washington to-day is remarkably quiet.

DISCIPLINE OF THE SEVENTH REGIMENT.

Major-General Lafayette McLaws led his Confederate division in an attack upon the Union Center at the Wheat Field.

BALTIMORE, Wednesday, July 1.

The discipline which is exercised in the New-York Seventh regiment is marked by such discrimination and prompt punishment, that that organization fully maintains its character. The regimental bulletin board at Fort Federal Hill to-day contained the following notice :

[*Extract from General Order.*]

Private W. E. KIDDER, of Co. A, having violated his pledge to return on the expiration of his furlough, is hereby dishonorably dismissed from further duty, and will not be allowed to rejoin his Company during their present term of service.

OUR SPECIAL ARMY CORRESPONDENCE.

Our Scouts in Hagerstown—The Departure of Gen. Hooker—Rapid Marches of our Troops—Gen. Meade's Staff—Doings of the Rebel Cavalry—No Telegraphic Communication with Washington, &c.

ARMY OF THE POTOMAC, Monday, June 29, 1863.

A party of Col. SHARPE's gallant scouts, only nine in number, headed by Sergt. M. W. KLINE, dashed into Hagerstown this morning, in the very rear of the enemy, and captured ten prisoners and a large rebel mail, which was on its way from the South to LEE's army.

Gen. HOOKER, accompanied by Maj. LAWRENCE and Capt. RUSSELL, his two personal Aids, left Frederick at noon, to-day, having been delayed by supposed trouble on the Baltimore and Ohio Railroad. His departure was entirely private.

The day has been wet and the roads heavy, but the troops are performing great feats of marching. They press forward with great vigor. When the history of this march is written people will be startled by the feats of endurance which our troops daily sustain.

I am very happy to say that the retirement of Gen. HOOKER has involved no material delay in the movement of the army. Gen. MEADE steps in vigorously, and applies himself with great energy to the task before him.

The entire Staff, save Gen. HOOKER's personal Aids, remains as heretofore for the present. Gen. MEADE adds three Aids, however, in the persons of Maj. BIDDLE and Capts. JAY and MEADE.

I should not be surprised if a great battle is fought on the Fourth of July, possibly sooner.

This is the important week of the war. The Army of the Potomac will do its duty.

MIDDLEBURGH, CARROLL CO., Md: Tuesday, June 30.

The presumption here is that the public are having a nice little excitement over the doings of the rebel cavalry in the rear of Washington. As that point is not exactly in my department, I cannot give you the particulars about the rampaging rebels down in that vicinity. We heard last evening that the rebel cavalry moving toward Annapolis, had struck and destroyed the Washington Branch of the Baltimore and Ohio Railroad at Laurel Factory, sixteen miles north of Washington. Where they went to from that point we have not fully learned, but an impression prevails that they steered for Ellicott's Mills on the main line, only ten miles distant by pike from Baltimore, and about fifteen by railroad.

Washington, we know, is not in telegraphic communication with us, and the only railroad in operation to-day is the Western Maryland Railroad, from Union Bridge to Baltimore. I sent a special messenger by that last evening, and he arrived in Baltimore safely.

The Frederick Road was not in operation. The regular morning train from Frederick, as also the special train with Gen. HOOKER, Gen. MARSTON, Col. HARDIE and others, were delayed at Monocacy Junction until after 12 o'clock, and I do not know that they left then. The telegraph line was not in operation and the road was being reconnoitered by a couple of engines, but with what success I did not learn.

The fact that Washington is absolutely cut off excites little sympathy in this army. If NERO could fiddle while Rome was burning, it is believed he finds his counterpart in the Commander-in-Chief, who cat-hauls the Army of the Potomac while the rebels are positively knocking at his own doors.

We have very little information from the enemy. The great distance between the two armies, and the rapid movement of both, have tended to lessen reports from the enemy. We shall, however, have definite information from the enemy in a day or two, and possibly a battle by the close of the week.

I am indebted to Capt. DAHLGREN, formerly of Gen. HOOKER's Staff, but now volunteer aid to Gen. PLEASANTON, for late Richmond and Charleston papers, which I forward herewith.

The dash into Hagerstown, yesterday, by Sergeant CLINE and eight scouts, was a very daring thing. They took more prisoners than they had men in their own party.

The public may be laboring under excitement now, because of recent bold movements of the enemy; but by the close of the week, if signs and plans do not fail, there will be cause for far greater perturbation of the public pulse. We all hope it may beat freer with the tidings of victory.

LATER.

TUESDAY, June 30—10 A. M.

The Western Maryland Railroad is also stopped, and the Army of the Potomac is without either telegraphic or railroad communication with Washington, or any other point. Blissful moment.

Rumors of a fight at Westminster prevailed last evening, but they proved to have been induced by the advance of our cavalry, some of them being taken for rebels by the citizens.

A few Baltimore papers of Monday have reached us, giving accounts of the rapid advance of the enemy along the Southern border of Pennsylvania, and the interruption of the Northern Central Railroad at York and Wrightsville. These things excite lively comment among the troops, and sharpen their appetites for the coming contest. We earnestly hope they will not fail to cross the Susquehanna and move on Philadelphia.

I sent a TIMES messenger by the Baltimore and Ohio Railroad from Frederick yesterday, but I am not at all sure that he got through. He had a full account of Gen. HOOKER's removal, and the causes thereof. I send another to-day through the country on horseback, and hope he will not fail. Communications are decidedly precarious.

If it will assure the public at all, I can say that the Army of the Potomac is in good position, full of spirit, and nerving itself for the great work before it. A feeling, based upon what it can do, pervades the army—that the time has now come for a change of the score from defeat to victory.

L. L. CROUNSE.

The New-York Times.

VOL. XII.—NO. 3674.   NEW-YORK, FRIDAY, JULY 3, 1863.   PRICE THREE CENTS.

VERY IMPORTANT NEWS

Further Particulars of the Battle Near Gettysburgh on Wednesday.

Gen. Reynolds' First Army Corps in the Advance.

An Attack by Longstreet and Hill.

THE ATTACK SUCCESSFULLY RESISTED.

CESSATION OF THE BATTLE AT 4 P. M.

The Whole Army of the Potomac on the Field on Wednesday Evening.

THE REBEL ARMY NOT CONCENTRATED.

Reported Capture of a Large Number of Prisoners.

2,400 OF THEM IN BALTIMORE.

Desultory Fighting All Day Yesterday.

THE DECISIVE BATTLE EXPECTED TO-DAY.

Repulse of a Rebel Attack on Carlisle.

EVACUATION OF MARYLAND HEIGHTS

BALTIMORE, Thursday, July 2—11 P. M.

I shall send you soon an account from the battle-field near Gettysburgh of yesterday's battle, which is *very favorable.*

Meanwhile, the cheering announcement has been made of *the capture of a large number of prisoners,* some of whom have arrived here and others are on the way. The number is stated at 6,000; but this may be an exaggeration. Gen. SCHENCK has just announced at the Eutaw House that 2,400 of them have already arrived.

LATEST FROM THE FRONT.
BALTIMORE, Thursday, July 2.

The *American* learns from parties who left Gettysburgh at noon to-day that everything was progressing favorably for the ultimate success of our arms. Up to that time they assert that 6,000 prisoners had been captured and sent to the railroad terminus at Union bridge, for transportation to Baltimore. The Seventh regiment have just gone to Belton depot to take charge of 800, already arrived, and Gen. SCHENCK has just announced from the Eutaw House that he then had in Baltimore and at the Relay House 2,400 in his possession.

We learn that nearly 1,000 of these prisoners were captured on Wednesday, by the Eleventh Army Corps, in their gallant charge on LONGSTREET's corps. They are said to have at first slightly faltered, but when Gen. HOWARD cried to them to "Remember Chancellorsville," they rushed into the fight like infuriated demons, and the whole line of the enemy gave way before them.

During the early part of to-day, up to noon, when our informant left, there had been no general battle, though heavy skirmishing had been going on all the morning, resulting in a heavy loss to the enemy, and the capture of over 5,000 more prisoners. In all these skirmishes, which were conducted under the direction of Gen. MEADE, our arms were entirely successful; but the enemy studiously avoided any general engagement, and it was thought there would be none before to-day, when it was said to be the intention of Gen. MEADE to press the enemy along the whole line.

The prudence and skill displayed by Gen. MEADE in the management of his army, and the strategy evinced by him in coping with LEE, had already won the confidence of his troops, and his presence drew forth the strongest demonstrations of attachment.

The army evinced the determination to win at all hazards, and had been strongly impressed by the officers with the dreadful consequences that would ensue to them and the country if disaster should occur to our arms in the coming conflict.

The enemy was rapidly concentrating troops yesterday, and Gen. MEADE's whole army had reached the field of battle.

Gen. COUCH was expected to press down through the Cumberland Valley on the enemy.

Eleven o'clock P. M.—Eight hundred and thirty rebel prisoners have just passed down Baltimore-street under guard. Among the number are Gen. ARCHER and seventy other officers.

BALTIMORE, Thursday, July 2.

The Baltimore *American* has the following in regard to the battle of Wednesday:

The body of Maj.-Gen. JOHN F. REYNOLDS, killed in the battle near Gettysburgh, arrived here this morning and was taken to the residence of his brother-in-law, Mr. GILDERSLEEVE.

We regret to learn from officers who brought down the body of Gen. REYNOLDS, that Brig.-Gen. PAUL was killed in the same fight in the south of Gettysburgh.

Gen. PAUL commanded the Third brigade of the First army corps.

Col. STONE and Col. WISTAR were both wounded and taken prisoners.

Col. WISTAR commanded the Bucktails—a Pennsylvania regiment.

Col. STONE also commanded a Pennsylvania regiment in the Second brigade of the First army corps, and was Acting Brigadier-General of the Second brigade.

Gen. NEWTON took command of the First Army Corps on the fall of Maj.-Gen. REYNOLDS.

LATER.

We learn from the officers of Maj.-Gen. REYNOLDS' Staff that our forces passed through Gettysburgh at 10 o'clock yesterday morning, and when a quarter of a mile west of the town, encountered Gens. LONG-STREET and HILL, who attacked the corps of Gen. REYNOLDS, which was in the advance.

This corps stood the force of the attack until it was relieved by the Third corps, and a commanding position secured.

The rebels made a strong attempt to flank the position we had gained, but were repulsed in the attempt.

Gen. REYNOLDS and Gen. PAUL fell under a volley from the rebel infantry. Both officers were mounted and at the head of their troops.

In the course of the conflict we fell back before superior numbers to a stronger position, and the fight ceased for the day at 4 o'clock.

At the close of the evening the whole Army of the Potomac had reached the field, and Maj.-Gen. MEADE had all the corps strongly posted for a renewal of the battle this morning.

The loss of the enemy was considered fully equal to ours.

The Army of the Potomac is in fine condition and very enthusiastic.

Our loss of officers is severe.

Cols. WISTAR and STONE were wounded when they fell into the hands of the rebels.

Our army is regarded as better concentrated than that of the rebels for the events of the day.

OFFICIAL DISPATCHES FROM GEN. MEADE.
WASHINGTON, Thursday, July 2.

The latest dispatches received from Gen. MEADE are dated last night. They state that the corps engaged with Gen. EWELL's army were Gen. REYNOLDS' and Gen. HOWARD's. Gen. PLEASANTON succeeded in inflicting severe injury upon STUART's cavalry. Gen. REYNOLDS was killed.

The reports received from all quarters are encouraging.

SPECIAL DISPATCH FROM WASHINGTON.
WASHINGTON, Thursday, July 2.

At the present hour, 9 P. M., no reliable advices have been received here from the Pennsylvania battle-field. It is generally felt that this is the crisis of the war. Intense anxiety prevails. The earliest information of yesterday's battle received here was L. L. CROUNSE's dispatch to the TIMES.

Profound sensation is excited here by the death of Gen. REYNOLDS, whose brilliant qualities as a soldier, and unvaried success as a brigade, division and corps commander, marked him for present and future distinction. The President, it is well known, hesitated long between the choice of him or Gen. MEADE as successor to Gen. HOOKER. Priority of rank finally determined the matter.

Eleven P. M.—At 10:30 P. M. no news had been received from the battle-field.

WASHINGTON, Thursday, July 2—Midnight.

Up to this hour the Government has not received any official details of yesterday's fight near Gettysburgh. The fact of its not being in immediate telegraphic communication with the Head-quarters of the Army of the Potomac will explain the non-receipt of dispatches.

It is very likely that our army has been engaged in combat with the enemy to-day, although if this be true, the War Department has no official notification of such fact.

JEFF. DAVIS IN PENNSYLVANIA.
PHILADELPHIA, Thursday, July 2.

A dispatch to the *Inquirer* says JEFF. DAVIS is at Greencastle.

TELEGRAMS FROM HARRISBURGH.
Special Dispatch to the New-York Times.
HARRISBURGH, Thursday, July 2.

Maj.-Gen. Governeur K. Warren

There has been no fighting of moment between Gen. SMITH's forces and the enemy to-day. I left Carlisle at 2 P. M., and since arriving here have seen some parties who left there later. Gen. SMITH occupies the town. The enemy has apparently gone in the direction of Gettysburgh. Our scouts are in pursuit.

Yesterday several houses were struck by rebel shells. Mr. J. H. YOUNG and others, of the United States Sanitary Commission, were with the troops, and gave aid to the wounded. The Dickinson College was used as a hospital. Our loss yesterday was one killed and sixteen wounded. After the fight at Oyster Point sixteen dead rebels were counted.

Annexed is the list of casualties:

Robert Walter, Co. I, 36th Penn. militia—killed.
Robert Wiley, Co. D, Blue Reserves—knee.
Morris Hunter, Co. B, 26th Penn.—contusion.
George McNult, Co. C, Blue Reserves—right leg.
Stuart Patterson, Co. A, 1st Philadelphia artillery—hand.
Lieut. W. Provost, Co. K, 37th New-York—hand.
H. C. Mecklen, Co. C, 37th New-York, knee.
J. Cowly, 37th New-York—contusion.
B. W. Walter, Co. H, Gray Reserves—face.
—— Ashmead, 1st Philadelphia artillery.
—— Blackinston, Co. D, Gray Reserves.
F. Croft, Co. H, 30th Pennsylvania—slight.
A. S. Hibbard, Co. K, 37th New-York—scalp.
P. Garrett, Co. G, Gray Reserves—slight.
C. W. Collady, Co. D, Gray Reserves—right leg amputated.
Ed. Colwell, Co. A, 1st Phila. artillery—ankle.
W. Scott, Co. A, 1st Philadelphia artillery—head.

There are under treatment a few cases of exhaustion. WHIT.

HARRISBURGH, Thursday, July 2.

The last of the rebels left Carlisle yesterday morning, and the town was occupied in the afternoon by a portion of our forces under Gen. SMITH.

About 5 o'clock in the evening the rebel cavalry appeared in large force, having come in on the York road.

A rebel officer sent in a flag of truce to Gen. SMITH, demanding the surrender of the town, which was refused.

The rebel officer, on receiving Gen. SMITH's reply, opened on the town with their artillery.

The rebel fire was promptly responded to by our forces.

The firing continued with intervals until about 10 o'clock, when the rebels fell back in the direction from whence they came.

The rebels burned the barracks, gas works and one dwelling.

Many buildings in the place also suffered from the rebel artillery.

The Court-house was struck several times.

When the rebels opened their fire on the town, the excitement among the citizens was very great.

The women and children fled in all directions, and hid themselves in cellars.

Our loss was three killed and eleven wounded.

The rebel loss is not known.

Previous to the retirement of the rebels they sent in another flag of truce, notifying the citizens to leave, as they intended to renew the attack to-day.

This morning the rebel pickets are again in sight.

HARRISBURGH, 12 o'clock noon.

Up to this hour no news has been received of a renewal of the attack on Carlisle by the rebels.

The barracks and gas-works which the rebels have burned are located a short distance outside of the town, which accounts for their being burned.

There is no news from any other quarter.

HARRISBURGH, Thursday, July 2.

Information received here shows that there is no enemy in Loudon or McConnellsburgh nor in that section of the country. They left this morning in the direction of Chambersburgh, taking a large amount of stolen property which they had collected.

The rebels in the neighborhood of Carlisle have all fallen back in the direction of LEE's army.

Heavy firing was heard to-day in the direction where Gen. MEADE's and LEE's armies are supposed to be.

As LEE's army is between here and the Army of the Potomac, we are not in a position to learn early news.

TELEGRAMS FROM PHILADELPHIA.

PHILADELPHIA, Thursday, July 2.

The *Bulletin* has the following special dispatch regarding the rebel attack on Carlisle:

HARRISBURGH, Thursday, July 2.

A demand was sent for an unconditional surrender of Carlisle by Gen. W. H. F. LEE.

Gen. SMITH promptly refused to give up the place, when the rebels placed a battery of six pieces in position to the left of the barracks and commenced to shell the town.

Gen. SMITH replied from his guns which were mounted in Main-street, near the centre of the town.

During the shelling the rebels made a detour around the railroad and fired the barracks.

The gas-works were also fired, sparks from which are said to have burned several lumber-yards, one private dwelling and several barns.

Some citizens are known to be injured.

The Court-house was damaged, and several shells fell upon the College building and grounds.

Gen. LEE then sent in another flag of truce, notifying the women and children to leave the town by 10 o'clock this morning.

Every confidence is had in Gen. SMITH's ability, not only to hold the place, but unless the rebels rapidly retire, his flanks and rear will be obstructed, and his force probably captured.

The citizens in the vicinity give Gen. LEE's force at 3,400 cavalry, and one battery of six guns, light 12-pounders.

TELEGRAMS FROM COLUMBIA.

PHILADELPHIA, Thursday, July 2.

The *Press*, of this city, has the following special dispatch:

COLUMBIA, Penn., Wednesday, July 1.

The Fifth New-York, the First Vermont, the First Virginia and the Eighteenth Pennsylvania cavalry regiments left Frederick on Saturday and moved forward to Hanover.

They arrived there on Tuesday morning, when they were charged upon in the rear by the rebel cavalry of STUART.

Major-General John F. Reynolds

The National forces numbered about 1,800, and the rebel force was nearly or quite 6,000.

The battle commenced at 9 o'clock in the morning, and continued until 7 o'clock in the evening.

The contest was a succession of charges, recharges, advances and repulses.

Our troops fought with desperate gallantry and daring, and gained a brilliant triumph.

We captured all the First South Carolina regiment except thirteen. The rebels, in turn, took but sixty prisoners.

A piece of artillery belonging to the First South Carolina is among our trophies.

The rebels lost beside one field-piece and one breech-loading steel rifled piece.

Our cavalry had no artillery.

Major-Gen. John F. Reynolds.

We have information by telegraph of the death Major-Gen. JOHN FULTON REYNOLDS, U. S. A., late commander of the First Corps of the Army of the Potomac, from a wound received on Wednesday in the battle near Gettysburgh, between the First and Eleventh corps and the rebel forces under Gens. LONGSTREET and HILL. Major-Gen. REYNOLDS was born in Pennsylvania about the year 1821, and entered the Military Academy at West Point in 1837. In 1841 he graduated and received his first commission as Brevet Second Lieutenant of the Third artillery. He served with distinction in the war with Mexico, being breveted Captain for gallant and meritorious conduct at Monterey, and again Major at Buena Vista. In 1852 he served as Aid-de-Camp on the Staff of Maj.-Gen. WOOL, and in 1855 received his rank as Captain. The following year he was sent to Oregon Territory, where he distinguished himself in several severe conflicts with the Indians, near Rogue River.

When the rebellion broke out Gen. REYNOLDS warmly espoused the cause of the Government, and, on the organization of the Pennsylvania Reserve Corps, he was appointed by Gov. CURTIN one of the brigade commanders. He took part with the Army of the Potomac in nearly all its actions, and so valuable were his services that the people of the State acknowledged them by the presentation of a sword.

At the commencement of the present year Gen. REYNOLDS was promoted to the Major-Generalship and command of the First Army Corps. After the removal of Gen. BURNSIDE from the office of Commander-in-Chief of the Army of the Potomac, the name of Gen. REYNOLDS was prominently mentioned for the succession, and again after the battle of Chancellorsville; but his own preferences were in favor of Gen. MEADE.

He fell while bravely leading his men, like LYON in Missouri, STEVENS and KEARNY at Chantilly, WILLIAMS at Baton Rouge, and other kindred spirits have nobly fallen. The country at large, as well as his associates in the army, will lament his death, but no one will feel a more poignant sorrow at this fortune of war than Maj.-Gen. MEADE, the new Commander of the Army of the Potomac. The deceased and he were bosom friends, and in the arduous and difficult duties that now devolve upon him he must have counted largely upon the aid and skill of the soldier who possessed his full confidence.

The body of Gen. REYNOLDS was yesterday taken to Baltimore.

The New-York Times.

VOL. XII–NO. 3675.   NEW-YORK, SATURDAY, JULY 4, 1863.   PRICE THREE CENTS.

THE GREAT BATTLES.

Our Special Telegrams from the Battle Field to 10 A. M. Yesterday.

Full Details of the Battle of Wednesday.

No Fighting on Thursday Until Four and a Half, P. M.

A Terrible Battle Then Commenced, Lasting Until Dark.

The Enemy Repulsed at All Points.

The Third Battle Commenced Yesterday Morning at Daylight.

THE REBELS THE ATTACKING PARTY.

No Impression Made on Our Lines.

The Death of Longstreet, and Barksdale of Mississippi.

Other Prominent Rebel Officers Killed or Wounded.

A LARGE NUMBER OF PRISONERS.

Gen. Sickles' Right Leg Shot Off.

OTHER GENERAL OFFICERS WOUNDED.

Special Dispatches to the New-York Times.

BATTLE-FIELD NEAR GETTYSBURGH,
Thursday 4:30 P. M.
Via BALTIMORE, Friday A. M.

The day has been quiet up to the present moment. The enemy are now massing a heavy force on our left, and have just began the attack with artillery. The probability is that a severe battle will be fought before dark.

The rebel sharpshooters have been annoying our batteries and men all day from the steeples of the churches in Gettysburgh.

We hold the Emmettsburgh and Baltimore roads.
L. L. CROUNSE.

BATTLE-FIELD NEAR GETTYSBURGH.
Friday morning July 3,—three A. M.
via BALTIMORE, one P. M.

At the close of my last dispatch at 4½ P. M. yesterday, the enemy had just opened a heavy attack by artillery on our left and centre. The tactics of the enemy were soon apparent—a massing of their main strength on our left flank, which covered the Frederick road, with the determination to crush it. So intent were the enemy on this purpose, that every other part of the lines was left alone.

The fighting was of the most desperate description on both sides. Our gallant men fought as they never fought before. We had against this great onslaught of the enemy three corps—the Second, Third and Fifth. The Third and Fifth joined hands, and fought heroically. The Second ably supported them, and at the same time held its own position. One division of the First was also engaged.

The fighting was so furious that neither party took many prisoners. We captured about 600 in one or two charges.

The losses, considering the duration of the conflict, are more than usually heavy on both sides. Many of our most gallant officers have fallen. Gen. SICKLES' right leg was shot off below the knee. Amputation has been performed, and he is doing well.

Late in the evening, Gen. MEADE called a council of his corps commanders, and it was resolved to continue the fight so long as there was any one left to fight.
L. L. CROUNSE.

BALTIMORE, Friday, July 3.
Via WASHINGTON, Friday, July 3.

Our correspondent has just arrived from the battle-field at Gettysburgh, having left there at 3 o'clock this morning. The reports of the occurrences in that vicinity, as thus far rendered in the Philadelphia and Baltimore papers, are almost totally incorrect. A brief and candid statement of the situation up to this morning is this:

In Wednesday's fight we were repulsed, simply because we were overpowered and outflanked. We fell back to the rear of Gettysburgh, and held that position. The action was not general, and was not intended to be by Gen. MEADE. It was brought on by Gen. REYNOLDS, under the impression that his force exceeded that of the enemy.

There was no fighting yesterday until 4½ o'clock, P. M. A bloody engagement was then fought, lasting until dark, *resulting in a substantial success to our forces, the enemy being repulsed with great loss.* The particulars I have already sent you by a special courier.

Neither Gens. WADSWORTH, VAN STEINWEHR nor DOUBLEDAY are wounded.

The total number of prisoners taken up to this morning was about fifteen hundred—eight hundred and fifty on Wednesday, and six hundred on Thursday. This is reliable.

The enemy made the attack yesterday. *It was terrific, and they threw their whole force into*

it, but they were finally repulsed with great slaughter.

At daylight this morning the battle was renewed, the cannonading being rapid and heavy. *It was the determination of our Generals to fight to the bitter end.* L. L. CROUNSE.

OFFICIAL DISPATCHES FROM GEN. MEADE.

WASHINGTON, Friday, July 3.

An official dispatch was received this afternoon from Maj.-Gen. MEADE, dated Headquarters Army of the Potomac, July 2, 11 o'clock P. M., which says:

"The enemy attacked me about 4 P. M. this day, and, after one of the severest contests of the war, was repulsed at all points. We have suffered considerably in killed and wounded. Among the former are Brig.-Gens. PAUL and ZOOK, and among the wounded Gens. SICKLES, BARLOW, GRAHAM and WARREN, slightly. We have taken a large number of prisoners."

SECOND DISPATCH.

WASHINGTON, Friday, July 3.

A later dispatch has been received from Maj.-Gen. MEADE, dated 8 o'clock this morning, which says:

"The action commenced again at early daylight upon various parts of the line. The enemy thus far have made no impression upon my position. All accounts agree in placing their whole army here. Prisoners report that LONGSTREET'S and A. P. HILL'S forces were much injured yesterday, and had many general officers killed. Gen. BARKSDALE, of Mississippi, is dead. His body is within our lines. We have thus far about 1,600 prisoners, and a small number yet to be started."

THE BATTLE OF WEDNESDAY.

Special Dispatch to the New-York Times.

BATTLE-FIELD NEAR GETTYSBURGH,
Thursday, 12 M., July 2. via Frederick, July 3.

The engagement yesterday was quite severe, though confined to our advance, the First and Eleventh corps ; the action being mainly fought by the First corps, under Gen. REYNOLDS, who was killed by a sharpshooter early in the fight. We first attacked the enemy's advance just beyond Gettysburgh, and repulsed it, when the whole corps became engaged, and subsequently the Eleventh corps, which came up to support by the Emmetsburgh road. The opposing forces were the rebel corps of HILL and EWELL. Our men gallantly sustained the fight, holding their own until 4 o'clock, when they retired to a strong position just to the eastward and southward of Gettysburgh. This was maintained until the arrival of reinforcements at night, and our lines are now well formed.

No general engagement has yet taken place, but the probability is that a great battle will be fought this afternoon or to-morrow. The enemy is in great force. Our troops are now all up and well in hand.

The battle yesterday was sanguinary in the extreme. WADSWORTH'S division sustained the early portion of it with great valor, charging the enemy and taking a whole regiment of prisoners with Brig.-Gen. ARCHER. We have taken fully one thousand prisoners and lost many, most of them being wounded and in Gettysburgh, the greater portion of which the enemy now hold.

The rebels occupy Pennsylvania College as an

hospital. ROBINSON's division and one brigade of DOUBLEDAY's supported WADSWORTH with great gallantry. The Eleventh corps, most of it fought well, and redeemed the disgrace of Chancellorsville. Among the general officers we lose beside Maj.-Gen. REYNOLDS, Gen. PAUL killed, and Gen. BARLOW wounded. Gen. SCHIMMELFENNIG is a prisoner. An estimate of yesterday's casualties cannot now be made.

Gettysburgh was injured by shells to a considerable extent. Most of the inhabitants remain in the burgh; many got away yesterday. It is a beautiful place, surrounded by a beautiful open and rolling country.

There has been more or less skirmishing all the morning, but no engagement of dimensions. Both parties are preparing for the great contest before them. Our troops are in splendid condition and fight like veterans.

REPORTS FROM PHILADELPHIA.

PHILADELPHIA, Friday, July 3.

The *Evening Bulletin* learns from parties who have arrived in this city the following particulars:

The fight opened at Gettysburgh on Wednesday, when our forces were about half a mile beyond the town.

But one brigade of the corps of Major-Gen. REYNOLDS was in position to do service at the opening of the struggle.

Gen. REYNOLDS gallantly pushed that brigade to a commanding position on Seminary Hill, and endeavored to hold it until the rest of the corps could come up.

Reinforcements were, however, delayed, and our forces subsequently fell back of the locality called Seminary Hill.

About 10,000 of our men in this fight were engaged with 30,000 of the enemy.

The last position taken by the Union forces was held up to the latest dates.

Gen. REYNOLDS was killed very early in the action, while placing the brigade in position.

During Wednesday night, about seventy-five thousand of Gen. MEADE's troops came up and took favorable positions for reopening the battle on Thursday morning, while at that period some twenty-five thousand other Union troops belonging to the Army of the Potomac were so near at hand as to be immediately available for the conflict.

The rebels had mainly concentrated their forces near Gettysburgh on Wednesday night, and there was but little doubt that the great battle of yesterday would involve every available man of both armies.

THE BATTLE OF THURSDAY.

Special Dispatch to the New-York Times.

BATTLE-FIELD NEAR GETTYSBURGH, Penn.,
Via BALTIMORE, Friday, July 3.

My brief dispatches regarding the desperate engagement of yesterday have hardly conveyed a true idea of its magnitude and character. We have now had two days' fighting. Nearly the whole of Wednesday was thus employed by the First and Eleventh Corps, with varying success, they finally being obliged to fall back before greatly superior numbers.

This morning there were strong premonitions of an early engagement with the enemy in force. but as the day wore away and no positive exhibition was made by the enemy. We began to think that perhaps there would be no immediate battle after all. We were hardly in a condition to give battle, as all our dispositions had not been made. Gen. MEADE not having arrived on the ground until 2 o'clock in the morning. The position of our forces after the fight of Wednesday was to the eastward and southward of Gettysburgh, covering the Baltimore Pike, the Taneytown and Emmittsburgh roads, and still being nearly parallel with the

latter. The formation of the ground on the right and centre was excellent for defensive purposes. On our extreme left the ground sloped off until the position was no higher than the enemy's. The ground in front of our line was a level, open country, interposed here and there with an orchard or a very small tract of timber, generally oak, with the underbrush cut away. During the day, a portion of the troops threw up temporary breastworks and an abbattis. Gen. MEADE's headquarters were at an old house on the Taneytown road, immediately in rear of the centre.

Our line was not regular in shape. Indeed the centre protruded out toward the enemy so as to form almost the two sides of a triangle. Before sundown Gen. MEAD's headquarters proved to be the hottest place on the battle-field, so far as careless shelling was concerned.

Gen. HOWARD occupied, with his corps, a beautiful cemetery on a hill to the south of Gettysburgh. Cannons thundered, horses pranced, and men carlessly trampled over the remains of the dead. From this hill a beautiful view could be obtained of the valley, and also of a goodly portion of the enemy's line of battle.

Our forces had all been concentrated on Tuesday night, save the Fifth and Sixth corps. The former arrived during the morning, and the latter soon after noon. They were all massed immediately behind our centre.

Whether or no it was Gen. MEADE's intention to attack, I cannot say, but he was hardly ready for it before the afternoon of yesterday. The day had become almost dull. Skirmishing was now and then brisk, and the sharpshooters in the steeples and belfreys of the churches persistently blazed away at officers and artillery horses. It was by a sharpshooter in a barn just opposite WADSWORTH's Division, yesterday, that Capt. STEVENS, of the Fifth

All four of these Union officers were wounded in action at Gettysburg. Seated is Winfield S. Hancock, commander of the II Corps. Standing, from left: General Francis Barlow, General David Birney, and General John Gibbon.

REPORTS FROM HARRISBURGH.

HARRISBURGH, Friday, July 3.

There is great excitement here to know the result of the battle fought yesterday and last night between Gen. MEADE and LEE's army.

Persons at Columbia and Bainbridge, and in the neighborhood of York, heard distinctly the roar of artillery. At times it was rapid and heavy.

At daylight this morning it was again renewed. The battle must have been in the neighborhood of Gettysburgh.

Telegraphic communication has been reopened with Baltimore, by way of the Northern Central Railroad.

There have been no movements in this Department worth mentioning.

HARRISBURGH, Penn., Friday, July 3.

The city is in the greatest state of suspense. All rebel infantry and detachments of cavalry, under JENNINGS, IMBODEN and FITZ HUGH LEE, have disappeared from the front, and travel has been resumed between this city and Carlisle. Nothing is yet known as to the result, but the impression prevails that the great decisive battle of the campaign has been fought in the neighborhood of Cashtown.

PHILADELPHIA, Friday, July 3.

A special dispatch to the Bulletin from Harrisburgh says:

Nothing is yet known as to results, but the impression prevails that the great decisive battle of the campaign, has been fought in the neighborhood of Cashtown, between Gettysburgh and Chambersburgh.

It is believed that we have suffered heavy losses in officers and men, but LEE is so crippled as to be placed on the defensive.

Yesterday Gen. MEADE assumed the offensive. The day before LEE had attacked MEADE, and was repulsed with heavy loss.

LEE holds a gap in South Mountain near Chambersburgh, through which he hopes to escape if defeated. A guard stationed at Bridge eighty-four on the Northern Central Railroad, heard firing in that direction like that of flying artillery, whence it is believed that PLEASANTON is again at work with his dashing cavalry, fighting for the possession of the Gap.

HARRISBURGH, Friday, July 3—Midnight.

A prominent citizen of Gettysburgh, who left there yesterday morning on a pass issued by Gen. EWELL to go to Heidleburgh, met STUART, FITZHUGH LEE and WADE HAMPTON, with what he estimated at 10,000 cavalry, who were moving in the direction of Gettysburgh.

Their officers told him that LEE had no intention of leaving Pennsylvania, but was going to remain here until his army was destroyed or victorious. He arrived here this evening, the enemy making no effort to detain him.

Two militia men from Susquehanna County were killed this evening at Camp Curtin by lightning.

A dispatch from Loudon this morning states that yesterday the rebels left Chambersburgh, taking the road in the direction of Gettysburgh. Before leaving, they burned the depot and workshops belonging to the railroad. Loudon is fourteen miles west of Chambersburgh.

The enemy also evacuated Shippensourgh yesterday, moving in the same direction.

Everything goes to show that LEE has his whole army concentrated between Cashtown and Gettysburgh.

The train that left Carlisle at seven o'clock this evening, brought down twenty-four rebel deserters who had come in from the mountains. They know nothing about the result of the battle, but state that both armies are fighting with great desperation.

Firing was heard from daylight up to three o'clock this afternoon, at different points down the river.

REPORTS FROM COLUMBIA, PENN.

PHILADELPHIA, Friday, July 3.

The Evening Bulletin has the following special dispatch:

COLUMBIA, Penn., Friday, July 3.

Capt. ROBERTS, of Philadelphia, who was captured near Gettysburgh and paroled, has arrived here.

He reports that yesterday, beyond York, a courier from Gen. MEADE to Gen. COUCH stopped at a house to have his horse fed.

The women in the house became alarmed, and blew a horn to collect the neighbors; when the courier, fearing that the noise would reach the rebels threatened them if they did not desist.

At this moment the owner of the house arrived, and, taking the courier for a rebel, drew a pistol and killed him.

The courier's dispatches were subsequently sent to Baltimore, very foolishly, instead of to Harrisburgh.

Capt. ROBERTS says that numbers of people in York and Adams Counties offered every possible assistance to the rebels, pointing out to them the property of Union citizens and of the Government, and showing them the roads.

Heavy and continuous artillery firing was heard yesterday afternoon and last night in the direction of Dover, eight miles northwest of York.

REPORTS FROM WRIGHTSVILLE, PENN.

PHILADELPHIA, Friday, July 3.

The Press, of this city, has the following special dispatch:

WRIGHTSVILLE, Penn, Thursday, July 2, Twelve o'clock—Midnight.

Our forces are known to have gained upon the enemy until 4 o'clock this afternoon.

Since 5 o'clock the firing has been much heavier and more rapid, indicating a general engagement between the entire armies.

The rebel force is concentrated on South Mountain, toward Carlisle, six miles north of Gettysburgh.

Gen. SEDGWICK's corps passed York, in the direction of Dover, at 4 o'clock this afternoon. It is in the rear of the enemy.

The Second army corps moved up from Hanover at 8 o'clock this morning.

The reported burning of Gettysburgh is unfounded.

REPORTS FROM BALTIMORE.

BALTIMORE, Friday, July 3.

A gentleman from Parkton, twenty-six miles from Baltimore, says that cannonading was heard there from noon yesterday until nine o'clock last night.

The cannonading was very heavy and was resumed again at daylight this morning with great fury.

It is positively known, however, that there was no engagement at Gettysburgh yesterday, up to 4 o'clock in the afternoon.

BALTIMORE, Friday, July 3.

The American has the following account of the battle:

WESTMINSTER, Md., Friday, July 3.

From the many reports brought here by parties from the battle-field, we make the following narration of the battle of Thursday:

Line of battle was formed about 4 o'clock A. M., our centre occupying the heights on this side of Gettysburgh at and near the cemetery. The Second and Third corps, Gen. SICKLES, formed the left wing; the First and Eleventh were on the right. Skirmishers were immediately thrown forward along the whole line in order to feel the enemy's position.

Our batteries also shelled the heights and woods, in order, if possible, to destroy the place where the enemy intended to mass his forces. We could elicit no reply from the rebel batteries. Their skirmishers were active and very often reinforced. The silence of the enemy was ominous.

Shortly after a terrific cannonade was opened on our centre and left, from the rebel batteries, which had been quietly placed in position, having been masked by woods and grain fields. Our rifled guns replied with awful power and telling effect for two hours.

A dead Confederate sharpshooter at Little Round Top.

The air seemed literally filled with screaming messengers of death. Old soldiers, who had heard the roar of cannon at Gaines' Mill, Malvern Hill, Fredericksburgh and Chancellorsville, declared the cannonading to be equal, if not greater than that of any of those engagements.

Suddenly a wild demoniac yell arose from thousands of rebel throats near the extreme left of our line to where the enemy were to make their great attack. SICKLE's corps sustained the first terrific onset of the rebel forces which had been massed on our right. The rattle of musketry now became incessant.

As soon as the design of the rebels became evident, a large number of pieces of the reserve artillery were massed in a splendid position to oppose the rebel infantry. At this time the centre and left centre advanced with loud cheers, pushing the rebels from point to point through the valley and up the heights beyond.

The enemy was secreted behind trees, rocks and ledges, and in many cases they were bayonetted by our troops or taken prisoners.

Night came at last, and with her sable closed the scene. The result of the day's work may be summed up briefly as follows: LEE had been attacked on his chosen ground, and our centre had driven the rebel lines more than one mile. The Army of the Potomac fought with a gallantry never before equalled during the war.

COL. CROSS, OF NEW-HAMPSHIRE, KILLED.

BALTIMORE, Friday, July 3.

The body of Col. CROSS, of the Fifth New-Hampshire Volunteers, arrived to-day, and will leave for New-Hampshire Saturday afternoon at 8 o'clock. He was killed on Thursday near Gettysburgh.

LATEST FROM YESTERDAY'S BATTLE.

The Rebel Army Driven in a North-westerly Direction.

MORE FIGHTING EXPECTED TO-DAY.

PHILADELPHIA, Saturday, July 4—3 A. M.

The following is a special to the Press:

HANOVER, Pa., Friday, July 3.

Early this morning the battle was renewed with increased vigor, and throughout this day has proved the most fearful of all the war.

The losses on both sides are very heavy. Among the casualties is Gen. BARLOW, severely wounded.

We captured more prisoners than the rebels.

Our officers are very enthusiastic in praise of the heroic conduct of our men. They never stood so like veterans before.

The enemy's entire force was engaged, and all our forces except Gen. COUCH's.

LATER.—To-night a messenger came from the battle-field, stating that up to 6 o'clock we had driven the enemy about three-quarters of a mile northwest.

All our men are confident of ultimate success. It is probable the battle will be renewed early to-morrow.

Maine Battery, got hit. A bullet passed through both legs below the knee, inflicting a severe, but not dangerous wound.

At 3½ o'clock, Gen. MEADE had received sufficient assurances to justify him in the belief that the rebels were concentrating their forces on our left flank, which all felt to be secure under the protection of the invincible Third corps. Our line was immediately strengthened on that flank, Gen. SICKLES' corps being sent to its support, and several batteries from the reserve being brought out and placed in position.

At about 4½ o'clock P. M., the enemy sent his first compliments by a salvo of artillery, his first shells falling uncomfortably near Gen. MEADE's Headquarters. From this hour forth to 8½ o'clock, occurred by all odds the most sanguinary engagements yet chronicled in the annals of the war, considering its short duration. The artillery attack which was made by the enemy on the left and centre was rapidly followed by the advance of his infantry. The Third corps received the attack with great coolness. The rebels at once made for our flank, and kept moving heavy columns in that a direction. This necessitated support, which was quickly given by the Fifth Corps. The division of Gen. BARNES being sent to the right, and that of Gen. AYRES, regulars, to the left, with Gen. CRAWFORD in reserve.

The battle now became perfectly fearful. The armies engaged each other at very short range, and for three long hours the war of musketry was incessant. I have heard more noise, louder crashes, in other battles, but I never saw or heard of such desperate tenacious fighting as took place on this flank. The enemy would often bring up suddenly a heavy column of men, and force our line back, only to be in turn forced back by our own line of glittering steel. Our gallant columns covered themselves with glory over and over again. They fought a superior force in numbers. The dispositions of the enemy were very rapid, for look where you would on that field a body of rebels would be advancing. Our dispositions were equally rapid, and the enemy found more than their equal in such gallant veterans as SICKLES and BIRNEY and HUMPHREYS. At half-past six Gen. SICKLES was struck in the right leg by a piece of shell, and borne from the field. The injury was so great that amputation became necessary, and it was performed successfully—the limb being taken off below the knee.

The struggle grew hotter and hotter. The Second corps was called on for aid, and though its own position was strongly threatened, yet the First division, formerly Gen. HANCOCK's flung themselves into the fight with desperation, and after a long and obstinate conflict the enemy slowly and sullenly gave way. In this last charge the brigade of Gen. CALDWELL, Second corps, and that of Col. SWITZER, from the Fifth corps, won great honors. The charges made by our men deserve mention, but want of time forbids. The rebels made frequent attempts to capture our artillery, and at one time had WATSON's battery in their possession, but it was retaken in a furious charge by BIRNEY's division.

The battle lasted till fully 8½ o'clock, when the enemy fell back to h ld position, and left our veterans the ensanguined victors of that field. Our pickets were thrown out, and our lines covered most of the field, including a great number of the enemy's dead and wounded.

I visited some portions of the line by moonlight and can bear personal witness to the terrible ferocity of the battle. In front of some of our brigades, who had good protection from stone walls or fences, the rebel dead laid piled in lines like winrows of hay. In front of Gen. WEBB's—the Philadelphia—brigade, they lay so thick as to literally cover the ground. Not far from here was found the body of Gen. BARKSDALE, that once haughty and violent rebel, who craved as a dying boon a cup of water and a stretcher from an ambulance-boy. He is literally cut to pieces with wounds, and must die.

A great and magnificent feature of this fight is the splendid use of artillery. Though our line of battle was only a mile and a half long, yet almost every battery belonging to the Army of the Potomac was more or less engaged. Every one of the reserve batteries was brought into action, the positions for use being numerous. The enemy also used artillery largely, but not to near so great an extent as we did. From this they suffered immensely, and specially on the left, where canister was largely used. I believe we lost no artillery, unless it was two or three disabled pieces, though it was very wonderful we did not considering how the enemy's forces were piled on to them. Some of their skirmishers were literally blown away from the muzzles of our guns.

Our losses at this hour cannot be computed, but for two days' fighting they are very heavy. We mourn the loss of many valuable officers, but they have been amply avenged in the hecatombs of rebel dead, who lie piled along the lines.

Between 10 o'clock and midnight a consultation was called by Gen. MEADE of all corps commanders, and after deliberation it was unanimously decided to maintain our present positions at all hazards, and fight as long as there was a man left.

The death of Lieut. Gen. LONGSTREET is reported by prisoners taken from his corps. I know of no other authority for it.

The enemy withdrew his forces from the City of Gettysburgh yesterday, and occupies it now only with skirmishers. Our skirmishers advanced into it a short distance last night, and now hold considerably more than they did.

There is much doubt whether the enemy will renew the attack at daylight, but the expression on all hands is, " we are ready."

Capt. DAHLGREN, Volunteer Aid to Gen. PLEASANTON, made a daring scout into Hagerstown yesterday with twenty picked men, and captured more prisoners than he had men in his party. He also captured a dispatch bearer from JEFF. DAVIS to LEE, with dispatches of the greatest importance, the nature of which cannot to-day be properly disclosed. They have an important bearing on " coming events."

L. L. CROUSE.

YESTERDAY'S BATTLE.

Our Special Telegrams from the Battle Field.

GETTYSBURGH, Friday, July 3.

The third day's battle began this morning at 4 o'clock. It is now 7 o'clock, and a circle of fire of musketry and artillery on the south side of Gettysburgh describes the field of contest. The musketry fight is wholly within the woods ; the artillery occupies the eminences shorn of timber.

The attack was commenced by the rebels on our right. The fight there has been unceasing, and the irregularity of the fire—slack and scattering for a while, and then heavy and continuous—indicates reinforcements of both sides.

The men at this hour are in the best of spirits, and the general officers feel confident of the result. The battle has been planned and thus far fought by Gen.

MEADE with equal prudence (ably and energetically assisted by Gen. BUTTERFIELD, who has not left the Army of the Potomac) and courage.

The day is now overcast, and the air damp and cool. The sky threatens rain, and a fog already obscures the outer edge of the field of battle.

QUARTER OF EIGHT, A. M.

Gen. BARKSDALE, of Miss., wounded yesterday, is lying dead within our lines. The rumor of the death of LONGSTREET, brought by rebel prisoners yesterday, is confirmed by prisoners taken this morning. LONGSTREET's and HILL's corps are said to be fighting on the right ; EWELL's in front.

10 O'CLOCK A. M.

Sixteen hundred prisoners, thus far during the engagement, have been sent to the rear, and more are here.

What the result may be to-day cannot now be predicted. HANCOCK, HOWARD, SLOCUM, WARREN, GIBBON and all the general officers have given the highest evidence to-day of capacity, energy and spirit.

Important dispatches have been captured by Capt. DAHLGREN and the gallant scout KLINE, from JEFF. DAVIS and COOPER to Gen. LEE. They indicate anxiety for the position of Richmond. Both decline to send LEE the reinforcements from BEAUREGARD he asked for. WILKESON.

NEWS RECEIVED IN WASHINGTON.

WASHINGTON, Friday, July 3.

The information received here is that the battle at Gettysburgh last night was extremely fierce and stubborn. Heavy and determined assaults were made by the rebels, which were gallantly met by our troops.

This morning at daylight the contest was spiritedly renewed. Our army drove the enemy, who in turn drove ours, the fighting being desperately severe, and the fiercest, probably, of the war.

Prisoners report that LONGSTREET was killed, and this seems to be confirmed by later intelligence.

Col. CROSS, of New-Hampshire, and Gen. ZOOK, of New-York, are among the killed.

Gen. SICKLES, it is said, was wounded, and had his leg amputated on the field.

Gen. BARKSDALE, of the rebel army, is killed, and his body is our possession.

The latest intelligence received here was up to 11 o'clock to day.

Rebel mail matter was captured. Among the letters, it is reported, is a letter from JEFF. DAVIS to LEE, saying he could send him no more troops as RICHMOND was seriously threatened.

WASHINGTON, Friday, July 3.

Gen. LONGSTREET is reported killed, but there is no confirmation.

NOTHING OF IMPORTANCE ADDITIONAL.

WASHINGTON, Saturday, July 4—2 A. M.

The latest official information received from Gen. MEADE is up to 12½ o'clock Friday noon. All was quiet at that hour.

Considerable firing both of artillery and infantry had taken place in various parts of our lines up to that time, and *several hundred prisoners had been taken since morning.*

NEWS RECEIVED IN PHILADELPHIA.

PHILADELPHIA, Friday, July 3.

A special dispatch to Forney's *Press* dated Hanover, 1 P. M., via Washington, July 3, says:

At 10 this morning our forces opened on about 5,000 rebels, who advanced on the field at daybreak, for the purpose of pillaging our dead.

The rebels hastily retreated. The fight thus far has been the most terrific of the war. The loss on both sides was heavy. Gen. SICKLES was wounded severely. His right leg was amputated, and he is doing well. A desperate battle rages.

THE ASSOCIATED PRESS DISPATCHES.

The New-York Times.

VOL. XII....NO. 3676.1   NEW-YORK, MONDAY, JULY 6, 1863.   PRICE THREE CENTS.

THE GREAT BATTLES.

Splendid Triumph of the Army of the Potomac.

ROUT OF LEE'S FORCES ON FRIDAY

The Most Terrible Struggle of the War.

TREMENDOUS ARTILLERY DUEL.

Repeated Charges of the Rebel Columns Upon Our Position.

Every Charge Repulsed with Great Slaughter.

The Death of Longstreet and Hill.

Our Cavalry Active on the Enemy's Flank.

THE REBEL RETREAT CUT OFF.

Chambersburgh in Our Possession.

Advance of the Militia under Gen. Smith to Important Positions.

The Rebel Pontoon Bridge at Williamsport Destroyed.

The Contents of the Captured Dispatches from Jeff. Davis to Lee.

A Peremptory Order for the Rebel Army to Return to Virginia.

OFFICIAL DISPATCHES FROM GEN. MEADE.

WASHINGTON, Saturday, July 4—10:10 A. M.

The following has just been received :

HEADQUARTERS ARMY OF POTOMAC,
NEAR GETTYSBURGH, Friday, July 3—8½ P. M.

Major-Gen. Halleck, Genneral-in-Chief :

The enemy opened at 1 P. M., from about one hundred and fifty guns, concentrated upon my left centre, continuin without intermission for

Major-General Daniel Sickles (left) lost his leg after being wounded by a Confederate frontal assault.

about three hours, at the expiration of which time, he assaulted my left centre twice, being, upon both occasions, handsomely repulsed, with severe loss to him, leaving in our hands nearly three thousand prisoners.

Among the prisoners is Brig.-Gen. ARMSTEAD and many Colonels and officers of lesser rank.

The enemy left many dead upon the field, and a large number of wounded in our hands.

The loss upon our side has been considerable. Maj.-Gen. HANCOCK and Brig.-Gen. GIBBON were wounded.

After the repelling of the assaults, indications leading to the belief that the enemy might be withdrawing, a reconnoissance was pushed forward from the left and the enemy found to be in force.

At the present hour all is quiet.

My cavalry have been engaged all day on both flanks of the enemy, harassing and vigorously attacking him with great success, notwithstanding they encountered superior numbers both of cavalry and infantry.

The army is in fine spirits.

GEORGE G. MEADE,
Maj.-Gen. Commanding.

WASHINGTON, Sunday, July 5—4 P. M.

The latest official dispatch received here, up to this hour, from Gen. MEADE, is dated at Headquarters Army of Potomac, 7 A. M., July 4, which merely states that the enemy had withdrawn from his position, occupied for attack, on Friday. The information in the possession of Gen. MEADE, at that hour, did not develop the character of the enemy's movement, whether it was a retreat or a manœuvre for other purposes.

Reliable information received here to-day asserts that Gen. LEE's Headquarters were at Cashtown yesterday afternoon, and further represents that the rebels were fortifying at Newman's Cut, in the South Mountains, apparently to cover a retreat.

Later official dispatches are expected this evening.

SECOND DISPATCH

HEADQUARTERS ARMY OF POTOMAC,
July 4—Noon.

Maj.-Gen. Halleck :

The position of affairs is not materially changed since my last dispatch of 7 A. M.

We now hold Gettysburgh.

The enemy has abandoned large numbers of his killed and wounded on the field.

I shall probably be able to give you a return of our captures and losses before night, and a return of the enemy's killed and wounded in our hands.

GEORGE G. MEADE, Major-General.

THIRD DISPATCH.

HEADQUARTERS ARMY POTOMAC,
July 4—10 P. M.

To Maj.-Gen. Halleck :

No change of affairs since my dispatch of noon.

GEO. G. MEADE, Major-General.

FOURTH DISPATCH.

WASHINGTON, Monday, July 6—12.30 A. M.

The following is the latest official dispatch :

HEADQUARTERS ARMY OF THE POTOMAC,
Sunday, July 5—8:30 A. M.

MAJOR-GEN. HALLECK : The enemy retired under cover of the night and the heavy rain, in the direction of Fairfield and Cashtown.

Our cavalry are in pursuit.

I cannot give you the details of our captures in prisoners, colors and arms.

Upward of twenty battle-flags will be turned in from one corps.

My wounded and those of the enemy are in our hands.　GEO. G MEADE, Major-General.

THE PRESIDENT TO THE COUNTRY.

WASHINGTON, D. C., July 4—10:30 A. M.

The President announces to the country that news from the Army of the Potomac, up to 10 P. M. of the 3d, is such as to cover that army with the highest honor; to promise a great success to the cause of the Union, and to claim the condolence of all for the many gallant fallen; and that for this, he especially desires that on this day He, whose will, not ours, should ever be done, be everywhere remembered and reverenced with profoundest gratitude.

(Signed)　　　　A. LINCOLN.

THE GREAT BATTLE OF FRIDAY.

Our Special Telegrams from the Battle-Field.

NEAR GETTYSBURGH, Saturday, July 4.

Another great battle was fought yesterday afternoon, resulting in a magnificent success to the National arms.

At 2 o'clock P. M., LONGSTREET'S whole corps advanced from the rebel centre against our centre. The enemy's forces were hurled upon our position by columns in mass, and also in lines of battle. Our centre was held by Gen. HANCOCK, with the noble old Second army corps, aided by Gen. DOUBLEDAY'S division of the First corps.

The rebels first opened a terrific artillery bombardment to demoralize our men, and then moved their forces with great impetuosity upon our position. HANCOCK received the attack with great firmness, and after a furious battle lasting until 6 o'clock, the enemy were driven from the field, LONGSTREET'S corps being almost annihilated.

The battle was a most magnificent spectacle. It was fought on an open plain, just south of Gettysburgh, with not a tree to interrupt the view. The courage of our men was perfectly sublime.

At 5 P. M. what was left of the enemy *retreated in utter confusion*, leaving dozens of flags, and Gen. HANCOCK estimated *at least five thousand killed and wounded on the field*.

The battle was fought by Gen. HANCOCK with splendid valor. He won imperishable honor, and Gen. MEADE thanked him in the name of the army and the country. He was wounded in the thigh, but remained on the field.

The number of prisoners taken is estimated at 3,000, including at least two Brigadier-Generals—OLMSTEAD, of Georgia, and another—both wounded.

The conduct of our veterans was perfectly magnificent. More than twenty battle flags were taken by our troops. Nearly every regiment has one. The Nineteenth Massachusetts captured four. The repulse was so disastrous to the enemy, that LONGSTREET'S corps is perfectly used up. Gen. GIBBON was wounded in the shoulder. Gen. WEBB was wounded and remained on the field. Col. HAMMELL, of the Sixty-sixth New-York, was wounded in the arm.

At 7 o'clock last evening, Gen. MEADE ordered the Third corps, supported by the Sixth, to attack the enemy's right, which was done, and the battle lasted until dark, when a good deal of ground had been gained.

During the day EWELL'S corps kept up a desultory attack upon SLOCUM on the right, but was repulsed.

Our cavalry is to-day playing savagely upon the enemy's flank and rear.　L. L. CROUNSE.

GETTSBUBGH, Friday, July 3.

The experience of all the tried and veteran officers of the Army of the Potomac tells of no such desperate conflict as has been in progress during this day. The cannonading of Chancellorsville, Malvern and Manassas were pastimes compared with this. At the headquarters, where I write, sixteen of the horses of Gen. MEADE'S staff officers were killed by shell. The house was completely riddled. The Chief of Staff, Gen. BUTTERFIELD, was knocked down by a fragment of case-shot. Col. DICKINSON, Assistant Adjutant-General, had the bone of his wrist pierced through by a piece of shell. Lieut. OLIVER, of Gen. BUTTERFIELD'S Staff, was struck in the head; and Capt. CARPENTER, of Gen. MEADE'S escort, was wounded in the eye.

While I write the ground about me is covered thick with rebel dead, mingled with our own. Thousands of prisoners have been sent to the rear, and yet the conflict still continues.

The losses on both sides are heavy. Among our wounded officers are HANCOCK, GIBBON and a great many others whose names I feel restrained from publishing without being assured that they are positively in the list of casualties.

It is near sunset. Our troops hold the field, with many rebel prisoners in their hands. The enemy has been magnificently repulsed for three days—repulsed on all sides—most magnificently to-day. Every effort made by him since Wednesday morning to penetrate MEADE'S lines has been foiled. The final results of the action, I hope to be able to give you at a later hour this evening.

S. WILKESON.

Editorials

GETTYSBURGH.—The rebels have fought their first battle on the soil of the Free States. It is rather likely to be their last. In its nature and results it has not been sufficiently encouraging for them to try it again.

The Triumph of the Army of the Potomac.

The Army of the Potomac, under its new leader, has won its greatest victory. The tremendous actions of the first three days of the month of July at Gettysburgh have been followed by the complete discomfiture of the entire rebel army, which so audaciously and exultingly crossed the Potomac, and planted itself on Pennsylvania soil less than a fortnight ago. Entertaining not a doubt of triumph, it advanced with flying banners, defiant shouts, and steady tread. From the Rappahannock to the Blue Ridge, from the mountains to the Potomac, from the Potomac to the Susquehanna, they swept unmolested over a distance of two hundred miles; and at the beginning of last week, were just preparing to consummate their triumphant campaign. They contemned the Army of the Potomac, sneered at its late leader, and boasted that they could kick him and his

The Iron Brigade, a distinguished Federal unit, suffered severely at Gettysburg.

army around the continent. Their commander had already led them in five great campaigns, two of them in their inception offensive, two defensive, and one what JOMINI styles offensive-defensive; and all of them they regarded as victorious. There were but three things more needed to insure their final success, and these were—to route the Army of the Potomac, capture Washington, and hold their army on our soil until they could dictate terms of peace and enforce the recognition of the Southern Confederacy. By the seizure of Philadelphia and Baltimore, they could also thoroughly humiliate us, and after the fashion they established at York, could fill the coffers of the Confederacy, and gratify their army with plunder. Their task was simple and their assurance unbounded.

So at least it appeared last Monday. So it appeared on the first day of the month of July.

But their lately exultant and defiant army of invasion—where is it, and what is it now?

Defeated in the very opening of the campaign. Defeated in three great battles in which their whole force of infantry, cavalry and artillery was engaged. Defeated by the Army of the Potomac. Defeated by Gen. MEADE, who then fought his first battle at the head of the army. Defeated with tremendous loss in killed and wounded, in prisoners and in artillery; and defeated when defeat was destruction. Defeated after struggling for three days with a fury more than mortal and an energy madder than that of despair.

Thus it stood on Friday night, and thus upon our army rose the Fourth of July, ghastly but glorious—gloomy as death for the rebellion, but bright with hope for the country.

We are not yet informed what has become of LEE and the remnant of his army since Friday night. We know that they have fled somewhere among the mountains, and are probably trying to make their way to the Potomac, over which they would now be glad to bear drooping the banners which but late they bore to this side proudly flaunting. We know that our army holds Gettysburgh, Chambersburgh—that an expedition has been sent out from Hagerstown, which has destroyed the pontoon bridge over the Potomac at Williamsport, and that the river has risen—perhaps so high as to make a sudden and successful fording of it impossible. We can only hope that our reserve force, the Pennsylvania militia and the troops of Gen. HEINTZELMAN will consummate the work so gloriously executed by Gen. MEADE, and see that this insolent army of invasion never gets

A Confederate sharpshooter killed at Gettsyburg lies peacefully behind a stone breastwork.

back to Richmond or offers us any more trouble.

Through the brief campaign Gen. MEADE's genius has shone resplendent. Taking the army at the most inauspicious moment, and under the most inauspicious circumstances, he has, within four days of that on which he assumed command, achieved these results. It is the work of eminent military genius—of genius such as has not heretofore been displayed in this war. His adversary was a good soldier, who had the prestige of past success—though we have never seen any reason to class him as a great military chief, as some have been so hasty to do. But his strategy on this occasion was bold, and was only defeated by the more masterly and heroic combinations of Gen. MEADE. The choice of the President and the officers of the army has been amply confirmed and approved by the result of this great battle. He also had able cooperation in his corps, and division and brigade commanders, and every one of them achieved undying honor, and proved himself worthy of his position.

The Army of the Potomac too, will now, more than ever, receive the admiration of the country. Its struggles for two years have been unparalleled, and often unsuccessful. But it has never lost its faith nor its valor, nor its inflexibility of purpose. It has been willing ever to serve and to struggle, to fight always, everywhere, and under all circumstances, to the death. To all its other and perhaps greater claims to admiration, it now adds that of the most honorable and complete success. Its heroic struggle during the three first days of July will forever adorn the annals of war, and of the American Republic.

POSTSCRIPT.

MONDAY, 5 O'CLOCK P. M.

LATEST FROM GETTYSBURGH.

The Retreat of the Rebel Army.

Lee Said to be Fortifying in the Mountains.

HARRISBURGH, Monday, July 6—1 A. M.

Official information leaves no doubt that LEE's army is in full retreat. The line of retreat is not definitely known. It is either through Cashtown or Fairfield; whichever way it is, Gen. MEADE appears to have the advantage, as he is posted at Gettysburgh, and is pushing out forces both toward Newman's Cut, directly west, and to Fairfield, southwest. Nothing is known as to the exact situation. LEE is probably trying to retreat by both routes.

It is supposed that he does not know of the destruction of the pontoon bridge.

The position of the rebel army last night was, with his left near Hunterstown, and his right across the Emmettsburg road, thus forming a semicircle around Gettysburgh. Gen. MEADE operates from the centre, and LEE on the arc of a circle.

No information can be sent as to the movements of our army, but all our Generals are vigilant, and the troops in the best of spirits.

The New-York Times.

VOL. XII—NO. 3678. NEW-YORK, WEDNESDAY, JULY 8, 1863. PRICE THREE CENTS

VICKSBURG.

VICTORY!

Gen. Grant's Celebration of the Fourth of July.

Unconditional Surrender of the Rebel Stronghold.

THE NEWS OFFICIAL.

Dispatch from Admiral Porter to the Navy Department.

Great Rejoicing Throughout the Country.

WASHINGTON, Tuesday, July 7—1 P. M.

The following dispatch has just been received:

U. S. MISSISSIPPI SQUADRON,
FLAGSHIP BLACK HAWK, July 4, 1863.

Hon. Gideon Welles, Secretary of the Navy:

SIR : I HAVE THE HONOR TO INFORM YOU THAT VICKSBURGH SURRENDERED TO THE UNITED STATES FORCES ON THE 4TH OF JULY.

Very respectfully,

Your obedient servant,

D. D. PORTER,

Acting Rear-Admiral.

UNOFFICIAL REPORTS FROM CAIRO.

CAIRO, Ill., Tuesday, July 7.

The dispatch boat has just arrived here from Vicksburgh. She left at 10 o'clock on Sunday morning.

The passengers announce that Gen. PEMBERTON sent a flag of truce on the morning of the 4th of July, and offered to surrender if his men were allowed to march out.

Gen. GRANT is reported to have replied that no men should leave, except as prisoners of war.

Gen. PEMBERTON then, after consultation with his commanders, unconditionally surrendered.

This news is perfectly reliable.

THE HERO OF THE MISSISSIPPI VALLEY.

Ever hopefully, but with feverish interest, the loyal people of the North have been watching more than seven weeks for the great news of the fall of Vicksburgh, that at last came yesterday as the crowning sheaf in the full harvest of Independence Day Victories. Now that the victory is assured, our readers will doubtless like to read somewhat of the history of the man who is the instrument of its achievement—Maj.-Gen. ULYSSES S. GRANT, in whom has centered so much of interest and of hope.

Gen. GRANT, whose brilliant exploits since the commencement of hostilities have fairly won for him the title of hero of the Mississippi Valley, was born at Point Pleasant, Clairmont County, Ohio, April 27, 1822, and entered West Point Military Academy, from his native State, in 1839, where he graduated with honors July 1, 1843, with the brevet rank of second lieutenant, receiving his appointment of Second Lieutenant of the Fourth Infantry Sept. 30, 1845. Though but 40 years old, he has been oftener under fire than any other man living on this continent, excepting that great chieftain now reposing on his laurels, Lieut.-Gen. SCOTT. He was in every battle in Mexico that was possible for any one man to be in. He followed the victorious standard of Gen. TAYLOR on the Rio Grande, and was in the battles of Palo Alto, Resaca de la Palma and Monterey. He was with Gen. SCOTT at Vera Cruz, and participated in every battle from the Gulf to the City of Mexico. He was breveted first lieutenant September 8, 1847, for gallant and meritorious conduct at the battle of Molino del Rey, and on the 13th of the same month he was breveted captain for gallant and meritorious conduct at the battle of Chepultepec. He has received the baptism of fire. No young officer came out of the Mexican war with more distinction than GRANT, and the records of the War Department bear official testimony of his gallant and noble deeds. He resigned the service on the 31st of July, 1854, being then full captain in the Fourth Infantry, and in 1860, he settled at Galena, Illinois.

At the breaking out of the rebellion he was one of the first to offer his services to the Government, saying that, as he had been educated by the Government, that Government was entitled to his services in its time of perils. He was appointed Colonel of the Twenty-first regiment Illinois Volunteers, and went into actual service in Missouri, remaining with his regiment until promoted a Brigadier-General, with commission and rank from the 17th of May, 1861. His commands in Missouri were important, and he discharged every duty with great fidelity and advantage to the public service. With a military head and a military hand he everywhere evoked order from chaos. Military discipline, order and economy traveled in his path. In time, he was made a Brigadier-General, and intrusted with the important command of the district of Cairo, and how diligently, how faithfully, how satisfactorily he discharged all his duties, is well known to the country. While in that command, learning of a movement about being made by the rebels at Columbus to send out a large force to cut off Col. OGLESBY, who had gone into Missouri after that roaming bandit JEFF. THOMPSON, by a sudden and masterly stroke he fell upon Belmont, and after a brilliant and decisive action, in which he and his troops displayed great bravery, he broke up the rebel camp with great loss, and then returned to Cairo. The expedition was broken up, OGLESBY's command was saved, and everything was accomplished that was expected.

In time came the operations up the Cumberland and Tennessee, rivers, and by a singular coincidence, on the 29th day of January, 1862, without any suggestion from any source, Gen. GRANT and Commodore FOOTE, always acting in entire harmony, applied for permission to move up those rivers, which was granted. The gunboats and land forces moved up to Fort Henry. After that fort was taken, it was determined to attack Fort Donelson. The gunboats were to go round and up the Cumberland River, while the army was to move overland from Fort Henry to Fort Donelson.

The roads were the worst ever known, and almost any other General, or any other troops, would have despaired of moving. But they did move. The country knows the result—Donelson fell. The enemy, 20,000 strong, behind his intrenchments, succumbed before the unrelenting bravery and vigor of our troops, no more than 28,000 being engaged. We took there, more than 16,000 prisoners.

While the capture of Donelson filled the country with joy, there was a cruel disposition to withhold from Gen. GRANT the meed of gratitude and praise so justly his due. Captious criticisms were indulged in that he did not make the attack properly, and that if he had done differently the work might have been better accomplished. Success could be no test of merit with him. And there was a more grievous suggestion touching his habits that has infused itself in the public mind everywhere. There never was a more atrocious slander upon a brave and noble-minded man, for he never indulges in the use of intoxicating liquor, and is an example of temperance. The battle of Pittsburgh Landing was his next engagement. This he fought with forty thousand men

Sketch by Theodore R. Davis shows General Pemperton (right) discussing surrender terms with General Grant.

Confederate artillery defending Vicksburg was well-entrenched.

against eighty thousand of the flower of the rebel army, led by their most distinguished generals. The contest, though a bloody one, resulted in a signal victory for our arms, as on the evening of the second day's fighting the enemy commenced a retreat, which soon degenerated into a perfect rout. Their loss was three to our two in men, and in much greater proportion in the demoralization of an army which follows a defeat.

The triumphal march of Gen. GRANT from Port Gibson to the Big Black, and his five great victories, as he swept through Jackson, the capital of Mississippi, prior to his investment of Vicksburgh, need not be a passing allusion. Every incident of the brilliant and rapid campaign is well remembered.

In the face of what seemed insurmountable obstacles, he has for weary weeks prosecuted the siege of this obstinately defiant city—conducting his operations with courage, sagacity and humility—until at last complete success has rewarded his energy, his genius and his skill.

Vicksburgh is taken—its strong garrison has unconditionally surrendered. All honor to Gen. GRANT and to the valorous army that he rasied to victory.

THE NEWS IN WASHINGTON.

Great Jubilation—Speeches by the President, Secretary Stanton, Gen. Halleck and Others.

Special Dispatch to the New-York Times.

WASHINGTON, Tuesday, July 7.

The Cabinet was in regular session to-day. Admiral PORTER's Vicksburgh dispatch was received by Secretary WELLES, and read to the President. The news immediately spread throughout the city, creating intense and joyous excitement. Flags were displayed from all the Departments and crowds assembled with cheers. Secretary STANTON issued an order for a salute of one hundred guns.

The fall of Vicksburgh, conjointly with the Gettys-

burgh successes, is regarded as the turning point in the war. The President and high officials express a determination that the campaign shall not slacken off in consequence, but be carried on with renewed vigor. This sentiment is urged upon them by Messrs. HAMLIN, WILSON, CHANDLER, WASHBURNE and other prominent loyalists now in town.

The President gratulates himself on his inflexible resistance to the efforts once made to induce him to remove Gen. GRANT. He always believed in GRANT's genius and energy, and is now rewarded for his decision in his favor. Hon. ELIHU WASHBURNE, GRANT's nearest personal friend, who defended him last Winter in the House, is overjoyed at the result of the siege.

REJOICING IN NEW-YORK.

ALBANY, Tuesday, July 7.

By order of the Adjutant-General, two salutes of thirty-four guns each were fired to-day—one in honor of our victory in Pennsylvania, and the other for the fall of Vicksburgh. To-night there is an impromptu demonstration by the citizens. Guns are exploding, bells ringing, and with music and fireworks, the demonstration will be kept up until a late hour by an immense gathering of both sexes.

SYRACUSE, Tuesday, July 7.

A grand impromptu celebration is taking place here, to-night, in honor of our victories. There is a mass-meeting in Hanover-square. A salute of 100 guns is thundering. All the bells of the city are ringing. There is a parade by the Davis Guards, and fireworks, bonfires, and illuminations flame in all the principal streets. Such a scene of enthusiasm and rejoicing was never known.

UTICA, Tuesday, July 7.

The fall of Vicksburgh has been celebrated here by the ringing of bells, firing of cannon, and every display of popular joy.

REJOICING IN NEW-JERSEY

BURLINGTON, N. J., Tuesday, July 7.

The glorious news of the surrender of Vicksburgh was received here amid the ringing of the church bells and a salute of one hundred guns. The most intense enthusiasm prevails. The Union League rooms and several private residences are illuminated.

REJOICING IN MASSACHUSETTS.

BOSTON, Tuesday, July 7.

The news of the surrender of Vicksburgh appeared to cause more joyous excitement in Boston than any previous event of the war. Bells were rung, cheers given, and congratulations exchanged generally.

At Newburyport the bells were rung, and a salute of one hundred guns fired.

Dispatches from many quarters describe similar demonstrations of joy and gratitude for the glorious result.

REJOICING IN PHILADELPHIA.

PHILADELPHIA, Tuesday, July 7—2 P. M.

The State House bell is ringing a joyful peal over the capture of Vicksburgh.

All the fire-bells in the city are also now ringing, by direction of the Mayor, sent through the police telegraph.

PHILADELPHIA, Tuesday, July 7.

The newspaper offices are illuminated this evening. The *Ledger* building has stars placed along the entire front. The *North American* has the word "Victory." The *Bulletin* and other offices are tastefully decorated in honor of the victory. Numerous private dwellings and other edifices are illuminated.

REJOICING IN NEW-HAVEN.

NEW-HAVEN, Conn., Tuesday, July 7.

There is great rejoicing in this city over the news of the capture of Vicksburgh.

A National salute is now being fired upon the Public Square by direction of the Mayor.

The New-York Times.

VOL. XII—NO. 3681.   NEW-YORK, SATURDAY, JULY 11, 1863.   PRICE THREE CENTS.

FROM THE SOUTH.

Rebel Reports of the Battle at Gettysburgh.

A Dispatch Worthy of Baron Munchausen.

The National Army One Hundred and Seventy-five Thousand Strong.

An Overwhelming Rebel Victory---40,000 Prisoners Captured.

Gen. Grant "Feeling the Pressure of Johnston's Iron Hand."

MOVEMENTS ON THE PENINSULA

BALTIMORE, Friday, July 10.

The Richmond *Dispatch*, of Wednesday, July 8, contains a leader on the battle of Gettysburgh. It says:

"We feel as well assured that Gen. LEE, if he has met the enemy in a pitched battle, has inflicted a terrible defeat upon them, as we do that we are living, breathing, sentient beings."

The *Dispatch* then alludes to a telegraphic dispatch announcing a great battle being fought on Sunday last, in which the Yankees were whipped with a loss of 60,000 men, and winds up as follows:

"We already begin to see glimpses of peace if this telegram only prove half true. But let us have no peace which we do not dictate ourselves."

The *Dispat* contains but one short editorial on Vicksburgh, which is as follows:

"It is evident that GRANT begins to feel the pressure of the iron hand which JOHNSTON has cast around him. Everything now depends on skill and valor, and in these qualities we have always been the master of the Yankees."

The following telegrams are also from the *Dispatch*. They are decidedly rich when the facts are taken into consideration:

MARTINSBURGH, Va., Monday, July 6.

On Saturday night our centre fell back, drawing the enemy from their works. Gens. EWELL and LONGSTREET flanked the enemy and gained the heights. A general fight ensued yesterday, in which the enemy were routed and LEE captured 40,000 prisoners, according to all accounts. Gen. KEMPER was killed. There is fighting at Williamsport, between IMBODEN's cavalry and several regiments of infantry, and a division of Yankee cavalry under PLEASANTON.

MARTINSBURGH, Va., Monday, July 6.

The latest, which seems to be reliable, is that the fight was continued on Sunday, and was the bloodiest of the war. Gen. HILL fell back in the centre, causing the enemy to believe that he was retreating. The enemy upon this advanced. Then EWELL and LONGSTREET advanced their right and left wings, surrounding the enemy. We then took the heights for which we have been contending, and captured 40,000 prisoners. They refused to be paroled. Gen. PICKETT's division is now guarding the prisoners to Martinsburgh.

The Richmond *Enquirer*, of the 8th inst., has received the following account of the battle of Gettysburgh:

THE BATTLE OF GETTYSBURGH.

Our loss is estimated at 10,000 at the battle of Get-

tysburgh. Between three and four thousand of our wounded arrived at Winchester, July 7. Gens. ARMISTEAD, BARKSDALE, GARNETT and KEMPER are killed. Gens. SCALES, PENDER, JONES, HETH, ANDERSON, HAMPTON and HOOD, are wounded. The Yankee army is estimated at 175,000 men. The fighting lasted four days and is regarded as the severest of the war, and the slaughter unprecedented. The enemy are said to have fought well. We captured 40,000 prisoners.

The following items are taken from the *Dispatch* of the 8th inst.:

FROM NORTH CAROLINA.

GOLDSBORO, N. C., Tuesday, July 7.

Letters from reliable sources, dated Winston last night, say that a courier who has just arrived reports an engagement progressing between the retreating enemy and our forces near Free Bridge. It is supposed that the enemy are cut off.

FROM VICKSBURGH AND VICINITY.

BOLTON STATION,
Via JACKSON, Miss., Sunday, July 5.

Yesterday, about 12 o'clock, the Yankee cavalry crossed the Big Black at Birdrong's Ferry, and advanced into the interior, but were promptly met by WHITFIELD's brigade, and driven back across the river.

A courier, just in from Edwards' Depot, says the entire command of Gen. OSTERHAUS crossed the Big Black near that place last night. If so we will have warm work to-day. GRANT is evidently feeling very uneasy in regard to events transpiring in his rear. There was very little firing at Vicksburgh yesterday.

[NOTE—I send the above to show how little they knew at Jackson on the 5th, what had really occurred at Vicksburgh on the 4th.—REPORTER.]

OUR FORCES ON THE PENINSULA.

The *Dispatch* says, speaking editorially of the movements around Richmond:

"The only information we have of the enemy's movements north of this city is that brought by the trains over the Fredericksburgh Road, which arrived last night for the first time for nearly a week past. They report that they could hear nothing of the Yankees either at Hanover Junction or at the South Anna Bridge, and that the roads, the Central and Fredericksburgh, are now unobstructed.

A citizen of King William County, who has been exiled from his home since its occupation by the band of marauders under DIX, went on a scout to that county on Monday last and obtained some interesting particulars of the whereabouts and movements of the Yankee army of plunderers. His statement is that their headquarters are at Mangolick Church, and that their squads of thieves are scattered throughout the country, taking whatever they can find, and destroying whatever is not convenient for them to remove. They are also endeavoring to incite the negroes to insurrection, promising to make them officers in company organizations as a temptation to them to quit their masters. The gentleman to whom we alluded learned that one of his own negro men had been tendered the command of a company as an inducement to quit his home. The negroes under these influences are said to be very insubordinate, and some are even boasting of their freedom and ability to maintain it.

FRESHET IN THE JAMES.

There is nothing of special interest in the local columns of the *Dispatch*, except an account of a heavy freshet in the James River. Nearly all the cellars on Main-street, opposite the market, are full of water.

The Richmond *Whig* of the 6th instant, contains some items of interest.

The *Whig* discredits entirely the Federal reports of a rebel reverse in Pennsylvania, insisting that from "the subdued tone" of our dispatches it is evident we have been "very seriously worsted." In another place the *Whig* facetiously calls the rebel offensive movement "a little summer tour of the boys into Maryland and Pennsylvania;" and adds that Richmond having been compelled, in the absence of troops, to defend herself, has "shown her teeth" in true mastiff style. Upon this point it continues:

RICHMOND SHOWING HER TEETH.

A party of Yankee rapscallions, hearing of her unprotected condition, have crept up to the White House with the intention of insulting and robbing

her. They don't know the old lady. Her quick ear caught the sound of their fumbling and fooling around her back yard, and being unwilling to part with her babies and niggers, besides having her meat-house broken open, she has bared her arm, caught up the broomstick and poker, and gone forth to meet the villains at the garden palings and knock them on the head. We saw her when she went out. She looked very unlike the quiet and genteel dame whom we have known for some years past. We may be mistaken, but the indications were that she had so far lost her temper that she intended to fight. Her teeth were set, her eye flashed, her nostrils were dilated, her brow was frowning. She looked glorious in her anger. In fact, she looked dangerous. We make no predictions, but we are really very much afraid that if the robbers don't go away she will hurt somebody.

MORALS IN RICHMOND.

The *Whig* upon another subject, is less facetious:

"Under the new policy of granting licenses indiscriminately to all who apply, a great number of drinking-houses have been established, in the evident detriment of public morals. They spring up like mushrooms in every corner, and in places where their presence is offensive to the refined portions of the community. It is even proposed to establish one on Governor-street, in the room formerly occupied by the High Constable. This street is much used by ladies, and one of the most quiet in the city."

THE FAMILY OF GEN. A. SIDNEY JOHNSTON.

The *Whig* says that Gen. GIDEON J. PILLOW has issued an appeal for aid to the family of Gen. A. SIDNEY JOHNSTON, who are in distress and destitution.

GEN. HOOKER.

The *Whig* has an article on Gen. HOOKER, from which we extract the following:

"A distinguished gentleman of the South had occasion some years ago to spend four months in the saddle on the Pacific coast. His business being of a public character, he was assigned a cavalry escort of 25 men, under charge of two United States officers. Those two officers happened to be HOOKER and STONEMAN, the one now commanding 'the finest army on the planet,' and the other at the head of all the cavalry in that army. With these officers he spent every hour of every day for the four months, and slept by their side on the grass at night. He necessarily came to know them about as well as it is possible for one person to know another. Mentioning the circumstance to us, he said of STONEMAN, that he was never more thoroughly convinced of anything connected with personal character than that he was a coward—an arrant coward. HOOKER he readily discovered to be a vain, conceited, pretentious, boastful fellow, of moderate capacity and astonishly ignorant. He had never seen a person of the education implied by graduating at West Point whose general information and scholarship were so limited. He knew nothing of the literature and history even of his own profession—of famous wars, campaigns and battles, ancient or modern, or of the most noted commanders or strategists. But he pretended to know everything, and always insisted that there was a better way of doing anything than the way in which it had been done or was proposed to be done. Not long after this excursion HOOKER resigned his commission in the army, and fell into such disreputable ways of life in San Francisco that the gentleman to whom we refer ceased to recognize him as an acquaintance."

THE REBELS AND ENGLAND.

The *Whig* has no hopes of help from Great Britain. In the course of a long article, after speaking of the hopes of British interference which were at first entertained, it says:

"The proportion of Confederates who could, until very recently, have been made to believe that English animosity to the South was so bitter as to override law, treaty stipulations, common justice and humanity, was as one to one million. Two years have produced a vast change. Admiration for England has died out utterly; respect is fast disappearing. With the facts before them, the people of the South are compelled to believe that the Government of Great Britain is hostile to them, and that the people of Great Britain, though aware of this hostility, prefer the Administration of Lord PALMERSTON to any other."

THE REBEL HOPES IN THE LATE CAMPAIGN.

A letter from a rebel officer in LEE's army, written at Williamsport, June 25, and published in the *Whig*, says:

"You may rely upon it that the deeds of this campaign will transcend in glory those of all others previous. Gen. LEE and his Lieutenants are said to be in a high flow of spirits.

The demonstrations favorable to us in Williamsport utterly astonished me. I was here in the Maryland campaign of last year. Then every house was shut, every door and window closed, and the place seemed possessed by solitude; but this evening the streets were literally lined with ladies and many men, who shouted and cheered and waved their handkerchiefs to every Confederate that passed.

You can form no idea of the immense droves of cattle and horses that are being sent to the rear from our advanced forces in Pennsylvania. The supplies in this country are represented to be nearly inexhaustible."

The New-York Times.

VOL. XII—NO. 3683.   NEW-YORK, TUESDAY, JULY 14, 1863.   PRICE THREE CENTS.

THE MOB IN NEW-YORK.

Resistance to the Draft—Rioting and Bloodshed.

Conscription Offices Sacked and Burned.

Private Dwellings Pillaged and Fired.

AN ARMORY AND A HOTEL DESTROYED.

Colored People Assaulted—An Unoffending Black Man Hung.

The Tribune Office Attacked—The Colored Orphan Asylum Ransacked and Burned—Other Outrages and Incidents.

A DAY OF INFAMY AND DISGRACE.

Unchecked mobs roamed the streets in New York in protest of the Union draft.

THE ATTACK ON THE ARMORY IN SECOND-AVENUE.

At about 4 o'clock the crowd proceeded from the scene of their exploits in Lexington-avenue and Forty-fourth-street, to the armory situated on the corner of Second-avenue and Twenty-first-street. The building was a large four-story one, and was occupied for the manufacture of rifles and carbines for the Government. In the early part of the day the Police authorities had placed in the building a large number of Policemen, consisting principally of the Broadway Squad. Their instructions were to protect the building and the property therein, and to resist with force any attempt of the invaders to enter the premises. The mob on Second-avenue, Twenty-first and Twenty-second streets rapidly increased, and at the time the first attempt was made to force the doors of the building, it amounted to from three to four thousand, the greater part of whom were boys. At this time some 18 or 20 men, followed by scores of youngsters, made an attempt to force the doors of the armory on Twenty-first-street. The doors were burst open by means of heavy sledges, and the crowd made a rush to enter the building. Those in charge of the building, acting under instructions, fired upon those who were entering, and four or five were wounded. One man, named MICHAEL VANEY, was shot through the heart, and died immediately. VANEY was a mechanic, and worked in the Morgan Iron Works. He was about 40 years of age, and resided in Twenty-third-street, between Avenues A and B. The other persons who were shot are not regarded as being seriously injured.

The shooting of VANEY, who was one of the ringleaders of the party making the attack, was the signal for a general onslaught upon the armory. Loud and deep were the curses uttered against the officers who had shot their leader, and for the next hour the paving-stones flew thick and fast, and not until the last pane of glass in the windows of the building had been broken, did they desist. It is proper to remark that nearly all those who threw the paving-stones were boys under twelve years of age. During all this time efforts of a desperate character were being made to fire the building. The doors on Second-avenue were finally forced open, and an excited multitude tried to effect an entrance. They were promptly repelled by those inside. Very soon they received reinforcements and again they made the attempt to enter, some of them with lighted torches in their hands. Meantime a dispatch was received by the officers of the Broadway Squad in charge of the building, from Police Headquarters, to the effect that inasmuch as it was impossible to reinforce them, and the attacking party so greatly outnumbered them, they must retire in the best manner they could. In a short time, they were all safely outside the building, with the exception of two of their number who were pelted on the head with brickbats; one of them was very seriously injured. The excitement against all policemen, at this time, ran so high that it was regarded a most hazardous undertaking for one to show himself to the excited populace. The fact that there was a private entrance in the rear was a most fortunate circumstance for them.

The police having vacated the premises, the mob found it comparatively an easy task to enter and fire the building. In fifteen minutes from the time the crowd had undisputed possession of it, the entire structure was a mass of flame. About half a dozen men remained inside as a sort of forlorn hope, and when all escape for them by the ordinary ways had been cut off by the flames, the poor fellows let themselves down from the windows of the third story in the best manner they could. One took hold of the window sill, and another slid down to his feet and then dropped to the pavement. In this way they all managed to escape; but two of them had each a leg broken, one had his skull so much fractured that he is not expected to recover, and another was so bruised and injured that when he was taken into a neighboring drug store life seemed extinct. Amid the excitement and confusion our reporter was unable to obtain the names of any of those who were thus injured.

BURNING OF THE ORPHAN ASYLUM FOR COLORED CHILDREN.

The Orphan Asylum for Colored Children was visited by the mob about 4 o'clock. This Institution is situated on Fifth-avenue, and the building, with the grounds and gardens adjoining, extended from Forty-third to Forty-fourth-street. Hundreds, and perhaps thousands of the rioters, the majority of whom were women and children, entered the premises, and in the most excited and violent manner they ransacked and plundered the building from cellar to garret. The building was located in the most pleasant and healthy portion of the City. It was purely a charitable institution. In it there are on an average 600 or 800 homeless colored orphans. The building was a large four-story one, with two wings of three stories each.

When it became evident that the crowd designed to destroy it, a flag of truce appeared on the walk opposite, and the principals of the establishment made an appeal to the excited populace, but in vain.

Here it was that Chief-Engineer DECKER showed himself one of the bravest among the brave. After the entire building had been ransacked, and every article deemed worth carrying away had been taken—and this included even the little garments for the orphans, which were contributed by the benevolent ladies of this City—the premises were fired on the first floor. Mr. DECKER did all he could to prevent the flames from being kindled, but when he was overpowered by superior numbers, with his own hands he scattered the brands and effectually extinguished the flames. A second attempt was made, and this time in three different parts of the house. Again he succeeded, with the aid of half a dozen of his men, in defeating the incendiaries. The mob became highly exasperated at his conduct, and threatened to take his life if he repeated the act. On the front steps of the building he stood up amid an infuriated and half-drunken mob of two thousand, and begged of them to do nothing so disgraceful to humanity as to burn a benevolent institution, which had for its object nothing but good.

He said it would be a lasting disgrace to them and to the City of New-York.

These remarks seemed to have no good effect upon them, and meantime, the premises were again fired—this time in all parts of the house. Mr. DECKER, with his few brave men again extinguished the flames. This last act brought down upon him the vengeance of all who were bent on the destruction of the asylum, and but for the fact, that some firemen surrounded him, and boldly said that Mr. DECKER could not be taken except over their bodies, he would have been dispatched on the spot. The institution was destined to be burned, and after an hour and a half of labor on the part of the mob, it was in flames in all parts. Three or four persons were horribly bruised by the falling walls, but the names we could not ascertain. There is now scarcely one brick left upon another of the Orphan Asylum.

ATTACK ON THE TRIBUNE OFFICE.

During the greater part of the day, a crowd, composed principally of overgrown boys, amused themselves by going around to the various newspaper offices down town, cheering the bulletins which announced the progress of the riot in the upper part of the City, groaning the editors of such journals as were deemed obnoxious by the mob, and chasing and beating every person of color who chanced to make his appearance. The *Tribune*, as a matter of course, came in for the principal share of the groans, and it is but fair to add, that the *Daily News* monopolized the cheers. Various hints were given out by the rioters that the *Tribune* would be attacked in the evening, but they were not credited, or if they were, no preparations appear to have been made to repel it. About 7 o'clock, however, the crowd of boys began to be swelled by a different class of roughs, who appeared on the ground with clubs in their hands, and from their appearance, had evidently been engaged in the more bloody work up town. They immediately gathered around the *Tribune* office and commenced a series of the most unearthly groans and demoniac yells. In a few moments one of the more forward among them commenced an attack upon the door of the publication office, which was locked, but which soon gave way to the pressure of the mob, who, amid the crashing of broken doors and windows, rushed in as quick as lightning. In a moment more files of the *Tribune* were thrown out to the crowd and torn and scattered to the winds. In less than five minutes the office was completely gutted, and the desks and counters upset and broken. At length a platoon of the First Ward Police came rushing up Nassau-street, and on seeing them the mob, which numbered not less than four hundred men and boys, ran like so many sheep, leaving Printing-house-square, in less than three minutes, almost as clear of people as it is of a Sunday morning. It was a striking illustration of the cowardice of a mob when confronted by a handful of determined officers of the law. Several shots were fired by the policemen at ringleaders of the mob—but, so far as is known, none of them took effect. One of the policemen was also shot at by a rioter, the ball taking effect in the back. The wound is serious, but it is thought not dangerous. Before leaving the office, the rioters set fire to the building, but it was extinguished by a policeman before much damage was done.

The New-York Times.

VOL. XII—NO. 3684.   NEW-YORK, WEDNESDAY, JULY 15, 1863.   PRICE THREE CENTS.

THE ESCAPE OF LEE.

Nearly His Whole Army Across the Potomac.

The Movement Effected Monday and Monday Night.

A Bridge of Flat-Boats the Means of Crossing.

His Intrenchments Found Evacuated Yesterday Morning.

PROMPT MOVEMENT OF KILPATRICK.

A Whole Brigade of Lee's Rear Guard Captured.

Two Pieces of Artillery Also Secured.

OFFICIAL DISPATCH FROM GEN. MEADE.

WASHINGTON, Tuesday, July 14.

The following dispatch has just been received:

HEADQUARTERS, ARMY OF THE POTOMAC, }
Tuesday, July 14—3 P. M. }

H. W. Halleck, General-in-Chief:

My cavalry now occupy Falling Waters, having overtaken and captured a brigade of infantry, 1,500 strong, two guns, two caissons, two battle-flags and a large number of small arms. The enemy are all across the Potomac.   G. G. MEADE.

SPECIAL FROM ST. JAMES' COLLEGE.

ST. JAMES' COLLEGE, }
FOUR MILES FROM WILLIAMSPORT, }
Tuesday Morning, July 14—10 A. M. }

The enemy has crossed the river.

This morning at daylight a scout came in and reported that the enemy had been crossing their troops all night.

His statement was not fully credited, but Gen. SEDGWICK'S corps on the centre was ordered to push forward. It advanced to the line of the enemy's works and found them empty.

At 5 A. M. Gen. KILPATRICK, anticipating his orders by two hours, moved out on the enemy's left and found their strong position, which commanded the Williamsport road, evacuated.

There has not been a gun fired. The wily rebel chieftain has crept stealthily away from under our very noses, while we were digging ditches for a line of defence.

The Second corps is now within two miles of Williamsport, and can throw shells into that place.

The rebels crossed on a bridge of flat boats, which they have built since they arrived at Williamsport. High water did not affect their proceedings. Their line of defence served them the excellent purpose of concealing their movement until they could safely retreat.   L. L. CROUNSE.

Federal troops arrive at the Potomac River, long after Lee's troops have escaped.

SPECIAL FROM HEADQUARTERS.

HEADQUARTERS ARMY OF THE POTOMAC, }
Tuesday, July 14—9 A. M. }

The enemy withdrew to the Virginia side of the river last night. Citizens state that all day Sunday he was getting over portions of his artillery and baggage trains.

The rebels crossed by means of bridges constructed of lumber taken from houses in Williamsport. Flat-boats were also used.

The various Union Corps Commanders reported, at an early hour this morning, that the enemy had evacuated their front. Cavalry reconnoissances were then immediately pushed forward.   WHIT.

FROM ANOTHER CORRESPONDENT.

HEADQUARTERS, ARMY OF THE POTOMAC, }
Tuesday, July 14. }

Lee's army withdrew from their position around Williamsport yesterday and last night, and recrossed the Potomac by a pontoon bridge at Falling Waters, and flat-boats at the Williamsport Ferry.

A portion of Gen. PLEASANTON'S cavalry entered Williamsport at 7 o'clock this morning, and captured many prisoners. LEE had previously sent over all his plunder, trains, &c.

A general movement was ordered this morning, and our columns were in motion at an early hour, but found the intrenchments vacated.   T. B.

THE POSITION ON MONDAY.

BALTIMORE, Tuesday, July 14.

A special dispatch from Hagerstown, dated July 13, P. M., says:

"No important change has occurred in the position of the armies. Our army has closely followed the rebels into their own position, and a battle may occur at any moment. It has rained heavily during yesterday and to-day, and there can be no abatement in the height of the river. Residents from the vicinity of Williamsport, who have reached here, say the rebels are building flatboats and have established a rope ferry across the river.

Gen. COUCH'S Pennsylvania troops are rapidly moving forward. Reinforcements from other points are also within reach. If a battle occurs at present it will undoubtedly be a severe one, and contested with savage resolution on both sides. The rebels keep very quiet, and, except the shelling of the woods and occasional picket firing, all is quiet.

KILPATRICK, in his dash into Funkstown yesterday, captured 200 prisoners who have been sent to Frederick.

The rebels shelled our pickets this morning, but no reply was made by us. Two of the Maryland brigade were wounded.

Our forces now hold a strongly intrenched position and Gen. MEADE can take his own time to give battle.

The rebels were driven yesterday out of some rifle pits and forced back into a thick wood on the Williamsport pike. To-day they occupied the woods in line of battle, with cannon in position.

The Seventh Maryland regiment, Col. WEBSTER yesterday participated in the charge on the rifle-pits. The Maryland brigade is incorporated with the First army corps. Gen. KENLY commands the Third division of that corps, and Gen. DUSHAW the brigade.

There is the strongest impression that the rebels cannot get across the river."

Editorials

The Raging Riot—Its Character, and the True Attitude Toward It.

The mob in our City is still rampant. Though the increasing display of armed force has done something to check its more flagrant outrages, it is yet wild with fury, and panting for fresh havoc. The very fact of its being withstood seems only to give it, for the time, new malignity; just as the wild beast never heaves with darker rage than when he begins to see that his way is barred. The monster grows more dangerous as he grows desperate. More than ever, everything depends on the energy and vigilance of the authorities, and the sustaining cooperation of all true men. Official duty and public spirit should supremely rule the hour. The man in public place, or in private place, who falters in this dread crisis should stand accursed.

We trust that Gov. SEYMOUR does not mean to falter. We believe that in his heart he really intends to vindicate the majesty of the law, according to his sworn obligations. But,

Governor Horatio Seymour

in the name of the dignity of Government and of pub'ic safety, we protest against any further indulgence in the sort of speech with which he yesterday sought to propitiate the mob. Entreaties and promises are not what the day calls for. No official, however high his position, can make them, without bringing public authority into contempt. This monster is to be met with a sword, and that only. He is not to be placated with a sop; and, if he were, it would only be to make him all the more insatiate hereafter. In the name of all that is sacred in law and all that is precious in society, let there be no more of this. There is force enough at the command of Gov. SEYMOUR to maintain civil authority. He will do it. He cannot but do it. He is a ruined man if he fails to do it. This mob is not our master. It is not to be compounded with by paying black mail. It is not to be supplicated and sued to stay its hand. It is to be defied, confronted, grappled with, prostrated, crushed. The Government of the State of New-York is its master, not its slave ; its ruler, and not its minion.

It is too true that there are public journals who try to dignify this mob by some respectable appellation. The *Herald* characterizes it as the people, and the *World* as the laboring men of the City. These are libels that ought to have paralyzed the fingers that penned them. It is ineffably infamous to attribute to the people, or to the laboring men of this metropolis, such hideous barbarism as this horde has been displaying. The people of New-York and the laboring men of New-York are not incendiaries, nor robbers, nor assassins. They do not hunt down men whose only offence is the color God gave them; they do not chase, and insult, and beat women; they do not pillage an asylum for orphan children, and burn the very roof over those orphans' heads. They are civilized beings, valuing law and respecting decency; and they regard with unqualified abhorrence the doings of the tribe of savages that have sought to bear rule in their midst.

This mob is not the people, nor does it belong to the people. It is for the most part made up of the very vilest elements of the City. It has not even the poor merit of being

what mobs usually are—the product of mere ignorance and passion. They talk, or rather did talk at first, of the oppressiveness of the Conscription law; but three-fourths of those who have been actively engaged in violence have been boys and young men under twenty years of age, and not at all subject to the Conscription. Were the Conscription law to be abrogated to-morrow, the controlling inspiration of the mob would remain all the same. It comes from sources quite independent of that law, or any other—from malignant hate toward those in better circumstances, from a craving for plunder, from a love of commotion, from a barbarous spite against a different race, from a disposition to bolster up the failing fortunes of the Southern rebels. All of these influences operate in greater or less measure upon any person engaged in this general defiance of law; and all combined have generated a composite monster more hellish than the triple-headed Cerberus.

It doubtless is true that the Conscription, or rather its preliminary process, furnished the occasion for the outbreak. This was so, simply because it was the most plausible pretext for commencing open defiance. But it will be a fatal mistake to assume that this pretext has but to be removed to restore quiet and contentment. Even if it be allowed that this might have been true at the outset, it is completely false now. A mob, even though it may start on a single incentive, never sustains itself for any time whatever on any one stimulant. With every hour it lives, it gathers new passions, and dashes after new objects. If you undertake to negotiate with it, you find that what it raved for yesterday, it has no concern for to-day. It is as inconstant as it is headstrong. The rabble greeted with cheers the suppliant attitude of Gov. SEYMOUR, and his promises with reference to the Conscription law, but we have yet to hear that they thereupon abandoned their outrages. The fact stands that they are to-night, while we write, still infuriate, still insatiate.

You may as well reason with the wolves of the forest as with these men in their present mood. It is quixotic and suicidal to attempt it. The duties of the executive officers of this State and City are not to debate, or negotiate, or supplicate, but to *execute the laws.* To execute means to enforce *by authority.* This is their *only* official business. Let it be promptly and sternly entered upon with all the means now available, and it cannot fail of being carried through to an overwhelming triumph of public order. It may cost blood—much of it perhaps ; but it will be a lesson to the public enemies, whom we always have and must have in our midst, that will last for a generation. Justice and mercy, this time, unite in the same behest :—*Give them grape, and a plenty of it.*

The Conscription Must be Enforced.

Not only must this infamous and dastardly mob be put down, but it must be balked in the object for which it was gotten up. It was ostensibly to defeat the enforcement of the Conscription. The Conscription is a necessity ; the Conscription is a law ; the Conscription is just. It is demanded for the suppression of the Southern rebellion; it

is needed to fill up our heroic but shattered regiments ; the country called for it, and acquiesced in its passage ; the army is a unit in urging its enforcement. It is the justest mode of raising an army—just to the people of every class and condition, poor and rich, black and white. No class or order of citizens is exempt from its operation—even poor clergymen, if drafted, being compelled to shoulder their musket.

This mob should in no way be allowed to interfere with its enforcement. If a few hundred desperadoes, backed up by a few thousand misguided and deceived men, may violently nullify a law of such grand and wide-spread scope and value as this—if they are permitted to nullify and violently overthrow any law of the land, then all law everywhere and finally is at an end. We have not only no Union, but no Government, no society, no civil order. We have anarchy in its most frightful form. We have the condition of things which this great City has suffered from for the last two days made permanent. We shall have faction giving battle to faction, class warring upon class, sect fighting sect, interest contending with interest, knavery with honesty, lawlessness with legality—not in the old arenas, not on the forum and through the Press, with the weapons of reason and justice, but with ball, bayonet, bowie-knife and slung-shot, amid blood, carnage and rapine.

We cannot afford to yield the Conscription to this mob. The mob is an additional argument for its enforcement. The Government cannot afford to suspend a general law, intended to apply to the whole country, because of a local riot sprang by a few bad schemers in this City. The Conscription has already been enforced in Massachusetts, Rhode Island and Connecticut ; and it is in the order of enforcement in every State of the Union. Can a scheme so extensive as this, so generally accepted everywhere, be thwarted by such a mob as has disgraced this City for two days?

We are astonished that Gov. SEYMOUR should hold out hopes that this will be the case. We are grieved that he should so far justify the mob as to admit that it will prove successful in its lawless object. In each of his three short speeches in the City yesterday he put forth that this would be the case. Gov. SEYMOUR is false to his responsibilities, to his duties, and to his office, in paltering with the mob in this way. He is false to the country of which he is a citizen, to the laws of which he is the constituted upholder, to public order of which he is the guardian. Such talk is an encouragement to this mob; it is an encouragement to all mobs. Coming from a man in his position, it foretokens no good to the City or the country. His duty is to enforce law and especially when there are organized attempts to overthrow it by violence.

The conscription, we repeat, cannot be abrogated in this City because of the mob. Its temporary suspense for a few days, until order is restored, is, of course, necessary. But, on the restoration of order, its execution must here be proceeded with at all hazards, as it has been successfully executed elsewhere.

The New-York Times.

VOL. XII—NO. 3685.   NEW-YORK, THURSDAY, JULY 16, 1863.   PRICE THREE CENTS.

ANOTHER DAY OF RIOTING.

CONTINUATION OF MOB RULE.

A PROCLAMATION FROM THE MAYOR.

A Morning and an Evening Fight--The Streets Raked with Canister.

A Large Number of Rioters Killed.

Several Soldiers Killed and Wounded.

THE EVENING MOB ARMED WITH RIFLES.

They Pick Off the Soldiers from the Housetops.

Citizen Volunteers Killed--Col. Jardine Wounded.

MORE NEGROES HUNG.

The Contagion Spreading---Riotous Demonstrations in Westchester County, Brooklyn, Jersey City, Staten Island and Jamaica.

Increased Preparations by the Authorities.

INCIDENTS, CASUALTIES, &c., &c.

The ravages of the mob which commenced its diabolical career on Monday are not yet ended, and it is impossible to say at the hour of going to press this morning whether the worst has yet been seen. All through Tuesday night marauding bands of plunderers in greater or less numbers, continued to commit their depredations in various parts of the City, but at daylight yesterday morning they had generally dispersed, and there was a fair prospect of a speedy restoration of quiet and order. The authorities, both State and military, appeared to consider the riot as substantially subdued, and after a consultation early in the forenoon, between Mayor OPDYKE, Gov. SEYMOUR and Gen WOOL, at the St. Nicholas Hotel, the following proclamation was issued from the Mayor's office:

PROCLAMATION OF THE MAYOR.

To the Citizens of New-York:

I am happy to announce to you that the riot which for two days has disgraced our City, has been in good measure subjected to the control of the public authorities It would not have interrupted your peace for a day but for the temporary absence of all our organized local militia. What now remain of the mob are fragments prowling about for plunder; and, for the purpose of meeting these, and saving the military and police from the exhaustion of continued movements, you are invited to form voluntary associations under competent leaders, to patrol and guard your various districts. With these exceptions you are again requested to resume your accustomed daily avocations. This is as necessary to your personal security as to the peace of the City.

The various lines of omnibuses, railways and telegraphs must be put in full operation immediately. Adequate military protection against their further interruption will be furnished on application to the military authorities of the State.

Fellow-citizens, the laws must and shall be obeyed; public order shall not be broken with impunity. Our first duty now is to restore the public peace and preserve it unbroken, and to pursue and punish the offenders against the majesty of the laws.

GEORGE OPDYKE, Mayor.

The Mayor also gave to the public, through the newspapers, the following

DISPATCH FROM SECRETARY STANTON:

WASHINGTON, July 14, 1863.

To Hon. George Opdyke, Mayor

Five regiments are under orders to return to New-York. The retreat of LEE, now become a rout, with his army broken and much heavier loss of killed and wounded than was supposed, will relieve a large force for the restoration of order in New-York.

Intelligence has just reached here of the auspicious commencement of Gen. GILMORE's operations against Charleston.

All but one fort on Morris Island have been captured, and that will speedily be reduced, after which Sumter must follow.

EDWARD M. STANTON, Secretary of War.

Our citizens, on reading the foregoing proclamation and the accompanying dispatch from the Secretary of War, felt a double pleasure in the prospect of an utter rout of the army of LEE on the Potomac, and his sympathetic band of coadjutors and thieves in this City, at one and the same time. How far these pleasant self-congratulations were warranted by the facts, our telegrams from the Potomac, published in another column, and the reports which follow of the doings of the mob up to a late hour last night, must determine.

THE ESCAPE OF LEE.

How the Movement Was Effected.

Our Army Just One Day too Late.

The Capture of the Enemy's Rear Guard at Falling Waters.

Death of the Rebel General Pettigrew.

About Two Thousand Prisoners Secured.

SPECIAL DISPATCH FROM FREDERICK.

FREDERICK, Md., Wednesday, July 15, 1863.

Your correspondent left headquarters at a late hour last night, after the final escape of LEE; the manner in which he did it, and the brief but brilliant fights with his rear guard at Falling Waters, had become fully known.

The history of our march and the minuter movements since both armies left Gettysburgh, I leave to be detailed hereafter. The manner in which the enemy escaped is of most interest at the present moment, and I add a few facts to what I have already forwarded.

Gen. MEADE had determined to feel vigorously of the enemy on Tuesday morning, and the corps commanders moved at an early hour. Gen. SEDGWICK, who held the centre, soon sent in word that there was nothing in his front. Gen. KILPATRICK, with his cavalry, had been ordered to move at 7 A. M. on the enemy's extreme left, but hearing reports that the enemy was leaving, he moved at 5 A. M., and soon was inside the rebel intrenchments, on the Williamsport road, a mile and a half west of Hagerstown. Thence he pushed rapidly to Williamsport, picking up a few stragglers on the way, but found the village vacated, with not a dollar's worth of rebel property left behind. About a hundred severely wounded men, most of them minus legs or arms, were left in the hospitals. These fell into our hands.

The manner in which the enemy crossed at Williamsport shows with what desperate energy they have striven to escape a doom which was considered almost certain. After the destruction of their bridge at Falling Waters by the scout GRENFELL and his party, (which really was destroyed, all other reports to the contrary notwithstanding,) the enemy had no means of crossing left, save the usual fords, which the heavy rains had made generally impracticable by the time he fell back on the river. A few pontoons were hurriedly brought up from Winchester, and with lumber and timber the bridge at Falling Waters was rebuilt. At Williamsport they made no endeavor to build a bridge, but constructed six or seven indifferent flatboats. On these they crossed their remaining wounded, their perishable supplies, and a portion of their ammunition and transportation. But most of their wagons, as well as all their cavalry, *forded the river at a point half a mile above Williamsport,* the water being about three and a half feet deep. A small number of their infantry also forded the river immediately at the Williamsport Ferry, *the water coming up to their shoulders.*

The main body of their infantry, however, as has already been stated, crossed on the precarious bridge at Falling Waters. They began to cross on Sunday night, continued it Monday and Monday night, their rear guard not getting over at all, but falling into our hands yesterday, at noon.

The people of Williamsport assert that the rebels were in a great state of trepidation on Monday, for fear that their movement would be discovered, and their divided army attacked and thoroughly beaten, *as it could have been.*

KILPATRICK found nothing in Williamsport, and so moved at once on Falling Waters, where the enemy was still crossing his forces. The first division of the Second corps, under Gen. CAULDWELL, moved rapidly to his support, and severe skirmishing began about 12 o'clock. Two of our batteries also went promptly to the front, and a sharp cannonade was at once opened. The enemy's rear guard was composed of one brigade of infantry, under Gen. PETTIGREW, of North Carolina, two regiments of cavalry, and a battery of artillery. They also had artillery posted on the south bank of the Potomac, and their troops hastily fell back to get under the cover of these guns. But our troops advanced on the double-quick, with great enthusiasm, the cavalry covering the flanks, and making frequent charges. A short engagement ensued, in which the rebels lost heavily, including Gen. PETTIGREW, who was killed by a musket ball and, being closed in on from both flanks, they speedily surrendered—to the number of fifteen hundred, being one entire brigade. We also captured two pieces of artillery, four caissons and about twenty wagons.

The New-York Times.

VOL. XII—NO. 3687. NEW-YORK, SUNDAY, JULY 19, 1863. PRICE FOUR CENTS.

THE FALL OF PORT HUDSON.

News via New-Orleans, by the Steamer Locust Point.

PARTICULARS OF THE SURRENDER.

Five Thousand Prisoners, Fifty Pieces of Artillery, Numerous Small Arms, &c.

The Garrison in a Ravenous Condition.

THE LAST MULE EATEN.

Details of the Siege to the Date of the Surrender.

The *Locust Point*, from New-Orleans on July 11, arrived at this port yesterday morning.

The *New-Orleans Era* has the following announcement of the fall of Port Hudson:

"The great stronghold of the Mississippi surrendered to the forces under Gen. BANKS at 7 o'clock on the morning of the 9th. GARDNER, the commander of the rebel fortress, had sent a flag of truce asking terms. The response was an unconditional surrender, and he was allowed twenty-four hours to consider. He did not take so much time, and at 7 o'clock on the morning of the 9'th, unconditionally surrendered the stronghold, with all it contained. There were 5,000 prisoners.

The moment the surrender was completed, the enemy sent out a request that six thousand rations should immediately be sent in, as the garrison had eaten its last mule. This was found to be literally the fact. The last mule at Port Hudson had been devoured.

The good old ship *Hartford* and the *Albatross* came down below Port Hudson at once, and were greeted with much enthusiasm after their glorious work.

The *Tennessee* is the flag-ship of Admiral FARRAGUT. She came down with a bearer of dispatches from Gen. BANKS to Gen. EMORY, and made the trip from Donaldsonville in *four hours and a half*. She reports all quiet in the river.

ADDITIONAL PARTICULARS.

The *Era* of the 11th inst. says, on Wednesday, the 8th, at 2 P. M., Gen. GARDNER, the rebel commander of Port Hudson, surrendered unconditionally to Maj.-Gen. BANKS. The rebel army was drawn up in line, stacked arms, and Gen. BANKS took possession of the place. Five thousand prisoners, fifty pieces of artillery, and all small arms, &c., have fallen into our hands.

A dispatch to the *Era*, dated on the morning of the 8th, from Port Hudson, says: "At 2 o'clock a parley was sounded from the fort, and being replied to, inquiry was made about the news from Vicksburgh. On being assured that it had fallen, Gen. GARDNER promised to surrender to-day. We entered the place at noon. The glorious event has filled our army with the wildest enthusiasm."

A subsequent account states that GARDNER sent a flag of truce, on the 8th, asking for terms, and Gen. BANKS responded, "Unconditional surrender," with twenty-four hours to consider. At 7 A. M., on the 9th, GARDNER unconditionally surrendered. The moment the surrender was completed the rebels sent a request for 6,000 rations, as the garrison had eaten its last mule. This was found to be literally true—they had devoured their last mule.

The news was brought to New-Orleans by the flag-ship *Tennessee*. One hundred guns were immediately fired by Gen. EMORY. The loyal citizens of New-Orleans were to have a torchlight procession, illumination, and a general joyful jubilation on the night the steamer sailed. The Secessionists in that city are represented as rather gloomy in countenance.

NATHANIEL HOBB, of Boston, gunner of the *Tennessee*, died of apoplexy.

The news of the capture of Vicksburgh, reached Port Hudson on the 7th, occasioning the greatest enthusiasm.

OUR PORT HUDSON CORRESPONDENCE.

The Approaching Fourth of July—Rebel Raid at Springfield Landing—Disgraceful Conduct of the Rhode Island Cavalry—Gallantry of the Blacks—A New Battery—A Rebel Explosion—Deserters—The Medical Department.

MAJ.-GEN. AUGUR'S HEADQUARTERS, }
REAR OF PORT HUDSON, Friday, July 3, 1863. }

To-morrow ushers in the Fourth July. Whether or not we shall, as we have been hoping, see the old flag waving upon the ramparts of Port Hudson on that eventful day, is what the next few hours—pregnant, it may be, with so much good or evil to our cause—will certainly determine.

In taking a comprehensive view of all that is passing around me, I confess that at this moment of writing—8 o'clock P. M.—I see and hear nothing at all to indicate an aggressive movement on our part to-night or to-morrow. But it will not do for me to judge by the appearances of things around me. Gen. BANKS is one of those men who keeps his own secrets so profoundly, that I should not be surprised at any moment to hear the order given for an advance. We can have very little more to do now in the way of approaching the enemy, for in some cases we are actually upon him.

THE SPRINGFIELD LANDING AFFAIR.

We had quite a day of excitement yesterday, the 2d inst., caused by an impudent raid of the rebel cavalry upon our depot at Springfield Landing, on the river below Port Hudson. When it is remembered that Springfield Landing is not only our chief depot for the transportation of all commissary stores, troops, ammunition, &c., but, as it were, the principal back door left open to us between here and New-Orleans, you can imagine what a commotion it made when we heard that the rebels had actually got in there.

At early dawn I was aroused from slumber in my tent, near the road, by the loud tramping of horsemen, and rising up to see what it was, found a large squad of our cavalry passing, and going along the Springfield road. This was the first indication we had that "something was up." Presently, we saw lots of empty wagons returning, the riders and horses fairly buried in dust, and each one—as is usual in all such cases—big with the most portentous intelligence of every sort of disaster, and each rebel, of course, magnified into at least twenty or thirty men in buckram.

Hurrying to headquarters as the best place to obtain correct information, I found that the wild rumors had reached there also. Our Generals were in close confab, couriers were constantly dashing up with information or being sent out in search of it, squads of cavalry were galloping off, and uninitiated individuals like myself had only to look on and wonder. When everybody was hurrying *from* Springfield Landing with hobgoblin stories, to go *to* it in search of news was even more enterprise than I thought you would require of your correspondent, and so I remained in the good company in which I found myself.

For two or three hours in the morning there was manifestly no little apprehension observable on the part even of those who tried to laugh the matter off as unimportant. But toward noon the affair began to clear up, and after it had been shorn of all exaggerations and fear-begotten coloring, this last piece of rebel impudence and daring turned out (for the *present*, at least) far more harmless than anybody had imagined.

THE SURRENDER OF VICKSBURGH.

Confederate General Frank Gardner surrendered his troops at Port Hudson to General Banks on July 9, 1863.

An Account from Another of Our Special Correspondents.

VICKSBURGH, Miss., Sunday, July 5, 1863.

I send greeting to all the loyal readers of the TIMES. No longer obliged to date my letters "above," "below," "opposite" or "near Vicksburgh," I salute them from the very Court-house—the heart and centre of the rebel Gibraltar on the Mississippi. Yes, Vicksburgh, with its accumulation of forts, traverses, rifle pits and magazines; its guns, large and small; its "whistling dicks" and "whispering jimmys;" its shattered and roofless houses; its skeleton walls and prostrate chimneys; its barricaded streets, dirt, rubbish and filth, its starved and vermin-devoured garrison—all are ours.

Twenty-eight thousand prisoners, including 8,000 to 10,000 in hospitals and convalescent camps;

Fifteen Generals and their Staffs;

Fifty thousand stand of arms, rifles and muskets;

Over one hundred siege guns;

Immense quantities of ammunition;

Sixty-three field pieces in the outer line; and

Fifty field pieces in the inner lines. Total, 113.

Four large foundries and machine-shops, literally full of shot and shell, all manufactured in the town—everything except provisions and the means of subsistence, are the trophies of this most desperate and protracted siege.

The entire army had been reduced to the greatest straits for food. There were twelve days' rations for the army inside when Gen. GRANT invested the place. These have been made to feed the stomachs, or rather to furnish mere subsistence, *for forty-five days*.

True to their declared purpose, the rebel army were subsisting upon mule meat when the act of surrender was signed. I saw one of the rebel officers—a very intelligent and apparently truthful man—not an hour ago, who told me that he had several mules slaughtered in his own command. I saw with my own eyes delicate rib pieces of mules lying about the streets, which had evidently been rejected by rebel stomachs and thrown away.

A woman living opposite a large rebel rendezvous, in Walnut-street, assured me that she had often seen the soldiers take *rats* from a trap, which had been caught for the purpose over night, and skin, fry and eat them for breakfast. As the mules and rats were giving out, the dogs were beginning to fall victims to insatiate rebel maws. Dog meat was getting high on the street, and good fat curs were in demand. I myself observed a great scarcity of the canine race; cats were also scarce in the town. But seriously, there probably was never seen a hungrier crowd of men than that which surrendered to the Union forces on the 4th of July. This was the last day of grace allowed by Gen. GRANT, and had not the surrender taken place the General would have "immediately moved upon their works."

The New-York Times.

VOL. XIII—NO. 3744.   NEW-YORK, WEDNESDAY, SEPTEMBER 23, 1863.   PRICE THREE CENTS.

THE GREAT BATTLES.

IMPORTANT DETAILS.

Substantial Successes for the Union Army.

HEROIC FIGHTING OF OUR TROOPS.

THE BATTLE ON SUNDAY.

Fierce Assaults on Our Left and Centre.

Repulse of the Enemy at all Points.

Our Army in Position at Chattanooga.

Casualties and Captures.

Special Dispatch to the New-York Times.
WASHINGTON, Tuesday, Sept. 22.

Shortly after noon to-day a dispatch was received here from an officer in command at Chattanooga, speaking in most encouraging terms of the general result of the actions of Saturday and Sunday last, wherein, according to his representations, the Union army achieved a substantial success instead of being beaten—the enemy being more damaged in killed, wounded, &c. On Sunday night Gen. ROSECRANS changed the position of his army to points near Chattanooga, with Gen. THOMAS' command still occupying the front, which shows how much less that officer's corps was crippled than the first newspaper accounts alleged. Our total loss in prisoners was but 2,000, while 1,300 rebel prisoners had been sent to the rear when the dispatch in question left Chattanooga, and more were being expected in from the front. The army is in excellent spirits, and the brightest anticipations are entertained.

REPORTS FROM WASHINGTON.
WASHINGTON, Tuesday, Sept. 22.

According to official dispatches received here, dated as late as 5 o'clock yesterday afternoon, Gen. ROSECRANS had information that LONGSTREET's corps had reinforced BRAGG before the battle of Saturday and it was subsequently stated by deserters from the rebel army that EWELL's corps had also come to his assistance.

A prisoner, taken from BRAGG's army, says that Mobile has been stripped of troops for BRAGG's army, and that some troops have been sent to him from Charleston; also that troops from LEE's army were in the late fight; in fact, that the whole Confederacy seemed concentrated there for that attack on ROSECRANS.

A rebel dispatch has been intercepted on the extreme front of the Army of the Potomac, wherein

A tough defensive line under General George H. Thomas allowed routed Federal troops to escape to Chattanooga. Later, U.S. Grant would place Thomas in command of the Army of the Cumberland.

the rebel commander of the Army of Northern Virginia-is informed from Richmond that BRAGG engaged ROSECRANS on Saturday and Sunday, capturing 20 pieces of artillery and 500 prisoners.

The *Star* and *National Republican*, in their late editions this afternoon, have accounts evidently derived from official sources. The longer one, from the *Evening Star*, is as follows:

On Saturday, the 19th, a demonstration was made by the rebels in strong force, which appears to have been repelled by the force under Gen. THOMAS, with the advantage on the Federal side.

On Sunday an engagement commenced late in the morning. The first gun was fired at 9 A. M., but no considerable firing took place until 10. Previous to 10 o'clock, Gen. ROSECRANS rode the whole length of our line. Soon after the battle commenced, Gen. THOMAS, who held the left, began to call for reinforcements. About 12 o'clock, word came that he had been forced to retire.

The second line of reinforcements were then sent to him, and McCOOK's whole corps, which was on the right, and as a reserve in the centre, was sent to his assistance. Gen. WOOD, of CRITTENDEN's corps, and VAN CLEVE, who held the front centre, were also ordered to the left, where the fury of the cannonade showed that the enemy's force was massed.

Their places were filled by DAVIS and SHERIDAN, of Gen. McCOOK's corps. But hardly had these divisions taken their places in the line, when the rebel fire, which had slackened, burst out in immense volleys upon the centre.

This lasted about twenty minutes, and then VAN CLEVE, on THOMAS' right, was seen to give way, but in tolerable order; soon after which the lines of

SHERIDAN and DAVIS broke in disorder, borne down by the enemy's columns, which are said to have consisted of POLK's corps.

These two divisions were the only divisions thrown into much disorder. Those of NEGLEY and VAN CLEVE were thrown into confusion, but soon rallied, and held their places—the first on the left, and the second on the right of THOMAS' corps. DAVIS and SHERIDAN, late in the day, succeeded in rallying about 8,000 of their forces, and joined THOMAS.

Gen. THOMAS finding himself cut off from the right, brought his divisions into position for independent fighting, his line assuming the form of a horseshoe along the crest of a wooded ridge. He was soon joined by GRANGER, from Rossville, with a division of Gen. McCOOK, and Gen. STEADMAN's division, and with these forces firmly maintained the fight until after dark.

Our troops were as immovable as the rocks they stood on. The enemy repeatedly hurled against them the dense columns which had routed DAVIS and SHERIDAN in the morning; but every onset was repulsed with dreadful slaughter. Falling first on one and then on the other point of our lines, the rebels for hours vainly sought to break them. Gen. THOMAS seemed to have filled every soldier with his own unconquerable firmness, and Gen. GRANGER, his hat torn by bullets, rode like a lion wherever the conflict was thickest. Every division commander bore himself gloriously, and among them Gens. TURCHIN, HAZEN, and PARKER, especially distinguished themselves.

TURCHIN charged through the rebel lines with the bayonet, and being surrounded, forced his way back again. PARKER, who had two horses shot under him,

Three Confederate veterans pose prior to Bragg's assault on Federal troops at Chickamauga.

Saturday, forming his men in one line, made them lie down until the enemy was close upon them, when suddenly they rose and delivered their fire, with such effect that the assaulting columns fell reeling back in confusion, leaving the ground covered with killed.

When night fell this body of heroes stood on the same ground occupied by them in the morning, their spirits being unbroken. Their losses are not yet estimated.

Gen. THOMAS telegraphs (Monday forenoon) that the troops are in high spirits. He brought off all his wounded. Of the sick and wounded at Crawfish Spring, including our main hospital, nearly all had been brought away.

The number of prisoners taken by the enemy will hardly surpass 2,000, besides the wounded, of whom not more than 1,000 could have fallen into their hands.

Of rebel prisoners we have sent 1,300 to Nashville. Most of our losses in artillery were occasioned by the killing of all the horses.

Gen. THOMAS retired to Rossville on Sunday night, after the battle had closed. Gen. ROSECRANS had issued orders for all his troops to be concentrated with the forces at Chattanooga.

In the last two assaults our troops fought with bayonets, their ammunition being exhausted.

The latest information that has reached this city is from Chattanooga last evening, and was to the effect that ROSECRANS would concentrate on Chattanooga last night. THOMAS had been engaged with the enemy prior to 5 P. M. yesterday, and it was therefore questionable whether he would be able to reach Chattanooga last night. There were indications that the army was contemplating a demonstration on another part of our line last evening.

FURTHER PARTICULARS OF THE CONFLICT.

[The following appeared in a part of our yesterday's edition.—ED. TIMES.]

CHATTANOOGA, Tuesday, Sept. 22.

The battle on the 19th resulted well for us, we having held our own as established on our left, and concentrated our forces during the day ; and on Sunday morning we held a handsome line, with our right on a ridge of hills and our left protected by rude works of logs thrown up during the night. Our left rested on the east side of Rossville and Lafayette, about four miles south of Rossville.

In the fight of the 19th we had lost about 600 killed and 2,000 wounded, and were ahead three pieces of artillery ; and the men were in splendid spirits.

The engagement was resumed at 9 o'clock on the morning of the 20th by attempts of the rebels to storm Gen. THOMAS' left and front. They were severely repulsed several times with heavy loss to them and very little to us. This fight lasted an hour and a half, and was the most terrific of the war, a continuous fire of musketry and artillery being kept up with deadly effect.

During this fight our right and centre were not engaged—our skirmishers keeping up a halting fire.

The enemy, finding their assaults vain, manœuvered to the left with the intention of throwing a force on the Rossville road and attacking THOMAS on the left flank. At this juncture THOMAS ordered Gen. BRANNAN, who had one brigade in reserve and two with REYNOLDS, holding the key of the position, which was THOMAS's right, to move to the left of the line, to protect the flank of Gen. ROSECRANS, and at the same time sent DAVIS and VAN CLEVE from the right and centre to support BRANNAN in the effort to hold the line to Rossville, and protect THOMAS's right.

On seeing the withdrawal of the skirmishers in front of the division, which was moving from the right and centre, the enemy made a vigorous attack on that part of the line, piercing the centre, cutting off DAVIS and SHERIDAN from the left, and driving the centre into the mountains, both right and centre being much scattered, without very serious loss in killed or wounded.

The right and centre gone, THOMAS' right became exposed to a most terrific flank attack, and REYNOLDS and BRANNAN, and the right of THOMAS' line was swung around. His extreme left being as at first, this also fell back a short distance on the Rossville road.

Parts of the centre were gathered up and reported to THOMAS, who made several stands, but was unable to check the rebel advance until the arrival of reinforcements. At 1 o'clock, Gen. GRANGER, with one division of reserves, came up, and was at once thrown into the centre, driving the enemy handsomely from his position on a strong ridge, with heavy loss. The fire from one of GRANGER's batteries mowed them down like grass.

This fight lasted about half an hour, with slight loss to us. Capt. RUSSELL, Gen. GRANGER's Adjutant, was killed before we had been ten minutes in the fight. After this bloody repulse the enemy remained quiet until 4 o'clock, persisting, however, in manœuvering on both flanks. Their full and correct information regarding this country enabled them to do so with great facility.

Having gotten again on our flank the enemy made a vigorous attack, and a fight ensued, which has no parallel in the history of this army.

Col. HARKER's brigade and Gen. WOOD's division distinguished themselves in the fight.

Gen. WOOD, Col. HARKER and Gen. GARFIELD were present, and with the remnant of Gen. JOHNSON's division held the left, and covered himself with glory.

On the right and centre, Gens. BRANNAN, BAIRD, REYNOLDS and PALMER, with parts of their divisions, fought most gallantly, while Gens. STEDMAN and GRANGER held the reserve, and drove the enemy at every point where they went in.

At 5 o'clock, Gen. THOMAS was still triumphant, and on the left held his line of the morning, but with the right of the enemy nearly back to his line, nearly at right angles with that of the morning. Two lines of retreat were open to Gen. THOMAS to Chattanooga, one of which he fell back to—to Rossville—during the night. Our losses have necessarily been heavy but the list of killed will be surprisingly light, and in the two days' engagement we have not suffered more in men than the enemy. In the charge by Gen. THOMAS, on the first day, the enemy lost as many in killed as we did in the whole day. What the losses in prisoners and material are cannot now be reported. Our killed will reach 1,200 ; our wounded will amount to 7,000—most of them slight wounds.

Among the general officers killed are Gen. Lyttle, Col. Key, Col. King, commanding brigade, and Col. Bartleton, of the One Hundred and First Illinois. Among the wounded are Gen. Morton, of Gen. Rosecrans' Staff ; Col. Craxter, Fourth Kentucky ; Col. Frankhouse, Ninety-eighth Illinois ; Lieut.-Col. Mudge, Eleventh Michigan ; Lieut.-Col. Hunt, Fourth Kentucky ; Col. Bradley, commanding brigade in Sheridan's division ; Col. Chas. Anderson, Sixth Ohio ; Maj. Mildman, Eighteenth Kentucky ; Lieut.-Col. Tripp, Sixth Indiana ; Lieut.-Col. Bryan, Seventy-fifth Indiana ; Col. Armstrong, Ninety-third Ohio ; Maj. Johnston, Twenty-second Illinois, and Lieut.-Col. Maxwell, of the Second Ohio—all slightly wounded.

Lieut.-Col. Vaughan, of the Seventh Kentucky ; Col. Stanley, of the Eighteeth Ohio, and Maj. Dawson, of the Nineteeth Infantry, were all slightly wounded.

Gen. John H. King is reported wounded and a prisoner.

We have captured Gen. Adams, of Texas, and 1,300 of his men.

The New-York Times.

VOL. XIII—NO. 3747.　　NEW-YORK, SATURDAY, SEPTEMBER 26, 1863.　　PRICE THREE CENTS.

FROM GEN. ROSECRANS' ARMY.

INTELLIGENCE TO THURSDAY NIGHT.

The Position Considered Impregnable.

The Enemy in Mass at Chickamauga Creek.

FURTHER DETAILS OF THE BATTLE

General McCook Said to be Responsible for Our Defeat.

IMPORTANT AND SUCCESSFUL RECONNOISSANCE

Anxiety Respecting Burnside's Army.

DETAILED ACCOUNTS OF THE BATTLES.

In the course of the 17th, already unmistakable signs indicated that the enemy had discovered the weak points of our position, and were massing their forces in front of our left centre and left, for the manifest purpose of crushing those parts of our lines, or getting between them and Chattanooga. A corresponding movement by the left flank was thence made by the whole army further down the West Chickamauga, so that on Friday morning our extreme left rested at Gordon's Mill, at the crossing of the Chickamauga by the Lafayette Pike, about 12 miles southwest of Chattanooga. On the morning of the 18th, (Friday,) a portion of the expected reinforcements, consisting of two brigades of the reserve corps, respectively commanded by Cols. McCook and Mitchell, made their appearance near Chattanooga, and were immediately ordered to make a reconnoissance toward Ringgold, and develop the intentions of the enemy from that quarter.

They came upon the advance of Longstreet's corps, pushed it back for some distance, took a number of prisoners from it, and fully established the anticipated concentration of the enemy in front of our left. All day Friday the cavalry, covering our front, skirmished with different bodies of the enemy issuing from the various gaps of the Pigeon Mountains and advancing upon and again retiring from our line. No serious collision however, occurred. It was evident the rebel Generals meant to create a false impression as to the points of our line against which they proposed to strike a blow with concentrated power. But Gen. Rosecrans was not deceived. The reports from the front all tended to confirm his previous impression that an onset in overwhelming numbers was contemplated upon our left flank, and that it had to be met by a still further shifting line toward Chattanooga.

Accordingly on Friday night the divisions of Brannan and Baird, formerly commanded by Gens. Rousseau and Reynolds, of Thomas' corps, together with Johnson's, of McCook's corps, moved from the centre to the left of Crittenden's corps. They were in their new positions at daybreak. The two other divisions of McCook's corps, Davis' and Sheridan's, were to move into the position abandoned by Thomas' corps, but had not time to assume it fully before the commencement of the action on the next morning. On the morning of Saturday our line then appeared as follows: On the extreme left Brannan, next Baird and Reynolds, with Johnson in reserve in the centre, Palmer on the

right of Reynolds, and Van Cleve on his left. The line, as already stated, was to be completed by Davis' and Sheridan's divisions, faced a little east of south. The scene of all the movements on the 17th and 18th was McLamore's Cave, previously described as the valley formed by the Missionary and Pigeon Mountains. The valley is washed for its greater part by the West Chickamauga, and traversed by two roads, one leading from Rossville, and the other from Chattanooga direct to Lafayette. The two roads run about two miles apart, and west of the Chickamauga where the battle of Saturday was fought.

The section of the valley bordered by the two roads is almost a plain, covered with thick woods, which rendered the field unfavorable for the effective use of artillery. The line proper, as given above, rested nearly at the base of the Missionary Mountains, some distance in advance of its right. Gordon's Mills, the point of intersection of the road from Chattanooga to Lafayette, and the Chickamauga aforementioned, was still held on Saturday morning by Wood's division of Crittenden's corps, supported by Negley's of Thomas'. Their position was a strong one; but at an angle with the line proper, appeared like a dangerous extension of the latter, and was proved such by subsequent events. It was meant to secure our right against turning manœuvres, but officers of good judgment entertained the belief that both greater compactness from closer contraction and perfect security of the right might have been obtained by posting the latter on the eastern abutments of Missionary Ridge.

The brigades of McCook and Mitchell of the reserve corps were ordered back to Rossville, on Friday afternoon, for the protection of our communication with Chattanooga, and hence were not to participate in the struggle of Saturday. The night had been frosty, and the troops not being permitted to kindle bivouac fires, the discomfort they experienced, together with the fatigue from marching and want of sleep, put them in a physical condition by no means as vigorous as it should have been for the severe work before them. Fortunately the sun rose clear, and, with its cheering rays, did much to revive the spirits of the army.

The early forenoon passed away without forewarning of the approaching conflict; but shortly before 11 o'clock the storm that had been brewing all the morning on the rebel side burst forth in the expected direction. At that time a long mass of rebel infantry was seen advancing upon Brennan's division on the extreme left. It first came upon the Second brigade, Col. Croxton commanding, and soon forced it back despite its determined resistance. The two other brigades of the division at once came to its assistance, and succeeded in checking the progress of the rebels and driving them back; but their column being in turn strongly reinforced, they advanced again with wild yells. So powerful was this assault, that they pushed Brennan back to and beyond his position in the line, and thus uncovered the left of Baird's division. Making prompt use of their advantage, they changed their course to the left, and speedily enveloped Scribner's and King's brigades—the latter of Regulars. They

Although General Braxton Bragg had led the Confederacy to a decisive victory at Chickamauga, he delayed in pressing the pursuit of fleeing Union troops. Instead he prepared to besiege Chattanooga.

were almost surrounded, but managed to disentangle themselves after fearful loss.

The crushing rebel masses next came upon JOHNSON's division, and rolled it upon REYNOLDS', which also became speedily involved in the desperate struggle. The stubborn resistance of these divisions, however, and the sweeping fire of some batteries posted under the personal supervision of Gen. ROSECRANS, arrested at last their sweeping advance.

The divisions of BRANNAN and BAIRD having been rallied, Gen. THOMAS ordered a general advance of the right, and soon the tide of battle was decidedly turned in our favor. With cheers our line advanced, halting only at times to shatter the enemy with musketry. Several times the latter's retreating line stopped and vainly tried to retain their gained ground; but steadily they were driven from position to position, and by 4 o'clock all the ground lost was nearly recovered. Several batteries belonging to Gens. BAIRD's and BRANNAN's divisions, whose horses had been killed and supports were swept away, were retaken, and several hundred prisoners captured. The enemy left all their dead and nearly all their wounded on the field. There were at least 500 of the former. The rebel troops engaging THOMAS belonged to BUCKNER's and LONGSTREET's commands.

At the time the struggle was turning in our favor on the left, BRAGG's army proper, consisting of the corps of POLK and HILL, (formerly HARDEE's,) moved to a most determined and well-executed attack upon PALMER's and VAN CLEVE's divisions in the centre. Its object was obviously to relieve the defeated rebel right. PALMER and VAN CLEVE soon found themselves overpowered and their divisions breaking. Their complete rout was imminent, when DAVIS' division came to their support on VAN CLEVE's right. The timely reinforcements at first had the effect of checking the enemy and restoring our line; but the rebel attack was speedily renewed with greater numbers, and the centre again compelled to yield. DAVIS was forced to the right and VAN CLEVE to the left, and the enemy advanced through the opening made in our line, threatening to take the centre and right by their flanks, as they had done on the left. At this critical juncture, SHERIDAN's division appeared, and was at once thrown upon the enemy. It stood its ground gallantly for a while, but becoming soon exposed to a destructive flank fire, was also compelled to fall back. Fortunately, the divisions of Gens. WOOD and NEGLEY, that had been easily withdrawn from Gordon's Mills when the rebel attack on the left threatened to be successful, now came to the rescue. After a brief contest, the rebels found themselves at last matched, and commenced giving away in their turn, REYNOLDS having also been sent to the assistance of the centre.

After the repulse of the rebel right an advance was ordered, and the original position regained about sunset.

About dark the enemy made another demonstration with a heavy artillery and musketry fire upon the centre, but eliciting a lively response, they soon abandoned this last effort of the day. Thus ended the battle of the 19th. It had been a defensive one on our part, and although we lost no ground, and probably less men and material than the enemy, its result could hardly be claimed as a triumph of Union arms. No substantial advantage had been won, and a large portion of the army was badly shattered. That the enemy, with his numerical superiority, would be able to offer again battle on the following day, could well be supposed. Gen. ROSECRANS anticipated a renewal of the struggle, and prepared for it.

During the night the disposition of our forces was changed. The line was made to rest along a cross-road running northeast and southwest, and connecting the Rossville and Lafayette Roads. By this disposition our extreme right was made to rest on Missionary Ridge. The new line was a mile shorter than that of the day before. The different divisions were disposed in this order: From right to left, one brigade of Negley's, Johnson's, Baird's, Palmer's, Reynold's, two brigades of Negley's, Wood's, Sheridan's and Davis'. Brannan's and Van Cleve's formed the reserve. The mounted brigades of Wilder and Minty covered the right flank.

Sunday morning broke upon the hostile armies as fair as that of the preceding day. Contrary to the universal expectation on our side, the enemy again allowed the early hours, so well suited to offensive manœuvres, to pass away undisturbed by the sounds of battle. The adaptation of their plan of attack to our new line, doubtless, necessitated this. About 9 o'clock a few shots were heard at various points of our front, but it was only a little before 10 that the report of whole volleys announced the resumption of the fight in good earnest. The firing that had begun upon our left, at once assumed the fiercest character. The enemy repeated the tactics of the previous day by throwing themselves first upon our extreme left, formed by Gen. BEATTY's brigade of NEGLEY's division. It stood the onset for some time, but finally retired.

Desiring to unite the two portions of Gen. NEGLEY's command, Gen. ROSECRANS ordered Gen. WOOD's division to take the position of the two brigades stationed further to the right. The rebels, perceiving the withdrawal of NEGLEY, and believing it to be a retreat in good earnest, quickly also moved upon the centre, and the action speedily became general. Finding themselves unable to make an impression on WOOD, the enemy, after the lapse of an hour or so, seemed to concentrate their main strength upon the centre, now again commanded by THOMAS.

During the night our troops had constructed along the line barriers of logs and fence-rails, and thus comparatively sheltered, they kept a continuous, murderous musketry fire upon the enemy. Our artillery was planted upon higher ground in the rear, and fired over the infantry. Destructive as our fire from small-arms and cannon was, it did not stay the advance of the rebels. At times they staggered, but only to rally and push again forward toward our line. With frantic yells, LONGSTREET's and HILL's corps both came rolling steadily on, in columns by battalions. Our centre, weakened to the extent of almost one-third, was not strong enough for success in this unequal contest. Closer and closer approached the shouting hostile masses, and at last forced BRANNAN's division to yield its position.

Meantime, as Gen. REYNOLDS was severely pressed, Gen. WOOD was ordered to march instantly by the left flank, pass Brennan, and go to his relief. DAVIS and SHERIDAN were to shift over the left, and thus close up the line. As the occasion was urgent, Gen. WOOD drew in his skirmishers with considerable haste, and the rebels for the second time, mistaking a withdrawal for a flight, pressed forward like a torrent, and poured musketry, canister and grape into the flank of the division, moving upon the double-quick. The men endeavored for a time to keep their files in order, but as the pitiless storm of lead and iron continued to be hurled against them, the regiments began to spread out like a fan wider and wider until finally they were torn to flinders. This was especially the case with the brigade commanded by Col. BUELL. PARKER's brigade alone passed on to its destination comparatively intact.

The battle now extended upon its most critical phase. The breaks, temporarily caused by the shiftings of divisions from one point of the line to another, were so promptly perceived and turned to advantage by the enemy, that they proved fatal, and cost the loss of the day. DAVIS' division, coming up to take WOOD's position on the extreme left, was taken with great suddenness and fury by the left flank, and pushed to the right in utter disorder. Simultaneously the weak remnants of VAN CLEVE's and PALMER's divisions, exposed by the withdrawal of DAVIS', were attacked with equal vehemence on the right, and forced back in great confusion. The rout of the left and the right was now complete, and even the exertions of Gen. ROSECRANS and his Staff, who, with drawn swords, attempted to restore order, were of no avail. Streams of demoralized, uncontrollable men, fleeing toward the rear, were all that remained of a large portion or the army.

After that fatal break, our line of battle was not again re formed during the day. The army was, in fact, cut in two, MCCOOK, with DAVIS, SHERIDAN and WILDER, being thrown off to the right; CRITTENDEN, except one brigade of WOOD's, being broken in pieces, and THOMAS, with his indomitable corps, and JOHNSON's division of MCCOOK's, remaining alone upon the left. THOMAS' divisions—NEGLEY's, BRANNAN's and BAIRD's—had been fearfully shaken and much scattered by the fight over the log works, and REYNOLDS' was the only one that retired in tolerable order. Retreat was now the only resort left, and the whole disorganized mass of our troops fell back over the road to Rossville. Crowds of stragglers, in mob-like disorder, made good speed toward Chattanooga, with the exception of SHERIDAN, DAVIS and WILDER, who, cut off from the centre, still straggled as best they could.

On the right the divisions of BAIRD, REYNOLDS, NEGLEY and BRANNAN, and HARKER's brigade of WOOD's division, alone retained cohesiveness, and took a position along the base of Missionary Mountains, where the Rossville road debouches from them, for another fight. The line was formed so that the left rested upon the Lafayette road, and the right at the gap represented an arc of a circle, and a southeast hill about its centre formed the key to the position. Between 2 and 3 o'clock the enemy appeared on the Lafayette road, and, moving by the left flank, soon formed for another attack.

At first they directed a heavy fire of musketry and artillery upon our position, as though meaning to dispirit its defenders before coming to an assault, but the 10,000 or 12,000 men that confronted them felt that the fate of the Army of the Cumberland and, in a great measure, that of the Union, depended upon the repulse of the enemy, and when the rebel lines finally came repeatedly to the attack, they advanced but to recoil with severe loss. Our troops were formed in two lines upon the crest, and firing one after the other, they kept up an unbroken fusilade with telling effect. The enemy, consisting of POLK's corps, were not only repelled, but thrown into such disorder that TURCHIN's brigade and other portions of the line followed, and took several hundred prisoners. Toward sunset the enemy were driven back to the position they took when filing out of the Lafayette road, and abandoned the contest.

When THOMAS' division were most sorely pressed during the afternoon, and it looked at one time as though they would again have to succumb to superior numbers, they were gladdened and encouraged by the advent, on the right, of MITCHELL's and WHITAKER's brigades, of the reserve corps, under the command of Gen. GORDON GRANGER, himself. With the accession of strength, our ability to maintain our position was no longer doubted. Soon after Gen. GRANGER had reported to Gen. THOMAS, his two brigades were sent out on the road, under command of Gen. STEADMAN, to retake an ammunition train that had fallen into the hands of the enemy. They came upon a large rebel force, and after a severe conflict, drove them away.

While Gen. THOMAS was making his gallant fight, SHERIDAN and DAVIS had managed, after being much cut up, to work their way to the Rossville Road with the remnants of their divisions, and fallen back in the direction of Chattanooga. At night Gen. THOMAS fell back to Rossville, four miles from Chattanooga, after bringing away all the wounded, transportation, and other material within reach.

While the struggle of Saturday ended in a drawn battle, that of Sunday resulted in a disastrous defeat. The failure of the first day was partly due to the greater numerical strength of the enemy, and partly to the deficient formation of our line of battle. That of the second is justly ascribed to improper tactics on the battle-field, and above all to the absence of command. The inspiring example set and influence exercised by the Commander-in-Chief at Stone River were wanting—he having been compelled to leave the field and return to Chattanooga before the action was over.

The early disappearance of two corps commanders from the field also made a demoralizing impression. The loyal people certainly have cause for self-congratulation that the Army of the Cumberland was not completely destroyed, and owes profound gratitude to Gen. THOMAS and those under him that saved it. Our losses are great. That in killed, wounded and missing will probably reach ten thousand. Of artillery, we are less some fifty pieces, mostly lost on Sunday. Of wagons, loaded with ammunition and supplies, ambulances, &c., we have also lost a great number. They were abandoned in the retreat on Sunday.

Gen. ROSECRANS and his lieutenants were busily engaged on Monday in strengthening their position by field-works, and reorganizing their commands. While the army itself may be considered safe enough, it is most certain that if the enemy have the advantage of greater numbers, flanking movements will compel ROSECRANS to retreat across the Tennessee, in case reinforcements should not promptly reach him.

The New-York Times.

VOL. XIII....NO. 3794.　　　　NEW-YORK, FRIDAY, NOVEMBER 20, 1863.　　　　PRICE THREE CENTS.

IMPORTANT FROM EAST TENNESSEE

The Rebels Advancing upon Knoxville.

THE PLACE COMPLETELY INVESTED.

HEAVY SKIRMISHING YESTERDAY.

The Position Very Strongly Fortified.

THE REBEL FORCES UNDER LONGSTREET.

KNOXVILLE, Thursday, Nov. 17.

The enemy began skirmishing from their position on Kingston Road, at 10 this morning. Our advance alone, composed wholly of mounted infantry and cavalry, occupied the position, under command of Gen. SANDERS, and each man fought like a veteran. At noon the enemy opened with artillery at short range, their battery protected by a large house. BENJAMIN's battery was the only one which replied, occupying the chief fortification, half a mile in front of and to the right of the town. A desperate charge was made by the enemy about 3 P. M. Our men were protected by rail barricades on the crest of the hill. Gen. SANDERS was severely wounded, and was borne from the field.

We yielded the position, and fell back about a third of a mile to a stronger one. We have lost about one hundred, one quarter of whom were killed. The enemy had completely invested the place, but Gen. BURNSIDE will defend it to the last man, and it is believed successfully. The troops are in the best spirits. Every important point is fortified, and confidence prevails that we shall whip the enemy out.

A MORE DETAILED ACCOUNT.

KNOXVILLE, Tenn., Tuesday, Nov. 17.

Gen. LONGSTREET, after crossing the Tennessee on Saturday morning, 14th inst., was attacked in the afternoon by Gen. BURNSIDE, who drove the advance guard back to within a mile of the river's edge by nightfall.

LONGSTREET crossed the remainder of his troops during the night, and on Sunday morning advanced in force.

Gen. BURNSIDE, finding it impossible to cope with him with the small force at his disposal, fell back to Lenoir, the rear guard skirmishing heavily with the enemy through the day.

Three desperate charges were made upon our positions during Sunday night, but they were handsomely repulsed.

On Monday morning Gen. BURNSIDE evacuated Lenoir, but owing to the energy with which the rebel pursuit was kept up, determined to give them a decided check, and accordingly came into line of battle at Campbell's Station, when a fight ensued, lasting from late in the forenoon until dark. Our first position commanding the road from both sides, the infantry deployed in front of this, and were soon attacked by the enemy, who made several gallant charges, and finally succeeded, by outflanking our men, in driving them to the cover of the batteries, which now opened a terrific and destructive fire. The rebels retired before it, gave way, and eventually fell back to the river.

It was now three o'clock in the afternoon. The rebels showing a desire to renew the attack, and having brought three batteries to their assistance, Gen.

BURNSIDE fell back to a more desirable position and again gave them battle. The contest continued, closing at nightfall, with our troops in possession of their own ground.

The object of the fight having been attained, and as the detention of the rebels had enabled our trains to get all in advance, our troops fell back during the night and early Tuesday morning reached Knoxville, where a great battle is expected to be fought to-morrow.

Yesterday the rebel advance guard attacked our outposts upon the Loudon and Clinton roads and heavy skirmishing continued all day.

This morning the attack was resumed when the fog which set in during the night had lifted. The rebels finding it impossible to drive our men with infantry, brought several guns into position, and poured in a flanking fire.

In the afternoon they brought forward a heavy force of infantry once more, and, after a brief skirmish, charged our position. A terrific hand to hand conflict occurred—both sabres and revolvers being used on both sides. Our men fought with the greatest gallantry; but at last were compelled to fall back about a third of a mile, to a strong line, which they hold to-night.

We have to regret the wounding of Gen. SANDERS and Capt. SIMMS, of the cavalry, who commanded the outpost. His condition is critical. Lieut.-Col. SMITH, of the Twentieth Michigan, was killed at Campbell's Station. Our loss in that fight was between two and three hundred. Our loss to-day will not exceed one hundred and fifty.

Our men are in the best of spirits and perfectly confident of success to-morrow.

THE HEROES OF JULY.

A Solemn and Imposing Event.

Dedication of the National Cemetery at Gettysburgh.

IMMENSE NUMBERS OF VISITORS.

A crowd gathers for the dedication of the military cemetery at Gettysburg.

Oration by Hon. Edward Everett—Speeches of President Lincoln, Mr. Seward and Governor Seymour.

THE PROGRAMME SUCCESSFULLY CARRIED OUT.

The ceremonies attending the dedication of the National Cemetery commenced this morning by a grand military and civic display, under command of Maj.-Gen. COUCH. The line of march was taken up at 10 o'clock, and the procession marched through the principal streets to the Cemetery, where the military formed in line and saluted the President. At 11¼ the head of the procession arrived at the main stand. The President and members of the Cabinet, together with the chief military and civic dignitaries, took position on the stand. The President seated himself between Mr. SEWARD and Mr. EVERETT after a reception marked with the respect and perfect silence due to the solemnity of the occasion, every man in the immense gathering uncovering on his appearance.

The military were formed in line extending around the stand, the area between the stand and military being occupied by civilians, comprising about 15,000 people and including men, women and children. The attendance of ladies was quite large. The military escort comprised one squadron of cavalry, two batteries of artillery and a regiment of infantry, which constitutes the regular funeral escort of honor for the highest officer in the service.

After the performance of a funeral dirge, by BIRGFIELD, by the band, an eloquent prayer was delivered by Rev. Mr. STOCKTON, as follows:

O God, our Father, for the sake of the Son, our Saviour, inspire us with thy spirit, and sanctify us to the right fulfillment of the duties of this occasion. We come to dedicate this new historic centre as a National Cemetery. If all the Departments of the one Government thou hast ordained over our Union, and of the many Governments which Thou has subordinated to the Union be there represented; if all classes, relations and interests of our blended brotherhood of people stand severally and thoroughly apparent in Thy presence, we trust it is because Thou hast called us, that Thy blessing awaits us, and that Thy designs may be embodied in practical results of incalculable, imperishable good. And so with thy holy Apostle and with the Church in all lands and ages,

The Gettysburg Address

Lincoln's "second draft" of the Gettysburg Address.

we unite in the ascription: Blessed be God, even the Father of Our Lord Jesus Christ, the Father of Moses, and the God of all comfort, who comforteth us in all our tribulation, that we may be able to comfort them which are in any trouble by the comfort wherewith we ourselves are comforted of God. In emulation of all angels, in fellowship with all saints, and in sympathy with all sufferers, in remembrance of Thy works, in reverence of Thy ways, and in accordance with Thy word, we love and magnify Thy infinite perfections, Thy creative glory, Thy redeeming grace, Thy providential goodness, and the progressive, richer and fairer development of thy supreme, universal and everlasting administration. In behalf of all humanity, whose ideal is divine, whose first memory is thy image lost, whose last hope is thy image restored: especially in behalf of our own nation, whose position is so peerless, whose mission is so sublime, and whose future is so attractive; we thank Thee for the unspeakable patience of thy compassion and for the exceeding greatness of thy loving kindness. In contemplation of Eden, Calvary and Heaven, of Christ in the God on the cross, and on the throne—nay, more—of Christ as coming again in all-subduing power and glory; we gratefully prolong our homage by this altar of sacrifice, on this field of deliverance, on this mount of salvation, within the fiery and bloody line of these mountains and rocks, looking back to the dark days of fear and of trembling, and the rapture of relief that came after, we multiply our thanksgivings and confess our obligations to renew and perfect our personal and social consecration to thy service and glory. O, had it not been for God! for our enemies, they came unresisted, multitudinous, mighty, flushed with victory and sure of success; they exalted on our mountains; they reveled in our valleys; they feasted, they rested, they slept, they awakened, they grew stronger, prouder and bolder every day; they spread abroad, they concentrated here; they looked beyond this horizon to the stores of wealth, to the haunts of pleasure and the seats of power in our Capital and chief cities; they prepared to cast the chain of Slavery around the form of freedom, and to bind life and death together forever. Their premature triumph was the mockery of God and man. One more victory, and all was theirs. But behind these hills was heard the feebler march of a smaller but still a pursuing host; onward they hurried, day and night, for their country and their God; footsore, wayworn, hungry, thirsty, faint, but not in heart; they came to dare all, to bear all, and to do all that is possible to heroes. At first they met the blast on the plain, and bent before it like trees; but then led by Thy hand to the hills, they took their stand on the these rocks, and remained as firm and immovable as they. In vain were they assaulted; all art, all violence, all desperation failed to dislodge them. Baffled, bruised, broken, their enemies retired and disappeared. Glory to God for this rescue! But, Oh! the slain, in the freshness and fulness of their young and manly life! with such sweet memories of father and mother, brother and sister, wife and children, maiden and friend.

From the coasts beneath the Eastern star; from the shores of Northern lakes and rivers; from the flowers of the Western prairies; from the homes of the midway and the border, they came here to die for us and for mankind! Alas How little we can do for them! We come with the humility of prayer, with the pathetic eloquence of venerable wisdom, with the tender beauty of poetry, with the plaintive harmony of music, with the honest tribute of our Chief Magistrate, and with all this honorable attendances; but our best hope is in Thy blessings. O Lord, Our God, bless us. O, Our Father, bless the bereaved, whether absent or present. Bless our sick and wounded soldiers and sailors. Bless all our rulers and people. Bless our army and navy. Bless the efforts to suppress this rebellion, and bless all the associations of this day, and place, and scene, forever. As the trees are not dead, though their foliage is gone, so our heroes are not dead though their forms have fallen. In their proper personality they are all with thee, and the spirit of their example is here. It fills the air, it fills our hearts, and as long as time shall last it will hover in these skies and rest on these landscapes, and pilgrims of our own land and of all lands, will thrill with its inspiration, and increase and confirm their devotion to liberty, religion and God.

Mr. EVERETT then commenced the delivery of his oration, which was listened to with marked attention throughout. [The oration of Mr. EVERETT will be found on our second page.]

Although a heavy fog clouded the heavens in the morning during the procession, the sun broke out in all its brilliancy during the Rev. Mr. STOCKTON's prayer and shone upon the magnificent spectacle. The assemblage was of great magnitude, and was gathered within a circle of great extent around the stand, which was located on the highest point of ground on which the battle was fought, A long line of military surrounded the position taken by the immense multitude of people.

The Marshal took up a position on the left of the stand. Numerous flags and banners, suitably draped, were exhibited on the stand among the audience. The entire scene was one of grandeur due to the importance of the occasion. So quiet were the people that every word uttered by the orator of the day must have been heard by them all, notwithstanding the immensity of the concourse.

Among the distinguished persons on the platform were the following: Governors Bradford, of Maryland; Curtin, of Pennsylvania; Morton, of Indiana; Seymour, of New-York; Parker, of New-Jersey, and Tod, of Ohio; Ex-Gov. Dennison, of Ohio; John Brough, Governor Elect, of Ohio; Charles Anderson, Lieutenant-Governor of Ohio; Major-Generals Schenck, Stahel, Doubleday, and Couch; Brigadier-General Gibbon; and Provost-Marshal-General Fry.

PRESIDENT LINCOLN'S ADDRESS.

The President then delivered the following dedicatory speech:

Fourscore and seven years ago our Fathers brought forth upon this Continent a new nation, conceived in liberty and dedicated to the proposition that all men are created equal. [Applause.] Now we are engaged in a great civil war, testing whether that nation, or any nation so conceived and so dedicated, can long endure. We are met on a great battle-field of that war. We are met to dedicate a portion of it as the final resting-place of those who here gave their lives that that nation might live. It is altogether fitting and proper that we should do this. But in a larger sense we cannot dedicate. We cannot consecrate, we cannot hallow this ground. The brave men, living and dead, who struggled here have consecrated it far above our power to add or detract. [Applause.] The world will little note nor long remember, what we say here, but it can never forget what they did here. [Applause.] It is for us, the living, rather to be dedicated here to the refinished work that they have thus so far nobly carried on. [Applause.] It is rather for us to be here dedicated to the great task remaining before us, that from these honored dead we take increased devotion to that cause for which they here gave the last full measure of devotion; that we here highly resolve that the dead shall not have died in vain; [applause] that the Nation shall under God have a new birth of freedom, and that Governments of the people, by the people and for the people, shall not perish from the earth, [Long continued applause.]

Three cheers were then given for the President and the Governors of the States.

After the delivery of the addresses, the dirge and the benediction closed the exercises, and the immense assemblage separated at about 4 o'clock.

About 3 o'clock in the afternoon, the Fifth New York regiment of heavy artillery, Col. MURRAY, was marched to the temporary residence of Gov. SEYMOUR, where they passed in review before the Governor, presenting a handsome spectacle. Upon the conclusion of this ceremony, which attracted quite a crowd of sight-seers. Gov. SEYMOUR presented a handsome silk regimental standard to the regiment, accompanying the gift with the following speech:

GOV. SEYMOUR'S SPEECH.

SOLDIERS OF NEW-YORK: We love our whole country, without reservation. But while we do so, it is not inconsistent with that perfect and generous loyalty to love and to be proud of our own State This day, when I took part in the celebration that was to consecrate yonder battle-field, while I felt as an American citizen, proud of my own country, and proud of the gallant services of her citizens, in every State, nevertheless my eye did involuntarily wander to that field where lie the glorious dead of our good and great State, and when I returned, to see marching before me your manly and sturdy columns, not knowing you belonged to New-York, my heart did quicken and my pulse tingle, to learn that you were acting commissions issued by myself I am most proud and most happy that I have have this opportunity, on behalf of the merchants of the great commercial City of New-York; to present to you this glorious banner, which has been sent as a token of their confidence in your loyalty and your courage, and your fidelity in the hour of danger. Sergeant, I place these colors in your hands in the firm confidence that they will be borne through every field of triumph, of toil and of danger, in a way that will do honor to yourselves, to the great State which you represent, and the still greater country, to which we all belong. My God bless you as you serve your country in the distant field of danger We find in those glorious fields you left behind you are not indifferent to this conflict; are not indifferent to the welfare of the whole Union. I do not doubt, therefore, that when you shall return from your dangerous fields of duty, you shall bring back this standard to place among the archives of our State with honorable mention of the services her sons have performed. I do not doubt that though it may perhaps be returned torn and stained, yet it will be still more glorious, and with glorious recollections clustering around it. In concluding these remarks, I ask in return of the men of New-York, to give three cheers for the Union of our country, and three cheers for the flag of our land.

Gen. SCHENCK followed in a short speech.

A subscription of $280 was made by the Marshals attending these ceremonies, to be devoted to the relief of the Richmond prisoners.

In the afternoon, the Lieutenant-Governor elect of Ohio, Col. ANDERSON, delivered an oration at the Presbyterian Church.

The President and party returned to Washington at 6 o'clock this evening, followed by the Governors' trains. Thousands of persons were gathered at the depot, anxiously awaiting transportation to their homes; but they will probably be confined to the meagre accommodations of Gettysburgh till tomorrow.

The New-York Times.

VOL. XIII—NO. 3799. NEW-YORK, THURSDAY, NOVEMBER 26, 1863. PRICE THREE CENTS.

GLORIOUS VICTORY !

GEN. GRANT'S GREAT SUCCESS.

Bragg Routed and Driven from Every Point.

SUCCESSFUL BATTLE ON TUESDAY.

Gen. Hooker Assaults Lookout Mountain and Takes 2,000 Prisoners.

General Sherman Finally Carries Missionary Ridge.

Gen. Thomas Pierces the Enemy's Centre.

Forty Pieces of Artillery Taken.

Five Thousand to Ten Thousand Prisoners Captured.

Flight of the Rebels in Disorder and Confusion.

Probable Interception of the Rebels at Rossville.

SPECIAL DISPATCH TO THE N. Y. TIMES.

WASHINGTON, Wednesday, Nov. 25.

Dispatches giving details of recent operations before Chattanooga were received to-night from Gen. GRANT. He is in happy spirits and confident of success.

Atlanta he declares to be a prize already within his grasp.

DISPATCHES TO THE ASSOCIATED PRESS.

CHATTANOOGA, Wednesday, Nov. 25.

We are completely victorious. The enemy is totally routed and driven from every position. Our loss is very small and the enemy's is heavy in prisoners. Finding Gen. HOOKER so successful in his movements against Lookout Mountain, the enemy evacuated that position during the night.

Gen. HOOKER took possession early this morning. The enemy moved south and got on Missionary Ridge on the battle-field somewhere near Chickamauga.

He is expected to intercept the flying foe. Gen. HOOKER is said to have captured 2,000 prisoners in his magnificent assault of Lookout Mountain.

Gen. SHERMAN being all prepared to begin an assault at 8 A. M. to-day, upon the strong position of the enemy at the north end of Missionary Ridge. He had the day before taken a hill near the position of the enemy, but commanded by their artillery. He had to descend into a valley, and he then made another ascent to the position held by the enemy. Two unsuccessful assaults were made by Gen. SHERMAN, but, with the coöperation of the centre, he ultimately gained the position, and completed the great victory.

The brigade of Gen. CARSE, with a portion of Gen. LIGHTFEWS brigade, composed the storming party in the first assault. They were repulsed with quite a heavy loss after an attack persisted in for an hour; but being reinforced they, were enabled to hold a part of the hills. In this attack Gen. CARSE was wounded quite severely in the thigh. The Thirty-seventh Ohio and Sixth Iowa and One Hundred and Third Illinois regiments were in the attack. A second assault was made at 3½ o'clock, in which MATHIAS', Loomis' and RAUL's brigades were engaged. The force reached within twenty yards of the summit of the hill and the works of the enemy, when they were flanked and broke, retiring to their reserves.

In this assault Gen. MATHIAS was wounded and Col. PUTNAM, of the Ninety-third Ohio, killed, their persistent efforts compelled the enemy to mass heavily on his right in order to hold the position of so much importance to him. About 3 o'clock Gen. GRANT started two columns against the weakened centre, and in an hour desperate fighting, succeeded in breaking the centre, and gaining possession of the ridge in which the enemy was posted, the main force was driven northward toward Gen. SHERMAN, who opened on them, and they were forced to break, and seek safety in disordered flight down the western slope of the Ridge, and across the western ridge of the Chickamauga. We have taken not less than 5,000 prisoners and perhaps 10,000. Gen. HOOKER will probably intercept the flying enemy in the vicinity of Rossville and the region east of it.

There are reports that we have taken a whole corps.

Among the casualties are Lieut.-Col. ESPY, of the Fifty-eighth Indiana regiment; Major McCAWLEY, of the Tenth Iowa; Col. OMARS, of the Ninetieth Illinois; Lieut.-Col. STUART, of the Ninetieth Illinois; Major WALKER, of the Tenth Missouri; Major WRISH, of the Fifty-sixth Illinois; Major INNISS, of the Sixth Iowa, wounded; Major IRWIN, of the Sixth Iowa, killed.

Full reports of the killed and wounded cannot be obtained, as most of the killed were in Gen. SHERMAN's corps, and remained at dark in the hands of the enemy. The list will be telegraphed to-morrow. The prisoners say that BRAGG was on the Ridge just before they were taken.

The successful storming parties consisted of WOOD's and BAIRD's divisions on the left centre and JOHNSTON's and SHERIDAN's on the right centre. Some of our wounded were left in the hands of the enemy after Gen. SHERMAN's unsuccessful assault, but were ultimately recovered.

CHATTANOOGA, Wednesday, Nov. 25—10 P. M.

The captured artillery is reported at about forty pieces. Gen. HOOKER captured five boxes of new muskets on Lookout Mountain.

We are in entire possession of the field. We have control over the railway and river to Bridgeport. Two boats came through this morning. Our loss will not amount to more than 300 killed and 250 wounded in the three days operations. The success has been most brilliant.

The enemy is reported to be bivouacking two miles beyond Missionary Ridge. Col. PHELPS, of the Thirty-eighth Ohio, and Major GLASS, of the Thirty-second Indiana, are killed. Gen. JOHN E. SMITH is reported wounded. Col. AVERY, of the One Hundred and Second New-York, lost a leg, and Major ELLIOTT is the same as dead.

REPORTS FROM WASHINGTON.

WASHINGTON, Wednesday, Nov. 25.

The following was received here this afternoon from a responsible source:

CHATTANOOGA, Wednesday, Nov. 25—11 A. M.

We have had a brisk engagement this morning, and have driven the enemy entirely off Lookout Mountain, a considerable portion of which they held up to this morning. We have also taken Missionary Ridge from him this morning, and the troublesome rifle-pits, in possession of which yesterday's engagement left them at the close.

All firing has ceased for a sufficient time to warrant the conclusion that BRAGG has retreated certainly, leaving all the ground and strong points in our possession for which we have been fighting for the last three days.

It is too early yet to enable me to state the casualties on either sides, which are not yet known. Our army is in glorious exultation indeed, over their series of victories.

WASHINGTON, Wednesday, Nov. 24.

Information has been received to-night at the War Department from Gen. GRANT of a great battle fought to-day, resulting in a complete victory over the rebels.

Our army has carried at the point of the bayonet Lookout Mountain Top, Missionary Ridge, and all the intrenchments and rifle-pits around Chattanooga. The bravery exhibited in this great contest by our troops has never been surpassed.

OFFICIAL REPORTS FROM GEN. THOMAS AND GEN. GRANT.

WASHINGTON, Wednesday, Nov. 25.

The following official dispatch from Maj.-Gen. GRANT has been received at the headquarters of the army here:

CHATTANOOGA, Tenn., Tuesday, Nov. 24—12 M.

Major-Gen. H. W. Halleck, General-in-Chief:

Yesterday, at 12½ o'clock, Gen. GRANGER's and Gen. PALMER's corps, supported by Gen. HOWARD's, were advanced directly in front of our fortifications, drove in the enemy's pickets, and carried his first line of rifle-pits between Chattanooga and Citer's Creek.

We captured nine commissioned officers and about 100 enlisted men.

Our loss is about 111.

To-day Gen. HOOKER, in command of Gen. GRANT's division, Twelfth corps; Gen. OSTERHAUS division, Fifteenth corps, and two brigades, Fourteenth corps, carried the north slope of Lookout Mountain, with small loss on our side, and a loss to the enemy of 500 or 600 prisoners; killed and wounded not reported.

There has been continuous fighting from 12 o'clock until after night; but our troops gallantly repulsed every attempt to take the position.

Gen. SHERMAN crossed the Tennessee River before daylight this morning, at the mouth of the South Chickamauga, with three divisions of the Fifteenth corps and one division of the Fourteenth corps, and carried the northern extremity of Missionary ridge.

Our success so far has been complete and the behavior of the troops admirable.

GEORGE H. THOMAS, Major General.

SECOND DISPATCH.

CHATTANOOGA, Tuesday, Nov. 24—6 P. M.

Maj.-Gen. Halleck. General-in-Chief, Washington :

The fighting to-day progressed favorably.

Gen. SHERMAN carried the end of Missionary Ridge, and his right is now at the Tunnel, and his left at Chickamauga Creek.

The troops from Lookout Valley carried the point of the mountain, and now hold the eastern slope and point high up.

I cannot yet tell the amount of casualties, but our loss is not heavy.

Gen. HOOKER reports 2,000 prisoners taken, besides which a small number have fallen into our hands from Missionary Ridge.

U. S. GRANT, Major-General.

REPORTS FROM REBEL SOURCES.

FORTRESS MONROE, Wednesday, Nov. 25.

The Richmond *Dispatch*, of Nov. 24, has the following :

MISSIONARY RIDGE, Monday, Nov. 23.

The enemy massed a heavy fire on our right this morning, and advanced at 2 o'clock, driving in our pickets. It is not certain yet whether they intend an attack in force, or to advance their lines.

There are various rumors of the occupation of Knoxville by our forces, but nothing official, however.

Two thousand Yankees passed Rogersville, and five regiments through Jacksborough, *en route* for Kentucky. Our forces are active in front.

President DAVIS arrived at Orange Court-house on Saturday. He is stopping with Gen. LEE.

MISSIONARY RIDGE, Nov. 23.

To Gen. Cooper :

We hold all the roads leading into Knoxville, except the one between Holsten and French Broad Rivers. Gen. JONES' cavalry might close that. The enemy's cavalry is most broken up. WHEELER cut off his train between Cumberland Gap and Knoxville.

(Signed,) BRAXTON BRAGG.

CAPT. MAURICE W. WALL A BRIGADIER-GENERAL.—A private dispatch from Washington states that Capt. MAURICE W. WALL, late acting as Adjutant-General of the Irish brigade, has been appointed a Brigadier-General of Colored Volunteers. to report immediately to Maj.-Gen. SCHOFIELD, of St. Louis, Mo. Capt. WALL is a veteran, having been in every engagement from Bull run the first to Gettysburgh.

FROM KNOXVILLE.

GEN. BURNSIDE'S POSITION SATISFACTORY

The Investment of the North Side of the Town Close.

Details of Three Days' Operations Before Knoxville.

CINCINNATI, Wednesday, Nov. 25.

The situation of Gen. BURNSIDE at Knoxville is perfectly satisfactory.

There was heavy firing west of the town on Saturday.

The investment of the north side of the town is close, but the south side is open.

Gen. BURNSIDE is confident of final success.

KNOXVILLE, Sunday, Nov. 22, 1863.

Thursday morning revealed a line of rifle-pits which the enemy had thrown up during the night. A house near our works was occupied by their sharpshooters, to the annoyance of our men, until our batteries shelled them out. During the day the rebels opened with a battery beyond the railroad depot, and threw a few shells. It was silenced by our guns.

On Friday a desultory fire was kept up between the skirmishers. Toward dusk the enemy opened with a new battery of six pieces and again threw a few shells. On the right a brilliant and successful sortie was made to burn a house on the Loudon road, which interfered with our range. The rebels were driven from their rifle-pits and the house burned, when our men came back, shelling them as they did so.

On Saturday a rain-storm set in, lasting nearly all day. The operations of the day were confined to skirmishing.

To-day skirmishing has been constant along the whole line. A few shots have been exchanged between the batteries. The enemy have invested the city with batteries. Their rifle-pits are quite close to our works, and sharpshooters occasionally pick off a man.

THE WAR IN SOUTH CAROLINA.

Dispatches via Richmond—Vigorous Shelling Continued.

FORTRESS MONROE, Wednesday, Nov. 25.

The Richmond *Dispatch*, of the 24th, contains the following from Charleston :

CHARLESTON, Monday, Nov. 23.

There was no shelling of the city last night, but a slow fire on Sumter.

The second dispatch says there has been a vigorous fire kept up between the enemy's batteries and ours all day. The enemy has not shelled the city to-day, but divided his attention between Sumter, Moultrie, Johnson and Simkins. They also threw a number of shells on James Island ; 290 shots were thrown in Sumter last night.

The Northwestern Convention of War Democrats.

CHICAGO, Ill., Wednesday, Nov. 25.

The Northwestern Convention of War Democrats organized this morning.

The business was transacted with closed doors.

None but accredited delegates were admitted.

All the States named in the call were represented.

Gen. JOHN A. McCLERNAND was chosen President of the Convention.

A Committee of nine, of which Judge LOVERIN, of Indiana, was selected as the Chairman, has been appointed to frame a platform or a call.

The Draft in Baltimore—Three Newspaper Reporters Drawn.

BALTIMORE, Wednesday, Nov. 25.

The draft is progressing in a most orderly manner. Three newspaper reporters were so fortunate as to be drawn this morning—one from the *American*, one from the *Clipper* and one from the *Daily Gazette*.

Quota in New-Hampshire.

A dispatch from Concord states that New-Hampshire is rapidly filling up her full quota of men by volunteers.

The Battle of Lookout Mountain

The New-York Times.

VOL. XIII—NO. 3801. NEW-YORK, SUNDAY, NOVEMBER 29, 1863. PRICE TWO CENTS.

GRANT'S VICTORY.

Detailed Official Report of the Operations.

Dispatch from Gen. Meigs to Secretary Stanton.

Graphic Accounts of the Three Days' Fighting.

The Preliminary Movements a Surprise to the Rebels.

The Best Directed and Best Ordered Battle of the War.

GLORIOUS CONDUCT OF OUR TROOPS.

Our Entire Loss Officially Reported at about Three Thousand.

OUR SPECIAL WASHINGTON DISPATCH.

WASHINGTON, Saturday, Nov. 28.

An official statement of our losses in the recent battles at Chattanooga was received here this morning. Our casualties in killed and wounded on the 23d, 24th and 25th, were but little over three thousand at the storming of Lookout Mountain, and at the assault upon Missionary Ridge about two hundred.

The report of our losses on the 25th is not yet received.

Our wounded are all under cover and well cared for. Hospital and all other supplies are abundant.

DETAILED OFFICIAL DISPATH.

HEADQUARTERS, CHATTANOOGA, Nov. 26, 1863.

Edwin M. Stanton, Secretary of War:

SIR: On the 23d instant, at 11½ A. M., Gen. GRANT ordered a demonstration against Mission Ridge, to develop the force holding it. The troops marched out, formed in order, and advanced in line of battle, as if on parade.

The rebels watched the formation and movement from their picket lines and rifle-pits, and from the summits of Mission Ridge, five hundred feet above us, and thought it was a review and drill, so openly and deliberately, so regular, was it all done.

The line advanced, preceded by skirmishers, and at 2 o'clock P.M. reached our picket lines and opened a rattling volley upon the rebel pickets, who replied and run into their advanced line of rifle-pits. After them went our skirmishers and into them, along the centre of the line of 25,000 troops which Gen. THOMAS had so quickly displayed, until we opened fire.

Prisoners assert that they thought the whole movement was a review and general drill, and that it was too late to send to their camps for reinforcements, and that they were overwhelmed by force of numbers. It was a surprise in open daylight.

At 3 P. M., the important advanced position of Orchard Knob and the lines right and left were in our possession, and arrangements were ordered for holding them during the night. The next day, at daylight, Gen. THOMAS had 5,000 men across the Tennessee, and established on its south bank, and commenced the construction of a pontoon bridge about six miles above Chattanooga.

The rebel steamer *Dunbar* was repaired at the right moment, and rendered effective aid in this crossing, carrying over six thousand men. By night-fall, Gen. THOMAS had seized the extremity of Missionary Ridge nearest the river, and was entrenching himself. Gen. HOWARD, with a brigade, opened communication with him from Chattanooga, on the south side of the river. Skirmishing and cannonading continued all day on the left and centre. Gen. HOOKER scaled the slopes of Lookout Mountain, and from the valley of Lookout Creek drove the rebels around the point. He captured some two thousand prisoners, and established himself high up the mountain side, in full view of Chattanooga. This raised the blockade, and now steamers were ordered from Bridgeport to Chattanooga. They had run only to Kelly's Ferry, whence ten miles of hauling over mountain roads and twice across the Tennessee on pontoon bridges brought us our supplies.

All night the point of Missionary Ridge on the extreme left and the side of Lookout Mountain, on the extreme right, blazed with the camp-fires of loyal troops.

The day had been one of dense mists and rains, and much of Gen. HOOKER'S battle was fought above the clouds, which concealed him from our view, but from which his musketry was heard.

At nightfall the sky cleared and the full moon, "the traitors doom," shone upon the beautiful scene, until 1 A. M., when twinkling sparks upon the mountain side showed that picket skirmishing was going on. Then it ceased. A brigade, sent from Chattanooga, crossed the Chattanooga Creek and opened communication with HOOKER.

Gen. GRANT'S headquarters during the afternoon of the 23d and the day of the 24th, were in WOOD'S redoubt, except when, in the course of the day, he rode along the advanced line, visiting the headquarters of the several commanders, in Chattanooga Valley.

At daylight on the 25th the Stars and Stripes were descried on the peak of Lookout. The rebels had evacuated the mountain.

HOOKER moved to descend the mountain, and strik-

Federal troops under General Thomas storm Missionary Ridge.

Missionary Ridge

ing Mission Ridge at the Rossville Gap, to sweep on both sides and on its summit.

The rebel troops were seen as soon as it was light enough, streaming regiments and brigades along the narrow summit of Mission Ridge, either concentrating on the right to overwhelm SHERMAN, or marching for the railroad, and raising the siege.

They had evacuated the valley of Chattanooga—would they abandon that of Chicamauga?

The twenty-pounders and four and a quarter-inch rifles of WOOD's redoubt, opened on Mission Ridge. Orchard Knob sent its compliments to the Ridge, which, with rifled Parrotts answered, and the cannonade thus commenced continued all day. Shot and shell screamed from Orchard Knob to Missionary Ridge, and from Missionary Ridge to Orchard Knob, and from WOOD's redoubt over the heads of Gens. GRANT and THOMAS and their Staffs, who were with us in this favorable position, from whence the whole battle could be seen as in an amphitheatre. The headquarters were under fire all day long.

Cannonading and musketry were heard from Gen. SHERMAN, and Gen. HOWARD marched the Eleventh corps to join him.

Gen. THOMAS sent out skirmishers who drove in the rebel pickets, and chased them into their intrenchments, and at the foot of Mission Ridge SHERMAN made an assault against BRAGG's right, intrenched on a high knob next to that, on which SHERMAN himself lay fortified. The assault was gallantly made.

SHERMAN reached the edge of the crest, and held his ground for (it seemed to me) an hour, but was bloodily repulsed by reserves.

A general advance was ordered, and a strong line of skirmishers, followed by a deployed line of battle, some two miles in length. At the signal of leaden shots from the headquarters on Orchard Knob, the line moved rapidly and orderly forward. The rebel pickets discharged their muskets and ran into their rifle-pits. Our skirmishers followed on their heels.

The line of battle was not far behind, and we saw the grey rebels swarm out of the ledge line of rifle-pits, in numbers which surprised us, and over the base of the hill. A few turned and fired their pieces, but the greater number collected into the many roads which cross obliquely up its steep face, and went on to their top. Some regiments pressed on and

swarmed up the steep sides of the ridge, and here and there a color was advanced beyond the lines. The attempt appeared most dangerous, but the advance was supported, and the whole line was ordered to storm the heights, upon which not less than forty pieces of artillery, and no one knew how many muskets, stood ready to slaughter the assailants. With cheers answering to cheers, the men swarmed upwards. They gathered to the points least difficult of ascent, and the line was broken. Color after color was planted on the summit, while musket and cannon vomited their thunder upon them.

A well-directed shot from Orchard Knob exploded a rebel caisson on the summit, and the gun was seen galloping to the right, its driver lashing his horses. A party of our soldiers intercepted them, and the gun was captured with cheers.

A fierce musketry fight broke out to the left, where, between THOMAS and SHERMAN, a mile or two of the ridge was still occupied by the rebels.

BRAGG left the house in which he had held his headquarters, and rode to the rear as our troops crowded the hill on either side of him.

Gen. GRANT proceeded to the summit, and there did we only know its height.

Some of the captured artillery was put into position. Artillerists were sent for to work the guns. Caissons were searched for ammunition.

The rebel log breastworks were torn to pieces and carried to the other side of the ridge, and used in forming barricades across.

A strong line of infantry was formed in the rear of BAIRD's line, hotly engaged in a musketry contest with the rebels to the left, and a secure lodgement was soon effected.

The other assault to the right of our centre gained the summit, and the rebels threw down their arms and fled.

HOOKER coming in favorable position, swept the right of the ridge and captured many prisoners.

BRAGG's remaining troops left early in the night, and the battle of Chattanooga, after days of manœuvring and fighting, was won. The strength of the rebellion in the centre is broken. BURNSIDE is relieved from danger in East Tennessee. Kentucky and Tennessee are rescued. Georgia and the south-

east are threatened in the rear, and another victory is added to the chapter of "Unconditional Surrender GRANT."

To-night the estimate of captures is several thousands of prisoners and thirty pieces of artillery.

Our loss for so great a victory is not severe.

BRAGG is firing the railroad as he retreats towards Dalton. SHERMAN is in hot pursuit.

To-day I viewed the battle-field, which extends for six miles along Mission Ridge and for several miles on Lookout Mountain.

Probably not so well directed, so well ordered a battle has been delivered during the war. But one assault was repulsed—but that assault by calling to that point the rebel reserves, prevented them repulsing any of the others.

A few days since BRAGG sent to Gen. GRANT a flag of truce, advising him that it would be prudent to remove non-combatants who might be still in Chattanooga.

No reply has been returned, but the combatants having removed from this vicinity, it is probable that non-combatants can remain without imprudence.

N. C. MEIGS, Quartermaster-General

GEN. BURNSIDE'S SITUATION.

Interesting Statements by Col. Leisure.

Col. LEISURE, of the Roundhead (Pa.) regiment, who left Knoxville on Nov. 11, has given the Pittsburgh *Chronicle* the following interesting information regarding BURNSIDE's situation.

"That General says that BURNSIDE has been all along aware that a movement was to be made against him, and that the late fight at Campbell's Station, and other points between Loudon and Knoxville, was not so much to allow his trains to get off as to afford his outlying posts, &c., to concentrate at Knoxville. This has been successfully done, and BURNSIDE's force now amounts, we are glad to say, to full 20,000 men. This includes, however, several new levies of East Tennesseeans, who, although individually brave, are ignorant, badly drilled, and generally unreliable when hard pressed. BURNSIDE has plenty of guns and ammunition, and can hold Knoxville against four times his numbers. Some of the best batteries in the service, including one of 20-pound Parrotts, is with him, while the formidable fortifications stretching in a semi-circle a couple of miles from the town, and constructed by the rebels against us, have been materially strengthened under directions of Col. POE.

It is a mistake to suppose Knoxville closely invested. LONGSTREET is only on the north side, while the south and all the region across the Holston River is open to us. This district is full of forage, corn, wheat, &c. BURNSIDE has all the mills. He has also fortified the heights immediately across the river, and his batteries command for four miles the only practicable roads of approach to the city on that side.

It is by this route BURNSIDE's telegraph to Cumberland Gap runs, by which he communicates with GRANT, and it is by this route he could retreat to Cumberland Gap if the rebels pressed him too hard. The most reliable troops with BURNSIDE are the Ninth army corps, now numbering about twelve thousand men. He has abundance of cavalry, under Gen. SHACKELFORD, the commander who chased MORGAN through Ohio, and altogether is able to give LONGSTREET a hard tussle.

Gen. LEISURE states that not only has BURNSIDE entire confidence in his position, but that his whole army have entire confidence in *him*, and will hear of his being relieved with great regret. It is probable that by this time the railroad between Cleveland and Loudon, by which LONGSTREET came, and must get all his supplies, has been cut either by GRANT's or BURNSIDE's cavalry; and if this be the case, LONGSTREET will have a 'very hard road to travel.' He has already been punished severely, and it will be a singular thing if, between SHERMAN and BURNSIDE, he be not caught in a trap which will finish his campaign for some time to come.

The troops which were probably intended to reinforce LONGSTREET from LEE, *via* Lynchburgh and Jonesboro, have doubtless been recalled to Gordonsville, by MEADE's threatened advance. MEADE is waiting on the banks of the Rapidan, to strike at LEE whenever that General shows any symptoms of weakening himself to strengthen either BRAGG or LONGSTREET, so that the situation appears to be satisfactory all around. LONGSTREET's force is composed chiefly of Alabamians and Georgians, but with the exception of HOOD's division, the rest are not the best troops in the South. Besides, even supposing his railroad communications uncut, he will have to wagon all his supplies over most wretched roads for over thirty miles. This he cannot do long, so that if he be not overwhelmed, we may soon expect to hear of his speedy retirement.

A DISPATCH FROM PARSON BROWNLOW.

The following dispatch appears in the Cincinnati *Gazette:*

CAMP LOUDON, Ky., Wednesday, Nov. 25.

Gen. BURNSIDE still holds Knoxville, and has held his position for ten days, against great odds. He is a moral and military hero, and has endeared himself to the Union men of East Tennessee as no man ever did, and deserves the honor and confidence of the whole country. My family are in Knoxville, and I am on my way to Cincinnati—advised to leave by the military authorities. I shall return by Chattanooga.

W. G. BROWNLOW.

The New-York Times.

VOL. XII — NO. 3802   NEW-YORK, MONDAY, NOVEMBER 30, 1863   PRICE THREE CENTS

Editorials

The Danger of Over Confidence.

It may not be amiss to caution the public against over-sanguine estimates of the recent victories of the Union arms. There seems to be no doubt that GRANT has achieved a very brilliant success, and has defeated BRAGG's army, which was the main strength of the rebellion in that quarter. It is not yet certain, however, that he has so routed and broken it as to prevent it from taking the field again, though it is not likely that its old strength can ever be renewed. BURNSIDE is still in a position of danger, though our latest advices indicate his ability to hold his ground until aid can reach him. MEADE, moreover, has commenced a movement against LEE, from which we may reasonably anticipate the best results, though it is well to remember that LEE is a much more formidable opponent to deal with than BRAGG.

If these movements are crowned with complete success, the back-bone of the rebellion will unquestionably be broken. We shall have seen the beginning of the end. But the end itself will not have been reached. Very much will remain to be done before resistance on the part of the rebels will cease, and the supremacy of the Constitution will be restored. There will still be elements of force scattered throughout the South powerful enough to require the presence and active efforts of a very large Union army, and to draw largely, for some time to come, upon the resources and the patience of the Government. For a long time, certainly for months and possibly for years, it will be necessary to maintain strong National garrisons in every part of the rebel States,—not only for the purpose of enforcing the authority of the National Government, but for the preservation of domestic peace. Our conquest, however complete, will leave society in the Southern States in a state of chaos and confusion. Its peace has rested hitherto solely on force,—on a system of repression more perfect in its details, and more rigid in its rule, than prevails in any other part of the world. This whole system will be overthrown, suddenly and by violence, and nothing is left to take its place. This lack must for a time, at least, be supplied by the National Government. The presence of very powerful Union armies will be absolutely essential in the Southern States for a long time after active hostilities against the National authority shall have ceased.

It must not be supposed, therefore, that the patriotic efforts of the friends of the Government can safely be relaxed. Every exertion must still be made to fill up the ranks of our armies. The volunteer movement should be pushed forward with steady and unremitted energy. The country will still have need of all the men it has called for. It must still expend enormous sums of money, and call upon the country for the largest contributions of men and means, to insure the complete and final overthrow of the rebellion.

The Union Victory in Georgia.

In the history of the military operations that have thus far marked the progress of the war, Gen. GRANT's operations of last week stand out in distinct relief as the one example, on either side, *of a victory followed up, and rendered decisive by the complete rout of the enemy.* It is this unique fact which forms the most striking characteristic in a success so magnificent in all the features of its planning and execution. Indeed, in the estimate of the great weight of debt under which Gen. GRANT has laid the nation by this victory, it is not easy to say whether we should set most by the material gain to the Union arms of this great blow inflicted on the enemy, or by the moral gain to the whole country of this inspiring example of unwonted military vigor and power. At a stroke, Gen. GRANT has brushed away the cobwebs of military pedantry, (dignified by the name of prudence,) which would make us believe that the pursuit of a defeated foe has become an impossibility; and in a country which accumulates in itself every condition unfavorable to pursuit (thus making it the more glorious) has ground to powder and scattered to the winds a great army of the rebellion, a week ago intrenched in a position so formidable by nature and art as to seem absolutely unassailable.

Gen. GRANT's victory has been so completely won "on the wing" that hardly a moiety of his captures in men and material have been made in battle. Indeed there has been throughout the week's operations, properly speaking, no great battle at all. GRANT caught BRAGG in the act of preparing for retreat, flung himself impetuously on the mountain lair, which the rebel Commander turned savagely to defend, routed him from it, and has since hung on his flanks and rear with the tenacity of a bloodhound. The first day's action, that of Monday, was for the enemy's advanced position, directly fronting Chattanooga, which was carried with trifling loss. Tuesday gave us the possession of the north slope of Lookout Mountain, carried by Gen. HOOKER, and the north slope of Mission Ridge, carried by Gen. SHERMAN. During the night of Tuesday, the rebels evacuated Lookout Mountain, and thereby the valley of Chattanooga. On Wednesday Gen. SHERMAN assaulted the rebel position on Missionary Ridge, and was repulsed, but a general advance of the whole line carried the Ridge. As the result of these three operations, between four and five thousand prisoners and forty pieces of artillery were taken. BRAGG's whole line, broken and shattered, fled during the night. "I believe," writes Gen. GRANT, "I am not premature in announcing a complete victory over BRAGG."

A General of the ordinary stamp would have rested abundantly satisfied with these three days' magnificent work. But GRANT is not a General of the ordinary stamp. Inspired with the Napoleonic maxim that nothing is done till all is done, *pursuit* presented itself as the next thing in order. "We will pursue the enemy in the morning," he writes on Wednesday night. Flying columns accordingly were promptly dispatched after the broken battalions of the enemy—HOOKER toward Ringgold, SHERMAN toward Redclay, and other corps wherever the enemy was to be found. This completed the work. It had been a defeat; it now became a rout, with all its attendant exhibitions. "It is a singular thing," says MARMONT, "the different impression produced upon the soldier when he looks the enemy in the face, and when he turns his back upon him. In the first case, he only sees what really exists; *in the second, his imagination increases the danger.*" All the powerful effects of this subtle metaphysical influence are fully displayed in the details which reach us of this wonderful flight and pursuit, continued for four days and perhaps not yet ended. Artillery, ammunition, caissons, wagons, arms, knapsacks, everything, in fact, that impeded their flight, was thrown away. "Wherever we reach portions of the rebel army," writes an eye-witness, "they instantly throw down their arms and scatter like frightened sheep. What is now left of BRAGG's boasted army is but a panic-stricken mob." The captures already have been immense—in men reaching probably ten thousand, in artillery at least sixty pieces.

Whether the blow which GRANT has inflicted on the army of BRAGG is to be counted as crushing as that which BLUCHER dealt the legions of NAPOLEON, can only be known when we are able to grasp the full scope of what has already been done, and when the work itself shall have been finished, which it is not as yet. There is every present appearance that when Gen. GRANT gets through with the business, the great rebel army of the Southwest will have ceased to exist: not, necessarily, that he will have "bagged" or butchered the whole host; but that its losses in men and material shall be so great, its disintegration and demoralization so complete, as to render it no longer available as an independent, effective army. The budget of rebel losses may show greater or less; but this, we believe, will be the net result. In doing this Gen. GRANT has done what no other Commander on either side has done during this war, and what has not very often been done in any wars.

HOOKER's BATTLE ABOVE THE CLOUDS.—Quartermaster Gen. MEIGS, in his lively account of the three days' conflict before Chattanooga, mentions the notable fact that in Gen. HOOKER's fight up the slopes of Lookout Mountain, "much of the battle was fought *above the clouds,* which concealed him from our view, but from which his musketry was heard." There is on record at least one parallel to this in the campaign of NAPOLEON in the Carnic Alps, in 1797. The battle of the Col de Tarvis, March 22, 1797, was fought above the clouds—the artillery thundering in the very laboratory of storms and arsenal of the electric batteries—while the cavalry charged and performed their evolutions on the ice, and the infantry floundered to the attack through snow three feet thick.

1864

The New-York Times.

VOL. XIII—NO. 3914. NEW-YORK, SATURDAY, APRIL 9, 1864. PRICE THREE CENTS.

FROM WASHINGTON.

The Anti-Slavery Amendment to the Constitution.

Passage of the Joint Resolution in the Senate.

SLAVERY TO BE TOTALLY ABOLISHED.

An Interesting Discussion in the House.

Views of One of Mr. Vallandigham's Friends on the War.

The Election Key-note of the Democratic Party.

SPECIAL DISPATCHES TO THE N. Y. TIMES.

WASHINGTON, Friday, April 8.

GEN. SEDGWICK'S TESTIMONY.

Gen. SEDGWICK testified to-day before the Committee on the Conduct of the War. He justified the conduct of Gen. MEADE at the battle of Gettysburgh, and was very severe on Gen. HOOKER in regard to the battle of Chancellorsville.. In reply to the question why Gen. HOOKER recrossed the river, he said he could give no reasons to justify such a step. He only did so after positive orders from Gen. HOOKER, which he exhibited to the committee. He also laid before the committee many other important orders in connection with that movement, which have never been made public.

THE REBEL DIPLOMATISTS IN EUROPE.

Advices received by the last steamer from Europe represent that the functions of the rebel diplomatists have materially changed within the past two months. MASON is in dignified retirement—a perfect anchorite—having shut himself out of sight of even his own cotemporaries.

SLIDELL is speculating, and has already obtained a notoriety among the gamblers of the Bourse. He has made money ; but he never touches Confederate securities, and, like SLIDELL, so are all his co-adventurers. It is noticeable that the rebel diplomats are far more successful as speculators than they were as plenipotentiaries.

PROCEEDINGS OF CONGRESS.

SENATE.

WASHINGTON, Friday, April 8.

THE TRANSFER OF SEAMEN FROM THE ARMY TO THE NAVY.

By unanimous consent Mr. HALE called up the bill to repeal the first section of the joint resolution of Feb. 24, 1864, relating to the transfer of persons from the military to the naval service, which was passed.

THE AMENDMENT TO THE CONSTITUTION.

The Senate then proceeded to the consideration of the joint resolution amending the Constitution.

Mr. SUMNER, of Massachusetts (Union.) said that the first thought that would strike an angel from the skies, or a stranger from another place, if either could be permitted to visit this earth, with surprise, after viewing the extent and resources of our people, would be the fact that there are four millions of human beings held in the most abject bondage, driven by the lash like beasts, and deprived of all rights, even that of knowledge and the sacred right of family. The stranger's astonishment would be doubly increased when he was pointed to the Constitution as the guardian of this many-headed wickedness. He would interpret the Constitution in its true sense, and say that Slavery could not exist by its positive text. He (SUMNER) contended that the words "slave" and "Slavery" did not appear in the Constitution, and if the pretension of property in man lurks anywhere in the Constitution, it was under a feigned name. He considered the preamble the key to open the whole instrument to freedom. He would call attention to those chain-breaking words, "No person shall be deprived of life, liberty or property, without due process of law." Scorning all false interpretations and glosses, which may have been fastened upon the Constitution as a support of Slavery, he would declare there was nothing in the text on which the hideous wrong could be founded. In dealing with this question in the past, it has not been the Constitution so much as human nature which has been at fault. Let the people change, and the Constitution would change also, for the Constitution was the shadow, while the people were the substance. Under the influences of the present struggle the people have changed, and in nothing so much as Slavery. Old opinions and prejudices have dissolved and the traditional foothold which Slavery once possessed has been weakening gradually, until now it scarcely exists. Naturally this change must show itself in the interpretation of the Constitution, and it is already visible in the concession of power; which were formerly denied, and the time has come when the Constitution, so long interpreted for Slavery, may be interpreted for Freedom. He contended, among the concessions for power over Slavery as a military necessity. Many join with PATRICK HENRY, who, in the Virginia Convention, declared the power of manumission was given to Congress in the Constitution, and argued against it on that ground. Slavery, receiving no support in the Constitution, he contended, was clearly under the control of Congress, under the giving Congress power to "provide for the common defence and general welfare." To all who would deny the power of Congress over Slavery, he referred to the words of PATRICK HENRY, when he said that on that subject the Constitution "speaks to the point." He contended that under the war power no one could deny its complete efficiency in enfranchising the soldiers-slave and his family. In the words of SHAKESPEARE, when he makes *Harry*, on the eve of the battle of Agincourt, say to his men to encourage them: "For he, to-day, that sheds his blood with me shall be my brother ; be he ne'r so vile, this day shall gentle his condition." He contended also that the clause guaranteeing a Republican form of Government to each State made it our plain duty to abolish Slavery, considering the essential elements that constitute it, as understood by our fathers. The clause that no person shall be deprived of life, liberty, or property, without due process of law, throws protection over every person without regard to color, class or condition. He held that this was not only a guarantee against, but a prohibition of Slavery. On the very face of the Constitution Slavery was an outlaw, and in its express provisions he had shown from sources of power, which, if executed, rendered it impossible. Nothing but hesitancy and delay in eradicating Slavery was unconstitutional. Slavery was not only a nuisance, but a public enemy and traitor in the rebellious States, lending succor to them, and holding out blue lights to encourage and direct their operations, and it must be abolished. In reference to the question of compensation, founded on the shameful assumption that there was property in man, there was a time when he was willing to pay money for emancipation. But it was as a ransom, and not compensation. Money was no longer needed for the purpose. The time had come for the old tocsin to sound, "Millions for defence ; not one cent for tribute." Millions of dollars and strong arms to defend our country against slave masters ; not one cent for tribute for them. Every dollar for compensation paid should go to the slave. He contended that the pretension to compensation for the renunciation of a system too disgusting to picture or detail, was odious. Slavery must be overthrown ; first, by the courts declaring and applying the true principles of the Constitution ; second, by Congress in the exercise of the powers which belong to it, and that by the people by amending the Constitution to that end. As the courts had failed to do their duty, Congress, by a single brief statute, will sweep Slavery out of existence. If Congress may not do this, let the Fugitive Slave Law be repealed and all others conflicting with the right of colored persons. But beyond all, the people must put the capstone on the glorious structure by an amendment to the Constitution. While he was desirous of seeing the great rule of freedom which we were about to ordain embodied in a text which should be like the precious casket to the more precious treasure, he was consoled by the thought that the most homely text containing such a rule would be more beautiful far than any passage of poetry or eloquence of words, and would be read with gratitude when the rising dome of this Capitol, with the statue of liberty which surmounted it, had crumbled into dust.

The discussion was further continued by Messrs. POWELL and DAVIS.

Mr. SAULSBURY, of Delaware, (Dem.,) proposed lengthy amendments and a substitute securing the liberty of the press and free speech, and reëstablishing the principles of the Missouri Compromise, which were rejected.

Mr. SUMNER withdrew his amendment, heretofore offered as a substitute, as he did not desire the committee's amendment in its passage.

Mr. McDOUGALL, of California, (Union,) said that the vote he should give against the measure was not from want of philanthropy to the slave, or from hatred to freedom. He had been the teacher of philanthropy to some of those who were now so blatant for freedom. He denied that the question of emancipation was germane to the present war, and had, therefore, declined to take part in it, believing that it tended to aggravate, rather than heal our wounds. Any effort to antagonize the blacks and whites must result in disaster to the former. As a true friend of the black race, he should vote against the measure.

The amendments, as reported from the Judiciary Committee, as a substitute for the original bill of Mr. HENDERSON, were then adopted.

YEAS—Messrs. Anthony, Brown, Chandler, Clark, Collamer, Conness, Cowan, Dixon, Doolittle, Fessenden, Foot, Foster, Grimes, Hale, Henderson, Howard, Howe, Johnson, Lane of Indiana, Lane of Kansas, Morgan, Morrill, Nesmith, Pomeroy, Ramsay, Sherman, Sprague, Sumner, Ten Eyck, Trumbull, Van Winkle, Wade, Wilkinson, Wiley, Wilson—38.

NAYS—Messrs. Davis, Hendricks, McDougall, Powell, Riddle, Saulsbury.

The following is the joint resolution as passed:

Be it Resolved, by the Senate and House of Representatives of the United States of America, in Congress assembled, two-thirds of both Houses concurring, that the following article be proposed to the Legislatures of the several States, as an amendment to the Constitution of the United States, which, when ratified by three-fourths of said Legislatures, shall be valid to all intents and purposes, as a part of the said Constitution, namely:

ARTICLE XIII, SECTION 1. Neither Slavery nor involuntary servitude, except as a punishment for crime whereof the party shall have been duly convicted, shall exist within the United States, or any place subject to their jurisdiction.

SEC. 2. Congress shall have power to enforce this article by appropriate legislation.

The Senate then adjourned until Monday.

THE WAR IN THE SOUTHWEST

A Rebel General's Order on the Repulse at Paducah.

WEST KENTUCKY TO BE HELD.

MISCELLANEOUS INTELLIGENCE.

The Rebel Forrest Leaving Kentucky.

PHILADELPHIA, Friday, April 8.

A special Cincinnati dispatch to the *Bulletin* says:

Notwithstanding the rebel BUFORD's assurance that he intends to remain permanently in Kentucky, it is reported that FORREST is manœuvering to get out of the State by dividing his forces into small detachments and slipping them off by byways.

THE LAST LOST REBEL RAM.

Sinking of the Great Iron-clad Rebel Ram Tennessee off Mobile.

The great rebel ram, off Mobile, which, according to Southern accounts, was to sink our whole fleet, has been sunk by a squall.

From the New-Orleans Era, March 29.

WEST GULF SQUADRON, Sunday, March 20, 1864.

On March 1 the *Kennebec* steamed up to Dauphine Island, to communicate with the vessels in the Sound. Several rebel gunboats, the *Tennessee* among them, were seen lying near Grant's Pass.

The day was squally, and at about 3 o'clock in the afternoon, the lookout on board the *Kennebec* sung out, "The *Tenneseee* is sinking!" All the officers on deck immediately looked toward the place where the *Tennessee* was lying, and, sure enough they saw her go down.

At the same time signals were seen on board the *Octarora*, lying in the Sound, and said signals interpreted, read: "The rebel ram *Tennessee* sunk."

It appears that a squall struck her, and, she being very low in the water, keeled over and went down.

Two feet of her smoke-stack can now be seen above the water, at the spot where the great ram once lay at anchor.

The New-York Times.

VOL. XIII—NO. 3920.   NEW-YORK, SATURDAY, APRIL 16, 1864.   PRICE THREE CENTS.

THE BLACK FLAG.

Horrible Massacre by the Rebels.

Fort Pillow Captured After a Desperate Fight.

Four Hundred of the Garrison Brutally Murdered.

Wounded and Unarmed Men Bayoneted and Their Bodies Burned.

White and Black Indiscriminately Butchered.

Devilish Atrocities of the Insatiate Fiends.

FROM CAIRO.

CAIRO, Thursday, April 14.

On Tuesday morning the rebel Gen. FORREST attacked Fort Pillow. Soon after the attack FORREST sent a flag of truce demanding the surrender of the fort and garrison, meanwhile disposing of his force so as to gain the advantage. Our forces were under command of Major BOOTH, of the Thirteenth Tennessee (U. S.) Heavy Artillery, formerly of the First Alabama Cavalry.

The flag of truce was refused, and fighting resumed. Afterward a second flag came in, which was also refused.

Both flags gave the rebels advantage of gaining new positions.

The battle was kept up until 3 P. M., when Major BOOTH was killed, and Major BRADFORD took command.

The rebels now came in swarms over our troops, compelling them to surrender.

Immediately upon the surrender ensued a scene which utterly baffles description. Up to that time, comparatively few of our men had been killed; but, insatiate as fiends, bloodthirsty as devils incarnate, the Confederates commenced an indiscriminate butchery of the whites and blacks, including those of both colors who had been previously wounded.

The black soldiers, becoming demoralized, rushed to the rear, the white officers having thrown down their arms.

Both white and black were bayoneted, shot or sabred; even dead bodies were horribly mutilated, and children of seven and eight years and several negro women killed in cold blood. Soldiers unable to speak from wounds were shot dead, and their bodies rolled down the banks into the river. The dead and wounded negroes were piled in heaps and burned, and several citizens who had joined our forces for protection were killed or wounded.

Out of the garrison of six hundred, only two hundred remained alive.

Among our dead officers are Capt. BRADFORD, Lieuts. BARR, ACKERSSTROM, WILSON, REVEL and Major BOOTH, all of the Thirteenth Tennessee Cavalry.

Capt. POSTON and Lieut. LYON, Thirteenth Tennessee Cavalry, and Capt. YOUNG, Twenty-fourth Missouri, Acting-Provost-Marshal, were taken prisoners.

Maj. BRADFORD was also captured, but is said to

have escaped; it is feared, however, that he has been killed.

The steamer *Platte Valley* came up at about half-past 3 o'clock, and was hailed by the rebels under a flag of truce. Men were sent ashore to bury the dead, and take aboard such of the wounded as the enemy had allowed to live. Fifty-seven were taken aboard, including seven or eight colored. Eight died on the way up. The steamer arrived here this evening, and was immediately sent to the Mound City Hospital, to discharge her suffering cargo.

Among our wounded officers of colored troops are Capt. PORTER, Lieut. LIBBERTS and Adjt. LEMMING.

Six guns were captured by the rebels, and carried off, including two ten-pound Parrotts and two twelve-pound howitzers. A large amount of stores was destroyed or carried away.

The intention of the rebels seemed to be to evacuate the place, and move on toward Memphis.

LATER.

CAIRO, Thursday, April 15.

Two negro soldiers, wounded at Fort Pillow, were buried by the rebels, but afterward worked themselves out of their graves. They were among those brought up in the *Platte Valley*, and are now in hospital at Mound City.

The officers of the *Platte Valley* receive great credit from the military authorities for landing at Fort Pillow, at eminent risk, and taking our wounded on board, and for their kind attentions on the way up.

REPORTS FROM ST. LOUIS.

ST. LOUIS, Friday, April 15.

The correspondent of the *Union*, who was on board the steamer *Platte Valley* at Fort Pillow, gives even a more appalling description of the fiendishness of the rebels than our Cairo dispatches.

Many of our wounded were shot in the hospital. The remainder were driven out, and the hospital was burned.

On the morning after the battle the rebels went over the field, and shot the negroes who had not died from their wounds.

Several of the guns captured by FORREST at Fort Pillow were spiked before falling into his hands. Others were turned upon gunboat No. 7, which, having fired some 300 rounds and exhausted her ammunition, was compelled to withdraw. Although a tin-clad, she received but slight injury.

Gen. LEE arrived and assumed the command at the beginning of the battle. Previous to which Gen. CHALMERS directed the movements. FORREST, with the main force, retired after the fight to Brownsville, taking with him the captured funds.

While the steamer *Platte Valley* lay under flag of truce, taking on board our wounded, some of the rebel officers, and among them Gen. CHALMERS, went on board, and some of our officers showed them great deference, drinking with them, and showing them other marks of courtesy.

Many of those who had escaped from the works and hospital, who desired to be treated as prisoners of war, as the rebels said, were ordered to fall into line, and when they had formed, were inhumanly shot down.

Of 350 colored troops not more than 50 escaped the massacre, and not one officer that commanded them survives. Only four officers of the Thirteenth Tennessee escaped death.

The loss of the Thirteenth Tennessee is 800 killed. The remainder were wounded and captured.

Gen. CHALMER told this correspondent that, although it was against the policy of his Government to spare negro soldiers or their officers, he had done all in his power to stop the carnage. At the same time he believed it was right.

Another officer said our white troops would have been protected had they not been found on duty with negroes.

While the rebels endeavored to conceal their loss, it was evident that they suffered severely. Col. REED, commanding a Tennessee regiment, was mortally wounded. There were two or three well filled hospitals at a short distance in the country.

FROM LOUISVILLE.

LOUISVILLE, Thursday, April 14.

Col. PRATT, commanding at Paducah, telegraphs that he is informed that Paducah has been attacked, and the town is full of rebels.

FURTHER FROM PADUCAH.

CAIRO, Friday, April 15.

No boats have been allowed to leave here for points below Columbus since the first news of the Fort Pillow affair.

The attack on Paducah yesterday proved to be a mere raid for plunder, made by a couple of hundred men, who were shelled out by the fort and gunboats after occupying a position of the city in squads.

About noon they left, taking away a number of horses and considerable plunder, and leaving behind about six of their wounded. No one was hurt on our side.

DEPARTMENT OF THE GULF.

Arrival of the Continental and George Washington from New-Orleans.

ALL QUIET AT ALEXANDRIA.

Gen. Banks Moving Up the Red River.

Our Land and Naval Forces Still Advancing.

AFFAIRS IN TEXAS.

THE CONSTITUTION CONVENTION IN SESSION.

THE "IRON-CLAD" TEST OATH OF LOYALTY.

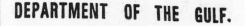

The steamer *Continental*, from New-Orleans on the 8th instant, arrived at this port yesterday morning. The *George Washington*, with New-Orleans dates to the 9th, also arrived yesterday. We are under obligations to Purser ALLEN for the prompt delivery of our files. The news is of only ordinary interest. Alexandria dates of the 5th instant report that Gen. BANKS and staff proceeded up the river and were reported to be at the Grand Ecore. All was quiet at Alexandria, and ample precaution taken against surprise by the enemy.

For the present Grand Ecore will be the headquarters of Gen. BANKS. The *Black Hawk*, on returning to Alexandria, when about twenty-five miles below Grand Ecore, was fired at by a party of about thirty guerillas, wounding Maj. E. GIFFORD, Paymaster United States army, the engineer, and a negress. Neither of the three was seriously injured, although Maj. GIFFORD had a narrow escape. He was struck in the arm by a buckshot, and a minie ball passed through and cut off some of his whiskers. The *Black Hawk* sustained but trifling injuries. Red River had fallen six feet at Alexandria, and was still receding. The heavy iron-clads had dropped down to Fort de Russy. There was still sufficient water for the gunboats and transports to cross the falls. The streets of Alexandria were barricaded in case of raids by the rebels. Some five hundred of the people have taken the oath under the President's Amnesty Proclamation. A Union meeting was held on the 4th inst.

The steamer *Luminary*, before reported destroyed, was above the Falls, uninjured.

The reports of a rebel attack on Alexandria are untrue.

The New-York Times.

VOL. XIII—NO. 3938.   NEW-YORK, SUNDAY, MAY 8, 1864.   PRICE FOUR CENTS.

THE BATTLE.

IMPORTANT NEWS FROM VIRGINIA.

A Great Battle Begun on Thursday.

Lee Confronts Grant with His Whole Army.

Severe Engagement Between Hancock and Longstreet.

HEAVY LOSS ON BOTH SIDES.

The Fifth Corps also Partly Engaged.

The Battle Renewed on Friday Morning.

Gen. Burnside's Corps on the Ground for Support.

STUART'S CAVALRY ROUTED BY SHERIDAN

The Troops Enthusiastic to a High Degree.

HIGHLY IMPORTANT FROM BUTLER'S ARMY

Very Successful Landing at City Point.

THE REBELS COMPLETELY SURPRISED.

Cavalry Expedition to Destroy the Richmond and Petersburgh Railroad.

Full Particulars from Our Special Correspondent.

WASHINGTON, Saturday, May 7.

The statements which were received here to-day, and which are entitled to belief, are that Gen. LEE made a tremendous and violent attack to pierce our centre, hoping thereby to divide our forces and to secure a victory; but Gen. HITCHCOCK's corps

Lieutenant-General Ulysses S. Grant, posing at his headquarters during the Wilderness Campaign.

came to the relief, and, amid a murderous fire, formed in line of battle, and thwarted the designs of the rebels. The loss was heavy on both sides.

Gen. SHERIDAN was profitably engaged in another part of the field, and sent the Chief in command a message that he had routed STUART's cavalry.

The attack of LEE was on our advancing columns, who doubtless anticipated a victory by his onslaught, before the main body could advance to the field of battle.

The appearances on Thursday were that the hostilities would be renewed on Friday.

A Battle Begun on Thursday—Grant Confronted by Lee's Whole Force—Severe Engagements Between Portions of Each Army—Hancock Engages Longstreet—The Battle-Ground near Chancellorsville.

From the Tribune.

UNION MILLS, Va., Friday, May 6—9 P. M.

The grand Army of the Potomac crossed the Rapi-

dan on Wednesday. The Second Corps moved on Tuesday to the Mills, opposite Ely's Ford. On Wednesday morning, at 4 o'clock, the cavalry crossed and drove the rebel pickets from the opposite heights, meeting with no opposition.

A position was gained and the corps moved on at 7 o'clock, taking the road to Chancellorsville, at which place Gen. HANCOCK would establish his headquarters.

The Fifth and Sixth Corps crossed at Germanna Ford in the course of the day, taking the road to the Wilderness.

On Wednesday night Gen. WARREN's headquarters were at the Wilderness, Gen. SEDGWICK on his right, and the general headquarters at Germanna Ford.

On Thursday morning the rebels pressed our pickets, and appeared to be in strong force on our right. The Fifth New-York Cavalry, skirmishing on the Orange Court house road, near Perkins' tavern, were driven in with a severe loss, leaving many wounded on the field. Gen. GRIFFITH's division was marched forward on our right about 11 o'clock to feel the enemy's position, and were met by the rebel Gen. A. P. HILL, supported by Gen. EWELL.

A severe action took place, in which we captured about 300 prisoners, though it is reported that we lost two guns. Meantime, Gen. HANCOCK marched his corps to the right to connect with WARREN, and had hardly got into position, his left resting on or near Chancellorsville, when he was attacked by LONGSTREET with his full corps, and a part of EWELL's.

Gen. HANCOCK, with the assistance of GETTY's division of the Sixth Corps, held his position under musketed fire of two and a half hours duration, in which his command suffered severely, inflicting much injury upon the rebels.

Other developments showed LEE to have his whole force in our front.

This knowledge of their position was, of course, highly important, and was thus obtained only by the greatest skill in the handling of our troops. It not being the purpose of Gen. MEADE to advance upon the enemy, he ordered the line of battle to be held till morning.

The position of our troops on Thursday night was parallel with and a little in advance of the road from Germanna Ford to Chancellorville, the two flanks resting on those points, and general headquarters at the Wilderness.

Meanwhile, in the afternoon the advance of the 9th Corps crossed Germanna Ford, taking position on our right flank.

Gen. BURNSIDE's rear arrived this forenoon.

It was understood that a general attack was to be made this morning, and heavy firing had commenced on our right when I had left, at 5 o'clock.

Heavy cannonading was heard when I passed Kelly's Ford, about 9 o'clock this forenoon, which leads me to believe that we had driven them to their defences, as no heavy guns could be brought into action on the former position.

There ought to be no doubt that there has been a grand victory, as Gen. MEADE showed his strength yesterday by a stubborn and gallant defence without using half the command that he has undoubtedly brought into the action to-day. The troops are in a high state of enthusiasm.

Reports from Washington—Doubtful Rumors—A Three Days' Battle Reported.
WASHINGTON, Saturday, May 7.

The *Republican* has the following:

"The Government has information this morning, whether from official sources or other we are unable to learn positively at the moment of going to press, that on Wednesday at daylight Gen. GRANT's whole army was entirely across the Rapidan. It marched to a plain a little beyond, and near the Chancellorsville battle-ground, when LEE was forced out of his works and offered battle, which was at once accepted. The fight became fierce, and lasted until dark, the enemy being forced back some distance, with great loss, leaving most of his killed and wounded in our hands.

The two armies lay on their arms all night Wednesday, and at daylight on Thursday the battle opened again, and raged with the greatest fury on both sides until dark, when it was found that the enemy had been forced back in the two days' fight about two miles and a half, leaving heaps of dying, killed and wounded on the field to be buried and taken care of by our troops. We have heard various estimates made of the number slaughtered, but at this moment it is useless to speculate on the subject. Everyone knows that it must have been terrible, and will speak to the senses when the facts are known.

On Friday morning, at 5 o'clock, the forces were marshaling for another conflict, Gen. GRANT moving on LEE's works.

Up to this time Gen. BURNSIDE's corps, numbering 30,000 men, had taken no part in the battle, but at half-past five was marching into position to engage in the bloody contest of the third day's battle.

Of the result of this day's battle we have no report up to the moment of going to press. The battle commenced at 6 o'clock in the morning. Unless LEE received reinforcements equal to BURNSIDE's corps, the battle of Friday must have proved terribly disastrous to him.

The fact that we have received no news of yesterday's fighting leads to the belief that LEE is endeavoring to get away to Richmond, and GRANT is in pursuit.

It is evident that the rebel forces about Richmond

Federal artillery crosses the Rapidan River as Grant launches his 1864 campaign against the Confederacy.

cannot be spared to reinforce LEE, as they have discovered ere this that they have enough to attend to there, probably from two attacks upon the city by Gen. BUTLER's force.

[The above dispatch is so extravagant in its statements, and corresponds so poorly with other and more reliable advices, that it is doubtless entitled to very little credit.—ED. TIMES.]

From Washington—Intense Excitement in the City—All Sorts of Reports, Rumors, &c.
WASHINGTON, Saturday, May 7.

The city has been intensely excited all day with the news from the Army of the Potomac, the early publications serving to excite the public curiosity concerning the military movements.

The bulletin boards of the newspapers attracted throngs of readers. Inquiries were repeatedly made of all who were supposed to have items of intelligence, while extra newspapers continued to be cried by the newsboys, and purchased in abundance.

Rumors of defeat and brilliant victories prevailed to a limited extent, but both classes of reports required authenticity to gain general belief.

The thoughtful, however, came to the conclusion that a single encounter would not determine the contest, and a series of battles may have to be fought before there can be any decisive result.

It was telegraphed hence by the Independent Telegraph Line, but refused by the other lines, doubtless for prudential reasons, that a great victory was achieved by Gen. GRANT on Wednesday and Thursday, he driving the rebels two and a half miles with immense loss, and that he was following up that victory on Friday morning by an assault on the rebel works.

The *Star*, in noticing a similar statement of an afternoon cotemporary, remarks:

"We should be very glad to be able to confirm this news, but have to say, after diligent inquiry, we are satisfied that the Government has received no such information, or any information of more decisive results than that furnished by the *Tribune* dispatch, elsewhere."

The fact that Gen. MEADE was able to stand the brunt of the Confederate onset with a portion of his command is considered a hopeful indication, and we hope soon to be able to announce a decisive victory; but we shall not trifle with our readers by manufacturing bogus victories for an hour's sensation."

The above contradiction of the *Star* is believed to be based on reliable information.

During the day many inquiries were made of officers of the Government, but without the satisfaction naturally desirable on the part of those who have impatient desires for early and complete success, and who forget that the work must be necessarily stubborn, heavy and persistent on both sides, owing to the great importance to each of the result.

The fragmentary information received from time to time shows nothing decisive, but serves to contradict many rumors and speculations concerning the

whereabouts and designs of the rebels which were so confidently asserted.

Further from Washington—No Later News Received by the Government up to 5 o'clock Last Evening.
WASHINGTON, Saturday, May 7.

Up to 5 o'clock this afternoon the Government had received no information of more decisive results than was furnished by dispatches published this morning. Therefore, the reports of a great victory achieved by Gen. GRANT on Wednesday and Thursday, and the pursuing of the enemy on Friday, etc., are, to say the least, not reliable.

WASHINGTON, Sunday, May 8—1 o'clock A.M.

It is said to-night that Gen. HAYS was killed in the fight on Thursday, and that several other generals were wounded.

Reported Casualties—Death of Brig.-Gen. Alexander Hays—Brig.-Gen. J. J. Bartlett and Col. Gurney Wounded.
PHILADELPHIA, Saturday, May 7.

A special dispatch to the *Evening Telegraph*, from Washington, says:

Gen. ALEXANDER HAYS was killed on Thursday, while deploying his troops as skirmishers.

Gen. BARTLETT and Col. GURNEY were severely wounded.

Gen. HAYS was a native of Pittsburgh.

The Forward Movement.
From the Washington Star, of Friday Evening.

We have information that up to 7 P. M. of Wednesday evening last no firing was heard in the direction taken by our Army of the Potomac the night before, and we have reason to believe that it was definitely known to Gen. GRANT that LEE had left his former positions before our advance took place. That up to this hour it is not known here by telegraph from Fortress Monroe, that LEE has attacked or confronted Maj.-Gen. "Baldy" SMITH's force, strikes us as embracing substantial proof that GRANT's pursuit commenced very shortly after LEE's movement—so soon after, as that, if he did move against our troops on the Peninsula, he could hardly open upon them before GRANT can attack his rear. But every succeeding hour of the absence of intelligence of a battle in that quarter strengthens the probability that LEE's movement was simply a retreat to get behind the Richmond fortifications; as by this time GRANT, if not seriously opposed, could have marched to within thirty or forty miles, at most, of the rebel capital, or to within supporting distance of where Gen. SMITH's army must be by this time, unless its advance has been delayed by the appearance of LEE in his front; in which case, GRANT's route to his support would be shorter than if his advance had been unopposed. Twenty-four hours at most must, however, solve all the so interesting questions as to what has happened in that quarter up to this time.

We have no fear of the success of any possible effort of LEE to attack and defeat Gen. SMITH's force before it can be amply sustained by the main army under GRANT, as we know many facts going to show that among Gen. GRANT's purposes is surely that of guarding against any disaster to SMITH's army that might otherwise result from LEE's movement.

The New-York Times.

VOL. XIII–3939. NEW-YORK, MONDAY, MAY 9, 1864. PRICE THREE CENTS.

GLORIOUS NEWS

Defeat and Retreat of Lee's Army.

TWO DAYS BATTLE IN VIRGINIA

Lieut.-General Grant Against Gen. Lee.

The Struggle of Thursday and of Friday in the Wilderness.

IMMENSE REBEL LOSSES.

Lee Leaves His Killed and Wounded in Our Hands.

OUR LOSS TWELVE THOUSAND.

GEN. BUTLER'S OPERATIONS.

Capture of City Point and Reported Occupation of Petersburgh.

Railroad Communication Destroyed.

Gen. Sherman's Movements in Georgia.

ADVANCE TO TUNNELL HILL.

Retreat of Joe Johnston's Army Toward Atlanta.

DISPATCHES FROM THE WAR OFFICE.

FIRST DISPATCH.

Gen. Grant Successful—Lee Reported to be Retiring—Gen. Sherman Advancing—Tunnel Hill Occupied.

To Gen. John A. Dix, New-York:

Washington, Sunday, May 8—9 A. M.

We have no official reports from the front, but the Medical Director has notified the Surgeon-General that our wounded were being sent to Washington, and will number from six to eight thousand.

The Chief Quartermaster of the Army of the Potomac has made requisition for seven days' grain, and for railroad construction trains, and states the enemy is reported to be retiring.

This indicates Gen. GRANT's advance, and affords an inference of material success on our part.

The enemy's strength has always been most felt in his first blows, and their having failed, and our forces not only having maintained their ground, but preparing to advance, lead to the hope of full and complete success, for when either party fails, disorganization by straggling and desertion commences, and the enemy's loss in killed and wounded must weaken him more than we are weakened.

Nothing later than my last night's dispatch has been received from Gen. BUTLER.

A dispatch from Gen. SHERMAN, dated at 5 o'clock P. M. yesterday, states that Gen. THOMAS had occupied Tunnel Hill, where he expected a battle, and that the enemy had taken position at Buzzard Roost Pass, north of Dalton. Skirmishing had taken place, but no real fighting yet.

Nothing later from Gen. BANKS.

You may give such publicity to the information transmitted as you deem proper.

It is designed to give accurate official statements of what is known to the department in this great crisis, and to withhold nothing from the public.

EDWIN M. STANTON, Secretary of War.

SECOND DISPATCH.

No Fighting on Saturday—The Wounded at Rappahannock Station—Severe Fighting by Gen. Butler's Army—The Richmond and Petersburgh Railroad Destroyed.

Washington, Sunday, May 8—5 P. M.

Major-Gen. John A. Dix, New-York:

We are yet without any official dispatches from the Army of the Potomac, except those referred to this morning from the Medical Director and Chief Quartermaster, and nothing additional has been received by the department from any other source. It is believed that no fighting took place yesterday.

A part of the wounded arrived in ambulances this morning at Rappahannock Station, and are on the way in by railroad. The department will probably receive dispatches by that train, which will arrive to-night.

A dispatch from Gen. BUTLER, just received, and which left him yesterday, states that a demonstration had been made by his forces on the railroad between Petersburgh and Richmond, and had succeeded in destroying a portion of it, so as to break the connection; that there had been some severe fighting, but that he had succeeded. He heard from a rebel deserter that HUNTER was dangerously wounded PICKETT also, and JONES and JENKINS were killed. Nothing has been heard from Gen. SHERMAN.

EDWIN M. STANTON, Secretary of War.

FRIDAY'S BATTLE.

FIRST DISPATCH.

Washington, Sunday, May 8, 1864.

Th latest news from the army received here is up to seven o'clock yesterday evening, at which time GRANT fully maintained his position. The fighting on Thursday and Friday was very severe, with skirmishing only on Saturday. LEE's first onset was made upon our left, but failing he then fell upon our centre and finally upon our right, where the hardest contest took place. Here the rebels charged upon our lines twice, but were repulsed each time with severe loss. HANCOCK's corps charged back twice, and at one time entered that portion of the enemy's entrenchments commanded by A. P. HILL, but were at length compelled to fall back. SEYMOUR's division of HANCOCK's corps was badly cut. Gens. WADSWORTH and BARTLETT were badly wounded, the former having been knocked off his horse by a spent minié ball. The rebels were reported retreating yesterday morning. The number of wounded is reported at about ten thousand; the killed at two thousand. The loss of the enemy exceeds this. He left his dead and disabled on the field, in our hands. The Ambulance Corps, with its admirable organization, is working up to its full capacity, carrying the wounded to Rappahannock Station. Sixteen trains of cars, dispatched from Alexandria to-day, will receive them. It is expected that they will return, with their bruised and mangled freight, about daylight. Several car-loads of ice were also sent down for the comfort of the wounded. The Sanitary and Christian Commissions are on the field, with a full force of assistants, and with plentiful supplies of everything necessary for the wounded. The Government has hospital accommodations here for thirty thousand, which will probably meet all demands.

SECOND DISPATCH.

Washington, Sunday, May 8—Midnight.

Your special correspondent, writing from headquarters at Wilderness Tavern, Friday evening, May 6, gives the following intelligence of the great battle on Friday:

The day has closed upon a terribly hard-fought field, and the Army of the Potomac has added another to its list of murderous conflicts. LEE's tactics, so energetically employed at Chancellorsville and Gettysburgh, of throwing his whole army first upon one wing and then upon another, have again been brought to bear, but I rejoice to say that the army of the Potomac has repulsed the tremendous onslaught of the enemy, and stands to-night solidly in the position it assumed this morning. The first attempt was made upon HANCOCK, upon the right, somewhat weakened in numbers by the battle of yesterday; but the iron old Second Corps nobly stood its ground; then the enemy hurled his battalions upon SEDGWICK, and once or twice gained a temporary advantage, but our veterans were nobly rallied, and the rebels repulsed with awful slaughter. About half-past four P. M., LEE made a feint attack upon the whole line, and then suddenly fell, with his whole force, upon SEDGWICK, driving him back temporarily, but the advantage was soon regained, and the rebels hurled back with great loss. Night had now come on, and it is believed at headquarters, at this hour, that LEE has withdrawn from our front. Although the nature of the ground has been of a terrible character, most of it being so thickly wooded as to render movements all but impossible, and to conceal entirely the operations of the enemy, yet he has been signally repulsed in all his attacks, and nothing but the nature of the battle-field has prevented it from being a crushing defeat. The loss on both sides has been very heavy, but at this hour of hasty writing, I cannot even give an estimate.

THURSDAY'S BATTLE.

FULL DETAILS.

WASHINGTON, Sunday, May 8.

The special correspondent of the Rochester *Democrat*, with the army, has arrived in Washington with the following account of operations up to Friday morning:

GEN. GRANT'S HEADQUARTERS, }
GERMANNA FORD, Wednesday, May 4—7 P. M.}

The whole Army of the Potomac to-day effected the passage of the Rapidan. Gen. WILSON's cavalry division forded the river at Germanna Ford, and Gen. GREGG's division at Ely's Ford, eight miles below, at daybreak. The few mounted pickets of the enemy that were watching the two points, scampered off before them. Double pontoon bridges were at once thrown across the river, and the infantry that had marched to the Ford during the night commenced crossing over at about 8 A. M. Gen. HANCOCK's corps and the reserve artillery crossed at Ely's Ford, and Gen. WARREN's at Germanna. SEDGWICK's corps followed the latter. The passage of the river continued all day at both points. All the troops are over at this hour. The trains will cross during the night. Gen. HANCOCK is encamped on the Chancellorsville battle-ground. Gen. WARREN is at the old Wilderness Tavern, and Gen. SEDGWICK at the tavern and Germanna Ford. Both Gen. GRANT and Gen. MEADE's headquarters are at this point for the night.

Not a shot was fired during the crossing. Immediately after reaching the south bank, Gen. WILSON's and Gen. GREGG's cavalry pushed forward, the former to Parker's Store, the latter some distance beyond Chancellorsville. They discovered nothing of the enemy but weak parties of cavalry, developing the fact that there was no strong rebel force south of us. About a dozen prisoners were taken by our cavalry, among whom were several couriers. One of the latter carried a dispatch from Gen. RHODES to Gen. EWELL, informing him that the Yankees had crossed in force at Germanna and Ely's Fords. There is absolutely nothing known of the movements of the enemy at headquarters to-night. It is supposed, however, that LEE is concentrating, and that we will meet him in force to-morrow. Efforts will be made, at all events, to ascertain his whereabouts. The army will be pushed southwestwardly to the open country beyond the Wilderness, provided developments in regard to the enemy do not necessitate a change of this purpose. The movements to-day were made in fine order, and with creditable precision. There was hardly any straggling, notwithstanding the hard work during the night and day. The troops are full of spirit; the most auspicious weather favors the advance. Gen. BURNSIDE's command, consisting of four (4) divisions, commanded by Gens. POTTER, FER-

RERO, WILSON and CRITTENDEN, is expected to come up with the army to-morrow afternoon.

Gen. GRANT'S HEADQUARTERS, May 5—8 P. M.

As expected, last night, the army came up with the enemy to-day. A battle has been fought between parts of it and the whole rebel army, but, as at Gettysburgh, the bloody scenes of this day were only a prelude to the bloody work, and it is to be hoped more auspicious results, to-morrow. Reveille was sounded at 3 A. M., and the whole army was again in motion at daylight. According to the order of the day, Gen. HANCOCK's corps was to march upon Chancellorsville, southwestwardly on the Pamunkey road to Grove Church, Gen. WARREN's from Old Wilderness Tavern to Parker's Store, on the Orange Courthouse plank road. SEDGWICK's corps was to follow behind WARREN's.

Gen. SHERIDAN was to concentrate the whole cavalry corps at Piney Branch Church, a few miles south of .Chancellorsville, and start upon a general hunt after STEWART's cavalry, the main body of which was reported to be concentrating for a fight. The different bodies had been in motion but a short time, when, at about 6 o'clock, reports came in from both turnpike and plank-road running almost parallel from this vicinity to Orange Court-house, that the enemy were advancing with infantry and artillery toward us from near Old and New Verdiersville. The evidence accumulating in the course of the next two hours that strong rebel columns were moving upon us from the directions mentioned, Gens. GRANT and MEADE came up from Germanna Ford, and orders were issued to halt the various columns of infantry, concentrate and form them for battle at this point. Commanding ridges running from the northwest to the southeast across both roads over which the enemy were advancing, about half a mile to the west of this point, offered a fine position for the formation of a battle front, and was selected for this purpose. SEDGWICK was ordered to take the right, WARREN the centre, and HANCOCK was expected to come up on the left. WARREN and SEDGWICK got into line about 11 o'clock, and soon after skirmishing was heard on the front. About noon Gen. WARREN was ordered to push GRIFFIN's division forward to the right and left of the turnpike, and ascertain what the enemy were about. BARTLETT's brigade moved up the left, and AYRES' regulars to the right of the road—SWEITZER'S following in reserve. After advancing about three-quarters of a mile, they suddenly found themselves confronted by a well-formed and strong rebel position on a thickly wooded ridge. A severe fight ensued. Our two brigades held their ground against evidently greater numbers for nearly an hour, when the enemy succeeded in overlapping AYRES' regular brigade, and forcing it back precipitately. The flank of BARTLETT's brigade being exposed, it was also soon forced back for some distance. Two pieces of the Third Massachusetts Battery had to be left behind in consequence of the killing of nearly all the horses, and fell into the hands of the enemy. SWEITZER's brigade, and WADWORTH's, of ROBINSON's division, were ordered forward, and relieved the two brigades. The enemy soon attacked these, but were held at bay. Brisk musketry and artillery firing were kept up for an hour longer, when the enemy drew off from that part of the line. Our loss in this affair was quite severe—AYRES' and BARTLETT's brigades principally suffering. No definite figures can now be given. But the total will probably not exceed six hundred in killed, wounded and missing.

Among the wounded are Gen. BARTLETT, slightly; Col. HAYES, Eighteenth Massachusetts, slightly; Col. GWYN, One Hundred and Tenth Pennsylvania; Col. GUINEY, Ninth Massachusetts; Col. LOMBARD, Fourth Michigan. We took about three hundred prisoners.

HANCOCK's corps had been ordered to turn off the road he had started out on, and march over a crossroad as rapidly as possible for this point, to complete the formation of the line of battle. About 3 o'clock in the afternoon, after the fight on the centre had closed, a movement by the enemy was discovered, evidently meant to throw a force between HANCOCK and the remainder of the army. GETTY's division of SEDGWICK's corps was ordered at once to stay this dangerous demonstration. HANCOCK's advance, MOTT's division, arrived just in time to form with GETTY's, to the left and right of the plank road leading directly from Chancellorsville to Orange Courthouse. Gen. GRANT ordered them to attack the advancing enemy, in order to give the remaining divi-

Brigadier-General James S. Wadsworth, one of the Union's more capable officers, was wounded in the Battle of the Wilderness on May 6. Captured by the Rebels, Wadsworth died two days later.

sions of HANCOCK's time to come up and form. They did so, and became at once hotly engaged in woods so thick that it was almost impossible to advance in line. BIRNEY's division of the Second Corps soon came up, and quickly formed on the right of GETTY. BURLOW's and GIBBONS' divisions formed a second line as they came up. The enemy in vast force pressed energetically and repeatedly upon the front, and a most furious musketry fight continued for nearly two hours. The heavy timber and dense undergrowth rendered the use of artillery impossible, and only a few rounds from heavy pieces were fired on either side, but as to violence, the musketry surpassed everything in the history of the Army of the Potomac. Our line steadily held its ground until the whole corps was forward, when nightfall prevented an advance on our part, and put an end to the fight. WADSWORTH's division and a brigade of ROBINSON's division, under command of Gen. ROBINSON, were ordered to take the enemy in front of HANCOCK by the right flank, but darkness also prevented the full execution of this fight. The loss on our left will probably reach one thousand, including Gen. ALEXANDER HAYS, killed; Cols. S. S. HICKS, CARRALL and TYLER among the wounded.

HANCOCK's men behaved most admirably. The Fifth New-York Cavalry, in advance on the road to Parker's Store, was attacked by superior force in the morning and driven back with considerable loss. Gen. SHERIDAN sent a message to Gen. MEADE in the evening, to the effect that he had met part of STUART's cavalry and was driving them in every direction. Gen. LEE made two attempts to cut our army in two, both on the right and left, by getting between the river and WARREN's and SEDGWICK's corps, with only part of BURNSIDE's across on the one side and between HANCOCK's corps and the remainder of the army on the other. That he was foiled in both purposes and that the army has been concentrated, notwithstanding his two well conceived attacks, constitutes a most substantial success for Gen. GRANT. Not quite one-half of the army was engaged to-day. To-night every corps is in proper position, BURNSIDE's being fully up and Gen. GRANT has at his command a force sufficient and will make a general attack upon the enemy at daylight. There was heavy firing on SEDGWICK's part of the line after dark, but it was of short duration. It is understood that it was brought about by an advance on our side to clear our front.

The New-York Times.

VOL. XIII....NO. 3942.   NEW-YORK, THURSDAY, MAY 12, 1864.   PRICE THREE CENTS.

THE GREAT CAMPAIGN.

ANOTHER TERRIFIC BATTLE.

Another Defeat of the Rebels.

THE REBEL RIGHT CRUSHED.

Three Brigades and Four Guns Captured.

The Rebel Intrenchments Occupied.

THE BATTLE NOT RENEWED YESTERDAY.

Authentic Details to Wednesday at 10 O'clock.

HANCOCK CROSSES THE RIVER PO.

The Rebel Army Becoming Disheartened.

Six Thousand Prisoners Captured.

Death of Brigadier-General Stevenson, of Massachusetts.

CONTINUED SUCCESS OF GEN. BUTLER.

Later Intelligence from General Sherman.

Reliable Details from the War Office and Our Special Correspondents.

DISPATCHES FROM THE WAR OFFICE.

Advices from Gen. Grant to Tuesday at Five o'clock—The Enemy Driven to their

Breastworks—Their First Line of Rifle-Pits Carried—The Wounded.

WASHINGTON, Wednesday, May 11.

Major-Gen. Dix:

Dispatches from the Army of the Potomac have just reached here, bearing dates to 5 o'clock P. M., of yesterday.

Both armies at that time held their positions at Spottsylvania Court-house, without any material change.

The enemy had been driven to their breastworks.

The Sixth Corps, under Gen. WRIGHT, had carried the first line of the enemy's rifle-pits.

There had been heavy skirmishing during the day.

Our wounded had reached Fredericksburgh, and during the night some were brought up to Washington.

The Surgeon-General reports that ample supplies of nurses, surgeons and medical stores have gone forward.

There has been nothing heard from Gen. SHERMAN or Gen. BUTLER since my last dispatch of yesterday.

EDWIN M. STANTON, Secretary of War.

Second Dispatch—Nothing Later from the Army of the Potomac nor from Gen. Butler— Intelligence from Gen. Sherman.

WASHINGTON, May 11, 1864.

To Maj.-Gen. Dix:

No intelligence has been received by this department from the Army of the Potomac since my dispatch of this morning.

A dispatch from Gen. SHERMAN, dated at Tunnel Hill, May 10, 7:30 P. M., states that MCPHERSON had not attacked the enemy at Resaca, having found their position strongly fortified, and had taken his position at Snake Creek Gap.

Gen. SHERMAN was in front of Buzzard Roost Gap, awaiting the arrival of a part of his forces.

This dispatch came by way of Knoxville and Cumberland Gap, having been delayed over twenty-four hours in consequence of a heavy storm that broke down all the lines south of Nashville.

No intelligence has been received to-day from Gen. BUTLER'S command, except that three hundred rebel prisoners, including one negro, had arrived at Fortress Monroe from City Point, in charge of a negro guard.

From Gen. BANKS' command nothing of recent date has been received.

E. M. STANTON, Secretary of War.

SPECIAL DISPATCHES TO THE N.Y. TIMES.

The Battle of Monday Evening—Hancock Crosses the River Po—Lee's Position and Line of Battle—Signs of Despondency on the Part of the Rebels—No Signs of Weariness in Grant's Army—Lee Out of Rations—Six Thousand Prisoners Captured.

WASHINGTON, Wednesday, May 11.

The latest news received here from Gen. GRANT's army relates to the operations of Monday and yesterday. The flight on Monday evening was very severe, inflicting a loss on our side of over two thousand men killed and wounded. It was brought on by HANCOCK, who, in his effort to take Spottsylvania Court-house, accomplished the crossing of the River Po under cover of a tremendous artillery fire, and established himself on the south bank.

LEE's army forms a line of battle immediately north of the Court-house. His left extends to Glady Run, and is protected by the block-house, curving northward. His centre occupies the high ground on the banks of the branch of the Po, with his right sweeping in similar curve north of this branch, and protected on its flank by the Ny River. His line presents the curves of capital letter B, with convex curves toward GRANT.

On yesterday morning SHERIDAN's cannons were heard away to the southward.

Although GRANT's losses are heavy his army presents no sign of weariness. All agree that he has handled his troops in a masterly manner.

LEE's men give unmistakable signs of despondency. They no longer cheer and fight, but charge or retreat in dogged silence. LEE's losses begin to tell on him. He flinches from direct assault, and has lost spirit. In an order to his army Monday, found on prisoners taken, he notified them that his communication with Richmond is broken, and no rations can be drawn from there.

He advises efforts to capture supplies from GRANT. So far his men have been unable to comply with this suggestion. They have not captured a pound of provisions.

GRANT, up to yesterday, had taken about 6,000 prisoners. A whole regiment was taken, the greater part of which was composed of men who had but a few weeks since been exchanged.

The Very Latest from the Battle-field—The Situation on Tuesday at 12 o'clock—Monday a Day of Quiet—Crossing of the Po by Hancock—Warren Advances His Line—The Prisoners—Rebel Dispatches—Averill's Raid.

WASHINGTON, Wednesday, May 11.

Your correspondent, WM. SWINTON, sends the following to this Bureau:

IN FRONT OF SPOTTSYLVANIA COURT-HOUSE, Va., TUESDAY, May 10, 1864.

The military situation at this hour (Tuesday, 12 M.) finds the line of the army drawn around Spottsylvania Court-house in the arc of a circle, the concave toward us. The enemy is in force at that point, and seems determined to dispute the passage. I mentioned in my letter of yesterday that the two armies ran a race from the Wilderness for Spottsylvania, but unfortunately the enemy won the race. This should not be interpreted as conveying any censure on the Army of of the Potomac, which has marched with a new inspiration and a rapidity never before seen in its history. But the very necessities of our condition as the invading party, with our old base abandoned and a new one not yet opened, obliges us to take immense trains, which, of course, retard the general movement of the army; the rebels constantly falling back on their base, and favored by their very poverty, can readily beat us on an equal start. It would certainly have been a great point gained had we been able to make Spottsylvania Court-house in advance of the enemy. An inspection of the map will show you that it is an important strategic point, being the point of divergence of the roads leading southward, both to the right and left. The enemy's command of it enables him to cover the withdrawal of his trains and at the same time bars our further advance, unless on the condition of an assault— which, in the country in which we are now fighting, is very destructive of life—or of a turning movement. It is probable that to-day will decide the question; and if, as we hope, it gives us Spottsylvania Court-house, we shall then be out of the Wilderness, and have a clear road on to Richmond.

Yesterday was intended to be a day of quietude, during which the army, fatigued by five days incessant marching and fighting, would have an opportunity to recuperate and renew the supplies of rations. Little occurred to interfere with this programme, although the rebels made an attack on WILCOX's Division of BURNSIDE's Corps, early in the afternoon. They were, however, handsomely repulsed, and BURNSIDE has the extreme left of our line, within a mile and a half of the Court-house.

About 6 o'clock last evening, Gen. HANCOCK, holding the right of our line, crossed Po Creek and seized the Block House Road, the direct line from Parker's Store to Spottsylvania Court-house. Immediately afterward, WARREN, who now has centre, advanced his line of battle, drove the rebels for a half a mile, and took up a strong position. Up to the present hour, the situation remains as here described.

The rebels have as yet shown no disposition to assume the offensive at this point. It was confidently expected on Sunday night that an attack would take place on HANCOCK's front, toward the Catharpen Road, and on a line with the Brock Road. The troops showed great diligence in throwing up breastworks, and a brigade was advanced out for a mile or more from the main front over some cleared land. About an hour before sunset this attack was made. Immediately upon the retirement of the advance brigade, the enemy charged toward our line, but never reached it. They put a few guns in position, and shelled the woods for a while, but did no harm. A small number of Gen. BIRNEY's troops, on whom the attack was principally made, were wounded by the enemy's musketry before they withdrew, having received more harm than they had done. Before this attack, our advance could see HILL's Corps marching south to join the main body, opposing our progress in front on the branch of the Po. As it was necessary to hold this position until it was certain the enemy were gone, Gen. HANCOCK did not stay the progress of the men engaged in forming breastworks, but added another line in the open ground around Todd's Tavern, a regiment of heavy artillery working all night to finish them. It was a very pretty sight. The lanterns of the workmen hung to the blossoming cherry-trees, and picturesque groups of soldiers digging and erecting the works, while batteries stood harnessed up, their cannoniers lying on the ground around the carriages, in wait for any emergency. At sunrise scouts advanced and found the enemy in small force; and about noonday Gen. HANCOCK left Gen. WARD's brigade to hold the position, and advanced with his corps toward the River Po, which by night he had, after considerable resistance, passed. Gen. BURNSIDE pushing out on the extreme left, advanced to a place in front of SEDGWICK's (now WRIGHT's) corps. A reconnoissance by two regiments was made. These advanced some distance without meeting much resistance. At the same time the cannonade along some portions of the front was quite brisk between ours and the rebel artillery.

The prisoners we have are in apparent good condition. One fellow, who was taken with much trouble, explained his determined efforts to avoid capture, on the ground that it was currently reported that we should massacre all our prisoners, in revenge for the slaughter of our negro soldiers.

We have fewer stragglers than usual, though not so few as might be. It is not easy to straggle in a country where there is no communication,

and guerrillas loaf around the army to pick up any waif or estray sleeping in the woods. The Provost-guard has all it can do, to keep the lingerers up to their duty.

Gen. PATRICK had quite a brigade of them one day, and I believe had serious thoughts of making a charge with them.

The same intolerable heat which we have had ever since this movement commenced still continues, and numerous cases of *coup de soleil* happen for the heat that it keeps the roads in excellent traveling condition, saving and excepting the dust, which is here of a most malignant type.

Gen. WRIGHT, who formerly commanded a division of the Sixth, is now in command of that Corps so grievously deprived of its head by the death of the beloved SEDGWICK, the details of which I yesterday sent you. The grief at this sad event intensifies as it becomes known throughout the army. An effort was at first made to keep the sad fact from the knowledge of his men. Gen. WRIGHT is an excellent soldier, and will command the Sixth well.

The road which our troops faced runs from Orange Court-house to Fredericksburgh, and is forty-one miles long. It crosses no river. Proceeding from Orange Court-house, we come at a distance of ten miles to Verdiersville; ten miles further brings us to Parker's Store; six miles further to Wilderness; five miles further to Chancellorsville; ten miles more to Fredericksburgh.

The following is published in the Richmond *Dispatch*, of the 7th inst., as the dispatch of its special correspondent, "Sallust," and gives an account of the second day's—Friday's—engagement:

ORANGE COURT-HOUSE, Friday, May 6.
The enemy renewed the attack this morning with great violence, attempting to turn our right and get between us and Richmond. Every attack of the enemy was repulsed. We have driven him some distance on the left, but he is very stubborn on the right, but is now giving way.

Lieut.-Gen. LONGSTREET had turned the enemy's left, and was steadily pushing him back, when he was severely wounded. He was shot *by Mahone's Brigade through mistake*. Gen. LONGSTREET is doing well. He and his command saved the day on the right. The artillery took but little part on either side on account of the woods and the nature of the ground. Our loss is very severe, including many valuable officers. Gen. WADSWORTH, of the Yankee army, was killed. The battle was fought in the wilderness, and will probably be designated as "the battle of the Wilderness." The enemy has been pushed back to-

ward Chancellorsville and Fredericksburgh. Everything looks well for our success.

To complete all the rebel material illustrations of the battle of the wilderness, I append a copy of a dispatch from Gen. JOHN PEGRAM to Gen. JEB. STUART, which was obtained by the capture of the courier carrying it, and which shows the important fact that LONGSTREET, after fighting our right under SEDGWICK in the morning, made a rapid march, united with A. P. HILL, and assisted in the tremendous effort made to roll up HANCOCK's left on the afternoon of the same day, all the circumstances of which I have detailed in former letters:

GENERAL: I learn from Gen. R. E. LEE that the enemy attacked EWELL early this morning, and were repulsed as usual. There was some confusion in HILL's Corps, but as soon as LONGSTREET came up, he commenced driving the enemy, and has been doing so up to this time, 7:20 P. M. Gen. LEE says you can render him very essential service by a vigorous attack on the enemy's left. PEGRAM.

Oddly enough, the attack was made near Toad's Tavern, but STUART was badly whipped by our cavalry, and the essential service was not rendered.

In regard to BUTLER's operations, the latest we have received here is from a dispatch of Gen. PICKETT, which I inclose:

The movements of the enemy on the south side are as yet but little known, with the exception of a general intention to flank Drewry's Bluff. A gentleman, who left City Point Thursday, about 8 o'clock, says that on that afternoon, about 4 o'clock, the enemy landed a force of some two thousand at City Point. The main bulk of the enemy's force proceeded to Bermuda Hundred, about three miles higher up James River, where they landed a force variously estimated at from ten to fifteen thousand men. Bermuda Hundreds is near the mouth of the Appomattox River, on its western bank, and but ten miles from Drewry's Bluff. It is also within two or three hours march of the Richmond and Petersburgh Railroad.

The following telegram was received here last night:

PETERSBURGH, May 6, 1864.
Our forces were skirmishing with the enemy's forces near Port Walthall Junction, at 6 o'clock this evening. G. E. PICKETT,
Major-General Commanding.

In regard to AVERILL's progress, the same journal gives the following:

LYNCHBURGH, Friday, May 6.
The *Virginian* has information that AVERILL has concentrated 8,000 cavalry and infantry at Kanawha Valley, with the intention of making a raid on the salt works in Washington County.

Just as I close this letter a heavy cannonading

Brushfires in the wilderness trapped many wounded men. This drawing by Alfred Waud depicts those injured who were fortunate enough to escape being burned to death.

has commenced in the front, for which I leave immediately.

News from Gens. Grant and Meade—Pursuit of the Rebels—Capture of Prisoners—The Stubborn Fight on Sunday—A List of Wounded.

WASHINGTON, Wednesday, May 11—8. A. M.

Dispatches have been received from Gens. GRANT and MEADE giving an account of operations up till dark on Monday. At that time our army was closely pressing LEE's retreating columns. Every inch of ground was stubbornly contested by the rebels. We have captured many prisoners. The loss on both sides is very heavy.

The fight on Sunday, near Spottsylvania, was desperate, and at its beginning was decidedly against us. Reinforcements, however, came up in time to save the day, and the enemy were handsomely repulsed.

The prisoners captured are about equal on both sides. In our present position artillery can be used with effect, which was impossible while we were in the Wilderness. Heavy and continuous cannonading, beginning at daylight on Monday, was heard at Fredericksburgh, in the direction of Spottsylvania Court-house—an evidence that the battle had been renewed.

The fighting up to noon yesterday had continued with vigor in the neighborhood of Spottsylvania Court-house. Our forces have intrenched themselves at that point, and though having fought five days and nights, aside from performing heavy marches under a broiling sun, they exhibit not the least willingness to give up, but encouraged by the successful termination of the battles in the Wilderness, from which they drove the enemy with great loss, and encouraged by the presence of Gen. GRANT and a determination to push to Richmond, they have thus far baffled all efforts of the enemy to drive them back or turn our flanks.

On Sunday morning, at 11 o'clock, the head of a column of ambulances and army wagons reached Fredericksburgh by the plank road from Chancellorsville. They comprised men who had been wounded in the battle in the Wilderness on Tuesday and Wednesday, and most of whom had lain in the field hospitals. The cases embraced mainly gunshot wounds in the lower limbs and body, the rebels having fired unusually low in this engagement.

A Day of Rest—The Army Sanguine—Gen. Lee Orders Supplies to be Captured from the Yankees—The Cavalry Operations—Particulars of Gen. Sedgwick's Death.

The following dispatch appeared in our Postscript edition of yesterday:

WASHINGTON, Wednesday, May 11—3 A. M.

The Army of the Potomac has had a portion of a day to recuperate.

Our army could not be in a more cheerful condition. All the men are sanguine of success, and they count the days when they shall in triumph enter the rebel capital.

Gen. LEE lately issued an order in relation to supplies, in which he said communication with Richmond was cut off, and it was impossible to furnish the men with stores. Gen. HILL's corps had no rations issued for three days. Gen. LEE enjoined upon his men the necessity of capturing supplies from the Yankees. Up to this moment they have failed to capture a single wagon.

The roads are in excellent traveling order, but very dusty.

All the battles thus far have been a series of attacks and repulses. Muskets were almost entirely used. The swampy nature of the ground rendered artillery impracticable.

LEE very absurdly claims a victory when he withdraws from our front and marches toward Richmond.

Gen. TORBETT's division of cavalry whipped the rebel cavalry near this place, and drove them from Spottsylvania Court-house, but being reinforced with infantry, they drove our cavalry a short distance. The Maryland Brigade, Fourth Division, Sixth

Union General John Sedgwick was the victim of an unknown Confederate sniper at Spotsylvania.

Corps, coming to their support, the fighting was exceedingly fierce. Gen. TORBETT and Gen. ROBINSON were both wounded, and are on their way to Washington.

Gen. SEDGWICK was shot through the head, Monday morning, whilst superintending the mounting of some heavy guns, in an angle the men had just prepared. There was no skirmishing at the time, but an occasional sharpshooter sent a bullet in that direction, which caused the men to be on the alert to dodge them. Gen. SEDGWICK, who was standing near them, was smiling at their nervousness, when a ball struck him in the forehead, the blood oozed from his nostrils, and he fell back dead into the arms of his Assistant Adjutant-General.

In Fredericksburgh, to-day, there were over 12,000 of our wounded, who have been crowding into the town since Sunday morning. When the first party of three hundred maimed and bleeding soldiers came into the city. Mayor SLAUGHTER and Mr. MAYER, a prominent citizen, rallied a few guerillas, and marched them into the rebel lines as prisoners of war. Mayor SLAUGHTER and his friends are now in the guardhouse of Fredericksburgh.

Pontoons have been laid across the Rappahannock below Fredericksburgh, over which there will be communication to Aquia Creek, where our transports lie, a distance of about eight miles from Fredericksburgh.

Guerillas abound throughout the country in our rear.

A report gained credence on Tuesday that our cavalry had captured at Guinney's Station a train of cars which had been sent from Richmond for the rebel wounded, and that they tore up the track there.

The bodies of Gens. SEDGWICK, WADSWORTH and HAYS reached Washington to-night.

A large number of wounded have arrived from Aquia Creek.

WASHINGTON, Wednesday, May 11—1 A. M.

The wounded are arriving in large numbers. The steamer *Keyport*, with nearly 600 on board, arrived here from Aquia Creek last night. Other vessels, freighted with wounded and dead, have just reached the wharf. The remains of Gens. SEDGWICK, HAYS and WADSWORTH were brought up on the *Keyport*. The following wounded General officers were also brought up; Gen. GETTY, wounded in the shoulder; Gen. TORBERT, of Cavalry Corps, wounded in abdomen; Gen. J. C. ROBINSON, in right leg; Gen. BAXTER, in right leg.

Rebel prisoners captured on Monday morning report LONGSTREET's death.

The Seventy-sixth New-York Regiment lost three entire companies, B, F and K, as prisoners. The loss of the regiment amounts entire to 300 men. Col. ROY STONE, of the Bucktail regiment, was injured in action by his horse falling, by which his wounds received at Gettysburgh were reopened, which so far disabled him as to cause his withdrawal from the field. Capt. CORT, A. A. G. to Gen. HAYS, prisoner; Act. Adjt.-Gens. NASH and LEE, of Gen. WARD's Staff, are missing; Col. CRAIG, One Hundred and Fifteenth Pennsylvania, wounded; Col. LEIDY, Fifty-seventh Pennsylvania, wounded; Lieut.-Col.

GREENWALT, commanding One Hundred and Tenth Pennsylvania, wounded; Major of the Third Maine, wounded; Maj. MATOX, First United States Sharpshooters, prisoner.

Gen. SEDGWICK was killed while occupied in making out a plan of the fighting-ground for his command. His staff were around him at the time, when a rebel sharpshooter fired three shots at him. One of his aids remarked that they were making a target of him, when he replied that there was no danger of his being hit at that distance. A moment after the fatal bullet struck him in the face, killing him instantly.

REPORTS FROM WASHINGTON.

Gen. Sedgwick Successor—No Movement on Monday—Rumors of Lee's Operations.

WASHINGTON, Wednesday, May 11.

Dispatches from the Army of the Potomac speak of Gen. WRIGHT, who succeeds the late Gen. SEDGWICK, as an able soldier, and who will not fail to secure the confidence of those over whom he is placed.

No movement of our army was intended to be made on Monday, but a brief period of rest given the soldiers after their heavy labors during the past week.

All was very quiet along the lines until late in the afternoon of Monday.

It was thought that the rebels were probably falling back, or that Gen. LEE had already gone to Richmond to meet Gen. SMITH, who was reported as being close to that place, and therefore a move was determined on on our part, and our forces commenced moving at 5½ o'clock on Monday evening.

The Battle of Tuesday—The River Po Crossed—The Enemy Forced Back Three-Fourths of a Mile—The Wounded Going to Belle Plain.

WASHINGTON, Wednesday, May 11—1 P. M.

Nothing has been received here of any reverse to Gen. GRANT's army.

The impression prevailed in the army yesterday that Gen. LEE was about to cross the North Anna River.

The entire line moved forward, the right consisting of Gen. BIRNEY's and Gen. GIBBONS' Divisions of the Second Corps, and Gen. CARROLL's Brigade on the left joined Gen. WARREN, the latter being in the centre with the Sixth Corps, forming the left.

The right crossed a branch of the River Po and charged on a light-horse battery, which was posted to cover a small bridge, but which quickly limbered up and started off, the skirmishers supporting it also retreating.

In the front of WARREN and on the left of HANCOCK, quite a lively engagement ensued, the shell and round shot from one of the enemy's batteries placed in the woods coming in rather close proximity to some lookers on in an open field, in the rear of Gen. WARREN's headquarters, and causing a stampede of the crowd there.

The enemy were driven back about three-fourths of a mile, and at dark the firing ceased.

A few prisoners were captured during this skirmish. They belonged to WILCOX's Division of Gen. HILL's Corps.

It is believed, however, that Gen. LONGSTREET's Corps was the only one in our front, and that he was left there to impede our progress as much as possible, while Gen. LEE was attending to Gen. SMITH.

A rebel cavalry brigade is reported as having been seen on the north side of the river Rapidan, on Monday, near Fredericksburgh.

As Fredericksburgh is in our possession the trains of the wounded have been sent thither to be forwarded to Bell Plain, and thence by transports to Washington.

Messengers were sent forward to stop all the boats going up the Potomac River that they might load up with the wounded.

Operations of Gen. Robinson's Division—The Bodies of Dead and Wounded Consumed by Fire—A Night's Fight with the Fifth Corps—A Terrible Reception of the Enemy.

THIRD DISPATCH.

WASHINGTON, Wednesday, May 11.

Gen. ROBINSON suffers much from his wound, which is in the knee.

His division was in the advance on the Spottsylvania road, from Todd's Tavern, with Gen. PHIL. SHERIDAN's cavalry, and had driven the rebels about six miles, carrying two positions they had endeavored to hold on to.

On reaching a cross road the rebels made a determined stand behind a temporary breastwork of rails and ties, and were massed in strong force, the greater part of their position being hid from view by dense woods.

An attempt was made to carry this position, but it failed, when Gen. ROBINSON rode up in front of his men and said, "The place must be ours," and asking the men to follow him.

The men replied with loud and enthusiastic cheers, and forming in line, rushed to the attack in most gallant style.

A terrible fire of musketry from the rebels met them in the face, and Gen. ROBINSON being wounded, and scarcely able to keep his seat in the saddle, the column was forced to fall back.

The whole affair cost us about three hundred men, and the loss of the services of one of the ablest and bravest Generals in the army.

The Pennsylvania Reserves were afterward led against the same position, but they met the same fate as Gen. ROBINSON's force, and the attempt was abandoned for the night.

Col. LOCKE, Assistant Adjutant to Gen. WARREN, was seriously wounded in the face on Sunday, while riding along the lines, delivering orders.

One of the most repulsive spectacles presented in the late encounters was that of some bodies found partially consumed by fire, the unfortunate men having been burned to death.

These fires were started by men who had been cooking, or through some heedless carelessness, and the leaves and husks lying around being very dry, the flames spread with great rapidity, extending over acres.

Of course the wounded left on the ground suffered the additional torture of death by fire.

A number of our wounded were on Monday still on the Wilderness battle-field.

IN THE FIELD, Tuesday, May 10—7 A. M.

Last night about 11 o'clock, the rebels in front of Gen. WARREN's Corps, made an assault on a line of rifle-pits, hastily constructed.

Our men gave them a volley and fell back, for the purpose of drawing them on to a second line. The ruse was successful, and as the rebels advanced they were received by a destructive fire, which drove them back in disorder; but finding our men still retiring, they followed them up, and charged on our third line. Here the whole line gave them such a raking fire as almost to demolish them, and, springing after them, charged and drove them back in disorder.

Their loss was very heavy, while our own was light. We took a number of prisoners.

The Army Advancing—Headquarters Beyond Spottsylvania—Capture of a Large Amount of Commissary Stores.

WASHINGTON, Wednesday, May 11.

It is reported that last night our headquarters were two miles in advance of Spottsylvania Court-house.

A general advance was ordered for five o'clock yesterday (Tuesday) evening, and the firing from that hour to sun-down is said to have been very heavy.

It is stated that GRANT has captured a large amount of rebel commissary stores.

The Body of Gen. Sedgwick.

WASHINGTON, Wednesday, May 11.

The body of Major-Gen. SEDGWICK arrived in town this morning, in charge of Major WHITTIER. It has been embalmed, and will leave to-night at 8 o'clock, for Connecticut. Major WHITTIER accompanies it.

VICTORY!

A Decisive Battle.

LEE'S ARMY ROUTED.

A Terrific Charge by General Hancock.

DESPERATE FURY OF OUR MEN.

Three Generals, 50 Officers, 3,000 Men and 12 Guns Captured.

Splendid News from General Sheridan.

Lee's Communications Totally Severed.

TRAINS AND SUPPLIES CAPTURED.

Over Five Hundred Union Prisoners Retaken.

WASHINGTON, Thursday, May 12.

News received to-day continues to be of a most satisfactory character.

Early in the day Secessionists were unusually exultant and open-mouthed. They claimed to have certain intelligence, by channels known only to the initiated, that GRANT was this side of the Rapidan, BURNSIDE had been cut to pieces, and black troops, who had caused all this disaster by dastardly conduct, were all captured. Evidence of falsity of such stuff accumulated during the morning so rapidly and irrepressibly, that nerves of the most timid individuals calmed down. Details of yesterday's fight have not reached here.

Fighting was renewed this morning at daylight by HANCOCK. In a most brilliant assault he fell upon A. P. HILL's division in its intrenchments, five miles below Spottsylvania

Court-house. HANCOCK was in his best mood, and as he led his eager men into the affray he is described as being the very impersonation of war. No mere flesh and bones could stand up before such a charge as was there made. The rebels broke in every direction, leaving trophies of victory in our hands—one Major-General, two Brigadiers, fifty officers, three thousand prisoners, and twelve pieces of artillery.

DISPATCHES FROM THE WAR OFFICE.

FIRST DISPATCH.

[OFFICIAL.]

WASHINGTON, Wednesday, May 11—11:30 P. M.
To Maj.-Gen. Dix:

Dispatches from Gen. GRANT, dated at 8 o'clock this morning, have just reached this department. He says:

"We have now ended the sixth day of very heavy fighting. The result to this time is much in our favor. Our losses have been heavy, as well as those of the enemy. I think the loss of the enemy must be greater. We have taken over 5,000 prisoners in battle, whilst he has taken from us but few except stragglers. I propose to fight it out on this line, if it takes all Summer."

The Government is sparing no pains to support him. EDWIN M. STANTON,
Secretary of War.

SECOND DISPATCH.

[OFFICIAL.]

WASHINGTON, May 12—8:15 P. M.
To Maj.-Gen. Dix:

No dispatches from the Army of the Potomac have been received since 11:30 o'clock last night.

Gen. SHERMAN has not been heard from, owing, probably, to the damage to the lines south of Nashville by the recent storm.

A dispatch from Gen. SHERIDAN, dated "Headquarters of the Cavalry Corps, May 10," states that he turned the enemy's right, and got into their rear, had destroyed from eight to ten miles of railroad, two locomotives and three trains, and a very large quantity of supplies; and that since he had got into their rear there was great excitement among the inhabitants and with the army. The enemy's cavalry had tried to annoy his rear and flank, but had been run off, and he had recaptured five hundred of our men—two of them Colonels.

No dispatches have been received for two days from Gen. BUTLER.

Dispatches received from Gen. STEELE report his command as having arrived at Little Rock. He had fought a superior force of the enemy, commanded by KIRBY SMITH in person, at Saline River, and defeated them.

A steamboat from Red River, arrived to-day at Cairo, reports reinforcements going up to Gen. Banks.

Gen. CANBY had passed Cairo on his way to Red River.

EDWIN M. STANTON,
Secretary of War.

The New-York Times.

VOL. XIII....NO. 3943.　　　　　NEW-YORK, FRIDAY, MAY 13, 1864.　　　　　PRICE THREE CENTS.

VICKORY!

A Decisive Battle.

LEE'S ARMY ROUTED.

A Terrific Charge by General Hancock.

DESPERATE FURY OF OUR MEN.

Three Generals. 50 Officers, 3,000 Men and 12 Guns Captured.

Splendid News from General Sheridan.

Lee's Communications Totally Severed.

TRAINS AND SUPPLIES CAPTURED.

Over Five Hundred Union Prisoners Retaken.

WASHINGTON, Thursday, May 12.

News received to-day continues to be of a most satisfactory character.

Early in the day Secessionists were unusually exultant and open-mouthed. They claimed to have certain intelligence, by channels known only to the initiated, that GRANT was this side of the Rapidan, BURNSIDE had been cut to pieces, and black troops, who had caused all this disaster by dastardly conduct, were all captured. Evidence of falsity of such stuff accumulated during the morning so rapidly and irrepressibly, that nerves of the most timid individuals calmed down. Details of yesterday's fight have not reached here.

Fighting was renewed this morning at day-light by HANCOCK. In a most brilliant assault he fell upon A. P. HILL's division in its intrenchments, five miles below Spottsylvania Court-house. HANCOCK was in his best mood, and as he led his eager men into the affray he is described as being the very impersonation of war. No mere flesh and bones could stand up before such a charge as was there made. The rebels broke in every direction, leaving trophies of victory in our hands—one Major-General, two Brigadiers, fifty officers, three thousand prisoners, and twelve pieces of artillery.

DISPATCHES FROM THE WAR OFFICE.

FIRST DISPATCH.

[OFFICIAL]

WASHINGTON, Wednesday, May 11–11:30 P.M.

To Maj.-Gen Dix:

Dispatches from Gen. GRANT, dated at 8 o'clock this morning, have just reached this department. He says:

"We have now ended the sixth day of very heavy fighting. The result to this time is much in our favor. Our losses have been heavy, as well as those of the enemy. I think the loss of the enemy must be greater. We have taken over 5,000 prisoners in battle, whilst he has taken from us but few except stragglers. I propose to fight it out on this line, if it takes all Summer."

The Government is sparing no pains to support him.　　EDWIN M. STANTON,

Secretary of War.

SECOND DISPATCH.

[OFFICIAL.]

WASHINGTON, May 12—8:15 P. M.

To Maj.-Gen Dix:

No dispatches from the Army of the Potomac have been received since 11:30 o'clock last night.

Gen. SHERMAN has not been heard from, owing, probably, to the damage to the lines south of Nashville by the recent storm.

A dispatch from Gen. SHERIDAN, dated "Head-quarters of the Cavalry Corps, May 10," states that he turned the enemy's right, and got into their rear, had destroyed from eight to ten miles of railroad, two locomotives and three trains, and a very large quantity of supplies; and that since he had got into their rear there was great excitement among the inhabitants and with the army. The enemy's cavalry had tried to annoy his rear and flank, but had been run off, and he had recaptured five hundred of our men—two of them Colonels.

No dispatches have been received for two days from Gen. BUTLER.

Dispatches received from Gen. STEELE report his command as having arrived at Little Rock. He had fought a superior force of the enemy, commanded by KIRBY SMITH in person, at Saline River, and defeated them.

A steamboat from Red River, arrived to-day at Cairo, reports reinforcements going up to Gen. BANKS.

Gen. CANBY had passed Cairo on his way to Red River.　　EDWIN M. STANTON,

Secretary of War.

REPORTS FROM WASHINGTON.

The Fighting Renewed on Wednesday—Our Lines Advance—A Flag of Truce from Gen. Lee—Wants Time to Bury His Dead—Grant says He Hasn't Time to Bury His Own Dead, and Proposes to Advance—Lee Withdraws His Centre—Evidences of a Retreat—Over Four Thousand Prisoners Captured on Tuesday and Wednesday—The Losses.

WASHINGTON, Thursday, May 12.

Yesterday morning the fighting was again renewed, and was continued with various success until about 11 o'clock, when our line was somewhat advanced.

At that hour a flag of truce is reported to have been sent by LEE, who asked for a cessation of hostilities for forty-eight hours, that he might bury his dead.

Gen. GRANT replied that he had not time to bury his own dead, and would advance immediately; and some parts of our line were therefore pushed forward.

It is stated that the woods were shelled, but no response was elicited from where the enemy's centre had been a few hours before.

The prisoners captured on Tuesday and Wednesday number over 4,000. The rebel dead and wounded were found covering almost every foot of ground wherever our troops surged forward and the rebels gave way.

The slaughter among our troops was terrific, but not so great as that of the enemy, and but few captures were made by the latter.

The Desperate Fighting of Tuesday—The Charge of the Sixth Corps—The Battle Probably Renewed Wednesday—Death of Gens. Rice and Stevenson—Incidents of the Battle.

WASHINGTON, Thursday, May 12.

Dispatches from the Army of the Potomac, dated Wilderness battle-field yesterday, say, probably the most desperate fighting of the past seven terrible days took place on Tuesday.

Believing the enemy to have sent a greater part of his troops to Richmond, an advance along the entire line was determined on at an early hour.

The Second Corps having the right of the line, had crossed the Po River the evening previous, and had met with but slight opposition.

In the morning the position of the enemy was found to be in the shape of a horseshoe, and on HANCOCK's troops advancing to attack they were compelled to fall back.

An attempt to break their centre was then ordered, and part of HANCOCK's men were sent to support WARREN in the movement.

Our right was also advanced, and the move was begun in the afternoon.

The enemy were driven into their intrenchments in gallant style, and UPTON's brigade of WRIGHT's division, Sixth Corps, got into the enemy's rifle pits, capturing twelve guns and about one thousand prisoners.

Not being supported by other portions of the line, who were unable to gain the tier of works in their front, this brigade was forced to evacuate its advanced position, leaving the captured guns, after spiking them, but bringing off all the prisoners.

The New-York Times.

VOL. XIII.—NO. 3952.　　　　NEW-YORK, TUESDAY, MAY 24, 1864.　　　　PRICE THREE CENTS.

THE GRAND CAMPAIGN.

The Situation in Virginia, Louisiana and Tennessee.

The Great Flank Movement Against Lee.

Our Army Rapidly Pressing Southward.

THE ADVANCE SOUTH OF THE MATTAPONY

Gen. Sherman Again in Pursuit of Johnston.

LATER FROM THE RED RIVER.

THE FLEET AND THE ARMY ALL SAFE.

How the Army is Being Reinforced and Supplied.

DISPATCH FROM SECRETARY STANTON.

Arrival of Admiral Porter at the Mouth of the Red River—The Fleet all Safe—Gen. Banks at Semmesport—Sherman Again in Pursuit of Johnston—The Way the Armies are Being Reinforced and Supplied.

[OFFICIAL.]

WASHINGTON, May 23.

Maj.-Gen. Dix:

Dispatches from Maj.-Gen. CANBY, dated mouth of the Red River, at midnight, May 15, state that "Admiral PORTER has just arrived. The remainder of the gunboats will arrive to-night. Gen. BANKS will probably reach Semmesport, on the Atchafalaya, to-morrow."

A dispatch from Admiral PORTER, dated on board the flagship _Black Hawk_, mouth of Red River, May 16 states that the portion of the squadron above the falls at Alexandria have been released from their unpleasant position, owing to the indefatigable exertions of Lieut.-Col. BAILEY, Acting Engineer of the Nineteenth Army Corps, who proposed and built a tree dam of six hundred feet across the river at the lower falls, which enabled all the vessels to pass in safety, the back-water of the Mississippi reaching Alexandria, and allowed them to pass over all the shoals and the obstructions planted by the enemy, to a point of safety. Lieut.-Col. BAILEY will be immediately nominated for promotion, for distinguished and meritorious services.

An unofficial report from Cairo, dated May 22, states that the army and gunboats were all safe at the mouth of the Red River and Semmesport.

Maj.-Gen. SHERMAN, by a dispatch dated 8:30 P. M.

last night, reports that he would be ready by the morning to resume his operations. Returned veterans and regiments, he says, have more than replaced all losses and detachments.

We have no official reports since my last telegram from Gen. GRANT or Gen. BUTLER.

Official reports of this department show that within eight days after the great battle of Spottsylvania Court-house, many thousand veteran troops have been forwarded to Gen. GRANT.

The whole army has been amply supplied with full rations of subsistence.

Upward of twenty thousand sick and wounded have been transported from the fields of battle to the Washington hospitals, and placed under surgical care.

Over eight thousand prisoners have been transported from the field to prison depots, and large amounts of artillery and other implements of an active campaign brought away.

Several thousand fresh cavalry horses have been forwarded to the army, and the Grand Army of the Potomac is now fully as strong in numbers and better equipped, supplied and furnished than when the campaign opened.

Several thousand reinforcements have also been forwarded to other armies in the field, and ample supplies to all.

During the same time over thirty thousand volunteers for a hundred days have been mustered into the service, clothed, armed, equipped, and transported to their respective positions.

This statement is due to the chiefs of the army staff and bureau, and their respective corps, to whom the credit belongs.

EDWIN M. STANTON,
Secretary of War.

THE FLANK MOVEMENT.

Lee's Right Flank Effectually Turned—Our Advance Eighteen Miles South of Spottsylvania on Saturday—Lee Falling Back—Hard Fighting Expected.

From Our Special Correspondent.

GUINEA'S STATION, Saturday, May 21—7 P. M.

The Army of the Potomac is again on the march toward Richmond. During the night, HANCOCK's corps, which had held the left of our lines in front of Spottsylvania Court-house, took up its march, moving on the road parallel with the Ny River. Early this morning it reached Guinea's Station, on the Fredericksburgh and Richmond railroad, twelve miles due south of Fredericksburgh. Thence it pushed onward, following the railroad, and to-night finds the head of HANCOCK's column at Bowling-green, eighteen miles south of Fredericksburgh. The other corps have been to-day following the same general line, and the Fifth is now passing the point at which this dispatch is dated. You will observe from these indications that the Commanding General has _effected a turning movement_ on the right flank of LEE, who is now hastily falling back to take up a fresh defensive position. It is expected that his next stand will be on the South Anna River, although he may endeavor to hit us while moving by the flank, just as he did when outflanked in his lines on the Rapidan.

Heavy firing, in fact, is this moment heard across the Ny, where one of our columns is moving. A mile south by west of Guinea Station is the point of confluence of the Po and Ny Rivers, and at this point the stream is crossed by Guinea's Bridge, which is in our possession. The river south of the junction of the Po and the Ny is called by the inhabitants of the country the

"Mattapony," although the Mat and Ta, its other two affluents, do not enter it till we reach a point a dozen miles south of this.

Our army is now all gone from the front it has held before Spottsylvania Court-house for the past two weeks, and the lines of Spottsylvania pass into history. They are associated with fighting as desperate as was ever made by embattled foes, and by the greatest valor on the part of both armies. Its woods sepulchre thousands of bodies of brave men, perished in the great cause for which this army marches and fights and suffers.

You will notice by the map that our present front, while it puts us in a very advantageous position in regard to the enemy, at the same time perfectly covers our communications, which are by way of Fredericksburgh and Acquia Creek. The railroad will soon be open from Acquia Creek to Fredericksburgh, and will doubtless be put in order south of that point as we advance. There are also several available points of water communication by the Rappahannock, as at Port Royal, &c., which will probably be used.

I should misrepresent the conviction of the soundest heads in this army if I should convey the impression that our progress is to be now only a triumphal march. We shall be met by the most obdurate resistance which skill and courage on the part of the enemy can command. But Gen. GRANT has given you the key-note of the sentiment of this army: we shall go through with this business, "if it takes all Summer to do it." SWINTON

GEN. BURNSIDE'S CORPS.

The Ten Days' Struggle—The Roads—The Prisoners—Reinforcements.

Correspondence of the New-York Times:

IN CAMP, NY RIVER, Monday, May 16, 1864.

After ten days' fighting, more terrible than the fighting on the Peninsula, at Antietam, or at Gettysburgh, we have driven the enemy to the heights lying on the north and northeast of Spottsylvania Court-house. But the struggle has cost us dear. One-third of the Army of the Potomac is _hors du combat_, and for a few days, before we again deliver battle, our brave and inspirited soldiers must be allowed to rest. Supplies also must be brought up from Belle Plain through Fredericksburgh, before the army can again move.

We have taken 18 guns from the enemy, 8,000 prisoners, and have inflicted on them a loss probably equal to our own. The military character of the Lieutenant-General, in this campaign at least, seems to be that of a man of untiring energy and of invincible determination. By dint of desperate fighting he intends to cut his way to Richmond.

The spirit of the army is high and confident. During the last three days I have talked constantly, by the roadside, around the camp fires, in the batteries and rifle-pits, in the hospitals, with hundreds of soldiers. "We are sure to win this time," are the words I have always heard. Their severe marching and fighting have not lessened, scanty rations and the pelting rain, have not diminished their assurance of final complete success.

This is the first clear day since the 11th. Daily rains have made almost impassable our roads of supply, the turnpike and the plank road to Orange Court-house, and the road to Spottsylvania Court-house. No one can form a correct notion of the condition of the highways except from personal observation. Even as I write, by the wooded roadside at headquarters, three horses of six, which are harnessed to an army wagon, are lying on their sides in the mud. The teamster is wading about, trying to unharness them; the roadmaster is helping him by giving contradictory orders, and by very loud and very vigorous cursing. Dead horses and broken down army wagons and ambulances one meets with nearly every mile, as well as occasionally the half-engulfhed body of a mule, which, getting cast in the traces, has been suffocated in the mud before he could be rescued. The soil af this portion of Virginia is sand or loam, and the three or four thousand army wagons which compose our supply train cut up the roads and the fields by the roadside whenever rain falls for a few hours. But on the other hand, the soil is porous, and two or three days of pleasant weather will enable our large train to bring up abundant supplies of hard bread, salt pork and salt beef.

At Fredericksburgh I chanced to see two thousand prisoners marching under escort to Belle Plain. They were a motley crowd, scantily dressed, and ununiformed. But I saw nothing in their countenances or in their movements which indicated lack of food in the rebel army. They were as vigorous and healthy in appearance as our own troops. I have made particular inquiries from our soldiers respecting the condition of the rebel prisoners when they were first taken. The result of these inquiries has convinced me that LEE has thus far been able to supply his army with sufficient food.

To-day the Ninth Army Corps lies about four miles from Spottsylvania Court-house. Batteries guard the crests of the ridge on which we lie. From a section of the battery of the Eleventh Massachusetts, whose guns are three-inch Parrotts, taken from us at the first Bull Run battle, and retaken by us at Bristoe Station, I have just looked over a portion of our extended lines. Sharpshooters lie in the edge of the woods which bound the horizon, and which conceal the rebel fortifications. The crack of their rifles is incessant. The rebel riflemen are equally on the alert. But casualties are few. Two wounded men of our own and one wounded man of the rebels, is the result, thus far, of the incessant picket-firing directly in our front. Within easy shelling range of the enemy's batteries, in a dense wood of pines and hemlocks, the headquarters of the Ninth Army Corps have been pitched. We change them, I trust, to-morrow. Not a hundred feet from the shelter-tent of Gen. BURNSIDE, a dozen cattle have been slaughtered for the use of the army. The offal lies festering in the sun, and last night the odor, blown through our camp, was exceedingly offensive.

On the left of our lines, just beyond our rifle-pits and in plain view, lie the bodies of several rebels, who were killed during the great battle of the 12th. One is the body of an officer. His gray coat is ornamented with gold lace, but the badges of his rank have been taken from his coat by our soldiers, as trophies or as mementos.

In the operations of the Ninth Army Corps the Third New-Jersey Cavalry, Col. MORRISON, have taken an arduous part. The duty assigned to this regiment was, and still is, to patrol the country on both sides of the Rapidan, from near its junction with the Rappahannock to Germanna Ford. On the 11th and 12th hourly reports were sent from the patroling lines to Gen. BURNSIDE. It was the assurance which these reports gave, that no enemy was in his rear, that enabled him to throw his whole force into the battle of the 12th. For the thorough manner in which this regiment did its duty on these days, Gen. BURNSIDE, in the presence of his staff, warmly thanked Col. MORRISON.

The army is cheered to-day with the news that reinforcements, large enough to fully supply our losses, have been landed at Belle Plain. In a few days we shall resume our advance. God give us a complete and final victory ! H. B.

FROM FREDERICKSBURGH.

Ewell's Attack Upon Our Right—Desperate Fighting of the Heavy Artillery Regiments.

From Our Own Correspondent.

FREDERICKSBURGH, Friday, May 20—6 A. M.

Yesterday our forces were massing on the left, and the enemy made a show of massing in the same direction by exposing their columns moving past Spottsylvania Court-house. Toward night a large force, said to be EWELL'S whole corps, made a demonstration upon our extreme right, and for a time cut off all communication between the army and Fredericksburgh. Our forces in that vicinity, composed largely of artillery, acting as infantry, were at first repelled, but upon receiving reinforcements

Surprisingly effective resistance from green Federal troops on May 19, 1864 cost General Ewell's seasoned veterans heavily, including the life of the soldier seen here.

from the Ninth Corps, promptly rallied, and in less than an hour the enemy was handsomely repulsed. Our loss was heavy, and so was that of the enemy, who made a desperate attempt to cut our communications.

Guerrillas hover on the road between Belle Plain and Fredericksburgh, and also between the latter place and the army. A party attacked some straggling teamsters night before last near Gen. HOOKER'S old headquarters, two miles from Falmouth, and beside capturing several horses, shot a teamster and then cut his throat. The Provost-Marshal of Fredericksburgh is arresting all citizens to-day, upon the supposition that they have furnished the enemy with information which led to the attack last night.

Lists of Casualties—Slaughter of the Rebels.

FREDERICKSBURGH, Saturday, May 21.

Inclosed you will find a pretty full list of men killed and wounded during Thursday evening, 19th, when EWELL attempted to flank us on the right. Most of the men who resisted this formidable attack never were in a fight before—artillerymen from the forts about Washington acting as infantry.

Our loss in that fight, which lasted about an hour and a half, will probably reach 1,000. But the enemy were fairly slaughtered. Some persons believe that they had as many killed as our total loss. The line has been advanced one and a half miles.

E. A. PAUL.

THE PIRATE FLORIDA.

Steering for the Track of Vessels from America to England.

The rebel steamer *Florida* sailed on the 14th from Bermuda, after landing an officer who was sick, and stood to the northward. She reported having burned a New-York ship from Callao about three weeks previous, and sent her crew to England on a foreign vessel.

From Newbern.

The North Carolina *Times* of the 21st is received. There is nothing very new in it.

The rebels in Little Washington set fire to the town on the 11th, destroying all but about twenty houses, and robbed all the women and children in the place.

The Wounded—The Fight of Friday.

FORTRESS MONROE, Saturday, May 21.

Three hundred wounded men were sent from the McClellan Hospital, to-day, to Philadelphia.

The weather is as yet very favorable for the patients in hospital, and most of them are doing well.

Gen. WISTAR has left for home sick.

Gen. DENNIS is at the Chesapeake Hospital, sick.

Yesterday noon the pickets on our left and near the Point of Rocks on the Appomattox, were driven in by the rebels and quite an engagement soon followed. As soon as the pickets reached our reserve force, two of our batteries opened on the enemy with a deadly fire, and they were so taken by surprise that they lost heavily in both killed and wounded.

The rebel Gen. WALKER is wounded and a prisoner, with many of his men.

The enemy got the worst of the skirmish and retired.

Picket skirmishing is going on much of the time along our lines.

There is heavy skirmishing this morning. Particulars are not yet received.

Attack on Fort Powhatan—Repulse of the Rebels.

BALTIMORE, Monday, May 23.

A letter from Fortress Monroe, of the 21st, states that the rebel cavalry had attacked Fort Powhatan, on the James River, making three charges, which were all reputed, with a heavy rebel loss and disorganization, and but slight loss on our side.

The New-York Times.

VOL. XIII—NO. 3961.   NEW-YORK, FRIDAY, JUNE 3, 1864.   PRICE THREE CENTS.

GRANT'S ARMY.

A BATTLE AT COLD HARBOR

The Commands of Gens. Wright and Smith Engaged.

The Rebels Driven from Their Works.

All Their Attempts to Regain Them Repulsed.

SEVERE CAVALRY BATTLE ON TUESDAY.

Encouraging Success at Every Point.

NEWS FROM GENERAL BUTLER.

Artillery Demonstrations Against His Lines.

News From Gen. Grant to 7 O'Clock Thursday Morning.

Union officers discuss plans for attack prior to the Battle of Cold Harbor. Grant, at the far left, is leaning over the back of a displaced pew to examine a map.

A Severe Cavalry Fight at Cold Harbor—Another at Hanover Court-house—The Rebels Severely Defeated in Each Instance—Our Centre Within One and a Half Miles of Mechanicsville.

[OFFICIAL.]

WASHINGTON, Thursday, June 2—12:15 P. M.

Major-Gen. Dix :

A dispatch from Gen. GRANT'S headquarters, dated yesterday, June 1, at 10 A. M., has been received by this department. It states that about 5 P. M. yesterday, (May 31,) Gen. SHERIDAN perceiving a force of rebel cavalry at Cold Harbor, which proved to be FITZ LEE'S division, attacked, and after a hard fight, routed it, together with CLINGMAN'S brigade of infantry, which came to LEE'S support. SHERIDAN remained in possession of the place. He reported at dark that he had a considerable number of prisoners, and that there were many rebel dead and wounded on the field. He was ordered to hold the position, and at 10 P. M., the Sixth Corps set out to occupy it. We have not yet heard from WRIGHT or Gen. SHERIDAN this morning, and do not know whether the former got his troops to their destination. SMITH must be close upon WRIGHT'S column.

This morning the enemy are also moving a heavy column in the same direction. The order has just gone to WARREN to fall upon their flank.

WILSON had a fight last evening near Hanover Court-house with YOUNG'S brigade of cavalry. He routed YOUNG, killing and capturing many, but there has been a good deal of artillery firing in that direction this morning.

WARREN reported last night that in his fight of Monday afternoon, near Bethesdy Church, Col. TYRELL, Thirteenth Virginia, and Col. WILLIS, commanding PEGRAM'S brigade, were killed. Col. CHRISTIAN, Forty-ninth Pennsylvania, was wounded and captured ; so was the Assistant Adjutant-General of RAMSAY'S brigade, name not reported. Ten other commissioned officers were captured and seventy privates. Sixty rebels were buried on the field.

On our centre BURNSIDE reports his advanced line as being this morning (1st) within a mile and a half of Mechanicsville.

No other military intelligence has been received by the department since yesterday.

EDWIN M. STANTON,
Secretary of War.

A Battle at Cold Harbor on Wednesday Evening—The Rebel Works Carried by the Sixth Corps—Several Hundred Prisoners Taken—The Rebels Repulsed in Their Attempts to Regain Their Works

[OFFICIAL.]

WAR DEPARTMENT.
WASHINGTON, June 2, 1864—9:30 P. M.

To Major-Gen. Dix :

A dispatch from Gen. GRANT, dated this morning, June 2, at Bethesda Church, 7 o'clock A. M., has just been received. It states that : " Yesterday afternoon an attack was ordered to be made on our left at Cold Harbor, by the Sixth Corps, and the troops under SMITH,—WARREN, BURNSIDE and HANCOCK being held in readiness, to advance in their respective fronts. The attack was made with spirit about 5 P. M., continuing until after dark, and resulting in our carrying the enemy's works on the right of the Sixth Corps, where we still hold them, and also the first line in front of SMITH. The latter, however, were commanded in the rear, which made those carried untenable. The enemy made repeated assaults on each of the corps not engaged in the main assault, but were repulsed with loss in every instance. Several hundred prisoners were taken, but I cannot say what number, nor estimate either our or the enemy's casualties. During the night the enemy made several assaults to regain what they had lost, but failed."

No dispatches from any other quarter have reached the Department to-day.

EDWIN M. STANTON, Secretary of War.

GEN. SMITH'S COMMAND.

The Death of Lieut. Hunt, U. S. A.—Communication with Gen. Grant—Movement of Gen. Smith's Command.

From our Special Correspondent.
WHITE HOUSE, Va., Tuesday, May 31, 1864.

I have just heard from Lieut. BEECHER, temporarily commanding Battery A, Fifth United States Artillery, particulars of the drowning of Lieut. HUNT, Commanding Battery L, Fourth United States Artillery. The accident occurred on Sunday night, about 11 o'clock, on the way down the James River, just below City Point. The cry was made, "A man overboard!" and the steamer was stopped at once, and a boat lowered. After the boat was manned, a cry was distinctly heard from the water, "I am drowning!" but the poor fellow could not be found. It was not known at this time who had fallen overboard, but upon calling the roll, Lieut. HUNT was missing. His bed was vacant, and the horrible truth forced itself upon the minds of his brother officers and men, by whom he was greatly beloved. It is believed that he walked overboard while asleep, as he was subject to fits of somnambulism. His loss is deeply felt by the whole command.

This morning Gen. SMITH will move with his command to Newcastle, in obedience to orders received last night from Gen. GRANT. GRANT's headquarters, late last night, were at Salem Church, and he will not force a fight until SMITH gets into position at the point designated. WARREN's corps had hard fighting yesterday, and pressed the enemy back to near Mechanicsville, four and a-half miles from Richmond. SHERIDAN also had two severe cavalry fights yesterday, losing about 300 men. H. J. W.

GEN. BUTLER'S ARMY.

Another Artillery Demonstration—The Reason of It—Few Casualties—Naval Attack on Rebel Fortifications.

From Our Own Correspondent.
IN THE FIELD, BERMUDA HUNDRED, }
Tuesday, May 31, 1864.

The enemy, evidently not contented with their lavish waste of ammunition yesterday, made another gunpowder-burning demonstration to-day. Opening heavily with their artillery on our centre, they gradually extended their fire in either direction until the fight was general along the whole line. Gen. TERRY, who has charge of the works, and who spared time to give me particulars, said it was impossible to give any plausible reason for the attacks of either yesterday or to-day. Our troops had not fired a shot until the enemy had shown a decided determination to be annoying, when they opened from all directions a well-concentrated fire of solid and other shot. The fight was maintained until toward evening, when the enemy ceased firing, and orders were issued to do likewise. While this artillery duel was in progress in our front, the enemy made a weak attack upon the works which Gen. HINCKS has built on Spring Hill, on the lower side of the Appomattox River. Gen. BUTLER, apprehending a greater demonstration, called in the services of the Seventh Independent New-York Battery, who he placed along the bluffs at Point of Rocks, and from where they completely covered the Spring Hill fortifications. No occasion was allowed them, however, for a display of their practice, as the enemy, after firing a few small arms, retired to the shelter of the woods.

Deserters who come in to-day report that the firing of yesterday was commenced in a moment of excitement, caused by the reception of news to the effect that LEE, after having been driven into his works around Richmond, repulsed an attack made by Gen. GRANT upon them, after which he drove him many miles. Upon the receipt, BEAUREGARD's men commenced a vociferous cheering, and rushing to the guns, opened upon our works. Gen. TERRY says he hasn't the most remote idea what their intentions really can be. The deserters further stated that

KEMPER's and H. B. JOHNSON's brigades had been sent from our front to join LEE. The gunboats were engaged both yesterday and to-day against a strong work on the Appomattox River. During the fight yesterday the *Commodore Perry* was struck thirteen times, and one man on board sustained the loss of a leg.

The inefficiency of the rebel artillery can be no better illustrated than by referring to our list of casualties. It shows that in both days' fight but six men were hurt, and three of these were wounded by our own shells yesterday. To-day, we lost Lieut. HULL, Co. G. Seventh Connecticut, who was killed outright, and Lieut. BALWIN and Private DOANE, of the same regiment, were wounded. I also saw a colored man who had been shot through the thigh. He was, I believe, a servant for some officer.

WEDNESDAY, June 1, 1864.

Terrific cannonading from the direction of the James River was heard last night; in fact the entire camp was awakened by it. The telegraph from Gen. BUTLER's headquarters to Gen. GILLMORE's, soon brought the facts that Commodore LEE had made a midnight attack on some batteries which the enemy had been erecting along the banks of the James. The rebels replied briskly, and for awhile affairs were quite exciting. Conjectures were rife regarding the cause of this firing, but when the facts were announced all turned in without further anxiety.

Significant Order from Gen. Butler—Naval Engagement in James River.

FORTRESS MONROE, Wednesday, June 1.}
VIA BALTIMORE, Thursday, June 2. }

An order has been issued by Gen. BUTLER, requiring that all rebel prisoners captured by Gen. WILD in the recent engagements on the James River, and forwarded by him to Fortress Monroe and thence to Point Lookout, shall be immediately returned to Gen. WILD's headquarters, for what purpose is not known.

Information has been received that colored troops captured from Gen. WILD's command have been shot by the rebels.

BERMUDA HUNDRED, Wednesday, June 1.

At 3 o'clock this morning a rebel iron-clad came down the James River, and attacked our monitors. The engagement continued upward of two hours, with continuous and heavy cannonading. The rebel iron-clad was then driven up the river. Further re-

sults were not known when the steamer *John A. Warner* left this morning.

Cannonading continued till that time, but it was supposed to be mostly on land.

Condition of the Wounded at Fortress Monroe.

FORTRESS MONROE, Wednesday, June 1.

The wounded officers and soldiers in the Chesapeake and Hampton Hospitals, in charge of Dr. McCLELLAN, are doing extremely well. The weather is very favorable. All the severest cases are in these hospitals, as the slightly wounded have been removed further north.

Lieut. HUNT, commanding Company L, HOWARD's battery, Fourth United States Artillery, was drowned in York River on the night of May 30, by falling overboard from the steamer which was conveying his battery to the White House. He was a brave and efficient officer.

NEWS FROM WASHINGTON.

Special Dispatches to the New-York Times.
WASHINGTON, Thursday, June 2.
THE NEW LOAN.

The Secretary of the Treasury is in conference with the House and Senate Finance Committees in reference to the proposed new loan. The reason assigned for the delay in placing the loan in the market is that Mr. CHASE has under consideration other schemes. Several members of the Ways and Means and Finance Committees have suggested to him to issue fifty millions Seven-thirty Legal-tender Notes, interest payable in currency. The impression, however, is that the Secretary, in case he puts any loan upon the market, will not go beyond six per cent.

COMMERCE BETWEEN THE STATES.

The Senate Committee on Commerce to-day reported the House resolution regulating commerce between the several States.

It will be taken up in the course of a few days and put upon its passage. The resolution is as follows: "That every railroad in the United States, whose road is operated by steam, its successors and assigns, be and is hereby authorized to carry upon and over its road, connections, boats, bridges and ferries, all freight property, mails, passengers, troops and government supplies on their way from any State to another State, and to receive compensation therefor."

Pontoon bridges such as this one were used by Grant's army to transport troops and supplies.

The New-York Times.

VOL. XIII—NO. 3963.   NEW-YORK, MONDAY, JUNE 6, 1864.   PRICE THREE CENTS.

THE ARMY.

STEADY PROGRESS.

Grant Moving on the Enemy's Works.

LEE NARROWING HIS LINE.

HEAVY LOSSES.

LARGE REINFORCEMENTS

SHERMAN PUSHING SOUTHWARD.

[OFFICIAL.]

WASHINGTON, Sunday, June 5—1 P. M.

To Major-Gen. Dix:

A dispatch from Gen. GRANT's headquarters, dated 8:30 o'clock last night has been received. It states that about 7 P. M. yesterday, (Friday, 3d of June,) the enemy suddenly attacked SMITH's brigade, GIBBONS' division. The battle lasted with great fury for half an hour. The attack was unwaveringly repulsed. SMITH's losses were inconsiderable.

At 6 P. M., WILSON, with his cavalry, fell upon the rear of a brigade of HETH's division, which LEE had thrown around to his left, apparently with the intention of enveloping BURNSIDE. After a sharp but short conflict, WILSON drove them from their rifle-pits in confusion. He took a few prisoners. He had previously fought and routed GORDON's brigade of rebel cavalry.

During these fights he lost several officers, among them Col. PRESTON, First Vermont Cavalry, killed; Col. BENJAMIN, Eighth New-York Cavalry, seriously wounded; Gen. STANNARD, serving in the Eighteenth Corps, was seriously wounded yesterday, (Friday.)

Our entire loss in killed, wounded and missing during the three days' operations around Cold Harbor, will not exceed, according to the Adjutant General's report, 7,500. This morning, (Saturday, June 4,) the enemy's left wing, in front of BURNSIDE, was found to have been drawn in during the night.

Col. CESNOLA, in command of 5,000 men, arrived here yesterday, having marched from Port Royal. [on the Rappahannock.]

Telegraphic communication between Cherrystone and Fortress Monroe continues uninterrupted.

A dispatch from Gen. SHERMAN, dated yesterday June 4, 8 A. M., thirteen miles west of Marietta, reports that his left is now well around, covering all roads from the south to the railroad about Ackworth. His cavalry has been in Ackworth and occupies in force all the Allatoona Pass. No other

View of the Bermuda Hundred Landing. Strategic Confederate defense "bottled up" General Butler's Army of the James, allowing more Rebel troops to combat Grant's offensive thrusts.

military intelligence has been received by the department.

EDWIN M. STANTON, Secretary of War.

A Battle on Friday—Combined Assault on the Rebel Works—No Decisive Advantage Gained—The Rebels Driven Within their Works.

[SATURDAY'S OFFICIAL DISPATCH.]

WASHINGTON, June 4, 1864.

To Major-Gen. Dix:

Dispatches from Gen. GRANT's headquarters, dated 3 o'clock yesterday, have just been received. No operations took place on Thursday. Yesterday, at 4:30 o'clock A. M., Gen. GRANT made an assault on the enemy's lines, of which he makes the following report:

"We assaulted at 4:30 A. M., driving the enemy within his intrenchments at all points, but without gaining any decisive advantage. Our troops now occupy a position close to the enemy, some places within fifty yards, and are remaining. Our loss was not severe, nor do I suppose the enemy to have lost heavily. We captured over three hundred prisoners, mostly from BRECKINRIDGE."

Another later official report, not from Gen. GRANT, estimates the number of our killed and wounded at about three thousand. The following officers are among the killed:

Col. HASKELL, Thirty-sixth Wisconsin.
Col. PORTER, Eighth New-York Heavy Artillery.
Col. MORRIS, Sixty-sixth New-York.

Among the wounded are Gen. R. O. TYLER—seriously—will probably lose a foot; Col. McMAHON, One Hundred and Sixty-fourth New-York; Col. BYRNES, Twenty-eighth Massachusetts—probably mortally; and Col. BROOKE, Fifty-third Pennsylvania.

EDWIN M. STANTON, Secretary of War.

FROM GEN. BUTLER.

Rebel Stories—Arrival of Prisoners at the White House.

FORTRESS MONROE, Saturday, June 4.

A rebel Major came into Gen. BUTLER's lines at Bermuda Hundreds yesterday, who says that the federal forces are at Secessionville, and threatening Charleston. The commander has telegraphed the rebel authorities for reinforcements, saying unless he receives them immediately Charleston is lost.

The steamer Manhasset, from White House, reports that the cannonading which had been heard very distinctly for nearly three days closed yesterday afternoon, and was not renewed this morning, at 8 o'clock.

One thousand prisoners had arrived at the White House, captured by Gens. SMITH and BURNSIDE.

The steamer Thomas Powell arrived from Bermuda Hundred at 4 P. M. There have been no active operations there since the last account.

The steamer May Flower was fired into, going up the James River, this morning. No damage was done.

Heavy cannonading was heard in the direction of Richmond, last night.

The Fight of Thursday—The Rebels Make a Dash at our Rifle-pits—How the Dash Was Circumvented and the Rebels Captured.

From Our Own Correspondent.

IN THE FIELD, BERMUDA HUNDRED, Friday, June 3, 1864.

We had quite a "brisk little time" here yesterday morning. The enemy made a dash at our pickets, with the intention of gaining possession of the entire line of rifle-pits, wherein our sentries "hide" themselves, as the rebs say. It will be remembered that they gained possession of a portion of these pits when they made their first attack on our position, but on TERRY's front they were unsuccessful. It seems they have, ignoring the commandment to the contrary, secretly coveted these pits from the very hour they were so decisively repulsed, and, if possible, determined to have them or, well, do something else. With this determination they attacked our lines yesterday morning, throwing forward their entire picket. Little did they dream of the treatment in store for them. That such an attack was expected at some time, is evident from the disposition made to meet it. The pickets of the right wing, holding the pits, were ordered to hold their position while the left should fall gradually back. It was hoped that the enemy, feeling exceedingly certain of bagging our retreating pickets, would not notice the gap which would thereby be caused in their line. And so it proved. On their left rushed, never noticing that the right had been checked, and they were not only detached, but gradually getting further and further within our lines. When they had got well into the trap, a part of the picket reserve slipped through the gap in behind the advancing foe. When fairly surrounded, they appreciated their danger, and tried to cut their way out, but 'twas no use. Their Colonel and many of his men having been killed, the remainder surrendered.

They proved to be a portion of the Twenty-second South Carolina Volunteers, Col. DANTZLER. The men who so neatly executed this well-devised plan, were dismounted cavalry, partly of the First District of Columbia Regiment. These men were armed with rifles shooting sixteen shots before they require loading.

Our loss was small—one killed, sixteen wounded; number of prisoners I have been unable to get.

After visiting all places of local interest, Mrs. Gen. BUTLER returned to Fortress Monroe to-day, by the steamer John A. Warner.

From Bermuda Hundred.

FORTRESS MONROE, Friday, June 3.

The enemy attacked Gen. BUTLER's lines of defence, above Bermuda Hundred, on Wednesday evening, at 9 o'clock, and made a charge with the evident intention of capturing our Parrott guns, but were repulsed with heavy loss. The fighting continued until near Thursday morning, when the enemy were driven back. Our loss was very slight.

FROM GEORGIA.

A Fierce Battle on May 25.

CINCINNATI, Sunday, June 5.

The Cincinnati *Commercial* has accounts from SHERMAN's army up to May 31.

There was a sharp and bloody fight, on the 25th of May, between HOOKER's corps and the rebel Gen. HOOD's command, near Dallas. The battle began at 5 o'clock in the afternoon. The Second Division, under Gen. WILLIAMS, drove the enemy from their first line of works for a distance of two miles.

This division was soon relieved by the First and Third Divisions, under Gens. GEARY and BUTTERFIELD, who advanced steadily, under a terrible musketry fire, and proceeded within forty yards of a concealed battery, which opened upon them a sudden and murderous discharge of grape and canister.

The First Division, in this charge, lost 900 men. The battery was finally silenced, and the enemy driven away. Few prisoners were taken on either side. Our loss was probably greater than the enemy's and amounted to about 1,500.

The substantial fruits of the day's work were the gain of two miles of ground, a favorable position, two pieces of artillery, and a better arrangement of our line for subsequent operations.

The Battle at Resaca—Bravery of Hooker's Troops—The Advance to Cassville.

Correspondence of the New-York Times:

CASSVILLE, Geo., Sunday, May 22, 1864.

For the past fifteen days the army under Gen. SHERMAN has been fighting its way into the heart of Georgia with unvarying success. It is now within sixty miles of Atlanta and about seventy from Chattanooga. The most obstinate resistance against our advance was made at Resaca, fifteen miles south of Dalton. JOHNSTON had fortified the heights northward from the town with great care, and having been joined by POLK's corps, was confident of success. The people were told that the "Yankee" army would here be signally defeated and its further progress rendered impossible. GEARY's division had, a few days before, attacked the enemy at Mill Gap, an impregnable position to the west of Dalton, and engaged their attention while McPHERSON had passed through Snake Gap in the Chattoogata Mountains, seven miles south, without opposition, and taken a position in their rear. Retreat became imperative, and accordingly JOHNSTON evacuated Dalton and fell back to Resaca. SHERMAN did not pause long before attacking the enemy at Resaca, and such was the vigor with which the Union troops assailed the rebel intrenchments that, one after another, they fell into our hands with comparatively small loss. The battle lasted for three days, but was at no time general. On the third and last day HOOKER's corps attacked their strongest position with great fury, and such was the enthusiasm of the troops under him that it was difficult to restrain them properly. No other troops were engaged on our side this day, and the larger portion of our splendid army held the position they had before gained and looked quietly on while the "Potomac men," as HOOKER's corps is called, were exhibiting their fighting qualities in a manner to excite the admiration of all. It was reserved for HOOKER's corps to carry their strongest position, and nobly was it done.

The battle-field was a succession of steep hills and intermediate ravines, densely wooded and almost impervious to the eye or foot of man. On the summits of the ridges the enemy had prepared formidable breastworks, with artillery planted on the commanding positions. A consultation was held in the morning by the leading Generals, among whom I saw Hooker, Howard, Scofield, Sickles, Williams, Geary, Ruger and Knipe, all sitting upon the trunk of a prostrate pine, and arranging the plan of battle. There were four double stars, and four single, all names that have become familiar in the history of the war.

Soon the columns of the Twentieth Corps were in motion, and with quiet yet energetic movement, entered the forest toward the rebel lines. All was hushed and the air seemed heavy with silence. The divisions of WILLIAMS, GEARY and BUTTERFIELD took their assigned positions as nearly as they were able, and the work of blood began. The enemy opened

Brevet Major-General Emory Upton

on us heavily with canister and musketry, but our men advanced steadily in columns of battalions, and with well directed volleys soon sent the enemy flying from their first line of works to the shelter of their artillery and supplementary lines. Immediately in front of BUTTERFIELD and GEARY, was a battery of four guns masked behind a thick undergrowth of scrubby oaks and protected by an earthwork. It annoyed us seriously.

Directly behind it, within fifty paces, was a rifle-pit on a slight elevation, which completely covered the guns and gunners. To capture this battery was very desirable, and the task was undertaken alternately by the men of both divisions. The contest was sharp and bloody. Our troops advanced to the roughly made fort and gained the base of the parapet, but as they showed their heads above it and endeavored to reach the guns, they were shot down by the men in the rifle-pits behind the battery. Thus the four brass pieces remained between the contending parties, inaccessible to either without almost certain death. Our men could put their hands upon the muzzles of the guns as they protruded through the embrasures, but no more. It was equally hazardous for the enemy to undertake to approach. Our forces just under and around the fort, were commanded by Col. COBHAM of GEARY's division, as brave an officer as ever drew a sword. Things remained in this condition for several hours until darkness approached. Col. COBHAM then consulted with Gen. GEARY, and was told that he must secure the guns at all hazards, but with as little loss as possible. A plan was devised by which the men dug away the earth on each side of the embrasures, and made an opening sufficiently wide to pass the guns out to the front. Ropes were attached to them, and some time after midnight they became ours. About this time the enemy gave us a parting volley, and their whole force retreated under cover of the night.

Our losses were considerable, particulars of which have doubtless reached you by telegraph.

Lieut.-Col. LLOYD, One Hundred and Nineteenth New-York Volunteers, was killed; and Col. IRELAND, commanding Third Brigade, GEARY's division, was severely but not dangerously wounded. Capt. WOELTON, One Hundred and Eleventh Pennsylvania Volunteers, was killed in the charge upon the battery.

When daylight came our whole force started in pursuit. We entered and passed through the town and station of Resaca, capturing considerable material and many prisoners. The enemy had burned the railroad bridge over the Oostanaula, but our men were quickly at work rebuilding it. The Oostanaula is a stream of about the same volume as the Rappahannock at Kelly's Ford. It is fordable at certain points at this season of the year. Our whole army was quickly crossed over—some by the various fer-

Confederate Major-General John C. Breckinridge was a presidential candidate in the election of 1860.

ries above and below Resaca, and others fording the stream.

The Twentieth and Twenty-third Corps moved on the left flank some distance east of the line of the railroad, while the Fourth and Fourteenth Corps were in the centre and on the right. We were fast penetrating into the more cultivated portions of Georgia, leaving the mountains behind us. Most of the inhabitants had fled. A few of the wiser remained to meet us, and hailed our advance with joy. Fine farms and plantations greeted our vision, with stately mansions surrounded by shady groves and disciplined shrubbery. From Resaca to Kingston it was a running fight of several days. The bulk of the rebel army was in front of the Twentieth and Twenty-third Corps. Approaching Cassville we found the enemy had made preparation for a determined resistance, and our arrangements were made to attack with vigor. There was considerable fighting on the 20th, but in the course of the night the enemy again fell back, and are now said to be fortifying the line of the Etowah.

Our battle of the 20th was in and around Cassville, the shire town of Cass County. It is a very pretty village, containing a college, several fine churches, hotels, &c. The town has suffered much from the battle in and around it. It lies in a beautiful valley, between two ranges of hills, and before war had laid its blighting hand upon it, was, doubtless, a pretty country village. There are several very fine private residences, giving evidence of former wealth and luxury. Rome, Kingston and Cassville, all lying on nearly the same parallel, are now in our possession, and our course is Gulfward. Our losses during the series of battles since we left Chattanooga, do not exceed 5,000 in the aggregate. Reinforcements are constantly coming up, and our army has largely increased since the commencement of the campaign.

We repair the railroad as we advance, and the trains keep close upon us with all needed supplies.

People in this vicinity have never seen a Union army before, and the national colors have not been unfurled to their astonished gaze for nearly three years. As they look upon our glorious old banner, their recollection of the prosperity and happiness they formerly enjoyed under its protection comes vividly before them, and many hail it with tears of joy.

"Remain with us," said an intelligent planter, "and let your flag and the bayonets of your men protect us from those who have worked our ruin." When the rebels evacuated Cassville and Kingston, our troops entered with colors flying and bands playing familiar patriotic airs. The surrounding hills seemed to rejoice as they echoed the music of the Union. Other hills and valleys southward are waiting for the advent of the starry flag of old, and the patriotic hearts that bear it onward. They shall not wait long.   NICKAJACK.

The New-York Times.

VOL. XIII–NO. 3964. NEW-YORK, TUESDAY, JUNE 7, 1864. PRICE THREE CENTS.

THE GRAND CAMPAIGN.

The Battle of the Chickahominy.

THE GREAT ACTION ON FRIDAY.

Gen. Grant's Object in the Movement.

Brilliant Assault on the Rebel Works.

The Enemy's Lines Carried in Front of Hancock and Wright.

The Rebels Rally and Retake Them.

TEN MINUTES OF HISTORY.

THE LOSS OF OUR KEY POSITION.

Incidents of the Afternoon's Work.

REBEL NIGHT ATTACK

THE RESULT OF THE DAY'S OPERATIONS.

Full and Thrilling Details of the Battle from Our Special Correspondent.

HEADQUARTERS, ARMY OF THE POTOMAC,
COLD HARBOR, NEAR THE CHICKAHOMINY,
Friday, June 3—10 P. M.

GENERAL VIEW OF THE BATTLE.

Judged by the severity of the encounter and the heavy losses we have experienced, the engagement which opened at gray dawn this morning and spent its fury in little over an hour, should take its place among the *battles* of the war; but viewed in its relations to the whole campaign, it is, perhaps, hardly more than a grand reconnoissance—a reconnoissance, however, which has cost us not less than *five or six thousand* killed and wounded.

The object of the action was to force the passage of the Chickahominy, on the north side of which, and covering the roads to Richmond, the rebels had planted themselves in a fortified line. What we have done is to *feel* this line by a vigorous attack, in which, though gaining some temporary successes, and at one or two points actually carrying the enemy's works, we have, on the whole, reached the conclusion that any victory that could here be won must cost too much in its purchase. I do not say this as speaking with any authority, but only as recording the general conviction of the army. Such conviction, however, when the common judgment of such men as have to-day led their lines against the enemy, is apt to be of itself *authority*, and hence I think I may safely predict that there will be *no renewal of the assault on the lines of the Chickahominy*; that we must look to the resources of strategy to plant this army in a position where, being at less of a disadvantage, its valor will have a better promise of adequate reward.

It is in this view that the action of to-day assumes to me the aspect of a great reconnoissance. But it might easily have been more. Were prudence not as much a characteristic of Lieut.-Gen. GRANT's mind as pluck, did he not know as well how and when to cry a halt as to order an advance, he might have pushed the action from a reconnoissance to a bloody battle; but to me it is clear we should have had only another Fredericksburgh and its useless slaughter. Gen. GRANT is not so poor in resource that he need do this; and I think already his eyes are turned away from the Chickahominy to lines and combinations more bold than any yet essayed.

TEN MINUTES OF HISTORY.

The metaphysicians say that time is naught, is but a category of thought; and I think it must be so, for into ten mortal minutes this morning was crowded an age of action. Ten minutes of the figment men call time, and yet that scant space decided a battle! There are a thousand details, ten thousand episodes, but the essential matter is this, that that first rush of advance carried our whole front butt up against a line of works, which we were unable to break through, or, breaking through, were unable to hold. Conceive of this in the large—the fierce onslaught amid deafening volleys of musketry and the thunder of artillery, and the wild, mad yell of battle, and see the ranks mown down, and the lines break here and there, and the sullen, obstinate retreat, every inch contested, and we shall then be able to descend to some of the points of action as they individualize themselves along the line.

THE LEFT—HANCOCK'S CORPS.

HANCOCK held the left of the whole line of battle; and of his three divisions, that of BARLOW held the extreme left of the army, that of GIBBON was drawn on the right of BARLOW's, while BIRNEY's division was held in reserve. Of the four brigades of BARLOW's division, BROOKS had the left and MILES the right—each brigade in double line of battle. SMITH, commanding the Irish Brigade, was placed in support. The left was protected by refusing it—the Third Brigade being disposed so as to cover that flank.

The formation of GIBBON's division on the right of BARLOW was similar, TYLER's brigade (heavy artillery) holding the right, SMITH's the centre and OWEN's the left—McKEAN in rear of TYLER's centre, in two lines. On HANCOCK's line there were but few places where artillery could be used with effect.

BARLOW had directed that his attacking brigades should, previously to the assault, be moved out, and formed just in rear of the picket line. From this point they advanced for half a mile through woods and over open intervals, under a severe fire, square up to the enemy's works. That portion of his front where the right of MILES' brigade joined with the left of BROOKS'—the same brigades that so brilliantly carried the famous salient in the lines of Spottsylvania—succeeded in a similar splendid *coup* here; they got over and into the enemy's parapet, capturing his guns, (four light 12-pounders,) his colors and five or six hundred prisoners, about 300 of whom were secured by promptly passing them to the rear. The storming column, in fact, were just turning the enemy's guns on the retreating rebels, when powerful reinforcements from the second rebel line appeared advancing. The first rebel line was held by BRECKINRIDGE's troops and was carried, but LEE is too good a General to leave a point so important thus weakly defended. BRECKINRIDGE's men were placed in the fore-front to receive the baptism of fire, but behind these lay the veterans of HILL's corps, and it is these we now see dashing forward to retrieve the honors we had snatched. BARLOW's brigades—stout hearts not used to pale before the greatest odds—could have held their own under conditions the least short of desperation, but the situation in which they now found themselves, o'erleaped its limits. It was not merely the overwhelming front that came pressing down upon them, of that they had no fear, but the position they had gained placed them in advance of the whole line of battle, and gave the rebel artillery the opportunity for a deadly enfilading fire. Beside this, they had lost the directing heads of two of the chief commanders. BROOKS and BYRNES, "souls of courage all compact," fell mortally wounded, and all the organizations had suffered fearfully from an unparalleled loss of officers. In this state of facts they fell back, bringing with them the prisoners they had taken and a captured color, but not the guns. They fell back, but not to their original position; to a position far in advance of that they had held, and at different points not more than fifty yards from the enemy. Here they intrenched, and here I leave them to pass on to GIBBONS' division of the same corps on the right, and which was engaged at the same time.

GIBBONS' advance was simultaneous with BARLOW's, but in moving forward, he came upon one of the swamps of the Chickahominy, which had to be turned or overpassed, in the process of which it became very difficult to establish the connection between different parts of his line. This overcome, however, his troops pressed forward with the same vigor that marked the conduct of their companion division on the left. Parts of the brigades of TYLER and OWEN gained the rebel works, but for reasons identical with those that forced back BARLOW's troops, they also were compelled to give up what they had won. GIBBONS' division, too, lost very heavily. Gen. TYLER, before reaching the works, was carried off the field, shot in the ankle. One of his regimental commanders, Col. PORTER, of the Eighth New-York Heavy Artillery, was killed; immediately after, the Lieutenant-Colonel (BATES) fell dead. Another of his regimental commanders, Col. McMAHON,

219

of the One Hundred and Sixty-fourth New-York, was struck while planting his colors on the rebel works, and was left a prisoner in the enemy's hands—his troops not supporting him after he was wounded. OWEN'S brigade lost two entire companies taken prisoners inside of the enemy's intrenchments. In giving way, GIBBONS' division also was far from losing all the ground it had gained. It took up an advanced position, close to the enemy, and just over the crest, the rearward slope of which was held by the rebels. This position it has retained during the day, and McKEAN'S brigade has held all day a position within *fifteen yards* of the enemy's works.

THE KEY-POINT OF THE BATTLE, AND HOW IT WAS LOST.

Not until the splendid attack of HANCOCK'S Corps had been made, not till after its blood-bought victory had been wrested from our hands, was he or any man in this army aware of the supreme importance of the position this morning carried and lost. The key-point in the battle of Gaines' Mills, two years ago, it is strange and mortifying that no one should have appreciated its value. This position is a bald hill, named "Watts' Hill," dominating the whole battleground, and covering the angle of the "Dispatch road." Along this ridge the rebel works formed a salient, and in front of it was a sunken road. Of this road HANCOCK got possession, and the brigades of MILES and BROOKS actually struck and carried the work directly on the salient! Had we held this point we would have had a position whence the entire rebel line might have been enfiladed; and I think it is not too much to say that the day would have been ours, and LEE pushed across the Chickahominy. Had we even known in advance its commanding importance, very different dispositions for attack would have been made: we would have massed on the left, and made the victory a certainty. These considerations certainly inspire bitter regrets ; but who does not know that it is on precisely such contingencies that the fate of battles often hangs?

THE LEFT CENTRE AND CENTRE.—WRIGHT AND SMITH.

Simultaneously with the attack of the Second Corps, the Sixth, under WRIGHT, connecting on the left with HANCOCK, made a general advance at a quarter before five o'clock—each division assaulting on the entire line. Of this corps, the Second Division, (McNEILL,) held the right, the Third Division, (RICKETTS,) the centre, and the First Division, (RUSSELL,) the left. Five batteries, under charge of the Chief of Artillery of the Second Corps, Col. TOMPKINS—namely : Adams' First Rhode Island Battery, Cowan's First New-York, (Independent,) Hahn's Third New-York, (Independent,) McCurtin's First Massachusetts, and Rhode's First Rhode Island, were planted in good positions and did effective service in covering the advance. The assault of the Sixth Corps was made with the utmost vigor, and succeeded in carrying the first line of rebel rifle-pits along its entire front, and got up within two hundred and fifty yards of the main works. SMITH'S Corps, connecting on the right with the Sixth, had advanced in conjunction with it; but the left division, that of MARTINDALE, who led the attack in heavy, deep columns, got disarranged, and was repulsed. Gen. SMITH made three different attacks to relieve MARTINDALE, but his last supports did not get up in time to allow him to hold on. The effect of this repulse on the left of SMITH had a disastrous effect on the position of WRIGHT. It uncovered the right flank of the Sixth, and exposed RICKETTS' Division, which was stoutly holding the advanced position, to a savage fire on the prolongation of its line. In this state of facts, to retain possession of a position somewhat in advance of his point of starting, was the utmost Gen. WRIGHT could possibly do.

OPERATIONS ON THE RIGHT AND RIGHT-CENTRE— WARREN AND BURNSIDE.

Operations along the fronts of WARREN and BURNSIDE were of an importance quite subordinate to that of operations on the left. No results were achieved except the carrying of the line of rifle-pits occupied by the rebel skirmishers. The Fifth and Ninth Corps nowhere struck the enemy's main work. BURNSIDE kept up a furious cannonade for some hours ; but it was nothing—*vox et preterea nihil.* From the tenor of one of BURNSIDE's morning dispatches, it was at one time hoped that he would be able to turn the enemy's left ; but this hope also was doomed to disappointment.

CHICKAHOMINY IN HISTORY.

Notwithstanding that the position of our own line would localize the action of to-day as the battle of Cold Harbor, I have called it the battle of the Chickahominy, for the double reason that this name marks the formation of the rebel line, which we assailed; and further, because the supreme object of to-day's action was to force the passage of that stream. In view of the failure to make good this purpose, the thought of the army and of the country will naturally be directed to the future moves on the great chess-board. It is a fact of which you may not have thought, that Lieut.-Gen. GRANT, in his advance on Richmond, has *crossed* every line of operations that has ever been planned with Richmond as the objective. He has adopted not ; he has bisected all. He is at present on the line of McCLELLAN's peninsular campaign ; but will he remain on it? May he not swing across that too? It would certainly be in the line of his mode of action to do so. But such considerations belong to an order of speculation in which extreme delicacy is an obligation of duty imposed upon every writer here. Accordingly, let the action of to-day pass into history to hold such relation with the whole campaign as the future may determine.

WILLIAM SWINTON.

A military bridge spans the Chickahominy River.

The New-York Times.

VOL. XIII—NO. 3965.   NEW-YORK, WEDNESDAY, JUNE 8, 1864.   PRICE THREE CENTS.

GRANT'S ARMY.

Intelligence Up to Tuesday Morning.

Three Rebel Night Assaults Repulsed.

A MIDNIGHT ATTACK ON BURNSIDE.

A FOGGY ATTACK ON HANCOCK.

The Enemy Driven Back with Heavy Loss.

GRANT BESIEGING LEE'S LINES.

Flags of Truce for the Care of the Dead and Wounded.

Late News from Gen. Grant—An Attack on Burnside Repulsed—Exchange of Flags of Truce in Reference to the Killed and Wounded—Grant Besieging Lee in his Lines.

[OFFICIAL.]

WAR DEPARTMENT,
WASHINGTON, June 7—10:15 P. M. }

Major-Gen. Dix:

Dispatches from headquarters, Army of the Potomac, dated 9 o'clock this morning, have been received. An assault was made on BURNSIDE about midnight, and successfully repulsed. In the preceding afternoon, a hundred picked men of the enemy made a rush to find out what was the meaning of HANCOCK'S advancing siege lines. Nine of the party were captured, and the rest killed or driven back.

Several letters have passed between Gen. GRANT and Gen. LEE in respect to collecting the dead and wounded between the two armies. Gen. GRANT in the closing letter, regrets that all his efforts "for alleviating the sufferings of wounded men left on the field, have been rendered nugatory."

Two rebel officers and six men, sent out to search for the wounded of their commands, were captured in consequence of the enemy not delivering Gen. LEE's letter until after the hour he had named had expired. Gen. GRANT has notified Gen. LEE that they were captured through a misunderstanding, and will not be held as prisoners, but will be returned.

No other military intelligence has been received.

EDWIN M. STANTON,

Secretary of War.

BATTLE OF SUNDAY.

Brevet Brigadier-General Thomas A. Smyth.

Special Dispatch to the New-York Times.

NEAR COLD HARBOR, Sunday Evening, June 5.

The enemy appear to be exceedingly anxious to break up our lines, particularly on the left, so as to cut off all communication with White House Landing. During the last three days they have made several assaults, but in each instance were repulsed with fearful loss. The last attempt of this kind was made just after dark this evening in front of SMYTHE' brigade, late CARROLL'S, of GIBBONS' Division, Second Army Corps. The weather was peculiarly favorable for the movement, as the rain of last night was succeeded by a hot murky day, and, in consequence, the whole lower strata of atmosphere was a dense mist. Under cover of this impenetrable fog the enemy advanced a strong line of battle, and succeeded in reaching a point within pistol range of our works before discovered by the advanced pickets. No sooner did the outpost give the alarm than one sheet of fire belched forth from our ranks in front and on both flanks of the enemy. In about half an hour he fell back, leaving the ground covered with his dead and wounded.

At a little later moment there was apparently a similar demonstration about to be made in front of Russell's Division of the Sixth Corps, but that was speedily checked.

These night attacks have got to be so frequent that they cease to create an alarm, for the whole army is always on duty, ready at any moment to meet any emergency. Gens. GRANT and MEADE are constantly on the alert, so that a surprise is practically an impossibility.

But while these attacks at night create no alarm there is something romantically interesting about them. It is a pyrotechnic display of gigantic proportion. The continued explosions of thousands of rockets would be no comparison.

The loss on our side in this last assault was small owing to the fact that the men were behind earthworks.

Lieut. McCUNE, Fifth Excelsior, of Gen. HANCOCK's Staff, had his leg shot off while standing near Gen. HANCOCK's headquarters.

The Second Cavalry Division, Gen. GREGG, gained an important position to-day on the left.

E. A. PAUL.

OPERATIONS OF SATURDAY AND SUNDAY.

Special Dispatch to the New-York Times.

ARMY OF THE POTOMAC, Sunday, June 5—P. M.

There has been no material change in the position of the Army of the Potomac since the close of the hard battle on Friday. On the left of our line, the Second Corps (HANCOCK's) still holds the ground, stretched along the road leading to Dispatch Station, and protected on the flank by SHERIDAN, whose dashing cavalry pickets the intervening region on the bank of the Chickahominy.

Our right wing is along the line of the Bethesda church road, and gradually pressing toward the left, thus rendering the army compact and firm.

WILSON's cavalry division, watchful and adventurous, covers the flank in this direction.

Our lines have moved forward a very little since Friday's costly struggle. Indeed the advance might be counted by inches.

The enemy, snugly covered inside his high breastworks, makes a vigorous defence to all our assaults, and shows no signs of yielding.

On our side, especially in front of the Sixth and Eighteenth Corps, the attack is sharp and urged onward with a full determination to win. By dint of pluck and sheer power of endurance, our lines have been pushed ahead inch by inch, almost solely by the use of the spade, the musket being simply an auxiliary, until at some points in front of MARTINDALE's Division of the Eighteenth Corps, they are not more than one hundred yards apart. This digging is done solely at night, and as the sappers advance, large numbers of the bodies, both rebel and our own, of those who fell on Friday, are reached and buried.

On both sides sharpshooters—fairly entitled to the name—perched in trees or hidden in pits, take grim delight in sending a bullet into any luckless individual whom incaution or duty exposes. This fact has been brought home to us quite painfully during the past few days by the loss of several excellent officers. Even this morning I was speaking to Capt. P. REED, Assistant Adjutant-General of the Staff of Brig.-Gen. BROOKS. Five minutes afterward a rebel rifleman, stationed nearly a mile distant to the right, succeeded in planting a minie ball in the Captain's leg, as he walked across the field in front of Gen. SMITH's Headquarters. These sharpshooting pests have disabled, at a low estimate, one hundred men per day, since Friday, in both the Sixth and Eighteenth Corps, while other organizations of the army have also not been exempt from their annoyance.

But the fighting has not been entirely confined to sharpshooting. There has been several artillery episodes, to vary with hoarser sounds, the lively, but not continuous, bang, bang on the skirmish line.

At 9½ o'clock last night, the rebels in front of the Eighteenth Corps attempted to thwart Gen. SMITH's settled purpose of relieving his troops in the rifle-pits. To do this they suddenly unmasked a battery about a mile distant from corps headquarters, sending their screeching voices through the air for a few minutes, with a rapidity that was quite demoralizing to everybody who listened, except, of course, the seasoned soldiers, to whom such harsh-voiced messages are familiar. The cannonade was accompanied by several sharp volleys of musketry, scattered shots of which clicked unpleasantly in the trees of the picturesque grove where

Union cavalry under Major-General Philip H. Sheridan (standing, at left of photo) harassed Confederates positions throughout the Richmond area. The other generals serving under Sheridan were, from left: J.I. Gregg, Wesley Merritt, Thomas C. Devin, and George A. Custer.

Gen. SMITH has cnosen to pitch his tents, causing leaves to fall in gentle showers. Capt. ELDER, Chief of Artillery of the Eighteenth Corps, speedily rebuked this presumption of the enemy. He massed his batteries on their position and blazed away so fiercely for a while that the very ground shook as he thundered. Silence thus secured, the remainder of the night passed away without disturbance.

There have been one or two animated artillery passages to-day also, in each of which Capt. ELDER grandly put a stop to the rebel demonstrations, by massing his pieces and firing with magnificent rapidity. The enemy lost his morale, and withdrew crestfallen. The few shots sent by the rebels were not, however, altogether harmless. There were three regiments in line near the edge of a piece of woods, about half a mile in the rear of our breastworks. These must have been observed, and doubtless drew the enemy's fire. Four of the shots went hissing, screeching overhead and cutting off tree-tops as they passed beyond. The fifth struck in the ranks of the Tenth New-York Heavy Artillery, completely disemboweling one man and injuring four others. A chance shot to-day also worked some mishhief in the Second Rhode Island Regiment. The term of the regiment has expired, and it was going from the front bound for home. Having got, as was supposed, well out of range, the order was given to halt, and a moment after came the rushing ball bringing its death message to two poor fellows who, after faithful service, having escaped all the dangers of the fight, were full of joyful anticipations at the speedy prospect of being home again. Their fate was doubly shocking.

About 7 o'clock to-night there was a furious fire suddenly opened on the left. For twenty minutes the rattling of musketry and roaring of artillery was kept up with a steadiness that is seldom equalled. Persons at a distance interpreted it into a determined attack by the rebels, with the view of turning HANCOCK'S position. The indications certainly pointed to something desperate, and the weakhearted made preparations for a skedaddle. Investigation has not made it precisely clear why so much noise was made. Some declare that the enemy attacked in force, attempting to break SMYTH's brigade of the Second Corps, while others insist that a scare was got up in the darkness, without any justification whatever. At any rate, our lines were preserved intact, and I must wait the developments of the morning for the facts.

Brig.-Gen. BARNARD was to-day assigned to duty as Chief Engineer of the Army of the Potomac.

H. J. W.

THE BATTLE OF FRIDAY.

Further Particulars—The Gallantry of Gibbons' and Barlow's Divisions—List of Casualties.

From Our Special Correspondent.

NEAR COLD HARBOR,
Friday, June 3—3 o'clock P. M.

Since my dispatch of 9 o'clock A. M., I have gathered some additional particulars of the contest this morning. Compelled to leave the field to get off that dispatch at the early hour I did, and not foreseeing that our troops might be compelled to give up a portion of the works they had won against such odds, makes my first account under present circumstances rather exaggerated; that is, the object of the movement on the left was not fully accomplished. True, the cavalry on the left of our line rests upon the Chickahominy, and this morning all felt confident that the left of the infantry line would certainly hold that position, by doing which the enemy, taken in flank, would have had their whole line on this side of the Chickahominy rolled up like a piece of parchment, and the entire demoralization of the enemy must have been the result. As it was, the success was only partial. Our extreme left (BARLOW's division of the Second Corps) advanced to within three-quarters of a mile of the river—an advance of nearly one mile. Of this gallant movement I wish to speak more in detail. Gen. BARLOW's division occupied the extreme left of the line—of the army, in fact; Gen. GIBBON's next, while Gen. BIRNEY's division was held in reserve. The movement was inaugurated by the advance of one-half of the first-named division. Gen. MILES' brigade, composed of the Fifth New-Hampshire, Sixty-first New-York, Eighty-first Pennsylvania, One Hundred and Fortieth Pennsylvania, One Hundred and Eighty-third Pennsylvania, Twenty-sixth Michigan and Second New-York Heavy Artillery, of BARLOW's division, occupied the extreme left; while BROOKS', brigade, of the same division, composed of the Fifty-third, One Hundred and Forty-fifth, One Hundred and Forty-eighth Pennsylvania, Sixty-sixth and Sixty-fourth New-York, Second Delaware and Seventh New-York Artillery, moved up on the right. The movement was commenced at precisely 4½ o'clock A. M. The One Hundred and Forty-eighth Pennsylvania, Col. BEAVER, deployed as skirmishers. At first the ground over which the command moved was covered with trees and an undergrowth of bushes, passing through which the command emerged into an open space, in full view of the enemy. At this moment a terrific fire was opened upon the devoted patriots—but they quailed not. Continuing to advance, one-half the command charged upon and obtained possession of the enemy's works. A battery of six guns was in our

hands, and just as Col. MORRIS, of the Second New-York Artillery, was in the act of turning the guns upon the foe, they advanced in overwhelming numbers, and the braves of the Union were compelled to fall back. The enemy did not then and have not since been able to use these guns. Our men (One Hundred and Forty-eighth Pennsylvania, Col. BEAVER,) hold a position within thirty-five yards, and every man is shot who attempts to approach the guns. The enemy, composed of HILL's and BRECKINRIDGE's troops, are behind a line of earthworks, on the crest of a roll of land, while our boys hold a similar position in a depression of the land, having thereby a little advantage as to position, as the reader will readily perceive, for to aim at our men a rebel must raise his head so far above the earthworks as to look down a hill, while ours look up at an angle of perhaps thirty degrees ; the enemy's flag floats defiantly over the parapet, and has been frequently shot away ; when this is done the boys banter the enemy to raise their "rag" again. Not a head or the least portion of a man's person can be exposed but what a dozen guns are instantly fired by our men ; and various are the expedients resorted to to induce some of the enemy to make a show of hands ; some of these which have been successfully used a number of times, are to give the word of command as though our men were to advance, about to be relieved, or reinforced ; being within within a few paces, the enemy hearing every word distinctly, in large numbers peer over their works to take advantage of the supposed order. Scores of them to-day have forfeited their lives by serving a bad cause with such alacrity. In the charge upon the works, Corp. TERRANCE BIGLER, Company D, Seventh New-York Heavy Artillery, snatched the State flag of the Twenty-sixth Virginia Infantry, from the hands of the bearer within the enemy's works, and carried it off triumphantly to the rear. The different temperament of men under the excitement of battle is strongly illustrated by the following incident : The Colonel of the Twenty-sixth Virginia was bayoneted on the spot by one of our men, while a Captain at his side was taken prisoner by another—all the work of a moment ; 15 commissioned officers and 215 non-commissioned officers and privates were captured by this division.

GIBBON's division, as I have before said, was at the right of Gen. BARLOW. His command also had a desperate conflict, assaulting the enemy's works several times, and gaining some ground and capturing about 150 prisoners. McKEAN's, OWEN's, SMITH's and TYLER's brigades were all in the fight. A portion of one brigade got so far within the enemy's works that it could not go either way, and there it remains at this moment. The men will be got out to-night.

The New-York Times.

VOL. XIII—NO. 3983.   NEW-YORK, WEDNESDAY, JUNE 29, 1864.   PRICE THREE CENTS.

THE GREAT CAMPAIGN.

News from Gen. Grant to Monday Evening.

General Wilson Tearing Up More Railroads.

Gratifying News from General Hunter.

The Complete Success of his Expedition.

Immense Destruction of Railroads and Supplies.

IMPORTANT FROM SHERMAN.

An Attack on the Rebels at Kenesaw Mountain.

Our Troops Repulsed with a Loss of 2,500.

THE ENEMY'S POSITION VERY STRONG.

WASHINGTON, Tuesday, June 28.

To Major-Gen. Dix:

A dispatch from Lieut.-Gen. GRANT, dated yesterday, the 27th, at 3·30 P. M., at his headquarters, reports no operations in front except from our own guns, which fire into the bridge at Petersburgh from a distance of two thousand yards. The dispatch gives the following intelligence from rebel papers. A Petersburgh paper of the 25th inst. states that Gen. HUNTER is striking for Jackson River depot, about forty miles north of Salem, and says that if he reaches Covington, which they suppose he will do with most of his forces, but with loss of material, he will be safe.

The same paper accuses Gen. HUNTER of destroying a great amount of private property, and stealing a large number of wagons, horses and cattle.

The same paper also states that Gen. WILSON destroyed a train of cars, loaded with cotton and furniture, burned the depot buildings, &c., at Burkesville, and destroyed some of the track, and was still pushing South. All the railroads leading into Richmond are now destroyed, and some of them badly.

A dispatch from Gen. SHERMAN, received this morning, reports that yesterday, June 27, an unsuccessful attack was made by our forces on the enemy's position, which resulted in a loss of between two and three thousand. The following particulars are given.

Pursuant to my orders of the 24th inst. a diversion was made on each flank of the enemy especially down the Sandtown road. At 8 A. M. Gen. McPHERSON attacked at the southwest end of Kensaw, and Gen. THOMAS at a point about a mile further south. At the same time the skirmishers and artillery along the whole line kept up a sharp fire. Neither attack succeeded, though both columns reached the enemy's works which are very strong.

Gen. McPHERSON reports his loss about 500, and Gen. THOMAS' about 2,000.

The loss is particularly heavy in general field officers. Gen. HARKER is reported mortally wounded; also, Col. DAN. McCOOK, commanding a brigade; Col. RICE, Fifty-seventh Ohio, very seriously Col. BAINDELL, Fortieth Illinois, and AUGUSTINE, Fifty-fifth Illinois, are killed,

Gen. McPHERSON took one hundred prisoners and Gen. THOMAS about as many, but I do not suppose we inflicted a heavy loss on the enemy, as he kept clear behind his parapets.

No other military intelligence has been received by the department.

EDWIN M. STANTON,
Secretary of War.

From Gen. Grant's Army.

HEADQUARTERS OF THE ARMY OF THE POTOMAC, Monday, June 27—5 o'clock A. M.

An attack was made on BURNSIDE'S line at about 11 o'clock on Saturday night, with the intention of driving back a working party who were engaged in digging intrenchments toward the enemy's front, so as to gain a better position in which to place guns to more effectually cover the rebel works. The firing was very brisk for about an hour, resulting in our men holding their ground and continuing their labors without any loss of consequence.

The usual amount of picket firing took place yesterday, it being a little more persistent in fron of the Ninth Corps than at any other point.

It is usual to relieve picket line shortly after dark, and the rebels being generally on the alert at the least noise, invariably open fire in hope of being able to pick off some men while the change is being made.

It is seldom any harm results from these attacks, as the men have become so careful to screen themselves that it is next to impossible for the rebel sharpshooters to get a range on them.

The health of the troops is in the main good, con-

General William T. Sherman was picked by Grant to command all Federal armies in the western theater of the war. Sherman's ultimate objective was to destroy the Confederate Army of Tennessee.

Raphael Semmes was the commander of the *Alabama*, credited with destroying 58 vessels in two years.

sidering the oppressively hot weather they have had to endure since their arrival here, and the scarcity of water in this section.

The Eighteenth Corps seem to have the greatest number of men in the hospital from the effects of the weather.

The colored troops are reported as being unaffected by the heat. Surgeon JACKSON, in charge of the Fourth Division Hospital, Ninth Corps, reports, that in that division only forty men out of four thousand were unfit for duty when they were put in front on Tuesday last to relieve the Second Corps. This tends to show how much better they can endure the scorching rays of the sun than white troops.

Appearances yesterday afternoon indicated that we should have a shower of rain. Black clouds appearing in the west, accompanied with a good deal of thunder, but we were disappointed. The storm passed off to the northeast, only a few drops falling in this vicinity.

EUROPEAN NEWS.

Arrival of the City of London and Hibernian, with Dates to June 17.

The Pirate Alabama Repairing at Cherbourg.

Burning of the Ships Tycoon and Rockingham.

Capt. Semmes Defends His Piratical Exploits.

Fresh Instructions from the British Government Regarding the Treatment of Prizes.

Forged Confederate Bonds in Circulation.

INTERESTING MISCELLANEOUS INTELLIGENCE.

FINANCIAL AND COMMERCIAL.

The *City of London* arrived at this port yesterday. She brings the summary of the *Sidon*, which left Liverpool June 14.

The steamship *America*, from New-York, arrived at Southampton on the 15th inst.

The Cunard screw steamer *Hecla* would leave Liverpool for New-York simultaneously with the *Arabia*, on the 18th of June, to accommodate the cargo intended for the *Persia*.

The United States steamer *Kearsage* was in Flushing Road on the 12th of June, and passed Deal June 13, bound west.

The United States corvette *St. Louis* sailed from Algesiras on the 3d of June, for the westward.

The steamship *Hibernian*, from Liverpool June 16, via Londonderry 17th, was boarded off Cape Race at 6 o'clock, Monday morning, on her way to Quebec.

The news is one day later than the *City of London's*.

The steamship *Westminster*, from New-York, arrived at London on the 17th.

The steamship *Caledonia*, from Quebec, arrived at Glasgow on the 17th.

AMERICAN TOPICS.

THE ALABAMA.

The notorious rebel cruiser *Alabama* arrived at Cherbourg, France, on the 11th of June, and was admitted to free *pratique*. She landed 40 prisoners—the crews of the ship *Tycoon*, Capt. AYRES, from New-York, bound to San Francisco, destroyed by the *Alabama*; and of the ship *Rockingham*, previously reported destroyed.

Capt. SEMMES has requested the *Times* to insert the reasons why the Confederate cruisers burn their prizes and his suggestion for a remedy. The communication, which the *Times* of course publishes, fills two columns and a half of the paper. He says it was his intention to have sent all his prizes for adjudication into the ports most convenient for the parties concerned, but this intention was frustrated by British order in council. Capt. SEMMES asks was it expected that he would abandon the right of capture altogether, or that he would be guilty of the child's play of capturing the enemy's ships with one hand and releasing them with the other? Further, he inquires what inconvenience to Great Britain, for example, could possibly have grown out of the fact of the captured vessels lying quietly in the port of Liverpool in charge of a ship-keeper and prize-agent until she could be adjudicated, and if she should be condemned, why should she not have been sold as quietly as if she had been seized and sold under any execution for debt. Capt. SEMMES takes credit to himself and his officers for every ship set on fire, insomuch as they sacrifice their chances of prize money to the good of the Confederate States.

The *Times* replies to Capt. SEMMES' arguments relative to the burning of ships, and shows them to be fallacious and judicially unsound.

Captain Winslow (third from left) and officers of the *U.S.S. Kearsarge*, who sank the Confederate privateer *Alabama* on June 19, 1864.

The New-York Times.

VOL. XIII.—NO. 4003.   NEW-YORK, SATURDAY, JULY 23, 1864.   PRICE FOUR CENTS.

ATLANTA.

A BATTLE ON THURSDAY.

THE ENEMY DEFEATED.

Our Forces Steadily Pushing the Rebels.

Railroad Communication with Richmond Completely Severed.

Only Two Routes of Retreat Open to the Rebels.

Telegraphic Communication with Atlanta.

WASHINGTON, Friday, July 22.

Official information from Gen. SHERMAN represents everything to be progressing in a manner highly satisfactory.

All-day before yesterday, our army was engaged with the enemy, and the rebels were steadily driven on into their intrenchments.

The city is in plain view of our troops, and our shells can reach it. Our army is in excellent condition.

Five miles of the railroad between Atlanta and Decatur have been destroyed, and thus the road is rendered useless to the rebels.

The *National Republican* has furnished the following, in advance of its publication:

" Official advices from Gen. SHERMAN received this morning, cover the operations down to last night. The work of investing the city was fast going on. There was hard fighting yesterday, which resulted in the repulse of the enemy in his efforts to dislodge our troops. Gen. PALMER advanced his line to a more advantageous position. Our loss during the day was small.

Gen. SHERMAN holds the railroad leading from Atlanta toward Richmond, so that JOHNSTON cannot escape by that route to reinforce LEE. His only means of leaving Atlanta are by two roads leading south to Macon, and southwest to West Point and Mobile. If JOHNSTON escapes with his army by either of these last-named routes, he will be obliged to move quickly. It is a well-settled opinion in military circles that the rebels can better afford to lose Atlanta than JOHNSTON'S army. It may possibly be true that LONGSTREET is already in command of it.

IMPORTANT REPORT.

Telegraphic Communication With Atlanta.

OFFICE ASSOCIATED PRESS, }
NEW-YORK, Friday, July 22. }

The Western Union Telegraph Company are in communication with Atlanta, Ga., to-day, messages

General Joseph E. Johnston had replaced Bragg as commander of the Army of the Tennessee, and was well liked by the troops. Johnston's defensive strategy was calculated to buy time for the South, discouraging Lincoln's re-election chances. Misunderstood by Jefferson Davis, Johnston himself was replaced.

from that place, of this date, having been transmitted over their wires.

No official announcement of the capture or occupation of Atlanta has been received at this office up to this hour, 3:30 P. M.

LATER.

WASHINGTON, Friday, July 22.

Dispatches received by the Government this afternoon announce that the rebel Gen. JOHNSTON has been superseded by Gen. HOOD, and that a battle has taken place between the two armies, in which Gen. SHERMAN defeated the enemy.

THE VERY LATEST.

WASHINGTON, Friday, July 22—11 P. M.

Nothing has been received by the Government in relation to the fall of Atlanta.

The Occupation of Decatur—Rebel Desertion.

LOUISVILLE, Ky., Friday, July 22.

The Nashville *Union*, of yesterday morning, states that on Monday morning Decatur, Ga., was occupied by our forces, thus cutting off all rebel communication with South Carolina by way of Macon. Deserters and stragglers had been coming into our lines in great numbers since our crossing the Chattahoochee. They represent that all hopes of saving Atlanta has disappeared.

ARMY OF THE POTOMAC.

Compliments to the Rebels in the Shape of 200-pound Mortar Shells—Important Movements on the Tapis—Gen. Smith Relieved.

From Our Own Correspondent.

HEADQUARTERS ARMY OF THE POTOMAC, }
Thursday, July 21, 1864—10 A. M. }

Yesterday was a day of more than usual activity at the front.

The enemy opened a battery upon our lines, but our Generals and men have not been idle notwithstanding the Maryland raid, and were prepared for them, returning the compliment with a 13-inch mortar, throwing a 200-pound shell, which blew up a rebel caisson, and silenced their most formidable battery. A new depot was discovered on the Weldon Railroad, which was burned by our shells. There were several officers and men wounded during the fight, which lasted four hours, among whom is Gen. WILCOX, slightly in the thigh, by a fragment of a rebel shell.

LATE SOUTHERN NEWS.

GEN. JOHNSTON RELIEVED FROM COMMAND.

General Hood Appointed to Succeed Him.

Gen. Sherman Cuts Communication Between Atlanta and Montgomery.

From Richmond papers of the 18th and 20th, we obtain the following interesting information:

FROM GEORGIA.

ATLANTA, Monday, July 18, 1864.

The army and public were surprised this morning by the announcement of the change of commanders—Gen. JOHNSTON being relieved, and Gen. HOOD receiving the command. The following is Gen. JOHNSTON'S farewell address to the troops:

HEADQUARTERS ARMY OF TENNESSEE, July 17, 1864.

In obedience to orders of the War Department, I turn over to Gen. HOOD the command of the Army and Department of Tennessee. I cannot leave without expressing my admiration of the high military qualities it has displayed so conspicuously—every soldier'y virtue, endurance of toil, obedience to orders, brilliant courage. The enemy move but to be severely repulsed and punished. You, soldiers, have never argued but from your courage, and never counted your fears. No longer your leader, I will still watch your career, and will rejoice in your victories. To one and all I offer assurances of my friendship, and bid an affectionate farewell.

(Signed)　J. E. JOHNSTON, General.

Gen. HOOD, on assuming command, issued the following address:

HEADQUARTERS ARMY OF TENNESSEE, July 18, 1864.
SOLDIERS: In obedience to orders from the War Department, I assume command of this army and department. I feel the weight of the responsibility so suddenly and unexpectedly devolved upon me by this position, and shall bend all my energies and employ all my skill to meet its requirements. I look with confidence to your patriotism to stand by me, and rely upon your prowess to wrest your country from the grasp of the invader, entitling yourselves to the proud distinction of being called the deliverers of an oppressed people.

(Signed)　J. B. HOOD, General.

Telegraphic communications with Montgomery was suspended last night near Notasulga. The interruption is supposed to have been caused by a portion of that part of the enemy who were reported to be at Talladega on Saturday. No train has arrived to-day from West Point. The main forces of the enemy crossed the Chattahoochee between Isham's Ford and Rosswell, and are slowly pushing forward. Cavalry skirmishing took place this morning at Buck Head, six miles from this place.

THE SITUATION.

From the Richmond Examiner, July 20.

Yesterday was a quiet day. There was no booming of cannon, no heavy masses of smoke on the Southern horizon, and no exciting rumors from any quarter. The fact that the flags of the Yankee shipping in James River were at half-mast on Monday caused many to give credit to the report of GRANT'S death, and this topic and the removal of Gen. J. E. JOHNSTON from the command of the Army of Tennessee, were the topics that chiefly occupied men's minds. Though no one believed his death would be of any great benefit to us, yet every one would have been glad, on general principles, to have been assured of his death. The Yankees think too much of him, and that is sufficient to make us rejoice over any misfortune that might befall him.

We have nothing later from our forces operating in Maryland than the news published yesterday. Other officers and men, wounded at Monocacy, arrived yesterday; but they bring nothing new, except that they estimate the number of horses obtained and secured by us in the raid at seven instead of five thousand.

The only news we have from Georgia is contained in the press dispatch, published in another column. From that it will be seen that affairs at Atlanta begin to wear a serious aspect. SHERMAN and his whole army has crossed to the east bank of the Chattahoochee River, and his cavalry were skirmishing with HOOD'S, within six miles of Atlanta. If Atlanta is to be defended a battle must be delivered within a

very brief period. If the enemy is allowed to intrench, having the larger army, he will immediately out-flank Gen. HOOD or oblige him to fall back. The eyes of the country are anxiously turned to this quarter. The dispatch alluded to says, "the army and the public were surprised by the announcement of the change of Commanders." The army and the public in Virginia have seen and experienced such strange things in the last three years, as to have lost the faculty of being surprised at anything done by those in authority.

From the Richmond Examiner.

* * * * The expedition has also shown how easily such things are done against an enemy that attempts enterprises beyond his strength, and strips his own capital of defenders to swell his armies sent against distant cities. Our troops are charmed, on the whole, with the little campaign. They consider that five or six thousand horses, two or three thousand cattle, and eight hundred prisoners, all brought safely across the Potomac (except FRANKLIN and TYLER) was no bad result of a few days' dash into Maryland. They won one small battle, and they lived well; the fighting was good, the eating and especially the drinking was "glorious," and in short, Mr. LINCOLN'S official organ declares that "the rebels are so flattered because they have put Washington and Baltimore in terror, that they will not hesitate to repeat the experiment." We think that extremely likely.

Possibly, too, our Government may at last—but of this we are not sanguine—find out that its duty to its own people does really require it to hurt a little the enemies of that people, when it has the power. And if not, then the people themselves will begin to conclude that the worst enemy they have is the Government which they established for their protection.

HOW TO PROTECT SOUTHERN RAILROADS.

From the Richmond Examiner, July 15.

Of such glorious rumors as those which pervaded the town on yesterday, it is best to decline discourse till we know whether they are truths or only illusions of hope. Let us attend to another report of a different character—that GRANT'S cavalry has started on a fresh raid against the Weldon Railroad.

One of the marked peculiarities of the people with whom we war is, that they publish their military intentions in newspapers before commencing their execution. One of the peculiarities of the singular breed of small politicians set over us at Montgomery, is a resolute disbelief in all information that comes to them through a plain, ordinary public channel. Although the result has a hundred times proven that the plan made public in the New-York paper was really the plan of the enemy's General or Government, they cannot comprehend the fact that the enemy does so give notice of their designs. The publication is to them a perfect proof that they are going to do something else.

They could not believe that this campaign in Virginia was intended, chiefly because the scheme was universally published. They pay as little attention to the plan now ascribed to GRANT by that same press. That plan is simple—to keep a large army close to Petersburgh and Lee, while cavalry raids cut the railroads leading into Richmond as fast as we can mend them.

This plan will be successfully executed if the Con-

federate authorities do not devise a method of defending the roads. It is useless to repair, if the cavalry can ride in about the time the work is completed and undo it in a couple of hours. They must defend the roads. They must defend the roads by other means than the single method hitherto attempted; because that method has proven utterly and invariably ineffectual—there has not been a solitary exception in the course of the war. The single method yet imagined or tried is, to send our Confederate cavalry in pursuit of the Yankee cavalry. But, as one body of horse will go as fast as another, those who have six hours start are not overtaken before the goal is reached. After the destruction is done and the Yankee raiders have to return, they are sometimes met and sometimes not. When collision occurs, our cavalry sometimes beats them, as they did the other day. But the railroad is broken, and the beating does not mend it.

The object being the salvation of the roads, it is clear that another means should be employed. It would seem to an observer that of all kinds of communication, a railroad should be the easiest to preserve and defend. Steam is stronger than horse flesh; locomotives move faster than cavalry; and a single train can transport a large body of troops to any point on the line in a few hours. But a large body of troops is not necessary to obstruct the advance of cavalry. A few hundred picked and well-mounted men can obstruct roads and bushwack the strongest raid till the pursuing cavalry overtakes and destroys it. Only these few hundred must be before and not behind it —and the railroad can put both them and their horses where they will get before it, if they and the train to convey them are kept in perpetual readiness at a depot. Hitherto the *militia* has been relied on for that work. Is it not time to discover that this expectation is a stupidity? The militia is composed of stiff-limbed old men and little boys, both equally unaccustomed to arms. Yet they are expected to perform the most dangerous as well as the most laborious service that can be demanded of the hardiest and most skillful soldier. To bushwhack is a military duty, requiring more confidence in one's weapon, greater strength of body and a cooler courage than any other whatever. The man, who does it, has to close alone with the enemy, and if caught is killed. For such a service thorough soldiers are required, and this or some other plan must be resorted to, if we would save our roads.

THE MARYLAND RAID.

From the Richmond Enquirer, July 18.

From three to five hundred prisoners have passed through Rockingham from Maryland, captured principally during the first of the invasion by our forces. They are principally Ohians, and nearly all were one hundred day men.

FROM THE INVASION.

Passengers from Staunton last night report that the "invaders" of Maryland were safely south of the Potomac, with a whole country crammed full of all sorts of live and vegetable plunder.

Sherman's first clash with the confederate army came at New Hope Church, where Rebel earthworks such as this one provided good cover against his advancing troops.

The New-York Times.

VOL. XIII.–NO. 4004. NEW-YORK, MONDAY, JULY 25, 1864. PRICE FOUR CENTS.

ATLANTA.

A Battle Before Atlanta on Friday.

RESULTS THUS FAR FAVORABLE.

Our Siege Guns Bearing on the City.

THE PLACE PARTIALLY AFIRE.

The Contest Still Progressing on Saturday.

A SAD LOSS TO OUR ARMS.

Death of the Great Soldier, Major-Gen. McPherson.

Details of Movements Preliminary to the Battle.

AFFAIRS IN THE ARMY OF THE WEST.

Special Dispatch to the New-York Times.

WASHINGTON, Sunday, July 24—10 P. M.

Official dispatches of another battle before Atlanta, fought on Friday, were received by the authorities last night. At the time of sending the dispatch the contest was still going on, but the results, so far as developed, were favorable. A position had been gained from which SHERMAN was able to bring his siege guns to bear on the city. Extensive fires were raging within its limits as though the rebels were burning stores, &c.

During this engagement Gen. MCPHERSON was killed. This sad report it was at first hoped might prove unfounded, but it has been fully confirmed. In this brilliant young officer the country loses one of its ablest Generals. Gen. GRANT has always placed the very highest estimate on his talent, and after the Vicksburgh campaign addressed him a letter, in which he stated that after SHERMAN, no man in his army had rendered him such service, and done so much for the success of the campaign as he.

Gen. McPherson's Death—A Battle on Friday —Fighting Still Going On.

LOUISVILLE, Sunday, July 23.

Major NORCROSS, local Paymaster at Chattanooga, telegraphs Major ALLEN, Chief Paymaster here, that Major-Gen. MCPHERSON was killed yesterday before Atlanta. Another correspondent says he was shot fatally through the lungs.

BALTIMORE, Sunday, uly 23.

A private dispatch received by a relative of Gen. MCPHERSON in this city last night, dated near Atlanta, July 23, announces that that gallant officer was killed in battle the day previous, and that his remains would be sent home in charge of members of his staff.

WASHINGTON, Sunday, July 24.

The latest official dispatches from Gen. SHERMAN represent repeated fighting, and give the circumstances attending the death of Gen. MCPHERSON, who fell in battle in the severe contest of Friday.

Gen. Hooker's Corps—Movements of the Army up to July 18—Kenesaw Mountain— Marietta—Chattahoochee River.

CHATTAHOOCHEE RIVER, Ga., Monday, July 18, 1864.

The first act of the grand drama which SHERMAN has been performing this Summer has been played. The Chattahoochee has been reached by the Army of the West. The curtain rests upon the stage, while the actors pause to take breath and arrange their costumes for the inauguration of Act II.— the struggle for Atlanta—which the distant booming of cannon announces is about to begin. That it will be prolific of battle scenes and bloody encounters none can doubt who reflect upon the importance of the position to be wrested from the foe.

Thus far Gen. SHERMAN's campaign has been mainly marked by irregular conflicts, prolonged skirmishing, by arduous marches, flanking operations, and the advance and attack of certain corps to conceal and protect the movements of others. Although the army has frequently been in line of battle and sometimes engaged for a week at a time in heavy skirmishing, if we except "Resaca" of the 14th and 15th of June, no general engagement has been fought between the opposing armies. But our columns have arrived at last at the river behind which the enemy has all along boasted that his main defence would be made. We are now so close to the city of Atlanta that the decisive conflict cannot be delayed much longer If the army moves at all beyond the river, the north bank of which is now its line, it will be a movement characterized by very heavy fighting.

In a previous letter the prediction was ventured that the most obstinate resistance to be encountered by our army, prior to crossing the Chattahoochee, would be in the vicinity of Kenesaw Mountain. Since that was written the position indicated has been occupied and maintained by JOHNSTON for two weeks against the most determined efforts of our combined armies. It was not without a severe struggle that he was driven from Pine Knob, where, on the 14th, 15th, and 16th ults., Gen. HOOKER, with his invincible corps, fought with great bravery. Gen. GEARY's division was chiefly engaged, losing 519 men in killed and wounded. The attack was continued until the desired position was attained, and the enemy retreated. On the 17th other divisions came to the active assistance of the heroic division which Gen. GEARY had handled with so much ability. The enemy was forced back through successive lines of works until the 20th, when Kenesaw and its adjacent ridges presented their stern front, bristling with guns and bayonets, to prevent the further progress of the hitherto triumphant army.

Kenesaw Mountain is a huge, isolated, double hill, rising boldly out of a country of almost uninterrupted forest-covered ridges—themselves of no mean elevation. In these ridges consist the peculiar adaptation of the country for defensive purposes. Aided by military science, they have been made by rebel engineering absolutely impregnable to direct assault. All the works I have seen partake of the same character. They consist of long lines of rifle-pits, elaborately constructed with good revetments of logs or fascines, and are well drained. These lines following the crests of the ridges, are occasionally broken by forts constructed on the most commanding elevations. The flanks are always well protected by strong forts. The woods in front of an intrenchment are generally cut down, so as to form an impenetrable abattis.

Major-General James B. McPherson, one of Sherman's ablest commanders, was killed in the Battle of Atlanta.

When their lines cross open fields, they are fully guarded by rows of sharpened stakes, driven firmly in the ground, at an angle calculated to impale a horse or man running upon them, and too closely set to permit of passage between. The villainous *chevaux de frise*, is also freely used, particularly on roads where our cavalry are expected to charge. This precaution is altogether unnecessary, as it is a well-known fact that we have no cavalry to hurl on rebel works. All we are required to defend the flanks and rear. Even in the construction of advanced works for skirmishers, the enemy seem to have bestowed time and care. Their forts and lines of intrenchments partake more of the aspect of permanent fortifications than field works for temporary use. The enemy has been driven from them by the flanking process which has been adopted by Gen. SHERMAN with so much success as to earn for him the suggestive appellation of "The Great Flanker."

I will not attempt to record a detailed account of the many assaults and conflicts that occurred between the two armies in the protracted struggle in front of Kenesaw. Suffice it to say that for two weeks Gen. SHERMAN vainly attempted this hill by direct assault. On the 27th of June a general attack was ordered, and in pursuance thereof the Fourteenth and Fourth Corps engaged the enemy's lines near the base of the mountain with great spirit, but could not drive them beyond their breastworks. During the battle, a furious cannonade was kept up on the mountain, enveloping its top and sides in the smoke of exploding shells. The other corps were in readiness to charge the moment the effort should show signs of success. But the attack was not a success, and soon developed the strong position of the foe, proving it to be folly to throw away lives in attempting to dislodge him by assault.

Gen. SHERMAN then turned his attention to other means, and applied to them his never-failing receipt for obstinacy—a flank movement. Supplies were replenished at Big Shanty, the new depot. Preparation was made to pass the entire army to the enemy's rear. As the movement contemplated would, if JOHNSON's lines did not fall back, necessarily leave the railroad at his mercy, the depot was ordered back to Alatoona Bridge. A strong column, SCHOFIELD's I believe, was sent westward on JOHNSTON's left, and on the 2d of July other corps followed. During the night of July 2d the enemy was ascertained to be again in retreat, after having obstinately held out against our assaults for two weeks. We pressed rapidly after them, passing through a series of works more formidable than any before captured. We again overtook them at night on the 3d of July, about two miles south of Marietta.

Marietta deserves more than a passing notice. Prior to the war it was noted throughout the South as one of the centres of Georgian wealth and refinement. Compared with a Northern town its proportions would be diminutive indeed; but in Georgia, with a population of two thousand, it ranked as the sixth town in size in the State. The period of its settlement dates anterior to that of Atlanta, which owes its superiority in size to the fact of its being a centre for several railroads. Marietta, with no commercial aspirations and no manufacturing interest, had, confessedly, a higher social grade than Atlanta, with all its teeming population, workshops and warehouses. It boasted a college of considerable importance—not widely known, but well patronized by those of the South, who preferred educating their sons in their own States to sending them to "Yankee" institutions to be "contaminated" by the enemies of "Southern principles." These watchful guardians of the morality of Southern striplings forgot that their own colleges were almost without exception officered by men of Northern birth and education.

As one might expect, the glory of Marietta College has departed. The buildings are standing gloomily enough upon the hill, from whence they overlook the town and beautiful gardens; but the pupils and teachers are gone; the former to the wars to destroy the Union of their fathers—the latter to their Northern homes to escape the persecution of their former pupils. This picture will answer for all Southern colleges. The war has closed their churches and their schools, with here and there a solitary exception.

Marietta presents a sad spectacle of war's devastating influences. Its fine mansions and lovely gardens, with their shaded walks and arbored seats, still remain, but not as they once were—the abode of a happy people, innocent of war. All these have left, and throngs of soldiers are now roaming over the half-destroyed gardens or strolling through the mutilated mansions, thrumming on the ruined pianos and lolling on the sofas abandoned by their wealthy proprietors. A few matrons—widowed relics of the war—and their half-scared daughters, still remain in the town. These, with a few old men, striplings and decayed servants, are all that are left of the denizens of the place. At one end of the town a half enclosed burial ground, with hundreds of newly made soldiers' graves, side by side, with marble monuments and mausoleums of the past, reveal the fact that Marietta's *dead* are more numerous than Marietta's *living*.

To resume our narrative from which we have digressed. On the 5th of July JOHNSTON moved still further southward, taking position on the railroad about two miles north of the Chattahoochee River. From the tops of the trees on the high hills occupied by the Twentieth Corps, we beheld Atlanta's glistening spires and housetops, seemingly about seven miles south of the river. On the 7th inst. the foe again retrogadred and assumed a new position, whose contracted limits were speedily ascertained to be in front of the railroad bridge, the flanks resting on the river on either side of the crossing. It was pretty evident that JOHNSTON was crossing his forces on the pontoons which we knew had been laid in that vicinity. The rebel front was as bold as ever, and no impression was made on their lines. By the morning of the 9th, the last skirmisher had disappeared from our front, and the railroad bridge was discovered to be in flames. We advanced through another series of fortifications to the river-bank, along which our line now rests. The enemy holds the opposite bank, and it is not an uncommon sight to see the soldiers of both armies meet in swimming parties and exchange tobacco and coffee, apparently as good friends as though a shot had never passed between them.

As it was currently reported that JOHNSTON commenced to cross the Chattahoochee on the 4th of July, it can be but a matter of surprise to many who view critically the movements of our armies, that he was not attacked at the time when he would have labored under the misfortune of having a river in his rear in very dangerous proximity. This has been a matter of much comment among officers and men, who will canvass such matters whenever opportunity occurs. A battle was pretty generally expected on the 4th, when it was stated that Gen. SHERMAN, in view of the golden opportunity thus presented by the situation of affairs, had ordered a general onslaught to be made by the whole army with a view to drive JOHNSTON in confusion to his crossings. Whether this attack was actually ordered, as the order countermanded, or for some cause rendered inoperative, is a matter for speculation. But one thing all unite in believing—that is—had a fight occurred on the "glorious Fourth" there would have been but two alternatives accepted by our army—"Victory or death." It would have fought as it never fought before, so eager and expectant for the fray were commanders and soldiers. There are many who regret the postponement of the battle, which they believe would have been decisive of the result of the campaign. They would have attacked at all hazards of life, though the enemy were never so firm and to all appearances secure in their fortifications. Whether these regrets are just or unjust time will develop. No inconsiderable number believe that JOHNSTON was allowed to cross the Chattahoochee in comparative security to insure important results from combined movements, of which we do not at present know, but in which other armies are supposed to be interested. All unite in indorsing the wisdom and generalship of SHERMAN, and willingly abide by any decision he may make, believing his conduct of the campaign to have been masterly, and productive of the most brilliant results.

Although the Chattahoochee River forms the main dividing line between the opposing armies, we have no inconsiderable force on the other side. Firing is occasionally heard from their direction. Supplies are being accumulated at Marietta, from which place they are distributed to the trains of the various corps. No effort is being made to rebuild the railroad bridge, for the reason that a strong fort on the rebel side of the river effectually commands the approaches to the old piers. A general movement to the south side of the river is daily expected. The army is resting and nerving for the severe struggle which will then, in all probability, begin.

Our expectations will be very agreeably disappointed, it the ten miles intervening between our present camp and Atlanta are not more difficult of accomplishment than the one hundred over which Gen. SHERMAN has so successfully led us since we left Chattanooga. J. G.

Preparing to Cross the Chattahoochee—Skirmishing—The Loss Between Marietta and the Chattahoochee—Interchange of Greetings—The Health of the Army.

HEADQUARTERS FOURTEENTH ARMY CORPS,
CHATTAHOOCHEE RIVER, Sunday, July 17, 1864.

As I write—it is a beautiful morning, by the way, made deliciously so by a ten minutes' shower—the entire army is upon the banks of the Chattahoochee River, a turbid, renegade-looking stream, which slices the country eight miles north of Atlanta.

We are on the *qui vive* this morning, as orders were issued last evening to HOOKER and PALMER to have their respective corps in readiness to move across the river at 9 o'clock. It is just 9, and JEFF. C. DAVIS' fine division is passing headquarters. An orderly from department headquarters, however, arrives, and immediately the three Division Commanders of this corps are ordered to halt until further advices. I learn that the particular reason for this "break" is that during the night the rebel forts destroyed the pontoon bridge. This was kind on their part, considing there were no soldiers or property of any description upon it. We shall probably get it ready for crossing before noon.

For the first time during the campaign the army has had a little rest. The last skirmish, in which infantry participated, occurred a few miles this side of Marietta, in which the brigade of regulars, under command of Gen. KING, particularly distinguished itself.

Nearly the whole brigade was acting as a grand skirmish line for the First Division. At an extraordinary juncture in the situation Capt. STETSON, of the Fifteenth Infantry, at the head of his company, dashed across an opening in the face of the enemy's infantry and artillery and took up a position in a clump of second growth and opened a handsome fire upon the enemy's cannoniers, compelling the rebel battery, after a couple of shots, to evacuate the premises. The whole brigade witnessed this exhibition of valor upon the part of Capt. STETSON and his men, and felt great concern in regard to the company's safety. As the line advanced the gallant Captain resumed his place in the battalion, with the loss of but one man wounded. It was a decidedly rash performance, but resulting as it did, reflected great credit upon the intrepid Captain and his troop.

During the advance of the army from Marietta to this point, as has, in fact, been the case since the opening of the campaign, the brigade of regulars has been in the advance, and has suffered to a great extent, one company in the Fifteenth losing as high as forty men in killed and wounded. Let me add, too, that during the seventy-five days' campaign this brigade has lost but one man as a prisoner, who was wounded upon the skirmish line at the base of Kenesaw, and subsequently captured. In the last skirmish Gen. KING in Gen. JOHNSTON's absence commanded the First Division, and Col. STOUGHTON, of the Eleventh Michigan, commanded the regular brigade.

During the last day of the skirmishing at the mouth of the river, Col. STOUGHTON carried the brigade into the hottest of the contest, succeeding many times in driving the whole of WALKER's division. It was while realizing the glory of the day that a shell severed the left leg from his body, and he was borne from the field. I cannot take my leave of the regulars without speaking a kind word in behalf of the gallant officers in it, all of whom are entitled to praise. I do not know young STETSON, but especially make mention of him, from the fact that his brother officers, in conversation, dwell at length upon his conduct upon the occasion which I have detailed above. Capt. MULLIGAN, of the Nineteenth, an officer of sterling ability, is still upon Gen. KING's Staff, and has acquitted himself admirably during the grand campaign between Chattanooga and the Chattahoochee.

Gen. JOHNSTON, who had his left side battered in by an ungenerous cannon ball near Kingston, and who was permitted to go home to recoperate, arrived yesterday and resumed command of his division, which is one of the finest in the army. It and JEFF. C. DAVIS' division did the main part of the fighting between Marietta and this place. The latter division takes the advance in the crossing of the river, and will, no doubt, have as much as it can possibly attend to. This division suffered frightfully at Kenesaw, and has experienced an awful thinning out during the last seventy days. Its Commander (JEFF. C. DAVIS) is universally admired, and enjoys the reputation of being one of the finest officers and one of the most accomplished gentlemen in the army. I do not believe there is an officer living who can move a division to better advantage than JEFF C. DAVIS. He fights his men, too, superbly, and performs his duties, whether in line of battle, or otherwise, with the coolness, skill, and unostentation characteristic of the true soldier.

During the entire skirmishing between Marietta and this point, we lost less than six hundred men in killed and wounded, and no prisoners. All along the route we picked up the enemy's stragglers and deserters, amounting, in the aggregate, since the occupation of Marietta, to between six and seven hundred.

So soon as the enemy had been thoroughly cleared out upon this side of the river, the respective corps of Gens. SCHOFIELD, BLAIR, LOGAN, DODGE, and HOWARD moved up the river on the left, to the distance of eight miles, and crossed, leaving Gens HOOKER and PALMER upon this side of the river, with the railroad in the centre. It is immediately in our front that the bulk of the enemy are disposed, within formed big earthworks on all sides. For the past three nights, our forces on this side of the river have been actively engaged in throwing up fortifications; and as I write, a fierce cannonading is being kept up by both parties.

The pickets of the contending parties are in force upon each side of the river, and do not fire upon each other. There is a continual conversation kept up, and temporarily the most friendly feeling exists. Each side allows no officers or groups of men to show themselves without being made a target. This is mutually understood, but I believe there is no official agreement for such proceedings. One of the happiest things that has occurred was told to me yesterday:

REBEL PICKET.—You can't come any further, boys. We've been reinforced. You'll never cross this river in the world.

FEDERAL PICKET.—O, I guess we'll come when we get ready.

REBEL.—No, Sir; we've been reinforced by LOGAN, and SCHOFIELD, and—

FEDERAL.—We'll send you over HOOKER in a few days.

I have heard several stories related in regard to the performances of the men, but they are of the same tenor, many times published. The above, however, was so good that I thought I would give it a hearing.

As a general thing, the parties upon each side banter each other, and call each other all kinds of names. According to the rebels' statements, they are particularly short of whisky, and, although they are continually begging newspapers, they never have any to give out. They say that there is but one paper published at Atlanta just now—the traveling Memphis *Appeal*.

CHICKAMAUGA.

The New-York Times.

VOL. XIII.–NO. 4005.   NEW-YORK, TUESDAY, JULY 26, 1864.   PRICE FOUR CENTS.

ATLANTA.

The Great Battle of Friday.

Official Statements from General Sherman.

Terrific Slaughter of the Rebels.

The Union Battle Cry, "Remember McPherson."

Sherman Shelling Atlanta, and the City on Fire.

The Rebel Loss Fully Seven Thousand.

General Sherman's Loss Less than Two Thousand.

WASHINGTON, Monday, July 25.

The *Republican*, extra, says:

Dispatches to the Government represent that a great battle was fought in Atlanta on Friday, resulting in a horrible slaughter and a complete repulse of the enemy at every point.

The rebels, holding the largest part of the city, assaulted our works on that day with great fury, evidently expecting to drive our forces out of the city. The Fifteenth Corps, commanded by Gen. FRANK BLAIR, seemed to be the special object of rebel wrath, as they massed against it in overwhelming force. The Fifteenth received the shock gallantly, and held its own until Gen. DODGE, with the Sixteenth Corps, came up, when the rebels were hurled back with great slaughter.

Gen. Logan, at the head of the Seventeenth Corps, went into battle with the rallying cry of "Remember McPHERSON."

This corps, as well as BLAIR's Fifteenth Corps, both constituting the army under Maj.-Gen. McPHERSON, fought desperately—the news of the death of their brave Commander having been communicated to them just before going into battle.

Gen. McPHERSON was shot while reconnoitering. He became separated from his staff for a moment, and a rebel sharpshooter shot him from an ambush.

The terrible struggle ended by repulsing the enemy at every point of the line.

It was arranged that on Saturday the dead of both armies should be buried and the wounded removed under a flag of truce.

Our troops buried one thousand rebels left on the field within our lines; besides which the rebels buried many of their own dead themselves near their works. Upon this basis, it is estimated that the rebel killed and wounded, on Friday, will exceed six thousand, the proportion of killed to wounded in battle being about one to seven.

Our loss will reach about 2,500 in killed and wounded. The Fifteenth Corps suffered severely, the enemy's troops having been massed against it. It was this act of the enemy in part that cost him such heavy loss.

While the work of burying the dead and removing the wounded was going on on Saturday, SHERMAN's heavy artillery was playing upon the city. At the same time large fires were observed in different parts of Atlanta, supposed to be caused by the destruction of supply depots and other rebel property, which the enemy could not carry off, and did not wish to fall into our hands. This is considered as evidence of their intending to evacuate the place.

Several rebel Generals are reported to be killed, but their names are not yet given.

FURTHER DETAILS.
WASHINGTON, Monday, July 25.

The enemy's cavalry at the outset turned our left flank, and the line at that point was driven back. One division retreated in some disorder. The troops were rallied there, however, and the rest of the line repelled the enemy. The enemy suffered seriously, but did not leave so many prisoners and wounded on our hands as on Thursday.

Before the attack was made, Gen. McPHERSON was killed by a sharpshooter, while reconnoitering alone in front of his lines, and some distance in advance even of his personal staff. Gen JOHN A. LOGAN succeeded to the command, and exercised it during the day.

Yesterday there was no general engagement, but Gen. THOMAS, who has established himself on the north and northeast, and within a mile and a half of Atlanta, bombarded that city continuously. No news of its positive capture has yet been received. Gen. HOOD's whole army is posted in and about the place.

LATER.
WASHINGTON, July 25, 1864.

A dispatch to-day from General SHERMAN states

Rebel fortifications defending Atlanta.

his loss in the battle of Friday at less than 2,000, while that of the enemy cannot be less than 7,000, owing to the advantage he took of their effort to turn his left column. There is no official information to show that our forces have entered Atlanta.

Special Dispatch to the N. Y. Times.
WASHINGTON, Monday, July 25.
THE BATTLES BEFORE ATLANTA.

Both engagements delivered before Atlanta, namely, that of Wednesday and that of Friday last, have been assaults on the part of the rebels. This is accounted for from the fact that Gen. HOOD, JOHNSTON's successor, has been throughout the campaign one of the most bitter opponents of JOHNSTON's retreating policy; and he felt impelled, the moment he was placed in command, to pitch in. It does not appear that he has gained any other result than to bring upon himself, in each instance, a loss thrice as heavy as that inflicted on the assailed party.

GEN. SHERMAN CONFIDENT OF SUCCESS.

Gen. SHERMAN's latest dispatches show an assured confidence in the capture of Atlanta, though the prize may not be won as speedily as the public had anticipated.

THE DEATH OF GEN. M'PHERSON.

Gen. SHERMAN's dispatches also express the most profound grief at the death of McPHERSON. That gallant soldier was killed about eleven in the forenoon, while riding in advance of his Staff to form a defensive line to meet the rebel attack. The severe fighting was done after McPHERSON's death, the engagement continuing until five in the afternoon.

THE LOSSES ON BOTH SIDES.

Gen. SHERMAN estimates the rebel loss at 7,000; our own at 2,000.

Destruction of Railroads—The Siege Progressing.

NASHVILLE, Monday, July 25.

Gen. GARRARD's expedition has been successful, destroying the bridges at Covington, forty miles east of Atlanta. The public stores at Covington and Conyear were also destroyed, with 2,000 bales of cotton, a locomotive and train of cars. Two hundred prisoners and a number of horses were captured.

Our loss in the recent battle will foot up something less than 2,000.

We have found over 1,000 dead rebels, which, with the usual proportion of wounded, will make their loss over 7,000.

Our army is in good condition, and the situation is favorable.

Official news is in from in front of Atlanta. It is meagre, but no reverses are reported. Gen. SHERMAN still maintains his position, and is vigorously advancing.

Gen. ROUSSEAU has successfully fulfilled his orders, and reports a loss of only 12 of his command.

Gen. McPherson's Remains.

NASHVILLE, Monday, July 25.

The remains of Gen. McPHERSON reached here at 9 A. M. to-day, and were escorted through to the Louisville depot by the Thirteenth Regulars. Capt. LAMONT, of the Tenth Tennessee Infantry, Col. SCULLY, of the Regular Artillery, Gens. McELROY and GILLOM, and Gov. JOHNSON and Staff were in the procession, which comprised all the officers of the different departments in the city.

The remains leave by special train, at 12 o'clock at noon, accompanied by a guard of the Thirteenth Regulars, of two officers and fifty men, to Sandusky, Ohio. The streets were thronged with citizens, and all the employes of the departments assembled to honor the remains of Gen. McPHERSON.

CAVALRY OPERATIONS OF GENERAL SHERMAN'S ARMY.

Important Raid on the Montgomery and West Point Railroad, by Gen. Rousseau—Complete Success of the Expedition.

The following has been received from Gen. ROUSSEAU's expedition:

MARIETTA, Ga., July 24, 1864.
To the Assistant Adjutant-General, District of Tennessee:

We arrived here day before yesterday, and have been eminently successful, and have executed the orders of Gen. SHERMAN to the letter. Our loss does not exceed twelve in killed and wounded. I start to-day for Nashville.

On the 22d Gen. SHERMAN announced, in a circular to his army, that Gen. ROUSSEAU had been entirely successful.

The important expedition against the Montgomery and West Point Railroad, the success of which is thus officially announced, was projected by Gen. ROUSSEAU, when Gen. SHERMAN was preparing to depart on his great raid through Mississippi, in the early part of this year; but for various military reasons, its execution was postponed until the present month. On the 30th ult., Gen. SHERMAN revived the project, as an important auxiliary to his grand movement upon Atlanta, his object being to cut the railroad between Columbus, Ga., and Montgomery, Ala., so effectually as to destroy permanently the rebel communications between these points. Abundant preparations were made for the destruction of the ties, rails, bridges, culverts, water-tanks, depot buildings, locomotives, arsenals, Government machine-shops, &c. Gen. ROUSSEAU was also ordered to destroy the town of Opelika, the point of junction of the road from Columbus with Atlanta, West Point and Montgomery road.

Gen. ROUSSEAU received his final orders on the 4th inst., and on the 8th, having completed his preparations, left Nashville with his staff. He was accompanied by Capt. J. C. WILLIAMS, Nineteenth United States Infantry, and Capt. ELKIN, Fifth Kentucky Cavalry, Aides-de-Camp; Capt. RUGER, Topographical Engineer; Capt. McCONNEL, Inspector, and several other officers. Capt. RUGER had been engaged for several months in preparing maps of the proposed route, and in gathering important information from Union refugees.

The force placed at the disposal of Gen. ROUSSEAU was limited to about 2,760 men, and consisted of the following regiments, which were concentrated at Decatur, Alabama: Fifth Indiana Cavalry, Col. T. J. HARRISON; Fifth Iowa Cavalry, Lieut.-Col. PATRICK; Second Kentucky Cavalry, Maj. EIFORT; Fourth Tennessee Cavalry and the Ninth Ohio Cavalry. The men composing this force were all veterans, well mounted and excellently armed. A thousand SPENCER repeating rifles, firing eight times and invaluable as a cavalry arm, were judiciously distributed among the men. Two light Rodman guns were also taken along.

Gen. ROUSSEAU moved from Decatur with his forces on the 10th inst., taking a southeasterly direction. The details of the expedition have not yet been received, but by referring to a good map of Alabama and Georgia it will be seen that the first important point on the route is Blountsville, about fifty miles from Decatur; the second Ashville, some thirty miles further on. He probably crossed the Coosa River somewhere in the vicinity of Broken Arrow, pushed on to Talladega, and thence to the Tallapoosa River, which he was to cross at the most convenient bridge or ford. This would bring him within thirty miles of the Montgomery road.

Eight important bridges carry this railroad over as many streams, between Opelika and Montgomery; and the thorough destruction of these was one of the principal objects of the raid. Having accomplished this work, and destroyed the workshops and other Government buildings at Opelika, and the bridges between that town and West Point, Gen. ROUSSEAU was ordered to move up on the west side of the Chattahoochee and join Gen. SHERMAN at some point between Marietta, Ga., and that river. That he has done his work effectually we know not only from Gen. SHERMAN's dispatch, but from the rebel acknowledgment that on the 17th inst. telegraphic communication was suspended between Atlanta and Montgomery, and that the railroad between the former place and West Point was not in working order.

Two frame houses stripped of wood for fortifications stand over Confederate earthworks.

Lieutenant-General John Bell Hood replaced Joe Johnston, and immediately engaged in combat with Sherman's forces. Hood defended Atlanta for nearly six weeks.

The New-York Times.

VOL. XIII.—NO. 4017.   NEW-YORK, TUESDAY, AUGUST 9, 1864.   PRICE FOUR CENTS.

GOOD NEWS.

Farragut's Attack on Mobile.

A GREAT NAVAL BATTLE

THE REBEL REPORT OF IT.

Our Fleet Passed Fort Morgan and Close to Mobile.

Dreadful Havoc Among the Rebel Gunboats.

The Iron-Clad Ram Tennessee Surrendered.

The Selma Captured, the Gaines Beached. the Morgan Trying to Escape.

The Rebel Admiral Buchanan Maimed and Captured.

Only One Union Monitor Reported Lost.

Official Dispatch from Secretary Stanton.

WAR DEPARTMENT, WASHINGTON, Aug. 8—9 P. M.

To Major-Gen. Dix, New-York:

The following announcement of the successful operations against Mobile, appears in the Richmond *Sentinel* of this date, and is transmitted by Major-Gen. BUTLER to the President,

FROM HEADQUARTERS OF GEN. BUTLER, }
MONDAY, Aug. 8—3 P. M. }

To His Excellency, A. Lincoln, President:

The following is the official report, taken from the Richmond *Sentinel* of Aug. 8:

B. F. BUTLER, Major-General.

"MOBILE, Aug. 5, 1864.

Hon. J. A. Seddon, Secretary of War:

Seventeen of the enemy's vessels, (fourteen ships and three iron-clads) passed Fort Morgan this morning. The *Tecumseh*, a monitor, was sunk by Fort Morgan. The *Tennessee* surrendered after a desperate engagement with the enemy's fleet. Admiral BUCHANAN lost

Major-General E. R. S. Canby was in charge of Army operations against Mobile.

a leg, and is a prisoner. The *Selma* was captured. The *Gaines* was beached near the hospital. The *Morgan* is safe and will try to run up to-night. The enemy's fleet has approached the city. A monitor has been engaging Fort Powell all day.

(Signed)   D. H. MAURY, Maj.-Gen."

Special Dispatch to the New-York Times.

WASHINGTON, Monday, Aug. 8.

GEN. BUTLER telegraphs that Richmond papers of Saturday, 6th inst., announce that our forces had taken possession of Dauphin's Island, at the extremity of which stands Fort Gaines, commanding one of the flanks of the entrance to Mobile Bay,

Should FARRAGUT not be willing to risk running the gauntlet of Forts Gaines and Morgan, and the obstructions, the landing on Dauphin's Island will afford a secure *point d'appui* for siege operations against both forts. The analogy between the positions thus gained and that of Gen. GILLMORE on Morris Island will be recognized. Up to the latest advices no naval attack had been made by Admiral FARRAGUT, nor had he attempted to force an entrance with his iron-clad fleet, but the grand *coup* was expected to come off on the 3d inst.

The Attacking Fleet.

We give below a list of the vessels understood to have been the fleet with which Admiral FARRAGUT attacked Mobile. These vessels are provided with the heaviest ordnance.

FLAGSHIP—Hartford, screw sloop, 20 guns.

Iron-clads.

Winnebago.........2 turret monitor..............	4 guns
Chickasaw.........2 turret monitor..............	4 guns
Tecumseh.........1 turret monitor..............	2 guns
Manhattan.........1 turret monitor..............	2 guns
Four Mississippi River iron-clads..............	10 guns

SCREW SLOOPS.

Richmond, 1st class......18	Oneida, 2d class...........10
Brooklyn, 1st class......24	Ossipee, 2d class...........13
Monongahela, 2d class...12	Galena, 2d class...........14
Lackawanna, 2d class....14	Genessee, 2d class......... 8

DOUBLE-ENDERS.

Metacomet..........Side-wheel...........10
Sebago..........Side-wheel...........10
Port Royal..........Side-wheel........... 8
Conemaugh..........Side-wheel........... 9

SCREW GUNBOATS.

Kennebec.............. 5	Pembina.............. 4
Itasca.............. 4	Penguin.............. 7
	Tennessee.............. 5

Besides these, there are five tugs, carrying two guns each.

Captain Percival Drayton

GENERAL SHERMAN'S ARMY.

Military Railroads—Farewell of Gen. Jo. Hooker—The Action of the 28th—Our Prospects for Atlanta.

Special Correspondence of the New-York Times.

CHATTANOOGA, Monday, Aug. 1, 1864.

Business of an important nature calling me from the front to this city, alone accounts for the date and place of this letter. I arrived here on Saturday, 30th ult., after a very tiresome ride on one of those modes of conveyance known as a military railroad—a mode of transportation excessively exhausting to feeble constitutions, and a horrible ordeal to men of a small amount of patience. It is the best, however, that Uncle Sam has for his children in this part of his territory; and, like an obedient son of a munificently-disposed parent, we will neither chide him nor find fault with his accommodations.

Thursday morning, the 28th ult., will not be soon forgotten by the Twentieth Army Corps. It was made memorable by the parting salutations of Major-Gen. HOOKER with the officers and men of the corps. The promotion of Major-Gen. HOWARD to the command of the Army of the Tennessee, seems to have been the cause of this change in the relations between Gen. HOOKER and the Western army. It was the ostensible, and, we presume, the substantial cause of Gen. HOOKER's asking to be relieved of his command. His request having been granted, on the morning of the 28th ult. he met the officers of the corps to bid them adieu. He said it had never been his lot to command as good an army as the one he had commanded in the West; and he never expected to command a better. He regretted very much the necessity of his parting with them, and assured them that if it was ever in his power to do anything for them, he would gladly do it. He highly commended the officers of the corps for the urbanity that had uniformly characterized their intercourse with him, and the unfeigned cheerfulness with which they had executed his commands; assuring them that he had never been so attached to any body of men as he was to them. He briefly reviewed the campaign, and the part his own command had taken in it. He said the number of casualties in any army is the measure of service it has rendered; and, during this campaign, they knew, as also did he, that his own command had not failed to render its full measure of service, for one-half of all the casualties in the campaign were in the Twentieth Corps. We have had hard service, and been in many tight places; but in what difficult place have we been put out of which we have not come all right?

These remarks, with many incidental interchanges of sentiment that occurred during the interview, unwound nature's sympathies, and tears were drawn from many eyes. Men in that assembly who could meet the enemy with an unblanching countenance, and a heart that never yields to fear in the presence of the forman, gave up their self-control, or rather had it taken from them in the mutual interchange of feeling that characterized the hour. It was a solemn parting, and one in which the silence was vocal and the nonutterance more pregnant with the meaning of the heart than what was said. Gen. HOOKER was a host in himself. His presence everywhere had something akin to magnetic power over the masses he commanded, and infused the breasts of his men with the same indomitable determination that stood out so boldly as a feature in his own military character. Whenever he passed along the lines he was hailed with the united applause of his whole command, while the men of other commands did not withhold from him kindred honors. He has gone from us, and the blessings of the entire corps are resting on his head, while every heart wishes him long life, a prosperous career and new glory in untried fields.

When I left the front, on Thursday evening, the 28th ult., things were assuming an important aspect. The Army of the Tennessee, under Maj.-Gen. HOWARD, had passed round from our extreme left to our extreme right, on the afternoon of Wednesday, the 27th ult., with the undoubted purpose of making important movements on the enemy's left, and, if possible, intercept his communications on the Macon and Western Railroad. On the day following, namely, 28th ult., these movements were made. The enemy detected the design at an early period of its development, concentrated his force, and made a rapid descent on our lines before, as he supposed, they were in a defensible posture. In this, however, he was egregiously deceived, for the General had been careful before advancing so to make his disposition as that, in the event of the enemy attacking him in the precise manner in which he did, the result should not be doubtful. The end of the engagement showed the wisdom of his plans. It was another victory for the Union arms. The battle lasted from 2½ to 6 o'clock P. M., and the enemy were repulsed, and four stands of colors were taken. There was a demonstration made all along the front. At 4 P. M. the whole front warmed into a perfect fusilade of artillery and musketry, and the whole line was in a sheet of flame and enveloped in smoke. No casualties of consequence occurred along our front, and but few elsewhere, except in the fight with the Army of the Tennessee. How great their loss was I have been unable to learn.

A pile of loose ammunition for BUNDY's battery, Thirteenth New-York Light Artillery, was shot into by a rebel shell, and exploded without personal injury to any one. The battle waned before night came on, and everything became quiet. Nothing but an occasional discharge of a big gun, and now and then a musket discharged, reminded us of the proximate presence of the foe. Hostilities had not been renewed when I left the Quartermaster's Department at the front, on Friday morning, the 29th ult.

Things are moving on steadily, and in the right direction here. The time cannot be distant when the city before which we have now set down will be numbered among the Union towns. A vigorous strike, a united and simultaneous advance of our whole army, while it would place many of our braves *hors du combat*, would result in our occupation of Atlanta, and that, too, in quick order. It has not, however, been the policy of the Commanding-General wantonly to expose his men, or for the sake of achieving for himself the reputation of a dashing and brilliant General to lay his troops on the altar of personal ambition and sacrifice them by thousands to gratify his aspiration. He has studiously sought out the most effectual way of routing the enemy from his stronghold with as little cost in human blood as possible, and how well he has succeeded in accomplishing his purpose, the history of the campaign is a proof.

Very many large fires have been seen in Atlanta since our advent to our present position, caused, it is presumed, by our shells, which are being constantly thrown into it. A citizen from the town who came into our lines to-day, told us that on the night of the 27th ult., one of its prettiest streets was burned. Many large fires, indicating buildings of large proportions, are frequently occurring, and during the night have illuminated the heavens from the horizon

Confederate cavalry led by Lieutenant-General Joseph Wheeler skirmished with Sherman's army in Georgia.

to the zenith in their immediate locality, and cast their reflection over our entire camp round about. The right and left wings of our vast army are now within three miles of making the circle complete around the fated city. Thus if the rebels attempt to escape, they are brought under our artillery from both flanks. A little while longer, and the great object of this campaign will be attained, and the nation's heart be gladhened. EPSILON.

Reported Capture of Gen. Stoneman Confirmed.

WASHINGTON, Monday, Aug. 8.

Information from Gen. SHERMAN's army leaves no doubt of the capture of Gen. STONEMAN with a portion of the forces under his command.

OPERATIONS IN VIRGINIA.

General Averill Overtakes the Enemy.

Reported Attack, and Capture of Rebel Artillery and 500 Prisoners.

Gen. Sheridan in Command on the Upper Potomac.

Official Dispatch from Secretary Stanton.

WASHINGTON, Monday, Aug. 8.

To Gen. John A. Dix, New-York:

Maj.-Gen. SHERIDAN has been assigned temporarily to the command of the forces in the Middle Military Division, consisting of the Department of Washington, the Middle Department and the Department of the Susquehanna and Southwest Virginia. He transmits the following intelligence:

"HEADQUARTERS MIDDLE MILITARY DEPARTMENT, HARPER's FERRY, Va., Monday, Aug. 8—8:40 P. M.

"*Maj.-Gen. Halleck, Chief-of-Staff:*

"Brig.-Gen. KELLY reports that a scout has just arrived at New Creek, and reports that Gen. AVERILL overtook the enemy near Morefield yesterday, and attacked him, capturing all of his artillery and five hundred prisoners. Nothing official has been received from Gen. AVERILL, however.

(Signed) "P. H. SHERIDAN, Maj.-Gen. Com."

EDWIN M. STANTON, Secretary of War.

PHILADELPHIA, Monday, Aug. 8.

The *Bulletin* of this city has the following special dispatch:

HARRISBURGH, Monday, Aug. 8.

Col. WM. H. BOYD, of the Twenty-first Pennsylvania Cavalry, took possession of Hagerstown yesterday.

The scene of the drama has been transferred from our border to that of rebeldom.

Later intelligence received this morning informs us that the rebels have retreated homeward.

They have again eluded the preparations made for their capture.

It is thought that under the new Commander the rebel inroads into our State will cease.

The members of the Legislature are beginning to make their appearance.

All Quiet on the Potomac.

HARRISBURGH, Penn., Monday, Aug. 8.

A dispatch received at headquarters here, at 9 o'clock this morning, from the military operator at Hagerstown, says:

All is quiet on the Potomac.

FROM PETERSBURGH.

THE BATTLE OF FRIDAY.

Desperate Charge of the Enemy—They Are Repulsed with Slaughter.

FORTRESS MONROE, Sunday, Aug. 7.

A terrific fight took place in front of Petersburgh on Friday afternoon, lasting from 5:30 to 7:30. It commenced by a charge from the enemy, which was repulsed with slaughter. They also exploded a mine, which done no damage to our troops or works, but killed some of the rebels. The fighting on our side was principally by the Ninth Corps, and was most desperate.

The Explosion of the Rebel Mine, &c.

WASHINGTON, Monday, Aug. 8.

A letter from the Army of the Potomac, dated Saturday evening, says:

"It is not generally believed that the purpose of the enemy on Friday was to blow up a fort in front of the Fifth Corps; but their intention was to damage a mine which they suspected was being dug in front of the Eighteenth Corps. Certain it is, there was an explosion, whatever may have been the object of it. Our men were considerably startled, and every one rushed to his post, when a rapid fire commenced from our line in the direction the enemy were supposed to be advancing. As soon as the smoke cleared away, the true state of affairs was discovered, and firing ceased.

A stray ball struck Col. STEADMAN, commanding Second Brigade, Second Division, Eighteenth Corps, inflicting a wound which soon after resulted in death. He was a gallant officer, and his services were highly appreciated."

A party of fifty deserters started to come into our lines yesterday morning at an early hour, when our gunners, not knowing their intention, opened fire upon them, killing and wounding about twenty. Nine of them arrived at headquarters on Saturday forenoon, some of them wounded. They represent the Confederacy as being in a bad way on account of the state of affairs at Atlanta, and tell how their army was frightened on the previous Saturday when the mine was sprung, all leaving their guns and running back some distance, fearing other explosions were going to occur along the line. But they soon regained confidence, and fell back into their former position in time to meet the attack, which, they say, was more than an hour and a half after the explosion.

These men say the reason why the soldiers do not exchange newspapers is, they are ordered not to do so. But this would be of no effect, if they could afford to buy them, the price being 40 cents apiece, and they have not been paid off for a long time.

Very little firing took place on Saturday.

The New-York Times.

VOL. XIII.—NO. 4022.　　　　NEW-YORK, MONDAY, AUGUST 15, 1864.　　　　PRICE FOUR CENTS.

MOBILE.

FARRAGUT'S VICTORY

Full Particulars From Eye-Witnesses.

PASSING THE FORTS.

The Capture of the Confederate Gunboats.

THE SURRENDER OF FORT GAINES.

FARRAGUT ON THE MAIN-TOP.

An Old Sea-Dog Directing the Fight.

Our New-Orleans files received yesterday by the steamship *Creole* contain ample and most interesting particulars of the victory of the gallant FARRAGUT and his fleet in Mobile Bay. The accounts of eye-witnesses, as they appear in the New-Orleans *Times*, *Era* and *Picayune*, are given with admirable clearness.

Farragut's Victories at Mobile.

NEW-ORLEANS, Sunday, Aug. 7.

Intelligence was received at headquarters yesterday, announcing that the fleet under Admiral FARRAGUT passed the forts at the entrance of Mobile Bay at 8 A. M., on the 5th inst.

The monitor *Tecumseh* was blown up by a rebel torpedo.

No other vessels were lost.

The rebel ram *Tennessee* surrendered after an obstinate resistance.

The rebel Admiral BUCHANAN lost a leg in the action, and is now a prisoner.

The land force under Maj.-Gen. GORDON GRANGER invested Fort Gaines, and with light batteries opened simultaneously with the passage of the forts by the fleet, taking the water batteries in reverse, and silencing them.

Our losses are not reported.

LATER.

Later advices from Admiral FARRAGUT's fleet may be summed up as follow:

Fort Gaines has surrendered.

Fort Powell was blown up by the rebels. [This was at Grant's Pass, at the opposite end of Dauphin Island from where the fight occurred.]

Four monitors went in first, followed by the steam war-vessels *Brooklyn, Hartford, Metacomet,* and others. The principal fighting was with the ram *Tennessee,* inside the bay.

The *Metacomet,* in attempting to ram the Ten-

Major-General Gordon Granger

nessee, struck the *Hartford,* and stove in her side timbers. The *Hartford* will go north for repairs.

The rebel gunboat *Selma* was sunk by the *Metacomet.*

The gunboats *Chickasaw* and *Winnebago* chased two rebel gunboats—the *Gaines* and *Morgan*—into Navy Cove, and they are blockaded there, without a chance of escape.

Only ten persons are known to have survived the destruction of the monitor *Tecumseh* by the torpedo.

The dispatch-boat *Philippi* was burned at sea while the fight was in progress.

Admiral FARRAGUT will push right on for Mobile City.

All the Texas coast, Brownsville included, has been evacuated, with the exception of Brazos Island. A small force is left there under Col. DAY, of the Ninety-third New-York.

Major-Gen. FRANK E. HERRON arrived from there yesterday, and is now at the St. Charles Hotel. His forces are there, and are going into camp above the city.

The rebels here are greatly excited over the Mobile news.

Politics is becoming lively and interesting. The Free State men are organizing for active duty, and the clubs of the last campaign are being revived. There is no doubt about the ratification of the new Constitution by the people. The city is full of people, notwithstanding the large numbers who have left for Northern watering-places.

The Mobile *News* of the 15th ult. boasts of the hanging of two colored soldiers and a cotton

speculator, near Vicksburgh, by WHITTAKER's guerrillas.

A number more of Union prisoners, recently exchanged, have arrived.

The Opening of the Ball.

WEST GULF BLOCKADING SQUADRON,
OFF FORT MORGAN, Aug. 3, 1864.

The fleet for the reduction of Mobile, commanded by Admiral FARRAGUT, and composed of the *Winnebago, Chickasaw, Manhattan* and *Tecumseh* of the monitor fleet, and the *Hartford,* (flagship,) *Brooklyn, Oneida, Itasca, Tennessee,* and *Metacomet,* of the wooden fleet, will commence to-morrow morning to pour their iron hail into the rebel Fort Morgan.

The ball was opened this afternoon by the monitor *Winnebago,* which steamed defiantly up to the fort and threw in a shell or two to give the rebs a taste of our quality. She is a splendid specimen of monitor naval architecture, and is as buoyant as a cork. On her your correspondent is located, and we expect to be first into the fight to-morrow. Her officers are every one of them gentlemen, and have afforded and will afford me every opportunity to witness the fight.

Capt. THOS. STENENS is well known as an officer "chock full of fight"; and he is ably seconded by Vol. Lieut. W. F. Shankland, Paymaster Girard, Chief Engineer Simon Shultes, 1st Assistant Engineer John Purdy, Ensigns Morrisey, Murphy and Whitworth, Acting-Master Megathlin, and Robert Sherman, gunner. To the latter gentleman I am indebted for favors to be remembered hereafter.

Of the fighting qualities of this noble vessel I shall speak more fully at some future time. The guns in her forward turret are worked by steam, and that they are terrible in execution the Rebels will bear me witness.

ON BOARD STEAMSHIP WINNEBAGO,
August 4, 1864.

This morning opened beautifully. Contrary to expectations, the land forces under Gen. GRANGER failing to co-operate, we did not attempt the reduction of the forts to-day. But Capt. STEVENS, determined not to be baulked of his share of the fight, steamed up in front of Fort Gaines, and at 11:30 o'clock this morning threw his first shell at the transport *Natchez,* which was unloading troops and ammunition at the landing in front of the fort. You should have seen her leave! In less than a minute after the shell burst in her neighborhood, the smoke of burning bacon and resin was plainly visible. We gave and received about a dozen shots, but nobody was hurt on our side.

That you may fully understand the position of affairs, let me explain: As we lay, head up the bay, Fort Morgan stands on our right, by and around the light-house, well known to many of your readers. Immediately opposite, and about five miles off, on the northeast end of Dauphin Island, is Fort Gaines. Running across from Morgan to Gaines is driven a tier of piles, fastened together by a net-work of chains. Opposite each fort a channel is left open, of about fifteen hundred yards in width, for the use of blockade-runners. In the channel, in front of Morgan, *were* placed a lot of buoys, on which the guns of her water battery are trained. I say *were,* for our boys destroyed about half of them last night. Outside of the piles are placed the torpedoes.

Just inside of the obstructions is lying the rebels' pride and hope—the ram *Tennessee*—and three gunboats. Neither of these have dared to show themselves outside while we were firing into their transports, but contented themselves with throwing a shot at us at long range—say about five miles—when they could have no hope of hitting us.

LATER.—Orders have just come aboard for us to go into the fight to-morrow, and from the quantity of fight in the Captain and officers of the *Winnebago,* and of the fleet generally, I can assure you we shall see fun.

Everything now betokens success on our part, and before this reaches you, Mobile, I am convinced, will have fallen.

WEDNESDAY, Aug. 5.

The glory is ours! The victory is with us! I have only time to say that we have passed Fort Morgan, and anchored in the bay.

The rebel ram *Tennessee* is ours, and also one of the gunboats. BUCHANAN, the rebel Commodore, is wounded, and I hear is dying.

The monitor *Tecumseh* was run on a torpedo opposite the obstructions and sunk immediately. All but eighteen of her officers and crew went down with her. Capt. CRAVENS, I believe, was her commander.

The *Chickasaw* is shelling Fort Powell. In the action to-day we have lost about 150 killed and wounded. Yours signally. C.

The bearer of the letter informs us that Fort Powell was blown up, and Fort Gaines taken. We learn from another source that the fleet which passed the forts consisted of fourteen gunboats and four monitors.

Another Account.

The following account is furnished by A. C. STERRETT, who was on board the gunboat *Port Royal* at the time of the fight :

FRIDAY, Aug. 7, 1864.

The fleet, consisting of the *Hartford, Brooklyn, Richmond, Lackawanna, Ossipee, Monongahela, Oneida, Galena, Port Royal, Metacomet, Octorora, Seminole, Itasca,* and the Monitors *Tecumseh, Manhattan, Chickasaw* and *Winnebago,* and the Admiral's steam barge *Loyal,* got under way at the anchorage off the entrance to Mobile Bay, at sunrise, the monitors in advance and the wooden vessels going together in pairs, the flag-ship taking the lead. When within point blank range of Fort Morgan, the vessels ahead were slowed down to enable the line to close up, and at this time the fort and rebel vessels opened fire on the fleet, which was returned from the 100-pounder Parrotts placed on the bows of our vessels in the advance.

The Admiral waited until directly abreast of Fort Morgan, when he delivered a succession of broadsides from the nine-inch guns of the *Hartford* with such precision and galling effect that the rebels were driven away from their guns, and the water battery and fort were silenced. At this time the monitors engaged the iron-clad ram *Tennessee,* which was discovered, laying in position to advance on our noble Admiral.

At this moment the monitor *Tecumseh* struck a torpedo and was seen to rise and disappear beneath the water almost instantly. The firing now became terrific, and the fleet, although steaming ahead at a full rate of speed, was completely enveloped in flame and smoke. The rebel ram made several attempts to run our passing vessels down, but failed to do so, and in the midst of all this a boat was lowered from the *Metacomet* to pick up the survivors of our ill-fated monitor. It was a beautiful and appalling sight to witness this boat rowing around on its sacred mission to rescue our drowning men, with its beautiful flag flowing to the breeze, and the missiles of death and destruction striking and ricocheting all around it. But the gallant officer (an ensign whose name I forget) heedlessly kept on his way, and succeeded in rescuing the pilot, one of the officers and three men, belonging to the *Tecumseh.*

With the exception of the monitor, our fleet had by this time succeeded in passing Fort Morgan, only to be subject to a galling, raking fire from the three rebel gunboats—*Selma, Morgan* and *Gaines.*

Our vessels, which were secured together in pairs, were now cast off, and the engagement became general, which in a short time resulted in driving the ram and two gunboats under the guns of Fort Morgan, whilst the *Selma* steamed up the bay with the evident intention of escaping to Mobile.

After a chase of about forty minutes the *Selma* hauled down her flag to Capt. DRUETT, of the *Metacomet.* On boarding her the cause of her surrender was soon apparent—their decks were covered with the dead and dying, and her scuppers were running with their blood. Among others I recognized the body of Lieut. COMSTOCK, with his bowels torn out and laying across the breach of a gun which he was engaged in sighting at the time of his death. He once belonged to our navy. Language is not adequate to describe the soul-stirring cheers which went up from the throats of our brave tars, and was reechoed from one vessel to another all through this terrible ordeal, and our brave, noble Admiral has exemplified in this fight that his theory of "iron hearts and wooden ships" is a correct one.

At this time, while our fleet, with a few exceptions, had collected together on the west side of the bay, in the direction of Fort Powell, and out of the range of Morgan's guns, the ram *Tennessee* was discovered steaming in the direction.

The monitors closed with her when in range, and one of the most interesting naval engagements of the war succeeded, and we, in the smaller wooden vessels, were the spectators.

A fight of some minutes ensued, when Admiral FARRAGUT, anxious to close the engagement in a summary manner, started toward the *Tennessee* at full speed; at the same time Capt. STRONG, in the *Monongahela,* struck the *Tennessee* amidships, and withdrew in time to give room to our Admiral to grapple his antagonist, BUCHANAN. When the smoke cleared away from the two vessels, a white flag was seen to wave from the *Tennessee's* pilot-house, in token of submission, and Capt. JEBAUD, who went in as a volunteer on the *Ossippee* as a representative of Admiral FARRAGUT, received the sword of Admiral BUCHANAN, and that terrible engine of destruction was ours, although gained at a great loss of life.

Our loss in this fight is about 240 killed and wounded, including the brave Capt. CRAVAN of the monitor, and 100 of his crew who went down with him. Admiral BUCHANAN of the *Tennessee* was shot through the leg below the knee, and the leg will have to be amputated.

Fort Powell, in Grant's Pass, was blown up last night after dark, and Fort Gaines will soon follow. The rebel gunboats, which sought protection under the guns of Morgan, will be destroyed or captured by our monitors to-day, and the investment and capture of Morgan must follow.

We have, by this great victory, effectually closed the port of Mobile, and its capture is only a question of time ; and Admiral FARRAGUT, and the gallant officers and men under his command, have established another claim to the admiration and respect of their countrymen and those who love liberty.

An Officer's Statement.

We are indebted to the courtesy of an officer of the navy, who witnessed the naval engagement in Mobile Bay, on Friday last, for the following interesting particulars :

Between 7 and 8 o'clock on that morning, the fleet moved in the following order : Four monitors and fourteen wooden vessels, the *Tecumseh* leading the former and the *Hartford* (flagship of Admiral FARRAGUT) the latter, advanced. The monitors were the *Tecumseh, Manhattan, Winnebago* and *Chickasaw.* The wooden vessels followed in pairs.

The rebel ram, the *Tennessee,* and gunboats *Selma, Morgan* and *Gaines,* were lying in wait under the guns of Fort Morgan, ready to attack the Federal fleet as it approached. It opened upon them with grape and canister—the *Hartford* and other vessels — with such severity that nothing could withstand the force of the terrific attack. The gunners of Fort Morgan, in the meantime, were driven from their guns, so fierce was the fire from the Federal fleet.

The *Tecumseh,* in passing the forts, was blown up by the explosion of a torpedo. The captain and all on board, with the exception of ten, sank with her. The Confederate ram *Tennessee,* after first attacking the fleet, as it advanced, seemed to return for shelter under the guns of Fort Morgan ; but, after the fleet had proceeded some distance up the bay, stood toward them, as if to give battle ; whereupon the *Hartford,* the monitors, and the wooden vessels of the fleet, stood for her, and a most terrible engagement commenced. The *Tennessee* was rammed by the *Hartford,* the *Lackawanna* and the *Monongahela*—the *Lackawanna* striking her under full headway, and all the vessels delivering a heavy fire at the same instant. The *Manhattan,* meantime, put one solid 15-inch shot at her, which penetrated her armor through and through and lodged on the opposite side.

Admiral FARRAGUT, during the engagement, was stationed in the maintop, where he had lashed himself in case be should receive a wound, communicating his orders below through speaking-tubes. After a most determined and gallant

A view of the deck of the *Hartford,* Admiral Farragut's flagship.

engagement, the *Tennessee* showed a white flag as a token of surrender. An officer of the Federal fleet then boarded the *Tennessee* and demanded the sword of Admiral BUCHANAN, which that officer surrendered, and it was taken on board the flagship. The Confederate Admiral was wounded severely, and will probably have to suffer the amputation of a leg.

The Confederate gunboat *Selma*, in the meanwhile, retreated up the bay, and was followed by the *Metacomet*, Lieut.-Commander JEWETT, and *Port Royal*, Lieut.-Commander GHIRARDI. The *Selma* surrendered to Lieut. JEWETT. The two other rebel gunboats, *Morgan* and *Gaines*, took refuge under the guns of Fort Morgan, and (says our informant) would probably be captured in the course of yesterday.

The U. S. monitor *Chickasaw*, Lieut.-Commander PERKINS, steered gallantly up to Fort Powell, and took in tow a steam barge from immediately under the guns of the fort. After taking the barge out of range, she returned and pelted the fort vigorously for half an hour with 11-inch shell. Fort Powell was finally evacuated, and at 11 o'clock at night was blown up by the rebels.

Of course, as the rebel vessels concentrated their fire principally upon her, she suffered the greatest loss. The total Federal loss, including that of the *Tecumseh*, (which was blown up by the torpedo and sunk,) in killed, wounded and missing, was about 240.

On the *Tennessee* there were twenty officers and about 120 men—Admiral BUCHANAN, commanding. Among the officers beside were Capt. JOHNSTON and Lieuts. BRADFORD and WHARTON.

Farragut's Own Account of the Fight.

From the New-Orleans True Delta.

Since the above was in type, Admiral PALMER has kindly read to us such portions of an official dispatch and private letter from Admiral FARRAGUT as he deems proper to make public. At an early hour on Friday, our fleet, lashed two and two, sailed into the Pass close up under the guns of Fort Morgan, pouring in broadside after broadside of grape and canister—thus driving the gunners of the fort from their pieces and leaving our vessels exposed only to the fire of Forts Gaines and Powell, which were, of course, less effective on account of distance. At the same time Gen. GRANGER'S land batteries enfiladed Gaines and caused the evacuation and blowing up of Powell. In passing the forts the *Oneida* received a shot which temporarily disabled her machinery, but she was safely towed through the fire by her consort.

Our monitor *Tecumseh* was one of the foremost. A torpedo, exploding beneath her bottom, she sunk almost instantaneously, carrying down all her officers, only ten of her crew escaping. She was commanded by Capt. LEWIS CRAVEN. Our loss on this vessel was about one hundred. The gunboats having passed the forts, and being out of their reach, were pursued by the formidable ram *Tennessee*, and three iron-clad gunboats—the *Selma*, *Gaines* and *Morgan*. Our vessels immediately attacked the ram, and battered him so effectually that he surrendered in a few minutes by hanging out the white flag. Admiral BUCHANAN, the Commander, lost a leg, and with all his crew, are prisoners in our hands. There were only 3 killed on the *Tennessee*. She was but slightly damaged, and it is probable that FARRAGUT has her fit for action by this time. We also captured the *Selma*, of which Capt. MURPHY was the commander. Lieut. PRENTISS, of the *Monongahela*, lost both legs. He is a gallant officer, and has a young wife in this city. Capt. MALANEY, of the *Oneida*, lost an arm. All the wounded will be sent to Pensacola. Our loss is two hundred and forty killed and wounded. The two remaining rebel gunboats fled under the guns of Fort Morgan for protection; one of them is aground, and the Admiral is confident that he can destroy them to-day. He has not the slightest doubt of his ability to reduce the forts. But their capture will not give us command of the city, which is extensively fortified at Dog River and elsewhere.

The *Hartford*, FARRAGUT'S flagship, was heavily engaged, losing one officer, HIGGENBOTTOM, Secretary to the Fleet Captain, killed, together with 20 of her crew, and 26 wounded. All our vessels were wooden except three.

Farragut and Granger Before Mobile.

From the New-Orleans Times.

Ever since the capture and occupation of this city by FARRAGUT and BUTLER the possession of Mobile by the Federal Government has been one of the principal objects of the desires of Union men, both here and at the North. Apart from its importance commercially to the Southern States, an importance which has not been lessened during the war, owing to the frequency with which rebel smugglers have evaded the cruisers of the blockading squadron off its harbor. Mobile, from its population and past importance, in a financial point of view, has been considered one of the chief jewels in the possession of the Confederacy. It has always been the opinion of rebels and loyal people that the fall of Mobile would be one of the most disastrous blows possible to the fortunes of the great insurrection which has deluged this country in blood, entailed upon it untold misery and an immense load of debt, diminished its national importance in the eyes of the world, and endangered the progress, the perpetuity even, of liberal principles in politics on the Western hemisphere.

The *Times* of yesterday evening announced the passage of the forts in Mobile harbor by Admiral FARRAGUT and his fleet, the capture of the rebel officer in charge of the Mobile naval defences, the investment of Fort Gaines by Gen. GRANGER, and the surrender of the much famed rebel ram, the *Tennessee*, on the 5th inst. We congratulate our Union population of the Crescent City on this great, glorious and most welcome intelligence. The whole country, outside the limits of rebeldom, and many a man within those hateful bounds, will unite in rejoicing over this magnificent exploit of the thrice-gallant FARRAGUT and the heroic GRANGER. Many a Union man, whose bosom swelled, and pulse beat hard, and eyes filled with tears of joy in New-Orleans on the day when scared rebels whispered the news from ear to ear of the passing of St. Philip and Jackson in April, 1862, felt a jubilant emotion like that which then raised his soul from the depth of despondency to the most delightful hopes and anticipations as he perused yesterday evening's *Times*. They said "God bless him!" of that daring, lion-hearted FARRAGUT, in the hour of their own greatest peril; and they now sympathize, with hearts full of devout thankfulness, with the Union men of Mobile, who have heard similar tidings, and are ready again with their invocations of blessings from on high to rest upon the head of the greatest naval commander of the age.

Perhaps, while we write, Mobile has fallen; but whether this is so or not, Mobile is sure to fall. The wise foresight of CANBY and FARRAGUT, the character of the men to whom the task has been devolved, the ample preparations that have been made, render the fall of the city an absolute certainty. There will be no backward step, no unnecessary delay; nothing but earnest action, guided by consummate skill, hard, telling blows, severely and effectively dealt, until the Stars and Stripes float in triumph over what is left of the metropolis of Alabama. Union men of New-Orleans! remember the feelings which swayed you when the fleet of the United States was forcing its way up the Mississippi, while you were surrounded by foes who would have hung you. Extend your heartiest sympathies to those men of Mobile who may be to-day rejoicing, and stifling their rejoicings, at the progress of the delivering arm of the nation.

With Atlanta partially within our grasp, if not entirely so; with the railroad connection between Atlanta and Mobile effectually severed; with Northern Alabama friendly to the Union cause; with GRANT at Petersburgh, holding before him the main force of the Confederates, tying them hand and foot before Richmond, totally unable to fly to the relief of any other section of the Confederacy; with the attention of the forces held to defend Charleston fully occupied by the gallant little band assailing that city day and night at every vulnerable point, what will prevent the success of the combined naval and land force at Mobile? Truly, "it is thundering all around," and is thundering to excellent purpose.

The brittle Confederacy is assailed at all points by forces that cannot help being successful. The officers in charge of the Union armies have been tried again and again without the discovery of a flaw; they have been winnowed until nothing but the true grain of gold remains. The armies of the United States are composed mainly of men to whom the noise of battle has grown a thing accustomed, and who have for months back carried the inspiring prestige of victory. The navy is coöperating wherever the brave sea-dogs can be of use; and the navy has never known aught but success. Truly, the end seems at hand, and is full of splendid promise.

ROUSSEAU'S raid, and the grand success of FARRAGUT and CANBY, are but the forerunners of the speedy return of Alabama to her place in the Union. A large part of her population did not approve secession. They did not vote for the secession ordinance, nor for the Confederate Constitution. The whole State voted against the immediate secession plan of YANCY. We have few fears for the future of Alabama.

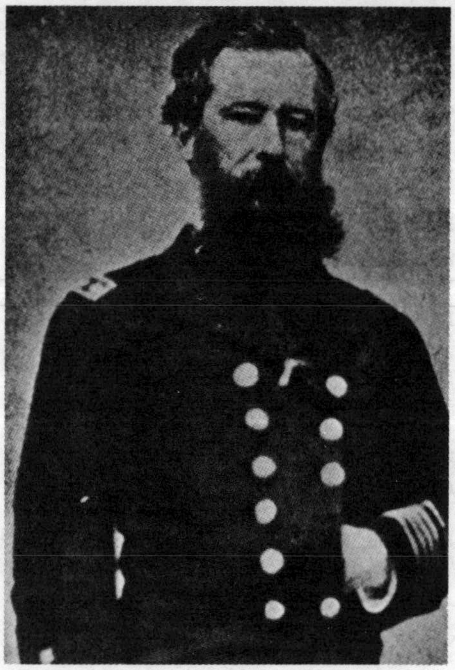

Captain Tunis A.M. Craven was lost as his ship *Tecumseh* was sunk by a mine.

Late Rebel News.

WASHINGTON, Sunday, Aug. 14.

The Richmond *Examiner*, of the 12th, has the following:

MOBILE, Tuesday, Aug. 9.

Hon. S. E. Mallory, Secretary of the Navy:

The enemy steamed in through the main entrance with four monitors and about sixteen heavy vessels of war. The *Tecumseh*, Commander T. A. M. CRAVEN, was sunk with nearly all her crew, and, also, another gunboat, the *Phillippi*, which I subsequently burned.

The *Richmond*, *Hartford* and *Brooklyn*, in line of battle, followed by the remainder of the fleet, pushed by Fort Morgan, under full headway, when they were encountered by the *Tennessee*, the *Morgan*, the *Gaines* and the *Selma*.*

The *Tennessee* and other vessels steamed in close range of the advancing force, and poured a heavy fire into the leading ships. After a desperate struggle between the fleets, the *Gaines* retired to Fort Morgan in a sinking condition.

The *Selma*, cut off, surrendered, and the *Morgan* escaped to Fort Morgan. The *Tennessee*, so far uninjured, steamed toward the whole fleet, and after an obstinate fight surrendered, her rudder disabled, her smoke stack carried away, and, as we suppose, her crew in an exhausted and smothering condition.

On the *Tennessee* Admiral BUCHANAN was severely wounded by a splinter in the leg. Two were killed and several wounded among her crew. On the *Gaines* two were killed and two wounded. On the *Morgan*, one was wounded.

On the *Selma* eight were killed, including her Executive officer, Lieut. J. H. COMSTOCK, and seven were wounded. The enemy suffered severely and requested permission to bury his dead. Respectfully, &c.,

G. W. HARRISON,
Confederate States Navy.

The *Examiner* also gives a list of the 28 Federal vessels engaged, having 212 guns, with the four Confederates, having 32 guns.

"It was a most unequal contest, in which our gallant little navy was engaged, and we lost the battle, but one ensign went down in a blaze of glory."

Up to Thursday night nothing of interest had occurred before Atlanta. Maj.-Gen. BATES received a flesh wound in the leg. The enemy is massing on our right and endeavoring to extend his lines in the direction of the Western Railroad.

A few shots were fired at the city yesterday, (9th.) Brisk shelling commenced at 11 o'clock last night, and continued four hours. No personal casualties are reported.

The New-York Times.

VOL. XIV.–NO. 4054.   NEW-YORK, WEDNESDAY, SEPTEMBER 21, 1864.   PRICE FOUR CENTS.

VICTORY!

Great Battle in the Shenandoah Valley.

The Rebels Defeated by General Sheridan.

THE BATTLE OF BUNKER HILL.

The Enemy Thoroughly Whipped.

They are Pursued Beyond Winchester.

Three Thousand Prisoners, Five Guns and Fifteen Battle-Flags Captured.

All the Rebel Dead and Wounded in Our Hands.

The Rebel Generals Gordon, Wharton, Rodes, and Ramsour Killed.

THE UNION GENERAL RUSSELL KILLED.

The Union Generals Chapman, Upton and Mackintosh Wounded.

THE OFFICIAL DISPATCHES,

SECRETARY STANTON TO GEN. DIX.

WAR DEPARTMENT,
WASHINGTON, Tuesday, Sept. 20—9:30 A. M.

Maj.-Gen. John A. Dix:

Yesterday, Maj.-Gen. SHERIDAN attacked EARLY, fought a great battle, and won a splendid victory.

Over 2,500 prisoners were captured.

Nine battle-flags and five pieces of artillery were captured.

The rebel Generals Gordon and Rhodes were killed and three other general officers were wounded.

All of the enemy's killed, and most of their wounded, are in our hands.

The details are stated in the following additional telegrams received by this department.

The department learns with deep regret, that we lost General Russell, killed.

GEN. STEVENSON'S FIRST DISPATCH.

HARPER'S FERRY, VA., Monday, Sept. 19—12 M.

Hon. Edwin M. Stanton, Secretary of War:

Gen. SHERIDAN moved on the enemy this morning at daylight. Soon after the movement commenced, there was heavy and continuous firing for two hours. It then ceased, apparently receding. It was resumed about nine o'clock, and has continued to this hour (12 M.,) apparently in the vicinity of Bunker Hill.

JOHN D. STEVENSON, Brig.-Gen.

GEN. STEVENSON'S SECOND DISPATCH.

HARPER'S FERRY, Monday, Sept. 19, 3 P. M.

Hon. E. M. Stanton, Secretary of War:

Just received report from signal officer as follows: Continuous firing between Opequan and near Winchester; very heavy since 10 A. M. Think the engagement is general. Line about 5 miles long.

AVERILL is heavily engaged with the enemy near Darkesville. I have sent a party of scouts and couriers to the front, and shall report promptly all reliable news.

JOHN D. STEVENSON, Brig.-Gen.

GEN. STEVENSON'S THIRD DISPATCH.

HARPER'S FERRY, Monday, Sept. 19—4:30 P. M.

Hon. E. M. Stanton, Secretary of War:

Fighting in the direction of Winchester much heavier. Our forces near Bunker Hill seem to be driving the enemy rapidly.

JOHN D. STEVENSON, Brig.-Gen.

GEN. STEVENSON'S FOURTH DISPATCH.

HARPER'S FERRY, Monday, Sept. 19—7 P. M.

Hon. E. M. Stanton, Secretary of War:

Just heard from the front. Our cavalry, under AVERILL and MERRITT engaged BRECKENRIDGE's corps at Darkesville at daylight, and up to 1 o'clock had driven him beyond Stevenson's Depot, a distance of seven miles, killing and wounding quite a number and capturing two hundred prisoners from GORDON's division.

On the centre and left the enemy were driven about three miles beyond the Opequan into a line of earthworks, our infantry attacking them in position. Since then, as the officer left, he could distinctly hear heavy musketry fire and continuous and heavy artillery firing as he came in. We have heard here heavy artillery firing, and still continuing to this hour. Every indication is most favorable to us.

JOHN D. STEVENSON, Brig.-Gen.

GEN. STEVENSON'S FIFTH DISPATCH.

HARPER'S FERRY, Tuesday, Sept. 20, 7:40 A. M.

Hon. E. M. Stanton, Secretary of War:

Just heard from the front that SHERIDAN has defeated the enemy, capturing 2,500 prisoners, five pieces of artillery, and five battle-flags. Rebel Generals GORDON and RHODES were killed, and YORK wounded. Our loss was about 2,000. Gen. RUSSELL, of the Sixth Corps, was killed. Gen. McINTOSH lost a leg. The enemy escaped up the valley under cover of night. SHERIDAN is in Winchester.

J. D. STEVENSON, Brig.-Gen.

Gens. UPTON, McINTOSH and CHAPMAN are wounded.

GEN. SHERIDAN TO GEN. GRANT.

Gen. SHERIDAN transmits to Gen. GRANT the following official report, which has just been received by the Department:

WINCHESTER VA., Sept. 19, 7:30 P. M.

Lieut.-Gen. U S Grant:

I have the honor to report that I attacked the forces of Gen. Early, over the Berryville pike, at the crossing of Opequan Creek, and after a most stubborn and sanguinary engagement, which lasted from early in the morning until five o'clock in the evening, completely defeated him, driving him through Winchester, capturing about 2,500 prisoners, five pieces of artillery, nine army flags, and most of their wounded. The Rebel Generals RHODES and GORDON were killed, and three other general officers were wounded. Most of the enemy's wounded and all their killed fell into our hands. Our losses are severe. Among them is Gen. D. A. RUSSELL, commanding a Division in the Sixth Corps, who was killed by a cannon ball. Gens. UPTON, McINTOSH, and CHAPMAN were wounded. I cannot tell our losses. The conduct of the officers and men was most superb. They charged and carried every position taken up by the rebels from Opaquan Creek to Winchester.

The rebels were strong in numbers, and very

The Union policy of scorching the Shenandoah Valley led to retaliation by Confederate cavalry. Chambersburg, Pennsylvania, was a victim of Rebel revenge.

obstinate in their fighting. I desire to mention to the Lieut.-Gen. Commanding the army, the gallant conduct of Generals WRIGHT, CROOK, EMORY, TORBERT, and the officers and men under their command. To them the country is indebted for this handsome victory. A more detailed report will be forwarded.

P. H. SHERIDAN,
Major-General, Commanding.

WAR DEPARTMENT, Tuesday, Sept. 20.
Full details of casualties will be given when received by the Department.

EDWIN M. STANTON, Sec'y of War.

SECRETARY STANTON'S SECOND DISPATCH

WAR DEPARTMENT,
WASHINGTON Tuesday, Sept. 20—12 M.

Maj.-Gen. John A. Dix:

The following dispatch has just been received giving further particulars of SHERIDAN'S great victory. A salute of one hundred guns has just been given.

HARPER'S FERRY, Tuesday, Sept. 20—11:40 A. M.
Hon. E. M. Stanton:

Just received the following official from Gen. SHERIDAN, dated 1 A. M. to-day:

GENERAL: We fought EARLY from daylight till between 6 and 7 P. M. We drove him from Opequan Creek through Winchester and beyond the town. We captured 2,500 to 3,000 prisoners, five pieces of artillery, nine battle-flags, and all the rebel wounded and dead.

Their wounded in Winchester amount to some three thousand. We lost in killed Gen. DAVID RUSSELL, commanding a division of the Sixth Army Corps, and wounded Gens. CHAPMAN, McINTOSH and UPTON. The rebels lost in killed the following General officers : Gen. RHODES, Gen. WHARTON, Gen. GORDON and Gen. RAMSEUR.

We have just sent them whirling through Winchester and we are after them to-morrow. This army behaved splendidly. I am sending forward all the medical supplies, subsistence stores and ambulances. (Signed,)

JNO. D. STEVENSON, Brig.-Gen.
EDWIN M. STANTON, *Secretary of War.*

SECRETARY STANTON'S THIRD DISPATCH.

WAR DEPARTMENT,
WASHINGTON, Monday, Sept. 20—7 P. M.

To Maj.-Gen. Dix, New York ;

The following is the latest intelligence received from Gen. SHERIDAN:

HARPER'S FERRY, VA.,
MONDAY, Sept. 20—8 P. M.

Hon. Edwin M. Stanton, Secretary of War:

The body of Gen. RUSSELL has arrived. As soon as it is embalmed, it will be forwarded to New-York. Gen. McINTOSH, with his leg amputated, has just come in, and is in good spirits.

Several officers from the front report the number of prisoners in excess of 3,000.

The number of battle-flags captured was fifteen, instead of nine.

All concur that it was a complete rout. Our cavalry started in pursuit at daylight this morning. SHERIDAN, when last heard from, was at Kearnstown. I sent forward this morning ample medical supplies. Full subsistence for the entire army goes forward. If you do not hear from me often, it will be because of the distance we are from the scene of action, and because I only send you such information as I esteem reliable.

JOHN B. RICHARDSON, Brig.-Gen.

The President has appointed Gen. SHERIDAN a Brigadier in the regular Army, and assigned him to the permanent command of the Middle Military Division.

Gen. GRANT has ordered the army under his command to fire a salute of one hundred guns at seven o'clock to-morrow morning in honor of SHERIDAN'S great victory.

Confederate Major-General Robert
E. Rodes

A dispatch just received from Gen. SHERMAN, at Atlanta, says :

"Everything continues well with us."

The reports of to-day show that the draft is proceeding quietly in all the States. In most of the districts vigorous efforts are continued to fill the quota by volunteers before the drafted men are mustered in.

EDWIN M. STANTON, Secretary of War.

DETAILS OF THE BATTLE.

BALTIMORE, Tuesday, Sept. 20—10 P.M.
The following is the *American's* special account of the great battle in the Shenandoah Valley:

HEADQUARTERS MIDDLE MILITARY DIVISION,
WINCHESTER, Va., Monday, Sept. 19—9 P.M.

Gen. SHERIDAN's army has this day fought one of the most successful and decisive battles of the war. Victory again perched on our banners, and the rebel army which so recently threatened the invasion of the loyal North, has been defeated and utterly routed, with the loss of at least three thousand killed and wounded including five Generals, namely, RHODES, WHARTON, BRADLEY, T. JOHNSON, GORDON, YORK and GODMAN, the first two of whom were killed, and the others badly wounded, and we have captured 2,500 prisoners, nine battle flags, representing nine different regimental organizations, five pieces of artillery with caissons.

The recital of the victory ought to make every loyal heart at the North glow with admiration and gratitude to the brave men and gallant officers who have achieved so signal success.

In order to more thoroughly understand the nature of the battle, with all the surrounding influences, it will be necessary briefly to refer to the operations of Sunday.

Sunday morning EARLY sent GORDON's division of rebel infantry from Bunker Hill, where it had been stationed for the past few days, to drive AVERILL out of Martinsburg and destroy the bridge on the Baltimore and Ohio R. R. across the Opequan, which they erroneously thought had been repaired. They occupied Martinsburgh for a short time, without doing any damage to the railroad, and were eventually driven by AVERILL as far as Darkesville.

Gen. SHERIDAN, learning their movements, ordered the whole command to break camp and prepare to march. Accordingly, at 3 o'clock on Sunday the tents were all struck and packed in wagons. The different divisions were all under arms, and prepared to move at a moment's notice, and remained in this state for about an hour, when the order came to go into camp for the night, and everything remained perfectly quiet. About 9 o'clock orders were received from SHERIDAN for the Sixth

and Nineteenth Corps to be ready to start at 3 o'clock, and the Army of Western Virginia, under CROOK, at 5 the following morning—the order of march to be as follows : The Sixth Corps to move out on the Winchester and Berryville pike, and move in two parallel columns on both sides of the road, with the artillery, ammunition and supply trains on the road ; the Nineteenth Corps to follow on the same road and in similar order ; the Army of Western Virginia, under CROOK, to move from its camping-ground in the vicinity of Summit Point, and striking across the country in a south-westerly direction, was ordered to form a junction at the crossing of the Opequan, on the Berryville and Winchester pike, and shortly after five o'clock WILSON's division of cavalry crossed the Opequan at the Berryville and Winchester pike. Moving his command rapidly along the road, driving in the enemy's skirmish line, he gallantly charged the enemy's field works with the first brigade, and carried them at the point of the sabre, capturing thirty prisoners. In this charge, Col. BRINTON, Eighteenth Pennsylvania cavalry, was wounded within a few feet of the enemy's works, whilst gallantly leading his regiment.

These field-works were constructed at the Opequan, and prevent our passage at that point. It will be seen how signally they failed to accomplish the object for which they were constructed.

Our cavalry having secured a safe passage for the infantry, the Sixth corps was moved across the Opequan, and along the pike toward Winchester, (leaving its train in part on the opposite side of the stream,) to a point about a mile and a half distant from the ford, where it formed in line of battle and threw out a strong skirmish line. At the same time the artillery opened on the woods into which the enemy's infantry had retired, and kept up an incessant cannonade, the enemy replying briskly with parts of two batteries.

There was a delay of at least two hours, caused by the non-arrival of the Nineteenth corps, who through misconception of orders, had failed to come up at the proper time. Gen. EMORY had moved his column to the rear of the baggage train of the Sixth corps instead of keeping his command closed up in the rear of the advancing column of the Sixth corps.

Gen. Sheridan having learned on Sunday that the main portion of Early's forces were encamped in the vicinity of Bunker Hill and Stephenson's Depot, resolved to mass his forces on the Winchester and Berryville pike, and by a rapid movement hurl them on Early's rear. There is no doubt but the enemy were surprised and outnumbered by Sheridan.

Whilst his different columns were being marched to the appointed place of rendezvous, a portion of our cavalry under Gen.'s. TORBETT and AVERILL kept up a strong picket line along the Opequan, and by demonstrating in force at Burn's ford kept a large portion of the enemy at that part of the field, which was nearly twelve miles distant from the point where it was intended our infantry should operate, and strike a blow which should result in the signal defeat of EARLY's army.

The delay in the arrival of the 19th Corps enabled EARLY to move GORDON's Division at the double quick from Bunker Hill, distant about ten miles, and bring it up in time to form in line of battle with BRECKENRIDGE's, RAMSEUR's, and RHODES' commands, who had already arrived, and were formed in a belt of woods skirting Berryville and Winchester.

As soon as the 19th corps arrived, it was formed in four lines of battle, about 300 yards apart, on the right of the 6th corps, and everything being in readiness, the advance was sounded at about 12 o'clock, and the different lines moved forward.

The two corps advanced in splendid style, and just as composedly as though marching at review or on parade, drums beating and colors flying, presenting such an imposing spectacle as has seldom been witnessed in the present war. In fact, some of the oldest and most experienced staff officers present declared they had never before witnessed so truly grand a spectacle.

The first line had not advanced more than two hundred yards before it became warmly engaged with the enemy, who were posted in line about six hundred yards distant. At the same time our artillery opened a furious cannonade, throwing shells and solid shot into the opposite woods, where the enemy could be distinctly seen moving up reinforcements. Our different lines of battle continued to advance steadily until within nearly two hundred yards of the enemy's line, when the rebels opened a furious canonade with grape and canister, from two batteries which they had previously kept secreted, and which ploughed through our advancing lines, mowing down large numbers of our men.

The first line was obliged to give way under so murderous a fire, and in retreating behing the second line, threw it into momentary confusion, and it also was compelled to fall back behind the third line, which had in the meantime been ordered to lie down, in order to avoid as much as possible the effects of the withring fire which the enemy's battery's were directing against our advancing lines.

The artillery was now brought up and posted on commanding positions, to silence these batteries of the enemy, which had caused us so much annoyance, and our line was reformed, and again moved forward, regaining the advanced position which they had held when they were obliged to fall back. But the success was not gained without the most obstinate resistance on the part of the enemy.

Gen. SHERIDAN had previously ridden along the lines, and was received everywhere by the men with the greatest enthusiasm, and when they advanced, it was with the terrible determination to do or die in the attempt.

Having regained the advanced position which we had previously occupied, the different lines of battle were ordered to lie down and wait the arrival of Gen. CROOK's Corps which was held in reserve on the eastern side of the Opequan. They were ordered up to take position on the extreme right of our line, and in order to counteract a movement on the part of the enemy who were massing troops on their left flank, with the view of turning our right.

Precisely at 3 o'clock, Gen. CROOK formed on the right of the Nineteenth Corps, his first division on the extreme right of our line, and the second division in the rear supporting a division of the Nineteenth Corps. Gen. CROOK, having formed his men, rode along the lines, and was received with most vociferous cheering, the men promising to go in and wipe out Winchester.

Gen. TORBETT, with MERRITT's and AVERILL's divisions of cavalry, having crossed the Opequan about 9 o'clock at BURN's and KNOX's Fords, had been hard at work all day, fighting considerable bodies of the enemy's infantry, and having been successful in steadily driving them before them, now arrived on our extreme right, and was prepared to take part in the final struggle which secured us the victory.

Gen. SHERIDAN rode out to where Gen. TORBETT was stationed, and after a consultation with him as to the part the cavalry were to take, ordered the final charge, which was made with an impetuosity which nothing could resist. Our line, extending nearly three miles in length, advanced, amid the cheers and yells, which could be distinctly heard far above the noise caused by the thunder of the artillery and the continuous roar of musketry, which, for its impetuosity, has seldom been exceeded in any battle of this war.

Our men determined to win the day, and nerved themselves accordingly for the coming struggle; and as our lines advanced closer and closer to those of the enemy, the battle became more and more fierce, until in point of desperate and fierce carnage, it will compare favorably with any similar contest of the war.

The slaughter now was truly awful. At every discharge men could be distinctly seen dropping all around, and the two contending lines at some points could not have been over two hundred yards apart.

Just at this critical period, above the roar of artillery, musketry and cheers, and the fiercer yells of the contending armies, could be distinctly heard the shrill notes of the cavalry bugle sounding the charge which was the death knell to EARLY's army. There could be seen the gallant CUSTER and MERRITT, each with headquarters flag in hand, and conspicuous amongst the advancing squadrons, gallantly leading the charge which in connection with the desperate courage of our infantry, secured us the victory. All honor to these gallant chiefs, who have done so nobly.

Those who have never witnessed a cavalry charge can form no idea of its magnificence, nor of the demoralizing effects when well executed, which it has on an enemy. The stubborn columns of EARLY's command were forced to give way and break before the fierce onslaught which our cavalry made upon them, who, with sabre in hand,

rode them down, cutting them right and left, capturing 721 privates and non-commissioned offices, with nine battle flags and two guns.

The broken and disorganised divisions comprising EARLY's command now fled in confusion, throwing away everything which could in any way impede their flight, and strewing the ground with their arms. Some made for the heights above Winchester, but they were speedily dislodged by AVERILL, and forced to beat an hasty and ignominious retreat up the valley, where such of EARLY's command as are left him are now scattered.

Our victory was a glorious one, and one well calculated to thrill the hearts of every loyal man with the impulses of sincere joy; but it has been well remarked that each joy has its attending amount of sorrow, and it is for our gallant dead and wounded who poured out their life's blood freely that this great and iniquitous rebellion be put down.

Amongst the killed I regret to announce the gallant RUSSELL, of the First Division, Sixth Corps, commanding. Fearless as was possible for man to be, brave unto rashness, he fell at the post of honor at the head of his division, while leading them in charge.

Gen. McINTOSH, commanding First Brigade, Third Cavalry Division, was wounded by a pistol ball in the leg, which necessitated amputation. He is doing very well.

Gen. UPTON, commanding division in Sixth Corps was also wounded, but not dangerously.

Of field and line officers I have been able to collect but few names who were killed or wounded. Among them are Col. BABCOCK, Seventy-fifth New-York, wounded in the thigh; Col. E. BAIGHT, One Hundred and Twenty-sixth Ohio. Third Division, Sixth Corps, killed; Capt. WRIGHT, Gen. DEVIN's Staff, killed; Capt. ROSENBAUGH, Second United States Cavalry, wounded in the arm; Capt. McGUIRE-TON, Second United States Cavalry, Aid to Gen. MERRITT, killed; Maj. VREDENBURG, Fourteenth New-Jersey, Third Division, Sixth Corps, killed.

Maj. DELLINGHAM, Tenth Vermont, Third Division, Sixth Corps, killed.

Lieut.-Col. BREWER, Seventh Michigan Cavalry, killed.

Lieut. JACKSON, First Michigan Cavalry, arm shot off.

Lieuts. MATHEWS and JOHN ALLEN, First Michigan Cavalry, killed.

The Michigan brigade, Gen. CUSTER's command, claim the honor of killing Gen. RHODES during the fierce conflict which ensued when they charged a portion of his division.

After the battle had been fought and won and while our troops were passing through the streets of Winchester, among them some of the best ladies residing in the town came out with Union flags in their hands, and bid our soldiers "Welcome back to Winchester."

The people of Winchester all agree in stating that EARLY's command is fearfully demoralized, and speak of his defeat as a disgraceful rout, in which both men and officers rushed frantically through the streets, throwing away everything which would in any way encumber them in their flight.

The City Hotel and the adjacent foundries, together with many private houses in Winchester, are full of rebel wounded. It is estimated there are at least 3,000 in Winchester. Allowing for those who were carried away in ambulances, and for those who were able to hobble along, it will be a small estimate to place their wounded at 4,000 and killed at 500, which with the prisoners already captured, numbering 3,000, will make their loss 7,500 in number, equal to one of their corps.

Of the Federal loss, it is impossible, at the time of writing this dispatch, to form any correct estimate; but from information at hand, together with personal observations on the field, I do not think it will exceed 500 killed and 2,500 wounded, if it amounts to that number.

Surely I am correct in stating that this has been one of the most sanguinary and decesive battles of the war, and reflects great credit on Gen. SHERIDAN, who was constantly at the front, exposing himself to the fire of the enemy's sharpshooters, and personally directing the movements of our army.

THE STRATEGY OF THE BATTLE.

Special Dispatch to the New-York Times.

WASHINGTON, Tuesday, Sept. 20,

Brevet Major-General David A. Russell

Gen. SHERIDAN's grand success near Winchester is noted as the first victory achieved by the national arms in the Shenandoah Valley. But it is so magnificent in its proportions as completely to wipe out the long series of reverses which have given to that region the designation of "The Valley of Humiliation." The loss to the enemy in killed, wounded and prisoners will, it is believed, reach not less than ten thousand, while the circumstances of the enemy's defeat leave EARLY's army in a condition little short of absolute rout and demoralization.

Popular logic will doubtless associate this brilliant exploit with the recent visit of the Lieutenant-General to the headquarters of Gen. SHERIDAN—an association so far correct, no doubt, that, had not Gen. GRANT authorized Gen. SHERIDAN to assume the offensive, we should not now have this victory to rejoice over. This does not, however, detract from the credit to which that gallant officer is entitled, and all the more so from the modest generosity with which he ascribes all the glory of the splendid achievement to his subordinate commanders.

The bearing of this operation on the greater problem immediately before Gen. GRANT, is of capital importance, and will go far to decide the fate of LEE's army and Richmond. The tremendous importance of Lynchburgh, as covering the now only remaining line of railroad communication with Richmond, has compelled LEE to retain in the valley full one-half of his entire force; and notwithstanding the terrible straits he has been put to for lack of troops to meet the movkeents of GRANT, the fatal menace which the presence of SHERIDAN's army in the Valley constantly held forth, has forced LEE to submit to them, on peril of the loss of Lynchburgh.

The army covering that point has, by SHERIDAN's splendid success, been disrupted and demoralized, and we may, at length, look for the execution of that movement in the Valley which has always been an integral part of Gen. GRANT's programme of operations for the capture of Richmond.

Other cooperative moves, not now proper for public mention, may be expected; and those best informed of all the elements of the military situation feel the most assurances that we shall have Richmond before the Presidential election.

The New-York Times.

VOL. XIV.–NO. 4055. NEW-YORK, THURSDAY, SEPTEMBER 22, 1864. PRICE FOUR CENTS.

SHERMAN VS. HOOD.

THE UNION OCCUPATION OF ATLANTA.

Reply of Gen. Sherman to Gen. Hood.

HOOD VERY BADLY BEATEN ONCE MORE.

Abstract of the Entire Correspondence.

WASHINGTON, Wednesday, Sept. 21.

The following is the reply of Gen. SHERMAN to Gen. HOOD's charge of "studied and ungenerous cruelty," and which was received in Washington today:

HEADQUARTERS MILITARY DIVISION OF THE MISSISSIPPI AND IN THE FIELD, ATLANTA, Ga., Sept. 10, 1864.

Gen. J. B. Hood, Commanding Army of the Tennessee Confederate Army.

GENERAL—I have the honor to abknowledge the receipt of your letter of this date at the hands of Messrs. BALL and CREW, consenting to the arrangements I had proposed to facilitate the removal south of the people of Atlanta who prefer to go in that direction. I enclose you a copy of my orders, which will, I am satisfied accomplish my purpose perfectly. You style the measures proposed "unprecedented," and appeal to the dark history of war for a parallel as an act of "studied and ungenerous cruelty." It is not unprecedented, for Gen. JOHNSTON himself very wisely and properly removed the families all the way from Dalton down, and I see no reason why Atlanta should be excepted. Nor is it necessary to appeal to the dark history of war when recent and modern examples are so handy. You, yourself, burned dwelling-houses along your parapet, and I have seen to-day fifty houses that you have rendered uninhabitable because they stood in the way of your forts and men. You defended Atlanta on a line so close to the town that every cannon-shot and many musket shots from our line of investments, that overshot their mark, went into the habitations of women and children. Gen. HARDEE did the same at Jonesboro, and Gen. JOHNSTON did the same last Summer at Jackson, Miss. I have not accused you of heartless cruelty, but merely instance these cases of very recent occurrence, and could go on and enumerate hundreds of others, and challenge any fair man to judge which of us has the heart of pity for the families of a "brave people." I say it is a kindness to these families of Atlanta to remove them now at once from scenes that women and children should not be exposed to, and the brave people should scorn to commit their wives and children to the rude barbarians who thus, as you say, violate the laws of war, as illustrated in the pages of its dark history. In the name of common sense, I ask you not to appeal to a just God in such a sacrilegious manner—you, who, in the midst of peace and prosperity, have plunged a nation into civil war, "dark and cruel war," who dared and badgered us to battle, insulted our flag, seized our arsenals and forts that were left in the honorable custody of a peaceful ordnance sergeant, seized and made prisoners of war the very garrisons sent to protect your people against negroes and Indians, long before any overt act was committed by the (to you) hateful Lincoln Government, tried to force Kentucky and Missouri into the rebellion in spite of themselves, falsified the vote of Louisiana, turned loose your privateers to plunder unarmed ships, expelled Union families by the thousand, burned their houses, and declared by ac of your Congress the confiscation of all debts due Northern men for goods had and received. Talk thus to the marines but not to me, who have seen these things, and who will this day make as much sacrifice for the peace and honor of the South, as the best born Southerner among you. If we must be enemies, let us be men, and fight it out as we propose to-day, and not deal in such hypocritical appeals to God and humanity. God will judge us in due time, and he will pronounce whether it be more humane to fight with a town full of women and the families of a "brave people" at our back, or to remove them in time to places of safety among their own friends and people.

I am, very respectfully,
your obedient servant,
(Signed) W. T. SHERMAN,
Major-Gen. Commanding.

Official copy: Signed L. M. DAYTON, A. D. C.

CORRESPONDEECE BETWEEN GEN. SHERMAN AND GEN. HOOD.

From the Richmond Examiner, Sept. 19.

The Georgia papers bring us a considerable mass of correspondence which has lately taken place between Gen. SHERMAN and Gen. HOOD. As we have not space to give this correspondence in full, we present an abstract of it, which will serve every purpose.

We have official copies of the correspondence in regard to the truce of ten days recently entered into by Gens. SHERMAN and HOOD. In his letter to Gen. HOOD, SHERMAN says that he "deems it the interest of the United States that the citizens now residing in Atlanta should be removed; those who prefer, to go South, the rest North;" and if HOOD consents, he (SHERMAN) offers to undertake the removal of families in Atlanta who prefer to go South, as far as Rough and Ready. In regard to the slaves, the correspondence mentions as one of its conditions that servants may be permitted to accompany their masters, provided no force be used toward them, one way or the other; if they wish to go with their masters and mistresses, they can do so; otherwise they are sent away or employed by the Quartermasters. To carry out this object SHERMAN proposes a truce of ten days.

HOOD replies, saying that he does not consider that he has any alternative in the matter, and that he accepts the proposition. In closing his letter Gen. HOOD protests "in the name of the God of humanity against the expulsion of the people of Atlanta from their firesides," and declares, while he accepts it, that SHERMAN's position "transcends the studied and ingenious cruelty of all acts ever before brought to the attention of mankind, even in the darkest history of war."

The subject of correspondence number two is in regard to the exchange of prisoners held on both sides. The first letter comes from HOOD. He proposes "an exchange of prisoners, officers and men, captured by both armies since the commencement of the present campaign; the exchange to be made man for man, and the equivalents to be allowed as regarded by the stipulations of the cartel." SHERMAN replies to this, informing HOOD that he accepts his offer; the basis of exchange to be the old cartel. This is quickly followed by another letter from SHERMAN, saying that he cannot recall those prisoners who may have reached beyond Chattanooga; that on arriving at Nashville they properly fall under the jurisdiction of the Commissioner, Col. HOFFMAN; but proposing to exchange such as he has on hand. He says he holds on the spot twenty-eight officers and seven hundred and eighty-two enlisted men, and en route for Chattanooga ninety-three officers and nine hundred and seven men, making one thousand, eight hundred and ten on hand, that he will exchange for a like number of his own men, captured by HOOD in this campaign, who belong to regiments with him, and who can resume their places at once. He takes it for granted HOOD will do the same with his. In other words, for these men he (SHERMAN) is not willing to take equivalents belonging to other armies than his own, or who belong to regiments whose times are out and who have been discharged. SHERMAN further says that by the laws of the Confederate States all men eligible for service are *ipso facto* soldiers, and if needed for civil duty they are simply detailed soldiers; that he found in Atlanta "about a thousand of these fellows," and that he is satisfied they are fit subjects of exchange, and proposes if HOOD will release an equal number of their prisoners at Andersonville, he (SHERMAN) will gather these together and send them as prisoners, and will take for them men belonging to any part of the United States army, subject to HOOD's control.

HOOD replies to this, reminding SHERMAN that he had previously accepted his offer "to exchange prisoners of war in hand at this moment"; that there was no condition attached to the acceptance on SHERMAN's part of his offer to exchange prisoners, and that he (HOOD) regards it as obligatory to the extent of the number of prisonerrs repesented by SHERMAN to be within his jurisdiction. He says that SHERMAN's refusal to receive in exchange his soldiers belonging to regiments whose times are out, and who have been discharged, discloses a fixed purpose on the part of his Government to doom to hopeless captivity those prisoners whose term of service has expired or will soon expire; that the new principle which SHERMAN seeks to interpolate upon the cartel of our recpective Governments, as well as upon the laws and customs of war, will not be sanctioned by him; that all captives taken in war who owe no obligation to the captors must stand upon the same equal footing; that the volunteer of a day and the conscript for the war, who may be captured in war, are equally subject to all of the burthens and equally entitled to all of the rights secured by the laws of nations; that this principle is distinctly conceded in the cartel entered into by our respective Governments, and is sanctioned by reason, justice and the public law of all civilized nations. Gen. HOOD further says that SHERMAN's avowal that this class of soldiers (those whose term of service had expired) will not be exchanged is deeply regretted by him, and that he hopes that this declared policy of SHERMAN's Government will be reconsidered, as it is unjustly oppressive to those whom the hazards of military service has rendered prisoners, and is violative of the well-understood obligations assumed by a Government toward those who are enlisted in its service.

HOOD further informs SHERMAN that his offer to him to effect an exchange of prisoners captured during this campaign, was not only approved, but that the Government placed at his disposal for immediate exchange, man for man, all the prisoners at Andersonville.

HOOD renews to SHERMAN his offer to exchange prisoners as proposed in his first communication, and here the matter ends.

IMPORTANT INTELLIGENCE.

LATE NEWS FROM THE SOUTH.

A PEACE CONFERENCE AT ATLANTA.

Sherman Corresponding with Leading Rebels.

An Exchange of Prisoners Between Sherman and Hood.

THE WAR NEWS.

From the Richmond Examiner, Sept. 19.

The following dispatch from General LEE, received on Saturday, contains the most agreeable news since Gen. HILL beat the Yankees at Reams' Station:

"HEADQUARTERS ARMY OF NORTHERN VIRGINIA, September 17, 1864.

"Hon. J. A. Seddon, Secretary of War:

"At daylight yesterday the enemy's skirmish line, west of the Jerusalem plank-road, was driven back upon his intrenchments along their whole extent. Ninety prisoners were taken by us in the operation.

At the same hour Gen. HAMPTON attacked the enemy's position north of the Norfolk Railroad, near Sycamore Church, and captured about three hundred prisoners, some arms and wagons, a large number of horses and twenty-five hundred cattle.

Gen. GREGG attacked Gen. HAMPTON on his return in the afternoon, at Belchess' Mill, on the Jerusalem Plankroad, but was repulsed and driven back. Everything was brought off savely. Our entire loss does not exceed fifty men. R. E. LEE."

We are informed that General Hampton started for a point on James river, south of City Point, where he had learned the cattle were on pasture; but while on the march he intercepted a letter addressed to Grant, which contained the information that the cattle had been removed to Sycamore church. The letter also assured Grant that the beeves were of a very superior quality, and expressed apprehensions that the grazing in Prince George would be insufficient. General Hampton changed his route according to the information given by the intercepted epistle.

The affair on Thursday, in which the enemy attempted a reconnoisance in the direction of Poplar Spring church, was much more inconsiderable and insignificant than we had been led to suppose. If any fighting took place on this part of the line—west of the Weldon railroad—it was of so trifling a character as to be beneath General Lee's notice.

FROM THE VALLEY.

We have no news from the Valley. Well-informed persons from that section say an able and enterprising leader like HAMPTON is much needed by our cavalry.

FROM GEN. HOOD'S ARMY.

The telegraph informs us that a partial exchange of prisoners has been agreed upon between Gens. HOOD and SHERMAN.

There were rumors in the army on Saturday that SHERMAN had sent an informal message, requesting Vice-President STEVENS, Gov. BROWN and Confederate States Senator JOHNSON to come to Atlanta, and confer with him on the subject of peace. If SHERMAN sent any such message, he must be deluded into the idea that in capturing Atlanta he has subjugated the State. We trust he will be soon roughly wakened from this delusion.

The New-York Times.

VOL. XIV.—NO. 4057.   NEW-YORK, SUNDAY, SEPTEMBER 25, 1864.   PRICE FOUR CENTS.

SHERIDAN'S GREAT VICTORY.

Additional Official Accounts.

How the Battle of Fisher's Hill was Fought and Won.

Magnificent Gallantry of Our Troops.

The Rebels Throw Down their Arms and Run.

Sixty-two Hundred Prisoners Accounted for by Gen. Stevenson.

REBEL ACCOUNTS OF THE BATTLE.

A Disastrous Defeat Admitted.

OFFICIAL ANNOUNCEMENT FROM GEN. LEE.

WAR DEPARTMENT, WASHINGTON, Sept. 24 —10 A. M.
Maj. Gen. D x:

The following official dispatch has just been received from Gen. SHERIDAN, detailing some of the particulars of the battle and victory at Fisher's Hill:

HEADQUARTERS MIDDLE DIVISION,
Woodstock, Va., Sept. 23—8 A. M.

To Lieut.-Gen. U. S. Grant, City Point:

I cannot as yet give any definite account of the results of the battle of yesterday. Our loss will be light. Gen. CROOK struck the left flank of the enemy, doubled it up, and advanced down their lines. RICKETT's division of the Sixth Army Corps swung in, and joined CROOK. GETTY's and WHEATON's divisions took up the same movement, followed by the whole line, and, attacking beautifully, carried the works of the enemy.

The rebels threw down their arms and fled in the greatest confusion, abandoning most of their artillery. It was dark before the battle ended. I pursued on after the enemy during the night to this point with the Sixth and Nineteenth Corps, and have stopped here to rest the men and issue rations.

If Gen. TORBERT has pushed down the Luray Valley according to my directions, he will achieve great results.

I do not think that there ever was an army so badly routed. The Valley soldiers are hiding away and going to their homes.

I cannot at present give any estimate of prisoners. I pushed on regardless of everything. The number of pieces of artillery reported captured is sixteen.

P. H. SHERIDAN, Major-General.

You are directed to cause a national salute of one hundred great guns to be fired for the victory.

Gen. STEVENSON reports that 3,000 prisoners from the field had reached Winchester last night.

Confederate Lieutenant-General Jubal A. Early struggled with Union forces for control of the Shenandoah Valley through the summer of 1864.

Reinforcements and supplies have been forwarded by Gen. SHERIDAN.

EDWIN M. STANTON, Secretary of War.

Semi-Official Particulars.

WASHINGTON, Saturday, Sept. 24—12:30 P. M.

The *Republican* extra makes the following announcement:—The Government received dispatches from Gen. STEVENSON this A.M., dated Harper's Ferry, announcing that 2,000 Strasburgh prisoners reached Winchester last night. He also states that 1,600 of the prisoners captured on the 19th inst., near Winchester, arrived at Harper's Ferry this morning, and that 1,600 more are yet to come. A later dispatch received from Gen. STEVENSON this forenoon, announces that 1,600 more prisoners, captured at Strasburgh on the 22d, reached Winchester this morning. When last heard from, EARLY's army was flying down the Valley, panic-stricken. SHERIDAN is hot in pursuit, and near Woodstock.

REBEL ACCOUNTS.

A Defeat Admitted—Death of Gens. Rodes and Godwin—Fitz Lee Wounded.

THE WAR NEWS.

From the Richmond Dispatch, Sept. 22.

A report was in circulation at an early hour yesterday morning that a fight occurred near Winchester, in the Valley of Virginia, on Monday last, which resulted disastrously to the Confederate arms. As usual, when any unfavorable news is afloat, the grossest exaggerations prevailed, until the following official dispatch from Gen. LEE was given out by the authorities:

HEADQUARTERS ARMY NORTHERN VIRGINIA.
Tuesday, Sept. 20.

Hon. James A. Seddon:

Gen. EARLY reports that on the morning of the 10th, the enemy advanced on Winchester, near which place he met his attack, which was resisted from early in the day till near night, when he was compelled to retire. After night he fell back to Newtown, and this morning to Fisher's Hill.

Our loss reported to be severe.

Major-Gen. RODES and Brig.-Gen. GODWIN were killed, nobly doing their duty.

Three pieces of artillery, of KING's battalion, were lost.

The trains and supplies were brought off safely.

(Signed,)   R. E. LEE.

Newton, the point to which our forces fell back on Monday night, is about eight miles this side of Winchester, at the intersection of the Valley turnpike and White Post roads. Fisher's Hill is adjacent

Colonel John S. Mosby, famed leader of "Mosby's Confederacy," a daring guerrilla cavalry band that plagued Federal troops throughout the Shenandoah Valley.

to Strasburgh, some eight miles south of Newtown. We have no further particulars of the battle than furnished by the official dispatch, except that Major-Gen. FITZ LEE received a painful, though not dangerous, flesh wound in the thigh.

SHERIDAN, having been reinforced from GRANT's army, was enabled to bring overwhelming numbers against the Confederates, who resisted nearly an entire day before falling back, and the fact that our trains and supplies were brought off safely, shows that it was no rout.

As in all other engagements of magnitude, we have to mourn the loss of many brave officers and men, the most prominent among whom is Maj.-Gen. ROBERT E. RODES, who fell nobly doing his duty. Maj.-Gen. RODES was born in Lynchburgh, Va.; was the son of DAVID RODES, and at the time of his death was about thirty-four years of age. He received a military education, and was for some time an assistant Professor in the Virginia Military Institute. Subsequently, in the capacity of Civil Engineer, he was engaged in the construction of various railroads in the South, and located at Tuskeegee, Ala., where he married. On the breaking out of the war, he came to Virginia as Captain of an Alabama company, and, winning distinction by meritorious conduct in the field, rose rapidly from this rank to that of Brigadier. In conformity with a dying request of Gen. T. J. JACKSON, he was subsequently made a Major-General, and appointed to the command of a division, a position which he has filled with honor to himself, and was justly esteemed as one of the most brave and gallant spirits of our army.

Brig.-Gen. ARCHIBALD C. GODWIN was a native of Nansemond County, Va. He was in California at the time of the breaking out of the war, but left for Virginia immediately upon her secession and offered his services to his country. He was assigned to the command of the military prison at Salisbury, N. C., and afterward had charge of the prison in Richmond. Receiving the appointment of Provost-Marshal of this city, he discharged the arduous duties of the position with much credit, but resigned and returned to Salisbury and raised the Fifty-seventh North Carolina Regiment, of which he was appointed Colonel. He led the command through many hard-fought battles, and was finally wounded and taken prisoner. Soon after his exchange he was made a Brigadier, and at once returned to the field, where he had been actively and arduously engaged up to the time of his death. His age was about thirty-six years. It is thought that his remains will be brought to Richmond for interment.

FROM PETERSBURGH.

On some portions of the lines in front of Petersburgh, within the past few days, the picket firing and mortar shelling have been quite brisk, and it is believed that a considerable number of the foe have fallen victims to the unerring aim of our sharpshooters. This was particularly the case on Tuesday, but beyond this nothing of importance occurred, nor was there any change in the general situation. The Yankees have heard of the capture of a large number of cattle by Gen. HAMPTON, and in their accounts are content with the reflection that "a large number of the raiders are reported to have been captured, with some of the cattle." It is said, however, that the Yankee officers are sorely nettled in consequence of the event, as good beef is scarce among them, and the chances of supplying the empty cattle-pens are slim indeed. Meanwhile our boys are enjoying the steaks and roasts, and unanimously vote Gen. HAMPTON a most skillful commissary.

On our extreme right—the enemy's left—both parties continue to watch one another with sleepless vigilance. Each returning day adds strength to the defensive works, and the tug of war, come when it may, will be one of the bloodiest of this very bloody contest.

It is a notorious fact that GRANT has, up to a very recent period, been giving his troops rations of whisky, and has frequently carried them into battle under the inspiration of this "Dutch courage," fearing to trust their natural qualities in this respect. We learn that he has changed his system entirely, and that an order has been issued positively prohibiting the bringing within the lines of the armies operating against Richmond of any spirituous, vinous, or malt liquors, except such as are brought by the commissary or medical departments. Probably GRANT thinks that he, with BUTLER's help, can do drinking enough for the whole army, and hence the withdrawal of the whisky rations from the "rank and file."

We perceive that the army commanded by Beast BUTLER, on the Southside, is now officially recognized by the Yankee War Department as the "Army of the James."

A report was brought over by the ambulance train last evening that the enemy yesterday made a feeble attack upon our advanced works and was repulsed. It is proper to state, however, that persons who arrived at a later hour had heard nothing of it. The usual cannonading took place on the lines yesterday morning.

FROM GEORGIA.

A letter from Lovejoy's Station, dated the 16th instant, gives the latest intelligence from Georgia as follows:

The court of inquiry in relation to the loss of stores at Atlanta has been concluded. There are rumors in camp of several important official changes, transfers, &c., of too visionary a nature to be made the subject of newspaper gossip. Major EUSTIS is temporarily acting chief of staff of this army.

A number of ladies arrived at headquarters, applicants for permits to go through the lines. The inspector-general's office is besieged daily with citizen visitors; and the acknowledged patience and good temper of that energetic official are sorely tried by a thousand and one importunities for personal favors from a thousand and one of the most impracticable and unreasonable sort of people.

The flag-of-truce letters sent forward under the auspices of Major CLAIR, Confederate truce officer, have been permitted to pass. Also, a few telegraphic dispatches have been permitted over the Federal wires to Nashville, and replies received within twelve hours.

An exchange of prisoners, two thousand on each side, has been effected between our Commissioner of Exchange, Col. G. A. HENRY, and Col. WARNER, of SHERMAN's army. After the necessary preliminaries, the two thousand Federal prisoners will be brought forward, and an equal number of Confederates from the other side, for exchange.

Gen. HOOD appears to be in as cheerful a flow of spirits as his brave and patriotic veterans. I saw him to-day surrounded by a group of major-generals and brigadiers, in social converse, under an oak tree. Where the next campaign will be is scarcely ever discussed. At present, there are no evidences of a movement. But I have reason to predict that before many moons have waned, the Federals will hear of HOOD and his army through quite a novel and unexpected channel.

FROM ATLANTA.

The Future of the Place—At what Cost it was Won—Col. Ireland.

Correspondence of the New York Times.

HEADQUARTERS 2D DIVISION, 20TH CORPS,
ATLANTA, GA., Sept. 10, 1864.

After a storm there comes a calm. Now that Atlanta is in our possession, and the famed city having passed through the ordeal of a months' shelling, has ceased to be an object of attack or defense, we may sit quietly within its shady precincts and talk of its value and its cost. The rebel army beaten and pursued thirty miles southward, will be "let alone" for a few days to enjoy its own reflections. We shall pause awhile to rest and estimate our gains. Deep into the central portion of the largest and most populous of the Gulf States the Union Army has penetrated and established itself securely. We have set up our tabernacle and hung out our banners on the outer walls of this city. Henceforth Atlanta shall be a Union city, for all its citizens who acknowledge sympathy for the Confederate cause must emigrate southward within a few days. So says Gen. SHERMAN, and he has excellent notions of what is best.

Four months of steady unremitting pursuit of a single object; of patient, intelligent toil and fighting; of sleepless nights and restless days, by an army of noble men under an able leader, have been crowned with a success of which we may well be proud, and for which our fellow citizens at home should rejoice with thanksgiving. Our losses have been heavy, but are not disproportionate to our gains.

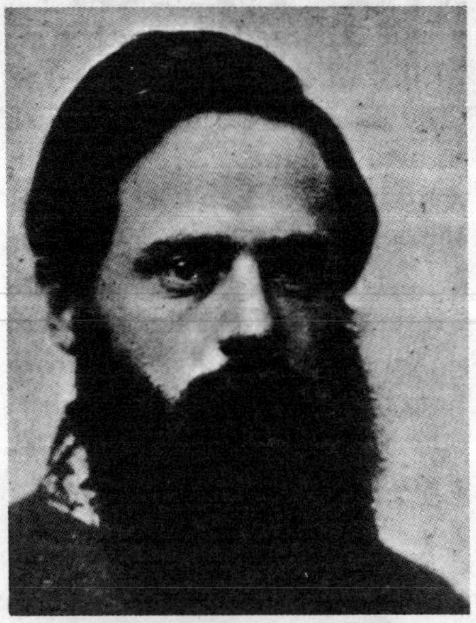

Major-General Fitzhugh Lee was a Confederate casualty at Fisher's Hill.

It is true that back over the bloody forest-path we have trodden for many leagues, fresh mounds of earth concealing lifeless forms of brave men are thickly scattered. In many a wild and dismal glen rearward,

"Each tree which guards its darkness from the day,
Waves o'er a warrior's tomb."

But the dead warriors are not all of one stripe. Beside the patriot in blue, there lies his traitor foe in garb of gray, all strife between them hushed. These are they to whom no sound of victory or defeat shall come; for whom peace shall bring no earthly blessing, and whose footsteps shall no more be heard on the threshold of home. Turn we then to the brighter side of the picture,—to that view of the "situation" which gives hope and good cheer to loyal, Union-loving citizens everywhere. The right arm of the iniquitous Confederacy is broken, its prospects gulfward are dark and threatening, and its inter-communication is severed. We desire no armistice, we cannot afford it; for the sword which we grasped to maintain our national honor and unity, shall in due time give us a lasting peace. We are ready to negotiate on the basis of submission to the government and laws of the United States. The graves of the dead shall be our shrine for repentance, and we will plant around them the cypress and yew trees, as emblems of our mourning.

Columns of Federal troops are entering the city or passing through hourly, accompanied by soul-stirring music and streaming banners. The ladies of Atlanta look on the war-stained heroes with much apparent interest and curiosity. As in HOMER's account of a bridal procession, so here it may be truthfully said:

"Through the fair streets the matrons in a row
Stand in the porches and enjoy the show."

Passing through one of the principal streets, today, I saw an old frame building, bearing a sign, on which, in large letters, were the words, "Auction Sales of Negroes." A shell had passed entirely through the edifice, making a hole into which a man could easily crawl. The spectacle suggested the thought that the Union gun which sent the angry messenger with command of thunder, was but uttering the condemnation of God and the civilized world, against the diabolical traffic. It was like a thunderbolt from Heaven speaking for humanity, and carrying destruction to the accursed tenement wherein the dearest rights of man had often been violated.

In the battle near 'Jonesboro', the gallantry of the Fourteenth Corps was especially marked. They charged upon and carried three lines of the enemy's works successively. After the series of battles at and near Jonesboro', and the surrender of Atlanta, our army was withdrawn from its advanced positions and is now being established in Atlanta and important points contiguous, for rest and recuperation. The rebel papers will doubtless chronicle this action on the part of Gen. SHERMAN, as a retreat from Jonesboro', resulting from a defeat at that place. Nothing could be further from the truth. We had captured Atlanta and had most seriously crippled HOOD's army, and these results accomplished, fortune, humanity and the welfare of his army dictated to Gen. SHERMAN the propriety of giving his veterans rest.

Four months of most arduous service have justly entitled them to a few weeks of relaxation, during which their rugged clothing may be put off for garments new and clean; shoeless feet may be comfortably shod, arms and accoutrements put in order for another campaign, and the paymasters have an opportunity to dispense their temporal blessings so well and nobly earned.

Col. DAVID IRELAND, for a long time commanding a brigade in GEARY's division, died of dysentery this morning.

Though much enfeebled, he lived to enter the city in triumph at the head of his brigade, and participate in the success to which he had so worthily contributed. He was formerly an officer in the Seventy-ninth New-York Volunteers, by whom he was much esteemed.

The officers of this corps who were so fortunate as to make the acquaintance of his young and accomplished wife, during her short stay with the command last Winter, take this opportunity to publicly express their condolence and sympathy for her in this bereavement.

The congratulatory orders of President LINCOLN, of Lieut.-Gen. GRANT, and last of all the admirable testimonial of Gen. SHERMAN to the troops of his command, have been most eminently gratifying to the whole army. NICKAJACK.

The Georgia State Troops.

IMPORTANT PROCLAMATION FROM THE GOVERNOR OF GEORGIA.

EXECUTIVE DEPARTMENT,
MILLEDGEVILLE, Sept. 10, 1864.

Gen. J. B. Hood, Commanding Army of Tennessee:

GENERAL: As the militia of the State were called out for the defence of Atlanta during the campaign against it, which has terminated by the fall of the city into the hands of the enemy, and as many of them left their homes without preparation, expecting to be gone but a few weeks, who have remained in service over three months, (most of the time in the trenches,) justice requires that they be permitted, while the enemy are preparing for the Winter campaign, to return to their homes and look, for a time, after important interests and prepare themselves for such service as may be required when another campaign commences against other important points in the State. I, therefore, hereby withdraw said organization from your command, in the hope that I shall be able to return it with greater numbers and equal efficiency, when the interests of the public service requires it. In this connection, I beg leave to tender to you, General, my sincere thanks for your impartiality to the State troops, and for your uniform courtesy and kindness to me individually. With assurances of my high consideration and esteem, I am, very respectfully, your obedient servant,

JOSEPH E. BROWN.

THE SOUTHERN MILITARY PRISONS.

Inquiry by the United States Sanitary Commission—Confirmatory Account of the Martyrdom of our Soldiers in the South.

From the Philadelphia Press, Sept. 24.

On May 19 last, Dr. VALENTINE MOTT, the eminent savant and medical professor; Dr. ELLERSLIE WALLACE, Professor in Jefferson College of this city; Dr. EDWARD DELAFIELD, President of the New-York College of Physicians; Hon. J. I. CLARK HARE, the distinguished Judge of the District Court; Rev. TREADWELL WALDEN, Rector of St. Clement's Church, of this city; and GOUVERNEUR MORRIS WILKINS, Esq., of New-York, were appointed a Committee of Inquiry by the United States Sanitary Commission to make investigation of the terrible reports of suffering which had reached the public from the prisons of the South, and to furnish to our people and the world an authentic statement of facts. This report is at length ready for the public in the remarkable pamphlet before us. It is the digested narrative of a volume of consistent testimony, which will be appended to the report of the Committee. Let us say here that the character of this body of gentlemen is eminently above reproach. They number three distinguished professors of medicine, one of our most estimable judges, and a well known minister of the Gospel.

THE RETURNED PRISONERS.

The condition of our prisoners at Annapolis has already been reported in these columns in a brief, but very suggestive communication from ELLERSLIE WALLACE, M. D., and by testimony of Miss DELIA DIX, whose noble ministration in our hospitals is well known. The present report intensifies the picture presented with so much feeling by Dr. WALLACE. "It was strange to find a Hercules in bones; to see the immense hands of a young giant pendant from *limbs thinner than a child's*, and that could be spanned with the thumb and finger. * * * Men in one part shriveled to nothing but skin and bones, and in another swollen and misshapen with dropsy or scurvy * * * the stomach fallen in, deep as a basin, and the bone protruding through a blood-red hole in the hip!" There were many like these, and even worse where all was so horrible and sickening, that the pen almost refuses its duty. The photographs of skeletons lately handed around through the North are only pictures of the hopeful cases. Hundreds died from utter weakness and starvation—scores grew insane or imbecile. There was a fearful *amount* of this ghastly and awful misery in the prisoners at Annapolis. In the countenances of some of the best cases there was a "look of utter desolateness, of settled melancholy, as if they had passed through a period of physical agony which had driven the smile from their faces forever." Contrast with this piteous picture the boasted chivalry of the South, and the civilization and Christianity of the age.

LIBBY PRISON.

The rooms are one hundred feet by forty. In six of these twelve hundred United States officers of all grades, from brigadier down, were confined for months. This was the almost incredible space allowed them in which to cook, eat, wash, sleep and take exercise. Ten feet by two claimed by each man for all the purposes of living! At one time they were not allowed benches or stools, or even to fold their blankets and sit upon them, but forced to huddle "like slaves in the middle passage;" at another only allowed to make stools out of the barrels and boxes they received from the North; at all times overrun by vermin, in spite of constant ablutions, no clean blankets ever being issued by the rebels; and lying down at night, according to Libby phrase, "wormed and dove-tailed together like fish in a basket." There were two stoves, and seventy-five windows, all broken, and in Winter the cold was intense. Every prisoner had a cough from the damp or cold. It was among the rules that no prisoner should go within three feet of the window, a rule extremely difficult to observe in the crowded prisons of the South. Often, by accident, or unconsciously, an officer would go near a window, and be instantly shot at. In the Pemberton Buildings, near by, as many as fourteen shots were fired in a single day, and very frequently a prisoner fell killed or wounded. It became a matter of sport to "kill a Yankee." Once the guard caught sight of Lieut. Hammond's hat through a boarded enclosure, where there were no windows, and came within an inch of murdering him. Major Turner, the keeper of Libby, remarked, "The boys are in want of practice." The sentry said "he had made a bet he would kill a d——d Yankee before he came off guard." Almost every prisoner had such an incident to tell. Throughout the Southern prison system it is a regular sport to kill Yankees. The guards were never reproved for their willingness to commit murder.

The daily ration in the officers' quarters of Libby Prison was a small loaf of bread, about the size of a man's fist, made of Indian meal. Sometimes it was made from wheat flour, but of variable quality. It weighed a little over half a pound. With it was given a piece of beef weighing two ounces. "I would *gladly*," said an officer, "have preferred the horse-feed in my father's stable." The corn bread began to be of the roughest and coarsest description. Portions of the cob and husk were often found ground in with the meal. The crust was so thick and hard that the prisoners called it iron-clad. To render the bread eatable they grated it, and made mush out of it, but the crust they could not grate. Now and then, after long intervals, often of many weeks, a little meat was given them, perhaps two or three mouthfuls. At a later period they received a pint of black peas, with some vinegar, every week. The peas were often full of worms, or maggots in a chrysalis state, which, when they made soup, floated on the surface.

Those who were entirely dependent on the prison fare, and who had no friends at the North to send them boxes of food, began to suffer the horrible agony of craving food, and feeling themselves day by day losing strength. Dreams and delusions began to distract their minds. "I grew so foolish in my mind," said Capt. CALHOUN, "that I used to blame myself for not eating more when at home. The subject of food engrossed my whole thoughts."

But the most unaccountable and shameful act of all was yet to come. Shortly after this general diminution of rations, in the month of January last, the boxes, which before had been regularly delivered, and in good order, were withheld. No reason was given. Three hundred arrived every week, and were received by Col. OULD, Commissioner of Exchange, but instead of being distributed, were retained, and piled up in warehouses near by, and in full sight of the tantalized and hungry captives, to the number of 3,000 at least. At length, five or six were distributed during the week! Scores were stolen.

For offences, trivial or serious, prisoners were consigned to cells beneath the prison, the walls of which were damp, green and slimy. They were never warmed, and often so crowded, that some were obliged to stand up all night. Dead bodies, too, were placed in the cellar, and very often were partly devoured by hogs, dogs, and rats. At the time of KILPATRICK's raid, some negroes pointed to the cellar: "Dug big hole down dar, massa—torpedo in dar, *sure!*" "Should KILPATRICK succeed in entering Richmond," said RICHARD TURNER, "the prison authorities would blow up the prison and all its inmates." "There is enough there to send every Yankee to hell," LIEUTENANT LATOUCHE was overheard to say. TURNER himself said, in the presence of Col. FARNSWORTH, in answer to the question, "Was the prison mined?" "Yes, and I would have blown you all to Hades before I would have suffered you to be rescued." The remarks of Bishop JOHNS is corroborative as well as curious, in reply to the question, "Whether it was a Christian mode of warfare to blow up defenceless prisoners?" "I suppose the authorities are satisfied on that point, though I do not mean to justify it." This passed comment. It is also well to remember that the Inspector of Libby, RICHARD TURNER, was a negro-whipper by trade.

BELLE ISLE.

Here is an inclosure variously estimated to be from three to six acres in extent, surrounded by an earthwork about three feet high, with a ditch on either side. The interior has something of the look of an encampment, a number of Sibley tents being set in rows, with "streets" between. These tents, rotten, torn, full of holes—poor shelter at any rate—accommodated only a small proportion. From ten to twelve thousand men have been imprisoned in this small space at one time, turned into the inclosure, like so many cattle, to find what resting-place they could. So crowded were they that, at the least, according to the estimated area given them, there could have been but a space two feet by seven, and, at the most, three feet by nine, per man—hardly a generous allotment even for a "hospitable grave."

Some were so fortunate as to find shelter in the tents, but even they were often wet with the rain, and almost frozen when Winter set in. Every day some places were made vacant by diseases or by death, as some were taken to the hospital, and some to burial. But thousands had no tents and no shelter of any kind. Nothing was provided for their accommodation. Lumber was plenty in a country of forests, but not a cabin or shed was built, or allowed to be built. Here thousands lay, with the sand for their beds and the sky for their covering, under fog, rain, cold, snow, hundreds blanketless, coatless and shoeless, others with ragged and rotten clothes. There were few fires and little shelter. A severe Winter came, in which the mercury was down to zero even at Memphis, and water left in buckets on Belle Isle froze two or three inches deep in the night. The snow lay deep on the ground around Richmond. The ice formed in the James and flowed in masses upon the rapids, on either side of the Island.

The men resorted to every expedient to keep from perishing. They lay in the ditch, as the most protected piece, heaped upon one another and lying close together, as one of them expressed it, "like hogs in Winter," taking turns as to who should have the outside of the row. In the morning, the row of the previous night was marked by the motionless forms of those "who were sleeping on in their last sleep"—*frozen to death!*

Every day, during the Winter season, numbers were conveyed away stiff and stark, having fallen asleep in everlasting cold. Some of the men dug holes in the sand in which to take refuge. All through the night crowds of them were heard running up and down, to keep themselves from freezing. And this fate threatened them even more than it would have threatened most men exposed to an equally severe temperature, even with such thin clothing and inadequate shelter—*for they were starving!*

Rock-like husky corn-bread (specimens of which we have seen,) meat often tainted, and suspiciously like mule meat; two or three spoonfuls of rotten beans; soup thin and briny, often with worms floating on the surface, made up their food. None of these were given together, and the whole ration was never one half the quantity necessary for bare life. Hear the words of the prisoners:

"There was no name for our hunger." "I was hungry; pretty nearly starved to *death*." "I waked up one night and found myself *gnawing my coat sleeve*." "I used to *dream* of having something good to eat." "I walked the *streets* for many a night; I could not sleep for hunger." "I lost flesh and strength for want of food." "*If I were to sit here a week I could not tell you half our suffering.*" These sentences form the very poem of misery and starvation.

"Lice were in all their quarters." Vermin and dirt incrusted their bodies. They were sore with lying in the sand. None, not even the sufferers with diarrhoea, were allowed to visit the sinks during the night, and in the morning the ground was covered and saturated with filth. The wells were tainted; the air was filled with disgusting odors.

Many were taken sick daily, but were allowed to suffer for days before they were removed to the hospitals; and when this was done, it was often so late that the half of them died before reaching it, or at the very moment their names were being recorded.

There was a hospital tent on the island, which was always full of the sick. It had no floor; the sick and dying were laid on straw, and logs were their only pillows. "If you or I saw a horse dying," said one, "wouldn't we put some straw under his head? Would we let him beat his head on a log in his agony?"

THE HOSPITALS.

The hospitals for our prisoners were virtually worse than the prisons themselves. Dr. FERGUSON testifies that, while the wounded were under treatment, the nourishment and stimulation they received were not sufficient to give them a proper chance for recovery. I am surprised that *more* do not die. Bedding and covering were very dirty and offensive. In three months, out of 2,800 patients, about 1,400 died. The hospitals were nothing less than hospitals for murder.

PHYSICAL CONDITION OF THE REBELS—THE PRISONS IN THE NORTH.

The investigations of the Commission, based on rebel and general testimony, conclusively show that no excuse can be found in the poverty and sufferings of the rebels for this fearful condition of things. The rebels have uniformly testified that they had, generally, good rations, and were well fed. It must be remembered that the cruelty of the rebel prisons is systematic, incessant and regular, however bad it may be. The rations of the rebel soldier was infinitely superior to that of Libby prison, or how could he have endured the marches, fatigue and hardships of so many severe campaigns? There is no room to doubt that the rebel army itself was fully if not abundantly supplied with the common necessaries.

The prisons of the North were next examined by the committee, and in this connection we have the copious and accurate observations of so respectable a gentleman as Judge HARR. We need not say that our rebel prisoners are well, and even kindly and carefully treated in all the particulars in which the rebel authorities are so barbarously cruel. The rations are better than those usually given to rebel soldiers. They have room to walk, to play and to live. Fort Delaware is but a common instance of this. The prisoners are required to be cleanly, and to bathe in squads in the river. They live in good health, and even in good humor, finding amusement in their condition, and a tolerable life among themselves. This part of the committee's inquiry is full and conscientious, and furnishes a strange and marvellous contrast to the treatment of our prisoners in Richmond. We may accept the report as history.

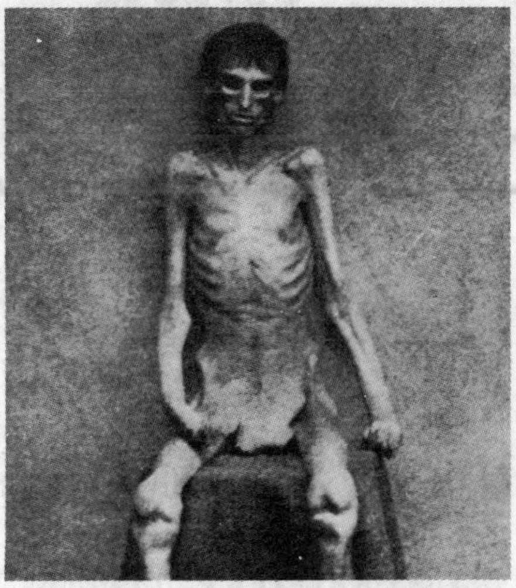

Reports of inhuman treatment of prisoners throughout Southern prisons were confirmed with photos such as this one, an emaciated captive in Andersonville, Georgia. Northern institutions were also far from perfect.

FROM NEWBERN.

Mails Received—Abatement of Fever—Arrival of Refugees—Federal Deserters in North Carolina.

NEW-YORK, Saturday, Sept. 24.

By the arrival of the United States steamer *Albany*, via Fort Monroe, we have North Carolina dates to the 22d inst.

The steamer *Fawn*, which was recently captured and burned by the enemy, contained the Boston mail of the 4th and 5th inst., and the New-York mail of the 5th and 6th inst., a large portion of which has been received from the wreck and brought to Newbern.

A flag of truce recently brought into Newbern a large number of refugees, many of whom belong to the first families of the State, who are on their way North, having lost all confidence in the Confederate cause since the fall of Atlanta. Among the number was the wife of the rebel Gen. MARTIN.

The Wilmington and Weldon Railroad advertise a dividend at 10 per cent.

The Salisbury (N. C.) *Watchman* has the following:

We protest against the inhuman treatment extended to the Yankee deserters, who are subjected to a course of treatment, which makes life far more uncertain than the battle field itself. A general pardon from LINCOLN would doubtless relieve the Confederacy of at least fifty thousand of these miserable beings, provided they have strength enough left to enable them to make their escape North.

"The five Federal officers, consisting of a Colonel, Lieut.-Colonel, Major and two Captains, who were dishonorably expelled by Gen. SHERMAN from the army, and sent into the rebel lines for speaking disrespectfully of the President of the United States in the presence of the enemy, while accompanying a flag of truce, have arrived in Richmond, where they are to be confined during the war, for fighting against their principles."

The sudden appearance of the congestive chills and billious fever in Newbern, has driven all the transient persons out of the department, including many established business men, who supposed they were fleeing from the yellow fever. Surgeon D. W. HAND, Medical Director, Surgeon R. J. METHINGER, Chairman of the Board of Health, and Dr. DOUGHERTY, Post Surgeon, including the other Surgeons at Newbern, who have been employed night and day, making every exertion possible to subdue the malady, are, through their skill and untiring labors, meeting with gratifying success, and now have the satisfaction of seeing a material abatement of this disease, which had assumed the form of an epidemic."

The New-York Times.

VOL. XIV.—NO. 4080.   NEW-YORK, FRIDAY, OCTOBER 21, 1864.   PRICE FOUR CENTS.

VICTORY!

Another Great Battle in the Valley.

Longstreet Whipped by Sheridan.

VICTORY WRESTED FROM DEFEAT.

The Rebel Attack at First Successful.

Timely Arrival of Gen. Sheridan.

THE REBELS THEN UTTERLY DEFEATED.

Forty-three Pieces of Artillery Captured.

Many Prisoners and a Large Number of Wagons Taken.

Gen. Bidwell Killed, and Gens. Wright, Ricketts and Grover Wounded.

The Rebel Gen. Ramseur Wounded and a Prisoner.

[OFFICIAL.]

War Department,
Thursday, Oct. 20—10.45 A. M.

A great battle was fought, and a splendid victory won by SHERIDAN over LONGSTREET, yesterday, at Cedar Creek.

Forty-three pieces of artillery were captured and many prisoners, among them the rebel General. RAMSEUR.

On our side Gens. WRIGHT and RICKETTS were wounded, and Gen. BIDWELL killed.

Particulars, so far as received, will be forwarded as fast as the operator can transmit them.

EDWIN M. STANTON,
Secretary of War.

SECOND DISPATCH.

[OFFICIAL.]

War Department, Washington,
Thursday, Oct. 20—10.45 A. M.

Maj.-Gen. Dix:

Another great battle was fought yesterday at Cedar Creek, threatening at first a great disaster, but finally resulting in a victory for the Union forces under Gen. SHERIDAN, more splendid than any heretofore achieved. The Department was advised yesterday evening of the commencement of the battle by the following telegrams:

Rectertown, Va.,
Wednesday, Oct. 19—4 P.M.

Maj.-Gen. H. W. Halleck, Chief of Staff:

Heavy cannonading has recommenced in the valley, and is now going on.

(Signed,) C. C. AUGUR, Major-General.

Harper's Ferry, Va.—6:40 P. M.,
Wednesday, Oct. 19.

Hon. E. M. Stanton, Secretary of War:

Firing at the front has been continuous during the day. The direction seemed at intervals to be to the left of Winchester, as if at Berry's Ferry. No news from the front.

(Signed,) JOHN D. STEVENSON,
Brigadier-General.

Harper's Ferry, Va.—8:45 P. M.,
Wednesday, Oct. 19.

Hon. Edwin M. Stanton, Secretary of War:

The enemy attacked our army with great impetuosity this morning at daylight.

The attack was made on the left of the Eighth Corps, and was at first successful, they capturing some guns, prisoners and wagons.

Our line was reformed and heavy fighting continued through the day.

SHERIDAN was reported at Winchester this morning, and went out to the front.

The particulars received are not official, and are not favorable, though no serious disaster could have occurred without direct news from SHERIDAN.

Respectfully,

(Signed) JOHN D. STEVENSON,
Brigadier-General.

Matters remain in the doubtful state represented by the foregoing telegrams until this morning, at 9:30, when the following telegram was received, unofficially, reporting the great victory won by SHERIDAN'S army:

Harper's Ferry, Va., Thursday,
Oct. 20—9:30 A. M.

News from SHERIDAN'S headquarters at midnight is to the effect that the enemy surprised our forces yesterday morning, driving the command in some confusion this side of Newtown, capturing artillery and prisoners.

SHERIDAN arrived in the field reorganized our forces, drove the enemy beyond Strasburg, capturing, it is reported, forty-three pieces of artillery, one hundred wagons and ambulances, and some two thousand prisoners.

The rout of the enemy is said to be complete. This is not official, but I think reliable.

(Signed) J. D. STEVENSON,
Brigadier-General.

A few minutes later the following official report of his victory was received from Maj. Gen. SHERIDAN:

Cedar Creek, Wednesday, Oct. 19, 10 P. M.

To Lieut. Gen. Grant, City Point:

I have the honor to report that my army at Cedar Creek was attacked this morning before daylight and my left was turned and driven in confusion.

In fact most of the line was driven in confusion, with the loss of twenty pieces of artillery.

I hastened from Winchester, where I was, on my return from Washington, and found the armies between Middletown and Newtown, having been driven back about four miles.

I here took the affair in hand, and quickly united the corps, formed a compact line of battle just in time to repulse an attack of the enemy, which was handsomely done at about 1 P. M.

At 3 P. M., after some changes of the cavalry from the left to the right flank, I attacked with great vigor, driving and routing the enemy, capturing, according to the last report, forty-three pieces of artillery and very many prisoners.

I do not know yet the number of my casualties or the losses of the enemy.

Wagons, trains, ambulances and caissons in large numbers are in our possession.

They also burned some of their trains.

Gen. RAMSEUR is a prisoner in our hands, severely and perhaps mortally wounded.

I have to regret the loss of Gen. BIDWELL killed, and Gens. WRIGHT, GROVER and RICKETTS wounded. WRIGHT is slightly wounded.

Affairs, at times, looked badly, but by the gallantry of our brave officers and men disaster has been converted into a splendid victory.

Darkness again intervened to shut off greater results.

I now occupy Strasburgh.

As soon as obtained, I will send you further particulars.

(Signed,) P. A. SHERIDAN, Maj. Gen.

The battle was fought on the same day, 19th of the month, that witnessed SHERIDAN'S victory in September.

What the numbers were opposed to Gen. SHERIDAN are not yet reported to the Department, but the boldness, vigor and success of the attack strongly indicate that a heavy reinforcement had been sent from Richmond, with the expectation of fulfilling LONGSTREET'S boast to smash up SHERIDAN.

LONGSTREET was known to be in the Valley, and had assumed command of the rebel army, and confident hopes of an overwhelming disaster to the Union army were boastfully expressed for several days back by the rebel adherents in Washington and Baltimore.

EDWIN M. STANTON,
Secretary of War.

THE LATEST.

Baltimore, Thursday, Oct. 20.

We have no additional particulars from the Valley; but all we hear is to the effect that SHERIDAN'S victory over LONGSTREET was most complete. The number of guns captured are understood to include the recapture of those which we lost in the morning.

The rebels are said to have continued their retreat rapidly up the Valley, being with their loss of trains and artillery in no condition to make a successful stand against SHERIDAN'S victorious troops.

THE ST. ALBANS' RAID.

Capture of a Portion of the Raiders—Recovery of $50,000.

Burlington, Thursday, Oct. 20.

Eight of the raiders who entered St. Albans and robbed the banks and murdered the citizens, have been caught, and $50,000 recovered. They were caught at Stanbridge and Farnham, Canada East. The remainder have been seen on the road and will probably also be arrested.

Rebel Raid into Vermont—Great Excitement at the Capital of the State—Organizing for Defence—The Legislature Enlist as Soldiers.

Correspondence of the New-York Times.

Montpelier, Vt.,
Wednesday, Oct. 19, 1864—6 P. M.

For the last two hours the most intense excitement has prevailed here, in consequence of news received by telegraph of a rebel raid into the village of St. Albans. St. Albans is about sixty miles north of Montpelier, and connected with it by mail and telegraph. The Legislature, now holding its annual session here, had just adjourned for the day when intelligence of the raid was received. The first appearance of anything unusual was the sight of the messengers, clerks, and various officials connected with the two Houses and the State offices, hurrying with rapid steps from hotel to hotel evidently in great haste and perturbation. The news soon got abroad that the Governor had received dispatches saying that a rebel force was burning and plundering St. Albans, the village, by-the-way, where he has his own residence and home. It was about 4 o'clock, or a little after, when the dispatch was received, and in a very few minutes the two Houses, in obedience to the summons of His Excellency, Gov. SMITH, had assembled in the Representatives Hall. They communicated to the dispatches arrived, which simply states that a party of rebels had robbed the banks of St. Albans, and were murdering its citizens. The Governor furthermore communicated the intelligence that issued orders for two hundred soldiers of the invalid corps stationed here and at Burlington, to go forward immediately, also that he had directed the citizens of Burlington (about thirty-five miles north of this place, and the largest and finest village of Vermont) to organize for defence. He furthermore added that he had ordered 2,000 stand of arms to be forwarded from Brottleboro, and had given authority for the immediate enlistment of a company here in Montpelia.

Under these circumstances, it may well be supposed there was a good deal of excitement. How great this rebel force might be was unknown. It might be large enough to advance, laying waste the finest portions of the State. The Legislature, considering that Gov. SMITH had taken prompt measures, resolved to do all they could to second his efforts. They adjourned their informal meeting, and I believe nearly all of them at once enlisted in the company gathered hastily here with the intention of moving forward to the scene of conflict. Up to 5 o'clock matters were in this position, and neither the Governor nor the telegraph operator could give any additional intelligence. The railroad trains were detained here, a portion of the soldiers of the Invalid Corps were hastened to the cars, and citizens of the town and members of the Legislature were in line, preparatory to as efficient organization as could be hastily made. The reasonable supposition was, that the wires of the telegraph had been cut by the raiding party near St. Albans, and the dispatches received were all that could be hurried through before the telegraph office was seized by the raiders.

At about 5 o'clock Gov. SMITH received further dispatches, stating that the raiding party was limited to forty men; that they had for some weeks been boarding at the hotels and boarding-houses in St. Albans; that having robbed the banks and murdered several citizens, they had taken horses wherever they could find them and made a hasty retreat. The Governor thereupon gave notice that the services of the citizens would not be required, and the hastily gathered company thereupon disbanded. Some of the soldiers have, I believe, been forwarded. The affair looks more like a robbery than a raid. It has, however, perhaps its origin among the rebel sympathizers gathered along the Northern border. It is still feared that it may be only the precursor of further outrages in northern Vermont, that is connected with a wide-spread conspiracy like that which came so near being successful on the western lakes.

The excitement still continues—7 P. M.—although less intense, by far, than two hours ago. Soldiers of the Invalid Corps are still in the streets, but citizens and members of Legislature, who an hour ago looked forward to doing soldiers' duty, and perhaps joining in a bloody fray, are now gathered in groups talking over the excitement.

It is generally predicted now that an efficient militia law will be enacted by this Legislature in the course of the present session.

Major-General Philip H. Sheridan

The New-York Times.

VOL. XIV.—NO. 4091.   NEW-YORK, THURSDAY, NOVEMBER 3, 1864.   PRICE FOUR CENTS.

THE REBEL RAM ALBEMARLE.

HOW SHE WAS DESTROYED.

A Bold, Daring and Romantic Feat.

Reports of Com. Macomb and Lieut. Cushing.

Particulars from our Own Correspondent.

WASHINGTON, Wednesday, Nov. 2.

Rear-Admiral PORTER has communicated to the Navy Department a copy of the report of Commander MACOMB, commanding the United States steamer *Shamrock*, dated October 29, from which it appears that on the night of the 27th inst., Lieut. W. B. CUSHING ascended the Roanoke in his torpedo boat, having the second cutter of this vessel in tow, for the purpose of blowing up the ram *Albemarle* at Plymouth. He passed the *Southfield* without being noticed, and arrived within a short distance of the ram before he was discovered, when he cast loose the cutter, ordering it to board the *Southfield* and capture the picket stationed there, while he attacked the ram with his torpedo.

Although the enemy kept up a severe fire of musketry and with howitzers mounted on the wharf, Lieut. CUSHING succeeded in exploding his torpedo under the *Albemarle*, at the same instant that the gun of that vessel, to which they were directly opposite, was fired on the torpedo boat, which immediately filled, and the Lieutenant ordered his officers and men to save themselves, and jumped overboard. He was picked up by the *Valley City* on the night of the 20th.

Report of Lieut. Cushing.

WASHINGTON, Wednesday, Nov. 2.

Admiral PORTER has communicated to the Secretary of the Navy the following interesting particulars from Lieut. CUSHING, in regard to the sinking of the rebel ram *Albemarle*:

ALBEMARLE SOUND, Oct. 30, 1864.

SIR: I have the honor to report that the rebel iron-clad *Albemarle* is at the bottom of Roanoke River.

On the night of the 27th, having prepared my steam launch, I proceeded up toward Plymouth, with thirteen officers and men, partly volunteers from the squadron.

The distance from the mouth of the river to the ram was about eight miles, the stream averaging in width some 200 yards, and lined with the enemy's pickets.

A mile below the town was the wreck of the *Southfield*, surrounded by some schooners, and it was understood that a gun was mounted there to command the bend.

I therefore took one of the *Shamrock's* cutters in tow, with orders to cast off and board at that point, if we were hailed.

Our boat succeeded in passing the pickets, and even the *Southfield* within twenty yards, without discovery, and we were not hailed until by the lookouts on the ram.

The cutter was then cast off and ordered below, while we made for our enemy under a full head of steam.

The rebels sprung their rattle, rang the bell, and commenced firing at the same time, repeating their hail and seeming much confused.

The light of a fire ashore showed me the iron-clad made fast to the wharf with logs around her about 30 feet from her side. Passing her closely, we made a complete circle so as to strike her fairly, and went into her bows on.

By this time the enemy's fire was very severe, but a dose of canister at short range seemed to moderate their zeal and disturb their aim.

Lieutenant William B. Cushing

Paymaster SWAN, of the *Otsego*, was wounded near me, but how many more I know not.

Three bullets struck my clothing, and the air seemed full of them.

In a moment we had struck the logs just abreast of the quarter-port, breaking them in some feet, our bows resting on them.

The torpedo boom was then lowered, and, by a vigorous pull, I succeeded in diving the torpedo under the over-hang, and exploding it at the same time that the *Albemarle's* gun was fired.

A shot seemed to go crashing through my boat, and a dense mass of water rushed in from the torpedo, filling the launch, and completely disabling her.

The enemy then continued his fire at fifteen feet range, and demanded our surrender, which I twice refused, ordering the men to save themselves, and removing my own coat and shoes.

Springing into the river I swam, with others, into the middle of the stream, the rebels failing to hit us.

The most of our party were captured, some were drowned, and only one escaped beside myself, and he in another direction.

Acting Master's Mate WOODMAN, of the *Commodore Hull*, met him in the water half a mile below the town, and assisted him as best he could, but failed to get him ashore.

Completely exhausted, I managed to reach the shore, but was too weak to crawl out of the water until just at daylight, when I managed to creep into the swamp close to the fort.

While hiding, close to the path, the *Albemarle's* officers passed, and I judged from their conversation that the ship was destroyed.

Some hours' traveling in the swamp served to bring me out well below the town, when I sent a negro in to gain information and found that the ram was truly sunk.

Proceeding through another swamp I came to a creek and captured a skiff belonging to a picket of

the enemy, and with this, by 11 o'clock the next night, I made my way out to the *Valley City*.

Acting Master's Mate WM. L. HOWETH, of the *Monticello*, showed, as usual, conspicuous bravery. He is the same officer who has been with me twice in Wilmington harbor. I trust he may be promoted when exchanged, as well as Acting Third Assistant Engineer STÖLSBURG, who, being the first time under fire, handled his engine promptly and with coolness.

All the officers and men behaved in the most gallant manner.

The cutter of the *Shamrock* boarded the *Southfield*, yet found no guns there. Four prisoners were taken there.

The ram is now completely submerged, and the enemy have sunk three schooners in the river to obstruct the passage of our ships.

I desire to call the attention of the Admiral and Department to the spirit manifested by the sailors in the ships in these sounds. But few hands were wanted, but all hands were eager to go into the action, many offering their chosen shipmates a month's pay to resign in their favor.

I am, Sir, respectfully, your obedient servant,
W. B. CUSHING, Lieut., U. S. N.

Rear-Admiral D. D. PORTER, Commanding North Atlantic Squadron.

The name of the man who escaped is WILLIAM HOFFMAN, seaman, on the *Chicopee*. He did his duty well and deserves a medal of honor.

Respectfully,
W. B. CUSHING, U. S. N.

KENTUCKY AND TENNESSEE.

Hood Reported to have Crossed the Tennessee River with 30,000 Men.

The Railroad from Louisville to Atlanta in Good Order.

Reported Defeat of Part of Forrest's Forces.

FROM LOUISVILLE.

LOUISVILLE, Ky., Tuesday, Nov. 1.

Rumor says that Gen. HOOD with thirty thousand men crossed the Tennessee River going Northward to-day.

The particulars and locality of the crossing are not stated, and are not attainable at present.

The railroad and telegraph from Louisville to Atlanta are now in good order.

The Henderson, Kentucky, *News* says that the great bulk of the drafted men in Kentucky are going into the Confederate service.

R. A. ALEXANDER's celebrated horse *Osterer*, valued at $18,000, was captured at Bloomfield, Kentucky, yesterday by the rebels.

SECOND DISPATCH.

LOUISVILLE, Wednesday, Nov. 2.

Reliable dispatches, received this morning, indicate that everything is all right along SHERMAN'S whole line.

FROM CAIRO.

CAIRO, Ill., Tuesday, Nov. 1.

Squads of FORREST's men, who passed through Dresden yesterday, stated that an engagement had occurred between a portion of FORREST's force and the forces under Cols. HATCH and SHELBY, last week, in which FORREST's men were routed, with the loss of their arms, ammunition, baggage and many horses.

The locality of the fight is not stated.

Strong reinforcements of mounted infantry have arrived at Paducah, Ky., which it is believed has caused Gen. FORREST to change his plan of operations. Johnsonville is now thought to be the place where the rebels will make their attack.

The rebel Gens. BUFORD, CHALMERS and LYON held a consultation at Paris, Tennessee, on Friday last.

All of Gen. FORREST's men furloughed or straggling through the country are ordered to rendezvous at Jackson, Tennessee.

The steamers *Oder Nanghock*, reported captured by the rebels on the Tennessee River, have arrived safely at Paducah.

The steamer capturned and burned by the rebels at Fort Herman, on the Tennessee River, on Saturday, was the *Mazeppa*.

She was a new steamer, and making her first trip. She had in tow a barge.

The *Mazeppa* was owned by R. C. LOVELL, of Cincinnati, and was valued at $40,000. Her cargo consisted of Government stores valued at $20,000, and considerable other freight.

Most of the clothing and blankets on board the *Mazeppa*, was taken to Fort Herman, by the rebels, before the boat was burned.

The fire from the gun-boat prevented the rebels from removing all the stores and forage from the river bank.

The fort was shelled by the gun-boat two hours, eliciting no reply, when the ammunition becoming exhausted, the gunboat withdrew, but previously to leaving, sent a party ashore and burned the forage oft by th e rebels on the river bank.

A rebel force, from Gen. BUFORD's command, had taken possession of Fort Herman the night previous. This force consisted of about four hundred men, and they had a battery of three guns, 12 and 18 pounders, masked on the river bank, completely commanding the river in each direction.

The officers and crew of the *Mazeppa* escaped to Pine Bluff, with the exception of Capt. PETTIS.

The steamer *Ann* was coming down the river four hours after the *Mazeppa*, and was fired on by another masked battery three miles above Fort Herman, but the *Ann* succeeded in passing the battery with but slight damage.

On passing the fort the *Ann* was again fired upon with shot and shell, completely riddling her upper-most works, and several shells penetrating her hull,

but she finally got out of the range of the rebel guns, and was taken in tow by a gunboat.

Forty-four rebel prisoners, including several officers, arrived from below to-day, and were sent to Chicago.

GEN. GRANT'S ARMY.

The Surprise of Our Pickets.

HEADQUARTERS OF THE ARMY OF THE POTOMAC,
Tuesday, Nov. 1.

The surprise and capture of a part of our picket line on Tuesday night occurred in front of Fort Davis, and the men taken belonged to the Sixty-ninth and One Hundred and Eleventh New-York regiments.

They were for the greater part new men and somewhat ignorant of their duties, and hence were not so watchful as the older troops, who have been on duty at this point of the line.

This is a place where our men, some time ago, played the rebels a similar trick, and the utmost vigilance has ever since been exercised on both sides to prevent a repetition of the occurrence; but when the late move commenced every man in the ranks left behind had to take his turn on picket, and some of these men, it is said, had never even loaded a gun.

It seems the rebels did not carry of a single musket belonging to our soldiers.

THE TALLAHASSEE AGAIN.

The Schooner Goodspeed Captured and Scuttled by the Tallahassee—Reported Destruction of Three Other Vessels—A Gunboat in Pursuit of the Pirate.

PROVIDENCE, R. I., Wednesday, Nov. 2.

The schooner *Goodspeed*, Capt. BAXTER, of and from Boston, via Newport, for Philadelphia, was boarded by the *Tallahassee*, seven miles south of Block Island, and scuttled. The Captain and the crew escaped to Block Island in a boat, and have reached Newport. The Captain reports that the *Tallahassee* scuttled another vessel within a short distance. The crew of the privateer said that they had the crews of three other vessels destroyed within a few days. The gunboat *Marblehead* left Newport in pursuit this evening.

From the West Gulf Squadron—Capture of Two Prizes by the United States Steamer Mobile.

PHILADELPHIA, Wednesday, Nov. 2.

The United States steamer *Bermuda* arrived off the Navy-yard last evening from the West Gulf Squadron. She brings 22 officers, and 188 sick and discharged seamen.

The *Bermuda* sailed from Galveston, Texas, on the 20th of October. She reports the capture of two prizes by the United States steamer *Mobile*, formerly the *Tennessee*, one with a cargo of cotton, and the other with an assorted cargo.

There is nothing of importance from Mobile Bay.

The following is a list of the vessels at present on that station:

The flagship *Hartford*, Rear-Admiral FARRAGUT; United States sloop *Richmond*, United States sloop *Lackawanna*; gunboats *Port Royal*, *Owasco*, *Metacomet*, and monitors *Manhattan*, *Chickasaw*, *Winnebago*, with a number of tugboats as tenders.

The *Bermuda* had as passengers, from Mobile Bay, Brig. Gen. J. NEWTON and staff, who has been ordered to command the forces at Key West.

The weather during the entire passage of the *Bermuda* has been very fine.

Confederate cavalry under Major-General Nathan B. Forrest plagued Union supply lines throughout Georgia and Tennessee.

The New-York Times.

VOL. XIV.–NO. 4116.   NEW-YORK, FRIDAY, DECEMBER 2, 1864.   PRICE FOUR CENTS.

TENNESSEE.

A Severe Battle at Franklin, Tenn.

HOOD DEFEATED BY THOMAS.

The Rebels Desperately Assault Our Works.

They are Repulsed with Fearful Carnage.

Six Thousand Rebels Killed and Wounded.

TWELVE HUNDRED PRISONERS CAPTURED

Our Loss Less than One Thousand.

MAGNIFICENT BEHAVIOR OF OUR TROOPS

Full and Graphic Account from Our Special Correspondent.

OFFICIAL ANNOUNCEMENT.

WASHINGTON, Thursday, Dec. 1.

The following official dispatch concerning the report of the victory in Tennessee, has been received at headquarters:

FRANKLIN, Tenn., Wednesday, Nov. 30.
FRANKLIN, Tenn., Wednesday, Nov. 30.

Major-Gen. Thomas:

The enemy made a heavy and persistent attack with two corps, commencing at 4 P. M., and lasting till after dark. He was repulsed at all points, with heavy loss—probably of five or six thousand men. Our loss is probably not more than one-fourth of that number. We have captured about one thousand prisoners, including one Brigadier-General.

(Signed,)   JOHN SCHOFIELD,
Major-General.

OUR SPECIAL ACCOUNT.

Special Dispatch to the New-York Times.
FOUR MILES SOUTH OF NASHVILLE, }
Thursday, Dec. 1. }

Gen. SCHOFIELD yesterday fought one of the *prettiest* fights of the war, resulting most disastrously to the rebels, with little loss to ourselves. After three days' skirmishing, the rebels crowded our first line of works yesterday afternoon, and at 4 P. M. made a most desperate attack on our right and centre, forcing our lines to our breastworks, which were thrown up from river to river in an open field on the Cumberland Pike, which ran through the centre of the field.

At least half the rebel force engaged en-

Troops under General John M. Schofield repulsed a Confederate assault by General Hood. Schofield was able to reach Nashville to combine forces with General Thomas.

deavored to pierce our centre, and come down viciously on WAGNER's Division, which, after desperate fighting, fell back, and MANY's rebel division, of FRANK CHEATHAM's corps, got inside our works and captured two guns. Our centre was not broken, however, and, better still, Gen. WAGNER successfully rallied his troops, who charged on the enemy, recaptured the two guns, and *drove the division over the breastworks, capturing one entire brigade and its commander.*

At 4:30 o'clock the battle was waged with unabating vigor, the enemy having made during a half hour several attempts to break our centre.

The Federal position was a magnificent one, and the result of these four days' work were magnificently grand.

All this while the rebels had appeared in front of our right. The plan was to pierce our centre and crush our right wing before dark. A portion of our infantry were engaged three-quarters of an hour firing on the rebel columns who stood their ground like madmen. During every charge made on our right and centre, volleys of grape and canister were hurled into their lines, and only darkness prevented their sacrifice being more awful. It is said that no canister shot was used by the rebels during the day, but fired shot and shell.

After the first break of WAGNER's division and its recovery, our line never budged a step. All was quiet after 10 P. M. It was not only one of the *prettiest* but *cleanest* battles of the war. The excessive slaughter of the enemy was owing to our wholesale use of canister and grape, and our selection of the ground. The battle was fought in an open field, with no trees or undergrowth, or other interruption. The enemy's loss in killed and wounded approximates 7,000, and we have over 1,200 prisoners, and one general officer and several field officers. The Colonel of the Fif-

teenth Mississippi, a Northern man, of Illinois, was wounded and taken prisoner. Four-fifths of his regiment were killed, wounded and captured. Our loss does not reach a thousand, *hors du combat.* Gen. BRADLEY, of Illinois, while gallantly leading his troops, was severely wounded in the shoulder. Our loss in field officers is very small. Our troops behaved handsomely. SCHOFIELD commanded on the field, STANLEY on the right, and COX on the left. Gen. STANLEY was wounded slightly in the neck, but remained on the field and is all right to-day.

I have told you all along the programme of Gen. THOMAS would electrify you, and this is but the epilogue of the battle to come off.

After our dead, wounded and prisoners were cared for, our army fell back to this point, and are in line of battle while I write. Up to this time, 3 P. M., the enemy has not made his appearance. The Third Corps of Veterans are in readiness, and a battle is expected before daylight to-morrow. All Government work is suspended, and all are under arms, from Gen. DONALDSON down to the unscientific laborers.

The falling back of our troops was accomplished at 8 o'clock this morning, and bridges burned across Harpeth River to retard the transportation of rebel supplies. The cavalry was handled prettily by Gen. WILSON, between Spring Hill and Triune.

A. J. SMITH's corps is in line of battle, and the situation is particularly grand. Forts Negley, Morton, Cairo and Houston are alive, and the infantry movements perfectly satisfactory. Something must immediately transpire, as Gen. THOMAS is ready to strike no matter how the rebels move.

BENJ. C. TRUMAN.

ANOTHER ACCOUNT.

NASHVILLE, Tenn., Thursday, Dec. 1—9:30 P. M.

About noon on Wednesday our main army reached Franklin, when Gen. SCHOFIELD prepared to give the enemy battle. There was very little skirmishing, as HOOD's object was to attack us before we had time to throw up defensive works.

About 4 o'clock the enemy commenced advancing on our lines, when the ball was opened by our batteries shelling their advance, and soon after a regular cannonading opened along the whole line. The rebels, who had been protected by woods, now emerged from cover, and opened with a fierce volley of musketry along the lines and then charged. For a moment part of our line wavered, and fell back before the desperate charge of the enemy. Gens. RUGER and Cox, however, rallied their men and charged the enemy, who had crossed over our abandoned line of works.

The rebels were now fighting with the desperation of demons, charging our lines furiously, some leaping our works and fighting hard.

Now was the critical moment, but our Generals, rallying their troops, swung on the rebel flank, doubling them in the centre, where our artillery and musketry mowed them down by hundreds.

The tide was now turned. Our men, inspired with success, gave a wild huzza and swept back on the rebel line like an avalanche, hurling the enemy back in the wildest disorder and confusion.

Night was now setting in, yet we followed up our advantage. What once threatened to be a disastrous defeat was thus turned into a glorious victory. The courage of our officers and the desperate bravery of our men was unexampled.

Our loss is about seven hundred killed and wounded. We captured over one thousand prisoners and eight battle-flags. Two rebel Brigadier-Generals are in our hands. A rebel Division-General was left on the field mortally wounded. The rebel loss in killed and wounded is estimated at three thousand.

The rebel Gens. CHEATHAM and LEE'S corps were engaged. The brunt of the battle on our side fell on the Second Division of the Fourth Corps.

Capt. COUGHLIN, of Gen. Cox's staff, was killed, and several regimental commanders and officers were killed and wounded, whose names have not been ascertained. Gen. STANLEY was slightly wounded in the neck, but did not leave the field.

Gen. Cox states that one could walk fifty yards on dead rebels in his front.

The excitement is allayed here by the knowledge of the above facts.

Our troops have taken position in a line of works between Nashville and Franklin.

Further Details.

NASHVILLE, Tenn., Thursday, Dec. 1.

The Federal forces under Gen. THOMAS retired from Franklin last night, and have taken position and formed in line of battle south of Nashville about three miles. Skirmishing has been going on all day about five miles south of here. Heavy cannonading can be distinctly heard in the city. No want of confidence is felt by the citizens in ultimate success by the Federals. The employes of the Quarter-Master's Department are under arms and in the trenches.

One hundred and seven Confederate officers, including one Brigadier-General and one thousand prisoners, arrived in the city this morning. They were captured in the fight last night near Franklin. A great battle may momentarily be expected.

A Most Desperate Attack by the Rebels—The Rebels Charge Our Masked Batteries—Terrible Loss of the Enemy—Forrest Reported Killed — Reinforcements for Schofield.

NASHVILLE, Thursday, Dec. 1.

Parties who have arrived from the front, and who witnessed the battle of yesterday, describe the attack of the rebel forces as desperate. Four charges were made upon the Federal masked batteries in columns four lines deep. Each time the rebels were repulsed with fearful loss.

The fort is on the north bank of the river, opposite the town, extending up the river, and encircling the town was the line of masked batteries. Eye-witnesses say that this engagement, in desperation and furious fighting, was hardly equaled by the battle of Stone River.

FORREST in person was on the field rallying his men. A rumor is in circulation that he was killed, but it lacks confirmation.

About 7 o'clock last night heavy reinforcements reached SCHOFIELD, which caused a complete rout of the rebel forces.

The city to-day is full of fleeing residents of Williamson and other counties south. They state HOOD is gathering up all the horses, hogs and mules that he can find, and sending them south.

There is great panic among the negroes in the counties south of Nashville. Numbers are fleeing to the city for protection.

THE VERY LATEST.

NASHVILLE, Thursday, Dec. 1.

HOOD'S Infantry force crossed the Harpeth River this morning, and he has not advanced that portion of his force since. His cavalry crossed Harpeth River on the fords above Franklin this morning at daybreak, closely following Gen. WILSON, who retired in this direction. Skirmishing with the advance has occurred all day. Gen. WILSON occupies a strong position a few miles south of Nashville, and is able to resist any force the rebels may bring against him.

The rebel General captured yesterday was Col. GORDON, of the Eleventh Tennessee, brevet Brigadier-General.

An officer who witnessed the fight yesterday, describes the battle as one of the most sanguinary of the war. The determined bravery of the rebels exceeded anything before seen. Although slaughtered by hundreds, they still advanced against our batteries. Within five hours, eleven distinct attacks were made against our works, each a failure.

The battle being ended our forces quietly withdrew from the town.

Among the casualties is Maj.-Gen. Stanley, wounded by a shot in the neck. The rebel Gen. Cheatham is reported wounded. Capt. Bissell, of the Twelfth Indiana, and Capt. Staley, One Hundred and Twenty-fourth Indiana, were killed; Capt. Hinton, One Hundred and Twenty-fourth Indiana, mortally wounded; Col. Lowrey, One Hundred and Seventh Illinois, killed; Capt. Coughlin, of Gen. Cox' Staff, was killed; Capt. Dowling, One Hundred and Eleventh Ohio, was wounded; Col. Walters, Third Brigade, First Division, was wounded in the shoulder; Col. Conrad, who commanded a brigade in the Second Division, was wounded.

The following are rebel casualties: Brig.-Gen. Adams, killed; Brig.-Gen. Scott, wounded. The enemy's total killed, wounded and prisoners are estimated at 4,000, 3,000 being either killed or wounded.

The Federal loss in killed and wounded was 700. The loss in prisoners is trifling.

Gen. BRADLEY is wounded and in the city.

COL. STOCKTON and Major JAMES, of the Seventy-second Illinois, are also wounded.

It is rumored this evening that HOOD is moving eastward, toward Murfreesboro'.

Rebel Speculations.

From the Richmond Whig, Nov. 29.

The care which the Yankee newspapers take to represent the movement of HOOD as ineffectual and despicable; the ridicule which they cast upon his present position; their constant declaration that THOMAS is more than a match for him, and that he has entirely failed, prove beyond a doubt that he has not failed. He has succeeded in placing SHERMAN in a most embarrassing situation, from which he could only escape by a desperate plunge, which he has taken, and the effect of which we shall very shortly witness.

The *Whig* of the 29th says Gen. RIPLEY has been placed in command of South Carolina.

GEORGIA.

LATER FROM GEN. SHERMAN.

Savannah and Augusta Papers to November 26.

Sherman Still Reported on the Oconee.

A PROBABLE MOVEMENT ON SAVANNAH.

Rebel Troops Concentrating at Augusta.

Bragg Brings Reinforcements from Wilmington.

A railroad depot in Atlanta, with soldiers of Sherman's army sitting atop the boxcars.

The Rebels Factories at Augusta Removed,

INTERESTING MISCELLANEOUS INTELLIGENCE.

From Our Special Correspondent.

SAVANNAH RIVER, Georgia, }
Sunday, Nov. 27, 1864. }

We are scarcely less excited here on the question of Gen. SHERMAN's movement than the rebels themselves, and we know that they are stirred as they never have been before at the boldness of his advance. The Savannah journals are not brought to us now until after they are two days old, for fear that we shall be too highly elated at the strait in which the Confederacy finds itself. The last authentic information from the rebels tells us that SHERMAN is advancing in three columns, with a force estimated at 60,000 men, at least one half of whom are cavalry and mounted infantry. The public buildings of Milledgeville, the capital of Georgia, have been burnt, and the Legislature, being in session at the time of SHERMAN's advance force entering the town, adjourned in confusion, some of the members paying as high as *one thousand dollars for transportation a distance of eight miles.* You will be able to form an idea of the reign of terror that now obtains in Georgia and South Carolina, from the files of newspapers which I forward. A levy en masse has been ordered, and BEAUREGARD is in command of the troops. There seems to be most perturbation because SHERMAN has shrouded his objective point in mystery, by sending out immense bands of mounted men to ravage the country on the flanks of his main columns. On Monday last he was at Gordon, with artillery, about fifteen miles from Milledgeville, and had fortified the Georgia Central Railroad between Gordon and Griswoldville, cutting off 2,500 of our prisoners that were to have been brought up from Camp Sumter, at Andersonville. To impede his progress, the bridges over the Oconee River have been destroyed and the country devastated in his front, so that he shall be unable to subsist upon it. The roads have been to a great extent rendered impassable by felled trees and pitfalls, and the rebels claim that during the past three days the progress of the Union troops eastward has not exceeded six miles. They also claim that their cavalry are picking up large numbers of our stragglers, by dashing upon our rear and flanks. From all that I can learn, I believe SHERMAN's main body to be within 125 miles of Savannah, with nothing to oppose him save the militia and such other unorganized forces as the emergency has brought together, and that the chances of his reaching the seaboard are at present altogether in his favor. Should he be delayed, by artificial obstructions of the road, long enough to detach a part of his army to confront him, GRANT in that case would be able to drive the rebels out of Virginia, and SHERMAN would doubtless find a mode of retreat, from the heart of rebeldom, southwestwardly to Mobile. A tremendously bold game is in progress on the military chess-board, and it is easy to see that the enemy believe it to be in our hands. H. J. W.

NEWS FROM REBEL SOURCES.

Our correspondent on the fleet in the Savannah River, Mr. H. J. WINSER, has supplied us with full files of Augusta and Savannah papers to the 26th ult., from which we glean the following intelligence about the campaign in Georgia:

WAR RUMORS
From the Savannah News, Nov. 24.
It was reported in the city yesterday, on the authority of a private dispatch, that Milledgeville had

When Sherman left Atlanta in mid-November 1864, his troops torched the city and destroyed any installations that were of military use. Here, the same railroad depot lies in ruins.

not been visited by the Yankees, and the capitol and other public buildings were still saf .

The Augusta *Register* of the 23d says: "The depot at Madison is burned, also all other depots on the road. The column advancing on the Georgia road is composed of SLOCUM's corps. It is attended by cavalry, variously estimated at from two to five thousand."

Reports from up the Central Railroad indicate that the right wing of the enemy are still advancing, but the exact progress made is not clearly understood. There is a report that they have crossed the Oconee, four miles below the railroad bridge, WHEELER is close on their rear. Our dispatches give some Yankee news of SHERMAN's intentions.

The Augusta *Constitutionalist* of Wednesday, Nov. 23, has the following :

"It is reported that the enemy has crossed the Oconee in force, near Milledgeville. This rumor, however, is strenuously contradicted by other parties. Milledgeville is reported as burned."

The column operating on the Georgia Road kept the western side, and struck off in the direction of Macon, as though contemplating a junction with the force in that vicinity.

Prisoners captured from the enemy on the Georgia Road state that the intention of SHERMAN was to avoid Augusta, and strike Macon probably—Savannah certainly. Atlanta is now in our possession. A strong force of cavalry is following SHERMAN, and it is not impossible that the invincible FORREST—SHERMAN's evil genius—may, ere long, hang like a wolf on his rear and flanks.

From the Augusta Register, Nov. 22.
We conversed with an intelligent gentleman who arrived last night by the passenger train up the Georgia Railroad.

He informed us that on Monday the Federals left the line of the Georgia road, going directly to Eatonton.

The only Yankees who came to Greensboro' were a few stragglers, who were captured.

The trains ran up to Greensboro' and Athens yesterday.

A portion of Maj. GRAHAM's command reached this city last night. They report that they visited Atlanta several days since and found it completely evacuated and burned. They state that the Federals took all the cattle and forage in their route, but did not molest those who staid at home.

They captured two or three hundred Yankee stragglers, who will probably reach here to-day.

They also corroborate the statement of the Federals leaving the Georgia Railroad and going in the direction of Eatonton.

THE WHEREABOUTS OF THE YANKEES.
From the Augusta Chronicle & Sentinel Nov. 25.
The whereabouts of the main body of the Yankee army is involved in mystery, and there is not a military man in this city that can definitely locate them, in our opinion. We should not be like Micawber, waiting for " something to turn up," but should "turn up something" ourselves.

CHEERING.
From the Augusta Constitutionalist, Nov. 23.
We have intelligence of the most important character, which we deem contraband at present. Suf-

fice it to say, that matters are beginning to assume a comfortable appearance, and Mr. SHERMAN had better keep his weather eye open, or mayhap he will get it closed.

What the Richmond Papers Say.
Special Dispatches to the New-York Times.
WASHINGTON, Thursday, Dec. 1.

Richmond papers of Tuesday, Nov. 20, received here to-day by the Philadelphia *Inquirer's* correspondent bring latest intelligence from Georgia. The theatre of war which now absorbs the attention of the whole country They break in some measure through their imposed reticence, on the pretence that SHERMAN has been baffled in his attempt to penetrate Georgia. The only instance, however, in which they actually localize his army, is in the statement that he is still on the west bank of the Oconee.

SHERMAN BAFFLED.
From the Richmond Enquirer, Nov. 29.

The fact that SHERMAN has been baffled thus far in his attempt to penetrate Georgia, has been well known in this city for several days, and further reticence on that score is unnecessary. He is floundering about now between the rapidly concentrating manœuvres of the State troops and such portions of the regular army as were not otherwise more advantageously employed, it having been deemed imprudent and, perhaps, unnecessary, to draw off troops from any of our frontier armies. Intelligence from Augusta on the 26th inst., states that the Macon train arrived on the previous night at the usual time, and that the rumor afloat, that the Central Road had been cut, was incorrect. Gen. HOOD, according to our last accounts, was already moving up into East Tennessee, and *rumor says he has encountered and defeated the opposing army.*

From the Richmond Examiner, Nov. 29.
The tenor of the news from Georgia, so far as it has reached us, is cheering. The *Examiner* closes a leader on the situation in Georgia with the following suggestion : " Why SHERMAN made his march southward an object to be gained by its reaching the seaboard. SHERMAN's army was insufficient to garrison and occupy a wide extent of country. But it might be used against Charleston and Savannah, or at least it might be employed after junction with GRANT against Richmond. Now the nearest road to Savannah, or Charleston, or Richmond, is precisely the road he has taken. By a march to Beaufort he reaches the fleet, which can land him without obstacle or danger on the banks of the James. In any event work for his army could only be found by directing his steps to the sea. His blows are not aimed at in- land villages, nor is the object of his march the separation of the Confederacy and those railroads which we can unite more rapidly than he can cut them."

The New-York Times.

VOL. XIV.—NO. 4132.　　　　NEW-YORK, WEDNESDAY, DECEMBER 21, 1864.　　　　PRICE FOUR CENTS.

NASHVILLE.

The Fruits of General Thomas' Splendid Victory.

Nine Thousand Prisoners Captured.

Sixty-one Pieces of Artillery Taken.

Three Thousand Rebel Wounded Captured at Franklin.

Our Loss Not Over Thirty-five Hundred.

Reported Defeat of Breckenridge by Stoneman.

Nearly All His Artillery Said to be Captured.

Murfreesboro, Chattanooga and Knoxville All Right.

Special Dispatch to the New-York Times.

NASHVILLE, Monday, Dec. 19.

THOMAS is pursuing the enemy to Duck River. We have nearly all HOOD's artillery, and his army is really fearfully demoralized. All the rivers are high, and all the bridges in HOOD's front destroyed. Our pontoons are up. We captured three thousand of the enemy's wounded at Franklin, Tenn. Since Thursday, we have captured and brought in just six thousand prisoners, making nine thousand, counting the wounded taken at Franklin. We have captured four Major-Generals, including Gens. JACKSON and JOHNSTON, as well as Brig.-Gens. SMITH and ROGER. HOOD had sixty-five pieces of artillery. We have captured fifty-four pieces. The enemy's killed and wounded is a little less than our own. Our entire loss will not reach 3,500.

None of our general officers were injured. This is the handsomest victory of the war.

FORREST gave Murfreesboro another trial, and was repulsed. ROUSSEAU and MILROY drove him from the town.

Our late victory at Franklin was not exaggerated in the least. The rebel Gen. JOHNSTON says that their loss was five thousand in killed and wounded. He states that six rebel Generals were killed and four wounded in that engagement. He saw Maj.-Gen. PAT CLEBURNE's body. He was shot through the heart. The whole rebel loss at Franklin, on the 30th ult., was 6,000. Ours is officially reported at 1,900.

STONEMAN has given BRECKINRIDGE a cleaning out in East Tennessee, near the Virginia line, routing his army, killing, wounding and capturing a large number, and getting most of his artillery.

Gen. ED. McCOOK is after Gen. LYON in Kentucky, and he cannot escape.

Murfreesboro, Bridgeport, Stevenson, Chattanooga and Knoxville all right.

BENJAMIN C. TRUMAN.

THE LATEST.

Hood Retreating Across Duck River—Capture of Three More Guns—Heavy Loss of Forrest at Murfreesboro.

NASHVILLE, Tuesday, Dec. 20.

An officer of Gen. ROUSSEAU's Staff, direct from the headquarters of Gen. THOMAS, arrived here last night. Our forces were then at Spring Hill, near Columbia. HOOD's army—the remnant of it—was at Duck River, which it was crossing as fast as possible.

All our wounded left at Franklin were recovered. We also captured there numbers of rebels, severely wounded, including Gen. QUARLES, of Tennessee, formerly Supervisor of the Banks of this State.

Yesterday morning Gen. HATCH captured three guns from the rebel cavalry force at Spring Hill. Our total captures of artillery from HOOD amount to 61 pieces.

The loss of FORREST, in his attack on Murfreesboro on Thursday last, is estimated at 1,500 killed and wounded, who fell into our hands.

The rebel army, from all accounts, has become utterly demoralized, is utterly unable to make a stand, and has scarcely any artillery left.

The telegraph is working to Spring Hill. Trains will run to Franklin this morning.

Gen. SCOFIELD was in Columbia this morning.

Our total loss in wounded in the battles of Thursday and Friday will reach but little over 2,000 men.

The river is rising rapidly, and there are fifteen feet of water on the shoals.

Capture of Three Thousand Rebel Wounded—The Rumored Defeat of Forrest by Rousseau, Near Murfreesboro—Heavy Rains.

NASHVILLE, Monday, Dec. 19.

A courier who left Franklin yesterday, reports the rebel forces in full retreat.

HATCH's cavalry attacked the rear guard of the rebels on Saturday, capturing large numbers of prisoners.

The Fourth Corps crossed the Harpeth River at Franklin on Sunday morning.

Franklin is reported full of rebel wounded—over 3,000 being left there on the retreat of the rebels.

Every church and public building there has been taken for hospitals and nearly all the churches of this city have been appropriated for our wounded.

It is rumored here that ROUSSEAU's command attacked and routed FORREST's force near Murfreesboro on the 15th inst.

There was a heavy fall of rain yesterday and last night.

The river is rising rapidly. Twelve feet of water is reported on the shoals.

THE PURSUIT ON MONDAY.

More Prisoners Captured—Losses and Incidents of the Fighting.

NASHVILLE, Monday, Dec. 19.

Our forces are advancing. This morning, at about 8 o'clock, they captured a body of rebel prisoners estimated at 3,000 in number. Among them are one General and a number of commissioned officers.

The capture was made between Brentwood, ten miles south of this city on the Franklin pike, and Harpeth River. An order for one thousand men to guard the prisoners has just been received by Gen. J. A. MILLER Commandant of this post.

They are expected to reach here during the day.

Col. SPAULDING and his brigade of Tennessee cavalry greatly distinguished themselves yesterday in the heat of the battle.

The Tenth and Twelfth Tennessee regiments contributed largely to the success of the day. The total number of rebel officers captured yesterday was as follows: Three Colonels, 1 Lieutenant-Colonel, 7 Majors, 46 Captains, 157 Lieutenants and 2 Surgeons.

Among the prisoners taken yesterday were three Brigadier-Generals not yet reported, viz: JOHNSON, SMITH and RUCKER.

All the rebel prisoners are corraled in the stone quarry, from which the material for building the Capitol was excavated, some few hundred yards from the Capitol, which is called Andersonville. The penitentiary and all the public buildings are full. Half the prisoners are barefooted, and all are sleeping on beds of rocks.

During the fight of Spring Hill, Maj. BOWDING, of the Twelfth Tennessee, was mortally wounded. His men swore to avenge his death, and they did it in yesterday's fight with desperate valor.

Gov. ANDREW JOHNSON was present on the field in the vicinity of the last bloody charge, which he watched with intense interest.

Additional particulars of yesterday's engagement are especially creditable to our cavalry, who contributed to the defeat of the rebels by their effective coöperation.

Gen. R. M. JOHNSON, instead of being killed, as reported, had turned the rebel flank and crossed the Harpeth River, eleven miles hence.

In the first charge made by the colored troops on the rebel ranks, the Thirteenth Regiment lost 256 men, and the Twelfth 119 men. Lieut. GEORGE TAYLOR, Thirteenth United States Colored Regiment, is killed.

The following officers of colored troops were wounded: Col. HALLENSTEIN and Lieut. BABBITT, Thirteenth Colored; Capts. WRIGHT and STRAIGHT and Lieut. GROSVENOR, One Hundredth Colored Regiment.

About 100 deserters came into our lines yesterday.

The army to-day is undoubtedly attacking the rear of the rebels, as heavy firing has been heard in the direction of their retreat early this morning. The total number of prisoners captured in the two days' fight is estimated at 6,500. HOOD's loss in men cannot be less than 15,000 since he advanced from Columbia toward Nashville.

Gen. THOMAS is determined to again give battle, and has ordered the pontoon trains forward, to cross the streams between this city and Columbia.

Reliable information confirms the conscription of several well known citizens residing near Nashville, among them Mr. GOOCH and JOHN and ARTHUR CHEATMAN, who have been forwarded to Nashville.

Among the incidents of yesterday's fight, may be narrated the following:

During a heavy artillery fire, about noon, the Sixth Ohio Battery, in two successive shots from their guns, blew up two caissons of a rebel battery, (STANFORD's, of Mississippi,) the whole of which was afterward taken by our forces in the last assault.

ARMY OF THE POTOMAC.

All Quiet—A Hundred-Pound Rebel Battery—Useless Shelling—A Salute in Honor of Thomas.

HEADQUARTERS ARMY OF THE POTOMAC, }
Sunday, Dec. 18, 1864, }

There is little of interest to report from this army, our Commanders seeming to be waiting for the result of SHERMAN's operations, as well as those of the fleet which lately sailed from Fortress Monroe.

A good deal of heavy firing has been going on at the Dutch Gap Canal during the past few days.

In front of Petersburgh the enemy a day or two ago opened a new 100-pound gun, and have since been industriously engaged in throwing shells at the railroad trains as they pass a certain point of the road in full view of their gunners; but they have done no damage whatever, nor are they likely to do so, unless they show more accuracy than they have done so far.

This morning a salute of one hundred guns was fired in honor of the great victory of THOMAS over HOOD.

The rebels sullenly threw a few shells in reply, but they did no damage.

Last night the pickets on the right of the line were very active keeping up an exchange of compliments all night.

W. D. McGREGOR.

Mutiny.

The ship *Mercury*, Capt. STETSON, sailed to-day for Havre, and when outside of Sandy Hook, the crew mutinied, and refused to go to sea in the vessel. The pilot, upon giving orders, was disobeyed and threatened, and upon the Captain remonstrating, he was attacked, badly beaten, and stabbed. The ship was put back, and anchored at Quarantine, where the revenue cutter at that station sent on board a boat's crew, and put the offenders in irons.

The New-York Times.

VOL. XIV.—NO. 4135.　　　　NEW-YORK, SATURDAY, DECEMBER 24, 1864.　　　　PRICE FOUR CENTS.

GEN. THOMAS' ARMY.

Particulars of Hood's Defeat and Flight.

Eighteen General Officers and Seventeen Thousand Men Disabled.

FIFTY-ONE CANNON CAPTURED.

Hood's Pontoons on the Tennessee Out of Reach of Our Gunboats.

OUR ARMY STILL PURSUING.

The Advance Across Duck River.

HOOD'S ADVANCE AT PULASKI.

Special Dispatch to the New-York Times.

FRANKLIN, TENN., Thursday, Dec. 22.

The rebel retreat from Franklin to Duck River beggars all description. HOOD told his Corps Commanders to get off the best way they could with their commands. FRANK CHEATHAM told his aunt, Miss PAGE, that HOOD was ordered to Nashville against his own wishes, but he blames HOOD for not attacking SCHOFIELD at Spring Hill. HOOD ordered BATE to attack at Spring Hill, and he didn't do it.

The rebel army is now beyond Columbia. During the rebel tarry in front of Nashville they captured but two locomotives and ten cars. The railroad is but little injured, and trains are running up to Spring Hill ; but two small bridges destroyed. Trains were run to Murfreesboro' on Sunday.

Telegraphic communication is all right with all points. But two small trestles are destroyed on the Johnsonville road. Johnsonville itself was not destroyed.

The rebel loss, during the campaign, was 17,000 men, fifty-one cannon captured and eighteen general officers. The killed, at Franklin, numbered 1,400 the wounded 3,800, and 1,000 prisoners were taken.

In the battles before Nashville and retreat to Columbia there were 3,000 killed [and wounded and 8,000 prisoners. The Federal loss in the battle at Franklin was 2,000, before Nashville not 4,000. The total Federal loss will not reach 7,000, with two generals slightly wounded.

HOOD has a pontoon bridge above the shoals on the Tennessee River, where our gunboats can't reach it.

HOOD marched on Franklin with 40,000 men, including cavalry, and 65 pieces of artillery. He lost just half his general officers, and counting in deserters which are coming in and stragglers which are being captured, he will lose nearly half his men. The rout is complete, although his army is not quite annihilated.

B. C. TRUMAN.

THE VERY LATEST.

A well-organized Federal force awaited Hood's army at Nashville.

NASHVILLE, Friday, Dec. 23.

The latest accounts from the front locate Gen. THOMAS' headquarters at Rutherford Hill, yesterday morning, eight miles this side of Columbia. Since that time our forces have crossed Duck River, and have moved to a point south of Columbia. Our cavalry forces crossed at Hunter's Ford, below Columbia, and dashed into the town, the enemy meanwhile retreating without firing a shot. We captured about fifty stragglers.

The rebel force was, at last accounts, at Pulaski, yesterday morning. They are probably some distance south of that place to-day. They are closely followed by our cavalry. No particular damage was done to the town of Columbia by the passage through it of the two armies.

At least one-third of HOOD's army are without arms and equipments, everything which impedes their flight having been thrown away. Rebel deserters and prisoners report the only effective corps of HOOD's army to be S. D. LEE's.

FORREST effected a junction with HOOD at Columbia on Tuesday evening.

The water on the Shoals is fifteen feet deep, and at a stand-still.

THE BATTLE OF NASHVILLE.

NASHVILLE, Friday, Dec. 16—Midnight.

The readers of newspapers do not know what correspondents suffer sometimes in mind. For instance, imagine a poor fellow taking the chances of a battle all day, then riding several miles in the dark, with mud up to his horse's belly, to find " the wires down east of Louisville." This has been the case with the subscriber, and others, for the past two days. The fighting yesterday and to-day, as I have stated in a telegram which, may be, you have never received, has been grander and more magnificent in

detail than anything I have ever witnessed upon a field of battle.

THURSDAY'S FIGHT.

Early in the morning the enemy's line of battle was within musket shot of Nashville, with both flanks resting upon the river, with Gen. FRANK CHEATHAM's corps on the rebel right, crossing the Lebanon, Murfreesboro and Nolensville Pikes; STEPHEN D. LEE's corps in the centre, crossing the Franklin, Granny White and Hillsboro Pikes, and STEWART on their left, crossing the Harding and Charlotte Pikes, and resting on the river a few miles south of the city, and commanded by HOOD in person.

Our forces were commanded by Gen. THOMAS, and moved upon the enemy in the following order: A. J. SMITH upon the right, STEEDMAN on the left, and WOOD in the centre, with SCHOFIELD in reserve, and most of our cavalry, under Gens. JOHNSON, HATCH and WILSON, on the right. Beside, we had gunboats assisting in the protection of our flanks, which rested on the river.

A. J. SMITH moved out the Sixteenth Corps about 8 o'clock, and skirmished with the enemy until a little before 1 o'clock, with little or no loss to either side, making about a mile in that time. WOOD moved out the celebrated Fourth Corps about the same time, and charged two lines of works and captured them before he took his dinner. Gens. BEATY's and ELLIOT's divisions charged with great fury and enthusiasm, and were received in gallant manner by the rebels, who fought with their accustomed desperation. But two rebel batteries were brought to bear upon the two divisions, while six batteries of field artillery, and all the big guns on Fort Negley, and guns upon Casino and Confiscation, for more than an hour, were employed in hurling destruction into the rebel ranks. Immediately in front of Mrs. ACKLIN's house the charge was made with unbounded spirit. Post's brigade and a battery of artillery piled into the lines head over heels, and captured one hundred men and a section of artillery. Gen. Steedman moved out his men, composed of a portion of his own division, detachments of troops belonging to the different corps with Sherman, and two brigades of colored troops, respectively commanded by Cols. Thompson and Morgan. Gen. Steedman's orders were to make a vigorous attack, for two reasons: Gen. Thomas desired to get possession of a nasty fort upon our extreme left, which commanded our line for two miles to the right, and further, to deceive Hood, as Smith and Schofield were to turn the enemy's left, had any attempt to crush Steedman taken place. But the rebels did not await the second charge of the two colored brigades, which went right up to the summit of the hill without much wavering, driving the enemy a quarter of a mile, and capturing nearly a hundred prisoners. Up to noon Steedman's troops were pretty actively engaged, the white and the black men, shoulder to shoulder, pitching in like fury, regardless of all considerations of color. At noon Steedman had moved nearly a mile and a half, and had commenced to swing his extreme left in a little from the river. On our extreme right, our cavalry had about all they could conveniently attend to during the forenoon, experiencing slight repulses, owing to the fine positions of the enemy. Our infantry and cavalry got some very rough handling just about this time, but were helped out of their dilemma by the gunboats, which came along in the nick of time. The *Carondelet* threw about fifty 64-pound shells into the rebel left, driving the troops resting on the river in great confusion, and silencing a battery of artillery.

In the afternoon Steedman was not so busily engaged as he had been during the early part of the day. His troops, however, were under fire all the while, and behaved with great gallantry. During all these charges, the colored troops hardly gave way. They were admirably handled by Cols. Thompson and Morgan, both brave young men, and as they tugged up the hill the white soldiers upon either side rent the air with vociferations. The negroes, too, as they dashed inside of the works, shouted, screamed, yelled and threw up their hats, notwithstanding they had left nearly two hundred of their comrades

behind, the bleeding victims of rebel shot and shell." As I said above, of the grand charge which I have described, Steedman moved with little opposition, as the rebels, in contracting their lines, necessarily abandoned some strong positions in his front. Wood's corps stood the brunt of the fight in the afternoon, and added new laurels to its well-known and well-earned fame. A little before 3 o'clock, the Second and Third Divisions made two glorious charges upon a long line of rude rifle-pits. An entire battery of brass guns were captured, but most of the troops ran away, and but few prisoners were captured. Before dark another line of works were taken, Wood's corps sustaining a loss of over one hundred men killed and wounded during the charge. He was above an hour from the commencement to the conclusion of this charge, during which time the enemy made very little use of his artillery. At dark the Fourth Corps was four miles from Nashville, having taken half a dozen lines of works, several cannon, and toward four hundred prisoners. Although Wood's corps did the hardest fighting in the afternoon, A. J. Smith, in conjunction with the cavalry and a portion of Schofield's corps, made a multiplicity of brilliant movements, resulting in the capture of two batteries of artillery, nearly a thousand prisoners, a wagon train, and Gens. Lee's and Chalmer's headquarters' trains. This was in a great measure owing to the sagacity and skill of Gen. A. J. Smith, who seems as much at home upon a field of action as one might well imagine. Portions of Schofield's corps were also eminently interested in the saking of the batteries, as were also Hatch's and Johnson's divisions of cavalry. The gunboats kept up their thundering all the latter part of the afternoon, and did considerable execution upon the enemy's left. At dark firing ceased, with the exception that our artillerists threw an occasional shell into the rebel lines. The enemy had been pushed over three miles all round since daylight, although at times the fighting was of the most stubborn character.

The victory was one of the superbest of the war. Our troops drove the enemy at all points, extending our territory three miles south of our position in the morning. Some five distinct lines of rebel works were taken on the left and centre, and the rebel left broken. We captured eighteen guns, with caissons,

&c., all in complete order. We also captured 1,600 prisoners, a large amount of small arms, and a number of wagons. It is believed that our own and the enemy's loss in killed and wounded, is about the same, each side losing between 1,200 and 1,500.

The rebels used very little artillery, but used what they did to a purpose. The captured guns were all smooth bores but four, and of excellent workmanship.

On account of the rolling condition of the country and the thinness of the forests, the movements of the troops upon both sides were witnessed to much advantage. At one time the entire front of Steedman's and Wood's troops and two corps of the enemy, could be seen distinctly from a safe position.

Gens. Thomas, Smith, Schofield, Wood, Steedman, Wilson and other general officers, were upon the field all day. No general officer was injured, although Wood like to have lost his head by a cannon ball twice.

FRIDAY'S FIGHT.

In point of splendor and magnificent results, to-day's affair was even more glorious than yesterday's. During the night, Gen. Hood contracted his lines in a remarkable degree, resting his right a short distance east of the Franklin pike, and his left on the Harding pike, making his line of battle less than four miles from flank to flank, although it was double that number of miles in extreme length, owing to its zig-zag order upon and near the Franklin pike. He also retired his army from a naturally weak position and disposed his forces at the base of a range of detached spurs of the Cumberland. It was evident that he intended to make another stand, and it was also evident that the preservation of his rear and his line of retreat upon the Franklin pike, were objects of his particular attention. Gen. Thomas evidently knew what Hood's programme was as well as Hood himself, and at daylight moved Steedman out rapidly upon the left, with orders to swing in and cross the Murfreesboro' and Nolensville pikes. This was done with rapidity, but no captures were made owing to the rebel evacuation of their works on our left during the night. Wood and A. J. Smith moved up to within musket shot of the rebel lines, while Schofield was held partly in reserve on the right and partly in a position to make

The state capitol of Tennessee was embellished with Federal batteries.

a rapid dash in conjunction with our cavalry, upon the enemy's left, should the situation suggest such a demonstration. All this transpired before 9 A. M. I went out upon the Granny White pike, a little before night, and watched the movements of our right and the enemy's left until noon.

The enemy had a very fine position at the base of a range of hills, extending from the Granny White to to the Harding pike. He was protected by a line of works which had been hastily constructed near the edge of the woods. GARRARD's and MCARTHUR's divisions had to advance through an open field over a mile in length. After getting within four hundred yards of the rebels our column went down upon their bellies, and crawled up some fifty or sixty yards closer. Three batteries followed up these two divisions, and when they halted commenced shelling the woods back of the rebel line and some houses on the pike, from behind which about fifty sharpshooters were banging away. Up to near 11 o'clock this was the order of things in front of SMITH. About that time the rebels showed their heads in great numbers above the works, and acted as though they intended to charge the three batteries. They came out of their works shortly after, and our batteries were retired temporarily to a safer position. Just before 12 SMITH's whole corps from right to left made a desperate charge, but could not carry the works. About half past 12 the attempt was again made, and a portion of the works were carried. MCARTHUR ordered up two six-gun batteries upon his left, and one battery upon the right of his division, his own and GARRARD's men made a charge, the three batteries being advanced so that an enfilading fire could be got in. The whole manœuvre was grand in projection and execution. The artillery did frightful work along the rebel line, our infantry carrying the works during a temporary panic, which was caused by the vigorous hurling of grape and canister into the rebel ranks. In this charge over two hundred of the enemy were captured. SMITH's whole line then advanced, his right swinging around a little from off the Hardin pike and a portion of the Twenty-third corps falling and making up the gap between the Sixteenth and HATCH's division of cavalry. It was now quite 1 o'clock, and a most terrible cannonading had opened all along our left and centre. Knowing that WOOD and STEEDMAN had a certain amount of work to perform to bring up with SMITH. I went over upon the left and centre, where I spent the afternoon until dark, and witnessed, in an unsafe position, more thrilling sights than I have ever seen before.

The rebel bullets were whizzing quite uncomfortably, but their artillery, which is the thing that generally produces the demoralization, remained comparatively quiet, and I, in company with two other correspondents, took the chances of the former.

The Sixth Ohio, and a battery of the Fourth Regular Artillery, took a position upon an open field, about fifty feet in the rear of our infantry; to the right of BEATTY's division a Michigan battery and two Ohio batteries, took up a position in an open field, near and upon WOOD's extreme right, while two batteries got in on the left. From 1 till 2 o'clock these thirty-six guns shelled the rebel position, which was very strong in WOOD's front, and particularly strong in front of STEEDMAN.

At precisely 2 o'clock it commenced to rain, and rained hard during the balance of the day. A little after 2 the Third and First Divisions of WOOD's corps made a desperate charge upon the rebel line which was located upon a slight elevation. The firing lasted fully twenty minutes, when the rebels retired in considerable disorder, leaving their dead and wounded and forty odd prisoners in our hands. The rebels had parallel works on this hill, and the two divisions, without orders, with the wildest enthusiasm, charged the other line of works in the face of a deadly volley of musketry and a shower of grape from four Napoleon guns. Really, I discovered no signs of wavering, and the whole drama was in full show. In ten minutes after they rushed into the works, captured three hundred men and the battery, which was a splendid one of four guns. Every member of the battery—the Second Louisiana—was either killed, wounded or captured.

SMITH and WOOD were now on an even line, and a frowning-looking eminence, topped with strong works, three regiments of Tennessee infantry and STAMFORD's Mississippi battery lie before STEEDMAN, who, at this juncture, was in conversation with WOOD. Capt. TRACY informed me that the two colored brigades would be ordered to storm the hill. I crossed the Franklin pike to see Col. THOMPSON, commanding one of the colored brigades, who is a particular friend of mine, when I heard the orders given for the assault. Immediately the two brigades of colored men started up the hill. I crossed back to the right of the Franklin pike, where I could see the whole movement, without placing myself in too great danger. When within about a hundred yards of the crest of the hill the four guns and the infantry poured a broadside into the negroes, when a frightful panic took place upon STEEDMAN's right, resting on the pike. The movement ceased for a few moments, when a couple of our batteries commenced an enfilading fire, and the assaulting party, with an additional brigade of white troops, again attempted the ascent. The rebel infantry blazed away at a fearful rate, and the artillery discharged sixteen shots of cannister, which made the assaulting column reel, waver and almost fall back. This was the most exciting picture I had ever seen so close, as I stood, in company with Capt. BOYD, of Gen. MILLER's Staff, about two hundred feet to the right of the assaulting party. After a manly struggle, with the loss of over two hundred men killed and wounded in the colored brigades, including eight officers; the party reached the top, and with a yell, went over the works, captured the entire battery and nearly three hundred prisoners. The guns were of the James pattern, were manufactured at Columbus, Ga., and were quite warm when I arrived. Every caisson had been smashed by our artillery, and most of the horses killed, although the guns were in good order. The men composing this battery stood like men to their post—32 out of 70 being killed and wounded. Every officer was killed. As soon as the hill was taken, the colored troops pitched after the retreating rebels, chasing them through a valley nearly a mile. Firing wholly ceased upon the left, which had swung around nearly a mile and a half in two hours. WOOD's corps carried another line of works, without much opposition, however, although POST's and STRAIGHT's brigades pitched in like good fellows.

This was a little before 4 o'clock, and, when all was quiet upon the left and centre, a tremendous crash took place upon the right. It only lasted about ten minutes, but the firing was awful during that time. I started to go over to the right, but when half way over, met Capt. BURROUGHS, of Gen. THOMAS' staff, who told me that SMITH had made a glorious charge, and with the assistance of SCHOFIELD, had taken twelve guns, two general officers, and fifteen hundred prisoners. As I told you in the start, SCHOFIELD had a certain plan to carry out if the opportunity presented itself. It did. While SMITH was making a charge, SCHOFIELD threw his whole corps away round to the right, and shut up toward A. J. SMITH's corps in front, the two corps grabbing the number of guns and prisoners stated above in the operation. Darkness came abruptly on, and hostilities ceased. As near as I can judge our loss is about two thousand in killed and wounded. The enemy's loss in killed and wounded is smaller. We captured about four thousand prisoners and two general officers. Gens. SMITH and SCHOFIELD captured 12 guns, and I saw WOOD's and STEEDMAN's corps capture a like number, while HATCH captured a section of artillery on our extreme right. I started for the city a little before 7 o'clock, at which time all was quiet at the front, and all of our dead, and our own and the rebel wounded had been cared for. Our front occupied a position between eight and nine miles from the city.

Rebel prisoners admit their defeat, and deplore their great loss in artillery and prisoners. Orders were issued last night for 5,000 rations for prisoners. Gen. JACKSON, captured by SMITH, is a Major-General, and is an old man. SMITH is a middle-aged man, and pays a high compliment to our troops, who, he says, are brave in a fight and magnanimous after victory.

LOSSES.

The following summing up of the relative losses of both armies during the two days' fight may be considered quite accurate:

Rebel killed and wounded, Thursday	1,500	
Rebel killed and wounded, Friday	2,000	3,500
Rebel loss in prisoners, Thursday	1,600	
Rebel loss in prisoners, Friday	4,000	5,600
and two general officers.		
Rebel loss of cannon, Thursday	18	
Rebel loss of cannon, Friday	26	44

The Federal loss in killed and wounded in the two days' fight, I think, will exceed the enemy's by a thousand. No prisoners are reported taken by the rebels.

Total rebel loss	8,160
Total Federal loss	4,600

Allowing our loss in killed and wounded to be one thousand more than the enemy's even, gives us the advantage of 3,600 men, 2 general officers, 44 cannon, 5,000 small arms, &c., &c.

BENJAMIN C. TRUMAN.

NEWS FROM REBEL SOURCES.

Special Dispatch to the New-York Times.

WASHINGTON, Friday, Dec. 23.

From the Richmond *Examiner* of Wednesday last, received at the office of the Philadelphia *Inquirer*, we extract the following editorial. No later news from Savannah or Wilmington, than that published to-day, is contained in any of the rebel papers of Wednesday:

A BITTER PILL FOR JEFF. DAVIS.

From the Richmond Examiner, Dec. 21.

The news from Tennessee is bad—the situation is bad,—but it is far from being irremediable. The army in Tennessee has been terribly misused, and has suffered awful injury; but it is not lost, and may be restored to full efficiency by the same hand which redeemed it after Missionary Ridge. But to change the fortunes of the country the Executive power and the Legislature must change their character and abandon the road to ruin, hitherto systematically pursued by both. The opening of this campaign found our two best men in real command and in the two principal positions. LEE in Virginia and JOHNSON in Georgia. The military condition of this country was never so prosperous as it was at Midsummer, for these two men had so done their work that it was then morally certain that the last supreme effort of the enemy was going to fail, and had it failed, it is impossible to doubt that this year would have been the last year of the war. The unexpected freak of the Executive in the removal of JOHNSTON, permitted in silence by the country, has produced fruits such as folly and subserviency never produced before. Although great evils might have been and were apprehended at the time, results have so much surpassed expectations, that they assume the appearance of judgments. But let the past go. The best remedy for the present evil is simply to stop the causes which have caused them. Let the Executive power cease to interfere with the armies; send JOHNSTON to the wreck of that army which he surrendered to HOOD in such magnificent conduct; give him *carte blanche* to do what he thinks proper for its salvation and for the defence of the country, and guarantee that neither his commission nor his plans will be any more meddled with. Give to BEAUREGARD complete discretion of action on the coast. Leave to LEE his whole army, and full powers in Virginia, and prosperity will return, good fortune will again befall the army of the South, and the great dangers which now menace the Confederacy will vanish like the clouds of the last rain.

But good sense, moderately and justly used, will never actuate the Executive power while Congress abdicates its functions and public opinion its rights. Nations will suffer just punishment whenever they intrust the power to puny hands, puff up the conceit, and encourage the passions of their rulers by fulsome flattery or silent submission. We have done so. The follies of the Government are manifest to all, but if any one who pays their share of the cost proposes opposition or even remonstrance, the amiable majority cry "Hush! Oh, hush! hush! We can't get rid of him, and he will do thus and so all the more if he is opposed. Don't say anything; we must have concord, unanimity, and there must be no opposition to the Government." Therefore the only voice which is heard at all is the voice of flattery—the voice of those who have neither head nor heart, neither knowledge nor principle. Hence the Executive power is encouraged to pursue its fancies, and although every military misfortune of this country is palpably and confessedly due to the personal interference of Mr. DAVIS, and the Legislature continued at each session to be his subservient tool, and to furnish new incentives to perversity, new means of mischief. Congress and the Southern public must change their attitude, adopt a more distinct and manly tone, deal with their own affairs with more resolution, keep the Executive power in the path of duty, and curb it with peremptory hands when it interferes with things beyond its capacity.

Great adversity has fallen upon us, but the power of the Southern States is not broken. Their resources are enormous, and on no side is the breach irreparable. Of all external dangers, there is not one that cannot be manfully met. *But greater danger is within.* Folly vested with license, and flattery to encourage folly. No calamity which has happened is in itself ruinous, but what will ruin us is this: that the Government should go on to do and continue the identical acts which have made the calamity by necessary sequence of cause and effect. The more harmony and more concord and more self-abnegation we evince under such circumstances, the more rapid is our progress to destruction. Let us determine that course of the ship shall be altered. *With that determination will be found means to compel change.*

The New-York Times.

VOL. XIV.....NO. 4155.   NEW-YORK, WEDNESDAY, JANUARY 18, 1865.   PRICE FOUR CENTS.

WILMINGTON.

Fort Fisher Carried by Assault.

Official Reports from General Terry and Col. Comstock.

Twenty-five Hundred Prisoners and Seventy-five Guns Captured.

Gen. Whiting and Col. Lamb Taken Prisoners.

OUR LOSS NINE HUNDRED.

ADMIRAL PORTER'S OFFICIAL REPORT.

General Grant Orders a Salute in Honor of the Victory.

REBEL ACCOUNT OF THE FIGHT.

Official Dispatch from General Lee.

[OFFICIAL.]

WASHINGTON, Tuesday, Jan. 17—10:40 A. M.

Maj.-Gen. J. A. Dix :

The following official dispatches have just been received at this department :

HEADQUARTERS UNITED STATES FORCES ON }
FEDERAL POINT, N. C., Jan. 15, }
via FORTRESS MONROE, Jan. 17. }

Brig.-Gen. J. A. Rawlins :

GENERAL : I have the honor to report that Fort Fisher was carried by assault, this afternoon and evening, by Gen. AMES' division and the Second Brigade of the First Division of the Twenty-fourth Army Corps, gallantly aided by a battalion of marines and seamen from the navy. The assault was preceded by a heavy bombardment from the Federal fleet, and was made at 3:30 P. M., when the First Brigade—CURTISS', of AMES' division—effected a lodgment upon the parapet, but full possession of the work was not obtained until 10 P. M. The behavior of both officers and men was most admirable. All the works south of Fort Fisher are now occupied by our troops. We have not less than 1,200 prisoners, including Gen. WHITING and Col. LAMB, the Commandant of the fort. I regret to say that our loss is severe, especially in officers. I am not yet able to form any estimate of the number of casualties. (Signed,) ALFRED H. TERRY,

Brev. Maj.-Gen., Commanding Expedition.

FORT FISHER, Monday, Jan. 16—2 o'clock A.M.

After a careful reconnoissance on the 14th it was decided to risk an assault on Fort Fisher. PAINE'S division with Col. ABBOTT'S brigade to hold our line, already strong, across the peninsula, and facing Wilmington against HOKE, while AMES' division should assault on the west end. After three hours of heavy navy firing, the assault was made at 3 P. M. on the 15th. CURTIS' brigade led, and as soon as it had made a lodgment on the west end of the land front it was followed by PENNYBACKER'S and the latter by BELL'S. After desperate fighting, gaining foot by foot, and severe loss, by 5 P. M., we had possession of about half the land front. ABBOTT'S Brigade was then taken from our line facing Wilmington, and put into Fort Fisher, and on pushing it forward, at 10 P. M., it took the rest of the work with little resistance—the garrison falling back to the extreme of the peninsular, where they were followed and captured, among others Gen. WHITING and Col. LAMB, both wounded. I think we have quite 1,000 prisoners. I hope our own loss may not exceed 500 ; but it is impossible to judge in the night. Among the wounded are the Commanders of the three leading brigades ; Gen. CURTISS being wounded, not severely ; but Cols. PENNYBACKER and BELL dangerously. The land front was a formidable one, the parapet in places, fourteen or fifteen feet high ; but the men went at it nobly, under a severe musketry fire. The marines and sailors went up gallantly ; but the musketry fire from the east end of the land front was so severe that they did not succeed in entering the work. The navy fire on the work, judging from the holes, must have been terrific. Many of the guns were injured. How many there were on the point I cannot say, perhaps thirty or forty.

(Signed)   C. B. COMSTOCK,

Lieutenant-Colonel A. D. C.,
and Chief Engineer.

THE NAVAL DISPATCH.

[OFFICIAL.]

FORTRESS MONROE, Jan. 17.

Hon. Gideon Welles, Secretary of the Navy :

The *Atlantic* is just in from Wilmington.

Fort Fisher and the works on Federal Point are in our possession.

The assault was made by the army and sailors on Sunday afternoon, and by 11 P. M. the works were ours.

The losses are heavy.

Lieuts. S. W. PRESTON and B. H. PORTER, of the navy, are killed.

Our captures were 72 guns and about 2,500 prisoners.

Gens. WHITING and LAMB, (rebels) are prisoners and wounded.

The *Vanderbilt* is on her way North with dispatches.

Two fifteen-inch guns burst on the monitors.

(Signed)   E. T. NICHOLS,

Commander.

THE REBEL ACCOUNT.

[OFFICIAL.]

WAR DEPARTMENT, Tuesday, Jan. 17—9 P. M.

Maj.-Gen. Dix, New-York :

The Richmond *Whig* of this morning contains the following account of the capture of Fort Fisher, by the naval and land forces of the United States :

FALL OF FORT FISHER.

The unwelcome news of the fall of Fort Fisher, commanding the entrance to Cape Fear River, was made this morning, and occasioned a sensation of profound regret. *The capture of this fort is equivalent to the closure of the harbor of Wilmington by the enemy's fleet.* It is situated about eighteen miles below the city, but was the main defence of the entrance to the river, and its fall, therefore, will prevent in future the arrival and departure of blockade-runners. How far this reverse may prove injurious to our cause, remains to be seen, but at present we regard it rather an unfortunate than a disastrous event. The following is the official report :

HEADQUARTERS NORTHERN VIRGINIA, }
Monday, Jan. 16. }

Hon. J. H. Seddon :

Gen. BRAGG reports that the enemy bombarded Fort Fisher furiously all day yesterday.

At 4 P. M. their infantry advanced to the assault, a heavy demonstration at the same hour being made against their rear by our troops.

A 6:30 P. M. Gen. WHITING reports that their attack had failed, and the garrison was being strengthened with fresh troops.

At about 10 P. M. the fort was captured with most of the garrison.

No further particulars at this time known.
(Signed,)   R. E. LEE.

No dispatches have been received from Gen. TERRY since that of Sunday night announcing the result of the assault.

C. A. DANA,
Assistant Secretary of War.

VERY LATEST FROM FORT FISHER.

The Bloody Nature of the Fight—The Rebel Gen. Whiting and Col. Lamb Both Wounded—Our Loss 900—The Rebel Pirates Chickamauga and Tallahassee Both Driven up the River—Accidental Explosion of Fort Fisher's Magazine.

BALTIMORE, Tuesday, Jan. 17.

The *American* has the following from its special correspondent with the Wilmington expedition, who has just arrived at Fortress Monroe.

FORTRESS MONROE, Tuesday, Jan. 17—6:30 P. M.

After three days and nights of bombardment, Fort Fisher is ours, with all the contiguous works commanding New Inlet. The assault was made by the army and the naval brigade at 3 o'clock on Sunday afternoon. One corner of the fort was secured in half an hour, but we had a hand-to-hand fight with the garrison, which lasted until 9 o'clock at night. It was a very stubborn and bloody resistance, and the fort and the approaches were strewn with dead. The garrison had been heavily reinforced. The number of prisoners taken was over 2,000. The number of guns captured was 72. All the forts, including Mound and Seeks Island batteries, surrendered.

The rebel loss in the assault was 500 dead, beside the wounded. Our loss (army and navy) is about 900 killed and wounded. Fleet-Lieut. PRESTON and Lieut. PORTER, commandant of the flagship, were both killed in the assault. Gen. WHITING and Col. LAMB are both prisoners and wounded.

The rebel pirates *Tallahassee* and *Chickamauga* were both in the fight, and were driven up the river. Our gunboats went up the river on Monday morning.

Our prisoners will be immediately sent North.

We had several days of delightful weather.

The magazine in the fort exploded by accident on Monday morning, killing and wounding two hundred of our men.

The *Santiago de Cuba* brings the bodies of Lieuts. PRESTON and PORTER, and the wounded of the navy.

The New-York Times.

VOL. XIV.....NO. 4167.　　　　NEW-YORK, WEDNESDAY, FEBRUARY 1, 1865.　　　　PRICE FOUR CENTS.

THE PEACE QUESTION.

ITS LATEST ASPECT.

Three Commissioners Coming from Richmond.

They Apply for Admission to General Grant's Lines.

A. H. Stephens of Georgia, R. M. T. Hunter of Virginia, and A. J. Campbell of Alabama.

A FLAG OF TRUCE AND A PARLEY.

General Grant in Communication with the Government.

Expected Arrival of the Commissioners at Annapolis.

Special Dispatch to the New-York Times.
WASHINGTON, Tuesday, Jan. 31.

In regard to the rebel Peace Commissioners, the following facts are known:

ALEXANDER H. STEPHENS of Georgia, R. M. T. HUNTER of Virginia, and A. J. CAMPBELL of Alabama, the latter formerly of the United States Supreme Court, arrived at Gen. GRANT's lines last Sunday afternoon and desired permission to come to Gen. GRANT's headquarters.

After considerable delay and parley they were allowed to come to Gen. GRANT's headquarters at City Point. It appears that Gen. GRANT immediately notified the Government of the fact, but up to this time we are not aware of the decision arrived at, though they are expected to reach Washington presently, via Annapolis.

FROM GEN. GRANT'S LINES.

The Commissioners Appear in Front of Petersburgh—Application for a Permit to Come Through—Scenes under the Flag-of-Truce—Excitement among the Soldiers.

From Our Special Correspondent.

HEADQUARTERS FIFTH ARMY CORPS,
Sunday, Jan. 29, 1864—10 A. M. }

For many days the weather has been intensely cold, and many cases of frost-bitten feet, ears, cheeks, &c., on our picket lines are reported. To-day the intense cold had moderated, and though the sun shone brightly and the air was calm, the roads were solid and travelers many.

In front of Col. HARRIMAN's brigade, of WILCOX's division, Ninth Corps, about noon to-day, a flag of truce was displayed on the parapet of the enemy's works, a few rods to the right of the crater. The bearer of the flag stated, that "Hon. ALEXANDER H. STEPHENS, Vice-President of the Southern Confederacy, and Hon. R. M. T. HUNTER, of Virginia, were desirous of proceeding to Gen. GRANT's headquarters; that they were expected, and would have approached our lines via the James River, but were unable to do so, owing to the ice in the stream."

The message sent by the bearer of the Confederate flag of truce was sent at once to the headquarters of the Ninth Corps.

The news that Messrs. STEPHENS and HUNTER were awaiting permission to enter our lines flew like wild-fire through the camps. They were distinguished men; they had made names for themselves before the war began, before acquiescing in the severance of the Republic, and the Union soldiers, who are reading men, knew it. Curiosity is one of the failings of the Union soldier, and, as the news of the flag passed from camp to camp, tents were evacuated, from bomb-proofs temporarily-buried soldiers emerged, pickets brought their rifled-muskets to an "order," and all, not otherwise engaged, covered the parapets of the works of the main and picket lines. As you know, for many days there has been a tacit understanding along this part of the line that there should be no firing; but, until to-day, the members of the corps did not think it conducive to their health to exhibit themselves prominently.

The white flag, however, brought both Unionists and Confederates within plain, point-blank shooting range of each other, and waiting for a reply to the rebel request, they showed themselves in clouds on the works of the contending armies. "How are you Fort Fisher!" says the Yanks; "Good-bye, European importations;" "Have you heard from HOOD?" "Did you know that your Virginian, THOMAS, had presented to Old ABE a 'worsted HOOD'?" and many other remarks of a like nature.

The "Confeds" seemed to take it all in good part, and made, in some instances, quite happy replies, such as, "Fort Fisher may be gone up, but why don't you take Fort Crater?" "GWIN's a fool, and we don't care a d—n for anything more from Europe;" and "HOOD's hoodwinked old THOMAS, and you'll hear from him directly, I reckon."

So they passed the time intervening before the reply came. Men who, a few moments later, might be engaged in mortal combat, whiled away the closing hours of the beautiful Sabbath in seemingly friendly intercourse. But does any one dream that, if in the midst of this sort of national gathering, the order had been given, "Prepare for action," any of the soldiers, so jocose and free from care, would have disobeyed the command? No! But, shoulder to shoulder, they would have repeated the lesson they have been endeavoring to teach the foes of their country for these long years. In the soldier's life there is sunshine and shadow, but, alas! the shadow predominates. The Union soldier lives on in the hope that through the shadow will finally break the sun of peace, reflecting against the bank of adversity's clouds a rainbow of victory, telling in unmistakable colors of a "Union" conquered and thereafter indivisible.

As the bright orb of day neared the western horizon, and glanced upon the lofty spires of the yet unconquered "Cockade City," an officer from the headquarters of the Ninth Corps neared our foremost line. All were on the tiptoe of excitement;

Confederate　Vice-President
Alexander H. Stephens

but, soldierlike, the gallant Colonel kept his own counsel; and, improvising a flag of truce from a white handkerchief, proceeded to scale the works; and, with one companion, advanced to the neutral ground.

After some minutes' waiting, he was met by four officers of the Confederacy, and a conference was held within a stone's throw of the scene of the terrible tragedy of the 30th of July last. What the result of this interview was, was not made public; but, it is believed that no word had been received from Gen. GRANT, and as a consequence, the "distinguished gentlemen" from Georgia and Virginia would have to bide their time, perhaps until to-morrow.

As the flags receded from each other, the thousands who covered the works suddenly disappeared, walking into their tents, crawling into their holes and descending into their bombproofs, to speculate upon the meaning of such a seemingly urgent desire on the part of the Vice-President and Ex United States Senator to enter the Union lines. Speculation upon this subject is not only rife among the soldiers, but among other thinking men, and the most extravagant propositions are put forth. Of course it is useless to speculate. It may be that the visit of these noted Southern gentlemen will be productive of good; but time alone will tell.　　　　G. F. WILLIAMS.

The New-York Times.

VOL. XIV.....NO. 4181.   NEW-YORK, FRIDAY, FEBRUARY 17, 1865.   PRICE FOUR CENTS.

SHERMAN'S MARCH.

Official Dispatches from the Army.

Particulars from Our Own Correspondents.

Interesting Reports from the Rebel Papers.

Branchville Evacuated by the Rebels.

Occupation of Orangeburg by Sherman.

Beauregard's Forces Retreating on Columbia.

THE OPERATIONS ON THE COAST.

Hardee in Command at Charleston.

Washington, Thursday, Feb. 16.

Maj. Stolbrand, Chief of Artillery of the Fifteenth Corps, of Gen. Sherman's army, has arrived here, bringing dispatches to the Government. He says that Gen. Sherman's plans are not generally known in his own army, although he has its entire confidence.

It was Gen. Blair's division which defeated the enemy at Rivers' Bridge, the soldiers wading to their waists to make the attack.

It is clear that Sherman is moving large columns to the right and left, or east and west, at Branchville.

A little to the northward of that point is a fine, high, fertile and productive section of country, easily traversed with good roads, and abounding in supplies.

If he is aiming at Columbia he will traverse the districts of Orangeburgh and Richland—a region unsurpassed in the whole land for wealth and abundance.

OPERATIONS BEFORE CHARLESTON.

Preliminary Movements—Our Forces Again on James Island—Gallant Capture of Rebel Works—Position of the Force under Gen. Hatch.

From Our Own Correspondent.

James Island, S. C., Saturday, Feb. 11, 1865.

The Northern District of the Department of the South, embracing the islands about Charleston harbor, is destined to become once more the scene of active operations. For some time past preparations have been in progress to attack the enemy, and the enemy, noticing the movements, has been busy at work to counteract them. On Friday, the 9th inst.,

Confederate Lieutenant-General Wade Hampton

a force of infantry and artillery, under the immediate command of Gen. Schimmelfennig, crossed over from Folly Island to James Island. This is the first time our troops have visited that locality since the demonstrations made on John's Island a few months ago, under the direction of Gen. Foster. It will be remembered that at that time, after having given the enemy a sound thrashing and driven him to his strong defences, our troops withdrew to their former positions on Folly and Morris Islands. The enemy then reoccupied the whole of James Island, and, in order to resist any future assault on our part, threw up additional earthworks at the southern end, and increased his force of men. The late attack was made in the afternoon, the troops having been occupied in the morning in disembarking

Everything being in readiness, a line of battle was formed on the southern end of the island, and a body of skirmishers sent forward to feel the enemy. They had advanced but about one mile when they discovered just in their front a long line of earthworks, behind which, it was subsequently ascertained, were posted 3,000 rebels. As our skirmishers advanced, fire was opened from a few pieces of light artillery which had been placed in position a short distance at the rear. The gunboat McDonough and the mortar schooner Smith moved up the Stono River, and joined in the fight by throwing shells into the woods where the rebels had formed their line of battle. The tin-clads Savannah and Augusta, under the command of Ensign Neil, also took an important part in the general movement. Late in the day, the howitzers were removed from the tin-clads and placed on shore; but unfortunately, while the men were hauling the pieces to the front, one of them became mired and could not be extricated in time to be brought into service that day. The remaining guns

were worked with good effect. The enemy having been shelled pretty thoroughly, a signal was given for our line of battle to advance and seize the outer works of the enemy. Away went the men with a bound and a yell, and in fifteen minutes time they had possession of three redoubts and taken thirty prisoners, including a Major of a South Carolina regiment. The force that defended the redoubts were infantry, nearly all of whom took to flight when our men made the dash upon them. Our loss was fifteen killed and thirty wounded. The enemy's loss in killed and wounded could not be ascertained.

The ground gained by the assault is held by our troops to-day, and it is quite possible that we may see some heavy fighting within a short time. The enemy have erected new and formidable works on the upper portion of James Island, but we believe that by proper management these works can be captured.

Maj.-Gen. Gillmore came up from Hilton Head early yesterday morning, and remained close to the scene of the fight during the day. This morning he had an interview with Admiral Dahlgren, when the plan for future operations was discussed and decided upon.

Brig.-Gen. Potter was also present yesterday. To-day he will take an active command on the shore.

Of course, it is impossible to tell what will be the result of these active movements, but one thing is certain, the enemy must be wary, or he may suddenly find himself without a Charleston.

The forces under Brig.-Gen. Hatch are bivouacked on the Charleston and Savannah Railroad, at the point where it crosses the Combahee River. They are steadily moving forward toward Charleston, the enemy, in the meantime, reluctantly retiring in the same direction.   WHIT.

The New-York Times.

VOL. XIV.....NO. 4182.   NEW-YORK, SUNDAY, FEBRUARY 19, 1865.   PRICE FOUR CENTS.

GLORIOUS NEWS

Triumphant March of Gen. Sherman.

Columbia, S. C., Occupied on Friday Morning.

Beauregard's Forces Retreat as Our Troops Enter the Town.

Large Quantities of Medical Stores Destroyed by the Rebels.

The "Cradle of Secession" Violently Rocked.

The Evacuation of Charleston a Military Necessity.

Speculations as to where Sherman will Next Strike.

He Lives on the Country and is Unopposed in His Advance.

OFFICIAL REPORTS FROM GENERAL GRANT.

[OFFICIAL.]
WAR DEPARTMENT,
WASHINGTON, D. C., Feb. 18, 1865.

Major-Gen. Dix:

The announcement of the occupation of Columbia, S. C., by Gen. SHERMAN, and the probable evacuation of Charleston, has been communicated to the department in the following telegram just received from Lieut.-Gen. GRANT.

EDWIN M. STANTON, Secretary of War.

CITY POINT, 4:45 P. M., Feb. 18, 1865.

Hon. E. M. Stanton, War Department:

The Richmond *Dispatch* of this morning says :—

SHERMAN entered Columbia yesterday morning, and its fall necessitates, it presumes, the fall of Charleston, which it thinks has already been evacuated.

U. S. GRANT, Lieutenant-General.

CITY POINT, Va., Feb. 18, 1865.

Hon. E. M. Stanton, War Department:

The following is taken from to-day's Richmond *Dispatch:*

THE FALL OF COLUMBIA.

Columbia has fallen. SHERMAN marched into and took possession of the city yesterday morn-

ing. The intelligence was communicated yesterday by Gen. BEAUREGARD in an official dispatch. Columbia is situated on the north bank of the Congaree River, just below the confluence of the Saluda and Broad Rivers.

From Gen. BEAUREGARD'S dispatch, it appears that on Thursday evening the enemy approached the south bank of the Congaree, and threw a number of shells into the city. During the night they moved up the river, and yesterday morning forded the Saluda and Broad Rivers. Whilst they were crossing these rivers our troops under Gen. BEAUREGARD evacuated Columbia. The enemy soon after took possession.

Through private sources we learn that two days ago, when it was decided not to attempt the defence of Columbia, a large quantity of medical stores, which it was thought it was impossible to remove, were destroyed. The female employes of the Treasury Department had been previously sent off to Charlotte, South Carolina, a hundred miles north of Columbia. We presume the Treasury lithographic establishment was also removed, although as to this we have no positive information.

The fall of Columbia necessitates, we presume, the evacuation of Charleston, which, we think likely, is already in process of evacuation.

It is impossible to say where SHERMAN will next direct his columns. The general opinion is that he will go to Charleston and establish a base there; but we confess that we do not see what need he has of a base. It is to be presumed he is subsisting on the country, and he has had no battle to exhaust his ammunition. Before leaving Savannah he declared his intention to march to Columbia, thence to Augusta, and thence to Charleston. This was uttered as a boast and to hide his designs. We are disposed to believe that he will next strike at Charlotte, which is a hundred miles north of Columbia, on the Charlotte and Columbia Railroad, or at Florence, S. C., the junction of the Columbia and Wilmington and the Charleston and Wilmington Railroads, some ninety miles east of Columbia.

There was a report yesterday that Augusta had been taken by the enemy. This we not believe.

We have reason to feel assured that nearly the whole of SHERMAN'S army is at Columbia, and that the report that SCHOFIELD was advancing on Augusta was untrue.

From the Whig.

The Charleston *Mercury* of Saturday announces a brief suspension of that paper, with a view to its temporary removal to another point. This is rendered necessary by the progress of military events, cutting it off from the mail facilities for distributing its paper to a large portion of its subscribers, while the lack of transportation renders its supply of paper precarious.

SEMMES has been made a Rear-Admiral, and

will take command of the James River Squadron.

U. S. GRANT, Lieutenant-General.

Rebel Reports.

From Richmond journals of the 16th, received yesterday at Washington, we get the following :

No official messages were received from any part of South Carolina yesterday.

At last accounts, as we stated in yesterday's paper, the enemy held Orangeburgh, on the Columbia branch railroad, and our forces were falling back toward Columbia.

There was a flying report yesterday, which we could trace to no reliable source, that there had been skirmishing on Tuesday morning, within four miles of Columbus.

Our troops abandoned Branchville last Sunday night.

WHEELER last Friday attacked and whipped KILPATRICK at Aiken, 15 miles northeast of Augusta, and drove him back five miles in the direction of Branchville.

The Augusta papers, of last Wednesday, state that at that time SLOCUM was at Windsor, ten miles east of Arpen, advancing on Augusta, his right flank being protected by the South Edisto, and his left by KILPATRICK's cavalry.

Two day's after this KILPATRICK was whipped by WHEELER. SLOCUM has with him the Fifteenth and Sixteenth Corps. The Fourteenth and Twentieth Corps comprise the force operating against Columbia and Charleston.

This leaves one corps of SHERMAN's accounted for. We presume it has been left at Savannah.

By the latest advices through Yankee papers we learn that SHERMAN was still at his headquarters at Beaufort.

Gens. S. D. LEE and WADE HAMPTON, recently appointed Lieut.-Generals, have been confirmed by the Confederate Senate.

The promotion of Gen. HAMPTON makes him rank Gen. WHEELER, and puts him in command of our cavalry now operating against Gen. SHERMAN.

The best events may be expected from this appointment. HAMPTON's presence will not fail to inspire confidence and enthusiasm.

THE CAMPAIGN IN SOUTH CAROLINA.

Interesting Facts Regarding Sherman's Movement—Strength of His Army—Plan of the Campaign—Character and Strength of the Adversary, Etc.

Correspondence of the Chicago Evening Journal.

NASHVILLE, Sunday, Feb. 12.

It would be folly for me here to repeat the statement that preparations are in progress for a grand campaign into Alabama, and that it is about to start, and that it would, ere this, have gone but for the inclemency of the weather; all these things have been told you, over and over; yet there is nothing else transpiring which would in the least interest the readers of the *Journal*, in this immediate locality. I must, therefore, be pardoned for going out of the department for my intelligence; and I am fortunately in possession of numerous facts relative to the situation in an important locality, which will be of interest, not only to every reader of the *Journal*, but to every patriot in the land.

The locality to which I refer is South Carolina, and the operations are those of SHERMAN and his adversary, in that stronghold of rebellion. Our army left Savannah strongly garrisoned with troops belonging to the Nineteenth Corps, so that SHERMAN set out at the head of the following force :

Fourteenth Corps	12,000
Twentieth Corps	19,000
Fifteenth Corps	16,000
Seventeenth Corps	18,000
Foster's army	22,000
Cavalry	16,000
Total	**103,000**

This may be regarded as a large force; but I am happy to say that it does not exceed, by one man, that number under command of SHERMAN; though in it are included some 10,000 negro troops, who will remain in the vicinity of Port Royal, so that the actual number moving northward is a little over 90,000, including cavalry. Of this number, nearly all the cavalry, and the Fourteenth and Twentieth Corps, in all from 42,000 to 45,000 men, passed through or by Robertsville, with a view to striking the Augusta and Charleston Railroad, some ten miles to the west of the Edisto River, whence they were to march directly upon the bridge

Columbia, South Carolina, felt the full fury of Sherman's troops as they swept into the "Cradle of Secession."

over that stream (which is a trestle structure of over seven hundred feet in length,) which is to be destroyed, thereby obviating all necessity for a detour to the west, with a view to the capture of Augusta. That place has lost all importance, since its shops and machinery were removed; and the only possible object SHERMAN could have in paying any attention to it would be to destroy the half mile of trestle-work over the Savannah River. But if he can succeed in cutting the bridge over the Edisto—and from a perfect knowledge of all the facts in the case, so far as developed, I am confident he has done that already—and then those over the Santee and Wateree Rivers, near Kingsville, and between Branchville and Columbia and Florence, then there is no necessity for the destruction of that at Augusta; and the three can be laid in ashes with less marching than would be required to reach the Savannah.

While these two corps and the cavalry are moving into Central South Carolina, the Fifteenth and Seventeenth Corps, and the greater part of FOSTER's white troops—all infantry, and numbering about 45,-000 men—are moving slowly, but surely upon Charleston. They were instructed to cross the Combahee, but to make no haste; but rather, by an appearance of hesitation and indecision, deceive the enemy and make him believe the whole thing a mere feint; and then, when it became apparent that he was concentrating in the vicinity of Branchville, to push rapidly on and invest the cradle of the rebellion, and let it have a taste of a little musketry, as well as artillery.

Some have conjectured that SHERMAN didn't care a fig whether Charleston was captured or not; that he proposed to isolate it, and then let the rebels either hold or evacuate it at their pleasure; but this is a serious mistake, as Charleston is too important a point of enport for any such trifling. He wants Branchville first, but he wants, and intends to take, Charleston also; and when once it falls into our hands he will move northward with the assurance that he has done his work well and released another large fleet which will not in the least detract from our moral force in dealing with our neighbors, whether on this Continent or in Europe.

In order to fully understand all these strategic points at which SHERMAN aimed on starting out, the reader should consult a map; without one, he will scarcely be able to fully appreciate the importance of the several movements I have indicated; but he has only to glance at a good atlas to perceive the grandness and magnitude of the present campaign, which cannot be otherwise than successful, with this present large army in the field.

BUT WHAT OF THE REBELS?

Are they idle? Let no one indulge the illusion that they are. What are the preparations which have been made to meet the invincible army of SHERMAN?

In the first place HARDEE, on evacuating Savannah, took with him about 6,000 veterans—the Georgia militia being no longer in the field. There were, in Georgia, at the same time, in scattered garrisons, some 5,000 more, and at Charleston 5,000 more, all of whom are now concentrated under the command of the rebel army of South Carolina, making in all about 16,000. To this must be added the following forces:

From Wilmington....................... 4,000
From Lee's army (5 divisions)................. 15,000
Add to the above........................... 16 000

Total.................................35,000

Of this number about five thousand are cavalry; and reinforcements to the number of five thousand more can be had if it is determined to evacuate Wilmington, which will probably be done. This force the rebels must continue to divide, if they propose to try to hold Charleston; but this I think they will scarcely do. In addition, a portion of Hood's old army, from eight thousand to ten thousand, have started in the direction of South Carolina. They are under command of CHEATHAM and S. D. LEE, but are not strictly their old corps—they are the picked men of the entire army, and are all of it who are worth the powder and lead it would take to kill them. But they commenced their peregrinations too late in the season. Had they started when HOOD was first driven across the Tennessee they could have been made available. But the first of them left Meridian, on the cars, on the 26th of January last; and the last not till the 4th of February, as transportation was exceedingly scarce; and after going to Talladega on the cars, they will be compelled to march overland 280 miles before they can be of any service, which is a month's journey at the least; so that they will not even set foot upon the "sacred soil" of South Carolina before the first of March; and long before that time SHERMAN will be out of the State and HARDEE's forces will be scattered.

It is useless to talk about the assistance which the militia will render to the regular rebel troops. The more of these in their army, the worse for the rebels. They are all old men and boys, and only valuable to consume commissaries which might otherwise fall into the hands of the "Yankees." Nor can LEE aid HARDEE, or BEAUREGARD, or whoever has command. He has but 35,000 infantry in the works at Richmond, and the late advance of GRANT evinces that he cannot hold his own, even with his present force; and as for his cavalry, they do not number 8,000 in all Virginia.

This, I repeat, is a correct statement of affairs in South Carolina; but of the results of these grand combinations, you will hear through another channel than Nashville—through Richmond and Washington.

HANDEL.

NEWS FROM REBEL SOURCES.

The Situation on the Appomattox—Reported Evacuation of Wilmington—Union Forces Concentrating at Newbern, &c.

WASHINGTON, Saturday, Feb. 18.

Richmond papers of the 16th inst. have been received here.

The Richmond *Dispatch* contains the following:

There was a cannonade of several hours' duration on our left, near the Appomattox, on Wednesday evening. With this exception, nothing of moment occurred. On the Petersburgh lines picket firing has, by tacit consent of both parties, very much slackened within the past few days. The enemy are quiet in their intrenchments on Hatcher's Run. Throughout Tuesday night the rumbling of wagons and artillery was heard on GRANT's lines in the neighborhood of Deep Bottom. It was supposed that GRANT was transferring a heavy body of troops to the north side. This may be simply the return of the troops sent over to Petersburgh to participate in the Hatcher's Run affair last Monday.

It was reported yesterday that our troops were evacuating Wilmington. The report is not confirmed, however, by official dispatches. The Yankee papers state that Gen. TERRY is still in the vicinity of Fort Fisher and waiting for Gen. HOKE.

Hitherto the Yankee press have represented Gen. TERRY as about to march toward Wilmington with the confident expectation of taking the place, but Fort Anderson has proved a more effectual obstruction than they had anticipated.

Gen. BAKER is in command of our forces at Goldsboro', and reports to the War Department that he has reason to believe that the enemy are concentrating at Newbern, and that they have with them materials for repairing the railroad from Newbern to Kinston.

Scouts who came into Kingston on the night of the 11th inst., report that Gen. FOSTER is in command at Newbern, and that 2,000 of the Eighteenth Army Corps have arrived there, making the number of troops at the post about 5,000.

It is reported and believed in Kinston that the enemy have landed two locomotives and two cargoes of railroad iron at Morehead City.

It is not apprehended in Kinston that the enemy design an early movement in that direction.

Col. ISAAC M. St. JOHN, at present Chief of the Nitre and Mining Bureau, has been appointed Commissary-General. He is by profession an engineer.

The New-York Times.

VOL. XIV.....NO. 4184.   NEW-YORK, TUESDAY, FEBRUARY 21, 1865.   PRICE FOUR CENTS.

GOOD NEWS.

CHARLESTON IN OUR POSSESSION.

The City Abandoned by the Rebels on Saturday Last.

Admiral Dahlgren Takes Possession on the Same Day.

SHERMAN'S GRAND TRIUMPH.

His March Still Onward and Victorious.

THE OCCUPATION OF COLUMBIA.

Advance Northward from that City.

News from Other Portions of the Field.

Rear-Admiral John A. Dahlgren

DISPATCH FROM ADMIRAL DAHLGREN.

WASHINGTON, Monday, Feb. 20.

The following dispatch has been received at the Navy Department:

FLAG-SHIP HARVEST MOON, REBELLION ROADS,
CHARLESTON HARBOR, Feb. 18, 1865,
VIA FORTRESS MONROE, Feb. 20—7 P. M.

Hon. Gideon Welles, Secretary of the Navy:

SIR: *Charleston was abandoned this morning by the rebels. I am now on my way to the city.*

I have the honor to be, very respectfully, your obedient servant,

JOHN A. DAHLGREN, Rear-Admiral.

[OFFICIAL.]

DISPATCH FROM SECRETARY STANTON.

WAR DEPARTMENT, WASHINGTON, Feb. 20—8 P. M.

Maj.-Gen. Dix, New-York:

The following details of military operations and the condition of affairs in the rebel States, taken from the Richmond papers of to-day have been forwarded by Gen. GRANT. This department has received no other intelligence in relation to the operations of our forces against Fort Anderson and Wilmington. A dispatch from Admiral DAHLGREN to the Secretary of the Navy, dated at Charleston Harbor, 18th, says *that the rebels were abandoning Charleston that morning, and he was now on his way to that city.*

EDWIN M. STANTON,
Secretary of War.

CITY POINT, Feb. 20.

Hon. Edwin M. Stanton, Secretary of War:

The following paragraphs are extracted from the Richmond papers of to-day:

We now know that Charleston was evacuated on Tuesday last, and that on Friday the enemy took possession of Columbia. It is reported that our forces, under Gen. BEAUREGARD, are moving in the direction of Charlotte. Official intelligence was recived at the War Office last night, that *Sherman was, on yesterday morning, advancing toward and was near Winsboro,* a point on the railroad leading to Charlotte and thirty miles north of Columbia. Charlotte is thronged with refugees from Columbia, who report that some of WHEELER'S cavalry plundered the city before the evacuation. Up to Tuesday last it was uncertain whether Columbia would come within the immediate range of SHERMAN'S purposes, and consequently the public mind was not prepared for such an early solution of the question. The Government had, however, just two weeks ago taken the precaution to remove its specie deposited there amounting to several millions of dollars, and within the past few days all of the dies and plates belonging to the Treasury Department, together with the supplies of Treasury notes on hand, were safely conveyed away. *The enemy being in possession of Branchville, Orangeburgh and Kingsville, precluded movements on the roads leading to Charleston,* and an unfortunate accident upon the Charlotte road from Columbia, prevented the authorities from making use of that avenue to save other valuable materials in the city. A large quantity of medical stores belonging to the Government were there, one-half of which were saved, and the rest, for want of time and transportation, was destroyed. The presses and fixtures for printing Treasury notes, in the establishments of EVANS & COGGSWELL, and KEATING & BALL, were necessarily abandoned, together with the other extensive machinery of those well known firms. The first-named establishment had one hundred and two printing presses, and was unquestionably the largest and best equipped publishing house in the South.

The enemy's forces operating west of Columbia, reached the banks of the Congaree, opposite the city, on Thursday evening, and threw in a number of shells, to which our batteries responded. A portion of this column moved up the river during the night, and crossed the Saluda and Broad Rivers, the main tributaries of the Congaree, which meet near Columbia, a few miles above the city. During the movement Gen. BEAUREGARD evacuated the city, and on Friday morning the enemy entered and took possession without opposition. Our troops were withdrawn to a position some twenty miles from Columbia, where they remained on yesterday.

The enemy's force, entering Columbia, consisted of SHERMAN'S main army, a large portion of which immediately moved up the Charlotte road, *while another portion moved down in the direction of Charleston. The latter city has doubtless ere this been evacuated.*

FROM CHARLESTON.

CHARLESTON, Tuesday, Feb. 14.

The enemy's gunboats and one monitor have been shelling our picket lines on James Island all day. All quiet in our immediate front. Nothing definite from above. The enemy keep up a steady shelling of the city.

CHARLESTON, Wednesday, Feb. 15.

All quiet along our lines. The enemy this morning are reported to be moving in force near Columbia, on the Lexington-road. It is reported that they crossed the Congaree to-day.

AFFRAY WITH REBEL DESERTERS.

A desperate affair occurred last Tuesday in Lunenburgh County between some deserters from the Confederate army and some of the Ninth Virginia Cavalry, aided by citizens. Several on both sides were wounded. The deserters were finally captured.

The New-York Times.

VOL. XIV.....NO. 4192.   NEW-YORK, THURSDAY, MARCH 2, 1865.   PRICE FOUR CENTS.

THE SOUTH.

Great Excitement in the Rebel Capital.

THE ABANDONMENT OF RICHMOND

The Removal of Guns and Military Stores in Progress.

CONSTERNATION OF THE CITIZENS.

Unseemly Flight of Rebel Congressmen ---Congress Reduced to a Mere Skeleton.

Extraordinary Article from the Richmond Examiner.

The Fall of Richmond the Fall of the Confederacy.

The Prospective Westward Flight of the Rebel Army.

VIRGINIA.

THE PROPOSED ABANDONMENT OF RICHMOND.

Special Dispatch to the New-York Times.

WASHINGTON, Wednesday, March 1.

Richmond papers of Monday contained very important admissions. The *Sentinel* admits that the removal of guns and stores from Richmond is going on, and endeavors to quiet the apprehensions of the people. The *Sentinel* says that the members of the rebel Congress have fled one by one until there is only a quorum left for business. Gen. LEE begs that Congress will not now adjourn, and leave his hands fettered and unprepared for further resistance.

From the Richmond Examiner, Feb. 27.

In the extraordinary message which Mr. DAVIS recently addressed to Congress he declared that "if the campaign against Richmond had resulted in success instead of failure ; if we had been compelled to evacuate Richmond as well as Atlanta, the Confederacy would have remained as erect and defiant as ever. Nothing could have been changed in the purpose of its Government, in the indomitable valor of its troops, or in the unquenchable spirit of its people. The baffled and disappointed foe would in vain have scanned the reports of your proceedings at some new legislative seat for any indication that progress had been made in his gigantic task of conquering a free people. There are no vital points, on the preservation of which the continued existence of the Confederacy depends. There is no military success of the enemy which can accomplish its destruction. Not the fall of Richmond, nor Wilmington, nor Charleston, nor Savannah, nor Mobile, nor of all combined, can affect the issue of the present contest." In the African Church, a fortnight ago, he

reiterated these extravagant propositions. Mr. BENJAMIN afterward took up the theme on the same rostrum, and spoke of evacuating this city with equal flippancy. Inconsiderate persons and newspapers, we observe with pain, repeat the same ideas ; as if they positively desired the country to be taught that the abandonment of this vital position would not only be of no injury to the Confederacy, but of positive advantage.

Let not this fatal error be harbored till it takes root in the imagination. *The evacuation of Richmond would be the loss of all respect and authority toward the Confederate Government, the disintegration of the army, and the abandonment of the scheme of an independent Southern Confederation. The war would, after that, speedily degenerate into an irregular contest, in which passion would have more to do than purpose ; which would have no other object than the mere defence or present safety of those immediately persisting in it. The hope of establishing a Confederacy and securing its recognition among nations, would be gone forever. The common sense of the country, the instinct of every man and woman in the land, contradicts the idea that any possibility of an independent South would remain after its capital was abandoned, its Government set adrift, and its army withdrawn into the solitudes of the interior.*

It is idle to pretend that Richmond is of no more importance than Savannah, Atlanta, Mobile or Norfolk, and that its fall would not be fatal to the Confederacy. If it had not been a vital point, why has so much effort been expended for its reduction and in its defence ? It has been the great objective point of the enemy through four successive campaigns. The Confederacy has spared no pains or exertions, no cost of blood or treasure to make good its defence. It is the capital of the last of the border States, commanding the entire portion of Virginia east of the Alleghanies, and the most important division of North Carolina. It is situated 140 miles from the sea, yet large ships can unload from its wharves. The occupation of Richmond in strong force by the enemy would necessarily drive the Confederate armies out of Virginia, and render all Eastern North Carolina untenable ; and, once gained by a power having command of the water, it could never, under any contingency, be recovered by the Confederacy.

Each contestant in the war has made Richmond the central object of all its plans and all its exertions. *It has become the symbol of the Confederacy. Its loss would be material ruin to the cause, and, in a moral point of view, absolutely destructive, crushing the heart and extinguishing the last hope of the country. Our armies would lose the incentive inspired by a great and worthy object of defence. Our military policy would be totally at sea ; we should be without a hope or an object ; without civil or military organization ; without a treasury or a commissariat ; without the means of keeping alive a wholesome and active public sentiment ; without any of the appliances for supporting a cause depending upon the popular faith and enthusiasm ; without the emblems of the semblance of nationality ;*

The withdrawal of the army from Richmond into the interior would so narrow the area of conscription as greatly to reduce our military strength. As the army would dwindle in numbers, *it would move more and more rapidly westward, and before reaching the banks of the Mississippi would have degenerated into a mere body guard for a few officials.* From the hour of giving up the seat of government, our cause would sink into a mere rebellion in the estimation of foreign Powers ; who would cease to accord to us the rights of belligerents ; while the enemy would be free to treat our officers and soldiers as traitors and criminals ; so that every " rebel " would fight thenceforward with a halter round his neck.

Virginia, though slow to come into the Confederacy, has been throughout the contest its main stay and support. It has borne the brunt of every campaign. It has suffered the ravages of war more severely than all the other States together. Every county in the State has felt the hand of the enemy. Its richest and best districts have been utterly desolated. Its sufferings have not only been severe beyond description, but continuous and unceasing. For four years it has been the common campaign and battle ground for the largest armies and bloodiest conflicts of modern times. No country in the world ever sustained as heavy losses or endured as hard a fate, with more heroism or fortitude. The evacuation of Richmond would be the abandonment of Richmond—forever—and without any rational hope of a return. Is it possible that such a desertion could be contemplated after the events of this war ? Even if the act were not suicidal in policy, could the Confederacy now consent to cast away this worn and devastated but still powerful Commonwealth as an old shoe that could be put to no further use ?

Aside from the disgrace that would attach to such ingratitude, the Confederacy could not afford to put Gen. GRANT into possession of Richmond, a depot and base a hundred and forty miles from the sea, and in the midst of Southern Virginia yet with water carriage to the door, and thus relinquish its last hold upon the last of the border States. It could not expect to continue the struggle with any hope of success, after abandoning States whence its most numerous recruits are obtained, a soil on which its arms have been uniformly victorious, and *withdrawing to States where defeat has*

constantly *attended them.* The abandonment of Virginia would be equivalent to executing a quit claim deed to all the border States, together with Tennessee and North Carolina. Two lines of railways radiate from here into the most populous and influential districts of this latter State, subjecting its best portions to the control of any considerable military power having its base at Richmond. Is the Confederacy's wealth in population and territory now so great that it can afford to make a voluntary donation of all this territory ; restricting its jurisdiction to the gulf States, and South Carolina, already overrun?

If Richmond be held but another six months, the fate of the Confederacy will have been favorably decided. The people will cling to the cause as long as the seat of Government is secure. Recent misfortunes will have awakened foreign Powers to the danger which would result to themselves from the restoration of the Union and pacification of this continent, now possessing a trained soldiery more numerous and formidable than any army in Europe. So long as Richmond and Virginia are ours, the very reverses which have been sustained will nerve our people to renewed exertion, and beguile the enemy into a false confidence. The war cannot be carried on much longer against us if we prove but true to ourselves ; *and the single test of success will be our determination and ability to hold Richmond.* Other cities may fall, the rest of the Confederacy may succumb ; but the cause still remains safe so long as Richmond and Virginia are held.

We have now before Richmond the best army which the Confederacy has ever possessed, impregnably posted, accustomed to victory and success. All its triumphs have been won in the defence of the Confederate capital. It has continued through every trial to make good that defence, and is honored throughout the Confederacy and the world for the prowess which it has exhibited in the successful effort. We have not the slightest belief or expectation that thoughtless friends or eager enemies will ever be gratified by the sight of such a national suicide as the evacuation of Richmond will be, while that noble army exists in any part ; but with the hope of putting an end to the fall of the idle and short-sighted on this matter, we throw out these hints as to the consequences of the act of which they speak so lightly.

WILD SKEDADDLE OF THE REBEL CONGRESS.

From the Richmond Examiner, Feb. 27.

During the last four weeks *wild apprehensions of danger have disturbed the minds of the timid. The enemy has lately thrown his forces across lines of easy Congressional retreat to the West, and South, and, since that time, Senators and Representatives have one by one fled the Capitol, leaving the skeleton of the Legislature rapidly diminishing to a minium number below a quorum.* It is true the President must stand firmer as national danger thickens ; it is true the scared army must bare their breasts to the storm with more heroic courage, as the columns of the enemy converge on the liberty and existence of the country. Should the President waver and imitate Congressional example *there will be no difficulty in finding instances in history to illustrate his disgrace.*

THE RICHMOND AND PETERSBURGH LINES.

From the Richmond Dispatch, Feb. 27.

GRANT has again been massing his troops on Hatcher's Run, on our extreme right, ten miles southwest of Petersburgh, and it is thought that another attempt by his columns to gain the Southside Railroad was prevented by the rain of Saturday. We think there can be little doubt that he will make this attempt so soon as the state of the roads will permit. In their present miry condition, the movement of artillery is out of the question. GRANT has enough of the gambler in his character for the disastrous failure of his last advance toward the railroad to make him the more impatient to renew the attempt. At present, the extreme left, which may properly be considered the advance of the Yankee army, occupies a position on the left or north side of Hatcher's Run, between nine and ten miles southwest of Petersburgh, and about five miles in a direct line from the Southside Railroad.

SOUTH CAROLINA.

THE SHELLING OF COLUMBIA.

From the Richmond Examiner, Feb. 27.

One of the most atrocious crimes perpetrated since the beginning of this war, says the Charlotte *Bulletin*, was the shelling of Columbia, S. C., by the enemy, without a moment's warning. We are justified by truth in saying that two batteries were placed at commanding points on the west side of the river, and a bombardment opened upon the city whilst it was filled with women and children. Many of the houses were perforated by the missiles, and the flying of women and children from the terror thus created is said to have been a most heart-rending sight. No demand had been made for the surrender of the city. On the contrary, the enemy's approach was silently and steadily conducted. Some eight or ten persons were killed by the fragments thrown into the midst of helpless non-combatants. We are informed, *also, that after the surrender of the place, squads of the enemy marched about the city shooting down such citizens as they could find, urging as an excuse that they might be stragglers from* BEAUREGARD'S *army.*

The New-York Times.

VOL. XIV.....NO. 4195.　　　　　NEW-YORK, MONDAY, MARCH 6, 1865.　　　　　PRICE FOUR CENTS.

GLORIOUS NEWS

A New Victory for Phil. Sheridan.

Capture of Gen. Early and His Entire Force.

Charlottesville Occupied by Our Troops.

Lieut.-Gen. Grant Co-operating with Sherman.

He Occupies Lee's Attention by Threatening Richmond from the Valley.

Lee Compelled to Send Forces to Defend Lynchburg.

Jeff. Davis' Lines of Retreat in Danger.

Sheridan Knocking at the Back Door to Richmond.

OFFICIAL DISPATCHES.

[OFFICIAL.]

SECRETARY STANTON TO GEN. DIX.

WAR DEPARTMENT, WASHINGTON, March 5.

To Maj.-Gen. Dix, New-York:

The following dispatches, in relation to the reported defeat and capture of Gen. EARLY by SHERIDAN, and the capture of Charlottesville, have been received by this department. Gen. SHERIDAN and his force commenced their movement last Monday, and were at Staunton when last heard from. Maj.-Gen. HANCOCK was placed in charge of the Middle Military Division during the absence of Gen. SHERIDAN, with headquarters at Winchester.

(Signed)　　　E. M. STANTON,
　　　　　　　Secretary of War.

FIRST DISPATCH FROM GEN. GRANT.

CITY POINT, Va., March 5—11 A. M.

Hon. Edwin M. Stanton, Secretary of War:

Deserters in this morning report that SHERIDAN had routed EARLY and captured Charlottesville. They report four regiments having gone from here (Richmond) to reinforce EARLY.

(Signed)　　　U. S. GRANT, Lieut.-General

SECOND DISPATCH FROM GEN. GRANT.

CITY POINT, Va., Sunday, March 5—2 P. M.

Hon. E. M. Stanton, Secretary of War:

Deserters from every point of the enemy's line confirm the capture of Charlottesville by Gen. SHERIDAN. They say he captured Gen. EARLY and his entire force, consisting of eighteen hundred men.

Four brigades were reported as being sent to Lynchburgh, to get there before Gen. Sheridan, if possible.

(Signed)　　　U. S. GRANT, Lieut.-Gen.

FROM WASHINGTON.

THE INAUGURATION CEREMONIES.

A Fine Display --- Enthusiasm Among the People.

Defective Arrangements for the Ceremonies.

SCENES AT THE CAPITOL--A GRAND CRUSH

The Inaugural Address of President Lincoln.

Graphic Account of the Proceedings of the Day.

WASHINGTON, Saturday, March 4.

President LINCOLN was inaugurated for another term of four years at twelve o'clock, noon, to-day.

Overhead the weather was clear and beautiful, and on account of the recent rains the streets were filled with mud. Despite this fact the crowd that assembled was exceedingly large, and thousands proceeded to the capital to witness the inauguration ceremonies.

The procession moved from Sixteenth-street and Pennsylvania-avenue at about 11 o'clock.

President LINCOLN had been at the capital all day, and consequently did not accompany the procession to the scene of the interesting ceremonies.

Several bands of music, two regiments of the Invalid Corps, a squadron of cavalry, a battery of artillery, and four companies of colored troops, formed the military escort.

The Mayor and Councilmen of Washington, visiting Councilmen from Baltimore, the firemen of this city and the visiting firemen from Philadelphia, the Good Will, Franklin and Perseverance companies, each company drawing its engine along, were also in the procession.

Among the benevolent societies present were Lodges of Odd Fellows and Masons, including a colored Lodge of the latter fraternity.

The public and principal private buildings along Pennsylvania-avenue were gaily decorated with flags, and every window was thronged with faces to catch a glimpse of the President elect.

The oath to protect and maintain the Constitution of the United States, was administered to Mr. LINCOLN by Chief-Justice CHASE, in the presence of thousands, who witnessed the interesting ceremony while standing in mud almost knee-deep.

The Inaugural was then read.

THE INAUGURAL ADDRESS.

FELLOW COUNTRYMEN: At this second appearing to take the oath of the Presidential office, there is less occasion for an extended address than there was at the first. Then a statement somewhat in detail of a course to be pursued seemed very fitting and proper. Now, at the expiration of four years, during which public declarations have been constantly called forth on every point and phase of the great contest which still absorbs the attention and engrosses the energies of the nation, little that is new could be presented.

The progress of our arms, upon which all else chiefly depends, is as well known to the public as to myself, and it is, I trust, reasonably satisfactory and encouraging to all. With high hope for the future, no prediction in regard to it is ventured.

On the occasion corresponding to this four years ago, all thoughts were anxiously directed to an impending civil war. All dreaded it; all sought to avoid it. While the inaugural address was being delivered from this place, devoted altogether to saving the Union without war, insurgent agents were in the city seeking to destroy it without war—seeking to dissolve the Union and divide the effects by negotiation. Both parties deprecated war, but one of them would make war rather than let the nation survive, and the other would accept war rather than let it perish, and the war came.

One-eighth of the whole population were colored slaves, not distributed generally over the Union, but localized in the Southern part of it. These slaves constituted a peculiar and powerful interest. All knew that this interest was somehow the cause of the war. To strengthen, perpetuate and extend this interest, was the object for which the insurgents would rend the Union even by war, while the Government claimed no right to do more than to restrict the territorial enlargement of it.

Neither party expected for the war the magnitude or the duration which it has already attained. Neither anticipated that the cause of the conflict might cease with, or even before the conflict itself should cease. Each looked for an easier triumph, and a result less fundamental and astounding.

Both read the same Bible and pray to the same God, and each invokes His aid against the other. It may seem strange that any men should dare to ask a just God's assistance in wringing their bread from the sweat of other men's faces, but let us judge not, that we be not judged. The prayers of both could not be answered. That of neither has been answered fully. The Almighty has his own purposes. "Woe unto the world because of offences, for it must needs be that offences come; but woe to that man by whom the offence cometh." If we shall suppose that American slavery is one of these offences, which in the providence of God must needs come, but which having continued through His appointed time, He now wills to remove, and that He gives to both North and South this terrible war as the woe due to those by whom the offence came, shall we discern therein any departure from those divine attributes which the believers in a living God always ascribe to Him? Fondly do we hope, fervently do we pray, that this mighty scourge of war may soon pass away. Yet, if God wills that it continue until all the wealth piled by the bondman's two hundred and fifty years of unrequited toil shall be sunk, and until every drop of blood drawn with the lash shall be paid with another drawn with the sword, as was said three thousand years ago; so, still it must be said, "The judgments of the Lord are true and righteous altogether."

With malice toward none, with charity for all, with firmness in the right, as God gives us to see the right, let us strive on to finish the work we are in, to bind up the nation's wounds, to care for him who shall have borne the battle and for his widow and his orphans, to do all which may achieve and cherish a just and a lasting peace among ourselves and with all nations.

After the delivery of the address a national salute was fired by a battery stationed east of the Capitol. The procession then again moved up Pennsylvania-avenue, the President being conveyed in an open barouche. Seated with him was his son and Senator FOSTER, of the Committee of Arrangements.

The President was escorted to the White-House; after which, the procession separated.

 The New-York Times.

VOL. XIV.....NO. 4203.   NEW-YORK, WEDNESDAY, MARCH 15, 1865.   PRICE FOUR CENTS.

PANIC IN RICHMOND.

DIRECT FROM THE REBEL CAPITAL

Intense Excitement and Alarm Caused by Sheridan's Operations.

Alarm Bells Rung---The Home Guards Called Out.

Sheridan Within Twenty Miles of Richmond on Saturday.

Destruction of the Beaver Mills Aqueduct.

Sheridan Believed to Have Crossed the James River at that Point.

THE DANVILLE ROAD IN DANGER

The Isolation of the Rebel Capital Nearly Completed.

SIGNS OF THE EVACUATION OF RICHMOND.

BALTIMORE, Tuesday, March 14.

A returned Union prisoner, who reached Annapolis to-day, direct from Richmond, communicates some interesting intelligence in relation to the state of affairs at Richmond and SHERIDAN'S movements. He says he was confined in Castle Thunder, and, through the friends of Union citizens incarcerated there, obtained much information relative to events transpiring, about which Richmond papers are silent.

On Saturday night last Richmond was thrown into a state of intense excitement, by the announcement that SHERIDAN was near the city. The alarm bells were rung, and all the Home Guards, and every available man that could be spared, was hurried off to repel the Yankees, who were said to be at Beaver Mills Aqueduct, on the James River, some twenty miles from the city, destroying the canal, the main feeder to Richmond. The excitement continued all night, and increased to a panic throughout Sunday, and down to Monday morning, when he left, the alarm still prevailed. It was understood that SHERIDAN had succeeded in the destruction of the aqueduct, blowing it up with gunpowder, and it would take at least six months to repair the damage done by him during Sunday afternoon. PICKETT's division passed Castle Thunder in great haste on the way to meet SHERIDAN. There was a ferry near the aqueduct, and it was believed that SHERIDAN's purpose was to cross the James, and strike the Danville road near the coal fields, where there is an expensive bridge,

A Southern cavalry victory over troops led by Major-General Judson Kilpatrick was eagerly welcomed by a Confederacy desperate for good news.

destroy that, and thus complete the destruction of communication of Richmond, and then make a junction with GRANT.

Movements indicating a preparation for an abandonment of Richmond have been in progress for some time. The heavy machinery for manufacturing iron has been removed ; also the machinery of their percussion-cap manufactory ; and all the carpenters in town were at work filling large Government orders for packing boxes.

The high water in the James had subsided so much that the boat which conveys prisoners from Richmond could not pass above Rockett's, as she had been doing previously. From this circumstance, it is hoped that SHERMAN will find less difficulty in crossing the streams in his line of march.

NEWS FROM REBEL SOURCES.

The Raiders Above Richmond—The Queer Victories of Bragg—The South Ready for a Dictatorship—Fast Day in Richmond.

We have received Richmond papers of Monday, the 13th inst. They contain very little of interest beyond what was published in the official bulletins yesterday morning. It is noticeable that they publish in full, from Northern papers, the accounts of SHERIDAN's victory over EARLY.

WAR NEWS.

SHERIDAN IN THE REAR OF RICHMOND.

From the Richmond Whig, March 13.

It is as well known to Grant as to our people that a considerable force of Yankee cavalry is raiding through some of the counties west of Richmond, and in the vicinity of the Central Railroad, but it is considered inexpedient by the military authorities to publish anything relating to their movements. At least this was the understanding several days ago, and we have not been apprised of any modification of the request communicated to the press. We mention this fact to explain to our readers the non-appearance in the Whig of intelligence from the country into which the enemy has penetrated.

THE QUEER VICTORIES OF BRAGG.

From the Richmond Whig, March 13.

The tide of fortune at last has turned. Good news has begun to reach us. Within the last two days we have received intelligence of two victories, which, although as to the number of the forces engaged and the losses, they may not approach the great battles of the war, are yet of immense importance, considered with relation to the existing and prospective military situation. Gen. Bragg's victory over the column of the enemy making its way out from Newbern, absolutely breaks

out one of the links of the much vaunted Yankee combination. The object of the enemy was, doubtless, to destroy the railroad in the neighborhood of Goldsboro, with an intention well understood by our Commanders. Gen. HAMPTON's victory over KILPATRICK is equally important, and will prove a heavy blow to SHERMAN. *We anticipate news of even more decisive results within a few days.*

FAST DAY IN RICHMOND.

From the Richmond Whig, March 13.

The President's appointment of Friday, the 10th inst., as a day of fasting, humiliation and prayer, was universally respected in this community, and, *by a large number*, was religiously and sincerely observed. All secular business was suspended, and the streets were almost deserted except by persons going to or returning from the religious services held at the various places of public worship and prayer.

The weather in the forenoon was wet, chilly and unfavorable, and to this circumstance we may attribute the lessened display of gaudy finery at the churches—which always seems indecorous on such occasions—but the congregations were large and attentive listeners to the appropriate discourses delivered during the day. It is to be hoped that the admonitions and "words of wisdom" uttered yesterday will be treasured in the memory of those who heard them, to the end that in the future they may all lead blameless lives, and whilst securing for themselves the incalculable advantage of well-doing, contribute to the righteousness of the nation, without which we cannot expect the favor of God.

NORTH CAROLINA.

IMPORTANT OFFICIAL BULLETIN.

SHERMAN HEARD FROM.

His Headquarters at Laurel Hill, N. C., March 8.

"We Are all Well, and Have Done Finely."

BRAGG IS FAIRLY BEATEN.

He Retreats Across the Neuse, at Kingston.

[OFFICIAL.]

WASHINGTON, D. C.—11 A. M., March 14.

Maj.-Gen. Dix :

Dispatches direct from Gens. SHERMAN and SCHOFIELD have been received this morning by this department.

Gen. SHERMAN's dispatch is dated March 8, at Laurel Hill, North Carolina. He says: "We are all well and have done finely."

Details are, for obvious reasons, omitted.

Gen. SCHOFIELD, in a dispatch dated at Newbern, March 12, states that on the night of the 10th, near Southwest Creek, BRAGG was fairly beaten ; that during the night he retreated across the Neuse at Kinston, and now holds the north bank of the river at that place.   EDWIN M. STANTON,

Secretary of War.

[Laurel Hill is a small town in Richmond County, North Carolina, about thirty miles southwest of Fayetteville, toward which point SHERMAN is evidently directing his march.—ED. TIMES.]

The New-York Times.

VOL. XIV.....NO. 4210.   NEW-YORK, THURSDAY, MARCH 23, 1865.   PRICE FOUR CENTS.

THE SOUTH.

JEFF. DAVIS AND HIS GOVERNMENT

The Rebel Senate in Judgment on the Rebel President.

THE REVELATIONS OF DESPAIR.

Scathing Commentary on the Dishonesty, Delays, and Disasters of the Davis Administration.

Conscription, Currency, Tax, and Impressment Bills Rejected by the Gross.

Lee the Forlorn Hope of the Rebels.

Address of the Rebel Congress to the People of the South.

Rodomontade and Misrepresentation.

THE REBEL CONGRESS ON JEFF. DAVIS.

From the Richmond Sentinel, March 20.

The following is the report of the Senate Committee on the recent message of President Davis. It was read and adopted in secret session, and the seal of secrecy removed on the 16th instant :

The Select Committee to whom was referred so much of the President's message of the 13th instant, as relates to the action of Congress during the present session, having duly considered the same, respectfully submit the following report :

THE RECOMMENDATIONS OF JEFF. DAVIS.

The attention of Congress is called by the President to the fact that, for carrying on the war successfully, there is urgent need of men and supplies for the army.

The measures passed by Congress during the present session for recruiting the army, are considered by the President inefficient ; and it is said that the results of the law authorizing the employment of slaves as soldiers will be less than anticipated, in consequence of the dilatory action of Congress in adopting the measure. That a law so radical in its character, so repugnant to the prejudices of our people, and so intimately affecting the organism of society, should encounter opposition and receive a tardy sanction, ought not to excite our surprise ; but if the policy and necessity of the measure had been seriously urged on Congress by an Executive message, legislative action might have been quickened.

THE POLICY OF ARMING SLAVES.

The President, in his official communication to Congress, has recommended the passage of a law putting slaves into the army as soldiers, and the message under consideration is the first official information that such a law would meet his approval. The Executive message transmitted to Congress on the 7th of November last, suggests the pro-

As the Confederacy crumbled, so too did support for beleaguered Jefferson Davis, loudly criticized by the Senate, the press, and the public.

priety of enlarging the sphere of employment of the negro as a laborer, and for this purpose, recommends that the absolute title to slaves be acquired by impressment, and as an incentive to the faithful discharge of duty, that the slaves thus acquired be liberated, with the permission of the States from which they were drawn. In this connection the following language is used :

"If this policy should recommend itself to the judgment of Congress, it is suggested that, in addition to the duties heretofore performed by the slave, he might be advantageously employed as *pioneer and engineer laborers;* and, in that event, that the number should be augmented to forty thousand. *Beyond this limit and these employments it does not seem to me desirable, under existing circumstances to go."*

In the same message, the President further remarks :

" The subject is to be viewed by us, therefore, solely in the light of policy and our social economy. *When so regarded, I must dissent from those who advise a general levy and arming the slaves for the duty of soldiers."*

It is manifest that the President, in November last, did not consider that the contingency had then arrived which would justify a resort to the extraordinary policy of arming our slaves. Indeed no other inference can be deduced from the language used by him ; for he says :

" These considerations, however, are rather applicable to *an improbable contingency of our need of resorting to this element of resistance than to our present condition."*

The Secretary of War, in his report, under date of

Nov. 3, seemed to concur in the opinion of the President when he said:

"While it is encouraging to know this resource for further and future efforts is at our command, *my own judgment does not yet either perceive the necessity or approve the policy of employing slaves in the higher duties of soldiers.*"

At what period of the session the President or Secretary of War considered the improbable contingency had arisen, which required a resort to slaves as an element of resistance, does not appear by any official document within the knowledge of your committee. Congress might well have delayed action on this subject until the present moment, as the President, whose constitutional duty it is "to give to the Congress information of the state of the Confederacy," has never asked, in any authentic manner, for the passage of a law authorizing the employment of slaves as soldiers. *The Senate, however, did not wait the tardy movements of the President.* On the 29th December, 1864, the following resolution was adopted by the Senate in secret session:

Resolved, That the President be requested to inform the Senate, in secret session, as to the state of finances in connection with the payment of the troops; the means of supplying the munitions of war, transportation and subsistence; the condition of the army, and the possibility of recruiting the same; the condition of our foreign relations, and whether any aid or encouragement from abroad is expected, or has been sought, or is proposed, so that the Senate may have a clear and exact view of the state of the country, and of its future prospects, and what measures of legislation are required.

In response to this resolution, the President might well have communicated to the Senate his views as to the necessity and policy of arming the slaves of the Confederacy, as a means of public defence. *No answer whatever has been made to the resolution.* In addition to this, a joint committee was raised by Congress, under a concurrent resolution adopted in secret session on the 30th December, 1864. That committee, by the resolution creating it, was instructed "by conference with the President, and by such other means as they shall deem proper, to ascertain what are our reliable means of public defence, present and prospective."

A written report was made by the committee on Jan. 25, 1865; and, although it had a conference with the President, no allusion is made in the report to any suggestion by him that the necessities of the country required the employment of slaves as soldiers. Under these circumstances, *Congress, influenced no doubt by the opinion of Gen. Lee, determined for itself the propriety, policy and necessity of adopting the measure in question.*

The recommendations of the President to employ 40,000 slaves as cooks, teamsters, and as engineer and pioneer laborers was assented to, and a law has been enacted at the present session for the purpose, without limit as to number.

All the measures recommended by the President, to promote the efficiency of the army, have been adopted except the entire repeal of class exemption; *and some measures not suggested by him—such as the creation of General-in-Chief—were originated and passed by Congress, with a view to the restoration of public confidence and the energetic administration of military affairs.*

THE SUBJECT OF EXEMPTIONS.

On the subject of exemptions, the President, in his message of Nov. 7, uses the following language:

"No pursuit nor position should relieve any one, who is able to do active duty, from enrollment in the army, unless his functions or services are more useful to the defence of his country in another sphere. But it is manifest that this cannot be the case with entire classes. All telegraph operators, workmen in mines, professors, teachers, engineers, editors and employes of newspapers, journeymen printers, shoemakers, tanners, blacksmiths, millers, physicians and numerous other classes mentioned in the laws, cannot in the nature of things, be either equally necessary in their several professions, nor distributed throughout the country in such proportions that only the exact number required are found in each locality."

The casual reader would infer that the laws, as they stood at the date of the message, exempted the classes enumerated by the President, as well as many other classes not mentioned by him. Such is not the fact. The only class exemptions allowed by the laws then in force were the following: Ministers of religion; superintendents and physicians of asylums for the deaf, dumb and blind, and of the insane; one editor for each newspaper, and such employes as the editor may certify on oath as indispensably necessary; the public printers of the Confederate and State Governments, and their journeymen printers; one skilled apothecary in each apothecary store, who was doing business as such on the 10th of October, 1862; physicians over thirty years of age, and for seven years in practice; presidents and teachers of colleges, seminaries and schools, and the superintendents, physicians and nurses in public hospitals; certain mail contractors, and drivers of post-coaches; certain officers and employes of railroad companies; certain agriculturists or overseers.

Officers of the State Government are not properly included among the exempted classes, because it is conceded that Congress has no constitutional power to conscribe them as soldiers. Nor are drunkards, Quakers, or other non-combatants, regarded as belonging to class exemptions, because, under the act of June 7, 1864, the exemption of these persons is subject to the control of the Secretary of War. The exemption of agriculturists or overseers, between the ages of 18 and 45, has been repealed at the present session. Tanners, shoemakers, millers, blacksmiths, telegraph operators, and workmen in mines, enumerated by the President as among the classes exempted, are not now, and have not been, since the passage of the act of 17th February, 1864, exempted as a class. If railroad officers and employes, and State officers who are not constitutionally subject to conscription, be excluded, the classes now exempted east of the Mississippi River embrace about 9,000 men—one-third of whom are physicians, and nearly another third are ministers of the Gospel; the remaining third is principally composed of teachers, professors, printers and employes in newspaper offices, and apothecaries.

DETAILED MEN.

In remarkable contrast to the number of persons relieved from military service by the exemptions above mentioned, the report of the Conscript Bureau exhibits the fact that east of the Mississippi River 22,035 men have been detailed by Executive authority. In consequence of this abuse of the power of detail, Congress, at its present session, passed an act revoking all details, and limiting the exercise of that power in the future. The third section of this act, exempting skilled artisans and mechanics from all military service, which is objected to by the President, and which has since been repealed, was originally adopted in consequence of suggestions contained in the report of the Secretary of War. In alluding to the embarrassments encountered by the administration's bureaus, the Secretary says:

"In addition, they have been constrained, by the stringent legislation of Congress, to relinquish their most active and experienced agents and employes, and substitute them from more infirm and aged classes."

Again:

"Interferences of this kind are inevitably so prejudicial and disturbing, that it is to be hoped a well-devised and permanent system of providing and retaining in continuous employment a sufficient number of artisans, experts and laborers, for all essential operations, may be devised and established."

The truth is, that the bill originally introduced into the Senate, exempting skilled artisans and mechanics, was actually prepared in one of the bureaus of the War Department. Congress, therefore, had reason to suppose that it would meet the sanction of the Executive.

CONSCRIPTION OF MINISTERS AND EDITORS.

To conscribe the ministers of religion, and require them to obtain details to preach the Gospel, would shock the religious sentiment of the country, and inflict a greater injury on our cause than can be described. The conscription of editors and of the printers necessary to the publication of newspapers would destroy the independence of the press, and subject it to the control of the Executive Department of the Government. The railroad officers and employes are as necessary to the prosecution of the war as the soldier in the field. Physicians and apothecaries are essential to the health of the people, and no complaint has reached Congress of abuses in this class of exemptions. If the education of youth be regarded as conducive to the maintenance of society and the preservation of liberty, it is not perceived that the exemption of professors of colleges and teachers of schools can be justly censured. The Senate passed a bill containing a section repealing the exemption allowed to mail contractors and drivers of post coaches; but, at a subsequent stage of proceedings, and on the recommendation of a committee of conference, based on the urgent remonstrances of the Postmaster-General, the section alluded to was stricken out.

CLASS EXEMPTIONS.

The subject of class exemptions was called to the attention of Congress by the Executive message of November last. It was carefully considered, and an act was passed expressive of the views of the legislative department of the Government. The message under consideration recurs to the same subject. It is to be regretted that the views of the legislative department of the Government have not met the favor of the Executive, and that he should deem it both necessary and proper to express dissatisfaction with the matured opinion of Congress.

NORTH CAROLINA.

PROGRESS OF SHERMAN'S CAMPAIGN.

Occupation of Goldsboro by Our Forces Confirmed.

Junction Between Sherman and Schofield.

Johnston Said to be Moving to Join Lee.

Sheridan Going to Look After Him.

INTERESTING REPORTS FROM KINSTON.

Special Dispatch to the New-York Times.

WASHINGTON, Wednesday, March 22.

A steamer arrived at Fortress Monroe yesterday afternoon, from Beaufort, N. C., on the evening of the 20th, bringing the intelligence that Gen. SHERMAN'S right wing occupied Golsboro on Sunday, the 19th. The Government has not yet received dispatches from Gen. SHERMAN at that point; but the information came from Gen. SCHOFIELD'S advance, which was moving on Goldsboro from Kinston, and is well authenticated.

SHERMAN left Fayetteville on the 14th, and was therefore six days in making the march, a distance of nearly sixty miles. Of course he could not have had much opposition.

SHERMAN'S left wing, it is known here, moved from Fayetteville in the direction of Mitchelop Station, where the railroad to Raleigh crosses the Neuse River a second time by a long and expensive bridge. This point is about twenty-five miles west of Goldsboro. Gen. SCHOFIELD, having no enemy in his front, would at once form a junction with Gen. SHERMAN, which is ere this undoubtedly accomplished.

The Neuse River is navigable for vessels of light draft as far as Goldsboro, but during the war none of our vessels have penetrated higher than Kinston, where the railroad bridge, which was without a draw, obstructed further progress. The completion of the railroad from Kinston to Goldsboro, together with the navigation of the Neuse to Kinston, will fully supply both SHERMAN and SCHOFIELD.

Both Beaufort and Newbern will be made bases of supplies. The steamer *Euterpe* sailed to-day for Beaufort with a cargo of clothing for SHERMAN'S army. Quartermaster-General MEIGS was a passenger on board.

REPORTS FROM WASHINGTON.

WASHINGTON, Wednesday, March 22.

The *Republican* extra says the Government has received intelligence that on Sunday last Gen. SHERMAN'S army entered Goldsboro, North Carolina. His march was unopposed.

The two armies of SHERMAN and SCHOFIELD have formed a junction.

The *Republican* extra further says SHERMAN'S present command is sufficiently formidable to confront LEE'S whole army in the open field, without the assistance of GRANT, and no force that the rebels may raise can impede SHERMAN'S triumphant march northward.

The story in the Richmond *Sentinel*, which we published yesterday, that four of SHERMANS' divisions were repulsed near Fayetteville turns out to be a rebel lie, as we stated.

REPORTS FROM PHILADELPHIA.

PHILADELPHIA, Wednesday, March 22.

A special from Washington to the *Evening Telegraph*, says a messenger arrived with news from Gen. SHERMAN to Monday, via City Point.

Goldsboro was occupied by our forces on Sunday, and the army moved immediately in pursuit of the enemy.

Refugees all report that JOHNSTON is moving to Richmond to join LEE, and that his army is really unfit for heavy fighting, and that HOPE'S troops are the only men that can be relied upon.

Raleigh will be captured with but little, if any, fighting.

Gen. SHERIDAN is off on another raid. It is said that he will intercept JOHNSTON in his retreat.

The Army of the Potomac is believed to be advancing West. A great battle is expected soon.

The New-York Times.

VOL. XIV.....NO. 4220.   NEW-YORK, TUESDAY, APRIL 4, 1865.   PRICE FOUR CENTS.

GRANT.

RICHMOND

AND

VICTORY!

The Union Army in the Rebel Capital.

Rout and Flight of the Great Rebel Army from Richmond.

Jeff. Davis and His Crew Driven Out.

Grant in Close Pursuit of Lee's Routed Forces.

Richmond and Petersburgh in Full Possession of Our Forces.

ENTHUSIASM IN THE REBEL CAPITAL.

The Citizens Welcome Our Army with Demonstrations of Joy.

RICHMOND FIRED BY THE ENEMY

Our Troops Save the City from Destruction.

THE EVACUATION OF PETERSBURGH.

FIRST DISPATCH.

[OFFICIAL.]

WAR DEPARTMENT,
WASHINGTON, April 3—10 A. M.

To Major-Gen. Dix:

The following telegram from the President, announcing the EVACUATION OF PETERSBURGH and probably of Richmond, has just been received by this department:

EDWIN M. STANTON, Secretary of War.

CITY POINT, Va., April 3—8:30 A. M.

To Hon. Edwin M. Stanton, Secretary of War:

This morning Lieut.-Gen. GRANT reports Petersburgh evacuated, and he is confident that Richmond also is.

He is pushing forward to cut off, if possible, the retreating rebel army.   A. LINCOLN.

THE CAPTURE OF RICHMOND.

SECOND DISPATCH.

WAR DEPARTMENT, WASHINGTON, D. C.,
April 3—10 A. M.

To Maj.-Gen. Dix:

It appears from a dispatch of Gen. WEITZEL just received by this Department, that our forces under his command ARE IN RICHMOND, having taken it at 8:15 this morning.

EDWIN M. STANTON, Secretary of War.

THIRD DISPATCH.

WAR DEPARTMENT, WASHINGTON,
Monday, April 3—12 o'clock noon.

Maj. Gen. Dix:

The following official confirmation of the capture of Richmond, and the announcement that the city is on fire, has been received.

E. M. STANTON, Secretary of War.

CITY POINT, Monday, April 3—11 A. M.

To Edwin M. Stanton, Secretary of War:

Gen. WEITZEL telegraphs as follows:

"We took Richmond at 8:15 this morning. I captured many guns. The enemy left in great haste. The city is on fire in one place. Am making every effort to put it out. The people receive us with enthusiastic expressions of joy."

Gen. GRANT started early this morning with the army toward the Danville road, to cut off Lee's retreating army, if possible.

President LINCOLN has gone to the front.

T. S. BOWERS, A. A. G.

E. M. STANTON.

OUR SPECIAL ACCOUNTS.

Movements by Gen. Sheridan—His Call for Reinforcements—Four Thousand Prisoners Captured—Operations on the Petersburgh Front—The Gunboat Fleet Doing Its Part.

From Our Own Correspondent.

HEADQUARTERS ARMY OF THE POTOMAC,
Sunday, April 2—6 A. M.

After we quitted the field on Friday evening the left of the Fifth Corps swung about half a mile further round, and drove the enemy before them. But intelligence being received from Gen. SHERIDAN that the condition of the ground on his front was such that he could not operate with cavalry, and his advance had, therefore, been compelled to fall back. The Fifth Corps was ordered to go to his assistance, in order to relieve it and prevent its withdrawal. Being perceived and taken advantage of by the enemy, Gen. MILES' division of the Second Corps was advanced by the left flank in its front, and it was

then withdrawn to the Boydtown road. Gen. MILES' division of the Second then fell back to a position on the plankroad behind a temporary embankment that had been thrown up on Wednesday, leaving in the line he recently occupied nothing more than skirmishers, who were directed to fall back if attacked. The Second Division of the Fifth Corps, Gen. AYRES, set out early this morning to support Gen. SHERIDAN, and the divisions of Gen. GRIFFIN and Gen. CRAWFORD followed it about noon. They all formed a junction with Gen. SHERIDAN's Corps at a distance of some five miles from the Mrs. Butler house, and a general engagement commenced there about 3 o'clock.

I was not able to go out, as the distance is too great for me to accomplish anything in time for the mail. I understand, however, that the combined forces of Gens. SHERIDAN and WARREN succeeded, after a hotly contested fight, in putting the enemy to flight. They captured four thousand prisoners, four batteries of artillery, a large train of loaded wagons and a number of cattle. The rebel loss in killed and wounded, as well as our own was very heavy, but I am unable to give any estimate of the number. On our lines during the day there was no fighting except on the Twenty-fourth Corps front. The rebels assaulted the pickets of that corps, and attempted to retake the picket line, from which they were driven yesterday. They were speedily repulsed with a loss of about twenty-five killed and wounded and sixty-four prisoners. Our loss was fifteen in the aggregate.

In the afternoon our troops were massed at three places in the Ninth Corps front, at two in the Sixth, and one in the Twenty-fourth, one in the Twenty-fifth, and two in the Second, with a view of making several demonstrations on the enemy's works and going through them, if necessary, for the complete development of the plan of attack. In pursuance with this design our artillery opened a furious cannonading along the entire front at about 11 P. M., which was continued with little intermission until 6 o'clock this morning. At 3 this morning, such of our troops as it was deemed proper to send in were got into position in front of our works and held ready to make the assault.

I have not yet had time to ascertain which troops were led to the assault, nor the results at different points, and am only able to speak of the Second Division, Gen. POTTER's, of the Ninth Corps. This division was posted on that part of the line between forts Sedgwick and Davis, and some time before the hour of attack arrived the Brigade Commanders Gens. GRIFFIN and CURTIN, perceiving the opportunity to do so without endangering their own men made a sortie and captured one hundred and thirty-three men and four officers of the rebel pickets.

His picket-line was completely surprised, and only knew of the attack when called upon to surrender. At this hour, 6 A. M., there is exceedingly heavy firing along the entire line from Deep Bottom to the Boydtown plank-road, and the fleet of gunboats on the James River are participating in it.

The assault on the enemy's works commenced at 4 o'clock in several places, and is still progressing, but with what success is not yet known. In the front of the Second Division of the Ninth Corps there seems to be more artillery engaged than elsewhere on the line, except at the

Federal troops huddle together prior to their attack on Confederate positions.

Much of Richmond succumbed to fire, adding to the destruction caused by artillery shelling. Incoming Union forces fought the blaze, with some success, but scenes such as this were commonplace.

W. H. F. LEE's cavalry, three brigades, was in front, but did not see fit to make a stand.

To-day, in an attempt to reach Supporty crossroads, some of PICKETT's command and LEE's cavalry formed a line of battle and held the ground. In the skirmish that took place the following named persons were wounded:

KILLED AND WOUNDED.

John Leonard, Company F, Sixth United States Cavalry, left thigh, flesh; James N. Glosswax, Company A, Sixth United States Cavalry, hip; John Thompson, Company M, Sixth United States Cavalry; Henry M. Feelan, First United States Cavalry; Patrick Germon, Company F, Sixth United States Cavalry; John Mooney, Company M, Seventh Michigan; Sergt. Marsh, First Michigan, killed; Sergt. J. L. Cullek, Seventh Michigan, foot; Sergt. R. Harris, Fifth United States Cavalry; J. B. Morril, Company M, Fifth United States Cavalry; Sergt. Thomas M. Welles, Company F, Sixth United States Cavalry; Sergt. James Homer; Corp. E. Leabe, Fifth United States Cavalry, arm, severe; Sergt. J. Miller, Sixth United States; J. Davidson, First Michigan; Maj. Duggin, First Michigan; William Sherburne, Twentieth Pennsylvania; D. Duggin, First Michigan; George Nash; Corp. George Derrick; Sergt. Robert Rordan, Sixth New-York; Corp. George B. Lott, Twentieth Pennsylvania.

E. A. PAUL.

Details of the Victory.

Dispatches to the Associated Press.

HEADQUARTERS ARMY OF THE POTOMAC,
Saturday, April 1.

The greater portion of the army has not been engaged with the enemy to-day. The time has been occupied in erecting works on the new line, and repairing the roads connecting the different corps. The late rains had rendered it impossible to move the wagon trains as fast as the troops advanced. One train took forty-eight hours to move five miles with the assistance of one thousand men. But through the untiring industry and perseverance of the officers in charge of the Quartermaster's and Commissary Departments, the army has been almost as well supplied as while in their old quarters.

When the news of SHERIDAN's repulse reached here last night, a part of the Fifth Corps was at once despatched to his aid, and it is expected that to-night or in the morning we shall receive good news from that quarter.

It appears that SHERIDAN was moving on the road leading to a place called the Three Forks, about three miles from the Southside Railroad, when two cavalry brigades of PICKETT's division, which had been moved out in a great hurry, came down on a road running from Sutherland Station. As SHERIDAN's cavalry had most of them passed the junction, this movement of the enemy threatened to cut him off. He, however, discovered his danger in time to get his command back with only a slight loss, at the same time taking about 100 prisoners. Both the LEES were present, but one of them was at a respectful distance.

On being reinforced this morning by the Fifth Corps, the enemy fell back so rapidly that their dead and many of their wounded fell into our hands, as well as those of our own that were unavoidably left behind yesterday afternoon.

The attack made on the enemy's line in front of the Twenty-fourth Corps was led by FOSTER's division, and about two hundred prisoners were brought in. the One Hundred and Forty-eighth New-York taking most of them. Some three hundred or four hundred yards of ground was taken from them, and our picket line so much further advanced.

At 4 o'clock this morning this position was assaulted, and a few of our men captured; but in a very short time it was retaken, with about sixty prisoners and a stand of colors.

Our losses up to the present time will not exceed twenty-five hundred; while those of the enemy, on some parts of the line, at least, were greater than our own; but, of course, the total cannot be given.

Major DIKEMAN, of the Fifteenth New-York Heavy Artillery, is reported wounded and a prisoner.

Three sharpshooters were brought into the Fifth

A Confederate defender lies peacefully after being killed in the assault of Petersburg. The Federal breakthrough led to the abandonment of Richmond.

Corps headquarters this morning, sixteen cavalrymen belonging to WM. HENRY LEE's command.

They had been on picket duty and were cut off by the force which went to the assistance of SHERIDAN.

SECOND DISPATCH.

HEADQUARTERS OF THE ARMY OF THE POTOMAC,
April 1—Midnight.

A courier from Major-Gen. SHERIDAN has just arrived with the most cheering news.

The combined forces of cavalry and Major-Gen. WARREN's infantry advanced against the enemy this afternoon, driving them several miles, and capturing about 4,000 prisoners and a number of pieces of artillery.

They retreated to Five Forks, where they were flanked by a part of the Fifth Corps, which had moved down the White Oak road. It was here the large number of prisoners were taken.

The rebels then retreated south along the White Oak road, and were vigorously pursued by Gen. SHERIDAN, while McKENZIE's cavalry from the Army of the James, advanced west on the Ford road toward the Southside road, and when the messenger left was only about three miles from it, and would undoubtedly reach it before morning.

Thus the last great line of railroad the rebels have to supply their capital and LEE's army by is about to be severed, and it is firmly believed that they will immediately leave their present position in Petersburgh and Richmond.

Sharp cannonading is now going on near the centre of the line, held by the left of the Sixth Corps.

REPORTS VIA BALTIMORE.

Capture of Forts Hell and Damnation—Heavy Losses.

Special Dispatch to the Evening Telegraph.

BALTIMORE, Monday, April 3.

The latest news here this morning is, that our forces had captured Fort Damnation last night, with all its armament and many prisoners. This fort is near Fort Hell, and one of the strongest and most important rebel forts.

It is also reported that Petersburgh has been captured.

The fighting has been terrible, and the losses heavy on both sides; but the rebel loss thus far is three times more than ours.

It is believed that SHERIDAN by this time has cut the Danville Railroad.

The Flood in the St. Lawrence—Submersion at Montreal—The Victoria Bridge in Danger.

MONTREAL, Monday, April 3.

The river rose several feet on Saturday and was piled with ice to a great heighth. One of the shoves came near striking a tube of the Victoria Bridge.

Yesterday morning, the river rose much higher, flooding William, Wellington and other streets. Between 5 and 6 o'clock in the evening, the ice shoved again and the water rushed over the revetment wall, flooding Commission-street. At about 11 o'clock, it again rose as high as St. Paul and St. Gill streets.

The Grand Trunk Railway track between Bonaventure and the tanneries is inundated.

The river rose a foot higher this morning.

The inundated parts of the city are covered with rafts formed with scows and boats.

At present, by far the greater part of the western end of the city is inaccessible except by boats.

The flood is causing the greatest suffering and distress.

Later—4 O'clock P. M.—The water is now slowly falling.

point where the gunboats are engaged. But Gen. POTTER and his two able Brigade Generals, GRIFFIN and CURTIN, are holding their men well up the work, and the determination is universal throughout the division to go through if required. Gen. POTTER and his staff are in the hottest part of the field, overseeing the assault in person. The General feels, no doubt, that his front is one of the most important positions on the whole line, and from its proximity to the rebel works, most liable to be broken through, except that opposite Fort Steadman, and he is consequently extremely solicitous respecting it. The front at Fort Steadman is ably defended by Gen. WILCOX.

LATER.

Part of the line on the left is said to have made a successful demonstration and captured a number of prisoners. If possible to get it through in time, I will send you particulars, dispatching it to City Point by express before the boat leaves.

Among the prisoners captured by the Ninth Corps are eight officers, one of them a Major. Col. GOWAN, of the Forty-eighth Pennsylvania, was badly wounded, as also Col. WINSLOW and Major STEINBERG, of the One Hundred and Sixth New-York ; Col. GREGG, One Hundred and Seventy-ninth New-York, badly wounded and reported dead. The fighting was so severe that the loss on both sides must necessarily be very heavy. The rebels fought our men hand to hand when we were about climbing the parapet of the fort, although lying down at the time to avoid the fire of our advancing line. Gen. GRIFFIN, of the Second Brigade of the Division, led the way into their works, and when Gen. POTTER sent to ask if he could hold the works, and if not to fall back, his reply was, " Tell Gen. POTTER I can hold the works. Send me more

men if you can ; but I will hold the works." He took command of the division on Gen. POTTER being wounded. Gen. CURTIN, of the First Brigade, also behaved with great gallantry, holding his men up to the works till an entrance was effected, and then dashing forward at their head driving the enemy before him. This fight, even if not ultimately successful, proves the old Ninth Corps to be equal to any emergency. The task set for it is the worst this army ever had to do, and so far it has accomplished the object unaided. Everybody here thinks those who are left of us will quarter in Petersburgh to-night, and that the old stars and stripes will wave over the cockade city ere the setting of the sun. In taking Petersburgh we draw the cord that will soon strangle the rebellion in Richmond.

Gen. WILCOX is also in the field with his staff. The lines here are also very close together, and if our forces should be repulsed and disordered, the enemy would have an excellent opportunity to inflict serious damage, and make us pay dearly for the temerity we have evinced in attempting to assault such almost impregnable works as those he occupies along this line.

Gen. HARTRANFT's Division is engaged in the assault, but I am not able to say at what particular point or with what success. It is composed wholly of new troops who have never been in any engagement but that of the 25th ult., but they behaved so nobly on that occasion that great things are expected of them. And they have such regard for their brave and noble Division Commander that they will no doubt strive hard for the sake of his reputation and their own. Gen. PARKE, the Corps Commander, is also near the scene of action with his staff and within range of the enemy's guns directing the operations.

From the present aspect of affairs he will have cause to be proud of his corps ere the day closes as we are no doubt already partially within the enemy's lines, strong as they are, whether we can hold them will soon be known. It is thought here that we can both take and hold them.

1 o'clock. A. M.—The demonstration in front of the Second division of the Ninth Corps promises to be a success. We have captured two of their forts, guns and all. and the line of works between and on either flank, and have taken two hundred more prisoners. The fight is still raging furiously. Our loss must be heavy, but at this hour it is impossible to give any estimate. We have succeeded in compelling them to bring their forces from the left and thus opened the way there for SHERIDAN and WARREN to operate successfully. Their force in this front, and which we are now fighting, is Gen. GORDON's corps, principally Southern troops from Alabama, Ga., and South Carolina. They have fought hard since the attack commenced, and still continue to dispute the ground inch by inch.

I regret to say that Gen. POTTER is severely wounded, being shot through the stomach. It is not classed as a mortal wound, but is highly dangerous.

I have not yet been able to learn how matters stand elsewhere, but we have now a strong force within their line of works and will hold them. By to-night, I hope to write you from Petersburgh.

H. H. YOUNG.

Skirmishing on March 30 Near Supporty Cross-Roads.

From Our Own Correspondent.

DINWIDDIE COURT-HOUSE, Va., Thursday, March 30. }
Via WASHINGTON, Monday, April 3—8:45 P. M. }

The advance of Gen. SHERIDAN's command crossed Hatcher's Run yesterday, meeting only slight opposition and annoyance at that place from the enemy's cavalry.

The New-York Times.

VOL. XIV—NO. 4221   NEW-YORK, WEDNESDAY, APRIL 5, 1865.   PRICE FOUR CENTS.

NEWS OF THE DAY.

THE REBELLION.

We give this morning, from our special correspondents, very interesting details of the recent battles for the possession of the rebel capital. The regular war dispatches also convey many important particulars, the wires being now working direct from City Point to Richmond. Gen. WEITZEL telegraphed early yesterday morning that he found 28 locomotives and 150 cars in the city. Gen. GRANT is said to have directed WEITZEL to allow No one to leave or enter the city except men connected with the army. On Sunday night, before the evacuation of Richmond, the rebels blew up their forts and rams on the James River, the explosion of which was terrible. Our gunboats have moved up the river, and are engaged in removing the obstructions. The rebels fired Petersburgh in several places before evacuating the town, but the fire was speedily extinguished. Gen. GRANT was, at 3¾ o'clock on Tuesday morning at Sutherland's Station, ten miles from Petersburgh, from which point he telegraphs that "SHERIDAN picked up twelve hundred prisoners to-day, and from three to five hundred more have been gathered by our troops. The majority of the arms that were left in the hands of LEE's army, are now scattered between Richmond and where his troops now are. The country is also full of stragglers. The line of retreat is marked with artillery, ammunition, burned or charred wagons, caissons, ambulances, &c." We are yet without definite knowledge of losses on either side, but our captures of prisoners are something wonderful. A Washington dispatch estimates that we had taken more than 25,000 up to Monday noon This figure is reduced by others to 20,000; others say 15,000 to 18,000. But this is, mainly, guesswork; GRANT has no time to make inventories. Many thousands of prisoners have already been received at City Point, and others are continually arriving. A sufficient number of troops could not be spared to guard them, and detachments of sailors and marines were taken from the gunboats and placed in charge. The destruction of property by the rebels is very great, but not equal to the general expectation. They burned some public buildings, but no attempt was made to convert Richmond into a Moscow; indeed, their haste was such that they lacked time for anything like systematic work. It is the general opinion, justified by GRANT's own position, that LEE is retreating upon the Danville Railroad, and that SHERIDAN is upon his flanks.

Editorials

The Capture of Richmond—What Next?

The capture of Richmond plucks out the very heart of the rebellion. It is not enough to say that the rebel capital has been taken. Richmond bore a much more important relation to the rebellion than that term would express. It was not merely the locality where rested the rebel government—as Washington is the seat of the Federal Government;—it was the great generator of the vital force of the Confederacy. The largest city in the Confederacy, since New-Orleans came into our possession; having an inherited prestige that no other could claim; the headquarters of the principal rebel army, as well as of the rebel civil administration; its press working for the rebel cause with a vehemence and a fire, and an effectiveness incomparably beyond anything displayed elsewhere in Southern journalism; and, what is most important of all, having been so attacked and so defended from the beginning of the war, that it is associated, the world over, with the very substance of the war, and bears, as no other spot does, its "form and impress,"—Richmond came to be the very vital source of all the material energy and all the moral power of the rebellion. Its collapse is the death of the rebellion. The confederacy will hereafter exhibit no activity or sign of life, except as it is galvanized.

Thus the question of pacification is at once brought home to us. It is the part of every loyal man now to consider how the priceless fruits of our victory can be quickest realized. We have been fighting this four years' war not from passion at the Fort Sumter outrage, nor from obstinacy that holds on, when once the hand is in for the mere sake of it, nor from a love of military fame, nor because of any glittering generality or chivalrous sentiment, but for the most practical and substantial of all ends—namely, the restoration of the blessings of the Union. All this immeasurable treasure and blood has been poured out for that object absolutely and alone. Nothing else ought now to be thought of. The fall of Richmond, much as it is calculated to stir every high emotion, should be estimated with particular reference to its being turned to practical account in speeding a cordial reunion between the North and the South. It is valuable just as in proportion as we so make use of it.

The event ought to be signalized by some demonstration from our Government that shall, if possible, reawaken loyalty on the instant. Every advance made by the President toward the Southern people, so long as Richmond defied him, would have been misconstrued into a bid for a compromise. This is now impossible. The power of our government to compel submission is now as manifest as the sun. No Southern mind can be so stupid as to impute an overture of kindness now to fear, or discouragement, or any other unworthy motive. It would be recognized as a pledge of good will, and, we believe, would forthwith rouse into life a reciprocal feeling. In a great crisis like that now existing in the South, the popular will often determines with an electric quickness. The Southern temperament is peculiarly susceptible to sudden accessions of new feelings and purposes. This was marvelously exemplified in the almost instantaneous firing of the Southern heart from which the rebellion first burst. Everything is just as favorable for a sudden influx of intense loyalty now, as of the contrary spirit then. We may say, vastly more so; for in the one case the impulse sprang from the imagination only, while in the other it comes from the most terrible experiences. The movement away from the Union was a relinquishment of great prosperity; if that could be speedily accomplished, we may look for quicker time yet in the movement back to the Union, from a state of immeasurable wretchedness. At all events, we trust our government will do its best to clear the way for it.

What is wanted is not so much a bald statement to the Southern people that they can have peace and protection by repudiating the Confederacy and resuming their true allegiance, as an appeal palpitating with brotherly regard. It is no longer necessary to dwell with emphasis upon the hard truth that the government cannot and will not give peace for anything less than unconditional submission. That is already well enough understood. The submission can be had. But if we want something more than submission, if we would have genuine, ardent, whole-souled loyalty, we should invite it in language calculated to reassure and ingratiate. ABRAHAM LINCOLN, notwithstanding all the abuse heaped upon him by the rebel leaders, is known through the South as well as in the North to be a thoroughly sincere man. Words of good will from him, assurances that his policy, so far as the body of the Southern people are concerned, will be to bury the past, to remove sectional distinctions, to secure the universal enjoyment of every national blessing, would challenge confidence at once, and we verily believe it would be followed by an enthusiastic response.

If this is ever to be done, now is the golden instant. The Southern mind is now in its most impressible mood. The fall of Richmond annihilates the last lingering trust in the Confederacy. Its suddenness intensifies the sensation. Every element of the Southern nature is most keenly alive to the question, what shall be done? A recoil that should send the Southern people back, at a bound, into the full embrace of the government, would come much more naturally now than after they had sunk, bewildered and nonplussed, into sullen apathy. The hour of victory is always the hour for clemency—always the hour for the easiest winning of the hearts of the vanquished. There are leaders, as all admit, who are beyond clemency either now or hereafter; and the Administration has done most nobly in so steadfastly refusing to grant them any stipulations or proffers. But the Southern people, in the mass, are bound to us by ties which we cannot sever if we would. They are our fellow-countrymen, who must not only live, but live with us. For our own sake, as well as theirs, they must have clemency. They must not be dragged back as vassals, but welcomed back as brothers. Our anxiety for this cannot be too quickly or too fully manifested.

The Completeness of the National Victory.

The material losses inflicted upon the rebel army around Petersburgh, in men, in the equipments and munitions of war, not less than in position, have not yet been so computed that their overwhelming weight can be made at once appreciable. A careful comparison of different data gave LEE, three months ago, an army of 85,000 men. Within that period there is superabundant evidence to prove to us that this force, so formidable in numbers, and, peradventure, scarcely less formidable in its tough experience, had lost full 15,000 men. We should clearly be under, rather than over the actual number, if we set down LEE'S losses, in killed and wounded, in the five day's engagements, at 10,000 more. And putting together all the returns of captured prisoners already received, we are unable, by the most moderate computation, to reduce their aggregate below 25,000. These deductions alone bring the relics of the rebel army of Virginia down to 35,000 men, without including the gangs of stragglers from that fugitive band, met with at every furlong of GRANT and SHERIDAN'S pursuit. If LEE to-day has even 30,000 in his immediate command he must have found material for conscription in the line of his inglorious flight. And each succeeding sunrise can but witness not only the decline of his army in bulk, but its rapid and irreclaimable demoralization as well.

The captures of guns in the storming of the right of LEE'S Petersburgh intrenchments and in the great field engagements, large as these are, represent—by accumulated testimony from every quarter of the field lately held by LEE—but a mere fraction of the war material sacrificed in the rebel flight. Not only are the lines of retreat strewed in all directions with abandoned arms of every variety and calibre, but so overwhelmingly sudden was

that swoop of our cavalry around and behind the right wing of LEE'S army, which gave GRANT the first signal and assurance of his victory, that there was not time left to the enemy to either use or destroy the railroad plant concentrated in Richmond, all of which was essential war material to the rebels only three days ago. Not only have we it reported on the authority of SHERIDAN—as the first experience of his pursuit of the rebels—that "the majority of the arms that were left in the hands of LEE'S army are now scattered between Richmond and where his troops now are ;" and that "the line of retreat is marked with artillery, ammunition, burned or charred wagons, caissons and ambulances,"—but the rolling stock of DAVIS' late military roads seems to have been abandoned as an utterly useless provision hereafter in the irregular warfare on which the remaining rebel force has fallen back.

With these material losses may be computed the loss of the best military position alike for offensive and defensive operations that remained to the Confederacy. To the value set upon that position, the countless battle-fields of Virginia, from Loudon Heights to the Rappahannock, the Chickahominy, and the Appomattox, bear grim proofs which permit neither of cavil or dispute. In that death-grapple of Sunday, around and beyond the forts at Petersburgh, the position thus cherished, thus clung to in the very agony of his desperate and hopeless situation, was abandoned by LEE, never to be retaken, till a 'more recreant race than ours shall control the power, and assume to uphold the honor of this Republic.

Yet, vast even almost beyond compute as are these immediate and palpable losses of the insurgent force, they cannot compare, in any rebel estimate to-day, with the overwhelming disaster which has overtaken the Confederacy as a political power. In the fall of Richmond every function it had exercised as a political combination ceased thenceforth and for all time. As an *organic* force it

passed out of existence, and lapsed incontinently into a mere insurrection. The flight of DAVIS from Richmond put an everlasting period to the relationship of his administration to every single one of the States that adhered to his political system. His spurious machinery of legislation became thereafter a by-word for history. His Executive Departments resolved themselves into visions of things spurious that *had been* but *should be* no more. His conscription appliances, his taxing agencies, his money-printing apparatus, his foreign relations—Heaven help them! —his postal system, his military tribunals, and his libel of a Constitution—all passed away like the spectral creations of some ugly dream. And what passed among the friendly crowd of on-lookers, but the other day, for the dignity and circumstance of an organized and permanently established power, was blown in a night to the winds by the hot breath of the avenging destroyer.

Were LEE'S armed bands, from the James to the Red River, twice as numerous and many times more faithful to the Confederacy than they, what compensation could it be for this utter demolition of the political structure in which the fortunes of the leading rebel gang had been staked? At best, these bands could but provide for their own sustenance and for escape from the immediate and condign punishment of the prime actors in this murderous league. At most they could play the *rôle* of banditti or guerrillas for a term which it would be altogether in the power of the supreme government to limit, with less exertion, probably, than has been expended on a single one out of a score of campaigns that have marked the past history of the war. With the disappearance, then, of all that gave cohesion and political vitality to this wretched Confederacy, goes all that made it formidable at home, or gave it informal recognition abroad.

Ruins of the State Arsenal in Richmond, Virginia.

The New-York Times.

VOL. XIV.....NO. 4223.   NEW-YORK, FRIDAY, APRIL 7, 1865.   PRICE FOUR CENTS.

THE REBEL ROUT.

Lee's Retreat Cut Off by Sheridan.

BURKESVILLE IN OUR POSSESSION

Lee's Army at Amelia Court House, East of Burkesville.

A Junction Between Lee's Forces and Johnston's Now Impossible.

Sheridan Hopes to Capture the Whole Rebel Army.

The Infantry Moving Rapidly to His Support.

General Grant at Sheridan's Headquarters.

[OFFICIAL.]

WAR DEPARTMENT, WASHINGTON, }
April 6, 1865—12 o'clock noon. }

Maj. Gen. Dix:

The following telegram announces the probable speedy destruction of Gen. LEE's army if our troops get up to support SHERIDAN, who has headed off the enemy.

EDWIN M. STANTON, Secretary of War.

JUNCTION SOUTHSIDE AND DANVILLE RAILROAD, }
BURKESVILLE, VA., April 5—10 o'clock P. M. }

Hon. Edwin M. Stanton, Secretary of War:

Lieut. Gen. GRANT received the following dispatch at 6:30 P. M., while on his way to this point, and at once proceeded to Gen. SHERIDAN's headquarters. Gen. GRANT desired me to transmit the dispatch to you, on the opening of the telegraph at this place, and to say that the Sixth Corps, without doubt, reached Gen. SHERIDAN's position within an hour or two after the dispatch was written. Two divisions of the Twenty-fourth Corps will encamp here to-night, and one division of the Twenty-fifth Army Corps at Black's and White's Station, Southside Railroad.

S. WILLIAMS, Brig.-Gen.

DISPATCH FROM GEN. SHERIDAN.

HEADQUARTERS CAVALRY, }
JETTERSVILLE, April 5—3 P. M. }

To Lieut. U. S. Grant:

GENERAL: I send you the enclosed letter, which will give you an idea of the condition of the enemy and their whereabouts. I sent Gen. DAVIES' brigade this morning around on my left flank. He captured, at Fame's Cross Roads, five pieces artillery, about two hundred wagons and eight or nine battle-flags, and a number of prisoners. The Second Army Corps is now coming up. I wish you were here yourself. I feel confident of capturing the army of Northern Virginia if we exert ourselves. I see no escape for LEE. I will put all my cavalry out on our left flank, except McKENZIE, who is now on the right.

(Signed,)   P. H. SHERIDAN, Major-General.

THE LETTER.

AMELIA COURT-HOUSE, April 5, 1865.

DEAR MAMMA: Our army is ruined, I fear. We are all safe as yet. SHYRON left us sick; JOHN TAYLOR is well; saw him yesterday. We are in line of battle this evening. Gen. ROBERT LEE is in the field, near us. My trust is still in the justice of our cause and in God. Gen. HILL is killed. I saw MURRAY a few moments since. Bernard Terry, it is said, was taken prisoner, but managed to get out. I send this by a negro, I see passing up the railroad to Michlenburgh. Love to all.

Your devoted son,

W. B. TAYLOR, Colonel.

THE PURSUIT OF LEE.

Evidences of the Precipitate Flight of the Enemy—The Roads Strewn with Arms, Caissons and Wagons—The Rebels Fighting without Spirit.

From Our Own Correspondent.

AURELIA COUNTY, VA., WINTACOMACK CREEK, }
ONE AND A HALF MILES SOUTH OF APPOMATTOX, }
Monday, April 3. }

This morning CUSTER's division left camp at a point several miles east of Namozine Creek, and made a rapid movement up what is called the Namozine road, leading into Aurelia County. At the ford on Namozine Creek the rebels were found to be strongly intrenched behind earthworks to cover the crossing. The Eighth New-York, Major BLISS, of WELLS' brigade, had the advance. A part of the First Vermont, under Capt. HAZELTINE, went up the stream a short distance and succeeded in effecting a crossing, flanking the enemy's position. LORD's section of artillery was brought up within easy range to the left of the ford, and simultaneously the ball was opened, firing grape shot at easy range. The enemy were so taken by surprise, they having supposed that the river was not fordable at any other place than where guarded, that they fled in the wildest confusion after a very brief skirmish. Col. WELLS continued the pursuit as rapidly as possible, the enemy endeavoring to obstruct the road by felling trees and piling the rails across, and at several points caissons were emptied, and the contents surrounded by fire, with the devilish hope that some of our daring riders in the advance might be killed.

The road bore abundant evidence of the haste the enemy were in. A number of caissons and wagons were overhauled, disabled, and arms, accoutrements, blankets, clothing and cartridges were to be seen on either hand. When near Namozine Church the enemy made a stand, and the whole Eighth New-York charged and carried the place, without materially interrupting the advance of the column. In this charge Capt. GOODRIDGE was mortally wounded; Capt. C. T. VAN DUZER received a flesh wound in the thigh; Corp. ELWOOD, Company B, was killed; Corp. GEORGE GRASS, Company H. flesh wound in forehead; H. H. FAIRBANKS, Company G, finger; P. M. BURTON, Company B, wounded in abdomen, dangerous, and OSCAR C. PALMER, Co. B, slightly in shoulder. The First Vermont, Lieut.-Col. HALL, being the advance regiment of the main column, supported the movement, and Sergt. JAS. BOHAN, Co. A, was mortally wounded, having received a ball through his right lung. The Fifteenth New-York, Col. COPPINGER, coming up also in support of the movement, had First Sergt. JOHN McGOUGH, Co. A, Capt. SKIFF, killed.

THE ATTACK ON MOBILE.

The Bombardment of the City Opened on March 30.

The Monitor Milwaukee Blown Up by a Torpedo.

Details of the Expedition from Our Own Correspondent.

The steamship Guiding Star, from New-Orleans, March 26, and Southwest Pass, the 28th, arrived yesterday.

The United States steamer Circassian arrived at Key West, April 2, and reported an attack of Union forces and gun-boats on Mobile, March 30. No particulars were obtained, except that the monitor Milwaukee was blown up off Dog River bar, by a torpedo.

The Guiding Star brings 2,794 bales cotton, 1,108 barrels flour, 1,000 sacks corn, 73 cases merchandise. The log reports: In consequence of detention by being run aground in Mississippi River by the pilot, had to stop at Key West to coal.

The steamer Empire City sailed from Key West, April 2; we passed her off Savannah, on the morning of April 4.

REPORTS FROM NEW-ORLEANS.

NEW-ORLEANS, Friday, March 31, }
Via CAIRO, Thursday, April 6. }

The Times and Delta say:

"Headquarters have received information that a portion of Gen. CANBY's army was within four miles of Mobile, and siege guns were in position, from which shells could be thrown into the suburbs of the city. The attack on Fort Bradley, the main defence of Mobile, had already commenced. MAURY commanded at Mobile, and Gen. DICK TAYLOR commanded the Spanish Fort. The bombardment of the latter commenced on the 28th. Gens. CANBY, GRANGER and SMITH were five miles up Fishing Creek on the 24th. There was heavy cannonading on the 22d, caused by the gunboats shelling the woods at the mouth of Fishing Creek."

NEW-ORLEANS, Saturday, April 1, }
VIA CAIRO, April 6. }

Gen. STEELE's command, from Pensacola, met with much opposition, but no regular battle was fought until it reached Mitchell's Fork, on the morning of the 27th ult., where the enemy, numbering about 800, made a stand, and, after a severe fight, were repulsed and scattered in the woods, many being captured.

The correspondent of the New-Orleans Times writing from the headquarters of the Thirteenth Army Corps, near Blakely, on the 28th ult., says a party of guerrillas made a dash upon a wagon train stuck in the mud near Fish River, and captured ten mules and eight drivers. But all the wagons and stores were brought in yesterday.

There has been much skirmishing, but no regular battle has taken place as yet. The bombardment of the Spanish fort progresses favorably. Torpedoes thickly stud the approaches to the fort. Our skirmishers are within 200 yards, and our artillery within 300 of the fort. We have it encompassed on three sides.

Their only chance of escape is by water, but if a gunboat can get up they cannot escape that way.

Gen. GRANGER and staff narrowly escaped being blown up by a torpedo placed in the road.

Col. BERTRAM's brigade captured a rebel telegraph office and dispatches showing that the rebels are fully posted in relation to all our movements, forces and places. Gen. STEELE captured two railroad supply trains at Pollard.

At last accounts our losses do not exceed 50 killed and 200 or 300 wounded.

Rebel steamers ply regularly between Mobile and the Spanish fort, conveying reinforcements and guns.

Two of our men have been injured by torpedoes near Mobile.

The New-York Times.

VOL. XIV..... NO. 4225.　　　NEW-YORK, MONDAY, APRIL 10, 1865.　　　PRICE FOUR CENTS.

HANG OUT YOUR BANNERS

UNION
VICTORY!

PEACE!

Surrender of General Lee and His Whole Army.

THE WORK OF PALM SUNDAY.

Final Triumph of the Army of the Potomac.

The Strategy and Diplomacy of Lieut.-Gen. Grant.

Terms and Conditions of the Surrender.

The Rebel Arms, Artillery, and Public Property Surrendered.

Rebel Officers Retain Their Side Arms and Private Property.

Officers and Men Paroled and Allowed to Return to Their Homes.

The Correspondence Between Grant and Lee.

OFFICIAL.

WAR DEPARTMENT, WASHINGTON, April 9, 1865—9 o'clock P. M.

To Maj.-Gen. Dix :

This department has received the official report of the SURRENDER, THIS DAY, OF GEN. LEE AND HIS ARMY TO LIEUT.-GEN. GRANT, on the terms proposed by Gen. GRANT.

Details will be given as speedily as possible.

EDWIN M. STANTON,

Secretary of War.

HEADQUARTERS ARMIES OF THE UNITED STATES, 4:30 P. M., April 9.

Hon. Edwin M. Stanton, Secretary of War :

GEN. LEE SURRENDERED THE ARMY OF NORTHERN VIRGINIA THIS AFTERNOON, upon the terms proposed by myself. The accompanying additional correspondence will show the conditions fully.

(Signed)　　U. S. GRANT, Lieut.-Gen'l.

SUNDAY, April 9, 1865.

GENERAL—I received your note of this morning, on the picket line, whither I had come to meet you and ascertain definitely what terms were embraced in your proposition of yesterday with reference to the surrender of this army.

I now request an interview in accordance with the offer contained in your letter of yesterday for that purpose.

Very respectfully, your obedient servant,

R. E. LEE, General.

To Lieut.-Gen. GRANT, Commanding United States Armies.

SUNDAY, April 9, 1865.

Gen. R. E. Lee, Commanding Confederate States Armies.

Your note of this date is but this moment, 11:50 A. M., received.

In consequence of my having passed from the Richmond and Lynchburgh road to the Farmville and Lynchburgh road, I am at this writing about four miles West of Walter's church, and will push forward to the front for the purpose of meeting you.

Notice sent to me, on this road, where you wish the interview to take place, will meet me.

Very respectfully, your ob'd't servant,

U. S. GRANT,

Lieutenant-General.

APPOMATTOX COURT-HOUSE, April 9, 1865.

General R. E. Lee, Commanding C. S. A. :

In accordance with the substance of my letters to you of the 8th inst., I propose to receive the surrender of the Army of Northern Virginia on the following terms, to wit :

Rolls of all the officers and men to be made in duplicate, one copy to be given to an officer designated by me, the other to be retained by such officers as you may designate.

The officers to give their individual paroles not to take arms against the Government of the United States until properly exchanged, and each company or regimental commander sign a like parole for the men of their commands.

The arms, artillery and public property to be packed and stacked and turned over to the officers appointed by me to receive them.

This will not embrace the side-arms of the officers, nor their private horses or baggage.

This done, EACH OFFICER AND MAN WILL BE ALLOWED TO RETURN TO THEIR HOMES, not to be disturbed by United States authority so long as they observe their parole and the laws in force where they reside.

Very respectfully,

U. S. GRANT, Lieutenant-General.

HEADQUARTERS ARMY OF NORTHERN VIRGINIA, April 9, 1865.

Lieut.-Gen. U. S. Grant, Commanding U. S. A. :

GENERAL : I have received your letter of this date, CONTAINING THE TERMS OF SURRENDER OF THE ARMY OF NORTHERN VIRGINIA, as proposed by you. As they are substantially the same as those expressed in your letter of the 8th inst., THEY ARE ACCEPTED. I will proceed to designate the proper officers to carry the stipulations into effect.

Very respectfully,

Your obedient servant,

R. E. LEE, General.

THE PRELIMINARY CORRESPONDENCE.

The following is the previous correspondence between Lieut.-Gen. GRANT and Gen. LEE, referred to in the foregoing telegram to the Secretary of War :

CLIFTON HOUSE, VA., April 9, 1865.

Hon. Edwin M. Stanton, Secretary of War :

The following correspondence has taken place between Gen. LEE and myself. There has been no relaxation in the pursuit during its pendency.

U. S. GRANT, Lieutenant-General.

APRIL 7, 1865.

Gen. R. E. Lee, Commanding C. S. A.:

GENERAL: The result of the last week must convince you of the hopelessness of further resistance on the part of the Army of Northern Virginia in this struggle. I feel that it is so and regard it as my duty to shift from myself the responsibility of any further effusion of blood, by asking of you the surrender of that portion of the Confederate States Army, known as the Army of Northern Virginia.

Very Respectfully,

Your obedient servant,

U. S. GRANT,

Lieutenant-General,

Commanding Armies of the United States.

APRIL 7, 1865.

General: I have received your note of this date.

Though not entirely of the opinion you express of the hopelessness of further resistence on the part of the army of Northern Virginia, I reciprocate your desire to avoid useless effusion of blood, and therefore, before considering your proposition, *ask the terms you will offer, on condition of its surrender.*

R. E. LEE, General.

To Lieut.-Gen. U. S. GRANT, Commanding Armies of the United States.

APRIL 8, 1865.

To Gen. R. E. Lee, Commanding C. S. A.:

GENERAL: Your note of last evening in reply to mine of same date, asking the conditions on which I will accept the surrender of the Army of Northern Virginia, is just received.

In reply, I would say that *peace being my first desire, there is but one condition that I insist upon, viz.:*

That the men surrendered shall be disqualified for taking up arms again against the Government of the United States until properly exchanged.

I will meet you, or designate officers to meet say officers you may name, for the same purpose, at any point agreeable to you, for the purpose of arranging definitely the terms upon which the surrender of the Army of Northern Virginia will be received.

Very respectfully, your obedient servant,

U. S. GRANT, Lieut.-General,

Commanding armies of the United States.

April 8, 1865.

GENERAL: I received, at a late hour, your note of to-day, in answer to mine of yesterday.

I did not intend to propose the surrender of the Army of Northern Virginia, but *to ask the terms of your proposition.* To be frank, I do not think the emergency has arisen to call for the surrender.

But as *the restoration of peace should be the sole object of all,* I desire to know whether your proposals would tend to that end.

I cannot, therefore, meet you with a view to surrender the Army of Northern Virginia, but *as far as your proposition may effect the Confederate States forces under my command, and tend to the restoration of peace, I should be pleased to meet*

Generals Lee and Grant agreed upon surrender terms at Appomattox Court House, Virginia.

you at 10 A. M., to-morrow, on the old stage road to Richmond, between the picket lines of the two armies.

Very respectfully, your obedient servant,

R. E. LEE,

General, C. S. A.

To Lieut.-Gen. GRANT, Commanding Armies of the United States.

APRIL 9, 1865.

General R. H. Lee, commanding C. S. A.:

GENERAL: Your note of yesterday is received. As I have no authority to treat on the subject of peace, the meeting proposed for 10 A. M. to-day could lead to no good. I will state, however, General, that *I am equally anxious for peace with yourself;* and the whole North entertain the same feeling. *The terms upon which peace can be had are well understood. By the South laying down their arms, they will hasten that most desirable event, save thousands of human lives, and hundreds of millions of property not yet destroyed.*

Sincerely hoping that all our difficulties may be settled *without the loss of another life,* I subscribe myself,

Very respectfully,

Your obedient servant,

U. S. GRANT,

Lieutenant-General United States Army.

THE VICTORY.

Thanks to God, the Giver of Victory.

Honors to Gen. Grant and His Gallant Army.

A NATIONAL SALUTE ORDERED.

Two Hundred Guns to be Fired at the Headquarters of Every Army, Department, Post and Arsenal.

[OFFICIAL.]

WAR DEPARTMENT, WASHINGTON, D. C., April 9, 1865—9:30 P. M.

Lieut.-Gen. Grant:

Thanks be to Almighty God for the great victory with which he has this day crowned you and the gallant armies under your command.

The thanks of this Department and of the Government, and of the People of the United States —their reverence and honor have been deserved— will be rendered to you and the brave and gallant officers and soldiers of your army for all time.

EDWIN M. STANTON, Secretary of War.

WAR DEPARTMENT, WASHINGTON, D. C., April 9, 1865—10 o'clock P. M.

Ordered: That a salute of two hundred guns be fired at the headquarters of every army and department, and at every post and arsenal in the United States, and at the Military Academy at West Point on the day of the receipt of this order, in commemoration of the surrender of Gen. ROBERT E. LEE and the Army of Northern Virginia to Lieut.-Gen. GRANT and the army under his command. Report of the receipt and execution of this order to be made to the Adjutant-General at Washington.

EDWIN M. STANTON,

Secretary of War.

The New-York Times.

VOL. XIV.....NO. 4226.   NEW-YORK, TUESDAY, APRIL 11, 1865.   PRICE FOUR CENTS.

Editorials

The New Epoch—The Advent of Peace.

This continent quivered yesterday as never since its upheaval from chaos. The lightning flashed peace, and from ocean to ocean, all minds thrilled with the sense of a new order of things. No more deluge of blood. No more whirls of ruin. No more brooding darkness. The republic rested again, and upon foundations as eternal as the hills. The whole heavens were spanned with the rainbow of promise, and every eye saw it.

This tremendous transition has been betokened latterly by many signs, yet its coming was sudden. The terrible trials of the war have weighed so heavily upon the land, and the people have been so often deceived by false appearances, that a confirmed impression existed that the deliverance, if it ever came, would come only with protracted tribulation. Even now, in spite of all we see, it is hard to realize that the rebellion has vanished. But just now it threatened to engulf the nation.

"Glory to the Lord of Hosts, from whom all blessings are." If ever a people under heaven was bound to prostrate itself in gratitude, it is the loyal people of this land. Had it been foretold to them four years ago what trials awaited them, there would have been a universal cry of despairing agony. Human history affords no instance of such a national ordeal. Never could we have endured it but for the strength given from on high, as we had need. The most capacious minds of Europe, schooled to the uttermost limit in all the wisdom of the past, called this war a madness. It was a madness, if estimated by any material standard. Eight millions of Anglo-Saxon rebels, compacted as one man, brave to the last pitch, inhabiting a country peculiarly defensible, having the encouragement of untiring faction beyond their bounds, and a moral alliance with nearly every Power in the Old World, according to all the ordinary rules of judging, would surely prevail. But we had a hidden strength which the world did not understand. It was Faith —a faith that first broke upon us with the first flash of Sumter's guns, and that ever afterward went on widening and deepening. The people came to feel as by an inspiration from heaven, that the moral elements of the national cause made it irresistible. They were penetrated with the feeling, that as sure as there was an Almighty Father, He could not permit the success of a rebellion that was made only for the benefit of human slavery. It was this which carried them through the struggle. Ten times their physical strength would not have kept them up, in the absence of this sovereign faith. The race of Titans could not have maintained this war, if, too, they had been a race of atheists.

That religious faith is fitly followed now by a religious gratitude. It is wonderful to mark the solemn character of the joy that now spreads the land. There are waving flags, ringing bells, booming cannon, and other national tokens of public gladness. But yet it is plain to see that the dominant feeling of the people is no ebullient exhilaration over human achievement, but a profound sense of a Divine blessing. The popular heart relieves itself, not so much in cheers and hurrahs as in doxologies. Never since the hosannas of that Palm Sunday in Jerusalem, has such irrepressible praise rolled up from a city street to the pure vault of heaven as from the great thoroughfare of money-changers in New-York at the tidings that the rebel capital had fallen. Yet that was but the key-note of the universal anthem. The enemies of this republic may talk as they please of its materializing tendencies, may to their heart's content stigmatize our people as worshipers of the "almighty dollar," they but waste their breath. Business activities, strenuous as they are, have not stifled the religious sentiment of the American heart. This has been demonstrated in ways without number, but never so grandly as now.

With this gratitude for deliverance is mingled a fresh assurance that Heaven has reserved our republic for a destiny more glorious than can yet be conceived. Americans now feel that it is less than ever a presumption in them to believe themselves a chosen people, appointed to school the world to new ideas of human capacities and human rights. The monarchs of the Old World are trembling with apprehension lest we shall be moved to repay our injuries by turning against them our arms. They have a thousand times greater reason to fear the moral force of our new position. We stand a living proof of the matchless potency of popular self-government. It rivets the attention of the whole civilized world. It will start new thoughts, will generate new purposes, will nerve to new acts. This is as sure as that the human reason shall continue to exist. It is this that the dynasties have need to fear; it is here that we expect our sweetest revenge.

Gen. Johnston's Army.

The most interesting question now is, what will Jo. Johnston do? He commands the only army of any magnitude now left in the Southern Confederacy. It is not a very formidable army in numbers, nor is it coherent in character. In every characteristic of an army, it is vastly inferior to that lately under Lee. It has never, as an army, fought a noteworthy battle. It has no traditions of success. It has no capable leaders. The troops of Hardee, who fled from Savannah and then from Charleston, form its nucleus, and to these have been added the tail of Hood's old army, the Wilmington force of Bragg, the picayune force of Beauregard, various feeble forces and garrisons picked up around, and a cavalry force under Wade Hampton and Wheeler. It is a piebald collection. Since its organization— such organization as it has—it has been steadily on the retreat; and the last we hear of it is that it has fled from Raleigh, and it must be now somewhere near the Southern border of Virginia. It was supposed that, in the last resort, Lee would try and effect a junction with it; but Johnston and his troops doubtless heard yesterday of the surrender of Lee and his whole army.

Opposed to Johnston is the powerful and magnificent army of Gen. Sherman. It is utterly impossible that Johnston should cope with it. He knows it would be ruin for him to try. He knows it would be madness.

In forming a judgment as to the possible course of Johnston in this emergency, we must take into consideration Johnston's hopeless prospect, as well as the great surrender of Sunday. We must take into account, too, the relations of Gen. Johnston to Jeff. Davis, and also his relations to Gen. Lee. For nearly two years Johnston and Davis have been in a state of bitter animosity with each other. They quarreled at the time of Grant's operations against Vicksburgh; and the Richmond rebel papers have often given us accounts of the depth of their mutual hatred. Twice has Davis removed Johnston from command; and on the last occasion, at Atlanta, it was under circumstances which stung Johnston to the quick. The whole press and people of the South clamored loudly for his reinstatement; but Davis was implacable. On the other hand, the relations of Johnston to Lee have always been those of mutual respect and friendliness. One of the first acts of Gen. Lee, when he received from the Confederate Congress the command of all the Confederate armies three months ago, was to put Johnston in command of the only army beside his own that existed in the South.

Now, under these circumstances, leaving out of view the hopeless prospect, it may be doubted whether Johnston will exhibit such devotion to the person and interests of Davis as to remain any longer in the field in his service. It is far more likely he will follow the example set him by his chief and friend, the Commander of the Confederate armies. If he does not do it quickly, Sherman will presently break him and his army to pieces. Then Jeff. Davis will be hardly able to get even a body-guard. This week will doubtless wind up Johnston, one way or another.

Rebel Surrenders.—Three rebel armies have surrendered to Gen. Grant—that under Buckner at Fort Donelson, on the 16th of February, 1862; that under Pemberton at Vicksburgh, on the 4th of July, 1863; and that under Gen. Lee, on the 9th of April, 1865. He is the only one of our Generals who has ever induced a rebel army to surrender; and he has induced three of them.

The New-York Times.

VOL. XIV.....NO. 4230.   NEW-YORK, SUNDAY, APRIL 16, 1865.   PRICE FOUR CENTS.

OUR GREAT LOSS

Death of President Lincoln.

The Songs of Victory Drowned in Sorrow.

CLOSING SCENES OF A NOBLE LIFE.

The Great Sorrow of an Afflicted Nation.

Party Differences Forgotten in Public Grief.

Vice-President Johnson Inaugurated as Chief Executive.

MR. SEWARD WILL RECOVER.

John Wilkes Booth Believed to be the Assassin.

Manifestations of the People Throughout the Country.

OFFICIAL DISPATCHES.

WAR DEPARTMENT, WASHINGTON, } April 15—4:10 A. M. }

To Major-Gen. Dix:

The President continues insensible and is sinking.

Secretary SEWARD remains without change.

FREDERICK SEWARD's skull is fractured in two places, besides a severe cut upon the head.

The attendant is still alive, but hopeless. Maj. SEWARD's wound is not dangerous.

It is now ascertained with reasonable certainty that two assassins were engaged in the horrible crime, WILKES BOOTH being the one that shot the President, and the other companion of his whose name is not known, but whose description

John Wilkes Booth

is so clear that he can hardly escape. It appears from a letter found in BOOTH's trunk that the murder was planned before the 4th of March, but fell through then because the accomplice backed out until "Richmond could be heard from." BOOTH and his accomplice were at the livery stable at six o'clock last evening, and left there with their horses about ten o'clock, or shortly before that hour.

It would seem that they had for several days been seeking their chance, but for some unknown reason it was not carried into effect until last night.

One of them has evidently made his way to Baltimore—the other has not yet been traced.

EDWIN M. STANTON, Secretary of War.

WAR DEPARTMENT, WASHINGTON, April 15.

Major-Gen. Dix:

ABRAHAM LINCOLN died this morning at twenty-two minutes after seven o'clock.

EDWIN M. STANTON, Secretary of War.

WAR DEPARTMENT, } WASHINGTON, April 15—3 P. M. }

Maj.-Gen. Dix, New-York:

Official notice of the death of the late President, ABRAHAM LINCOLN, was given by the heads of departments this morning to ANDREW JOHNSON, Vice-President, upon whom the constitution devolved the office of President. Mr. JOHNSON, upon receiving this notice, appeared before the Hon. SALMON P. CHASE, Chief Justice of the United States, and took the oath of office, as President of the United States, assumed its duties and functions. At 12 o'clock the President met the heads of departments in cabinet meeting, at the Treasury Building, and among other business the following was transacted:

First—The arrangements for the funeral of the late President were referred to the several Secretaries, as far as relates to their respective departments.

Second—WILLIAM HUNTER, Esq., was appointed Acting Secretary of State during the disability of Mr. SEWARD, and his son, FREDERICK SEWARD, the Assistant Secretary.

Third—The President formally announced that he desired to retain the present Secretaries of departments of his Cabinet, and they would go on and discharge their respective duties in the same manner as before the deplorable event that had changed the head of the government.

All business in the departments was suspended during the day.

The surgeons report that the condition of Mr. SEWARD remains unchanged. He is doing well.

No improvement in Mr. FREDERICK SEWARD.

The murderers have not yet been apprehended.

EDWIN M. STANTON, Secretary of War.

THE ASSASSINATION.

Additional Details of the Lamentable Event.

WASHINGTON, Saturday, April 15.

The assassin of President LINCOLN left behind him his hat and a spur.

The hat was picked up in the President's box and has been identified by parties to whom it has been shown as the one belonging to the suspected man, and accurately described as the one belonging to the suspected man by other parties, not allowed to see it before describing it.

The spur was dropped upon the stage, and that also has been identified as the one procured at a stable where the same man hired a horse in the evening.

Two gentlemen who went to the Secretary of

War to apprize him of the attack on Mr. LINCOLN met at the residence of the former a man muffled in a cloak, who, when accosted by them, hastened away.

It had been Mr. STANTON's intention to accompany Mr. LINCOLN to the theatre, and occupy the same box, but the press of business prevented.

It therefore seems evident that the aim of the plotters was to paralyze the country by at once striking down the head, the heart and the arm of the country.

As soon as the dreadful events were announced in the streets, Superintendent RICHARDS, and his assistants, were at work to discover the assassin.

In a few moments the telegraph had aroused the whole police force of the city.

Maj WALLACH and several members of the City Government were soon on the spot and every precaution was taken to preserve order and quiet in the city.

Every street in Washington was patrolled at the request of Mr. RICHARDS.

Gen. AUGUR sent horses to mount the police.

Every road leading out of Washington was strongly picketed, and every possible avenue of escape was thoroughly guarded.

Steamboats about to depart down the Potomac were stopped.

The Daily *Chronicle* says:

"As it is suspected that this conspiracy originated in Maryland, the telegraph flashed the mournful news to Baltimore and all the cavalry was immediately put upon active duty. Every road was picketed and every precaution taken to prevent the escape of the assassin. A preliminary examination was made by Messrs. RICHARDS and his assistants. Several persons were called to testify and the evidence as elicited before an informal tribunal, and not under oath, was conclusive to this point. The murderer of President LINCOLN was JOHN WILKES BOOTH. His hat was found in the private box, and identified by several persons who had seen him within the last two days, and the spur which he dropped by accident, after he jumped to the stage, was identified as one of those which he had obtained from the stable where he hired his horse.

This man BOOTH has played more than once at Ford's Theatre, and is, of course, acquainted with its exits and entrances, and the facility with which he escaped behind the scenes is well understood.

The person who assassinated Secretary SEWARD left behind him a slouched hat and an old rusty navy revolver. The chambers were broken loose from the barrel, as if done by striking. The loads were drawn from the chambers, one being but a rough piece of lead, and the other balls smaller than the chambers, wrapped in paper, as if to keep them from falling out.

CLOSING SCENES.

Particulars of His Last Moments—Record of His Condition Before Death—His Death.

WASHINGTON, Saturday, April 15—11 o'clock A. M.

The *Star* extra says:

"At 7:20 o'clock the President breathed his last, closing his eyes as if falling to sleep, and his countenance assuming an expression of perfect serenity. There were no indications of pain, and it was not known that he was dead until the gradually decreasing respiration ceased altogether.

Rev. Dr. GURLEY, of the New-York-avenue Presbyterian Church, immediately on its being ascertained that life was extinct, knelt at the bedside and offered an impressive prayer, which was responded to by all present.

Dr. GURLEY then proceeded to the front parlor, where Mrs. LINCOLN, Capt. ROBERT LINCOLN Mrs. JOHN HAY, the Private Secretary, and others, were waiting, where he again offered a prayer for the consolation of the family.

The following minutes, taken by Dr. ABBOTT, show the condition of the late President throughout the night:

11 o'clock—Pulse 44.
11:05 o'clock—Pulse 45, and growing weaker.
11:10 o'clock—Pulse 45.
11:15 o'clock—Pulse 42.
11:20 o'clock—Pulse 45; respiration 27 to 29.
11:25 o'clock—Pulse 42.
11:32 o'clock—Pulse 48. and full.
11:40 o'clock—Pulse 45.
11:45 o'clock—Pulse 45; respiration 22.
12 o'clock—Pulse 48; respiration 22.
12:15 o'clock—Pulse 48; respiration 21—echmos both eyes.
12:30 o'clock—Pulse 45.
12:32 o'clock—Pulse 60.
12:35 o'clock—Pulse 66.]
12:40 o'clock—Pulse 69; right eye much swollen, and echmoses.
12:45 o'clock—Pulse 70.
12:55 o'clock—Pulse 80; struggling motion of arms.
1 o'clock—Pulse 86; respiration 30.
1:30 o'clock—Pulse 95; appearing easier.
1:45 o'clock—Pulse 86—very quiet, respiration irregular.
Mrs. LINCOLN present.
2:10 o'clock—Mrs. LINCOLN retired with ROBERT LINCOLN to an adjoining room.
2:30 o'clock—President very quiet—pulse 54—respiration 28.
2:52 o'clock—Pulse 48—respiration 30.
3 o'clock—Visited again by Mrs. LINCOLN.
3:25 o'clock—Respiration 24 and regular.
3:35 o'clock—Prayer by Rev. Dr. GURLEY.
4 o'clock—Respiration 26 and regular.
4:15 o'clock—Pulse 60—respiration 25.
5:50 o'clock—Respiration 28—regular—sleeping
6 o'clock—Pulse failing—respiration 28.
6 30 o'clock—Still failing and labored breathing.
7 o'clock—Symptoms of immediate dissolution.
7:22 o'clock—Death.

Surrounding the death-bed of the President were Secretaries Stanton, Welles, Usher, Attorney-General Speed, Postmaster-General Dennison,

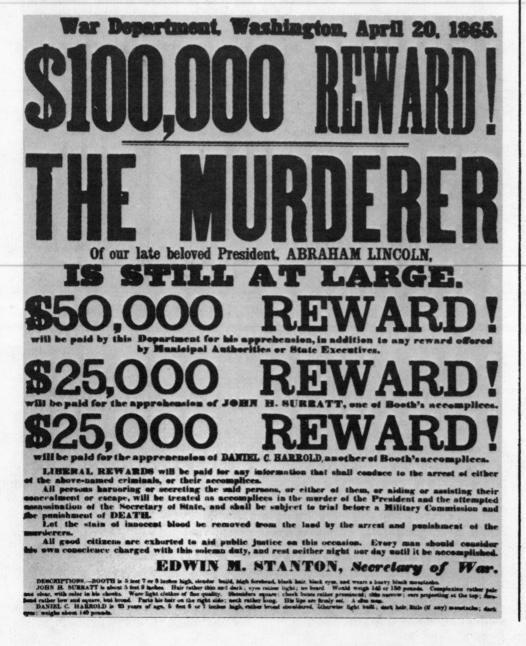

M. B. Field, Assistant Secretary of the Treasury; Judge Otto, Assistant Secretary of the Interior; Gen. Halleck, Gen. Meigs, Senator Sumner, R. F Andrews, of New-York; Gen. Todd, of Dacotah; John Hay, Private Secretary; Gov. Oglesby, of Illinois; Gen. Farnsworth, Mrs. and Miss Kenney, Miss Harris, Capt. Robert Lincoln, son of the President, and Doctors E. W. Abbott, R. K. Stone. C. D. Gatch, Neal Hall, and Mr. Lieberman. Secretary McCulloch remained with the President until about 5 o'clock, and Chief-Justice Chase, after several hours' attendance during the night, returned early this morning.

Immediately after the President's death a Cabinet meeting was called by Secretary STANTON, and held in the room in which the corpse lay. Secretaries STANTON, WELLES and USHER, Postmaster-General DENNISON, and Attorney-General SPEED, were present. The results of the conference are as yet unknown.

Removal of the Remains to the Executive Mansion—Feeling in the City.
WASHINGTON, Saturday, April 15.

The President's body was removed from the private residence opposite Ford's Theatre to the executive mansion this morning at 9:30 o'clock, in a hearse, and wrapped in the American flag. It was escorted by a small guard of cavalry, Gen. AUGUR and other military officers following on foot.

A dense crowd accompanied the remains to the White House, where a military guard excluded the crowd, allowing none but persons of the household and personal friends of the deceased to enter the premises, Senator YATES and Representative FARNSWORTH being among the number admitted.

The body is being enbalmed, with a view to its removal to Illinois.

Flags over the department and throughout the city are at half-mast. Scarcely any business is being transacted anywhere either on private or public account.

Our citizens, without any preconcert whatever, are draping their premises with festoons of mourning.

The bells are tolling mournfully. All is the deepest gloom and sadness. Strong men weep in the streets. The grief is wide-spead and deep and in strange contrast to the joy so lately manifested over our recent military victories.

This is indeed a day of gloom.

Reports prevail that Mr. FREDERICK W. SEWARD, who was kindly assisting the nursing of Secretary SEWARD, received a stab in the back. His shoulder blade prevented the knife or dagger from penetrating into his body. The prospects are that he will recover.

A report is circulated, repeated by almost everybody, that BOOTH was captured fifteen miles this side of Baltimore. If it be true, as asserted, that the War Department has received such information, it will doubtless be officially promulgated.

The government departments are closed by order, and will be draped with the usual emblems of mourning.

The roads leading to and from the city are guarded by the military, and the utmost circumspection is observed as to all attempting to enter or leave the city.

AUTOPSY UPON THE BODY OF ABRAHAM LINCOLN.
WASHINGTON, Saturday, April 15.

An autopsy was held this afternoon over the body

Co-conspirator Lewis Paine wounded Secretary of State Seward. Planned attempts on Vice-President Johnson and General Grant were never carried out.

of President LINCOLN by Surgeon-General BARNES and Dr. STONE, assisted by other eminent medical men.

The coffin is of mahogany, is covered with black cloth, and lined with lead, the latter also being covered with white satin.

A silver plate upon the coffin over the breast bears the following inscription:

ABRAHAM LINCOLN,
SIXTEENTH PRESIDENT OF THE UNITED STATES,
Born July 12, 1809,
Died April 15, 1865.

The remains have been embalmed.

A few locks of hair were removed from the President's head for the family previous to the remains being placed in the coffin.

THE ASSASSINS.

Circumstances Tending to Inculpate G. H. Booth—Description of his Confederate in the Crime.

WASHINGTON, Saturday, April 15.

There is no confirmation of the report that the murderer of the President has been arrested.

Among the circumstances tending to fix a participation in the crime on BOOTH, were letters found in his trunk, one of which, apparently from a lady, supplicated him to desist from the perilous undertaking in which he was about to embark, as the time was inauspicious, the mine not yet being ready to be sprung.

The *Extra Intelligencer* says: "From the evidence obtained it is rendered highly probable that the man who stabbed Mr. SEWARD and his sons, is JOHN SURRATT, of Prince George County, Maryland. The horse he rode was hired at NAYLOR's stable, on Fourteenth-street. SURRATT is a young man, with light hair and goatee. His father is said to have been postmaster of Prince George County."

About 11 o'clock last night two men crossed the Anacostia Bridge, one of whom gave his name as BOOTH, and the other as SMITH. The latter is believed to be JOHN SURRATT.

Last night a riderless horse was found, which has been identified by the proprietor of one of the stables previously mentioned as having been hired from his establishment.

Accounts are conflicting as to whether BOOTH crossed the bridge on horseback or on foot; but as it is believed that he rode across it, it is presumed that he had exchanged his horse.

From information in the possession of the authorities it is evident that the scope of the plot was intended to be much more comprehensive.

The Vice-President and other prominent members of the Administration were particularly inquired for by suspected parties, and their precise localities accurately obtained; but providentially, in their cases, the scheme miscarried.

A boat was at once sent down the Potomac to notify the gunboats on the river of the awful crime, in order that all possible means should be taken for the arrest of the perpetrators.

The most ample precautions have been taken, and

It is not believed the culprits will long succeed in evading the overtaking arm of justice.

The second extra of the *Evening Star* says:
"Col. INGRAHAM, Provost-Marshal of the defences north of the Potomac, is engaged, in taking testimony to-day, all of which fixes the assassination upon J. WILKES BOOTH.

Judge OLIN, of the Supreme Court of the District of Columbia, and Justice MILLER, are also engaged to-day, at the Police Headquarters, on Tenth-street, in taking the testimony of a large number of witnesses.

Lieut. TYRELL, of Col. INGRAHAM's staff, last night proceeded to the National Hotel, where BOOTH had been stopping, and took possession of his trunk, in which was found a Colonel's military dress-coat, two pairs of handcuffs, two boxes of cartridges and a package of letters, all of which are now in the possession of the military authorities.

One of these letters, bearing the date of Hookstown, Md., seems to implicate BOOTH. The writer speaks of "the mysterious affair in which you are engaged," and urges BOOTH to proceed to Richmond, and ascertain the views of the authorities there upon the subject. The writer of the letter endeavors to persuade BOOTH from carrying his designs into execution at that time, for the reason, as the writer alleges, that the government had its suspicions aroused. The writer of the letter seems to have been implicated with BOOTH in "the mysterious affair" referred to, as he informs BOOTH in the letter that he would prefer to express his views verbally; and then goes on to say that he was out of money, had no clothes, and would be compelled to leave home, as his family were desirous that he should dissolve his connection with BOOTH. This letter is written on note paper, in a small, neat hand, and simply bears the signature of "Sam."

At the Cabinet meeting yesterday, which lasted over two hours, the future policy of the government toward Virginia was discussed, the best feeling prevailed. It is stated that it was, determined to adopt a very liberal policy, as was recommended by the President. It is said that this meeting was the most harmonious held for over two years, the President exhibiting throughout that magnanimity and kindness of heart which has ever characterized his treatment of the rebellious States, and which has been so lily requited on their part.

One of the members of the Cabinet remarked to a friend he met at the door, that "The government was to-day stronger than it had been for three years past."

WASHINGTON, Saturday, April 15—3:30 P. M.

To-day no one is allowed to leave the city by rail conveyance, or on foot, and the issuing of passes from the Headquarters of the Department of Washington has been suspended by Gen. AUGUR.

Probable Attempt of the Assassins to Escape into Canada—Order from the War Department.

[CIRCULAR.]

WAR DEPARTMENT,
PROVOST MARSHAL-GENERAL'S BUREAU,
WASHINGTON, D. C.—9:40 A. M., April 15.

It is believed that the assassins of the President and Secretary SEWARD are attempting to escape to Canada. You will make a careful and thorough examination of all persons attempting to cross from the United States into Canada, and will arrest all suspicious persons. The most vigilant scrutiny on your part, and the force at your disposal, is demanded. A description of the parties supposed to be implicated in the murder will be telegraphed you to-day. But in the meantime be active in preventing the crossing of any suspicious persons.

By order of the Secretary of War.

N. L. JEFFERS, Brevet Brig. Gen.,
Acting Provost-Marshal General.

MR. SEWARD AND SON.

Secretary Seward will Recover—Frederick Seward Still Very Low.

Special Dispatch to the New-York Times.
WASHINGTON, Saturday, April 15.

Mr. SEWARD will recover.

FREDERICK SEWARD is still unconscious. He

breathes calmly and has an easy pulse. His head is dreadfully contused and lacerated.

An invalid soldier nurse saved Mr. SEWARD's life.

GEN. GRANT'S MOVEMENTS.

PHILADELPHIA, Saturday, April 15.

Gen. GRANT arrived in this city late last night on his way to Jersey, but was intercepted on his way to Walnut-street wharf, by a dispatch from the office of the Associated Press, and it is supposed he he returned to Washington immediately.

His Return to Washington—Dispatch from Mrs. Grant.

BURLINGTON, N. J., Saturday, April 15.

Lieut.-Gen. GRANT left Burlington for Washington, at 6 o'clock this morning.

MRS. U. S. GRANT.

WASHINGTON, Saturday, April 15.

Gen. GRANT, who left yesterday for New-Jersey, and who was informed of the assassination as he was leaving Philadelphia this morning, arrived here in a special train about noon, and immediately proceeded to the President's house.

The Theatres.

Dispatches from Boston announce that all the theatres in that city will be closed until further notice.

In this city a movement of the same kind has been inaugurated. Fox's Old Bowery Theatre will be closed this evening.

Editorials

The Murder of President Lincoln.

The heart of this nation was stirred yesterday as it has never been stirred before The news of the assassination of ABRAHAM LINCOLN carried with it a sensation of horror and of agony which no other event in our history has ever excited. In this city the demonstrations of grief and consternation were without a parallel. Business was suspended. Crowds of people thronged the streets—great gatherings sprung up spontaneously everywhere seeking to give expression, by speeches, resolutions, &c., &c., to the universal sense of dismay and indignation which pervaded the public mind.

Perhaps the paramount element in this public feeling was evoked by personal regard for ABRAHAM LINCOLN. That a man so gentle, so kind, so free from every particle of malice or unkindness, every act of whose life has been so marked by benevolence and good-will, should become the victim of a cold-blooded assassination, shocked the public heart beyond expression. That the very moment, too, when he was closing the rebellion which had drenched our land in blood and tears—by acts of magnanimity so signal as even to excite the reluctant distrust and apprehensions of his own friends—should be chosen for his murder, adds a new element of horror to the dreadful tragedy.

But a powerful element of the general feeling which the news aroused was a profound concern for the public welfare. The whole nation had come to lean on ABRA-HAM LINCOLN in this dread crisis of its fate with a degree of confidence never accorded to any President since GEORGE WASHINGTON. His love of his country ardent and all-pervading,—swaying every act and prompting every word,—his unsuspected uprightness and personal integrity,—his plain, simple common sense, conspicuous in everything he did or said, commending itself irresistibly to the judgment and approval of the great body of the people, had won for him a solid and immovable hold upon the regard and confidence even of his political opponents. The whole people mourn his death with profound and sincere appreciation of his character and his worth.

ANDREW JOHNSON, of Tennessee, is now the President of the United States. We have no doubts and no misgivings in regard to the manner in which he will discharge the duties which devolve so suddenly upon him. This country has no more patriotic citizen than he—no one among all her public men who will bring to her service a higher sense of his responsibilities, a sounder judgment in regard to her interests, or a firmer purpose in the maintenance of her honor and the promotion of her welfare. He has suffered, in his person, his property and his family relations, terribly from the wicked rebellion which has desolated the land; but he is not the man to allow a sense of personal wrong to sway his judgment or control his action in a great national emergency. Traitors and rebels have nothing to expect at his hands, but strict justice, tempered with such mercy only as the welfare of the nation may require.

In this hour of mourning and of gloom, while the shadow of an awful and unparalleled calamity hangs over the land, it is well to remember that the stability of our government and the welfare of our country do not depend upon the life of any individual, and that the great current of affairs is not to be changed or checked by the loss of any man however high or however honored. In nations where all power is vested in single hands, an assassin's knife may overthrow governments and wrap a continent in the flames of war. But here the PEOPLE rule, and events inevitably follow the course which *they* prescribe. ABRAHAM LINCOLN has been their agent and instrument for the four years past; ANDREW JOHNSON is to be their agent for the four years that are now to come. If the people have faith, courage and wisdom, the result will be the same.

YESTERDAY.—It would be presumptuous to attempt to express in words the deep sorrow with which the death of our noble President has filled all hearts. To the honor of our people be it said, that, with a few unimportant exceptions, the nation's heart throbs with the profoundest grief, and the utterances of the nation's voice are all in accord in lamentation. The great calamity was scarcely known, and where known, was hardly believed, at the late hour of its announcement on Friday night. But, early yesterday morning we were assured of the mournful truth. As one man the people put on the habiliments of mourning, and the glad songs of triumph over the anticipated advent of peace were subdued to the wail of such grief as only a nation can feel. All day the stunned and bewildered citizens were putting forth the emblems of mourning. Business was almost entirely suspended. Sorrow was visible on every face, not seldom varied with an expression that partook of revenge. The low, earnest conversation of friends, the almost tearful greetings of acquaintances, the entire absence of the ordinary hum and bustle of business, fittingly marked the people's appreciation of their bereavement. It was a day never paralleled, and never to be forgotten.

The Rebel Leaders and the Treatment they Should Receive.

The men who have filled prominent positions in the rebel army have, as a general rule, had no share in getting up the rebellion. They drew the sword in it, after the politicians had decreed it should take place, many of them, no doubt, from a mistaken sense of allegiance to their respective States, and others in the hope of more rapid promotion than they were likely to have in the United States army; and others again, for mere love of excitement, or from a feeling of sympathy with their neighbors. In the large majority of cases, if not in all, these men are sufficiently punished by their total defeat, by the hardships of the last four years, and by the loss of their commanders. It may, therefore, be expedient to let them go home quietly, and chew the cud of bitter fancy. Their memories of the rebellion during the remainder of their lives are not likely to be agreeable.

But the projectors of the attempt at revolution, the men who have during the last ten or fifteen years preached it, prepared the minds of the Southern people for it, devised and put in motion the machinery necessary to bring it on, and who have during the last four years directed the affairs of the Confederacy, do not deserve, and, we sincerely hope, will not receive, at the hands of the government, or of any portion of the public, the smallest commiseration or indulgence. They stand in an entirely different category from the military men; and, in fact, the army may be said to have been the blind and unhappy instruments of their will. They have for years deliberately plotted the overthrow of the United States Government. Many of them used the power placed in their hands by their occupation of official positions in its service, to help on the preparations made for its destruction. Among these stand DAVIS, BRECKINRIDGE and COBB. Others have since devoted their best energies to blackening the national reputation abroad, and persuading European monarchies to interfere by armed force in our affairs. Prominent among these are SLIDELL, MASON, and DUDLEY MANN. Amongst the others who served in any capacity in which they could do much mischief, were TOOMBS, of Georgia, and that astute and disinterested friend of freedom, JUDAH P. BENJAMIN.

We are strongly opposed, as our readers know, to anything like general vengeance. We desire that, as regards the people of the Confederate States, by-gones shall really be by gones. We pity the man who supposes that any penalty we now could inflict, would have many terrors for a people whose young men are dead or crippled, half of whose women and children are widowed, orphaned and impoverished, whose homes and fields lie desolate, whose quays and streets are grass-grown. The scenes which were witnessed last Sunday in the Richmond churches—congregations composed almost exclusively of women, dressed in black, and weeping through the liturgy—tell of themselves an awful story; and they will doubtless be repeated to-day in every city of the South. There is in truth hardly a house all over the land from which husband, son, or brother has not perished in this unnatural strife. Surely, for the Southern people the bitterness of death is past. Their crime has been great, but since Gaul, long prostrate under the sword of JULIUS CÆSAR, no nation has ever paid a penalty so terrible. Religion and humanity, as well as sound policy, demand that as far as they are concerned, we should do everything in our power to remove all traces of the terrible convulsion from which they are emerging, except the memory of the folly and wickedness which brought it on.

But as regards the leaders, there is a very different course marked out for us. We have urged the infliction of condign punishment on DAVIS, if he should ever fall into our hands; and condign punishment in his case can be nothing less than the penalty assigned by law to the offence of which he has been guilty. We say to-day that there is at least a dozen of his associates, TOOMBS, MASON, SLIDELL, BENJAMIN, BRECKINRIDGE, VANCE, COBB, TRENHOLM, and others, who cannot possibly remain hereafter in the United States. A "decent regard for the opinion of mankind," as well as self-respect, and respect for order, law and morality, forbid that they should ever find shelter or protection under the national flag, or that even their bones should find a resting-place in our soil.

We have for four years been making the world ring with our stories of the wickedness of the rebellion, of the perfidy and barbarity of its authors. We have exhausted the resources of invective in holding them up to the reprobation of foreign nations, and we have professed to be shocked to the last degree by the welcome with which they have been greeted in Europe at the hands of

"Christians and gentlemen." After all this, we cannot possibly receive them back into citizenship; we cannot even suffer their presence in our streets or courts or capitols, without stultifying ourselves most painfully, without presenting ourselves to the world as cheats and humbugs, or worse. What will people think of our denunciations of crime when they see us next day associating with the criminals? What can they think of us, if they see MASON or TOOMBS in our Senate, or even in our parlors, except that we are a race of jugglers and impostors—men to whom truth and falsehood, treason and loyalty, are but empty sounds, used to adorn stump speeches and befog foreign simpletons? What can they think of our war except that it was what these Southern conspirators represented, a vast crusade instigated by greed and treachery, and led by hypocrites and knaves?

Distinctions we know are sometimes made by moralists between the crime and the criminal, and some of them have professed themselves able to abhor the one while justifying and even lauding the other. But this is very much too fine-drawn for ordinary human use, and any attempt on the part of the great mass of mankind to adopt it, would assuredly result in the obliteration of the moral sense. The world believes, and it is a belief which is justified both by philosophy and experience, that a man who loves the society of thieves, and is content to be surrounded by them as his equals, cannot have any great horror of theft.

We "lost our heads" when we began this war; went into it with a wild burst of enthusiasm, which worked up the lesson of experience, and almost refused even to take count of the laws of the natural world. The result was Bull Run. There is now some danger that we will rush crazily into peace, singing, dancing and hurrahing, and forgetting in our jubilation, both what we owe to ourselves and our children, and what we owe to the memory of the great army of the dead, who have laid down their lives that we might see this great salvation. And as might be expected, it is those who were most frantic and excited in 1861, who supposed the South could be overrun by an undisciplined mob, and whose wild preaching plunged the nation into the greatest humiliation that has ever overtaken it, who are now trying to betray us into the still greater humiliation of embracing and receiving back to our firesides the desperadoes who plotted our destruction, and whose garments have been rolled in the blood of the flower of our young men.

THE LAST BRITISH PROPHECY.—Our readers may have noticed that latterly we have taken no notice of the ponderous and pretentious letters of the London *Times'* special correspondent, and, indeed, have only brought the "Thunderer's" own pompous malice before our readers, when to do so was necessary to give to the public information as to the current of opinion abroad in regard to our affairs. It has long been noticed that whenever the London *Times* uttered one of its solemn prophecies with judicial air, the paper con-

taining it was sure to arrive here either just after or just before the occurrence of an event directly in the face of the prediction. In these performances the special correspondent has beaten the home editor always, out and out; and has prophesied the thing that did not happen, and asserted "the thing that is not" twice to his principal's once. The following passage in his letter last arrived is too good to be passed over under the circumstances:

"LEE, however, it is known to the Federal Government, if not to the Federal people, commands an army of nearly 100,000 men, of whom four-fifths are veterans, and can *defy any assault* upon any side of Richmond that GRANT may make with *a third of the number.* He can consequently *spare a respectable army* from the defences of the capital to reinforce Gen. J. E. JOHNSTON, or dispatch it to any other point at which it may seem more advisable to strike a blow. Gen. GRANT has about 125,000 men—not all veterans of the old Army of the Potomac, but fully 40,000 of them recruits, and continually calls upon the government to supply him with better men. I learn on good authority that he is quite *convinced that Richmond is impregnable* unless by a combined military and naval assault, both to be made by a colossal force, and that he has persuaded the President, Mr. STANTON and Mr. WELLES to place at his disposal a strong fleet of gunboats, iron-clads, and monitors, to be commanded by Admiral FARRAGUT, and force the passage of the James River to within shelling distance of Richmond."

As this letter, by the inevitable fatality aforesaid, happened to arrive here between the defeat of Gen. LEE's entire forces by Lieut.-Gen. GRANT, with their consequent flight from Petersburgh and Richmond, and the subsequent total rout of LEE, and his surrender of the remnant of his army, the perusal of this passage by the writer of it must have been an amusingly rueful performance. Of what value the letters in question have been to their British readers, we leave it to them now to judge. Yet we will say that they have afforded us infinite amusement. To reassure us as to the favorable issue of any movement on foot, it was only necessary to receive the London *Times*, with the special correspondent's prediction of failure.

A NATION IN MOURNING.—Of the twenty millions of people in the loyal and border States, perhaps more than one-half were yesterday apprized of the violent death of President LINCOLN. The telegraph brings us brief notices of their feelings upon this dreadful catastrophe. There is but one expression in its silent flashes. Sorrow, deep and unfeigned sorrow, that words cannot fitly shadow forth, fills every hamlet and every heart from the Madawaska to the Pacific; a sorrow that is only beginning, and will be felt and expressed for months and years to come.

A FRIENDLY WORD FROM A NEIGHBOR.—Yesterday was the time appointed for the official promulgation of laws in Nova Scotia, but the Governor, with a delicacy and feeling that does him great honor, announced that in consequence of the shocking intelligence of the assassination of President LINCOLN he should postpone the ceremony. The people most cordially responded to his manly expression, and the naval authorities gave further proof of brotherly feeling by ordering the flag of a rebel vessel lying in Halifax harbor to be hauled down. Such tokens fall like cooling dew upon the nation's burning sorrow.

The New-York Times.

VOL. XIV.....NO. 4232.   NEW-YORK, TUESDAY, APRIL 18, 1865.   PRICE FOUR CENTS.

CAPTURE OF MOBILE.

The Last of the Coast Cities in Our Possession.

The News Officially Confirmed.

The City Surrendered on the 9th inst. to Our Forces.

OVER FIVE THOUSAND PRISONERS.

Large Quantities of Ordnance Stores Taken.

FULL DETAILS OF PREVIOUS OPERATIONS.

NEW-ORLEANS, Monday, April 10, via CAIRO, Sunday, April 16.

The *Times* publishes an official dispatch of the capture of Spanish Fort, and of the town of Blakeley.

The former was captured at 10:30 on the morning of the 9th, with 700 prisoners.

The letter was captured on the same day by assault, with over 5,000 prisoners and a large amount of ordnance stores.

Our gunboats and troops were proceeding unresisted toward Mobile, which place was captured last evening by a portion of Gen. SMITH's command, assisted by the light-draught gunboats, after a short resistance by the enemy.

IMPORTANT FROM GEN. SHERMAN.

Negotiations with Johnston in Progress.

Probable Surrender of the Rebel Army.

WASHINGTON, Monday, April 17.

Information has been received by the government from Gen. SHERMAN that he was in communication with Gen. JOHNSTON, with a view to the surrender of the latter.

Gen. SHERMAN would offer the same terms that Gen. GRANT did to Gen. LEE, and it was supposed they would be accepted.

THE ASSASSINATION.

Condition of Secretary Seward Improving.

NEW FACTS ABOUT THE MURDERERS.

Preparations for the President's Funeral.

Official Directions from Heads of Departments.

DESCRIPTION OF THE ASSASSINS.

Reward of Thirty Thousand Dollars Offered for Their Apprehension.

Additional Details of the Conspiracy.

APPEARANCE OF THE CITY.

WASHINGTON, D. C.
Tuesday, April 17—9:20 P. M.

The city has to some extent resumed its wonted appearance, though the great grief is still uppermost in all hearts, and its signs are appearent on every hand. Every yard of black fabric in the city on Saturday, was bought up at an early hour on that day, and hundreds of persons who wished to testify their grief by draping the residences were unable to do so. This morning, however, further supplies arrived here, and this afternoon many more houses have been draped in mourning.

Business has been partially resumed, though large numbers of stores have simply contented themselves with opening their doors and not taking down their shutters. In the Public Departments some work has been done during the day, but business generally will not be resumed therein till after the funeral.

THE NEWS IN RICHMOND.

The news of the murder of the President was received in Richmond during the evening of Saturday, by special telegram to Gen. ORD's headquarters. It created great alarm and consternation, and the first feeling among the officers who learned it Saturday evening was, that swift justice should be meted out to the authors.

THE FLAG TORN BY THE ASSASSIN.

The National flag draped round the box at the theatre, occupied by the President, belonged to the Treasury Department Regiment. It was torn by the spur of the assassin as he leaped to the stage.

CONDITION OF SECRETARY SEWARD AND SON

At 10:30 o'clock to-day, Secretary SEWARD was represented to be in an improving condition, though he rested rather uncomfortably last night from mental excitement, caused by conversation with friends in relation to recent events.

His son FREDERICK has partially recovered consciousness, and his symptoms are otherwise somewhat favorable.

MR. HANSELL IS BETTER.

Mr. HANSELL, the Messenger of the State Department, who was stabbed in the back at the same time, is a great sufferer, but believed to be out of danger.

A GRAY COAT STAINED WITH BLOOD FOUND.

WASHINGTON, Monday, April 17.

Yesterday a grey coat stained with blood, and which evidently had been worn as an overcoat, was found near Fort Bunker Hill, just back of Glenwood Cemetery. In the pocket was a false moustache, a pair of riding gloves, and a slip of paper, upon which was "MARY E. GARDNER, 419." The coat is supposed to have been worn by the man who attacked Secretary SEWARD, although the weight of the evidence indicates that all the conspirators took the same route—that of the navy-yard bridge.

BOOTH'S RECENT BEHAVIOR.

The *Evening Star* says on Friday last, BOOTH was about the National Hotel, as usual, and strolled up and down the avenue several times. During one of these strolls he stopped at the Kirkwood House, and sent to Vice-President JOANSON a card, upon which was written:

"I do not wish to disturb you. Are you in?
     J. WILKES BOOTH."

A gentleman of BOOTH's acquaintance at this time met him in front of the Kirkwood House, and in the conversation which followed, made some allusion to BOOTH's business, and, in a jesting way, asked: "What makes you so gloomy? Have you lost another thousand in oil?" BOOTH replied he had been hard at work that day and was about to leave Washington never to return. Just then a boy came out and said to BOOTH: "Yes, he is in his room." Upon which the gentleman walked on, supposing BOOTH would enter the hotel. About 7 o'clock Friday evening he came down from his room at the National, and was spoken to by several concerning his paleness, which, he said, proceeded from indisposition. Just before leaving, he asked the clerk if he was not going to Ford's Theatre, and added: "There will be some very fine acting there to-night." The doorkeeper at the theatre noticed BOOTH as he passed in, and shortly after the latter entered the restaurant and in a hurried manner called for "Brandy, brandy, brandy," rapping at the same time on the bar.

The *Star* also contains the following article, headed, "A Clue to the Assailant of Mr. SEWARD:"

About three weeks ago, a man named ATZERARD, represented as being a merchant at Brigantown, Charles Co., Md., went to the stables of THOMPSON NAYLOR, corner of Thirteen and a half and E streets, for the purpose of selling a stallion, and a brown horse blind in one eye. ATZERARD made several attempts to sell the horses to the government, but without success, and finally disposed of the stallion to Mr. THOMPSON NAYLOR, stage contractor to Port Tobacco. He continued to visit Mr. NAYLOR's stables, however, and in a short time reported that he had also sold his brown horse.

On Friday afternoon a man named HARLD, who appeared to be intimate with ATZERARD, came to the stable and hired a roan pacing horse, and shortly afterward ATZERARD appeared with a bay horse, which he left, telling the hostler to have it ready for him at 10 o'clock. Upon calling for the horse at the appointed time, the hostler asked what had become of his friend HARLD and the roan, to which ATZERARD replied: "Has he not returned yet? He'll be here directly." Some time after the hostler heard the pace of the roan coming down from the direction of the Treasury, and went out to meet him, but the rider, apparently to avoid the hostler, turned up Fourteenth and then down F-street. The latter went back to the stable, and feared HARLD intended to make off with the horse, saddled another, and followed him to the Navy Yard Bridge. Where, in answer to his inquiries, the guard stated that a man riding such a horse had passed over, and was probably about a quarter of a mile in advance. He was told that he might go over, but could not return before morning. He then came back to the stable, and, hearing that a horse had been picked up in the street by the detectives, made inquiries, and after giving his statement to the Provost-Marshal, was shown a saddle, which he identified beyond doubt as the one used on the brown horse when at NAYLOR's stable, which ATZERARD said he had sold.

This forenoon several prisoners from Prince George's County were brought to Washington. As they were being taken to the Old Capitol from Provost-Marshal INGRAHAM's office a large crowd followed, increasing in numbers at every corner, although, as a precautionary measure, the route taken was down the back streets. The crowd was a motly one, of all ages and colors. It being represented, and the report that the parties were BOOTH and SURRATT gaining credit, as they reached the Baltimore depot, the cry was raised, "Hang them." "kill them," and at the same time the prisoners were attacked with stones, who were struck several times, as were also the guard. Some orderly persons attempted to quiet the crowd by remonstrating with them and assuring them that they were mistaken, but they failed to stop the riotous proceedings, which, however, were soon quieted. After the guard were struck a number of times, they faced about and made ready to defend themselves with their muskets. The prisoners were delivered to the superintendents of the prison, each of them having been somewhat bruised by the flying missiles.

Among other arrests to-day were, it is said, several men in female apparel.

The New York Times

THE GOLDEN ANNIVERSARY OF PEACE WITHIN THE UNION

AN INTERPRETATIVE HISTORY OF THE CIVIL WAR
WRITTEN FOR THE NEW YORK TIMES BY CHARLES WILLIS THOMPSON

(Copyright, 1915, by The New York Times Company.)

SECTION SEVEN   NEW YORK, APRIL 4, 1915   TWENTY-FOUR PAGES

THE BLUE AND THE GRAY

BY FRANCIS MILES FINCH ~

*In 1869 the women of Columbus, Miss., * * * strewed flowers alike on the graves of the Confederate and of the National soldiers.*

By the flow of the inland river,
　Whence the fleets of iron
　　have fled,
Where the blades of the grave-
　grass quiver,
　Asleep on the ranks of the dead;
Under the sod and the dew,
　Waiting the Judgment Day;
Under the one the Blue,
　Under the other the Gray.

These in the robings of glory,
　Those in the gloom of defeat,
All with the battle-blood gory,
　In the dusk of eternity meet:
Under the sod and the dew,
　Waiting the Judgment Day;
Under the laurel the Blue,
　Under the willow the Gray.

From the silence of sorrowful hours,
　The desolate mourners go,
Lovingly laden with flowers,
　Alike for the friend and the foe:
Under the sod and the dew,
　Waiting the Judgment Day,
Under the roses the Blue,
　Under the lilies the Gray.

So, with an equal splendor,
　The morning sun rays fall,
With a touch impartially tender,
　On the blossoms blooming for
　　all:
Under the sod and the dew,
　Waiting the Judgment Day;
Broidered with gold the Blue,
　Mellowed with gold the Gray.

So, when the Summer calleth,
　On forest and field of grain,
With an equal murmur falleth
　The cooling drip of the rain:
Under the sod and the dew,
　Waiting the Judgment Day;
Wet with the rain the Blue,
　Wet with the rain the Gray.

Sadly, but not with upbraiding,
　The generous deed was done;
In the storm of the years that are
　fading,
　No braver battle was won:
Under the sod and the dew,
　Waiting the Judgment Day;
Under the blossoms the Blue,
　Under the garlands the Gray.

No more shall the war cry sever,
　Or the winding rivers be red;
They banish our anger forever
　When they laurel the graves of the dead!
Under the sod and the dew,
　Waiting the Judgment Day;
Love and tears for the Blue,
　Tears and love for the Gray.

FIFTY YEARS SINCE APPOMATTOX

(April 9, 1865)

The Union Became a Fact When Grant and Lee Met—The Efforts Made in the North and South to Reach an Agreement.

FIFTY years ago this week the war between the North and South ended. Last Friday, April 2, was the fiftieth anniversary of the fall of Richmond. Fifty years ago next Friday, April 9, Grant and Lee met under the apple tree at Appomattox and the greatest war ever fought on this continent came to its end, though Johnston did not surrender to Sherman until April 27. There still remained two armies in the West, but Richard Taylor surrendered all the Confederate troops east of the Mississippi to Canby on May 4, and E. Kirby Smith the troops west of the river to the same officer on May 26. But with that meeting under the apple tree the war was over.

Why was this mighty war fought? It is not until long after a war that its real causes emerge; that things that seemed of vast moment at the time sink out of sight, and the true perspective is reached. The vulgar belief that the war was fought for the abolition of slavery is unfounded. It was the slavery question that brought about the collision, but the cause lay in the different interests and aims of the two sections.

The South seceded because of the election of Lincoln, but the Republican Party was not an abolition party. Its aim, it proclaimed, was to keep slavery in the South and out of the territories; yet almost its first act after Lincoln's election was to organize the Territories of Colorado, Dakota, and Nevada, with no provision whatever regarding slavery; and it passed this act unanimously—Sumner, Stevens, Wade, Chandler, Lovejoy, and all the other radicals approving.

"I have no purpose, directly or indirectly," announced Lincoln in his inaugural address, "to interfere with the institution of slavery where it exists. I believe I have no lawful right to do so, and I have no inclination to do so." But his party had already put itself on record much more emphatically. A committee of thirty-three, headed by Thomas Corwin of Ohio, had reported to the House, before Lincoln's inauguration, a resolution providing for a Thirteenth Amendment to the Constitution, to the effect that "no amendment shall be made to the Constitution which will authorize or give Congress the power to abolish or interfere within any State with the domestic institutions thereof, including that of persons held to labor or service by the laws of said State." It passed the House by a vote of 133 to 65. In the Senate only twelve of the twenty-five Republicans voted against it. In its original form it had been moved in the committee by Charles Francis Adams of Massachusetts. His proposition was that no anti-slavery amendment to the Constitution should originate in any anti-slavery State or be valid without the assent of every one of the slave States, a proposition more radically pro-slavery than any that had ever been submitted by a Democrat or a Southern man.

The amendment as passed by Congress was hardly less extreme. It would have made slavery perpetual. It made slavery part of the organic law of the land; it set slave property apart and above all other kinds of property. Among those who voted for it were

Sherman, Adams, Colfax, and Windom. Thus did the Republican Party declare its position on slavery just before the war. The amendment was never ratified, because the war intervened before the States could take it up, and the Thirteenth Amendment that was adopted four years later, at the instance of James M. Ashley, was vastly different. The Republican Party had changed its attitude by that time.

One of the chief reasons why Seward failed of the Republican nomination in 1860 was that he was thought to be too radical on the slavery question. The party was conservative. After the firing on Fort Sumter the President summoned the Thirty-seventh Congress in extra session, and as soon as it met John J. Crittendon in the House and Andrew Johnson in the Senate offered a resolution declaring the object of the war. It included a statement that it was not waged for "the overthrowing or interfering with the rights or established institutions"—that is, slavery—"of those States, but to defend and maintain the supremacy of the Constitution," and that "as soon as these objects are accomplished the war ought to cease." The House adopted it without debate, and in the Senate only five votes were cast against it, four of them those of Democrats from Missouri and Kentucky. "It was the voice of the Republican Party, with no one openly opposing it in either branch of Congress," says Blaine.

"My paramount object," wrote Lincoln to Greeley on Aug. 22, 1862, "is to save the Union, and not either to save or destroy slavery. If I could save the Union without freeing any slaves I would do it;

if I could save it by freeing all the slaves I would do it, and if I could save it by freeing some and leaving others alone I would do it." Two years before Wendell Phillips, the abolitionist, had called him "the slave hound of Illinois."

Nor did the Confederates regard the war as one for abolition, however their demagogues may have misled the people by using that shibboleth. Many of them, perhaps a majority if we include the dumb rank and file of poor whites in the army, considered it a minor issue, and were willing to give up the institution if necessary. Prince Polignac, a French officer serving under General E. Kirby Smith, in 1864 visited Gov. Allen of Louisiana, a Confederate General up to the time of his election to that office. He found the Governor full of a plan to arm the slaves, enlist them in the Confederate Army, and emancipate them as a reward.

In 1863 General William C. Oates, afterward Governor of Alabama, had brought the same proposal to the attention of General Ewell, who replied, "I think that you are right. Young man, the need of additional troops will bring us to it later." Oates visited Richmond and urged his plan on members of Congress, and found favor among the members from the border States, but not from those further south. Representative Pugh said that to free the negroes would be "simply throwing aside the bone of contention." Says Gov. Oates:

I replied that if the Confederate Government would send an authorized agent to Lee's army and let him proclaim to every regiment in it that the war was being fought solely for the maintenance of slavery, it would close in ten days; that two-thirds of the men in

the ranks never owned a slave, and they would not offer their lives as a sacrifice for that consideration. * * * Such a proclamation, "that the war was being fought alone for slavery," would have caused a disbandment of the armies. The soldiers could not have been held together. The men would have laid down their arms and gone home.

But the most important attempt at emancipation by the Confederates was made by General Patrick R. Cleburne, who on Jan. 1, 1864, drew up a paper advocating enlistment and emancipation and addressed it to the Generals and regimental commanders in the Army of Tennessee. He pointed out that this would not only give the South armies numerically superior to those of the North and enable it to take the offensive, but would deprive the North of European sympathy based on "bitter prejudices with which foreigners view the institution."

This paper was presented to the Brigadiers in Cleburne's division. Generals Polk, Lowrey, Govan, and Granbury, who all approved it. Later General Johnston called a meeting of the general officers of the army. He and Hardee were favorably disposed—in fact, Johnston had already suggested the enlistment idea to President Davis, without mentioning emancipation—but several disapproved. Johnston declined to forward it to the War Department because it was of a political, not a military, nature; but General W. H. T. Walker, who violently disapproved it, did forward a copy, with Cleburne's permission. President Davis sent it back with the following indorsement:

While recognizing the patriotic motives of its distinguished author. I deem it inexpedient, at this time, to give publicity to this paper, and request that it be suppressed.

Later in the war the Administration began to yield, and at Mr. Davis's instance Congress passed a bill for the enlistment of slaves; but this was in 1865, just before the end came, and nothing was ever done. Enlistment would undoubtedly have been followed by emancipation. As Gov. Allen said, there was no way out of it.

What changed the attitude of the Republican Party toward slavery? It did change mightily from the day, in 1861, when Charles Francis Adams, advocating the abortive Thirteenth Amendment, said to his Democratic adversaries: "We offer to settle the question finally in all of the present territory that you claim by giving you every chance of establishing slavery that you have any right to require of us."

Hardly had the Johnson-Crittenden resolution disclaiming any intention to interfere with slavery been passed when it was found that thousands of slaves were being employed in the construction of earthworks, driving teams, in the general work of the Quartermaster and Commissary Departments, and in other military services for the Confederacy. This simply added 4,000,000 to the Confederate population available for military service. As soon as it became certain that slavery was a military factor a different face was put on the situation.

This first became apparent when Congress passed, in 1861, a law "to confiscate property used for insurrectionary purposes," including slave property; and from that time on, step by step, bill by

Telegram Written by General Grant Announcing the Surrender at Appomattox.

bill, the Government was forced forward until the last steps were taken in the Emancipation Proclamation and the Thirteenth Amendment—Ashley's, not Corwin's. How Lincoln viewed it is shown in a letter he wrote in 1862 to a Louisiana Unionist, who urged him not to issue the proclamation. "You must not expect me to give up this Government without playing my last card."

The South, Europe, and a large part of the North believed in 1860 that the Union was not a nation but a partnership, from which any of the partners had a right to withdraw whenever it saw fit. "Few," says Goldwin Smith, "who have looked into the history can doubt that the Union originally was, and was generally taken by the parties to it to be, a compact, dissolvble perhaps, most of them would have said, at pleasure, dissoluble certainly on breach of the articles of union." And Senator Lodge, in his life of Webster, says:

When the Constitution was adopted by the votes of States at Philadelphia, and accepted by the votes of States in popular convention, it is safe to say that there was not a man in the country, from Washington and Hamilton on the one side, to George Clinton and George Mason on the other, who regarded the new system as anything but an experiment entered upon by the States, and from which each and every State had the right peaceably to withdraw, a right which was very likely to be exercised.

But—"however it may have been in 1788, in 1860 a nation had grown into existence," said the Charles Francis Adams who died last month, the son of him who moved in the Thirty-sixth Congress to make slavery perpetual. And that explains the war. From the moment the Fathers made what they regarded as a compact, it began to grow into a nation. Marshall and Webster were its chief architects; but it was the conditions that made a nation inevitable. The Fathers had sought to create a divided sovereignty, divided between nation and States; sovereignty cannot be divided, as Mr. Adams points out. The country had to make its choice.

Economic conditions created a divergence between the choice made by the North and that made by the South. The North was a manufacturing, the South an agricultural community. The North lived by machinery, the South by slaves. At the beginning there was no reason to expect such a divergence; one section might as well have been expected to be a mechanical centre as the other. Slavery had died out in the North, and was expected to die out in the South. But Eli Whitney's invention of the cotton gin in 1793 made slave labor profitable and turned the South permanently in the agricultural direction.

The conflict of interests between North and South was almost immediately evident. **The manufacturing North needed a tariff; this taxed the South for the North's benefit. It was a contest between two industrial systems. The first blow was aimed by the North, when the growth of the slave-labor system was proscribed by the Missouri Compromise. This prohibited slavery north of the latitude of 36 degrees 30 minutes, and thus circumscribed the increase of the South's industrial system. The South retaliated with nullification—an attempt to cripple the tariff system on which the North depended; and that was when the civil war began. It continued for forty years and ended in bloodshed.**

The Northern population grew and became enormous, so that the North was sure of controlling the House. The South clung desperately to the Senate, and when new States were admitted it insisted on offsetting every free State with a slave State. But it was a losing game. The end was in sight when California, admitted on the supposition that it would be a slave State, turned out to be a free one; the discovery of gold had brought to her a great rush of Northern men. The balance of power was gone; it was only a question of a few years when the North would be in control of the whole Government. The time came ten years after the admission of California, when Lincoln was elected President on a platform declaring against the extension of slavery. South Carolina seceded and dragged nearly all the rest of the South after her.

It is true that the South had dominated the Government from the first. But the end had come. She seceded, not so much **because of anything that had been done as because of what she foresaw would be done. There was, as Commodore M. F. Maury** says in an able paper setting **forth the Southern view,** "cumulative **dissatisfaction in the Southern** mind **toward the Federal Government,** and **Southern men began to ask each other,** 'Should we not be better off out of the Union than we are in it?'" But while this might have taken South Carolina and some other **radical States out of the** Union, it **would not have taken many; it** was "the fear **of something yet to come" that caused the South, still holding to the** "compact" **idea of the Union, to withdraw from it. The North did not believe** in or understand **the "compact" idea. Webster and Marshall had taught her otherwise, and the railroad had abolished State lines, and machinery and immigration had made a nation.**

HOW THE GREAT STRUGGLE BEGAN

The Mistake of Jefferson Davis Which Consolidated the North Against His Cause, and the Vain Protest of Toombs.

IF Jefferson Davis had not ordered General Beauregard to fire on Fort Sumter, which he did fifty years ago on April 12 next, nothing is more probable than that the Southern Confederacy would have been firmly established and the Union broken. That act doomed the Southern cause; the Confederacy became, as Colonel A. K. McClure says, "a colossal suicide."

The Confederacy had been safely organized and in peaceful control of its territory for two months. There was no disposition in the North to coerce it, except among a minority. "If the cotton States shall decide that they can do better out of the Union than in it, we insist on letting them go in peace," said Horace Greeley in the leading Republican organ, The New York Tribune. "Wayward sisters, go in peace," said General Scott, the commander of the American Army. If Mr. Lincoln had fired on the Confederates, half of the North would have risen against him.

What united the North, brought Democrats and Republicans together, united the abolitionists of Massachusetts with the pro-slavery men of Delaware, and called the border slave States to the colors was the assault on the American flag. Jefferson Davis had done what Abraham Lincoln could not do; he had solidified the divided North.

It is hard for us now to get into the atmosphere of those days; the Union is so fixed a thing that we can hardly realize the 1860 frame of mind. The South was solid, the North fluid; the South was moving on irresistibly in the erection of the new nation, the North was paralyzed and incoherent and appalled. The predominant sentiment North was that nothing could be done, and that the South was acting within its rights, however it might be regretted.

James Buchanan has been hardly dealt with. He was not a strong man, but he was a patriot. His Administration did drift helplessly, but so did Lincoln's for two months after the inauguration. Neither had a policy; both were awaiting events. Lincoln had a loyal Cabinet; Buchanan had a disloyal one, which betrayed him, spied on him, and misled him. The main difference between the two was that Lincoln was unalterably resolved to hold on to the Government property which the secessionists had not yet captured, and he did not come to that resolution decidedly until Francis P. Blair, Sr., had argued the case with him. Lincoln had a freer hand; Buchanan, whose Administration was ending, could not plunge the country into war in his last days and turn the terrible legacy over to his successor.

Buchanan did not believe he had the power to coerce the South, in which most of the North agreed with him. His devotion to the Union disgusted the South, where he was more hated and despised than in the North. Northerners and Southerners declined to shake hands with him; on New Year's Day hardly any of the customary calls were made on him. "I have tried," he said to Senator Fitzpatrick, "to do my duty to both sections, and have displeased both; I am isolated in the world." He feared assassination, and not unreasonably; assassination was in the air; there were plots to murder Lincoln, from which he narrowly escaped; and a distinguished Senator of the United States, Alfred Iverson of Georgia, speaking from his place in the Senate, said of Sam Houston, the Union Governor of Texas: "If he does not yield to public sentiment, some Texan Brutus will arise to rid his country of the hoary-headed incubus that stands between the people and their sovereign will." Says Draper:

(Buchanan) was living in an atmosphere of treason; his Cabinet was disorganized; its confidential policy was repeatedly betrayed; a ship could not be ordered on secret service without the telegraph at once giving information to the secession conspiracy. All Washington was converted into a whispering gallery; what was uttered in secrecy in its council chamber was instantly reverberated to Montgomery. Conclaves were held under the very shadow of the Capitol for the seizure of forts, arsenals, Custom Houses, and for the organization of conventions to insure secession in the distant States—the telegraph and the Post Office were tampered with.

The Government itself was secretly disarmed; its munitions of war were transferred to its assailant; its troops, under specious pretensions, were sent off to the frontiers, there to be entrapped; its navy was treacherously dispersed all over the ocean; its finances, with atrocious skill, were brought apparently into irremediable ruin. The public offices were swarming with disloyal men, and even of many of those who were loyal, the wives and daughters were not to be trusted. Nothing could be hidden from the female spies who pervaded society in Washington, through and through.

Meanwhile, Congress, in a panic, was trying to conciliate the South by granting everything it demanded and more; was trying to amend the Constitution so as to make slavery perpetual. All through the North there was dismay and irresolution, fully as great as that in Buchanan's circle. "The Southern States," says Blaine, "were going further than the people had believed possible. The wolf which had been so long used to scare seemed at last to have come."

Throughout the North meetings to save the Union by surrendering every principle at issue were held. In Boston a police escort had to take Wendell Phillips home to protect him from the mob after he had made a no-surrender speech. Philadelphia had voted for Lincoln by a vast majority, but now George William Curtis was warned by the Republican Mayor that it would not be safe for him to come there and speak.

Mayor Wood of New York submitted to the Common Council a proposal that since the Union was now broken and each must look out for his own interests, this town should secede and organize itself as a free city. Gov. Hicks of Maryland wrote to Gov. Burton of Delaware proposing a Central Confederacy, consisting of their two States, Virginia, Kentucky, Missouri, and Tennessee, and if possible North Carolina and Georgia. The Republican Party was demoralized and voiceless. General Twiggs surrendered the whole army in Texas to the Confederacy, and arsenals, navy yards, forts, and Custom Houses were taken over by them without **a protest. The foreign Ministers gave their Governments to understand that the Union was at an end; even the friendly British Minister, Lord Lyons, began referring to this country as a** "confederation" **in his official dis**patches.

At this point Buchanan **reorganized his** Cabinet and put men loyal to the Union in the places held by the men who had betrayed him. There was an immediate change. South Carolina sent Commissioners to treat with him; Judge Black, the new Secretary of State, threatened to resign unless Buchanan refused their demand for the surrender of the Charleston forts. Buchanan yielded and permitted Black, Holt, and Stanton to frame his reply.

The policy of surrender was halted. Secretary of the Treasury Dix sent an agent to New Orleans to save some revenue cutters from seizure by ordering them to New York. The Captain of one of them replied to the agent, "Your letter, with one of Jan. 19 from the Honorable Secretary of the Treasury, I have duly received, and in reply refuse to obey the order." This answer was telegraphed to Dix, who answered: "Tell Lieut. Caldwell to arrest Capt. Breshwood, assume command of the cutter. and obey the order through you. If Capt. Breshwood, after arrest, undertakes to interfere with the command of the cutter, tell Lieut. Caldwell to consider him as a mutineer, and treat him accordingly. If any one attempts to haul down the American flag, shoot him on the spot." The Southerners side-tracked the telegram, it was never received, and the cutter fell into their hands.

The President, refusing to give up Fort Sumter, sent a merchant steamer, the Star of the West, with supplies for it. The vessel was fired upon and had to return. Thus South Carolina fired the first shot against the American flag and began the war which brought so terrible a retribution upon her. How did South Carolina know the destination and purpose of the Star of the West? Jacob Thompson of Mississippi, who had not yet yielded his place as Secretary of the Interior in Buchanan's Cabinet, went straight from the Cabinet meeting at which it had been decided to dispatch her, and notified the South Carolina authorities.

To such a situation Lincoln succeeded on March 4. He faced a united South with a divided North; and his own section was cold to him. He was little known and generally believed to be weak; he was not trusted. His party was eaten with a desire for spoils, and the White House was overrun with office-seekers who took up most of his time. Seward was supposed to be running the Administration, and thought so himself.

Throughout the Winter Seward had been in communication with leading secessionists, and had come to an understanding with them that Fort Sumter was not to be attacked if no attempt was made to reinforce it. Buchanan was to keep this agreement, and when his term ended Seward was to continue it. Why? Because if the fort was not relieved famine must force its surrender; bloodshed would be avoided, and the issue could be postponed. General Scott acquiesced in the agreement. At first Seward prevailed on Lincoln to follow this policy, whereupon Postmaster General Montgomery Blair wrote out his resignation; but he never had to present it. His father, Francis P. Blair, Sr., visited the President and opened his eyes to the weakness and danger of the Seward-Scott plan, and Lincoln changed his attitude.

The Confederacy sent commissioners to Washington to negotiate for the surrender of Fort Sumter. They negotiated with Seward through Justice John A. Campbell of the Supreme Court, and through him Seward promised that no attempt would be made to relieve Sumter without due notice to South Carolina. At that very time, April 1, Lincoln was planning a relief expedition. Seward in vain tried to dissuade him. The commissioners accused Seward of bad faith, and on April 7 he wrote to Campbell significantly, "Faith as to Sumter kept; wait and see." The day before he sent this note he had, without Lincoln's knowledge, detached the Powhatan, the vessel which was to carry soldiers, and sent her to Pensacola.

In these machinations, Seward thought he was serving his country by preventing bloodshed. Instead he was injuring it; nothing but an attack on the American flag could ever have brought the North together. But that was not the most dangerous feature of the situation; Europe was preparing to recognize the Confederacy as a nation, would surely have done so by Summer if the Confederacy had gone unchallenged that long, and then it would have been virtually impossible to save the Union. It was essential to the cause of the Union that there should be war, but the Government could not fire first, for that would have alienated half the North and all the border. Seward was blindly fighting against his country, not for it.

Fortunately the South cut the knot; and the hasty and reckless State which had precipitated the whole trouble destroyed the Confederacy. It was the pressure from South Carolina which forced Davis to give the suicidal order. He was warned; his Cabinet was summoned to discuss the question, and Robert Toombs, the Secretary of State, told him vehemently, "The firing upon the fort at this time is suicide, murder, and will lose us every friend at the North. You will wantonly strike a hornets' nest which extends from mountain to ocean, and legions now quiet will swarm out and sting us to death. It is unnecessary; it puts us in the wrong; it is fatal."

But South Carolina overcame him; Davis gave the order, Sumter was fired on, and Toombs's prophecy was instantly fulfilled. From mountain to ocean the hornets poured forth. On April 14 the fort capitulated; on April 15 Lincoln called for 75,000 troops. The whole North arose as one man, all differences forgotten, and more troops were offered than could possibly be accepted.

South Carolina was drunk with joy. The story of her spectacular celebration sounds like a page from the days of the French Revolution festivals. There had been a sharp competition over who should have the honor of firing the first shot against the flag, and Beauregard had conferred it upon an aged civilian from Virginia, Edmund Ruffin. Two years later Charleston was in ruins; and on June 17, 1865, Edmund Ruffin blew his brains out, leaving a note in which he said, "I cannot survive the liberties of my country." He was then almost eighty years old.

The South also sprang to arms. It was sure of the result. The belief was general that the Northerners were cowards and "mudsills" and would not fight; that "one Southerner could whip five Yankees." One man, at any rate, did not agree with this estimate, and he had fought side by side with the Yankees and knew. A young staff officer remarked to General Albert Sidney Johnston, with the usual Southern certainty, "The Yankees will not stand cold steel." He was dumfounded to hear Johnston reply, in his deliberate manner: "If we are to succeed, what we do must be done quickly. The longer we have them to fight, the harder they will be to defeat." He knew the North.

Bombardment of Fort Sumter.

HOW NORTH AND SOUTH MADE PEACE

Events Leading Up to Historic Meeting of Grant and Lee--- Surrender of Johnston and Last Confederates in the Field.

MOST wars leave behind them a legacy of hate that lasts long, often for centuries. Civil wars are proverbially the bitterest of all. It is not often that the hatred dies away in the lifetime of the participants. But when the veterans of North and South met at Gettysburg two years ago to celebrate in unison the fiftieth anniversary of the battle, no one who was there can doubt the reality of the reunion. When the survivors of Pickett's men "charged" again up Cemetery Ridge, and the survivors of Webb's forces bent down over the old stone wall and helped them up where fifty years ago they shot their comrades down, it was as thrilling a sight to those who saw it as the original charge could have been.

It will be fifty years next Friday since the war ended with the meeting under the Appomattox apple tree. Peace had long been talked of; there had been sporadic efforts by well-meaning persons, chiefly Northerners, to bring it about. Horace Greeley bothered Lincoln with proposals to send peace commissioners to Niagara Falls to confer with the Confederate leaders there, until the President got rid of him by appointing Greeley himself; he went, and speedily found that it was easier to talk about peace than to make terms. Colonel Jaquess and James R. Gilmore, the writer, whose pen name was "Edmund Kirke," pestered the President until he let them go to Richmond and make their peace proposals to President Davis. They came to nothing, of course; Davis would treat on no basis except that of Southern independence. Both these incidents happened early in 1864, and they were followed by the Democratic nomination of General McClellan for President on a peace platform that declared the war a failure--a platform which McClellan instantly repudiated.

But all the peace talk in 1864 did not come from the North. There was a strong demand for peace emanating from Georgia, North Carolina, and other sections of the South. Georgia was greatly disaffected toward the Confederate Government, and there were even intimations that, under Governor Brown's lead, she might rebel against the Confederacy. This disaffection, which had grown to a considerable height by the end of 1864, finally had its effect on Davis, and it is probably due to this that he paid more attention than was usual with him to the proposal of Francis P. Blair, Sr., which led to the famous Hampton Roads Conference.

Lincoln had already declared his disbelief in the utility of trying to negotiate with Davis. He had set forth his reasons in his message on Dec. 6, saying: "He [Davis] would accept nothing short of severance of the Union, precisely what we will not and cannot give. * * * He does not attempt to deceive us. * * * It is an issue which can only be tried by war and decided by victory." But when Blair sought permission to visit Davis with a proposal, Lincoln, who had great confidence in him, yielded and

gave him a pass, on condition that Blair should not tell him what the proposal was. He was determined not to let even Blair approach Davis as an authorized messenger from him.

Blair told Davis that the war was over as far as slavery was concerned, and his plan was to find a meeting-ground for the two sections. He found it in the French aggression on Mexico. He proposed a suspension of hostilities while the Southern Army, aided by Union soldiers, rescued Mexico from French bayonets. Probably Davis never seriously considered this scheme, but with Georgia worrying him he was willing to accept an excuse for a peace conference; and he appointed Alexander H. Stephens, John A. Campbell and R. M. T. Hunter as commissioners.

Lincoln sent Seward and Major Thomas T. Eckert to meet them. They demanded to see Lincoln himself. The President had no faith in the conference, and was about to summon Seward and Eckert home when Stanton received a telegram from General Grant assuring him that the Commissioners were sincere and their intentions good, and regretting that Lincoln would not meet them. The President changed his mind and went to Hampton Roads, where the conference was held on Feb. 3, 1865.

It was fruitless. A romantic story gained currency and was long believed that Lincoln wrote the word "Union" on a piece of paper and said to Stephens, "Alex, if you will subscribe to that you can fill up the rest of the paper to suit yourself," and that Stephens refused. It was not true. The President refused to consider any proposition except that of unconditional surrender. He promised "clemency," but refused to define it, except to say that he would execute the confiscation and other penal acts with the utmost liberality, and that he would favor indemnifying the South for its slaves. But he refused again and again to make any promises, and he would not hear of granting independence. When the Commissioners left Stephens was the last to go; and as he retired the President said (or so Stephens told Senator Vest):

"Stephens, you are making a great mistake. You Government is a failure, and when the crash comes, as it soon must come, there will be chaos, and disaster which we cannot now foresee must come to your people."

He had mentioned the sum of $400,000,000 as a possible figure for the slavery indemnity. Three days later he brought up the subject before his Cabinet, and proposed the payment of that sum. The Cabinet was against it, and Lincoln dropped the matter for the time. He was assassinated before he found an opportunity to revive it.

The issue, Lincoln had said, must be "tried by war and decided by victory"; and the decision was not far off. Fleeing after the crushing defeat of Five Forks and the surrender of Ewell at Sailor Creek, in a desperate effort to escape from Grant, Lee found his retreat cut off, knew that he was in a trap, and surrendered. On April 9 Ord's infantry

had made a forced march and joined forces with Sheridan's cavalry. The battle was about to begin when an officer waving a white flag rode out from the Confederate lines and asked for a truce

Alexander H Stephens

until terms of surrender could be agreed upon. The officer was a member of General Gordon's staff and the white flag was a towel.

The contrast between the two Generals was an epitome of the whole war, of the two contending sections. Lee, tall, handsome, soldierly, the picture of a modern knight in his handsome uniform; by his side the short, stubby figure of Grant, wearing a private soldier's blouse, not even buttoned; trousers tucked in boots that were splashed high with mud; not wearing a sword, but sticking his swordhand in his trousers pocket. The "mudsill" North and the "chivalric" South were face to face.

And the characteristics of the North were irresistibly shown in the ordinary, business-like, commonplace way in which Grant did the splendidly knightly acts which did so much to bring North and South together. No heroics, no dramatics, nothing imposing or impressive; he did them as if he were making out a bill of lading. "Let them keep their horses; they will need them for the Spring plowing," and so on.

There were still three armies in the field, and many in the Confederacy had no idea that the war was over. Davis had not; he started immediately to make his way to the Mississippi to organize resistance in Texas. Johnston long afterward wrote to Beauregard of this time that the Confederates could have continued the war "only as robbers or guerrillas," but many welcomed that prospect with fierce joy. General Lee's own son, who was not included in the surrender, hastened to join Davis, "not believing for an instant," as he said, "that our struggle was over." Whether there should be a long and ferocious guerrilla struggle was a question that hung in the balance. Had the South foreseen the years of outrage that were to follow in the name of reconstruction, it is hardly to be doubted that the decision would have been for war.

It would not have been ferocious on the Southern side alone; for on April 14 Lincoln was assassinated, and Carl Schurz, then a Major General in the Union Army, says:

The soldiers admired their great Generals, and often saluted some of them with enthusiastic acclamations. But their President, their good "Father Abraham," they loved. Him they carried in their hearts as their personal friend and the friend of their homes and families. When the foul deed by which he had been taken off was made known to them, they did not vent their feelings in loud tones of anger and vengeance, but they sat around their campfires either silent or communicating their wrathful grief to one another in grim murmurs. But as I went around among them, and here and there caught their utterances, it occurred to me that now it was the highest time that the war should cease. If it had continued, and if these men had once more been let loose upon "the enemy's country," there would have been danger of vengeance taken for Abraham Lincoln's blood that might have made the century shudder.

On April 18 Sherman and Johnston met to arrange terms of surrender for the latter's army. Sherman, who had been merciless in war, was generous in peace. His terms were the immediate admission of the seceded States into the Union just as they had left it, with no "reconstruction" inferno to pass through, with their own State Governments, and with a general amnesty. Reagan, the Postmaster General of the Confederacy, had drawn up a memorandum to some such effect, but Sherman made it fuller and more sweeping.

When these terms reached Washington there was a storm. Sherman, in drawing up this generous paper, had been guided by his memory of what he had heard President Lincoln say concerning his own intentions in the treatment of the fallen enemy, and was trying to carry out Lincoln's ideas as he understood them. This was precisely what Secretary Stanton did not want. He had always opposed Lincoln's clement plans, and now that the President was dead he saw a chance to triumph. He obtained the support of Attorney General Speed, and produced the paper at the Cabinet meeting. Speed informed the Cabinet that in his opinion Sherman was plotting to place himself, "at the head of his victorious legions," in control of the Government and become a dictator, and that this was the first step. The denunciations of Stanton and Speed carried the Cabinet off its feet; Sherman's action was unanimously disapproved, and Stanton not only sent Sherman a sharp rebuke, but published the whole transaction, in a somewhat garbled form, if Secretary Welles is right in his account of it.

Meanwhile the Cabinet had ordered Grant to convey to Sherman its disapproval, and that true friend of Sherman's decided to take the message in person. Sherman was instantly appeased and ready to follow Lincoln in this, as he had in the other matter; and on April 29 Johnston surrendered on the same terms on which Lee had surrendered to Grant.

Canby received, on May 4, the surrender of General Richard Taylor's army, all the Confederate forces east of the Mississippi, and on May 26 of Kirby Smith's forces west of the river.

GRANT AND LEE, THE RIVAL CHIEFTAINS

Striking Contrast Between the Leaders---Each Typified His Section and the Cause for Which He Fought.

THERE could not be a greater contrast than that between the two great chieftains of the war; and each typified his section and his cause. Lee personified that gallant gentlehood which was the South's ideal, and personified it visibly, so that in seeing him one seemed to see the South as it saw itself. Grant, too, the plodding, pondering, taciturn man, suggesting more the business man than the soldier, but transcendently efficient, visibly personified the North. And while each suggested to his section the genius of that section, the likeness was equally evident to the other, the hostile one; so that the North as well as the South saw the South in Lee, and the South instantly recognized the North in Grant.

Both were great Generals, undeniably—undeniably now, that is; for a fashion grew up in the North of denying Grant's greatness. The reason was political, and Lee had the good fortune to encounter no politics; otherwise there would have been denial of his greatness, too. Even while the war was going on the decrying of Grant began, for it was a political necessity with a large party to minimize the successes of the Union so as to prevent the Administration from becoming too popular; so Grant was a "hammerer," a "butcher," who knew nothing of strategy and could only understand the value of superior numbers. Afterward, when Grant himself entered politics and became a party leader, there was ten times more reason to discredit him. No party and no faction had any reason for dimming the fame of Lee. Grant is dead now, the factions and issues of his day are in the grave, too, and no one seriously disputes his greatness any more.

Had these two great Generals changed places, it is doubtful whether they would have won such fame. "Had Grant," says Colonel A. K. McClure, "been a Confederate soldier he would probably have developed into a great Lieutenant of the type of Stonewall Jackson, but had he been in command of a Confederate army his aggressive qualities would not have prevented him from fighting against odds and advantages, and he would have been a failure." "Lee's weak side," says General Longstreet, "was in delivering offensive battle. His military reputation must, I think, finally rest almost wholly upon his qualities as a defensive General." Hence, if he had been in Grant's place, he would have won no fame, for he would have been required to be continually on the offensive.

"Lee," says President Davis, "was always daring, but never reckless of the lives of his men." It was charged against Grant that he was reckless in that respect. But to Lee, with a smaller army and no way of enlarging it, it was a military necessity to save his men as much as possible, just as to Grant it was a military necessity to grind Lee down without regard to the loss of life involved. On occasion, where something was to be gained by it, Lee could be prodigal of life; as, for instance, when he sent Pickett's men across that open field to Cemetery Ridge. Longstreet said that Lee's characteristic fault was "headlong combativeness; he chafed at inaction, always desired to beat up the enemy at once and have it out."

Lee's men loved him; Grant's men did not love him, at least as they had loved McClellan, but they trusted him. Lee was aloof from the soldiers of his army; there was no comradeship, no intimacy, nothing to endear him; yet they loved him. "A word from him," says General Oates, "would calm the fiercest passions and allay all contentions and conflicts among his subordinates." He never court-martialed an officer, nor did he ever sanction the death penalty either upon one of his own soldiers or one of the enemy, not even a spy. When, at a crisis in the Wilderness, he placed himself at the head of Hood's Texans to lead them in a charge, they surrounded his horse, shouting, "No, no! Lee to the rear! Lee to the rear!" and would not stir a step until he had yielded and ridden out of harm's way. Then, with the rebel yell, they dashed furiously on the Union intrenchments amid a hail of bullets. One cannot easily imagine a similar scene if it had been Grant

When the war was over Lee's example did much to save the country from the horror of irregular or guerrilla warfare, which was a real danger and was made more real by President Davis's attempt to escape to Texas and continue hostilities. "I think it the duty of every citizen," Lee wrote, "in the present condition of the country, to do all in his power to aid in the restoration of peace and harmony, and in no way to oppose the policy of the State or general government directed to that object." Again "All should unite in honest efforts to obliterate the effects of war, and to restore the blessings of

Ulysses S. Grant.   Robert E Lee

peace. They should remain, if possible, in the country; promote harmony and good feeling; qualify themselves to vote" (that is, take the oath of allegiance to the Federal Government) "and elect to the State and general Legislatures wise and patriotic men, who will devote their abilities to the healing of all dissensions." We may never know how much the United States owes to General Lee for this unselfish and generous attitude.

Yet, with incredible meanness and even more incredible blindness to the welfare of the nation, the Government, under the guidance of the implacable Stanton, made preparations to arrest and try this great and good man as a traitor; and nothing short of the gallows was intended for him. It is here that the strong likeness in the fundamental things between Lee and Grant, wide apart as they were in externals, shines forth even more brightly than in the memorable scene at Appomattox, when Grant ordered that the Confederates should keep their horses "for the Spring plowing." For Grant, hearing of Stanton's purpose, immediately called on that statesman and informed him, in sharp, crisp words, that the contemplated infamy must not be committed. He had accepted Lee's surrender; his honor was engaged; he would be dishonored if the man who had yielded to him were molested. It is said that he closed by announcing his intention to resign from the army and let the people know why he resigned. For once, Stanton was cowed; Grant was the head of the army, and fear of what the army might do was an ever-present bugbear with Stanton. He cringed before the soldier's honest anger, and Lee went unharmed.

Longstreet, drawing a distinction between the art of war and its science,

asserted that Lee was vastly the superior of his adversaries in the latter but not in the former. He was, Longstreet said, "of great and profound learning in the science of war." In all strategical movements he handled his army with "comprehensive ability and signal success." "But," said Longstreet, "of the art of war, more particularly that of giving offensive battle, I do not think General Lee was a master." In this he considered Grant and other Union officers as Lee's equals; which was perhaps not the word he really had in mind. "His impatience to strike, once in the presence of the enemy, whatever the disparity of forces or relative conditions, I consider the one weakness of General Lee's military character."

Longstreet may be considered a questionable witness. But Davis, always loyal to Lee, said in his defense against Lord Wolseley's attack, "A charge against him for risking too much could be better sustained than for over-caution and neglect of opportunities."

Grant's method was vastly different from Lee's. But there were times when Grant "risked too much"; when he hurled his army against Lee in that useless and suicidal attack at Cold Harbor, for instance. It was exactly what Lee did at Gettysburg, except that it was on a vaster scale and that the slaughter was greater and more horrifying.

Grant made his own strategy. "Some of our Generals," said he, "failed because they worked out everything by rule. They knew what Frederick did at one place, and Napoleon at another. They were always thinking about what Napoleon would do. Unfortunately for their plans, the rebels would be thinking about something else. * * * While our Generals were working out problems of an ideal character, problems that would have looked well on a blackboard, practical facts were neglected. Even Napoleon showed that; for my impression is that his first success came because he made war in his own way, and not in imitation of others."

His Vicksburg campaign was a masterpiece of bold conception and perfect execution, and Grant himself said it was the only one of his campaigns with which, looking back, he had no fault to find. It is the final answer to those who called him simply a "hammerer," with no notion of strategy. If he "hammered" in Virginia and did not hammer in Mississippi, it was because hammering was the right tactics in the one place and not in the other. But his Virginia campaign was not one of hammering alone; it was based on a steady slanting movement which finally brought the sea behind him and made it his base of supplies; and his rapid manoeuvres at Spottsylvania are unsurpassed by any in the war.

After the Wilderness a roar of rage rose all over the North; it was declared that Grant was destroying the army with his butcheries, that he had no plan, and that the Union downfall was at hand. There were two men who did not agree with this view; one was Grant and the other was Lee. Delegations visited Lincoln demanding Grant's removal before he could do any more harm. It was not the first time; after Shiloh the same demand had been made, and Lincoln had replied, "I can't spare this man; he fights." Now he said:

Grant is the first General I have had. You know how it has been with all the rest. As soon as I put a man in command of the army he'd come to me with a plan of campaign and about as much as to say: "Now, I don't believe I can do it, but if you say so I'll try it on," and so put the responsibility of success or failure on me. They all wanted me to be the General.

Now, it isn't so with Grant. He hasn't told me what his plans are. I don't know, and I don't want to know. I am glad to find a man that can go ahead without me. When any of the rest set out on a campaign they would look over matters and pick out some one thing they were short of and they knew I couldn't give 'em, and tell me they couldn't hope to win unless they had it; and it was

most generally cavalry. Now, when Grant took hold, I was waiting to see what his pet impossibility would be, and I reckoned it would be cavalry, of course, for we hadn't horses enough to mount what men we had. There were 15,000 or thereabouts up near Harper's Ferry and no horses to put them on. Well, the other day Grant sends to me about those very men, just as I expected; but what he wanted to know was whether he could make infantry of them or disband 'em.

Grant recognized from the first the truth that Lincoln had long ago tried to impress on Hooker: that his true objective was Lee's army. McClellan had committed the same mistake that the British did in the Revolution. Their true objective was Washington's army, yet they spent much labor in capturing points like Philadelphia because it was the capital, and rejoiced greatly when they had taken such places, which were of no use to them. So McClellan expended much intellectual effort figuring how to take Richmond and other strategic

points. Grant bothered so little about Richmond that when he took it he never entered it, not even after the surrender.

Certainly the officers opposed to him did not think him merely a "butcher," or doubt his generalship. "It is arrant nonsense," wrote D. H. Hill to Beauregard on June 11, 1864, "for Lee to say that Grant can't make a night march without his knowing it. Has not Grant slipped around him four times already?" Lincoln knew instantly that he had got a General at last. "It had been the habit," says Schurz, "of the Generals commanding the Army of the Potomac to cross the Rappahannock, to get their drubbing from Lee, and then promptly to retreat and recross the Rappahannock again. Grant crossed the Rappahannock, got his drubbing from Lee, but did not recross the Rappahannock again in retreat."

Lee saw the difference as quickly as Lincoln did, and knew that the end was coming. The one-sidedness of the war had ended already; there had been only one great Captain, but now there were two. They were matched at last; and the strength of numbers was with the newcomer. And now the character of the war changed; it is not the Virginia campaigns of 1864 and 1865 that figure in song and story, though they were so much more important than the others.

"With Grant's coming," says a Northern critic, "the civil war ceased to be a splendid and stirring spectacle, a contest in which chivalry, individual gallantry, even collective military superiority, played the decisive and the conspicuous rôle. It became a business, the brutal, grim business of battering to pieces a brave opponent inferior in numbers and resources."

FIVE UNLUCKY UNION COMMANDERS

Misfortune Pursued Army of the Potomac's Leaders, Even Him Who Won War's Decisive Battle, Until Advent of Grant.

Maj-Gen John Pope

FIVE men in succession commanded the Army of the Potomac, and misfortune dogged the steps of all; all came out of the war disappointed men, nearly all with reputations tarnished, some justly tarnished and some unjustly. A single battle apiece was enough to ruin three of them; a fourth, a great defensive General, was misplaced in an offensive campaign; the fifth, after winning the decisive battle of the war, lost the confidence of the Administration, ended the war as a subordinate, and was slighted and passed over that a favorite of the commanding General might be rewarded. There was a sixth, who commanded a part of the Army of the Potomac, who met the fate of an incompetent and a braggart, John Pope, and who deserved to meet it.

When the war broke out the opinion was general, both North and South, that it would be over in a jiffy. In the Union Army one battle was expected to settle it; hence there was just rivalry for the command, since whatever glory was to be won would have to be won in a single fight. The winner was Major Irvin McDowell of Scott's staff; he

fought his one battle; it was Bull Run. The expected glory changed to disgrace. Yet it was not General McDowell's fault. General Sherman, who commanded a brigade in that battle, said, "It was one of the best-planned battles, but one of the worst fought."

It is usually described as a collision between two armed mobs, in which one mob got scared before the other, but that is not the whole truth. McDowell's army was composed of raw and untrained volunteers. Many of them had enlisted only for three months; their term of enlistment was up, and numbers of them marched away from the field with the sound of Beauregard's shells in their ears as the battle began. This created an immense and disastrous impression in Europe; Palmerston told Minister Adams that the defeat, even the stampede, was nothing, for that could be ascribed to the greenness of soldiers who might afterward fight well; but the lack of interest which these three months' men took in the war was not to be explained away.

McDowell's purpose was to attack Beauregard's army and defeat it, while Johnston's army was held back by General Patterson. There was no flaw in his plan, and at first the battle went all McDowell's way. The Confederates were beaten by the middle of the afternoon; but Patterson failed to hold Johnston, who eluded him, marched to Beauregard's aid, and fell like a thunderbolt with his fresh troops on McDowell's raw recruits. The stampede followed. The fault was Patterson's, not McDowell's, but McDowell was the commander and bore the blame. The storm that raged around him was terrific; he was charged with treason, with being drunk on the battlefield (though he was a total abstainer.) He served in subordinate commands through the rest of the war, and never had another opportunity for distinction.

His successor, McClellan, was the only Union commander who had won any victories at that time. He had cleared the Confederates out of West Virginia. He was brilliant, magnetic, and popular. But two things stood in

his way, one to his credit and one not. He had the good sense to understand that if the North was to win it must give up trying to fight by means of an armed mob, and must organize an army. The impatient North wanted him to hurl his untrained greenhorns on the vast and almost invulnerable territory of the South and had no idea of the uses of organization; it had learned nothing from Bull Run. The other difficulty was that McClellan had no aggressiveness; the bent of his mind was all toward the defensive. He would have made an admirable Confederate General, but his abilities were not those needed in an army which must be perpetually on the offensive.

He was, however, one of the two or three men who won the war for the North; for it was McClellan who created that magnificent army. To the end of the war it remained in all essentials just what he had made it. Meade used to say, "Had there been no McClellan there could have been no Grant, for the army made no essential improvement under any of his successors," of whom Meade was one. Having done this, his work was done; thenceforward he acted always as if he were on the defensive. When he really was on the defensive, as in his retreat on the Peninsula, his talents shone brilliantly.

On the offensive he was a failure; the bent of his mind was such that the mere fact of being on the offensive made him timid, hesitant, and disposed to "see things." Gurowski, the bitter Polish railer who spread denunciation of the men of the hour, spoke truly of McClellan's wonderful faculty for "realizing hallucinations." He was obsessed at all times with the idea that he was greatly outnumbered and must proceed with extreme caution to escape being overwhelmed, when he should have known that the Confederates could not possibly bring even an equal force against him. Carl Schurz speaks of this as McClellan's "morbid delusion," and he never freed himself from it. The plan of his peninsular campaign was a good one, but his excessive caution made it a failure, and with great self-com-

placency he congratulated himself on "saving" his great army.

He quarreled violently with Lincoln and Stanton and addressed insubordinate language to them. As to Stanton, McClellan was not to be blamed; for at the very time when that statesman was sending McClellan letters full of fulsome adulation and protestations of affection he was secretly moving heaven and earth to destroy him. "I ever will hereafter trust your judgement about men," wrote McClellan to his wife. "Your woman's tact and your pure heart make you a better judge than my dull apprehension. I remember what you thought of Stanton when you first saw him. I now know you were right. Enough of the creature!"

Lincoln, with his usual utter absence of personal feeling, bore with McClellan's complaints and tart language long after any other President would have removed him. "If I save this army now," wrote McClellan to Stanton after the Seven Days' Battles, "I tell you plainly that I owe no thanks to you or to any other persons in Washington. You have done your best to sacrifice this army." Not even this affront moved the patient President. But after Antietam, which Lee called "a drawn battle," but which the North regarded as a victory, McClellan, with his fatal propensity for acting as if he were on the defensive, made no move, despite Lincoln's efforts to get the army into motion again. Meanwhile Lee was sending Stuart north on one of his famous raids. The President at last removed McClellan from the command.

Critics have dealt harshly with McClellan, lightly with Burnside, though Burnside was the most colossal failure of the war. Political partisanship has something to do with it, and it is perhaps attributable, too, to Burnside's winning character, his bluff manliness, his honesty and good heart. McClellan's faults, however, were venial beside Burnside's; no such horrible and useless massacre as Burnside inflicted on his men at Fredericksburg is recorded anywhere else in the history of the war, for even Cold Harbor had a

Maj. Gen. Geo. B. McClellan

Brig. Gen. Irvin McDowell

Maj. Gen. Joseph Hooker

Maj. Gen. Ambrose E. Burnside

Maj. Gen. George G. Meade

purpose. McClellan had been condemned for inaction; Burnside determined to be very active. His idea of how to do it was to go wherever the Confederates were and attack them immediately, with or without prospect of success. He found them intrenched behind a stone wall at the top of a steep hill; and he sent his army of martyrs again and again to sure death. The Confederates, almost invisible, almost invulnerable, massacred them by the thousand. Burnside learned nothing, and after the massacre had been repeated to a surfeit, he was planning to order a repetition of it the next day when his Generals revolted and begged him not to continue the senseless slaughter. He was surprised, but he meekly yielded.

Burnside manfully shouldered the whole responsibility, blaming himself and no one else. But the army had lost confidence in him; his Colonels began to resign and the privates deserted in great numbers. Before he gave up the command 85,000 men were reported as "absent without leave." Burnside desperately determined to retrieve his reputation, and ordered another forward movement. A heavy rain set in, his artillery could not be moved, and his infantry floundered in mud nearly to their waists. The country was fairly covered with mired wagons, ambulances, pontoons, and guns. "Burnside stuck in the mud" became a common street expression. He went back as best he could, but the country had lost all confidence in him. He did not seem to know it, and just before his removal he went to Lincoln with a request that Hooker and two other Generals be dismissed from the army for intriguing against him, and that Franklin, "Baldy" Smith, and several other Generals be relieved. He was vastly surprised to receive an order directing him to turn over the command to Hooker and take a command in the West.

His later career was of a piece with the earlier; a career of honest bungling and unreadiness. He was always too late; and his final demonstration of this quality was when his tardiness ruined the plans for the Wilderness and Spottsylvania battles. He was tried by a court-martial, which found him "answerable for the want of success" in those battles, and Burnside was not heard of again in a post where he could do any harm.

It is the highest tribute that can be paid to the Army of the Potomac to say that these experiences did not demoralize it. It kept its morale and fought magnificently, and not even failure and the rapid change of commanders could daunt

it. Its Generals, as Charles Francis Adams says, were outclassed by Lee and Jackson, "sometimes terribly, sometimes ludicrously, always hopelessly," but it remained undiscouraged. For this much of the credit is due to McClellan; he had made it an army, he had made soldiers of greenhorns. A Confederate soldier, Stiles, in his "Four Years Under Marse Robert," records the amazement of the Southern troops "that an army could maintain even so much as its organization under the depressing strain of those successive appointments and removals of its commanding Generals." That it did preserve its cohesion and fighting power he regards "as furnishing impressive demonstration of the high character and intense loyalty of our historic foe, the Federal Army of the Potomac."

Lincoln was under no misapprehension about Hooker's qualities. Some time before when he was proposed for the command, the President said, "I think as much as you or any other man of Hooker, but—I fear he gets excited." He knew that Hooker had been advocating seizing the Government and establishing a military dictatorship. He knew that Hooker was accused of having played Burnside false; and Postmaster General Blair had told him that Hooker was "too great a friend of John Barleycorn." But he had to take the best material he could find. He wrote to Hooker telling him that he knew of his dictatorship talk, and saying: "Of course it was not for this but in spite of it that I have given you the command. Only those Generals who gain success can set up dictators. What I now ask of you is military success, and I will risk the dictatorship."

It is universally conceded that the plan

of the Chancellorsville campaign was perfect, and that up to the moment of battle it was well executed. But as soon as Hooker got across the Rappahannock a strange paralysis fell upon his faculties. He sat motionless in the Wilderness, while Lee, with incredible audacity, divided his small army and sent Jackson marching around the supine Hooker. Hooker had left his right wing "in the air," as the military phrase goes, and Jackson fell upon it and smashed it while Lee attacked in front. Hooker was warned again and again, but he laughed at the warnings and did nothing, while all day long Jackson marched around him to fall on him at sunset; and 120,000 men fled back across the Rappahannock, disgracefully defeated by 39,000. Yet Hooker actually issued an order congratulating his army on its achievements and on the fact that when it retreated "not a rebel dared to follow." This order overwhelmed him with ridicule.

Why Hooker's brilliantly executed forward movement should have ended in the strange lassitude that resulted in this disaster has been eagerly debated. It is the misfortune of all men who drink that every mistake of theirs is at once attributed to that cause, often with great injustice, and Hooker suffered this detraction. He had, however, been knocked insensible by a piece of a pillar broken by a cannon ball, and for some time after he recovered was in no condition to give orders; and it has been conjectured that the confusion in his brain caused by this injury lasted throughout the day.

There are other explanations. "Whether," says Thomas Nelson Page

in his life of Lee, "the Federal commander was momentarily overcome by the magnitude of Lee's fame, or whether by the terrifying mystery of the shadowy silences stretching before him, from which no word had come since he crossed the Rappahannock and turned southward, or whether there was a personal reason, all of which have been asserted, he halted." General Stoneman gave what may be the real reason. He had often played poker with Hooker, and he said "Hooker could play the best game of poker I ever saw until it came to the point when he should go a thousand better, and then he would flunk."

Hooker asked to be relieved on the eve of the battle of Gettysburg, and Meade was put in his place four days before the fight. It was a terrifying position; put in command of an army only one corps of which knew him and of whose management he knew nothing, and asked to win the decisive battle of the war when his opponent was already staging it. Meade did it, however, but he did not win the glory he should have received, because he did not follow up the victory. In the Cabinet the successful General was more bitterly denounced than any of his unsuccessful predecessors had been. "Oh," groaned the President, "it is terrible, terrible, this indifference of our Potomac Generals, with such armies of good and brave men." Welles suggested that he get rid of Meade. "What can I do," asked the President, "with such Generals as we have? Who among them is any better than Meade?"

Meade developed greatly after the terrible test placed upon him at Gettysburg. "Meade's swift tactical manoeuvres to meet Lee's flank movement toward Washington early in the Fall of 1863 showed the most decided ability to handle a large army," says Longstreet. At Gettysburg, he says, Meade, only four days in command, "had not yet acquired that grasp of his army, that personal confidence, which he subsequently manifested."

He looked forward to a Lieutenant Generalship as the reward of his great victory, when the war ended and such rewards were to be bestowed. But it was one of Grant's traits, manifested to his great harm in the Presidency, to pick favorites and stand by them. Sheridan was one of his favorites; when Grant was made General he procured the jump of Sheridan to the Lieutenant Generalship over Meade's head, and the victor of Gettysburg died a disappointed man, believing that he had been the victim of a conspiracy. His fate was not so hard as those of some of his predecessors, but to a man of his sensitive nature it was as bitter as gall.

BEST GENERALS ON BOTH SIDES

Other Military Geniuses Besides Grant and Lee Were Jackson, A. S. Johnston and Forrest—High Generalship Also Shown by Sherman and Thomas.

Gen. Stonewall Jackson

Gen. N. B. Forrest

Gen. William T. Sherman

Lieut. Gen. P. H. Sheridan

GRANT and Lee are universally and properly recognized as the two great captains of the war; but there were other men who, if they had been placed in the positions held by Grant and Lee, would doubtless have made as great a reputation. There were more such men on the Southern side than on the Northern. Thomas, and perhaps Sherman, are the only names that come to mind on the Northern side; on the Southern there is no doubt that Jackson, Albert Sidney Johnston, and Forrest were not merely good Generals, but military geniuses. Indeed, it is a favorite subject for armchair debate whether Jackson was not a greater General than Lee. Certain it is that the Army of Northern Virginia never began to give ground until Jackson's death, and began to do so immediately after it; and Lee was speaking with sad sincerity when he said to his dying lieutenant, "Could I have directed events, I should have chosen, for the good of the country, to have been disabled in your stead." It is conceivable that had Jackson been in command Gettysburg might have ended differently; for the mistakes that lost the battle to the Confederates were precisely the mistakes which Jackson could not possibly make.

Jackson was an Ironside; there was something Cromwellian about him. He has been compared to Grant in his whole-hearted devotion to the cause and his utter indifference to the individual. He thought of nothing but the goal. After he received the wound that killed him, General Pender said, "General, I doubt my ability to hold my position." "You must hold it, Sir," was the last command Jackson ever gave. A Federal officer displayed such extraordinary gallantry that the Confederate officer in command gave orders not to fire upon him; he was too brave to be killed. Jackson heard of

it and was displeased. "It is the brave men we want to kill," was his rebuke. General D. H. Hill sent word to Jackson that his ammunition was wet by the rain and that he thought he had better fall back. "Give my compliments to General Hill," said Jackson, "and tell him that the Yankee ammunition is as wet as his; to stay where he is." He never held councils of war; he was sufficient unto himself; he exacted obedience, not counsel.

There is not anywhere a flaw in the record of his achievements; there is not a failure or a mistake to his discredit. His campaigns were not only brilliant, but something new in warfare. One of his cardinal principles, he told General Imboden, was to mystify, mislead, and surprise the enemy; the secret of success was "to move swiftly, strike vigorously, and secure all the fruits of victory." Of all his wonderful operations, his Valley campaign was the most dazzling. That excellent political essayist whose pen name is "Savoyard" sums up this campaign admirably:

Jackson's Valley campaign will always be regarded as one of the most startling prodigies of military genius. In conception and in execution it rivals Bonaparte's first Italian campaign. He opposed several armies, each equal to his own in numbers, and scattered them to all points of the compass. He threatened Washington and Baltimore and carried terror as far north as New York. He kept 50,000 reinforcements from McClellan. His infantry, the best in the world, was called "foot-cavalry." Its rapidity of movement and prowess in battle bewildered the Federal commanders, and before they had recovered from their stupor Jackson was on McClellan's flank, dealing those blows that made the first campaign against Richmond a lamentable failure.

His lightninglike movements and his superb plan of campaign left the several armies which he encountered no choice but flight. The dismay in Washington approached horror; when Banks, by desperate marching, barely escaped him and he threatened Harper's Ferry the dis-

may became panic. It was his plan that gave Lee the victory at Chancellorsville. In that battle the bullets of his own men closed a career, one of the most wonderful in military history. What would have been the story of the war had Jackson lived?

The war was slow in developing its military geniuses. Lee and Jackson were recognized before the first year of fighting had ended, but the war was near its close before men began to understand what could have been done had Thomas or Forrest been in high command from the beginning. It was not until the last year of the war that Sheridan was recognized, and he would not have been then if Grant had not forced him upon a surprised and reluctant country.

Forrest never had a high command and has gone into tradition only as a dashing cavalry raider. But military critics, analyzing his work in subordinate commands, detect in them powers not inferior to those of the great Generals of history, and speculate on what he might have done had his great qualities been understood at Richmond. Lord Wolseley speaks of his "genius," and ranks him among the great soldiers of the world. Dr. Johnston, a nephew of General J. E. Johnston, asked his uncle whom he considered the greatest soldier of the war. "Forrest," answered Johnston instantly, "who, had he had the advantages of a military education and training, would have been the central figure of the civil war." (Wolseley did not make even that qualification, but asserted that Forrest's military instinct supplied the lack of military education.) General Johnston then reviewed Forrest's campaign, gave Lee and Jackson their full measure of credit, but ended by pronouncing Forrest "the greatest soldier the war produced."

General Beauregard said that "For-

rest's capacity for war seemed only to be limited by the opportunities for its display," which sufficiently disposes of those who saw in him only a daring trooper. In 1864 Sherman said that "the death of Forrest was so essential to the success of the Union cause that 10,000 lives and the expenditure of limitless means were as naught to its accomplishment." After the war Sherman called Forrest "the most remarkable man our civil war produced on either side." And Sherman added:

He had never read a military book in his life, knew nothing about tactics, could not even drill a company, but he had a genius for strategy which was original, and to me incomprehensible. There was no theory or art of war by which I could calculate with any degree of certainty what Forrest was up to. He seemed always to know what I was doing or intended to do, while I confess I could never tell or form any satisfactory idea of what he was trying to accomplish.

"The trouble was," said President Davis after the war, "that the Generals commanding in the Southwest never appreciated Forrest until it was too late. Their judgment was that he was a bold and enterprising partisan raider and rider. I was misled by them, and I never knew how to measure him until I read his reports of his campaign across the Tennessee River in 1864. This induced a study of his earlier reports, and after that I was prepared to adopt what you are pleased to name as the judgment of history." He was speaking to ex-Gov. Porter of Tennessee, who had said history would name Forrest as "one of the half dozen greatest soldiers of the country."

Forrest was almost illiterate. At Fort Donelson he charged a Union cavalry regiment and got into a hand-to-hand conflict. The two regiments became mixed together, and Forrest tried to think of the command to give his men. He should have ordered "Right thrust," but he could not think of it; so he yelled, "Punch 'em, boys; damn 'em, punch 'em!" This unusual order worked quite as successfully as the correct one would have done. He somewhat resembled the Union General, Frank Wolford, the Kentucky mountaineer, who gave orders to his men such as "Huddle up thar!" "Scatter out thar!" "Form a line of fight!"

Thomas, a General who never made a mistake and whose specialty was the saving of the Union Army in desperate situations, never was appreciated until the end of the war. He saved the army at Murfreesboro in 1862; his great exploit, however, was saving it not only from defeat but from destruction at Chickamauga. That battle was a Confederate victory, but Thomas made it barren; when all the rest of the army was in flight he stood his ground, held the Confederates off, and won his sobriquet of "The Rock of Chickamauga."

Yet, even as Forrest won only the reputation of a cavalry raider until it was too late, these great deeds of Thomas's won him only the reputation of a defensive General. The war was ending before it dawned on the country that Thomas was as great on the offensive as on the defensive. When Hood took his army to Tennessee to attack him in 1864, Thomas was still so little understood that great apprehension was felt concerning his ability to make an attack; his ability to defend was conceded. Thomas refused to attack until the conditions were right, and Grant, after a number of impatient dispatches, relieved him from the command.

Some misgiving prompted Grant later to restore him; but even then he was uneasy, and sent Logan to Nashville to supersede him. Then his growing anxiety led Grant to go himself; but before either he or Logan could get there he received news of the rout of Hood. Thomas had attacked him and obtained one of the most complete and decisive victories of the war. It was the utter destruction, so far as any opportunity of effective fighting was concerned, of the fine army Johnston had commanded; and Lee was left at Grant's mercy. Then Thomas proceeded to prove that he was not only a master if offense and defense but energetic in pursuit.

The complaint against Meade had been that he did not follow up his victory at Gettysburg; Thomas followed up Nashville with such terrible effectiveness that, but for Forrest, Hood's army would have been annihilated. "Heretofore," says George Cary Eggleston in his "History of the Confederate War," "no chase of a defeated Southern army by Northern soldiers had been so vigorous and effective, despite the inclement weather and bad roads."

It was by superhuman exertions that Forrest saved it. "The Army of Tennessee," Forrest wrote, "was badly defeated, and is greatly demoralized, and to save it during the retreat from Nashville I was compelled almost to sacrifice my command."

Sheridan was more fortunate than either Forrest or Thomas; but had it not been for Grant he, too, would have failed of recognition until the end of the war. His own expectations never reached a Generalship. When he heard that war had broken out he threw up his cap and shouted, "Here's for a Captain's commission or a soldier's grave!" When Grant took command in the East he astonished the War Department and most of the Eastern military men by calling Sheridan to the command of the cavalry. They had paid no attention to Sheridan; but Grant had. What had attracted his attention was the charge up Missionary Ridge in 1863. The Union commanders had no idea of storming that eminence, but to their amazement they saw the soldiers suddenly charge forward, drive the Confederates from their defenses at the base of the ridge, follow them up the hill, drive Bragg from his position at its top, and rout his army. "Who ordered that charge?" demanded Grant, as it began. "Not I," said his Generals, one after another. "But," said General Granger, "I tell you, they're going to the top!" Grant saw that Sheridan was the inspiration and driving force of the charge and the victory, and he kept his eye on him from that time forward.

Sheridan was a merciless fighter. On

Sept. 8, 1870, he was Bismarck's guest at dinner. The Franco-German war was going on. To Bismarck and his guests the American said.

The proper strategy consists, in the first place, in inflicting as telling blows as possible upon the enemy's army, and then in causing the inhabitants so much suffering that they must long for peace and force their Government to demand it. The people must be left nothing but their eyes to weep with over the war.

"Somewhat heartless, it seems to me," wrote Busch in his diary after the dinner, "but perhaps worthy of consideration."

Sherman and Grant were both misunderstood in the early stages of the war, and demands were made for the removal of both; but Sherman was in more danger than Grant, for he was sincerely believed to be crazy. This was because, while not the only. General to see that conquering the Confederacy would be difficult, he was the only one to proclaim his belief. "Why," said Secretary Cameron, who had visited Sherman's camp after hearing the rumors of his insanity, "Sherman wants 60,000 troops to hold Kentucky, and says that not less than 200,000 can conquer the rebellion in the Southwest." He reported at Washington that Sherman was "gone in the head," and the General was promptly relieved from his command and ordered to report at the St. Louis barracks, where he wore his heart out for months. He might have stayed there throughout the war if Grant had not insisted on having him assigned to his army. Thus Grant gave both Sherman and Sheridan to the Union.

Grant and Sherman were one to the end of the war. "Admiral Porter," says Welles, "has always said there was something wanting in Grant which Sherman could always supply, and vice versa as regards Sherman, but that the two together made a very perfect general officer, and they ought never to be separated." "There was a difference," said Sherman, "between Grant's and my way of looking at things. Grant

never cared a damn about what was going on behind the enemy's lines, but it often scared me like the devil."

It was Sherman who finally silenced Europe. Our war had never been understood there. Moltke said he "did not have time to devote to the study of the combats of two armed mobs." Charles Lever described it as resembling two lunatics playing chess. "There are the two madmen engaged in a struggle, not one single rule nor maxim of which they comprehend." The comment in the European newspapers was equally contemptuous. Suddenly Sherman appeared on the Georgia coast, Savannah fell, and the army and navy struck hands. "The announcement," says Adams, "seemed absolutely to take away the breath of the foreign critics—social, military, journalistic. An undeniably original and brilliant strategic blow had been struck; an operation, the character of which could neither be ignored nor mistaken, had been triumphantly carried through to a momentous result; the thrust—and such a thrust!—had penetrated the vitals of the Confederacy—what next? Europe recognized that a new power of unknown strength but undeniable military capacity was thenceforth to be reckoned with." He attributes to this the change in the European attitude toward America as a nation which has been so evident ever since; the passing of that "certain condescension," which Lowell had noticed in them.

Albert Sidney Johnston fought but one battle and lost his life in it; yet he impressed himself indelibly on American history, and there is nowhere any doubt that had he lived he would have been one of the greatest figures of the war; perhaps have challenged Lee's lonely place on the Confederate side. Joseph E. Johnston was a great General, but unlucky; misfortune dogged his steps, ably assisted by the narrow prejudice President Davis had toward him. Again and again, on the eve of triumph, the cup was snatched from his lips. War is capricious in its choice of favorites.

WOMEN WHO FOUGHT AS SOLDIERS

Many Enlisted Either by Stealth or Openly on Both Sides and Fought Bravely Shoulder to Shoulder with Men.

IN the war now being fought over in Europe women get into men's uniforms and fight battles. For instance, there is one girl by the name of Tomaszeff who made a wonderful record in the Russian Army; and many a woman like her has won similar fame. Yet there has been no war in which girls and women have not won this kind of celebrity. The civil war was certainly no exception.

There were many girls who fought through the war on both the Union and Confederate sides. For example, Dr. Mary E. Walker received a commission as Assistant Surgeon, and went through the war with it, but there were many women who enlisted and went through hard service without making Dr. Walker's reputation. For example, there was Frances Hook, a fourteen-year-old girl, who enlisted with her brother at Chicago. The two enlisted in the Sixty-fifth Illinois and were mustered out after three months. Frances Hook, wearing male clothes, enlisted in the Nineteenth. Her brother was killed

at Shiloh, but the girl, still wearing clothes of a man, fought through the war until Chickamauga, when she was captured and shot through the leg in an attempt to escape. While she was a prisoner in Atlanta Jefferson Davis is said to have offered her a Lieutenancy if she would join the Confederate forces. Frances, it is said, replied to President Davis's offer that she would let herself be hanged before she would take up arms against the Union. She had enlisted under the name of Frank Miller.

In one of the regiments from Ohio a girl enlisted. She was the sister of a member of the regiment. While at Camp Jackson and Camp Dennison she handled lumber, performed sentry duty, and did other work of that sort. It was two weeks before she learned that there were two Camp Dennisons, and that her brother was at the other one. Straightway she made application for a transfer and failed. She wanted to go to the Pennsylvania Camp Dennison, and she wanted to go badly. The Colonel of the regiment, a

good sort of fellow named Morrow, talked to the girl for some time and made her confess that she was flying under false colors. Without much ceremony she was dismissed and sent home.

Just after the battle of Chickamauga, Colonel Burke of the Tenth Ohio exchanged a large number of prisoners with the Confederates. He noticed a particularly clever and able young man among the prisoners he received—a boy who gave the name of Frank Henderson. The Colonel became interested enough to inquire who Frank was, and found out that he was a girl. He, or rather she, had enlisted with her brother at the outbreak of the war. They were orphans, and were devoted to each other, and she could not bear the thought of being separated from him. He had been her only companion from babyhood.

At the expiration of her enlistment for three months in the regiment she was mustered out, and next enlisted in another regiment from Southern Illinois,

where her sex was not discovered. She was wounded two or three times, discharged and sent home, and enlisted again in the Nineteenth Illinois. She was finally captured, and a bullet wound in her leg led to the discovery of her sex.

There is no braver story in all the annals of war than that of Mary Owens. She came from a place called Danville, in Pennsylvania. Her husband decided to enlist. Mary went with him; she and he went to the front together; she had eloped with him, and now she was ready to carry their decision to the limit. Man and wife, they fought together until a bullet put the man out of the running; and even then the woman fought on. A Southern bullet struck her in the chest and she went to the hospital, but on the record were written the words, "A more faithful soldier never shouldered a musket."

In Brooklyn, N. Y., a girl enlisted and fought to the finish through the war until she was mortally wounded in Hooker's advance on Lookout Mountain.

Fanny Wilson enlisted in the Twenty-fourth New Jersey in order to follow her sweetheart, who was a member of the same regiment, into the field. He knew nothing of her action, but she saw him every day and came near being assigned to the same mess tent with him. At Vicksburg Miss Wilson was shot. So was the young man; and Miss Wilson, who nursed him, did not reveal her identity to him until just as the boy was dying. She stayed by him, closed his eyes, and then went to Cairo and got an engagement as a chorus girl. A little while later she enlisted again, still in male clothes, as a member of the Third Illinois. She was taken to the headquarters of the commanding officer, it being suspected that she might be a Confederate spy, but she made it clear that she was a good, loyal Federal soldier.

In one of the Pennsylvania regiments a bright little girl of twelve years enlisted as a drummer boy. She gave the name of Charles Martin, and she appeared to be a clever little fellow and made herself useful to the officers of the regiment in the capacity of a clerk. She was in five battles, but always escaped without a bullet wound. Her superior officers never suspected her sex for a moment. It was not until she was taken to a hospital in Philadelphia suffering from typhoid fever that her sex was discovered.

An officer of the Seventeenth Illinois, by the name of Reynolds, had his wife made a Major. Reynolds himself was a Lieutenant. She was a scout and spy and made no effort to conceal her sex.

A girl named Annie Lillybridge of Detroit became betrothed to a Lieutenant in the Twenty-first Michigan and decided to put on soldier's clothes and serve with him until the end of the war. She enlisted in the same regiment without his knowledge and carefully hid her identity. She even went so far as to enlist in a different company from his. One of her comrades, after several months, became aware of the secret of her sex, and when he was killed in battle the girl found his body in the field. She was finally disabled by a shot in the arm and, her sex being discovered, she was sent home.

Major Pauline Cushman was one of the cleverest servants the Union Army had throughout the war. She was an actress who lived in Cleveland and was employed as an officer of the Union Army. As scout, spy, and soldier, the girl Major made a reputation second to none in the Northern army. Pauline Cushman has left a reputation only second to that of Belle Boyd, to whom Stonewall Jackson wrote that she had saved his army.

Mary Siezgle, the wife of a soldier in the Forty-fourth New York, enlisted with him and fought in the battle of Gettysburg. She served for a while as a nurse, but afterward put on male clothes and did her share in actual fighting.

One little heroine of the war had the honor of being complimented in general orders. She was a fifteen-year-old girl named Schwartz, living in a farm house about twelve miles from Jefferson City, Mo. On the night of Aug. 6, 1863, a party of bushwhackers who had heard that it was a rendezvous of Union men, attacked it. There were four men in the house, one being the child's father; they all fled and left her alone to confront the guerrillas. The little girl intrepidly opened the door with a revolver in her hand which the men had abandoned in their flight and said, "Come on, if you want to. Some of you will fall or I will." The bushwhackers told her that if she did not leave the doorway they would kill her. "The first one who takes a step toward this door dies," was the girl's response, and the marauders left.

VICTIMS OF UNDESERVED DISGRACE

Fitz-John Porter, Stone, Warren and Others Came Out of Civil War with Sullied Reputations Through No Fault of Their Own.

THE list of the war's victims was not confined to those who fell. Many a reputation was tarnished, and in almost all cases undeservedly. Fitz-John Porter, Stone, G. K. Warren, and many another suffered condemnation at the hands of their country, and it took many weary years before justice was laggardly done.

The Fitz-John Porter case was the most notable of all. He was a splendid soldier, whose abilities were lost the Union because of the political antipathy to McClellan in Washington. It is hard for us now to get into the frame of mind which possessed the country in 1862; the North was swarming with traitors, and every failure or slow approach was attributed to treason. Porter was unable to reach Pope at Manassas, and the fevered North jumped to the conclusion that he had deliberately betrayed that foolish and incompetent General.

Pope had started his campaign by announcing that he had never seen anything but the backs of his enemies, and that his headquarters were in the saddle. When this vainglorious boasting met its proper rebuke at Bull Run, Pope looked for a victim and found him in Porter. Porter was thoroughly loyal to McClellan, who at that time was out of favor; indeed, the second Bull Run was fought only a short time before McClellan was relieved from command. Politics was stronger at Washington then than military achievement, and Porter, the friend of the Democratic commander, was tried by a court studiously organized by Stanton to convict him. Lincoln hesitated long before he gave his assent to the verdict of the court-martial and afterward sincerely regretted it. Nevertheless, Porter was dismissed from the army and the Union cause lost the services of a patient and skillful officer.

For twenty-three years Porter devoted all his energy to a reversal of this unjust verdict. He finally enlisted Grant in his cause, and in 1886 a bill was passed restoring him to his original rank as Colonel in the United States Army.

The cruelest case that arose during the war was that of General Charles P. Stone. In 1861 both sides believed that the war would be over in a jiffy; Davis proclaimed on his way to Montgomery that it was only a question of a short time when the Confederate armies would be in possession of the North, and Seward believed that the war would be over in sixty days. Any defeat to either army was regarded by public opinion as inexcusable and necessarily the result of treason. At the beginning of the war a rash Senator who had been made a Colonel charged up a cliff known as Ball's Bluff and was wiped out. The North was not so seasoned as it afterward became to the loss of gallant men, and the death of Senator Baker raised a howl all over the country. As usual when there is a disaster, whether it be a fire or a railroad collision, nobody thought it was an unavoidable calamity, and there was a demand for a victim. Stone was selected for the sacrifice. Though Baker's mad move had been made on his own responsibility, he was represented as having been sent to his death, and the whole North believed that as he marched to the battlefield he said, "I will obey General Stone's orders, but it is my death warrant."

Stone was summoned before a Congressional committee and testified frankly. The testimony against him was frivolous, but Stanton ordered McClellan to arrest him. He was imprisoned in Port Lafayette, his money taken from him, an armed sentinel placed before his door, and no letter allowed to reach him; he was in solitary confinement. To his repeated demands to know what the charge against him was, no answer was returned. At last he was released, still without knowing what charge was laid at his door; he applied repeatedly for permission to serve the Union as an officer of the army, but never could get it.

Long after the war General Lew Wallace demanded a Court of Inquiry to investigate his conduct at Shiloh. It was not granted. He failed to come to the rescue of the surprised Union Army until the second day's fighting was about to begin, and for a long time Wallace was blamed for the defeat which unquestionably was the result of Johnston's fierce attack on the first day. Wallace, however, did not get the order until the battle had begun and was then misled by his guide into a circuitous route. Grant, bitter at not receiving the support he had expected, made a sharp report to the War Department, but in his memoirs he made amends to Wallace. He always regarded Wallace's choice of routes as a mistake, but he admitted it to have been merely a pardonable error of judgment.

Aside from the case of Fitz-John Porter, the saddest instance of injustice done to a brave and faithful officer in the civil war is that of General Gouverneur K. Warren, the man who made possible the victory of Gettysburg. At the Battle of Five Forks his slowness to execute the orders he had received led to Sheridan's relieving him of command in the midst of the fighting. "Sir," said Sheridan, to Warren's adjutant, "tell General Warren he wasn't in the fight." "Shall I tell him that, Sir? I can hardly take a verbal message of that kind to him," said General Locke, who was a gentleman. "Then write it," said Sheridan. "Tell him he wasn't at the front."

The Union Army was being crowded. Officers jammed themselves around Sheridan. He raised his hat high above his head and yelled, "We've got a record to make before sunset that'll make hell tremble, and I want you to be there." "They took him at his word," says General Joshua L. Chamberlain, who was there; "at any rate, they took the shortest way to death."

Warren rode back to the White Oak Road, where he received Sheridan's order relieving him of command. He took it to Sheridan and asked that he take time to reconsider it. "Reconsider!" shouted Sheridan; "reconsider! hell, I never reconsider!" And Warren rode slowly to the rear, his head bent and his heart broken. Long after the war he asked for a court of inquiry and got it, but the blemish stayed on his fame.

No question arising out of the war has been so bitterly debated as Lee's conduct at Gettysburg and during the movement that preceded the battle. Colonel Mosby has published a book defending the performance of Stuart that left Lee destitute of cavalry at the beginning of the northern march, but history inexorably places that among Lee's mistakes. The actual fighting of the battle was full of blunders on the Confederate side; it was well planned, but, as Thomas Nelson Page says, "On the part of Lee's corps commanders it was the worst fought battle of the war." The corps commanders, he says, "not once, but again and again," failed Lee and "threw away every chance of victory and left the honors of all but valor to the Union General." Yet Lee took the blame himself, refused even to criticise the reluctant Longstreet, and placed his resignation at Davis's disposal. For once Davis was great; he refused to accept it.

No misunderstanding of the war has been more cruel or unjust than that which arose out of the conduct of the Eleventh Corps at Chancellorsville. The North, still more or less under the sway of the Know-Nothing agitation, which had placed an ex-President of the United States in the running only four years before, was still prejudiced against immigrants; and the belief that Howard's corps was largely composed of Germans undoubtedly emphasized the violence with which its defeat was commented on. Three-fifths of the corps was American by birth, so that the criticism was unjust; it was further unjustified by the fact that this doomed corps was the only one in the Federal Army which foresaw Jackson's move and tried to forestall it, and that it fought bravely to prevent it, while Hooker lay placid and idle.

THE GREAT CAMPAIGNS OF THE WAR

Succession of Moves on Part of North, Not Due to Any One Leader, Which Nevertheless Formed Comprehensive Plan.

Commodore A.H.Foote.

THE civil war had no Napoleon, no one genius, to lay out a plan and pursue it. Yet the North did pursue a Napoleonic plan, even though no one man can take credit for it. Spenser Wilkinson, the English military critic, asks us to suppose that a master mind like Napoleon's had been charged with the direction of the Federal operations, and had been able from the beginning to grasp the nature of the advantages the Confederates possessed and the difficulties in the way. What would such a master mind have done? Wilkinson answers:

He would have seen that it would not be possible, as it had been in Europe at the beginning of the century, to break down the Confederacy by the crushing defeat of a single army, followed by the occupation of the capital, but that it would be necessary to defeat one army after another, and to exhaust the resources of the enemy by the occupation of the whole of his territory. Such a mind, devising a grand and comprehensive plan, might have seen that the first and most effective blow would be struck if it were possible to close the sea to the shipping of the Confederacy, and thus to isolate the enemy's territory from the rest of the world. That, this accomplished, the next step would be, while holding the Confederate armies on the frontier between the their forces there fully occupied, to take possession of the great highway of the Mississippi, and thus to cut off from the main body of the Confederacy all those territories which lay to the west of that river.

That, this accomplished, the third move would be to strike at the middle of the Confederacy by the avenue of the Cumberland and Tennessee Rivers, and then to pass an army from Chattanooga along the great central railway to Atlanta, from which radiated all the communications of the Southern States. And that then, if any army were collected at Atlanta and pushed across the State of Georgia, the granary of the Confederacy, to the sea, it could sweep up through the seaboard States, until it could take in the rear the last Confederate army, still held in the grip of the Federal forces, based upon Washington. Such a plan would have been a work of genius, for it would have exactly met all the conditions which had to be considered.

This plan, this "work of genius," is in fact the plan that was carried out, even though no single mind ever devised it. "In the American civil war," says Wilkinson, "may be said to have been fulfilled the prophecy enunciated more than thirty years before by the Prussian General, Clausewitz, that, whenever a war should be the affair of a whole nation deeply stirred by the cause of quarrel, the operations would be sure to reveal a great and comprehensive plan."

The first part of the plan, the closing of the sea to the shipping of the Confederacy, was begun by Secretary Welles six days after the fall of Sumter; but the blockade was not effective for many months. The operations of Flag Officers Stringham and Goldsborough—until the beginning of the war the navy was so little thought of that the highest rank in it was that of Captain, and the commander of a squadron could only be designated as "Flag Officer"—took Hatteras Inlet and Roanoke Island away from the Confederates, and it was only then that the South began to feel the first slow movement of the thing that was to suffocate and strangle it and leave it a prey to the Northern armies.

So far as ending the war is concerned, the campaign in Virginia was, as Wilkinson says, the holding of the Confederate armies and keeping them occupied. The fall of Richmond, on which McClellan concentrated his energies, would have left the Confederacy still lusty and fighting. At this time, the Winter of 1861-2, he had not begun it; he was busy organizing his men and transforming them from a crowd into an army; and the first step in the great plan that was made on land was made in the West. It was the first movement to "strike at the middle of the Confederacy by the avenue of the Cumberland and Tennessee Rivers."

Grant himself conceived the attack on Forts Henry and Donelson and spent weeks urging that he be permitted to make it. At first Halleck, whose narrow stupidity did so much to thwart his Generals and wreck his cause, told Grant to mind his own business, but at last he gave a grudging assent, and Grant, with 15,000 men, afterward increased to 27,000, advanced into a territory held by 45,000 to capture two supposedly impregnable forts. He did it. "For physical dimensions," says John Fiske, "it was the greatest military achievement that The American Continent had yet witnessed; but its strategical value was not to be measured by its physical dimensions. Two great rivers were laid open for hundreds of miles, so that Union gunboats sailed far into Alabama. * * * The first Confederate line was shattered throughout its whole length." Grant wanted to complete the work by marching to Nashville, which lay helpless before him and was of great strategic value, but Halleck refused to permit it.

These two forts had given the South control of the Cumberland and the Tennessee, and these rivers served the Confederates as roads of approach to important strategic positions. Grant's plan was to make them roads for the Federals into the heart of the Confederacy. He believed that if Halleck had allowed him to follow up his victory he could have ended the war then.

Now was taken the first step toward taking possession of the Mississippi, and thus cutting off the eastern part of the Confederacy from the western. On April 7, 1862, the capture of Island No. 10 opened the river to Memphis, which fell into Union hands on June 6. The next step was taken from the south. On April 24 came that great naval exploit of Farragut's, the passing of Forts Jackson and St. Philip, immortal under the name of the "River Fight." The Confederate fleet was destroyed, the forts passed, and New Orleans surrendered to Farragut, to remain in Union hands till the end of the war. But between New Orleans and Memphis the great Confederate highway was still in Confederate hands.

Meanwhile McClellan was in motion at last for the capture of Richmond. He advanced up the peninsula and got within twenty-four miles of the Confederate capital. He had 120,000 men, and J. E. Johnston had 50,000. McClellan reckoned on getting 40,000 more from McDowell, but Stonewall Jackson suddenly dashed into the Shenandoah Valley and McDowell was called back to defend Washington. McClellan, always filled with his absurd delusion that he was outnumbered, did not move forward, but fortified himself and asked for reinforcements. Suddenly Johnston attacked him and nearly cut his army in two at Seven Pines. In the midst of the battle Johnston received one of the thirteen wounds which he got during the war—General Scott described him as "a most capable officer, who had the bad habit of getting himself wounded"—and two days later Lee took the command he was never to relinquish

McClellan's army was divided on the two sides of the Chickahominy; Jackson now suddenly emerged from the valley and appeared on his right flank, and Stuart appalled him by raiding completely around his army. The Seven Days' Battles ended in the escape of McClellan from the inferior force opposed to him. Lee had raised the siege of Richmond. His next problem was to prevent Pope from effecting a union with McClellan, and this he did by inflicting on that vainglorious boaster the defeat known as the second battle of Bull Run. McClellan had now been manoeuvred out of Virginia, and Lee determined on an aggressive campaign. He moved into Maryland, where McClellan encountered him at Antietam and foiled his purpose of transferring the seat of war to the North.

That part of the Northern plan which included the control of the Tennessee and Cumberland Rivers now entered upon a new phase. The strategic importance of Chattanooga was immense; its possession gave the Confederates several easy roads into Kentucky, made probable their conquest of the eastern part of that State and the reconquest cf the two rivers, and threatened Grant with having to fall back to the Ohio. If the Federals could take it they would save Kentucky to the Union and recover Tennessee. But Halleck delayed, while Bragg was hurrying to throw an army into Chattanooga, and it fell into the hands of the Confederates. After a futile attempt to attack Louisville, Bragg determined to take Nashville, and had moved as far as Murfreesboro when Rosecrans attacked him and foiled his intention.

Now, late in 1862, began in earnest the execution of the plan to cut the Confederacy in two and deprive the east of its food supplies from the west by capturing the Mississippi. The fall of Memphis had left the Confederates in possession only of that part of the river between Vicksburg and Port Hudson. After an eight months' campaign Grant took Vicksburg, Port Hudson surrendered five days later, and, as Lincoln said, "the Father of Waters once more flows unvexed to the sea."

Thus two of the cardinal points in the Union plan had been attained—the Confederacy had been split and the blockade, now in full swing, was starving it to death.

Grant's Vicksburg campaign is admitted to have been excellently planned and finely carried out. His march around Johnston, who was at Jackson, Miss., and his throwing himself on Vicksburg, leaving the outmanoeuvred Johnston behind him, is called by Colonel McClure "the boldest military manoeuvre ever executed by Grant" and "one of the boldest and grandest strategic movements of the war." So daring a deed was it and so novel in warfare that General Sherman before it was begun handed to Grant a written protest against it, pointing out that it must surely fail. Grant put the paper in his pocket. After the victory he quietly handed it back to Sherman without a word.

Meanwhile Burnside and Hooker had in turn advanced on Lee in Virginia and been terribly defeated, and the Army of the Potomac was as far away from Richmond as ever. Again did Lee decide to carry the war into the North. His plan was nothing less than to threaten not only Washington but Philadelphia and New York. He had hardly got into Pennsylvania, however, before he was overtaken and driven back by Meade at Gettysburg. Nothing more of any importance happened in Virginia in 1863, but in the West the great Northern plan was rapidly unfolding.

Chattanooga, thanks to Halleck's dilatoriness, was still in Confederate hands. Before the great movement to rend the Confederacy from west to east, as it had been rent from north to south, could begin, Chattanooga must be taken. Bragg's position was impregnable to direct assault; but Rosecrans drew him out of it by threatening an invasion of Georgia, the same which Sherman in fact afterward made. Finding that all Rosecrans wanted was Chattanooga, Bragg, reinforced by Longstreet, undertook to force him out of the city and retake it. The result was the battle of Chickamauga; a Confederate victory on the field, (for Rosecrans was driven off, and, but for Thomas's valiant resistance, would have been completely routed,) but a Union victory in its results. For, after it was all over, Rosecrans still held Cahttanooga. Subsequent Confederate defeats at Missionary Ridge and Lookout Mountain forced Bragg out of Tennessee and into Georgia, and J. E. Johnston took his place at the head of the army.

At the beginning of 1864 the Federals had conquered a large part of the West, but in Virginia they were just where they had been when the war began. Grant now took command of all the armies. He was the only man who saw what the problem was; he was, says Eggleston, "a man capable of clearly seeing and perfectly understanding that the Confederate strength lay in the fighting force of the Southern armies rather than in the possession of strategic positions." Lincoln, indeed, had seen this, but had never been able to convince his Generals, with their eyes fixed on the strategy of campaigns fought in Europe under entirely different conditions by Napoleon, Frederick, and Marlborough.

Grant, then, determined to destroy the resisting force of Lee's army by hurling a superior force upon it, and at the same time to prevent any reinforcement of Lee by active movements against all the other Confederate armies simultaneously. He gave orders to this effect, but he was not always well served, and many of his subordinates failed utterly to keep their adversaries employed. In his own movement against Lee he planned at first to use three armies—Meade was to engage Lee, while Butler was to move on Richmond and threaten Lee's communications, and Burnside was to lie in reserve behind Meade. The incompetent Butler, haughtily rejecting the advice of his Generals, allowed himself to be "bottled up," as he himself expressed it, by an inferior force under Beauregard, at the very time Grant was fighting his desperate and unavailing battle in the

Wilderness, and the well-laid plan went to pieces. Sigel failed in his part of the great forward movement, which was to advance up the Valley of Virginia and break the communications between Tennessee and the Confederate capital, and Halleck telegraphed Grant: "Sigel is in full retreat on Strasbourg. He will do nothing but run, never did anything else." Banks failed to place his army of 40,000 men at New Orleans in time to help in the grand strategy Grant had laid out. But Sherman and Grant's other subordinates carried out the plan as he had made it.

In Virginia, Grant moved continually to the left, with his face toward Richmond, until, instead of having his back to Washington, he had his back to the

sea, which became his base of supplies. In June he had reached the point aimed at by McClellan two years before. He was baffled by Lee at Spottsylvania and Cold Harbor, and, though he said that he would "fight it out on this line if it takes all Summer," he did not. Instead, he undertook to capture Petersburg and cut off Lee's communications.

Meanwhile Sherman was carrying out the fourth number on the great program of the North—to move from Tennessee to Atlanta, from which radiated all the communications of the Southern States. Hampered and harassed by Johnston, he yet reached Atlanta and took it; and now the war was to enter on its last phase—his army was to sweep through Georgia, "the granary of the Confederacy," to the

sea and up through the seaboard States until it could take the last effective Confederate army in the rear. Hood made a desperate effort to divert him by invading Tennessee, hoping to draw Sherman after him; but Thomas encountered and crushed Hood at Nashville, and Sherman went his way. Lee, too, tried to divert Grant by sending Early into the Valley, but Sheridan drove him back. By the Spring of 1865 Sherman was in North Carolina, Lee's lines at Petersburg were broken, and he was obliged to retreat, and at last, finding himself nearly surrounded, he surrendered. The great Napoleonic plan, the work of no one Napoleon, had succeeded despite all the blunders that so often nearly wrecked it.

SIX MOST FAMOUS BATTLES OF THE WAR

Only One Was Victory for Federals, Though Two More Left Advantage on Their Side---Rest Were Clean-Cut Confederate Triumphs.

OF the six most famous battles of the war only one, Gettysburg, was admittedly a Union victory. Antietam was claimed by the Confederates as a drawn battle, though both it and Chickamauga ended by leaving all the solid results of the fighting in Federal hands. Fredericksburg, Chancellorsville, and the three battles of the Wilderness, Spottsylvania and Cold Harbor, which were all one battle so far as the purpose and result are concerned, were Confederate victories.

Antietam is a historic battle, partly because it foiled the first of Lee's attempts to transfer the fighting to the North, but chiefly because it enabled President Lincoln to issue his Emancipation Proclamation. Gettysburg foiled the second and last of Lee's attempts on the North and broke the back of the Confederacy. Chickamauga gave Tennessee to the Union and made possible Sherman's march through Georgia and the Carolinas and the splitting of the Confederacy from the Mississippi to the sea. The Wilderness, Spottsylvania, and Cold Harbor foiled Grant's plan to "fight it out on this line if it takes all Summer," and postponed the end of the war until Petersburg could be taken. Chancellorsville was the repulse of a great effort to move on Richmond, and opened the way for Lee's invasion of Pennsylvania. As for Fredericksburg, it settled nothing; its interest is that horrified interest which attaches to a massacre.

Justly does Carl Schurz call Antietam "one of the landmarks of human history," because its consequence was emancipation. On July 22, 1862, Lincoln read to his Cabinet the draft of what is called the "Monitory Emancipation Proclamation," and said he proposed to issue it. Seward urgently protested; McClellan had just suffered his defeat on the Peninsula, and the North was plunged in gloom. "It may be viewed," said Seward, "as the last measure of an exhausted Government, a cry for help; the Government stretching forth her hands to Ethiopia, instead of Ethiopia stretching forth her hands to the Government. It will be considered our last shriek on the retreat." He urged the President to withhold it until a victory had been won. This view of the case had not occurred to the President, but he saw the force of it, and he put the proclamation aside. On Sept. 17 came the battle

of Antietam; Lee retreated from Maryland, and on Sept. 24 the Monitory Proclamation was issued, to be followed next January by the final and decisive proclamation.

Lee began his invasion of Maryland on Sept. 3, and was well advanced before he informed Davis of his purpose. He was across the Potomac before Davis could interfere if he had wanted to. In three days Jackson was entering Frederick, where the Barbara Frietchie incident did not take place. Nor would Stonewall Jackson, always religiously chivalrous toward women, have ordered his men to fire because a Union flag "met his sight." In fact, while he was passing through Middletown two pretty girls rushed out and waved Union flags in his face. He bowed, raised his hat to them, and said, with a smile to his Staff: "We evidently have no friends in this town." However, there was a foundation for the story. It was not Barbara, but Mrs. Mary Quantrell, a neighbor, who fastened a flag to her porch. General A. P. Hill asked her politely if she would not take it down, but she refused, and he rode on; but some private soldiers came along afterward and tore it down, breaking the staff. Mrs. Quantrell put out another. The soldiers were tearing that down, too, when General Hill learned what was going on and sent orders that the offenders let her alone, and that they be arrested if they annoyed her any further. One Cornelius S. Rainsford heard the story, and also a story about how Barbara Frietchie had hung out a flag when the Union troops marched through. He got the two stories mixed, told Mrs. Southworth, the novelist, the story as he understood it, and she sent the supposed facts to Whittier.

While Lee was threatening Washington, Baltimore, and even Harrisburg and Philadelphia, Bragg was threatening Louisville and Cincinnati, and the consternation in the North was great. McClellan, always at his best on the defensive, met Lee at Antietam. Both sides claimed the victory; but Lee had to give up his invasion and return to the South. He had hoped to raise Maryland against the Union, and had issued an address to the people, saying that he had come "to aid you in throwing off this foreign yoke." But Maryland did not rise; it liked the foreign yoke; and Lee lost more men by desertion than he gained in recruits. His campaign was a failure.

The Administration was dissatisfied because McClellan did not follow Lee up. He continued to quarrel violently with Stanton, and even with Lincoln, and at last he was relieved from command and Burnside put in his place. That gallant and honest gentleman did not want the command; he must have known himself unfit for it. "It seems," says Rhodes in his history of the United States, "that incompetence attends his every movement." He determined to attack Lee wherever he could be found; and Lee was found at Fredericksburg.

The battle, or rather the wholesale slaughter, took place on Dec. 13, 1862. "The pictures of Burnside on Dec. 12," says Rhodes, "are those of a General bewildered in the undertaking of a larger enterprise than he had the ability and nerve to carry through. It is impossible to discover that he had a well-defined plan of operation." The only chance of success was in attacking Lee's right, and Burnside at first had some notion of doing this. But, as he failed to explain himself fully to his subordinates, Franklin sent Meade's division to make the attack alone; it was not properly supported, and was driven back by Stonewall Jackson. "The only bright Union spot in the disastrous day at Fredericksburg," said Longstreet, "was Meade's work as a Division Commander. He broke Jackson's line and for a brief hour made things look dangerous on our right. But there Meade was not promptly supported and our people soon recovered their ground after sustaining heavy losses."

Then Burnside committed the incredible folly of attacking Lee's left, posted on Marye's Heights, crowned with batteries. To attack such a position as Burnside did was to attempt an impossibility; but this was not all. The hill, looked at from below, seemed to present a smooth surface, but, in fact, well down the slope there was a sunken road faced with a stone wall, forming a perfect breastwork, and into this sunken road Lee threw 2,000 riflemen. They were perfectly concealed and were ordered to withhold their fire until the enemy, charging up in the face of the terrible cannonade from the heights above, should be within twenty yards of the sunken road, when they could be swept away like dust. It was a perfect trap. "A chicken could not live on that field when we open on it," reported Longstreet's Chief of Artillery.

French's division made the first attack; it was being decimated by the fearful fire from the hilltop when it came upon the sunken road and was blown back, leaving half its number on the field. Burnside ordered Hancock forward; he left 2,000 of his 5,000 on the hill when he was driven back. "Oh, great God!" cried General Couch. "See how our poor fellows are falling! It is only murder now." It was evident enough

Maj. Gen. O. O. Howard.

that human beings could not take that hill; but Burnside sent forward another, and another, and another division, to see them all melt in that inferno and come back wrecked. At last he ordered Hooker forward. This was the sixth assault; five other divisions had made the useless attacks. Hooker begged him to spare the lives of his men, showing him the uselessness of the horrible sacrifice. "In a blind rage," says Eggleston, "Burnside seemed unable to comprehend what his subordinates saw clearly enough. He insisted upon sending Hooker's command also into that slaughter pen." It rushed into the jaws of death, and in a few minutes half the division was lying on the hill and the rest were coming back.

Burnside had lost 12,653 of his best men. He was overwhelmed with grief. "Oh, those men! those men over there!" he said, pointing to the hill where his victims lay, "I am thinking of them all the time." Nevertheless, he planned to

Pickett's charge at Gettysburg.

The Remnant Through the Batteries Broke and Crossed the Works with Armistead.

renew the assault next day, and this time to lead it in person. Not yet had the idea dawned on him that the taking of the hill was impossible. Sumner, Franklin, and other Generals labored with him through the night and finally got him to give up the idea. It ended his standing with the army. Soon afterward, at a review of the Second Corps, he was received with such coldness that General Sumner asked Couch to call for cheers for him. Couch and other Generals rode along the lines; waving their caps and calling for cheers, but the veterans stood grimly silent; the only answer was a few derisive cries. The correspondent of The London Times at Lee's headquarters wrote that Dec. 13 would be "a memorable day to the historian of the Decline and Fall of the American Republic."

Burnside was relieved from the command, which was given to his severest critic, Hooker.

That General planned the Chancellorsville campaign excellently. His dispositions were such that it was hard to see how Lee could avoid having his left turned and being forced either to retreat or give battle in the open with inadequate forces. Hooker crossed the Rappahannock—surprising Lee, who was not expecting him—and had already ordered a rapid move toward Fredericksburg when he changed his mind and countermanded the order. After that he did nothing; he sat there in the Wilderness waiting for Lee to move. And Lee moved!

He and Stonewall Jackson sat down on a couple of cracker boxes and consulted. "The result of their meditations," says Rhodes, "evinced their supreme contempt for the generalship of their opponent." For, though Lee had only 55,000 and Hooker 131,000, Lee decided to divide his little force in the presence of his enemy. Jackson took 30,000 of them and on May 2, 1863, tranquilly began a march around Hooker's army. He marched all day, and

Hooker lay there motionless all the time.

The Eleventh Corps, Howard's, composed Hooker's right, and it was left up in the air, with nothing to lean upon. Jackson, from a good vantage point, looked down upon the doomed corps playing cards, sleeping, or butchering beeves, in serene unconsciousness of what eyes were fixed upon them. Yet Carl Schurz caught a glimpse of Jackson's men through the forest, immediately surmised who they were, and reported what he had seen to Howard, urging him to make a new disposition so that his corps could face the attack instead of having it come on the flank. Howard scouted the idea, saying that both he and Hooker believed Lee was in full retreat. General Schimmelfennig, Col. Gilsa, and other officers on the ill-fated right wing saw more and more of Jackson's advance, which he hardly seemed to try to conceal in his contempt for his adversary, and reported what they saw; but Hooker and Howard, filled with their delusion that Lee was retreating, refused to credit it or take any steps to avert it. Hooker, in his folly, believed that the Confederates these officers had seen were the head of the retreating army.

At nearly 6 o'clock rabbits came bounding through the woods in terror—the first intimation that the storm was about to break; and after them came Jackson like a whirlwind. The Eleventh Corps, so posted that it could not confront the enemy, fought as well as it could, but to fight was hopeless. Brigade after brigade was crumpled up, and the Federals were streaming through the forest in disorder; arms, accoutrements, knapsacks caught on branches, artillery wagons overturned between trees or jammed in the jungle, and Jackson's yelling veterans dashing after in hot pursuit. Throughout this wild charge Jackson was frequently seen to stop, raise his eyes to heaven, and pray.

But night had fallen, and in the ardor of the pursuit and the mazes of the Wilderness the Confederate divisions and brigades were getting mixed together. Jackson saw the danger and ordered a halt to re-form his lines. This took him about two hours, and at 10 o'clock he rode out of his lines to reconnoitre. The two armies were so close together that soldiers were taken prisoners in each other's lines, supposing that they were in their own. Jackson rode back into his own lines at the very moment when two regiments were exchanging a volley, and the Southern regiment, seeing several horsemen riding toward it through the forest in the dense gloom, apparently coming from the Federal lines, thought it was being charged, and fired. The men were North Carolina mountaineers, dead shots, and every man of Jackson's escort was swept from his saddle. He himself kept his seat, but he had been mortally wounded, and he died eight days later. The troops who killed him were under the command of General James H. Lane, who had been one of his students when he was a college professor.

Hooker did not attempt to keep Lee's army divided; instead he acted wholly on the defensive. Jackson's men, under Stuart, completed the work begun the day before, while Lee attacked in front, and Hooker was soon flying across the Rappahannock.

Lee's men now believed themselves invincible. He and Davis determined to invade the North, in the belief that by overrunning Pennsylvania and threatening Washington they would put such a weapon in the hands of the Northern peace party that public sentiment would force Lincoln to give in, and that Europe would recognize the Confederacy and intervene. Besides, they were disturbed over Grant's steady advance to success before Vicksburg, and wished to achieve a victory so spectacular as to overcome the bad effect that would be created if

Vicksburg should fall.

They entered Pennsylvania without being stopped. Neither Lee nor Meade intended to fight at Gettysburg; in fact, it was long before Lee knew that the Union Army was on his track. He had committed the mistake of permitting Stuart, his cavalry commander, to exercise his own discretion in his movements; and Stuart, who had no discretion to exercise, chose to make a dramatic and picturesque cavalry raid in the neighborhood of Washington. This deprived Lee of "the eyes of the army," and he was left in the dark concerning his enemy's movements. When he finally learned them, he chose Cashtown as the scene of the impending battle, while Meade pitched on Pipe Creek as the field.

But General Heth, whose soldiers had worn out their shoes on the march, decided to enter Gettysburg and get some. His men ran into General Buford's Union cavalry, who were making a reconnoissance; there was a fight; hearing the firing, other troops on both sides hurried up, and soon both armies were grappling in the deadly contest of July 1, 2, and 3, 1863. "What are you fighting there?" asked the puzzled Lee, who had ordered Ewell forward to sweep away the Union cavalry, supposing they were the only Federal soldiers there. "The whole Yankee army, I think," answered Ewell.

The first day's fighting ended in the driving of the Federals out of the immediate neighborhood of Gettysburg, and under Hancock's direction—Meade had sent him to the field to take command—they took up a strong position on Cemetery Ridge. Lee put his forces on Seminary Ridge, which faces the other and is about a mile away from it. Owing to the accidental way in which the invading and pursuing armies had stumbled on each other their armies were scattered, but by the afternoon of July 2 both had their whole forces on the field. Lee ordered an attack, the effect of which was lost owing to a wholly unexpected circumstance. Sickles, in disregard of Meade's plan of battle, had moved out slightly in front of the Union lines, and the Confederate attack fell upon him. His men resisted with stubborn valor, and in trying to get Sickles out of the way the Confederates spent themselves and left the second day's battle still undecided. Meanwhile one of the most desperate fights of the war had been going on for the possession of Little Round Top, an eminence at the end of Cemetery Ridge and rising above it and commanding it. In the end the Federals held the hill. At the other end of the ridge a battle for the possession of Culp's Hill had ended in the same way.

On the third day Pickett's charge was made. It was preceded by a bombardment of the Federal lines by 150 guns. This lasted for an hour, its purpose being to silence the Federal artillery. For that purpose it was a failure; but Lee believed, when the Federals stopped returning the fire, that he had succeeded, and the divisions of Pickett, Wilcox, and Pender were ordered to charge across that open ground, a mile across, and take Cemetery Ridge. When the artillery fire fell upon them they knew that Lee had been mistaken in thinking he had silenced the Federal guns; but they did not falter, nor did they when Hancock's men opened a terrific fire of small arms. The column, said General Sickles, "was torn by our artillery and crushed by the fire of Hancock's infantry, and disappeared like ocean waves dashing against a rock-ribbed shore."

Pickett himself halted at a barn about 300 yards from the Union position; but one of his brigade commanders, Armistead, actually ascended the ridge, crossed the stone wall behind which Hancock's men were posted, put his hand on a Federal cannon, waved his sword with his hat on it, and shouted, "Give them the cold steel, boys!" The next instant he fell mortally wounded. Some of his men had poured in after him—only a handful—and they were all killed or captured. The rest of the assailants were hurled back. The spot where Armistead fell is about fifty yards inside the stone wall, and there is a stone monument marking the place which bears the words, "High-water mark of the rebellion." It was, indeed; from that moment the Confederate cause, hitherto in the ascendant, began to decline until it reached Appomattox.

Chickamauga was on both sides the most merciless and ferocious battle of the war. Men fired cannon at each other at a distance of 100 yards. Trees were shot down and wounded men burned to death in blazing woods.

It was a battle of blunders and lost opportunities, also, on both sides. Rosecrans had manoeuvred Bragg out of Chattanooga and complacently supposed that the Confederate General was in full retreat. Under this delusion he started to pursue, and in crossing mountains far apart separated widely his corps and divisions. This gave Bragg a great opportunity, but at first he did not know it. The lack of information concerning the enemy which was the case in both camps seems surprising now, but a remark of Bragg's explains it. Pointing to the Cumberland range, he said to General D. H. Hill:

> It is said to be easy to defend a mountainous country, but mountains hide your foe from you, while they are full of gaps through which he can pounce upon you at any time. A mountain is like the walls of a house full of rat holes. The rat lies hidden at his hole, ready to pop out when no one is watching. Who can tell what lies hidden behind that wall?

On Sept. 12, 1863, Rosecrans suddenly awoke to his peril; Bragg was concentrating in front of his centre, and his army was scattered. He wrought with the fury of desperation to bring it together. His reserve under Granger was at Chattanooga, Crittenden's corps was at Ringgold, McCook's at Alpine, and Thomas's in the valley known as McLemore's Cove. McCook's corps was ten miles from Thomas, part of Crittenden's twenty miles, and the rest fifteen miles.

Bragg was in easy reach of Thomas, who was in a trap. McLemore's Cove was six miles wide, hemmed in by two precipitous mountains, Pigeon and Lookout. It was a blind alley, a cul-de-sac. There was no escape except through a narrow defile leading to the summit of Lookout Mountain. Thomas was apparently lost. Bragg ordered Hindman to attack him at daybreak, and Cleburne to await the sound of Hindman's guns and then attack. Hindman did not move, and all that morning and most of the afternoon Thomas was madly moving his troops up the defile, screened by the trees in the cove. Late in the afternoon Bragg ordered D. H. Hill to make the attack; it fell on the last of Thomas's rear guard, just moving up into the defile, and amounted to nothing. Thomas had been within an ace of utter destruction, but he had saved his corps. Hindman was arrested; he produced Bragg's order, and it appeared that, instead of being mandatory, it left it to Hindman's discretion whether to attack or not. Why he did not use his discretion in favor of assaulting instead of lying idle was never explained. But it does not excuse Bragg; he could have reached Hindman by courier within an hour or two at any time; yet he saw that the expected attack was not made, and yet did not inquire the reason or take any steps at all until late in the afternoon. He lost the opportunity to wreck the Union cause in the West.

Rosecrans, as he afterward said, recognized that it was "a matter of life and death" to get his army together. It took him nearly a week of frenzied work to do it; "but," says Rhodes, "the loss of sleep, the fear that Bragg might crush, one after another, his different detachments, as some now think he had it in his power to do, the intense anxiety on two successive nights for the safety of one of his corps, all these combined to unnerve the Union commander, who, in the opinion of his army, was whipped before he went into the battle."

Meanwhile Bragg had ordered Polk to attack Crittenden, who had not yet joined the rest of the army, but the order was not obeyed, and by Sept. 18 the army was united, except for Granger's reserve, which never was in the fight. Bragg ordered Polk to attack at daybreak on Sept 19, but he did not; and it was 9:30 before the first gun was fired by Breckinridge. Bragg intended to fall upon and crush the Federal left, bend back the line and place himself between the Federal army and its base; but instead of sending forward men who were used to this sort of fighting—Longstreet's veterans, who had just come from the Gettysburg field to join him—he sent Polk's men; and it was the great Thomas they had to face.

Thomas not only resisted effectively but made counter-attacks and deranged Bragg's plans. On the next day, Sept. 20, Rosecrans became imbued with the idea that Bragg was hurling his whole army on Thomas, and gave several orders which destroyed himself. He began changing the dispositions of his forces under fire, and weakened his centre to send troops to Thomas, at the same time moving other bodies of troops to different

Gen W S Hancock

places. The moment he chose for this fatal action was just before Longstreet was about to burst upon him like a storm. Longstreet fell upon the marching brigades and divisions, caught them on the flank and in motion, burst them asunder, and pierced the right centre. They were swept before him like leaves before a gale.

The rout was like that at Chancellorsville. Men cut horses from gun carriages and caissons, mounted them, and fled; the roads were choked with flying troops; infantrymen threatened with their bayonets officers who tried to stop the stampede. Rosecrans sat his horse crossing himself—a companion piece to Jackson's stopping to pray during his charge at Chancellorsville—but he was carried away in the crowd of fugitives. At Chattanooga he telegraphed to Halleck that he had been overwhelmed, and Assistant Secretary of War Charles A. Dana, who had also been "swept bodily off the field by the panic-stricken rabble," telegraphed, "Chickamauga is as fatal a name in our history as Bull Run."

But Rosecrans and Dana were premature. They did not see the end of the battle. "In spite of the fact, clearly apparent to him," says Eggleston, "that Rosecrans was defeated and three-fifths of his army destroyed, Thomas continued the bloody contest with a fury that knew no flinching, and hesitated at nothing of human sacrifice in the achievement of its purposes." With 25,000 men he held his ground against the furious assaults of double his number, fighting in the open and behind log breastworks, and when night fell he was still immovable. Next day he leisurely retreated; he had saved the army and won the title of "The Rock of Chickamauga."

In May, 1864, Grant began his advance into Virginia. He crossed over into the Wilderness, intending to move around Lee and get between him and the Confederate capital. He had no intention of fighting in the Wilderness, but Lee detected his purpose and assailed him there on May 5. It was not like any other battlefield of the war. The trees had been cut down for fuel many years before, and there was a tangled mass of second growths, complicated with thickets and brush. Men could not see their opponents a hundred feet away. No regularity of formation was possible. No regiment or division could tell what its allies were doing. Officers had no way of telling whether they were supported or not, and no alignment could be made. A forest fire broke out, and Longstreet and Hancock fought in the flames and smoke. They had to leave their wounded amid the blazing brush.

There is no doubt that Lee expected his opponent to retreat after he had failed to win the battle, as former commanders of the Army of the Potomac had done. He doubtless thought Grant's western victories had been due to the inferiority of his opponents; indeed, the same belief existed in the North, where it was said Grant "would find Bobby Lee a different customer from the pigheaded Bragg or the weak Pemberton." His soldiers, accustomed to Generals who ordered a retreat after a defeat, questioned when they were ordered to march whether they were to go northward and recross the river. When they found their faces turned to the South they were overjoyed; they sang and cheered as they marched. Lee, discovering to his surprise that Grant was still in his front, is said to have remarked to his officers, "Gentlemen, at last the Army of the Potomac has a General."

Grant determined to seize Spottsylvania Court House as the best chance for getting between Lee and Richmond; but again Lee penetrated his design and was ready for him. The fighting here lasted a week, and is memorable particularly for the bloodshed at the Bloody Angle. This was a salient. It projected toward the Federal lines, so that an attacking force could fire upon it both from the front and the two sides. Hancock carried it, capturing Edward Johnson's force, and pushed on; but he was repulsed at a second line of intrenchments, and then the Confederates undertook to recapture the Angle.

Under a fearful enfilading fire they assaulted the salient five times. They reached the embankment and fought hand-to-hand with Hancock's men. Sometimes men on either side thrust their bayonets through the crevices in the logs and ran each other through. At every point before and behind the embankment men lay piled five deep on each other. An oak tree nearly two feet thick was cut down by bullets, and fell with a crash, killing the Confederates who were fighting beneath it.

After this unsuccessful battle Grant kept moving by the left, his favorite manoeuvre in this campaign, until he and Lee came face to face at Cold Harbor. That useless assault was made on June 3. The soldiers knew it was hopeless and murderous, and the night before they were busy pinning on their coats slips of paper carrying their names and home addresses; they knew they were doomed to death. Cold Harbor was a frontal assault on an intrenched enemy. Lee concentrated troops on the extremely short front where the fighting was to take place; they stood six deep in the breastwork, the men in the rear loading rifles and passing them to those in front. The fighting lasted only twenty minutes, but in that time Grant lost 10,500 men, or nearly ten men per second. Lee sent a messenger to General A. P. Hill for a report. Hill pointed to the dead bodies of Union soldiers piled high upon each other, and said, "Tell General Lee it is the same all along my front." The Confederate loss was 1,000.

There was a story, long believed, that Grant ordered another assault, and that the troops refused to move; a mutiny of the Army of the Potomac. It was not true. But all over the North there rose a storm of terrible indignation, and a demand for Grant's removal. It was this battle that gave him the name of "the Butcher," and in spite of the great skill with which he had manoeuvred throughout the campaign up to this point, the impression was created that he had no science, and was simply a "hammerer." It was, however, his only mistake of that kind. He recognized it as a mistake himself, deplored it, and in his memoirs said: "No advantage whatever was gained to compensate for the heavy loss we sustained." He had learned his lesson; his next move was to sit down before Lee and begin the siege of Petersburg.

HOW THE NAVY STRANGLED THE SOUTH

Confederacy Fell Because Federal Ships Prevented It From Getting Indispensable Supplies, Especially Food and Ammunition, From Outside Sources.

THE Confederacy was not shot to death. It was strangled to death. What killed it was the United States Navy. It was regarded in Europe as a foregone conclusion that the South could not be conquered, and its fall created great surprise. The territory of the South was, in a military sense, almost unlimited and unassailable; its defensive position was an offset to the North's numerical superiority; its defenders, as soldiers, were at least the equals of those who attacked it. It fell because it could not get food, clothing, ammunition, rolling stock, money. It was the navy that prevented it from getting these things.

The blockade goes unsung. It was prosaic work, with few spectacular features. But it was the decisive factor in the fall of the Confederacy; it was what made the South's cause a Lost Cause. It held the Confederacy by the throat while Grant and Sherman pounded that helpless prisoner to death. "The Confederacy collapsed from inanition," says Charles Francis Adams, in his "Studies Military and Diplomatic." "Suffering such occasional reverses and defeats as are incidental to all warfare, it was never crushed in battle or on the field, until its strength was sapped away by want of food. It died of exhaustion—starved and gasping!"

The distinguished English military critic, Spenser Wilkinson, in his essays on "War and Policy," also finds the blockade the fundamental explanation of the Confederacy's fall. He says:

The effect of the blockade was, first of all, to put an end to exports and imports. Neither cotton nor other produce could be sold, for it could not be delivered to the foreign markets. Provisions and manufactured goods could no longer be bought, for in the absence of exports there were no funds wherewith to pay for them, and if bought they could not be delivered.

Thus the Confederacy was affected in three ways. It was impoverished at the very time when money was needed as the sinews of war. Its military resources were crippled by the impossibility of obtaining from abroad arms, clothing and machinery. In the second place, mechanical skill and machine making industries were almost unknown in the South. The railways, therefore, could not be supplied with new rolling stock, while that in hand at the outbreak of the war was used up. Shipbuilding, unknown at the South before the war, could not be established, and steamers could neither be built nor provided with engines. The blockade made it impossible to create a navy, in the absence of which the blockade could neither be prevented nor broken. Lastly, the closing of the sea threw the South upon its own resources for food, and as cotton and tobacco had no longer any value when the markets were inaccessible, it became necessary to abandon their culture and substitute that of corn and other foodstuffs.

"Aptly did camp slang name the blockade the 'Conda,'" says a Southern writer. "It was the crush of the Conda that squeezed us to death." It was the maritime supremacy of the North that made possible Grant's movement through Virginia and Sherman's march to the sea. The Confederacy had two frontiers, one on the land and one on the sea. The land frontier was in contact with Northern territory at every point, and hence closed for export and import. Only by the seaboard was communication with the outside world possible, and when this was closed the South was stifled. The South thus held helpless, the greater strength of the North was irresistible.

A blockade had been believed impossible, and certainly this was the greatest blockade in the world's history. The entire length of beaches under guard was

Admiral David G. Farragut.

exactly 11,593 miles. In 1858 Senator James H. Hammond of South Carolina, addressing his Northern colleagues, said:

We have 3,000 miles of continental seashore line so indented with bays and crowded with islands that when their shore lines are added we have 12,000 miles. * * * Can you hem in such a territory as that? You talk of putting up a wall of fire around 850,000 square miles so situated! How absurd!

The blockade was declared six days after the fall of Fort Sumter, but for a long time it was ineffective, chiefly because the United States had no navy adequate for the task and had to make one under fire. The blockade runners made full use of the inlets along the coast, especially that of North Carolina. The capture of Hatteras Inlet by Stringham and Butler, and of Roanoke Island by Goldsborough and Burnside, was the first sign that the "Conda" was stretching his coils around the South. For a time after this blockade runners made great profits, but the high prices they received significantly showed how scarce the goods they brought were getting to be.

The creation of the new navy was a great example of American energy. When Secretary Welles took office there was only one armed vessel of any importance on the Atlantic Coast, the steam frigate Brooklyn, which had lately arrived after a three years' cruise. There was no time to build vessels for the immediate needs of the war, and Welles began by buying them. He bought even

Brooklyn ferryboats, and at first Flag Officer Stringham spent about half his time reporting the breakdown of vessels. Not only was the Government short of ships, but it was short of men; it had on March 4 only 207 men in all the ports and receiving ships on the Atlantic Coast. Welles called not only for ships but for men. By the end of 1863, during which time the Government had been furiously building ships, it had 600 vessels; before the end of the war, 700. Of them seventy-five were ironclad. One man, James B. Eads, furnished in less than 100 days an armored squadron of eight ships, in the aggregate of 5,000 tons burden, capable of steaming nine knots per hour. At the time Eads closed the contract with the Government the timber from which the ships were to be made was still standing in the forest, and the machinery with which the armor was to be rolled was not constructed.

The building of the Monitor revolutionized naval warfare; yet she was built amid a storm of obloquy and ridicule. Secretary Welles and Admiral Smith, unmoved by it, went calmly ahead with their experiment. On the very eve of the Monitor's engagement with the Merrimac, Secretary Stanton, at a Cabinet meeting, panic-stricken by the havoc the Merrimac was making, sneered at Welles for his folly and covered the Monitor with contempt. The navy was stained by none of the blunders and incapacities that damaged so many reputations in the army. Com-

mander Preble was disgraced for not being able to hit the Florida, but it does not seem to have been his fault; and Admiral Du Pont was relieved from command at Charleston for being too forceless and unready. But there were no Burnsides, no Hallecks, no Hookers, in the navy; the navy never had a Fredericksburg or a Chancellorsville.

Much of the credit for this must be given to Secretary Welles, who made no mistakes in the selection of his officers and who could not be cajoled or threatened into giving up one he had selected. It was the business of Welles and Stanton to pick out the right men for command; Welles did, and Stanton did not. "While the War Department," says John T. Morse, Jr., "was painfully learning on many a lost and bloody battlefield who could not command victory, the Navy Department sent well-chosen Captains from one success to another."

An instance is the case of Farragut. Just as Welles stood inflexibly by Ericsson and the Monitor in the face of the scorn of "practical seamen," so he picked Farragut and stood by him in defiance of the protest that his choice aroused. Senator Hale, the Chairman of the Naval Affairs Committee, warned him that Farragut was "Southern born, a Southern resident, with a Southern wife." Congressmen flocked to him to tell him that Farragut was an unknown officer, who should not be placed in high command. None of the Cabinet, but Seward, (who was not consulted,) knew Farragut. Lincoln was perturbed; he inquired if Farragut was equal to the task, and if it would not be better to give it to Du Pont.

When Welles appointed Du Pont to command a squadron, the whole navy applauded. Du Pont was the navy's pet. "But," says Welles in his diary, "no cheering response was made to the appointment of Farragut." Naval officers generally doubted his ability to exercise high command. They were all wrong, both as to Farragut and Du Pont, and on Sept. 2, 1864, Welles had the satisfaction of making this entry in his diary:

No one can now hesitate to say which is the real hero; yet three years ago it would have been different. Farragut is earnest, unselfish, devoted to the country and the service. He sees to every movement, forms his line of battle with care and skill, puts himself at the head, carries out his plan, if there is difficulty leads the way, regards no danger to himself, dashes by forts and overcomes obstructions. Du Pont, as we saw at Sumter, puts himself in the most formidable vessel, has no order of battle, leads the way only until he gets within cannon-shot range, then stops, says his ship would not steer well, declines, however, to go to any other, but signals to them to go forward without order or any plan of battle, does not enjoin upon them to dash by the forts; they are stopped under the guns of Sumter and Moultrie, and are battered for an hour, a sufficient length of time to have gone to Charleston wharves, and then they are signaled to turn about and come back to the Admiral out of harm's way.

He was not, however, charging Du Pont with cowardice. He called him "a polished naval officer, selfish, heartless, calculating, scheming, but not a hero by nature though too proud to be a coward." What first attracted his attention to Farragut was an incident at the time the Virginia Convention voted for secession. Farragut, a Southern man living in Virginia, boldly denounced the act without regard to the consequences, declared in the presence and to the faces of the secessionists that he would live and die under no flag but that of the Union, and left the State next day—left also his home and property. This led Welles to make inquiries concerning him, and what he learned fixed his decision and gave Farragut's name to the roll of American naval heroes.

Aside from the deeds of the Merrimac and the battle of Mobile Bay, the record fo the Confederate navy is chiefly that of the privateers. (It is curious, by the way, that the same man commanded in both the actions mentioned; Franklin Buchanan was the Captain of the Merrimac and the Confederate Admiral at Mobile Bay.) But the valor of the privateers sheds lustre on the American name. "Raphael Semmes," says Spears in his history of the American navy, "earned the right off Cherbourg to have his name inscribed in the list of the sea heroes of America." Knowing that his force was inferior, he sailed forth to meet his enemy, fought a duel with him until his ship was shot from under his feet, hurled his sword into the sea and sprang after it just as the Alabama's stern disappeared under the waves and her bow rose in the air, and swam to a British boat rather than surrender. And John Newland Maffitt, Captain of the Florida, facing two Union ships at 300 yards distance; sick with fever, sitting on his deck during the fight, because he was too ill to stand; alone save for the man at the wheel; he is worthy to stand with Semmes.

It was Farragut as well as Grant who opened the Mississippi and split the Confederacy; it was Foote as well as Grant who cleared Western Tennessee of the Confederates, an event made illustrious by Walke's daring passage of Island No. 10. The battle of Mobile Bay was not one of the major operations of the war, but it stands high above many that are because of the heroism of the Admiral who "damned the torpedoes" and led the way, and the immortal chivalry of Capt. Craven of the Tecumseh. His ship blown up by a torpedo, Craven and the pilot met at the head of the ladder in the pilot-house. There was only room for one. "After you, pilot," said the Captain, courteously stepping back. The pilot went down the ladder and escaped; the ship sank, and Craven with it. Nor can any American, North or South, fail to thrill at the story of the Confederate ram Tennessee, under Admiral Buchanan, dashing into the heart of the Union squadron, running amuck there, doomed by her own act, but determined to take as many of the enemy with her as she could, and fighting a titanic fight until she was shot to pieces, the Admiral severely wounded, the men still alive suffocating in the smoke with which she was filled. The battle of Mobile Bay was a combat of heroes.

DARING RAIDS AND THEIR LEADERS
Exploits of Mosby, Morgan, Stoneman and Others Which Won Them Enduring Fame—Peaceful Vermont's Taste of War.

SOME of the greatest achievements of both the Federal and Confederate armies were conducted by raids; and in the enumeration of the great actions conducted by the Generals on both sides something of the glory that attached to the daring and adventurous cavalrymen has been neglected. Nevertheless, such men as Morgan, Stuart, and Mosby on one side, Grierson, Wilson, and Stoneman on the other, played their part, and a very large part, in bringing the war to an end.

Of all the raiders, the most sentimental interest attaches to J. J. Andrews. He was the man who captured the locomotive. He rounded it up at Big Shanty with twenty-one men and carried the engine from Marietta, Ga., down South. Andrews actually had the nerve to drive that engine as far south as Ringgold. He was hanged in Knoxville, and seven of his men suffered the same fate. Many of them escaped and were never captured. All things considered, Andrews's raid was the most daring exploit of the civil war.

The most famous exploit in that line, however, was General John H. Morgan's raid into Ohio. It was really a part of Bragg's Tennessee campaign; he had decided to make a diversion on the north and sent Morgan into Ohio for that purpose. Morgan raided the southern and central part of Ohio and worried the North. He was captured and confined in the Ohio Penitentiary. In the latter part of 1863 Capt. Tom Hines and several other officers tunneled their way out of the penitentiary, found a train for Cincinnati, and boarded it. Morgan and Hines took the train as far as the Kentucky shore, where they paid a boy $2 to row them across the river.

In 1864 Morgan was killed by a Confederate soldier. This man, whose name was Campbell, had deserted from the Second Arkansas, and when Johnston surrendered General Govan recognized him among the soldiers who were receiving the captive Confederates. Govan afterward met Campbell in Arkansas, and the soldier said that he had desert-

James J. Andrews

ed because of some injustice done him by his Captain. As the story is told by Capt. Irving A. Buck in his history of "Cleburne and His Command," it is to this effect:

On Sept. 4, 1864, his command was in the vicinity of Greenville, Tenn., and he was informed by a woman that General Morgan and staff had quartered for the night at a house in town, unguarded, and his command was some distance away. Campbell's company surrounded the house, and at about dawn demanded surrender. He observed a man attempting to escape through the shrubbery in the garden, who refused to stop when ordered, upon which Campbell fired and the man fell. In the dim light of breaking dawn the body was not first recognized as that of General Morgan. Campbell asserted that when he fired he had no idea as to whom it was he was shooting at. It is singular that the gallant Morgan should have fallen by the hand of a Confederate deserter.

One of the most astonishing raids of the war was that made on St. Albans, Vt., in 1864. Colonel Bennett H. Young, now or recently the head of the United Confederate Veterans, was the inspiration of the movement. Twenty-one men conducted it, and they went from Canada to St. Albans. Jacob Thompson, who had been Secretary of the Interior in Buchanan's Cabinet, was their inspiration. There were five banks in St. Albans. Young's men divided their party and walked into each bank at a fixed hour, (2:30 in the afternoon.) Each group leveled a revolver at the cashier and demanded all the money in the place. "We are from the Confederacy," they said, "and we'll just take charge of this bank and run it."

The amazed and unarmed bankers handed over $243,000 to the raiders, and that money meant close to a million in view of the exhausted state of Confederate finances. In order to secure themselves, the raiders captured all the men they met, and without firing a shot they marched 300 prisoners to the centre of the town.

Twenty-one men had raided a town of 7,000. The Governor of Vermont offered a reward of $50,000 for the capture of the raiders, dead or alive,

John H. Morgan.

but they all reached Canada in safety, bringing with them the $243,000. Thirteen of them were prosecuted under the neutrality laws; Colonel Young was not indicted, but, hearing that his men were under arrest, he walked into Montreal and gave himself up. It is hardly necessary to say that he was not convicted.

A hapless raider was Colonel Streight, who was sent to cope with Forrest. At the beginning of Sherman's campaign through Georgia he sent Streight on a raid for the purpose of crippling the Confederate cavalry. Forrest met him and destroyed him.

Streight had tried to march around Bragg's army and cut off his communications. Forrest followed him for almost a month and finally demanded his surrender. Streight surrendered only to learn after the capitulation had been made that he outnumbered Forrest. Forrest boasted afterward that he had "won by a pure bluff."

The raids of Grierson, Stoneman, and Wilson are too familiar to need repetition. Grierson's wonderful cavalry movement around the Confederate communications was one of the great deeds of the war; and Wilson's great achievement, if it had been fought in the first year, would have made a deathless name, but by 1864 men had ceased to think of individual accomplishments, and neither Wilson, Stoneman, nor Grierson ever won the fame they deserved.

The Confederate raiders, especially Morgan and Mosby, won a disproportionate eminence. There is one black outstanding record against the Confederacy—Quantrell's raid on Lawrence, Kan., a massacre. It was probably no worse than many of the raids by Union Jayhawkers along the border; the barbarities of that border conflict have never been told and never will be. Nevertheless, the Lawrence raid stands out in history. The brutalities in Missouri and Kansas shamed the war in the East.

Gen. George Stoneman

No partisan ranger in Virginia, on either side, was guilty of the atrocities that were the daily story north of 36:30. Missouri was the Belgium of 1861.

FAMOUS SECRET SERVICE AGENTS

How Belle Boyd Won a Victory for Stonewall Jackson—Exploits of Timothy Webster—Lizzie Van Lew in Richmond—The Boy Spy of the Confederacy.

STONEWALL JACKSON'S Valley campaign was one of the great deeds of history. Not since Napoleon's time have men been so dazzled as they were by that great exploit of his. Yet Stonewall might have gone down the Valley in defeat had it not been for a little college girl named Belle Boyd. On May 23, 1862, after Jackson had routed Banks and driven him in confusion up the line of the Shenandoah, he wrote this letter:

"Miss Belle Boyd: I thank you for myself and for the army for the immense service that you have rendered your country today."

The Union General Shields was quartered at Miss Boyd's house. He held a council of war there. Miss Boyd bored a hole in the floor of her chamber, which was over Shields's room, and lay there with her ear to it throughout the night. The next morning Stonewall Jackson was in full possession of the plans for a great battle, and was able to defeat the Union army.

She kept up her valiant work for the Confederacy until the Union officers began to suspect her, and Jackson ordered her to move from her Shenandoah home to Winchester. She had been arrested by the Federals and had flirted her way to liberty—for she was a pretty girl, despite the libelous photographs of her. In Winchester Jackson conferred upon her a commission as Captain in the Confederate Army. By this time the whole North had become aware of the services she was rendering the Confederacy, and every officer and private was on the alert to get her. Yet she escaped until 1864, when she was caught on a blockade runner. Her captor lost his heart to her, deserted the navy, and married her, and the Prince of Wales, afterward Edward VII., attended the wedding.

Belle Boyd is the most famous of the spies, but there are many others who deserve at least as much fame as she won. One of them was Elizabeth B. Van Lew, who had the incredible courage to act as a Union spy in Richmond throughout the war. There was not a moment during those four years when Lizzie Van Lew could hear a step behind her on the street without expecting to have somebody tap her on the shoulder and say, "You are my prisoner." She did not confine her activities to spying and reporting what she had discovered to the Union Generals; she hid escaped prisoners in her house, she dealt out messages to soldiers in Libby from their homes; her resources were endless. One of her favorite devices was a metal platter with a double bottom, in which she used to pretend to convey food to the prisoners. Once a Confederate soldier, whose suspicion had been aroused, insisted on examining it; but that day Lizzie, who had been expecting some move of this kind, had filled the false bottom not with secret messages but with scalding water, and the soldier dropped it with a shriek.

Lizzie Van Lew had a secret recess in her house, a hiding place for dispatches. Sometimes she would move a hand idly toward this recess, and an hour or two later some old negress, apparently dusting the room, would slip her hand back of the mantel and find a dispatch which would go to Grant that day. It was Lizzie Van Lew who stole the body of Colonel Ulric Dahlgren and smuggled it out of Richmond, one of the most daring exploits of the war.

Rosa B. Greenhow was a Confederate spy in Washington who dazzled the Union in the early days of the war. It was one of her assistants, a Miss Duval, of Washington, who brought Beauregard the first news of McDowell's advance and enabled him and Johnston to foil the Federal plans for the campaign of Bull Run. Mrs. Greenhow sent Miss Duval to Beauregard on July 10, giving him the first news of the contemplated advance, and on July 16 she sent him word of the forces and the contemplated movement of the Union army. He promptly wired the information to Davis, and the word was sent to Johnston, which resulted in his advance and the terrible downfall of the Northern cause.

The Northern Secret Service was technically under the direction of General Lafayette C. Baker, a man without scruple. After the war Baker insisted on taking to himself most of the credit for what had been done in detective work, but as a matter of fact the best work done in the war was done by volunteers, men and women, who were willing to risk a shameful death to serve their country. Many of them were private soldiers; some were enlisted among Allan Pinkerton's detectives. Of these the most famous was Timothy Webster, one of the greatest detectives who ever lived. Webster succeeded in getting the South to believe in him to such an extent that he came near being made the Colonel of an Alabama regiment, and in Baltimore he was a member of the Knights of Liberty. He even became a trusted emissary of the Confederate War Department at Richmond, and at Pittsburgh a Union mob tried to lynch him as a Confederate spy. Nothing saved him but the arrival of Allan Pinkerton, with a drawn revolver, and Webster and Pinkerton backed against the wall and stood off the mob until help arrived. Webster was finally captured in Richmond, and was betrayed by one of his associates, who confessed to a man he supposed to be a Catholic priest. The man was not a priest, but a disguised Confederate soldier. The secrets of the confessional, of course, did not apply in such a case, and the brave spy was hanged. Hattie Lewis, Webster's sweetheart, got an audience with Mrs. Jefferson Davis and begged her, with tears in her eyes, to save the man she loved. Instead, Hattie Lewis herself was convicted of being a Union spy and served a year's imprisonment.

There was one girl who won the rank of Major in the Union Army. She was Pauline Cushman, an actress, who became one of the best and most famous spies in the Union Army. Often and often Major Pauline acted as a sort of advance guard to the Federal Army, Twice the Confederates captured her, but on both occasions she escaped. The first time she came near being released after a first search, but a second revealed the fact that in a hidden recess in her garters there were orders from Thomas. She was about to be hanged when Thomas captured Nashville and saved her. Secretary Stanton commissioned her as Major in the Union Army, and she was the only woman who held that rank except Major Belle Reynolds, the wife of a Captain in the Seventieth Illlinois, who went to the war with her husband and performed such prodigies of valor that Stanton honored her with a commission.

Sam Davis, the boy spy of the Confederacy, left an imperishable record of heroism. He was only 14 when he joined the Confederate service, at first as a private soldier. His talents as a spy were great, and throughout Bragg's long warfare in Tennessee he continually made use of the brave little fellow. Davis was finally betrayed and captured in Nashville. He was taken before General Grenville M. Dodge, whose story of the hearing makes a companion piece to the last days of Nathan Hale. Here is the story as General Dodge tells it:

I took him to my private office and told him it was a very serious charge brought against him; that he was a spy, and from what I found upon his person, he had accurate information in regard to my army, and I must know where he obtained it. I told him he was a young man and did not seem to realize the danger he was in. Up to that time he had said nothing, but then he replied in a most respectful and dignified manner:

"General Dodge, I know the danger of my situation, and I am willing to take the consequences."

I asked him then to give the name of the person from whom he got the information; that I knew it must be some one near headquarters who had given him the plans of the Federal Army. He replied:

"I know that I'll have to die, but I will not tell where I got the information. And there is no power on earth that can make me tell. You are doing your duty as a soldier, and I am doing mine. If I have to die, I do so feeling that I am doing my duty to God and my country."

I pleaded with him and urged him with all the power that I possessed to give me some chance to save his life, for I had discovered that he was a most admirable young fellow,

Miss Pauline Cushman   Miss Lizzie van Lew   Miss Belle Boyd   Allan Pinkerton

with the highest character and strictest integrity. He then said, "It is useless to talk to me. I do not intend to do it. You can court-martial me, but I will not betray the trust reposed in me." He thanked me for the interest I had taken in him, and I sent him back to prison. I immediately called a court-martial to try him.

Even then the boy received offers of liberty if he would betray his confederate. He would not. The only thing he wrote was a short note to his mother saying that he had been captured and was to be hanged and was not afraid to die. As he stood on the scaffold a messenger arrived from General Dodge promising him immunity if he would reveal the identity of his confederate. The rope was around his neck: the boy answered:

"If I had a thousand lives I would lose them all here before I would betray my friends or the confidence of my informant."

Then he turned to the executioner and said casually, "I am ready." The trap was sprung and one of the heroes of the Confederacy was dead. He was then 16 years old.

There was an underground railroad of Confederate sympathizers running through Maryland and Virginia, headed by Custis Grymes of Virginia. He came of the family which gave a wife to George Washington, and many of his emissaries were high-born women. One was a clergyman, the Rev. Dr. Stuart, an irreproachable Episcopalian. When the dashing but hopeless raid on Vermont by a Confederate force in Canada was ordered in 1864 Grymes sent a girl named Olivia Floyd, who concealed the order in her hair. It was the fashion then for women to wear a curly net over their locks, and Olivia hid the documents there and made a wild ride on

a bitter cold night into the lines, where she delivered the orders that resulted in the attack of St. Albans.

General Jim Lane had a woman spy named Elizabeth W. Stiles, whose husband was murdered before her eyes by Quantrell's guerrillas in 1862. Border warfare was merciless; there was something Indian about it. Mrs. Stiles devoted her life to vengeance. She was quite deliberate about it. She went East and put her children in school, and then came back to the West and put herself under Lane's orders. She faced death many a time; once she was arraigned before Sterling Price himself, but she made him believe she was a Confederate spy, and he gave her a horse and firearms and sent her on her way.

One Union spy, Mack Williams, found himself in the Confederate line face to face with his own brother, a Confederate

soldier. "I'm a Yankee spy," said Williams; "you're a rebel. Betray me if you want to; it's your duty." It was a hard and delicate question, but the ties of nature won out over patriotism, and Mack Williams went back into the Union lines unscathed.

General Baker has recorded the fact that for two years a farm near Fairfax Court House was frequented by Union officers, none of whom had the least suspicion that a daughter of the house was a Confederate spy. She was, Baker says, "a young and decidedly good-looking woman, with pleasing, insinuating manners." She appeared to be a violent Union sympathizer, yet at night she used to go out and meet Colorel Mosby and give him the information she had gained from the credulous Union officers. Baker finally caught her by sending a woman spy who gained her confidence.

PROBLEMS THAT CONFRONTED LINCOLN
Taught by Staggering Difficulties of Early Part of His Term, He Became the One Tremendous Figure That Dominated His Epoch.

ONE cannot fully realize the difficulties that beset Abraham Lincoln without taking into account the political situation. To confront such a gigantic disaster as the war would have tried the quality of any man to the utmost. But Lincoln confronted it at the head, not of a disciplined and seasoned party, but of a new party, a heterogeneous mass with no history or traditions and hardly any organization; a wrangling crowd of former enemies, united only on one question; a conglomeration of Whigs, Democrats and Know-Nothings. It is as if the Populists of our time had suddenly been put in power to confront a war. Included in the ranks were all the cranks and fanatics in the land, and all those demagogues and self-seekers who flock to a new party because they are too well known and understood to get offices out of the old one. So far as Lincoln came in contact with it during his early months in Washington, it presented itself to him chiefly as an appetite; and it so beset him with demands for office at that time that he had little time left to consider the needs of the country. Its leaders, newly brought together from the wreck of hostile parties, suspected and plotted against each other, and all sought Lincoln's ear.

He himself was not the Lincoln he became. He was inexperienced and made many mistakes; but his greatness largely consisted in the power to grow, and the bungling novice of 1861 grew colossal in the flames of war; "iron-like, his temper grew by blows," as Tom Taylor said of him in that never-to-be-forgotten confession of Punch's. But at the beginning an inexperienced President, ignorant of much that an older statesman would have known, met the greatest peril his country ever faced at the head of a confused and gelatinous party.

Naturally he fell at once into the hands of his Secretary of State, Seward, and for awhile was guided by a man greatly his inferior in wisdom, but universally supposed to be his superior. Yet, even at the beginning, he gave signs of the Lincoln he was to become. Toward the close of his first month in office Seward drew up a paper in which he proposed that Lincoln should turn the Government

Abraham Lincoln

over to him. It did not occur to Seward that there was anything surprising about the proposal; he assumed, as did everybody else, that Lincoln was not only inexperienced, but weak and helpless, and would be only too glad to have the responsibility taken off his shoulders. He

also suggested in this paper that the impending war with the South be headed off by a war with France and Spain, perhaps with England and Russia as well, on the theory that a foreign war would reunite the nation.

Lincoln answered this paper the same

day, meeting Seward's propositions with a gentle refusal. The final proposal, that Seward should take the direction of the Government out of Lincoln's hands and carry out the policy he outlined, Lincoln met with the simple words, which nevertheless carried a hint of the coming Lincoln with them, "If this must be done, I must do it." Seward had his lesson; he never brought the subject up again, and from that time he was a loyal and faithful subordinate.

Not all of the Cabinet were that. Three of them—Seward, Smith, and Bates—had been Whigs; four—Chase, Cameron, Welles, and Blair—Democrats. All came into the Cabinet viewing the President with curiosity and aloofness. Lincoln knew the character of Cameron when he appointed him; he told Gustave Koerner and Norman B. Judd that to refuse the War portfolio to Cameron would alienate Pennsylvania, whose votes he needed. Koerner told him that Cameron was a corrupt and tricky politician. "I know, I know," groaned Lincoln, "but how am I to get along if that State should oppose my Administration?" "He was very much distressed," records Koerner in his memoirs.

Getting rid of Cameron and appointing Stanton in his place was almost the first sign the President gave of the new Lincoln. "Conscious," says Henry Greenleaf Pearson, in his life of Wadsworth, "of the train of blunders into which his administrative inexperience and insecurity had led him, he had now, at the long last, turned into the upward path." He knew, undoubtedly, of the fierce contempt that Stanton entertained for him, but he knew that Stanton could serve the country, and with no personal feeling whatever he appointed him. Stanton had been writing letters to Buchanan portraying "the painful imbecility of Lincoln" and the "venality and corruption" in the departments, which could not be altered "until Jeff Davis turns out the whole concern." "In less than thirty days," he told Buchanan, "Davis will be in possession of Washington." He had been writing to McClellan urging him to seize the Government and proclaim himself dictator. After he entered the Cabinet he still abused Lincoln in private for awhile. Colonel Lamon says Stanton "usually spoke of Lincoln to public men with a withering sneer." "I found him a low, cunning clown," said Stanton. This abuse was echoed in the Republican Party. Once Lamon found the President lying on a sofa, greatly disturbed. Jumping to his feet, he cried out, "You know it was always my ambition to be President, but look at me! I wish I had never been born! I would rather be dead than thus abused in the house of my friends!"

The Cabinet was at swords' points. Blair told Lincoln he must get rid of Cameron at once, that he was unfit and incompetent; but when he did, Blair was so disgusted that, instead of getting a man like Ben Wade, "he picked up this black terrier," Stanton. Blair was true and loyal to Lincoln, as were Bates, Welles and Usher, who succeeded Smith. But Seward and Chase distrusted each other deeply. Stanton, who had urged McClellan to become dictator, now intrigued against him constantly, while writing him gushing letters; and Seward became McClellan's champion. At last, in September, 1862, Seward was overborne by Stanton's vehemence and consented to sacrifice the General.

In December, 1862, a caucus of Republican Senators formulated a demand that Seward be forced to resign, and that the policy of the Government be decided in future by a majority vote of the Cabinet. They believed that Seward was running the Government, and that the President was his puppet. A committee, headed by Senator Collamer of Vermont, waited on the President with this demand, and Seward immediately resigned. Lincoln, manifesting no anger, asked the committee to meet the Cabinet next day, Dec. 20. They did so, and Senator Fessenden of Maine bluntly told the President that "no one in particular should absorb and direct the whole executive action." Collamer said the Senate wanted "united counsels, combined wisdom and energetic action"; Grimes, Sumner and Trumbull demanded Seward's head.

Postmaster General Blair spoke out manfully, telling the Senators that the President had the responsibility, and should have the right to ask the opinions of all his Cabinet, of some of them, of one of them, or of none at all, as he saw fit. Secretary Chase felt himself in a false position; he saw that he might be suspected of engineering this amazing performance, and he tendered his resignation. The President was delighted. "I see my way clear," he said. Stanton offered his resignation, too, to be in fashion. "You may go to your department," said the President cavalierly; "I don't want yours." Three days later he rejected the resignations of Seward—and Chase. By thus putting them in the same boat he drew the fangs of Chase's friends in the Senate; they could not pursue the matter further.

By the beginning of 1863 the Cabinet had discovered that the mild-mannered President was their master. When Hooker was removed from the command of the Army of the Potomac the President asked the Cabinet to suggest a successor. Various names were suggested and discussed, but the Cabinet soon learned that the order putting Meade in command had already been issued. "We were consulted after the fact," grimly recorded Secretary Welles in his diary, with, however, an evident relish. At the end of that year, summing it up, Welles declared that the Cabinet, if discordant with itself, was united as regarded the President.

He was not quite right. Chase was scheming to get the Presidential nomination. He had already said that no President should have more than one term, and that qualities different from Lincoln's would be needed in the next four years. In February there was published a secret circular sent out by Senator Pomeroy of Kansas in the interest of the Chase boom. The President was hurt, though Chase tried to make it appear that he knew nothing of it.

This publication killed the boom; the circular was meant to aid. In Chase's State, Ohio, the Legislature immediately passed resolutions indorsing Lincoln for another term. Thus repudiated at home, Chase was obliged to take himself out of the race. At this time the self-contained and silent Attorney General, Bates, unbosomed himself to Welles on the subject of his colleagues, declaring that Seward "had much cunning but little wisdom, was no lawyer and no statesman," and that Chase was "not well versed in law principles even— was not sound nor of good judgment."

Soon after Chase left the Cabinet the President asked his own loyal and devoted friend, Blair, for his resignation. Blair cheerfully surrendered his office, since his chief desired it. Long afterward the President told Welles that it was done to bring Chase's friends into line; they were sulking in the campaign because Chase was out of the Cabinet and Blair, his enemy, remained in it. There were moments when Chase seemed to understand Lincoln a little better. Once he wrote to a friend that if to his kindliness and good sense the President joined "strong will and energetic action, there would be little left to wish for in him." But these lapses into clear vision were rare with Chase.

Blair and his father directed the campaign for Lincoln's renomination. Their plan was to have every State declare for Lincoln in advance of the convention, thus pre-empting the field and concentrating attention on a single candidate. This manoeuvre outgeneraled the opposition, and Lincoln swept the convention. The malcontents held a third party convention and nominated General Frémont, but it was soon evident to him that his candidacy could only result in a Democratic victory, and he withdrew.

In the Summer of 1864 a secret movement was started in the Republican Party to compel the withdrawal of both Lincoln and Frémont and the nomination of a new candidate. It was still sincerely believed that Lincoln was irresolute and weak, and this movement enlisted many of the leading men of the party, honest but mistaken patriots. Horace Greeley, Whitelaw Reid, Richard Smith, Charles Sumner, Lucius Robinson, and many other names of light and leading are to be found in this list. Sherman's capture of Atlanta summarily ended their endeavor, and all the Union men fell in line behind Lincoln.

One day in April, 1865, Assistant Secretary of War Dana received a telegram from Portland, Me., saying that Jacob Thompson, the Confederate Envoy in Canada who had instigated the raid on St. Albans, Vt., would pass through Portland that night. It came from the Provost Marshal, who asked for orders.

When this telegram was shown to Stanton, he said, "Arrest him," and then added, "No, better ask the President."

"No, I rather think not," was Lincoln's answer. "When you have got an elephant by the hind leg, and he is trying to run away, it is best to let him run." Dana reported this answer to Stanton, who angrily snorted, "Oh, stuff!" That night Dana was awakened by an official, who said, "Mr. Dana, the President is dead, and Mr. Stanton directs you to arrest Jacob Thompson." Mr. Stanton, in issuing this reversal of the President's wishes, must have just come from that scene at Lincoln's death-bed, where he had dramatically said, laying down the dead man's hand which he had been holding, "He had belonged to the ages." It is gratifying to know that his order came too late; Thompson had escaped.

With the President there was only one question: how can the Union be saved? To save it he made every sacrifice to hold the border States in line. He was bitterly abused by the abolitionists and Eastern radicals generally, but he was vindicated by the result; the border States had such faith in him that not even the preliminary emancipation proclamation of 1862 could disturb it, and when the five leading free States, including the President's own, deserted him in the election of that year, a Union majority in the House was secured by the votes of the border States and New England.

To save the Union he did not scruple to play politics. When the Thirteenth Amendment was trembling in the balance, he obtained the votes of three Democrats by sending Dana to them with a promise that they should have anything they wanted. Two demanded Internal Revenue Collectorships, one an office in the New York Custom House. The demands were granted; the amendment passed. It had to be ratified by two-thirds of the States, and the Administration was short one State. Nevada was admitted to the Union to furnish the necessary vote. Some who knew what kind of territory Nevada was protested. "It is easier," answered Lincoln inflexibly, "to admit Nevada than to raise another million of soldiers."

SOUTHERN GOVERNMENT'S PROBLEMS

Jefferson Davis and His Colleagues, Though Not Confronted by Opposition Party as Was Abraham Lincoln, Had Other Difficulties in Their Paths.

THE Southern Government had its own troubles and defects, and they had a great deal to do with the fall of the Confederacy, but they were not similar to the Northern Government's. President Davis did not have to contend with the same difficulties that beset President Lincoln—hostility in Congress, division in the Cabinet, and an anti-administration party at the polls. Though, in his conversation with Surgeon Craven in his prison after the war, he talked of "the anti-administration party," there was none.

There were individuals who disapproved his policy, but there was no party. The situation in the Confederacy resembled that in the Colonies at the time of the Revolution; the thoughts and energies of the population were taken up with the war, and there were no party divisions. Only once was there any approach to a political test of the Administration's standing. That was when a distinguished South Carolinian, ex-Senator Robert Barnwell Rhett, ran for Congress in Charleston on a platform hostile to Davis; he was defeated.

Vice President Stephens was antagonistic to the President, and in his State, Georgia, political sentiment was largely with him. The friends of General Joseph E. Johnston resented the President's treatment of that officer, and many of the Confederate statesmen criticised Davis in private. But there was little public criticism of him, and no party or faction against him.

The mistakes of the Northern Administration were as much those of the Cabinet as of Lincoln; those of the Southern Administration rest on the shoulders of Davis, for he was supreme. His Cabinet consisted chiefly of mediocre men, who obeyed him and did not dare to advise him (Benjamin being a shining exception); the Confederate Congress simply registered his decrees and had no ideas of its own. The history of the Confederate Government is a history of the acts and policies of one man, President Davis.

Before the war Davis was popular with the Northern Democracy, his popularity was growing, and he was likely to be President of the United States. Indeed, as Blaine points out in his "Twenty Years of Congress," he might have been nominated in 1860 but for the split in the party. "No man," says Blaine, "gave up more than Mr. Davis in joining the revolt against the Union. In his farewell words to the Senate there was a tone of moderation and dignity not unmixed with regretful and tender emotions." He was universally regarded as a statesman and a great man, and the defects of character which the Presidency subsequently disclosed were unknown. There was no opposition to his election first as Provisional President and then as Constitutional President of the Confederacy. In the short time that elapsed between the two elections nothing had occurred to shake the popular confidence in him.

"He would have made an admirable President in time of peace," says General Oates, in his "War Between the Union and the Confederacy." "He had not the peculiar gifts or traits of genius essential to success as President of the Confederacy."

The chief of his defects were his unyielding obstinacy and his resentment of advice. When to these were joined a judgment not always correct and the government of his mind by prejudice, not even his pure and unselfish devotion to his cause and his honest determination to serve it to the utmost could save him from mistakes injurious to that cause. Stephens, in the diary he kept in prison after the war, wrote:

He proved himself deficient in developing and directing the resources of the country, in finance and diplomacy, as well as in military affairs. His greatest failure in statesmanship was either in not understanding the popular aim and impulses, or in attempting to direct the movement to different ends from those contemplated by the people who had intrusted him with power.

After the Battle of Bull Run, Davis was at the head of a united people, while there was discontent at the North with the policy of the Lincoln Administration. "At that time," says Stephens, "if Mr. Davis had had those high qualities that mark the great statesmen, how easily he could have controlled events." The South, he says, had no desire for independence except as a last resort, and if Davis had been a statesman he could "have shaped events so as to effect a settlement that would have been satisfactory to the great majority of the people of both sections."

Instead, one of the first things he did was to follow Lincoln's example, and ask for a suspension of the writ of habeas corpus, the very thing that was doing much to alienate the North from Lincoln. Then he demanded a conscription, and in thus following the example of the North, according to Stephens, he dissipated the difference which existed in the popular mind, North and South, between the two Governments.

But the chief trouble was temperamental. "I wish my friends would cease to advise me," he cried, before the war had well begun, and he acted on that wish more and more as it went on. Th Cabinet, says John W. Du Bose in his life of Wheeler, "soon and easily learned to know the unconquerable aversion of their chief to the opinions of other men." Pollard, in his "Lost Cause," declares that Davis was governed by his wife, and tells how she caused him to dismiss the Quartermaster General because his wife had criticised Mrs. Davis's figure. "Those who knew Mr. Davis best," says Pollard, "testified that he was the weakest of men, on certain sides of his character, and that he had a romantic sentimentalism, which made him the prey of preachers and women."

Weak on other sides of his character he certainly was not. He had, as Pollard admits, "certain elegant an ' brilliant accomplishments, which dazzled the multitude, confused the world in its judgment of his merits, and gave him a singular reputation, in which admirers and censors were strangely mingled." One of the qualities of greatness is the ability to choose good subordinates; this Davis had and Lincoln had not. Except in a few cases, such as that of Hood, Davis made no mistakes in the selection of his generals, as Lincoln so often did; and among all his appointees there was not a single instance of treachery.

Seward has been ridiculed for believing that the war would last only a few weeks, but Davis had the same idea. As he went to Montgomery to take the Provisional Presidency he made speeches announcing with calm certitude the invasion and destruction of the Northern cities, where, he said, "food for the sword and torch await our armies."

His unyielding stubbornness at first served his cause well. When Albert Sidney Johnston abandoned Tennessee a howl rose against that splendid general from all over the western part of the Con-

Jefferson Davis.

federacy. He was denounced as an incompetent, and delegations visited Davis demanding his head. The President listened calmly, and firmly replied: "If Sidney Johnston is not a general, I have none to give you." There were similar denunciations of Lee, but they fell on the President like waves on a rock.

The conscription bore with fearful severity upon the South. From it were exempted all men who owned fifteen or more slaves, and even men who did not have so many, but had means and influence, could get themselves detailed in various ways so as to escape the conscription. The soldiers in the ranks growled, and there were murmurs that it was a "rich man's war and a poor man's fight."

The Confederate currency was ruined, and General Oates charges that its ruin was hastened by "an unpatriotic speculation" on the part of Secretary of War Seddon:

Virginia had commissioners to assess the value of things taken from persons by the Government. They had been assessing values at twenty to one and the producers seemed satisfied to let their produce go at that. But Mr. James A. Seddon, the Secretary of War, directed or suggested to the commissioners to appraise wheat at $40 per bushel, instead of $20, and they did it. He sold a large crop of wheat which he himself had grown on his plantation on the James River at $40 a bushel, and several of his neighbors followed his example. This action of the War Minister in Davis's Cabinet sent prices skyward, making the price of every commodity at $40 in Confederate money for one dollar of real value. This was in August, 1864, and in the month of January, 1865, the currency had depreciated, until it was sixty to one. It would take $60 of Confederate money to pay for a breakfast at an ordinary hotel.

When the collision between Grant and Pemberton in Mississippi was becoming imminent, Joseph E. Johnston advised the President to transfer Holmes's army, 50,000 strong, from Arkansas to Mississippi. Pemberton had 25,000 and Grant only 46,000, and Holmes and Pemberton could fall on Grant and crush him. Pemberton could then hold the Mississippi and Holmes could invade Missouri with excellent prospects.

Though Holmes's army was idle, no enemy confronting it, Davis rejected the suggestion. If he had accepted it, the Vicksburg campaign might have ended very differently. Instead, he detached 9,000 men from Bragg's army in Tennessee, which was already much weaker than the Union Army confronting it, and sent them to Pemberton over Johnston's protest. They never did Pemberton any good, only weakened Bragg still further. Davis, unfortunately, believed himself a general; in fact, he had accepted the Presidency with reluctance, preferring a command in the field.

But the army did not fully lose confidence in the Administration until Davis's fatuous and suicidal error in the case of Joseph E. Johnston. That General had managed with consummate skill, as all his Union adversaries testify, the campaign through Georgia. He had worn and harassed Sherman, fighting him continually, but always avoiding a decisive battle, and now the time was coming toward which all the movements of his artful campaign had been directed. Sherman was close to Atlanta, and about to cross Peachtree Creek. Johnston knew

Sherman's methods, and knew that he would scatter his army in motion. He prepared to assail the parts that were crossing the stream, drive them into it, and then hurl his whole army upon the other parts. His first assault was to be delivered upon the part commanded by Thomas. His preparations were all made, and Hardee and Hood had received orders to be ready to attack at a moment's notice. At this crisis Johnston received the following telegram from Adjutant General Cooper:

I am directed by the Secretary of War to inform you that as you have failed to arrest the advance of the enemy to the vicinity of Atlanta, far in the interior of Georgia, and express no confidence that you can defeat or repel him, you are hereby relieved from the Army and Department of Tennessee, which you will immediately turn over to General Hood.

"Thus perished the Southern Confederacy," sadly comments John W. Du Bose. "One of the most prominent historians of the Confederacy," says General Hooker, "ascribes the misfortunes of the Lost Cause to the relief of General Johnston. I do not think this, but it certainly contributed materially to hasten its collapse." Sherman was delighted. He afterward wrote:

At this critical moment the Confederate Government rendered us a most valuable service. Being dissatisfied with the Fabian policy of General Johnston, it relieved him, and General Hood was substituted to command the Confederate Army. The character of the leader is a large factor in the game of war, and I confess I was pleased at this change.

Hood did not want it; he, with two of his three corps commanders, Hardee and Stewart, united in a telegram begging Davis to put off the change until after the battle, but Davis never took advice. Hood, who was not a Fabian, made his assault, and Sherman defeated him and entered Atlanta. Later Hood conceived the mad idea that he could lure Sherman away from Georgia by marching up to Tennessee and attacking Thomas. Sherman paid no attention to the move, and Thomas met the enfeebled and shrunken Confederate Army and pulverized it. After that everybody could see that the war was virtually over.

Davis, of course, was as blindly confident as ever, and as sure that his acts were superlatively wise. He visited the army, to be greeted with cries of " Give us Johnston! " He made a speech to the soldiers, predicting that McClellan would be elected President, that as a result the North would be divided between the East and West, and that thus the war would end, leaving the Confederacy triumphant. On his return trip he met his brother-in-law, General Richard Taylor, who had been traveling through the Gulf States. Taylor was blunt and candid. He said he had found the citizens "universally depressed and disheartened," and the soldiers dissatisfied both with Johnston's removal and the subsequent conduct of affairs. Davis was surprised and resentful, but did not change his policy, though Gov. Brown, Vice President Stephens and Robert Toombs were on the point of mutiny, and their State, Georgia, was threatening to call a Constitutional Convention, recall her citizens from the army and break with the Confederate Government.

Congress plucked up courage to pass a resolution calling for Johnston's restoration, but the President merely wrote a message, saying that Johnston would never have another command. He did not send it, however, and afterward, when Hood's wild move on Nashville had ruined and all but destroyed the army, he had to restore Johnston because there was nothing else to do. It was too late; the Confederacy was dead. It had become indeed the Lost Cause.

FOREIGN ENEMIES OF THE UNION

Napoleon III. Most Menacing Among Them, Though England Has Received Credit for Heading Foes of North in Europe.

ONE of the greatest perils that confronted the Union in the early stages of the war was European recognition of the independence of the Confederacy; and as time went on it became evident that intervention on behalf of the South would immediately follow. The peril did not begin to fade until after the Battle of Gettysburg; and in 1862 we were within an ace of it; it was touch-and-go. Napoleon III. was the enemy of the Union fully as much as Jefferson Davis, and was fully as dangerous.

He was the head and front of the European conspiracy against the North. In what has been written of that phase of the war the part played by England looms disproportionately large, but the reason is simple, and it is not that England's part was the leading one. It is that the United States had expected England's sympathy, and was outraged at not receiving it. Hence the indignant writers and orators who have dealt with the question have exhausted language concerning England's attitude and have dismissed France's attitude briefly.

At the beginning Lord Palmerston's attitude toward this country was one of complete indifference; he cared not which side won. There were even some evidences of a carelessly kindly feeling toward the North in Lord John Russell's attitude. These two men headed the Ministry; they had agreed in 1859 that whichever of them was made Prime Minister should send for the other, who was pledged to serve under him. The sentiment in the English aristocracy favored the South, that in the middle and lower classes favored the North.

But Napoleon from the first was actively hostile, and he devoted much energy to getting England and Russia to join him in what he described as mediation " on a basis of separation "—in other words, intervention, for the purpose of establishing the Confederacy; or, in plain words, war, for that is what it would have come to. The Palmerston-Russell Ministry early agreed to act in concert with France on all matters connected with the United States, and when Napoleon broached this plan it readily assented; but Russia refused. Not only did Russia refuse, but Alexander II. ranged himself definitely on the side of the Union and made a significant and threatening gesture toward the other powers by ostentatiously sending two fleets to American waters. This hint was not to be mistaken, and the French ardor cooled.

We had another ally besides Alexander II.; we had the working classes of England. Charles Francis Adams, the younger, says that one of the greatest battles of the war was fought in Lancashire, where the Confederacy met a fatal defeat. The struggle in Lancashire decided the supremacy of the Union. The Lancashire workmen and their families were among the unnamed heroes of the war. The great Lancashire cotton famine, caused by the blockade of the South, lasted three years; cotton was at a premium of 200 in Liverpool; the looms were idle and men saw their wives and children brought to the verge of starvation; but they stood by the Union, though the war measures of the Union were destroying them, and stood by it

Emperor Alexander II

Henry John Temple, Lord Palmerston

for no other reason than that they believed in the abolition of slavery. And, with this menace behind him and the Czar's guns scowling at him from New York and San Francisco, Palmerston found his enthusiasm for Napoleon's policy fading away.

Over and over again Napoleon tried to convert the Czar and spur England to his aid, and in the latter object he came close to success; he never had a chance with the first. Unable to carry out his project alone, he did the next best thing; he defied the Monroe Doctrine and took advantage of our preoccupation with the South to land an army in Mexico, found an empire there and place the Austrian Archduke Maximilian on the throne, supported by French bayonets.

As early as February, 1861, Russell was on the lookout for a rupture. "Supposing," he wrote Lord Lyons, the British Minister, " that Mr. Lincoln, acting under bad advice, should endeavor to provide excitement for the public mind by raising questions with Great Britain, Her Majesty's Government need feel no hesitation as to the policy they would pursue." He then outlined that policy; he would " warn a government which was making capital out of blustering demonstrations that

our patience might be tried too far."

This dispatch is a mystery. Nothing in Lord Lyons's communications had supplied the least warrant for it. Yet Lord John Russell wrote like a prophet. A month later Lincoln was in office and was receiving that " bad advice " which Russell anticipated; Seward was instructing him, in a patronizing way, that he should, in Russell's words, " provide excitement for the public mind by raising questions with Great Britain "—even by declaring war upon her. Lincoln had the wisdom to disregard the " bad advice." Had Russell received from private sources information of which Lyons was ignorant concerning Seward's intentions?

The European nations made great haste to recognize the belligerency of the Confederates. England, with great discourtesy, recognized them on the day before the American Minister, Charles Francis Adams, arrived on her shores to present the Union case. The Czar stood out and refused recognition.

On Nov. 9, 1861, an event occurred which brought England and America to the verge of war—the famous " Trent Affair." James Murray Mason and John Slidell, Confederate envoys to England, were voyaging thither on the British mail steamer Trent, when she was overhauled

by the San Jacinto, an American war vessel. The American commander, Charles Wilkes, was a headstrong, illbalanced, egotistical officer. He searched the British ship, took the envoys prisoners, with their two secretaries, and carried them to Boston, where they were imprisoned in Fort Warren.

Instantly England was aflame with anger. "The people," wrote Charles Mackay to Seward, "are frantic with rage, and were the country polled I fear nine hundred and ninety-nine men out of a thousand would declare for war. Lord Palmerston cannot resist the impulse if he would. If he submits to the insult to the flag his Ministry is doomed—it would not last a fortnight." There was no cable in those days, and nothing was known of the English fury on this side of the water. Here the people were equally excited; no battle of the war was received with more uproarious joy than Wilkes's foolish act. He was the hero of the hour; Secretary Welles congratulated him, and the House of Representatives passed a joint resolution asking the President to give him a gold medal, and other resolutions asking the President to order Mason and Slidell into close confinement in retaliation for similar treatment inflicted by the Confederates on Colonels Michael Corcoran and A. M. Wood. The Senate shelved them.

Russell's first dispatch to Lord Lyons on receiving the news of this event was so violent and provocative that Prince Albert, when the dispatch was submitted to the Queen, toned it down. It was the last public act the Prince ever performed. Lord Lyons, always the staunch friend of the United States, acted with his customary judgment and delicacy; he refrained from calling on Seward and saw no American official, so that there would be no chance of any awkward discussions or explanations, until he could hear from home. He would make no demand on the United States for fear that it would increase our difficulties.

When he did hear from Earl Russell, it was to the effect that this country must immediately surrender the envoys and make a suitable apology, and seven days were given us; at the end of that time, if the United States had not complied, he was to leave the country. Meanwhile, the Palmerston Government, though this Russell did not say, was making active preparations for war.

Yet Russell's action was not as provocative as might appear. He instructed Lyons not to take this demand to Seward nor read it to him, but to communicate its purport informally in conversation. Lyons was so much our friend that he was sure to do this in the gentlest and most tactful way, and this he did. He told Seward that he hoped the United States would of its own accord, and without demand from England, offer the proper reparation; "and that it was in order to facilitate such an arrangement," as he wrote Russell, in reporting the conversation, "that I had come to him without any written demand, or even any written paper at all, in my hand; that if there was a prospect of attaining this object I was willing to be guided by him as to the conduct on my part which would render its attainment most easy."

Seward seems to have had doubts

from the first about the correctness of Wilkes's performance, though Postmaster General Blair was the only member of the Cabinet who had raised his voice in condemnation of it; all the others were enthusiastic over it. He "received my communication seriously and with dignity, but without any manifestation of dissatisfaction," Lyons wrote. Just as the seven days were expiring he made the required explanation (it was scarcely an apology) and surrendered the envoys.

From that time the attitude of the English Government was hostile to the North, and became increasingly so throughout 1862. Confederate privateers, including the famous Alabama, were fitted out in English ports and sent from there to prey on American commerce. Meanwhile, Spain was going as far as she dared in embarrassing and thwarting our attempt to maintain the blockade, letting blockade runners into her Cuban ports while denying their pursuers the right to enter, and doing other annoying things. By 1863 she went so far as to give notice of her intention to extend her jurisdiction six miles from the Cuban coast instead of the customary marine league. Seward replied that we "could not submit to a menace, especially at such a time as this," and as the battle of Gettysburg and the English change in attitude happened just at this time Spain did not press the point.

After McClellan's defeat on the Peninsula, Palmerston and Russell gradually yielded to Napoleon's views. A Cabinet meeting was called for Oct. 23, 1862, at which the subject of intervention was to be taken up in earnest. The United States was never in such danger on the eve of any battle; and nothing saved us from intervention except the jealousy between Palmerston and Gladstone, the Chancellor of the Exchequer. They were rivals and on bad terms, and Gladstone had repeatedly been on the point of resignation. Gladstone, knowing of what was going to happen on the 23d, made his celebrated speech at Newcastle on the 7th, in which he said: "Jefferson Davis and the other leaders have made an army; they are making, it appears, a navy; and they have made what is more than either, they have made a nation."

This was taken everywhere as foreshadowing intervention, just as Gladstone meant it to be. When intervention came, he would get the credit, not Palmerston; and meanwhile, as a member of the Government, he had committed Palmerston to intervention beyond recall. Palmerston determined to checkmate him; the Premier abandoned the intervention policy on the spot and sent Sir George Lewis, the Minister of War, to Hereford as his spokesman. There Lewis made a speech flatly controverting Gladstone; the Chancellor's speech promptly lost all its significance and became an individual indiscretion in the public mind; and the Cabinet meeting of the 23d was never held. It had been a close call for the Union.

The danger was over only for the moment, but now Russia took decisive action on behalf of the Union. She had been our steady friend throughout. It was from the Czar that Lincoln first learned of the efforts of Napoleon to form a coalition against us, early in 1861. He then told us that we could rely on his friendship; he had refused to enter the coalition, as he did every time Napoleon proposed it. In October, 1862, Napoleon changed the form of his proposal, suggesting mediation and a truce, but again the Czar broke up the scheme. On June 25, 1862, Seward exultantly wrote to John Bigelow:

Between you and myself alone, I have a belief that the European State, whichever one it may be, that commits itself to intervention anywhere in North America, will sooner or later fetch up in the arms of a native of an Oriental country not especially distinguished for amiability of manners or temper * * * It might perhaps be well if it were known in Europe that we are no longer alarmed by demonstrations of interference.

Soon after this, according to Andrew G. Curtin, American Minister to Russia, to whom Prince Gortchakoff showed the correspondence in the imperial archives at St. Petersburg, the Czar became more definite in his expressions. In a letter which Curtin saw he informed Napoleon that not only would he join no coalition, but that he would reserve freedom of action to proceed as he deemed necessary under the circumstances. Following this, in the Winter of 1863, a Russian fleet appeared in the harbor of New York and another in the harbor of San Francisco, bearing sealed orders.

There was no doubt anywhere in the North what this meant, and the nation went wild with joy. The Russian officers were feasted and honored and paraded about with the utmost ostentation, for the impressment of whom it might concern. From that time on the talk of intervention began to vanish.

What the sealed orders were will probably never be officially made known; it makes little difference, since the effect desired by the Czar was produced on England and France. But Admiral Farragut and the Russian Admiral became friends, and in the course of a conversation during his stay in New York Harbor the Russian told Farragut that his orders were to break the seals the moment the United States became involved in war with any European nation. To Bayard Taylor, who was Secretary of Legation in St. Petersburg at this time, Gortchakoff showed an order, written in the Czar's own hand, directing the Admiral to report to President Lincoln in that contingency. President Lincoln told one of his confidants, Senator Harlan, that he had sought early in 1862 to learn the Czar's attitude in case we were attacked by England or France, and that to his envoy, Simon Cameron, the Czar replied that in such a case the friendship of Russia for the United States would be shown "in a decisive manner." "We desire," said the Czar on another occasion, "above all things the maintenance of the American Union as one indivisible nation."

The gratitude of the United States continued throughout the war and for some time afterward. When the Czar narrowly escaped assassination, in 1866, a naval vessel was sent to Russia, bearing Assistant Secretary of the Navy Fox with a resolution of Congress congratulating him on the escape. Oliver Wendell Holmes wrote his stirring poem, "Who Was Our Friend When the World Was Our Foe?" Russia wished to get rid of Alaska, then supposed to be a barren waste, and we took it off her hands. But the debt was too great; we never really discharged it.

TWO FAMOUS PROSE DESCRIPTIONS

What Carl Schurz Saw at Gettysburg as Told by Himself —Draper's Picture of the Devastated South After the War.

GETTYSBURG.
From "The Reminiscences of Carl Schurz."

AND then came that interval of perfect stillness of which most of the descriptions of the battle of Gettysburg has so much to say. That the battle should have come to a short stop would have surprised nobody. But when that stop lengthened from minute to minute, from half hour to half hour, and when it settled down into a tranquillity like the peaceful and languid repose of a warm midsummer morning in which one might expect to hear the ringing of the village church bells, there was something ominous, something uncanny, in these strange, unexpected hours of profound silence so sharply contrasting with the bloody horrors which had preceded and which were sure to follow them.

Even the light-hearted soldiers, who would ordinarily never lose an opportunity for some outbreak of a hilarious mood, even in a short moment of respite in a fight, seemed to feel the oppression. Some sat silently on the ground munching their hardtack, while others stretched themselves out seeking sleep, which they probably would have found more readily had the cannon been thundering at a distance.

The officers stood together in little groups discussing with evident concern what this long-continued calm might mean. Could it be that Lee, whose artillery in long rows of batteries had been silently frowning at us all the morning, had given up his intention to make another great attack? If not, why had he not begun it at an earlier hour, which unquestionably would have been more advantageous to him?

Suddenly the riddle was solved. About 1 o'clock the long hush was broken by the booming of two guns fired in rapid succession on the enemy's right, where Longstreet's corps stood. And at once this signal was answered by all the batteries of the Confederate Army, about 130 cannon, that could be brought to bear upon Cemetery Hill and the ridge joining it to the Round Tops. Instantly about eighty pieces of our artillery—as many as could usefully be posted in our line facing west and northwest—took up the challenge, and one of the grandest artillery duels in the history of wars followed.

All that I had ever read in battle stories of the booming of heavy guns outthundering the thunders of heaven and making the earth tremble, and almost stopping one's breath by the concussions of the air—was here made real, in terrific effect. The roar was so incessant and at times so deafening that when I wished to give an order to one of my officers I had to put my hands to my mouth as a speaking trumpet and shout my words into his ear.

Fortunately the enemy had aimed their artillery a little too high, so that most of its missiles passed over our heads. But enough of them struck the ground in the cemetery and exploded there, to scatter death and destruction among the men immediately around, and to shatter gravestones and blow up ammunition caissons. But as most of them flew over us, rushing, screaming, whirring, and as they burst above, and sent down their deadly fragments, they added to the hellish din a peculiarly malicious noise of their own.

How would the men endure this frightful experience? One of the hardest trials of the courage and steadfastness of the soldier is to stand still and be shot at without being able to reply. This ordeal is especially severe when the soldier is under a heavy artillery fire, which, although less dangerous than that of musketry, is more impressive on the nerves. It bewilders the mind of the bravest with a painful sense of helplessness as against a tremendous power, and excites to peculiar vivacity the not unnatural desire to get into a safer place out of range.

As a matter of course we ordered the troops to lie down flat on the ground, so as to present the smallest possible target. But when I observed the effect of the dropping of a shell right into the midst of a regiment which caused some uneasy commotion, I thought it my duty to get upon my feet and look after it. I found that it had a very steadying and cheering effect upon the men to see me quietly walking up and down in front smoking a cigar. I could not speak to them, for the incessant roar of the cannonade would not let them hear me. But I noticed that many of them returned my smile in a sort of confidential way when I happened to catch their eyes, as if to say: "It is not jolly, but we, too, will not be frightened by it."

Indeed, it was not jolly, for I felt as if the enemy's projectiles rushing over me were so near that I might have touched them with my riding-whip held up at full length of my arm. But, observing the good effect of my promenade in front, I invited, by gesture, some of the regimental officers to do likewise. They promptly obeyed, although, I suppose, they liked the stroll no more than I did.

* * * * * *

And then came forth that famous scene which made the battle of Gettysburg more dramatic than any other event of the civil war, and which more nearly approached the conception of what a battle is in the imagination of persons who have never seen one. I will describe only what we observed of it from the crest of Cemetery Hill.

From a screen of woods opposite our left centre emerged a long line of Confederate infantry, mounted officers in front and behind; and then another, and another—about 15,000 men. The alignment was perfect. The battle flags fluttered gayly over the bayonets glittering in the sunlight. The spectacle has often been truly likened to a grand holiday parade on a festive ground. A mile of open field separated them from our line of defense.

They had hardly traversed one-tenth of that distance when they became fully aware that those of them who had counted upon our artillery having been much disabled had grievously deceived themselves. No sooner had the attacking column appeared on the open than our batteries, which had in the meantime been re-formed and well supplied with ammunition, opened upon them from the front and from the right and left, with a terrific fire. Through our fieldglasses we could distinctly see the gaps torn in their ranks and the ground dotted with dark spots—their dead and wounded. Now and then a cheer went up from our lines when our men observed some of our shells striking right among the advancing enemy and scattering death and destruction around. But the brave rebels promptly filled the gaps from behind or by closing up on their colors, and unshaken and unhesitatingly they continued their onward march.

Then the Confederate artillery behind them, firing over their heads, tried to silence our batteries or at least to attract their fire so as to divert it from the infantry masses advancing in the open field. But in vain. Our cannon did not change their aim, and the number of dark spots dotting the field increased fearfully from minute to minute. So far not a musket had been discharged from behind the stone fences protecting our regiments.

Now the assailants, steadily marching on, seemed to disappear in a depression of the ground where they stopped for a little while to readjust their alignment. But when they emerged again, evidently with undismayed courage, and quickened their pace to make the final plunge, a roar of cannon and a rattle of musketry so tremendous received them that one might have thought any force coming against it would have been swept from the face of the earth.

Still the attacking lines, although much thinned and losing their regularity, rushed forward with grim determination. Then we on the cemetery lost sight of them, as they were concealed from our eyes by the projecting spur of the ridge I have already spoken of.

Meanwhile a rebel force, consisting apparently of two or three brigades, supporting the main attack on its left, advanced against our position on Cemetery Hill. We had about thirty pieces of artillery in our front. They were ordered to load with grape and canister, and to reserve their fire until the enemy should be within four or five hundred yards. Then the word to fire was given, and when, after a few rapid discharges, the guns "ceased" and permitted the smoke to clear away, all we saw of the enemy was the backs of men hastily running away, and the ground covered with dead and wounded. Our skirmishers rushed forward, speeding the pace of fugitives and gathering in a multitude of prisoners.

But on our left the struggle, which from the cemetery we could not see, still

Carl Schurz.

continued. We could only hear a furious din which seemed to be stationary. Could it be that the rebels were breaking our lines? With nervous anxiety we turned our eyes upon the valley behind us. But there we saw, not fugitives or skulkers from our positions, but columns of troops hurrying to the scene of the decisive conflict. This was reassuring. At last, looking again at the field which had been traversed by the splendid host of assailants, we saw, first little driblets, then larger numbers, and finally huge swarms of men in utter disorder hurrying back the way they had come, and then, soon after, in hot pursuit, clouds of blue-coated skirmishers from our front rushing in from both sides, firing, and capturing prisoners.

This spectacle could have but one meaning. The great attack had failed disastrously. That magnificent column that had so proudly advanced upon us was not only defeated but well-nigh annihilated. A deep sigh of relief wrung itself from every breast. Then tremendous cheers arose along the Union lines, and here and there the men began to sing "John Brown's Soul." The song swept weirdly over the bloody field.

AFTER THE WAR.
From "The History of the American Civil War"—Draper.

A REIGN of terror, a vision of independence, appeals to patriotism, the novel excitement of military life, a prospect of placing the slave institution beyond the reach of abolitionists, soon gave unanimity to the South. Her journalism was disgraced by unscrupulous misrepresentations and by an unparalleled gasconade. An illiterate people was made to believe that it was the most enlightened, the most religious, the most polite, the most chivalrous community on earth. One Southern soldier was equal in battle to five Yankees; many were of opinion that that number was too small, and were rather disposed to put it at ten. The sentiment of "indignant virtue,"

which had originated in Charleston, and had caused so much amusement in Europe, spread like a delusion of insanity through the South. Forgetting her conspiracy of thirty years, which had culminated in her firing on the national flag, she actually persuaded herself, before many months were gone, that "the North was the aggressor, through jealousy of her superior civilization and virtues and the purer and more pious life of her society."

Her politicians had more than accomplished their purpose of firing the Southern heart. They had ignited the whole country. Everything was in a dance of excitement, like the quivering of objects seen over a hot surface. The deceitful mirage of independence loomed up in the distance, but, like the mirages of Sahara, was destined never to be reached. The sky was full of parhelions of delusive glory. The women, blazing with treason, flitted about like fireflies on an Autumn night.

Not a doubt was anywhere entertained that the passage of an ordinance of secession was equivalent to the establishment of a great slave empire. Up to this time, in America, everything had been settled by voting, and why not this? And up to this time, in happy America, no one knew what was truly meant by that little but most awful monosyllable —war. When the President of the United States called for 75,000 soldiers, the news was received in Montgomery with screams of derisive laughter. There are many mourning and ruined families in America who know what war means now.

In Charleston that dreadful arbitrament was first invoked. Crowds of beautiful ladies and gallant gentlemen went out to see the cannons fired. When the American flag was hauled down in Fort Sumter it was a gala day—a day of champagne, conviviality, chivalry.

Let us read what is written by an eye-witness who walked through Charleston after an avenging American army had raised again that insulted flag.

The wharves looked as if they had been

deserted for half a century—broken down, dilapidated; grass and moss peeping up between the pavements, where once the busy feet of commerce trod incessantly. The warehouses near the river, the streets as we enter them, the houses, and the stores, and the public buildings—we look at them and hold our breath in utter amazement. Every step we take increases our astonishment.

No pen, no pencil, no tongue can do justice to the scene; no imagination can conceive the utter wreck, the universal ruin, the stupendous desolation. Ruin, ruin, ruin, above and below, on the right hand and on the left, ruin, ruin, everywhere and always—staring at us from every paneless window, looking out at us from every shell-torn wall, glaring at us from every battered door, pillar, and veranda, crouching beneath our feet on every sidewalk.

Not Pompeii, nor Herculaneum, nor Tadmor, nor the Nile, have ruins so complete, so saddening, so plaintively eloquent, for they speak to us of an age not ours and long ago dead, with whose people and life and ideas we have no sympathy whatever; but here, on these shattered wrecks of houses—built in our own style, many of them doing credit to the architecture of our epoch—we read names familiar to us all, telling us of trades and professions and commercial institutions which every modern city reckons up by the hundred —yet dead, dead, dead; as silent as the graves of the Pharaohs, as deserted as the bazaars of the merchant princes of old Tyre.

If that wayfarer had followed the baleful path of secession through these now blasted but once beautiful provinces of the sun he would have seen the footprints of retribution everywhere—retribution on those who, for the sake of ambitious ends, bring upon their country the greatest of all curses—civil war.

In Columbia, where the convention first met and whence it was driven by a loathsome pestilence, stark chimneys point out where family hearthstones once were. If he inquired in Charleston for St. Andrew's Hall, where the ordinance was passed, or for the institute in which it was signed, some emancipated black would point out to him piles of charred rubbish. The tomb in St. Philip's Churchyard he would find had been violated by the friendly hands of a sad remnant of those who had once made obeisance before it—a remnant spared from the hospital and the sword —and the ashes of the great teacher of secession piously secreted from a conqueror's wrath. He would see the prophetic threat from a State in the far North had come to pass: "The rebellion, which was where Charleston is, shall end where Charleston was."

Had that awe-stricken traveler gone into the border States he would have found retribution in Rolleston, the home of that Governor of Virginia who put to an ignominious death, by hanging, the brave old fanatic, John Brown, for trying to liberate slaves; in that home he would have seen "a Yankee school-marm" teaching negroes to read the Bible, and that "school-marm" the daughter of "Old John Brown."

In the once picturesque but now desolated woods of Arlington, that City of the Silent, the shades of ten thousand American soldiers, whose ghastly corpses lie under its grassy lawns, are flitting in the midnight moonshine and beckoning its master to come—not to the fantastic dance of its gay and glittering halls, but to the dread tribunal of that inexorable Judge who will demand why these men were deprived of light and life. It is the unearthly welcome of Warwick and the Prince to Clarence in his dream.

Can any one doubt that there is retribution when he sees the once imperious master of many hundred slaves now lowly bending his forehead on the footstool of a "poor white"—who in his early life gained his bread by the humblest industry—and submissively supplicating for pardon, waiting in hope for permission to touch the tip of the outstretched sceptre of clemency?

The stars in their courses in the heavens are guided by immutable law, and the families of men upon earth are judged with unswerving equity. For her participation in the great American crime the North has had mourning sent into tens of thousands of her families, and the wealth she has wearied herself in acquiring is wrung from her by remorseless taxation.

Her more guilty sister, the South, has in bitterness of soul surrendered far more than her firstborn; and as the African many a time fainted under the lash of a cruel taskmaster, so now she faints under the lash of the Angel of Retribution. In her former days of peace she hugged slavery to her bosom, and now that peace is at last given back to her, she is condemned to be chained with adamant to that black and festering carcass.

Guilty, then—both of us—in the sight of God, let us not vex each other with mutual crimination, but bear with humility our punishment, though it may be, as our Chief Magistrate once told us, the hard penalty, that for every tear the black man has shed the white man shall pay a drop of blood.

There is another people whose day of retribution is not far off—who brought the course of slavery on this nation; who, for the sake of gain, armed it and strengthened it in its dying battle; who abetted it in its treason, and encouraged it in its fratricidal strife.

Shall he who writes the story of this hideous war hide from his reader its fearful lesson? Shall he not remember that on this widespread continent climate is making us a many-diversified people. That, in the nature of things, we must have our misunderstandings and our quarrels with one another?

If, in the future, there should be any one who undertakes to fire the heart of his people, and to set in mortal battle a community against the nation, let us leave him without the excuse which the war-secessionist of our time may perhaps not unjustly plead, that he knew not what he did. Let us put our experience in the primer of every child; let us make it the staple of the novel of every school-girl; let us tear from this bloody conflict its false grandeur and tinsel glories, and set it naked in the light of day—a spectacle to blanch the cheek of the bravest man, and make the heart of every mother flutter as she sits by her cradle.

THREE GREAT WAR-TIME ORATIONS

Speeches by Lincoln, Wendell Phillips, and Henry Ward Beecher Which Splendidly Reflect Civil War Days.

ABRAHAM LINCOLN.
Speech at Gettysburg.
November 19, 1863.

FOURSCORE AND SEVEN years ago our fathers brought forth upon this continent a new nation, conceived in liberty, and dedicated to the proposition that all men are created equal. Now we are engaged in a great civil war, testing whether that nation, or any nation so conceived and so dedicated, can long endure. We are met on a great battlefield of that war. We have come to dedicate a portion of that field as a final resting place for those who here gave their lives that that nation might live.

It is altogether fitting and proper that we should do this. But, in a larger sense, we cannot dedicate, we cannot consecrate, we cannot hallow this ground. The brave men, living and dead, who struggled here, have consecrated it far above our power to add or detract. The world will little note, nor long remember, what we say here, but it can never forget what they did here. It is for us, the living, rather to be dedicated here to the unfinished work which they who fought here have thus far so nobly advanced. It is rather for us to be here dedicated to the great task remaining before us, that from these honored dead we take increased devotion to that cause for which they gave the last full measure of devotion; that we here highly resolve that these dead shall not have died in vain; that this nation, under God, shall have a new birth of freedom, and that government of the people, by the people, and for the people, shall not perish from the earth.

HENRY WARD BEECHER.
The Martyr President.
Brooklyn, April 15, 1865.

EVEN he who now sleeps has, by this event, been clothed with new influence. Dead, he speaks to men who now willingly hear what before they refused to listen to. Now his simple and weighty words will be gathered like those of Washington, and your children, and your children's children, shall be taught to ponder the simplicity and deep wisdom of utterances which, in their time, passed, in party heat, as idle words. Men will receive a new impulse of patriotism for his sake and will guard with zeal the whole country which he loved so well. I swear you, on the altar of his memory, to be more faithful to the country for which he has perished. They will, as they follow his hearse, swear a new hatred to that slavery against which we warred, and which, in vanquishing him, has made him a martyr and a conqueror. I swear you, by the memory of this martyr, to hate slavery with an unappeasable hatred. They will admire and imitate the firmness of this man, his inflexible conscience for the right; and yet his gentleness, as tender as a woman's, his moderation of spirit, which not all the heat of party could inflame, nor all the jars and disturbances of his country shake out of its place. I swear you to an emulation of his justice, his moderation, and his mercy.

You I can comfort; but how can I speak to that twilight million to whom his name was as the name of an angel of God? There will be wailing in places which no minister shall be able to reach. When, in hovel and in cot, in wood and in wilderness, in the field throughout the South, the dusky children who looked upon him as that Moses whom God sent before them to lead them out of the land of bondage, learn that he has fallen, who shall comfort them? O, Thou Shepherd of Israel, that didst comfort thy people of old, to thy care we commit the helpless, the long-wronged, and grieved.

And now the martyr is moving in triumphal march, mightier than when alive. The nation rises up at every stage of his coming. Cities and States are his pall-bearers, and the cannon beats the hours with solemn progression. Dead, dead, dead, he yet speaketh! Is Washington dead? Is Hampden dead? Is David dead? Is any man that ever was fit to live dead? Disenthralled of flesh, and risen in the unobstructed sphere where passion never comes, he begins his illimitable work. His life now is grafted upon the infinite, and will be fruitful as no earthly life can be. Pass on, thou that hast overcome! Your sorrows, O people, are his peace! Your bells, and bands, and muffled drums, sound triumph in his ear. Wail and weep here; God made it echo joy and triumph there. Pass on!

Four years ago, O Illinois, we took from your midst an untried man, and from among the people. We return him to you a mighty conqueror. Not thine any more, but the nation's; not ours, but the world's. Give him place, O ye prairies! In the midst of this great continent his dust shall rest, a sacred treasure to myriads who shall pilgrim to that shrine to kindle anew their zeal and patriotism. Ye winds that move over the mighty places of the West, chant his requiem! Ye people, behold a martyr whose blood, as so many articulate words, pleads for fidelity, for law, for liberty!

WENDELL PHILLIPS.
The War for the Union.
Boston, December, 1861.

I KNOW how we stand today, with the frowning cannon of the English fleet ready to be thrust out of the port-holes against us. But I can answer England with a better answer than William H. Seward can write. I can answer her with a more statesmanlike paper than Simon Cameron can indite. I would answer her with the Stars and Stripes floating over Charleston and New Orleans, and the itinerant Cabinet of Richmond packing up archives and wearing apparel to ride back to Montgomery. There is one thing, and only one, which John Bull respects, and that is success.

It is not for us to give counsel to the Government on points of diplomatic propriety, but I suppose we may express our opinions, and my opinion is that, if I were the President of these forty-four States, while I was, I should want Mason and Slidell to stay with me.

I say, then, first, as a matter of justice to the slave, we owe it to him; the day of his deliverance has come. The long promise of seventy years is to be fulfilled. The South draws back from the pledge. The North is bound, in honor of the memory of her fathers, to demand its exact fulfillment, and in order to save the Union, which now means justice and peace, to recognize the right of four millions of its victims. This is the dictate of justice—justice, which at this hour is craftier than Seward, more statesmanlike than Cameron; justice, which appeals from the Cabinets of Europe to the people; justice, which abases the proud and lifts up the humble; justice, which disarms England, saves the slaves from insurrection, and sends home the Confederate army of the Potomac to guard its own hearths; justice, which gives us four millions of friends, spies, soldiers in the enemy's country, planted each one at their very hearthsides; justice, which inscribes every cannon with "Holiness to the Lord" and puts a Northern heart behind every musket; justice, which means victory now and peace forever. To all cry of demagogues asking for boldness, I respond with the cry of "justice, immediate, absolute justice!" And if I dared to descend to a lower level, I should say to the merchants of this metropolis, "Demand of the Government a speedy settlement of this question."

Wendell Phillips.

PUNCH'S NOBLE APOLOGY TO LINCOLN

YOU lay a wreath on murdered Lincoln's bier,
> *You*, who, with mocking pencil,
> wont to trace
Broad for the self-complacent British
sneer,
His length of shambling limb, his fur-
rowed face,

His gaunt, gnarled hands, his unkempt,
bristling hair,
> His garb uncouth, his bearing ill at
> ease,
His lack of all we prize as debonair,
> Of power or will to shine, of art to
> please;

You, whose smart pen backed up the pencil's laugh,
> Judging each step as though the way
> were plain,
Reckless, so it could point its paragraph,
> Of chief's perplexity or people's pain—

Beside this corpse that bears for winding sheet
> The Stars and Stripes he lived to rear
> anew,
Between the mourners at his head and
feet,
> Say, scurrile jester, is there room for
> *you?*

Yes, he had lived to shame me from my
sneer,
> To lame my pencil, and confute my
> pen;
To make me own this hind of Princes
peer,

This rail-splitter, a true-born king of
men.

My shallow judgment I had learned to
rue,
> Noting how to occasion's height he
> rose,
How his quaint wit made home truth
seem more true,
> How, iron-like, his temper grew by
> blows;

How humble, yet how hopeful, he could
be;
> How, in good fortune and in ill, the
> same;
Nor bitter in success, nor boastful he,
> Thirsty for gold, nor feverish for fame.

He went about his work—such work as
few
> Ever had laid on head and heart and
> hand—
As one who knows, where there's a task
to do,
> Man's honest will must Heaven's good
> grace command;

Who trusts the strength will with the
burden grow,
> That God makes instruments to work
> His will,
If but that will we can arrive to know,
> Nor tamper with the weights of good
> and ill.

So he went forth to battle on the side
> That he felt clear was Liberty's and
> Right's,
As in his peasant boyhood he had plied

His warfare with rude Nature's
thwarting mights—

The uncleared forest, the unbroken soil,
> The iron bark that turns the lumber-
> er's axe,
The rapid that o'erbears the boatman's
toil,
> The prairie, hiding the mazed wan-
> derer's tracks,

The ambushed Indian and the prowling
bear—
> Such were the needs that helped his
> youth to train:
Rough culture—but such trees large fruit
may bear,
> If but their stocks be of right girth and
> grain.

So he grew up, a destined work to do,
> And lived to do it: four long-suffering
> years'
ill-fate, ill-feeling, ill-report, lived
through,
> And then he heard the hisses changed
> to cheers,

The taunts to tribute, the abuse to
praise,
> And took both with the same unwaver-
> ing mood;
Till, as he came on light, from darkling
days,
> And seemed to touch the goal from
> where he stood,

A felon hand, between the goal and him,
Reached from behind his back, a trig-
ger pressed—

And those perplexed and patient eyes
were dim,
> Those gaunt, long-laboring limbs were
> laid to rest.

The words of mercy were upon his lips,
> Forgiveness in his heart and on his pen,
When this vile murderer brought swift
eclipse
> To thoughts of peace on earth, good
> will to men.

The Old World and the New, from sea
to sea,
> Utter one voice of sympathy and
> shame.
Sore heart, so stopped when it at last
beat high!
> Sad life, cut short just as its triumph
> came!

A deed accursed! Strokes have been
struck before
> By the assassin's hand, whereof men
> doubt
If more of horror or disgrace they bore;
> But thy foul crime, like Cain's, stands
> darkly out,

Vile hand that brandest murder on a
strife,
> Whate'er its grounds, stoutly and no-
> bly striven,
And with the martyr's crown, crownest a
life
With much to praise, little to be for-
given.

TOM TAYLOR, in Punch, 1865.

CELEBRATED POEMS OF THE WAR

Battle Hymn of the Republic

By Julia Ward Howe.

MINE eyes have seen the glory of
the coming of the Lord:
He is trampling out the vintage
where the grapes of wrath are
stored;
He hath loosed the fateful lightning of
His terrible swift sword:
> His truth is marching on.

I have seen Him in the watchfires of a
hundred circling camps;
They have builded Him an altar in the
evening dews and damps;
I can read His righteous sentence by the
dim and flaring lamps.
> His day is marching on.

I have read a fiery gospel, writ in bur-
nished rows of steel:
"As ye deal with My contemners, so with

you My grace shall deal;"
Let the Hero, born of woman, crush the
serpent with His heel,
> Since God is marching on.

He has sounded forth His trumpet that
shall never call retreat;
He is sifting out the hearts of men before
His judgment seat;
Oh! be swift, my soul, to answer Him! be
jubilant, my feet!
> Our God is marching on.

In the beauty of the lilies Christ was
born across the sea,
With a glory in His bosom that transfig-
ures you and me;
As He died to make men holy, let us die
to make men free,
> While God is marching on.

Romance

By William Ernest Henley.

The last of the Confederate Army—"Dixie's bottom dollar"—leaving Charleston in
1865, after Sherman took Columbia.

TALK of pluck!" pursued the Sailor,
Set at euchre on his elbow,
> "I was on the wharf at Charles-
> ton,
Just ashore from off the runner.

"It was gray and dirty weather,
And I heard a drum go rolling,
Rub-a-dubbing in the distance,
Awful dour-like and defiant.

"In and out among the cotton,
Mud, and chains, and stores, and anchors,

Tramped a squad of battered scare-
crows—
Poor old Dixie's bottom dollar!

"Some had shoes, but all had rifles,
Them that wasn't bald was beardless,
And the drum was rolling 'Dixie,'
And they stepped to it like men, Sir!

"Rags and tatters, belts and bayonets,
On they swung, the drum a-rolling,
Mum and sour. It looked like fighting,
And they meant it, too, by thunder!"

From "John Burns of Gettysburg"

By Bret Harte.

JUST where the tide of battle turns,
Erect and lonely, stood old John
Burns.
How do you think the old man was
dressed?
He wore an ancient, long buff vest,
Yellow as saffron—but his best;
And, buttoned over his manly breast,
Was a bright blue coat with a rolling
collar,
And large gilt buttons—size of a dol-
lar—
With tails that country folk called
"swaller."
He wore a broad-brimmed, bell-crowned
hat,
White as the locks on which it sat.
Never had such a sight been seen
For forty years on the village green,
Since old John Burns was a country
beau,
And went to the "quiltings" long ago.

Close at his elbows all that day,
Veterans of the Peninsula,
Sunburnt and bearded, charged away;
And striplings, downy of lip and chin—
Clerks that the Home Guard mustered
in—
Glanced, as they passed, at the hat he
wore,
Then at the rifle his right hand bore;
And hailed him, from out their youthful
lore,
With scraps of a slangy repertoire:
"How are you, White Hat?" "Put her
through!"
"Your head's level!" and "Bully for
you!"
Called him "Daddy"—begged he'd dis-
close
The name of his tailor who made his
clothes,

And what was the value he set on those;
While Burns, unmindful of jeer or
scoff,
Stood there picking the rebels off—
With his long brown rifle, and bell-
crowned hat,
And the swallow tails they were laugh-
ing at.

It was but a moment, for that respect
Which clothes all courage their voices
checked;
And something the wildest could under-
stand
Spake in the old man's strong right
hand,
And his corded throat, and the lurking
frown
Of his eyebrows under his old bell-
crown;
Until, as they gazed, there crept an
awe
Through the ranks in whispers, and
some men saw,
In the antique vestments and long white
hair,
The Past of the Nation in battle there;
And some of the soldiers since declare
That the gleam of his old white hat
afar,
Like the crested plume of the brave Na-
varre,
That day was their oriflamme of war.

So raged the battle. You know the rest:
How the rebels, beaten and backward
pressed,
Broke at the final charge and ran.
At which John Burns—a practical
man—
Shouldered his rifle, unbent his brows,
And then went back to his bees and
cows.

Laus Deo!

By John Greenleaf Whittier.

(On hearing the bells ring on the passage of the Constitutional Amendment abolishing slavery.)

IT is done!
  Clang of bell and roar of gun
  Send the tidings up and down.
How the belfries rock and reel!
How the great guns, peal on peal,
Fling the joy from town to town!

  Ring, O bells!
  Every stroke exulting tells
Of the burial hour of crime.
  Loud and long, that all may hear,
  Ring for every listening ear
Of Eternity and Time!

  Let us kneel:
  God's own voice is in that peal,
And this spot is holy ground.
  Lord, forgive us! What are we,
  That our eyes this glory see,
That our ears have heard the sound?

  For the Lord
  On the whirlwind is abroad;
In the earthquake has He spoken;
  He has smitten with His thunder
  The iron walls asunder,
And the gates of brass are broken!

  Loud and long
  Lift the old exulting song;
Sing with Miriam by the sea,
  He has cast the mighty down;
  Horse and rider sing and drown;
" He hath triumphed gloriously!"

  Did we dare,
  In our agony of prayer,
Ask for more than He has done?
  When was ever His right hand
  Over any time or land
Stretched as now beneath the sun?

  How they pale,
  Ancient myth and song and tale,
In this wonder of our days,
  When the cruel rod of war
  Blossoms white with righteous law,
And the wrath of man is praise!

  Blotted out!
  All within and all about
Shall a fresher life begin;
  Freer breathe the universe
  As it rolls its heavy curse
On the dead and buried sin!

  It is done!
  In the circuit of the sun
Shall the sound thereof go forth.
  It shall bid the sad rejoice,
  It shall give the dumb a voice,
It shall belt with joy the earth!

  Ring and swing,
  Bells of joy! On morning's wing
Send the song of praise abroad!
  With a sound of broken chains
  Tell the nations that He reigns
Who alone is Lord and God!

O Captain! My Captain!

By Walt Whitman (1865.)

O CAPTAIN! My Captain! Our fearful trip is done,
  The ship has weather'd every rack,
    the prize we sought is won,
The port is near, the bells I hear, the people all exulting,
While follow eyes the steady keel, the
    vessel grim and daring;
  But O heart! heart! heart!
    O the bleeding drops of red,
  Where on the deck my Captain lies,
    Fallen cold and dead.

O Captain! My Captain! Rise up and
    hear the bells;
Rise up—for you the flag is flung—for
    you the bugle trills,
For you the bouquets and ribbon'd
    wreaths—for you the shores
    a-crowding,

For you they call, the swaying mass,
    their eager faces turning;
  Here Captain! dear father!
    This arm beneath your head!
  It is some dream that on the deck
    You've fallen cold and dead.

My Captain does not answer, his lips are
    pale and still,
My father does not feel my arm, he has
    no pulse nor will,
The ship is anchor'd safe and sound, its
    voyage closed and done,
From fearful trip and victor ship comes
    in with object won;
  Exult O shores and ring O bells!
    But I with mournful tread,
  Walk the deck my Captain lies,
    Fallen cold and dead.

Lines on a Confederate Note

These lines were written by Major A. S. Jonas, a native of Mississippi and a member of the staff of General Stephen D. Lee. Being paroled, he went to Richmond to secure transportation home.
At the Powhatan Hotel the company met a Miss Anna Rush, a young girl from the North, who was visiting in Richmond. Conversing with officers, she showed them a batch of Confederate notes printed on one side, which, she said, she was taking home as souvenirs. Handing one to each officer, she requested them to write something on the back. The officers complied, and this poem was Major Jonas's contribution:

REPRESENTING nothing on God's
    earth now,
  And naught in the waters below it,
As the pledge of a nation that's dead and
    gone,
Keep it, dear friend, and show it.
Show it to those who will lend an ear
  To the tale that this paper can tell
Of Liberty born of the patriot's dream,
  Of a storm-cradled nation that fell.

Too poor to possess the precious ores,
  And too much of a stranger to borrow,
We issued today our promise to pay,
  And hoped to repay on the morrow.
The days rolled by and weeks became
    years,
  But our coffers were empty still;
Coin was so rare that the treasury'd
    quake
  If a dollar should drop in the till.

But the faith that was in us was strong,
    indeed,
  And our poverty well we discerned,
And this little check represented the pay
  That our suffering veterans earned.
We knew it had hardly a value in gold,
  Yet as gold each soldier received it;
It gazed in our eyes with a promise to
    pay,
  And each Southern patriot believed it.

But our boys thought little of price or
    of pay,
  Or of bills that were over-due;
We knew if it brought us our bread today,
  'Twas the best our poor country could do.
Keep it, it tells all our history o'er,
  From the birth of our dream till the
    last;
Modest, and born of the angel Hope,
  Like our hope of success, it passed.

The Conquered Banner

By Abram Joseph Ryan.

FURL that Banner, for 'tis weary;
    Round its staff 'tis drooping
    dreary;
  Furl it, fold it—it is best;
For there's not a man to wave it,
And there's not a sword to save it,
And there's not one left to lave it
In the blood which heroes gave it,
And its foes now scorn and brave it;
  Furl it, hide it—let it rest!

Take that Banner down! 'Tis tattered;
Broken is its staff and shattered;
And the valiant hosts are scattered,
  Over whom it floated high.
Oh, 'tis hard for us to fold it,
Hard to think there's none to hold it,
Hard that those who once unrolled it
  Now must furl it with a sigh!

Furl that Banner—furl it sadly!
Once ten thousands hailed it gladly,
And then thousands wildly, madly,
  Swore it should forever wave;
Swore that foeman's sword should never
Hearts like theirs entwined dissever,
Till that flag should float forever
  O'er their freedom or their grave!

Furl it! for the hands that grasped it,
And the hearts that fondly clasped it,
  Cold and dead are lying low;
And that Banner—it is trailing,
While around it sounds the wailing
  Of its people in their woe.

For, though conquered, they adore it—
Love the cold, dead hands that bore it,
Weep for those who fell before it,
Pardon those who trailed and tore it;
And Oh, wildly they deplore it,
  Now to furl and fold it so!

Furl that Banner! True, 'tis gory,
Yet 'tis wreathed around with glory,
And 'twill live in song and story
  Though its folds are in the dust!
For its fame on brightest pages,
Penned by poets and by sages,
Shall go sounding down the ages—
  Furl its folds though now we must.

Furl that Banner, softly, slowly!
Treat it gently—it is holy,
  For it droops above the dead.
Touch it not—unfold it never;
Let it droop there, furled forever,
  For its people's hopes are fled!

INTERESTING STATISTICS OF THE WAR

Figures Which Show the Number of Men Engaged and the Appalling Cost of the Struggle in Lives and Money.

THE great war between the States brought into action on the Union side approximately 2,772,000 men, while those who fought for the Confederacy have been variously estimated to have totaled between 700,000 and 1,500,000, and by some authorities at an even higher figure than the last given. It is certain that more than 3,500,000 Americans were called to arms in the great struggle. Conservative and presumably authentic figures compiled in the effort to reach the exact total engaged on the side of the Union places the number at 2,772,408 men. Major Thomas L. Livermore, one of the most eminent of civil war statisticians, has

even placed it as high as 2,898,304 men, which total he explains in his statistical history of the war includes " about 230,000 militia and emergency men."

Here are the various estimates that have been made of the fighting strength of the Confederacy:

Marcus J. Wright........600,000 to 700,000
Early, Stephens and Jones..........600,000
Estimate from census..............1,234,000
Estimate from the number and average strength of regiments ....1,227,890 or 1,406,480
Estimate War Records Office......1,000,000
Casselman's estimate..............1,500,000

The above table indicates how difficult a matter it is to correctly estimate the number of men who fought under Lee

and his Generals. The most conservative estimate would appear to be somewhere between 800,000 and 1,000,000.

Here are the losses of the Union armies as compiled in the office of the Adjutant General of the Army in Washington:

Killed in battle.................... 67,058
Died of wounds 43,012
Died of disease 199,720
Other causes 40,154

Total 349,944

The Confederate losses, as compiled by the Adjutant General, U. S. A , are:
Died of wounds or disease, 133,821.

The above casualties, due to wounds

and disease and other causes, total 483,765 men.

The number of Union troops captured during the war was 212,608, while the number of Confederates taken by the Union armies, including the surrenders at the end of hostilities, totaled 476,169 men. The number of Union troops paroled by the Confederates was 16,431 and the number of Confederates paroled by the Union commanders was 248,599. The number of Union troops who died while prisoners was 30,156 and the number of Confederate prisoners who died, 30,152. The largest army assembled by the Union was the one that fought at the Wilderness, and the largest Confederate force was the one engaged in the seven days' fighting in Virginia.

The first blood of the war was shed in the streets of Baltimore, April 19, 1861. The war may be said to have actually begun with the bombardment of Fort Sumter, in Charleston Harbor, on April 13, and it practically ended with the surrender of General Lee at Appomattox on April 9, 1865. General J. E. Johnston surrendered April 26, and General Kirby-Smith surrendered the last of the detached commands in May.

The cost of the war to the North has been conservatively estimated at about $12,500,000,000, and of this amount about $4,500,000,000 has been paid in pensions to Union veterans of the war. The cost of the war to the South has been estimated to have been in excess of $4,000,000,000, which would bring the total cost to about $16,500,000,000.

The number of deserters from the Union army was 199,105, and the total of those who deserted the Confederate side, 104,428.

The losses of the Union and Confederate Armies in the various battles of the civil war, given in the table below, were taken in part from Major Thomas L. Livermore's statistical record of the civil war, and in part from Capt. Frederick Phisterer's statistics. These two are among the best of the civil war statisticians, and for years following the civil war both devoted their time to gathering of the data upon which they subsequently based their estimates of the Union and Confederate casualties in the various battles of the war. It is pointed out by both that the Union records are much more complete than are those of the Southern armies. As a matter of fact in many instances all data except estimated totals are missing in the Confederate records. In the table the battles citied are those in which one or both sides suffered losses in killed, wounded, missing, or prisoners of a total of over 500 men.

Tables of Losses Over 500 on Both Sides in the Principal Battles.

Place and Date.	Union Killed.	Union Wounded and Missing.	Union Total.	Confederate Killed.	Confederate Wounded and Missing.	Confederate Total.
1861.						
Bull Run, Va., July 21	481	2,227	2,768	387	1,594	1,981
Wilson's Creek Mo., Aug. 1	223	1,012	1,235	257	927	1,184
Lexington, Mo., Sept. 12-20	....	....	1,774	....	....	100
Ball's Bluff, Va., Oct. 21	....	....	894	....	....	302
Belmont, Mo., Nov. 7	....	....	498	....	....	966
1862.						
Fort Donelson, Tenn., Feb. 12-16	500	2,332	2,832	2,000	14,623	16,623
Pea Ridge, Ark., March 7	203	1,081	1,284	600	200	800
New Berne, N. C., March 14	....	....	557	....	....	583
Winchester Va., March 23	....	....	567	....	....	691
Shiloh, Tenn., April 6-7	1,754	11,293	13,047	1,723	8,971	10,694
Williamsburg, Va., May 4-5	456	1,783	2,239	*1,570	133	1,703
Front Royal, Va., May 23	....	....	904	....	....	....
Winchester, Va., May 25	....	....	900	....	....	....
Fair Oaks, Va., May 31-June 1	790	4,241	5,031	980	5,154	6,134
Cross Keys, Va., June 8	....	....	625	....	....	287
Fort Republic, Va., June 9	....	....	1,002	....	....	657
James Island, S. C., June 16	....	....	685	....	....	204
Oak Grove, Va., June 25	....	....	516	....	....	541
Mechanicsville, Va., June 26	49	312	361	*1,484	....	1,484
Gaines's Mill, Va., June 27	894	5,943	6,837	*8,751	....	8,751
Peach Orchard, Savage Station, White Oak Swamp, Glendale, and Malvern Hill, June 29-30 and July 1	724	7,312	8,036	*8,602	875	9,477
Murfreesboro, Tenn., July 13	....	....	895	....	....	150
Cedar Mountain, Va., Aug. 8	314	2,039	2,353	231	1,107	1,338
Guerrilla campaigns in Missouri, July 20 to Sept. 20	....	....	580	....	....	2,886
Manassas and Chantilly, Aug. 27 to Sept. 2	1,724	14,330	16,054	1,481	7,716	9,197
Richmond, Ky., Aug. 29-30	206	5,147	5,353	78	373	451
Harper's Ferry, W. Va., Sept. 12-15	*500	13,000	13,500	....	....	500
South Mountain, Md., Sept. 14	325	1,488	1,813	325	2,360	2,685
Mumfordsville, Ky., Sept. 14-16	....	....	3,616	....	....	714
Antietam, Md., Sept. 16-17	2,108	10,302	12,410	2,700	11,024	13,724
Iuka, Miss., Sept. 19-20	....	....	782	....	....	1,516
Corinth, Miss., Oct. 3-4	355	2,165	2,520	473	3,760	4,233
Big Hat-Chie River, Miss., Oct. 5	....	....	500	....	....	400
Perryville, Ky., Oct. 8	845	3,396	4,241	510	2,886	3,396
Prairie Grove, Ark., Dec. 7	175	1,076	1,251	164	1,153	1,317
Hartsville, Tenn., Dec. 7	....	....	1,855	....	....	149
Foster's Expedition to Goldsboro, N. C., Dec. 12-18	....	....	577	....	....	739
Fredericksburg, Va., Dec. 13	1,284	11,369	12,653	595	4,714	5,309
Chickasaw Bayou and Bluff, Tenn., Dec. 27-29	208	1,568	1,776	63	144	207
Elizabethtown, Ky., Dec. 27	....	....	500	....	....	....
Stone's River, Tenn., Dec. 31 to Jan. 1, 1862	1,667	11,229	12,896	1,294	10,445	11,739
1863.						
Galveston, Texas, Jan. 1	....	....	600	....	....	50
Arkansas Post, Ark., Jan. 11	134	927	1,061	28	4,872	4,900
Thompson's Station, Tenn., March 4-5	....	....	1,706	....	....	600
Streight's Raid into Georgia, April 27 to May 3	....	....	1,547	....	....	....
Port Gibson, Miss, May 1	....	....	853	....	....	1,650
Chancellorsville, Va., May 1 to 4	1,575	15,270	16,845	1,665	11,099	12,764
Champion Hill, Miss., May 16	410	2,031	2,441	381	3,470	3,851
Assault on Vicksburg, Miss., May 22	502	2,697	3,199	*2,340	....	2,340
Assault on Port Hudson, La., May 27	293	1,702	1,995	*235	....	235
Milliken's Bend, La., June 6-8	....	....	492	....	....	725
Brandy Station, Va., June 9	....	....	500	....	....	700
Winchester, Va., June 13-15	....	....	3,000	....	....	850
Assault on Port Hudson, La., June 14	203	1,589	1,792	22	25	47
Rosecran's Campaign, Murfreesboro to Tullahona, Tenn., June 23-30	....	....	560	....	....	1,634
Gettysburg, Penn., July 1-3	3,155	19,894	23,049	3,903	24,160	28,063
Jackson, Miss., July 9-16	....	....	1,000	....	....	1,339
Assault on Fort Wagner, S. C., July 18	246	1,269	1,515	36	138	174
Chickamauga, Ga., Sept. 19-20	1,657	14,513	16,170	2,312	16,142	18,454
Grand Coteau, La., Nov. 3	....	....	726	....	....	445
Rogersville, Tenn., Nov. 6	....	....	667	....	....	30
Chattanooga, Tenn., Nov. 23-25	753	5,071	5,824	361	6,306	6,667
Mine Run, Va., Nov. 27-Dec. 1	173	1,480	1,653	110	635	745
Bean's Station, Tenn., Dec. 14	....	....	700	....	....	900
1864.						
Olustee, Fla., Feb. 20	203	1,658	1,861	93	841	934
Sabine Cross Roads, La., April 8	....	....	2,900	....	....	1,500
Pleasant Hill, La., April 9	150	1,219	1,369	*1,000	500	1,500
Fort Pillow, Tenn., April 12	....	....	574	....	....	80
Plymouth, N. C., April 17-20	....	....	574	....	....	80
Jenkins's Ferry, Ark., April 30	....	....	1,155	....	....	80
Wilderness, Va., May 5-7	2,246	15,420	17,666	1,900	5,850	7,750
Engagements near Dalton, Ga., May 5-9	....	....	837	....	....	600
Spottsylvania, Va., May 10	753	3,347	4,100	....	....	No r'c'd
Swift Creek, Va., May 9-10	....	....	490	....	....	500
Spottsylvania, Va., May 12	*6,020	800	6,820	*5,000	4,000	9,000
Drewry's Bluff, Va., May 12-16	390	3,370	4,160	355	2,151	2,506
Resaca, Ga., May 13-16	....	....	2,747	....	....	2,800
New Market, Va., May 15	....	....	920	....	....	405
Bermuda Hundred, Va., May 16-30	....	....	1,200	....	....	3,000
N. Anna River, Va., May 23-27	....	....	1,973	....	....	2,000
Dallas, Ga., May 25-June 4	....	....	2,400	....	....	3,000
Cold Harbor, Va., June 1-3	*12,000	....	12,000	....	....	1,700
Piedmont, Va., June 5	....	....	780	....	....	2,970
Guntown, Miss., June 10	....	....	2,240	....	....	606
Kellar's Bridge, Ky., June 10	....	....	767	....	....	No r'c'd
Trevellian Sta., Va., June 11-12	....	....	735	....	....	336
Petersburg, Va., June 15-18	*8,150	....	8,150	*2,970	....	2,970
Lynchburg, Va., June 17-18	....	....	400	....	....	200
Trenches in front of Petersburg, Va., June 20-30	....	....	1,418	....	....	No r'c'd
Kennesaw Mount'n, Ga., June 27	1,999	52	2,051	270	172	442
Chattahoochee River, Ga., July 6-10	....	....	730	....	....	600
Monocacy, Md., July 9	....	....	1,959	....	....	400
Tupelo, Miss., July 13-15	77	597	674	210	1,116	1,326
Peach Tree Creek, Ga., July 20	*1,600	....	1,600	*2,500	....	2,500
Atlanta, Ga., (Hood's Attack,) July 22	430	3,292	3,722	*7,000	1,000	8,000
Winchester, Va., July 24	....	....	1,200	....	....	600
Stoneman's Raid, Ga., July 26-31	....	....	1,000	....	....	No r'c'd
McCook's Raid, Ga., July 26-31	....	....	600	....	....	No r'c'd
Atlanta, Ga., July 28	*559	73	632	*4,100	200	4,300
The Mine, Va., July 30	*2,864	929	3,793	*1,200	....	1,200
Deep Bottom, Va., Aug. 14-19	328	2,573	3,294	....	....	No r'c'd
Weldon Railr'd, Va., Aug. 18-21	198	4,257	4,455	*1,200	....	1,200
Jonesborough, Ga., Aug. 31	*179	....	179	*1,725	....	1,725
Jonesborough, Ga., Sept. 1	223	1,051	1,274	....	....	No r'c'd
Winchester, Va., Sept. 19	697	4,321	5,018	276	3,645	3,921
Athens, Ala., Sept. 23	....	....	950	....	....	30
Chaffin's Farm and Forts Harrison and Gilmer, Sept. 29-30	383	2,944	3,327	377	....	No r'c'd
Price's Invasion of Missouri, Sept. 24-Oct. 28	....	....	506	....	....	No r'c'd
New Market Heights, Va., Sept. 28-30	....	....	2,429	....	....	2,000
Altoona, Ga., Oct. 5	....	....	706	....	....	1,142
Cedar Creek, Va., Oct. 19	644	5,021	5,665	320	2,590	3,910
Hatcher's Run, Va., Oct. 27	....	....	1,902	....	....	1,000
Boydton Plank Road, Va., Oct. 27-28	166	1,592	1,758	....	....	No r'c'd
Fort Kelly, W. Va., Nov. 2	....	....	700	....	....	5
Franklin, Tenn., Nov. 30	189	2,137	2,326	1,750	4,502	6,252
Broad River, S. C., Nov. 30	....	....	711	....	....	No r'c'd
Deveaux's Neck, S. C., Dec. 6-9	....	....	627	....	....	400
Nashville, Tenn., Dec. 15-16	387	2,674	3,061	No r'c'd	4,462 (captured)	No r'c'd
1865.						
Beverly, W. Va., Jan. 11	....	....	608	....	....	No r'c'd
Fort Fisher, N. C., Jan. 13-15	....	....	955	....	....	2,483
Hatcher's Run, Va., Feb. 5-7	170	1,342	1,512	....	....	1,200
Wise's Fork, N. C., March 8-10	....	....	1,101	....	....	1,500
Averysboro, N. C., March 16	....	....	554	....	....	865
Bentonville, N. C., March 19	139	964	1,103	195	1,923	2,118
Fort Steadman, Va., March 25	....	....	911	....	....	2,681
Spanish Fort, Ala., March 26-April 8	....	....	795	....	....	552
Wilson's raid in Alabama and Georgia, March 22-April 24	....	....	725	....	....	8,020
Dinwiddie C. H. and White Oak Road, Va., March 29	*2,198	583	2,781	....	....	No r'c'd
Five Forks, Va., April 1	....	....	884	....	....	8,500
Fall of Petersburg, April 2	625	3,515	4,140	....	....	3,000
Sailors Creek, Va., April 6	....	....	1,180	....	....	7,000
High Bridge, Va., April 6	....	....	1,041	....	....	No r'c'd
Farmville, Va., April 7	....	....	655	....	....	No r'c'd
Fort Blakely, Ala., April 9	....	....	629	....	....	2,900
Surrender of Gen. Lee, April 9	....	....	....	....	....	26,000
Surrender of Gen. Johnston, Apri 26	....	....	....	....	....	29,924
Surrender of Gen. Taylor, May 4	....	....	....	....	....	10,000
Surrender of Sam Jones, May 10	....	....	....	....	....	8,000
Surrender of Jeff Thompson, Surrender of Gen. Kirby-Smith, May 26	....	....	....	....	....	20,000

*Includes wounded.